Nineteenth-Century Literature Criticism

Guide to Gale Literary Criticism Series

For criticism on	Consult these Gale series
Authors now living or who died after December 31, 1959	*CONTEMPORARY LITERARY CRITICISM (CLC)*
Authors who died between 1900 and 1959	*TWENTIETH-CENTURY LITERARY CRITICISM (TCLC)*
Authors who died between 1800 and 1899	*NINETEENTH-CENTURY LITERATURE CRITICISM (NCLC)*
Authors who died between 1400 and 1799	*LITERATURE CRITICISM FROM 1400 TO 1800 (LC)* *SHAKESPEAREAN CRITICISM (SC)*
Authors who died before 1400	*CLASSICAL AND MEDIEVAL LITERATURE CRITICISM (CMLC)*
Black writers of the past two hundred years	*BLACK LITERATURE CRITICISM (BLC)*
Authors of books for children and young adults	*CHILDREN'S LITERATURE REVIEW (CLR)*
Dramatists	*DRAMA CRITICISM (DC)*
Hispanic writers of the late nineteenth and twentieth centuries	*HISPANIC LITERATURE CRITICISM (HLC)*
Native North American writers and orators of the eighteenth, nineteenth, and twentieth centuries	*NATIVE NORTH AMERICAN LITERATURE (NNAL)*
Poets	*POETRY CRITICISM (PC)*
Short story writers	*SHORT STORY CRITICISM (SSC)*
Major authors from the Renaissance to the present	*WORLD LITERATURE CRITICISM, 1500 TO THE PRESENT (WLC)*

ISSN 0732-1864

Volume 67

Nineteenth-Century Literature Criticism

Excerpts from Criticism of the Works of Novelists, Poets, Playwrights, Short Story Writers, Philosophers, and Other Creative Writers Who Died between 1800 and 1899, from the First Published Critical Appraisals to Current Evaluations

Denise Evans
Editor

GALE

DETROIT · NEW YORK · LONDON

STAFF

Denise Evans, *Editor*

~~Jelena Krstovic~~, Marie Lazzari, Daniel G. Marowski, *Contributing Editors*
Amy K. Crook, *Associate Editor*
Ira Mark Milne, *Assistant Editor*
Aarti D. Stephens, *Managing Editor*

Susan M. Trosky, *Permissions Manager*
Kimberly F. Smilay, *Permissions Specialist*
Steve Cusack, Kelly A. Quin, *Permissions Assistants*

Victoria B. Cariappa, *Research Manager*
Julia C. Daniel, Tamara C. Nott,
Tracie A. Richardson, Cheryl L. Warnock, *Research Associates*
Jeffrey Daniels, *Research Assistant*

Mary Beth Trimper, *Production Director*
Deborah L. Milliken, *Production Assistant*

Ninette Saad, *Desktop Publisher Assistant*
Randy Bassett, *Image Database Supervisor*
Robert Duncan, Michael Logusz, *Imaging Specialists*
Pamela A. Reed, *Imaging Coordinator*

Library of Congress Catalog Card Number 84-643008
ISBN 0-7876-1907-8
ISSN 0732-1864
Printed in the United States of America

10 9 8 7 6 5 4 3 2 1

Contents

Preface vii

Acknowledgments ix

Preface

S ince its inception in 1981, *Nineteenth-Century Literature Criticism* has been a valuable resource for students and librarians seeking critical commentary on writers of this transitional period in world history. Designated an "Outstanding Reference Source" by the American Library Association with the publication of its first volume, *NCLC* has since been purchased by over 6,000 school, public, and university libraries. The series has covered more than 300 authors representing 29 nationalities and over 17,000 titles. No other reference source has surveyed the critical reaction to nineteenth-century authors and literature as thoroughly as *NCLC*.

Scope of the Series

NCLC is designed to introduce students and advanced readers to the authors of the nineteenth century, and to the most significant interpretations of these authors' works. The great poets, novelists, short story writers, playwrights, and philosophers of this period are frequently studied in high school and college literature courses. By organizing and reprinting commentary written on these authors, *NCLC* helps students develop valuable insight into literary history, promotes a better understanding of the texts, and sparks ideas for papers and assignments. Each entry in *NCLC* presents a comprehensive survey of an author's career or an individual work of literature and provides the user with a multiplicity of interpretations and assessments. Such variety allows students to pursue their own interests; furthermore, it fosters an awareness that literature is dynamic and responsive to many different opinions.

Every fourth volume of *NCLC* is devoted to literary topics that cannot be covered under the author approach used in the rest of the series. Such topics include literary movements, prominent themes in nineteenth-century literature, literary reaction to political and historical events, significant eras in literary history, prominent literary anniversaries, and the literatures of cultures that are often overlooked by English-speaking readers.

NCLC continues the survey of criticism of world literature begun by Gale's *Contemporary Literary Criticism (CLC)* and *Twentieth-Century Literary Criticism (TCLC),* both of which excerpt and reprint commentary on authors of the twentieth century. For additional information about *TCLC, CLC,* and Gale's other criticism series, users should consult the Guide to Gale Literary Criticism Series preceding the title page in this volume.

Coverage

Each volume of *NCLC* is carefully compiled to present:

- criticism of authors, or literary topics, representing a variety of genres and nationalities
- both major and lesser-known writers and literary works of the period
- 5-8 authors or 4-6 topics per volume
- individual entries that survey critical response to an author's work or a topic in literary history, including early criticism to reflect initial reactions, later criticism to represent any rise or decline in reputation, and current retrospective analyses.

Organization

An author entry consists of the following elements: author heading, biographical and critical introduction, list of principal works, excerpts of criticism (each preceded by a bibliographic citation and an annotation), and a bibliography of further reading.

- The **Author Heading** consists of the name under which the author most commonly wrote, followed by birth and death dates. If an author wrote consistently under a pseudonym, the pseudonym will be listed in the author heading and the real name given in parentheses on the first line of the biographical and critical introduction. Also located at the beginning of the introduction to the author entry are any name variations under which an author wrote, including transliterated forms for an author whose language uses a nonroman alphabet.

- The **Biographical and Critical Introduction** outlines the author's life and career, as well as the critical issues surrounding his or her work. References are provided to past volumes of *NCLC* in which further information about the author may be found.

- Most *NCLC* entries include a **Portrait** of the author. Many entries also contain reproductions of materials pertinent to an author's career, including manuscript pages, title pages, dust jackets, letters, and drawings, as well as photographs of important people, places, and events in an author's life.

- The list of **Principal Works** is chronological by date of first publication and identifies the genre of each work. In the case of foreign authors with both foreign-language publications and English translations, the English-language version is given in brackets. Unless otherwise indicated, dramas are dated by first performance, not first publication.

- **Criticism** in each author entry is arranged chronologically to provide a perspective on changes in critical evaluation over the years. All titles of works by the author featured in the entry are printed in boldface type to enable the user to easily locate discussion of particular works. Also for purposes of easier identification, the critic's name and the publication date of the essay are given at the beginning of each piece of criticism. Unsigned criticism is preceded by the title of the journal in which it appeared. Publication information (such as publisher names and book prices) and some parenthetical numerical references (such as page and line references to specific editions of works) have been deleted at the editors' discretion to provide smoother reading of the text. Footnotes that appear with previously published pieces of criticism are reprinted at the end of each essay or excerpt. In the case of excerpted criticism, only those footnotes that pertain to the excerpted text are included.

- A complete **Bibliographic Citation** provides original publication information for each piece of criticism.

- Critical excerpts are prefaced by **Annotations** providing the reader with a summary of the critical intent of the piece. Also included, when appropriate, is information about the critic's reputation, individual approach to literary criticism, and particular expertise in an author's works, as well as information about the relative importance of the critical excerpt. In some cases, the annotations cross-reference excerpts by critics who discuss each other's commentary.

- An annotated list of **Further Reading** appearing at the end of each entry suggests secondary sources on the author. In some cases it includes essays for which the editors could not obtain reprint rights.

Cumulative Indexes

■ Each volume of *NCLC* contains a cumulative **Author Index** listing all authors who have appeared in Gale's Literary Criticism Series, along with cross-references to such biographical series as *Contemporary Authors* and *Dictionary of Literary Biography.* Useful for locating authors within the various series, this index is particularly valuable for those authors who are identified with a certain period but who, because of their death dates, are placed in another, or for those authors whose careers span two periods. For example, Fyodor Dostoevsky is found in *NCLC,* yet Leo Tolstoy, another major nineteenth-century Russian novelist, is found in *TCLC* because he died after 1899.

■ Each *NCLC* volume includes a cumulative **Nationality Index** which lists all authors who have appeared in *NCLC*, arranged alphabetically under their respective nationalities.

■ Each new volume in Gale's Literary Criticism Series includes a cumulative **Topic Index**, which lists all literary topics treated in *NCLC, TCLC, LC 1400-1800*, and the *CLC* Yearbook.

■ Each new volume of *NCLC*, with the exception of the Topics volumes, contains a **Title Index** listing the titles of all literary works discussed in the volume. In response to numerous suggestions from librarians, Gale has also produced a **Special Paperbound Edition** of the *NCLC* title index. This annual cumulation lists all titles discussed in the series since its inception. Additional copies of the index are available on request. Librarians and patrons have welcomed this separate index: it saves shelf space, is easy to use, and is recyclable upon receipt of the following year's cumulation. Titles discussed in the Topics volume entries are not included in the *NCLC* cumulative index.

Citing *Nineteenth-Century Literature Criticism*

When writing papers, students who quote directly from any volume in Gale's Literary Criticism Series may use the following general forms to footnote reprinted criticism. The first example pertains to material drawn from periodicals, the second to material reprinted from books:

[1]T.S. Eliot, "John Donne," *The Nation and Athenaeum*, 33 (9 June 1923), 321-32; excerpted and reprinted in *Literature Criticism from 1400-1800,* Vol. 10, ed. James E. Person, Jr. (Detroit: Gale Research, 1989), pp. 28-9.

[2]Clara G. Stillman, *Samuel Butler: A Mid-Victorian Modern* (Viking Press, 1932); excerpted and reprinted in *Twentieth-Century Literary Criticism,* Vol. 33, ed. Paula Kepos (Detroit: Gale Research, 1989), pp. 43-5.

Suggestions Are Welcome

In response to suggestions, several features have been added to *NCLC* since the series began, including annotations to excerpted criticism, a cumulative index to authors in all Gale literary criticism series, entries devoted to criticism on a single work by a major author, more illustrations, and a title index listing all literary works discussed in the series.

Readers who wish to suggest authors, single works, or topics to appear in future volumes, or who have other suggestions, are cordially invited to write: The Editors, *Nineteenth-Century Literature Criticism,* 835 Penobscot Bldg., 645 Griswold St., Detroit, MI 48226-4094; call toll-free at 1-800-347-GALE; or fax to 1-313-961-6599.

Acknowledgments

The editors wish to thank the copyright holders of the excerpted criticism included in this volume and the permissions managers of many book and magazine publishing companies for assisting us in securing reproduction rights. We are also grateful to the staffs of the Detroit Public Library, the Library of Congress, the University of Detroit Mercy Library, Wayne State University Purdy/Kresge Library Complex, and the University of Michigan Libraries for making their resources available to us. Following is a list of the copyright holders who have granted us permission to reproduce material in this volume of. Every effort has been made to trace copyright, but if omissions have been made, please let us know.

PHOTOGRAPHS AND ILLUSTRATIONS APPEARING IN *NCLC,* VOLUME 67, WERE RECEIVED FROM THE FOLLOWING SOURCES:

Huxley, Thomas Henry (seated), sketch.—Huxley, Thomas Henry (head and shoulders), photograph. Archive Photos, Inc. Reproduced by permission.—Huxley, Thomas Henry (standing near table), photograph. Corbis-Bettmann. Reproduced by permission.—Huxley, Thomas Henry (seated with hands in lap), photograph. Corbis-Bettmann. Reproduced by permission.—Kant, Immanuel (head and shoulders), engraving. Corbis-Bettmann. Reproduced by permission.—Kant, Immanuel (seated at desk with quill pen in hand), engraving. Corbis-Bettmann. Reproduced by permission.—Kant, Immanuel (facing forward, head and shoulders), engraving. Archive Photos, Inc. Reproduced by permission.—Nerval, Gerard De (sitting, hands in lap), engraving. The Library of Congress.—Norcom, Dr. James, Sr., photograph. Courtesy of the North Carolina Division of Archives and History, Raleigh.

T. H. Huxley

1825-1895

English biologist, philosopher, social critic, lecturer, essayist, and nonfiction writer.

INTRODUCTION

Tenacious and articulate, Huxley became the Victorian era's popularizer of Darwinian evolution, the most fiercely debated issue of his generation. Called "Darwin's Bulldog," Huxley was one of the theory's first adherents and, in such works as *Evidence as to Man's Place in Nature*, made the first clear statements as to man's place in the evolutionary scheme.

Biographical Information

Born on May 4, 1825, in Ealing, Middlesex, near London, Thomas Henry Huxley was the seventh child of George Huxley, a rural schoolmaster. Although he received only two years of formal education during his childhood, he read science, history, and philosophy voraciously; by the time he received a medical apprenticeship to Charing Cross Hospital at the age of 15, he had mastered German, French, and Italian and had read Charles Lyell's *Principles of Geology* (1830-33), William Hamilton on logic, and much of Thomas Carlyle. After studying as a free scholar at Charing Cross, Huxley received top honors in chemistry, anatomy, and physiology and took his medical degree from the University of London in 1845, having published his first article—the identification of a structure in the human hair membrane, still known as Huxley's layer. At 21, he became assistant surgeon on the Royal Navy frigate the H. M. S. *Rattlesnake*, which charted the waters between the Great Barrier Reef and the Australian coast. During the nearly five-year journey Huxley collected and closely studied specimens of marine invertebrates. The research results were regularly contributed to the *Westminster Review* and, when he returned to England, Huxley found that he had become accepted into scientific circles. He became lecturer on natural history at London's School of Mines and shortly sent for and married his fianceé Henrietta Heathorn, whom he had met in Sydney, Australia.

In 1859, following the birth of his first son and after recovering from an illness which took him to Switzerland, Huxley finally saw the publication of *The Oceanic* Hydrozoa, a description of his observations during the *Rattlesnake* voyage. In that same year, in the

Proceedings of the Royal Society, he published his 1858 Croonian lecture, "On the Theory of the Vertebrate Skull," and was appointed secretary of the Geological Society. However, far more significant in terms of his long-term reputation were his 1859 and 1860 reviews of Darwin's *On the Origin of Species* in the London *Times* and *Westminster Review*. Darwin's book stated convictions toward which Huxley himself had been leaning, and it soon became a significant influence upon his career as a lecturer and writer. Huxley began publicly to advocate Darwin's theory of evolution. In June 1860 at the British Association meeting at Oxford, Huxley debated Archbishop Samuel Wilberforce, advancing Darwinian evolution as the best explanation for species-diversity, and in 1862 he gave a series of lectures on Darwin's theories to an audience of workingmen at the Royal School of Mines; shorthand notes of these lectures would later be published as *On Our Knowledge of the Causes of the Phenomena of Organic Nature* (1862).

The following decades showed his abilities as a preacher of the gospel of evolution coupled with a credo based upon a view toward traditional religious belief that Huxley called "agnostic"—a term coined by him to describe his position against holders of orthodox faith. In the decade following the publication of his first full-length book in 1863, *Evidence as to Man's Place in Nature*, Huxley found increasing popularity as a lecturer, educator, and public advocate for the emerging new science; this led to his winning numerous offices and honors and to the writing of several essays. One of his most significant achievements in 1864 was his helping to organize with eight fellow scientists, including John Tyndall, Joseph Hooker, and Herbert Spencer, a dinner group known as the X Club. For nearly thirty years they gathered before each meeting of the Royal Society to discuss and plan the politics for the advancement of English science. Known as the "inner cabinet of science," they virtually shaped the direction of scientific affairs in mid-Victorian England and insured continuing contact among eminent researchers and educators.

As Huxley became an eminent member of the scientific community, his commitments grew. In addition to his salaried appointments as inspector of salmon fisheries and as dean of the Royal College of Science, Huxley was also a fellow of the Royal Society, the Linnean Society, the Zoological Society, and the Royal College of Surgeons, as well as an honorary member or fellow of a dozen or more other scientific societies. At various times he was president of the Royal Society, the office that he ranked as his highest honor, of the Geological Society, the Paleontographical Society, the Ethnological Society, and the British Association. He was elected to London's first school board and served as a trustee of the British Museum, received the distinguished Copley and Darwin medals, and started a science column in the *Saturday Review* that gave rise to two influential journals, the *Natural History Review* and *Nature*.

In the midst of rapidly increasing professional responsibilities, including ongoing research and writing of textbooks, Huxley continued writing in such varied areas as biology and evolution, zoology, education reform, and politics. Recurring problems of ill health worsened, however, until 1885, when continuing illness forced his retirement from all official appointments. The writings that followed, such as *Evolution and Ethics* (1893), take on a pessimistic tone; this quality is noted by several modern critics, including James G. Paradis, who, in *T. H. Huxley: Man's Place in Nature* (1978), finds that Huxley's "philosophical outlook underwent a gradual transition from youthful Romanticism, . . . toward increasing determinism at mid-career, to his final and startling *fin de siècle* declaration, almost on his deathbed, that man's hope lay in his revolt against nature." Huxley supervised the publication of his *Collected Essays* during 1893 and 1894, preparing prefaces to each of the nine volumes, and died shortly afterward, on June 29, 1895.

Major Works

Huxley was a prolific writer whose contributions to Victorian culture and science span anatomy, marine biology, zoology, and paleontology, as well as philosophy, religion, education and politics. Throughout his career, he contributed substantially to facilitating the kind of scientific education he espoused through the publication of textbooks, such as his *A Manual of the Anatomy of Vertebrated Animals* (1871), which remained the standard text for over twenty-five years. But his *Evidence as to Man's Place in Nature* (1863), which appeared five years after Darwin's *Origin of Species*, is one of his most important and influential works. In it, Huxley combines comparative anatomy, embryology, and paleontology to demonstrate man's kinship with lower animals, especially apes. *Evidence as to Man's Place in Nature* extended Darwin's ideas in remarkably simple layman's language and, for the first time, explicitly applied evolutionary theory to human beings, which Darwin, for the most part, had avoided. Huxley attacked views such as those of Lamarck and Robert Chambers, but he also critiqued Darwin's view that evolution is a gradual process. Rather, Huxley thought that an evolving lineage may undergo rapid "saltations." One of the first to suggest the reptilian ancestors of modern day birds, Huxley claimed that such drastic shifts occurred in the descent of birds from dinosaurs.

Huxley also explored the ethical implications of his and Darwin's theories. His lecture "On the Physical Basis of Life," given before an Edinburgh audience at the heart of Scotch Presbyterianism, flatly rejects all theories of vitalism and spontaneity by declaring that all life forces are determined by chemical ones; a combination of elements produces protoplasm, the physical basis for life, and the mind itself is but "the result of molecular forces." However, he leaves the door open to ethical responsibility by declaring that apparent natural law is only a probability and that matter is unknown, subject to the skeptic's questioning. Indeed, later writings such as *Science and Morals* (1888) proclaim the unromantic view that morality actually resists the natural order, that it is "a real and living belief in that fixed order of nature which sends social disorganization on the track of immorality."

Critical Reception

Although he denied being a materialist and said that he used materialistic terminology only as a tool to express scientific ideas, Huxley faced criticism for seemingly implying the absence of ethical responsibility. Huxley frequently locked horns with the orthodox religious establishment and was known as the "bishop eater" for his provocative and challenging attacks on defenders of biblical literalism; many—most notably Dr. Henry Wace, Archbishop Wilberforce, and W. C. Magee, bishop of Peterborough—criticized his position on religion. But Huxley's strong impact upon English education and his effective leadership among his fellow scientists were recognized throughout his career. He was acquainted with such figures as Joseph Hooker, Charles Lyell, Herbert Spencer, and Charles Darwin, and his leadership in the English scientific community and as a popularizer of science shaped modern science and scientific practice.

PRINCIPAL WORKS

On the Educational Value of the Natural History Sciences (nonfiction) 1854
The Oceanic Hydrozoa: *A Description of the* Calycophoridae *and* Psysophoridea *Observed During the Voyage of H.M.S. "Rattlesnake," in the Years 1846-1850* (nonfiction) 1859
On Our Knowledge of the Causes of the Phenomena of Organic Nature (philosophical prose) 1862
Evidence as to Man's Place in Nature (philosophical prose) 1863
Elementary Atlas of Comparative Osteology (drawings) 1864
Lectures on the Elements of Comparative Anatomy (lectures) 1864
A Catalogue of the Collection of Fossils in the Museum of Practical Geology (catalogue) 1865
An Introduction to the Classification of Animals (nonfiction) 1869
Lay Sermons, Addresses and Reviews (essays) 1870
Lessons in Elementary Physiology (nonfiction) 1871
A Manual of the Anatomy of Vertebrated Animals (nonfiction) 1871
Critiques and Addresses (essays) 1873
A Course of Practical Instruction in Elementary Biology [with H. N. Martin] (nonfiction) 1875
The Evidence of the Miracle of Resurrection (philosophical prose) 1876
American Addresses, with a Lecture in the Study of Biology (lectures) 1877
A Manual of the Anatomy of Invertebrated Animals (nonfiction) 1877
Physiography: An Introduction to the Study of Nature (nonfiction) 1877
Hume (philosophical prose) 1878
The Crayfish: An Introduction to the Study of Zoology (nonfiction) 1879
Introductory Science Primer (nonfiction) 1880
Science and Culture, and Other Essays (essays) 1881
An Introduction to the Study of Zoology, Illustrated by the Crayfish (nonfiction) 1884
Science and Morals (philosophical prose) (1888)
The Advance of Science in the Last Half-Century (history) 1887

"Autobiography" (autobiography) 1890; published in *From Handel to Hallé: Biographical Sketches with Autobiographies of Professor Huxley and Professor Herkomer*
Social Diseases and Worse Remedies (philosophical prose) 1891
Essays on Some Controverted Questions (essays) 1892
Evolution and Ethics (philosophical prose) 1893
Collected Essays 9 vols. (essays) 1893-94
The Scientific Memoirs of T. H. Huxley 5 vols. (memoirs) 1898-1903
Life and Letters of Thomas Henry Huxley [edited by Leonard Huxley] (letters and memoirs) 1900
T. H. Huxley's Diary of the Voyage of H. M. S. Rattlesnake (diary) 1935

CRITICISM

Henry F. Osborn (essay date 1895)

SOURCE: "Memorial Tribute to Professor Thomas H. Huxley," in *Transactions of the New York Academy of Sciences*, Vol. XV, November 11, 1895, pp. 40-50.

[*In the following essay, Osborn surveys Huxley's career and pays tribute to his lasting influence.*]

All the members of this Academy, all men of science in America, in fact, are in different ways indebted to the late Professor Huxley. We would be ungrateful, indeed, especially in this section of the Academy, if we failed to join in the tributes which are being paid to him in different parts of the world.

In his memory I do not offer a formal address this evening, but as one of his students, would present some personal reminiscences of his characteristics as a teacher, and some of the most striking features of his life and work.

Huxley was born in 1825. Like Goethe, he inherited from his mother his brilliantly alert powers of thought, and from his father, his courage and tenacity of purpose, a combination of qualities which especially fitted him for the period in which he was to live. There is nothing striking recorded about his boyhood as a naturalist. He preferred engineering, but was led into medicine.

At the close of his medical course he secured a navy medical post upon the "Rattlesnake." This brought with it, as to Darwin, the training of a four years voyage to the South Seas off eastern Australia and west Guinea—a more liberal education to a naturalist than any university affords, even at the present day. This voyage began at twenty-one, and he says of it: "But, apart from experience of this kind and the opportunity offered for scientific work to me, personally, the cruise was extremely valuable. It was good for me to live under sharp discipline, to be down on the realities of existence by living on bare necessities, to find out how extremely worth living life seemed to be, when one woke from a night's rest on a soft plank, with the sky for a canopy and cocoa and weevily biscuit the sole prospect for breakfast, and more especially to learn to work for what I got for myself out of it. My brother officers were as good as sailors ought to be and generally are, but naturally, they neither knew nor cared anything about my pursuits, nor understood why I should be so zealous in the pursuit of the objects which my friends, the middies, christened 'Buffons,' after the title conspicuous on a volume of the *'Suites a Buffon,'* which stood in a prominent place on my shelf in the chart-room."

As the result of this voyage of four years numerous papers were sent home to the Linnæan Society of London, but few were published; upon his return, his first work, *Upon the Anatomy and Affinities of the Medusæ,* was declined for publication by the Admiralty; a fortunate circumstance, for it led to his quitting the navy for good and trusting to his own resources. Upon publication (1849) this memoir at once established his scientific reputation at the early age of twenty-four, just as Richard Owen had won his spurs by his 'Memoir on the Pearly Nautilus.' In 1852 Huxley's preference as a biologist was to turn back to physiology, which had become his favorite study in the medical course. But his fate was to enter and become distinguished in a widely different branch which had as little attraction for him as for most students of marine life, namely, palæontology. He says of this sudden change of base:

"At last, in 1854, on the translation of my warm friend, Edward Forbes, to Edinburgh, Sir Henry de la Beche, the Director General of the Geological Survey, offered me the post Forbes had vacated of Palæontologist and Lecturer on Natural History. I refused the former point-blank, and accepted the latter only provisionally, telling Sir Henry that I did not care for fossils and that I should give up natural history as soon as I could get a physiological post. But I held the office for thirty-one years and a large part of my work has been palæontological."

From this time until 1885 his labors extended over the widest field of biology and of philosophy ever covered by any naturalist, with the single exception of Aristotle. In philosophy Huxley showed rare critical and historical power; he made the most exhaustive study of Hume, but his own philosophical spirit and temper was more directly the offspring of Descartes. Some subjects he mastered, others he merely touched, but every subject which he wrote about he illuminated. Huxley did not

discover or first define protoplasm, but he made it known to the English-speaking world as the physical basis of life—recognizing the unity of animal and plant protoplasm. He cleared up certain problems among the *Protozoa.* In 1849 appeared his great work upon the oceanic *Hydrozoa,* and familiarity with these forms, doubtless suggested the brilliant comparison of the two-layered gastrula to the adult hydrozoa. He threw light upon the Tunicata, describing the endostyle as a universal feature, but not venturing to raise the Tunicata to a separate order. He set in order the cephalopod mollusca, deriving the spiral from the straight shelled fossil forms. He contributed to the Arthropoda; his last word upon this group being his charming little volume upon the "Crayfish," a model of its kind. But think of the virgin field which opened up before him among the vertebrata, when in 1859 he was the first to perceive the truth of Darwin's theory of descent. Here were Cuvier's and Owen's vast researches upon living and extinct forms, a disorderly chaos of facts waiting for generalization. Huxley was the man for the time. He had already secured a thoroughly philosophical basis for his comparative osteology by studying the new embryology of Von Baer, which Richard Owen had wholly ignored. In 1858 his famous Croonian lecture on the **"Theory of the Vertebrate Skull,"** gave the death blow to Owen's life work upon the skull and vertebral archetype, and to the whole system of mystical and transcendental anatomy; and now Huxley set to work vigorously to build out of Owen's scattered tribes the great limbs and branches of the vertebrate tree. He set the fishes and batrachia apart as the *Icthyopsidan* branch, the reptiles and birds as the *Sauropsidan* in contrast with the *Mammalian,* which he derived from a pro-sauropsidan or amphibian stem, a theory which with some modification has received strong recent verification.

Prof. Owen, who had held undisputed sway in England up to 1858, fought nobly for opinions which had been idolized in the first half century, but was routed at every point. Huxley captured his last fortress, when, in his famous essay of 1865, **"Man's Place in Nature,"** he undermined Owen's teaching of the separate and distinct anatomical position of Man. We can only appreciate Huxley's fighting qualities when we see how strongly Owen was intrenched at the beginning of this long battle royal; he was director of the British Museum and occupied other high posts; he had the strong moral support of the government and of the royal family, although these were weak allies in a scientific encounter.

Huxley's powers of rapid generalization of course betrayed him frequently; his *Bathybius* was a groundless and short lived hypothesis; he went far astray upon the phylogeny of the horses. But these and other errors were far less attributable to defects in his reasoning powers than to the extraordinarily high pressure under which he worked for the twenty years between 1860 and 1880, when duties upon the Educational Board, upon the Government Fisheries Commission and upon Parliamentary committees crowded upon him. He had at his command none of the resources of modern technique. He cut his own sections. I remember once seeing some of his microscopic sections. To one of our college junior students working with a Minot microtome Huxley's sections would have appeared like a translucent beefsteak—another illustration that it is not always the section which reveals the natural law, but the man who looks at the section.

Huxley was not only a master in the search for truth, but in the way in which he presented it, both in writing and in speaking. And we are assured, largely as he was gifted by nature, his beautifully lucid and interesting style was partly the result of deliberate hard work. He was not born to it; some of his early essays are very labored; he acquired it. He was familiar with the best Greek literature and restudied the language; he pored over Milton and Carlyle and Mill; he studied the fine old English of the Bible; he took as especial models Hume and Hobbes, until finally he wrote his mother tongue as no other Englishman wrote it. Take up any one of his essays, biological, literary, philosophical, you at once see his central idea and his main purpose, although he never uses italics or spaced letters as many of our German masters do to relieve the obscurity of their sentences. We are carried along upon the broad current of his reasoning without being confused by his abundant side illustrations. He gleaned from the literature of all time until his mind was stocked with apt similes. Who but Huxley would have selected the title **"Lay Sermons,"** for his first volume of addresses; or, in 1880, twenty-one years after Darwin's work appeared, would have entitled his essay upon the influence of this work: **"The Coming of Age of the Origin of species."** Or to whom else would it have occurred to repeat over the grave of Balfour the exquisitely appropriate lines: "We mourn for Lycidas—Dead before his prime." Who else could have inveighed thus against modern specialization: "We are in the case of Tarpeia, who opened the gates of the Roman citadel to the Sabines and was crushed by the weight of the reward bestoyed upon her. It has become impossible for any man to keep pace with the progress of the whole of any important branch of science. It looks as if the scientific, like other revolutions, meant to devour its own children; as if the growth of science tended to overwhelm its votaries; as if the man of science of the future were condemned to diminish into a narrower specialist as time goes on. It appears to me that the only defense against this tendency to the degeneration of scientific workers lies in the organization and extension of scientific education in such a manner as to secure breadth of culture without superficiality; and, on the other hand, depth and precision of knowledge without narrowness."

Huxley's public addresses always gave the impression of being largely impromptu, but he once told me; "I always think out carefully every word I am going to say. There is no greater danger than the so-called *inspiration of the moment,* which leads you to say something which is not exactly true, or which you would regret afterward. I sometimes envy your countrymen their readiness and believe that a native American, if summoned out of bed at midnight, could step to his window and speak well upon any subject." I told him I feared he had been slightly misinformed; I feared that many American impromptu speeches were more distinguished by a flow of language than of ideas. But Huxley was sometimes very impressive when he did not speak. In 1879 he was strongly advocating the removal of the Royal School of Mines from crowded Jermyn Street to South Kensington, a matter which is still being agitated. At a public dinner given by the alumni of the School, who were naturally attached to the old buildings, the chairman was indiscreet enough to make an attack upon the policy of removal. He was vigorously applauded, when, to every one's consternation, Huxley, who was sitting at the chairman's right, slowly rose, paused a moment, and then silently skirted the tables and walked out of the hall. A solemn pall fell over the remainder of the dinner and we were all glad to find an excuse to leave early.

In personal conversation Huxley was full of humor and greatly enjoyed stories at his own expense. Such was the following: "In my early period as a lecturer I had very little confidence in my general powers, but one thing I prided myself upon was clearness. I was once talking of the brain before a large, mixed audience and soon began to feel that no one in the room understood me. Finally I saw the thoroughly interested face of a woman auditor and took consolation in delivering the remainder of the lecture directly to her. At the close, my feeling as to her interest was confirmed when she came up and asked if she might put one question upon a single point which she had not quite understood. 'Certainly,' I replied. 'Now Professor,' she said, 'is the cerebellum inside or outside of the skull?'" A story of his about babies is also characteristic: "When a fond mother calls upon me to admire her baby I never fail to respond, and, while cooing appropriately, I take advantage of an opportunity to gently ascertain whether the soles of its feet turn in and tend to support my theory of arboreal descent."

Huxley as a teacher can never be forgotten by any of his students. He entered his lecture room promptly as the clock was striking nine, rather quickly and with his head bent forward "as if oppressive with its mind." He usually glanced attention to his class of about ninety and began speaking before he reached his chair. He spoke between his lips, but with perfectly clear analysis, with thorough interest and with philosophic insight, which was far above the average of his students.

He used very few charts, but handled the chalk with great skill, sketching out the anatomy of an animal as if it were a transparent object. As in Darwin's face, and as in Erasmus Darwin's or Buffon's, and many other anatomists with a strong sense of form, his eyes were heavily overhung by a projecting forehead and eyebrows and seemed at times to look inward. His lips were firm and closely set, with the expression of positiveness, and the other feature which most marked him was the very heavy mass of hair falling over his forehead, which he would frequently stroke or toss back. Occasionally he would lighten up the monotony of anatomical description by a bit of humor. I remember one instance which was probably reminiscent of his famous tilt with Bishop Wilberforce at the meeting of the British Association in 1860. Huxley was describing the mammalian heart and had just distinguished between the tricuspid valve on the right side of the heart and the bicuspid valve on the left, which you know resembles a bishop's mitre, and hence is known as the mitral valve. He said, "It is not easy to recall on which side these respective valves are found, but I recommend this rule; you can easily remember that the mitral is on the left, because a bishop is never known to be on the right."

Huxley was the father of modern laboratory instruction, but in 1879 he was so intensely engrossed with his own researches that he very seldom came through the laboratory, which was ably directed by T. Jeffrey Parker, assisted by Howes and W. Newton Parker, all of whom are now professors, Howes having succeeded to Huxley's chair. Each visit therefore inspired a certain amount of terror, which was really unwarranted, for Huxley always spoke in the kindest tones to his students, although sometimes he could not resist making fun at their expense. There was an Irish student who sat in front of me, whose anatomical drawings in water color were certainly most remarkable productions. Huxley, in turning over his drawing-book, paused at a large blur under which was carefully inscribed "sheeps' liver" and smilingly said, "I am glad to know that is a liver; it reminds me as much of Cologne cathedral in a fog, as of anything I have ever seen before." Fortunately the nationality of the student enabled him to fully appreciate the humor.

The greatest event in the winter of 1879 was Darwin's first and only visit to the laboratory. They came in together, Huxley leading slowly down the long narrow room, pointing out the especial methods of teaching which he had originated and which are now universally adopted in England and in this country. Darwin was instantly recognized by the class as he entered and sent a thrill of curiosity down the room, for no one present had ever seen him before. There was the widest possible contrast in the two faces. Darwin's grayish-white hair and bushy eyebrows overshadowed the pair of deeply-set blue eyes, which seemed to image his wonderfully calm and deep vision of nature, and at the same time to emit benevolence. Huxley's piercing black eyes and determined and resolute face were full of admiration, and at the same time protection of his older friend. He said afterwards, "you know I have to take care of him, in fact I have always been Darwin's bulldog," and this exactly expressed one of the many relations which existed so long between the two men.

Huxley was not always fortunate in the intellectual calibre of the men to whom he lectured in the Royal School of Mines. Many of the younger generation were studying in the universities, under Balfour at Cambridge and under Rolleston at Oxford. However, Saville Kent, C. Lloyd Morgan, George B. Howes, T. Jeffrey Parker and W. Newton Parker are representative biologists who were wholly trained by Huxley. Many others, not his students, have expressed the deepest indebtedness to him. Among these especially are Prof. E. Ray Lankester, of Oxford, and Prof. Michael Foster, of Cambridge. Huxley once said that he had "discovered Foster." He not only singled men out, but knew how to direct and inspire them to investigate the most pressing problems of the day. As it was, his thirty-one years of lectures would have produced a far greater effect if they had been delivered from an Oxford, Cambridge or Edinburgh chair. In fact, Huxley's whole life would have been different, in some ways more effective, in others less so, if the universities had welcomed the young genius who was looking for a post and even cast his eyes toward America in 1850, but in those early days of classical prestige both seats of learning were dead to the science, which it was Huxley's great service in support of Darwin to place beside physics, in the lead of all others in England. Moreover, Oxford, if not Cambridge, could not long have sheltered such a wolf in the fold.

What Haeckel did for evolution in Germany, Huxley did in England. As the earliest and most ardent supporter of Darwin and the theory of descent, it is remarkable that he never gave an unreserved support to the theory of natural selection as all-sufficient. Twenty-five years ago, with his usual penetration and prophetic insight, he showed that the problem of variation might, after all, be the greater problem; and only three years ago, in his **"Romanes Lecture,"** he disappointed many of the disciples of Darwin by declaring that natural selection failed to explain the origin of our moral and ethical nature. Whether he was right or wrong, we will not stop to discuss, but consider the still more remarkable conditions of Huxley's relations to the theory of evolution. As expositor, teacher, defender, he was the high priest of evolution. From the first he saw the strong and weak points of the special Darwinian theory; he wrote upon the subject for thirty years, and yet he never contributed a single original or novel idea to it; in other words, Huxley added vastly to the demonstration, but never added to the sum of either theory or working hypothesis, and the contemporary history of the theory proper could be written without mentioning his name. This lack of speculation upon the factors of evolution was true throughout his whole life; in the voyage of the "Rattlesnake" he says he did not even think of the species problem. His last utterance regarding the causes of evolution appeared in one of the Reviews as a passing criticism of Weismann's finished philosophy, in which he implies that his own philosophy of the causes of evolution was as far off as ever; in other words, Huxley never fully made up his mind or committed himself to any causal theory of development.

Taking the nineteenth century at large, outside of our own circles of biology, Huxley's greatest and most permanent achievement was his victory for free thought. Personally we may not be agnostic; we may disagree with much that he has said and written, but we must admire Huxley's valiant services none the less. A reformer must be an extremist, and Huxley was often extreme, but he never said what he did not believe to be true. If it is easy for you and for me to say what we think in print and out of print now, it is because of the battles fought by such men as Huxley and Haeckel. When Huxley began his great crusade the air was full of religious intolerants, and, what is quite as bad, scientific shams. If Huxley had entered the contest carefully and guardedly he would have been lost in the enemies ranks, but he struck right and left with sledge hammer blows whether it was a high dignity of the Church or of the State. Just before the occasion of one of his greatest contests, that with Gladstone in the pages of the *Contemporary Review,* Huxley was in Switzerland, completely broken down in health and suffering from torpidity of the liver. Gladstone had written one of his characteristically brilliant articles upon the close correspondence between the Order of Creation as revealed in the first chapter of Genesis and the Order of Evolution as shown by modern biology. "When this article reached me," Huxley told me, "I read it through and it made me so angry that I believe it must have acted upon my liver. At all events, when I finished my reply to Gladstone I felt better than I had for months past."

Huxley's last public appearance was at the meeting of the British Association at Oxford. He had been very urgently invited to attend, for, exactly a quarter of a century before, the Association had met at Oxford and Huxley had had his famous encounter with Bishop Wilberforce. It was felt that the anniversary would be an historic one and incomplete without his presence, and so it proved to be. Huxley's especial duty was to second the vote of thanks for the Marquis of Salisbury's address—one of the invariable formalities of the opening meeting of the Association. The meeting proved to be the greatest one in the history of the Association. The Sheldonian theatre was packed with one of the most distinguished scientific audiences ever brought

together, and the address of the Marquis was worthy of the occasion. The whole tenor of it was the unknown in Science. Passing from the unsolved problems of Astronomy, Chemistry and Physics, he came to Biology. With delicate irony he spoke of the *"comforting word, evolution,"* and passing to the Weismannian controversy implied that the diametrically opposed views so frequently expressed nowadays threw the whole process of evolution into doubt. It was only too evident that the Marquis himself found no comfort in Evolution, and even entertained a suspicion as to its probability. It was well worth the whole journey to Oxford to watch Huxley during this portion of the address. In his red doctor-of-laws gown, placed upon his shoulders by the very body of men who had once referred to him as "a Mr. Huxley," he sank deeper into his chair upon the very front of the platform and restlessly tapped his foot. His situation was an unenviable one. He had to thank an ex-Prime Minister of England and present Lord Chancellor of Oxford University for an address the sentiments of which were directly against those he himself had been maintaining for twenty-five years. He said afterwards that when the proofs of the Marquis's address were put in his hands the day before he realized that he had before him a most delicate and difficult task. Lord Kelvin (Sir William Thompson), one of the most distinguished living physicists, first moved the vote of thanks, but his reception was nothing to the tremendous applause which greeted Huxley in the heart of that University whose cardinal principles he had so long been opposing. Considerable anxiety had been felt by his friends lest his voice would fail to fill the theatre, for it had signally failed during his Romanes Lecture delivered in Oxford the year before, but when Huxley arose he reminded you of a venerable gladiator returning to the arena after years of absence. He raised his figure and his voice to its full height, and, with one foot turned over the edge of the step, veiled an unmistakable and vigorous protest in the most gracious and dignified speech of thanks.

Throughout the subsequent special sessons of this meeting Huxley could not appear. He gave the impression of being aged but not infirm, and no one realized that he had spoken his last word as champion of the law of Evolution. He soon returned to Eastbourne. Early in the winter he contracted the grippe, which passed into pneumonia. He rallied once or twice and his last effort to complete a reply to Balfour's "Foundations of Belief" hastened his death, which came upon June 29th, at the age of seventy.

I have endeavored to show in how many ways Huxley was a model for us of the younger generation. In the central hall of the British Museum of Natural History sits in marble the life size figure of Charles Darwin; upon his right will soon be placed a beautiful statue of Richard Owen, and I know that there are many who will enjoy taking some share in the movement to complete this group with the noble figure of Thomas Henry Huxley.

P. Chalmers Mitchell (essay date 1900)

SOURCE: "Citizen, Orator, and Essayist," in *Thomas Henry Huxley: A Sketch of His Life and Work,* G. P. Putnam's Sons, 1900, pp. 204-17.

[*In the essay that follows, Mitchell examines Huxley's rhetorical style and his involvement in scientific organizations.*]

A great body of fine work in science and literature has been produced by persons who may be described as typically academic. Such persons confine their interest in life within the boundaries of their own immediate pursuits; they are absorbed so completely by their avocations that the hurly-burly of the world seems needlessly distracting and a little vulgar. No doubt the thoughts of those who cry out most loudly against disturbance by the intruding claims of the world are, for the most part, hardly worth disturbing; the attitude to extrinsic things of those who are absorbed by their work is aped not infrequently by those who are absorbed only in themselves. None the less it is important to recognise that a genuine aversion from affairs is characteristic of many fine original investigators, and it is on such persons that the idea of the simple and childlike nature of philosophers, a simplicity often reaching real incapacity for the affairs of life, is based. There was no trace of this natural isolation in the character of Huxley. He was not only a serious student of science but a keen and zealous citizen, eagerly conscious of the great social and political movements around him, with the full sense that he was a man living in society with other men and that there was a business of life as well as a business of the laboratory. We have seen with what zeal he brought his trained intelligence to bear not only on his own province of scientific education, but on the wider problems of general education, and yet the time he gave to these was only a small part of that which he spared from abstract science for affairs. In scientific institutions as in others, there is always a considerable amount of business, involving the management of men and the management of money, and Huxley's readiness and aptitude led to his being largely occupied with these. For many years he was Dean of the Royal College of Science at South Kensington, and for a considerable time he served the Geological Society and the Royal Society as secretary. In all these posts, Huxley displayed great capacity as a leader of men and as a manager of affairs, and contributed largely to the successful working of the institutions which he served.

In England, when troublesome questions press and seem to call for new legislation, it frequently happens that the collection and sifting of evidence preliminary to legislation is a task for which the methods and routine of Parliament are unsuitable. The Queen, acting through her responsible advisers, appoints a Royal Commission, consisting of a small body of men, to which is entrusted the preliminary task of collecting and weighing evidence, or of making recommendations on evidence already collected. To such honourable posts Huxley was repeatedly called. He served on the following Commissions: 1. Royal Commission on the Operation of Acts relating to Trawling for Herrings on the Coast of Scotland, 1862. 2. Royal Commission to Enquire into the Sea Fisheries of the United Kingdom, 1864-65. 3. Commission on the Royal College of Science for Ireland, 1866. 4. Commission on Science and Art Instruction in Ireland, 1868. 5. Royal Commission on the Administration and Operation of the Contagious Diseases Acts, 1870-71. 6. Royal Commission on Scientific Instruction and the Advancement of Science, 1870-75. 7. Royal Commission on the Practice of Subjecting Live Animals to Experiments for Scientific Purposes, 1876. 8. Royal Commission to Enquire into the Universities of Scotland, 1876-78. 9. Royal Commission on the Medical Acts, 1881-82. 10. Royal Commission on Trawl, Net, and Beam-Trawl Fishing, 1884. This is a great record for any man, especially for one in whose life work of this kind was outside his habitual occupation. It was no doubt in special recognition of the important services given his country by such work, as well as in general recognition of his distinction in science, that he was sworn a member of Her Majesty's Privy Council, so attaining a distinction more coveted than the peerage.

The voluminous reports of the Commissions shew that Huxley, very far from being a silent member of them, took a large part in framing the questions which served to direct witnesses into useful lines, and that his clear and orderly habit of thought proved as useful in the elucidation of these subjects as they were in matters of scientific research. For the most part, the problems brought before the Commissions have lost their interest for readers of later years, but there are matters still unsettled on which the opinions of Huxley as expressed then remain useful. The Commission of 1876, for instance, dealt with vivisection, a matter on which the conscience of the ordinary man is not yet at rest. Although Huxley was intensely interested in the problems of physiology, and although at one time he hoped to devote his life to them, fortune directed otherwise, and the investigations for which he is famed did not in any way involve the kind of experiments known as vivisection. The greater part of his work was upon the remains of creatures dead for thousands of years or upon the lifeless skeletons of modern forms. On the other hand, he was keenly interested in the progress of physiological science, he had personal acquaintance with most of the distinguished workers in physiology of his time at home and abroad, and from this knowledge of their character and aspirations he was well able to judge of the wholesale and reckless accusations brought against them. He was a man full of the finest humanity, with an unusual devotion to animals as pets, and with knowledge of the degrees of pain involved in experimenting on living creatures. He insisted strongly on the necessity of limiting or abolishing pain, where-ever it was possible; he agreed that any experiments which involved pain should not be permitted for the purpose of demonstrating known elementary facts. But, from his knowledge of the incalculable benefits which had been gained from experimental research, and from his confidence in those who conducted it, he declined to give support to the misguided fanatics who desired to make such experimental research a penal offence, even when conducted by the most skilled experts for the highest purposes.

Huxley contributed his share to the great questions which agitated the public not only by service on Commissions, but by delivering a large number of public addresses and writing a large number of essays on topics of special interest. Much of his work on scientific, educational, and general subjects took its first shape in the form of addresses given to some public audience. University audiences in England, Scotland, and America were familiar to him, and from time to time he addressed large gatherings of a mixed character. But probably his favourite audience was composed of working men, and he had the greatest respect for the intelligence and sympathy of hearers who like himself passed the greater portion of their time in hard work. Professor Howes, his pupil, friend, and successor, writes of him:

> He gave workmen of his best. The substance of *Man's Place in Nature,* one of the most successful and popular of his writings, and of his *Crayfish,* perhaps the most perfect zoölogical treatise ever published, was first communicated to them. In one of the last communications I had with him, I asked his views as to the desirability of discontinuing the workmen's lectures at Jermyn Street, since the development of workmen's colleges and institutes was regarded by some as rendering their continuance unnecessary. He replied, almost with indignation, 'With our central situation and resources we ought to be in a position to give the workmen that which they cannot get elsewhere,' adding that he would deeply deplore any such discontinuance.

Huxley had no natural facility for speech. He tells us that at first he disliked it, and that he had a firm conviction that he would break down every time he opened his mouth. The only two possible faults of a public speaker which he believed himself to be without, were "talking at random and indulging in rhetoric." With practice, he lost this earlier hesitancy, and before long became known as one of the finest speakers of his time. Certain natural gifts aided him; his well-set fig-

ure and strong features, of which the piercing eyes and firm, trap-like mouth were the most striking, riveted attention, while his voice had a wide range and was beautifully modulated. But it was above all things the matter and not the manner of his speech that commanded success. He cared little or nothing for the impression he might make—everything for the ideas which he wished to convey. He was concerned only to set forth these ideas in their clear and logical order, convinced in his own mind that, were the facts as he knew them placed before the minds of his hearers, only one possible result could follow. The facts had convinced him: they must equally convince any honest and intelligent person placed in possession of them. He had not the smallest intention of overbearing by authority or of swaying by skilfully aroused emotion. Such weapons of the orator seemed to him dishonest in the speaker and most perilous to the audience. For him, speaking on any subject was merely a branch of scientific exposition; when emotion was to be roused or enthusiasm to be kindled the inspiration was to come from the facts and not from the orator. The arts he allowed himself were those common to all forms of exposition; he would explain a novel set of ideas by comparison with simpler ideas obvious to all his listeners; and he sought to arrest attention or to drive home a conclusion by some brilliant phrase that bit into the memory. These two arts, the art of the phrase-maker and the art of explaining by vivacious and simple comparison, he brought to a high perfection. The fundamental method of his exposition was simply the method of comparative anatomy, the result of a habit of thinking which makes it impossible to have any set of ideas brought into the mind without an immediate, almost unconscious, overhauling of the memory for any other ideas at all congruous. In a strict scientific exposition Huxley would choose from the multitude of possible comparisons that most simple and most intelligible to his audience; when in a lighter vein, he gave play to a natural humour in his choice. Instances of his method of exposition by comparison abound in his published addresses. Let us take one or two. In the course of an address to a large mixed audience so early in his public career as 1854, in making plain to them the proposition, somewhat novel for those days, that the natural history sciences had an educational value, he explained that the faculties employed in that subject were simply those of the common sense of every-day life.

> The vast results obtained by Science are won by no mystical faculties, by no mental processes other than those which are practised by every one of us, in the humblest and meanest affairs of life. A detective policeman discovers a burglar from the marks made by his shoe, by a mental process identical with that by which Curvier restored the extinct animals of Montmartre from fragments of their bones. Nor does that process of induction and deduction by which a

lady, finding a stain of a peculiar kind on her dress, concludes that somebody has upset the inkstand thereon, differ in any way, in kind, from that by which Adams and Leverrier discovered a new planet.

In one of his addresses to working men on ***Man's Place in Nature*** he shewed that from time to time in the history of the world average persons of the human race have accepted some kind of answer to the insoluble riddles of existence, but that from time to time the race has outgrown the current answers, ceasing to take comfort from them.

> In a well-worn metaphor a parallel is drawn between the life of man and the metamorphosis of a caterpillar into a butterfly; but the comparison may be more just as well as more novel, if for its former term we take the mental progress of the race. History shews that the human mind, fed by constant accessions of knowledge, periodically grows too large for its theoretical coverings, and bursts them asunder to appear in new habiliments, as the feeding and growing grub, at intervals, casts its too narrow skin and assumes another, itself but temporary. Truly, the imago state of man seems to be terribly distant, but every moult is a step gained, and of such there have been many.

As another instance, the following from his address on a **"Liberal Education"** may be taken. He had been discussing the intellectual advantage to be derived from classical studies, and had been comparing, to the disadvantage of the latter, the intellectual discipline which might be got from a study of fossils with the discipline claimed by the ordinary experts upon education to be the results of classical training. He wished to anticipate the obvious objection to his argument: that the subject-matter of palæontology had no direct bearing on human interests and emotions, while the classical authors were rich in the finest humanity.

> But it will be said that I forget the beauty and the human interest, which appertain to classical studies. To this I reply that it is only a very strong man who can appreciate the charms of landscape as he is toiling up a steep hill, along a bad road. What with short-windedness, stones, ruts, and a pervading sense of the wisdom of rest and be thankful, most of us have little enough sense of the beautiful under these circumstances. The ordinary schoolboy is precisely in this case. He finds Parnassus uncommonly steep, and there is no chance of his having much time or inclination to look about him till he gets to the top. And nine times out of ten he does not get to the top.

The last example we shall take comes from a speech made after dinner at a much later period of his life. The occasion was a complimentary dinner to the editor of the English scientific periodical *Nature,* which had been for long the leading semi-popular journal of En-

glish science. Huxley, in proposing the health of the editor, declared that he did not quite know how to say what he wanted to say, but that he would explain by a story.

> A poor woman . . . was brought into one of our hospitals in a shockingly battered condition. When her wounds had been cleaned and sewn, and when the care of the surgeons had restored her to comparative comfort, someone said to her, 'I am afraid your husband has been knocking you about.' 'What!' she said, 'my Jim bash me? no it worn't by him; he's always been more like a friend to me than a husband.' That . . . is what I wish to say about our guest of to-night. In all our intercourse with him he has been more like a friend to us than an editor.

It is impossible to make a real distinction between the essays and the addresses of Huxley. Many of the most important of his addresses, as for instance his Romanes lecture on **"Evolution and Ethics,"** were written and printed before he delivered them; most of them were carefully prepared, and revised and printed after delivery. It is therefore not remarkable to find a close resemblance in matter and manner between what was originally spoken and what was published without a *vivâ voce* delivery. Everything that may be said of the one set applies with an equal fitness to the other set. There are many who assert with confidence that Huxley is one of the great masters of English, and although an examination of this opinion involves discussion of the elusive quality termed "style," it is necessary to attempt it.

In that totality which consists of an essay or of a printed address, and of which we are, most of us, ready to discuss the style, there are at least three separable elements, each contributing after its kind to the effect on our minds. When the general effect is to throw us into a state of pleasure, it is our habit to qualify the style with an adjective of praise, selecting the adjective according to the degree of restraint or of enthusiasm with which we are accustomed to express our emotions; when the general effect is to throw us into a condition of boredom or of distaste, we make a corresponding choice of appropriate adjectives. When we wish to be specially critical we pass a little way beyond an empirical judgment by pleasure or annoyance and take into account the degree of harmony between matter and manner. In such a frame of mind we discount the pleasure obtained from verbal quips, if these occur in a grave exposition, or that received from solemn and stately harmonies of language if these be employed on insignificant trifles. In a condition of unusual critical exaltation we may even admit an excellence of language and phrasing though these have as their contents ideas which we dislike, or press towards conclusions from which we dissent. But if we desire to make an exact appreciation of literary style, it is requisite to examine separately the three elements which contribute to the effect produced on us by any written work. These three elements are the words or raw materials employed, the building of words into sentences and of sentences into paragraphs, which may be designated as the architectural work, and, finally, the ideas conveyed, that is to say, the actual object of the writing.

Huxley was a wide and omnivorous reader, and so had an unusually large fund of words at his disposal. His writings abound with quotations and allusions taken from the best English authors, and he had a profound and practical belief in the advantage to be gained from the reading of English. "If a man," he wrote, "cannot get literary culture out of his Bible, and Chaucer, and Shakespeare, and Milton, and Hobbes, and Bishop Berkeley, to mention only a few of our illustrious writers—I say, if he cannot get it out of these writers, he cannot get it out of anything." He had at least a fair knowledge of Greek in the original, and a very wide acquaintance with Greek phrasing and Greek ideas derived from a study of Greek authors in English versions. He had an unusual knowledge of Latin, both of the classical writers and of the early Church fathers and mediæval writers on science and metaphysics. French and German, the two foreign languages which are a necessary part of the mental equipment of an English-speaking man of science, were familiar to him. Finally, he had of necessity the wide and varied vocabulary of the natural and technical sciences at his disposal. From these varied sources, Huxley had a fund of words, a store of the raw material for expressing ideas, very much greater and more varied than that in the possession of most writers. You will find in his writings abundant and omnipresent evidence of the enormous wealth of verbal material ready for the ideas he wished to set forth: a Greek phrase, a German phrase, a Latin or French phrase, or a group of words borrowed from one of our own great writers always seemed to await his wish. General Booth's scheme for elevating the masses by cymbals and dogma was "corybantic Christianity"; to explain what he thought was the Catholic attitude to the doctrine of evolution, he said it would have been called *damnabilis* by Father Suarez, and that he would have meant "not that it was to be damned, but that it was an active principle capable of damning." Huxley was like a builder who did not limit himself while he was constructing a house to the ordinary materials from the most convenient local quarry, but who collected endlessly from all the quarries and brickfields of the world, and brought to his heaps curiously wrought stones taken from a thousand old buildings. The swift choice from such a varied material gave an ease and appearance of natural growth to his work; it produced many surprising and delightful combinations, and it never sacrificed convenience of expression to exigencies of the materials for expression. On the other hand, Huxley lacked the sedulous concern for words themselves as things valuable and delightful; the de-

light of the craftsman in his tools; the dainty and respectful tribute paid to the words themselves; in fine, he took little pleasure in words themselves and used them as counters rather than as coins. Careful reflection and examination will make it plain that the pleasure to be got from Huxley's style is not due in any large measure to his choice and handling of words. There is no evidence that he deliberately and fastidiously preferred one word to another, that he took delight in the savour of individual words, in the placing of plain words in a context to make them sparkle, in the avoidance of some, in the deliberate preference of other words,—in fact, in all the conscious tricks and graces that distinguish the lover of words from their mere user.

A close examination discovers a similar absence from Huxley's work of the second contributory to the total effect produced by written words. Anything that may be said about absence of artistry in the use of words, may be said as to absence of artistry in building of the words into sentences, of the sentences into paragraphs and pages. In the first place, actual infelicities of sentence-building are frequent. Clause is piled on clause, qualifying phrases are interpolated, the easy devices of dashes and repetitions are employed wherever convenience suggests them. It is striking to find how infrequent is the occurrence of passages marked in any way by sonorous rhythm or by the charm of a measured proportion. The purple passages themselves, those which linger in the memory and to which the reader turns back, linger by their sense and not by their sound. For indeed the truth of the matter is that Huxley's style was a style of ideas and not of words and sentences. The more closely you analyse his pages the more certainly you find that the secret of the effect produced on you lies in the gradual development of the precise and logical ideas he wished to convey, in the brilliant accumulation of argument upon argument, in the logical subordination of details to the whole, in fact, in the arts of the convinced, positive, and logical thinker, who knew exactly what he meant you to know and who set about telling you it with the least possible concern for the words he used or for the sentences into which he formed his words. The ideas and their ordering are the root and the branches, the beginning and the end of his style. To put it in another way: it would be extremely easy to translate any of Huxley's writings into French or German, and they would lose extremely little of the personal flavour of their author. The present writer has just been reading French translations of Huxley's **Physiography** and **Crayfish,** made at different times by different translators. At first reading it seems almost miraculous how identically the effect produced by the original is reproduced by the French rendering, but the secret is really no secret at all. Huxley produced his effects by the ordering of his ideas and not by the ordering of his words. From the technical point of view of literary craftsmanship, he cannot be assigned a high place; he is one of our great English writers, but he is not a great writer of English.

Oliver Lodge (essay date 1906)

SOURCE: An introduction to *Man's Place in Nature and Other Essays,* by Thomas Henry Huxley, J. M. Dent & Sons, Ltd., 1906, pp. ix-xvii.

[*In the following essay, Lodge distinguishes Huxley's scientific materialism from naturalized philosophies, claiming that his heroic efforts in favor of the former did not imply the latter.*]

Forty years ago the position of scientific studies was not so firmly established as it is to-day, and a conflict was necessary to secure their general recognition. The forces of obscurantism and of free and easy dogmatism were arrayed against them; and, just as in former centuries astronomy, and in more recent times geology, so in our own lifetime biology, has had to offer a harsh and fighting front, lest its progress be impeded by the hostility born of preconceived opinions, and by the bigotry of self-appointed guardians of conservative views.

The man who probably did as much as any to fight the battle of science in the nineteenth century, and secure the victory for free enquiry and progressive knowledge, is Thomas Henry Huxley; and it is an interesting fact that already the lapse of time is making it possible to bring his writings in cheap form to the notice of a multitude of interested readers. The pugnacious attitude, however, which, forty years ago, was appropriate, has become a little antique now; the conflict is not indeed over, but it has either totally shifted its ground, or is continued on the old battlefield chiefly by survivors, and by a few of a younger generation who have been brought up in the old spirit.

The truths of materialism now run but little risk of being denied or ignored, they run perhaps some danger of being exaggerated. Brilliantly true and successful in their own territory, they are occasionally pushed by enthusiastic disciples over the frontier line into regions where they can do nothing but break down. As if enthusiastic worshippers of motor-cars, proud of their performance on the good roads of France, should take them over into the Sahara or essay them on a Polar expedition.

That represents the mistake which, in modern times, by careless thinkers, is being made. They tend to press the materialistic statements and scientific doctrines of a great man like Huxley, as if they were co-extensive with all existence. This is not really a widening of the materialistic aspect of things, it is a cramping of everything else; it is an attempt to limit the universe to one of its aspects.

But the mistake is not made solely, nor even chiefly, by those eager disciples who are pursuing the delusive gleam of a materialistic philosophy—for these there is hope,—to attempt is a healthy exercise, and they will find out their mistake in time; but the mistake is also made by those who are specially impressed with the spiritual side of things, who so delight to see guidance and management everywhere, that they wish to blind their eyes to the very mechanism whereby it is accomplished. They think that those who point out and earnestly study the mechanism are undermining the foundations of faith. Nothing of the kind. A traveller in the deckcabin of an Atlantic liner may prefer to ignore the engines and the firemen, and all the machinery and toil which is urging him luxuriously forward over the waves in the sunshine; he may try to imagine that he is on a sailing vessel propelled by the free air of heaven alone; but there is just as much utilization of natural forces to a desired end in one case of navigation as in the other, and every detail of the steamship, down to the last drop of sweat from a fireman's grimy body, is an undeniable reality.

There are people who still resent the conclusions of biology as to man's place in nature, and try to counteract them; but, as the late Professor Ritchie said ("Philosophical Studies," page 24)—

It is a mistake, which has constantly been made in the past by those who are anxious for the spiritual interests of man, to interfere with the changes which are going on in scientific conceptions. Such inter-ference has always ended in the defeat of the sup-porters of the quasi-scientific doctrines which the growing science of the time has discarded. Theology interfered with Galileo, and gained nothing in the end by its interference. Astronomy, geology, biol-ogy, anthropology, historical criticism, have at dif-ferent periods raised alarm in the minds of those who dread a materialistic view of man's nature; and with the very best intentions they have tried to fight the supposed enemy on his own ground, eagerly welcoming, for instance, every sign of disagreement between Darwinians and Lamarckians, or every dispute between different schools of historical critics, as if the spiritual well-being of mankind were bound up with the scientific beliefs of the seventeenth, or even earlier, century, as if *e.g.* it made all the difference in man's spiritual nature whether he was made directly out of inorganic dust or slowly ascend-ed from lower organic forms. These are questions that must be settled by specialists. On the other hand, philosophic criticism is in place when the scientific specialist begins to dogmatize about the universe as a whole, when he speaks for example as if an accurate narrative of the various steps by which the lower forms of life have passed into the higher was a sufficient explanation to us of the mystery of existence.

Let it be understood, therefore, that science is one thing, and philosophy another: that science most properly concerns itself with matter and motion, and reduces phenomena, as far as it can, to mechanism. The more successfully it does that, the more it fulfils its end and aim; but when, on the strength of that achievement, it seeks to blossom into a philosophy, when it endeavours to conclude that its scope is complete and all-inclusive, that nothing exists in the universe but mechanism, and that the aspect of things from a scientific point of view is their only aspect,—then it is becoming narrow and bigoted and deserving of rebuke. Such rebuke it received from Huxley, such rebuke it will always receive from scientific men who realize properly the magnitude of existence and the vast potentialities of the universe.

Our opportunities of exploration are good as far as they go, but they are not extensive; we live as it were in the mortar of one of the stones of St. Paul's Cathedral; and yet so assiduously have we cultivated our faculties that we can trace something of the outline of the whole design and have begun to realize the plan of the building—a surprising feat for insects of limited faculty. And—continuing the parable—two schools of thought have arisen: one saying that it was conceived in the mind of an architect and designed and built wholly by him, the other saying that it was put together stone by stone in accordance with the laws of mechanics and physics. Both statements are true, and those that emphasize the latter are not thereby denying the existence of Christopher Wren, though to the unwise enthusiasts on the side of design they may appear to be doing so. Each side is stating a truth, and neither side is stating the whole truth. Nor should we find it easy with all our efforts to state the whole truth exhaustively, even about such a thing as that. Those who deny any side of truth are to that extent unbelievers, and Huxley was righteously indignant with those shortsighted bigots who blasphemed against that aspect of divine truth which had been specially revealed to him. This is what he lived to preach, and to this he was faithful to the uttermost.

Let him be thought of as a devotee of truth, and a student of the more materialistic side of things, but never let him be thought of as a philosophical materialist or as one who abounded in cheap negations.

The objection which it is necessary to express concerning Materialism as a complete system is based not on its assertions but on its negations. In so far as it makes positive assertions, embodying the result of scientific discovery and even of scientific speculation based thereupon, there is no fault to find with it; but when, on the strength of that, it sets up to be a philosophy of the universe—all inclusive, therefore, and shutting out a number of truths otherwise perceived, or which appeal to other faculties, or which are equally true and are not really contradictory of legitimately materialistic statements—then it is that its insufficiency

and narrowness have to be displayed. As Professor Ritchie said:—"The `legitimate materialism of the sciences' simply means temporary and convenient abstraction from the cognitive conditions under which there are `facts' or `objects' for us at all; it is `dogmatic materialism' which is metaphysics of the bad sort."

It will be probably instructive, and it may be sufficient, if I show that two great leaders in scientific thought (one the greatest of all men of science who have yet lived), though well aware of much that could be said positively on the materialistic side, and very willing to admit or even to extend the province of science or exact knowledge to the uttermost, yet were very far from being philosophic materialists or from imagining that other modes of regarding the universe were thereby excluded.

Great leaders of thought, in fact, are not accustomed to take a narrow view of existence, or to suppose that one mode of regarding it, or one set of formulæ expressing it, can possibly be sufficient and complete. Even a sheet of paper has two sides: a terrestrial globe presents different aspects from different points of view; a crystal has a variety of facets; and the totality of existence is not likely to be more simple than any of these—is not likely to be readily expressible in any form of words, or to be thoroughly conceivable by any human mind.

It may be well to remember that Sir Isaac Newton was a Theist of the most pronounced and thorough conviction, although he had a great deal to do with the reduction of the major Cosmos to mechanics, *i.e.,* with its explanation by the elaborated machinery of simple forces; and he conceived it possible that, in the progress of science, this process of reduction to mechanics would continue till it embraced nearly all the phenomena of nature. (See extract below.) That, indeed, has been the effort of science ever since, and therein lies the legitimate basis for materialistic statements, though not for a materialistic philosophy.

The following sound remarks concerning Newton are taken from Huxley's **"Hume,"** p. 246:—

> Newton demonstrated all the host of heaven to be but the elements of a vast mechanism, regulated by the same laws as those which express the falling of a stone to the ground. There is a passage in the preface to the first edition of the 'Principia' which shows that Newton was penetrated, as completely as Descartes, with the belief that all the phenomena of nature are expressible in terms of matter and motion:—
>
> 'Would that the rest of the phenomena of nature could be deduced by a like kind of reasoning from mechanical principles. For many circumstances lead me to suspect that all these phenomena may depend upon certain forces, in virtue of which the particles

of bodies, by causes not yet known, are either mutually impelled against one another, and cohere into regular figures, or repel and recede from one another; which forces being unknown, philosophers have as yet explored nature in vain. But I hope that, either by this method of philosophizing, or by some other and better, the principles here laid down may throw some light upon the matter.'

Here is a full-blown anticipation of an intelligible exposition of the Universe in terms of matter and force—the substantial basis of what smaller men call materialism and develop into what they consider to be a materialistic philosophy. But there is no necessity for any such scheme; and Professor Huxley himself, who is commonly spoken of by half-informed people as if he were a philosophic materialist, was really nothing of the kind; for although, like Newton, fully imbued with the mechanical doctrine, and of course far better informed concerning the biological departments of nature, and the discoveries which have in the last century been made,—and though he rightly regarded it as his mission to make the scientific point of view clear to his benighted contemporaries, and was full of enthusiasm for the facts on which materialists take their stand,—he saw clearly that these alone were insufficient for a philosophy. The following extracts from the Hume volume will show that he entirely repudiated materialism as a satisfactory or complete philosophical system, and that he was especially severe on gratuitous denials applied to provinces beyond our scope:—

> While it is the summit of human wisdom to learn the limit of our faculties, it may be wise to recollect that we have no more right to make denials, than to put forth affirmatives, about what lies beyond that limit. Whether either mind or matter has a 'sub-stance' or not, is a problem which we are incom-petent to discuss: and it is just as likely that the common notions upon the subject should be correct as any others. . . . 'The same principles which, at first view, lead to scepticism, pursued to a certain point, bring men back to common sense' (p. 282).

> Moreover, the ultimate forms of existence which we distinguish in our little speck of the universe are, possibly, only two out of infinite varieties of existence, not only analogous to matter and analogous to mind, but of kinds which we are not competent so much as to conceive,—in the midst of which, indeed, we might be set down, with no more notion of what was about us, than the worm in a flower-pot, on a London balcony, has of the life of the great city (p. 286).

And again on pp. 251 and 279:—

> It is worth any amount of trouble to . . . know by one's own knowledge the great truth . . . that the honest and rigorous following up of the argument which leads us to 'materialism' inevitably carries us beyond it.

> To sum up. If the materialist affirms that the universe and all its phenomena are resolvable into matter and motion, Berkeley replies, True; but what you call matter and motion are known to us only as forms of consciousness; their being is to be conceived or known; and the existence of a state of consciousness apart from a thinking mind is a contradiction in terms.

> I conceive that this reasoning is irrefragable. And, therefore, if I were obliged to choose between absolute materialism and absolute idealism, I should feel compelled to accept the latter alternative.

Let the jubilant but uninstructed and comparatively ignorant amateur materialist therefore beware, and bethink himself twice or even thrice before he conceives that he understands the universe and is competent to pour scorn upon the intuitions and perceptions of great men in what may be to him alien regions of thought and experience.

Let him explain, if he can, what he means by his own identity, or the identity of any thinking or living being, which at different times consists of a totally different set of material particles. Something there clearly is which confers personal identity and constitutes an individual: it is a property characteristic of every form of life, even the humblest; but it is not yet explained or understood, and it is no answer to assert gratuitously that there is some fundamental substance or material basis on which that identity depends, any more than it is an explanation to say that it depends upon a soul. These are all forms of words. As Hume says, quoted by Huxley with approval, in the work already cited, p. 194:—

> It is impossible to attach any definite meaning to the word 'substance,' when employed for the hypothetical substratum of soul and matter. . . . If it be said that our personal identity requires the assumption of a substance which remains the same while the accidents of perception shift and change, the question arises what is meant by personal identity? . . . A plant or an animal, in the course of its existence, from the condition of an egg or seed to the end of life, remains the same neither in form, nor in structure, nor in the matter of which it is composed: every attribute it possesses is constantly changing, and yet we say that it is always one and the same individual (p. 194).

And in his own preface to the Hume volume Huxley expresses himself forcibly thus—equally antagonistic as was his wont to both ostensible friend and ostensible foe, as soon as they got off what he considered the straight path:—

That which it may be well for us not to forget is, that the first-recorded judicial murder of a scientific thinker [Socrates] was compassed and effected, not by a despot, nor by priests, but was brought about by eloquent demagogues. . . . Clear knowledge of what one does not know is just as important as knowing what one does know. . . .

The development of exact natural knowledge in all its vast range, from physics to history and criticism, is the consequence of the working out, in this prov-ince, of the resolution to 'take nothing for truth without clear knowledge that it is such'; to consider all beliefs open to criticism; to regard the value of authority as neither greater nor less, than as much as it can prove itself to be worth. The modern spirit is not the spirit 'which always denies,' delighting only in destruction; still less is it that which builds castles in the air rather than not construct; it is that spirit which works and will work 'without haste and without rest,' gathering harvest after harvest of truth into its barns, and devouring error with un-quenchable fire (p. viii).

The harvesting of truth is a fairly safe operation, for if some falsehood be inadvertently harvested along with the grain we may hope that, having a less robust and hardy nature, it will before long be detected by its decaying odour; but the rooting up and devouring of error with unquenchable fire is a more dangerous enterprise, inasmuch as flames are apt to spread beyond our control; and the lack of infallibility in the selection of error may to future generations become painfully apparent.

The phrase represents a good healthy energetic mood however, and in a world liable to become overgrown with weeds and choked with refuse, the cleansing work of a firebrand may from time to time be a necessity, in order that the free wind of heaven and the sunlight may once more reach the fertile soil.

But it is unfair to think of Huxley even when young as a firebrand, though it is true that he was to some extent a man of war, and though the fierce and consuming mood is rather more prominent in his early writings than in his later work.

A fighting attitude was inevitable forty years ago, because then the truths of biology were being received with hostility, and the free science and philosophy of a later time seemed likely to have a poor chance of life. But the world has changed or is changing now, the wholesome influences of fire have done their work, and it would be a rather barbarous anachronism to apply the same agency among the young green shoots of healthy learning which are springing up in the cleared ground.

Thomas Henry Huxley's evaluation of himself, given to Francis Galton in 1873:

Strong natural talent for mechanism, music and art in general, but all wasted and uncultivated. Believe I am reckoned a good chairman of a meeting. I always find that I acquire influence, generally more than I want, in bodies of men and that administrative and other work gravitates to my hands. Impulsive and apt to rush in-to all sorts of undertakings without counting cost or responsibility. Love my friends and hate my enemies cordially. Entire confidence in those whom I trust at all and much indifference towards the rest of the world. A profound religious tendency capable of fanaticism, but tempered by no less profound theological scepticism. No love of the marvellous as such, intense desire to know facts; no very intense love of my pursuits at present, but very strong affection for philosophical and social problems; strong constructive imagination; small foresight; no particular public spirit; disinterestedness arising from an entire want of care for the rewards and honours most men seek, vanity too big to be satisfied by them.

Thomas Henry Huxley, quoted in Cyril Bibby,
T. H. Huxley: Scientist, Humanist and
Educator, *Watts, 1959.*

Walter E. Houghton (essay date 1949)

SOURCE: "The Rhetoric of T. H. Huxley," in *The University of Toronto Quarterly,* Vol. XVIII, No. 2, January, 1949, pp. 159-75.

[*In this essay, Houghton contends that, contrary to traditional appraisals, Huxley used a variety of rhetorical tools to advocate his agnosticism.*]

For anyone so obviously devoted to controversy and propaganda, Huxley enjoyed a reputation for candour and sincerity that seems almost incredible. We can scarcely believe that the self-appointed champion of science, writing in an age of bitter religious controversy, and endowed with both pugnacity and a flair for style, could have resisted the temptation to use rhetorical sophistries of one kind or another. And use them he did, and with all the more success because, by great good luck, he had managed to acquire a reputation for simple honesty and plain speech which disarmed the usual caution of critics, as well as of general readers, on approaching polemical literature.

This good fortune (is there any better, or rarer, for a partisan?) was ultimately derived from his well-known championship of freedom of inquiry, and his complementary scorn of hypocrisies and evasions.[1] He became something like an apostle of veracity to a generation which found itself caught between belief and unbelief, and often forced, by social pressures or psychological fears, into insincerities as distasteful to them as they now seem to us. His enthusiastic reception in America in 1876 was primarily given to the champion "of freedom and sincerity in thought *and word* against shams and self-deceptions of every kind. It was not so much the preacher of new doctrines who was welcomed, as the apostle of veracity."[2] This conception of his style, no less than of his thought, was explicitly affirmed by James Routh in 1902: "The most marked thing about his style is its clearness and sincerity. The man looks you straight in the eyes and speaks with a frankness and an earnestness which come from the bottom of the soul and carry conviction—a conviction of the absolute truthfulness of the man, if not of the soundness of his doctrine."[3] Clearness, and therefore sincerity, that is a second clue to Huxley's reputation. It is because his writing seems, and often is, so lucid and direct in diction and structure, so apparently free from artifice and elaboration, that it escapes the suspicion of rhetorical motivation. In Leonard Huxley's account of his father's style, we can see the identification of honesty and clarity which is now so firmly established in Huxleyan criticism.

> Have something to say, and say it, was the Duke of Wellington's theory of style; Huxley's was to say that which has to be said in such language that you can stand cross-examination on each word. Be clear, though you may be convicted of error. If you are clearly wrong, you will run up against a fact some time and get set right. If you shuffle with your subject, and study chiefly to use language which will give a loophole of escape either way, there is no hope for you.

> This was the secret of his lucidity. . . . In him science and literature, too often divorced, were closely united; and literature owes him a debt for importing into it so much of the highest scientific habit of mind; for showing that truthfulness need not be bald, and that real power lies more in exact accuracy than in luxuriance of diction.[4]

It is not surprising that this passage was quoted with approval in Aldous Huxley's lecture of 1932 on "T. H. Huxley as a Man of Letters," for that paper, though otherwise an able analysis of Huxley's style, is, in this respect, uncritically traditional:

> His passion for veracity always kept him from taking any unfair rhetorical advantages of an opponent. The candour with which he acknowledged a weakness in his own case was always complete, and though he made full use of a rich variety of literary devices to bring home what he wanted to say, he never abused his great rhetorical powers. Truth was more important to him than personal triumph, and he relied more on a forceful clarity to convince his readers than on the brilliant and exciting ambiguities of propagandist eloquence.[5]

Finally, it is not difficult to support this association of honesty, clarity, and rhetorical restraint from Huxley's own remarks. For one thing, he was always quick to condemn the use of oratorical devices by any of his contemporaries. The *Quarterly* reviewer of *The Origin of Species* dealt with Mr. Darwin, he charged, "as an Old Bailey barrister deals with a man against whom he wishes to obtain a conviction, *per fas aut nefas,* and opens his case by endeavouring to create a prejudice against the prisoner in the minds of the jury."[6] Of Mr. Balfour, apropos of *The Foundations of Belief,* Huxley observed that he was a good debater who knew "the value of a word. The word 'Naturalism' has a bad sound and unpleasant associations. It would tell against us in the House of Commons, and so it will with his readers."[7] Mr. Gladstone forgot that the "rhetorical artifices" which had brought him "fame and honour" in politics, had long ceased to take effect in "the region of letters or of science," where readers now find that "mere dexterity in putting together cleverly ambiguous phrases, and even the great art of offensive misrepresentation, are unspeakably wearisome."[8] The implied difference from Huxley's own methods is affirmed in a number of protestations. He has had to be content through life, he confesses in the **"Autobiography,"** "with saying what I mean in the plainest of plain language."[9] When W. S. Lilly accused him of gilding his teaching with rhetorical ornaments, he replied with righteous indignation that "rhetorical ornament is not in my way, and that gilding refined gold would, to my mind, be less objectionable than varnishing the fair face of truth with that pestilent cosmetic, rhetoric."[10] Such pronouncements, coming as they do from one whose reputation for sincerity was so well established, naturally added their weight to the critical tradition, and confirmed the impression of candour which the apparent simplicity of his style so readily produces.[11]

Not, of course, that this impression is always wrong. It is right enough in such descriptive essays as **"A Piece of Chalk," "A Lobster,"** or **"Animal Automatism."** But when Huxley turned from straight exposition to generalizations about the values of science or religion, usually their relative values, and to cognate passages on scientists and clergymen, he was by no means reluctant to bolster a shaky or a biased argument, or even to support a good one, with the extra-emotional influence of rhetorical methods. Broadly speaking, he makes use of two in particular, exaggeration and insinuation.

I

For illustration of the former, we may turn first to some passages on science from the lecture **"On the Advisableness of Improving Natural Knowledge."** Huxley's main thesis is introduced as follows:

. . . if the noble first President of the Royal Society could revisit the upper air . . . he would find himself in the midst of a material civilisation more different from that of his day, than that of the seventeenth was from that of the first century. And . . . he would need no long reflection to discover that all these great ships, these railways, these telegraphs, these factories, these printing-presses, without which the whole fabric of modern English society would collapse into a mass of stagnant and starving pauperism,—that all these pillars of our State are but the ripples and the bubbles upon the surface of that great spiritual stream. . . .[12]

When the effect of losing its inventions is made to show the value of applied science, the loss is nothing less than the collapse of the whole fabric of society, and into a state, no, a mass, of stagnant and starving pauperism—though we are tempted to ask, with the eighteenth century in mind, if that would, in fact, be the permanent condition of an England without railroads and telegraphs. Then the hyperboles are doubled, in reverse. These great inventions, which are the very pillars of our State, are nothing but ripples and bubbles on the great spiritual stream of science. Two particular words show the broad character of this rhetoric. "Stagnant" pauperism is hardly a precise epithet, but the "st" alliteration resounds with emphasis in "starving," and presently, though we are not conscious of it, the contrast of "stagnant" life without science and the great "stream" of science carries its effective influence. Second, although the primary meaning of "spiritual" is "incorporeal," "mental," "pertaining to moral and intellectual life," can we—should we—suppress the overtones of "holy" and "pure"? Or even the reassuring sense that somehow science is spiritual, as is religion? Certainly it would not be out of character for Huxley to claim for science a term commonly used by his clerical adversaries in scorn of science, to describe areas far beyond its low material sphere. Turning the flank of the enemy by appropriating religious, biblical, or doctrinal phraseology, is a minor, but very effective, element in his rhetoric. We shall meet it again later on.

This passage, however, is not up to Huxley's standard: the loose development of metaphor ("pillars" becoming "ripples") and the hackneyed "noble" and "great" are unworthy of his talents. We can study a superior example a few pages below, where Part I of the essay comes to a triumphant climax, in the Macaulay manner on the Macaulay theme of progress:

It is very certain that for every victim slain by the plague, hundreds of mankind exist and find a fair share of happiness in the world by the aid of the spinning jenny. And the great fire, at its worst, could not have burned the supply of coal, the daily working of which, in the bowels of the earth, made possible by the steam pump, gives rise to an amount of wealth to which the millions lost in old London are but as an old song.[13]

This, of course, brings down the house. But Huxley's thesis is, "that the improvement of natural knowledge . . . has not only conferred practical benefits on men [discussed in Part I], but, in so doing, has effected a revolution in their conceptions of the universe and of themselves, and has profoundly altered their modes of thinking and their views of right and wrong" (now to be discussed in Part II).[14] This latter discussion, however, does not commence until four initial paragraphs have been devoted to the important job of reorienting the reader's whole state of mind. Not only must he now be made to feel that the material values of science are, after all, inferior to its philosophical values; he must, if possible, even be made to feel repelled by the very worship of progress in which he has just been indulging. In short, he must be swung right-about-face, so that when Huxley comes to listing the higher values of science, the reader will accept them at once and without hesitation. This process begins in the opening sentence—and dramatically, indeed melodramatically. The fantastic praise of spinning jennies and steam pumps is still ringing in our ears as Huxley suddenly turns round and says:

But spinning jenny and steam pump are, after all, but toys, possessing an accidental value; and natural knowledge creates multitudes of more subtle con-trivances, the praises of which do not happen to be sung because they are not directly convertible into instruments for creating wealth. When I contemplate natural knowledge squandering such gifts among men. . . .

At this point we are not merely aware that scientific inventions are trivial, but we even feel a little ashamed of caring for such things, mere toys (and we, supposedly, adults), and instruments for creating wealth. The last word now carries a connotation of covetousness and waste which was quite lacking a moment ago, but is now elicited by the notion of science squandering such gifts among men. Already, therefore, we are backing away from the very object which we had just been ardently approaching.

Then Huxley introduces his thesis with a brilliant simile:

When I contemplate natural knowledge squandering such gifts among men, the only appropriate comparison I can find for her is, to liken her to such a peasant woman as one sees in the Alps, striding ever upward, heavily burdened, and with mind bent only on her home; but yet without effort and without thought, knitting for her children. Now stockings are good and comfortable things, and the children will undoubtedly be much the better for them; but surely it would be shortsighted, to say the least of it, to depreciate this toiling mother as a mere stocking-machine—a mere provider of physical comforts?

This simile not only gives form to Huxley's abstract idea of the relative values of science, "spiritual" and material, but, more important, it makes full use of all the latent attractions of the image. There is the elemental appeal of presenting science in terms of mother, home, and children. There is the added advantage of making the mother a peasant, with its affective associations of sturdy endurance and existence close to the soil, far from the artificial life of wealth just referred to. Finally, the mother is not merely a peasant, but an Alpine peasant, and at this particular moment climbing to her mountain home, so that she can be presented as striding ever upward, and, though heavily burdened with household supplies, uncomplaining, her mind unselfishly bent on her home. In this way Huxley can identify science and the scientist with all the heroic qualities, inherent in the imagery, of struggle and courage, unselfish devotion to humanity, and striving upward towards the Ideal. After which, the notion of mother science as a mere stocking-machine is, of course, indignantly repudiated, and the reader is well prepared to hail her influence upon the minds and morals of her children. We may note, in passing, how effectively Huxley withholds the epithet "toiling" until the end of the paragraph. Since it cannot apply to the knitting, which is "without effort," it must and does apply to the striding upward towards home. The heroic suggestions are therefore recalled in the final sentence.

With his idea and its imagery sketched out, Huxley proceeds to expand the implications, and intensify the emotional pattern of repulsion and attraction:

> However, there are blind leaders of the blind, and not a few of them, who take this view of natural knowledge, and can see nothing in the bountiful mother of humanity but a sort of comfort-grinding machine. According to them, the improvement of natural knowledge always has been, and always must be, synonymous with no more than the improvement of the material resources and the increase of the gratifications of men.

> Natural knowledge is, in their eyes, no real mother of mankind, bringing them up with kindness, and, if need be, with sternness, in the way they should go, and instructing them in all things needful for their welfare. . . .

The rhetorical development is striking. The peasant mother shades easily into the bountiful mother of humanity (the remote suggestion of "mother earth" is active here); and she in turn becomes, almost without our being aware of it, so neatly is the exaggeration made under guise of mere repetition, the *real* mother of mankind, bringing up her children in *the* way they should go, and instructing them in *all* things needful for their welfare. Were religion and moral philosophy ever more cunningly disposed of?

In the meanwhile, the lower values of applied science, which were "placed" by the knitting-machine, are again attacked on the lines initiated by the opening sentence on toys and instruments of wealth, only now with more irritation because Huxley shifts his attention, and ours, from technology itself to the men who see no other values in science. These blind leaders of the blind (good oratorical stock-in-trade) cannot recognize the bountiful mother, the real mother, and so on. They can only see, at first, a comfort-grinding machine (the connotations of sensual gratification and luxury show that this is not a synonym for knitting-machine), and then suddenly they do see a mother—of a strikingly different kind:

> Natural knowledge is, in their eyes, no real mother of mankind . . . but a sort of fairy godmother, ready to furnish her pets with shoes of swiftness, swords of sharpness, and omnipotent Aladdin's lamps, so that they may have telegraphs to Saturn, and see the other side of the moon, and thank God they are better than their benighted ancestors.

This, of course, builds on the implications we found in the opening sentence of Part II. The toys, which at first were only trifles, are now toys indeed, the toys of the rich, who look to science for the same "luxury" emotions of wonder and power which children find in magic sets and wooden soldiers; with the further appeal of enjoying the fine sense of superiority which they can assume toward their benighted ancestors.

Thus, as we finish the third paragraph, we are far from thinking that the technological values of science are merely inferior to its philosophical values. The former have been belittled and debased until, at this point, we feel that no self-respecting, intelligent person (like me) would think of giving more than a moment's thought to material progress. And consequently, since science is valuable, it must be for higher things—things as high and precious as those we have all received from our mothers. Then, in the next remark, comes the pay-off:

> If this talk were true, I, for one, should not greatly care to toil in the service of natural knowledge.

The tone of righteous superiority is, we feel, entirely justified, very much to Huxley's credit (we'd feel the same way if we were scientists). And by the astute repetition of the word "toil," Huxley beautifully identifies himself with the heroic mother of humanity striding ever upward. Who would not listen with confidence and admiration to such a man?

In its way this is certainly a brilliant piece of rhetorical writing; and yet the truth is that it will not bear scrutiny. The passage is blurred and confused, because Huxley is saying two things at once: first, that the material values of applied science are inferior, though none the less genuine (the children will be much the better for the stockings), to the moral and intellectual values of pure science; second, that scientific inventions are mere toys which people prize for what they can get out of them—money, or physical luxuries, or the thrill of "Popular Mechanics," or the mean complacency of feeling superior to their ancestors. And this second estimate is in striking contradiction not only to the first, but to the whole essay up to this point.

The fact is that Huxley shared the optimistic pride of the Victorians in the vast commercial and industrial progress of England, and he was ready enough to salute the great middle class which directed it.[15] But at the same time, he was very much irritated both by middle-class ambitions to grow rich and buy a peerage,[16] and by middle-class suspicion of science as "speculative rubbish"—at the worst, on grounds that "rule of thumb" had been the source of past prosperity and would suffice "for the future welfare of the arts and manufactures"; at the best, because "scientific knowledge of direct practical use" is alone valuable, and "can be studied apart from another sort of scientific knowledge, which is of no practical utility, and which is termed 'pure science.'"[17] Both of Huxley's attitudes, enthusiasm for industrial progress and scorn for the crass ambitions and intellectual blindness of "practical men," are exactly what we might expect from a popular champion of science, himself of the middle class, but a scientist who happened to be well over on the theoretical side. This explains what happened at the turning-point of the essay. As Huxley's mind shifted from the praise of applied science, sincerely given, to the greater glories of pure science, he thought of those stupid business men making large fortunes out of the former, and going about disparaging the latter. And with characteristic pugnacity he tore after them, only to strike, in his irritation, at the whole world of applied science, and talk as though steam pumps and spinning jennies were for every one no better than comfort-grinding machines or telegraphs to Saturn. In short, the rhetoric is not under control, or, to put it differently, it is not being used simply to sway the reader and make him feel the inferior status of technology; rather it serves mainly to release Huxley's personal annoyance, and thereby accidentally and inconsistently to rouse the reader's disgust with applied science in general.

What has happened here is fairly common in Victorian writing. The rhetoric tends to get out of hand because the writer is suddenly swept by a gust of personal emotion which he cannot check or cannot master sufficiently to integrate it with his theme. The difficulty stems from an inability to stand far enough off, with enough detachment to contemplate different and perhaps mutually exclusive elements in a given situation at one and the same time. Arnold observed "our want of flexibility . . . our inaptitude for seeing more than one side of a thing . . . our intense energetic absorption in the particular pursuit we happen to be following";[18] or, one might add, in a new idea that crosses our path. Why this was so is too large a question to pursue in

this paper. But whatever its ultimate cause, the Victorian sensibility has a tendency to jump from point to point, one might say from passion to passion, with the result that two attitudes which are not compatible, or at any rate not co-ordinated, are sometimes expressed at the same time.

In the passage we have just examined, the shift of focus from principles to persons is characteristic, especially where Huxley is on the attack. He knew that because our antipathies are much more readily aroused by men than by doctrines, he could strike more effectively at a creed by exposing its disciples than by attacking it directly. This can be illustrated by two passages on the same subject, the bibliolatry which appealed to plenary inspiration against the unbiblical truths of the new science. The first deals with the topic ideologically, and by doing so comes close to what we should expect from the Huxleyan tradition of sincerity and clarity:

> Wherever bibliolatry has prevailed, bigotry and cruelty have accompanied it. It lies at the root of the deep-seated, sometimes disguised, but never absent, antagonism of all the varieties of ecclesiasticism to the freedom of thought and to the spirit of scientific investigation. For those who look upon ignorance as one of the chief sources of evil; and hold veracity, not merely in act, but in thought, to be the one condition of true progress, whether moral or intellectual, it is clear that the biblical idol must go the way of all other idols. Of infallibility, in all shapes, lay or clerical, it is needful to iterate with more than Catonic pertinacity, *Delenda est*.[19]

No one, of course, would imagine that this was unbiased writing, but we may grant that in this instance Huxley is presenting his side of the case without taking "unfair rhetorical advantages of an opponent." But that is hardly true of the second passage where he concentrates on the Bibliolaters themselves:

> In this nineteenth century, as at the dawn of modern physical science, the cosmogony of the semi-barbarous Hebrew is the incubus of the philosopher and the opprobrium of the othodox. Who shall number the patient and earnest seekers after truth, from the days of Galileo until now, whose lives have been embittered and their good name blasted by the mistaken zeal of Bibliolaters? Who shall count the host of weaker men whose sense of truth has been destroyed in the effort to harmonise impossibilities—whose life has been wasted in the attempt to force the generous new wine of Science into the old bottles of Judaism, compelled by the outcry of the same strong party?[20]

Here, in comparison, our feelings are brought far more sharply into play, because Huxley has shifted his focus from opposing principles to contending parties, and presented the parties in black-and-white antithesis. Our sense of justice, with the complementary emotions of pity for the wronged and anger for the perpetrators, is finely, and extravagantly, outraged. The lives of men (good men, too, patient and earnest seekers after truth) were *embittered* and *wasted,* their good names *blasted,* their sense of truth *destroyed.* And not a few men either: they were beyond number, beyond count, and all of them, it is implied, men like Galileo. The one, and only, example could hardly be better chosen, with its nice suggestion of the Inquisition.

Before leaving this passage, one minor technicality is worth noticing for its evidence of how closely Huxley studied his effects. The explosive disgust of the alliterative "b," announced when the semi-barbarous Hebrew accepts what is the incubus of the philosopher and the opprobrium of the orthodox, and then intensified when lives are embittered and good names blasted by Bibliolaters, is still active when we reach the old bottles of Judaism.

II

In the examples so far considered, Huxley's method may be loosely described as exaggeration or hyperbole. In those that follow we can study a more subtle technique, that of insinuation. This is intimately related to his agnosticism.

In considering Huxley's "evil" influence upon religious vitality, Wilfred Ward once suggested that it should be charged not so much to what he said as to the way he said it. His agnosticism made him willing, officially, to admit that theism, in one form or another, was a possibility, and certainly to reject dogmatic atheism, but "his anti-Christian rhetoric was calculated . . . to destroy religious belief wholesale, including positions which the writer himself, to say the least, considered quite tenable."[21] But considered tenable in what sense? In the sense, I think, that he thought them safe from logical attack, but not in the sense that he himself really thought them credible. We have to remember that Huxley was not a genuine agnostic, but only a polemical agnostic. The genuine agnostic is really in doubt: he is searching for a religious truth which he considers entirely possible. But the polemical agnostic is an atheist, or at any rate a naturalist, at heart. He has no doubts. He does not believe, as Huxley confessed for himself, that there is "any justification for cutting the Universe into two halves, one natural and one supernatural."[22] He has no faith in immortality, and none in either a personal God or a divine spirit immanent in the universe. But to deny the possiblity of such things would be naïve. They had best be treated agnostically, which will mean admitting that their truth is tenable, but at the same time betraying one's real denial of them, both consciously and unconsciously, through one's language. I think that Ward took Huxley's admissions too seriously because he did not distinguish

between polemical and genuine agnosticism;[23] but he was dead right about the anti-religious rhetoric.

The essay **"On Improving Natural Knowledge,"** which is so rich in rhetorical play, ends with a passage on the foundation of the new morality which is being laid down by science:

> And as regards the second point—the extent to which the improvement of natural knowledge has remodelled and altered what may be termed the intellectual ethics of man,—what are among the moral convictions most fondly held by barbarous and semi-barbarous people?

> They are the convictions that authority is the soundest basis of belief; that merit attaches to a readiness to believe; that the doubting disposition is a bad one, and scepticism a sin; that when good authority has pronounced what is to be believed, and faith has accepted it, reason has no further duty. There are many excellent persons who yet hold by these principles, and it is not my present business, or intention, to discuss their views.[24]

In the last sentence the polite irony of "excellent," which means "stupid if respectable," is followed by one of Huxley's typical refusals to take issue with principles which, it is implied, he could of course demolish if he wanted to—and which, in point of fact, he always proceeds at once to do, if he has not done so already.[25] But the apparent refusal is well calculated to put the reader off his guard. If by any chance he finds himself judging and condemning, he must be doing so on his own account: he is not being influenced or prejudiced—how could he be?—by a man who is not discussing the matter. A second glance would show, of course, that Huxley has already judged and condemned these principles by associating their "excellent" upholders with barbarous and semi-barbarous people; but our reading habits, especially of prose, are far too rapid to make such a second glance a possibility that Huxley need consider. "All I wish to bring clearly before your minds," he continues blandly, as though off in another direction, "is the unquestionable fact. . . ." But before we let Huxley state this "fact," let us consider the sentence which he *would* have written had he really been dropping the authoritarian beliefs of these excellent persons:

> All I wish to bring clearly before your minds is the unquestionable fact, that the improvement of natural knowledge is effected by methods which follow just the opposite convictions, and assume the exact reverse of each.

That, I suppose, is an unquestionable fact. Huxley would there be talking only of science. He would not be saying or implying that these authoritarian principles might not be quite right and proper in other areas of thought, in religion, for instance. Certainly, many really excellent persons, John Henry Newman for one example, believed that the authority of divine revelation, preserved in the creeds or in the Bible, was the soundest basis of belief. But not Huxley—as we see from the sentence which he *did* write:

> All I wish to bring clearly before your minds is the unquestionable fact, that the improvement of natural knowledge is effected by methods which directly give the lie to all these convictions, and assume the exact reverse of each to be true.

This, of course, is quite different—not, perhaps, in what Huxley could claim he was saying, but certainly in what he is implying. The clauses could be interpreted as meaning that scientific methods "give the lie to these convictions in the field of natural knowledge, and assume the exact reverse of each to be true for scientific purposes." But at this point, with the reader conditioned as he is, they can only mean "give the lie to these convictions and prove them to be false," period. With our critical intelligence neutralized, and our knowledge that these are the convictions of barbarous and semi-barbarous people, we are helpless. We can only say, no wonder modern science gives them the lie.

Then, in the next paragraph Huxley adds insult to injury. In describing the method of science he largely follows a negative formula: it is not this, it does not assume that, and so forth, but in each case the negative idea is expressed in authoritarian and religious terms. In this way he seems to be setting up a contrast between science and religion; and since what he claims for science is obviously true, religion is made to seem obviously false.

> The improver of natural knowledge absolutely refuses to acknowledge authority, as such. For him, scepticism is the highest of duties; blind faith the one unpardonable sin. And it cannot be otherwise, for every great advance in natural knowledge has involved the absolute rejection of authority, the cherishing of the keenest scepticism, the annihilation of the spirit of blind faith; and the most ardent votary of science holds his firmest convictions, not because the men he most venerates hold them; not because their verity is testified by portents and wonders; but because his experience teaches him that whenever he chooses to bring these convictions into contact with their primary source, Nature—whenever he thinks fit to test them by appealing to experiment and to observation—Nature will confirm them. The man of science has learned to believe in justification, not by faith, but by verification.

The final epigram is masterful, and crystallizes the method. All that Huxley *says,* of course, is that the scientist must not rest upon faith, but must verify his hypotheses by observation and experiment. But because

of the theological diction, and the emotional bias he has already set up in the reader from the previous paragraph, he can insinuate that whoever believes any longer in justification by faith is just a bit of a fool, to put it mildly. One must hear the sarcastic tone in the phrase "not by faith," followed by the triumphant "but by verification."

The fact is that there is not one argument in the whole passage which has any logical bearing on religious authoritarianism or religious faith or religious people; and yet we find ourselves at the end looking at all three with the gravest suspicion. To appreciate how devastating this rhetoric is, we have only to compare a passage by G. H. Lewes on the same subject:

> The Faith of Theology and the Faith of Science are very different in their credentials. The former is reliance on the truth of principles handed down by Tradition, of which no verification is possible, no examination permissible; the latter is reliance on the truth of principles which have been sought and found by competent inquirers, tested incessantly by successive generations, are always open to verification in all their details, and always modifiable according to fresh experiences.[26]

We are left in no doubt about Lewes' own preference, but, beyond that, the religious attitude is not even challenged, let alone rendered contemptible.

My last example of Huxley's rhetoric is taken from the introductory paragraphs of the Prologue to ***Essays on Some Controverted Questions***. His thesis is that the intellectual history of man has shown a constant growth in naturalism accompanied by a co-ordinate elimination of supernaturalism. He has therefore first to show that this is true, and then close his introduction with the key question, "How far is this process to go?"—that being "the Controverted Question of our time." And if that were all that he did, we would not be concerned with the passage. But how could it be, with that question coming up? To Huxley, of course, there was no doubt of the right answer: "the further the better." It was imperative, therefore, that the reader should be so conditioned by the previous paragraphs that that answer should come with the speed and thought-lessness of a reflex the moment the crucial question was put.

The success of naturalism is first announced:

> . . . so far as men have paid attention to Nature, they have been rewarded for their pains. They have developed the Arts which have furnished the conditions of civilised existence; and the Sciences, which have been a progressive revelation of reality and have afforded the best discipline of the mind in the methods of discovering truth.[27]

Here again one is impressed by the slippery use of language. Huxley does not exactly, specifically, say that reality is what science reveals, or that truth is discoverable only by the scientific method, but both are well implied. Then, to the claim of progress, he adds the claim of agreement:

> They have accumulated a vast body of universally accepted knowledge; and the conceptions of man and of society, of morals and of law, based upon that knowledge, are every day more and more, either openly or tacitly, acknowledged to be the foundations of right action.

After this defence, Huxley can turn confidently to the record of supernaturalism:

> History also tells us that the field of the supernatural has rewarded its cultivators with a harvest, perhaps no less luxuriant, but of a different character. It has produced an almost infinite diversity of Religions. These, if we set aside the ethical concomitants upon which natural knowledge also has a claim, are composed of information about Supernature; they tell us of the attributes of supernatural beings, of their relations with Nature, and of the operations by which their interference with the ordinary course of events can be secured or averted. It does not appear, however, that supernaturalists have attained to any agreement about these matters, or that history indicates a widening of the influence of supernaturalism on practice, with the onward flow of time. On the contrary, the various religions are, to a great extent, mutually exclusive; and their adherents delight in charging each other, not merely with error, but with criminality, deserving and ensuing punishment of infinite severity.

Sleight-of-hand could hardly be more skilful. All that Huxley says, in the next to last sentence, is that supernaturalists have not agreed about these matters and that the influence of supernaturalism has declined. But what he insinuates is that this fact is a test of value, so that we find ourselves condemning supernaturalism on a basis which, were it brought into the open, we would be quick to challenge. Disagreement and decline may be regrettable matters of fact; they are scarcely proofs of the inferiority of supernaturalism to a contrary outlook that happens to have enjoyed greater agreement and popular success. And yet, though we know that that is true, we are ready at this point to reject any philosophy which has to make such a confession, so neatly has Huxley's previous paragraph associated the great achievements of science with agreement and progress. To resist the appeal would require far more caution than we think necessary in reading Huxley, and far slower habits of reading in general than we have acquired. In any case, the final clause is so damaging that we are in no mood to give religion its due. For Huxley does not say that some religious people have charged each other with error and criminality, and that even a few, here and there, have found a sadistic delight in doing so. That would be a fair state-ment—but a minor blunder, given his intention of determining in advance what answer we shall make to the culminating question. What he actually says, therefore, is that "their adherents delight in charging each other" with error and criminality. That's religious people for you! Thank God, religion is declining! At which point, we are literally unable to remember the many thousands of adherents, in all ages, who have found spiritual and moral strength in a supernatural theology. Needless to say, Huxley was well aware of that historical fact. On another occasion he could admit that anyone who recalled the "ethical purity and nobility [of Christianity], which apostles have pictured, in which armies of martyrs have placed their unshakable faith" was not "likely to under-rate the importance of the Christian faith . . . in human history."[28] But that, as I say, was on another occasion. This occasion called for the suppression of any such evidence in favour of supernaturalism—which incidentally shows us that "the candour with which he acknowledged a weakness in his own case" was not, as Aldous Huxley imagined, "always complete."

He next proceeds to press home the argument that the facts of growth and decline are unquestionable standards of value:

> In singular contrast with natural knowledge, again, the acquaintance of mankind with the supernatural appears the more extensive and the more exact, and the influence of supernatural doctrines upon con-duct the greater, the further back we go in time and the lower the stage of civilisation submitted to investigation. Historically, indeed, there would seem to be an inverse relation between supernatural and natural knowledge. As the latter has widened, gained in precision and in trustworthiness, so has the former shrunk, grown vague and questionable; as the one has more and more filled the sphere of action, so has the other retreated into the region of medita-tion, or vanished behind the screen of mere verbal recognition.

Again, Huxley seems merely to be stating a fact which no one is likely to question. The word "historically," placed conspicuously at the beginning of the middle sentence, serves to place his remarks in the neutral area of established truth. Hence the general attitude aroused is one of agreement, though what we are admitting is, of course, not simply the fact of change, but that the change has been progress. For supernaturalism is first associated with the lower stage of civilization, and is then said to have "retreated" before the advance of naturalism, where the connotation of "defeat" by the stronger (because more enlightened) power is patent. (We must remember the enormous difference the Victorian assumed between savages and Englishmen, before later research suggested another point of view, as in Ruth Benedict's *Patterns of Culture.*) Then, his case made, Huxley blandly continues:

Whether this difference of the fortunes of Naturalism and of Supernaturalism is an indication of the progress, or of the regress, of humanity; of a fall from, or an advance towards, the higher life; is a matter of opinion. The point to which I wish to direct attention is that the difference exists and is making itself felt.

Could anything be more bare-faced? He will not debate the matter; he is only concerned to show that a difference exists! The hesitant reader is thus reassured that Huxley is merely stating a fact and not a judgment; if the reader has made up his mind he has done so for himself. Once that is established, Huxley can add the weight of his own authority, offered with due modesty:

> Men are growing to be seriously alive to the fact that the historical evolution of humanity, which is generally, and I venture to think not unreasonably, regarded as progress, has been, and is being, accompanied by a co-ordinate elimination of the supernatural from its originally large occupation of men's thoughts. The question—How far is this process to go?—is, in my apprehension, the Controverted Question of our time.

To which question, the reader instantly answers, "The further the better." We cannot help recalling the reviewer of *The Origin of Species* in the *Quarterly* who was so justly reproved by Huxley for opening "his case by endeavouring to create a prejudice against the prisoner in the minds of the jury."

III

In thus attempting to qualify the notion of Huxley as a man of simple honesty and plain speech by showing that he was not always a lover of truth and a hater of rhetoric, but sometimes almost the reverse, I have no intention of blackening his character. To expect that any man could spend a lifetime in controversy and never use the weapons of controversy would be naïve. When Frederick Rogers spoke of a certain Dr. W. as an "unscrupulous controversialist," Newman answered: "I dare say he is. But who is not? . . . I declare I think it is as rare a thing, candour in controversy, as to be a Saint."[29] In a sense, this opinion is confirmed by the fact that the only Victorian who was genuinely candid in controversy, and whose style was completely lacking in rhetorical colouring, was the saint of rationalism, J. S. Mill. At any rate, if Huxley was no saint, neither was he a sinner. His misrepresentations are not, I think, vicious or unscrupulous, and much of the time he was kept from taking "unfair rhetorical advantages," not so much by his passion for veracity as by his love of humour, since laughter dissipates the anger that can lead so easily to distortion. Moreover, no one would say, apropos of his anti-religious rhetoric, that Huxley

had not some cause for irritation. He was brought up in Evangelical circles to believe in "the necessity, on pain of reprobation in this world and damnation in the next, of accepting, in the strict and literal sense, every statement contained in the Protestant Bible"; and to think of anyone who trusted for interpretation to "carnal reason" as almost belonging to the criminal classes.[30] This bigotry, as it seemed to him once he was "emancipated," was something he could never forget or forgive. And the latent bitterness it fostered was then increased a hundred fold by the frightened and ignorant outcry which too many of the clergy, led by Samuel Wilberforce, raised in the sixties against science in general, and against Darwin and Huxley in particular. Indeed, Huxley had only to read *The Origin of Species* to foresee the coming battle, and to prepare to give blow for blow. In November, 1859, he wrote to Darwin: "As to the curs which will bark and yelp, you must recollect that some of your friends, at any rate, are endowed with an amount of combativeness which . . . may stand you in good stead. I am sharpening up my claws and beak in readiness."[81] If we have more admiration for Darwin's dignified silence in the face of attack, we are far from blaming Huxley for sharpening up his rhetoric.

For this remark is an admission that he could enjoy using controversial methods rather different from "saying what I mean in the plainest of plain language." Still better, one may cite against his denials, a passage from the Prologue to *Controverted Questions:*

> If I may judge by my own taste, few literary dishes are less appetising than cold controversy; moreover, there is an air of unfairness about the presentation of only one side of a discussion, and a flavour of unkindness in the reproduction of "winged words," which, however appropriate at the time of their utterance, would find a still more appropriate place in oblivion. Yet, since I could hardly ask those who have honoured me by their polemical attentions to confer lustre on this collection, by permitting me to present their lucubrations along with my own; and since it would be a manifest wrong to them *to deprive their, by no means rare, vivacities of language of such justification as they may derive from similar freedoms on my part;* I came to the conclusion that my best course was to leave the essays just as they were written. . . .[32]

Our conclusion is, that if Huxley's style reveals a bias, a failure to recognize both sides of an issue, a play of exaggeration and insinuation calculated to impose on unwary readers and critics, this is not because he was simply a slick politician with a party platform to defend. His anti-religious rhetoric had its source in a firm belief that the term "'Nature' covers the totality of that which is,"[33] and that the religious view of man and the universe was not only an illusion, but that in the hands of its official upholders it was an obstacle to the advancement of scientific truth. His advocacy, therefore, as Wilfred Ward has noticed, "was not special pleading to order, but the outcome of deep conviction." "But none the less," Ward adds at once, "his method was distinctly that of the able and lucid exponent of one side."[34]

Notes

[1] See, for example, his "Autobiography," in *Method and Results* (New York, 1898), 16; his famous letter to Charles Kingsley, in Leonard Huxley, *Life and Letters of Thomas Henry Huxley* (New York, 1901), I, 237-8; or, for a typical sentence, "Universities: Actual and Ideal," in *Science and Education* (New York, 1898), 205: "The very air he breathes [the student in an ideal university] should be charged with that enthusiasm for truth, that fanaticism of veracity, which is a greater possession than much learning; a nobler gift than the power of increasing knowledge; by so much greater and nobler than these, as the moral nature of man is greater than the intellectual; for veracity is the heart of morality."

[2] Leonard Huxley, in *Life and Letters,* I, 494. The italics are mine.

[3] James E. Routh, Jr., "Huxley as a Literary Man" (*Century Magazine,* LXIII, 1902, 393).

[4] *Life and Letters,* I, 319-20. The same point of view is echoed through the textbooks and anthologies: see, for example, Hugh Walker, *The Literature of the Victorian Era* (Cambridge, 1940; 1st ed., 1910), 233-4; *Readings from Huxley,* ed. Clarissa Rinaker (New York, 1934; 1st ed., 1920), xxiii-xxiv; *Essays by Thomas H. Huxley,* ed. Frederick Barry (New York, 1929), xvii; Julian M. Drachman, *Studies in the Literature of Natural Science* (New York, 1930), 292. Justin McCarthy, *A History of Our Own Times, from the Accession of Queen Victoria to the General Election of 1880* (New York, n.d.), II, 634, found Huxley's style "free from any effort at rhetorical eloquence"; but that it had "all the eloquence which is born of the union of deep thought with simple expression and luminous diction." The extreme position is taken by P. C. Mitchell, *Thomas Henry Huxley* (New York and London, 1900), 216: "The more closely you analyse his pages the more certainly you find that the secret of the effect produced on you lies in the gradual development of the precise and logical ideas he wished to convey, . . . in fact, in the arts of the convinced, positive, and logical thinker, who knew exactly what he meant you to know and who set about telling you it with the least possible concern for the words he used or for the sentences into which he formed his words." This is fantastic. It would be much truer to say that Huxley relied on "the arts of the convinced, positive, *rhetorical* thinker" and that he took "the *greatest* possible concern for the words he used."

[5] 14. The lecture, which was originally printed separately in London, 1932, has been included in the *Huxley Memorial Lectures, 1925-1932,* edited by the Imperial College of Science and Technology (London, 1932).

[6] From "Mr. Darwin's Critics" in *Darwiniana* (New York, 1898), 184.

[7] *Life and Letters,* II, 419.

[8] From "Illustrations of Mr. Gladstone's Controversial Methods," in *Science and the Christian Tradition* (New York, 1898), 413-14.

[9] *Method and Results,* 3.

[10] From "Science and Morals," in *Evolution and Ethics* (New York, 1898), 128. When G. K. Chesterton quoted the remark in *The Victorian Age in Literature* (New York and London, 1913), 39, he continued, "which is itself about as well-plastered a piece of rhetoric as Ruskin himself could have managed." Needless to say, Chesterton is an exception to the critical tradition I have been describing. The only other scholar I know who has recognized the power and extent of Huxley's rhetoric is Wilfred Ward in his valuable essay on Huxley in *Problems and Persons* (London, 1903), 233, 241, and 244.

[11] This influence is revealed by the fact that Aldous Huxley, on pp. 13-14 of his lecture, quotes the comments on Gladstone and Balfour to support the conclusion that Huxley, by contrast, relied on "forceful clarity to convince his readers."

[12] *Method and Results,* 25.

[13] p. 29. The passage I am discussing is on pp. 29-31.

[14] p. 31.

[15] See, for example, "The Progress of Science," in *Method and Results,* 42; "A Liberal Education; and Where to Find It," in *Science and Education,* 94.

[16] See "Administrative Nihilism," in *Method and Results,* 252-3.

[17] From "Science and Culture," in *Science and Education,* 137 and 155.

[18] From "Sweetness and Light," in *Culture and Anarchy* (New York, 1901), 13.

[19] From the Preface to *Science and the Hebrew Tradition* (New York, 1898), ix-x.

[20] From "The Origin of Species," in *Darwiniana,* 52.

[21] *Problems and Persons,* 241.

[22] In the Prologue to *Essays on Some Controverted Questions,* reprinted in *Science and the Christian Tradition,* 39 n.

[23] Cf. a similar distinction made by E. B. Bax, *Reminiscences and Reflections of a Mid and Late Victorian* (New York, 1920), 189-95, where he discusses the meaning of the term "agnostic" as used in Huxley's period.

[24] *Method and Results,* 39-40. The entire passage I am discussing is on pp. 39-41.

[25] See, for example, *Method and Results,* 39, lines 6-9 from the bottom, and cf. the previous paragraph; *Science and Education,* 394; *Science and the Hebrew Tradition,* 288.

[26] "On the Dread and Dislike of Science" (*Fortnightly Review,* XXXIII n.s., 1878, 811).

[27] *Science and the Christian Tradition,* 5-6. The complete passage I am dealing with is on pp. 5-7.

[28] From "Agnosticism," in *Science and the Christian Tradition,* 254.

[29] *Letters and Correspondence of John Henry Newman,* ed. Anne Mozley (London, 1891), II, 324.

[30] From the Prologue to *Controverted Questions,* in *Science and the Christian Tradition,* 21-2.

[31] *Life and Letters,* I, 189.

[32] *Science and the Christian Tradition,* 2. The italics are mine.

[33] In the Prologue to *Controverted Questions,* in *Science and the Christian Tradition,* 39 n.

[34] *Problems and Persons,* 233.

Oma Stanley (essay date 1957)

SOURCE: "T. H. Huxley's Treatment of 'Nature'," in *Journal of the History of Ideas,* Vol. 18, January, 1957, pp. 120-27.

[*In the following essay, Stanley claims that Huxley's early, romantic view of nature differs from his later, scientific philosophy. Stanley suggests that the shift may have occurred as a result of John Stuart Mill's essay "Nature."*]

The reader of Thomas Henry Huxley may be puzzled in observing the contradictory points of view toward Nature embodied in the various essays. In any one essay the view is consistent. But in one piece Nature appears as a loving mother heaping rich gifts upon her children *if* they obey her rules. And in another Nature is the non-moral sum of all phenomena. That is, in one essay Huxley is romantic; in another, scientific. An effort to explain this opposition required first an examination of Huxley's writings in chronological order. This inspection revealed that in all discussions of Nature made before 1871, Huxley treated the subject from the romantic point of view; and that from 1876 onward, his attitude was scientific. Between 1870 and 1876 Huxley did not discuss the topic. The two periods are separated by an event which may have some significance; namely, the posthumous publication in 1874 of John Stuart Mill's essay "Nature," which had been completed in 1854. The possible relevance of this essay to Huxley's later treatment of Nature will be discussed in due course.

In the early period Huxley discusses Nature four times: once each in 1866 and 1868 and twice in 1870. In the later period I have found eight instances, but two of these are brief and incidental. They occur once each in the years 1876, 1878, 1880, 1888, 1890, 1892, 1893, 1894. In my own exposition of this topic I shall begin with one of the examples from 1870 because in it Huxley comments on his romantic attitude. Then I shall go back to 1866 and move along from there in an orderly fashion.

Writing to his friend Dr. Anton Dohrn on January 30, 1870, Huxley said: "Do you know I did a version of his [Goethe's] *Aphorisms on Nature* into English the other day. It astonishes the British Philistines not a little. When they began to read it they thought it was mine, and that I had suddenly gone mad!"[1]

Huxley had translated Goethe's rhapsody for the first number of *Nature,* November 4, 1869. The piece is indeed an extravaganza of poetic prose in which Nature parades as a living, breathing matron, active, purposeful, wise, and beneficent. Goethe had composed it about 1786. A few quotations from Huxley's translation will show its character:

> The one thing she [Nature] seems to aim at is Individuality; yet she cares nothing for individuals. She is always building up and destroying; but her workshop is inaccessible.
>
> She performs a play; we know not whether she sees it herself, and yet she acts for us, the lookers-on.
>
> She has always thought, and always thinks; though not as a man, but as Nature. She broods over an all-comprehending idea, which no searching can find out.
>
> Mankind dwell in her and she in them. With all men she plays a game for love, and rejoices the

Huxley, a noted zoologist, in his youth.

more they win. With many her moves are so hidden that the game is over before they know it.[2]

". . . She is beneficent. I praise her and all her works. She is silent and wise." ". . . She is cunning, but for good ends, and it is best not to notice her tricks."

Commenting on his translation, Huxley said:

> When my friend, the editor of *Nature*, asked me to write an opening article for his first number, there came into my mind this wonderful rhapsody on 'Nature' which has been a delight to me from my youth up. It seemed to me that no more fitting purpose could be put before a Journal, which aims to mirror the progress of that fashioning by Nature of a picture of herself, in the mind of man, which we call the progress of Science. . . . Supposing, however, that critical judges are satisfied with the translation as such, there lies beyond them the chance of another reckoning with the British public, who dislike what they call 'Pantheism' almost as much as I do, and who will certainly find this essay of the poet's terribly Pantheistic. In fact, Goethe himself almost admits that it is so.[3]

If the British Philistines had been familiar with Huxley's own writing about Nature up to this time, they might still have been justified in thinking that he had gone mad. They would have seen his derangement, however, not as a sudden collapse but as the climax of a process that had been going on for some time. For Huxley, though not so extravagant as Goethe and others, had written of Nature as an animate being all along and was to continue to do so until 1876, when he first had occasion to treat the subject after the publication of Mill's essay on "Nature" in 1874.

The earliest instance of Huxley's metaphorical view of Nature as animate, to my knowledge, occurs in the essay **"On the Advisableness of Improving Natural Knowledge,"** written in 1866. In this Huxley says that in the eyes of the blind leaders of the blind,

> Natural knowledge is no real mother of mankind, bringing them up with kindness, and, if needs be, with sternness, in the way they should go, and instructing them in all things needful for their welfare; but a sort of fairy godmother, ready to furnish her pets with shoes of swiftness, swords of sharpness, and omnipotent Aladdin's lamps, so that they may have telegraphs to Saturn, and see the other side of the moon, and thank God they are better than their benighted ancestors.[4]

Huxley's next exposition of Nature occurs in **"A Liberal Education and Where to Find It,"** written in 1868. Here Huxley maintains that education is knowledge of the laws of Nature. In the game of chess, man plays for his life, fortune, and happiness *against* Nature, whose "play is always fair, just, and patient," and who "never overlooks a mistake, or makes the smallest allowance for ignorance." Originally this piece was a lecture delivered to working men who had little or no mental training. In this, as in other talks to similar groups, Huxley suited his expository method to his audience. He states in the essay that he is using a metaphor. Nevertheless it is a figure which embodies the old pathetic fallacy of the romantic poets. And Huxley emphasizes it by recalling Retzsch's painting of Satan playing at chess with a man for his soul. Huxley suggests that if a "calm, strong angel who is playing for love" be substituted for the fiend—an angel who "would rather lose than win,"—one would have an acceptable image of human life. Other figurative uses are seen in the following: "Nature would begin to teach him,"—i.e., a man created adult. "Nature took us in hand,"—i.e., all born into the world. "Nature is still continuing her patient education of us. . . ." "Nature's pluck means extermination."

Man brings himself into "harmony with Nature" through training and self-discipline: he has trained his passions to come to heel by a vigorous will. Huxley goes so far as to say here that the moral laws of men are grounded in Nature:

> . . . there lies in the nature of things a reason for every moral law, as cogent and as well defined as

that which underlies every physical law; that stealing and lying are just as certain to be followed by evil consequences, as putting your hand in the fire, or jumping out of a garret window.[5]

Nature again appears fully personified in 1870 in Huxley's essay, **"On the Formation of Coal"**: "Nature is never in a hurry and seems to have had always before her eyes the adage, 'Keep a thing long enough, and you will find a use for it.'" Nature has

> kept her beds of coal many millions of years without being able to find much use for them; she has sent them down beneath the sea, and the sea-beasts could make nothing of them; . . . and it was only the other day, so to speak, that she turned a new creature out of her workshop, who by degrees acquired sufficient wits to make a fire, and then to discover that the black rock would burn.

> The English people grew into a powerful nation, and Nature still waited for a full return of the capital she had invested in the ancient club-mosses.

> Thus, all this abundant wealth of money and of vivid life is Nature's interest upon her investment in club-mosses, and the like so long ago. But what becomes of the coal which is burnt in yielding this interest? Heat comes out of it, light comes out of it; and if we could gather together all that goes up the chimney, and all that remains in the grate of a thoroughly-burnt coal-fire, we should find ourselves in possession of a quantity of carbonic acid, water, ammonia, and mineral matters, exactly equal in weight to the coal. But these are the very matters with which nature supplied the club-mosses which made the coal. She is paid back principal and interest at the same time; and she straightway invests the carbonic acid, the water, and the ammonia in new forms of life, feeding with them the plants that now live. Thrifty Nature! Surely no prodigal, but most notable of housekeepers![6]

Though an examination of the *Life and Letters* and other possible sources[7] has disclosed no direct evidence of Huxley's having read John Stuart Mill's essay, "Nature," Huxley's own handling of the subject before and after the appearance of Mill's essay strongly suggests that he knew it and that he changed his way of writing about Nature partly as a result of reading Mill. He knew Mill's other writings and had a high opinion of them, or at least of some of them, and of Mill as a man of parts. So it seems unlikely that Huxley would not have read Mill's "Nature" when it appeared in 1874, the year following Mill's death.

It will suffice to quote the concluding paragraphs of Mill's essay:

> The word Nature has two principal meanings: it either denotes the entire system of things, with the aggregate of all their properties, or it denotes things as they would be, apart from human intervention.

> In the first of these senses, the doctrine that man ought to follow nature is unmeaning; since man has no power to do anything else than follow nature; all his actions are done through, and in obedience to, some one or many of nature's physical or mental laws.

> In the other sense of the term, the doctrine that man ought to follow nature, or in other words, ought to make the spontaneous course of things the model of his voluntary actions, is equally irrational and immoral.

> Irrational, because all human action whatever, consists in altering, and all useful action in improving, the spontaneous course of nature:

> Immoral, because the course of natural phenomena being replete with everything which when committed by human beings is most worthy of abhorrence, any one who endeavoured in his actions to imitate the natural course of things would be universally seen and acknowledged to be the wickedest of men.

> The scheme of Nature regarded in its whole extent, cannot have had, for its sole or even principal object, the good of human or other sentient beings. What good it brings to them, is mostly the result of their own exertions. Whatsoever, in nature, gives indica-tion of beneficent design, proves this beneficence to be armed only with limited power; and the duty of man is to co-operate with the beneficent powers, not by imitating but by perpetually striving to amend the course of nature— and bringing that part of it over which we can exercise control, more nearly into conformity with a high standard of justice and goodness.[8]

Huxley's first occasion to comment on Nature after the publication of Mill's essay came in 1876. Huxley was now 51 years of age. The essay is **"The Three Hypotheses Respecting the History of Nature."** Here Huxley speaks of Nature as "a system of things of immense diversity and perplexity"; and of the "conception of the constancy of the order of Nature," which, he says, has become the dominant idea of modern thought.[9]

There is no direct evidence in this essay that Huxley had read Mill. But, though he does not define Nature any further than stated above, his point of view is scientific, not at all romantic. His next discussion, however, seems to reflect Mill clearly. This occurs in *Hume, With Helps to the Study of Berkeley,* written in 1878. On p. 154 Huxley says in part:

"The definition of a miracle as a 'violation of the laws of nature' is, in reality, an employment of language which, on the face of the matter, cannot be justified. For `nature' means neither more nor less than that which is; the sum of phenomena presented to our experience; the totality of events past, present, and to come. Every event must be taken to be a part of nature until proof to the contrary is supplied. And such proof is, from the nature of the case, impossible."

In this passage, the words "sum of phenomena" are those Mill used—though Mill had said "sum of all phenomena."[10] The whole sentence in which the phrase occurs, however, reflects Mill.

In **"Science and Culture,"** Huxley seems to have suffered a momentary lapse into the earlier point of view expressed in **"A Liberal Education and Where to Find It,"** discussed above. For in **"Science and Culture,"** written in 1880, he says: "They [both capitalist and operative] must learn that social phenomena are as much the expression of natural laws as any others. . . ."[11]

In **"The Struggle for Existence in Human Society,"** however, written in 1888, Huxley clearly maintains the scientific attitude, when he speaks of "the vast and varied procession of events, which we call Nature." In demonstrating his thesis that Nature is "neither moral nor immoral, but non-moral," Huxley uses the deer and the wolf as examples. The deer has skill which enables it to escape from the wolf; the wolf has skill which enables it to track and finally bring down the deer. Viewed under the dry light of science, says Huxley, they are alike admirable. But the deer suffers; the wolf inflicts suffering. This engages *our* moral sympathies. *We* call the deer good, the wolf bad; men who are like the deer we call innocent and good; men who are like the wolf, malignant and bad. But if we transfer these judgments to nature outside the world of man at all, we must do so impartially. Thus nature is *non*-moral.[12]

Another significant passage in the same essay reads as follows:

> In the strict sense of the word 'nature,' it denotes the sum of the phenomenal world, of that which has been, and is, and will be; and society, like art, is therefore a part of nature. But it is convenient to distinguish those parts of nature in which man plays the part of immediate cause, as something apart; and, therefore, society, like art, is usefully to be considered as distinct from nature. It is the more desirable, and even necessary, to make this distinc-tion, since society differs from nature in having a definite moral object; whence it comes about that the course shaped by the ethical . . . necessarily runs counter to that which the non-ethical man—the primitive savage . . . —tends to adopt. The latter fights out the struggle for existence to the bitter end, like any other animal; the former devotes his best energies to the object of setting limits to the struggle.[13]

This material is clearly reminiscent of Mill, whose essay contains at least two passages which treat the opposition of Nature to Art (cf. Mill's essay, "Nature," 7-8, 20-21). In the latter, Mill says: "Everybody professes to approve and admire many great triumphs of Art over Nature. . . ." And two years later, in a letter of October 27, 1890, to Mr. W. Platt Ball, Huxley states his position even more pointedly and explicitly. "Of moral purpose I see no trace in Nature," he says. "That is an article of exclusively human manufacture—and very much to our credit."[14]

In the **"Prologue"** to *Science and Christian Tradition,* written in 1892, there is no reflection of Mill. The following passage is worth including, however, because in it Huxley describes the conception of nature and the "supernatural" held by undeveloped minds, and in doing so he avoids all romantic pitfalls. In a situation which might easily have tempted him to personify nature, he speaks plainly and factually:

> Experience speedily taught them [i.e., "thinking men"] that the shifting scenes of the world's stage have a permanent background; that there is order amidst the seeming confusion, and that many events take place according to unchanging rules. To this region of familiar steadiness and customary regularity they gave the name Nature. But, at the same time, their infantile and untutored reason, little more, as yet, than the playfellow of the imagination, led them to believe that this tangible, commonplace, orderly world of Nature was surrounded and interpenetrated by another intangible and mysterious world, no more bound by fixed rules than, as they fancied, were the thoughts and passions which coursed through their minds and seemed to exercise an intermittent and capricious rule over their bodies. They attributed to the entities, with which they peopled this dim and dreadful region, an unlimited amount of that power of modifying the course of events of which they themselves possessed a small share, and thus came to regard them as not merely beyond, but above, Nature.
>
> Hence arose the conception of a 'Supernature' antithetic to 'Nature'—the primitive dualism of a natural world 'fixed in fate' and a supernatural, left to the free play of volition. . . . [15]

In a footnote on page 39 of this **"Prologue"** Huxley comments significantly on his use of the words "Supernature" and "Supernatural." "I employ the words 'Supernature' and 'Supernatural'," he says, "in their popular senses. For myself, I am bound to say that the term 'Nature' covers the totality of that which is. The world of psychical phenomena appears to me to be as much part of 'Nature' as the world of physical phenomena: and I am unable to perceive any justification for cutting the Universe into two halves, one natural and one supernatural."

In **"Evolution and Ethics,"** the Romanes Lecture of 1893, Huxley was mainly concerned with the development of ethical standards. However, he does refer significantly to Nature, even though his treatment is brief and incidental. "The thief and the murderer," he says, "follow nature just as much as the philanthropist." This, I think, is a strong echo of Mill's treatment of his first definition of Nature: everything that is.

Throughout this essay Huxley seems to be most careful of his words in his references to Nature. He speaks of "cosmic nature" and "the cosmic process." Nowhere is there a suggestion of consciousness or purpose in Nature. Social and moral progress results from man's checking of the cosmic process. But this process, as he uses the phrase, is not a process carried on by a conscious cosmos. All that Huxley says in this essay about the development and practice of ethics against the cosmic process reflects Mill's discussion of his second definition of Nature, that is, things as they would be without human intervention.[16]

Huxley discusses Nature in greater detail in **"Evolution and Ethics, Prolegomena,"**[17] which he wrote in 1894, the year before his death. It appears in the published works as a sort of introduction to, or first half of, the Romanes Lecture of the previous year. Throughout this essay Huxley maintains the scientific attitude toward Nature. For example: "That the state of nature, at any time, is a temporary phase of a process of incessant change, which has been going on for innumerable ages, appears to me to be a proposition as well established as any in modern history."[18] It is in this essay that Huxley uses his famous illustration of the garden in discussing the intervention of man in the state of nature. The whole treatment calls to mind Mill's second definition of Nature: "things as they would be, apart from human intervention." A "state of Art," Huxley says, is created by man and sustained by him. The state of nature is hostile to the state of art. "Even in the state of nature itself, what is the struggle for existence but the antagonism of the results of the cosmic process in the region of life, one to another?"[19] And finally,

> That which lies before the human race is a constant struggle to maintain and improve, in opposition to the State of Nature, the State of Art or an organized polity; in which, and by which, man may develop a worthy civilization, capable of maintaining and constantly improving itself, until the evolution of our globe shall have entered so far upon its downward course that the cosmic process resumes its sway; and, once more, the State of Nature prevails over the surface of our planet.[20]

The conclusion may be brief.

I have found no statement by Huxley that he had read Mill's essay "Nature." And certainly he might have arrived at his later conception, and probably would have, if Mill had never written "Nature." The changing intellectual climate, the general shift of informed opinion toward scientific views, especially after the publication of Darwin's *Origin* in 1859, would have been enough in itself to impel Huxley to speak precisely rather than colorfully, even in popular lectures. Also, Huxley's whole treatment of Nature, early and late, might have sprung from some of the Greek and Latin writers who had dealt with the subject.[21] In the absence of conclusive evidence, therefore, Mill's influence must remain conjectural. There are two facts, however, which I think form reasonable props to my surmise that Huxley revised his conception of Nature under the influence of Mill's essay. These are (1) that Huxley did not manifest the scientific attitude to Nature until 1876, two years after Mill's essay was published; and (2) that Huxley's later discussions reflect Mill clearly, sometimes to the extent of employing the same words, whereas the ones prior to 1874 portray Nature as an animate being.

Notes

[1] Leonard Huxley, *Life and Letters of Thomas Henry Huxley* (London, 1900), I, 326-327.

[2] This looks like the source of Huxley's famous game-of-chess illustration in his essay, "A Liberal Education and Where to Find It," of which more anon.

[3] The excerpts from Huxley's translation, and Huxley's comment, are taken from Wolfgang von Goethe and Thomas Henry Huxley, "'Nature'; A Literary Find," *Living Age,* 330 (1926), 681-683.

All students of the 19th century are familiar with Mr. Joseph Warren Beach's study, *The Concept of Nature in Nineteenth Century English Poetry* (New York, 1936). In this book Mr. Beach gives a superlative treatment of the romantic attitude toward Nature as shown in the poetry of the period. It may be pertinent, however, to quote from what a later writer has to say about Matthew Arnold in this connection. Mr. Lionel Trilling, in his *Matthew Arnold* (New York, 1949), says in part (89f.):

> The Art of Goethe, the Beauty of Keats, Love, History, Mind, Self, Society—all had been used to reanimate the world, and of all the new myths perhaps the most successful had been the myth of animate Nature, of which Wordsworth had been the chief exponent. However frequently Arnold may recur to the Spinozistic simplicity that Nature is without mind or personality, he is ever trying some new subtlety to deny what he has affirmed. He has not yet come to his mature sense of 'what pitfalls there are in that word Nature!'

Indeed, in his poetical youth the variety of meaning Arnold gives to the treacherous word is in itself sufficient justification for Mill's famous essay "Nature". If, in one sonnet, he cries, 'one lesson, Nature, let me learn of thee'—the lesson of quiet work—in another, 'To an Independent Preacher Who Preached That We Should Be "In Harmony With Nature",' he furiously attacks the shallowness of the preacher's sentiment." Here Mr. Trilling quotes the last eight lines of the poem, in which occur the statements that Nature is cruel, stubborn, fickle; and that she forgives no debt and fears no grave. He continues by commenting on Arnold's similar treat-ments of Nature in "Religious Isolation," "Morality," and "In Utrumque Paratus."

These comments help to show how widespread the addiction to the pathetic fallacy was at the time. It is no wonder that even scientifically minded people like Huxley fell under such a pervasive spell. Even Mill, it will be remembered, found solace for a time in the poems of Wordsworth. Apparently, however, he finally realized how absurd the current attitude toward Nature was and in his essay "Nature," written in 1854 when the reaction to the Wordsworthian pantheistic spiritu-alization of Nature was at its height, set himself the task of establishing a reasonable view.

[4] *Method and Results* (New York, 1897), 30. Huxley's use of "natural knowledge" instead of "Nature" in this passage suggests a momentary confusion of terms. In the preceding paragraph he speaks of natural knowledge as the "bountiful mother of humanity." This follows his reference to the peasant woman knitting stockings for her family while climbing the mountain to her home. Surely, Huxley says, one does not think of this toiling mother as a mere stocking-machine. In the passage quoted, it seems reasonable to surmise that he had "Nature" in mind when he used "natural knowledge." Regardless of the term meant, however, the personification is there.

[5] The quotations from this essay may be found in *Science and Education* (N.Y., 1897), 80-88. The italics for *against* are mine. With reference to the quotations in the last paragraph above, Huxley's change of view later will be treated below.

[6] All quotations are from *Discourses Biological and Geological* (N.Y., 1897), 159-161.

[7] Specifically, Clarence Ayres' biography, Michael St. John Packe's recent biography of Mill, and Houston Peterson's *Huxley, Prophet of Science* (New York, 1932). Though Peterson does not mention noticing Huxley's shift in point of view, he does say (283) that Huxley's essay, "Evolution and Ethics," is "little more than a restatement of Mill's essay on nature in the language of a later generation nourished on *The Origin of Species.*" That is, Peterson noted the similarity be-tween Huxley's later view and Mill's treatment in the essay, "Nature." But he did not mention Huxley's shift, though he did note (166) Huxley's earlier contribution to the magazine *Nature,* cited above.

[8] J. S. Mill, *Nature, The Utility of Religion, and The-ism* (London, 1874), 64-65.

[9] *Science and Hebrew Tradition* (N.Y., 1897), 46-47.

[10] *Op. cit.,* 5. The *Hume* was published in 1896.

[11] *Science and Education,* 158.

[12] *Evolution and Ethics,* 195, 197. Italics mine.

[13] *Ibid.,* 202-203.

[14] *Life and Letters,* II, 268.

[15] *Science and Christian Tradition* (N.Y., 1900), 3-4.

[16] *Evolution and Ethics,* 80-81f.

[17] *Evolution and Ethics,* 1-45.

[18] *Ibid.,* 5.

[19] *Ibid.,* 13.

[20] *Ibid.,* 44-5.

[21] Arthur O. Lovejoy and George Boas, *Primitivism and Related Ideas in Antiquity* (Baltimore, 1935). See espe-cially meanings of "Nature," 14-17 inclusive, 448-449.

Sir Michael Foster's high opinion of Huxley, as expressed in his obituary in the Proceedings of the Royal Society:

Whatever bit of life he touched in his search, protozoan, polyp, mollusc, crustacean, fish, reptile, beast, and man— and there were few living things that he did not touch— he shed light on it, and left his mark. There is not one, or hardly one, of the many things which he has written which may not be read again to-day with pleasure and with profit; and, not once or twice only in such reading, it will be felt that the progress of science has given to words written long ago, a strength and meaning even greater than that which they seemed to have when first they were read. There is not a biologist of the latter half of this century who has not been helped on his way, directly or indirectly, by some research or by some word of Huxley's. And though those who are coming after can never be fully aware of how great was the personal influence of the man outside his recorded words, the writings which do remain will serve to keep alive the memory of one who, while with his own hand he added many chambers to the growing building of biologic science, did almost as much by a life which taught both his comrades and lookers on, the beauty, dignity and power of natural knowledge.

Sir Michael Foster, quoted in Huxley: Prophet of Science, *edited by Houston Peterson, Longmans, Green and Co., 1932.*

Charles S. Blinderman (essay date 1962)

SOURCE: "T. H. Huxley's Theory of Aesthetics: Unity in Diversity," in *Journal of Aesthetics and Art Criticism,* Vol. 21, Fall, 1962, pp. 49-55.

[*In the following essay, Blinderman examines Huxley's art criticism as it bridges the gap between science and humanities and explicates his literary powers.*]

Leonardo Da Vinci, painter and inventor, and Albert Einstein, violinist and mathematician and social critic, were geniuses of Protean talent, creative in art and science. Another such figure whose works are illuminated by the creative imagination which makes for constant contemporaneity was Thomas Henry Huxley. He is less well known than these two epitomes of human power, but he was a spokesman of the Victorian New Reformation, a prophet of science, and a critic of art. Huxley's unpublished papers confirm the conviction of students familiar with his published volumes that he was more than Darwin's bulldog—though his efforts as a popularizer of Darwinism need not be belittled. In addition to being a scientist of noteworthy repute, he was an artist in prose, a point generally conceded even by those victim to his episcophagous appetite. He was, furthermore, a critic of art whose commentaries upon structure are valuable in at least two respects. First of all, these commentaries indicate that a sense of structure pervaded his thinking, manifesting itself in his scientific research, in his philosophical excursions, and in his literary endeavors. In a wider dimension, they lead towards a synthesis which demonstrates that the bridging of the gap between the "two cultures" of science and the humanities can be achieved through an engagement with form as well as through that commitment to man's welfare which is, I believe, the ultimate responsibility of both. From a presentation of Huxley's commentaries upon art we may extrapolate that unity.

Although this paper will be primarily devoted to a presentation and analysis of his commentaries upon aesthetics, a brief discussion of his scientific and philosophical work will illustrate the first thesis, namely, that in both disciplines the architectonic faculty was the operative agent. E. Ray Lankester, one of Huxley's laboratory protégés, wrote of his teacher that he dealt with form not only as an engineer but also as an artist, "a born lover of form, a character which others recognize in him though he does not himself set it down in his analysis."[1] This is slightly inaccurate: Huxley did in fact set it down in his autobiography, where he confesses that as a medical student he cared little for medicine as the healing art, but much about physiology (uniquely defined by him as "the mechanical engineering of living things"); little for species work, but much for "the architectural and engineering part of the business, the working out the wonderful unity of plan in the thousands and thousands of diverse living constructions, and the modifications of similar apparatuses to serve diverse ends." In a comparable autobiographical note for Francis Galton's study of famous men, Huxley observed that he had a "Strong natural talent for mechanism . . . ,"[2] a talent which was first revealed when as a boy he attempted to invent a perpetual motion machine. Unlike Darwin, Huxley was not a field naturalist; he was a morphologist, and it is in morphology, significantly enough, that he made a number of original contributions to biology.

Early in his career, Huxley discerned a conflict between the scientific view of the universe, with its imposition of mechanism, and the religious view, with its imposition of a transcendental designer. In an essay written during his early years, he exclaimed, without thinking clearly about the matter:

> In traveling from one end to the other of the scale of life, we are taught one lesson, that living nature is not a mechanism but a poem; not a rough engine-house for the due keeping of pleasure and pain machines, but a palace whose foundations, indeed, are laid on the strictest and safest mechanical principles, but whose superstructure is a manifestation of the highest and noblest art.[3]

He later recognized that such a view, specifically antagonistic to Darwinian utilitarianism, had to be modified; that emphasis had to be placed upon the machine aspect and not upon the poetic nature of the cosmos. As a scientist, he found himself daily occupied with investigating homologues and tracing them to an archetypal origin, as he did in his vital research on the Labyrinthrodont, birds, and the horse. This first paper, in fact, which won for him acceptance into the Royal Society and its medal, was a clarification of the systematics of coellenterate and related animals.

Though he refuted the accusation that his philosophy was one of materialism, Huxley was a materialist in the classic sense—a follower of Democritus, inspired by atomism, mechanism, and determinism—and in the Victorian sense—a follower of Darwin, inspired by a totally natural sequence of development. He went further than Darwin in adapting materialistic principles to Victorian science, popularizing the abominable (to some critics) notion that in his living activities man is a machine. He asserted that we shall discover a mechanical equivalence for consciousness as we have discovered one for heat. To Alfred Whitehead and to most critics of a fundamentalistic bent, materialism is a dull and senseless philosophy; but to Huxley, the operation of discrete mechanisms to produce unified behavior was a scene of intense, and, furthermore, reasonable, activity.

As Lankester suggests, others have recognized in Huxley a born lover of form. His scientific colleagues were enthusiastic in their praise of this quality: one noted that Huxley was a "master of intellectual design," another that he had a profound" passion for logical symmetry," and a third (a literary critic this time) that Huxley's prose style is comparable to a building "destitute of ornament, but beautiful by reason of its outline and proportion."[4] The Positivist Frederic Harrison once wrote, in a passage I quote at length because it is a perceptive analysis not only of the way in which Huxley structured a scientific-philosophical argument but also because it illustrates the contention that Huxley was an influential force in Western thought:

> In consequence of the way the Bishop of Oxford attacked Huxley, he has determined to popularize the question, and has devoted this course to the "relation of man to the quadrumana."

> Last night's lecture I thought a type of popular exposition, central, broad, clear, positive, suggestive, and elementary. It at once took one into the radical ideas of biology and handled them from a social and practical point of view. It was on the development of the embryo as seen by comparative physiology from impregnation to parturition. He took a frog (by diagrams) and detailed the outline of this process, then ran down the scale of life into plants, showing an identical process less developed throughout, then up the scale of life, showing the same in gradually increasing complexity. Having carried the inquiry to the mammalia he analyzed in detail the process in the dog, then came to his last stage by exhibiting identical and scarcely distinguishable processes in man, showing that the changes from the dog to man are infinitely less than from the frog to the dog, etc., etc. Thus in the cardinal idea of life he established one grand analogy, delicately graduated through the whole scale of life, from the lowest plant to man himself.

> The proposition to which his six lectures are devoted is this, "Biology shows less structural difference between man and the higher apes than between the higher and lower apes; and far less than between the higher apes and inferior animals." This is the *provocatio ad populum* with a vengeance. . . . It will want many sermons to undo last night's work.[5]

In a sense, nature itself provided the organization for this lecture; Huxley in proceeding from the lowest forms of life to the highest through embryological development simply recapitulated phylogeny. But even when a definite structure was not implicit in the matters which he treated, as was the case with philosophical and religious disquisitions, he invariably located a unifying principle and presented it with its adumbrating illustrations in such a manner that the chaos of natural phenomena or of philosophical controversy was reduced to a cosmos. This reduction of chaos to cosmos, this discovery of a unifying principle, seems to have been characteristic of things other than scientific exercises

or literary popularizations. Wilfred Ward pointed out that Huxley's conversation was "singularly finished, and . . . clean cut; never longwinded or prosy; enlivened by vivid illustrations"; Sir William Flower recollected in a statement which in its import is similar to that of Ward's, "In dissecting, as in everything else, he was a very rapid worker, going straight to the point he wished to ascertain with a firm and steady hand, never diverted into side issues, nor wasting any time in unnecessary polishing up for the sake of appearance." P. Chalmers Mitchell, isolating the single rein which enabled Huxley to ride in admirable concord the contentious Pegasuses of science and literature, wrote:

> The fundamental method of his exposition was simply the method of comparative anatomy, the result of a habit of thinking which makes it impossible to have any set of ideas brought into the mind without an immediate, almost unconscious overhauling of the memory for any other ideas at all congruous.[6]

Huxley recognized the fact that there was a similarity in the approach of scientist and artist, a similarity predicated upon the discernment by both of what Walter Pater called "mind in style," of what Dewey was alluding to in commenting upon the "ordering" of "energies," of what Lipps meant in speaking of "unity in variety," of what DeWitt H. Parker called "evolution," of what Huxley himself termed "unity in diversity."

In an undated fragment in which he discussed the province of science, Huxley wrote that "In the great majority of our thoughts . . . the scientific and the aesthetic elements are inseparably commingled." He was here referring in part to the fact that certain men of science, such as himself, and certain men of letters, such as Charles Kingsley, shared certain social and philosophical values. It should not be forgotten that Huxley disdained a program of science for science's sake and art for art's sake, that for him both science and art were means towards the end of a reconstructed society; he said once that we value great literature not only for its artistic form but also for its intellectual content. But when he reminded his audience that Aristotle, Galileo, and Descartes were artists as well as scientists, he had in mind something other than their common possession of the great ideas; he had in mind their ambition to structure the universe. If we do not assume this, then his further remark that "there is hardly a work of art which does not contain a scientific element—hardly a great artist who is not in the broad sense of the word a man of science"[7] becomes fatuous.

The rapprochement between science and art through the discovery of symmetry or through the imposition of order was a favorite subject for Huxley's commentary upon aesthetics. He returned to unity in diversity when he spoke of music, of architecture, of drawing and painting, and of literary style. Both a general statement of his theory of aesthetics and a specific application of that theory are evident in this passage, from **"On Science and Art in Relation to Education"**:

> I cannot give you any example of a thorough aesthetic pleasure more intensely real than a pleasure of this kind—the pleasure which arises in one's mind when a whole mass of different structures run into one harmony as the expression of a central law. . . . it has often occurred to me that the pleasure derived from musical compositions of this kind [Bach's fugues] is essentially of the same nature as that which is derived from pursuits which are commonly regarded as purely intellectual. I mean, that the source of pleasure is exactly the same as in most of my problems in morphology—that you have the theme in one of the old master's works followed out in all its endless variations, always appearing and always reminding you of unity in variety. So in painting: what is called "truth to nature" is the intellectual element coming in, and truth to nature depends entirely upon the intellectual culture of the person to whom art is addressed.

Again, this time from a technical essay in *Scientific Memoirs,* he developed an extended metaphor to communicate the idea:

> Flowers are the primers of the morphologist; those who run may read in them uniformity of type amidst endless diversity, singleness of plan with complex multiplicity of detail. As a musician might say, every natural group of flowering plants is a sort of visible fugue, wandering about a central theme which is never forsaken, however it may, momentarily, cease to be apparent.[8]

As Laurence Buermeyer wrote of a symphony—that it must have variety and unity, but that it must also have a recognizable theme amidst variations—so Huxley, the morphologist, wrote of flowers.

To turn to the other three arts, those of a visual nature, we see the same general principle underlying his unsys-tematized theory of aesthetics. In a little-known article written in 1887 for *The Youth's Companion,* Huxley traced the evolution of building types from the hut to the pantheon much as he traced embryological development in the lecture noted earlier. In the course of this article on architecture occurs this redaction of his thesis:

> Beauty, as a general rule, implies simplicity; I do not mean the simplicity of monotony, but the simplicity of unity. That which is highly and nobly beautiful always conveys an impression of balance, harmony, or rhythm; the parts, however various they may be, are related in a way which produces an intellectual satisfaction. Mind agitates the mass of sensible impressions; the inner order shines through them and appeals to the reason.[9]

Huxley's activities were so varied and extensive, that one is in danger if he flatly states that Huxley was not a practicing architect. He was, however, a practicing artist. His *Rattlesnake* memoirs contain dozens of closely representational sketches of natives, tools, vessels, marine fauna, sketches which in their clarity and precision are the envy of those uninitiated who can no more make a sketch look like what they are looking at than they can fly. As a teacher Huxley delighted his students with blackboard caricatures of so provocative a nature that students in later years recalled this visual aid as one of the more memorable aspects of the course. The drawings in his zoological notebooks are so admirably executed that they have elicited from biological illustrators the criticism that they are "illuminated by the fascination which the structure of animals held for him."[10]

Huxley once remarked that a competent artist could discover without prior instruction the essential resemblances between a bird skeleton and a mammalian skeleton, for the artist, like the osteologist, has been trained to seek "unity in diversity." He gave the highest praise to the artist, first by continually insisting that training in drawing should be part of the student's liberal education, second by such compliments as this one, delivered at a Royal Academy meeting in 1876:

> I will be generous, and acquaint you with a fact not generally known; to wit, that the recent progress of biological speculation leads to the conclusion that the scale of being must be thus stated—minerals, plants, animals, men who cannot draw—artists. Thence I conclude, sir that you, as President of the Academy, are the crown and summit of creation. My statement, however complimentary, may be a little startling, and you will, therefore, I hope, permit me to state the grounds on which it takes rank as scientific truth. We have been long seeking, as you may be aware, for a distinction between men and animals. The old barriers have long broken away. Other things walk on two legs and have no feathers, caterpillars make themselves clothes, kangaroos have pockets. If I am not to believe that my dog reasons, loves, and hates, how am I to be sure that my neighbour does? Parrots, again, talk what deserves the name of sense as much as a great deal which it would be rude to call nonsense. Again, beavers and ants engineer as well as the members of the noblest profession. But, as a friend of mine discovered a few years ago, man alone can draw or make unto himself a likeness. This, then, is the great distinction of humanity, and it follows that the most pre-eminently human of creatures are those who possess this distinction in the highest degree.[11]

The study of a lobster's body rings illustrates "unity of plan, diversity in execution"; so does the study of flowers; of music; of the pantheon; of drawings; and so does the study of literary style. It is with respect to this point that Huxley penned his most thorough exposition of his theory of aesthetics. In criticizing the writing of his friends, he was concerned more with organization—structure—than with any other single quality. Thus, aware of the superlative significance of "literary form and logical structure," he complained of German writers that "most of them have no notion of style, and seem to compose their books with a pitchfork"; he observed of Darwin's style: "Exposition was not Dar-win's *forte*—and his English is sometimes wonderful. But there is a marvellous dumb sagacity about him—like that of a sort of miraculous dog—and he gets to the truth by ways as dark as those of the heathen Chinee"; and he advised one of his laboratory assistants:

> From a literary point of view, my dear friend, you remind me of nothing so much as a dog going home. He has a goal before him which he will certainly reach sooner or later, but first he is on this side of the road, and now on that; anon, he stops to scratch at an ancient rat-hole, or maybe he catches sight of another dog, a quarter of a mile behind, and bolts off to have a friendly, or inimical sniff. In fact, his course is . . . (here a tangled maze is drawn) not———

In his own writing, Huxley strove above all for direction, unity, structural integrity, and such eager responses as that of artisans who were pleased by "a regular logical argument" over which he had labored reinforced his decision to enable his audience to discover, as he had done, "unity in diversity."[12]

Huxley considered clear language and emotive language contradictory states of writing, though he indulged in both at the same time; he also advised writers not to emulate models. But even in commenting upon these points, he returned to that unity the ascertainment of which gave a feeling of pleasure and power. Incompetent writing, however important the subject matter, was not good enough:

> If the name of literature may be applied to all the publications which owe their origin to the activity of scientific investigators and thinkers there can be no question that the magnitude and importance of the scientific literature of the present day has no precedent in human history.

He went on, in this unpublished paper on literary style, to declare that though scientific blue books cannot be reckoned as literature there is, however,

> a portion of scientific work which seems to me to have an indisputable claim to the title of literature. I mean the work of the popular expositor—of the man who being a well qualified interpreter of nature translates that interpretation out of the hieratic language of the experts into the demotic vulgar tongue of all the world. I call this literature for it seems to me to be the essence of literature that it embodies great emotions and great thoughts, in such form that they touch the hearts and reach the apprehensions not merely of the select few but of all mankind.

That is the work which lies before every man of science who is worthy of the name, who addresses a popular audience. He should be mindful of the maxims of one of the greatest philosophers and perhaps the greatest popularizer of the last century. That every subject is a unity and however vast it may be may be embraced by a single discourse; that full and familiar knowledge is the condition of successful exposition; that every sentence should be a link in a chain of ideas; that entire good faith is the best way of shewing respect for one's hearers or readers and that nothing comes of imitation but that every man's style should express his own individuality.[13]

In a second undated paper, this one in printed form, Huxley answered the question posed by a symposium topic, "Good writing: a gift or an art?," by summarizing his principles of literary style, bringing together in a single long passage his ideas on the necessity of clear thinking (by which may be understood knowledge of subject-matter and ability to structure that knowledge), the value of appropriate language, and the primacy of the architectonic sense, here conceived of as an innate quality:

> They [Defoe, Hobbes, and Gibbon] were great writers, in the first place, because, by dint of learning and thinking, they had acquired clear and vivid conceptions about one or other of the many aspects of men or things. In the second place, because they took infinite pains to embody these conceptions in language exactly adapted to convey them to other minds. In the third place, because they possessed that purely artistic sense of rhythm and proportion which enabled them to add grace to force, and, while loyal to truth, make exactness subservient to beauty.

> I cannot say that the principles I have laid down have been my own guides; they are rather the result of a long experience. A considerable vein of indolence runs through my composition, and forty years ago there was nothing I disliked so much as the labour of writing. It was a task I desired to get over and done with as soon as possible. The result was such as might be expected.

> If there is any merit in my English now, it is due to the fact that I have by degrees become awake to the importance of the three conditions of good writing which I have mentioned. I have learned to spare no labour upon the process of acquiring clear ideas—to think nothing of writing a page four or five times over if nothing less will bring the words which express all that I mean, and nothing more than I mean; and to regard rhetorical verbosity as the deadliest and most degrading of literary sins. Any one who possesses a tolerably clear head and a decent conscience should be able, if he will give himself the necessary trouble, thus to fulfill the first two conditions of a good style. The carrying out of the third depends, neither on labour nor on honesty,

but on that sense which is inborn in the literary artist, and can by no means be given to him who has it not as his birthright. I should so much like to flatter myself that I am one of the "well-born" in this respect that I dare not speculate on the subject. Vanity, like sleeping dogs, should be let lie.[14]

Huxley hoped that the natural sciences would "furnish that common ground upon which Men of Science and Men of Letters are most disposed to meet," meaning by this that science deals with those "great thoughts" which become the "great emotions" of literature and that both are in pursuit of "unity in diversity." The following quotation—again from an unpublished manuscript—and the two previous long quotations together comprise the closest statement one can get of Huxley's theory of art. At a meeting of the Royal Academy in 1887, Huxley spoke of

> the undying instinct of curiosity in mankind, in part the sense of symmetry and beauty, and in part the instinct which is so characteristic of man to do that which Faust in his despair refused to do—to say to the moment, "Stop," and to arrest in forms intelligible by the feelings or by the intellect the different phases of that astonishing and continually marvellous flux of phenomena which passes before the eyes of the lower forms of life unnoticed, uncounted, and unregarded. I imagine that it is the business of the artist and of the man of letters to reproduce and fix forms of imagination to which the mind will afterwards recur with pleasure; so, based upon the same great principle by the same instinct, if I may so call it, it is the business of the man of science to symbolize, and fix, and represent to our mind in some easily recallable shape, the order, and the symmetry, and the beauty that prevail throughout nature.

> I am not sure that any of us can go much further from the one to the other. We speak in symbols. The artist places his colours upon the wall; the colours have no relation to the actual objects, but they serve their purpose in recalling the emotions which were present when the scenes which they depict were acted. I am not at all sure that the conceptions of science have much more correspondence with reality than the colours of the artist have; but they are the symbols by which we are constantly recalling the order and beauty of nature, and by which we by degrees force our way further and further into her penetralia, acquiring a greater insight into the mystery and wonder which are around us, and at the same time, by a happy chance, contributing to the happiness and the prosperity of mankind. . . .art and literature and science are one.[15]

Huxley's talent as an artist in prose has led some critics to contend that, in the words of the unsympathetic G. K. Chesterton, "Huxley . . . was much more a literary man than a scientific man," or, in the stronger statement of the sympathetic H. L. Mencken, Huxley

was "a master-writer even more than a master biologist, one of the few truly great stylists that England has produced since the time of Anne."[16] To Leonard Huxley, literature owes T. H. Huxley a debt because he imported into it the scientific habit of mind; to George Gissing, the twentieth century should be grateful that Huxley's "remarkable combination of powers" has enabled the "plainest of the plain" to read his works; to a writer in *The Spectator,* a contemporary journal, the reason for all this adulation is that Huxley had a "passion for completeness of logical sequence which is as clearly the distinctive note of the thinker, as the yearning for completeness of aesthetic harmony is the distinctive note of the artist"[17]—in which statement the writer fails to appreciate the fact that a "passion for completeness of logical sequence" and "the yearning for completeness of aesthetic harmony" may be alternative descriptions of the same agency. That agency—the structuring of chaos—which can almost be said to have been an element of his personality, is the theme which signalizes his research in science, which for the most part was morphological; his philosophy, founded upon materialism; and his various artistic enterprises.

Although Huxley's work in science, his original discoveries and his popularization of the discoveries of others, is of importance in the history of science, it was his genius as a creator of order which contributed to his fame. He used to amuse his children by carving, out of a shapeless peel of an orange, a pig. Once he sent a specimen to a daughter to illustrate

> the heights to which the creative power of the true artist may soar. I call it a "Piggurne, or a Harmony in Orange and White."

> Preserve it, my dear child, as evidence of the paternal genius, when those light and fugitive productions which are buried in the philosophical transactions and elsewhere are forgotten.[18]

The allegory implicit in Huxley's Piggurnes is valuable both for an appreciation of his labors in the cause of enlightenment for a method by which to forge from two cultures one community.

Notes

[1] E. Ray Lankester, "Huxley's Collected Essays," *Nature,* XLIX (1894), 311.

[2] T. H. Huxley, *Collected Essays* (London, 1893), I, 7; and Karl Pearson, ed., *The Life and Labours of Francis Galton* (London, 1914), II, 178.

[3] Michael Foster, and E. Ray Lankester, eds., *The Scientific Memoirs of Thomas Henry Huxley* (London, 1898), I, 27.

[4] H. E. Armstrong, *Our Need to Honour Huxley's Will* (London, 1914), p. 2; Edward Clodd, *Professor Huxley* (Edinburgh, 1905), p. 127; and Hugh Walker, *The Literature of the Victorian Era* (Cambridge, Eng., 1913), p. 233.

[5] Frederic Harrison, *Autobiographic Memoirs* (London, 1911), I, 283-84.

[6] Wilfred Ward, *Problems and Persons* (London, 1903), p. 233; and Sir William Flower, quoted in Leonard Huxley, ed., *The Life and Letters of Thomas Henry Huxley* (New York, 1900), I, 255; and P. Chalmers Mitchell, *Thomas Henry Huxley* (New York, 1900), pp. 209-10.

[7] "The Huxley Papers," XLII, 147. Material from this collection is quoted by permission of the Governors, Imperial College of Science and Technology.

[8] *Collected Essays,* III, 177 and 178; and Foster and Lankester, *Scientific Memoirs,* IV, 666.

[9] "The Huxley Papers," XXXIII, 191. Huxley also spoke here of the beauty of Euclidean axioms.

[10] D. R. Newth, and E. R. Turlington, "The Drawings of T. H. Huxley," *Medical and Biological Illustration,* VI (1956), 73 and 74.

[11] "The Huxley Papers," XLIX, 36.

[12] *Collected Essays,* IX, 121; L. Huxley, *Life and Letters,* II, 382, II, 203, and I, 447; and "The Huxley Papers," XV, 81-81v.

[13] "The Huxley Papers," XLIX, 55-57.

[14] *Ibid.,* 59-60.

[15] *Ibid.,* XLIX, 37.

[16] G. K. Chesterton, *The Victorian Age in Literature* (London, 1928), p. 39; and H. L. Mencken, *A Book of Prefaces* (New York, 1916), p. 74.

[17] George Gissing, *Autobiographical Notes* (Edinburgh, 1930), p. 12; and "Professor Huxley on the Charities of London," *The Spectator,* 2238 (1871), 598.

[18] L. Huxley, *Life and Letters,* II, 457-58.

Joseph H. Gardner (essay date 1970)

SOURCE: "A Huxley Essay as 'Poem'," in *Victorian Studies,* Vol. XIV, No. 2, December, 1970, pp. 177-91.

[*In the essay that follows, Gardner explores the literary devices used by Huxley to support his claim that "On the Physical Basis of Life" is poetry.*]

Of all the acknowledged nineteenth-century masters of non-fictional prose, Thomas Henry Huxley raises in its most acute form the critical problem of justifying non-fiction as "literature" and "art." As scientist, educator, and agnostic, Huxley more than makes good a claim to significance as "background" and grist for the mills of intellectual and social history. Nor would many deny that his writings—whether they be treatises addressed to the Royal Society or essays published in the *Fortnightly*—are remarkable for their clarity, forcefulness, and grace of style. But on what grounds can any of them be termed "literature" and in what sense can their author be called an "artist?" The very people who conscientiously include him in their syllabuses may very well be those who most enjoy the joke of Dickens's including *The Collected Poems of T. H. Huxley* among the false book-backs with which he decorated his study at Gadshill. Even the very texts out of which Huxley is taught in literature courses prejudice his right to be considered by English departments at all. One, for example, compares him to Mill, concluding that both "enter only a little way into the 'domain of art proper.' They were both scientific rationalists and as such devoted first of all to 'the literature of fact,' not to 'the literature of the imaginative sense of fact.'... So far as their prose styles go, therefore, Mill and Huxley were 'journeymen' of a high order, but journeymen nonetheless."[1] Even laying aside the fact that these remarks ignore what Huxley himself held to be the close relationship between (or even identity of) scientific rationalism and "the imaginative sense of fact," they can be refuted, in the case of at least one of his essays, by a close analysis of the writing itself, an analysis that will reveal a solid basis for a claim for Huxley as "poet."

Such an analysis need rest only on two widely held assumptions. One assumption is that in practical criticism the traditional distinction between "rhetoric" and "poetry" is most easily made by examining the way in which a given author uses metaphor in any given work. In rhetoric metaphor plays a secondary, subservient role, either 1) illustrating or clarifying a meaning pre-established by discursive modes; or 2) by its appeal to the emotions predisposing the audience toward a desired action; or both. But in poetry its role is primary; the metaphor *is* the message. It is at once the mode of cognition by which meaning is discovered, the linguistic form in which it is embodied, and the vehicle by which it is conveyed.[2] The other assumption is that poetry and rhetoric can be further distinguished by a difference between the relationship, in each, of meaning to action. In rhetoric meaning is prior to action; the one adheres to the writer and the other to the audience. In poetry meaning and action are fused; both adhere to the writer, being expressed in and by the composition, which the audience merely contemplates formally. Elder Olsen has reminded us that in dramatic poetry a character's speech is both *lexis* and *praxis,* meaning and action: "What the poetic character says in the mimetic poem is speech and has meaning; his *saying* it is action, an act of persuading, confessing, commanding, informing, torturing, or what not." Hence metaphor as action leads us through itself to the speaker as acting. "For metaphor is not simply a figure of diction in poetry; it is also someone's thinking, significantly, that something resembles something; it is the thought, that is, of a certain character in a certain situation, and it is significant of these things."[3]

Clearly Huxley does frequently use metaphor rhetorically, either to illustrate and clarify[4] or to incite to action.[5] But with equal frequency—as, for example, in one of his most celebrated paragraphs—his use of metaphor involves complexities that rhetorical principles cannot unravel. In his inaugural address as principal of the South London Workingman's College Huxley observes that, were our lives to depend upon our ability to play chess, no father would allow his children nor any state its citizens to grow up without at least knowing a pawn from a knight:

> Yet it is a very plain and elementary truth, that the life, the fortune, and the happiness of every one of us . . . do depend upon our knowing something of the rules of a game infinitely more difficult and complicated than chess. It is a game which has been played for untold ages, every man and woman of us being one of the two players in a game of his or her own. The chessboard is the world, the pieces are the phenomena of the universe, the rules of the game are what we call the laws of Nature. The player on the other side is hidden from us. We know that his play is always fair, just, and patient. But we also know, to our cost, that he never overlooks a mistake, or makes the smallest allowance for ignorance. To the man who plays well, the highest stakes are paid, with that sort of overflowing generosity with which the strong shows delight in strength. And one who plays ill is checkmated—without haste, but without remorse.[6]

To a certain degree the metaphor does function rhetorically, but as rhetoric it is ultimately unsuccessful because it, in itself, raises difficult problems of meaning. What, or more accurately, Who, is the hidden chess player? How literally are we to take him either allegorically or anthropomorphically? And which? Huxley's own attempt to explicate does not help us very much:

> My metaphor will remind some of you of the famous picture in which Retzsch has depicted Satan playing at chess with man for his soul. Substitute for the mocking fiend in that picture, a calm, strong angel who is playing for love, as we say, and would rather lose than win—and I should accept it as an image of human life.[7]

The introduction of the "calm, strong angel" expands the anthropomorphism into definite suggestions of theism.

And if the angel is playing for love, how then are we to account for the ruthlessness of his play and the remorselessness of his victories? I do not offer to answer these questions. The point is simply that the passage does raise problems of meaning that puzzle precisely because the available answers seem to run counter to the discursive argument of the essay in which the metaphor appears and to the major patterns of thought in Huxley's work as a whole. Put in different terms, the chess metaphor disturbs because Huxley has shifted from a rhetorical mode to a poetical mode without, perhaps, being himself aware of the shift, and certainly without providing his auditors clues that they must make an appropriate shift in response. Nor are the two modes integrated into any unified vision.

Neither in the chess metaphor do we see illustrated a meaning that will serve as a prior cause to a posterior effect: our being moved to revamp curricula to include large doses of scientific instruction. We are not so moved because the metaphor does not invite our attention to focus upon its "objective" accuracy as an analogy descriptive of an external reality, "nature," so much as it lures us into attempting a specifically "literary" explication to grasp Huxley's "subjective" understanding of a symbolic force or entity *called* "nature." (Accordingly, we do not overlook the capital "N" that graces the word throughout the essay.) The metaphor does not tell us as much about "nature" as it does about Huxley. It is mimetic, not dialectic, since it imitates a state of a human mind just as Hamlet's celebrated "ulcer" metaphor is not an objective description of the political state of Denmark at a given point in history: it is an imitation of a response of a human spirit to the human condition. Unlike Hamlet's, Huxley's metaphor is unsatisfying because it betrays deep-seated and unacknowledged contradictions in the state of mind it imitates, contradictions that are not to be interpreted organically as characteristics of that which it attempts to reproduce. We cannot balance or reconcile the discords struck when the anthropomorphic theism implied by the hidden chess player is juxtaposed to the agnostic skepticism dramatized in other Huxley essays.[8]

Arguing that his highest ideals in writing were accuracy and veracity, Aldous Huxley observes that his grandfather used metaphors "seldom and only with the greatest caution" since while "ideas can be vividly expressed in terms of metaphor and simile . . . analogies are rarely complete [and their] vividness is too often achieved at the cost of precision."[9] Ironically, Aldous presents Thomas Henry not "as a literary man" but only as a rhetorician; he becomes a "poet" when metaphor displaces discursive logic as mode of cognition and structural principle in his writings, as it does take in at least one of his most significant, most characteristic, and best known essays, the lay sermon delivered in Edinburgh, 8 November 1868, and later published, with great sensation, in the *Fortnightly* as **"On the Physical Basis of Life."**

Like much "poetry" Huxley's essay is devoted to the examination of a paradox, what he calls the "union of materialistic terminology with the repudiation of materialistic philosophy."[10] And like most "poetry" it can be submitted to "prose" explication, *i.e.,* a discursive "meaning" can be extracted from it in the form of a paraphrased "argument": The ultimate nature of both matter and spirit is unknowable; as Hume has demonstrated, both "materialism" and "spiritualism" lie outside the limits of philosophical inquiry (162). However, "the order of Nature is ascertainable by our faculties to an extent which is practically unlimited" (163), but we must remember that order does not, logically, imply necessity. Order is ascertained by manipulating symbolic systems or terminologies, and "if we find that the ascertainment of the order of nature is facilitated by using one terminology, or one set of symbols, rather than another, it is our clear duty to use the former; and no harm can accrue, so long as we bear in mind that we are dealing merely with terms and symbols" (164). Thus we may exploit the usefulness of materialistic terminology without becoming materialists. The paraphrase, of course, is based upon explicit, rhetorical statements Huxley makes in his concluding paragraphs, just as a satisfactory paraphrase of Shakespeare's "Sonnet 73" could be based upon the explicit rhetoric of its concluding couplet. Accordingly, it bears the same relationship to the total essay as the statement "the older you see me grow, the more you love me" bears to all fourteen lines of the sonnet. To grasp some sense of the totality of Shakespeare's poem we usually begin by examining its metaphors, their meanings, their structural relationships and functions, and their significance as verbal actions. The same method applied to Huxley's essay will reveal that the total essay is built upon a complex cluster of metaphors that 1) emphasizes the symbolic nature of all knowledge; 2) equates all symbolic systems with religious myths and evaluates their validity; while, 3) chastising man's eternal penchant for philosophical error.

Huxley leads his audience into the cluster of metaphors that is both the discovery of the essay and the determinant of its structure by dramatizing a suppositional situation: "Let us suppose that knowledge is absolute, and not relative, and therefore, that our conception of matter represents that which it really is" (158). The materialistic assumption will then bring with it as its necessary correlate determinism, and "as surely as every future grows out of past and present, so will the physiology of the future gradually extend the realm of matter and law until it is coextensive with knowledge, with feeling, and with action":

> The consciousness of this great truth weighs like a nightmare, I believe, upon many of the best minds of these days. They watch what they conceive to be the progress of materialism, in such fear and powerless anger as a savage feels, when, during an eclipse,

the great shadow creeps over the face of the sun. The advancing tide of matter threatens to drown their souls; the tightening grasp of law impedes their freedom; they are alarmed lest man's moral nature be debased by the increase of his wisdom.

> (159-160)

The elaborate rhythmical pattern of Huxley's celebrated "caesura sentences,"[11] their muted hints of alliteration and assonance, and their intricate manipulation of parallelism, balance, and antithesis all serve to fuse into one complex whole a series of three closely related images, related in that all involve acts of oppression and obliteration which carry with them intense emotional responses, since each is totally beyond the power of conscious control of those they affect. It is through this metaphor-cluster that Huxley discovers the paradox that is the essay's "meaning." Nightmares, eclipses, and tides are "real"; they are "facts" of experience just as the statements of physiologists about protoplasm are demonstrably "real" and "factual." But they are not "great truths." For, after all, one does, eventually, awaken from a nightmare. No eclipse lasts forever, and tides ebb as well as flow. The impotent fear and frustrated anger of dreamer, savage, and drowning man result from the false supposition that a temporary state represents permanent and necessary reality.[12] Materialistic philosophy, correspondingly, depends upon the equally false supposition that "our conception of matter represents that which it really is." By bringing us to realize this, Huxley has shown us how the light of truth can be eclipsed by the shadow of error and how it can be brought out again on the other side. But, paradoxically, the truth is that there is no truth; we are enlightened by discovering that the ultimate nature of matter and spirit is eternally shrouded in darkness.

Huxley's thinking on this point, his idea, is fused throughout the essay with his image, the eclipse metaphor and its correlate figures. (In addition to being tied to the "nightmare" and "tide" metaphors, the "eclipse" metaphor itself contains two more or less distinct, though obviously related patterns of imagery—light and darkness images on the one hand and images of reduction, engulfing, and swallowing up on the other. I stress the "eclipse" as overriding because it involves all these image patterns at once.) Acknowledging that he derives his philosophical skepticism from Hume, he questions the appropriateness of the term skepticism: "If a man asks me what the politics of the inhabitants of the moon are, and I reply that I do not know; that neither I, nor any one else, has any means of knowing; and that, under these circumstances, I decline to trouble myself about the subject at all, I do not think he has any right to call me a skeptic" (162). Huxley's choice of lunar politics as an example of the unknowable is not accidental; it is determined by the eclipse metaphor. In a solar eclipse the moon interposes itself between the earth and the sun. The physical darkness of the savage results when in the place of the sun he sees only the moon. Correspondingly, mental darkness results when we turn our eyes from those things which can illuminate us and look toward that which is forever in obscurity. Hence our "fear and powerless anger" at lunar darkness is just as irrational as that of the savage witnessing an eclipse—and just as fruitless, just as spiritually and morally misguided. For in Huxley's imaginative vision, the state of Victorian man is metaphorically equated with that of the savage. "We live," he says with quiet force, "in a world which is full of misery and ignorance." The illumination brings with it a corresponding moral imperative: "the plain duty of each and all of us is to try to make the little corner he can influence somewhat less miserable and somewhat less ignorant than it was before he entered it" (163). But how can we brighten the corner where we are if we interpose the moon and its politics between ourselves and our source of light? We will see the light only when we accept the usefulness of materialistic terminology in clarifying the order of nature; "the alternative, or spiritualistic terminology, is utterly *barren* [like the moon?] and leads to nothing but *obscurity*" (164; italics mine). But we should never equate "usefulness" with "truth."

The religious implications of the eclipse metaphor hinted at in the preceding paragraph are explored throughout the essay. The "fear and powerless anger" of the savage are to be considered the response of a man who sees his god being destroyed. Recognizing the sun as his primary source of light, warmth, and ultimately life itself, the savage imputes to it supernatural powers and worships it as a mighty god. An eclipse can only mean that his god has either forsaken him or has been swallowed up by another god whose characteristics and powers must be antithetical to those of the sun: darkness replaces light, evil triumphs over good, death usurps life, the light of the world falls before the imp of darkness. The keystone of his whole sense of order and meaning in nature crumbles away. Huxley has carefully prepared us to recognize these implications in the metaphor. In the paragraph immediately preceding that in which it is introduced, he writes: "what is the difference between the conception of life as the product of a certain disposition of material molecules, and the old notion of an Archaeus governing and directing blind matter within each living body, except this—that here, as elsewhere, matter and law have devoured spirit and spontaneity?" (159). The reference to Archaeus serves to reduce spiritualistic interpretations of nature to the level of primitive superstition, preparing us for the even greater primitivism of the savage, while at the same time clearing the way for the ultimate point that all our conceptions of nature are—and can be—only symbols and myth. Moreover, Huxley's phrasing encourages us to transfer the epithet "blind" from "matter" to "the old notion of Archaeus" and to glimpse, however faintly, a hint of the light and

darkness, illumination and obscurity images that control the essay. The operative word in the remaining portion of the sentence is the verb "devoured," which anticipates the eclipse swallowing the sun and the tide eating away at the land. But to conceive of matter and law devouring spirit and spontaneity is, ironically, to duplicate the mental processes of the savage, to interpret nature by the anthropomorphizing mechanisms of myth. Hence the irony of the sentence undercuts not only the spiritualistic notion of an Archaeus, but also the materialistic notion that life is "the product of a certain disposition of material molecules." It too is only superstition, myth, false religion, the mental state of a savage, since it depends upon the fallacy of assuming that "our conception of matter represents that which it really is."

The exposure, through metaphor, of both spiritualism and materialism as false religions constitutes the essay's most elaborate motif. If the patterns of irony in the Archaeus metaphor prepare us for the nightmare-eclipse-tide paragraph, a subsequent passage makes its implications even more explicit:

> For, after all, what do we know of this terrible "matter," except as a name for the unknown and hypothetical cause of states of our own consciousness? And what do we know of that "spirit" over whose threatened extinction by matter a great lamentation is arising, like that which was heard at the death of Pan, except that it is also a name for an unknown and hypothetical cause, or condition, of states of consciousness? In other words, matter and spirit are but names for the imaginary substrata of groups of natural phaenomena.
>
> (160)

The reference to Pan not only parallels the earlier reference to Archaeus but also ties eclipse (matter "extinguishes" spirit) to nightmare just as the word "devoured" in the Archaeus sentences emphasizes the link between eclipse and tide. In Roman myth Pan and his cohorts, the Panisci, cause bad dreams. Nor would it be too far-fetched to see another set of associations being exploited in the references to Pan. Huxley's essay was published in 1868, less that two years after the *succés-de-scandale* of Swinburne's *Poems and Ballads,* a volume which included a poem devoted, precisely, to recording the lamentations heard at the death of Pan. One of the effects of the "Hymn to Proserpine"—perhaps *the* effect as far as outraged Victorians were concerned—was to reduce Christianity to the same status (in degree as well as kind) as heathen myth and to assert that of the two superstitions, the pagan is in many ways superior. Huxley's essay is just as blasphemous, and it makes a similar point. The pale Galilean killed Pan; materialistic science is killing Christ, and to lament the death of the one is as irrational an expression of savage superstition as to mourn the passing of the other. Moreover, we are again reminded of

Huxley's over-arching meaning: if Christ is equated with Pan, materialism itself is also a form of superstitious myth. The reduction of the figures of Judeo-Christian tradition to the equivalents of such heathen gods as Archaeus and Pan lends additional force to the labelling elsewhere in the essay of Auguste Comte as "a modern Agag." Samuel hewed Agag into pieces because he worshipped false gods; Huxley's metaphors have established materialistic positivism as a false religion. Hence there is more than merely a clever rhetorical joke in his celebrated assertion that "in fact, M. Comte's philosophy . . . might be compendiously described as Catholicism *minus* Christianity" (156).

Similar functionings of the eclipse metaphor to equate materialism with savage superstition, pagan myth, and Christianity as false religions can be found elsewhere in the essay. When Huxley says that in accepting the most elementary conclusions of materialistic physiology "you are placing your feet on the first rung of a ladder which, in most people's estimation, is the reverse of Jacob's and leads to the antipodes of heaven" (153-154), he is using Jacob in much the same way that he later uses Archaeus, Agag, and Pan, while at the same time reinforcing the links between his controlling metaphors. Like the eclipse, the new Jacob's ladder leads from the light of heaven into the darkness of hell; in other words, the prophet's dream becomes a nightmare. Additionally, the metaphorical concept of materialism as superstition and false religion controls much of the diction in which he describes the structure of the materialistic myth. "Protoplasm, simple or nucleated," he says, "is the formal basis of all life. It is the clay of the potter: which, bake it and paint it as he will, remains clay, separated by artifice, and not by nature, from the commonest brick or sun-dried clod" (142). The strategem here is transparent; Huxley takes the one metaphor of Judeo-Christian tradition most popularly used in the literature of his day and appropriates it to explicate the scientific myth. But given the paradox embodied in most of the metaphors of **"On the Physical Basis of Life,"** we are not bothered by the potter as we are by the hidden chess player in **"A Liberal Education."** In *Isaiah* the identity of the potter is established explicitly: "But now, O Lord, thou art our father; we are the clay and thou our potter; we are all the work of thy hand." The ramifications of the eclipse metaphor have shown Isaiah's Lord to be a creature of myth, the equivalent of Archaeus, Pan, and the sun-gods of savages; accordingly, the materialist's potter is also the mythological god of a false religion. Elsewhere Huxley speaks of single-celled organisms, "multitudes of which could in fact dance upon the point of a needle" (132); he describes the "thaumaturgy" of plants (149), and explains digestion as the process by which we "transubstantiate sheep into man"; the lobster we sup upon, he says, undergoes "the same wonderful metamorphosis into humanity" (147). Apparently the religion of materialism has its own panoply of angels, its own doctrine of incarnation, its own eucharistic sacraments.

More complex is a passage in which Huxley explains that scientists must believe that the properties of water in all its forms result from the properties of its component elements, hydrogen and oxygen:

> We do not assume that a something called "aquosity" entered into and took possession of the oxidated hydrogen as soon as it was formed, and then guided the aqueous particles to their places in the facets of the crystal, or amongst the leaflets of the hoarfrost. On the contrary, we live in the hope and in the faith that, by the advance of molecular physics, we shall by and by be able to see our way as clearly from the constituents of water to the properties of water, as we are now able to deduce the operations of a watch from the form of its parts and the manner in which they are put together.

> Is the case in any way changed when carbonic acid, water and nitrogenous salts disappear, and in their place, under the influence of pre-existing living protoplasm, an equivalent weight of the matter of life makes its appearance?

> (152)

Certainty is always impossible in matters of religion: like the spiritualists, the devotés of materialism live only by "hope" and "faith," fed by the same deductive processes as those of many Victorian Christians. Huxley is speaking to an audience suckled on Paley's *Evidences* and the argument from design: by the analogy of the watch Victorian Christians were invited to deduce the existence of God. Huxley uses the analogy to deduce matter as the ultimate reality and prime mover of the universe. But he is not simply turning the devices of the spiritualists against themselves, transforming their concept of a watchmaker God into the petard by which they can be hoist for ridicule. Rather, by equating the hopes and faiths of the materialists with those of their spiritualistic contemporaries and implying that both are sustained by identical logical processes, he is once more illustrating that both are false religions. Hence there is little strain in seeing the watch analogy give way to yet another version of the essay's controlling metaphor. The component elements of protoplasm "disappear" and "an equivalent weight of the matter of life makes its appearance." Ironically, this "eclipse" may clarify rather than obfuscate the "order of nature"—but only in terms of the materialistic myth.

If we say on the one hand that the eclipse metaphor exposes both spiritualism and materialism as false religions—and, on the other, maintain that the kind of "poetry" Huxley is writing has as its final end truth, clarification, or vision, metaphor serving as the cognitive mode by which truth is discovered—then we can properly ask of the essay: what is *true* religion? To label something false is to imply that something else is true; the sun does not remain obscured forever but reappears on the other side of the eclipse with new clarity. The metaphors in **"On the Physical Basis of Life"** imply that at this stage in his development Huxley elevated Agnosticism to the status of True Religion with the Unknowable as its god. Nowhere in the essay is this made explicit, but the eclipse metaphor practically demands it. In his after years he himself seems to have become aware of where his metaphors had taken him. Twenty years later he observes in **"Agnosticism and Christianity"** that "the extent of the region of the uncertain, the number of the problems the investigation of which ends in a verdict of not proven, will vary according to the knowledge and the intellectual habits of the individual Agnostic. I do not very much care to speak of anything as 'unknowable.'" On incorporating the essay into the collected edition, he added a footnote: "I confess that, long ago, I once or twice made this mistake; even to the waste of a capital 'U.'"[13]

Poetry fuses idea with image; if Huxley's metaphors control his thinking, his thinking also controls his metaphors. His lay sermon is intended to bring comforting words to those of his contemporaries who felt themselves gripped by the nightmare of despair as materialism eclipsed those spiritual lights that had given order and meaning to their lives. In other words, it was the very eclipse Huxley describes that had contributed to the "darkling" of the Victorian plain. **"On the Physical Basis of Life"** was written within a year of both the appearance of "Dover Beach" in the *New Poems* of 1867 and the blossoming of Huxley's friendship with its author. Arnold had despaired at the ebbing of the sea of faith; Huxley's drowning man founders in the rising tide of materialism. But Huxley himself knows that his founderer is only "threatened," only thinks he is going to drown. Inspired by the light of his true religion, he knows that no tide stands still; knows that materialism itself may ebb, leaving the possibility open for the Sea of Faith to flow—a possibility that Arnold has notoriously overlooked. Moreover, he is himself indifferent to the tides because he realizes that they do not represent ultimate reality. Spiritualistic faith he denigrates to the status of a savage superstition that is useless as a symbolic system; materialism and its sister-god, determinism, he deals with as the High Priest of Agnosticism who has seen the light on the other side of darkness: "For my part, I utterly repudiate and *anathematize* the intruder. Fact I know; and Law I know; but what is this Necessity, save an empty *shadow* of my own mind's throwing?" (161; italics mine). But the High Priest is not always the agent of a wrathful god; in his kinder moments he has his own saints in his own heaven whom he can invoke to intercede for those who follow strange gods in the temple of materialism: ". . . could David Hume be consulted, I think he would chide them for doing even as the heathen, and falling down in terror before the hideous idols their own hands have raised" (160).

In discussing Huxley's use of metaphor as mode of cognition and vehicle for embodying and conveying meaning, I have necessarily implied much about how metaphor also operates as structural principle. Only a few further remarks need to be made. Huxley begins the essay by describing the "nightmare" world created by the notion that there is such a thing as "*the* physical basis or matter of life" (131). The notion itself is nightmarish enough to besieged Victorian idealists; Huxley is merciless in depicting the kind of bad dream in which everything turns into something else, in which images of beauty corrode into visions of horror and loathsomeness. Since they are all composed of protoplasm, giant Sequoyahs dissolve into the microscopic fungi multiplying "into countless millions in the body of a living fly" (131); great Finner whales fade into phosphorescent plankton (132); the golden hair of a young girl is transmuted into a jellyfish (132), and the ceaseless whirling of cellular matter transforms "the wonderful noonday silence of a tropical forest" into "the roar of a great city" (136-137). Even the principle governing the actions of protoplasm is itself nightmarish. Physiology, Huxley tells us, "writes over the portals of life—'Debemur morti nos nostraque.'" Granted that rare visionaries like Lucretius or Whitman could elevate such a principle into the basis of an optimistic faith; Huxley makes no attempt to do so. Protoplasm is for him merely the physiological equivalent of Balzac's *peau de chagrin* (145-47). But he does not intend that we remain paralyzed by bad dreams forever; hence he shifts from the nightmare to the eclipse as his governing metaphor. I propose, he says, "to lead you through the territory of vital phaenomena to the materialistic slough in which you find yourselves now plunged, and then to point out to you the sole path by which, in my judgment, extrication is possible" (155).

On the surface it would seem that Huxley has introduced a new metaphor. But upon consideration we note that the pattern of action embodied in the slough metaphor is identical with that of the eclipse: in one side and out on the other. This pattern governs the remainder of the essay both as a whole and in its individual parts. One example can stand for many. In a passage referred to earlier, Huxley says:

> *If* scientific language is to possess a definite and constant signification . . . it seems to me that we are logically bound to apply to protoplasm . . . the same conceptions as those which are held to be legitimate elsewhere. If the phaenomena exhibited by water are its properties, so are those represented by protoplasm, living or dead, its properties.

> *If* the properties of water may be properly said to result from the nature and disposition of its component molecules, I can find no intelligible reason for refusing to say that the properties of protoplasm result from the nature and disposition of its molecules.

> But I bid you beware that, in accepting these conclusions, you are placing your feet on the first rung

of a ladder which . . . is the reverse of Jacob's and leads to the antipodes of heaven. It may seem a small thing to admit that the dull vital actions of a fungus, or a foraminifer, are the properties of their protoplasm and are the direct results of the nature of the matter of which they are composed. *But if . . . their protoplasm is essentially identical with, and most readily converted into, that of any animal, I can discover no logical halting-place between the admission that such is the case, and the further concession that all vital action may . . . be said to be the result of the molecular forces of the proto-plasm which displays it. And if so, it must be true . . .* that the thoughts to which I am now giving utterance, and your thoughts regarding them, are the expression of molecular changes in that matter of life which is the source of our other vital phaenomena.

(153-4; italics mine)

In a sense the passage is highly rhetorical, but the rhetoric is governed and controlled by the eclipse metaphor. The relentless progression of "if's" dupli-cates the action of the eclipse, each conditional sen-tence swallowing up more and more of the spiritu-alistic light until it is blotted out altogether. The remorseless logic proceeding from an axiom we cannot possibly deny—and would not choose to since we do not know where it is leading us—leaves us as impotent in our fear and anger as the savage watch-ing the extinction of the sun. Moreover, our frus-trated emotions blind us to the fact that the steps in the logical process are, precisely, conditionals, no more necessarily representing ultimate reality than the darkness of the eclipse. When, one page later, Huxley explains that the obscurity of materialism involves "grave philosophical error," the true light begins to emerge from the other side. The pattern exhibited in these paragraphs is the pattern of the essay as a whole.

If this explication of **"On the Physical Basis of Life"** seems somewhat long and detailed, hopefully it will also suggest the kind of riches with which Huxley can repay us if we approach him not as a rhetorician but as a poet. The particular Huxley essay is not unique in the canon; while it is beyond the scope of the present essay to treat any of his other writings, many could be analyzed by the same method here applied to only one and could equally be shown to be "poetry," lacking only the superficial form of verse.[14] However, even on the basis of only one essay it is possible to make gen-eralizations above and beyond the statement that Huxley at his best is indeed a "poet" and not merely a journey-man of letters. Earlier I cited Elder Olsen's observa-tion that metaphor is not solely a statement that some-thing resembles something else but that it is also someone's thinking, significantly, a similarity between two things exists. I return to it now *a propos* a remark by a man who knew Huxley as well as anyone of our time, William Irvine:

For Huxley, writing was always an instrument . . . Literature in the narrow sense could hardly have claimed him, partly because he was too practical and utilitarian to care for mere art and partly because he was not sufficiently interested in its characteristic subject matter, which is man as such. He could become absorbed in man as a physical mechanism, as an anthropoid ape, as a citizen and social animal, as a delicate machine for the discovery of scientific truth; but not in man as a personality and a human being. With all his splendid talents for friendship and affection, he remained, from the deeper psycho-logical point of view, indifferent to people. In fact . . . he was not even interested in himself. Seldom has so vivid and articulate a writer had so little of importance to say, even in his most intimate letters, about himself.[15]

If by "literature in the narrow sense" Irvine means "poetry" as I have attempted to define it, then I cannot agree less. Few writers of the nineteenth century have given us a more fruitful or insightful glimpse of the state of mind of Victorian man as such than Huxley does in the cluster of metaphors that lie at the heart of **"On the Physical Basis of Life."** And by working out the meanings inherent in those metaphors he drama-tizes the responses of one human spirit to the human condition more fully than any volume of intimate cor-respondence ever could. If he himself may never have claimed to be a man of letters, literature can surely claim him.

Notes

[1] William E. Buckler, "Introduction," *Prose of the Victorian Period* (Boston, 1958), p. xx. The internal quotations are from Pater.

[2] The distinction goes back at least as far as Aristotle and is still very much alive, forming, for example the ultimate basis for Levine and Madden's distinction between "practical prose" and "aesthetic prose"—*The Art of Victorian Prose* (Oxford, 1968), pp. vii-xxi. Moreover, both the distinction itself and the method for applying it were readily available to Huxley and his contemporaries. For example it can be found in two theoretical works highly influential in nineteenth-century aesthetic thought. In his *Lectures on Rhetoric and Belles Lettres* Hugh Blair clearly relegates meta-phor to a secondary role; it is simply "a great branch of the ornament of Style." The discursive meaning, or idea, is always primary: "the figure is only the dress" (Facsimile Edition, ed. H. F. Harding, 2 vols. [Carbon-dale, 1965], I, pp. 272, 277). In the *Biographia Liter-aria,* on the other hand, Coleridge asserts that true poetry need not display the superficial form of verse; it need only maintain an organic relationship between its parts and its whole and result from the operation of the "esemplastic power" of the poetic imagination, which "blends and . . . fuses, each into each, . . . the

idea with the image." While poetry "subordinates . . . the manner to the matter," it does so, paradoxically, by fusing the idea with the image so that the idea is the image, the image the idea. (Ed. J. Shawcross, 2 vols. [Oxford, 1907], II, pp. 9-12.) But despite the currency and general acceptance of these notions they seem curiously hard to hold on to when it is Huxley who is under the critical microscope. Even his most knowledgeable, perceptive, and sympathetic critics are capable of such juxtapositions as that contained in these two sentences: "Huxley strove after the *forcible* as well as the clear expression of ideas and it is in this striving that he exploited the poetic potentialities of language. There is in Huxley's writing . . . the existence of the rhetorical statement, which sacrifices 'clarity' to 'effectiveness.'" The same essay goes on to quote Huxley himself on rhetoric: "gilding refined gold would, to my mind, be less objectionable than varnishing the fair face of truth with that pestilant cosmetic, rhetoric." (C. S. Blinderman, "Semantic Aspects of T. H. Huxley's Literary Style," *Journal of Communication,* XII [1962], 174-75.) It does not seem to me too much to say that in his metaphors of refined gold and pestilant cosmetics Huxley himself both implies and illustrates the distinction between poetry and rhetoric I am invoking.

[3] "William Empson, Contemporary Criticism, and Poetic Diction," *Critics and Criticism,* ed. R. S. Crane (Chicago, 1952), pp. 54-56.

[4] As in the comparison of the internal workings of a crayfish to the whirlpool at the base of Niagara quoted in Aldous Huxley, "T. H. Huxley as a Literary Man," *The Olive Tree* (New York and London, 1937), pp. 77-78.

[5] As in the comparison of a "man of high natural ability, who is both ignorant and miserable" to "a rocket without a stick" in the essay "Administrative Nihilism," *Methods and Results* (New York, 1898), pp. 255-56.

[6] "A Liberal Education and Where to Find It," *Science and Education* (New York, 1897), p. 82.

[7] Pp. 82-83.

[8] Again Huxley himself indicated that he was at least preconsciously aware of the kind of distinction I make. One of his students reports him as saying "Here in my teaching lectures, I have time to put the facts fully before a trained audience. In my public lectures I am obliged to pass rapidly over the facts, and I put forward my personal convictions. And it is for this that people come to hear me." (Blinderman, "Sematic Aspects," 177.)

[9] *The Olive Tree,* p. 77.

[10] *Methods and Results,* p. 155. Subsequent references to this edition will be indicated by page number in the text.

[11] So-called by Aldous Huxley, *The Olive Tree,* pp. 74-77.

[12] Notice that Huxley underlines the savage's philosophical error by making him guilty of a scientific one: it is the earth, not the sun, that is enshadowed by an eclipse.

[13] *Science and Christian Tradition* (New York, 1898), p. 311.

[14] Again I am echoing Coleridge's distinction between "poetry" and "poem," a distinction that allows Coleridge to label as poetry the prose of Taylor, Burnet and the unknown author of *Isaiah.* I have felt it much better to try to make my point here by treating only one essay in detail than by attempting a survey of metaphoric patterns in the *Collected Essays* as a whole. But such a survey cries out to be done. Oma Stanley has remarked upon Huxley's tendency in his early work to "romantically" personify "nature." ("T. H. Huxley's Treatment of Nature," *JHI,* XVIII [1957], 120-27.) As my remarks on the chess metaphor in "A Liberal Education" indicate, this seems a logical place to begin.

[15] "Carlyle and T. H. Huxley," *Victorian Literature: Modern Essays in Criticism,* ed. Austin Wright (New York, 1961), pp. 197-98.

Adrian Desmond on Huxley's tenacity and agnosticism:

My good & kind agent for the propagation of the 'Gospel', Darwin called him, 'ie the Devil's gospel'. Thomas Henry Huxley became Darwin's Rottweiler, instantly recognizable by his deep-set dark eyes and lashing tongue. Where Darwin held back, Huxley lunged at his limping prey. It was he, not Darwin, who enraptured and outraged audiences in the 1860s with talk of our ape ancestors and cave men. Listeners were agog in a prim, evangelical age. These were terrifying, tantalizing images. 'It is not the bishops and archbishops I am afraid of', Samuel Butler once said. 'Men like Huxley . . . are my natural enemies'. No one stirred passions like Thomas Henry Huxley.

Huxley was one of the founders of the sceptical, scientific twentieth century. We owe to him that enduring military metaphor, the 'war' of science against theology. He coined the word 'agnostic'—and gave the West its existential crisis. All of this makes him look so modern that we want to snatch him from his age. Today his agnostic stand seems obvious. But yesterday it was an immensely daring, motivated, ideological position. That plodding zoological autocrat, Richard Owen, called him a pervert with 'some, perhaps congenital, defect of mind' for denying Divine will in Nature. Who can realize the prissy, patronage-based, undemocratic, sermon-dominated, Anglican-controlled, *different* society Huxley faced, and faced squarely?

Adrian Desmond, in Huxley: The Devil's Disciple, *Michael Joseph, 1994.*

James G. Paradis (essay date 1978)

SOURCE: *T. H. Huxley: Man's Place in Nature,* University of Nebraska Press, 1978, pp. 1-9, 11-45, 165-96.

[*In the following excerpts, Paradis examines Huxley's early, romantic scientific view and his later view that man's hope lies in his moral objection to natural determinism. Paradis also explores Huxley's conception of the role of the scientist in understanding humankind's existential condition, comparing it specifically with Matthew Arnold's view as expressed in* Culture and Anarchy.]

Introduction

> Nothing great in science has ever been done by men, whatever their powers, in whom the divine afflatus of the truth-seeker was wanting.
>
> T. H. Huxley, "The Progress of
> Science: 1837-1887"

The Victorian debate over the challenge offered by the new science to traditional concepts of man and man's place in nature found its most prophetic focus in the clear, forceful argument of T. H. Huxley's generalist or popular essays. Huxley, whose professional reputation as a British anatomist and physiologist was well established and growing, undertook a second career, that of an essayist and cultural critic of mid-Victorian England, in the full recognition that technology had proved itself a force to alter society and that theoretical science was proving itself a force to alter assumptions as fundamental as man's conception of himself. This characteristically modern appreciation of the power of theoretical science to define sets Huxley apart from other major essayists of the Victorian period. In such works as *Lay Sermons* (1870), *Critiques and Addresses* (1873), *Science and Culture* (1881), and *Evolution and Ethics* (1893), he made important critical examinations of the new relationship that was being negotiated between man and nature through the intervention of modern science and technology. Few Victorian cultural or social values would remain unaffected by this new relationship. Concepts of human identity, of ethical law, of modern culture as a force for reconciling the progress of the present with the values of the past, would all be profoundly influenced by the new concept of man as a force in nature.

I have been drawn to the study of Huxley's thought and vision because he was a Victorian critic of unique accomplishments who brought the perspective of the scientific professional to bear on a society that was itself under the growing influence of science and technology. The nineteenth century was an age, as A. N. Whitehead has observed, which invented the method of invention.[1] But while the new knowledge had brought new power, it also brought a new and perplexing ignorance; while

it exerted considerable influence on traditional cultural values and assumptions, it manifested itself intellectually in systems which frequently passed beyond the competence of thinkers and critics of the age. One of the great examples of Victorian interdisciplinary ability, Huxley combined a literary sensitivity and talent with an intimate understanding of the great theoretical and practical developments in nineteenth-century British and continental science. He had made important contributions himself, his research in invertebrate anatomy having earned him entry into the Royal Society at the age of twenty-six and the Royal Medal in physiology a year later, in 1852. From earliest youth he had pursued studies in the history of science and in a variety of literary and philosophical subjects, making his special interest the interrelationship between science and society.

Huxley struggled to comprehend the enigma of the increasing intersections of cultural and natural history, in which ideas of man, nature and deity had come to be defined by conflicting concepts of truth. Natural and supernatural explanations had become attached to identical processes, often creating a debilitating sense of dualism such as is found in much of Victorian literature. In a work like Tennyson's *In Memoriam,* the elemental force of death gave rise to a shartering ambivalence, new and indeed peculiar to Victorian culture, as to the causes and destinies of things. Naturalism and supernaturalism struggled bitterly over the self throughout the dozen years or so that Tennyson devoted to the poem. Critics like Walter Houghton have found that "bourgeois industrial society and widespread doubt about the nature of man, society, and the universe" were main determinants of the Victorian frame of mind.[2] Such doubt revealed that Victorian culture was hard pressed to forge a new synthesis, to discover what Matthew Arnold in the preface to the 1853 edition of the *Poems* had called the "spirit of the whole." Earlier, the Romantic synthesis had taken the form of "natural supernaturalism," Carlyle's term for the fusion of natural and divine. The bridge of self was able to span the great chasm that had begun to loom between a physical nature, ever more clearly defined, and a supernature which had begun to seem somewhat vague and abstract by comparison. For Victorians, the fusion of nature and supernature was more difficult to achieve, for the concreteness with which researchers were documenting physical nature had created a compelling sense of verifiable reality which no evidence in support of divinity could easily match. This growing relativity of truth, as we shall see, was best captured in Huxley's term, "agnosticism," which was more a Victorian than a philosophical word. Victorians discovered, ironically, that the products of scientific precision and certitude could inspire doubt as readily as optimism.

Huxley's maturation as an essayist and critic is particularly instructive in this respect, for, as I shall attempt to show, his philosophical outlook underwent a gradual transition from youthful Romanticism, influenced by writers like Carlyle and Goethe, toward increasing determinism at mid-career, to his final and startling *fin-de-siècle* declaration, almost on his deathbed, that man's hope lay in his revolt against nature. Thus, while in Huxley's essays we witness the transition from "supernaturalism" to "natural supernaturalism," as identified by critics like M. H. Abrams, carried its inevitable step further to Victorian "naturalism," we also find, somewhat paradoxically, the great summation of the Victorian disillusionment with and revolt against nature.[3] The last essays, looking boldly out from behind the wall of civilization to an empty, hostile universe, bridge the Victorian and modern sensibilities.

The shaping of a new critical consciousness which would defer to scientific thought and ideals was no casual scientism on Huxley's part, but a carefully considered effort to integrate the forces of Victorian science and culture. It was a Victorian commonplace that the transition occurring in all facets of society had taken a course whose logic few could explain. Like other Victorian critical essayists, Huxley aspired to a theory of transition which would illuminate the great social changes occurring throughout England by revealing the principles of their order. In 1873, he wrote his wife:

> We are in the midst of a gigantic movement greater than that which preceded and produced the Reformation, and really only the continuation of that movement. But there is nothing new in the ideas which lie at the bottom of the movement, nor is any reconcilement possible between free thought and traditional authority. One or other will have to succumb after a struggle of unknown duration, which will have as side issues vast political and social troubles. I have no more doubt that free thought will win in the long run than I have that I sit here writing to you, or that this free thought will organise itself into a coherent system, embracing human life and the world as one harmonious whole.
>
> [Leonard Huxley, *Life and Letters of Thomas Henry Huxley*, 2 vols., New York: D. Appleton, 1900; hereafter *LL*, 1:427-28]

Like Matthew Arnold, Huxley dreamed of the "harmonious whole," doubting, however, the powers of Victorians or their immediate twentieth-century descendants to achieve it. Nevertheless, he invested considerable energy in an attempt to discover the outline of a "coherent system" which would unify "human life and the world," and set out to enlist the scientist as an ally of intellectual freedom in the archetypal struggle between free thought and traditional or ideological authority. Such a unity, he had hoped early in his career, might take the form of a naturalistic system in which ethical order was established as the premise of social order, historical processes of nature and human society were shown

to be uniform, and the universal order of nature was accepted by all as the great absolute of existence. Extensive notes Huxley left behind in his manuscripts reveal that his system would have borrowed from Greek Stoical thought and from the philosophy of Spinoza, incorporating the principle of evolutionary progression as the driving force of the whole. But Huxley's system, for reasons which we shall explore, failed to develop beyond the planning stages.

The alternatives which presented themselves to Victorians in their quest for order were those of vision and system, the twin aspects of unity. Each presented possibilities which had a strong attraction for Huxley, the systematic approach appealing to his rationalist appreciation for the formal architectonic, the visionary possibility appealing to his vivid sense of value.[4] The attraction of a system like Herbert Spencer's synthetic philosophy to a scientist like Huxley was considerable, since Spencer offered a systemic unity, formulated along lines of evolutionary development, in which to orient the facts and phenomena of social and historical transition. Karl Marx offered much the same—an ordered theory of historical process which achieved the dimensions of a philosophical system and claimed allegiance to the new science. The systems of Spencer and Marx were great Victorian efforts at synthesis, but Huxley held aloof from Marxist theory and rejected Spencer on the basis of his a priori methodology. A priori thought, divorced as it was from verifiable experience, was of a similar intellectual structure to the "traditional authority" Huxley held to be locked in perpetual conflict with free thought. Its assumptions were frequently vast; its logic was sometimes impervious to fact: "Spencer's idea of a tragedy," Huxley had observed, "is a deduction killed by a fact."[5]

While the scientist might find the alternatives to overt system unattractive, since what was not capable of systematic representation could have little experimental validity, the critic and man of letters operated in a world of value and tradition where the ceremony of consistency was not always stood upon. Experience was important in the critical writings of men like Carlyle, Arnold, and Ruskin, but it rarely assumed the schematized patterns into which the scientist's experience was organized. For the cultural critic, valid experience could also be expressed in moral and emotional modes which originated internally in the personal vision. In his writings, the critic sought to reveal the personal experience of self amid culture, thinking of culture as an organic entity, its complexities not reducible to quantities, whether economic, historical, or biological. Lionel Trilling has observed that "to think in cultural terms is to consider human expressions not only in their overt existence and avowed intention, but in, as it were, their secret life, taking cognizance of the desires and impulses which lie beyond the open formulation."[6] The Victorian cultural critic sought the inward experience that described the sensation of living at a particular moment in history, the frustrations and inspirations of a unique cultural period. In undertaking to consider how the activity of science was influencing Victorian culture, Huxley found himself turning increasingly toward the secret life of Victorian science, seeking to discover the impulses which could be seen as the aspirations of a unique culture. In this critical context, Huxley argued that scientific ideals and accomplishments could furnish material and spiritual means to implement a moral and intellectual revolution such as society had never experienced. In his vision, Huxley dreamed the Baconian dream of a science which, guided by some worthy human aspiration, could shape society anew.

In lieu of realizing his system, Huxley steadily built up a critical edifice from which to view the intersection of science and society, the voices of critic and scientist inevitably becoming one. The result of this union was the creation of a unique cultural agent—the scientist—whom Huxley installed as the primary intelligence of his essays. Essentially a persona, a second self extracted from professional experiences, historical antecedents, and personal ideals, Huxley's idea of the scientist generated a unified vision which lent the essays their consistencies of tone, perspective, and value, or what Oliver Elton has called their "noble unity of mental temper."[7] The scientist figure became Huxley's most significant literary creation, for it allowed him to formulate and sustain what amounted to a scientific world view—a critical consciousness that was able to range freely over diverse materials and to judge them according to ideals and standards it associated with science. The scientist-as-critic, however, added an important dimension to all this, for he was willing to express moral and emotional sensations, to register opinion and to admit error. He was flexible, embracing both the imaginative and the rational, embodying the human element of science, revealing, ideally, the self amid the system.

With origins in the old Baconian vision of the seer, whose methodology filled him with the power of transformation and enabled him to manipulate nature, and with other roots in the Enlightenment, with its cynical regard for authority and its worship of reason, Huxley's man of science was a complicated idea with an interesting intellectual pedigree. He was an adventurer, setting out on his quest in nature in order to confront the unknown, with an almost Puritan sense of mission to bring order to the wilderness:

> In fact, the history of physical science teaches (and we cannot too carefully take the lesson to heart) that the practical advantages, attainable through its agency, never have been, and never will be, sufficiently attractive to men inspired by the inborn genius of the interpreter of Nature, to give them

courage to undergo the toils and make the sacrifices which that calling requires from its votaries. That which stirs their pulses is the love of knowledge and the joy of the discovery of the causes of things sung by the old poet—the supreme delight of extending the realm of law and order ever farther towards the unattainable goals of the infinitely great and the infinitely small, between which our little race of life is run. In the course of this work, the physical philosopher, sometimes intentionally, much more often unintentionally, lights upon something which proves to be of practical value. Great is the rejoicing of those who are benefited thereby; and, for the moment, science is the Diana of all the craftsmen. But, even while the cries of jubilation resound and this flotsam and jetsam of the tide of investigation is being turned into the wages of workmen and the wealth of capitalists, the crest of the wave of scientific investigation is far away on its course over the illimitable ocean of the unknown.

[1:53-54]

The quest theme was essential to Huxley's vision; the man of science sought experience in nature so as to extend the "realm of law and order" even further. One can also detect at such junctures an imperialist element in Victorian science which was consonant with the historical aspirations of the time, the quest for empire, the concern to institute a British order in unknown lands, the romance with the unexplored. Darwin and Huxley, each in his youth, had sailed out from England aboard Her Majesty's ships, the *Beagle* and the *Rattlesnake,* over the "illimitable ocean of the unknown" to return with plans which would bestow order on whole biological realms, Huxley with his rationale for invertebrate classification, Darwin with his theory of natural selection.

We return, then, to the question of man's place in nature, for just as the dynamic between man and nature had always been a subjective one, the definition of the one influencing that of the other, so was the new Victorian extension of law to biological nature to have serious implications for the cultural concept of man and the personal idea of self. Such works as Huxley's **Man's Place in Nature** (1863), Lyell's *The Antiquity of Man* (1863), and Darwin's *The Descent of Man* (1871), brought Victorians face to face with their biological selves, an encounter which proved startling to most, establishing a new concept of self as a physical entity. Because of the Victorian inability to reconcile him with traditional assumptions of self, biological man emerged as yet another version of Victorian dualism. The question of man's place in nature, as Victorians phrased it to themselves, became in this way not only one of the central concerns of several biological sciences—physical anthropology, embryology, physiology, comparative anatomy—but it also found its inevitable way to the center of things, to the human image itself, around which cultures must always be organized.

In the study of Huxley's thought and cultural criticism which follows, I have set out to explore the network of ideas, the vision, in which Huxley labored, concentrating on his special concern with the locus of man amid the powers of nature. In order to examine his vision, I have pursued a series of inquiries which I believe describe the outlines of Huxley's thought, each inquiry cutting across his concern with the human figure in its existential condition. I have also followed a rough chronological pattern in tracing Huxley's intellectual development, beginning with the genesis of his concepts of science and the scientist and concluding with a consideration of his broad critical approach to the problems of Victorian culture and society. Throughout, I have attempted where appropriate to compare Huxley's ideas with those of his leading Victorian antagonists and counterparts so as to weave his thought into the fabric of his era; for Huxley defined and personally symbolized an intellectual and social development which contributed strikingly to Victorian culture.

Victorian culture and science had become deeply, if not consciously, integrated. It was Huxley's critical insight to understand the historical significance of this union and to attempt to raise the relationship to a more conscious level of thought in the minds of his contemporaries. There were those, then as now, whose ideal science was a hidden science, either submerged in an unseen service to society, challenging neither the intellectual discipline nor the cultural tradition, or held aloft from the uninitiated, above the common reach of the masses. Huxley spent a considerable amount of his life's energy arguing the danger, not to mention the intellectual contemptibility, of such positions. If science were merely the slave to the material appetites of humanity, he declared, it were better to do without. And to the Brahmans, scientific and historical, he observed:

> I have not been one of those fortunate persons who are able to regard a popular lecture as a mere *hors d'oeuvre,* unworthy of being ranked among the serious efforts of a philosopher; and who keep their fame as scientific hierophants unsullied by attempts—at least of the successful sort—to be understood of the people.
>
> [8:v]

Always Huxley envisioned science as a great social and intellectual venture, a synthesis of knowledge in an endeavor that had been vital to humanity since the beginning of civilization.

Chapter I: The Idea of The Scientist

i. the new victorian

If Mary Shelley presented the nineteenth century with the figure of the obsessed man of science, and Charles Dickens and George Eliot created images of the in-

tense young researcher and physician, it was Huxley who formulated for the cultural imagination the ideal scientist as moral figure, prophet of order, and relentless seeker after truth. Selecting almost at random from Huxley's essays, one finds the general outlines and characteristics of the new man of science in the frequent references to what the scientist is, what he is concerned with, and how he carries out his quest for truth, in the voice and assumptions of the essays themselves. Whether the scientist is directly mentioned or not, he is nearly always present by virtue of the fact that a Huxley essay has been written self-consciously by a man of science. This particular perspective, created by a continual scientific presence and voice, characteristically accompanies Huxley's critical essays and constitutes one of their most effective unifying threads.

As a term, "scientist" was a Victorian contribution to the language, coined by William Whewell in his important work *The Philosophy of the Inductive Sciences* (1840), where he set it in contrast to "artist":

> We need very much a name to describe a cultivator of science in general. I should incline to call him a *Scientist.* Thus we might say, that as an Artist is a Musician, Painter, or Poet, a Scientist is a Mathematician, Physicist, or Naturalist.[1]

Apparently taking up Whewell's suggestion, David Scott, a Romantic artist, contributed an essay to the August 1840 issue of *Blackwood's;* looking back to the Renaissance, he compared Leonardo to Correggio by declaring: "Leonardo was mentally a seeker after truth—a scientist: Correggio was an asserter of truth—an artist."[2] And he considered at some length the difference in methodologies between scientist and artist, emphasizing the urge of Leonardo to experiment, his restless drive to perceive anew. For both Whewell and Scott, the scientist or man of science was one who cultivated the pursuit of knowledge with all the determination and intensity of the artist. Whewell's term signaled the scientist's advancing social and cultural status, even though the term "scientist" would not come into common usage until the end of the century. The scientist was becoming a new Victorian professional who lived by means of his intellect, seeking to extend the borders of his discipline, filled with what Whitehead, in referring to the new character of nineteenth-century science, called the "self-conscious realisation of the power of professionalism in knowledge . . . and of the boundless possibilities of technological advance."[3]

The scientist's greatest critic and explicator, his enthusiast, champion, and most visible Victorian representative, in some sense his creator, was Thomas Huxley. For Huxley, the concept of the man of science furnished the foundation for a world view. It had deep personal significance just as it had a vital new cultural implication. A personal and professional concept, it defined Huxley's relationship to his age on both emotional and intellectual planes.

In essays like **"On the Advisableness of Improving Natural Knowledge"** (1866) and **"On the Method of Zadig"** (1880), the scientist surfaces as an ancient and honored type; Huxley examines methods, values, and attitudes toward experience which characterize sound scientific thought. Zadig, a mythical figure, becomes the prototypical scientist by virtue of his elegant and superior use of empirical method to extract from mere evidence the attributes of creatures and phenomena he has never seen. In **"Joseph Priestley"** (1874), **"Charles Darwin"** (1882), and in essays on Harvey and Des-cartes, Huxley explored the idea of the scientist through biographical portraits. Priestley emerges as a model of piety and sincerity, who repudiates the myth of amorality which had commonly been evoked to indict the godless scientist. Darwin, "the incorporated ideal of a man of science," is the truth seeker, the great spirit pursuing his vision amid the storm of controversy (2:245). And in yet other essays such as **"On a Piece of Chalk"** (1868) and in the public Working Men's Lectures, beginning in the 1850s, the featured scientist is none other than Huxley himself, fact and ideal merging on stage at the Huxley theater as he addresses his vast audiences from the halls of Victorian industrial cities.

Letters and journals reveal that even in his earliest years Huxley found a potent personal image in the man of science. Speaking of science as a way of life, a conviction, Huxley generalized on his struggle to become a professional scientist and recorded decisive turns in his scientific career. With reverence for his scientific vocation, he examined the purity of his intentions in a journal entry in 1848: "Have I the capabilities for a scientific way of life or only the desire and wish for it springing from a flattered vanity and self-deceiving blindness?"[4] One is reminded here of a religious novice, preparing for his final vows. The scientist, priest of reason, espoused what Huxley saw as the rationalist commitment and a way of life which promised a unity between belief and deed. Confronting the apparent irrationality and disorder of phenomena, the man of science sought their logic according to his own faith in the ultimate rationality of the natural world.

As a young man, Huxley felt an intense need to find the logic of experience, for his own early life had been a period of disorder and debilitating mental conflict, brought on by what he once referred to as having had his "household gods early overturned & scattered by mis-fortune."[5] Possessed by periodic mental depression and by a terrible sense of his own instability, Huxley appears to have found in the scientist an alternate identity in which he could overcome the anxieties of his youth. We find him at twenty-two, assistant surgeon and unofficial ship's naturalist aboard H.M.S. *Rattlesnake,* writing in his journal as he journeyed on a mapping voyage to Australia and New Guinea in 1846: "In the region of the intellect alone can I find free and innocent play for such faculties as I possess. And it is well for me that my way of life allows me to get rid of the 'malady of thought' in a course of action so suitable to my tastes, as that laid open to me by this voyage."[6] The course of action to which Huxley was referring was not his medical duties, which he found mostly a burden, but his work with South Sea invertebrates, research involving the study of anatomical structure and the search for archetypal anatomical plans. These were suitable objects for his faculties, opening him a path around the "malady of thought," a condition of anxiety which, while vague and diffuse, remained, as we shall see, a lifelong companion. In the same journal entry, written on his twenty-second birthday, he reflected on his birth into the world as a "pulpy mass of capabilities, as yet unknown and save by motherly affection uncared for," and wondered whether it were not better to have been "crushed and trodden out at once." Strident statements like these often punctuate Huxley's early correspondence and suggest that a deep sensitivity and turmoil lay beneath his aggressive rationalism. Some forty years later, Beatrice Webb, fascinated with Huxley while interviewing him about his old associate Herbert Spencer, recorded in her journal: "Huxley, when not working, dreams strange things: carries on lengthy conversations between unknown persons living within his brain. There is a strain of madness in him; melancholy has haunted his whole life."[7] It was a shrewd observation. Huxley's chronic mental depressions and collapses, his sense of isolation and trauma when speaking of his past, suggest that his intense commitment to the rationalist world view, which he identified as the fundamental view of the scientist, was in important ways generated by the impulse to seek and to create external order in the face of impending personal disorder.

From his earliest youth, when he had set out to organize the disciplines of knowledge into objective and subjective categories, to his final years, when he set the human order at odds with the natural order, Huxley was fascinated by philosophical architectonics. "What I cared for," he pointed out in his **"Autobiography,"** "was the architectural and engineering part of the business, the working out the wonderful unity of plan in the thousands and thousands of diverse living constructions, and the modifications of similar apparatuses to serve diverse ends" (1:7). Science opened a bridge between the external world of phenomena and the internal world of intellect and emotion. Writing to Kingsley in 1860, Huxley, emotionally wrought over the death of his son Noel, declared:

> Science seems to me to teach in the highest and strongest manner the great truth which is embodied

in the Christian conception of entire surrender to the will of God. Sit down before fact as a little child, be prepared to give up every preconceived notion, follow humbly wherever and to whatever abysses nature leads, or you shall learn nothing. I have only begun to learn content and peace of mind since I have resolved at all risks to do this.

[*LL,* 1:235]

Thus it was that death and the apparent irrationalities of the world were brought into rational perspective by the outlook of the man of science. Just as his son Noel had surrendered to the ultimate fact of death, so Huxley resolved to sit down before the same fact and to surrender his will to the reality of the boy's death. It was an act of courage and deep emotion. Like a true Stoic, Huxley sought to live according to the truths of science, believing that they were the truths of life itself, that the work of the scientist was a progressive revelation of the nature of things not only in the laboratory but in the world.

ii. science and self

Huxley's idea of the scientist originated during a period of personal struggle and unrest, when he was uncertain of the direction his life was to take. Born in 1825, the sixth child in an impoverished and factious family, Huxley found his early years full of conflict. For while very early he was keenly interested in acquiring an education as a guide into the world of intellect, he was for the most part left to drift. With little family support and only a year of formal education, he was forced to secure his education through a self-motivated and self-directed process of study, which, while made somewhat easier by his intellectual enthusiasm, was to succeed only through long, grueling lessons in self-discipline. Considering the rigorous educations of his Victorian counterparts, John Stuart Mill and Matthew Arnold, Huxley could only look back on his earlier years with a sense of bitter failure. In 1845, reflecting in a journal on the previous five years of his life, the time of his medical apprenticeship and his study at Charing Cross Hospital in London, he wrote of pain and neglect:

I hardly care to look back into the seething depths of the working and boiling mass that lay beneath all this froth, and indeed I hardly know whether I could give myself any clear account of it. Remembrances of physical and mental pain . . . absence of sympathy, and thence a choking up of such few ideas as I did form clearly within my own mind.

[*LL,* 1:15]

The period remained permanently embroiled in a feeling of despair; it had been a struggle to assemble ideas amid anxieties and circumstances which he would recall in later life with a sense of lonely isolation.

The loss of educational opportunity left Huxley with a sense of intellectual disenfranchisement. While his early journal, **"Thoughts and Doings,"** reveals him at work among studies and experiments in physiology, chemistry, and electricity; readings in English and German Romantic authors like Carlyle, Novalis, and Lessing; and language studies in Greek, Latin, German, and Italian; Huxley was keenly aware that he was without guide and that his studies were often random and incomplete. Left to his own devices in determining his educational program, he found himself ranging over widely diverse materials, and often out of his depth. His future was determined by the fact that his brothers-in-law were medical doctors and that he was expected to follow them; but he demonstrated only slight interest in medicine, devoting much time to the study of his favorite authors, Goethe and Carlyle, and to his readings in philosophy and theoretical science. He managed, in the "boiling mass" of his early years, to obtain a preliminary certificate in medicine at London University in 1845, and a naval position the following year as assistant surgeon aboard H.M.S. *Rattlesnake;* yet he remained anxious, convinced he had wasted his abilities and lost his opportunity. At sea in 1849, writing to his Australian fiancée, Henrietta Heathorn, whom he had met less than a year after he set out on his voyage to Australia and New Guinea, Huxley struck out at his past and expressed his sense of neglect:

I believe that I possess powers which might by proper training have been made a good deal of. I believe that I have a somewhat acute logical mind and strong appreciation of the Beautiful in whatever shape—I might have made a good critic and an accomplished man. As it is, what am I? A hotch-potch of knowledge and ignorance—facts and fictions picked up from all the highways & byways of knowledge, cheek by jowl with the most absurd ignorance at which a schoolboy might blush. My knowledge is mostly the result of thought and reasoning, whereas all that shows in the world is learning—the result of a good memory and superficial aptness.[8]

Running through the passage is a clash between fact and aspiration, a sense of having fallen far short of capacity. But Huxley's was an exaggerated sense of inferiority—while he had not acquired a classical British university education, he had nevertheless developed his powers of "thought and reasoning" considerably in his struggle to educate himself, and he had read widely, if not systematically, in several disciplines. At the very time he wrote to Henrietta, he was studying ocean invertebrates, research which would prove to be highly innovative and original. It appears, however, that Huxley initially desired a literary rather than a scientific career, and much of his discontent may have arisen from the absence of any choice in his life. His enthusiasm for criticism, the feeling that he might have made a good critic, was undoubtedly inspired by his readings in Carlyle, whose critical essays and *Sartor Resartus* were Huxley's intimate voyage companions. He quoted them and read them for solace; he found Carlyle's essays on Jean Paul deeply appealing, since the conditions of the young Richter's life, the lack of tutors, the neglect by the father of the sons' education, the poverty and struggle, all ran so parallel to his own.[9] Huxley found his own long, introspective flights and depressions considerably amplified and defined by the unrest he encountered in the worlds of Carlyle, Goethe, and the other Romantics whom he read widely. The "malady of thought" he often referred to as his persistent shadow and persecutor was a term used by Carlyle in his essay "Goethe" to describe that Byronic and Goethean sense of despair about the "whole scene of life" which had become barren of belief and hope.[10] It was the "life-weariness" of *Manfred,* the "moody melancholy" of *Werther.* Huxley felt it in his own deep disappointment with the conditions of life, in his sense of alienation, his faltering belief.

The personal struggles of childhood influenced, perhaps even instigated, Huxley's slow synthesis of a professional identity. Few ideals were to be gleaned from the adult models of his early life, and Huxley, precocious, sensitive, and frequently demoralized by a sensation of being entirely alone and adrift, felt a powerful urge to seek out his own. Writing to Kingsley in 1860, he recalled how he had been "kicked into the world a boy without guide or training," and how few men had "drunk deeper of all kinds of sin" than he (*LL,* 1:237). The past was a barrier, complicated with vague yet intense guilt feelings which had their origins at once in childhood incidents and in a diffuse, Romantic sense of sin and alienation, a Byronic *Weltschmerz.*[11] Like Byron's Cain, whose profound discontent with the conditions of human mortality and misery led him to ponder his sleeping child Enoch with the thought that it would have been better to have "snatch'd him in his sleep, and dash'd him 'gainst / The rocks"; Huxley wondered whether it had not been better had he at birth been "crushed and trodden out at once."[12] A similar enmity for experience underlay Huxley's sense of alienation.

Writing to Henrietta Heathorn from 1847, the year they were engaged in Australia, to 1854, the year they were reunited and married in London, Huxley frequently spoke of his past, his painful experiences in the world of men, his private solace in the world of dream and intellect.[13] It was a period of great uncertainty and his letters were often anxious and deeply introspective, at times almost confessional. They revealed a young man, now in his twenties, who had long been alone with his thoughts and who lived intensely in the self. His new love for Henrietta had opened a vista into the external world, much as his scientific research aboard the *Rattlesnake* had been doing. Some letters disclose that as a child he had felt such a burning conflict with the conditions of his life that he had fled inward, constructing a wall between his own mental and the outer physical worlds. In a dream state of consciousness, he had found a personal refuge, away from events which were sources of anxiety and pain. Writing to Henrietta while at sea in December 1848, Huxley spoke of mental and social isolation:

> I fear I have nothing of that fine feeling called "love for one's species." The actions of human beings whether now around me or as they are recorded in history for the most part touch my intellect but not my heart. I like to watch them as I should like to see a play—but I always feel the spectator. It may be Tragedy or Comedy—my feelings may be pain-fully or pleasantly excited—but I feel more among men than of them. Even among the most real occur-rences a dreamy feeling creeps over me—I feel like a man who believes his dream and yet knows he is dreaming.
>
> I fancy that people must occasionally think me very unstable and indeed heartlessly indifferent. I am apt to enter into men's ways and feelings with a certain warmth and enthusiasm which is for the time perfectly real—but in fact only skin deep—and which I fear makes people fancy that I have a feeling of friendship for them when none exists. I go away and forget all about the matter and am as much surprised at their claim of friendship as I should be if, after weeping over the sad fortunes of King Lear, his majesty should doff his robes and beard and request me to back a bill for him on the strength of my sympathy. This may seem hard hearted, but so it is with me. Men's actions often interest me but their motives are either laughable for their folly or contemptible for their selfishness—that is to say, in general, god forbid that I should slander humanity so far as to say that this is universally the case.
>
> I believe that I owe many of these feelings to my early life. My life from eight years age up to manhood was made up of two sets of feelings—joys and anticipations derived from the inward world, those such as a student only knows (and however ill-directed my energies or misspent my time still I *was* a student from my childhood); and sorrows and misfortunes coming from the outward world upon all those whom I had reason to love and value most. Then, too, I was one of the most sensitive, thin-skinned mortals in the world. I had little pleasure in the general pursuits of boys of my own age, cared only for the society of men, and yet was too proud to be treated as one whit of less importance than they—so that I had hardly any friends. There was absolutely nothing to bring me into contact with the world—and I hated and avoided it. Its good was not my good, its ends not my ends, and so I saw it pass before me, little recking, and dreaming my own dreams.
>
> Since then I have indeed had a few shakes, enough to rouse the dead. But I still fear I am occasionally no better than a somnambulist.[14]

The world was, then, often a stage for the young Huxley, who remained apart, dreaming and yet awake, among men but not of them; he was surprised when their existence was affirmed through the breaking of the frame and he was called upon to respond. As a child, to insulate himself from harm, he drew his energies inward to a place where he might control events as the world passed before him in the distance. He lived with a separate mental convention which systematically disembodied the external world of its materiality and, hence, of its power to inflict pain. Like a dreamer, he saw with the objectivity of one removed, of a keen observer who sees the performances of men fall far short of possibility.

The clash of the real and the ideal in Huxley's youthful mind had its origin in events which were not covered in Leonard Huxley's *Life and Letters*. Very little is known about the Huxley family when Thomas was a child, other than that it was often in desperate financial straits, that it had a history of severe mental disorder, and that factiousness reigned during Huxley's early and later years. It was an atmosphere which bred the permanent rupture between members of the family and the older brother, William, who remained estranged for thirty years because of a family quarrel over the marriage of his brother George. "You will think it strange," Thomas wrote to Henrietta about William, "that you have hardly heard me mention his name before, although he lives in London. But he is completely alienated from the rest of us. You will, I fear, think that we are a very strange set and it is very true. For some inscrutable reason we seem to me to get on with everybody but one another."[15] Exceptions were Thomas and his older sister, Lizzie, who was in many ways his surrogate mother. Of the six children, Thomas Huxley wrote to Lizzie, they were the only two "who seemed to be capable of fraternal love."[16] Beset with financial difficulties, the family was driven inward upon itself, with little guidance from George Huxley, the uncommunicative father who by the time of Thomas's youth was probably slipping into the mental isolation which was well advanced by the time Huxley returned from his *Rattlesnake* voyage in 1850. In an atmosphere of tension and anxiety, and, unable to maintain his equilibrium, the young Huxley withdrew into the private world of dream and intellect.

Huxley's early clash with the world of experience was symbolized by his famous encounter with the corpse in the post mortem scene of his "**Autobiography**." Written in 1889 when he was nearly sixty-four, Huxley's account of himself follows a pattern beginning with childhood anecdote and ending with a reflection over the most important goals of his scientific life. Midway through the autobiography, he recounts his grim rite of passage from childhood to maturity, the tableside witness, when he was a boy of thirteen or fourteen, of a post mortem dissection. Death was the ultimate reality, the great fact of life which none could escape. There on the table, stiff and grotesque, lay a body before a young man who had had nothing to bring him into contact with the external world, the place of pain and sorrow, and who "hated and avoided" it. Yet, fascinated, Huxley indulged his curiosity for two to three hours in a state of profound but momentarily controlled mental agitation. His recollection that he did not suffer a cut implies that he may even have used the scalpel, perhaps probing and exploring to satisfy his own curiosity after the major dissection had been completed. The scene is full of irony, for while Huxley was actively confronting the fact of death, he was simultaneously submitting to its powerful reality. The corpse belonged to a world he had half disbelieved in, a world of shadows and figures, now suddenly materialized by death. Huxley left to go home in what appears to have been a state of shock and with the feeling of having been "poisoned" (1:8). Sinking into a "strange state of apathy," he languished at home for days.

The family atmosphere was unable to revive him, since it was itself a source of insecurities and the sense of neglect epitomized by the corpse. The corpse, a human figure no longer having an identity, isolated and utterly powerless, was a symbol not only of human materiality, but of human alienation as well. Huxley remained in this strange state of isolated depression until he was removed from home to "the care of some good, kind people . . . who lived in a farmhouse in the heart of Warwickshire"; the following day he arose from the dead, or the very nearly dead: "I remember staggering from my bed to the window on the bright spring morning after my arrival, and throwing open the casement. Life seemed to come back on the wings of the breeze" (1:8). Huxley himself seems to have undergone the experience of death and been reborn with a new knowledge of good and evil.[17]

The experience was important in another sense, for in confronting death Huxley had, if only momentarily, triumphed over his own anxiety. The motivation behind the act of dissection goes to the core of Huxley's thought. The self-destructive impulse to shrink from experience, to exist in dream isolation, was overcome by the scientific necessity to confront the world of fact. There at the dissecting table, the factual curiosity of the aspiring man of science enabled Huxley to control his anxieties and to confront his ultimate fate. As the researcher, he was able to distance himself and to control the object, death, by rendering it the passive subject of his rational intelligence. Science provided a framework in which one might achieve an attitude toward experience which amounted to a negation of the self. In effect, it provided a center of indifference, for its business was with phenomena only insofar as they might be quantified. The flow of consciousness was thus outward and not inward.[18] Confrontation with reality was to become the prime object of Huxley's man of science, and his childhood encounter at the dissecting table would find its ultimate justification in the conclusion of the **"Autobiography,"** which argued that alleviation for the sufferings of mankind could come only through "the resolute facing of the world as it is when the garment of make-believe by which pious hands have hidden its uglier features is stripped off" (1:16).

Death remained for Huxley a vivid symbol of reality, of corporality, a symbol which concentrated all the contingencies which seemed to threaten him as a child. The same vision of mortality which haunted Byron's Manfred and Cain haunted Huxley's private, introspective hours. In a letter to Henrietta written in May 1849, he saw death as a reality against which all ideals seemed impotent:

> In my many solitary hours—in this my hermitage— strange thoughts rise in my mind. A weary sense of the vivid emptiness of life—a scorn of my own occupations & the petty aims after which I and others struggle—a miserable feeling of the short coming of all efforts after the noble ideal which now & then for a few bright moments seems so near—so easily attainable. And under all these, as a dark background, showing forth more vividly their lurid colours—the certainty of death. I do not mean in its hackneyed sense. All men tell you they are certain of death as they tell you that they are sinners. But with me this certainty at times assumes a vividness such as I can hardly describe—I see it rather than feel it.[19]

Huxley's vision had likely been intensified by his actual encounters with death in the course of his medical studies, but long before his study at Charing Cross Hospital he had felt the force of death as a threat to his childhood security. Speaking of his mother in a letter to Henrietta, he recalled: "As a child my love for her was a passion—I have lain awake for hours, crying, because I had a morbid fear of her death."[20] His childhood fears must often have bordered on hysteria. Even his love for Henrietta was menaced in his imagination by death: "Will you believe it when I tell you that my foolish fancy carries me to so far as to even imagine you ill, or dying, or even forever . . . parted from me? My imagination has always a pictoral distinctiveness, and I see myself heading over to Holmwood on the day of our return, and hearing that you are no longer mine—no longer of this earth."[21] Reality often seemed to threaten its worst, to dissolve these intangible, emotional attachments in a show of superior force. Given to carrying on long dialogues with the self, Huxley found the private, internal world as threatening as the world without, for there was no insulation from the morbid imagination.

Huxley's early Romantic sense of alienation was thus a distillation of his very real childhood anxieties over death, neglect, and isolation—the "seething depths" and the "boiling mass" he had looked back over in his journal entry of 1845. The Romantic, introspective movement inward, the sullen alienation of Byron's Cain contemplating the injustice of having been called into the world of life only to suffer and die, the sense of dignity in intellectual rebellion, and the enmity toward experience, all conformed to Huxley's youthful sensibilities and conditions. Yet he had also begun to find avenues outward: in his research aboard H.M.S. *Rattlesnake* from 1846 to 1850, in his relationship with Henrietta Heathorn beginning in 1847, and in his increasing grasp of the Carlylean doctrines of antiself-consciousness and work. Each of these broadened and strengthened his interests in the external world. Research aboard the *Rattlesnake* carried him deeper into the physical world where he found himself increasingly at home in the material world of experience. Living aboard ship for four years brought him into steady contact with a harsh physical world whose laws he disciplined himself to abide by. His work countered his tendency to withdraw, for the labor of the field researcher was among facts which had to be obtained in physical nature. Above all, in the methods of the sciences one found a rational framework in which to approach the phenomena of the external world, even death, since all were a part of the great natural pattern. Science, Huxley declared to Kingsley in 1860, had taught him to "sit down before fact as a little child," and to "follow humbly wherever and to whatever abysses nature leads" (*LL,* 1:235). Only then had he begun to "learn content and peace of mind."

Huxley's conversion from self-centeredness to antiself-consciousness was a gradual one, and appears to have occurred in the years immediately after his return to London in 1850. He devoted himself intensively to his scientific research for more than four years. Not only did science offer a rational framework in which to view the struggles and pains of life; it also hinted that they were essentially just, since they were universal, without malice, and to varying degrees predictable. "I cannot but think," Huxley reflected in his 1854 essay **"On the Educational Value of the Natural History Sciences"** "that he who finds a certain proportion of pain and evil inseparably woven up in the life of the very worms, will bear his own share with more courage and submission" (3:62). In spite of pain, one found "the predominance of happiness" among living things, and a "secret and wonderful harmony" in nature. Science offered a Carlylean center of indifference from which to view the whole, for one's obligation was to seek a self-annihilating disinterestedness with which, without fear, one could look upon the worst. "The intellectual perception of truth," Huxley wrote to Henrietta in 1851, "and the acting up to it is so far as I know the only meaning of the phrase 'one-ness with God.' So long as we attain that end, does it matter much whether our small selves are happy or miserable?"[22] It was Carlyle who had cautioned against the morbid introspection, the "malady of thought," that drove one to an inner fury and agony:

> "What is this that, ever since earliest years, thou hast been fretting and fuming, and lamenting and self-tormenting, on account of? Say it in a word: is it not because thou are not HAPPY? Because the THOU (sweet gentleman) is not sufficiently honoured, nourished, soft-bedded, and lovingly cared-for? Foolish soul! What Act of Legislature was there that *thou* shouldst be Happy? A little while ago thou hadst no right to *be* at all . . . Art thou nothing other than a Vulture, then, that fliest through the Universe seeking after somewhat to *eat;* and shrieking dolefully because carrion enough is not given thee? Close thy *Byron;* open the *Goethe.*"[23]

The vast scope of the scientific vision served for Huxley as the infinitude in which to dwarf the problems and anxieties of the self. And his Romantic sense of alienation gradually evolved into the "scientific Calvinism" which he identified in a letter to his friend Dyster as the philosophy underlying his 1854 essay. "Pain being everywhere is inevitable," he confided, "and therefore like all other inevitable things to be borne" (*LL,* 1:122). To reach the higher truth, one had to learn the lesson of renunciation, and Huxley found Carlyle's argument compelling enough to list *Sartor Resartus* as one of the "agents" of his redemption (*LL,* 1:237).

The steady confrontation of harsh reality became a high priority of Huxley's intellectual vision, giving rise to his new scientific Calvinism. It was in many ways a fierce vision, a determined commitment to confront, at whatever cost, the abyss that loomed in the world "when the garment of make-believe by which pious hands have hidden its uglier features is stripped off" (1:16). And yet there was a dignity, a courage, in the confrontation that promised a new human possibility and truth. Typically, the confrontation took the form of analysis. Huxley's observation in the 1854 essay **"On the Educational Value of the Natural History Sciences"** that the real advantage in the *"trained and organised common sense"* of the scientist was the same as that of the "point and polish of the swordsman's weapon" over the "club" of the savage, demonstrated that he still was at battle with the powers of the earth (3:45). Rebellion was part of his character, and renunciation came much easier to him than submission. His doctrine of confrontation found one of its classic expressions in his 1868 essay **"A Liberal Education; and Where to Find it,"** where death was the outcome of a neglected reality, and science the proper instrument for the confrontation of that reality. He characterized life as a game of chess played against nature by men according to rules which were identical to the laws of nature. While the opponent, nature, was not sinister, but rather a "calm, strong angel," the stakes were high. Those who could not learn to play the game were

"plucked," and Huxley carefully pointed out that "Nature's pluck means extermination" (3:85). Death remained the old adversary.

Huxley's 1854 essay was his unofficial inaugural essay. He delivered it at St. Martin's Hall in London on July 22, only a few days after he had been appointed Lecturer in Natural History at the Government School of Mines, replacing his close friend Edward Forbes. For the first time since he had returned to London in 1850, he was able to contemplate a scientific career with some confidence. He had fought for a position in scientific London, but found it difficult to penetrate the inner circle where professional positions were controlled by an intimate polity of researchers and specialists, and very scarce. The pressure was intensified by the absence of Henrietta, whom Huxley could not bring over from Australia until he had a dependable income. The four years from 1850 to 1854 were not unproductive, however, for he earned admission to the Royal Society in 1851, and the society's Royal Medal the following year for his research among ocean invertebrates; he was also earning a reputation as a talented writer and speaker. By midyear 1854, he had published more than twenty papers on technical subjects, including a brilliant study, **"On the Morphology of the Cephalous Mollusca,"** in which he had begun to renovate British theories of anatomy and classification; he had translated and edited, in collaboration with George Busk, Kölliker's *Handbuch der Gewebelehre des Menschen (Manual of Human Histology);* and he had begun to write scientific columns and reviews for George Eliot in the *Westminster Review,* contributing regularly from 1852 to 1854. He was thus growing familiar with both scientific and literary circles in London, and coming into contact with the main ideas and intellectual trends of his time.

During the four years after his return to London, Huxley's growing commitment to scientific life and work helped him to consolidate his idea of the scientist. But he found a new pattern of adversity dominating his life: the personal alienation of his youth he now saw being recapitulated in the public alienation of the scientist as a type in Victorian society. Huxley's individual struggle formed a basic pattern which was strikingly representative of professional scientists who sought to earn their livings by means of scientific pursuits. In a letter to Henrietta, Huxley wrote in 1851:

> To attempt to live by any scientific pursuit is a farce. Nothing but what is absolutely practical will go down in England. A man of science may earn great distinction, but not bread. . . . A man of science in these times is like an Esau who sells his birthright for a mess of pottage.
>
> [*LL,* 1:72]

In a somewhat different way, Huxley's struggle typified that of Victorian science to become accepted as an intellectual force and a professional body of knowledge. Livings were not often to be made in pure science, although medals and professional plaudits were common enough, for the simple reason that science had yet to be recognized as a social, economic, and cultural force. It remained the amateur's field, that of the gentleman researcher who, like Darwin, might divert himself for years with little concern for income. Huxley wrote, "My opportunities for seeing the scientific world in England force upon me every day a stronger and stronger conviction. It is that there is no chance of living by science. . . . There are not more than four or five offices in London which a Zoologist or Comparative Anatomist can hold and live by. Owen, who has a European reputation, second only to that of Cuvier, gets as Hunterian Professor £300 a year! which is less than the salary of many a bank clerk" (*LL,* 1:74). Professional scientific specialization in England began and developed in a pattern and schedule that roughly paralleled Huxley's professional career.

The search for employment, which for Huxley recalled the childhood anxieties over instability, helped him to formulate a broad notion of the scientist. He was also able to generalize from his own experience to the common experiences of men of science whom he began to characterize as a type in his personal letters. Facing a long period of poverty, continued separation from Henrietta, and uncertainty about his future, Huxley had to consider carefully his motivation for pursuing the way of the scientist, and he began to construct out of his own ideals and those of the men with whom he associated a representative concept of the profession. Looking around him, he found numerous "first-rate men—men who have been at work for years laboriously toiling upward—men whose abilities, had they turned them into many channels of money-making, must have made large fortunes. But the beauty of Nature and the pursuit of Truth allured them into a nobler life" (*LL,* 1:74). In the same letter, written on his twenty-sixth birthday, less than a month after he had been elected a member of the Royal Society, he confided to Henrietta:

> A man who chooses a life of science chooses not a life of poverty, but, so far as I can see, a life of *nothing,* and the art of living upon nothing at all has yet to be discovered. You naturally think, then, "Why persevere in so hopeless a course?" At present I cannot help myself. For my own credit, for the sake of gratifying those who have hitherto helped me on—nay, for the sake of truth and science itself, I must work out fairly and fully complete what I have begun.
>
>   [*LL,* 1:74-75]

Six months later, Huxley declared that the "real pleasure, the true sphere" of his ambition, lay "in the feeling of self-development—in the sense of power and of growing *oneness* with the great spirit of abstract truth" (*LL,*

1:75). The idealistic dedication to beauty and truth was tempered by an awareness of personal and social conflict. The struggle of the scientist, linked as it was to both truth and adversity, became symbolic for Huxley in a personal as well as a professional sense. It became part of the nobler life, the life which death and childhood misfortunes had often seemed to threaten before they met with the force of his own intellectual enthusiasm. In 1853, he wrote, "I have become almost unable to exist without active intellectual excitement" (*LL,* 1:91). In the scientist, Huxley's personal struggles and values had found their intellectual, public equivalent. In 1860, when he was thirty-five, he confided to Kingsley that he had come to feel as one who had been redeemed from himself. He identified his three "agents . . . of redemption" as *Sartor Resartus,* science, and his love for Henrietta Heathorn (*LL,* 1:237). Carlyle's work had led him from his early alienated scepticism, a Cain-like antipathy for the world that sin had spawned, to the recognition that a "deep sense of religion was compatible with the entire absence of theology." In science he had found an appropriate and constructive resting place for his intellectual rebellion against "authority and tradition." And love had taught him of the "sanctity of human nature" and of the duties and responsibilities of human relationships. Huxley's early Romantic sense of alienation had found its Victorian solution.

iii. the lower world

The idea of a scientist developed into one of the controlling unities of Huxley's nontechnical essays. Exploring the man of science as a type, Huxley investigated his moral, intellectual, and social profile against the Victorian cultural background. As a fusion of personal vision, extracted from Huxley's private experience, and professional generalization, derived from his familiarity with scientists past and present, Huxley's man of science took on the dimensions of a broad ideal. It was an unusual ideal, however, for its preoccupation was with physical reality. Like the poet and the artist, the scientist immersed himself in nature, but in a physical nature where his business was as often as not in the bowels of the earth. As a result, his findings frequently held little aesthetic appeal; they were less likely to reflect the realm of human ideal than to contribute to the book of physical law. The scientist was codifying nature. He was not, as Ruskin had urged, simply the eagle, acting in the conviction that "the glory of the higher creatures is in ignorance of what is known to the lower."[24] While Ruskin argued that great knowledge, "sophia," forbade men to bury themselves in "the mole's earthheap," Huxley held that the pursuit of coarse and inelegant fact was the source of the scientist's power. For Ruskin man had the choice of "stooping in science beneath himself, and striving in science beyond himself," while for Huxley the system of nature was of such unity that the lowliest fact led to the most exalted vista.[25]

In an unpublished, undated fragment, Huxley traced the development from Greek thought to modern thought of the concept of "sophos":

> The early Greeks called a skillful craftsman, one who excelled his fellows, *Sophos;* and hence the term easily extended to cover the shrewd & intelligent in general whence there lay but a step to the men of deep knowledge & wisdom or even of mere worldly wisdom. In fact the fate of the word was pretty much that of our "cunning."[26]

He went on to argue that "sophos" and "sophia" originally meant the craftsman and his skill, but that gradually they came to refer to the wise man and his wisdom, and later to the pedantic art of argumentation. The "philosophos," he noted, was originally the self-designation of one who did not claim to be a "sophos"— a skilled artificer, artist or thinker—but only a lover of such. Only gradually did "philosophos" come to mean the skilled and authoritative wise man. "Sapientia" and "scientia," Huxley observed, were the Latin equivalents of the Greek "sophia," and they had undergone "a most unfortunate narrowing" in modern thought until they were specifically applied to disciplines of chemistry, biology, physics, and mathematics, when in fact they should apply to "organised knowledge whatever its subject matter." For Huxley, the pedigree of human knowledge could be traced back to the precision and skill of the craftsman, whose mastery of detail and preoccupation with materials of the earth, with forging the tools for survival, earned him the admiration of his fellows. Greek technology and science, that is, organized knowledge, laid the foundations for Greek philosophy. Thus while Ruskin's great lectures in *The Eagle's Nest* were delivered at Oxford, Huxley's lectures were given more frequently at working men's clubs; these were the respective symbolic centers of their separate concepts of "sophia."

For Huxley the idea of the scientist had strong proletarian roots. In his address **"Technical Education"** (1887), he described himself as a teacher of handicrafts, a manual laborer, and emphasized the egalitarian basis of scientific knowledge. Speaking before the Working Men's Club and Institute in London, he referred to anatomy as his "handicraft," and argued that the sciences all required a manual dexterity similar to that of the anatomist, whose skill enabled him to dissect, "say, a blackbeetle's nerves" (3:406). Huxley was careful to emphasize that he meant the comparison in a literal sense, and while his claim seemed somewhat exaggerated, he quite properly drew upon the relationship between the crafts and the laboratory, an association which had endured since the Renaissance. "Doing" was essential to scientific investigation, for the sciences demanded constant verification, and, like the craftsman, the scientist was required to remain in touch with the crude realities of daily experience.

Huxley as a young man (1857).

Huxley went on to suggest that the bond between the cobbler and the anatomist lay in their common "contact with tangible facts" (3:407). At the same time, he set in opposition to the scientist and craftsman certain "learned brethren, whose work is untrammelled by anything 'base and mechanical'" (3:408). These were the intellectuals whose histories edified and whose poems charmed; their work illustrated "so remarkably the powers of man's imagination." Yet they were removed from the world of "mother wit" and physical, manual skill. They were the inhabitants of the "empyreal kingdom of speculation," where there were distinct prejudices against mere "grovelling dissectors of monkeys and blackbeetles" (3:408). In his solidarity with his craftsman audience, Huxley gave rein to his sense of antagonism toward the humanities. He emasculated the liberal arts through stereotype: "Mother Nature is serenely obdurate to honeyed words" (3:408). He claimed for the scientist and the craftsman a higher sense of reality and therefore a greater power over nature. The scientist, he argued, is tied to the reality of physical fact by a logic no less compelling than that which demands the attention of the British working classes. For both, it is a matter of survival which, although often prosaic, yields rewards in the increased awareness of physical reality.

Huxley was oversimplifying in identifying the scientist so literally with the working man; in many other essays he had claimed the kingdom of speculation for scientists as well as for intellectuals. Yet he believed that the distinctive character of scientific knowledge and work was their preoccupation with physical nature. The process of accumulating experience had its counterpart in the process of recording factual data. Huxley had formulated reality out of hard, sometimes harsh facts; it was the fundamental lesson of his youth. Imagination and speculation were frequently suspect as pleasant, even lurid, indulgences that for all their edification and charm were not essential to survival. The craftsman's knowledge had its primary value in enabling him to manipulate and thereby change physical reality, to make with his own hands "a veritable chair" (3:407). The man of science had a similar power, only on a larger scale. In his famous lay sermon **"On the Advisableness of Improving Natural Knowledge"** (1866), Huxley pointed out that natural knowledge had become so fundamental that it had been "incorporated with the household words of men, and . . . supplied the springs of their daily actions" (1:28). He was referring to the largely unconscious behavior of Londoners which averted catastrophes like the great plague and the great fire. The scientist, not the theologian or politician, delivered men from natural catastrophe. Like the working man, he labored in a hidden world, grappling with realities no one else cared to contemplate. Their alliance was a natural one, even to the extent that they suffered in common a certain taint of servility as a consequence of their common residence in lower worlds of fact and utility.

Huxley's belief in the bond between scientists and the working class remained strong throughout his life. His working men's lectures, his energetic pioneering work in technical education and universities for the working classes, suggests a deeply felt identification. British science and labor had secured a close, if stormy, relationship in their shared concern with technology. One remembers the strong ally Dickens finds for the working class in the technology of the Rouncewell iron factory in *Bleak House,* and Carlyle's ambition for British industry.[27] Not only did technology, with its fusion of science and the crafts, supply new possibilities for the British laboring classes, as Huxley noted in his essay on improving natural knowledge, it promised a new independence and dignity. For Marx and Engels, the subjection of nature's forces, resulting from the application of new technology, had revealed that unsuspected "productive forces slumbered in the lap of social labor."[28] Technology promised power for the working classes, even if its exploitation was in the hands of another class. The vast new laboring forces in textiles, commerce, and mining, as Marx had pointed out, promised a new locus of power. The underlying themes of Huxley's working men's lectures and essays treating education, while not Marxist, appreciated simi-

larly the physical power men were exercising over nature. Technical knowledge was that of force and power; it was the new learning which would ultimately revolutionize all human knowledge and human society.

Huxley's thrust in essays like **"A Liberal Education; and Where to Find It"** and **"Technical Education"** was the reverse of John Henry Newman's, for Newman's idea of knowledge as its own end rejected the notion that education must have a practical application. Indeed, such knowledge as could be put to distinct use was considered "servile" by Newman to the degree that its worth was to be measured in terms of the efficacy of the particular action it inspired.[29] Newman sought to liberate knowledge from utilitarian standards of value. Liberal knowledge justified itself by fulfilling the basic need of human nature to know. Ruskin, too, found the university the center of "conception" rather than "skill": "The object of University teaching is to form your conceptions;—not to acquaint you with arts, nor sciences. It is to give you a notion of what is meant by smith's work, for instance;—but not to make you blacksmiths."[30] The drive of Newman and Ruskin toward *gnosis,* the contemplative sphere of knowledge, contrasted dramatically with Huxley's advocacy of *praxis.* Scientist and working man were, in their different capacities, oriented toward action. Both were members of "Nature's university," learning to survive and operate in a world that functioned according to natural principle. Physical science was the proletarian of the intellectual world.

Of Huxley's portraits of scientists, fictitious or real, none is more compelling than Zadig in his unique combination of perceptual acumen and that "coarse commonplace assumption, upon which every act of our daily lives is based," the reasoning from effects to causes (4:7). In this 1880 lecture delivered at the Working Men's College, Huxley went to considerable lengths to establish Voltaire's well-known character as a prototype of the modern scientist. Using the "unconscious logic of common sense," Zadig surmises that the king's lost horse has a tail three and a half feet long because the dust of the trees had been disturbed on either side of a narrow, seven-foot alley (4:8). "Nothing can be more hopelessly vulgar," Huxley pointed out, "more unlike the majestic development of a system of grandly unintelligible conclusions from sublimely inconceivable premises" (4:8). Huxley deliberately set off the portrait in prosaic, even primitivistic, terms, calling Zadig's insight "methodized savagery" (4:8). The point of the portrait was to domesticate the scientist figure, to show that his activities were natural and fundamentally concerned with natural processes, that they were human and "nothing but the method of all mankind" (4:8). Certainly, as Phyllis Rose has suggested, Huxley was over-simplifying the nature of the scientist, but at the same time he was demonstrating the essential human impulse behind the great disciplines that had developed out of empirical investigations.[31] Huxley wished to proclaim the democracy of scientific knowledge by characterizing Zadig as a kind of scientific Everyman. Throughout the essay, the clarity and simplicity of Zadig's method is contrasted with the a priori stances of "magian wisdom, with all its lofty antagonism to everything common" (4:7). Scientific knowledge drew its strength from its vulgar simplicity, its dismissal of intellectual pretension.

Not only was Zadig a plucky antiauthoritarian, like Huxley's scientific Everyman, he served to universalize intellectual procedures commonly associated with scientific method. Precisely because he was not a professional scientist Zadig gave legitimacy to the nineteenth-century scientist, for he illustrated that the scientist had his roots in the distant past, that the unadorned search for fact had moral force, and that the process of scientific method was simple, common, and human. The need to recast the figure of the scientist as a socially responsible being had to be met before science could be taken seriously by society as a means of progress. One suspects that Huxley had something similar to Mary Shelley's *Frankenstein* in mind when he asserted that "Science is not, as many would seem to suppose, a modification of the black art, suited to the tastes of the nineteenth century" (3:45). The gothic obsession of Frankenstein's hideous labor in his isolated laboratory, already by 1823 a popular melodrama in London, presents an interesting contrast to the elegant rationality of Zadig.

Zadig and Dr. Frankenstein belong to different worlds. The science of Frankenstein is a nineteenth-century version of the murky machinery of Cornelius Agrippa, scholar and broker of occult powers over nature. It is a science that still hopes for fabulous "secrets" which promise prodigious power. "I succeeded in discovering the cause of generation and life; nay, more, I became myself capable of bestowing animation upon lifeless matter," records Frankenstein.[32] Mary Shelley attempted to give a solid scientific base to Frankenstein's work, yet for all that, he emerges as the magus, obsessed with his great opus. And it is this isolation while in possession of obscure and demonic power which makes Frankenstein so frightening. By contrast, Zadig's powers appear benign. There is no mystery to them, nor is Zadig outside of society or reason. With his "mere carnal common sense," the common intellectual tool of mankind, he seeks out the obvious in a natural setting. What Zadig discovers is apparent to all; what Frankenstein discovers is shrouded in mystery. In Frankenstein's world, Zadig would seem narrow and dull; in Zadig's world, Frankenstein would seem excessive and mad.

Huxley's essay on Zadig goes on to suggest that Cuvier, the great French naturalist, had used precisely the same method of reasoning from effects to causes to reconstruct the past from the fossil remains of the present.

It was, Huxley rightly noted, a demonstrative triumph over the limitations of time; method, it turned out, sought prophecy. The essential characteristic of prophecy, Huxley suggested, is the "apprehension of that which lies out of the sphere of immediate knowledge," in essence, the perception of that which, due to the limitations of time, is no longer physically apparent to the observer (4:6). Cuvier's was a form of "retrospective prophecy" in that his insights, based solidly on evidence gleaned from the present, moved backward into dim epochs of prehistorical time. Interweaving Voltaire's *Zadig* with Cuvier's *Recherches sur les ossemens fossiles,* Huxley eloquently demonstrated not only Cuvier's use of Zadig's method, but the affinities between the French Enlightenment with its philosophical rationalism and nineteenth-century science with its empirical method. Huxley's scientist is very much an offspring of the Enlightenment, bound to an egalitarian ideal by Huxley's continual assertions that his mind and method were essentially the apparatus of all humanity. The great existential constant, "the common foundation of all scientific thought," was the axiom of "the constancy of the order of nature" (4:12). Working on this assumption, the scientist could move not only into the past but into the future. Science offered prophetic powers to laborer and merchant alike. All men were equal before scientific fact; all men stood to gain through scientific knowledge. Prophecy and significant knowledge were democratized.

The simplicity of scientific method was an important issue. In the Zadig essay Huxley was not making claims for the simplicity of actual scientific disciplines, for these involved technical language and a complexity of detail that were the product of extensive intellectual effort. But the basic idea underlying the scientist and his work remained a very simple one: his faith in the constancy of the natural order was justified by daily experience (5:37). The soundness of scientific thought might be demonstrated to all who were prepared to listen to reason. Huxley's scientist had a profound appreciation for order and reason, and he rejected that problematic ingredient, deity. It was an order that was antiauthoritarian, antitraditional, and sometimes even antiintellectual. But even as he was undermining the concept of authority, Huxley was combing tradition for scientific predecessors.

iv. the Huxley theater

If the Zadig essay featured Huxley's scientific Everyman expatiating on the simplicity of scientific method, the lead performer and featured scientist of many essays was none other than Huxley himself. His ability to project to the untutored mind a vision of the new science was nothing short of remarkable. On many a night Huxley's public performances as the new man of science unfolding the great drama of Victorian scientific discovery must have been the best theater in town.

As early as 1860 at the famous Oxford clash with Wilberforce over Darwin's *Origin,* Huxley had established his dramatic mettle by challenging and, thought many, defeating Wilberforce at a public forum tailored to the latter's intellectual and oratorical genius. The same projection of self and ideas lifts the Huxley essay to the level of fine dramatic art. Controversy counted for part of the drama, but beyond controversy there was an electrifying motion of ideas, a theatrical clash between tradition and new knowledge, a glimpse into the strange new universe that Victorian science had been quietly assembling. This was Huxley's proletarian theater, frequently offered exclusively to working men with proof of occupational status the condition for entry. "Here he is, this working man, whom I have so often sought and found not," commented Bernard Becker, author of *Scientific London,* as he recounted an evening's performance of Huxley: "His place is not usurped by smug clerks and dandy shopmen."[33]

The drama of Huxley's lectures and essays is frequently achieved through two techniques he relied on consistently. The first involves a process which might be referred to as the dramatization of material entities. It is a theatrical treatment of physical entities and objects whereby Huxley, as scientist-choreographer, presents us with a dance of the material universe. Using such unpromising subjects as chalk, lobsters, coal, yeast, and protoplasm, Huxley describes patterns and rhythms shared between organic and inorganic forms of existence. In such presentations, the boundaries between living and inanimate entities cease to be distinct. Huxley was fascinated by the common organizational principles of the material and the organic universe, and in essays such as **"On a Piece of Chalk"** and **"On the Physical Basis of Life"** he probed continually for insights into the shared character of matter and life. The intellectual process becomes dramatic when he begins to call forth and spotlight his entities. "Sit down before fact as a little child, . . . or you shall learn nothing," Huxley had declared in his letter to Kingsley (*LL,* 1:235). And in the Huxley theater one must sit down before the facts and objects which actually seem to perform under the discipline of Huxley's voice. The other dramatic technique Huxley frequently used in his lectures and essays is the projection of the self as scientist-choreographer. The self, as scientist, becomes a stage manager of the material world, demonstrating within the artistic frameworks of stage and essay a variety of existential truths.

Huxley typically designed his performances for a working class audience as in **"On a Piece of Chalk,"** delivered in 1868 to the working men of Norwich. In this famous lecture, subsequently published in *Macmillan's Magazine,* Huxley refers to his presentation as "making the chalk tell us its own history" (8:6). We begin with a descent under the city of Norwich, soon finding ourselves in a great layer of chalk that extends north to Yorkshire, south to Dorset, links London to Paris,

runs through Europe and parts of Asia and Africa. "A great chapter of the history of the world is written in the chalk," Huxley declares. It is a history that will give a man "a truer, and therefore a better, conception of this wonderful universe, and of man's relation to it, than the most learned student [will have] who is deep-read in the records of humanity and ignorant of those of Nature" (8:4). A piece of chalk, so common that every carpenter carries it in his pocket, suddenly comes to life as we discover that it is organic, composed of *Globigerinae, Radiolaria* and diatoms, the remains of which have formed vast deposits beneath the surface of the earth and under the ocean floor. Through simple detail and geographical panorama, Huxley slowly assembles his heroic vision: "the earth, from the time of the chalk to the present day, has been the theatre of a series of changes as vast in their amount, as they were slow in their progress" (8:29). The world is the stage of a great drama. One learns not only of buried forests and gradually evolving forms of reptiles sunk in layers of chalk, but that the chalk itself has arisen and descended at least four times relative to sea level. Land and ocean are merely conditions of time. What makes the essay particularly dramatic is Huxley's continual use of active verbs in describing the processes involved in the piece of chalk's history. The essay is alive with motion. Time and its inexorable impress on the material of nature are manifested in vast processes of sedimentation, uplifting, and concretion. The very ground under one's feet must have felt strange after hearing Huxley tell how once it was all the floor of an immense sea.

"A small beginning has led us to a great ending," Huxley notes in his final paragraph (8:36). The piece of chalk is given visionary significance as he observes that if one were to subject it to a flame of burning hydrogen it would glow like the sun, a physical metamorphosis that "is no false image of what has been the result of our subjecting it to a jet of fervent, though nowise brilliant, thought to-night" (8:36). The chalk, then, becomes "luminous," a lantern lit by the intellect of Huxley as scientist, "its clear rays, penetrating the abyss of the remote past" (8:36). It becomes a complex agent which under the influence of the scientist's controlling intellect leads us into the distant past. Its relationship to the scientist is very nearly that of the relationship of Coleridge's aeolian harp to the "intellectual breeze." The piece of chalk, as an image of both common material and the intellectual lantern, carries the significance of being the product of both inorganic and organic forces in nature. At the same time it functions as a dramatic entity within the framework of the essay, performing in a variety of ways to the proddings of Huxley's flames, acids, and pulverizers. It has a story "to tell," and under Huxley's careful direction, the story which began with Norwich well diggers striking a white substance in their downward progress ends with a vision of the eternal process of time.

The organizing voice of the scientist in the chalk essay plays a significant role not only in the stage-management of material entities, but in creating a sense of control, both intellectual and physical, over the entire material world. It is the guiding force of the scientific intellect that irradiates what seems at first so pedestrian a subject. "A small beginning has led us to a great ending," Huxley observes. The scientific mind moves from the common object to reflections that embrace the cosmos, bestowing dignity on rude entities by connecting them with the great network of all things. For Huxley, it was a theatrical process. Who but the scientist could show the way? And yet the way, once seen, was incredibly simple. Huxley's essays reflect that simplicity in their patient reconstruction of fact, always in the simplest and most concrete language he could summon. Observed Professor Howes of the Royal College of Science:

> As a class lecturer Huxley was *facile princeps,* and only those who were privileged to sit under him can form a conception of his delivery. Clear, deliberate, never hesitant nor unduly emphatic, never repetitional, always logical, his every word told. Great, however, as were his class lectures, his working-men's were greater. Huxley was a firm believer in the "distillatio per ascensum" of scientific knowledge and culture, and spared no pains in approaching the artisan and so-called "working classes." He gave the workmen of his best.
>
> [*LL,* 2:438]

Huxley's working men's lectures, models of simplicity and yet full of detail and substance, seemed to proclaim a democracy of knowledge, if only because they were consistently woven around the common objects of experience. The first and final court of intellectual appeal became the great "University of Nature." And this placed a new emphasis on hard physical realities and on an intimate knowledge of the material world.

The Huxleyan "I" looms large in the famous *Six Lectures to Working Men* delivered in 1862 and collected in 1863. It is the "I" of both Huxley the man and Huxley the representative scientist. The first lecture—**"The Present Condition of Organic Nature"**—makes such extensive use of the first-person pronoun that we cannot read it without sensing an organizing and explicit consciousness at work among diverse materials, the same consciousness that lavished its attention on the piece of chalk. This essay concerns itself with explaining and demonstrating that inorganic and organic forms of existence are composed of the same basic materials, guided by the same physical forces, and engaged in a continual conversion of one into the other. Huxley selects the horse, "an extremely complex and beautifully-proportioned machine, with all its parts working harmoniously together" (2:313), as a model with which to demonstrate a number of his most important ideas. The entire presentation is, again, dramatic in Huxley's mode; it is filled with physical description and motion as the scientific consciousness works on its object: "if I were to saw a dead horse, across, I should find that . . ."; "now, suppose we go to work on these several parts,—flesh and hair, and skin and bone, and lay open these various organs with our scalpels" (2:308-9). What makes the essay more than mere demonstration is the manner in which Huxley has thrust his scientist on stage along with the various objects of demonstration. We are watching the scientist perform. There is a dramatic relationship between him and the materials he examines, a dynamic relationship for which the image of Victor Frankenstein laboring to bring forth life from the inanimate is not entirely inappropriate. But for Huxley the romantic impulse to recreate the external world in the image of the self is absent; Huxley's mind breathes life into its material so as to create a lamp, to return to the chalk example, that is capable of illuminating fundamental principles of natural order. Life itself is a form, but not the apex, of natural order.

Huxley went on in the other lectures of this working men's series to present a primer of Victorian life sciences, discussing a variety of scientific theories and examining the work of such scientists as Darwin, Pasteur, and Harvey. Darwin is central and his evolutionary hypothesis becomes the subject of the last three lectures, with Huxley always pressing, however, toward his larger themes of the ultimate order and unity of nature and the rational vision of the scientist. Darwin's model is a "hypothesis," yet it will remain "the guide of biological and psychological speculation for the next three or four generations" (2:475). Abstract concepts are continually made visual for the audience, traced to their manifestations in the concrete patterns of daily existence. To illustrate the intricacy of evolutionary success, Huxley uses as an example a frail historian who, retreating with Napoleon's troops from the advancing Russian army, grabs on to the cloak of a hearty French cuirassier, who at first curses and cuts at the historian and then, in order to save himself, struggles across the single narrow bridge amid the general panic, dragging the historian along (2:443). The simplicity of experimental method is enacted in a little drama between shopkeeper and customer in which after twice testing specimens from a batch of apples the customer generalizes that those apples which are hard and green are also sour (2:365-67).

The Huxley theater has, indeed, many qualities in common with the old morality play, in its careful acting out of ideas, its props, its homely, simplifying anecdote.[34] In the second lecture, **"The Past Condition of Organic Nature,"** Huxley evokes the image of the history of nature against which "mere human records sink into utter insignificance," only to turn and tell his audience that the record of nature's history is formed in "mud":

You may think, perhaps, that this is a vast step—of almost from the sublime to the ridiculous—from the contemplation of the history of the past ages of the world's existence to the consideration of the history of the formation of mud! But, in Nature, there is nothing mean and unworthy of attention; there is nothing ridiculous or contemptible in any of her works."

[2:333-34]

We return to the humblest of materials, ordinary mud, for our lesson on the heroic past of earth's slow, elemental change, its ceaseless alteration by unseen forces, the growth of its many life forms. It is a lesson on causality and its subject is life; but no deity lingers in the essay. Sealed in the mud are the imprints and fossil remains of plants and animals, many extinct, many still thriving in the modern world. Examining simple materials, we achieve what few disciplines of knowledge can offer—a physical vision into the past that dwarfs in time and magnitude the mere human present. The vision of the sublime is achieved through the humble contemplation of the ridiculous. The lesson of basic science is a lesson in humility and in the dignity of the material world.

Huxley's lectures were issued in pamphlet form under the title ***On Our Knowledge of the Causes of the Phenomena of Organic Nature,*** and became an immediate and large-scale success. Ultimately, the Huxley theater was as popular with professional scientists as it was with the working classes. Like Dickens, Huxley produced material that transcended class boundaries, which made him one of the most widely read essayists of his day. He had reason to seek a wide audience. From his earliest to his final essays, he expressed the conviction that while many were content to assimilate the material achievements of physical science into the basic patterns of their lives, they often lagged dangerously behind in their grasp of scientific method and knowledge. This was true not only of the public, but in the intellectual centers of England as well. The Oxford confrontation with Wilberforce at the British Association meeting in 1860, when Wilberforce asked Huxley whether his ancestry with the ape was to be traced on his grandmother's or his grandfather's side, was an incident which in many ways epitomized the collision of two kinds of knowledge, two habits of thought, two realities which ultimately split the Victorian mind in two. Wilberforce, a subtle and highly intelligent man, had misjudged not only the moral force behind the scientific quest for truth but the substance and magnitude of scientific knowledge. The question he posed about Huxley's ancestry was precisely the question Victorians wanted answered. Given the religious perspective and the perspective of the intellectual tradition of England, who would believe that at ancient Oxford this new science, with its tinge of the ridiculous, its apes, mud and a thousand other materials from the "mole's earthheap," would presume to

contemplate itself with such gravity? The clash would echo, again tinged with absurdity, in Huxley's duel with Gladstone in the mid 1880s and the early 1890s, over such things as the legalities of Christ's destruction of the Gadarene swine. Rarely were the details of these controversies of more than incidental interest; more gripping was the conflict of visions, of concepts of human knowledge, conflicts so fundamental that they created an aura of profound absurdity and high intellectual comedy. It was a comic clash which would find expression in the plays of Shaw, and also in the shrewd wit of Shaw's critic William Irvine in *Apes, Angels, and Victorians.*

Huxley declared to Matthew Arnold in 1880 that it was a mistake to attempt a criticism of life without knowing what science had achieved over the past half century. It was not merely a matter of being ignorant of a new fund of knowledge; it was, more seriously, a misapprehension of the very foundations of one's own society. To devalue or underestimate the fundamental role of physical science in society and culture was to alienate oneself from vital realities that supported one's own existence. Culture, in the sense of its being a criticism of life, was important for assessing such realities in order to influence the course of human affairs. It was not merely a problem of misconception, but one of misperception. Modern technology and theory were elements of reality. The great object of his life, Huxley declared in his **"Autobiography,"** was "to promote the increase of natural knowledge and to forward the application of scientific methods of investigation to all the problems of life" (1:16). It was, Huxley believed, the only true possibility for the "alleviation for the sufferings of mankind." Huxley's was a deeply human and moral ambition, yet it was locked in conflict with traditions many saw as the mainstays of morality and culture. Huxley found a more receptive, though not more avid, audience among colleagues and workers than among intellectuals and divines.

The mythos of Huxley's science, the legend of his scientist, and the vindication of his own personal struggle from childhood to forge a vision worthy of his ideals were all concentrated in the remarkable Cinderella metaphor which appeared at the end of his 1886 essay **"Science and Morals."** Here lay the story of Victorian science, and of Huxley himself, contemplating intellectual disenfranchisement. The essay had been written in answer to W. S. Lilly's charges, made in the November issue of the *Fortnightly,* that modern science had inspired materialism, fatalism, and was causing the erosion of morality. Huxley responded to Lilly, who was John Henry Newman's advocate and compiler, with the claim that the only axiom held by the scientist was "the universality of the law of causation," and that this implied neither materialism, atheism, nor fatalism, but only a determinism which was not even inconsistent with the theological notion of an omniscient deity or with predestination (9:141-44). Huxley summed up his position at the end of the essay by constrasting the youthful Cinderella of Victorian science with her two elder sisters, philosophy and theology:

> Cinderella is modestly conscious of her ignorance of these high matters. She lights the fire, sweeps the house, and provides the dinner; and is rewarded by being told that she is a base creature, devoted to low and material interests. But in her garret she has fairy visions out of the ken of the pair of shrews who are quarrelling down stairs. She sees the order which pervades the seeming disorder of the world; the great drama of evolution, with its full share of pity and terror, but also with abundant goodness and beauty, unrolls itself before her eyes; and she learns, in her heart of hearts, the lesson, that the foundation of morality is to have done, once and for all, with lying; to give up pretending to believe that for which there is no evidence, and repeating unintelligible propositions about things beyond the possibilities of knowledge.

> She knows that the safety of morality lies neither in the adoption of this or that philosophical speculation, or this or that theological creed, but in a real and living belief in that fixed order of nature which sends social disorganisation upon the track of immorality, as surely as it sends physical disease after physical trespasses. And of that firm and lively faith it is her high mission to be the priestess.
>
> [9:146]

Cinderella was science and Huxley at once; a potential queen, she labored at providing for the common needs of others. But as she worked in the prosaic world of physical reality, she had visions of the great cosmic order, of the vast drama of evolutionary terror and beauty. These visions, while they suggested metamorphosis, a future in which scientific knowledge would blossom into something beautiful, as Cinderella had in the fairy tale, asserted with equal strength the existence of an ultimate, macrocosmic order pervading the universe. The vision of "the order which pervades the seeming disorder of the world" was basic to Huxley's thought and faith. Cinderella was the scientist whose solemn quest was to discover, to whatever extent possible, the complexion of the natural order. . . .

. . . . .

Chapter V: Science and Culture

i. science and criticism

Huxley's state of art was the concept of a critic and moralist who believed that the principle of society must have a rational and ethical basis. At the same time, he held that society required a clear empirical foundation on which to build. He believed such a foundation could be established on a principle of scientific naturalism which set rigorous empirical standards as the conditions for assent. His problem was that in order to assert the existence and value of human critical reason, after Descartes, while verifying the methodological standards of the empiricists, he was obliged to find a meeting ground for two traditions which were at odds on several philosophical premises. Science, he believed, could furnish the required critical and integrative activity which would effect the fusion of rationalist sources of value with empiricist standards for assent.

Huxley consciously sought to establish his new scientific perspective at the broad Victorian forum on culture, where the concept of social and cultural criticism, initiated, as Mill had pointed out, by Bentham and Coleridge, had begun to flourish. The essays and studies of Carlyle, Mill, Ruskin, and Arnold moved within a common sphere of critical activity, examining the ethics and mechanics of society by exploring the meanings and traditions of culture. To this debate, Huxley brought a broad awareness of developments in scientific thought in an effort to furnish a fresh basis for examining Victorian social and cultural issues, many of which had been raised by the frenetic activity within his own scientific disciplines. Matthew Arnold believed that the nineteenth century was a critical age in which there was a pressing need for the establishment of a new order of ideas. It was the object of the critical power "in all branches of knowledge, theology, philosophy, history, art, science to see the object as in itself it really is."[1] Criticism could establish an "intellectual situation of which the creative power can profitably avail itself."[2] To Huxley, seeing the object as it really is was a particular specialty of the scientific mind, scientific naturalism having as its goals the elimination of preconceptions and the critical isolation of its object. "The essence of the scientific spirit is criticism," he declared in his essay, **"The Coming of Age of *The Origin of Species*"** (1880). And in his Birmingham address in October of the same year, **"Science and Culture,"** he agreed with Arnold that a criticism of life was the essence of culture, but observed that "an army, without weapons of precision and with no particular base of operations, might more hopefully enter upon a campaign on the Rhine, than a man, devoid of a knowledge of what physical science has done in the last century, upon a criticism of life" (3:144). The scientist, with his tool of method; his distinterestedness, with his solid base in the physical world, was potentially an ideal critic.

Just as Matthew Arnold's "best self" in *Culture and Anarchy* identified the cultural center, the intellectual and moral ideal Arnold wished to associate with sound cultural criticism, Huxley's man of science was the rationalist with a deeply ethical cultural ambition. He was what Arnold would have found an incurably infected Hebraist, with a passion for law, a prejudice toward action, and the strictest of moral consciences. These sprang from values which had a high personal significance for Huxley as well.

More deeply, Huxley associated the scientific frame of mind with an innocence he identified in the process of sitting down before fact as a "little child," in the model of childlike simplicity he found in Darwin's mind, in the innocent Cinderella at the end of **"Science and Morals,"** alone in her garret, contemplating the great natural order of existence. From this haven of innocence, where the self often existed in meditative disembodiment from the world, Huxley drew inner moral resources to prepare for the confrontation with material phenomena and the clash of instinct and consciousness. The scientific haven of innocence was also the state of art of **"Evolution and Ethics"** where one could operate insulated from the struggle going on in brute nature. While its psychic origins seem clearly to have been established in Huxley's childhood mode of withdrawal from the world of men and experience, of which he spoke to his fiancée, Henrietta Heathorn, its primary cultural metaphor Huxley identified in the **"Prolegomena"** to **"Evolution and Ethics"** with the colony set up in a hostile environment to make moral law prevail over instinctual or natural law, civilization prevail over nature. The dark side of this vision was its consuming fear of disorder, its sometimes frantic belief that man can create human community through the establishment of law in all quarters of existence. Its hope lay in the unpretentious rationalism of Huxley's scientist, who doggedly resisted the utopian trend toward absolutism and who sought to establish the free expression of thought as the ethical obligation of society.

Huxley's essays established the critical voice and perspective of the scientist-rationalist, just as Huxley molded the essay itself into a lean and versatile literary instrument with which to dissect chosen features of English culture and society. Always clear, direct, and bold, yet gifted in his use of irony and metaphor, he constructed terse and tightly organized essays which reflected in the simplicity of their literary form a simplicity of values and ideals.[3] He began, like Ruskin, with the materials of his specialty, then expanded his considerations into general subjects and, inevitably, into the still broader scope of cultural and social criticism. His insistent appeal to experiment and observation and his views on the duties of scepticism made him, as Walter Houghton has shown, one of the representative voices of the Victorian critical spirit.[4] Uttered with legendary economy, his criticism was rarely subtle, but nearly always of basic importance. His ultimate appeal was neither to utility nor to empirical standards of verification, but to reason, which as he used the term meant the faculty of judgment that integrated experience with permanent value, whether culturally or intuitively derived. This rationalist appeal was a key to his success as an essayist and controversialist. One after

another, great spokesmen for differing traditions, Wilber-force, Gladstone, Argyll, A. J. Balfour, rose up to attack what seemed to be an indiscriminate assault on authority, only to find their own positions opposed from the stronghold of reason and morality. Of Huxley's critics, only Matthew Arnold seemed fully to comprehend the basis of his critical appeal, and he responded by seeking a wider perspective in which to interpret the idea of reason, which was still much valued by Victorians.

Few words were more important or more elusive in the Huxley lexicon than "reason." It was consistently placed strategically in his important essays. It dominated his definitions of agnosticism; it was integral to his definition of agnosticism; it typically formed the conceptual bridge in his essays between the activities of science and culture. Huxley identified reason with "private judgment" in his 1892 **"Prologue"** to *Controverted Questions* (5:9). He assumed that the faculty of reason functioned in a commonsensical manner, that it was self-evident, and that it furnished an innate and sufficient intellectual means for the individual to form a private judgment on the truth of an idea. Its most compelling modern tool was empirical method, which for Huxley was the systematization of common human patterns of experience. Reason was superior to but not independent of sense experience, since sensory data established the bridge between mind and nature. Informed by the data of sensation, it justified assent or doubt and negotiated value through processes which were partially intuitive, since they were not entirely represented in the consciousness. Unlike empirical method, in which the mind consciously and methodically constructed inductive and deductive logical sequences in the formal structuring of experience, reason often made rapid unconscious judgments that could not be fully accounted for by explicit logic and in detail. Conviction and doubt, Huxley observed in a fragment, arose from a complex of intellectual materials which were not fully represented in the consciousness:

> The essence of what we call reason in man is the logical process, not the state of consciousness by which sometimes, and more or less partially, the man becomes aware of the process. The essential operations of induction and deduction, the operations which have the effect of what we call generalization and syllogistic reasoning are performed by quadrupeds and by savages as much as by ourselves. But the quadruped has no or next to no representations in consciousness of these operations; the savage very few; the majority more or less of civilized men not many more; and even the most perfected self analyst constantly drops many, and as we say jumps to a conclusion without the least consciousness [of] most of the work that has been done to get him there.[5]

Human reason, then, shared fundamental characteristics with the intuitive mental processes of lower forms of life, although in the human intellect the processes were more complex and better represented in the consciousness. Aware of his reason, man could externalize it with his experimental method.

Huxley considered science the product of an evolved human consciousness which enabled the intellect to direct and control its own operations more deliberately. Science was a refinement of common sense, where method reconstructed experience in such a way as to reproduce the quasi-conscious and more complex operations of reason. In 1886, late in his career and deep in controversy with Gladstone over Genesis, Huxley gave this definition of science: "To my mind, whatever doctrine professes to be the result of the application of the accepted rules of inductive and deductive logic to its subject-matter; and which accepts, within the limits which it sets to itself, the supremacy of reason, is Science" (4:193). Reason and method were in this way interdependent, but with reason as the ultimate justification for assent. Similarly, in **"Science and Culture,"** his essay addressed to Arnold six years earlier, Huxley had associated reason with method: "We falsely pretend to be the inheritors of [Greek] culture, unless we are penetrated, as the best minds among them were, with an unhesitating faith that the free employment of reason, in accordance with scientific method, is the sole method of reaching truth" (3:152). Huxley's emphasis on method, an explicitly patterned form of consciousness, countered Arnold's stress in *Culture and Anarchy* on spontaneity and the free play of consciousness. While both he and Arnold were strong advocates of reason, Huxley, with his Hebraic love of law, considered reason the faculty for eliminating error in logic and for integrating the results of empirical effort with standards of value, while Arnold frequently used the word in close association with the imagination.

In his essay, "Heinrich Heine," Arnold associated "idea" and "reason" intimately with one another: "The enthusiast for the idea, for reason, values reason, the idea, in and for themselves; he values them irrespectively of the practical conveniences which their triumph may obtain for him."[6] While reason was associated with an antidogmatic principle for Huxley, it was associated with an anti-Philistinic principle for Arnold, the Philistine being one who was willing to tolerate the absence of reason and ideas in exchange for practical convenience. Reason was associated with method for Huxley, and this combination laid a heavy stress on order and on the logical arrangement of parts. Science was, above all, an order-seeking activity in pursuit of law and causation. In Arnold's thought, reason, associated with imagination or ideas, was manifested in balance or harmony, that is, an order that would appeal to the aesthetic sense rather than to standards of inductive or deductive logic. This would account, in part, for the concern with wholeness and harmony characteristic of Arnold's thought.[7]

This contrast extended to the two concepts of criticism Huxley and Arnold supported. Arnold's criticism aspired to inclusiveness, the collection of the best that is known and thought about a given question. Huxley's criticism stressed exclusiveness, the elimination of erroneous and undemonstrable assumptions. The scientific spirit was identical to the critical spirit, its method was empirical, and its ultimate appeal was to the reason:

> The scientific spirit is of more value than its products, and irrationally held truths may be more harmful than reasoned errors. Now the essence of the scientific spirit is criticism. It tells us that whenever a doctrine claims our assent we should reply, Take it if you can compel it. The struggle for existence holds as much in the intellectual as in the physical world. A theory is a species of thinking, and its right to exist is coextensive with its power of resisting extinction by its rivals. [2:229]

While Huxley had rejected social laissez-faire, he embraced its intellectual equivalent in the spirit of Mill's *On Liberty*. Truth was the product of competitive struggle, various theories and ideas vying for supremacy as each stood equal before the reason. The compelling truth was the one that could be traced to its origin via an empirical structure. And since "irrationally held truths may be more harmful than reasoned errors" the means—properly, empirical—of arriving at truth might be more important than the truth itself, truthfulness becoming as important as truth. For Arnold, methodology, whatever its efficacies, was clearly not to be stressed; the important critical object was, through disinterestedness and free play of imagination, to seek and to establish a sense of the whole. Like Huxley, Arnold believed that reason was self-evident and compelling: "But the prescriptions of reason are absolute, unchanging, of universal validity; *to count by tens is the easiest way of counting*—that is a proposition of which every one, from here to the Antipodes, feels the force."[8] While Huxley found specialist knowledge compelling to the reason, knowledge, for example, of Darwin's great argument, Arnold found generalist knowledge compelling to the reason. These attitudes formed the separate foundations of their critical theories.

In **"On the Method of Zadig,"** which also appeared in 1880, Huxley went to considerable lengths to show that "Zadig's method was nothing but the method of all mankind" (4:8). The argument, reminiscent of his early declaration in 1854 that science was nothing but *"trained and organised common sense,"* suggested that science was an exact body of knowledge which had been forged through the power of human reason (3:45). Science conferred upon human kind the power to construct a whole from a part, just as Zadig, reasoning from evidence to origins, described physical phenomena which he had never witnessed. Like his famous detective ancestor, Cuvier began with a fragment—a mere bone, perhaps—and through a careful process of induction and deduction synthesized a whole (4:18). The implication behind Huxley's Zadig essay was that scientific thought was essentially a refinement of common sense, and that scientific theory aimed at defining reality rather than at the accumulation of a distinct, independent, and self-consistent body of thought. An important question was whether the primary allegiance of a theory was to its own internal consistency or to an external reality. Few modern theorists would unreservedly support Huxley's position that the theoretical whole was an accurate representation of external reality or that scientific thought was common-sensical.[9]

On the other hand, Huxley's **"The Progress of Science: 1837-1887"** (1887), a key late Victorian essay, revealed that his theory of the relationship between scientific construct and external reality was more complex than has often been supposed. He made several important observations on science which anticipated modern attitudes. He rejected the idea that science was a process of discerning truth in which the methodological interventions of man led by rote from fact to discovery:

> It is a favourite popular delusion that the scientific inquirer is under a sort of moral obligation to abstain from going beyond that generalisation of observed facts which is absurdly called "Baconian" induction. But any one who is practically acquainted with scientific work is aware that those who refuse to go beyond fact, rarely get as far as fact; and any one who has studied the history of science knows that almost every great step therein has been made by the "anticipation of Nature," that is, by the invention of hypotheses, which, through verifiable, often had very little foundation to start with. [1:62]

Huxley rejected the idea that scientific activity was a kind of mechanized arranging of factual data to achieve a routine, determined result, emphasizing, rather, the elements of chance and creativity upon which discovery depended. Furthermore, scientific generalizations and hypotheses were neither absolute nor uniform, but were only useful and accurate within defined limits, and therefore could be accepted only under conditions as truth (1:64). Verifiable hypotheses were to be considered "not as ideal truths, the real entities of an intelligible world behind phenomena, but as a symbolical language, by the aid of which Nature can be interpreted in terms apprehensible by our intellects" (1:65). Each of these observations dismissed the idea of an absolute correlation between the scientific description of nature or process and the reality, such as it might be, of physical nature. This insight was important, for, while the popular imagination frequently considered scientific principle as absolute in some rigid and undeniable sense, often by extension thinking of the scientist himself as an absolutist, the reverse was actually the case: the scientist's success depended on his recognition of a given system's limitations. The "scientific 'criticism of life,'" Huxley declared in **"Science and Culture,"** appealed not to authority but to nature: "It admits that all our interpretations of natural fact are more or less imperfect and symbolic, and bids the learner seek for truth not among words but among things. It warns us that the assertion which outstrips evidence is not only a blunder but a crime" (3:150).

ii. naturalism

In his effort to identify the bond between science and culture, Huxley searched for a critical concept which would establish significant common ground occupied by science and society. By 1892, when he wrote his **"Prologue"** to *Controverted Questions,* he had long dissociated natural and social order and was preparing for his Romanes lecture, **"Evolution and Ethics,"** in which he was to formulate his declaration of ethical independence. While his earlier speculations on natural order had often been geared to the discovery of a principle which would unify natural law with social law, he abandoned the attempt sometime between 1869 and 1871, when he wrote **"Scientific Education"** and **"Administrative Nihilism,"** respectively. In **"Scientific Education,"** he declared that there was a "struggle for existence, which goes on as fiercely beneath the smooth surface of modern society, as among the wild inhabitants of the woods" (3:114). Scientific knowledge strengthened one's powers of attack. Two years later in **"Administrative Nihilism,"** written in support of Forster's Education Act, he launched a vigorous attack on what he identified as social "laissez-faire," or the unrestricted pursuit of self-interest. He quoted widely from Locke, Hobbes, Humboldt, and Kant, but even so, his laissez-faire sounded most like Arnold's "doing as one likes" in *Culture and Anarchy.*

Arnold's essays appeared as an edition in 1869, and it would be difficult to imagine Huxley, with all his enthusiasm and, indeed, anxiety, over order, not picking up a major new work by Arnold with "anarchy" in its title. He had jokingly referred to the Bishop Wilson of *Culture and Anarchy* in a note to Arnold in July 1869, in which he sought the return of an umbrella he had left at Arnold's house (*LL,* 1:335). Most likely the two had discussed *Culture and Anarchy* at some length during the visit. Huxley's **"Administrative Nihilism"** made a dramatic departure from his earlier essays, becoming the first of a series of essays on political and social thought which culminated in his final attack on social laissez-faireism in **"Evolution and Ethics."** Huxley argued the need to curtail self-interest and pointed out the superior virtues of social cooperation over social competition. The target was Herbert Spencer, who had systematically borrowed constructs from the biological sciences to fashion his models for society. Spencer more than anyone else showed Huxley the overwhelming problems entailed in using scientific systems, a priori, as models for society. This included Darwinian natural selection. By 1871, Huxley had taken up a position in opposition to the new naturalism. Nevertheless, he maintained that the natural order was a vital factor in the state of art and that it must remain the focus of significant human activity.

That Huxley was constantly searching for critical principles which linked natural order with society and culture is suggested by the large number of critical terms he adopted. Of the three main critical principles he followed over a period of fifty years, the earliest was the "thätige Skepsis" which he borrowed from Goethe and which emphasized a kind of Romantic doubt or scepticism, stressing the unceasing effort to overcome, attaining a positive, if conditional, principle of belief. Inside the back cover of his voyage diary, Huxley wrote:

> "Thätige Skepsis." "An *Active Scepticism* is that which unceasingly strives to overcome itself and by well directed research to attain to a kind of conditional certainty."[10]

Well before the mid-fifties, he had seen in scientific research a possible avenue to the conquest of doubt. The term appeared again in his essay, **"On Descartes' 'Discourse Touching the Method of Using One's Reason Rightly and of Seeking Scientific Truth'"** (1870), an essay Arnold admired and one Huxley regarded as central to his own critical theory. Descartes was the first modern, he declared, to make it a matter of religious duty "to strip off all his beliefs and reduce himself to a state of intellectual nakedness, until such time as he could satisfy himself which were fit to be worn" (1:170). The object of such doubt was not to destroy, but, as Goethe had observed, to arrive at foundations and to conquer itself. Again, in 1892, Huxley used the term in **"An Apologetic Irenicon"** to counter the charge of Frederic Harrison that, unlike positivism, agnosticism did not attempt to reconstruct what it dismantled. The spirit of the agnostic position, Huxley declared, was contained in Goethe's "thätige Skepsis," which "enjoins the clearing of the ground, not in a spirit of wanton mischief, not for destruction's sake, but with the distinct purpose of fitting the site for those constructive operations which must be the ultimate object of every rational man."[11]

Along with "thätige Skepsis," Huxley's "agnosticism" functioned as a critical principle which urged the use of empirical method to tutor the reason. It was a somewhat more conservative term since it suggested the withholding of assent, the suspension of belief, as well as the innate human limitation for determining truth. Even more significant was the implication that belief or faith should not influence action, since they had no basis in verifiable reality. The sole basis of behavior, Huxley argued, should be consistent with verifiable

truth. The central problem raised by the agnostic principle was, predictably, the ethical question. Huxley's early alternative to the connection of faith and ethics was to urge a morality based on reason and natural law. As he came to believe that nature was amoral, he was forced to conclude that ethics was based on paradox, having evolved with human consciousness as an independent force that functioned in opposition to the cosmic processes of nature. Consciousness made will capable of revolting against the tyranny of nature through substitution of ethical law for natural law.

In his reexamination of the concept of agnosticism in the 1889 essays, Huxley again closely associated reason and method. Agnosticism was not a creed but a "method," the essence of which was expressed by Socrates and which could be summed up in "Try all things, hold fast by that which is good" (5:245). Positively expressed, the agnostic principle could be stated as: "In matters of the intellect, follow your reason as far as it will take you, without regard to any other consideration" (5:246). But it was never entirely clear what he meant when he advised one to follow reason "as far as it will take you." He did not explore in any detail the precise relationship between reason and method. Certainly if Socrates is to be seen as an agnostic, then Cartesian rationalism, to say nothing of various nineteenth-century methodologies, is not essential to the "method" or to the "reason" of agnosticism. Indeed, if the agnostic method may be summed up in "Try all things, hold fast by that which is good," then Huxley was not referring to a specific method such as induction or deduction at all, for the concept of "good" is of a different order. The good is above all an idea of value, which can only be formed by making value judgments. It cannot be formulated by means of a rigorous methodology unless one defines it in terms of process, equating it, for example, with "consistency." Reason, however, as the faculty of judgment, can make evaluatons methodologies are powerless to determine. Given an idea of the good which in **"Evolution and Ethics"** Huxley identified with both human sympathy and aesthetic intuition, reason could examine methodological efforts in terms of that idea. This seems to be what Huxley was suggesting when he declared that agnosticism was a method which appealed to the reason. In this sense, agnosticism was the fusion of method and reason.

Huxley's reluctance to clearly define what he meant by reason and method had a complicating effect on his thought in general. It did not strengthen its theoretical base; many critics have encountered a fundamental vagueness when confronting ideas such as Huxley's agnosticism from a theoretical point of view. As A. W. Benn and D. W. Dockrill have both found, there is a certain amorphousness to the term "agnosticism," an apparent clash and confusion between the metaphysical, methodological, and moral implications it held for

Huxley at various times.[12] "Science" is another of Huxley's terms which slips from one's grasp if examined too closely, again because it is difficult to understand precisely what he meant by telling us that we must accept the supremacy of reason in our use of method. If by "reason" we understand him to mean a partially intuitive process of evaluation, a private response to external facts, systems, and phenomena; and by "scientific method" we take him to mean the formal, specialized, yet creative processes governed by induction and deduction, we come closest to the twin aspects of his science and agnosticism. His real aim appears to have been to accommodate two philosophical traditions—the rationalist tradition which, as A. W. Benn notes, made reason the "supreme regulator" of belief and action, and the empiricist tradition which held that knowledge was derived from sensory experience alone.[13] Chesterton considered Huxley one of the most devoted and consistent of Victorian rationalists.[14] Wanting very much to link science with reason, Huxley set out, sagelike, to unify them through his own powers of rhetoric in an attempt to establish a vision of order which could assimilate scientific definition without itself being reduced to an arrangement of scientifically defined parts. Unable to achieve a formal philosophical system equal to his vision—a common enough Victorian predicament—Huxley chose what to him was the only worthwhile alternative: the rhetorical affirmation of a complex vision, which he was unable theoretically to define.[15]

Of his rhetorical objectives, the foremost was to communicate the *value* of scientific activity, not merely as a means to material improvement, but as a way of seeing things, of perceiving truth, however limited. He believed that science was a progressive, if necessarily approximate, revelation of reality. When he declared that agnosticism was a method, he was identifying it as a quantifying process involving induction and deduction. But when he observed that it could be expressed in that most ancient principle, "Try all things, hold fast by that which is good," he was aligning it with the qualitative process of evaluation, of judgment. In this way, he could accept Darwinian theory as the great discovery of the century, yet reject it, as he did in **"Administrative Nihilism"** (1871) and **"Evolution and Ethics"** (1893), as the dynamic for human society. It was an important function of reason to prevent the methodological extension of empirical results to the region of the absolute:

> Rational doubt—doubt as a means to the attainment of certainty, either of knowledge or of no knowledge—has been the fire of the intellectual world—the great agent not merely of destruction but of construction. For it is out of doubt of the old that the new springs; and it is doubt of the new that keeps innovation within rational bounds.[16]

Huxley considered agnosticism an antidogmatic principle, aimed against the dogmas of materialism and naturalism as well as those of traditional theology. Indeed, agnosticism was attacked as strenuously by the materialists as by the traditional theologians. In his introduction to the English edition of *Socialism: Utopian and Scientific,* Engels in 1892, made a sweeping polemical attack on agnosticism, arguing that it was nothing but "'shamefaced' materialism."[17] And he went on to claim the mantle of science for historical materialism.

Huxley's critical theory assumed the "scientific naturalism" of his 1892 **"Prologue"** to **Controverted Questions**. As he had done in coining the term "agnosticism," he conceived his scientific naturalism as an antithesis, this time of "super-naturalism." The qualification "scientific" was necessary to distinguish his conception of naturalism from Spencer's a priori version. Associating scientific naturalism with the ideal of intellectual freedom, he argued that naturalism, with its reference to physical nature and to empirical standards of independence, elevated private judgment to a higher social and cultural truth than public judgment, which he identified with all authoritarian structure. Law, whether scientific or civil, was based on human experience and reason, and was a great cultural inheritance, the only force capable of opposing the dogmas of public judgment and imposed definition, whether formulated by religious or by civil authority.

Scientific naturalism, Huxley argued, was the intellectual descendant of "private judgment" or reason; these had become historical forces through the evolving human consciousness which created opposition to dogmas imposed by authorities of given historical periods (5:38). Scientific naturalism was in this sense a historical term, the logical outcome of a cultural evolution which found its most immediate origin in the Renaissance with the rejection of the old medieval standard of Church authority. The historical progress of private judgment was an intellectual evolution which Huxley believed advanced in an almost deterministic pattern, comparable to the historical dialectic of Marx. The intellectual tyranny of dogma was for Huxley an antiprogressive historical force equivalent to Marx's concept of economic tyranny. But Huxley's criticism applied to proletarian as well as to religious dogma; Marxist societies forged through the regimented imposition of definition would ultimately generate the opposition such historical phenomena had always inspired. The issue of private judgment would inevitably rise anew as a powerful historical force.

"The goal of the humanists," Huxley maintained, "whether they were aware of it or not, was the attainment of the complete intellectual freedom of the antique philosopher" (5:14). By intellectual freedom, he meant the speculative freedom which he associated with Greek philosophy, as opposed to the intellectual serfdom he associated with the "dogmas of mediaeval Super-naturalism" and subsequent Protestant authoritarianism (5:12). Nineteenth-century science had inherited the Renaissance humanistic tradition in the sense that it advocated the use of human reason in the examination of nature as the avenue to truth. The "New Reformation" of modern science was to continue where the old Reformation had failed; it would advance the rule of reason over human affairs. While Erasmus was the "arch-humanist" and the spiritual father of the nineteenth-century spirit of scientific inquiry, Descartes was the first to formulate a clear method for pursuing the essential goals of the humanists:

> It is important to note that the principle of the scientific Naturalism of the latter half of the nineteenth century, in which the intellectual movement of the Renascence has culminated, and which was first clearly formulated by Descartes, leads not to the denial of the existence of any Supernature; but simply to the denial of the validity of the evidence adduced in favour of this, or of that, extant form of Supernaturalism.
>
> [5:38-39]

Scientific naturalism provided the basis for human knowledge of nature, revolutionizing traditional fields of knowledge, often times shriveling them to mere bits and fragments of ideas. "Scientific historical criticism" had "reduced the annals of heroic Greece and regal Rome to the level of fables"; "scientific literary criticism" had assailed the "unity of authorship of the *Iliad*," not to mention the Bible; "scientific physical criticism" had reduced the earth to a satellite, and the solar system "to one of millions of groups of like cosmic specks, circling, at unimaginable distances from one another through infinite space" (5:32-33). Natural explanation was replacing supernatural explanation; but the cost to tradition was monumental.

Having coined "scientific naturalism" as an antithetical term to "supernaturalism," Huxley was caught off guard two years later by A. J. Balfour who, in his *The Foundations of Belief,* attacked the concept of naturalism and classed Mill, Spencer, and Huxley together as its advocates.[18] While all three could be said to hold that phenomena must be traced to natural causes, they differed widely in their general theories. Spencer's naturalism was older and formulated in different philosophical terms than Huxley's scientific naturalism, and while Huxley had borrowed substantially from Mill, he was more a rationalist than a utilitarian.[19] Balfour's attack and Huxley's two replies, the second of which was never published in his lifetime, demonstrated that the concept of naturalism had become complicated and that a struggle had taken shape to forge a controlling theory through which to channel the tremendous social and cultural forces generated by Victorian science and technology.

While Spencerian naturalism had rejected supernaturalism, Spencer's organic theory elevated evolutionary development, including Darwinian natural selection, to the region of the absolute. It was a "universal" and "necessary" principle, the very foundation of reality: "The universal and necessary tendency towards supremacy and multiplication of the best, applying to the organic creation as a whole as well as to each species . . . tends ever to maintain those most superior organisms which, in one way or another, escape the invasions of the inferior."[20] Man was an animal in the natural world and, guided primarily by instinct, a creature with an impotent will, responding to environmental force as formulated along the lines of Darwin's *Origin*. Progress, Spencer declared in *The Principles of Sociology,* was the product of "universal conflict" leading to greater diversity and higher organization.[21] Huxley found methodological fault with the notion that the biological laissez-faire of Darwin could be transposed to history or society. The real difference between the naturalism of Huxley and Spencer is that for Huxley scientific naturalism was a critical principle; for Spencer, naturalism was a theory of reality, an ontology.

While he placed a fundamental value on the importance of private judgment and intellectual freedom, Huxley was most insistent in his opposition to the concept of natural rights, arguing that rights were the result of laws rather than of abstract systems formulated according to what man was ideally supposed to be. In 1890, he wrote a series of political essays which appeared in four of the early issues of the *Nineteenth Century*. Together, they reflected a somewhat complicated effort to attack Rousseau and Henry George for their a priori defenses of "natural rights," to defend the right of property ownership on the basis of its legal sanctions, to reject the principle of social laissez-faire, and to emphasize the value of the communal effort and the advantages of a strong central government.[22] As a political thinker, Huxley escapes most conventional definitions. He leaned toward the conservative side in his strong emphasis on social order and rationalism; yet his rejection of laissez-faire and his stress on communal effort often seem to place him within the progressive camp. Certainly he was not radical. In his **"On the Natural Inequality of Men,"** he argued that men were born with unequal abilities; although primitive men did not appear to have owned land privately, they were not therefore equal, because they governed by the laws of physical strength. Social organization diminished the sway of the powerful over the weak. Huxley argued that human society was a construct of human consciousness, and that law and ethics had no justification in nature. Like Mill, he rejected Rousseau's concepts of natural and social man as based on a false premise of the benevolence of primitive man. Huxley defended property ownership with the explanation that the right to property was originally established in a condition of social laissez-faire, and that it was the inevitable result of a primitive situation in which men were naturally unequal in their abilities (1:334). Thus while he defended private ownership as a social reality, he did not defend it as an ideal.

Again in his **"Capital—the Mother of Labor: An Economical Problem Discussed from a Physiological Point of View,"** Huxley took what at first seemed a conservative approach to the labor theory of value advocated by the socialists. However, upon close examination of his essay, one finds not an argument that the capitalist system of economics is the sound alternative approach to the distribution of wealth, but a reminder that "vital capital," the essential energy of living organisms, is impossible for the human organism to produce. Green plants alone were "the chief and, for practical purposes, the sole producers of that vital capital which we have seen to be the necessary antecedent of every act of labour" (9:155). The essay is an interesting, if somewhat bizarre, approach to the economics of capital and labor; in it Huxley's primary objective was to establish the likelihood that the classical socialist and capitalist economic duality of capital and labor is itself a fallacy, since the true capital of society is its vital capital, the physiological energy which drives the human organism. Huxley rejects the labor theory of value and denies that financial capital is able to produce "vital capital." He concludes by asserting that both capital and labor in their traditional senses are inconsistent with the more fundamental physiological realities of life.

Huxley's series of political essays suffers from the lack of a thesis. He was not sympathetic to traditional conservative thought and value; and he criticized socialist politics by associating them with regimentation. His desire for social and political order led him to reject the program of revolution advocated by the Marxists, and his high esteem for freedom of speech and individual liberty led him to oppose the tyranny of the majority. On the other hand, his belief that government itself was an instrument which should promote the general well-being of society against the privilege of the few convinced him of the importance of a strong central government which would function as a progressive organ for the improvement of the whole. His ethical vision, in its emphasis on social cooperation, on strengthening the polity through diminishing competition among individuals, had definite socialist overtones. In **"Government: Anarchy or Regimentation"** (1890), he attacked both laissez-faire individualism, which he equated with anarchy, and "'regimental' Socialism," which he identified with the Communist International and with the forceful use of the state as an instrument for the organization of men (1:393). This was a force which would ultimately destroy individual liberties and establish an "artificial equality" at the expense of natural inequalities manifested in varieties of human talent

and taste. "But there is no necessary connection between socialism and regimentation," he added, and he accepted in principle the possibility of men voluntarily organizing according to socialist ideals. Ultimately, Huxley emerges as a political critic without a true political conviction or philosophy, a fatal flaw which lessened the impact and influence of his political thought as a whole.

By 1894, Huxley had long thought in terms of two separate worlds, each with its own history. These were the worlds of "civil history" and "natural history" which, in a fragment written after **"Evolution and Ethics,"** he suggested were discrete but interlocking spheres of activity:

> In the Romanes Lecture I use the term "Natural History" as correlate and complement of "Civil History"—which I conceive to be its received & proper sense. Civil history deals with man in the state of art or civilization; natural history with man & the rest of the world in the state of nature. I have said that the ethics of evolution . . . is applied Natural History because it supposes that the struggle for existence on which progress in the "Natural History" world depends goes on & is the condition of progress in civil society.

> The complete logical consequence of that doctrine is the ultra individualism of the philosophical anarchists—the half way to it is the "astynomocracy" of laissez faire philosophy. Practical results of it are seen in the ignoring of the value of the state; the denial of its authority & of the duties of the individual toward it; which seems to me quite as mischievous as the antique errors in the other direction—perhaps more so.[23]

The distinctions he was making had particularly important implications for his critical theory, for if natural history were a "world" distinct from civil history, then values, insights, and laws that described one world would be independent of those that described the other. Progress was not simply the extension into society of the evolutionary principle of natural history. There was in fact, a clash, between social progress and progress in nature. Radical individualism or doing as one likes was consistent with natural law; but civil history began with "self-renunciation" or "abstinence by the individual from executing some of his possibilities of action."[24]

In his two histories theory, Huxley had given up his earlier tendencies to see natural law as a great existential unity.[25] The investigation of nature through the activity of research had not produced the values that Huxley in his youth had looked forward to so confidently. He did not reject the validity of his earlier determinism or abandon the idea of the great, universal order of nature. Indeed, as cited earlier, he had argued in the last days of his life to Balfour that rather than denying the existence of reason in the universe, natural science had to regard it as "reason *in excelsis*," far superior to that incarnate in man.[26] But whatever it was that bound the ethical process to its antagonistic parent, the cosmic process, remained to be disclosed. Years later Whitehead would reassert the primary ethical value of human cooperation in the creation of a state of art:

> The other side of the evolutionary machine, the neglected side, is expressed by the word *creativeness*. The organisms can create their own environment. For this purpose, the single organism is almost helpless. The adequate forces require societies of coöperating organisms. But with such coöperation and in proportion to the effort put forward, the environment has a plasticity which alters the whole ethical aspect of evolution.[27]

The communal effort to create, numerous organisms working together to establish the State of Art, these also were Huxley's final great objects. Humanity must forge its own ethical environment; it must create value.

iii. science and humanism

Three interrelated aspects of Huxley's thought aligned him with the humanistic tradition: his steady focus on man as the reference for significant knowledge, his emphasis on the reasoning faculty as the ultimate basis for knowledge of the external world, and his insistence on the dignity and uniqueness of man as a civilized and ethical being. He was not oriented within the classical humanist tradition of England, however: his notions of curriculum were decidedly at variance with that tradition, whose outstanding Victorian representative was Matthew Arnold. Huxley's debate with Arnold over the relative merits of scientific and classical humanistic studies was significant, for both men were professionally concerned with English education and understood the historical origins of their debate.

Like Arnold, Huxley had read widely in classical literature, seeking a more penetrating insight into the present by studying the history of Western thought and culture. Fascinated with Greek Stoical thought, he had long-lived ambitions to establish a modern philosophical system which would synthesize the bold Stoical monism, with its epistemological triad of physics, logic, and ethics, with the ethical system of Spinoza and the methods of Victorian science and technology. Huxley looked to Greek rationalism for a new morality and world view; he found a direct connection between the Stoical Logos and Spinoza's deity. This in turn inspired the great kaleidoscope that Huxley, in **"Scientific and Pseudo-Scientific Realism,"** imagined as the true macrocosmic symmetry. His notebooks were filled with elaborate notes from Anaximander, Diogenes, and other speculative thinkers who had struggled to pen-

etrate the mystery of the material universe. In private a passionate metaphysical speculator, Huxley found a powerful stimulus for his imagination in the enthusiasm of classical thought for its science, its impassioned yet methodical study of physical nature, its unflinching certainty that to grapple with the problems of material nature was to begin the gaining of wisdom and knowledge. This had been the path of such learned men as Empedocles, Heraclitus, Zeno, Socrates, and Aristotle, all of whom had been sophisticated and shrewd observers of material phenomena.

Huxley, however, was unable to accept the theodicy which enjoined men to see the ultimate good in social laissez-faire, and he was unable to confirm an alternative, ideal entity or structure in which to posit ultimate truth. He was left with the final philosophical impasse, from which he was unable to discover a systematic exit, of a macrocosm which was "reason *in excelsis*" and a cosmic process bearing grimly down, as in **"Evolution and Ethics,"** in opposition to all that was essential to human civilization. In his own philosophical terms, to combat the cosmos was to struggle against reason itself.

From his studies in Greek thought, however, Huxley discovered the historical dimension of scientific speculation and discovered as well that natural philosophy frequently provided the foundation upon which other cultural efforts were based. Cultures grew from shared assumptions on the character of man's intersection with nature, an intersection which was thought of as reality; and the most basic constructs of a given culture could be said to begin with the physical speculation of those who belonged to its scientific tradition. While Huxley had found that natural order itself had no moral content, he was still able to assert without contradiction that scientific naturalism was an effective critical method, based on the axiom that "nature is the expression of a definite order with which nothing interferes, and that the chief business of mankind is to learn that order and govern themselves accordingly" (3:150). This assertion, which was the central argument of his **"Science and Culture,"** raised the formal issue with Arnold over education and curriculum—the classical humanistic concerns. More fundamentally, it raised the question of what knowledge would enable the individual to enter into a valid criticism of modern life.

Arnold himself had great reservations about the possibilities of finding an ethical value in nature, and, like Huxley, was inclined to locate the moral center in human reason. The same alien cosmos loomed before his Empedocles, whose deep insight into the order of physical nature could not stir the hope which ultimately justified his continuing existence. An interesting equivalent to Huxley's ideal of the man of science, Empedocles was Arnold's dramatization of the purely rational vision; stoical intellect and moral insight were unable to compensate for the increased agony of a consciousness unable to escape itself. Arnold overlooked, however, the spontaneity and creative impulse that accompanied the scientific quest, the escape from self that scientific critics like Huxley and, more recently, George Sarton, identified with the scientific vision:

> When this scientific objectivity is carried high enough it leads to a particular kind of disinterestedness which is more fundamental than the disinterestedness of the most generous man. It is not so much a matter of generosity as of forgetfulness and abandonment of self. Every scientist (as every artist or saint) who is sufficiently absorbed in his task reaches sooner or later that stage of ecstasy (unfortunately imperma-nent), when the thought of self is entirely vanished, and he can think of naught else but the work at hand, his own vision of beauty and truth, and the ideal world which he is creating. In comparison with such heavenly ecstasy, all other rewards—such as money and honors—become strangely futile and incongruous.[28]

Empedocles, unable to escape from self into the imagination, struggled, via the consciousness, to contend with conditions that were beyond the influence of human will:

> In vain our pent wills fret,
> And would the world subdue.
> Limits we did not set
> Condition all we do;
> Born into life we are, and life must be our
>   mould.[29]

Having lost the vision of beauty in the macrocosm, he was left only with a rational consciousness, "a naked, eternally restless mind," which now, for lack of an object, preyed inward upon him.

Certainly, as Arnold had admitted, Empedocles presented few solutions to the dilemma of existence. But Arnold also understood the necessity of learning the physical conditions which defined the human "mould." To Huxley's query in **"Science and Culture"** of how one was to formulate an adequate criticism of life without consulting the ideas of men of science, Arnold did not hesitate to respond that he had, indeed, included the great scientific trends of thought in his cultural program of sweetness and light. In *Culture and Anarchy,* he had identified the "genuine scientific passion" with a curiosity he described as "a desire after the things of the mind simply for their own sakes and for the pleasure of seeing them as they are."[30] This impulse was part of the human passion for culture, the desire to augment the excellence of one's own nature which was, in effect, the source of Empedocles' drive toward perfection. However, there was another source of culture, Arnold argued, more properly described as a *"study of perfection,"* and which had predominantly "social" motives.[31] This realm of culture extended beyond that of Empedocles, the isolated intellect, and was preferred by Arnold to other concepts of culture as the "more interesting and far-reaching." Social perfection was the fundamental idea of culture, social perfection which went beyond mere individual accomplishment to the notion of cultural accomplishment; this was to be sought in "the idea of perfection as an inward condition of the mind and spirit."[32]

In **"Science and Culture,"** Huxley acknowledged Arnold's breadth of cultural appreciation, but he was convinced that Arnold's intention in *Culture and Anarchy* was to establish the classical subject matter of conventional British education as the exclusive educational curriculum. In an argument that he recognized was opposed to the traditional humanist ideal, he declared that modern social conditions made it desirable to abandon the study of Greek and Latin texts; furthermore, "for the purpose of attaining real culture, an exclusively scientific education is at least as effectual as an exclusively literary education" (3:141).

The distinctive character of Victorian times, Huxley held, "lies in the vast and constantly increasing part which is played by natural knowledge" (3:149). There were two propositions in Arnold's critical theory: "The first, that a criticism of life is the essence of culture; the second, that literature contains the materials which suffice for the construction of such a criticism" (3:143). Huxley agreed to the first proposition: "Culture certainly means something quite different from learning or technical skill. It implies the possession of an ideal, and the habit of critically estimating the value of things by comparison with a theoretic standard. Perfect culture should supply a complete theory of life, based upon a clear knowledge alike of its possibilities and of its limitations" (3:143). Huxley went on to trace the development of humanism in the Renaissance, arguing that it presented to the European mind, just emerging from the Middle Ages, a new art and a new science, imported through studies of classical thought. Humanism provided an example of "perfect intellectual freedom—of unhesitating acceptance of reason as the sole guide to truth and the supreme arbiter of conduct" (3:148). This, he agreed, had a profound effect on Renaissance education, and became the guiding spirit of humanist culture. The new humanists failed to understand, however, that the knowledge furnished by the study of classical texts had long since ceased to be the broadening and liberating force it had once been to a culture just emerging from the medieval period. The languages of Greek and Latin, which were formerly the sole avenues to the liberation of the intellect had become highly specialized studies in a modern age which possessed the widest range of knowledge ever before available to mankind.

Huxley's final argument against classical humanism would be voiced in his **"Prologue"** to *Controverted*

Questions (1892), where he maintained that "the goal of the humanists, whether they were aware of it or not, was the attainment of the complete intellectual freedom of the antique philosopher" (5:14). Humanism sought above all to liberate through knowledge, to provide the rational insight which would set the intellect free. In **"Science and Culture,"** he had declared that the great advantage of the "scientific 'criticism of life'" was that it appealed "not to authority, nor to what anybody may have thought or said, but to nature" (3:150). In essence, scientific criticism supplied a reference independent of human authority and human subjectivity.

By contrast, Arnold believed freedom was implicitly conferred on the intellect which had grasped the vision of wholeness that had inspired the Greek mind. In his Rede lecture, which was printed in the *Nineteenth Century* in August 1882, Arnold challenged Huxley's **"Science and Culture"** and addressed the issue of classical humanism. Certainly not a less brilliant controversialist than Huxley, Arnold, disarming his readers with modest references to the "poor humanist," turned defense to offense by observing that Huxley had confused literature with *"belles lettres."* He agreed with Wolf, the critic of Homer, who held that "all learning is scientific which is systematically laid out and followed up to its original sources, and that a genuine humanism is scientific."[33] The scientific study of cultures demanded that one attend to them in their original languages. Arnold thus laid claim to a scientific basis for humanistic education.

He went on to argue that the force of the humanistic approach could be traced to the ancient argument of Socrates, contained in the Diotimian monologue of the *Symposium,* that man felt as his fundamental desire the need for the good. Arnold converted this argument into a naturalistic thesis by equating the notion of fundamental desire to the biological concept of "instinct." According to Arnoldian naturalism:

> Following our *instinct* for intellect and knowledge, we acquire pieces of knowledge; and presently, in the generality of men, there arises the desire to relate these pieces of knowledge to our sense for conduct, to our sense for beauty,—and there is weariness and dissatisfaction if the desire is baulked. Now in this desire lies, I think, the strength of that hold which letters have upon us.[34]

In this move, Arnold sought to link the human quest for perfection with human instinct for the good, suggesting that civilization had an organic, biological basis. He identified the instinct for the good with the fundamental biological instinct of self preservation:

> As before, it is not on any weak pleadings of my own that I rely for convincing the gainsayers; it is on the constitution of human nature itself, and on

the *instinct* of *self-preservation* in humanity. The *instinct* for beauty is set in human nature, as surely as the *instinct* for knowledge is set there, or the *instinct* for conduct.[35]

Scientific knowledge, Arnold held, as Wordsworth had in his preface to the *Lyrical Ballads,* would ultimately be humanized for all through the force of literature; but for the uninitiated it remained raw, inorganic knowledge, removed from the great human instincts. It was analytical and fundamental, but as yet unassimilated, valued by virtue of the intellect, but not by virtue of the emotion. "Humane letters," by contrast, engaged the instincts because they appealed to emotion, to beauty, and to conduct. This, Arnold declared, was the great source of appeal of medieval knowledge; it answered to the instinctual need for the good that was itself part of the human identity. Man was not man without these things; and "Man's happiness consists in his being able to preserve his own essence," as Spinoza had once declared.[36] Thus the notion of self-preservation was to be taken in the sense of preserving one's essence as well as existence. Scientific knowledge was fundamental to physical self-preservation; for some, it was a great emotional and imaginative realm as well. But humane letters, history, literature, philosophy had the explicit responsibility of spiritual self-preservation, the preservation of human nature and identity. In the end, this must be accounted the more fundamental need.

The humanistic pursuit of Greek letters carried the instinct for beauty and knowledge and conduct to its epitome, since it alone presented the vision of harmony that answered to the deepest needs of men, the desire for wholeness. Leonardo himself, artist and archscientist of the Renaissance, by his own admission, Arnold pointed out, lacked the "antique symmetry," and felt this his one great fault. The ultimate end of the study of classical civilization, Arnold held, was to deliver to the modern mind a vision of symmetry in beauty, knowledge, and conduct which it then would apply to its own conditions and surroundings.

Arnold and Huxley remained at odds on the issue of humanistic education in England. The correspondence between the two men, however, was intimate and good humored, and while they recognized their fundamental differences, they also recognized the profound similarities in their general values. Neither sought, although Huxley has often been accused of seeking, the kind of disciplinary exclusivity that would become more common in the following century.[37] Although Josiah Mason had excluded "mere literary instruction and education," Huxley pointed out, the new school was to provide instruction in English, French, and German; these would open the way to the "three greatest literatures of the modern world" (3:140, 150). It is worth remembering that Huxley had had only a year of general instruction at Ealing School where Latin and Greek grammar were central to the curriculum. This was the school he had once characterized as having been run by "baby-farmers" (1:5). In spite of this, he had learned, through private effort, Greek and Latin, Italian, French, and German, and had read widely in the literature and philosophy of both modern and ancient civilizations. He questioned the value of the classical humanistic education, not only because he had never experienced its possibilities, but because he had acquired his own knowledge through independent study and research. Arnold, the product of private tutors, Winchester College, Rugby, and Oxford, a living representative of English humanism, saw differently, for his family had long been intimately associated with classical education in England. Huxley placed little value on tradition; his success and rise to influence had come through the new knowledge of Victorian science, and he sought to justify its independent value as a social and cultural activity.

With some concern over the possible misunderstanding of his **"Science and Culture,"** Huxley wrote a second essay, **"On Science and Art in Relation to Education,"** which was delivered at the Liverpool Institute in early 1883 after Arnold had presented his "Literature and Science" as the Rede lecture at Cambridge.[38] While neither an exclusively literary nor scientific education was the ideal, the sciences, if one were to insist on disciplinary exclusivity as so many traditionalists had indeed been doing, were as useful and enlightening a basis in the preparation of one for a criticism of life as the literary arts could be. He agreed with Arnold, however, that it was not a question of whether men of science or of art should dominate; they should, above all, understand one another (3:179). The proper philological study of ancient Greek civilization, he admitted, "affords a splendid and noble education," but it still was incomplete and beyond the practical means of most (3:182). Modern education was obliged to give due attention to the realities of the present which it should strive to alter, as far as possible, for the better. The Greek genius had been one of symmetry, it was true, but a symmetry conceived in the context of its own present, an integration of its science, philosophy and letters. The classical humanistic ideal of Victorian England, Huxley argued, provided an education which lacked the very spirit of symmetry it sought in Greek civilization, for it had abandoned the present for a harmonious vision of the past.

Literature and art, Huxley concluded, were justly esteemed as great emotional and imaginative realms of humanity; the best literature, such as that of Shakespeare, "satisfies the artistic instinct of the youngest and harmonises with the ripest and richest experience of the oldest" (3:179). Huxley had always been sensitive to artistic beauty; in his "Universities: Actual and Ideal" (1874), he had observed, perhaps even thinking of Arnold's *Culture and Anarchy:*

But the man who is all morality and intellect, although he may be good and even great, is, after all, only half a man. There is beauty in the moral world and in the intellectual world; but there is also a beauty which is neither moral nor intellectual—the beauty of the world of Art. There are men who are devoid of the power of seeing it, as there are men who are born deaf and blind, and the loss of those, as of these, is simply infinite. There are others in whom it is an overpowering passion; happy men, born with the productive, or at lowest, the appreciative, genius of the Artist.

[3:205]

He took pains that his advocacy of scientific education not be interpreted to mean that he believed literary education should be weakened. He believed that both curricula were capable of being taught without sacrificing one to the other. Furthermore, science and art were not discrete intellectual and aesthetic entities, as they were commonly regarded. In a fragment manuscript, he had written:

In the great majority of our thoughts, however, the scientific and the aesthetic elements are inseparably commingled. . . . There is hardly a work of art which does not contain a scientific element—hardly a great artist who is not in the broad sense of the word a man of science—while the greatest works of art might be characterized as science . . . moulded by feeling. . . . If culture is the even and balanced development of all our faculties and if education is the means of obtaining culture then it is absurd to imagine that there can be any antagonisms between science and art or between science and literature as art.[39]

Huxley's thought consistently returned to his focus in *Man's Place in Nature:* "The question of questions for mankind—the problem which underlies all others, and is more deeply interesting than any other—is the ascertainment of the place which Man occupies in nature and of his relations to the universe of things" (7:77). He insisted that the answer had to be sought in physical nature itself. This was the central idea behind his critical terms, *thätige Skepsis,* agnosticism, and scientific naturalism. And it was an important source for his grandson's "scientific humanism":

Scientific Humanism is a protest against supernaturalism: the human spirit, now in its individual, now in its corporate aspects, is the source of all values and the highest reality we know. . . . It insists on human values as the norms for our aims, but insists equally that they cannot adjust themselves in right perspec-tive and emphasis except as part of the picture of the world provided by science.[40]

For Julian Huxley, as for his grandfather, the sciences were to provide insights into the structure of external reality, which were then to be modified according to values, presumably rationalist, derived from the human spirit. This looked back to Huxley's fusion of method and reason. Scientific thought was not, according to Julian Huxley, to set itself up "as an external code or framework as did revealed religion in the past."[41] The same distinction moved Thomas Huxley to seek a critical function for the scientific vision: to join reason with method was to protect humanity from absolutist systems, whether scientifically or religiously inspired.

While Huxley and Arnold were close and kindred spirits, drawn together by their shared sense of value in their broad humanist outlooks, deep divisions between them remained. Striving for a concept of critical reason that would reflect their personal visions, both sought to throw new light on the changes that appeared to be transforming their society into something entirely new. For Huxley imagination fulfilled a role subordinate to reason, however, while for Arnold it was reason's equal. In **"Scientific and Pseudo-Scientific Realism"** (1887), Huxley had declared that "if imagination is used within the limits laid down by science, disorder is unimaginable" (5:73). This also meant the end of the miraculous. One remembers how Browning's Arab physician, Karshish, "the not-incurious in God's handiwork," good-natured scholar that he was, could not escape the rational prejudice of his method.[42] For him, the structure of the perception had become the essence of its reality: face to face with divinity, he saw only irregularity. The goodness and beauty of the idea, the simple yet wonderful harmony implicit in the miraculous possibility of Lazarus' cure, was not enough to override the earnest physician's reason, though it nearly succeeded—"The very God! think, Abib."

Arnold associated reason closely with imagination, conceiving of them, although not very coherently, as a single, continuous faculty. This established a dual guardianship over the mind, where neither the purely imaginative nor the purely rational construct was to be accepted. "The main element of the modern spirit's life," he declared, "is neither the sense and understanding, nor the heart and imagination; it is the imaginative reason."[43] Fruitful, harmonious thought, Arnold believed, was achieved through a combination of reason and emotion, sense and imagination; it was the humanization and personalization of knowledge. Searching for a way to avoid what he believed was the dilemma of Empedoclean speculation divorced from emotion, he urged the establishment of an alternative cultural ideal modeled on that of Hellenic harmony and spontaneity. Huxley, in his different way, sought unity as well. His impassioned dream of "reason *in excelsis*" was not in the end so different from Arnold's imaginative reason.

Accepting the new relationship between man and nature constituted the most difficult of Victorian adjustments, since it considerably altered the most fundamental of cultural ideas—the human self-image. Huxley and Arnold both experienced the widening of the chasm between natural process and traditional ideas of self with a growing sense of alienation, a fact which moved them to the search for sources of human value and dignity consonant with the new realities of the coming era. It is in this light that Huxley's call for revolution against nature needs to be understood, for he was revolting against a lifeless paradigm he had constructed himself—that of the cosmic kaleidoscope and of biological man—in the interests of humanly-centered ideas of reason, ethics and community. If to moderns his call for revolution against nature sounds ominous, it is partly because we no longer share in his conception of cosmic organization; more deeply, it is because we fear a Pyrrhic victory over nature. Whether, as Freud asserted, we are still and necessarily in open revolt remains a question, and one which, given our growing technological potency, we can ignore only at our profound peril.

The observations and insights of Huxley and Arnold are of prime significance to the modern age, for both men, in a striking anticipation of modern sensibility, sought ways of locating centers of value and independence in an age that seemed to be losing, amid the confusion of social transition, its sense of restraint and liberty. The independent locus of human dignity, standards of value to modify raw social, political, and economical forces, were found by both men in the humanist values of the past, Huxley locating them in the speculative tradition of science, and Arnold locating them in the syncretic traditions of classical literature. In the Renaissance, the dignity of human knowledge found eloquent spokesmen like Galileo and Bacon, just as in Greek civilization it was expressed in the speculative rapture of the rationalist inquiry into nature. In modern thought, we refer to Einstein and Eliot, to Sakharov and Solzhenitsyn, in our search for the loci of free, spiritual thought amid absolutism. Science and art have always provided humanity with twin refuges—centers of value which are free, when genuine, from dogma and public authority. Both flourish in spite of doctrine, for both celebrate the freedoms of imagination, speculation, and emotion. In science and the rigor of its independent appeal to nature, Huxley found a witness to the mystery and enactment of human intellectual freedom; and this became the frame and measure for his own human identity.

Notes

notes for introduction

[1] Alfred North Whitehead, *Science and the Modern World,* p. 141.

[2] Walter Houghton, *The Victorian Frame of Mind, 1830-1870,* p. 22.

[3] M. H. Abrams, *Natural Supernaturalism,* pp. 66-69.

⁴ See, for example, Charles S. Blinderman, "T. H. Huxley's Theory of Aesthetics," p. 51.

⁵ Quoted in William Irvine, *Apes, Angels, and Victorians,* p. 30.

⁶ Lionel Trilling, "Science, Literature and Culture," p. 475.

⁷ Oliver Elton, *A Survey of English Literature, 1780-1880,* 3:77.

notes for chapter I

¹ William Whewell, *The Philosophy of the Inductive Sciences,* 1:cxiii.

² David Scott, "On Leonardo Da Vinci and Correggio," *Blackwood's Magazine* 48 (August 1840): 273.

³ Alfred North Whitehead, *Science and the Modern World,* p. 142.

⁴ *T. H. Huxley's Diary of the Voyage of H. M. S. Rattlesnake,* p. 99.

⁵ 2 July 1849, T. H. Huxley, Correspondence with Henrietta Heathorn: 1847-1854, fol. 70, Imperial College of Science and Technology, London. Material from this collection is quoted with permission from the Governors, Imperial College of Science and Technology. In quoting from Huxley's manuscripts, I have made minor alterations in the punctuation.

⁶ *T. H. Huxley's Diary,* p. 26.

⁷ Beatrice Webb, *My Apprenticeship,* p. 28.

⁸ 2 July 1849, Huxley-Heathorn Correspondence, fol. 70.

⁹ See Thomas Carlyle, *The Works of Thomas Carlyle,* ed. Henry Duff Traill, vol. 27, *Critical and Miscellaneous Essays* (1904), pp. 112-13.

¹⁰ Ibid., vol. 26, *Critical and Miscellaneous Essays* (1904), pp. 17-18.

¹¹ See also Cyril Bibby, *T. H. Huxley,* pp. 12-13.

¹² George Gordon Byron, *Cain, A Mystery,* in *The Complete Poetical Works of Byron,* ed. Paul E. More, p. 648. See also *T. H. Huxley's Diary,* p. 26.

¹³ For a catalogue of the Huxley-Heathorn correspondence for this period, see Jeanne Pingree, *Thomas Henry Huxley: List of His Correspondence with Miss Henrietta Heathorn, 1847-1854.*

¹⁴ 31 December 1848, Huxley-Heathorn Correspondence, fol. 40.

¹⁵ 18 August 1851, Huxley-Heathorn Correspondence, fol. 162.

¹⁶ Quoted in Bibby, *T. H. Huxley,* p. 5.

¹⁷ Cf. Houston Peterson, *Huxley, Prophet of Science,* pp. 14-15.

¹⁸ See also William Irvine, "Carlyle and T. H. Huxley," pp. 198-99.

¹⁹ 12 May 1849, Huxley-Heathorn Correspondence, fol. 57.

²⁰ 7 May 1851, Huxley-Heathorn Correspondence, fol. 147.

²¹ 2 September 1848, Huxley-Heathorn Correspondence, fol. 37.

²² 23 September 1851, Huxley-Heathorn Correspondence, fol. 166.

²³ Thomas Carlyle, *Sartor Resartus,* ed. Charles F. Harrold, pp. 191-92.

²⁴ John Ruskin, *The Works of John Ruskin,* ed. E. T. Cook and Alexander Wedderburn, vol. 22, *The Eagle's Nest: Ten Lectures on the Relation of Natural Science to Art* (1906), p. 138.

²⁵ Ibid. See also Walter F. Cannon, "The Normative Role of Science in Early Victorian Thought," p. 500.

²⁶ The Huxley Papers, Imperial College of Science and Technology, London, 45:86. Material from this collection is quoted with permission from the Governors, Imperial College of Science and Technology.

²⁷ Charles Dickens, *The New Oxford Illustrated Dickens,* vol. 3, *Bleak House* (1948), pp. 845-47.

²⁸ Karl Marx and Friedrich Engels, *The Communist Manifesto,* in *The Essential Works of Marxism,* ed. Arthur P. Mendel, p. 18.

²⁹ John Henry Cardinal Newman, *The Idea of a University, Defined and Illustrated,* pp. 106-7.

³⁰ Ruskin, *Eagle's Nest,* p. 135.

³¹ Phyllis Rose, "Huxley, Holmes, and the Scientist as Aesthete," p. 22.

³² Mary Shelley, *Frankenstein or the Modern Prometheus,* ed. James Rieger, p. 47.

³³ Quoted in Bibby, *T. H. Huxley,* p. 98; see also pp. 96-101.

[34] The term "Huxley theater" is not used in comparative reference to the critical study by Robert Garis, *The Dickens Theatre* (Oxford: Clarendon Press, 1965).

. . . . .

notes for chapter V

[1] Matthew Arnold, "The Function of Criticism at the Present Time," in *Complete Prose Works,* vol. 3, *Lectures and Essays in Criticism,* p. 261.

[2] Ibid.

[3] Several studies have been made of Huxley's style and rhetoric, including Walter Houghton's "The Rhetoric of T. H. Huxley," pp. 159-75, and Aldous Huxley's "T. H. Huxley as a Literary Man," *The Olive Tree,* pp. 47-83. Aldous Huxley examines a number of his grandfather's rhetorical techniques, rejecting, however, Chesterton's claim that Huxley was more a literary than a scientific man. See G. K. Chesterton, *The Victorian Age in Literature,* p. 26. Charles S. Blinderman argues in "T. H. Huxley's Theory of Aesthetics," pp. 54-55, that it was Huxley's "genius as a creator of order which contributed to his fame." Blinderman also cites H. L. Mencken's claim that Huxley was "one of the few great stylists that England has produced since the time of Anne." Joseph Gardner, in "A Huxley Essay as 'Poem,'" argues that Huxley's "On the Physical Basis of Life," which is often cited as a classic of Victorian materialism, has a complex metaphorical structure which repudiates materialism.

[4] Walter Houghton, *The Victorian Frame of Mind,* pp. 94-95.

[5] The Huxley Papers, Imperial College, London, 47:122-23. See also Huxley's "Mr. Balfour's Attack on Agnosticism: II," p. 317.

[6] Arnold, "Heinrich Heine," in *Complete Prose Works,* 3:113.

[7] See, for example, Arnold, *Culture and Anarchy,* in *Complete Prose Works,* 5:94. "But, finally," Arnold observes, "perfection—as culture from a thorough disinterested study of human nature and human experience learns to conceive it,—is a harmonious expansion of *all* the powers which make the beauty and worth of human nature, and is not consistent with the over-development of any one power at the expense of the rest."

[8] Arnold, "The Function of Criticism at the Present Time," p. 264.

[9] See, for example, Thomas S. Kuhn, *The Structure of Scientific Revolutions,* 2nd ed., pp. 206-7. Werner Heisenberg, in his *Physics and Philosophy;* p. 200, points out that scientific concepts are "idealizations" and that "through this process of idealization and precise definition the immediate connection with reality is lost." In a different but relevant context, A. N. Whitehead in his *Science and the Modern World,* pp. 23-24, declares that "Science has never shaken off the impress of its origin in the historical revolt of the later Renaissance. It has remained predominantly an antirationalistic movement, based upon a naïve faith. What reasoning it has wanted, has been borrowed from mathematics which is a surviving relic of Greek rationalism, following the deductive method. Science repudiates philosophy. In other words, it has never cared to justify its faith or to explain its meanings; and has remained blandly indifferent to its refutation by Hume."

[10] *T. H. Huxley's Diary,* p. 278.

[11] T. H. Huxley, "An Apologetic Irenicon," p. 565.

[12] A. W. Benn, *The History of English Rationalism in the Nineteenth Century,* 2:453. See also D. W. Dockrill, "T. H. Huxley and the Meaning of Agnosticism," p. 465.

[13] Benn, *History of English Rationalism,* 1:1. See note 19 below.

[14] G. K. Chesterton, *The Victorian Age in Literature,* p. 127.

[15] See John Holloway, *The Victorian Sage,* pp. 10-12.

[16] The Huxley Papers, 45:10.

[17] Friedrich Engels, "Introduction [to the English edition of 1892]," *Socialism: Utopian and Scientific,* trans. Edward Aveling, p. 18.

[18] Arthur J. Balfour, *The Foundations of Belief,* pp. 124-25.

[19] Huxley's rationalism adheres to values generally expressed by A. W. Benn in chapter 1 of his *History of English Rationalism in the Nineteenth Century,* pp. 1-15: "Rationalism might be defined as the method and doctrine of those who strive to make reason the supreme regulator of their beliefs and of their actions; who try to think and speak in terms to which fixed and intelligible senses are attached" (p. 1). Benn considered agnosticism an intimate philosophical relative to rationalism, observing that Huxley's definition of agnosticism "covers rationalism in the wide sense," but that it admits to an ignorance that the rationalist is unaware of. For both rationalist and agnostic, however, "the appeal is to reason, and to reason alone. But reason in the hands of the agnostic is applied to the destruction of non-religious metaphysics rather than to the destruction of religious belief" (p. 14). Yet, "of those who in England accept the extreme results of

rationalism, the immense majority call themselves, and are called by others, agnostics."

[20] Herbert Spencer, *The Principles of Biology,* 1:355.

[21] Herbert Spencer, *The Principles of Sociology,* 2:240.

[22] The essays were: "The Natural Inequality of Men"; "Natural Rights and Political Rights"; "Capital, the Mother of Labor"; and "Government: Anarchy or Regimentation," in order of appearance. For a discussion of conservative trends in Huxley's political thought see William Irvine, *Apes, Angels, and Victorians,* pp. 334-36. See also Cyril Bibby, *T. H. Huxley: Scientist, Humanist and Educator,* pp. 51-63.

[23] The Huxley Papers, 45:42-43.

[24] Ibid., 45.

[25] For an important critical essay on Huxley's final philosophical position, see John Dewey, "Evolution and Ethics." Dewey, who knew Huxley's Romanes lecture intimately, recalls that "many felt as if they had received a blow knocking the breath out of their bodies. To some it appeared that Mr. Huxley had executed a sudden *volte-face* and had given up his belief in the unity of the evolutionary process." Dewey argues that aggressive forms of "self-assertion" are transformed in society into positive factors in the ethical process (p. 330). He rejects the notion that there can be any opposition between natural and moral processes (pp. 334-36).

[26] T. H. Huxley, "Mr. Balfour's Attack on Agnosticism: II," p. 317.

[27] A. N. Whitehead, *Science and the Modern World,* pp. 164-65.

[28] George Sarton, *The History of Science and the Problems of To-day,* pp. 27-28. Arnold's expertise in science was slight, as Fred A. Dudley has argued in "Matthew Arnold and Science." His concept of science was framed more in classical natural speculation, just as his critical theory looked to classical notions of symmetry and harmony. Huxley was deeply versed in the classical idea of science as well, which gave his debate with Arnold a distinct historical context.

[29] Arnold, "Empedocles on Etna," in *Poems,* p. 164.

[30] Arnold, *Culture and Anarchy,* p. 91.

[31] Ibid.

[32] Ibid., p. 95.

[33] Arnold, "Literature and Science," in *Complete Prose Works,* 10:57.

[34] Ibid., p. 62. (Italics are mine.)

[35] Ibid., pp. 70-71. (Italics are mine.)

[36] Ibid., p. 67.

[37] See also Cyril Bibby, "Thomas Henry Huxley and University Development," p. 107.

[38] For an examination and dating of the public platform behind the Huxley-Arnold debate, see David A. Roos, "Matthew Arnold and Thomas Henry Huxley: Two Speeches at the Royal Academy, 1881 and 1883," pp. 316-24.

[39] The Huxley Papers, 42: 147-48.

[40] Julian Huxley, *What Dare I Think?,* pp. 180-81.

[41] Ibid., p. 182.

[42] Robert Browning, "An Epistle, Containing the Strange Medical Experience of Karshish . . . ," *The Complete Poetical Works of Browning,* ed. Horace E. Scudder, pp. 338-41.

[43] Arnold, "Pagan and Mediaeval Religious Sentiment," in *Complete Prose Works,* 3:230.

Selected Bibliography

Abrams, M. H. *Natural Supernaturalism: Tradition and Revolution in Romantic Literature.* New York: Norton, 1973.

Arnold, Matthew. *The Complete Prose Works of Matthew Arnold.* Edited by R. H. Super. 11 vols. Ann Arbor: University of Michigan Press, 1960-77.

————. *The Poems of Matthew Arnold.* Edited by Kenneth Allott. London: Longmans, 1965.

Balfour, Arthur J. *The Foundations of Belief.* New York: Longmans, Green, 1895.

Benn, A. W. *The History of English Rationalism in the Nineteenth Century.* 2 vols. New York: Longmans, Green, 1906.

Bibby, Cyril. *T. H. Huxley: Scientist, Humanist and Educator.* New York: Horizon, 1960.

————. "Thomas Henry Huxley and University Development." *Victorian Studies* 2 (1958): 97-116.

Blinderman, Charles S. "T. H. Huxley's Theory of Aesthetics: Unity in Diversity." *Journal of Aesthetics and Art Criticism* 21 (1962): 49-56.

Browning, Robert. *The Complete Poetical Works of Browning.* Edited by Horace E. Scudder. Cambridge Edition. Boston: Houghton Mifflin, 1895.

Byron, George Gordon. *The Complete Poetical Works of Byron.* Edited by Paul E. More. Cambridge, Mass.: Houghton Mifflin, 1933.

Cannon, Walter F. "The Normative Role of Science in Early Victorian Thought." *Journal of the History of Ideas* 25 (1964): 487-502.

Carlyle, Thomas. *Sartor Resartus: The Life and Opinions of Herr Teufelsdröckh.* Edited by Charles F. Harrold. New York: Odyssey Press, 1937.

———. *The Works of Thomas Carlyle.* Edited by Henry Duff Traill. Edinburgh Edition. 30 vols. New York: Scribner's, 1903-4.

Chesterton, G. K. *The Victorian Age in Literature.* 1913. Reprint. London: Oxford University Press, 1946.

Dewey, John. "Evolution and Ethics." *Monist* (Chicago), 8 (1898): 321-41.

Dickens, Charles. *The New Oxford Illustrated Dickens.* 21 vols. London: Oxford University Press, 1948-58.

Dockrill, D. W. "T. H. Huxley and the Meaning of 'Agnosticism.'" *Theology* (London), 74 (October 1971): 461-77.

Dudley, Fred A. "Matthew Arnold and Science." *PMLA,* 57 (March 1942), 275-94.

Elton, Oliver. *A Survey of English Literature, 1780-1880.* 4 vols. New York: Macmillan, 1920.

Engels, Friedrich. "Introduction [to the English Edition of 1882]." *Socialism: Utopian and Scientific.* Translated by Edward Aveling. Chicago: Charles H. Kerr, 1908.

Gardner, Joseph H. "A Huxley Essay as 'Poem.'" *Victorian Studies,* 14 (1970): 177-91.

Heisenberg, Werner. *Physics and Philosophy: The Revolution in Modern Science.* 1958. Reprint. New York: Harper and Row, 1962.

Holloway, John. *The Victorian Sage: Studies in Argument.* 1953. Reprint. New York: Norton, 1965.

Houghton, Walter. "The Rhetoric of T. H. Huxley." *University of Toronto Quarterly* 18 (1949): 159-75.

———. *The Victorian Frame of Mind: 1830-1870.* New Haven: Yale University Press, 1957.

Huxley, Aldous. *The Olive Tree.* New York: Harper and Brothers, 1937.

Huxley, Julian. *What Dare I Think?* New York: Harper, 1931.

Huxley, Leonard. *Life and Letters of Thomas Henry Huxley.* 2 vols. New York: D. Appleton, 1900.

Huxley, Thomas Henry. "An Apologetic Irenicon." *Fortnightly Review* 58 (1892): 557-71.

———. "Mr. Balfour's Attack on Agnosticism: II." In *Huxley: Prophet of Science,* by Houston Peterson, pp. 315-27. New York: Longmans, Green, 1932.

———. *T. H. Huxley's Diary of the Voyage of H. M. S. Rattlesnake.* Edited by Julian Huxley. Garden City, N.Y.: Doubleday, Doran, 1936.

Irvine, William. *Apes, Angels, and Victorians: The Story of Darwin, Huxley and Evolution.* New York: McGraw-Hill, 1955.

———. "Carlyle and T. H. Huxley." In *Victorian Literature: Modern Essays in Criticism.* Edited by Austin Wright, pp. 193-207. New York: Oxford University Press, 1961.

Kuhn, Thomas. *The Structure of Scientific Revolutions.* 2d ed. Chicago: University of Chicago Press, 1973.

Marx, Karl, and Engels, Friedrich. *The Essential Works of Marxism.* Edited by Arthur P. Mendel. New York: Bantam, 1971.

Newman, John Henry Cardinal. *The Idea of a University, Defined and Illustrated.* New York: Longmans, Green, 1931.

Peterson, Houston. *Huxley: Prophet of Science.* New York: Longmans, 1932.

Pingree, Jeanne. *Thomas Henry Huxley: List of His Correspondence with Miss Henrietta Heathorn, 1847-1854.* London: Imperial College of Science and Technology, 1969.

Roos, David. "Matthew Arnold and Thomas Henry Huxley: Two Speeches at the Royal Academy, 1881 and 1883." *Journal of Modern Philology* 74 (1977): 316-24.

Rose, Phyllis. "Huxley, Holmes, and the Scientist as Aesthete." *Victorian Newsletter* 38 (Fall 1970): 22-24.

Ruskin, John. *The Works of John Ruskin.* Edited by E. T. Cook and Alexander Wedderburn. 39 vols. London: George Allen, 1903-12.

Sarton, George. *The History of Science and the Problems of To-day.* Washington, D.C.: W. F. Roberts, 1935.

Scott, David. "On Leonardo Da Vinci and Correggio." *Blackwood's Magazine* 48 (1840): 270-80.

Shelley, Mary. *Frankenstein or the Modern Prometheus.* Edited by James Rieger. New York: Bobbs-Merrill, 1974.

Spencer, Herbert. *The Principles of Biology.* 2 vols. New York: D. Appleton, 1871.

————. *The Principles of Sociology.* 3 vols. New York: D. Appleton, 1900-1901.

Trilling, Lionel. "Science, Literature and Culture: A Comment on the Snow-Leavis Controversy." *Commentary* 33 (June 1962): 461-77.

Webb, Beatrice. *My Apprenticeship.* New York: Longmans, Green, 1926.

Whewell, William. *The Philosophy of the Inductive Sciences, Founded upon Their History.* 2 vols. London: John Parker, 1840.

Whitehead, Alfred North. *Science and the Modern World.* New York: Macmillan, 1925.

Ed Block, Jr. (essay date 1986)

SOURCE: "T. H. Huxley's Rhetoric and the Popularization of Victorian Scientific Ideas: 1854-1874," in *Victorian Studies,* Vol. 29, No. 3, Spring, 1986, pp. 363-86.

[*In this essay, Block explores Huxley's rhetorical style and the extent to which he shaped modern scientific writing.*]

The most recent books treating Thomas Henry Huxley make a strong claim for the impact that his work had on developing a sense of "man's place in nature" and his place in science during the nineteenth century.[1] Critics agree that many of Huxley's essays remain important landmarks and persuasive defenses of Victorian science. Yet few have sought to describe precisely how Huxley's drive for "unity in diversity" developed,[2] or how his fabled "clarity of expression"[3] effectively accommodated itself to the lesser knowledge and stronger prejudices of his different audiences. I propose to sketch briefly the evolution of Huxley's rhetorical strategy in some of his popular scientific essays. I shall also demonstrate the extent to which these and all Huxley's major essays are motivated by a peculiar sense of structure and certain characteristic modes of development. I shall then show how Huxley employed this rhetoric in a specific phase of the popular debate over evolutionary theory: the mind-matter debate that developed following his famous 1868 Edinburgh address, **"On the Physical Basis of Life."** Adapting his style and focus to the individual opponents and the issues they had raised, he extended his own rhetorical depth and range. He also further refined a style that became a standard for popular scientific writing which has lasted into the twentieth century.

Sorting through the complexities of catastrophism, progressionism, uniformitarianism, and the durability of species, Huxley adopted a coherent theory with which to comprehend and interpret the world (di Gregorio, *Huxley's Place,* p. 58). Reacting to the sometimes humdrum argumentative and descriptive rhetoric of William Whewell and Richard Owen, he molded a style full of intensity, vividness, and coherence. He harnessed the obsessive hypothetical and deductive method of Charles Darwin and made it serve more limited tasks of argumentation.[4] Shaped and worked into the more concentrated form of the lecture or essay, Huxley's rhetorical gift developed a form which enabled him to answer if not always clearly defeat increasingly more difficult and more varied opponents like Owen (summarized in di Gregorio, *Huxley's Place,* pp. 186-187) and St. George Mivart. Deploying this form in a varied range of periodicals and for a variety of Victorian audiences, Huxley earned a permanent place in the ranks of imaginative and powerful rhetorical writers.

Huxley openly acknowledged the philosophical heritage of René Descartes, Thomas Hobbes, John Locke, Bishop Berkeley, David Hume, and William Hamilton, and the heritage of the great biologists from Georges Cuvier and Georges Buffon to Darwin. From the way he defends the rational empiricism and the application of scientific method in these men's work, it is little wonder that Huxley's own scientific writing reinforces a number of striking scientific features found in the genre of the popular scientific essay. If it is fair to say that the orientation of the "Romantic," or what Dwight Culler has called the "Christian-Humanist," essay is either temporal, sequential, and narrative, or logical and symbolical;[5] then Huxley's "Utilitarian" and scientific essays often introduce a significant contrapuntal theme. Whereas the essays of Francis Jeffrey, Thomas Carlyle, and T. B. Macaulay most often take their predominant structure from history or biography, Huxley uses chronology sparingly, as a way, for example, to sketch the vastness of geologic time. Whereas John Henry Newman, John Ruskin, and Charles Swinburne use description and discursive logic to argue a logical point or a symbolic insight, Huxley emphasizes experiment and observation in the service of scientific logic. Even into essays otherwise conventionally structured, he introduces in contrastively effective ways the atemporal, the ahistorical, and the impersonal.

Formed first by the rigorous conventions of anatomy and physiology,[6] and then by the habits of the lecture hall, the classroom, and the periodical press, his essays became subtle models of effective logical structure, capitalizing on the importance of audience, and acknowledging the effectiveness of classical ideals of aesthetic completeness. The reassurance and sense of formal security which observance of these conventions conveys accounts in part for their unquestioned effect on the Victorian public. His gifts as describer, classifier, and expositor of experimental method, on the other hand, make him a mediator between distinct intellectual and rhetorical traditions. His scientifically nurtured sense of analogy and synecdoche gives specific passages and sometimes whole essays a peculiarly pure and unusual poetic quality.[7]

I

To suggest that there is something innovative in most ordinary scientific writing—especially nineteenth-century scientific writing—is far from my purpose. Huxley's early scientific papers, like the lesser papers of Darwin, Owen, and John Tyndall, are models of conventional scientific structure. They tend to be full of meticulous technical descriptions, careful surveys of existing research, and modest generalizations from the facts described. But Huxley's early scientific papers also contain what Walter Weimer identifies (in other scientific writers) as a peculiar, and philosophically important linguistic feature, the injunctive mode. Paraphrasing G. Spencer Brown's *Laws of Form* (1972), Weimer says: "Scientific communication becomes a set of commands that will enable the researcher to have the appropriate experience: 'Do this, and you will experience the world correctly!' The descriptive commentary of the scientific report becomes a description only within this injunctive framework."[8] These features, description, survey, and generalization, along with the records of experiments or "injunctive" directions as to what to see in a specimen, have a significant impact on Huxley's later, more popular works. In his scientific work before 1859, however, Huxley also mobilizes his fabled analogizing power and employs with more conscious polemical purpose than might be expected the deductive-inductive method which is the scientist's stock in trade. He also acknowledges the importance of imagination in scientific endeavor. In retrospect, these features anticipate techniques used effectively in the popular scientific lectures.

One striking feature of Huxley's early scientific essays is their descriptive vividness, their representational dimension. Huxley's capacity for drawing implies acute and synthetic powers of observation.[9] In the following brief opening passage from **"Lacinularia Socialis"** (1851), reminiscent of Darwin's famous "tangled bank,"[10] Huxley assumes the tone and stance of the eighteenth-century natural historian, and from a quick, vivid look at some relevant and irrelevant conditions of the rotifer's existence, he moves to the introduction of his main point:

> The leaves of the Ceratophyllum, which abounds in the river Medway, a little above Farleigh Bridge, are beset with small, transparent, gelatinous-looking, globular bodies, about 1/15th of an inch in diameter. These are aggregates of a very singular and beautiful Rotifer, the Lacinularia socialis of Ehrenberg. On account of their relatively large size, their transparency, and their fixity, they present especial advantages for microscopic observation; and I therefore gladly availed myself of a short stay in that part of the country to inquire somewhat minutely into their structure, in the hope of being able to throw some light on the many doubtful or disputed points of the organization of the class to which they belong.[11]

The passage clearly takes its focus from the audience for which it was intended, the Microscopial Society of London. There is also rhetorical subtlety in beginning a refutation of prior research with the almost pastoral details of the opening description. What the passage teaches us chiefly, however, is that Huxley's descriptions, even relatively early in his career, have the capacity to render the detail as well as the flux of phenomena with a sense of locale, immediacy, and vigor. This capacity, developed, enlarged, and made even more sensitive to differing audiences, contributes to the effect of his later scientific lectures.

We find Huxley's analogizing capacity most prominent in essays like **"On the Anatomy and the Affinities of the Family of the Medusae"** (1849) (*Memoirs,* I, 9-32), **"Lacinularia Socialis,"** and **"On the Development of the Teeth"** (1853). In all three, Huxley corrects mistaken biological classifications by reference to Owen's relatively new ideas of homologous organs or functions. In **"Medusae"** he uses the careful comparison of organs to distinguish and relate five forms of jellyfish. This scientific effort, along with the others produced while a naval surgeon on the *HMS Rattlesnake,* earned him a membership in the Royal Society. In **"Lacinularia Socialis"** he shows that the rotifer—a common microscopic aquatic animal—forms a link between two species not formerly related. In **"On the Development of the Teeth,"** he demonstrates the homologues of human teeth. This essay concludes in a characteristically forceful manner: "The true homologues of the teeth in man are, I think, the hairs. As Hildebrandt says, "As the hairs in their bulb (sac), so the Teeth are developed in their capsules' . . . Substitute corneous matter for calcerous, and the Tooth would be a Hair. The cortical substance of the hair contains canals not unlike those of the dentine; its relation to a dermal papilla is the same as that of the dentine . . . Hairs and teeth, then, are organs in all respects homologous, and true dermal organs. Under the same category, probably, will come Feathers and Scales of fishes" (*Memoirs,* I, 239). In its balanced structure, its injunctive emphasis on what to see in a given anatomical feature, and its deft use of authority and example, this passage reflects Huxley's mature expression as well as his ability to perceive and articulate important comparisons. Employed to achieve the mundane purposes of clarifying an aspect of human anatomy, this passage has little of the stunning insight or wide-ranging persuasive power of the comparisons in **"On a Piece of Chalk,"** but it does indicate the way in which Huxley learned to exercise his analytical and comparative powers of observation and expression. This passage, too, shows that it is really misleading to call Huxley's mode "analogical," for Huxley himself, in **"Lacinularia Socialis,"** distinguishes between the analysis and comparison of homologous organs and the discovery of "mere analogies" or "superficial" resemblances between the rotifers and the polyzoa to which previous scientists had linked it. Huxley scorns the looser, merely classificatory concept of analogy as William Sharp MacLeay and other earlier natural historians had used it. Huxley's observation and subsequent practice show, even more forcefully than his later assertion to that effect, that imagination is a component of scientific, as much as it is of literary, creativity. The concept of homologous organs is after all, founded on the ability to perceive similarities. The discovery of "true homologues"—as Huxley's sometimes revolutionary classifications demonstrate—implies the ability to see essential similarities of anatomy or structure. In this light the poet's purely "ornamental" analogies are deficient only because they depend on the perception of random, subjective comparisons. Perception of homologous features and expression of genuinely revelatory poetic "analogies," however, require the ability to perceive and articulate essential similarities.

Huxley's polemical inductive-deductive method manifests itself early in his career in his incisive use of Mill's Canons.[12] This technique appears with particular prominence in a review essay, **"The Cell-Theory,"** published in 1853. In this essay Huxley weighs the competing theories of Theodor Schwann and Caspar Friedrich Wolff as to cell structure and function and concludes, after rigorous inductive argument, that: "We have failed to discover any satisfactory evidence that the endoplast, once formed, exercises any attractive, metamorphic, or metastatic force upon the periplast, and we have therefore maintained the broad doctrine established by Wolff, that the vital phenomena are not necessarily preceded by organization, nor are in any way the result or effect of formal parts, but that the faculty of manifesting them resides in the matter of which living beings are composed, as such— or, to use the language of the day, that the 'vital forces' are molecular forces" (***Memoirs,*** I, 277). Having thoroughly examined and weighed the evidence for Schwann's theory of cell function, Huxley confidently rejects its assertion of some immaterial "force" operating in cells, and thus anticipates **"On the Physical Basis of Life"** in which he affirms a purely molecular explanation of the cell's functioning. The later essay, in turn, anticipates the later development of Huxley's "mechanistic" explanation of mental processes.

Particularly interesting in light of Huxley's conclusion was the way his statement of principle earlier in the essay wedded logical and imaginative faculties. "In biology," he says, "as in all the more complicated branches of inquiry, progress can only be made by a careful combination of the deductive methods with the inductive, and by bringing the powerful aid of the imagination, kept of course, in due and rigid subordination, to assist the faculties of observation and reasoning; and there are periods in the history of every science when a false hypothesis is not only better than none at all, but is a necessary forerunner of, and preparation for, the true one" (***Memoirs,*** I, 248-249). The importance of this admission, that imagination and error are essential to scientific discovery, deserves careful examination. The passage implies two rather modern notions of scientific method. The first, that scientists make use of imagination, has become a truism since the advent of modern physics and astrophysics. The second, that wrong hypotheses are better than no hypotheses, is a striking feature of recent research in the history and philosophy of science (Weimer, "Science," p. 5). Huxley tacitly acknowledges that scientific investigation needs the context which a theory provides. The facts to which Huxley was always adverting are not, in themselves, significant. As perceptual and gestalt psychologists have shown, what a person believes or expects is constitutive of what he or she actually perceives. For the purposes of coherent scientific investigation, then, Huxley assumed the theory he was testing in order to analyze the theory in the light of what the facts could confirm or deny. To understand the place of the rotifers in the order of living beings, he needed a Linnaean classification, even an inaccurate one. To come to an understanding of the specific parts and functions of the cell, he must have a theory of cell vitalism or other organizing hypothesis which could then be tested and—as in the case of Schwann—rejected.

For our purposes, Huxley's statement is important in one further way. With a principle of developmental to explore, Huxley can test and retest its applicability on a number of specific examples, from the common horse to the coalfields of Bradford. It is Huxley's later adoption of the evolutionary hypothesis which makes possible the brilliant popular scientific lectures. Each essay is an attempt to extend the applicability of the hypothesis by means of rigorous inductive and deductive reasoning, imaginatively linked by complex comparisons of process and morphology to the objects of earlier research.

II

If the conventions which Huxley employed in his scientific essays included technical description, the survey of research, argumentation, and a keen comparative sense, the classroom and the lecture hall taught him a sense of audience, impressed upon him the importance of clear logical structure, and accentuated the tendency to vivid description and apt analogy. In his lectures and periodical essays, Huxley began to define a persona and an audience upon which he could rely as he began to explore with the educated Victorian reader the intricacies of nineteenth-century biological thought.

Huxley gave his first important public lecture at the Royal Institution in 1852, "before the best audience in London" and revelled in the chance to have stood "in the place of Faraday."[13] In 1854 he began teaching in London at the Government School of Mines, Jermyn Street. In a surprisingly short time, he had become astute in assessing and adjusting to the knowledge of his audiences, and skilled in the various conventional arrangements of lecture material. He notes as early as 1854 that his audiences of working men stimulate his efforts, saying they "are as attentive and as intelligent as the best audience I have ever lectured to. . . . I have studiously avoided the impertinence of talking down to them."[14] In an early lecture like **"On the Educational Value of the Natural History Sciences"** (1854), we can see the adaptation of Huxley's scientific attitude and style to the level of knowledge and the expectations of his audience.

The introductory partition of **"On the Educational Value of the Natural History Sciences"** exemplifies the obvious structure of his early popular essays:

Regarding Physiological Science, then, in its widest sense—as the equivalent of *Biology*—the Science of Individual Life—we have to consider in succession:

1. Its position and scope as a branch of knowledge.

2. Its value as a means of mental discipline.

3. Its worth as practical information.

And lastly,

4. At what period it may best be made a branch of Education.

(***Essays,*** III, 38-39).

He then contrasts what different phenomena the physicist or chemist observes when a lump of gold is dropped in water to what "the student of life" sees when a microscopic Euglena is placed in the same vessel of water. The exemplary comparison, which reads like a highly simplified experiment, leads Huxley to conclude that "whatever forms the Living Being may take on, whether simple or complex, *production, growth, reproduction* are the phenomena which distinguish it from that which does not live" (***Essays,*** III, 44). Huxley acknowledges this "totally new order of facts" but goes on to demonstrate painstakingly, by the canons of logic,

that the methods and results of biological science are exactly comparable to those in other sciences. He founds his method on more accurate and precise application of common sense, clinching his statement of principle with the first of a long line of military figures which occur in his collected essays: "Science is, I believe, nothing but *trained and organized common sense,* differing from the latter only as a veteran may differ from a raw recruit: and its methods differ from those of common sense only so far as the guardsman's cut and thrust differ from the manner in which a savage wields his club" (***Essays,*** III, 45).

The remainder of the lecture fulfills the other three partitions, closing with a stirring peroration that summarizes the effects of not teaching science; effects carefully coordinated with the four headings under which he began the lecture. **"On the Educational Value of the Natural History Sciences"** manifests a rigidly logical form, replete with argument, example, refutation, and perorational flourish. With many of the early essays, however, it suggests at least implicitly that Huxley's sense of an audience and its expectations has still not been honed as sharply as it will be by the 1860s. The deficiency may be explained by Huxley's vacillating between writing to an imagined general audience and addressing a real and therefore more particularized and stimulating audience. Even as late as 1859 and 1860, while defending Darwin's *Origin of Species in The Times* and the *Westminster Review,* he demonstrates a rather crude, highly oratorical sense of audience. The result of assuming a generalized audience is sometimes pompous syntax, highly polemical diction, and consequently a somewhat blurred point.

The immediate remedy for this insufficiently refined sense of particular audience came in his series of controversies with Richard Owen. These controversies culminated in Huxley's refutations of Owen in ***Man's Place in Nature***. Owen, representative of the scientific establishment, had denied certain anatomical similarities between human beings and apes, thus denying the implication that Darwin's *Origin of Species* could be applied to human beings. Huxley, the young scientific challenger, sought to extend the application of Darwin's principles. In the process, Huxley refined his own sense of audience by having to deal with a well-informed and antagonistic audience, namely Owen himself. **"On the Zoological Relations of Man with the Lower Animals"** (1861), the first of the scientific memoirs to become part of ***Man's Place in Nature,*** effectively refutes Owen's conclusions about human cerebral structure (see di Gregorio's summary, *Huxley's Place,* pp. 136-139). He points out Owen's errors in classification, anatomy, and consequently refutes Owen's conclusions about physical anthropology. The essay is characterized by an obvious emphasis on clear logical structure and the usual detailed examination of specific homologues and general structural similarities in men and apes. Huxley answers objections, and he introduces a number of powerful rhetorical effects. Most notable is the famous "clay modeller" metaphor (*Essays,* VII, 85) which poetically implies a shaping force behind nature, like that in the writings of David Hume, and which distracts the general audience's attention from Huxley's otherwise rather obvious materialism.

Huxley almost literally took this anti-Owenist argument into the streets. He first delivered a course on anthropology for working men; then he delivered a lecture in Edinburgh on the **"Relations of Man to the Lower Animals"** (di Gregorio, *Huxley's Place,* p. 138). When he published **Man's Place in Nature** in 1863, he acknowledged the importance of the controversies and the help that his various audiences had given him. In the preface to **Man's Place in Nature** he says: "Some experience in popular lecturing had convinced me that the necessity of making things plain to uninstructed people, was one of the very best means of clearing up the obscure corners in one's own mind. So, in 1860, I took the Relation of Man to the Lower Animals, for the subject of the six lectures to working men which it was my duty to deliver. It was also in 1860, that this topic was discussed before a jury of experts, at the meeting of the British Association at Oxford" (*Essays,* VII, ix). In the advertisement to **Man's Place in Nature,** Huxley also uses his audience's response as proof of his argument's clarity, saying that "the readiness with which my audience followed my arguments, on these occasions, encourages me to hope that I have not committed the error, into which working men in science so readily fall, of obscuring my meaning by unnecessary technicalities" (*Essays,* VII, xv).

Despite these obvious indications that Huxley had refined his sense of audience in controversy with Owen, a final proof of his as yet not fully developed sense of a specific reading public was his investment of time and energy in the *Natural History Review.* This periodical, which he founded, saw the first publication of **"On the Zoological Relations of Man with the Lower Animals"** and other anthropological essays, but it scarcely outlived the furor of the Huxley-Owen debates. After the demise of the *Natural History Review,* Huxley returned to publishing his popular and polemical scientific essays in the standard middle-range and upper-range Victorian periodicals, using now one forum and now another to make his point and keep his message before different facets of the Victorian reading public.

III

Whatever the rigidities and flaws of his early rhetorical approach, by 1861 Huxley was well on the way to developing the right sense of audience, and with that discovery he found the first of a variety of more innovative ways to select and arrange his material. From

the thorough exposition and careful definition of its exordium to the reasoned distinction of its partition of the biological sciences, **"A Lobster: or, the Study of Zoology,"** respects its audience's intelligence as it gently defines the conventional role which the audience is to assume. By invoking these initial conventions, Huxley "creates" an audience along roughly classical lines. He establishes a contract with his audience for a fairly conventional logical structure and a fairly conventional mode of response. When he formally introduces the exemplary lobster, however, Huxley transforms his audience into something like a biology class. But because the lobster itself—like the horse, the coal, the yeast, or the oyster of later essays—is so much a part of the audience's everyday world, Huxley also manages to sustain a sense in which the audience is merely an alert but otherwise ordinary observer: "Let us turn away then from abstract definitions. Let us take some concrete living thing, some animal, the commoner the better, and let us see how the application of common sense and common logic to the obvious facts it presents, inevitably leads us into all these branches of zoological science" (*Essays,* VIII, 199-200). Here Huxley proposes to illustrate the important principles of common sense and logic that he had presented virtually without example in **"On the Educational Value of the Natural History Sciences."** As a result of the changed strategy, however, he creates in the remainder of the lecture what turns out to be a consciously designed model of the pedagogical form he is endorsing. From the moment that Huxley states: "I have before me a lobster," he is imitating the scientist doing science, in the conventional situation of the classroom laboratory demonstration. He merges the injunctive mode (Weimer, "Science," pp. 11-13) of scientific writing and teaching with the more mimetic and hortatory mode of the public lecturer.

As we would expect of what is still a relatively early essay, the examination of the lobster's anatomy and physiology follows a clear pattern to an equally predictable and characteristic conclusion. The steps of the examination are exactly those outlined in **"On the Educational Value of the Natural History Sciences"**: observation, comparison, classification, and deduction. Only the relative proportion of injunctive technical description and striking comparisons has increased. The resoundingly general conclusion, that "unity of plan everywhere lies hidden under the mask of diversity of structure," (*Essays,* VIII, 206) has been reached as a culmination of an injunctive and presumed communal effort of observation, analysis, and comparison. In this guided tour of the lobster, Huxley has conveyed both the ease and the arduousness which attend scientific discovery. It is rhetorically significant, too, that Huxley chose a subject with a mixture of strangeness and familiarity. The alien, almost prehistoric appearing crustacean is still a part of the audience's experience. Furthermore, it exhibits an easily analyzed and pictured bilateral symmetry. Huxley's articulation of the lobster's symmetrical structure mixes the straightforwardness of the scientist with something like the legerdemain of the performer.

"The Lobster" presents a clear and more developed model of Huxley's oratorical structure than any of his earlier pieces. Those who wish to evaluate it according to a strict standard of Aristotelian argument will find that the essay employs all but one of the most discretionary parts, the narration.[15] Even refutation is present, though not in the prescribed position. Yet while it is exemplary of many of Huxley's popular scientific lectures, **"The Lobster"** is not the only or even the best example of Huxley's later work. Its clarity, vividness, and immediacy are characteristic. The underlying scientific principles anticipate such famous essays as **"On a Piece of Chalk," "Yeast,"** and **"The Formation of Coal."** But the overtness and conventionality of the essay's pedagogic method are perhaps too prominent for the essay to be taken as the sole model for the later scientific and philosophical lectures.

As a second example, then, I would like to re-examine briefly the essay with which the late Walter Houghton initiated modern academic analysis of Huxley's style.[16] The lay sermon, **"On the Advisableness of Improving Natural Knowledge"** (1866), is a *tour de force;* its exaggeration and its insinuation are both illuminating and characteristic of Huxley's work from **"The Cell-Theory"** to the *Westminster Review* essay, **"The Origin of Species."** The peasant woman metaphor, too, is astounding in the way it envisions science, using a significant strain of Romantic imagery (Houghton, "The Rhetoric," p. 166). But the essay is also paradigmatic in more important, structural ways.

The purpose of **"On the Advisableness of Improving Natural Knowledge"** is essentially that of **"On the Educational Value of the Natural History Sciences."** Its methods, on the other hand, are in sharp contrast to the 1854 essay. Its subject matter combines features of the more purely educational essays like **"Science and Culture"** with those of the popular scientific lectures. Its rhetorical structure is more innovative and difficult to follow (at least for the casual auditor) than **"The Lobster."** As such it engages the reader in a way more complex and more characteristic of later essays.

Huxley defends the proposition that "the improvement of natural knowledge, whatever direction it has taken, and however low the aims of those who may have commenced it—[sic] has not only conferred practical benefits on men, but, in so doing, has effected a revolution in their conceptions of the universe and of themselves, and has profoundly altered their modes of thinking and their views of right or wrong" (*Essays,* I, 31). The remainder of the essay develops the clear but more subtly stated partitions implicit in this thesis. How-

ever, what occurs in the thirteen or so pages before the statement of purpose marks this essay as an important innovation, combining as it does the persuasive techniques of the prose essayist and the logical techniques of the scientific expositor.

Huxley omits a formal exordium and opens with a narration which in its evocation of place and immediacy of focus brings the London plague and fire of 1664-1666 vividly before the audience:

> This time two hundred years ago—in the beginning of January, 1666—those of our forefathers who inhabited this great and ancient city, took breath between the shocks of two fearful calamities: one not quite past, although its fury had abated; the other to come.

> Within a few yards of the very spot on which we are assembled, so the tradition runs, that painful and deadly malady, the plague, appeared in the latter months of 1664; and, though no new visitor, smote the people of England, and especially of her capitol, with a violence unknown before, in the course of the following year.
>
> (*Essays,* I, 18).

He follows this sketch with a more subdued recital of the founding of the Royal Society "some twenty years before" the plague. The purpose of this juxtaposition is to dramatize the different explanations that the ordinary seventeenth-century citizen and the scientist might give of calamities such as the plague and the fire. He first presents the ordinary, religious, view of the events: "Our forefathers had their own ways of accounting for each of these calamities. They submitted to the plague in humility and in penitence, for they believed it to be the judgment of God" (*Essays,* I, 19). This view he contrasts with that of an at first anonymous, prophetic view: "It would, I fancy, have fared but ill with one who, standing where I now stand . . . should have broached to our ancestors the doctrine which I now propound to you—that all their hypotheses were alike wrong; that the plague was no more, in their sense, Divine judgment, than the fire was the work of any political, or of any religious, sect; but that they were themselves the authors of both plague and fire" (*Essays,* I, 20). This exaggerated and moralistic version of the modern scientific view then affords a subtle transition to the story of the founding of the Royal Society. The whole technique of the opening is actually an innovative adaptation of a conventional feature in Huxley's scientific papers. The conventional historical survey of wrong hypotheses becomes here a skillful and purposeful recounting of two divergent histories, two divergent explanations of the same natural events. A similar technique occurs in **"The Cell-Theory," "On the Natural History of the Man-like Apes,"** and **"On Some Fossil Remains of Man."** In the later essays like **"On the Study of Biology,"** the convention often solidifies into a mere history of modern science from Descartes to Darwin. But even at its most conventional, this imaginative use of the *narratio* has the effect of re-interpreting the audience's world in the same way that the striking juxtaposition of religious and scientific world-views revises the 1866 audience's interpretation of the plague. Huxley dramatizes the difference, made possible by a spirit symbolized in the Royal Society, which an advance in natural knowledge has made: "We have learned that pestilences will only take up their abode among those who have prepared unswept and ungarnished residences for them. Their cities must have narrow, unwatered streets, foul with accumulated garbage. Their houses must be ill-drained, ill-lighted, ill-ventilated. Their subjects must be ill-washed, ill-fed, ill-clothed. The London of 1665 was such a city" (***Essays,*** I, 27). The powerful anaphora of the middle three sentences, aided by the injunctive syntax—here raised to an ironic imperative—drives home a sense of the real causes which modern science has discovered.

The further uses of narrative technique in this essay confirm the extent to which Huxley has hit upon a truly innovative technique. After stating the proposition, Huxley retells the progress of natural knowledge from "when the savage first learned that the fingers of one hand are fewer than those of both" to the founding of mathematics, astronomy, physics, and medicine, including religion as another important construct of the human mind (***Essays,*** I, 32, 35-38). Recounting the development of these sciences, Huxley presents a further series of comparisons meant to create a parallel sense of the immensity of the macrocosm and the minute complexity of the microcosm. This impression has the effect of re-interpreting the audience's normal, historical sense of the world's development. In describing the advances of astronomy, for instance, Huxley concludes by depicting the heavens as space "filled by an infinitely subtle matter whose particles are seething and surging, like the waves of an angry sea; which opens up to us infinite regions where nothing is known, or ever seems to have been known, but matter and force, operating according to rigid rules" (***Essays,*** I, 35). In the discussion of medicine, on the other hand, Huxley notes that:

> If the astronomer has set before us the infinite magnitude of space, and the practical eternity of the duration of the universe . . . the workers in biology have not only accepted all these, but have added more startling theses of their own. For, as the astronomers discover in the earth no centre of the universe, but an eccentric speck, so the naturalists find man to be no centre of the living world, but one amidst endless modifications of life; and as the astronomer observes the mark of practically endless time set upon the arrangements of the solar system so the student of life finds the records of ancient forms of existence peopling the world for ages, which, in relation to human experience, are infinite.
>
> (***Essays,*** I, 37-38).

These increasingly schematic and truncated instances of narrative technique, combined with Huxley's descriptive powers, transform a normal sense of human history into an ever more impersonalized and abstract "history" of the world's development. From the causes of the plague to the knowledge of stars, and cells, and the origin of species, the picture of the world becomes increasingly logical, interpretable as the results of the operation of "rigid laws." In the process, man's own experience of himself and his history becomes alien, and distorted by the immense expanses of time which Huxley asks the audience to imagine.[17] In the structure of **"On The Advisableness of Improving Natural Knowledge,"** this three-fold narrative re-interpretation of the Victorian audience's world is both condition and confirmation of the thesis that natural knowledge has "effected a revolution in their [human beings'] conception of the universe and of themselves." The narrative techniques are rhetorical in the narrowest sense, seeking by arrangement as well as mode to persuade the audience as it appeals simultaneously to reason, imagination, and emotion.

IV

From this analysis, the nature and stages of development in Huxley's rhetoric should be fairly clear. All that remains is to show how Huxley employed this rhetoric in a specific aspect of the debate over evolutionist research and the conclusions drawn from that research. In doing so, we shall also see how the periodical context of debate defined issues, further shaped Huxley's rhetoric, and determined the field of battle for the next decade and more. If we also take Huxley's part in the mind-matter debate as representative of how some scientific ideas were transmitted and transformed in the Victorian dialogue over evolutionary principles, we learn a good deal about that process. Stated succinctly, Huxley popularized scientific ideas by imposing new and persuasive interrelationships among some keywords that were part of popular discussion. In the mind-matter debate specifically, he adopted current senses of "matter," "force," and "law" and sought to relate them to the realm of "knowledge," "feeling," and "action," Huxley sought to explain current notions of "molecular force" by applying them to ever wider areas.

Huxley's part in the mind-matter debate may be precisely the special case necessary to isolate Huxley the polemicist and "educationalist crusader" (di Gregorio, *Huxley's Place,* p. 197) from Huxley the scientist. Such a distinction may further separate and help highlight a few of the closely intertwined strands of his variegated career at the same time it clarifies his relation to the popularizations of science and philosophy taking place in the periodicals of the time. When Huxley joined battle with critics of **"On the Physical Basis of Life,"** his purely scientific interests lay in a direction other than the relation of brain function to thought. He was, in fact, engaged in showing how Darwinian principles explained the development of the dinosaurs, and in discovering the genealogy of primitive birds, two tasks for which he is still given considerable credit in scientific circles. His bibliography during these years reflects the rather sharp distinction of interests. Papers on birds and dinosaurs appear in such places as *The Proceedings of the Zoological Society*. His contributions to the mind-matter debate, on the other hand, appear in the more popular *Contemporary Review* and *Macmillan's Magazine* (see di Gregorio, *Huxley's Place,* chap. 3, and his bibliography of Huxley's writings, pp. 213-214).

When in his November 1868 lecture in Edinburgh, **"On the Physical Basis of Life,"** Huxley asserted that "the thoughts to which I am now giving utterance . . . are the expression of molecular changes in that matter of life which is the source of all our other vital phenomena" (*Essays*, I, 154), he was not uttering a revolutionary idea, even for the journal-reading audience of the time. The prominent psychologist, Alexander Bain, had sought to summarize the relation of "matter, force and law" in a review-article that referred, in turn, to Dr. Frankland's Royal Institute lectures of 1866.[18] The thrust of Bain's argument was to distinguish the different kinds of force, mechanical force, molecular force, "vital force," and "nerve force," and relate them in terms of "the doctrine called the Correlating Persistence, Equivalence, Transmutability, and Indestructability of Force" (Bain, "Correlation," pp. 372, 373). Bain's essay was published in the same month that John Tyndall delivered a lecture on "Matter and Force" to the "Working-Men of Dundee."[19] In his essay, Tyndall too relied upon the relatively recent notion of the conservation of energy.

Huxley's essay, subsequently published in the *Fortnightly Review,* evoked a storm of criticism that earlier essays on similar topics had not. Many of these criticisms appeared in one of the more important philosophically inclined quarterlies of the time, the *Contemporary Review.* The rejoinders to Huxley, some of the most significant ones from fellow-members of the recently formed Metaphysical Society, specified the terms of the mind-matter debate.[20] To this somewhat select audience and their general position Huxley addressed his responses in the next four to five years. The terms of the debate were relatively simple. Huxley argued that mind and its operations, including volition, were explicable in terms of brain function, "molecular changes," or what we might call mechanistic causes. The opponents: liberal, clerical, and philosophical, argued that man and particularly his will were unique. To defend his position, Huxley became a philosophical polemicist and used his intellectual powers and the various periodical forums familiar to him to argue his position.

From 1869 into the mid-1870s he waged a strenuous battle in the periodical press. In this battle he focused his attack and enlarged the field of engagement in a way uncharacteristic of his publication record before or after this period. His topics became the scientific outlook generally and the mind-matter debate specifically. In these years he also extended his appeal—one must conclude it was deliberate—from the intellectually high level of journalism in the quarterly and monthly reviews like the *Contemporary* and the *Fortnightly* to the liberal "middle-range" journalism of the magazines and weeklies. He wrote to the middle classes, the magazine and review readers, as he remained aware of attackers in the *Contemporary* and elsewhere. He spoke to the YMCA in Cambridge, made after-dinner speeches, addressed the British Association, and debated in the Metaphysical Society, defending the materialistic interpretation of mind that had stirred readers and hearers of "On the Physical Basis of Life." While purporting to speak to working-class audiences (witness the titles of his published **Lectures for Working Men** and **Science Lectures for the People**) and casual lay readers—like those at his after-dinner speeches—as well as self-improving audiences like the YMCA and the British Association, he really assumed and targeted a largely middle-class liberal audience.

Because some critics might argue that Huxley began his educationalist crusade before **"On the Physical Basis of Life,"** I shall, before continuing to examine the mind-matter debate itself, digress briefly to discuss the "Clergy and Science" debate. This lesser controversy precedes the greater debate, but by 1870 the greater argument over mind and matter had absorbed the terms and issues of the earlier argument, and had amalgamated the audiences of both. Yet, at its inception, the audience and the chosen forum of discussion for this lesser debate, too, contribute to our knowledge of Huxley's polemical method and the ways in which he at all times kept his message before as broad and yet as specific an audience as possible.

In **"Scientific Education: Notes of an After-Dinner Speech"** (1869), Huxley argues the usefulness of a knowledge of matter and force and scientific law. He notes that even clerics should have such scientific knowledge (*Essays,* III, 118). As a matter of fact, this essay is replete with evidence that Huxley is contributing to an on-going debate on the merits of teaching clerics the fundamentals of science. This on-going debate is one which appeared in the *Contemporary Review* under the general title, "Clergy and Science," from 1867 to 1869. Huxley's **"Scientific Education: Notes of an After-Dinner Speech,"** published in *Macmillan's Magazine,* is a response to the debate, as was **"A Liberal Education and Where to Find It"** (1868), Huxley's first essay published in *Macmillan's* since a review of Darwin's *Origin of Species* in 1859. Huxley's two magazine articles and the responses in the *Contemporary Review* focus on the advisableness of acquiring natural knowledge, but also upon the possibil-

Huxley at work.

ity of knowing anything about the spiritual world. Huxley's position is clear. He is for clerics having accurate and verifiable natural knowledge. He is less concerned about the other issue. Opponents like John Hannah and E. W. Farrar complain about "a gospel of spiritual nescience" (*Contemporary Review,* 9, [1868], 404) and chafe at the likely effects of the scientists' mechanistic thinking. It is clear from this exchange that Huxley's "educationalist crusade" was already well underway even before he delivered **"On the Physical Basis of Life,"** and that his return to *Macmillan's* before delivery of that lecture was implicitly an attempt to reach an audience which, if it includes later critics in the *Contemporary Review,* is also broader than and was prior to that which included the *Contemporary Review* critics of **"On the Physical Basis of Life."**

Having once reappeared in the pages of *Macmillan's,* this "middle to upper class, Broad Church or even agnostic . . . Liberal" magazine,[21] Huxley made it (with one exception in 1871) the chosen middle-ground forum for the mind-matter debate until 1874. In **"Scientific Education: Notes of an After-Dinner Speech"** (1869), **"On Descartes' 'Discourse on Method'"** (1870), and **"Bishop Berkeley on the Metaphysics of Sensation"** (1871), we see Huxley developing the implica-

tions of **"On the Physical Basis of Life,"** choosing the most advantageous ground as he kept an eye on the arguments of his clerical and philosophical opponents. He also returned to other weeklies for the first time since 1861 (when he had attacked Owen in the *Athenaeum*). Between 1868 and 1874 he published not only in *Macmillan's Magazine,* but in the *Academy, Good Words,* and the newly founded *Nature.*

In all the essays devoted to the mind-matter debate, Huxley played to what G. M. Young, in "The New Cortegiano" has called the "common stock of reference and allusion" of his middle-class reading public.[22] Discoursing in clear, straightforward, but oratorical fashion, he presumed "a certain unitary quality of doing, thinking, and appreciating" that Young has identified as characteristic of the middle range of Victorian journalism at the time (Young, *Daylight,* p. 146). But instead of focusing the audience's curiosity on "what had always been, its most obvious food, the art, the literature, the memorials of the past" (Young, *Daylight,* p. 148), Huxley—as I have already shown—chose instead to emphasize the concepts and discoveries of science, especially those which were verifiable by observation or experiment.

In **"On Descartes' 'Discourse on Method'"** Huxley refers to "matter and force" in a manner familiar from contemporary essays in *Macmillan's.* He uses these mechanistic concepts to reduce the notions of "self" and "voluntary action" to proportions manageable in experimental terms. In **"Bishop Berkeley on the Metaphysics of Sensation,"** he poses the hypothetical case of a human being deprived of all senses except those in the palm of his hand. This supposed case helps him to argue that the sense of self depends upon—if it is not actually constituted by—physical sensation and brain function. In **"Darwin's Critics"** his refutation of St. George Mivart's review of *The Descent of Man*— Huxley's one sally published in the *Contemporary Review*—he relies on the description of another hypothetical experiment to show that "consciousness and molecular action are capable of being expressed by one another, just as heat and mechanical action are capable of being expressed in terms of one another" (***Essays,*** II, 162).[23]

Huxley made his strongest argument in the mind-matter debate when he chose that topic, instead of his old standby, "development" or evolution, for his evening address at the Belfast meeting of the British Association, 24 August 1874. His eleventh hour change of topic is chronicled in Leonard Huxley's ***Life and Letters*** (II, 128-132). **"On the Hypothesis that Animals are Automata and Its History"** clearly acknowledges its debt to earlier essays in the educationalist crusade. It is an extensive revision of a paper read to the Metaphysical Society (**"Has the Frog a Soul, and of What Nature is that Soul, Supposing it to Exist"**). It also incorporates aspects of the YMCA talk on Descartes. Happening upon a real case study of brain-injury such as he had proposed in **"Bishop Berkeley on the Metaphysics of Sensation"** and **"Darwin's Critics,"** he uses this study to question the role of consciousness and the nature of human autonomy. The continued debate over volition, selfhood, and freedom versus necessity which animated discussion in the periodicals through the 1870s and beyond owes at least part of its impetus to Huxley's strenuous engagement with opponents on this occasion. Though Huxley turned to other issues after this essay, he was himself clearly affected by the debate, and his darkening view of nature has generally been taken as a consequence of his metaphysical-psychological speculations.

As interesting as the essay's impact and complex intertextuality are, however, even more important for our purpose is Huxley's concern for the essay's currency. Reports or transcripts of the lecture appeared in no fewer than three places: the *Northern Whig, Nature,* and the *Fortnightly Review.* Huxley personally supervised its first setting up for the *Northern Whig* (***Life and Letters,*** II, 136); he also wrote John Morley, editor of the *Fortnightly,* about publication there (***Life and Letters,*** II, 150). He thus assured the lecture's having a broad professional and lay audience in the weekly and monthly press, in addition to the audience made up of members of the British Association who actually heard the speech in person. After **"On the Hypothesis that Animals are Automata and Its History,"** Huxley's "educationalist crusade" generally took a more pragmatic turn, concentrating on the change of institutions which would make increased, quality scientific education possible. But though he turned from explicit treatment of the mind-matter issue, its defense from 1868 to 1874 had important effects on Huxley's notion of his audience, and on his manner of popularizing more specific though less inflammatory issues in science.

Even from this somewhat selective survey of the mind-matter debate, it becomes evident how Huxley popularized certain current scientific ideas. In the mind-matter debate, he is consciously engaged in exploring and extending the implications that stem from theories concerning the conservation of matter and force, and which were expressed in contemporary references to "molecular" and other "forces" at work in different physical, biological, and even mental phenomena. Adopting the contemporary explanations of "molecular force" applied in physical and chemical contexts to description of biological action, he seeks to counter arguments about "vital forces" (see William Carpenter's 1851 *Manual of Physiology*) and give an exclusively mechanistic cast to his physiological and psychological explanations. For seven years Huxley refined and extended these mechanistic explanations, seeking to make them prevail in the dialogue over mind in matter, and in the arguments over "matter, force, and law" generally. In time he also made deliberate and implicit

use of the already noted experiments with the central nervous system (called "nerve force" in Bain's essay), reports of "alternating consciousness," and speculations about "unconscious cerebration"[24] to find that "mechanical equivalent of consciousness" he had referred to in **"Descartes"** (***Essays,*** I, 191) and which echoed Tyndall's "mechanical equivalent of heat" (Tyndall, "The Constitution of Nature," *Fragments,* p. 28).

In light of the dialogue over "molecular force" and its correlation with mind, **"On the Hypothesis that Animals are Automata"** is only the latest of Huxley's contribution to this transformation and reformulation of the Victorian applications to which "molecular forces" may be put. It is notable for its use of the experimental clinical evidence. It proceeds little further, however, than **"Darwin's Critics"** in its assertion of the central argument. Its contribution to the popularization of scientific ideas is proven, however, by noting the long shadow cast by its central suggestion. "Automatism" as an issue in physiological and psychological discussions of mind occurs from the time of William Carpenter's response to Huxley, right into the 1890s.[25]

In later essays from **"On the Study of Biology"** through **"Science and Culture"** to **"On Oysters and the Oyster Question,"** Huxley continued to offer varied attractions to his audiences. If his essays were not mini-travelogues or mini-encyclopedias, they were histories of science abbreviated to make the most of his polemical point. Among the most strikingly modern of Huxley's methods of proof is the hypothetical argument or example referred to in the mind-matter debate. On a number of occasions he proposes something like the "possible worlds" of the twentieth-century biologist, J. B. S. Haldane, an imaginative construct meant to provide unconventional thinking about alternative consequences of certain kinds of reasoning.[26] From merely imagining what a coral reef would look like were the sea drained from around it,[27] to speculating on the possible sensations of a "rational piano" (***Essays,*** VI, 283-284), Huxley makes use of the quasi-fictional technique that he had used more humorously in the "prophet" and "revenant" figures of **"On the Advisableness of Improving Natural Knowledge"** or the deathwatch beetles speculating on their world in **"The Genealogy of Animals"** (***Essays,*** II, 111-112). In using metaphor, diagram, map, or hypothetical argument, Huxley shows his clear preference for analogical, spatial, and hypothetical techniques. These techniques punctuate the already richly various structure of individual essays and point to a fundamentally imaginative mode of perception and thought which puts the stamp of originality on Huxley's work. But whatever their polemical point, these essays always provide in easily digestible form that "modicum of instruction" that Young sees as proof of the existence of a general level of culture to which Victorian middle-range journalism appealed (Young, *Daylight,* p. 148). Huxley, as di Gregorio observes, had for his part developed a certain "skill in keeping on the right side of his audiences" (di Gregorio, *Huxley's Place,* pp. 188, 189). His audience, in turn, responded positively because of his sense of journalistic decorum and because he provided in some measure what they wanted, and not merely because "his audience held their scientific intelligentsia in esteem."[28]

Paradoxically, Huxley's popular lectures on important scientific and philosophical topics—like protoplasm, materialism, cerebral injury, and the mind-matter controversy generally—also made increasingly imminent the "two cultures" division of the Victorian and modern world. He is responsible with earlier scientists like Sir Humphry Davy, David Faraday, Charles Lyell, Charles Darwin, and John Tyndall for expanding the middle-class public's awareness of and interest in philosophical and scientific issues, and for shrinking it. After him, few if any scientists could move as easily as he through the thickets and thorny pathways of scientific debate, handling difficult issues and still clearly appealing to a general middle-class audience by the clarity, vividness, and forcefulness of argument. Of course the fault was also with increasing readership and declining curiosity. The boosters of the "press terrorists of higher culture" were responsible as well (Young, *Daylight,* p. 151). But with the exception of H. G. Wells and perhaps J. B. S. Haldane—each of whom is clearly situated on Huxley's side of the two cultures barrier—few writers of quality could appeal to both lay audience and specialists.

T. H. Huxley's work represents one of the most significant and enduring Victorian perspectives on humanity's place in nature and society, and on the ways in which the nature of humanity's knowledge and use of language explores, affirms, and creates a coherent sense of that place. In assessing the contribution of his popular scientific essays to developing that perspective, it should be amply clear what they are and what they are not. They are rhetoric in the service of science. While not directly "scientific," they effectively communicate and popularize the findings with the excitement of scientific discovery, imitating as they do the structures and strategies of scientific investigation. They are schematic, selective, and specially organized strategies of persuasion. They are really small paradigms which reflect aspects of an emerging world view. They create the impression of the scientist doing science; they also create an audience that is to conceive of itself as an observer employing only precise and organized common sense. In that double creation is a large part of the essays' persuasive power. They create a coherent scientific world never before so fully or carefully imagined and described in so short a space. Narrative surveys, descriptive density, and rigorous logic effectively diminish the individual human being's sense of self and self-importance. If in Young's view "Mr. [H. G.] Wells has done more than any man to adjust the

modern imagination to the materiality of its framework" (Young, *Daylight,* p. 157), it was Huxley who had in part made the later Victorian imagination vividly aware of this materiality and had drawn out some of the implications for individuals and for society through his popular essays on scientific subjects. Huxley acknowledged that language was merely an interpretation of the facts of nature (***Essays,*** III, 279-282), an inadequate instrument for translating the multitude of impressions which at best only suggest the nature of reality. Yet his essays are effective strategies because through their use of language they successfully re-interpret the world, before the periodical audience's eyes, giving that world greater coherence and solidity. Because of their relation to the prevailing scientific paradigm, these strategies continue to exert their force.

Notes

[1] James G. Paradis, *Man's Place in Nature* (Lincoln: University of Nebraska Press, 1978), and Mario A. di Gregorio, *T. H. Huxley's Place in Natural Science* (New Haven: Yale University Press, 1984). Paradis discusses Huxley's development as an essayist, but his focus is not the rhetorical aspects of Huxley's work by itself.

[2] Charles S. Blinderman, "T. H. Huxley's Theory of Aesthetics: Unity in Diversity," *Journal of Aesthetics and Art Criticism,* 21 (1962), 49, 51.

[3] Loren Eiseley, "Introduction" to *On a Piece of Chalk,* ed. Loren Eiseley (New York: Charles Scribner's Sons, 1967), pp. 10, 12.

[4] Critics have made much of Huxley's acceptance and defense of Darwin's evolutionary hypothesis. Recently, di Gregorio has shown that until the late 1860s Huxley was less an adherent of Darwin than of the German embryologist, K. E. von Baer. I choose to see his adoption of von Baer's and subsequently Darwin's theory as a rhetorical as well as a practical, scientific necessity. Science requires a hypothesis, a paradigm. Until Huxley had an "Archimedean point" from which to interpret all his research, he might have remained little more than a gifted anatomist, taxonomist, or physiologist.

[5] A. Dwight Culler, "Method in the Study of Victorian Prose," *Victorian Newsletter* (1956), pp. 1-4, introduced this useful threefold distinction.

[6] Cyril Bibby, *Scientist Extraordinary* (New York: St. Martin's Press, 1972), chapters 2 and 3.

[7] Joseph Gardner, "A Huxley Essay as Poem," *Victorian Studies,* 14 (1970), 177-191, and Charles S. Blinderman, "Semantic Aspects of T. H. Huxley's Literary Style," *Journal of Communication,* 12 (1962), 177.

[8] Walter B. Weimer, "Science as a Transaction: Toward a Nonjustificational Conception of Rhetoric,"

Philosophy and Rhetoric, 10 (1977), 12. See also Norwood Russell Hanson, "A Picture Theory of Theory Meaning," in *The Nature and Function of Scientific Theories,* ed. Robert G. Colodny (Pittsburgh: University of Pittsburgh Press, 1970), pp. 233-237.

9 T. H. Huxley, *Autobiography in Collected Essays of Thomas Henry Huxley,* 9 vols. (1898; rpt. ed., New York: Greenwood Press, 1968), I, 4; and Bibby, *Scientist Extraordinary,* p. 7).

10 Darwin's famous description, at the conclusion of his *Origin of Species,* in *Darwin,* ed. Philip Appleman, 2d ed. (New York: Norton, 1979), p. 131, is really less vivid than it is merely specific; more an example of process and argument than it is of locale, context, and immediacy. Yet Darwin's descriptive powers continue to attract critical attention while Huxley's receive little notice.

11 T. H. Huxley, *Scientific Memoirs,* 5 vols. (London: Macmillan's, 1898-1903), I, 126.

12 Mill's Canons, the method of agreement, the method of difference, the joint method of agreement and difference, the method of residues, and the method of concomitant variation are treated in J. S. Mill's *System of Logic* (1843) and are summarily explained in the *Dictionary of the History of Science,* ed. W. F. Bynum, E. J. Browne, and Ray Porter (Princeton: Princeton University Press, 1981). p. 269. Huxley probably first learned the use of these logical canons of causation not from the man from whom they get their name, but from Sir Hamilton, one of the more skilled logicians of the early nineteenth century. See Bibby, *Scientist Extraordinary,* p. 51 and Paradis, *Man's Place,* p. 92.

13 Leonard Huxley, *Life and Letters of Thomas Henry Huxley,* 2 vols. (London: Macmillan, 1903), I, 144-145.

14 Quoted in Cyril Bibby, *Thomas Henry Huxley: Scientist, Educator and Humanist* (New York: Horizon Press, 1960), pp. 97-98.

15 Aristotle, *The Works of Aristotle,* ed. W. Rhys Roberts, 11 vols. (Oxford: Clarendon Press, 1946), XI, book III, chap. 14. For another application of Aristotelian rhetorical distinctions to Victorian prose, see Martin J. Svaglic, "Classical Rhetoric and Victorian Prose," in *The Art of Victorian Prose,* ed. George Levine and William Madden (New York: Oxford University Press, 1968), p. 270.

16 Walter Houghton, "The Rhetoric of Thomas Henry Huxley," *University of Toronto Quarterly,* 18 (1948), 161.

17 See Loren Eiseley, *Darwin's Century* (Garden City, New York: Doubleday, 1958), chapters 2 and 3, "The Time Voyagers" and "The Pirate Chart" for an intima-tion of something like this. See also Howard E. Gruber, "Darwin's 'Tree of Nature' and Other Images of Wider Scope," in *On Aesthetics in Science,* ed. Judith Wechsler (Cambridge, Massachusetts: MIT Press, 1978), pp. 121-142.

18 Alexander Bain, "On the Correlation of Force in Its Bearing on Mind," *Macmillan's Magazine* 16 (1867), 372-383.

19 John Tyndall, "Matter and Force," in *Fragments of Science* (New York: D. Appleton, 1875), pp. 71-94.

20 In the replies of John Young, "Professor Huxley and 'On the Physical Basis of Life,'" *Contemporary Review* 11 (1869), 240-263; Henry Calderwood, "Professor Huxley's *Lay Sermons,*" *Contemporary Review,* 15 (1870), 195-207; and "Present Relations of Physical Science and Mental Philosophy," *Contemporary Review,* 16 (1871), 225-238; Charles Pritchard, "Spectrum Analysis," *Contemporary Review,* 11 (1869), 481-490; Alfred Barry, "The Battle of Philosophies: Physical and Metaphysical," *Contemporary Review,* 12 (1869), 232-244; and Anon., "Nature Development and Philosophy," *Contemporary Review,* 14 (1870), 173-191, the issues became not merely molecular force and relation of organic and inorganic (Pritchard, p. 487) but the effects of Huxley's views on the emerging "philosophy of mind" (Barry, p. 239) and the place of design and volition (Anon., pp. 184, 186) in the physiology and psychology of human affairs.

21 Alvar Ellegård, *The Readership of the Periodical Press in Mid-Victorian Britain* (Goteborg, Sweden: Goteborgs Universitets Arsskrift, 1957), p. 34.

22 G. M. Young, *Daylight and Champagne* (London: Jonathan Cape, 1937), p. 145.

23 T. H. Huxley, "Darwin's Critics," *Contemporary Review,* 18 (1871), 443-476 responds to St. George Mivart's "Descent of Man," *Quarterly Review,* 131 (1871), 47-90.

24 Frances Power Cobbe and the renowned physiologist, W. B. Carpenter, exchanged views on "unconscious cerebration" and its relation to human freedom in the pages of *Macmillan's Magazine* and the *Contemporary Review:* Frances Power Cobbe, "Unconscious Cerebration," *Macmillan's Magazine,* 23 (1870), 24-37, 512-523; W. B. Carpenter, "The Physiology of the Will," *Contemporary Review,* 17 (1871), 192-217.

25 Among contributions to the "automatism" and "two-minds" debate are the following: R. A. Proctor, "Have We Two Brains," *Cornhill Magazine,* 31 (1875), 149-166, and "Dual Consciousness," *Cornhill Magazine,* 35 (1877), 86-105; George Henry Lewes, "Conscious and Unconscious," *Mind,* 2 (1877), 157-167; C. E.

Brown Sequard, "Have We Two Brains or One," *Forum,* 9 (1890), 627-643; Max Dessoir, "The Magic Mirror," *Monist,* 1 (1890), 87-117; R. Meade Bache, "The Question of Duality of Mind," *Monist,* 1 (1891), 362-371; and A. Seth, "The New Psychology and Automatism," *Contemporary Review,* 63 (1893), 555-574. George Croom Robertson, editor of *Mind,* reports on an article, "Double Consciousness with Periodic Loss of Memory," by M. Azam, *Revue Scientifique* (20 May 1876) in *Mind,* 1 (1876), 414-416, 553. He also reports on an article, "Double Memory," by M. Dufay in *Revue Scientifique* (15 July 1876) in *Mind,* 1 (1876), 552-553.

[26] J. B. S. Haldane, *Possible Worlds* (London: Chatto and Windus, 1927), pp. 260-286. Perhaps the original for all such suppositions is Descartes' own supposition of an evil spirit deluding the human senses in his *Meditations on First Philosophy* (1641).

[27] T. H. Huxley, "On Coral and Coral Reefs," in *Critiques and Addresses* (New York: D. Appleton, 1873), p. 121.

[28] Peter Morton, *The Vital Science: Biology and the Literary Imagination, 1860-1900* (London: George Allen and Unwin, 1984), p. 43.

James Paradis (essay date 1989)

SOURCE: "*Evolution and Ethics* in its Victorian Context," in *Evolution & Ethics: T. H. Huxley's Evolution and Ethics, With New Essays on its Victorian and Sociobiological Context,* Princeton University Press, 1989, pp. 3-55.

[*In this essay, Paradis discusses the social and political implications of Huxley's "Prolegomena" and "Evolution and Ethics."*]

In the summer of 1892, three years before his death, an ailing T. H. Huxley wrote the celebrated lecture **"Evolution and Ethics,"** which he delivered at Oxford University the afternoon of May 18, 1893. The lecture, together with the **"Prolegomena,"** an introductory essay completed in June of 1894, set traditional humanistic values in direct conflict with the physical realities revealed by nineteenth-century science. The forces of nature, seen by Huxley in terms of powerful material and instinctual laws, were poised, he now argued, against civilization and the future of humanity.

Huxley built his two essays on a domestic foundation, using a wealth of autobiographical themes and images. The struggle against odds, the need for self-restraint, the summoning of courage to strip off the veil of nature and remove the garment of make-believe, all lifelong personal themes, were transformed in the manner of

Montaigne into dimensions of the human condition. Willingly or not, we are all controversialists in a transitory universe:

> The more we learn of the nature of things, the more evident is it that what we call rest is only unperceived activity; that seeming peace is silent but strenuous battle. In every part, at every moment, the state of the cosmos is the expression of a transitory adjustment of contending forces; a scene of strife, in which all the combatants fall in turn. (p. 49)

Here, in the depths of the aging Huxley's dynamism, lies a symbol of the Victorian age itself, like Huxley, tottering at the edge of the abyss its science had so irrevocably revealed. This sense of peril is reflected in the images of the colony that Huxley used in his two essays to characterize the polity, civilization, and England itself.

The prolific garden imagery of the **"Prolegomena"** had an origin in Huxley's recent occupation of a small house, Hodeslea, he had built for his retirement on the windswept chalk downs above the sea at Eastbourne, a fitting outpost for the author of **"On a Piece of Chalk"** (1868). Gardening had become, along with controversy, his occupation, leading him to cite Voltaire's Candide as his own—and civilized man's—proper spiritual mentor; "Cultivons notre jardin" (Huxley 1892, 564). The wall of civilization inscribing the artificial world that Huxley described in the **"Prolegomena"** had its physical analogue in his own garden wall; he wrote that out his study window beyond his garden he could see the "state of nature" to which all was destined eventually to return. These personal images gave Huxley's essays the intensity and clarity that moved Leslie Stephen at a meeting of the Huxley Memorial Committee to place Huxley among the greatest of English prose artists (Stephen 1895).

It is well to recall that Huxley wrote *Evolution and Ethics* at a time when it was not clear what role, if any, the forces of science had to play in the framing of social policy—a peculiarly modern ambiguity. As Burrow (1966), Young (1985), and Stocking (1987) have shown, writers like Herbert Spencer and Walter Bagehot had broadly integrated popular biology and contemporary anthropology with social argument, often through the vehicles of comparison and metaphor. At the same time, the natural sciences had undermined many traditional cultural assumptions concerning the natural order, causing politicians, clergy, and intellectuals alike to reexamine the sources of social, intellectual, and moral authority (Manier 1978; Moore 1979).

This search for authority was not merely academic. Voting suffrage, extended first to urban laborers and then to miners and farm laborers in the Second and Third Reform Bills of 1867 and 1884, had dramatically expanded the English electorate and redistributed political power. In addition, as Steadman Jones has demonstrated (1971), London in the 1880s and 1890s was a scene of cyclic economic depression attended by great poverty and social unrest. If the century had been "predominantly a history . . . of emancipation, political, economical, social, moral, intellectual," as William Gladstone observed soon after resigning his fourth premiership in March of 1893, that same emancipation, he added, was opening "a period possibly of yet greater moral dangers; certainly a great ordeal for those classes which are now becoming largely conscious of power, and never heretofore subjected to its deteriorating influences" (Reid 1899, 2:732). This sense that new social forces had been unleashed was felt throughout British society.

Huxley, Gladstone, and their aging contemporaries saw the social speculation of the time as competing for the hearts and minds of the emerging voters. A great variety of radical political movements had asserted themselves, each with its unique program and future: Henry Hyndman's Social Democratic Federation, General William Booth's Salvation Army, Fabian socialism, Henry George's Single Land Tax movement, Francis Galton and Karl Pearson and the Eugenics movement. Books published in the years leading up to Huxley's *Evolution and Ethics* included Arnold Toynbee's *The Industrial Revolution* (1884), the English edition of Friedrich Engels's *The Condition of the Working-Class in England* (1892), the second edition of Galton's *Hereditary Genius* (1892), George's *Progress and Poverty* (1877-79), General Booth's *In Darkest England* (1890), Edward Bellamy's *Looking Backward: 1888-2000* (1888), and Spencer's *Principles of Ethics* (1892-93), not to mention William Gladstone's *Impregnable Rock of Holy Scripture* (1890)—all works considering the values and measures that might secure the future of society. This bookish activism, avidly followed by Huxley, had its social counterpart in the atmosphere of conflict in London in the 1880s and 1890s, the years of economic instability that witnessed the 1886 Riot, Bloody Sunday (1887), and the Dock Strike (1889), as well as innumerable lesser social tremors and the vast political controversy over Irish Home Rule.

In the most important study to date of the social context of Huxley's *Evolution and Ethics,* Michael Helfand has rightly argued that Huxley, struck by the radical political agitation of the 1880s and 1890s, had an overt political motivation for writing the two essays. Helfand, however, has constructed an elaborate texture of "hidden" intention that makes Huxley over into a repressive partisan of the status quo. Against formidable intellectual evidence to the contrary, Helfand is obliged to argue an externalist thesis that Huxley's "real" view of contemporary society was actually a "disguised" Spencerian laissez-faire dynamic of struggle for existence (Helfand 1977, 160-61). Huxley's motivation under this interpretation was to defend an en-

trenched middle class against the rising working classes and their anti-imperialist champions, Henry George and Alfred Wallace. This conspiratorial thesis of class conflict, aside from giving more political unity and credibility to Huxley's opponents than is perhaps justified, is too reductive for an individual of Huxley's experience and complexity.

To be sure, Huxley, formerly a middle-class administrator in London, was dismayed by the social volatility of contemporary London, which seemed to him to threaten the institutions that protected society from anarchy. A recognized reformer, Huxley was also a social realist who had spent innumerable hours on public commissions and institutional committees. As a practitioner familiar with the demands of social change, he saw social stability as the condition of social amelioration. Revolution in the cause of speculative political theory went against Huxley's most fundamental convictions and training. His opposition to groups of radicals, from anarchists and Salvation Army members to eugenicists, was a protest against the exotic utopian character of their programs. His objections in earlier essays to the sweeping anti-Malthusianism of George's *Progress and Poverty* had been much more elaborately articulated in Toynbee's widely-known criticisms of George in *The Industrial Revolution.*

In an essay on Charles Darwin's theory of natural selection, Huxley had once observed, "The struggle for existence holds as much in the intellectual as in the physical world. A theory is a species of thinking, and its right to exist is coextensive with its power of resisting extinction by its rivals" (1893-94 2:229). The 1880s and 1890s furnished graphic evidence of this conceptual struggle, which Huxley took up by writing on social issues from his own professional and personal perspective. Given populist politics, given the power of the later industrial revolution, and given the intellectual and social implications of contemporary evolutionary theory, anthropology, and biblical criticism, how, Huxley asked, are we to affirm an ethical principle for human society? His answer was to reassert, in a series of essays culminating with *Evolution and Ethics,* a modified Malthusian argument based on the natural inequality between the forces of population and production.

Huxley wrote the two essays of *Evolution and Ethics* in imitation of Malthus for precisely the reasons that Malthus had written *An Essay on the Principle of Population* (1798)—to refute, by reference to natural material and instinctual constraints, the romantic a priori arguments of the social idealists. Like many fin-de-siècle Victorians, Huxley feared that violent revolution might be at hand (Jones 1971, 290). In an introduction to the English translation of Théodore Rocquain's anticlerical history of the French Revolution, *The Revolutionary Spirit,* he had written:

The grave political and social problems which press for solution at the present day are the same as those which offered themselves a hundred years ago. Moreover, the a priori method of the *Philosophes,* who, ignoring the conditions of scientific method, settled the most difficult problems of practical politics by fine-drawn deductions from axiomatic assumptions about natural rights, is as much in favor at the end of the nineteenth, as it was in the latter half of the eighteenth century. (Huxley 1891, vii-viii)

But Huxley's reservations about radical political theory did not make him an advocate of social status quo or a partisan of Spencerian laissez-faire. Unlike Malthus, he had witnessed the material powers of the industrial revolution. If human society were governed by an evolutionary dynamic, that society's abilities to transform its conditions of existence might go far in neutralizing the formidable natural constraints on the individual. This theme of social transformation is the burden of *Evolution and Ethics*.

In education and human artifice, Huxley found two principles of transformation by which the so-called state of art supplanted the strictly evolutionary dynamic of the state of nature. The key to Huxley's political philosophy, if we may call it that, is education. Although this philosophy is not elaborated in the two essays of *Evolution and Ethics,* it is spelled out in detail in such essays as **"A Liberal Education and Where to Find It"** (1868), **"The School Boards: What They Can Do, and What They May Do"** (1870), **"Universities: Actual and Ideal"** (1874), and a dozen other essays on educational topics, collected in volume 3 of his *Essays*. Huxley wrote the classic nineteenth-century essays on science education, which he viewed as the means to transforming society, liberating individuals, and establishing a free market of merit and ideas—a theme that was to figure prominently in John Dewey's philosophy. This was for Huxley a profoundly autobiographical theme, reflecting upon his meteoric rise from Free Scholarship student at Charing Cross Hospital in 1842-1845 to president of the Royal Society from 1883-1885. Yet education, seen within the evolutionary dynamic, was also the social vehicle that transmitted human experience, the source of society's power to transform its surroundings (Noland 1964).

Huxley's Romanes Lecture and **"Prolegomena,"** with all their political and autobiographical elements, were preeminently Huxley's final defense of Victorian naturalistic thought (Barton 1983). Anchored in eighteenth-century ethical categories derived from Malthus, Hume, and Hartley, the two essays invoked a Victorian anthropological perspective to argue that ethical behavior was part of a universal cultural dynamic that both depended upon physical and biological circumstances and sought to break free of them. In this dynamic, the biological and sociocultural implications of ethics were

not easily reconciled. Physical nature, operating outside the compass of ethics, which was decidedly a human cultural artifice, could not furnish a norm for ethics. From the moralist's practical perspective, the cosmic background was not simply neutral, but embodied forces that effectively, although not intentionally, frustrated human ethical intent. It was antagonistic in the sense of tragedy, in which unknown forces within and without the individual bring forth chaos. The ethical individual was, therefore, knowingly or not, in revolt against the macrocosm. Human artifacts played a decisive role in this struggle, a role greatly magnified by the powers of the industrial revolution. With this reasoning, Huxley denied the romantic impulse to spiritualize the natural and pitted science and consciousness against nature and instinct. In these two major essays of his late career, Huxley achieved a plausible intellectual and social synthesis consistent with Victorian evolutionary, anthropological, and technological developments, a synthesis that explains his appeal and modernity as a Victorian man of letters.

Huxley and Eighteenth-Century Naturalistic Thought

In *Evolution and Ethics,* Huxley locates the historical origins of Victorian ethical naturalism in the diffuse speculative traditions of the previous century. Two of these traditions made natural process the a priori metaphor of morality (Lovejoy 1936, 289). The familiar literary neoclassicism of such figures as John Dryden, Joseph Addison and Henry Steele, and Alexander Pope, promoted as both social and aesthetic truth the old stoical injunction, *live according to nature* (p. 73). This aphorism's social validity is a matter to which Huxley's two essays continually return. A second, equally prominent, line of British ethical naturalism was established by the physicotheologians, who in the analogical tradition of the great natural philosophers John Ray, Robert Boyle, and Isaac Newton, celebrated the fruits of natural inquiry as evidence of the great cosmic order of the Creator. Within this tradition, which continued unabated through William Paley's *Natural Theology* (1802) to Robert Chambers's *Vestiges of the Natural History of Creation* (1844), physical nature, duly schematized and interpreted, furnished a value-laden social norm that proclaimed the very moral codes of established religion (Gillispie 1951; Hankins 1985). As both neoclassical and physicotheological traditions thus vigorously appealed to physical nature as the standard of reason and morality, so, too, did they certify the existing social order, all of which led Basil Willey to characterize them as philosophies of "cosmic Toryism" (1940, 34-36, 55).

Developing somewhat in counterpoint to this eighteenth-century literary naturalism, however, was a third, equally bold trend of viewing human behavior from the normative perspective of populations. Assuming unity of kind in causes and effects, Jeremy Bentham, David

Hume, Adam Smith, and Thomas Malthus all deliberately softened the distinctions between humans and brute animals in order to fix the individual on a material grid whose abstract terms would support a new kind of social analysis. Adam Smith, for example, argued in his *Wealth of Nations* (1776) that any "species" of animal, including humans, "multiplies in proportion to the means of [its] existence," child mortality being one of the key factors of social adjustment (1776, 1:97). Smith extrapolated the systematic consequences of group behavior in the notion of an *economy*—a closed, material, self-adjusting system. This material view of humankind was central to Malthus's study of population. In *An Essay on the Principle of Population* (1798), Malthus derived from the material circumstances of both animals and humans laws, based on populations, that identified certain forces irresistibly influencing individual behavior, including moral behavior. These forms of analysis, which derived norms of behavior from representative circumstances, established a new methodological naturalism that found its ultimate Victorian expression in the population statistics of the Belgian astronomer Adolphe Quételet and the evolutionary speculation of Darwin (Ghiselin 1969, 49; Schweber 1977, 287-93; Ruse 1979, 145-46).

Huxley's *Evolution and Ethics*, appearing at the end of the nineteenth century, reflected back on the naturalisms that had contributed so considerably to the achievements of Darwin and his contemporaries, including Huxley himself. Malthus had stated in the clearest terms that the dilemma of an ethical society is biological. The Malthusian inequality between population and production—a secular analogue to fallen nature—remained the central ethical obstacle recognized by Huxley nearly a century later. From Hume, on the other hand, Huxley borrowed moral categories and arguments, especially the instinctual category of *sympathy*—similar, in some respects, to Christian grace—that he had originally established in his full-length critical monograph, *Hume* (1878). Finally, in Hartley's associationist psychology, Huxley found a precedent for a physiological explanation of moral development that suggested a material basis for the evolution of ethical behavior.

The driving energies of Huxley's *Evolution and Ethics* derive from the Malthusian "natural inequality" between population and production, which is to say between nature and humans. In both men's works, biological limits give rise to and yet threaten mind and society. Both Malthus and Huxley sought to expose the methodological weaknesses of contemporary a priori social speculators. Malthus, in the naturalistic language of his contemporary, the geologist James Hutton, cited the "constancy of the laws of nature and of effects and causes" in opposition to the "conjectures" of Condorcet and Godwin concerning the perfectibility of humans as organic and moral beings (1798, 126, 162). Huxley,

likewise, appealed to natural process in order to expose the fallacies of "modern speculative optimism, with its perfectibility of species, reign of peace, and lion and lamb transformation scenes" (p. 78). His adversaries—laissez-faire social speculators such as Spencer and Petr Kropotkin, and social idealists such as George and General William Booth—might as easily have been Malthus's own targets.

For Malthus, the resources of nature were unequal to the needs of its progeny, which made nature impossible to accept as a social and ethical norm. From the Renaissance through the eighteenth century, the concept of the natural was richly invested with standards of order and harmony. *"Nature,"* Lovejoy once remarked, "[was] the chief and most pregnant word in the terminology of all the normative provinces of thought in the West" (1948, 69). But Malthusian nature, as recent commentators have observed, with its "natural inequality of the two powers of population and production," constituted a physical and psychical environment of enduring conflict (Young 1985; Kohn 1980; Ospovat 1981). Such conflict led to a social dilemma of profound human proportions.

The Malthusian view thus ruptured the traditional myths and ideologies of the natural, which had for centuries found a worthy moral and artistic referent in the order and permanence of the natural world (Tillyard 1942; Willey 1940; Gillispie 1951). A destabilized physical nature of the kind Malthus had imagined in his *Essay on Population* had little capacity to furnish an ethical norm:

> Necessity, that imperious all pervading law of nature, restrains [all existence] within the prescribed bounds. The race of plants and the race of animals shrink under this great restrictive law. And the race of man cannot, by any efforts of reason, escape from it. Among plants and animals its effects are waste of seed, sickness, and premature death. Among mankind, misery and vice. . . . The ordeal of virtue is to resist all temptation to evil. (1798, 20)

In the Malthusian world, where the human conditions of existence are not significantly alterable, humanity must look elsewhere than to nature for its ethical ideal. Malthus could only resolve this dilemma with the aid of theodicy. If there was little moderation in nature, the burden of moral restraint was shifted to the individual. Morality was not the emulation of natural processes; rather, the moral individual must transcend natural circumstances, including instincts.

In Huxley's *Evolution and Ethics*, the physical conditions manifesting the "cosmic process" have the same destructive potential for the individual and for society. Malthusian necessity, however, despite Darwin's powerful generalizations of its applications, seemed only half the law for Huxley, as for many Victorians. Although governed by the realities of a physical world, society could exert a material influence over the conditions of existence so as to soften their impact. "The whole meaning of civilization is interference with this brute struggle," wrote Toynbee in his posthumously published Oxford lectures, *The Industrial Revolution:* "We intend to modify the violence of the fight, and to prevent the weak being trampled under foot" (1884, 59). Huxley likewise reaffirmed Malthus, only to call for human intervention: "Let us understand, once for all, that the ethical progress of society depends, not on imitating the cosmic process, still less in running away from it, but in combating it" (p. 83). Hence, in Huxley's concept of society, humans challenge the Malthusian landscape of conflict, not simply by individual restraint, as for Malthus, but by social and technological initiative.

Both Malthus and Huxley see the individual as a compound being, driven by instinct as well as by reason. For Malthus, the powerful organic cravings of the individual can be expected to oppose the general interests of society (1798, 163-64). Huxley likewise argues that the conflict between instinct and civil behavior remains an enduring challenge to civilization. But for Malthus, such disharmony furnishes a creative tension by which the individual is transformed in a teleology of self-transcendence: "Evil seems to be necessary to create exertion, and exertion seems evidently necessary to create mind" (1798, 204). The imperfections of nature are "admirably adapted to further the high purpose of the creation and to produce the greatest possible quantity of good" (ibid., 212). Malthus argues by theodicy that evil has purpose and is a necessity. In *Evolution and Ethics,* Huxley unceremoniously discards this teleological superstructure ordained by final end. He cannot understand why "among the endless possibilities open to omnipotence, that of sinless, happy existence among the rest, the actuality in which sin and misery abound should be that selected" (p. 72). The disharmonies of nature may drive human ingenuity and awaken the will to struggle against the cosmos, but there is no intelligence behind the reality. Evil is not the necessary source of greatest good, but only the origin of prodigious waste. England is not now, nor ever destined to be, the best of possible worlds.

Within the Malthusian conflict in the physical world of *Evolution and Ethics,* Huxley derived his rationale for ethics from the naturalistic categories of Hume. In his monograph *Hume* (1878), Huxley had traced his own agnosticism to Hume's skepticism, which demanded "the limitation of all knowledge of reality to the world of phenomena revealed to us by experience" (1893-94, 6:71). This pragmatic philosophy of experience had once obliged Huxley and his physiological colleague William Carpenter to dwell on Darwin's lack of physiological evidence for natural selection (1893-94, 2:16-18, 72-76; Carpenter, 1889, 109; see also Hull 1973, 49-50;

Bartholomew 1975; Ghiselin 1969; and di Gregorio 1984). And it appears intact in *Evolution and Ethics* in Huxley's conclusion that the facts of daily life confirmed the logical absurdity that humans and nature are antagonists. Huxley had always elevated experience over logic and theory. In *Hume* he had highlighted Hume's call for thinking individuals to "reject every system of ethics, however subtle or ingenious, which is not founded upon fact and observation" (1893-94, 6:230; Hume 1777, 174-75). Hume's attack on systems is reiterated in Huxley's relentless attacks on utopian ethical theory in *Evolution and Ethics.* To Huxley, society is a built-up, makeshift, and therefore contractual affair, quite beyond the deliberate constructions of human method.

Ignoring the religious sanction for morality, Hume had naturalistically derived the moral sense from an innate sympathy, which in the social sphere took the utilitarian form of justice (Hume 1977, 180). "Crime or immorality," he wrote, "is no particular fact or relation, which can be the object of the understanding, but arises entirely from the sentiment of disapprobation, which, by the structure of human nature, we unavoidably feel on the apprehension of barbarity or treachery" (ibid., 292-93). Justice was a social concept, and hence artificial. As societies developed, Hume pointed out, mutual agreements would give advantages to those that functioned best as wholes (1893-94, 6:232). This notion of innate sympathy was adopted by Smith and Darwin as the likely origin of moral behavior, whose considerable utility in strengthening society would naturally lead humans to reinforce and codify sympathy in a system of justice (Smith 1759, 87-89; Darwin 1871, 84-85; see also Ruse, 1986).

Sympathy, innately received, likewise furnishes the intuitive source of moral behavior in both essays of *Evolution and Ethics* (pp. 28-30, 79). In the "instinctive intuitions," Huxley found a unification of biology and philosophy. He incorporated Hume and Darwin in the argument that moral behavior was based on the intuitive responses of an evolved psychological faculty. "Cosmic evolution," he argued, "may teach us how the good and the evil tendencies of man may have come about; but, in itself, it is incompetent to furnish any better reason why what we call good is preferable to what we call evil than we had before" (p. 80; cf. Hume 1777, 214). And he went on to associate human notions of the good with the "evolution of aesthetic faculty," which by intuition—and not understanding— distinguished what is beautiful from what is ugly. As Darwin had done in his *Descent of Man,* Huxley cited Smith's *Theory of Moral Sentiments,* which made the innate human sympathy borrowed from Hume the coin of the ethical realm (p. 28; Darwin 1871, 81). Smith, Darwin, and Huxley all treated sympathy as an instinct, and hence, a source of pleasure (Smith 1759, 3, 7; Darwin 1871, 81).

To the two naturalistic principles of Malthus's natural inequality and Hume's socially redeeming sympathy, Huxley joined Hartley's doctrine of association to suggest a dynamic principle of psychological change. Huxley's philosophical views had always been distinguished by his interests as a physiologist in reflex action and instinct. He had published two textbooks on physiology, *Elementary Lessons in Physiology* (1866) and *The Crayfish: An Introduction to the Study of Zoology* (1879). His *Crayfish,* a classic of nineteenth-century physiology, was written at midcareer, roughly at the time he was writing his monograph *Hume* (1878) and its companion piece, **"On Sensation and the Unity of Structure of Sensiferous Organs"** (1879). In the latter article, he argued that sensations were modes of motion initiated from outside the body, that the brain was modified epithelium, and that "our sensations, our pleasures, our pains, and the relations of these, make up the sum total of the elements of positive, unquestionable knowledge" (1893-94, 6:318). This theme of the material basis of mind permeated Huxley's more sensationalist essays, such as **"On the Physical Basis of Life"** (1868) and **"On the Hypothesis that Animals are Automata"** (1874), in which he had argued that mental phenomena are known to us primarily, if not exclusively, by means of material phenomena.

Hartley's materialistic theory of individual moral growth by nervous association of experiences suggested a physiological basis for the evolution of ethical behavior in both individuals and society. In Hartley's theory of moral development, the social self emerged by degrees with the suppression of one's own natural cravings—which Huxley had identified with "original sin" (1892). In his *Observations on Man,* for example, Hartley had spoken of the "method of destroying the self, by perpetually substituting a less and purer self interest for a larger and grosser," in a process of associationist sensation building by degrees to morally more complex ideas (Hartley 1749, 2:282). The accumulated nervous experiences of the organism led to forms of more complex behavior, moral sense developing from simple sensations (Willey 1940, 137). A nineteenth-century physiologist like Huxley, contemplating evolutionary process, could interpret this process as adaptive.

Beginning with Hartley's view that the self was destroyed as the consequence of acculturation, Huxley went on in *Evolution and Ethics* to argue that the individual suppressed instinct by denying expression to an authentic part of the natural self. He characterized this process in terms of Smith's "ideal man within the breast"—the cultivated "artificial personality" of civilization (Smith 1759, 208; p. 30). In Hartley's idea of self-destruction, Huxley saw a principle of evolution of the artificial personality, in which benevolence is by degrees associated with perceived self-interest and becomes a source of the polity. Children, he noted,

always come into the world entirely selfish, in the primitive manner of ancestral or savage humankind, but they gradually accept new social priorities: "every child born into the world will still bring with him the instinct of unlimited self-assertion. He will have to learn the lesson of self-restraint and renunciation" (p. 44).

In framing his naturalism in the context of the eighteenth-century thought of Malthus, Hume, and Hartley, Huxley attempted to reveal the historical depths of the intellectual and social tradition of which he considered himself a part. With Malthus's secularization of fallen nature in the so-called natural inequality, Hume's naturalization of grace in sympathy, and Hartley's physiological theory of individual moral development, Huxley built a formidable naturalistic framework for the emergence of human ethical behavior. He used eighteenth-century thought most systematically to displace classical Christian theological speculation about the ethical dilemma of humankind. This displacement, suggesting the historical failure of Christian ethical theology, fit the model of uniformitarian overtaking catastrophic causal explanation (See also Barton 1983).

Huxley's elaborate secularization by means of systematic intellectual displacement was so thorough that Lightman has been moved to argue, in a fascinating tu quoque retort, that Huxley, in replacing one set of middle-class religious orthodoxies with another set of scientific orthodoxies, was formulating a new "religion," complete with a "holy trinity" (Lightman 1987, 176). In this view, which does some reductive violence to the concept of religion, Huxley's naturalistic scheme merely supplants a theological theodicy with a secular one that argues for status quo. The effort, Lightman argues, is "to reconcile people to the existing social order by conceiving of society as an organism that should be allowed to develop on its own accord, since it is slowly progressing and growing due to the irresistible movement of natural laws" (1987, 117-18). This laissez-faire argument of irresistible progress, long associated with Spencer, was explicitly rejected by Huxley in 1871 and thereafter on a regular basis (1893-94, 1:268-70). We must also keep in mind that Huxley's systematic and frequent use of religion as a comparative frame of reference for his own naturalistic thought was a rhetorical device for ridicule that served to juxtapose, in elaborate mock-heroic fashion, the sacred and the secular.

Huxley and the Victorian Anthropological Perspective

While drawing on eighteenth-century thought to frame his own naturalistic world view, Huxley shared with many of his contemporaries the understanding that cultures were dynamic. An important Victorian ethnologist in his own right, Huxley viewed civilization not as a fixed state, as Malthus, Hume, and Hartley had, but as a process that continually transformed the conditions of the natural world. In asserting the naturalistic basis of cultural evolution, Huxley both intensified the polarities between the primitive and civilized human and bound the two together in an unprecedented physical and psychological intimacy.

Huxley's ideological origins derived partly from the thought of the bourgeois historian François Guizot, whom Huxley, in his retrospective essay **"Agnosticism"** (1889), rated one of the most important influences on his thinking (1893-94, 5:235). Agnosticism, Huxley argued, was a product of the intellectual progress Guizot identified with history itself. Guizot had argued that civilization was "properly a relative term" that implied "both a state of physical well-being and a state of superior intellectual and moral culture" (Guizot 1828, 1:18). Propelled by the innately motivated desire of humanity for "political liberty" and "free inquiry," civilization was also attended by certain necessary restrictions of individual freedom (ibid., 1:74, 265, 290).

This theme of progressive civilization and its attendant restrictions runs through Huxley's entire program of cultural criticism, reaching its summit in *Evolution and Ethics*. On the one hand, the argument of the improved "external" condition of humans conformed to the social rationale of his essays on the progress of science; on the other hand, the theme of the progress of the intellect fit Huxley's model of an increasingly rational and competent society, founded on naturalism and physical science. These concepts gave a social and intellectual legitimacy to science, locating the man of science within the texture of history and furnishing him with an essential role in contemporary culture (see Turner 1974, 10-13). Guizot's ideology of transition enabled Huxley, in such essays as his **"Prologue to Controverted Questions"** (1892), to view science as the logical extension of the humanist critical spirit (1893-94, 5:14, 41).

For Guizot, civilization was "an improved condition of man resulting from the establishment of social order in place of individual independence and lawlessness of the savage or barbarous life" (1828, 1:18). His antithesis of the civilized and savage life, identical in some respects to the dynamic views of his British counterparts Edward Gibbon and Henry Buckle, was easi-ly transformed to a conflict between mind and nature. In their inductive histories, Gibbon and Buckle, by a massive coordination of facts derived from long-term conflicts, identified historical process with natural and social processes that operated over extensive periods. Gibbon's Rome succumbed to physical and social antagonisms, including "the injuries of time and nature" and "the use and abuse of materials," "which continued to operate in a period of more than a thousand years" (Gibbon 1901, 3:863). John Stuart Mill's brilliant essay, "Nature," had appeared in 1874, arguing that "nature impales man,

breaks him as on the wheel" (Mill 1969, 375). Buckle argued, in his naturalistic *History of Civilization in England* (1857-61), that "man is affected by four classes of physical agents; namely climate, food, soil, and the general aspect of nature" (Hanham 1970, xv). Gibbon's "injuries of time and nature," Mill's antagonistic forces of nature, and Buckle's "general aspect of nature" were opposed to human constructs in precisely the way that in *Evolution and Ethics* Huxley's cosmic process, manifested socially in the forces of instinctual aggression and physically in those of nature, opposed human artifice (see also Stanley 1957).

The process historians' concepts of physical agency were reinforced in many ways by the emerging work of British ethnologists and anthropologists at mid-century, work in which Huxley himself had played a significant role. These movements, secure in the assumption of British cultural superiority, contained seeds of this assumption's destruction in the naturalistic view that humans and their cultures, whether contemporary British or ancient Hindu, were material constructs that yielded much to comparative analysis. Such were the insights brought through empire.

Huxley's earliest work as a morphologist fitted solidly into the emerging disciplines of comparative zoology—morphology, physiology, and embryology—rising from the work of Buffon, Cuvier, Von Baer, Richard Owen, and E. Geoffrey Saint-Hilaire. In spite of themselves, these individuals often projected humans solely as physical entities (Greene 1959a). In *Man's Place in Nature,* Huxley maintained the psychical unity of humans with lower animals, as well as the monogenist racial theory of the common origin of man, which led Darwin in his *Descent of Man* to cite Huxley's volume extensively in support his own evolutionist view of humans (Darwin 1871, 13-17, passim; cf. Di Gregorio 1984, 153-58).

In midcentury London, the emergency and amalgamation of the ethnological and anthropological societies established new approaches to the study of cultures (Burrow 1966; Stocking 1971). In contrast to the humanistic study of classical cultures on the basis of texts, the new cultural anthropology now empirically examined actual societies for insights into physical and prehistoric culture (Stocking 1987). Darwin, Alfred Wallace, and Huxley all helped to legitimize this trend in their voyage narratives and studies. Darwin's Fuegians in the *Journal of Researches* (1839) had become standards of savage behavior, to which Darwin would ultimately return in his *Descent of Man* (1871). Wallace had written extensively about native peoples in papers, as well as in his *The Malay Archipelago* (1869). Huxley, during his voyage on HMS *Rattlesnake,* (1846-1850), had filled numerous notebooks with ethnological observations and drawings of native peoples in New Guinea and Australia, which he turned to account in his Fullerian Lectures on ethnology at the Royal Institution in 1866-1867. In a key paper, **"On the Methods and Results of Ethnology,"** he assessed the state of the field in 1865 as an ethnologist in the Darwinian cast who considered humans an evolved form and held to the monogenist theory of human origins (1893-94, 7:248-52).

The new approaches to historical and anthropological analysis acted synergistically to establish a powerful new Victorian critical perspective, in which cultures, despite assumptions of English superiority, were seen relativistically as human constructs. Combining empirical observation with the comparative method and growth analogy, the new anthropologists brought the human physical species increasingly into phase with civilization. "The thing that has been will be," wrote Edward Tylor, "and we are to study savages and old nations to learn the laws that under new circumstances are working for good or ill in our own development" (1871 1:158-59). John Lubbock held that the conditions and habits of savages resembled those of ancestors and helped to reveal how current customs and ideals were lodged in the mind "as fossils are imbedded in the soil" (1869, 1).

Efforts to join present to past naturalized the contents of the mind by associating them with the primitive, prehistoric past. Tylor wrote, in the uniformitarian language of Charles Lyell: "The savage state in some measure represents an early condition of mankind, out of which the higher culture has gradually been developed or evolved, by processes still in regular operation as of old, the result showing that, on the whole, progress has prevailed over relapse" (1871 1:32). For Tylor, Victorian culture could be linked in fundamental and revealing ways with primitive cultures: "The civilized mind still bears vestiges neither few nor slight, of a past condition from which savages represent the least and civilized man the greatest advance" (ibid., 1:68-69). Although this view assumed a hierarchy of social and cultural characters with Victorian civilization at the apex, it nevertheless made the psychological connection between all humans (see also Bowler 1986, 78-80). Civilization was a fluid state, manifested in different degrees and modes by all societies, which were now, in some sense, on a par. Civilization, always in flux, could either grow or atrophy.

These lines of nineteenth-century historical and anthropological thinking were incorporated by Huxley into *Evolution and Ethics,* with its naturalistic themes of the dynamic interaction of nature and culture, the physical status of the human animal, and the evolution of religion and morals. To derive the moral categories of Hume, given the destabilized physical nature of Malthus and Darwin, Huxley imagined a psychically divided individual who incorporated the innate aggressive impulses of the ancestors with the acquired social restraint of the cultured being. He used faculty psychology to incorporate two versions of humanity into the same mind.

Huxley's view of nature in *Evolution and Ethics* is darker, more pessimistic, than it had been in his early career. This shift, which can be traced to several political, personal, and intellectual factors, was by no means straightforward. In his essay, **"A Liberal Education and Where to Find It"** (1868), he had optimistically personified nature as the "calm strong angel" who was playing at chess with man and who would "rather lose than win" (1893-94, 3:82). Still, Nature opposes the individual. The prototype of his angel had been the fiend in the famous painting of the German artist Moritz Retzsch, mockingly playing at chess with man for his soul. Three years later, in his essay **"Administrative Nihilism,"** Huxley rejected the nature-as-norm concept insofar as it implied laissez-faire principles of society. Human aggression, he held, was a natural component of human nature and required social amelioration. Huxley's views of human nature here were possibly influenced by Bagehot's *Physics and Politics* (1869), in which the natural human was little more than an abject, aggressive brute.

In **"Science and Morals"** (1886), Huxley returned to the argument that "the safety of morality" lay not in theological creeds, but rather "in a real and living belief in that fixed order of nature which sends social disorganization upon the track of immorality, as surely as it sends physical disease after physical trespass" (ibid., 9:146). If the implication here was to follow nature, his 1888 essay, **"The Struggle for Existence in Human Society,"** abandoned this last vestige of teleological speculation. In this essay, Huxley firmly seized upon the Malthusian factor of overpopulation as the fundamental destabilizing force of society and history (ibid., 9:208). Nature from the perspective of the primitive individual was the personification of Istar, the bloodthirsty goddess, who "wants nothing but a fair field and free play for her darling, the strongest" (ibid., 9:207). Yet, from the perspective of modern science, nature was a process of material logic:

> If we desire to represent the course of nature in terms of human thought, and assume that it was intended to be that which it is, we must say that its governing principle is intellectual and not moral; that it is a materialized logical process, accompanied by pleasures and pains, the incidence of which, in the majority of cases has not the slightest reference to moral desert. (ibid., 9:202)

Huxley now removed the moral content he had once invested in natural process. As Hume had long before argued, nature could be considered the term for that which *is* but not a term for that which *ought* to be (Hume 1739, 469). In virtue of its uniformity, natural process was open to logical analysis and manipulation, but the collective forces known as nature were nonteleological, without moral purpose. Hence, the ethical law could not be identified with the physical law. Ethics, Huxley went on to argue in *Evolution and Ethics,* cannot be "applied natural history" (p. 74).

Various personal, political, and intellectual factors all help to explain these shifts in Huxley's views. His daughter Marian's death in late 1887, two months before he wrote **"The Struggle for Existence,"** must have had some effect on Huxley's state of mind. Not only had this favorite, much-animated, daughter been happily married and possessed of considerable artistic talent, but her long suffering could hardly have had anything to do with individual moral desert. Huxley's essay also reflected contemporary social unrest. Mob rule in the West End of London after the riot of February 8, 1886, attended by looting and robbery, was followed by several days of panic among Londoners, fueled by rumors of wandering hordes of toughs and impending revolution (Jones 1971, 291-93). This anarchy was repeated in the fall of 1887, at the height of the depression, with the Trafalgar Square riot, not only impressing upon middle-class Londoners the implausibility, not to mention danger, of laissez-faire social policy, but also inspiring a great round of speculative programs. A direct reflection upon these events, Huxley's **"Struggle for Existence"** essay asserts not only that humans are subject to the same destructive impulses witnessed in the natural world, as they seek to fulfill fundamental needs, but also that society must be a collective effort to substitute a state of mutual peace for one of war (1893-94, 9:204). The destabilizing element Huxley identified in his essay was the Malthusian tendency toward overpopulation, which was based on a universal human instinct.

Huxley's view of the natural human as beast played an important polarizing role in the social construction of his state of art, by identifying a naturalistic source for the antisocial tendencies of the individual. This comparative thesis of innate aggressiveness had a certain autobiographical cogency, given Huxley's own confrontational personality and sense of youthful vulnerability (1900, 1:5). Victorian social theory was often compounded partly of autobiographical elements, not merely in the projection of one's own personality, but also because narrative was a formidable means of constructing possible chains of causality (Landau 1984; Beer 1983). "The simplest study of man's nature," Huxley assured the largely Christian audience of his *Man's Place in Nature* (1863), "reveals, at its foundations, all the selfish passions and fierce appetites of the merest quadruped" (1893-94, 7:155). These moral dualisms appeared in many forms familiar to Victorians. Bagehot, who had drawn on Huxley's notion of artificial reflex actions as a means by which humans "stored faculty and acquired virtue," had argued in *Physics*

and Politics that among primitive humans "the strongest killed out the weakest, as they could" (1869, 6, 18). In the **"Struggle for Existence"** essay of 1888, Huxley considered the ethical individual to be exposed to the "deep-seated organic impulses which impel the natural man to follow his non-moral course"; unremitting human misery inevitably brought humans to the verge of a "chaos of savagery" (1893-94, 9:205, 214).

Huxley's natural human made his final appearance in *Evolution and Ethics* as the brute, a deterministic instrument of instinct, with little independent will or consciousness, a "superb animal" who owned his success in the savage state to "his exceptional physical organization; his cunning, his sociability, his curiosity, and his imitativeness; his ruthless and ferocious destructiveness when his anger is roused by opposition" (pp. 51-52). The Victorian natural man was, in fact, the personification of contemporary naturalism, an embodiment of the forces that Darwin, Lubbock, Bagehot, Mill and others had in their diverse ways imagined in the prehistoric landscape. This fascinating if threatening new version of humanity was usually some blend of personal experience and the contemporary "savage," who was seen as an entity of instinct and expediency. Darwin concluded in *The Descent of Man* that primal man was a "savage who delights to torture his enemies, offers up bloody sacrifices, practises infanticide without remorse, treats his wives like slaves, knows no decency, and is haunted by the grossest superstitions" (1871, 2:405). These strains all reflected the vast, dizzying fall, via Victorian ethnology, of natural man from his heights of romantic innocence to a new natural state of brutish "innocence."

In *Evolution and Ethics,* Huxley reconciled the natural with the ethical individual by merging them through the agency of society. Tylor had argued in 1871 that the civilized mind still bore vestiges of a primal past: "How direct and close the connexion may be between modern culture and the condition of the rudest savage" (1871, 159). Huxley argued that violent cosmic nature had been internalized as a psychical force, "born with us," the product of "millions of years of severe training." Hence, ethical nature may count on having a "powerful enemy as long as the world lasts" (p. 85).

This affiliation of primitive and modern mentalities lent considerable importance to human constructive efforts to maintain the social whole, for it removed all sense that culture was inevitable. Such a theme had been taken up by Huxley's protégé E. Ray Lankester in his provocative monograph *Degeneration: A Chapter in Darwinism* (1880), which evoked the biological phenomenon of devolution as a metaphor for what might happen to civilizations. Using Gibbon's Roman Empire as a case in point, Lankester warned that humanity could "degenerate" into a contented life of material enjoyment accompanied by ignorance and superstition. At the beginning of the **"Prolegomena"** Huxley argued that progress is relative (p. 4). If human culture could progress, it could also persist, unchanged, just as it could degenerate. There was neither necessity nor unified purpose to evolution. These themes, which introduced new biological metaphors of instability to cultural discourse, are sources of the pervasive feeling of impermanence that suffuses Huxley's *Evolution and Ethics*.

Huxley, Darwin, and the Ethics of Utility

In *Evolution and Ethics,* Huxley challenged utilitarian moral theory and its related late nineteenth-century theories of eugenics. What seems to have concerned him most was the threat to ethical codes posed by the convergence of (1) classical utilitarian theories holding behavior to be motivated by self-interest and pleasure, and (2) evolutionary theory and its utilitarian cycles of struggle and self-aggrandizement. This convergence could—and did for some, like Spencer and Galton—justify the radical pursuit of self-interest as a legitimate social doctrine.

"Blessings are provided for offspring by due self-regard," argued Spencer in his *Principles of Ethics* (1897, 1:222). The phrase "ethics of evolution," Huxley countered, was ambiguous, because it suggested that a code of ethical behavior could be based on the view that "fittest" was "best." But "fit" had no moral authority, since what was fittest depended entirely on the conditions of existence (pp. 80-81). This uncoupling of the fit and the moral put Huxley in conflict not only with Spencer and Galton, but also, to a considerable extent, with his own early view that nature was just.

Victorians widely associated the adaptive operations of evolution with the principle of utility (Wallace 1900; Richards 1982, 48, 50; Bowler 1984, 144-45; Young 1985, 3, 261-62), although many, including Darwin, had trouble accepting a strict utilitarian rationale for moral behavior. The broad social utility of moral behavior was rarely at question, since the stable, self-restrained community founded on mutual regard promised collaborative advantages in adaptation. More problematic was the individual basis of utilitarian morality, which was associated with ideas of pleasure, self-interest, and expediency.

Pleasure, as a general animal experience, a biological universal, so to speak, had provided a powerful conceptual tool for viewing human morality as an extension of animal behavior. But how could the pleasure-pain dynamic account for the renunciation required of an ethical individual in pursuit of the ideal signalled by *ought?* This key Victorian moral dilemma was faced by Darwin, Huxley, and Spencer alike, with very different results.

The deeply naturalistic tendencies of eighteenth-century ethical speculation nicely converged with the biological thinking by which Victorians like Darwin, Spencer, and Huxley absorbed classical debates over ethics in a new behavioral terminology of instinct and habit (see Moore 1979, 156; Richards 1982). For many, the biological universals of pleasure and pain, when associated with repetitive actions, introduced principles of reinforcement and habit that justified increasingly complex social behaviors, whether in the long-term sense of the development of species or in the short-term sense of the education of the individual.

Two assumptions found throughout Darwin's *Descent of Man,* Huxley's *Evolution and Ethics,* and Spencer's *Principles of Ethics* set the behavior of humans and animals on a continuum out of which a principle of behavioral development could be extracted: the unity and variability of animal and human faculties. Darwin argued in specific terms that the mental faculties of higher animals and humans were identical: "Man and the higher animals, especially the primates, . . . have the same senses, intuitions, and sensations—similar passions, affections, and emotions, even the more complex ones" (1871 48-49). This linking of the mental faculties of humans and animals, together with the principle of variability, supported a naturalistic concept of cultural evolution consistent with the thought of anthropologists like Tylor and Lubbock, whom Darwin cited frequently.

In his *Descent,* Darwin derived moral behavior from a "complex" of mental and social factors grounded in "the social instincts [which] lead an animal to take pleasure in the society of its fellows, to feel a certain amount of sympathy for them, and to perform various services for them" (ibid., 72). Citing Hume and Smith, Darwin argued that sympathy had distinct adaptive value, for those communities which included the greatest number of sympathetic members, would flourish best and rear most offspring (ibid., 81-82, 85; see also Schweber 1977; Manier 1978). Yet, as Darwin also understood, these two principles embodied a potential conflict between the individual and the community (see Richards 1982). Behavior that was adaptive for the community as a whole was not necessarily beneficial or pleasurable for the individual; the reverse was true, as well. If individual instinct was the driving force of moral behavior, Darwin concluded, communal opinion, in directing that instinct, must often deflect it (1871, 72, 93, 98-99).

Darwin clearly saw the conflict between various human instincts, but he viewed this conflict as one that steadily diminished with experience and culture. This primeval conflict in humans was still part of civilized experience: "At the moment of action, man will no doubt be apt to follow the stronger impulse, and though this may occasionally prompt him to the noblest deeds, it will far more commonly lead him to gratify his own desires at the expense of other men" (ibid., 91). The processes by which behavioral priorities passed from the individual to the community thus became central to Darwin's theory of moral development:

> With increased experience and reason, man perceives the more remote consequences of his actions, and the self-regarding virtues, such as temperance, chastity, &c., which during early times are, as we have before seen, utterly disregarded, come to be highly esteemed or even held sacred. . . . Ultimately, a highly complex sentiment, having its first origin in the social instincts, largely guided by the approbation of our fellow men, ruled by reason, self-interest, and in later times by deep religious feelings, confirmed by instruction and habit, all combined, constitute our moral sense or conscience. (ibid., 165-66)

This series of increasingly directive, institutionally reinforced moral behaviors suggests the gradual overtaking of instinct by consciousness. It further suggests the eventual conversion of individual priorities into those of the generalized whole or community. Darwin concludes, in optimistic, even utopian language, that the struggles in men "between higher and lower impulses" will with generations become less severe and "virtue will be triumphant." The "Golden Rule" is the natural outcome of social instinct, aided by "active intellectual powers and effects of habit" (ibid., 104, 106; see also Greene 1977).

Darwin's formula for the evolution of the moral sense or conscience in humans has a distinct strain of anthropomorphism—if not outright autobiography—that suggests the educational narrative of a Victorian youth raised in affluence. For Darwin, as for Huxley, the moral development of the individual—partly conceived in terms of one's own biography—recapitulates the psychological and cultural development of the race. In the infant, Darwin observed, "we may trace the perfect graduation from the mind of an utter idiot, lower than that of the lowest animal, to the mind of a Newton" (ibid., 106). To a considerable extent—with due regard for available facts—moral development seems to have been imagined by Darwin and his Victorian counterparts by reading personal experiences and values into the processes of nature so as to derive "naturalistically" their own culture and moral norms (see Landau 1984; Flew 1967; Beer 1983).

Despite his general agreement with utilitarian moral theory, Darwin explicitly rejected J. S. Mill's view in *Utilitarianism* that the moral sense was acquired and not innate (1871, 71). If moral behavior had evolved partly by the natural selection of instincts, one could answer the moral dilemma of *ought*—actions that often went against the individual's immediate interests—for the evolution of complex instincts through the natural selection of variations in simpler instincts would

establish a nonconscious basis of moral behavior. Such a phenomenon could explain how more complex social instincts developed in "sterile worker-ants and bees, which leave no offspring to inherit the effects of experience and modified habits" (ibid., 38). The same phenomenon might explain a high standard of morality that gave slight or no advantage to the individual and his offspring over members of the same tribe, but gave advantages over other tribes. Hence, Darwin argued, "with strictly social animals, natural selection sometimes acts indirectly on the individual, through the preservation of variations which are beneficial only to the community" (ibid., 155). In the evolution of nonconscious human drives, the selection unit might be identified with the group (see also Ruse 1986, 218-19).

Huxley must have returned to the *Descent of Man* as he was writing **Evolution and Ethics,** for he took up the same issues he had considered in 1871, when defending Darwin's new volume against St. George Mivart and Alfred Wallace (Hull 1973; Wallace 1864). We find the same issues Darwin had taken up—the Malthusian pressures, the unity of human and animal faculties, the instinctual basis and utility of morality, behavioral mimicry, and sympathy. The faculty of moral sense, Huxley argued, is heightened through "mutual affection of parent and offspring, intensified by the long infancy of the human species," and socially generalized by the tendency of the individual "to reproduce in himself actions and feelings similar to, or correlated with, those of other men" (p. 28). The human individual, the most consummate of all mimics in the animal world, is also an emotional chameleon, who feels and needs sympathy and regards peer opinion as essential to his own well-being. Here, as in Darwin, we find strong biographical themes, blended with Hux-ley's distinctive behavioralist emphasis. Huxley gave more emphasis than most to nonconscious, irrational sources of human motivation. The themes of animal automation had long preoccupied him, especially the notion, pursued in his 1874 Belfast Address, **"On the Hypothesis that Animals are Automata,"** that nonconscious, non-purposive psychic components contributed substantially to human behavior (1893-94; 1:199-250).

In **Evolution and Ethics,** the themes of autonomic behavior resurface in Huxley's argument that the evolution of nonconscious behavior helps to explain the emergence of the moral sense. Criticizing Adam Smith for insisting on justifying social behavior on the basis of reason, Huxley retrieves Darwin's example of bee society to argue that complex social organization can develop through the evolution of nonconscious instinct. A thoughtful drone, he pointed out, "must needs profess himself an intuitive moralist of the purest water":

> He would point out, with perfect justice, that the devotion of the workers to a life of ceaseless toil for a mere subsistence wage, cannot be accounted

for either by enlightened selfishness or by any other sort of utilitarian motives; since these bees begin to work, without experience or reflection, as they emerge from the cell in which they are hatched. (p. 25)

This "automatic mechanism" hammered out by natural selection, motivates behavior advantageous to the group, but not necessarily to the individual. Therefore, it cannot be justified solely by utility, contrary to the theories of Mill and Spencer. At base, Huxley speculates, human society was "as much a product of organic necessity as that of the bees" (p. 26).

For Huxley, as for Darwin, the development of moral behavior had two distinct components—instinctive behavior, reinforced by conscious intelligence, and acquired reflex. In his *Expression of Emotion in Animals,* Darwin drew on Huxley's distinctions between *natural* and *artificial* reflexes (Huxley 1866) to explain instinctual and habitual expressive behavior that was beyond volition. Darwin, however, took the Lamarckian view that acquired behaviors could be inherited, a view which Huxley and his former associate Lloyd Morgan rejected (Morgan 1896, 252). "Some actions," Darwin noted, "which were at first performed consciously, have become through habit and association converted into reflex actions, and are now so firmly fixed and inherited, that they are performed, even when not of the least use, as often as the same causes arise, which originally excited them in us through volition" (1872 39-40). Such reflex actions, he went on, "gained for one purpose might afterwards be modified independently of the will or habit, so as to serve for some distinct purpose" (ibid., 41). These Lamarckian tendencies were clear in Darwin's thought, although Darwin also argued that human expressive emotions could be based on nonconscious elements subject to selection.

Where Darwin accepted a Lamarckian mechanism for the migration of behavior toward the altruistic end of the moral spectrum, Huxley, with his faculty psychology and its material, autonomic components, divided the human mind against itself. This view provided Huxley the foundation for his thesis in *Evolution and Ethics* that innate determinants of behavior must coexist in the mind in considerable tension, not only with one another, but also with acquired behaviors. Such antagonism is the source of the dualism of *Evolution and Ethics* that troubled so many of Huxley's commentators (Stephen 1893; Dewey 1898).

Huxley accepted the notion of inherent human conflicts in motivation because certain contents of the mind were beyond the shaping influences of self or group. The human organism owed its success in the cosmos—not to mention in Victorian London—to faculties expressed in aggressive drive, quite as much as to those manifested in cooperative skills. Unlike Spencer and Darwin, who assumed that antisocial impulses would

by degrees be converted into the substance of ethical behavior, Huxley argued that self-restraint and self-assertion were instincts with equal claims upon the normal, thriving individual and its society:

> Just as the self-assertion, necessary to the maintenance of society against the state of nature, will destroy that society if it is allowed free operation within, so the self-restraint, the essence of the ethical process, which is no less an essential condition of the existence of every polity, may, by excess, become ruinous to it. (p. 31)

The impulses of aggressive behavior remained essential sources of human drive—the will with which the individual combated the cosmos (cf. Helfand 1977, 176). Hence, virtue was not likely to "triumph," as Darwin had suggested. The Golden Rule, strictly observed, Huxley noted, subverts the interests of society because it refuses to punish law-breakers.

Huxley's anti-utilitarian sentiment is felt throughout the two essays of *Evolution and Ethics* in pervasive references to the pain and suffering of human existence. In Huxley's view, the pressures of social life require that individuals relinquish the prerogative of acting out their instinctive impulses. The very refinements among humans of emotion and intellect are attended by a proportional enlargement in the capacity for suffering. And, once again reflecting on themes of considerable personal import, he adds, "the divine faculty of imagination, while it created new heavens and new earths, provided [man] with the corresponding hells of futile regret for the past and morbid anxiety for the future" (p. 55).

This denial of the sufficiency of utility as a moral principle was directed at Herbert Spencer and his laissez-faire social policies. Spencer had linked ethical behavior, as had Mill, with the higher pleasures of self-sacrifice. To Spencer, the individual organism advanced by experience, which accumulated biologically through the generations. Although Spencer repudiated an absolute laissez-faire doctrine (1893 2:601), his social and ethical philosophy was rigorously anti-interventionist on the biological assumption that struggle was a means of adjusting and strengthening society. With his Lamarckian views that acquired behaviors could be transmitted, Spencer applied biological metaphors to society to derive a self-adjusting organism. He had increasingly less sympathy for the interventionist spirit of meliorative social policy (Burrow 1966, 206).

Spencer's theories, despite their elaborate tissue of doubtful biological metaphor, were often original and provocative, a fact that was not lost on Huxley. Spencer had grasped, for example, the idea that the preservation of biological essence through the generations was somehow tied up with the axioms of behavior for all organisms, including humans (1897 1:221). Thus, the superior claims of egoism were that they increased the chances of one's offspring's success. For Spencer, excessive altruism and self-denial led to such social evils as mental illness and the production of "relatively weak offspring" (ibid., 1:225-227). Huxley had once half-jokingly written to Spencer on Spencer's philosophy: "No objection except to the whole" (1900, 2:185).

The core of Spencer's ethical thesis is his identification of "survival of the fittest" with "utility" and hence, pleasure (1892, 1:352). Where the utilitarian ethics of Bentham and Mill had assumed the stability and universality of human nature, Spencer now saw it as variable and progressive (Greene 1959b, 432). Accepting the principle of greatest happiness as the basis of human motivation, Spencer argued that pleasure, variously secured, was the basis of the adaptive behavior by which humans had constructed a democratic society. By the progress achieved as individuals, constantly adjusted to new conditions of existence, egoistic and altruistic behaviors were found increasingly to converge. Hence, although Spencer held with Darwin and Huxley that altruistic and egoistic behaviors had evolved simultaneously, he argued further that "every species is continually purifying itself from the unduly egoistic individual, while there are being lost to it the unduly altruistic individuals" (1892, 1:234). By degrees, Spencer speculated, with only the vaguest Lamarckian mechanism in mind, egoism and altruism were to merge at higher stages of evolution in what he called the paradox that "the pursuit of the altruistic pleasure has become a higher order of egoistic pleasure" (ibid., 1:325).

Spencer's concept of behavior assumed a transformational dynamic that Huxley's did not. That is, new behaviors transformed the primal sources of motivation, and instincts were converted to the substance of ethical behavior. This view, central to John Dewey's interventionist thought and philosophy of education, led in Spencer to the conviction that conditions left to themselves were most likely to produce the human adaptive behaviors that would improve upon human nature itself.

A stark contrast emerges between Huxley's and Spencer's views in their respective concepts of humanity's future. Where Huxley stoically envisions society in the present as an imperfect but still effective instrument of ethical collaboration, attended by the pains of necessary renunciation, Spencer looks to the attainment of a future society in which the egos of individuals merge in the interests of the whole. For Spencer, the human is "undergoing transformation from a nature appropriate to his aboriginal wild life, to a nature appropriate to a settled, civilized life" (1897, 1:24). For Huxley, human nature is for all intents and purposes biologically fixed, given the slowness of evolutionary change; meaningful improvements must therefore be sought in the environment, transformed by human intervention

into the state of art. Hence, for Huxley, laissez-faire policy *is* the essence of the struggle for existence; for Spencer, laissez-faire policy promotes conditions under which the human organism advances in perfection. Spencer's hope is in the change of human nature; Huxley's hope is in the change in human conditions.

Huxley thus concludes his **"Prolegomena"** with the observation that the "political animal" is "susceptible of a vast amount of improvement, by education, by instruction, and by the application of his intelligence to the adaptation of conditions of life to his higher needs." Yet the individual remains forever outside the best of possible worlds, "compelled to be perpetually on guard against the cosmic forces, whose ends are not his ends, without and within himself." And the prospect, Huxley concludes, "of attaining untroubled happiness, or of a state which can, even remotely, deserve the title of perfection, [is] as misleading an illusion as ever was dangled before the eyes of poor humanity" (p. 44). It is this final stoicism uttered by the companion of mortality, not some bourgeois political ambition on behalf of status quo, that ultimately moves Huxley to reject political radicalism.

Huxley's vision makes a revealing contrast with Spencer's curious alter ego, the human of the future:

> Bounding out of bed after an unbroken sleep, singing or whistling as he dresses, coming down with beaming face ready to laugh on the smallest provocation, the healthy man of high powers, conscious of past successes and by his energy, quickness, resource, made confident of the future, enters on the day's business not with repugnance but with gladness; and from hour to hour experiencing satisfactions from work effectually done, comes home with an abundant surplus of energy remaining for hours of relaxation. (1897, 1:220)

One is struck by the mechanical, formulaic quality of this futuristic figure, by the utter failure of realism, by the emotional sterility of Spencer's imagination. Such was the Victorian divergence in naturalistic concepts of the moral human individual.

In Spencer's naturalism, we see Lamarckian biology in service of the ideal human, yet another version of Quételet's average man of the future. It is a two-dimensional figure, the leader-on-the-poster, gazing amicably in the foreground of a flag. For Bagehot, it was the "national character" who, by some "'chance predominance' made a model, and then invincible attraction, the necessity which rules all but the strongest men to imitate what is before their eyes, and to be what they are expected to be, molded men by that model" (1869, 26-27). It is classless man. In Huxley's non-Lamarckian naturalism, however, we see realistic, material man, struggling with his own imperfections against forces he only partly comprehends (1893-94, 9:ix). Huxley's is the "eternally tragic" figure, as seen in Oedipus or in Jude Fawley of Thomas Hardy's *Jude the Obscure*.

Art, Artifice, and the Artificial World

Huxley's view of human nature as virtually fixed shifted the burden of progress to the transformation of environment. This transformation of the human conditions of existence, demonstrably made possible by artifacts, was one of the striking instances in which Victorian evolutionary and anthropological theory converged. The biological role played by technological intervention elevated human artifice to the status of a elemental force against what to Malthus had seemed a cosmic background of irresistible natural process. These newly apparent powers of transformation inspired an important line of Victorian social speculation concerning the manner in which humans routinely helped to shape their own destinies. Huxley not only participated in this discussion, but his *Evolution and Ethics* may be seen as its Victorian culmination, finding in the progress of human material construction one of the great social hopes of the future.

The role of human artifice was greatly magnified in Huxley's view by the increasing technological prowess of the industrial being. The argument of **"Evolution and Ethics"** is nested in the fable of Jack and the beanstalk, which Huxley made over into an allegory of the cyclical ebb and flow of civilizations. Out of a primary world of forces and matter rises a superstructure, a "world composed of the same elements as that below, but yet strangely new" (p. 46). This artificial world is none other than English industrial civilization, which Huxley in his famous essay, **"The Progress of Science, 1837-1887,"** had presented as the "new nature, begotten by science upon fact." In Huxley's robust industrial optimism, we see a distillation of the Baconian transformation of the world, with one important difference. Progress, perpetually at odds with fundamental physical and instinctual forces, is not inevitable, nor is it toward anything of remotely millenial proportions. Thus, it is nonteleological. Victorian civilization is not the best of possible worlds, and its existence, given physical reality, must eventually cease.

The antithesis Huxley posed between society and the cosmic background made a paradox of humanity that troubled many commentators, including Spencer and Dewey. How could humans, the products of the cosmos, revolt against the cosmic force? Were they not, as Mill observed in his essay "Nature," physical beings and necessarily extensions of nature? (Mill 1969). Huxley's Promethean call for the revolt against na-ture must have seemed to many an expression of hub-ris—the unthinking arrogance of human technological intervention.

The notion of humans as independent, transforming agents in nature was forcefully spelled out in the first chapter of Darwin's *Origin of Species,* "Variation Under Domestication," with which Huxley, Wallace, and many other Victorians were familiar. Huxley's references throughout the **"Prolegomena"** to the "horticultural process" suggest that he had reread Darwin's chapter. Humans, the subjects of selection, had also become creative forces in nature. As artificers of life forms, they could adapt the accidents of nature to their own ends (Darwin 1859, 30; see also Ritvo 1987). Darwin's use in the *Origin* of artificial selection as the conceptual template for natural selection is well known (Young 1985; Ruse 1979; Kohn 1980). Alfred Wallace and, more recently, Robert Young have drawn attention to certain fallacies implicit in Darwin's active metaphors for nature as an agent of "selection" (Wallace 1864; Young 1985). We can see in Darwin's thinking at the very beginning of the *Origin* an incipient dualism in which the human intervention through horticultural art becomes the allegory of natural process. Human designs guided by human purposes provide the model for, and hence systematically shift, the nonteleological processes of nature. An anthropomorphic analogy presides over the stringent naturalism of Darwin's *Origin of Species* (Beer 1983).

The theme of human transformation in the first chapter of the *Origin* thus contrasts with the natural world in the remainder of the volume in ways that shed light on Huxley's dualistic argument in the two essays of *Evolution and Ethics*. In Darwin's domestic world of the English countryside, husbandry bends nature to human ends, whereas in the natural world beyond, environment is governed absolutely by the laissez-faire dynamics of struggle for existence. It is the very contrast Huxley made between the state of art and the state of nature, governed respectively by the horticultural and the cosmic processes. Hence, while Darwin's intentions in the *Origin* were not even remotely Huxley's in *Evolution and Ethics,* they both promoted the common theme of the power of artificial process to reconstruct material reality.

The power of artificial processes to supplant natural processes was a theme that many of Darwin's mid-century contemporaries explored as nature became increasingly difficult to accept as a social and cultural norm. For Alfred Wallace, who had trouble deriving human culture solely on the principle of natural selection, the dualism implicit in "natural selection" suggested a principle of cultural development. Unlike brutes, whose harmony with their surroundings was perpetually destabilized by new conditions of existence and variability in generations, humans fashioned tools to mediate their fit with the natural world.

> [Man] is, indeed, a being apart, since he is not influenced by the great laws which irresistibly modify all other organic beings. Nay more: this victory which he has gained for himself gives him a direc-

ting influence over other existences. Man has not only escaped "natural selection" himself, but he actually is able to take away some of that power from nature which, before his appearance, she universally exercised. We can anticipate the time when the earth will produce only cultivated plants and domestic animals; when man's selection shall have supplanted "natural selection"; and when the ocean will be the only domain in which that power can be exerted, which for countless cycles of ages ruled supreme over all the earth. (1864, p. 168)

Human directive will, made possible by conscious mind, could substitute human purpose for natural process and allow man with an unchanged body to alter the conditions of existence with increasing effectiveness, an argument Darwin followed in his *Descent* (1871, 158-59). Thus, we see the makings of a new teleology, by which material reality is permanently molded by human artifice (Turner 1974, 76-78).

Such transformational optimism promised a kind of utopian control that would redeem the natural world. Marrying the dynamic of evolutionary progress with the Baconian theme of the advancing human control of nature through new knowledge, many Victorian intellectuals, the young Huxley included, were inclined to read into the human condition a necessarily higher destiny. This ideological construction also correlated with the Marxist view of the conquest of nature through human labor amplified by technique (Engels 1927; Williams 1980). Indeed, it furnished an array of social theorists with the notion that humans, restored to their natural rights within less artificial social structures, and supported by material progress, could attain a civilization of near-millenial proportions.

Yet Victorian transformist ideology also delivered a hidden problem of self-restraint that was not seen very clearly by Wallace or his scientific and political counterparts. The problem, as the American philologist and diplomat George Perkins Marsh showed in his *Man and Nature* (1864), was that human intervention was not only more powerful than either Darwin or Wallace had imagined; it was also pathological. Human action upon nature, Marsh suggested, differs in essential character from animal action because "it is guided by a self-conscious and intelligent will aiming as often at secondary and remote as at immediate objects" (1864, 41). The human tenacity of purpose had a troubling potency: "There are parts of Asia Minor, of Northern Africa, of Greece, and even of Alpine Europe," Marsh noted, "where the operation of causes set in action by man has brought the face of the earth to a desolation almost as complete as that of the moon . . ." (ibid., 42). Marsh documented the creation of deserts, the extinction of animal populations, and vast alterations of geological structures, impressing Lyell with his evidence for the magnitude of the human capacity to alter geological nature. But Marsh could not explain the pathology of the human war against its environment.

This awareness that human powers of transformation were steadily advancing against nature moved the romantic humanist John Ruskin to near-hysteria in his attacks against profane utilitarian science (Sawyer 1985, 217-246). But transformist ideology continued to gain ground in the 1860s and 1870s among those who sought no normative referent in nature. In Darwin's thought and in the industrial revolution, both human and material nature had been seen to offer vast potential for transformation. W. K. Clifford, for example, wrote in his remarkable 1877 essay, "Cosmic Emotion": "Human nature is fluent, it is constantly, though slowly changing, and the universe of human action is changing also" (1877, 420). These instabilities offered an advantage to human enterprise, for if nature was uniform, collective human effort could aspire to control. "How far away is the doctrine of uniformity from fatalism!" Clifford wrote. "It begins directly to remind us that men suffer from preventable evils, that the people perisheth for lack of knowledge" (ibid., 417). To Clifford, evolution supplied the key to ethics: "My actions are to be regarded as good or bad according as they tend to improve me as an organism, to make me move further away from those intermediate forms through which my race has passed, or to make me retrace those upward steps and go down again." Drawing on Spencer's concept of the social organism, Clifford declared that human collective action—or "Band Work"—enabled the social whole to "'originate events independently of foreign determining causes,' or to act with freedom" (ibid., 423). This notion of environmental plasticity under the collaborative stress of human intervention reemerged in the work of John Dewey (1920) and Alfred North Whitehead (1925). The Kingdom of Man was at hand.

Huxley's **Evolution and Ethics** was the product of the same tradition of transformational speculation that had followed in the wake of Darwin's *Origin of Species*. But by the 1890s, Huxley was reflecting back across an economic and social landscape in considerable disarray, as the result of the severe depression in England. The idea that social amelioration was to emerge in any automatic manner by the maintenance of laissez-faire social policies was no longer acceptable. Rejecting religion as a human effort to manipulate, by theodicy, the *concept* of reality rather than the reality itself, Huxley looked once more to science, which offered a means of neutralizing the mechanisms of natural selection. He accordingly rejected the theodicy—the assumption that this is the best of possible worlds—and challenged the cosmic process.

Huxley argued, as Wallace, Clifford, and Mill had, that modern humans construct an artificial world. Intervention and transformation were the great objects of civilization. By artifice, humans modified, albeit temporarily, the forces of nature and helped in the making of their own destiny. "The history of civilization details the steps by which men have succeeded in building up an artificial world within the cosmos. . . . In virtue of his intelligence, the dwarf bends the Titan to his will" (pp. 83-84). This argument drew on Huxley's 1887 essay, **"The Progress of Science,"** in which he spoke of "a new Nature, the existence of which is dependent upon men's efforts, which is subservient to their wants, and which would disappear if man's shaping and guiding hand were withdrawn" (1893-94, 1:51). He identified the transformation as the "new birth of time"—the divergence of civil from natural history.

Huxley had difficulty, as did Lyell and Wallace, accepting the gradualist view of cultural development promoted by Tylor, Lubbock, and Darwin. For Huxley, this was because of the brevity of civil history, given the great cultural differences between the primitive being of his *Man's Place in Nature* (1863) and the modern intellect that worked the miracles of his essay, **"The Progress of Science."** Moreover, there was little evidence in historical time that the human mind was evolving (p. 77-78). In his essay **"Administrative Nihilism"** (1871), Huxley had thus argued a theory of cultural saltation, suggesting that some primordial "aggregation," a term he borrowed from Walter Bagehot and Henry Maine, might precipitate a condition or state of cooperative culture (1893-94, 1:274-75; Bagehot 1869, 17).

Huxley's state of art in **"Evolution and Ethics"** is a psychological construct, an existential condition engendered by a shared mentality, a social consciousness devoted to the persistence of humans both as material and as ethical beings. As Morgan pointed out, Huxley recognized in culture the emergence of a psychological principle of "mental evolution," which enabled conscious choice to displace natural selection as the primary agent of change (Morgan 1896, 334-36). Ethics, like art, worked in "harmonious contrast" with the forces of nature; both were governed by an innate aesthetic sense of the good or beautiful; both were secured at the expense of considerable self-restraint (pp. 31, 35, 80). Interventionist in spirit, these products of the human consciousness sought to manipulate the forces of the cosmos and subordinate them to human purpose. What is neutral in nature—for example, the innate self-centeredness of the biological individual—becomes culpable in the state of art. Neutral physical force and circumstance become tragic within the consciousness of art. Oedipus cannot exist outside the state of art, nor, for that matter, can Thomas Hardy's tragic figures. The ritual of human suffering reveals the very norm of nature, the cosmic process intruding upon the human condition (p. 59).

Thus Huxley, eschewing the unthinking anthropomorphism of religions, consciously reconstructs an anthropomorphic state of art, where the human becomes the moral center of existence. This is the object of all artifice. Huxley's psychological theory of culture as a

mental state was consistent with contemporary Victorian speculation. Walter Bagehot, for example, had argued that humans exercised an increasing mental control over their physical limitations. This idea led to Bagehot's notion of the "age of discussion," in which static civilizations based on set customs were supplanted by progressive civilizations that placed priority on the exercise of intelligence—presumably in English parliamentary democracy (1869, 119). Similar but much more psychologically developed ideas were explored in Lloyd Morgan's theories of mental evolution. Morgan argued that ideas evolved not by selection but by the elimination of incongruity with other similar ideas in a cultural environment, which was wholly a psychic construct (1891, 485-94). D. G. Ritchie, in his *Darwinism and Politics,* explicitly extended themes of struggle he had found in Huxley's essay, **"The Struggle for Existence in Human Society,"** to the domain of institutions. To Ritchie, institutions were artificial constructs that behaved as instruments of Lamarckian evolution, shifting the burden of transmission from biology to social artifices. "Natural selection operates in the highest types of human society as well as in the rest of the organic realm; but it passes into a higher form of itself, in which the conflict of ideas and institutions takes the place of the struggle for existence between individuals and races" (1891, 106). By such means, Ritchie argued, the well-being of society as an ethical end was substituted for the individualist conception of a balance of pleasures and pains (ibid., 106).

Huxley's psychological dualism accommodated a naturalistic, more complexly monistic concept of the civilized individual, who now emerged as both egoistically aggressive and altruistically selfless, irrational and reasoned. The social individual lived in considerable psychological tension, just beyond the sway of the instinctual self. One might thus reconcile the natural history of Darwin with the civil history of Gibbon.

Such psychological realism also revealed a pathological dimension of culture that Huxley was well aware of. The pervasive references throughout the two essays of *Evolution and Ethics* to the pains of renunciation were analogous to a feeling of illness, which Huxley's own long mental suffering, now augmented by the onset of heart failure and the loss of his daughter Marian, must have made palpable. Huxley had been attracted in his essay **"Administrative Nihilism"** by Immanuel Kant's theory in *Idea for a Universal History* (1784) that art was the product of the "unsocial sociability" of humankind. Huxley quoted at length from Kant's essay the argument that society "originated by a sort of pathological compulsion, [which became] metamorphosed into a moral unity." Kant had concluded that "all culture and art which adorn humanity, the most refined social order, are produced by that unsociability which is compelled by its own existence to discipline itself, and so by enforced art to bring the seeds implanted by nature into full flower" (1893-94, 1:277). In **"Evolution and Ethics,"** Huxley modernized this argument: the civilized being necessarily denied expression to instincts that in a state of nature were fundamentally adaptive. In surpressing the "qualities he shares with the ape and the tiger," the divided individual had taken on the burden of pain, which reached its summit in quality and intensity among members of the organized polity (p. 51). Humans were thus compelled to live in the state of art at the expense of their own instinctual lives, living paradoxes, unable to reach under natural conditions the full potential of their powers.

The concept of human artifice as adaptive neither originated nor ended with Huxley. Yet Huxley transformed it into a dualistic principle familiar in twentieth-century organic theories of culture promulgated by individuals like Sigmund Freud and Konrad Lorenz. Freud, whose *Civilization and Its Discontents* took the theme of the irremediable antagonism between the demands of instinct and the restrictions of civilization, concluded his work in 1931 by observing:

> The fateful question for the human species seems to me to be whether and to what extent their cultural development will succeed in mastering the disturbance of their communal life by the human instinct of aggression and self-destruction. . . . Men have gained control over the forces of nature to such an extent that with their help they would have no difficulty in exterminating one another to the last man. They know this, and hence comes a large part of their current unrest, their unhappiness and their mood of anxiety. And now it is to be expected that the other of the two "Heavenly Powers," eternal Eros, will make an effort to assert himself in the struggle with his equally immortal adversary. But who can foresee with what success and with what result? (1931, 92)

In *Evolution and Ethics,* Huxley brought the logic of his generation to the verge of the considerable dilemma, also identified in the work of George Perkins Marsh, of humans at war with the cosmos, instinct joining with artifice against their fellows and environment.

The Reception of "Evolution and Ethics"

To many former associates accustomed to Huxley's robust team spirit in controversies with orthodoxy, **"Evolution and Ethics"** seemed an abandonment of the old "conspiracy" to translate questions into the monistic terms of scientific naturalism while invoking agnostic brackets for the larger ontological questions. Henry Drummond, the Scottish naturalist and evangelical writer, noted the widespread surprise at Huxley's dualistic drift: "For, by an astonishing *tour de force*—the last, as his former associates in the evolutionary ranks have not failed to remind him, which might have been expected of him—[Huxley] ejects himself from

the world order, and washes his hands of it in the name of Ethical Man" (1894, 22). Others, like Lloyd Morgan, the comparative psychologist, found in Huxley's views a crucial new distinction between human conscious choice and natural selection as agents of change (1896, 336).

Leslie Stephen, St. George Mivart, Herbert Spencer, John Dewey, Karl Pearson, and Petr Kropotkin, as diverse an assembly of late Victorian philosophical and social speculators as one could summon, all agreed that inconsistency had overtaken Huxley's thinking. With the exception of Mivart, the Roman Catholic evolutionist, they flatly rejected Huxley's psychological dualism, which set the instinctual content of the primitive mind against its transformed version in the social self and made humans the antagonists of nature. Psychological dualism, which Huxley had derived from nineteenth-century physiology and ethnology, recognized a complexity in the mind that others like Sigmund Freud would ultimately transform into a rich source of oppositions and submerged complexes. This idea of self-opposition naturalized the irrational and shattered one of the great dreams of Victorian social speculators, including Huxley himself: to unify the laws of nature and society under the principles of reason and utility.

Objections voiced both by Leslie Stephen and St. George Mivart in reviews of the Romanes Lecture demonstrated how thoroughly Huxley had confounded the proponents of liberalism and orthodoxy. Stephen held to the utilitarian line of his own *Science of Ethics* (1882), arguing that moral behavior was a product of evolution. He rightly noted that Huxley's metaphorical language anthropomorphically invested natural process with negative qualities—"ferocity," "evil," and "titan"—that infused nature with an intentionality it could not, in fact, support. Huxley's argument that the social individual was at odds with the natural individual was "awkward," Stephen suggested politely, for Huxley had introduced a developmental gap between the cosmic and horticultural processes that had no logical explanation. To Stephen, the social utility of virtue was identical with its evolutionary utility, making virtue the logical product of self-evident natural forces (1893, 164). If suffering, as Huxley had argued, was indeed a perennial companion of the higher organism, that pain was also a source of well-being. Stephen thus embraced theodicy: "the sheep may be, on the whole, the better for the wolf" (1893, 160).

As Stephen thus clung to his utilitarianism, so the Catholic evolutionist Mivart rejoiced in Huxley's restoration of the gap between brutes and humans. Mivart, once the rising Huxley's anatomical assistant in the preparation of **Man's Place in Nature** (1863), had burned his professional bridges in a review of Darwin's *Descent of Man* that challenged Darwin's theory of the unity of human and animal faculties (Hull 1973, 372-75, 414; James R. Moore 1979, 120-21). Mivart had insisted in *The Genesis of Species* (1871) on a qualitative gap between the instinctive social behavior of animals and the conscious moral behavior of humans. Huxley had patronizingly dismissed Mivart's theistic morality and argued that both animal and human psychology reflected a utilitarian ethical strategy (1893-94, 2:170-71). But six years later, Huxley argued against strict utility that moral sense, like aesthetic sense, was intuitive (Huxley et al. 1877, 536-37).

In his 1893 review of Huxley's Romanes Lecture, "Evolution in Professor Huxley," Mivart noted with irony that Huxley's thought was itself "evolving." For Huxley was now challenging utilitarian ethics and insisting on an unexplained gap between natural process and human conscious will, between the cosmic and ethical process, between nature and man. Mivart, as he had done for twenty years, thrust God into this gap: "So great, indeed, is the contrast and distance between man and the world of irrational nature, that it suggests now, as it suggested of old, . . . a mode of being which is raised above all human nature, as man himself is raised above all infrahuman nature" (1893, 330). This was classical theistic argument. Merely beneficial social behavior, Mivart held in contrast to Stephen, could not be equated with conscious virtue. Rather, a new principle must come into play. Others thought similarly. The philosopher William Courtney argued approvingly that Huxley had left break enough between nature and humans for a spiritualist interpretation (Courtney 1895, 320-22). And an anonymous reviewer in *The Atheneum* marveled at Huxley's dexterity in promulgating a doctrine that made no mention of Christianity, yet "in its essential character was an approximation to the Pauline dogma of nature and grace" ("Evolution" 1893a, 119; see also Lightman 1987).

The shifts in Huxley's thinking detected by Stephen and Mivart were especially bitter to the embattled Herbert Spencer, whose Lamarckian theories of social progress came under increasing attack in the 1880s and 1890s by liberals, socialists, and physiologists alike. To Spencer, Huxley was deceitfully abandoning a tacit alliance that had served both men for a generation. **"Evolution and Ethics,"** he reasoned in characteristic a priori fashion, could hardly be considered an attack against himself, since he and Huxley held identical views, and he had preceeded Huxley as a philosopher. It was unlikely that Huxley intended to teach him his own theories (1893, 184). Huxley, the same old utilitarian monist he had associated with for more than forty years, was evidently attacking the extreme anarchists. The footnotes of Huxley's published version of *Evolution and Ethics,* Spencer insisted, belied the insistent dualism of the main text. Huxley had stated in note 20 that "strictly speaking, social life, and the ethical process in virtue of which it advances towards

perfection, are part and parcel of the general process of evolution, . . . just as the 'governor' in a steam engine is part of the mechanism of the engine" (Spencer 1893, 193-94; p. 114-15). Huxley, Spencer insisted, held views so similar to his own that the final paragraph of **"Evolution and Ethics"** expressed the very sentiment of the final paragraph of his own two-volume *Principles of Ethics,* which, Spencer noted pregnantly, Huxley had had in his hands some two weeks before he delivered the Romanes Lecture (1893, 194).

The long and fruitful association of Huxley and Spencer was too widely known for anyone to be surprised by Spencer's claim. As late as 1878 Huxley had written of his fellow X Club member for the ninth edition of *Encyclopedia Britannica:* "The profound and vigorous writings of Mr. Spencer embody the spirit of Descartes in the knowledge of our own day, and may be regarded as the 'Principes de la Philosophie' of the nineteenth century" (1893-94, 2:213). This was hardly the language of an antagonist, especially in view of the profound regard Huxley had for Descartes as the prototypical truth seeker (ibid., 5:166-98).

However, mutually supportive scientific naturalists as they were from a distance, Spencer's a priori method had always been at odds with Huxley's own stringent empiricism. For thirty years, their opinions had steadily widened over issues long identified with Spencer, which Huxley attacked in *Evolution and Ethics*: the law of progress, the perfectibility of man, laissez-faire social policy, radical individualism, and utilitarian ethics. In such seminal articles as "Progress: Its Law and Cause" (1857) and "The Social Organism" (1860), Spencer had made evolution and human social development parts of the same necessity, on the a priori assumptions that every force had multiple effects and therefore contributed to a growing heterogeneity that was the essence of progress, whether organic or social (Spencer 1904, vol. 1; Bowler, 1984).

In contradiction of the laissez-faire individualism such views inspired, Huxley promulgated theories of persistence, waged a vast campaign for public education and for improving natural knowledge, rejected the analogy of state and organism, attacked radical individualism, and finally discredited nature as an ethical model (see also Desmond 1982, 97-101). Indeed, Huxley's two essays, with their emphasis on environmental rather than organic change, were fundamentally at odds with the Lamarckian dynamic of Spencer's social views. Even Spencer's ardent Chinese disciple Yen Fu considered Huxley the antagonist and translated *Evolution and Ethics* into classical Chinese so as to provide a foil to the master's philosophy (Schwartz 1964).

What most troubled Spencer and other contemporaries about *Evolution and Ethics* was Huxley's final—and, really, quite characteristic—agnostic refusal to rationalize away the apparent gap between civilization and nature, ethics and instinct. Where Victorians had routinely invoked theodicies or teleological speculations to explain, justify, or diminish the discontinuity, Huxley agnostically abandoned the effort to provide it with a specific logic or faith, a point first noted by Lloyd Morgan (1923, 206). "If the conclusion that the [cosmic and horticultural processes] are antagonistic is logically absurd," Huxley had written, "I am sorry for logic, because, as we have seen, the fact is so" (p. 12). He thus accepted the concept of the irrational that others denied. Spencer had found in the gap teleological evidence for the "making of man," Darwin had normalized it with the principle of unity of mental faculties, Stephen had justified it in a theodicy, Mivart had cited it as evidence of spiritual intervention. But Huxley denied it an explanation.

In a letter of March, 1894, he observed:

> There are two very different questions which people fail to discriminate. One is whether evolution accounts for morality, the other whether the principle of evolution in general can be adopted as an ethical principle.

> The first, of course, I advocate, and have constantly insisted upon. The second I deny, and reject all so-called evolutionary ethics based upon it. (1900, 2:360)

In his refusal to fill in the gap between the realms of biological determinism and human purpose, Huxley denied nineteenth-century theories of biological process the role of furnishing a social praxis (Himmelfarb 1968, 332; 1986, 79). But he did not suggest that there were no connections between the two realms, for instinct and physical nature were integral to the dynamic of which modern humanity was an inescapable part. The two essays of *Evolution and Ethics,* although based on Malthusian principles, sought to deny these primary roles in human society.

Huxley's social meliorism drew criticism from the nascent British eugenics movement. Leslie Stephen, oddly enough, was the first to raise eugenic objections to Huxley's call in **"Evolution and Ethics"** for the equipping of as many as possible to survive. Citing Karl Pearson on the struggle for existence among races of men, Stephen argued in his review of **"Evolution and Ethics,"** "We give inferior races a chance of taking whatever place they are fit for, and try to supplant them with the least possible severity if they are unfit for any place" (1893, 170). In what appears to be an impressionistic blend of Spencer, Bagehot, Quételet, and Galton, Stephen spoke confidently, if theoretically, of developing the "best stock" of the race in a future "average man" who would combine great intellectual power with physical vigor: "We are engaged in working out a gigantic problem: What is best, in the sense of the most efficient, type of human being?" (ibid., 168; see also Quételet 1835, 96-97).

Huxley's anti-eugenicist **"Prolegomena,"** although partly a response to Stephen's review of **"Evolution and Ethics,"** broadly criticized the growing eugenics movement. Galton's *Hereditary Genius,* which appeared in its second edition in 1892, classified humans by qualities that Galton argued were transmitted among human "breeding groups" through the generations. Denying a role to nurture and giving all to nature in the physical and mental constitution of the individual, Galton raised hereditary transmission to a social absolute (Kevles 1985). He sought to formalize and "humanize" the "survival of the fittest" in a deliberated public policy of hereditary transmission. An oligarchy of breeding experts might manipulate—ever so slightly—conditions of human existence, so as to vary the birth and death rates of favored groups and thus improve the physical and mental qualities of the average human (Galton 1892, 27, 41). The purifying role of Spencer's laissez-faireism was thus supplanted by Galton's artificial selection.

Huxley concluded that the social interventions of the eugenicists, despite their Platonic concerns for the ideal individual, failed to imagine the brutal consequences for the real individual. The selection of humans by other humans, he argued, would destroy the bonds of sympathy that held society together, without which "there is no conscience, nor any restraint on the conduct of men" (pp. 36-37). Huxley's own family history of mental instability would not have entitled him to any favors in a Galtonian eugenicist state, as Huxley was well aware (Paradis 1978). "One must be very 'fit,' indeed," he noted, not to know of an occasion or two "when it would have been only too easy to qualify for a place among the 'unfit'" (p. 39). Huxley's anti-eugenicist stance was challenged by Karl Pearson in an address delivered at the Oxford University Junior Science Club nearly fourteen years later to the day, on May 17, 1907. The conflict between the ethical and cosmic processes, Pearson argued, was in reality a conflict between "human sympathy" and "racial purification." Human sympathy, he noted without a hint of irony, was overwhelming English society: "One factor—absolutely needful for race survival—sympathy, has been developed in such an exaggerated form that we are in danger, by suspending selection, of lessening the effect of those other factors which automatically purge the state of the degenerates in body and mind" (1907, 25). Huxley's state of art, by suspending selection and meliorating the physical conditions of existence, was to Pearson the certain source of physical, mental, and moral degeneration.

John Dewey, another avid Huxley-watcher, took the themes of environmental transformation and social intervention by education not as liabilities but as central arguments in a new philosophical scheme. The antagonism that Huxley saw between humans and their environment was a dualism that could be recast both as a dialectic between fact and ideal and as a source of social drive. Humans progressed, the young Dewey agreed, by reconstructing a part of the natural environment, not so much in rebellion against nature as "to relate a part of nature more intimately to the environment as a whole" (Dewey 1898, 326). Themes of transformation, both material and social, permeated Dewey's later philosophy of reconstruction. Nature was "something to be modified, to be intentionally controlled. It is material to act upon, so as to transform it into new objects which answer to our needs" (1929, 80-81; see also 1920, 116). But Dewey rejected what he saw as Huxley's dualistic view that brute self-assertion remained a determinant of human behavior. Rather, "the natural process, the so-called inherited animal instincts and promptings, are not only the stimuli, but also the materials, of moral conduct" (1898, 332-33). Like Spencer, Dewey believed that the animal impulses were not just deflected but actually eliminated by transformation. Dewey substituted for Huxley's gap between natural and ethical humans his own monistic behavioral gap between "habit and aim," arguing that the social priority was to transform the former to the latter (ibid., 335).

Demonstrating the formidable plasticity of biosocial theory itself, Petr Kropotkin, geographer, anarchist, and social theoretician, launched an ambitious frontal attack on Huxley's assumptions by reconstructing a non-Malthusian nature with the assistance of Darwinian principles. Kropotkin felt morally outraged by Huxley's Malthusian essay, **"The Struggle for Existence in Human Society"** (1888), in which Huxley had argued that the natural state for all organisms was a Hobbesian war of each against all. "From the point of view of the moralist," Huxley had argued, "the animal world is on about the same level as a gladiator's show . . . the strongest, the swiftest, and the cunningest live to fight another day . . . [and] no quarter is given" (1893-94, 199-200).

Kropotkin's response—eight articles written between 1890 and 1896 on collaboration as a universal adaptive strategy—was collected in 1902 under the title *Mutual Aid: A Factor of Evolution.* Recounting how during his own extensive travels in Siberia he had witnessed not struggle but solidarity among organisms, Kropotkin drew on Darwin's thesis of the adaptive function of intraspecies cooperation. Kropotkin contested Huxley's—and Darwin's own—Malthusian assumption that in nature the combined destabilizing pressures of population growth and variability in inheritance tended to force species into a natural state of individualistic, aggressive self-aggrandizement. Who are the fittest? Kropotkin asked: those continually at war with each other, or those who support each other? (1914, 14). Darwin's references to individual struggle, Kropotkin argued, were mainly metaphorical, for Darwin had produced little empirical evidence of severe struggles among individuals and varieties of the same species.

Kropotkin's ingenious blend of biological and social discourse, developed in defense of a radical laissez-faire theory of human society, reanimated the romantic view of primitive human innocence and benevolence. Prehistoric society was a state of "primitive communism" and "tribal solidarity" later corrupted by the development of the modern nuclear family (ibid., 94-97). Thus, Kropotkin read community, not individualism, from the natural state. He exaggerated Darwinian struggle—and Hobbesian war—to mean continual, visible confrontation, rather than the more subtle but still fatal strategies by which some organisms dominated food supply and breeding privilege. Hobbes had not meant by *war* literal battle among individuals or groups. "For Warre," he had insisted, "consisteth not in Battell onely, or the act of fighting; but in a tract of time, wherein the Will to contend by Battell is sufficiently known. . . . So the nature of War, consisteth not in actuall fighting; but in the known disposition thereto, during all the time there is no assurance to the contrary" (Hobbes 1651, 1:185-86). War did not mean for Hobbes, just as struggle did not mean for Darwin, literal confrontation to the death, but rather the disposition to use force as a utilitarian strategy of securing an individual end.

Despite Kropotkin, Huxley's confrontationist themes were taken up with renewed force by his former protégé E. Ray Lankester, the Oxford morphologist, in the Romanes Lecture of 1905, titled "Nature's Insurgent Son." Lankester, president of the British Association for the Advancement of Science and an intimate of H. G. Wells, Huxley's former student, hammered on the theme, consistent with Marxist ideology, that "the knowledge and control of nature is Man's destiny and his greatest need" (1907, 60). Author of a volume on *Extinct Animals* (1905), Lankester referred to the "unobtrusive, yet tremendous slaughter of the unfit which is incessantly going on" (ibid., 13). Reiterating some of the themes of his earlier volume, *Degeneration,* he argued that humans had begun a process of revolt against nature from which they could no longer withdraw without immense and catastrophic consequences to civilization.

Huxley's rejection of strict ethical utilitarianism opened up questions that continued to be debated in the terms of *Evolution and Ethics.* Some, like George E. Moore, sought to weaken what they saw as the metaphorical authority Victorian biology had assumed over ethics. In his *Principia Ethica* (1903), for example, Moore explored the so-called naturalistic fallacy, by which Bentham and Spencer had identified the good with natural process and pleasure (Moore 1903, 48-50; see also Huxley, p. 74). The *facts* of evolution were assumed to be the rules of natural process and, by theodicy, of ethical behavior. Pointing to the fallacy that "more evolved" meant "higher," he observed, as Huxley had, that an alteration in the earth's conditions would mechanically change the significance of "more evolved"

(Moore 1903, 47; Huxley, pp. 4-5, 80-81; see also Richards 1987, 323-25).

Yet the rapidly developing fields of behaviorism and psychology could draw on a body of developing knowledge that had far more subtle explanatory potential than Spencer's simple analogical naturalism, as both Ruse and Richards have attempted to demonstrate (Ruse 1986; Richards 1987). In "Evolutionary Ethics," his own Romanes Lecture of 1943, Julian Huxley patronizingly dismissed his grandfather's misplaced Victorian moral standards as no longer self-evident. Sounding rather like Spencer, Julian Huxley sought to unify cosmic and ethical process by once more causally subordinating ethics to natural principles (Huxley and Huxley, 1947, 131; see Toulmin 1982, 53-71). Rejecting intuitive theories of the good, he declared ethics to be a loose term for conventions of rightness and wrongness. "Ethical realism" was the key, the degree to which ethical judgments conformed to external facts of experience. The greater the knowledge, the greater the degree of realism and good. Even Nazi indulgence of aggression and violence towards Jews was an example of ethical behavior, albeit a "grossly unrealistic one" (Huxley 1947, 123). Evolutionary advantages accrued to groups that could pool experience and coordinate actions that were based on a higher order of reality.

In the reception of Huxley's *Evolution and Ethics,* we find an intellectual and social divide. Older Victorian ethical naturalisms, including those of Spencer, Darwin, Clifford, and Stephen, tended to locate a direct operational analogy for ethical behavior in evolutionary utility. That is, the evolutionary process was conceived as the model of the ethical process. Individuals with these views sought explanatory parallels between human and animal behavior and saw Huxley's Romanes Lecture as dualistic and therefore inconsistent with his own naturalism. In a sense, they were right, for Huxley had once been a partisan of such naive analogical naturalism. On the other hand, Huxley did not reject evolutionary principles as the basis for the emergence of morality. Rather he concluded that evolutionary principles were not themselves to be taken as ethical principles.

Conclusion: The Human Colony

Huxley's Romanes Lecture was pronounced "one of the most brilliant gems in the prose literature of the nineteenth century" by the *Oxford Magazine* ("Evolution," 1893b). Yet it was an essay about limitation and failure: the profound physical limits experienced by the human organism, and the failure of simple naturalism to light the way through the gathering social conflicts of the Victorian twilight. If Huxley self-critically pondered the metaphorical excesses of the century's biological speculators, his haunting image of human isolation remained the naturalistic product of Victorian

scientific cosmology. But now the human colony, contending against entropy and instinct in an alien cosmic milieu, could seek little reassurance in the once-familiar equation "follow nature" (see Meyers 1985). Huxley had few answers, concluding his essay conservatively with a wistful backward glance at Tennyson's "Ulysses," and calling upon his fellows "To play the man 'strong in will / To strive, to seek, to find, and not to yield'" (p. 86). The Victorian ship was setting sail.

In the sequestered human culture Huxley imagined as a colony apart from the natural realm, we find one extreme of the secularization of human ends that had so tortured the nineteenth-century sensibility. The immediate ends of the individual and contemporary society had effectively displaced from Huxley's cultural agenda all theoretical futures—whether Christian, pantheist, evolutionary, or Marxist. "It is not clear," he had observed sarcastically in 1888, "what compensation the *Eohippus* gets for his sorrows in the fact that, some millions of years afterwards, one of his descendents wins the Derby" (1893-94, 9:199). Human purpose, if partly determined by instinct, had through consciousness and culture taken as its object the shaping of human conditions of existence according to an ethical ideal. But there were no teleological consolations, no evidences of a design, no unfolding necessities in nature, no meaningful hopes of a dramatically higher human destiny. Huxley adopted, rather, the practical demotic object of constructing by human artifice more humane, if necessarily temporary, terms of existence. This isolationist view of the human condition was a Victorian product that was to become familiar as a modern version of the cosmological picture, haunted by the prospect of Heat Death and isolated consciousness (Barrow and Tipler 1986).

Isolationism meant for Huxley the collapse of the explanatory biological analogy he had once championed with Spencer, Stephen, and other naturalists. Such Victorian analogical naturalism, as epitomized in Spencer's work, had endeavored to explain complex social processes by reference to specific physiological, embryological, and evolutionary processes. Even Darwin, somewhat in spite of himself, had thought of the increasing complexity of species as a natural progress toward what was innately *higher* rather than simply better suited to current conditions of existence (Ospovat 1981, 228). For Huxley, this effort to derive human terms of social existence from evolutionary process had come to seem a dangerous exercise. "It is very desirable," he now observed in his **"Prolegomena,"** "to remember that evolution is not an explanation of the cosmic process, but merely a generalized statement of the method and results of that process" (p. 6). No longer did the evolutionary transformation of humankind loom as an end immanent in nature, with a theodical basis in the argument that continuous transmutation supported a pervasive progressive momentum from the lower to the higher. In Huxley's *Evolution and Ethics,* the Victorian dream of an "ideal man" was thus discarded.

In rejecting naive analogical naturalism, Huxley did not abandon the empirical principles of scientific naturalism or the assumption that culture and mind were the natural products of some unknown physical process. The divided individual could be seen in the demonstrated conflict of consciousness with instinct. Huxley's dualism was thus naturalized in the psychological division that he now viewed as the fundamental truth of human existence. As a characteristic of the brain, such internal human conflict was for all practical purposes permanent. Hence, environment and society became the only remaining domains of human adjustment, a view comprehensively developed by Huxley's former associate Lloyd Morgan in *Habit and Instinct:*

> Evolution has *been transferred from the organism to his environment.* There must increment somewhere, otherwise evolution is impossible. In social evolution on this view, the increment is by storage in the social environment to which each new generation adapts itself, with no increased native power of adaptation. In the written record, in social traditions, in the manifold inventions which make scientific and industrial progress possible, in the products of art, and the recorded examples of noble lives, we have an environment which is at the same time the product of mental evolution, and affords the condition of the development of each individual mind to-day. (1896, 340)

This attractive yet problematic theme that humans can effectively influence their collective destiny by altering environment, so prominent in the thought of Wallace, Darwin, Clifford, Huxley, Freud, Whitehead, Dewey, Julian Huxley, and many others, was reinforced by the Baconian view of science as control. It is a theme that has found recent expression in René Dubois's *The Wooing of Earth* (1980).

In Huxley's two essays, Victorian technological man became at once the personification of artifice and the gardener-force of the evolutionary world view. Although he could not effectively select, his powers were the very greatest to which humans could aspire, for he could alter conditions of existence—the strong force of Darwin's evolutionary dynamic. This unprecedented human competency, identified with the man of science, whom Huxley had championed among Victorians, gave considerable social consistency to Huxley's lifelong efforts on behalf of science education. It also brought upon Huxley the charge of petty liberal elitism, of seeking the marriage of science and capital on behalf of the captains of industry (Helfand 1977). Yet, the political intent of Huxley's **"Evolution and Ethics"** and **"Prolegomena,"** as was clear in previous essays, including **"Government: Anarchy or Regi-**

mentation" (1893-94, 1:383-430), was to seek some political middle ground from which to advance common social causes and exploit the growing "dominion over Nature" (ibid., 1:423). To Huxley, socialism overlooked the more fundamental problem of Malthus in favor of the secondary problem of distribution; on the other hand, laissez-faire individualism acquiesced to the status quo (ibid., 1:427-28).

The successes of the industrial revolution had made possible a new nature, "begotten by science upon fact." Such Baconian transformism, made more forceful by the industrial revolution, was blind to the equilibrium of environment (see Leiss 1972; Worster 1977). Huxley's colony distilled from Victorian culture the virtues of self-sufficiency and human enterprise amid the alien internal and external forces of the physical world. But in its imperial and single-minded drive to neutralize the forces of the antagonist, it demonstrated little sensitivity to the dependencies of humankind in the fabric of nature. Huxley had little sense of the ecological whole. If he was more realistic in his views of human limits than many of his contemporaries, his program was also ambiguous, for it implied the apotheosis of control in a war against the self and nature that none dare win.

Bibliography

Bagehot, Walter. 1869. *Physics and Politics.* Reprint. 1956. Boston: Beacon Press.

Barrow, John D, and Frank J. Tipler. 1986. *The Anthropic Cosmological Principle.* New York: Oxford University Press.

Bartholomew, Michael. 1975. "Huxley's Defence of Darwin." *Annals of Science* 32:525-35.

Barton, Ruth. 1983. "Evolution: The Whitworth Gun in Huxley's War for the Liberation of Science from Theology." In *The Wider Domain of Evolutionary Thought,* ed. D. Oldroyd and I. Langham, 261-87. Dordrecht: Reidel.

Beer, Gillian. 1983. *Darwin's Plots: Evolutionary Narrative in Darwin, George Eliot, and Nineteenth-Century Fiction.* London: Routledge and Kegan Paul.

Bowler, Peter J. 1984. *Evolution: The History of an Idea.* Berkeley: University of California Press.

———. 1986. *Theories of Human Evolution: A Century of Debate, 1844-1944.* Baltimore: Johns Hopkins University Press.

Burrow, J. W. 1966. *Evolution and Society: A Study in Victorian Social Theory.* Cambridge: Cambridge University Press.

Carpenter, William. 1889. *Nature and Man: Essays Scientific and Philosophical*. New York: Appleton.

Clifford, W. K. 1877. "Cosmic Emotion." *Nineteenth Century* 1:411-29.

Courtney, William L. 1895. "Professor Huxley as a Philosopher." *Fortnightly Review* 64:17-22.

Darwin, Charles. 1859. *The Origin of Species . . . a Variorum Text*. Ed. Morse Peckham. 1959. Philadelphia: University of Pennsylvania Press.

————. 1871. *The Descent of Man and Selection in Relation to Sex*. Ed. John Tyler Bonner and Robert M. May. 1981. Princeton: Princeton University Press.

————. 1872. *The Expression of the Emotions in Man and Animals*. Reprint. 1955. New York: The Philosophical Library.

Desmond, Adrian. 1982. *Archetypes and Ancestors: Paleontology in Victorian London, 1850-1875*. Chicago: University of Chicago Press.

Dewey, John. 1898. "Evolution and Ethics." *Monist* 8:321-41.

Dewey, John. 1920. *Reconstruction in Philosophy*. Enlarged ed. 1948. Boston: Beacon Press.

————. 1929. *The Quest for Certainty: A Study in the Relation of Knowledge and Action*. Vol. 4 of *The Later Works of John Dewey*. Ed. Jo Ann Boydston; intro. Stephen Toulmin. 1984. Carbondale: Southern Illinois University Press.

di Gregorio, Mario A. 1984. *T. H. Huxley's Place in Natural Science*. New Haven: Yale University Press.

Drummond, Henry. 1894. *The Ascent of Man*. 7th ed. 1898. New York: James Pott and Company.

Dubois, René. 1980. *The Wooing of Earth: New Perspectives on Man's Use of Nature*. New York: Scribner's.

Engels, Friedrich. 1927. *Dialectics of Nature*. Trans. and ed. Clemens Dutt. 1940. New York: International Publishers.

"Evolution and Ethics," by T. H. Huxley. Review. 1893a. *The Atheneum*, no. 3430:119-20.

"Evolution and Ethics," by T. H. Huxley. Review. 1893b. *Oxford Magazine* 11:380-81.

Flew, Anthony. 1967. *Evolutionary Ethics*. New York: St. Martin's.

Foster, Sir Michael. 1896. Obituary Notice for Thomas Henry Huxley. *Proceedings of the Royal Society of London* 59:xlvi-lxvii.

Freud, Sigmund. 1931. *Civilization and its Discontents*. Trans. and ed. James Strachey. 1962. New York: W. W. Norton.

Galton, Francis. 1892. *Hereditary Genius: An Enquiry into its Laws and Consequences*. Ed. C. D. Darlington. 2d ed. 1962. New York: World Publishing Company.

Ghiselin, Michael T. 1969. *The Triumph of the Darwinian Method*. Reprint. 1984. Chicago: University of Chicago Press.

Gibbon, Edward. 1901-02. *The History of the Decline and Fall of the Roman Empire*. Ed. John Bury. 2d ed. 7 vols. London: Methuen.

Gillispie, Charles C. 1951. *Genesis and Geology: The Impact of Scientific Discoveries upon Religious Beliefs in the Decades before Darwin*. New York: Harper and Row.

Gladstone, William E. 1892. "An Academic Sketch." First Romanes Lecture, October 24, 1892. Oxford: Clarendon Press.

Greene, John C. 1959a. *The Death of Adam: Evolution and Its Impact on Western Thought*. Ames: Iowa State University Press.

————. 1959b. "Biology and Social Theory in the Nineteenth Century: Auguste Comte and Herbert Spenser." In *Critical Problems in the History of Science,* ed. Marshall Clagett, 419-47. Madison: University of Wisconsin Press.

————. 1977. "Darwin as Social Evolutionist." *Journal of the History of Biology* 10:1-27.

Guizot, François Pierre Guillaume. 1885. *History of Civilization from the Fall of the Roman Empire to the French Revolution*. Trans. William Hazlitt. 2 vols. London: Macmillan.

Hanham, Harold. 1970. "Introduction." In *On Scotland and the Scotch Intellect,* xiii-xxxvii. Chicago: University of Chicago Press.

Hankins, Thomas L. 1985. *Science and the Enlightenment*. Cambridge: Cambridge University Press.

Hartley, David. 1749. *Observations on Man, His Frame, His Duty, and His Expectations*. Reprint. 1966. Gainesville: University of Florida Press.

Hearnshaw, F.J.C., ed. 1933. *The Social and Political Ideas of Some Representative Thinkers of the Victorian Age*. Reprint. 1967. New York: Barnes and Noble.

Helfand, Michael S. 1977. "T. H. Huxley's 'Evolution and Ethics': The Politics of Evolution and the Evolution of Politics." *Victorian Studies* 2:159-77.

Himmelfarb, Gertrude. 1968. *Victorian Minds*. New York: Knopf.

———. 1986. *Marriage and Morals among the Victorians*. New York: Knopf.

Hobbes, Thomas. 1651. *Leviathan, or The Matter, Forme, & Power of a Common-wealth, Ecclesiasticall and Civill*. Ed. C. B. MacPherson. 1968. New York: Penguin.

Hofstadter, Richard. 1955. *Darwinism in American Thought*. Revised ed. Boston: Beacon Press.

Hull, David. 1973. *Darwin and His Critics*. Chicago: University of Chicago Press.

Hume, David. 1739-40. *A Treatise of Human Nature*. Ed. L. A. Selby-Bigge. 2d. ed. 1978. Oxford: Oxford University Press.

———. 1777. *Enquiries Concerning Human Understanding and Concerning the Principles of Morals*. Ed. L. A. Selby-Bigge. 3d ed. Revised P. H. Nidditch. 1975. Oxford: Oxford University Press.

Huxley, Julian. 1948. "Eugenics and Society." *Man in the Modern World: Selected Essays*. New York: New American Library.

Huxley, Julian, and Thomas H. Huxley. 1947. *Touchstone for Ethics: 1893-1943*. New York: Harper and Brothers.

Huxley, Leonard. 1900. *Life and Letters of Thomas Henry Huxley*. 2 vols. New York: Appleton.

Huxley, Thomas H. 1866. *Lessons in Elementary Physiology*. New ed. 1881. London: Macmillan.

———. 1879. *The Crayfish: An Introduction to the Study of Zoology*. Reprint. 1974. Cambridge: MIT Press.

———. 1891. Introduction to *The Revolutionary Spirit*, by Théodore Rocquain, trans. J. D. Hunting. London: Swan, Sonnenschein.

———. 1892. "An Apologetic Irenicon." *The Fortnightly Review* 52:557-71.

———. 1893. "Evolution and Ethics." The Second Romanes Lecture. London: Macmillan.

———. 1893-94. *Collected Essays*. 9 vols. London: Macmillan.

———. 1936. *T. H. Huxley's Diary of the Voyage of HMS Rattlesnake*. Ed. Julian Huxley. Garden City, New York: Doubleday.

Huxley, Thomas H. et al. 1877. "A Modern Symposium: The Influence upon Morality of a Decline in Religious Belief." *Nineteenth Century* 1:531-46.

Irvine, William. 1955. *Apes, Angels, and Victorians: The Story of Darwin, Huxley, and Evolution*. New York: McGraw-Hill.

Jones, Gareth Steadman. 1971. *Outcast London: A Study in the Relationship between Classes in Victorian Society*. Reprint. 1984. New York: Penguin.

Kevles, Daniel J. 1985. *In the Name of Eugenics: Genetics and the Uses of Human Heredity*. Reprint. 1986. Berkeley: University of California Press.

Kohn, David. 1980. "Theories to Work By: Rejected Theories, Reproduction, and Darwin's Path to Natural Selection." *Studies in the History of Biology* 4:67-170.

Kropotkin, Petr. 1914. *Mutual Aid: A Factor of Evolution*. Reprint. 1955. Boston: Extending Horizons Books.

Landau, Misia. 1984. "Human Evolution as Narrative." *American Scientist* 72:262-68.

Lankester, E. Ray. 1880. *Degeneration: A Chapter in Darwinism*. London: Macmillan.

———. 1907. *The Kingdom of Man*. London: Archibald Constable.

Leiss, William. 1972. *The Domination of Nature*. New York: Braziller.

Lightman, Bernard. 1987. *The Origins of Agnosticism: Victorian Unbelief and the Limits of Knowledge*. Baltimore: Johns Hopkins University Press.

Lovejoy, Arthur O. 1936. *The Great Chain of Being*. Cambridge: Harvard University Press.

———. 1948. *Essays in the History of Ideas*. New York: G. P. Putnam's Sons.

Lubbock, John. 1870. *The Origins of Civilization and the Primitive Condition of Man*. London: Longmans, Green, and Company.

Malthus, Thomas R. 1798. *An Essay on the Principle of Population as it Affects the Future Improvement of Society and An Essay on the Principle of Population . . . and A summary View of the Principle of Population*. Ed. Anthony Flew. 1970. New York: Penguin.

Manier, Edward. 1978. *The Young Darwin and His Cultural Circle*. Dordrecht: Reidel.

Marsh, George Perkins. 1864. *Man and Nature; or, Physical Geography as Modified by Human Action,* ed. D. Lowenthal. Reprint. 1965. Cambridge: Harvard University Press.

Meyers, Greg. 1985. "Nineteenth Century Popularizations of Thermodynamics and the Rhetoric of Social Prophecy." *Victorian Studies* 29:35-66.

Mill, John Stuart. 1969. *Essays on Ethics, Religion, and Society.* Vol 10 of *Collected Works of John Stuart Mill.* Ed. J. M. Robson. Toronto: University of Toronto Press.

Mivart, St. George. 1871. "Darwin's *Descent of Man.*" In *Darwin and His Critics.* Ed. David Hull. 1973. Chicago: University of Chicago Press.

———. 1893. "Evolution in Professor Huxley." *Popular Science Monthly* 44:319-33.

Moore, George E. 1903. *Principia Ethica.* Reprint. 1984. Cambridge: Cambridge University Press.

Moore, James R. 1979. *The Post-Darwinian Controversies: A Study of the Protestant Struggle to Come to Terms with Darwin in Great Britain and America, 1870-1900.* Cambridge: Cambridge University Press.

Morgan, C. Lloyd. 1891. *Animal Life and Intelligence.* London: Edward Arnold.

———. 1896. *Habit and Instinct.* London: Edward Arnold.

———. 1923. *Emergent Evolution.* New York: Henry Holt.

———. 1933. *The Emergence of Novelty.* London: Williams and Norgate.

Noland, Richard. "T. H. Huxley on Culture." *The Personalist.* 45:94-111.

Ospovat, Dov. 1981. *The Development of Darwin's Theory: Natural History, Natural Theology, and Natural Selection, 1838-1859.* Cambridge: Cambridge University Press.

Paradis, James. 1978. *T. H. Huxley: Man's Place in Nature.* Lincoln: University of Nebraska Press.

Pearson, Karl. 1907. "On the Scope and Importance to the State of the Science of National Eugenics." 2d ed. 1909. London: Dulau and Company.

Quételet, Lambert Adolphe. 1835. *A Treatise on Man and the Development of His Faculties.* Trans. R. Knox. 1842. Reprint. 1968. New York: Burt Franklin.

Reid, Sir Wemyss, ed. 1899. *The Life of William Ewart Gladstone.* 2 vols. New York: G. P. Putnam's Sons.

Richards, Robert. 1981. "Instinct and Intelligence in British Natural Theology: Some Contributions to Darwin's Theory of the Evolution of Behavior." *Journal of the History of Biology* 14:193-230.

———. 1982. "Darwin and the Biologizing of Moral Behavior." In *The Problematic Science: Psychology in Nineteenth-Century Thought,* ed. William R. Woodward and Mitchell G. Ash, 43-64. New York: Praeger.

———. 1987. *Darwin and the Emergence of Evolutionary Theories of Mind and Behavior* Chicago: University of Chicago Press.

Ritchie, D. G. 1891. *Darwinism and Politics.* 2nd ed. London: Swan Sonnenschein.

Ritvo, Harriet. 1987. *The Animal Estate: The English and Other Creatures.* Cambridge: Harvard University Press.

Ruse, Michael. 1979. *The Darwinian Revolution: Science Red in Tooth and Claw.* Chicago: University of Chicago Press.

———. 1986. *Taking Darwin Seriously: A Naturalistic Approach to Philosophy.* New York: Blackwell.

Sawyer, Paul. 1985. "Ruskin and Tyndall: The Poetry of Matter and the Poetry of Spirit." In *Victorian Science and Victorian Values: Literary Perspectives,* ed. James Paradis and Thomas Postlewait, 217-46. New Brunswick: Rutgers University Press.

Schwartz, Benjamin. 1964. *In Search of Wealth and Power: Yen Fu and the West.* Cambridge: Harvard University Press.

Schweber, S. S. 1977. "The Origin of the *Origin* Revisited." *Journal of the History of Biology* 10:229-316.

Smith, Adam. 1759. *The Theory of Moral Sentiments.* Reprint. 1976. Oxford: Oxford University Press.

———. 1776. *An Inquiry into the Nature and Causes of the Wealth of Nations.* Reprint. 1976. 2 vols. Oxford: Oxford University Press.

Spencer, Herbert. 1851. *Social Statics.* Revised ed. 1892. New York: Appleton.

———. 1893. "Evolutionary Ethics." *The Atheneum,* no. 3432:193-94.

———. 1897. *The Principles of Ethics.* American ed. 2 vols. Reprint. 1978. Indianapolis: Liberty Classics Press.

———. 1904. *Essays: Scientific, Political, and Speculative.* 3 vols. New York: Appleton.

Stanley, Oma. 1957. "T. H. Huxley's Treatment of Nature." *Journal of the History of Ideas* 18:120-27.

Stent, Gunther S., ed. 1980. "Introduction." In *Mortality as a Biological Phenomenon: The Presuppositions of Sociobiological Research.* Berkeley: University of California Press.

Stephen, Leslie. 1893. "Ethics and the Struggle for Existence." *The Contemporary Review* 64:157-70.

———. 1895. "The Huxley Memorial." *Nature Magazine* 53:183-86.

Stocking, George, W., Jr. 1971. "What's in a Name? The Origins of the Royal Anthropological Institute (1837-71)." *Man* 6:369-91.

———. 1987. *Victorian Anthropology.* New York: Free Press.

Tillyard, E.M.W. 1942. *The Elizabethan World Picture.* New York: Random House.

Thomas, Keith. 1983. *Man and the Natural World.* New York: Pantheon Books.

Toulmin, Stephen. 1982. *The Return to Cosmology: Postmodern Science and the Theology of Nature.* Berkeley: University of California Press.

Toynbee, Arnold. 1884. *The Industrial Revolution.* Reprint. 1956. Boston: Beacon Press.

Turner, Frank. 1974. *Between Science and Religion: The Reaction to Scientific Naturalism in Late Victorian England.* New Haven: Yale University Press.

Tylor, Edward. 1871. *Primitive Culture.* 2 vols. London: John Murray.

Wallace, Alfred. 1864. "The Origin of Human Races and the Antiquity of Man Deduced from the Theory of Natural Selection." *Journal of the Anthropological Society* 2:58-88.

———. 1900. "The Problem of Utility: Are Specific Characters Always or Generally Useful?" In *Studies, Scientific and Social.* 2 vols. London: Macmillan.

Whitehead, Alfred North. 1925. *Science and the Modern World.* New York: New American Library.

Willey, Basil. 1940. *The Eighteenth-Century Background: Studies on the Idea of Nature in the Thought of the Period.* Boston: Beacon Press.

Williams, Raymond. 1980. *Problems in Materialism and Culture: Selected Essays.* London: Verso.

Worster, Donald. 1977. *Nature's Economy: A History of Ecological Ideas.* Cambridge: Cambridge University Press.

Young, Robert. 1985. *Darwin's Metaphor: Nature's Place in Victorian Culture.* Cambridge: Cambridge University Press.

FURTHER READING

Biography

Ashforth, Albert. *Thomas Henry Huxley.* New York: Twayne Publishers, Inc., 1969, 182 p.

Brief biography of Huxley that evaluates his contributions in light of modern science.

Bibby, Cyril. *T. H. Huxley: Scientist, Humanist and Educator.* London: Watts, 1959, 330 p.
Biography of Huxley that emphasizes his eclectic interests.

Desmond, Adrian. *Huxley: The Devil's Disciple.* London: Michael Joseph, 1994, 475 p.
Biography of Huxley focusing particularly on his agnosticism and social criticism, and the extent to which he ushered in "the great Victorian crisis of faith."

Irvine, William. *Thomas Henry Huxley.* London: Longmans, Green & Co., 1960, 40 p.
Brief biography of Huxley published for the British Council and the National Book League.

Peterson, Houston. *Huxley: Prophet of Science.* London: Longmans, Green and Co., 1932, 334 p.
Discusses Huxley's literary prowess as well as his advances in biology and how they shaped modern science.

Criticism

Band, Henretta Trent. "Thomas Henry Huxley's Opposition to Evolutionary Ethics." *Michigan Academician* 23, No. 4 (Fall 1991): 345-67.
Uses the backdrop of the New Kantian communism to evaluate Huxley's view of the relationship between cultural evolution and ethical behavior.

Bartholomew, Michael. "Huxley's Defense of Darwin." *Annals of Science* 32, No. 6 (Nov. 1975): 525-35.
Surveys Huxley's theories before and after his introduction to Darwin and discredits his arguments on Darwin's behalf.

di Gregorio, Mario A. "The Dinosaur Connection: A Reinterpretation of T. H. Huxley's Evolutionary View." *Journal of the History of Biology* 15, No. 3 (Fall 1982): 397-418.

Contends that Huxley only adopted Darwin's position as a working hypothesis because he never fully accepted the theory of natural selection.

————. *T. H. Huxley's Place in Natural Science*. New Haven: Yale University Press, 1984, 253 p.

Evaluates Huxley's contributions to modern science, emphasizing his zoological and ethnological theories.

Eisen, Sydney. "Huxley and the Positivists." *Victorian Studies* 7, No. 4 (June 1964): 337-58.

Contrasts Huxley's agnosticism with the views of the religious positivists, who discredited both scientific and religious claims to complete systems of belief.

Helfand, Michael S. "T. H. Huxley's 'Evolution and Ethics': The Politics of Evolution and the Evolution of Politics." *Victorian Studies* 20, No. 2 (Winter 1977): 159-77.

Contends that traditional analyses of *Evolution and Ethics* incorrectly interpret Huxley's thesis. Helfand contends that "Huxley introduced the fulcrum of the theory of natural selection, Malthusian theory, to justify his political position and to dismiss as unrealistic the socialist theories of George and Wallace."

Irvine, William. *Apes, Angels, and Victorians: The Story of Darwin, Huxley, and Evolution*. New York: McGraw-Hill Book Company, 1955, 399 p.

Historical discussion of the development of the theory of evolution in the nineteenth century, focusing specifically on the lives and writings of Darwin and Huxley.

Parker, T. Jeffery. "Professor Huxley: From the Point of View of a Disciple." *Natural Science* 8, No. 49 (March 1896): 161-67.

Describes the character of Huxley as a teacher and lecturer.

Richards, Evelleen. "Huxley and Woman's Place in Science: The 'Woman Question' and the Control of Victorian An-thropology." In *History, Humanity and Evolution: Essays for John C. Greene*, edited by James R. Moore, pp. 253-84. Cambridge: Cambridge University Press, 1989.

Examines Huxley's position on women in anthropology, claiming that "Huxley excluded women from science in the name of science and redefined that science to ratify their exclusion."

Spencer, Herbert. Review of *Evolution and Ethics*. *The Athenaeum* (Jul.-Dec. 1893): 119-20, 193-94.

Evaluates the arguments and style of Huxley's lectures collected in *Evolution and Ethics*.

Wells, H. G. "Professor Huxley and the Science of Biology." In *Experiment in Autobiography: Discoveries and Conclusions of a Very Ordinary Brain (Since 1866)*, pp. 159-65. New York: Macmillan Company, 1934.

Memoir of Wells's time in an Elementary Biology class taught by Huxley.

Additional coverage of Huxley's life and career is contained in the following sources published by Gale Research: *Dictionary of Literary Biography*, Vol. 57.

Harriet Jacobs

c. 1813-1897

(Also wrote under the pseudonym of Linda Brent) American autobiographer.

INTRODUCTION

Harriet Jacobs's slave narrative, *Incidents in the Life of a Slave Girl, Written by Herself* (1861), stands out from the male-dominated slave narrative genre in its unique point of view and especially in its focus on the sexual exploitation of the female slave. Soon after the publication of *Incidents*, which Jacobs penned under the pseudonym Linda Brent, questions arose regarding the text's authenticity. Many believed the book to have been written by its white abolitionist editor, Lydia Maria Child. Doubts about the narrative's veracity and its true author persisted into the twentieth century, and *Incidents* consequently was neglected by historians and critics alike. In 1981, however, Jean Fagan Yellin discovered Jacobs's correspondence with Child, and with another abolitionist friend, Amy Post. The letters, along with the rest of Yellin's research, assured the authenticity of Jacobs's narrative; and since then *Incidents* has received its due critical attention. Modern criticism has focused largely on Jacobs's exploitation of the sentimental domestic genre and on the differences between Jacobs's work and slave narratives such as Frederick Douglass's *Narrative of the Life of Frederick Douglass, an American Slave* (1845).

Biographical Information

Jacobs was born a slave in North Carolina. Her parents were both slaves, but her grandmother had been emancipated and owned her own home, earning a living as a baker. When Jacobs was six years old, her mother died, and she was sent to the home of her mother's mistress, Margaret Horniblow. Horniblow taught the young Jacobs to read, spell, and sew; she died when Jacobs was eleven or twelve and willed Jacobs to Mary Matilda Norcom, Horniblow's three-year-old niece. While living in the Norcom household, Jacobs suffered the sexual harassment of Dr. James Norcom, Mary's father and a prominent physician. Dr. Norcom threatened Jacobs with concubinage when she was sixteen years old. Rather than submit to the doctor, Jacobs became the mistress of a white slave-holding neighbor of the Norcoms and soon announced that she was pregnant. She bore two children, both fathered by this white neighbor. At the age of twenty-one, Jacobs ran away, believing that Norcom would sell the chil-

dren in her absence. In her narrative, Jacobs, as Linda Brent, wrote that at this time she hid for seven years in an attic crawlspace in her grandmother's home, where her children lived unaware of their mother's presence. The children were purchased by their father shortly after Jacobs went into hiding; they were allowed to continue living with their grandmother. Jacobs finally succeeding in fleeing North in 1842. There she reunited with her children and tried to establish a home for her family. In 1850, the passage of the Fugitive Slave Law (which stated that anyone caught aiding a fugitive slave was subject to punishment) threatened her safety and Jacobs once again went into hiding. In 1852 her employer, Mrs. Nathaniel Parker Willis, purchased Jacobs for three hundred dollars in order to free her. Soon after, Jacobs was urged by Amy Post to write her life's story, and spent five years doing just that. After three years of trying to get her book published, Jacobs finally succeeded in 1861. Throughout the Civil War and Reconstruction, Jacobs and her daughter continued to fight for the rights of African Americans. Jacobs died in 1897.

Major Works

Incidents in the Life of a Slave Girl details the horrific experiences endured by Jacobs. In the preface to the book, Jacobs, as Linda Brent, states that her "adventures may seem incredible," but assures readers that her "descriptions fall short of the facts." Brent describes her life as a slave from her early years, when she did not even know she was a slave, to the violence and exploitation she endured as a teenager at the hands of her master, and finally to her repugnance at the thought of her well-meaning employer purchasing her in order to free her. Although Jacobs wrote *Incidents* in the style of the sentimental novel, she seems to argue against the conception of womanhood that the sentimental novel conventionally upheld. While appealing to a Northern, white, female audience at a time when "true womanhood" meant chastity and virtue, Jacobs urges that slavery makes it impossible for a black woman to live a virtuous, chaste life. As she upholds some of the conventions of the sentimental genre by emphasizing the primacy and significance of motherhood and domesticity, Jacobs also demonstrates how the institution of slavery threatens and destroys white and black women alike. In these respects, *Incidents* differs markedly from typical, male slave narratives, which emphasize the ways in which slavery destroys masculinity. Yet a common factor among male slave narratives and Jacobs's *Incidents* is the sense of triumph the writer describes as he or she reclaims a sense of self.

Critical Reception

Incidents received little critical attention until Yellin's research revealed the authenticity of the narrative. This research established Jacobs as the sole author of *Incidents* and clarified Child's limited role as editor. Since then, critical studies usually discuss the way in which *Incidents* uses or exploits the conventions of one of two genres: domestic literature or slave narrative. Minrose C. Gwin argues that Jacobs was influenced by sentimental literature in that Jacobs felt compelled to apologize for and explain her reasons for her sexual experiences. Gwin goes on to state that whereas sentimental literature advanced ideals such as virtue and sensibility, Jacobs shows that such ideals were incompatible with the slave woman's experience. While Thomas Doherty identifies the shortcomings of *Incidents* as a work of sentimental literature, he argues that the book moves "women's literature" into the realm of politics. Similarly, Jean Fagan Yellin suggests that *Incidents* is designed to prompt women to political action. Elizabeth Fox-Genovese contends that in writing to an audience of free, Northern women, Jacobs uses the style of sentimental domestic fiction, but the tone and content of the book differ considerably from other works of domestic fiction. While Fox-Genovese states that *Incidents* depicts slavery as a violation of womanhood, Hazel V. Carby argues that Jacobs appropriates the conventions of the sentimental genre in order to examine the standards of female behavior and the relevance of such standards to the experience of black women in particular. Similarly, Valerie Smith demonstrates that although Jacobs uses the rhetoric of sentimental fiction, the author transcends the constraints of the genre in order to express the "complexity of her experience as a black woman." Mary Helen Washington, on the other hand, views *Incidents* more as a slave narrative than a sentimental novel. Washington argues that as a slave narrative, *Incidents* surpasses gender boundaries; Washington emphasizes the significance of the reclamation of the self in *Incidents* and in other slave narratives. Sarah Way Sherman also examines *Incidents* as a slave narrative, discussing the ways that the book differs from Douglass's *Narrative*. Sherman specifically emphasizes the differences between Douglass's and Jacobs's upbringing as well as the obvious difference in gender. Furthermore, Sherman notes that the nineteenth-century's conception of domesticity is challenged by Jacobs in *Incidents*. Like Sherman, Carolyn Sorisio examines *Incidents* in terms of both the slave narrative and the sentimental domestic genre and concludes that Jacobs's story— which, Sorisio contends, focuses most heavily on the issue of identity and the conception of self—cannot fit into either of the genres Jacobs has used to tell it.

PRINCIPAL WORKS

Incidents in the Life of a Slave Girl, Written by Herself [as Linda Brent] (autobiography) 1861

CRITICISM

Lydia Maria Child (essay date 1861)

SOURCE: "Introduction" to *Incidents in the Life of a Slave Girl, Written by Herself,* by Harriet A. Jacobs, edited by L. Maria Child (1861), new edition edited and introduced by Jean Fagan Yellin, Harvard University Press, 1987, pp. 3-4.

[*In the introduction that accompanied* Incidents in the Life of a Slave Girl *upon its publication in 1861, Child attests to the veracity and purpose of the text.*]

The author of the following autobiography is personally known to me, and her conversation and manners inspire me with confidence.[1] During the last seventeen years, she has lived the greater part of the time with a distinguished family in New York, and has so deported herself as to be highly esteemed by them. This fact is sufficient, without further credentials of her character. I believe those who know her will not be disposed to doubt her veracity, though some incidents in her story are more romantic than fiction.

At her request, I have revised her manuscript; but such changes as I have made have been mainly for purposes of condensation and orderly arrangement. I have not added any thing to the incidents, or changed the import of her very pertinent remarks. With trifling exceptions, both the ideas and the language are her own. I pruned excrescences a little, but otherwise I had no reason for changing her lively and dramatic way of telling her own story.[2] The names of both persons and places are known to me; but for good reasons I suppress them.

It will naturally excite surprise that a woman reared in Slavery should be able to write so well. But circumstances will explain this. In the first place, nature endowed her with quick perceptions. Secondly, the mistress, with whom she lived till she was twelve years old, was a kind, considerate friend, who taught her to read and spell. Thirdly, she was placed in favorable circumstances after she came to the North; having frequent intercourse with intelligent persons, who felt a friendly interest in her welfare, and were disposed to give her opportunities for self-improvement.

I am well aware that many will accuse me of indecorum for presenting these pages to the public; for the experiences of this intelligent and much-injured woman belong to a class which some call delicate subjects, and others indelicate. This peculiar phase of Slavery has generally been kept veiled; but the public ought to be made acquainted with its monstrous features, and I willingly take the responsibility of presenting them with the veil withdrawn. I do this for the sake of my sisters in bondage, who are suffering wrongs so foul, that our ears are too delicate to listen to them. I do it with the hope of arousing conscientious and reflecting women at the North to a sense of their duty in the exertion of moral influence on the question of Slavery, on all possible occasions. I do it with the hope that every man who reads this narrative will swear solemnly before God that, so far as he has power to prevent it, no fugitive from Slavery shall ever be sent back to suffer in that loathsome den of corruption and cruelty.

Notes

[1] Lydia Maria Child (1802-1880), author, editor, abolitionist, and reformer, met Harriet Jacobs in 1860. Child was excluded from polite literary circles after she called for the immediate abolition of chattel slavery in her *Appeal in Favor of that Class of Americans Called Africans* (1833). In the years that followed, she edited numerous antislavery pamphlets and books. Although she continued to produce novels, short stories, and poems, as well as histories and biographies, Child's strongest writings are the polemics and newspaper articles she wrote for the abolitionist movement. Jacobs to Post, Oct. 8 [1860], IAPFP [Isaac and Amy Post Family Papers. Department of Rare Books, Manuscripts, and Archives, University of Rochester Library, Rochester, N.Y.] #1259, BAP [Black Abolitionist Papers. Seventeen reels with a published guide and index. New York: Microfilming Corporation of America, 1981-83: Ann Arbor: University Microfilms International, 1984-.] 16: 686-688 (Letter 13); *Lydia Maria Child: Selected Letters, 1817-1880,* ed. Milton Meltzer and Patricia G. Holland (Amherst: University of Massachusetts Press, 1982).

[2] Child to Jacobs, Aug. 13, 1860, IAPFP #1330, LMCP [Lydia Marie Child Papers. *The Collected Correspondence of Lydia Marie Child, 1817-1880,* ed. Patricia G. Holland and Milton Meltzer. Millwood, N.Y.: Kraus Microform, 1980.] 46: 1243 (Letter 11); and Sept. 27, 1860, IAPFP #1338, LMCP 46: 1255 (Letter 12).

Jean Fagan Yellin (essay date 1981)

SOURCE: "*Written by Herself*: Harriet Jacobs' Slave Narrative," in *American Literature,* Vol. 53, No. 3, November, 1981, pp. 479-86.

[*In the following seminal study, Yellin reveals the existence of a "cache of [Jacobs's letters]" that attests to the authenticity of* Incidents, *establishes Jacobs as the author, and illuminates the editorial role of Lydia Maria Child. This discovery, Yellin emphasizes, transforms "a questionable slave narrative into a well-documented pseudonymous autobiography."*]

I

Your proposal to me has been thought over and over again, but not without some most painful remembrance. Dear Amy, if it was the life of a heroine with no degradation associated with it! Far better to have been one of the starving poor of Ireland whose bones had to bleach on the highways than to have been a slave with the curse of slavery stamped upon yourself and children. . . . I have tried for the last two years to conquer . . . [my stubborn pride] and I feel that God has helped me, or I never would consent to give my past life to anyone, for I would not do it without giving the whole truth. If it could help save another from my fate, it would be selfish and unChristian in me to keep it back.[1]

With these words, more than a century ago the newly emancipated fugitive slave Harriet Jacobs expressed conflicting responses to a friend's suggestion that she make her life story public. Although she finally succeeded in writing and publishing her sensational tale, its authenticity—long questioned—has recently been denied. Jacobs' *Incidents in the Life of a Slave Girl: Written By Herself* has just been transformed from a questionable slave narrative into a well-documented pseudonymous autobiography, however, by the discovery of a cache of her letters.[2]

This correspondence establishes Jacobs' authorship and clarifies the role of her editor. In doing so, it provides us with a new perspective on an unlikely grouping of nineteenth-century writers—Nathaniel P. Willis, Harriet Beecher Stowe, William C. Nell, and L. Maria Child—and enriches our literary history by presenting us with a unique chronicle of the efforts of an underclass black woman to write and publish her autobiography in antebellum America.

II

The appearance of Jacobs' letters has made it possible to trace her life. She was born near Edenton, North Carolina, about 1815. In *Incidents,* she writes that her parents died while she was a child, and that at the death of her beloved mistress (who had taught her to read and spell) she was sent to a licentious master. He subjected her to unrelenting sexual harassment. In her teens she bore two children to another white man. When her jealous master threatened her with concubinage, Jacobs ran away. Aided by sympathetic black and white neighbors, she was sheltered by her family and for years remained hidden in the home of her grandmother, a freed slave. During this time the father of her children, who had bought them from her master, allowed them to live with her grandmother. Although later he took their little girl to a free state, he failed to keep his promise to emancipate the children.

About 1842, Harriet Jacobs finally escaped North, contacted her daughter, was joined by her son, and found work in New York City. Because the baby she was hired to tend was the daughter of litterateur N. P. Willis, it has been possible to use Willis' materials to piece out—and to corroborate—Jacobs' story.[3] In 1849 she moved to Rochester, New York, where the Women's Rights Convention had recently met and where Frederick Douglass' *North Star* was being published each week. With her brother, a fugitive active in the abolitionist movement, she ran an antislavery reading room and met other reformers. Jacobs made the Rochester Quaker Amy Post, a feminist and abolitionist, her confidante; her letters to Post date from this period. In September 1850 Jacobs returned to New York and resumed work in the Willis household. When she was again hounded by her owner, she and her children were purchased and manumitted by Willis.

It was following this—between 1853 and 1858—that Jacobs acquiesced to Post's urgings; after a brush with Harriet Beecher Stowe, she wrote out the story of her life by herself. With the help of black abolitionist writer William C. Nell and white abolitionist woman of letters L. Maria Child (whose correspondence, too, corroborates Jacobs'), her narrative was finally published early in 1861.[4] As the national crisis deepened, Jacobs attempted to swell sentiment for Emancipation by publicizing and circulating her book. During the Civil War she went to Washington, D.C., to nurse black troops; she later returned South to help the freedmen. Jacobs remained actively engaged for the next thirty years. She died at Washington, D.C., in 1897.

III

The primary literary importance of Harriet Jacobs' letters to Amy Post is that they establish her authorship of *Incidents* and define the role of her editor, L. Maria Child. They also yield a fascinating account of the experiences of this underclass black female autobiographer with several antebellum writers.

Jacobs' letters express her conviction that, unlike both his first and his second wife, Nathaniel P. Willis was "pro-slavery," and writings like his picturesque 1859 account of slave life entitled "Negro Happiness in Virginia" must have confirmed her judgment.[5] Because of this—although she repeatedly sought help to win the time and privacy to write, and even requested introductions to public figures in hope that they would effect the publication of her book—Jacobs consistently refused to ask for Willis' aid. She did not even want him to know that she was writing. For years, while living under his roof, she worked on her book secretly and at night.

Her brief involvement with Harriet Beecher Stowe was decisive in the genesis of *Incidents.* When Jacobs first agreed to a public account of her life, she did not plan to write it herself, but to enlist Stowe's aid in helping her produce a dictated narrative. To this end, Jacobs asked Post to approach Uncle Tom's creator with the suggestion that Jacobs be invited to Stowe's home so they could become acquainted. Then, reading in the papers of the author's plan to travel abroad, Jacobs persuaded Mrs. Willis to write suggesting that Stowe permit Jacobs' daughter Louisa to accompany her to England as a "representative southern slave."

Harriet Beecher Stowe evidently responded by writing to Mrs. Willis that she would not take Jacobs' daughter with her, by forwarding to Mrs. Willis Post's sketch of Jacobs' sensational life for verification, and by proposing that if it was true, she herself use Jacobs' story in *The Key to Uncle Tom's Cabin,* which she was rushing to complete. Reporting all of this to Post, Jacobs suggests that she felt denigrated as a mother, betrayed as a woman, and threatened as a writer by Stowe's action.

> [Mrs. Stowe] said it would be much care to her to take Louisa. As she went by invitation, it would not be right, and she was afraid that if . . . [Louisa's] situation as a slave should be known, it would subject her to much petting and patronizing, which would be more pleasing to a young girl than useful; and the English were very apt to do it, and . . . [Mrs. Stowe] was very much opposed to it with this class of people. . . .

> I had never opened my life to Mrs. Willis concerning my children. . . . It embarrassed me at first, but I told her the truth; but we both thought it wrong in Mrs. Stowe to have sent your letter. She might have written to inquire if she liked.

> Mrs. Willis wrote her a very kind letter begging that she would not use any of the facts in her *Key,* saying that I wished it to be a history of my life entirely by itself, which would do more good, and it needed no romance; but if she wanted some facts for her book, that I would be most happy to give her some. She never answered the letter. She [Mrs. Willis] wrote again, and I wrote twice, with no better success. . . .

> I think she did not like my objection. I can't help it.[6]

Jacobs later expressed her racial outrage: "Think, dear Amy, that a visit to Stafford House would spoil me, as Mrs. Stowe thinks petting is more than my race can bear? Well, what a pity we poor blacks can't have the firmness and stability of character that you white people have!"[7]

Jacobs' distrust of Willis and disillusionment with Stowe contrast with her confidence in William C. Nell and L. Maria Child. After the Stowe episode, Jacobs decided to write her story herself. She spent years on the manuscript and, when it was finished, more years trying to get it published in England and America. Finally, in a letter spelling out the cost of her lack of an endorsement from Willis or Stowe, she reported to Post that Nell and Child were helping arrange for the publication of her autobiography.

> Difficulties seemed to thicken, and I became discouraged. . . . My manuscript was read at Phillips and Sampson. They agreed to take it if I could get Mrs. Stowe or Mr. Willis to write a preface for it. The former I had the second clinch [?] from, and the latter I would not ask, and before anything was done, this establishment failed. So I gave up the effort until this autumn [when] I sent it to Thayer and Eldridge of Boston. They were willing to publish it if I could obtain a preface from Mrs. Child. . . .

> I had never seen Mrs. Child. Past experience made me tremble at the thought of approaching another satellite of so great magnitude . . . [but] through W. C. Nell's ready kindness, I met Mrs. Child at the antislavery office. Mrs. C. is like yourself, a whole-souled woman. We soon found the way to each other's heart. I will send you some of her letters. . . .[8]

Accompanying this correspondence are two letters from L. Maria Child to Harriet Jacobs. These, I believe, resolve the questions historians have repeatedly raised concerning the editing of Jacobs' manuscript. Child begins the first by describing her editorial procedures in much the same way she later discussed them in her Introduction to *Incidents.*

> I have been busy with your M.S. ever since I saw you; and have only done one-third of it. I have very little occasion to alter the language, which is wonderfully good, for one whose opportunities for education have been so limited. The events are interesting, and well told; the remarks are also good, and to the purpose. But I am copying a great deal of it, for the purpose of transposing sentences and pages, so as to bring the story into continuous *order,* and the remarks into *appropriate* places. I think you will see that this renders the story much more clear and entertaining.

Child's second letter is a detailed explanation of the publisher's contract.[9]

Jacobs' letters are also of value in providing a unique running account of the efforts of this newly emancipated Afro-American woman to produce her autobiography. After deciding to write the manuscript herself, she followed the long-standing practice of sending apprentice pieces to the newspapers. In style and in subject, her first public letter reflects her private correspondence and prefigures her book by using the language of polite letters to discuss the sexual exploitation of women in slavery. Jacobs begins with an announcement of her newly found determination to tell her tale by herself. Then—as in the letters and the

book—she expresses the pain she feels as she recalls and writes about her life.

> Poor as it may be, I had rather give . . . [my story] from my own hand, than have it said that I employed others to do it for me. . . .

> I was born a slave, raised in the Southern hot-bed until I was the mother of two children, sold at the early age of two and four years old. I have been hunted through all of the Northern States—but no, I will not tell you of my own suffering—no, it would harrow up my soul. . . .[10]

Encouraged by the publication of this letter, Jacobs secretly composed others. Her correspondence during this period reveals that she was at once determined to write, apprehensive about her ability to do so, and fearful of being discovered: "No one here ever suspected me [of writing to the *Tribune*]. I would not have Mrs. W. to know it before I had undertaken my history, for I must write just what I have lived and witnessed myself. Don't expect much of me, dear Amy. You shall have truth, but not talent."[11]

The letters record other pressures. During the years Jacobs composed her extraordinary memoirs, Mr. and Mrs. Willis moved into an eighteen-room estate and added two more children to their family; Jacobs' work load increased accordingly. Writing to Post, she voiced the frustrations of a would-be writer who earned her living as a nursemaid: "Poor Hatty's name is so much in demand that I cannot accomplish much; if I could steal away and have two quiet months to myself, I would work night and day though it should all fall to the ground." She went on, however, to say that she preferred the endless interruptions to revealing her project to her employers: "To get this time I should have to explain myself, and no one here except Louisa knows that I have ever written anything to be put in print. I have not the courage to meet the criticism and ridicule of educated people."[12]

Her distress about the content of her book was even worse than her embarrassment about its formal flaws. As her manuscript neared completion, Jacobs asked Post to identify herself with the book in a letter expressing her concern about its sensational aspects and her need for the acceptance of another woman: "I have thought that I wanted some female friend to write a preface or some introductory remarks . . . yet believe me, dear friend, there are many painful things in . . . [my book] that make me shrink from asking the sacrifice from one so good and pure as yourself."[13]

IV

While *Incidents* embodies the general characteristics of the slave narrative, it has long been judged a peculiar example of this American genre. It is not, like most, the story of a life but, as its title announces, of incidents in a life. Like other narrators, Jacobs asserted her authorship in her subtitle, wrote in the first person, and addressed the subject of the oppression of chattel slavery and the struggle for freedom from the perspective of one who had been enslaved. But in her title she identified herself by gender, and in her text addressed a specific aspect of this subject. *Incidents* is an account by a woman of her struggle against her oppression in slavery as a sexual object and as a mother. Thus it presents a double critique of our nineteenth-century ideas and institutions. It inevitably challenges not only the institution of chattel slavery and its supporting ideology of white racism; it also challenges traditional patriarchal institutions and ideas.

Publication of this book marked, I think, a unique moment in our literary history, *Incidents* defied the taboos prohibiting women from discussing their sexuality—much less their sexual exploitation—in print. Within its pages, a well-known woman writer presented to the public the writing of a pseudynomous "impure woman" on a "forbidden subject." Here a black American woman, defying barriers of caste and class, defying rules of sexual propriety, was joined by a white American woman to make her history known in an attempt to effect social change. It is ironic that this narrative, which was painfully written in an effort to give "the whole truth," has been branded false. Now that the discovery of Harriet Jacobs' letters has established that her book was indeed *Written By Herself*, we can reexamine its place within women's writings, Afro-American literature, and the body of our national letters.

Notes

[1] This passage comes from one of thirty letters from Harriet Jacobs to Amy Post in the Post Family Papers recently acquired by the University of Rochester Library. Labeled n.d. #84, it was probably written at the end of 1852 or the beginning of 1853. All of the letters cited from Jacobs to Post are in this collection. Most note only day and month; my attempts to supply missing dates may be in error. Editing Jacobs' letters, I have regularized paragraphing, capitalization, punctuation, and spelling, but not otherwise tampered with text.

I hasten to record my considerable debt to Dorothy Sterling who includes some of Jacobs' letters in *A Woman and Black* (Norton, in press) and with whom I am writing a book on Jacobs; to Karl Kabelac of the University of Rochester Library; and to Patricia G. Holland, co-editor of *The Collected Correspondence of Lydia Maria Child, 1817-1880* (Millwood, N.Y.: K.T.O. Microform, 1979).

[2] [Harriet Jacobs], *Incidents in the Life of a Slave Girl. Written by Herself.* Ed. L. Maria Child (Boston: For the Author, 1861). An English edition appeared the following year: [Harriet Jacobs], *The Deeper Wrong: Or, Incidents in the Life of a Slave Girl. Written by Herself.* Ed. L. Maria Child. (London: W. Tweedie, 1862).

Examining *Incidents* in a discussion of "fictional accounts . . . in which the major character may have been a real fugitive, but the narrative of his life is probably false," John Blassingame recently judged that "the work is not credible." See *The Slave Community* (New York: Oxford Univ. Press, 1972), pp. 233-34.

[3] Willis referred to Jacobs directly—though not by name—in a *House and Home* column reprinted in *Outdoors at Idlewild* (New York: Scribner's, 1855), pp. 275-76.

[4] Nell reviewed *Incidents* in *The Liberator*, 25 Jan. 1861. Other reviews include *The National Anti-Slavery Standard*, 23 Feb. 1861, and *The Weekly Anglo-African*, 13 April 1861. Relevant passages from Child's correspondence are cited below.

[5] For Jacobs on Willis, see Jacobs to Post, Cornwall, Orange County (late 1852-early 1853?) n.d. #84. Child commented on Jacobs' relationship with Willis in a letter to John G. Whittier dated 4 April 1861, now in the Child Papers, Manuscript Division, the Library of Congress. Willis' article was anthologized in *The Convalescent* (New York: Scribner's, 1859), pp. 410-16.

[6] My discussion of Jacobs and Stowe is based on five letters from Jacobs to Post: Cornwall, Orange County (late 1852-early 1853?) n.d. #84; 14 Feb. (1853?); 4 April (1853?); New Bedford, Mass. (Spring, 1853?) n.d. #80; 31 July (1854?) n.d. #88. The lengthy quotation is from Jacobs to Post, 4 April (1853?). I have been unable to locate any letters to Stowe from Post, Cornelia Willis, or Jacobs, or from Stowe to Cornelia Willis.

[7] Jacobs to Post, New Bedford, Mass. (Spring, 1853?) n.d. #80.

[8] Jacobs to Post, 8 Oct. (1860?). I have not been able to document a second attempt to gain Stowe's backing. Jacobs discusses her efforts to publish her book abroad in letters to Post dated 21 June (1857?) n.d. #90; New Bedford, 9 August (1857?); 1 March (1858?); and Cambridge, 3 May (1858?) n.d. #87.

[9] Child to Jacobs, Wayland, 13 August 1860; and Wayland, 27 Sept. 1860. Any remaining doubts concerning Child's role must, I think, rest on an undated plea for secrecy from Jacobs to Post: "Please let no one see these letters. I am pledged to Mrs. Child that

I will tell no one what she has done, as she is beset by so many people, and it would affect the book. It must be the slave's own story—which it truly is." To my mind, this reflects an effort to shield Child from interruption while she edits the manuscript, not an attempt to hide editorial improprieties. Also see Child to Lucy [Searle], 4 Feb. 1861 in the Lydia Maria Child Papers, Anti-Slavery Collection of Cornell University Libraries.

[10] "Letter From a Fugitive Slave," New York *Tribune*, 21 June 1853. Jacobs' second letter appeared on 25 July 1853.

[11] Jacobs to Post, 9 Oct. (1853?) n.d. #85. Also see Jacobs to Post, Cornwall, 25 June (1853?).

[12] Jacobs to Post, Cornwall, 11 Jan. (1854?).

[13] Jacobs to Post, 18 May and 8 June (1857?). Post's signed statement in the Appendix to *Incidents* was written in response to this request.

An excerpt from a letter Jacobs wrote to Amy Post, c. 1852:

Your proposal to me [for Jacobs to write about her life in Slavery] has been thought over and over again but not with out some most painful rememberances dear Amy if it was the life of a Heroine with no degradation associated with it far better to have been one of the starving poor of Ireland whose bones had to bleach on the highways than to have been a slave with the curse of slavery stamped upon yourself and Children your purity of heart and kindly sympathies won me at one time to speak of my children it is the only words that has passed my lips since I left my Mothers door I had determined to let others think as they pleased but my lips should be sealed and no one had a right to question me for this reason when I first came North I avoided the Antislavery people as much as possible because I felt that I could not be honest and tell the whole truth often have I gone to my poor Brother with my gurived and mortified spirits he would mingle his tears with mine while he would advise me to do what was right my conscience approved it but my stubborn pride would not yeild I have tried for the past two years to conquer it and I feel that God has helped me or I never would consent to give my past life to any one for I would not do it with out giving the whole truth if it could help save another from my fate it would be selfish and unchristian in me to keep it back. . . .

Harriet A. Jacobs, in a letter to Amy Post, c. 1852, reprinted in Incidents in the Life of a Slave Girl, *edited by Jean Fagan Yellin, Harvard University Press, 1987.*

Minrose C. Gwin (essay date 1985)

SOURCE: "Green-Eyed Monsters of the Slavocracy: Jealous Mistresses in Two Slave Narratives," in *Conjuring: Black Women, Fiction, and Literary Tradition,* edited by Marjorie Pryse and Hortense J. Spillers, Indiana University Press, 1985, pp. 39-52.

[*In the following essay, Gwin examines the way in which the stereotypes and relationships of white and black women within the "slavocracy" of the South inform Jacobs's work. Gwin also demonstrates how Jacobs's narrative was influenced both by the conventions of the sentimental genre and by her white female audience, pointing out that the ideals of virtue and sensibility advanced by sentimental literature were incompatible with the experience of slave women.*]

Historians of the southern experience have observed volatile psychological and sociological connections between the white man's sexual exploitation of the slave woman and the evolution of the white woman's pedestal.[1] It is not the smallest irony of the slavocracy that its codes of conduct demanded moral superiority from white women and sexual availability from black, yet simultaneously expected mistress and slave woman to live and work in intimate physical proximity. As Katherine Fishburn points out, southern *mythos* denied women of both races sexual self-determination: "Whereas the lady was deprived of her sexuality, the black woman was identified with hers." White women were characterized by their "delicate constitutions, sexual purity and moral superiority to men," while southern mythology cast black women into roles of "subhuman creatures who, by nature, were strong and sexual."[2]

The virgin/whore dichotomy that was imposed upon white and black southern women deeply affected their images of themselves and of each other. Yet one of the most obvious but seldom asked questions about slavery and the southern racial experience—and certainly one of the least satisfactorily answered—concerns the explosive psychological realities of the relationships between these women of the mid-nineteenth century. Placed as they were in an opposing but a similarly dehumanizing mythology, how did the stereotypical sexual roles and obverse images assigned them by white males affect their relationships with one another? In cases of miscegenation, a white wife might be expected to react with terrible vengeance and intense sexual jealousy toward a coerced slave woman, seeing in her, perhaps, something of a lost female sexuality which she herself had been denied. Powerless against a lustful husband and blind to the harsh realities of chattel slavery, the enraged wife often vented her jealous rage upon the one person whom she *could* control, the black woman. The slave woman thus became a double victim of the two-headed monster of the slavocracy, the lecherous master and the jealous mistress. The white man demeaned and controlled her through what Angela Davis calls "an institutionalized pattern of rape";[3] his enraged wife punished the victim instead of the victimizer.

In the mistress-slave relationship the white woman exerted ultimate power, and that power could transform sexual jealousy into intense cruelty. The abolitionists' slogan that complete power corrupts is nowhere more apparent than in the relationships between these southern women, whose common bonds of suffering and dehumanization might have bound them in mutual compassion. Stephen Butterfield points out that black autobiography is often a "mirror of white deeds";[4] and it is in the slave narratives, not in the white women's journals and reminiscences, that the jealous mistress springs to life in all of her fury and perversity. Particularly in two women's narratives of the 1860s, the jealous mistress becomes a symbol of the narrators' past powerlessness and of the terror and degradation perpetrated under the South's "peculiar institution." Harriet Jacobs's *Incidents in the Life of a Slave Girl* (1861) and Elizabeth Keckley's *Behind the Scenes: Thirty Years a Slave and Four Years in the White House* (1868), perhaps the two best-known women's book-length slave narratives of the nineteenth century, depict former mistresses as cruel, jealous, vindictive women. Yet, in remaking their own lives in language, both Jacobs and Keckley exert upon these white women the control that they as mistresses formerly exerted upon them as slaves. In this sense these narratives become avenues of self-determination and of emotional freedom from the specter of slavery. As Jacobs and Keckley reshape their lives as slaves and reenact the cruelties of their jealous mistresses, they remake and strengthen themselves as ontological beings in a free world where cross-racial female bonds are possible.

The two black women write of their resentments against their mistresses, but not with as much total condemnation as a contemporary reader might expect. As Frances Foster points out, writers of the slave narratives, both men and women, were writing to a white audience.[5] In the antebellum and Civil War periods, the slave narratives were designed first of all to convince a white northern audience that slavery was wrong—not just for the slave but for everyone. Wronged mistresses were depicted as cruel and vindictive, but they were also construed as victims themselves of an institution which allowed sexual degradation of black women and forced an acceptance of the double standard for white women. As Harriet Jacobs writes of her perversely vindictive mistress Mrs. Flint, " . . . I, whom she detested so bitterly, had far more pity for her than [her husband] had, whose duty it was to make her life happy."[6] When the subject matter of the narratives changed during and after Reconstruction, deemphasizing the horror of slavery and concentrating

instead on the contributions of blacks,[7] freedwomen such as Kate Drumgoold in 1898 and Annie Burton in 1909 wrote of their former mistresses with affection and emphasized female nurturance in the slave-mistress relationship.

The autobiographical writings of Jacobs and Keckley may thus reflect their relationships to white women in ways limited by diverse purposes of the writings, by the contingencies of genre, and particularly by the need to define and assert selfhood in the face of repression and denial. As a genre, the slave narrative became a means of asserting black humanity and identity. The narratives were, as Foster puts it, "retrospective endeavors which helped narrators define, even create, their own identities."[8] This should be particularly true for the black woman writer, yet out of thousands of slave narratives, written and orally transmitted by blacks,[9] there are fewer than thirty written by black women and published as books during their lifetimes.[10] Although scholars have raised questions about the extent of editorial involvement in many of these volumes, some were undoubtedly written by black women and are products of conscious literary endeavor that the transcribed oral accounts do not reflect. All of these women's books were written or dictated by former slaves who had either escaped or been manumitted.

In this fact we find one reason for their scarcity. Only those who went north, whether as fugitives or freedwomen, could find resources to produce such books. With such notable exceptions as Harriet Tubman, Harriet Jacobs, and Ellen Craft, most slave women were so tied to their children that they found the harrowing journey north impossible. Though theories that slaves lived essentially in a matriarchal society have been disproven in recent years,[11] the black mother did have enormous responsibility for child care, simply because her children were owned by her master and were usually kept with her in their early years. From the 1830s through the war years, the anti-slavery press and the northern public turned avidly to the adventurous slave narratives both as testimonials of the evils of slavery and as exciting, sensational, even titillating reading. When black women did write or tell of their experiences, they were meant to be and often *were* particularly vivid testimonials of sexual exploitation and disruption of family ties, the two greatest evils of slavery for the American Victorian mind. These emphases in the women's narratives set them apart, not because they gave more accounts of sexual coercion and family disruption than the men's narratives did, but because they rendered these accounts from the female viewpoint of the rape victim, the bereft mother, the grieving wife.

This point of view was not without conflicts and problems. Though, as Marion Starling suggests, "the helplessness of the slave woman depicted in the slave narrative might serve as a galvanizing agent, spurring luke-warm sympathies into active anti-slavery ferment,"[12] the black woman wrote in a tradition of sentimental litera-ture in which her experiences and life situations were anomalies. In a number of ways the slave narrative does represent, as Sidonie Smith suggests, "a spiritual tran-scendence over the brutalizing experience of slavery."[13] Often, however, the black woman found herself in the difficult position of writing to Victorian audiences and attempting to explain how and why she felt it necessary to succumb to the repeated sexual blandishments of white men rather than to remain chaste—in the tradition of the sentimental heroine—though refusal meant rape, death, or severe abuse. Foster shows that the period 1831-1865, which saw the height of popularity and literary achievement of the slave narrative, was characterized by sentimental literature which "emphasized the culti-vation of sensibility, the glorification of virtue, the pres-ervation of family life, the revival of religion, and the achievement of a utopian society."[14] The ideals of sen-sibility and virtue were incompatible with the slave woman's experience. The black woman was indeed measured by the standards of the nineteenth-century Cult of True Womanhood, as Erlene Stetson suggests,[15] but her situation of enslavement prevented her from being able to live up to the Victorian ideal of chastity. Many of her comments about sex in the narratives seem at-tempts to explain why her experiences did not lend them-selves to Victorian behavior and how, as Bell Hooks puts it, "passive submission" to the white man's sexual demands should not be viewed as complicity.[16] If the black woman had any choices at all, often they were merely the lesser of evils.

At fifteen, for example, Harriet Jacobs became the mistress of a white man quite simply to escape the clutches of her lecherous master. Nonetheless, in writ-ing her ***Incidents in the Life of a Slave Girl,*** she re-mains apologetic about the affair and attempts to de-fend her decision to give up her chastity:

> But, O, ye happy women, whose purity has been sheltered from childhood, who have been free to choose the objects of your affection, whose homes are protected by law, do not judge the poor desolate slave girl too severely! (p. 54)

After explaining the hardships of slave girls which made them "prematurely knowing, concerning the evil ways of the world," Jacobs acknowledges that her decision to submit was motivated by the fact that "it seems less degrading to give one's self, than to submit to compul-sion. There is something akin to freedom in having a lover who has no control over you, except that which he gains by kindness and attachment" (p. 54). The black woman might be expected to view the southern white female as someone who had choices she did not have and as the embodiment of a respectability nur-tured by that freedom of choice.

Writing within this tradition of the sentimental novel, the black woman also adhered to the demands of the period and the genre in which she told her story. Al-though a detailed analysis of the slave narrative would not be relevant to my argument,[17] depictions of cross-racial female relationships were surely influenced by the distinctive structures and purposes of the genre, which changed when the abolitionist impulse no longer motivated the narratives but they rather became tracts for continued black progress in the late nineteenth and early twentieth centuries.[18] Jacobs's portrait of the horrific Mrs. Flint who exudes evil from every pore is obviously tied to the intense anti-slavery sentiment of the late 1850s, just as Drumgoold's love of her "white mother" in *A Slave Girl's Story* of 1898 stresses Chris-tian endurance and cross-racial female nurture.

In all types of slave narrative the primary purpose was, as Charles Nichols points out, quite simply to show "what it feels to be a slave."[19] Such autobiographical writings lend themselves to an episodic structure and a focus on external details. A peculiar tension arises from the conflicting purposes of the narrative. The narrator may write out of a need to assert an individual identity, to exert her own ordering power over the chaos which has been her life. Yet in this process of self-definition she must also accept the demands of the genre that she become the Everywoman of the slave experience. As Butterfield points out, this tension be-tween communal and individual self is apparent in all slave narratives.[20] It is perhaps most acute in the au-tobiography of the former slave woman who was sub-jected to all the labor and punishments of the male slaves but was in addition sometimes subjected to denial of self-determination in sexual choice. Jacobs's ges-ture of taking a white lover, is, in this sense, a grand show of choice, as she herself emphasizes. In a literary remaking of her life as a slave, the black woman sees herself dually as an individual with a burgeoning sense of self and as a symbol of former powerlessness. Both as black self and as black symbol, she ponders the relationship with the white female other and either accepts or rejects the ideal of mutual female nurturance.

One aspect of the study of women's autobiographies about the slavery experience involves the issue of authenticity and the meaning of the term *autobiogra-phy.* Roy Pascal separates autobiography from mem-oirs, diaries, and reminiscences by its emphasis on self-examination.[21] By this definition few if any of the women's slave narratives may be considered true au-tobiography. The issue is clouded further by the fact that, as Starling notes, the autobiographer sometimes needed editorial assistance[22] and the extent of that as-sistance is often a matter of conjecture. One can only accept, as does Nichols,[23] Lydia Maria Child's asser-tion that her editorial changes of Jacobs's manuscript were made "mainly for purposes of condensation and orderly arrangement."[24] But it has been speculated that abolitionist editors such as Child and the unnamed editor of *Aunt Sally* may have had essential shaping influences upon the narratives. In the early and later years of the narratives, evangelical northern ministers like G. W. Offley molded women's accounts of slave life as *exempla* of Christian endurance and triumph over great suffering.[25]

Despite the many textual questions concerning the autobiographies of black southern women published directly before, during, and well after the Civil War, several book-length reminiscences are purported to have been written by literate freedwomen of the region and relate in first-person accounts these former slaves' experiences with white women in a southern setting. Among those are Jacobs's *Incidents* and Keckley's *Behind the Scenes,* which were both prepared with editorial assistance. Child edited *Incidents,* and James Redpath is believed to have helped Keckley prepare her book. As mentioned, Child writes that her impact was minimal. There is no such statement by Redpath.[26] We can only assume that these are stories of the experiences of articulate black women and should be critically approached as such. Jacobs's narrative was closely tied to the abolitionist movement through the involvement of Child, who edited the *National Anti-Slavery Standard,* a weekly published in New York, and who wrote *Appeal in Favor of that Class of Americans called Africans* which won many to the antislavery cause.[27] Although Keckley's *Behind the Scenes* was published after the war and written mainly to relate her association with the Lincolns, the early chapters about her lurid experiences as a slave woman show the influence of antebellum antislavery writings such as Theodore Weld's *American Slavery As It Is* and the essays, travel books, and journals of Frances Kemble, the Grimké sisters, and Harriet Martineau.

In each of these two autobiographies the white women's sexual jealousy becomes perverse cruelty, and the black women are victimized again and again by their mistresses' displaced rage at their husbands' lechery. In describing these white women as enraged monsters, these two early women writers seem to view their mistresses as specters of slavery itself. Far from adhering to the code of the Cult of True Womanhood, which demanded piety and morality, the white women become evil creatures, nurtured by the institution which allows them and their husbands absolute power over other human beings. It is as if white women perceive the slave woman's stereotypical association with sexuality to mock her mistress's socially imposed purity. Therefore Keckley's and Jacobs's autobiographies portray the white southern woman as defiled not only by her husband's sexual misdeeds but by her own acts of cruelty to the black woman.

Jacobs's Mrs. Flint is particularly cruel and Jacobs's depiction of her evil mistress deeply ironic. Yet this demonic portrait is drawn against a background of the slave girl's early happiness with a mistress who taught her to read and write and who was "so kind . . . that I was always glad to do her bidding" (p. 10). Actually, though, even this kind mistress fails her because, at the white woman's death when Jacobs is twelve, the slave girl is bequeathed to the five-year-old daughter of her former mistress's sister, the ogress Mrs. Flint. Jacobs had hoped to be freed by her kind mistress and feels the provisions of her will a direct personal betrayal. She writes bitterly:

> My mistress had taught me the precepts of God's Word: "Thou shalt love thy neighbor as thyself." "Whatsoever ye would that men should do unto you, do ye even so unto them." But I was her slave, and I suppose she did not recognize me as her neighbor. I would give much to blot out from my memory that one great wrong. As a child, I loved my mistress; and, looking back on the happy days I spent with her, I try to think with less bitterness of this act of injustice. (p. 6)

This same "kind" mistress also reneged on a promise to young Linda's grandmother that, upon her death, the old slave woman should be freed. Instead, when the estate is settled, Dr. Flint, the old mistress's brother-in-law, dispatches "Aunt Marthy" to the auction block where, luckily, a family member buys her for fifty dollars and sets her free.

It is small wonder that Jacobs has a difficult time forgiving her former mistress's "one great wrong." From the time she is sent to the Flints, her young life becomes a nightmare punctuated by Dr. Flint's lechery and his wife's jealousy. To maintain some control over her life, young Linda, then fifteen, takes a white lover and has two children whom Mrs. Flint immediately assumes are her husband's own offspring. When the Flints decide to "break in" her children on the plantation, Jacobs, realizing that they are being punished because of her, runs away, hides in the home of a sympathetic white woman, and then is concealed in a casketlike space of a shed attached to the roof of her grandmother's house through which she bores a peephole in order to watch her children as they play. After seven years of this living death, Jacobs manages to escape to Philadelphia—a physical and emotional wreck.

Motivated as she was to write her narrative by abolitionist supporters and by her own outrage, Jacobs is scathingly ironic in her discourse, particularly as it applies to Mrs. Flint. In the actions of her mistress toward her and toward other black women, Jacobs sees not only the cruelty perpetrated by the system but also the hypocrisy of the slavocracy. Jacobs has a strong sense of the moral responsibilities of women in an immoral society, and her vivid depictions of Mrs. Flint's immorality are designed to shock those who believed that the plantation mistress was, as Catherine Clinton puts it, "the conscience of the slave South."[28] She describes Mrs. Flint as "totally deficient in energy" but with "nerves so strong, that she could sit in her easy chair and see a woman whipped, till the blood trickled from every stroke of the lash" (p. 10). The white woman's Christianity is a sham: with biting irony Jacobs writes that Mrs. Flint

> was a member of the church; but partaking of the Lord's supper did not seem to put her in a Christian frame of mind. If dinner was not served at the exact time on that particular Sunday, she would station herself in the kitchen, and wait till it was dished, and then spit in all the kettles and pans that had been used for cooking. She did this to prevent the cook and her children from eking out their meagre fare with the remains of the gravy and other scrapings. (pp. 10-11)

Mrs. Flint's sins are cataloged in horrendous detail throughout *Incidents*. Like Prue's fictional mistress in *Uncle Tom's Cabin,* she locks the cook away from a nursing baby for a whole day and night. Jacobs relates an incident in which her mistress makes her walk barefoot on a long errand through the snow. Later in the narrative, Jacobs gives an account of Mrs. Flint's treatment of her aunt, who, although she had many miscarriages, is forced to lie at her mistress's door each night to listen for the white woman's needs. When Aunt Nancy dies, a victim of mistreatment all of her life, Jacobs writes with the deepest irony, "Mrs. Flint took to her bed, quite overcome by the shock." The mistress "now [becomes] very sentimental" and demands that the body of the black woman whose health she has wrecked "by years of incessant, unrequited toil, and broken rest" be buried "at her feet" in the white family plot. Though dissuaded from that wish by a minister who reminds her that the black family might wish to have some say in the matter, "the tender-hearted Mrs. Flint" makes a pretty picture at Aunt Nancy's funeral "with handkerchief at her eyes" (pp. 148-50).

Mrs. Flint's most memorable characteristic, though, is the jealous rage which she directs toward young Harriet, the hapless victim of Dr. Flint's lust. Her mistress's behavior bears brutal testimony to Jacobs's plaint: "I would rather drudge out my life on a cotton plantation, till the grave opened to give me rest, than to live with an unprincipled master and a jealous mistress" (p. 49). Jacobs paints Mrs. Flint's jealousy as a kind of madness brought on by the institution of slavery and sees herself, the beleaguered slave girl, and the scorned white woman as its mutual victims. She feels a kinship for her mistress: "I never wronged her, or wished to wrong her; and one word of kindness from her would have brought me to her feet" (p. 31). Yet that kinship is not reciprocated. Like many southern white women whose husbands were guilty of philandering with slave women,

Mrs. Flint is totally blind to the plight of the female slave. "She pitied herself as a martyr," writes Jacobs, "but she was incapable of feeling for the condition of shame and misery in which her unfortunate, helpless slave was placed." Mrs. Flint "would gladly have had me flogged . . . but the doctor never allowed anyone to whip me" (p. 33).

When Jacobs's first child is conceived, Mrs. Flint, thinking it is her husband's offspring, vows to kill the young woman. The jealous Dr. Flint, whose injunction against violence does not extend to his own, throws Harriet down a flight of stairs, shears her hair, and beats her. In her account of Mrs. Flint, Jacobs stresses also the woman's desire to dominate. When she is sent away to the plantation of Dr. Flint's son and has worked there for five years, Jacobs must wait on the table at which the visiting Mrs. Flint is served. "Nothing could please her better than to see me humbled and trampled upon," the black woman writes. "I was just where she would have me—in the power of a hard, unprincipled master. She did not speak to me when she took her seat at table; but her satisfied, triumphant smile, when I handed her plate, was more eloquent than words" (p. 95). When Jacobs runs away, the enraged Mrs. Flint is reported to have said, "The good-for-nothing hussy! When she is caught, she shall stay in jail, in irons, for one six months, and then be sold to a sugar plantation. I shall see her broke in yet" (p. 105). Throughout Jacobs's account, Mrs. Flint is depicted as struggling for control of young Harriet, and later of her children. The white woman equates these blacks to animals to be conquered and tamed. As Jacobs depicts her, Mrs. Flint is at the same time horribly vindictive and pitifully weak. She longs to control her husband's sexual appetites, but cannot. Instead she transfers her rage to Jacobs and her children and attempts, also unsuccessfully, to control them as symbols of the lust which her husband embodies.

Jacobs writes so bitterly and so thoroughly about Mrs. Flint that she seems at times to transform *Incidents* into a vehicle of rage directed toward her former mistress. If the slave narrative is indeed a means of controlling past experiences and asserting personal order upon social indignity, then *Incidents* is surely the artifact created by Jacobs's impulse to control and dominate, in language, those who controlled and dominated her. She imbues her descriptions of Mrs. Flint with terrible irony and bitterness. In so doing, she, as narrator, dominates and manipulates Mrs. Flint. She herself becomes the old slave woman with a dead, cruel mistress about whom she relates an anecdote. When the mistress dies, Jacobs writes, the old slave woman who has borne the brunt of her many beatings and cruelties steals into the room where the dead woman lies. "She gazed a while on her, then raised her hand and dealt two blows on her face, saying, as she did so, 'The devil is got you now!' " (p. 48). Like the old slave, Jacobs flogs her powerless former mistress over and over throughout her narrative. At long last the slave woman controls the plantation mistress, and the vehicle of that domination, language, becomes infinitely more powerful and more resonant than the lash or the chain could ever be.

Unlike Jacobs, Keckley dispenses with her years of bondage in the early part of her autobiography. Yet her focus, like Jacobs's, centers on the brutality of a southern mistress with "a cold jealous heart." Keckley is more reticent than Jacobs about her master's sexual coercion, which resulted in the birth of her only child. But it is easy to read between the lines. Like Jacobs, young Keckley was sent to a new master and mistress when she was in early puberty. When she was eighteen and had grown into "strong, healthy womanhood," her master Mr. Burwell, a Presbyterian minister, and his "helpless" ill-tempered wife moved from Virginia to Hillsboro, North Carolina, taking Keckley, their only slave, with them.

It is at this point that Keckley's tortures begin. Her mistress, Keckley writes, "seemed to be desirous to wreak vengeance on me for something," and "Mr. Bingham, a hard, cruel man, the village schoolmaster" became Mrs. Burwell's "ready tool" (p. 32). At her mistress's behest, Keckley undergoes a series of savage beatings and personal exposure at the hands of the sadistic schoolmaster. In addition, Keckley suffers violent abuse in the Burwell home—in which she has a chair broken over her head. When even the perversely cruel Bingham refuses to whip the black woman again, Mrs. Burwell urges her husband to "punish" her. Mr. Burwell, Keckley writes with grim irony, "who preached the love of Heaven, who glorified the precepts and examples of Christ, who expounded the Holy Scriptures Sabbath after Sabbath from the pulpit," cuts the heavy handle from an oak broom and beats her so brutally that her bloodied condition, she writes, touched even the "cold, jealous heart" of her mistress (p. 37). (Mrs. Burwell's "pity" more likely was motivated by the probability of losing a valuable piece of property, her only maid.)

Up to this point in Keckley's narrative the Burwells' sadism appears motiveless. Keckley writes only that the beatings were to "subdue [her] pride" (p. 38). But their motives, particularly Mrs. Burwell's, crystallize as the black woman admits that the savage actions of owners "were not the only things that brought me suffering and deep mortification" (p. 38). In her half-apologetic account of her own sexual coercion Keckley chooses her words carefully. Her hesitant, tentative story shows above all a continuing psychological enslavement to the white man and to a cardinal rule that the black woman must never reveal the name of the father of her mulatto child. It also paints the minister Burwell as even more of a perverse monster. Not only

does he force sex upon the slave woman; he beats her savagely even after his cruel wife begs him to desist. Burwell is a prime example of Davis's and Hooks's theory that sexual domination of female slaves was an avenue to power for the white male and that rape became in the slave South a symbol of white man's total dominance over blacks and over women.[29] Burwell dominates Keckley through sex and through violence; and although the hesitancy in her account of sexual coercion may be partly ascribed to nineteenth-century reticence on such topics, it is also testimony to a prevailing fear of the immense power of the southern white man:

> I was regarded as fair-looking for one of my race, and for four years a white man—I spare the world his name—had base designs upon me. I do not care to dwell upon this subject for it is one that is fraught with pain. Suffice it to say, that he persecuted me for four years, and I—I—became a mother. The child of which he was the father was the only child that I ever brought into the world. If my poor boy ever suffered any humilating pangs on account of birth, he could not blame his mother, for God knows that she did not wish to give him life; he must blame the edicts of that society which deemed it no crime to undermine the virtue of girls in my then position.
>
> Among the old letters preserved by my mother I find the following, written by myself while at Hillsboro'. In this connection I desire to state that Robert Burwell is now living at Charlotte, North Carolina. (p. 38)

In this account and in the letter which follows it, Keckley mentions "griefs and misfortunes" which result in family disapproval. From her specific mention of Burwell, we can infer that he was the father of her child. Keckley's account of Burwell's sexual aberrations restores, by contrast, a more sympathetic view of her mistress. It is she who finally falls on her knees and begs her husband to stop beating Keckley. Faint glimmerings of a sympathetic portrait emerge from this part of the narrative. In her former mistress Keckley shows us a white woman warped by her husband's perverse will to sexually dominate a female slave. Her sadism is horribly engendered by his lust for power.

We wonder how representative Mrs. Flint and Mrs. Burwell are. An unpublished study of the role of plantation mistresses in the lives of slaves shows mistresses to have been responsible for only a small portion of punishments inflicted upon slaves. Yet the study, in which Elizabeth Craven surveyed nineteenth- and twentieth-century slave narratives, also shows that many incidents involving the cruelty of a mistress also concerned a female slave's alleged intimacy with the master. Clinton, who cites the study in *The Plantation Mistress*, summarizes Craven's findings: "When [male] slaveowners sexually harassed or exploited female slaves, mistresses sometimes directed their anger, not at their unfaithful husbands, but toward the helpless slaves."[30] In writing about the white women who transferred their jealous rages to them, Jacobs and Keckley evoke the autobiographical process as an avenue toward understanding and order. It is only through confrontation with the human evil of slavery that the freed woman can reorder experience, redefine her place in the world, and assert her human rights. Keckley and Jacobs see their relationships with their former mistresses as paradigmatic of the essential evil of slavery—the perversity of that "peculiar institution" which transformed victim into victimizer and severed potential bonds of sisterhood. By recreating Mrs. Flint and Mrs. Burwell and their "cold, jealous heart[s]," these two black women writers rise in language from the ashes of their enslavement and create themselves anew—as ontological selves, as nonvictims.

Notes

[1] See, for example, John W. Blassingame, *The Slave Community: Plantation Life in the Antebellum South* (New York: Oxford University Press, 1972); W. J. Cash, *The Mind of the South* (New York: Knopf, 1941); Catherine Clinton, *The Plantation Mistress: Woman's World in the Old South* (New York: Pantheon, 1982); Angela Davis, *Women, Race & Class* (New York: Random House, 1981); Herbert G. Gutman, *The Black Family in Slavery and Freedom, 1750-1925* (New York: Pantheon, 1976); Bell Hooks, *"Ain't I a Woman?": Black Women and Feminism* (Boston: South End, 1981); Anne Firor Scott, *The Southern Lady: From Pedestal to Politics 1830-1930* (Chicago and London: University of Chicago Press, 1970); Kenneth Stampp, *The Peculiar Institution: Slavery in the Ante-bellum South* (New York: Knopf, 1956); C. Vann Woodward, *The Burden of Southern History* (Baton Rouge: Louisiana State University Press, 1960).

[2] Katherine Fishburn, *Women in Popular Culture: A Reference Guide* (Westport, Conn.: Greenwood, 1982), pp. 10-11.

[3] Davis, p. 23.

[4] Stephen Butterfield, *Black Autobiography in America* (Amherst: University of Massachusetts Press, 1974), p. 3.

[5] Frances Foster, *Witnessing Slavery: The Development of Antebellum Slave Narratives* (Westport, Conn.: Greenwood, 1979), p. 65.

[6] Harriet Jacobs [Linda Brent], *Incidents in the Life of a Slave Girl,* ed. L. Maria Child (1861; rpt. New York: Harcourt Brace Jovanovich, 1973), p. 31. Subsequent references will be designated parenthetically.

[7] Foster, pp. 60-61.

[8] Foster, p. 3.

[9] Marion Starling lists more than 6,000. See "The Slave Narrative: Its Place in American Literary History," Diss. New York University, 1946.

[10] For separate bibliographies of women's slave narratives, see Erlene Stetson, "Studying Slavery," in *But Some of Us Are Brave,* ed. Gloria Hull, Patricia Bell Scott, and Barbara Smith (Old Westbury, N.Y.: The Feminist Press, 1982), pp. 82-84 (contains several errors); Stetson, "Black Women In and Out of Print," in *Women in Print—I,* ed. Joan Hartman and Ellen Messer-Davidow (New York: MLA, 1982), p. 97 (a more selective, but also more accurate listing). Marion Starling in "The Slave Narrative," Francis Foster in *Witnessing Slavery,* and Charles Nichols, *Many Thousand Gone,* 2nd ed. (Bloomington: Indiana University Press, 1969) all list female and male narratives together. For collected excerpts of some women's narratives, see Bert Loewenberg and Ruth Bogin, *Black Women in Nineteenth-Century American Life* (University Park: Pennsylvania State University Press, 1976).

[11] See, for example, Blassingame and Gutman.

[12] Starling, p. 294.

[13] Sidonie Smith, *Where I'm Bound: Patterns of Slavery and Freedom in Black American Autobiography* (Westport, Conn., and London: Greenwood, 1974), p. 10.

[14] Foster, p. 64.

[15] Stetson, "Studying Slavery," p. 79.

[16] Hooks, p. 26.

[17] See Starling, Foster, Nichols, and Butterfield.

[18] Foster makes these distinctions in *Witnessing Slavery,* p. 150.

[19] Nichols, ix.

[20] Butterfield, p. 3.

[21] Roy Pascal, *Design and Truth in Autobiography* (Cambridge: Harvard University Press, 1960), pp. 3-5.

[22] Starling, p. 311.

[23] Nichols, xi.

[24] Lydia Maria Child, "Introduction," *Incidents,* xi.

25 See, for example, *Narrative of Jane Brown and Her Two Children* (Hartford: Published for G. W. Offley, 1860).

26 Dorothy Porter, "Introduction," in Elizabeth Keckley, *Behind the Scenes or, Thirty Years a Slave, and Four Years in the White House* (1868; rpt. New York: G. W. Carleton, 1968), pp. i-ii. *Behind the Scenes* was initially recalled from the market at the request of Robert Lincoln, who rebuked Keckley for publishing his mother's letters. In 1935 an Associated Press story credited Jane Swisshelm, a Washington reporter, with authorship of the book and denied the existence of Elizabeth Keckley. John Washington, author of *They Knew Lincoln,* soundly refuted this report. The extent of Child's and Redpath's assistance is not known. (Subsequent references to this edition are designated parenthetically.)

27 Walter Tenner, "Introduction," *Incidents,* x.

28 Clinton p. 189.

29 Davis, p. 23; Hooks, p. 27.

30 Clinton, p. 188.

Thomas Doherty (essay date 1986)

SOURCE: "Harriet Jacobs' Narrative Strategies: *Incidents in the Life of a Slave Girl,*" in *Southern Literary Journal,* Vol. XIX, No. 1, Fall, 1986, pp. 79-91.

[*In the following essay, Doherty examines Jacob's use of the conventions of the sentimental genre and describes the shortcomings of* Incidents *as a sentimental novel. Rather, he argues that Jacobs "ingeniously inducts 'women's literature' into the cause of women's politics."*]

In 1853, the fugitive slave Harriet Jacobs confided her literary ambitions to the poet and abolitionist Amy Post. "Don't expect too much of me, dear Amy," she cautioned, "You shall have truth but not talent" (Sterling 79). Jacobs' modest opinion of the work that became *Incidents in the Life of a Slave Girl,* published in 1861 under the pseudonym Linda Brent, has generally accorded with critical opinion. When noted at all, it has been valued primarily as a historical document, one of the precious few antebellum slave narratives written by a woman—and even then, until quite recently, a text considered of dubious authenticity.[1] Likewise, its formal virtues have received scant consideration, Jacobs' stylistic debt to the sentimental novel typically warranting her the bemused appellation "the Pamela of the slave narratives" (Bayliss 108, Foster 58-59).

Though the dearth of historical and literary regard has lately been somewhat remedied, *Incidents in the Life of a Slave Girl* is still more apt to be taken as a generic anomaly filling the affirmative action slot of English Department book lists than as a complex creative act deserving scrutiny in its own right. Like Jean de Crevecoeur's naive Farmer James in *Letters from an American Farmer,* the author's guileless persona has too effectively masked her literary sophistication. Prefatory claims of authorial innocence and creative "deficiencies" (xiii) aside, Jacobs ingeniously inducts "women's literature" into the cause of women's politics in her tale of sex-determined destiny under slavery. Seldom has an American writer so ably put popular art to a polemical purpose.

Even by the standards of slave narratives, *Incidents in the Life of a Slave Girl* relates an incredible story. Linda, the author's autobiographical persona, is orphaned in childhood and reared by her kindly manumated grandmother, a community matriarch of no little authority in her Carolina county. In early adolescence, the precocious slave girl is made servant to the lecherous Dr. Flint, a hypocrite with all the unholy passions and none of the capacity for moral regeneration of the sentimentalist seducers of the era's best-selling fiction. As Linda grows to womanhood, Flint's sexual harassment becomes increasingly persistent and aggressive, but despite threats and temptations, she steadfastly repulses the advances of her ostensible master. When she cheekily confesses her love for a free-born "young colored carpenter" (36), Flint rages like a jealous suitor, striking Linda and forbidding her marriage.

Shortly after the ill-starred romance, and seemingly more in willful defiance of Flint than from any infatuation of her own, Linda succumbs to the attentions of a prominent white man, by whom she eventually bears two children. Again, Flint is furious and abusive, though (curiously) his violence always stops short of rape. Unable any longer to bear his persecutions, Linda goes into hiding, leading Flint and his slavehunters to believe she has fled North. However, unbeknownst even to her children, Linda is actually concealed in the tiny attic of her grandmother's house. She spends seven years in this crawlspace, a "garret . . . only nine feet long and seven wide. . . . (with) no admission for either light or air" (117). Ultimately, fearing discovery, Linda secures passage North. In New York City, she finds successive employment and sisterly succor with two exemplary mistresses. With their help, and through her own unwavering efforts, she obtains legal freedom for her children and herself. At the narrative's close, she reports, with satisfaction, the news of Flint's death and notes pointedly, "Reader, my story ends with freedom; not in the usual way, with marriage" (207).

Throughout, as per generic convention, Jacobs interweaves her story with long stretches of anti-slavery rhetoric, much valuable ethnography, and some solid history (especially the chapter "Fear of Insurrection" (64-69), which is vivid testimony to the panic among Southern whites wrought by Nat Turner's uprising in 1831). But what lends this narrative unique and immediate appeal is, of course, sex—the sex of the narrator, of the audience, and in the story.

From the outset, Jacobs is gender specific about her audience and cause:

> I do earnestly desire to arouse the women of the North to a realizing sense of the conditions of two millions of women at the South, still in bondage . . . (xiv).

The strategy is both demographically and rhetorically astute. Northern women, largely from leisured middle-class households, were among the abolitionist movement's most dedicated participants. As Frederick Douglass declared in a famous tribute to their "agency, devotion, and efficiency in pleading the cause of the slave," women gave the anti-slavery crusade much of its moral force, social legitimacy, and practical effectiveness. "When the true story of the anti-slavery cause shall be written," Douglass predicted, "women shall occupy a large space in its pages; for the cause of the slave has been peculiarly women's own" (472, 469; see also Lutz, Sillen).

To be sure, the active participation of women in the great debate over slavery was an unprecedented break with the sexual status quo; within the abolitionist movement itself, their efforts often met with fierce opposition. Though they were less likely to be the target of outright physical assault, female abolitionists faced a special measure of public resistance, ridicule, and censure. Those who presumed to enter the fray possessed a courage and commitment not wholly typical of their gender and class. Catherine Beecher, the famous apostle of wifely domesticity, probably spoke for the common rung when she placed anti-slavery agitation "entirely without the sphere of female duty" (104-105).

For a great many women, however, the anti-slavery cause was a matter of conscience that overrode convention. Like Lydia Maria Child, Jacobs' editor and literary sponsor, they felt its removal required "every heart and head in the community" (226). Angelina Grimke's *An Appeal to the Women of the Nominally Free States,* an influential pamphlet issued in 1837 by an anti-slavery convention of American women, expressed the special sense of responsibility and commitment these women brought to "the cause of immediate, unconditional, and universal emancipation," condemning the "vast system of oppression and robbery and heathenism" that was chattel slavery and suggesting how best to combat it. Above all, Northern women were advised to educate themselves to the true nature of slavery by reading and subscribing to anti-slavery publications:

> Be not satisfied with merely setting your names to a constitution—this is a very little thing: read on the subject—none of us has yet learned half the abominations of slavery. . . . Anti-slavery publications abound: and *no intelligent woman ought to be ignorant of this great subject—no Christian woman can escape the obligation now resting upon her, to examine it for herself.* . . . Read, then, beloved sisters. ([58-59, emphasis in the original)

For the Northern woman who took up the challenge, the basic text, after the Bible, was the slave narrative. With the sensational melodrama they inspired, Harriet Beecher Stowe's *Uncle Tom's Cabin* (1852), slave narratives were the most telling weapons in the abolitionist arsenal. As political argument, the simple fact of a slave autobiography, with the assurance "written by himself" on the title page, was a rejoinder to racist ideology. As marketable literature, the built-in potential for adventure and melodrama lent a dramatic edge guaranteed to stir the pulse and pull the hearstrings of the Northern reader. Blending the high moral purpose of religious testimony with the entertainment appeal of escapist fiction, the slave narrative was a truly "good read" for the conscientious, middle class woman who made the slave's cause her own. Whether a true believer or a potential convert, the "virtuous reader" (56) whom Jacobs straightforwardly addresses is a female who will listen to the slave girl's tale in "true womanly sympathy" (185). "Oh, you happy free women," she writes in a characteristic oratorical flourish, "contrast *your* New Year's Day with that of the poor bondwoman!" (14) Like Sarah Forten, whose poem served as an epigraph for Grimke's *Appeal,* the authorial presumption is "our skins may differ, but from thee we claim / a sister's privilege and a sister's name."

Having defined what a modern publisher would call her "target group," Jacobs adopts suitable rhetorical strategies. Always, she speaks to the reader as a (sexual) equal; always, she plays on values and emotions having a special force and immediacy for female readers. "Slavery is terrible for men," she declares, "but it is far more terrible for women. Superadded to the burden common to all, *they* have wrongs, and sufferings, and mortifications peculiarly their own" (79).

Foremost among these mortifications is the sexual subservience sanctified by law. When Linda enters her fifteenth year, Dr. Flint assumes his prerogatives:

> My master began to whisper foul words in my ear. . . . He tried his utmost to corrupt the pure principles my grandmother had instilled. He peopled my young mind with unclean images, such as only a vile monster could think of. . . . He told me that I was

his property; that I must be subject to his will in all things. My soul revolted against the mean tyranny (26).

Thus begins the duel of wills, the bent "romance" that is the narrative's central conflict. Henceforth, Flint and Linda will act out a drama of seduction well-known to the woman well-read in mid-nineteenth century American fiction.

Throughout the 1850s, concurrent with the composition of Jacobs' autobiography, the slave narrative and the sentimental novel freely—and lucratively—engaged in a promiscuous cross-pollination of influences. Exotic in setting and replete with real-life melodrama, the peculiar institution provided the raw material for squadrons of successful "scribbling women". (Indeed, in the bogus *Autobiography of a Female Slave* (1857), Mattie Griffiths performed a wholesale theft of the genre.) In turn, the skillful slave narrator drew on the conventions of popular literature to render more movingly the stock situations—family separations, assaults on virtues, and unrequited love—that were to him only too real. The sentimental novel's *sine qua non* was the seduction motif, a moral conflict that might seem especially well-suited for abolitionist exploitation. A theme as old as the novel itself, it received its first and definitive treatments in Samuel Richardson's *Pamela* (1740) and *Clarissa* (1747-48), the two great sources for the best-selling fiction of antebellum America. Referring to the "appalling popularity of the seduction motif" in the popular sentimental literature of the time, Herbert Ross Brown, the genre's best critic, observed that "no other theme was able to provoke more purple patches or inspire more poetic flights" (44). Similarly, seduction is the one indispensible element in Leslie Fiedler's definition of the early novel: "a prose narrative in which Seducer and Pure Maiden were brought face to face in ritual combat destined to end in marriage or death" (62). But despite its twin potential for plot and polemics, the seduction theme appears only rarely in antebellum slave autobiographies—after all, the narrators were overwhelmingly male.[2] It was left to Jacobs to exploit the propagandistic possibilities of the form's characteristic moral confrontation. By couching her personal narrative in the familiar terms of formula fiction, she appropriated its popularity while undercutting its presumptions.

In her opening chapters, Jacobs paints the contestants in primary sentimentalist colors: Linda, the steadfast maiden of low estate; Flint, the slimy reprobate from the upper orders. To Flint's first proposition, Linda responds in ripe Richardsonian tones:

> When he told me I was made for his use, made to obey his command in *every* thing; that I was nothing but a slave, whose will must and should surrender to his, never before had my puny arm felt half so strong. . . . The war of my life had begun; and

though one of God's most powerless creatures, I resolve never to be conquered. Alas, for me! (16, 17)

Described as a villain "whose restless, craving, vicious nature roved about day and night, seeking whom to devour" (16), Flint also fulfills generic expectations. Jacobs gives him the dialogue required of the role: " 'Curse you!' " he mutters through clenched teeth, "'You obstinate girl! I could grind your bones to powder!' " (59) Like the most sinister of the sentimentalist seducers, Flint demands his victim's willing complicity, favoring psychological, not physical, pressure. Thus, though "(he) sought in every way to render (Linda) miserable, . . . he did not resort to corporal punishment, but to all the petty tyrannical ways that human ingenuity could devise" (17).

Having cast her characters in stark (and stock) opposition, Jacobs advances the abolitionist argument in "Sketches of Neighboring Slaveholders" (45-53), a striking chapter aimed directly at the female reader. The author describes the state of women—slave and free—within an institution as patriarchal as it is peculiar. The familiar appeals to interracial sympathy are not slighted:

> No pen can give adequate description of the all-pervading corruption produced by slavery. The slave girl is reared in an atmosphere of licentiousness and fear. The lash and foul talk of her master and his sons are her teachers (51).

However, in emphasizing just how pervasive the corruption can be, Jacobs crosses the color line:

> Nor do the master's daughters always escape. . . . The white daughters early hear their parents quarreling about some female slave. Their curiosity is excited, and they soon learn the cause. They are attended by the young slave girls whom their father has corrupted; and they hear such talk as should never meet youthful ears, or any other ears. They know that the women slaves are subject to their father's authority in all things; and in some cases they exercise the same authority over the men slaves. I have seen the master of such a household whose head was bowed down in shame; for it was known in the neighborhood that his daughter had selected one of the meanest slaves on his plantation to be the father of his first grandchild (52).

In one sense, Jacobs is simply employing basic rhetorical strategy: know your audience and play to it. Having few illusions about the white Northerner's capacity for interracial compassion, slave narrators typically waged a campaign on two fronts, attacking slavery as a system corrupting white and black alike. Always in tune with her readership, Jacobs consistently stresses the insidious influence of slavery on the sacred relations between the white husband and wife, the white parent and child. More to the point, she also suggests relations that are not confined by color: the bond between women, black or white. "Reader," she insists, "it is not to awaken sympathy for myself that I am telling you truthfully what I suffered in slavery. I do it to kindle a flame of compassion in your hearts for my sisters who are still in bondage, suffering as I once suffered" (28). Certainly—but her confessions spark a kindred recognition that the singular possessive is too exclusive, that her sisters are the *reader's* as well. Further, by cataloging the uniquely female burdens of slavery, the author has provided her virtuous readers with a metaphor for their own sex-determined condition in the nominally free North.

Jacobs makes the comparison explicit in a cautionary tale (50-51) told just prior to the one cited above. A "good mistress" who "taught her slaves to lead pure lives, and wished them to enjoy the fruit of their own industry,. . . . cherished an unrequited passion for a man who had resolved to marry for wealth." The pious young lady marries the fortune hunter, and the "new master" quickly undoes her good work, selling some slaves down the river and debauching others. Legally, the wife has no recourse against the husband's disposition of her—now his—property. "I no longer have the power I had a week ago," she tells a black father who implores her intercession. The mistress can only render her slaves such kindnesses as her "unfortunate circumstances" permit, before passing peacefully away, "glad to close her eyes on a life which had been made so wretched by the man she loved." The moral of the story is so unmistakable that Jacobs' final comment is either diversion or misinterpretation: "Had it not been for slavery, he would have been a better man and his wife a happier woman." Clearly, she faults her wrong patriarchal institution; marriage, not slavery, is the true culprit.

For reasons of cultural necessity, Jacobs' treatment of marriage can only be equivocal. In purely dramatic terms, Linda's duel with Flint is accordingly very much in the Richardsonian tradition. However, for the sentimental heroine so beset, the traditional reward for moral constancy and unwarranted suffering is either marriage (*Pamela*) or heaven (*Clarissa*), the classic culmination having the girl either wedded to her (redeemed) seducer or triumphant over him in the next, better world. For the slave heroine, neither ending is possible if the author is to remain true to her abolitionist mandate. Jacobs may appropriate the trappings of sentimental fiction, but not its secure moral universe. Thus, she offers the reader a third alternative: personal autonomy.

Whether from the vantage of the sentimental novel or the slave narrative, Jacob's most striking generic departure is Linda's extraordinary sense of self, her maintainence of an autonomous identity seemingly impervious to assault. As singular as she is single-minded, Linda has a strength of character and consistency of personality more worthy of note than her creator's gender. To say the least, the peculiar institution bequeathed to its victims an understandable reticence about personal revelation and the assertion of self. Concealment and deception defined the slave's relationship to the white world, duplicity being both a strategy for survival and a means of escape. As Stephen Butterfield argues in *Black Autobiography in America*:

> To avoid punishment the slave has to learn to wear a mask, to seem as if he fits the owner's conception of 'the nigger.' At the same time, he has an identity of his own that must be hidden, because it is a threat to the slave system. In effect, he maintains a double identity and shifts between the two according to the occasion (20).

Certainly identity is too fragile a concept actually to be donned and discarded like a mask—at some point, the actor becomes the role—but Butterfield's metaphor properly evokes the two-faced nature of slave behavior. The songs, stories, and jokes of slave folklore confirm and celebrate such deceits, as do the slave narratives themselves. For example, the tobacconist Lunsford Lane, whose existence as a slave was relatively easy, wisely concealed his rising fortune, finding "it politic to go shabbily dressed, and to appear poor" (16). Likewise, Solomon Northup, a New York freeman kidnapped into slavery, quickly learned his "true policy" was to keep quiet about his background because "it would but expose (him) to maltreatment, and diminish the chances of liberation" (250).

The role of deception, the donning by the black narrator of a mask that accords with white society's racist expectations, is the first consideration when examining the slave narrator's autobiographical self. Indeed, as public manifestoes directed at a white audience, the narratives might appear to be intrinsically compromised documents. However, after a lifetime of compromised identity, slave narrators generally turned to the autobiographical act not as a way to assume yet another mask, but as an occasion for self-examination and revelation. Though they may, like Lane and Northrup, recall past disguises, their present presentation of self needs no costume; in the slave narrative, the political mandate for anti-slavery testimony accords perfectly with the autobiographical mandate for frank confession.[3] By these lights, Jacobs' presentation of self (Linda Brent) is still more unusual for, past as well as present, she is only herself.

This is not to say that Linda is above some strategic trickery ("slaves," she observes by way of explanation, "being surrounded by mysteries, deceptions, and dangers, early learn to be suspicious and watchful, and prematurely cautious and cunning" [159]). To facilitate her escape, she disguises herself as a sailor and, during the long confinement in her grandmother's attic, she engages in an extended "competition in cunning" (130-135), diverting her pursuers with letters postmarked from New York. But face to face with Flint, she plays neither fool nor coquette. She wears no mask.

The singleness of identity reinforces the singleness of purpose. Jacobs expresses an acute awareness and profound abhorrence of the double-dealing pretenses intrinsic to slavery. She tells of the gullible Northern clergyman on his first visit to a Southern plantation, "easily blinded" by the false performances of slaveholder and slave alike:

> (The clergyman) walks around the premises, and sees the beautiful groves and flowering vines, and the comfortable huts of favored household slaves. The southerner invites him to talk with these slaves. He asks them if they want to be free, and they say, "Oh, no, massa" (76).

Similarly, the "grand funeral" of a beloved slave matriarch, complete with dramatic effusions of grief from Dr. and Mrs. Flint, is treated as a piece of theater:

> Northern travellers . . . might have described this tribute of respect to the humble dead as a beuatiful feature in the "patriarchal institution"; a touching proof of the attachment between slaveholders and their servants; and tender-hearted Mrs. Flint would have confirmed this impression, with handkerchief at her eyes. We could have told them a different story (150).

Bitterly conscious of the harm such play-acting does to the abolitionist cause, Jacobs takes every opportunity to expose the reality behind appearances. Linda herself offers the best occasion: consistently "one-self," she takes no part in the broad shams of slave life.

Linda's refusal to compromise, and insistence on asserting, her "self" makes the slave girl's relationship with her obsessed master more nearly one of psychological equality. It often gives Linda the edge. Nowhere is this more evident than in the pair's dramatic confrontation over Linda's pregnancy (54-57). Determined not to fall prey to Flint's seductive machinations, Linda resolves to do "anything, everything, for the sake of defeating him." Her subsequent "plunge into the abyss," an affair with a certain "white unmarried gentleman," is shameful to relate and doubtless shocking to a readership "whose purity has been sheltered from childhood," but Linda makes clear that she was no deceived maiden, that this admittedly illicit relationship had her willing participation. (Her confession is downright boastful: "I knew what I did, and I did it with deliberate calculation.") Significantly, she rationalizes her action in terms of personal autonomy:

> It seems less degrading to give one's self, than to submit to compulsion. There is something akin to freedom in having a lover who has no control over you, except that which he gains by kindness and attachment (55).

She is honest enough to own up to another, equally personal motive: spite. "I knew nothing would enrage Dr. Flint so much as to know that I favored another; and it was something to triumph over my tyrant even in that small way," she admits.

For his part, Flint acknowledges both the terms of the competition (a duel of wills, not arms) and its prize (Linda's identity, not her "honor"). He seeks to break down his opponent with incessant verbal and occasional physical abuse (most memorably, when he crops her hair after being informed of her second pregnancy), but he never carries his assault to its logical conclusion. Rape will not confer the victory he craves. "Dr. Flint loved money, but he loved power more" (81), Linda observes, and that power is emphatically psychological. Linda knows very well what the real stakes are and what her advantage is:

> . . . I thought how completely I should be in his power and the prospect was appalling. Even if I should kneel before him, and implore him to spare me, for the sake of my children, I knew he would spurn me with his foot, and my weakness would be his triumph (86).

And again:

> I had a women's pride, and a mother's love for my children; and I resolved that out of the darkness of this hour a brighter dawn should rise for them. My master had power and law on his side; I had a determined will. There is might in each (87).

Linda is handicapped in her battle—and Jacobs in her narrative—by the female's usual complication, children. The slave husband or father who left his family to escape North could justify his desertion as a necessary tactical and personal move. In freedom, he could better fight slavery, more easily earn the money to emancipate his family, and, above all, be his own man. A woman who did likewise was not granted the same latitude. Speaking the harsh truth, Linda's grandmother reminds her of the double standard: " 'Nobody respects a mother who forsakes her children' " (93). If Linda is to escape slavery unburdened by guilt, and if Jacobs is to retain the reader's unqualified sympathy, she must first faithfully discharge her maternal responsibilities.

Linda earns her maternal credentials most impressively through the seven long years she spends hidden in the tiny crawlspace above her grandmother's shed, her dismal "loophole of retreat" (117-120). This extraordinary confinement, Jacobs knows, will strain credulity ("I hardly expect the reader will credit me . . ." [151]), so in keeping with generic convention she attaches confirming testimony in a brief appendix. As an indictment of slavery and an expression of the lengths its victims will go to escape it, the ordeal speaks for itself, but the episode serves at least two additional, narrative functions. First, it is a ready metaphor not only for the prison of slavery but for the restrictions of domestic life. Linda spends perhaps one fourth of the narrative literally imprisoned in the female's traditional sphere of influence, the household, initially in the attic of a white benefactress ("For that deed of Christian womanhood, may God forever bless her!" [103]) and later in the loophole. Watching, waiting, sometimes plotting against Flint, Linda lives an almost wholly vicarious existence. Though the author herself may not be conscious of the associations, she describes this circumscribed life in terms a wifely readership might find evocative:

> Sometimes it appeared to me as if ages had rolled away since I entered upon that gloomy, monotonous existence. At times, I was stupified and listless; I became very impatient to know when these dark years would end, and I should again be allowed to feel the sunshine, and breathe the pure air (152).

The episode has a second, more certain narrative purpose: it verifies and accentuates Linda's maternal commitment. Her domestic imprisonment has one compensation: " . . . I was not comfortless. I heard the voices of my children" (117). As a cynical strategic device, the bond between mother and child promises an emotional force, and hence a propagandistic pull, to which an audience of "happy free women" is especially susceptible. For Jacobs, the opportunity to enhance antislavery politics with the power of familial melodrama is irresistible:

> Season after season, year after year, I peeped at my children's faces, and heard their sweet voices, with a heart yearning all the while to say, "Your mother is here" (152).

If the narrative strategy is cold-blooded, the execution is not. Jacobs' tearful declarations are obviously heartfelt and the scenes between mother and child inspire her most heartrending prose. Typically, she expresses "such feelings as only a slave mother can experience" in language equal parts affection and abolitionism. "Never should I know peace till my children were emancipated with all due formalities of law" (140). Or: "Always I was in dread that by some accident, or some contrivance, slavery would succeed in snatching my children from me" (153). Necessarily, her ultimate decision to escape comes only after her daughter has been sent North and the imminent threat of discovery jeopardizes the welfare of her son and grandmother. Once in the comparative safety of New York, Linda's first thoughts are dutifully maternal: "I was impatient to go to work and earn money, that I might change the uncertain position of my children" (172). Assisting Linda is her employer, the kindly Mrs. Bruce, a woman of true Christian sympathy and a exemplary model for like-minded readers.

Jacobs' concluding chapter, "Free At Last" (200-208), does double duty as narrative closure. Throughout *Incidents in the Life of a Slave Girl,* the author has drawn on the conventions of one prose narrative form (the sentimental novel) for the purposes of another (the slave narrative). Though her authorial allegiance has never been in doubt, she cannot complete the course of one narrative (slavery to freedom) without ending the other (the maiden versus the seducer). Despite everything, it is her former master whose presence animates Linda's story; the reader demands a final accounting and Jacobs can do nought but provide one. In a letter from her grandmother, Linda at last receives the news: " 'Dr. Flint is dead.' " She comments:

> I cannot say, with truth, that the news of my master's death softened my feelings towards him. There are wrongs which even the grave does not bury. The man was odious to me while he lived, and his memory is odious now (201).

With the book closed on Flint, Jacobs turns to the remaining unfinished business, the long-negotiated purchase of "legal" freedom for her children and herself. Once the necessary document is signed ("future generations will learn from it that women were articles of traffic in New York, late in the nineteenth century of the Christian religion . . ." [206]), the author bluntly sums up her narrative, and political, priorities: "Reader, my story ends with freedom; not in the usual way, with marriage." Perhaps only Jacobs' modern readers can appreciate the many meanings of that declaration.

Notes

[1] Citing a discovery of a cache of Jacobs' letters, Jean Fagin Yellin convincingly asserts that *Incidents in the Life of a Slave Girl* "has just been transformed from a questionable slave narrative into a well-documented pseudonymous autobiography" (479). The contribution of editor Lydia Maria Child, long thought crucial, is deemed to be precisely what she affirmed in her introduction: "mainly for purposes of condensation and orderly arrangement" (p. xii).

[2] Male slave narrators did comment occasionally on seduction. See Nichols (36-40).

[3] For another reading see Minter.

Works Cited

An Appeal to the Women of the Nominally Free States: Issued by an Anti-Slavery Convention of American Women, 2nd Edition. Boston: Isaac Knapp, 1838; rpt. Freeport, New York: Books for Libraries Press, 1971.

Bayliss, John F., editor. *Black Slave Narratives.* New York: The McMillan Company, 1970.

Beecher, Catherine. *An Essay on Slavery and Abolitionism, with Reference to the Duty of American Females.* Philadelphia: Henry Perkins, 1837.

Brent, Linda. *Incidents in the Life of a Slave Girl* [1861]. New York: Harcourt Brace Jovanovich Publishers, 1973.

Brown, Herbert Ross. *The Sentimental Novel in America, 1789-1860.* Durham, North Carolina: Duke University Press, 1940.

Butterfield, Stephen. *Black Autobiography in America.* Amherst: University of Massachusetts, 1974.

Child, Lydia Maria. *An Appeal in Favor of That Class of Americans Called Africans.* Boston: Alklen and Ticknor, 1833.

Douglass, Frederick. *The Life and Times of Frederick Douglass* [1892]. New York: McMillan Publishing Company, 1962.

Fiedler, Leslie. *Love and Death in the American Novel.* New York: Stein and Day Publishers, 1960.

Foster, Francis Smith. *Witnessing Slavery: The Development of the Ante-bellum Slave Narrative.* Westport, Connecticut: Greenwood Press, 1979.

Lane, Lunsford. *Narrative of Lunsford Lane* [1842]. Rpt. in Katz, William Loren, editor. *Five Great Slave Narratives.* New York: The Arno Press, 1969.

Lutz, Alma. *Crusade for Freedom: Women of the Anti-Slavery Movement.* Boston: Beacon Press, 1968.

Minter, David. "Conceptions of Self in Black Slave Narratives." *American Transcendental Quarterly* 24 (1974): 62-68.

Nichols, Charles H. *Many Thousands Gone: The Ex-Slaves' Account of Their Bondage and Freedom.* Leiden, Netherlands: E.J. Brill, 1963.

Northrup, Solomon. *Twelve Years a Slave: The Narrative of Solomon Northup* [1853]. Rpt. in Osofsky, Gilbert. *Puttin' on Ole Massa.* New York: Harper and Row, 1969.

Sillen, Samuel. *Women Against Slavery.* New York: Massesfd and Mainstream, 1955.

Sterling, Dorothy, editor. *We Are Your Sisters: Black Women in the Nineteenth Century.* New York: W.W. Norton and Company, 1984.

Yellin, Jean Fagin. "Written By Herself: Harriet Jacobs' Narrative." *American Literature* 25 (1981): 479-486.

Elizabeth Fox-Genovese (essay date 1987)

SOURCE: "To Write My Self: The Autobiographies of Afro-American Women," in *Feminist Issues in Literary Scholarship,* edited by Shari Benstock, Indiana University Press, 1987, pp. 161-80.

[*In the following excerpt, Fox-Genovese explores the differences in tone and content between* Incidents *and other works* of *sentimental domestic literature.*]

. . . Harriet Jacobs, in ***Incidents in the Life of a Slave Girl,*** left no doubt about whom she thought she was writing for: "O, you happy free women, contrast *your* New Year's day with that of the poor bond-woman!" (14).

Jacobs wrote, at least in part, to introduce the world to the special horrors of slavery for women. To achieve her goal, she sought to touch the hearts of northern white women and, accordingly, wrote to the extent possible in their idiom. She so doggedly followed the tone and model of sentimental domestic fiction, that for a long time it was assumed that her editor, Lydia Maria Child, had written the book. Jacobs's surviving correspondence proves that she, not Child, wrote her own story, as she claimed in its subtitle "written by herself."[21] And Jacobs's text differs significantly in tone and content from other examples of domestic fiction. She casts her withering indictment of slavery as the violation of womanhood. Time and again she asserts and demonstrates that if slavery is bad for men, it is worse for women. Thinking that she understands the northern middle-class female audience, she depicts the horrors of slavery for women as specifically related to the assaults upon female chastity and conjugal domesticity. Linda Brent, Jacobs's self in the narrative, grows up in the shadow of her master's determination to possess her sexually. She claims to fend off his advances as an affront to her chastity. Ultimately, her determination to avoid him leads her, after her master has prohibited her sale and marriage to the free black man she loves, to accept another white man as a lover and to bear him two children. One important strand of her story concerns the ways in which she atones for this "fall" and, especially, regains the respect and love of her own daughter. In some sense, Jacobs attempts to present her resistance to her master as a defense of her virtue, even though that defense leads her into a loss of "virtue" by another route. Jacobs does not fully resolve the contradictions in her behavior and principles at this level of discourse, however hard she tries. Ultimately, she throws herself on the pity— and guilt—of her readers, as she threw herself on the pity of her daughter. But Jacobs's text also invites another reading or, to put it differently, conceals another text.

Jacobs begins her narrative: "I was born a slave; but I never knew it till six years of happy childhood had passed away"(3). The claim not to have recognized one's condition—of race or of enslavement—until six or seven years of age is common among Afro-American authors.[22] For Jacobs, that opening sentence underscores the difference between condition and consciousness and thereby distances the self from the condition. But Jacobs never suggests that the condition does not, in some measure, influence the self. She insists that her father "had more of the feelings of a freeman than is common among slaves," thereby implicitly acknowledging the difference between slavery and freedom in the development of an independent self. In the same passage, she reveals how heavily slavery could weigh upon the slaves' sense of manhood. On one occasion Jacobs's father and mistress both happened to call to her brother at the same moment. The boy, after a moment's hesitation, went to the mistress. The father sharply reproved him: "You are *my* child . . . and when I call you, you should come immediately, if you have to pass through fire and water" (7). The father's desire to command the primary obedience of his own child flows from his feelings of being a free man and contradicts the harshest realities of slavery. Slavery stripped men of fatherhood. Even a free father could not call "his" child by a slave wife his own, for the child, following the condition of the mother, remained a slave. Jacobs is, surely not by accident, depicting a spirit of manliness and an instinctive grasp of the virtues of freedom in her father as the introduction to her own story of resistance.

Jacobs's narrative rests upon every conceivable element of fantasy and ambiguity. If her father had the feelings of a free man, both of her parents were mulattoes who lived a model of conjugal domesticity, and her maternal grandmother was the daughter of a South Carolina planter who apparently had inherited The Chivalry's own sense of honor—more than could be said for her owners. Jacobs, in other words, endows herself with a pedigree of physical, mental, and moral comeliness. She is not like the other slaves among whom she lives. She has the capacity to rise above her condition. Her sense of herself in relation to the other slaves leaves something to be desired for an opponent of slavery, or, worse, it reflects either her assimilation of "white" values or her determination to play to what she takes to be the prejudices of her audience. Jacobs offers a confused picture of the relation between the identity and behavior of Afro-Americans, including herself, and the effects of slavery. If slavery is evil, it has evil consequences. If those evil consequences include a breaking of the spirit of the enslaved, then how can slaves be credited with character and will? The questions circle on and on, admitting of no easy answers. They clearly plague Jacobs.

These difficult questions do not seriously cloud Jacobs's sense of her self. They affect her sense of how best to present that self to others, her sense of the relation between her self and her gender, her sense of the relation between self and social condition. The awareness of white readers deeply influences the ways in which she depicts life under slavery. But under, or woven through, the discourse for the readers runs a discourse for herself. For Jacobs, the issues between her and her master did not primarily concern virtue, chastity, sexuality, or any of the rest. They concerned the conflict of two wills. Having described her master's foul intentions towards her, she adds that he had told her "I was made for his use, made to obey his command in *every* thing; that I was nothing but a slave, whose will must and should surrender to his . . ." (16). The words make her "puny" arm feel stronger than it ever had: "The war of my life had begun; and though one of God's most powerless creatures, I resolved never to be conquered. Alas, for me!" (17). The "alas for me" should not be read as some regret about her determination or any acknowledgement that such willful feelings might be inappropriate for a woman, but as a confirmation that everything that follows follows directly from her determination not to be conquered.

Jacobs's narrative of her successful flight from slavery can be read as a journey or progress from her initial state of innocence through the mires of her struggle against her social condition, to a prolonged period of ritual, or mythic, concealment, on to the flight itself, and finally to the state of knowledge that accompanies her ultimate acquisition of freedom. The myth or metaphor of the journey to selfhood is as old as culture, although it has carried a special resonance for Western Christian, notably Protestant, culture. Jacobs, in some respects like Harriet Wilson, registers the end of the journey as a rather bleak dawn on a troubled landscape. Here is no pot of gold at the end of the rainbow. The self-knowledge that accrues consists above all in the recognition that there is no resting place for the fugitive. The struggle for the dignity of the self persists. Insult and injury abound in freedom as under slavery, albeit in different forms. Life remains a war. But the focused struggle of wills with the master has given way to a more generalized struggle to affirm the self in a hostile, or indifferent, environment. . . .

Notes

[21]Jean Fagan Yellin, "Texts and Contexts of Harriet Jacobs' *Incidents in the Life of a Slave Girl: Written by Herself*," in Charles Davis and Louis Henry Gates, eds., *The Slave's Narrative* (New York: Oxford University Press, 1985), pp. 262-82; and her "Written By Herself: *Harriet Jacobs' Slave Narrative*," *American Literature* 53, no. 3 (November 1981), 479-86. For Jacobs's own account of her experience and authorship, see her correspondence, University of Rochester Library, Post Family Papers. Dorothy Sterling has reprinted some of Jacobs's letters in her excellent anthology, *We Are Your Sisters: Black Women in the Nineteenth Century* (New York: Norton, 1984), pp. 73-84. On the general tradition of the slave narratives, see, among many, Marion Wilson Starling, *The Slave Narrative: Its Place in History* (Boston: G. K. Hall, 1981); John Sekora and Darwin T. Turner, eds., *The Art of Slave Narrative* (Macomb: Northern Illinois University Press, 1982); James Olney, " 'I Was Born': Slave Narratives, Their Status as Autobiography and as Literature," in Davis and Gates, eds., *The Slave's Narrative*, pp. 148-75; Houston A. Baker, Jr., "Autobiographical Acts and the Voice of the Southern Slave," *loc. cit.*, pp. 242-61; and Charles T. Davis, "The Slave Narrative: First Major Art Form in an Emerging Black Tradition," in his *Black Is the Color of the Cosmos: Essays on Afro-American Literature and Culture 1942-1981*, ed. Louis Henry Gates (New York: Garland Publishing, 1982), pp. 83-119. As a rule, the general treatments of slave narratives take little or no account of any female perception, in part because so few women either escaped or wrote narratives.

[22] See, among many, Zora Neale Hurston's *Their Eyes Were Watching God* (Urbana: University of Illinois Press, 1978; orig. ed. 1937), p. 21: "Ah was wid dem white chillun so much till Ah didn't know Ah wuzn't white till Ah was round six years old."

Mary Helen Washington (essay date 1987)

SOURCE: "Meditations on History: The Slave Woman's Voice," in *Invented Lives: Narratives of Black Women, 1860-1960*, Anchor Press, 1987, pp. 3-15.

[*In the following essay, Washington analyzes Jacobs's use of the sentimental domestic genre, noting that this was "a poor choice for her story," and emphasizes that* Incidents *reads more as a slave narrative than a sentimental novel, particularly in the way in which it transcends the boundaries of gender.*]

In 1861, with the help of two white abolitionists, Amy Post and Lydia Maria Child, Harriet Jacobs, abolitionist and exslave, published under the pseudonym, Linda Brent, an account of her life in slavery called *Inci-dents in the Life of a Slave Girl,* one of the few slave narratives written by a woman.[1] Working in New York as a nurse for the well-known magazinist, Nathaniel Parker Willis, Jacobs had to write her autobiography secretly at night when she could steal the time from her duties taking care of four small children in an eighteen-room house. The Willis' demanding social schedule exhausted everyone in the house. Jacobs wrote to Amy Post in 1853 that despite these continual interruptions, she was determined to get her story written: "Poor Hatty's name is so much in demand that I cannot accomplish much; if I could steal away and have two quiet months to myself, I would work night and day though it should all fall to the ground . . . As yet I have not written a single page by daylight."[2]

Twenty years after her escape from slavery, Harriet Jacobs published what may very well be the only slave narrative that deals primarily with the sexual exploitation of slave women. Linda Brent deliberately chooses to bear two children by a white man in order to escape the sexual harassment of her legal master, Dr. Flint, a choice that labels her a disgrace in the eyes of her family and her community and herself. Harriet Jacobs's narrative is unique in still other ways. Brent does not follow the usual pattern of the male fugitive slave who flees to freedom, leaving behind kith and kin. She is so reluctant to leave her children and grandmother that she hides out in a tiny garret at the top of her grandmother's house for several years. Nor is there any man-to-man physical confrontation between Brent and her owner; she exerts her power against Flint in more covert and clandestine ways.

And when she comes to write her story, she encounters a problem that no male slave autobiographer had to contend with. The male narrator was under no compulsion to discuss his sexuality or his sex life; he did not have to reveal the existence of children he may have fathered outside of marriage. However, neither Linda Brent's sexual exploitation nor her two half-white children could be ignored in the story of her bondage and her freedom. The male narrator could write his tale as a reclamation of his manhood, but under the terms of white society's ideals of chastity and sexual ignorance for women Brent certainly cannot claim "true" womanhood.[3] By the hypocritical standards of nineteenth-century Victorian morality, Brent was a scandalous woman with a disgraceful past. This question of a woman's shame over her sexuality is central to our understanding of Brent's narrative; for, unlike male slave narrators who wrote to show that they had the qualities valued and respected by other men—courage, mobility, rationality, and physical strength—Harriet Jacobs wrote to confess that she did not have the qualities valued in white women.[4] Writing again to her trusted friend, Amy Post, Jacobs struggled with her feelings of humiliation about her past life and anguished over whether she should expose herself by writing her life story:

Your proposal to me has been thought over and over again, but not without some most painful remembrance. Dear Amy, if it was the life of a Heroine with no degradation associated with it! Far better to have been one of the starving poor of Ireland whose bones had to bleach on the highways than to have been a slave with the curse of slavery stamped upon yourself and Children. . . . I have tried for the last two years to conquer [my stubborn pride] and I feel that God has helped me on. I never would consent to give my past life to anyone without giving the whole truth. If it could help save another from my fate it would be selfish and unchristian in me to keep it back.[5]

Though she is unable to say so directly, Brent was a sexually experienced woman even at the age of fifteen. She tries to explain her sexual maturity discreetly: "The influences of slavery had had the same effect on me that they had on other young girls; they had made me prematurely knowing, concerning the ways of the world. I knew what I did, and I did it with deliberate calculation" (p. 56).

But Brent cannot savor the satisfaction of her actions because the very act of taking control of her life is also, for a woman, a fall from grace. Her grandmother nearly disowns her, Brent herself feels degraded, and, when she comes to write her story, she chooses to tell it in a form that made it impossible for her to discuss her sexual abuse openly.

Writing in the nineteenth century and in the form of the domestic sentimental novel, Brent had to observe conventions of decorum which demanded virginity, modesty, and delicacy of women.[6] Locked into these conventions, Brent presents Dr. Flint as a jealous lover and herself as a vulnerable, young woman undergoing a "perilous passage" rather than a slave whose sexual exploitation was legally sanctioned. Her use of romantic language seems more suited to a story of seduction than to the slave woman's life. As contemporary critics of the Brent narrative have demonstrated, Brent was obviously reaching for a form that would help her to establish rapport with her Northern white women readers, and they would most certainly have been familiar with the domestic novel. It was, in almost every way, a poor choice for her story; for a novel that described the perfect woman as the submissive, pious, and devoted wife of a white man "mocked the condition of the female slave."[7] If the domestic novel of sentiment and melodrama helped Brent to reach an audience of women who were familiar with this form, it also severely limited her ability to produce a written account of her life as profound as her own experiences.

But Harriet Jacobs did not allow the sentimental novel to reenslave her as some critics have said.[8] Her contemporary interpreters, Jean Fagan Yellin, Hazel Carby,

Valerie Smith, and Joanne Braxton have demonstrated conclusively Brent's struggle to resist the ideological implications of the sentimental novel and the cult of true womanhood. It is an ideology, writes Carby, "that would deny her very existence as woman and as mother."[9] Yellin argues further that the Brent narrative actually defies the domestic novel's rules of sexual propriety:

Despite her language (and what other one wonders was available to her?) this narrator does not characterize herself conventionally as a passive female victim. On the contrary, she asserts that she was—even when young and a slave—an effective moral agent, and she takes full responsibility for her actions.[10]

Brent's deliberate and knowing choice to take a white lover and to bear two children by him in order to foil Dr. Flint's plans to make her his mistress is, in some ways, an act of emancipation. That she sees it as a means to free herself is clear: "It seems less degrading to give one's self than to submit to compulsion. There is something akin to freedom in having a lover who has no control over you, except that which he gains by kindness and attachment" (p. 55).

Yellin also invites us to consider that "extraordinary sentence" in *Incidents* in which Brent, refusing to be bound by the standards and morality of white women, "proposes a new definition of female morality grounded in her own experience."[11] Having confessed her sexual experience and her willful use of it, Brent concludes, "Still, in looking back calmly, on the events of my life, I feel that the slave woman ought not to be judged by the same standard as others" (p. 56). These are neither the words nor the sentiment, nor the rhetoric, of the domestic novel or the novel of seduction.[12] The sentence is direct, powerful, unadorned; and it separates Linda Brent from the women of sentimental fiction. Brent makes that separation even more explicit when, at the end of her story, she eschews the sentimental novel's passive stance for one of power and autonomy: "Reader, my story ends with freedom; not in the usual way, with marriage. I and my children are now free."

In spite of Harriet Jacobs's twenty-year struggle to write her story; in spite of her status as social activist—she worked in the antislavery office and reading room in Rochester where she met Amy Post and other abolitionists—in spite of her work as a teacher and nurse with the newly freed people in Virginia, where she and her daughter Louisa organized sewing circles and schools; in spite of the book's enthusiastic reception at the time of its publication, Harriet Jacobs's narrative was considered by many twentieth-century scholars to be a fraud In his 1972 edition of his landmark study of slave narratives, *Slave Testimony,* John Blassingame dismisses Jacobs's story as too melodramatic to be authentic. Using the male slave narrative as the standard, Blassingame cannot accept this "non-standard" female slave narrative with its peculiar form, the many examples of "miscegenation and outraged virtue, unrequited love, and planter licentiousness [which] appear on practically every page." But, as Hazel Carby argues in her study of female slave narratives, this rejection of the female story is based on criteria that exclude the female experience:

> . . . issues of miscegenation, unrequited love, outraged virtue and planter licentiousness, are found foregrounded in diaries by southern white women while absent or in the background of the records of their planter husbands. Identifying such a difference should lead us to question and consider the significance of these issues in the lives of women as opposed to men not to the conclusion that the diaries are not credible because they deviate from the conventions of male authored texts.[13]

Black women wrote about 12 percent of the total number of extant slave narratives, but none of these is as well known as the narratives by men. The result has been that the life of the male slave has come to be representative, even though the female experience in slavery was sometimes radically different, as the Jacobs narrative documents.[14] What is also different—often radically—is the written form of their narratives. In male narratives, women play subordinate roles. Men leave them behind when they escape to the North, or they are pitiable subjects of brutal treatment, or benign nurturers who help the fugitive in his quest for freedom, or objects of sentimentality. Or, as in the case of the Frederick Douglass *Narrative,* they are simply rendered invisible. Douglass tells the story of his escape as though he were a solo artist—self-initiating, self-propelling, and self-sustaining—making the plunge into the dark night of freedom alone and unassisted. The testimony of his eldest daughter, Rosetta, tells quite a different story: that one Anna Murray, a free black woman of Baltimore, welcomed Frederick Bailey (as he was then known) into her circle of friends, that a romance developed between them, that not only did Anna make the sailor suit that Douglass wore in his daring escape disguised as a sailor, but that she used funds from her savings as a valued household worker to help him get safely to New York and, a week after his arrival, "she confidently joined in matrimony, this man, this escaped slave with a price on his head and then went on to face with him the double uncertainty of life in the North."[15] I have often wondered why none of this critical information about Anna Murray Douglass found its way into Douglass's poignant story. Like the Douglass *Narrative,* the plot of the standard male narrative, Valerie Smith points out, is not only "the journey from slavery to freedom, but also the journey from slavehood to manhood." She comments, "By mythologizing rugged individuality, physical

strength, and geographical mobility, the narratives of men enshrine cultural definitions of masculinity."[16]

Narratives by women play an important part in allowing us to hear the voices of slave women; they show women as active agents rather than objects of pity, capable of interpreting their experiences and, like men, able to turn their victimization into triumph. Hazel Carby makes the point that women slave narrators describe their victimization in a context that also shows them fighting back:

> Narratives by black women foreground their active tales as historical agents as opposed to passive subjects, acting upon their own visions they make decisions over their own lives. They do also document their sufferings and brutal treatment *but in a context that is also the story of resistance* [emphasis mine].[17]

The Linda Brent narrative is such a story about a woman in the act of resistance. Her resistance took bizarre forms, but, however melodramatic her autobiography may seem by contemporary standards, we now know that the facts of her life presented in *Incidents* are irrefutable. According to Yellin, there is enough external evidence to establish beyond a doubt the truthfulness of Jacobs's account of her life.

In 1982 Yellin went to North Carolina, interviewed local historians, and worked in the state archives which enabled her to identify nearly all of the people and places in *Incidents,* including "Dr. Flint," who was a prominent North Carolina doctor, and, according to Yellin's findings, evidently capable of just the sort of tyranny presented in *Incidents.* Walking through Edenton, Yellin found the town exactly as Jacobs described it, the historic area where Jacobs lived so compact that it would be possible to look out of an attic window and observe many of the town's activities. Yellin says she has absolute faith in Jacobs's reconstruction of events in *Incidents:* "You can trust her. She's not ever wrong. She may be wrong on incidentals like the birth order of her mistress's children—after all she was a woman in her forties trying to remember what happened to her as a teenager—but she's never wrong in substance."[18]

Furthermore, the discovery of a cache of her letters showing her in the act of creating her narrative also proves that *Incidents* was indeed written by Harriet Jacobs. Through these letters we discover, for example, that, though she refused the aid of her proslavery employer, Nathaniel Willis, Jacobs did ask Harriet Beecher Stowe to help her write her manuscript. Stowe, the prominent author of *Uncle Tom's Cabin,* suggested that she use Jacobs's story in *The Key to Uncle Tom's Cabin,* which Stowe was rushing to complete. Jacobs was firmly opposed to that idea and determined to be the author of her own life. She requested her employer, Mrs. Willis, to write to Stowe, saying "that I wished it to be a history of my life entirely by itself, which would do more good, and it needed no romance; but if she wanted some facts for her book, that I would be most happy to give her some."[19]

We know also from these letters and from her preface that Jacobs was embarrassed about the revelations of her sexual life. She expressed to Post her need for a woman to write an introduction to the book that would justify its sensational contents: "I have thought that I wanted some female friend to write a preface or some introductory remarks . . . yet believe me, dear friend, there are many painful things in . . . [my book] that make me shrink from asking this sacrifice from one so good and pure as yourself."[20] Jacobs was able to persuade Lydia Maria Child, another abolitionist, to write an introduction that was intended to influence white Northern women to accept her story in spite of its "indecorum." Child accepted the responsibility of presenting slavery "with the veil withdrawn" for the greater purpose of arousing Northern white women to exert their influence against slavery. And Jacobs finally agreed to publish her story that was "no fiction" in order to expose not just her own suffering, but "the condition of two millions of women at the South, still in bondage, suffering what I suffered, and most of them far worse" (p. xi).

While much of the current criticism and analysis of *Incidents* focuses on its relationship to the domestic novel and its subversion of that form, my own reading of *Incidents* would connect it to the tradition of the Afro-American slave narrative. For me, the pivotal moment in the Brent text, one consistently overlooked in feminist readings, is one that transcends the boundaries of gender and unites Brent with both male and female slave narrators determined to affirm a self in a world equally determined to annihilate that self. Near the end of her story, Brent becomes enraged when she learns that Mrs. Bruce has arranged to buy her from Dr. Flint. The buying and selling of Linda Brent— even if Mrs. Bruce's ultimate goal is to give her her freedom—is an act that demonstrates the white woman's power and the black woman's powerlessness; and Brent deeply resents being forced to acknowledge herself as chattel:

> The more my mind has become enlightened, the more difficult it was for me to consider myself an article of property; and to pay money to those who had so grievously oppressed me seemed like taking from my suffering the glory of triumph. I wrote to Mrs. Bruce, thanking her, but saying that being sold from one owner to another seemed too much like slavery; that such a great obligation could not be easily cancelled; and that I preferred to go to my brother in California. (p. 205)

This demonstration of anger, outrage, and obstinacy, as Brent calls it, is the moment of real triumph in the text. Brent refuses the role of pathetic victim as well as the role of grateful slave rescued by noble benefactor. Furthermore, her defiance links Brent to the tradition of narrators who finally throw off all the shackles of slavery and exert control over their own voice. As Marilyn Richardson says in her review of *Our Nig* (1859), the confrontation by which the black character claims a distinct sense of self "is one of the classic recurring scenes in all early black writing."[21] Brent's sense of herself as too enlightened to consider herself a piece of property reminds me of that turning point in Frederick Douglass's *Narrative* after which he tells us he could no longer consider himself a slave, even though legally he was still owned by a white man. Even when he is working for a "good" master, Douglass, like Brent, is beyond the point where he can consider anyone his "master": "I will give Mr. Freeland the credit of being the best master I ever had, till I became my own *master* . . . by this time I began to want to live *upon free land* as well as *with Freeland;* and I was no longer content, therefore, to live with him or any other slaveholder."[22]

The rhetoric in the Brent passage is also reminiscent of Douglass's *Narrative.* The balanced parallel phrases ("The more my mind had become enlightened, the more difficult it was for me to consider myself an article of property"); the powerful active voice ("I preferred to go to my brother in California"); the desire to claim her own moment of glory ("to pay money to those who had so grievously oppressed me seemed like taking from my suffering the glory of triumph")—these rhetorical patterns connect Brent to all those other figures in the slave narrative tradition who recreated a self and a voice in order to challenge a system that meant to destroy them.

Harriet Jacobs/Linda Brent was subjected to many kinds of imprisonment. She deliberately confined herself to a cramped attic space for many years in order to achieve freedom; she was confined by a slave narrative tradition that took the male's experiences as representative and marginalized the female's experiences; and she was rendered nearly invisible by a fictional tradition that made white skin a requirement for womanhood. She resisted all of these imprisonments to create a document that helps to answer the question, What was it like to be a *female* slave? In spite of the constraints against a black woman that made it nearly impossible for her to achieve authority in her own life as well as in the retelling of that life, Jacobs, nonetheless, succeeded in doing both.

Notes

[1] Harriet Jacobs, *Incidents in the Life of a Slave Girl* (New York: Harcourt Brace Jovanovich, 1973). Subsequent references will be to this edition.

[2] Dorothy Sterling, ed., *We Are Your Sisters: Black Women in the Nineteenth Century* (New York: W. W. Norton Company, 1984), p. 80.

[3] Barbara Welter describes the nineteenth-century notion of true womanhood in her essay, "The Cult of True Womanhood," *Dimity Convictions: The American Woman in the Nineteenth Century* (Athens: Ohio University Press, 1977), pp. 21-41.

[4] As Jean Yellin points out in her reading of this essay, Jacobs's emphasis on herself as a devoted mother feeds into the Victorian idolatry of motherhood. While her sexual involvement precludes her from claiming true womanhood, her devotion to her children partly reclaims her. *Women and Sisters* (New Haven: Yale University Press, forthcoming).

[5] Sterling, *We Are Your Sisters,* p. 75.

[6] I do not wish to join the list of critics who have traditionally maligned the "domestic" or "sentimental" novel. The new scholarship on nineteenth-century American women's writing challenges the gender politics which has made terms like *sentimental* and *domestic* pejorative buzzwords used to ridicule and dismiss nineteenth-century women. Judith Fetterly's *Provisions: A Reader from 19th Century American Women* (Bloomington: Indiana University Press, 1985) and Lucy Freibert and Barbara A. White's *Hidden Hands; An Anthology of American Women Writers, 1790-1870* (New Brunswick, N.J.: Rutgers University Press, 1985) offer reassessments of the domestic novel which suggest that nineteenth-century women writers were no more sentimental or melodramatic than the men of their era, that, in fact, women were predominantly realistic writers, more overtly concerned with social and political issues than nineteenth-century American [white] men. (Qualification mine.)

[7] Annette Niemtzow, "The Problematic of Self in Autobiography: The Example of the Slave Narrative," in *The Art of Slave Narrative: Original Essays in Criticism and Theory,* ed. John Sekora and Darwin T. Turner (Macomb, Ill.: Western Illinois University, 1982), p. 105.

[8] In their essays in *The Art of Slave Narrative* both Niemtzow and Raymond Hedin conclude that Harriet Jacobs is unable to triumph over the conventions of the sentimental novel. In "Strategies of Form in the American Slave Narrative," Hedin says women narrators had less reason than did men to undercut the genre of the sentimental novel because the vulnerable woman image could elicit the emotional responses they wanted from their largely female readers. Niemtzow says in "The Problematic of Self in Autobiography" that in her attempt to gain the virtues of true womanhood, Linda Brent allows the domestic novel to consume her

authentic voice. I agree with Jean Fagan Yellin, Hazel Carby, and Valerie Smith who have conclusively proved that Brent does triumph over the limits of the form she has chosen.

[9] Hazel Carby, *Reconstructing Womanhood: The Emergence of the Afro-American Woman Novelist* (New York: Oxford University Press, 1987).

[10] Jean Yellin, "Text and Contexts of Harriet Jacobs's *Incidents in the Life of a Slave Girl: Written By Herself,*" in *The Slave's Narrative,* ed. Charles T. Davis and Henry Louis Gates, Jr., (New York: Oxford University Press, 1985), p. 273.

[11] Ibid., p. 274.

[12] Jean Yellin makes a distinction between the novel of seduction and what Nina Baym calls "women's fiction." Baym argues that "women's fiction," also called the domestic or sentimental novel, does show women as active. Women as passive victims are found more often in the novel of seduction.

[13] In *Reconstructing Womanhood,* Hazel Carby rejects the notion of a representative narrative based on the male slave narrative. She argues that John Blassingame's *The Slave Community: Plantation Life in the Antebellum South* (New York: Oxford University Press, 1979), as well as other studies that exclude the female narrative are limited because they rely on a set of assumptions based on the experiences of men, pp. 74-75.

[14] Sekora and Turner, *The Art of Slave Narrative,* a recent book of critical essays on the slave narrative, features a cover designed by Preston Jackson. Representing the slave is a large muscular man in a loincloth, his head bent from the weight of a heavy burden, his muscles straining to carry the load. Blassingame's *Slave Testimony* also features a picture of a man on the inside front page. As these images indicate, many interpretations and/or critical studies of the slave narrative imagined the representative slave as a man.

[15] Sylvia Lyons Render, "Afro-American Women: The Outstanding and the Obscure," *The Quarterly Journal of the Library of Congress* (October 1975): 308.

[16] Valerie Smith, "Narrative Authority in Twentieth-Century Afro-American Fiction" (Cambridge: Harvard University Press, 1987), forthcoming.

[17] Carby, *Reconstructing Womanhood,* p. 22.

[18] Telephone conversation with Jean Fagan Yellin, August 26, 1985. Yellin's first documentation of the authenticity of *Incidents* was the essay, "Written by

Herself: Harriet Jacobs' Slave Narrative," *American Literature* 53 (November 1981): 479-86. She has done an annotated edition of *Incidents,* that establishes the real names of the people in the narrative and further documents the authenticity of Jacobs's autobiography (Cambridge: Harvard University Press, 1987).

[19] Sterling, *We Are Your Sisters,* p. 77.

[20] Yellin, "Written by Herself," pp. 485-86.

[21] Marilyn Richardson, "The Shadow of Slavery," *The Women's Review of Books* 1, no. 1 (October 1983): 15.

[22] Benjamin Quarles, ed., *Narrative of the Life of Frederick Douglass: An American Slave Written by Himself* (Cambridge: Harvard University Press, 1979), p. 116.

An excerpt from Jacobs' preface to *Incidents in the Life of a Slave Girl* (1861):

Reader, be assured this narrative is no fiction. I am aware that some of my adventures may seem incredible; but they are, nevertheless, strictly true. I have not exaggerated the wrongs inflicted by Slavery; on the contrary, my descriptions fall far short of the facts. I have concealed the names of places, and given persons fictitious names. I had no motive for secrecy on my own account, but I deemed it kind and considerate towards others to pursue this course. . . .

I have not written my experiences in order to attract attention to myself; on the contrary, it would have been more pleasant to me to have been silent about my own history. Neither do I care to excite sympathy for my own sufferings. But I do earnestly desire to arouse the women of the North to a realizing sense of the condition of two millions of women at the South, still in bondage, suffering what I suffered, and most of them far worse. I want to add my testimony to that of abler pens to convince the people of the Free States what Slavery really is. Only by experience can any one realize how deep, and dark, and foul is that pit of abominations. May the blessing of God rest on this imperfect effort in behalf of my persecuted people!

LINDA BRENT.

Harriet A. Jacobs, preface to Incidents in the Life of a Slave Girl, *edited by L. Maria Child, 1861, reprinted and edited by Jean Fagan Yellin, Harvard University Press, 1987.*

Hazel V. Carby (essay date 1987)

SOURCE: " 'Hear My Voice, Ye Careless Daughters': Narratives of Slave and Free Women before Emanci-

pation," in *Reconstructing Womanhood: The Emergence of the Afro-American Woman Novelist,* Oxford University Press, 1987, pp. 40-61.

[*In the following essay, Carby explores the influence of the nineteenth-century conception of "true womanhood" on* Incidents *and contends that Jacobs used the events of her life to "critique conventional standards of female behavior and to question their relevance and applicability to the experience of black women."*]

A survey of the general terrain of images and stereotypes produced by antebellum sexual ideologies is a necessary but only preliminary contribution to understanding how the ideology of true womanhood influenced and, to a large extent, determined the shape of the public voice of black women writers. What remains to be considered is how an ideology that excluded black women from the category "women" affected the ways in which they wrote and addressed an audience. The relevance of this question extends beyond the writing of slave narratives, and I will first examine texts written by free black women living in the North before turning to a slave narrative, Harriet Jacobs's ***Incidents in the Life of a Slave Girl***.

In 1850, Nancy Prince published in Boston her *Life and Travels.* A free woman, Nancy Prince declared that her object in writing was not "a vain desire to appear before the public"; on the contrary, her book was the product of her labor by which she hoped to sustain herself. In other words, Prince regarded her writing as her work. The publication of her *Life and Travels* was the occasion for an assertion of Prince's intention to retain and maintain her independence:

> The Almighty God our heavenly father has designed that we eat our bread by the sweat of our brow; that all-wise and holy Being has designed and requires of us that we be diligent, using the means, that with his blessing we may not be burdensome, believing we shall be directed and go through.[1]

But this statement was double-edged: it was at once an assertion of her present condition and a comment on her history which was retold in the main body of the text. Prince's assertion appealed to the values of the "Protestant ethic," while the opening pages of her text were an apt demonstration of economic racial discrimination; however hard the young Nancy and her family labored in the North, the fruits of that society were not granted to them. At fourteen years old, Nancy replaced a sick friend in service and "thought herself fortunate" to be with a religious family, as she herself had received religious instruction and had been taught "right from wrong" by her grandfather. Prince recounted the details of her arduous duties and cruel treatment and then interrogated the hypocritical religion of her employers:

> Hard labor and unkindness were too much for me; in three months, my health and strength were gone. I often looked at my employers, and thought to myself, is this your religion? I did not wonder that the girl who had lived there previous to myself, went home to die. They had family prayers, morning and evening. Oh! yes, they were sanctimonious! I was a poor stranger, but fourteen years of age, imposed upon by these good people. (11-12)

After seven years of "anxiety and toil," Prince married and went to live in Russia, where her husband was employed and where there was "no prejudice against color" (20-23). Prince established her international perspective in a section which detailed life in Russia and then condemned the racism which permeated the United States, North and South. In a direct address to her audience, which Prince considered to be primarily a Northern readership, she described how, upon her return to her own country, "the weight of prejudice . . . again oppressed [her]," even while she retained her belief in ultimate justice:

> God has in all ages of the world punished every nation and people for their sins. The sins of my beloved country are not hid from his notice; his all-seeing eye sees and knows the secrets of all hearts; the angels that kept not their first estate but left their own habitations, he hath reserved in everlasting chains unto the great day. (43)

By extending the logic of religious conviction, Prince revealed the hypocrisy at the heart of American society. Her thinly veiled threat of revenge gained additional power from her earlier, obviously sympathetic response to those she had witnessed rebelling against the injustices of Russian society.

The dignity and power of Prince's narrative was gained from her position at once inside and outside the society she wished to condemn. Her narrative voice was given strength through her presentation of herself as a true practitioner of Christian principles who was able to comment on the hypocritical attitudes and forms of behavior that she saw practiced throughout the country. Prince used her knowledge of other societies to compare and contrast with her own. Somewhat ironically, she commented that she "may not see as clearly as some" because of the weight of oppression, but, of course, this rhetorical device revealed exactly how appropriate a witness and how effective a narrator of racist practices she was (42). Prince made clear her double position inside U.S. society as a citizen and outside it as an outcast because of her color; her final narrative position, however, was above "this world's tumultuous noise," at the side of the ultimate judge (89).

In her narrative, one action in particular used, but also questioned, a fundamental attribute of true womanhood:

the possession of sexual purity. Having discovered that her eldest sister had been "deluded away" into a brothel and become a prostitute, Prince responded: "[t]o have heard of her death, would not have been so painful to me, as we loved each other very much" (12). This statement was in accord with conventional expectations of the importance of sexual purity; death was easier to accept than loss of virtue. However, Prince did not continue to follow the conventional pattern of regarding her sister as "lost" forever but searched for, found, and rescued her. Far from seizing the narrative opportunity to condemn her sister, Prince claimed her "soul as precious" and revealed the contradiction of a sexual ideology that led her sister to feel she was neither "fit to live, nor fit to die." Returning her sister to the bosom of a family Prince declared not shame but a sense of "victory" (13-16). As author, Prince used the structure of spiritual autobiography not to conform to a conventional representation of experience but to begin to question the limits of those conventions as they contradicted aspects of her own experience. *A Narrative of the Life and Travels of Mrs. Nancy Prince. Written by Herself* is an early example of a black woman who attempted to use a conventional narrative form, spiritual autobiography, in unconventional ways.[2] Princes's adoption of a public voice assumed and asserted the authority of her experience.

The conviction that writing was work was attested to by another free black woman, Harriet Wilson, in her narrative *Our Nig; or, Sketches from the Life of a Free Black* (1859).[3] A comparison of Wilson's motives for writing with those of Prince is fruitful. Wilson stated in her preface:

> In offering to the public the following pages, the writer confesses her inability to minister to the refined and cultivated, the pleasure supplied by abler pens. It is not for such these crude narrations appear. Deserted by kindred, disabled by failing health, I am forced to some experiment which shall aid me in maintaining myself and my child without extinguishing this feeble life.

Prince established that her book was the product of her labor, and Wilson appealed to her audience to buy her narrative as a product of her labor so that she and her son could survive. But, unlike Prince, Wilson sought her patronage not from a white Northern audience but from her "colored brethren." Wilson attempted to gain authority for her public voice through a narrative that shared its experience with a black community which she addressed as if it were autonomous from the white community in which it was situated.

In his introduction to Wilson's text, Henry Louis Gates, Jr., calls it the first novel by a black writer because of its use of the plot conventions of sentimental novels (xiii). But the use of these particular conventions can be found not only in the novel but also in many slave narratives. I would argue that *Our Nig* can be most usefully regarded as an allegory of a slave narrative, a "slave" narrative set in the "free" North. The first indication of the possibility of an allegorical reading occurs in the subtitle, "Sketches from the Life of a Free Black, in a Two-Story White House, North. Showing That Slavery's Shadows Fall Even There." Wilson used her voice as a black woman addressing a black audience to condemn racism in the North and criticize abolitionists. This placed Wilson in a position similar to that of Prince, both inside and outside the society subject to critique. Whereas Prince gained narrative dignity and power from her experience of other countries, her outcast status, and her "true" religious principles, Wilson's narrative authority derived from an assertion of independence from the patronage of the white community. Her narrative was written apart from any links to the abolitionist movement, and her direct appeal to the black community marginalized a white readership.

The "two-story white house" can be interpreted initially as the equivalent of the Southern plantation, in which the protagonist, Frado, was held in virtual slavery. Scenes of punishment and brutality, whippings, and beatings were evoked, as in a conventional slave narrative, to document the relentless suffering and persecution to which the slave was subject. The Northern house, like its Southern counterpart, was the sovereign territory of a tyrant, ruled by a mistress whom Wilson described as being "imbued with *southern principles*" (preface). Mrs. Bellmont, the white mistress, was described as having power over the whole family—husband, sons, daughters, and Frado—and was symbolic of the power of the South. The domestic realm, within which Wilson represented Mrs. Bellmont as the ultimate power, was the terrain of struggle over the treatment of Frado in which debates about the position and future of blacks in the United States are re-created. Sensitivity and compassion were to be found in some members of the family, including Mr. Bellmont and one of his sons, but their protests were ignored; the power of the mistress, like the power of the South, was never effectively challenged. The actions of Mrs. Bellmont determine and structure the overall pattern of her slave's life in the house; a house which increasingly resembles the nation, as the resolve of Mrs. Bellmont's opponents to improve Frado's conditions disintegrated at the slightest possibility of conflict. Mr. Bellmont was portrayed as preferring to leave the house to the tyrannical rages of his wife, hiding until the recurring ruptures receded and Frado had again been punished. In a close resemblance to the position of many abolitionists, Mr. Bellmont and his son offered sympathy and loud protestations but were unwilling to assert the moral superiority of their position by fighting the mistress, the South, and imposing an alternative social order. Both men merely dressed Frado's

wounds and turned their backs when battles were renewed. The two-story house was an allegory for the divided nation in which the object of controversy and subject of oppression was *Our Nig*. Like Prince, Wilson gained her narrative authority from adapting literary conventions to more adequately conform to a narrative representation and re-creation of black experience. It is important to identify the source of many of these conventions in the sentimental novel and also to recognize that Wilson's particular use of sentimental conventions derives from the sentimental novel via slave narratives to produce a unique allegorical form. That *Our Nig* did not conform to the parameters of contemporary domestic fiction can be attributed to this cultural blend.

The issue of conformity to conventions has been linked to questions concerning the authenticity of slave narratives by historians, particularly in the case of Harriet Jacobs's narrative, ***Incidents in the Life of a Slave Girl*** (1861).[4] Arguing, convincingly, that historians need to recognize both the "uniqueness" and the "representativeness" of the slave narrative, John Blassingame, in *The Slave Community,* concluded that Jacobs's narrative is inauthentic because it does not conform to the guidelines of representativeness.[5] Blassingame questioned the narrative's orderly framework and the use of providential encounters and continued:

> the story is too melodramatic: miscegenation and cruelty, outraged virtue, unrequited love, and planter licentiousness appear on practically every page. The virtuous Harriet sympathizes with her wretched mistress who has to look on all of the mulattoes fathered by her husband, she refuses to bow to the lascivious demands of her master, bears two children for another white man, and then runs away and hides in a garret in her grandmother's cabin for seven years until she is able to escape to New York. . . . In the end, all live happily ever after.[6]

With regard to internal evidence and the question of the authority of the public voice, the critique that Blassingame offers focuses heavily, though perhaps unconsciously, on the protagonist, Linda Brent, as conventional heroine.

In comparing slave narratives to each other, historians and literary critics have relied on a set of unquestioned assumptions that interrelate the quest for freedom and literacy with the establishment of manhood in the gaining of the published, and therefore public, voice. The great strength of these autobiographies, Blassingame states, is that, unlike other important sources, they embody the slaves' own perception of their experiences. Yet it is taken for granted that this experience, which is both unique and representative, is also male:

> If historians seek to provide some understanding of the past experiences of slaves, then the

autobiography must be their point of departure; in the autobiography, more clearly than in any other source, we learn what went on in the minds of *black men*. It gives us a window to the "inside half" of the slave's life which never appears in the commentaries of "outsiders." Autobiographers are generally so preoccupied with conflict, those things blocking their hopes and dreams, that their works give a freshness and vitality to history which is often missing in other sources.[7]

The criteria for judgment that Blassingame advances here leave no room for a consideration of the specificity and uniqueness of the black female experience. An analogy can be made between Blassingame's criticism of *Incidents* as melodrama and the frequency with which issues of miscegenation, unrequited love, outraged virtue, and planter licentiousness are found foregrounded in diaries by Southern white women, while absent or in the background of the records of their planter husbands. Identifying such a difference should lead us to question and consider the significance of these issues in the lives of women as opposed to men, not to the conclusion that the diaries by women are not credible because they deviate from the conventions of male-authored texts. Any assumption of the representativeness of patriarchal experience does not allow for, or even regard as necessary, a gender-specific form of analysis. Indeed, the criteria chosen by Blassingame as the basis for his dismissal of the narrative credibility of Jacobs's narrative are, ideologically, the indicators of a uniquely female perspective.

Jean Fagan Yellin, a literary historian, critic, and biographer of Jacobs, has (from external evidence) established the authenticity of Jacobs's narrative.[8] Jacobs wrote under the pseudonym Linda Brent. *Incidents in the Life of a Slave Girl* was first published in Boston in 1861, under the editorship of Lydia Maria Child, and a year later it appeared in a British edition.[9] In the discussion that follows, the author will be referred to as Jacobs, but, to preserve narrative continuity, the pseudonym Linda Brent will be used in the analysis of the text and protagonist.

Incidents in the Life of a Slave Girl is the most sophisticated, sustained narrative dissection of the conventions of true womanhood by a black author before emancipation. It will be the object of the following analysis to demonstrate that Jacobs used the material circumstances of her life to critique conventional standards of female behavior and to question their relevance and applicability to the experience of black women. Prior to a close examination of the text itself, it is necessary to document briefly the conditions under which Jacobs wrote her autobiography and gained her public voice.

At the time of writing, Jacobs worked as a domestic servant for and lived with Nathaniel P. Willis and his second wife, the Mr. and Mrs. Bruce of the text. Unlike either his first or second wife, Nathaniel Willis was proslavery. Against Jacobs's wishes but to protect her from the fugitive slave law, the second Mrs. Willis persuaded her husband that Jacobs should be purchased from her owners and manumitted by the family. Because of her suspicions of Nathaniel Willis, Jacobs did not want him to be aware that she was writing of her life in slavery; the need for secrecy and the demands of her domestic duties as nurse to the Willis children forced Jacobs to write at night.[10] Jacobs recognized that the conditions under which she lived and wrote were very different from those under which other female authors were able to write and under which her audience, "the women of the North," lived. In her preface, Linda Brent stated:

> Since I have been at the North, it has been necessary for me to work diligently for my own support, and the education of my children. This has not left me much leisure to make up for the loss of early opportunities to improve myself; and it has compelled me to write these pages at irregular intervals, whenever I could snatch an hour from Household duties. (xiii)

Unlike her white female audience or contemporary authors, Jacobs had neither the advantages of formal education nor contemplative leisure. She contrasted both her past life as a slave and her present condition, in which the selling of her labor was a prime necessity, with the social circumstances of her readership. Jacobs thus established the context within which we should understand her choice of epigram, from Isaiah (32: 2): "Rise up, ye women that are at ease! Hear my voice, Ye careless daughters! Give ear unto my speech" (iv). Jacobs had achieved her freedom from slavery, but she was still bound to labor for the existence of herself and her children.

The closing pages of *Incidents* contrasted the "happy endings" of the conventional domestic novel with the present condition of the narrator, Linda Brent:

> Reader, my story ends with freedom; not in the usual way with marriage. . . . We are as free from the power of slaveholders as are the white people of the north; and though that, according to my ideas, is not saying a great deal, it is a vast improvement in *my* condition. (207)

Contrary to Blassingame's interpretation, *Incidents* does not conform to the conventional happy ending of the sentimental novel. Linda Brent, in the closing pages of her narrative, was still bound to a white mistress.

Jacobs's position as a domestic servant contrasted with the lives of the white women who surrounded and befriended her. Mrs. Willis, though she was instrumental in gaining her manumission, had the power to buy her and remained her employer, her mistress. Jacobs's letters to Amy Post, although to a friend, revealed her consciousness of their different positions in relation to conventional moral codes. Desiring a female friend who would write some prefatory remarks to her narrative, Jacobs consulted Post, but the occasion led her to indicate that the inclusion of her sexual history in her narrative made her "shrink from asking the sacrifice from one so good and pure as yourself."[11] It was as if Jacobs feared that her own history would contaminate the reputation of her white friend. Lydia Maria Child, who became Jacobs's editor, and Harriet Beecher Stowe, with whom Jacobs had an unfortunate brush, were both described by her as "satellite[s] of so great magnitude."[12] This hierarchy in Jacobs's relations with white women was magnified through the lens of conventional ideas of true womanhood when they appeared in print together, for Jacobs's sexuality was compromised in the very decision to print her story and gain her public voice. As she wrote to Post, after Post had agreed to endorse her story, "Woman can whisper her cruel wrongs into the ear of a very dear friend much easier than she can record them for the world to read."[13] Jacobs had children but no husband and no home of her own. In order to be able to represent herself in conventional terms as a "true" woman, Jacobs should have had a husband to give meaning to her existence as a woman. As I described in the previous chapter, any power or influence a woman could exercise was limited to the boundaries of the home. Linda Brent, in the concluding chapter of her narrative, recognized that this particular definition of a woman's sphere did not exist for her, and this factor ensured her dependence on a mistress. She stated, "I do not sit with my children in a home of my own. I still long for a hearthstone of my own, however humble. I wish it for my children's sake far more than my own" (207).

The ideological definition of the womanhood and motherhood of Linda Brent (and Jacobs) remained ambivalent as Linda Brent (and Jacobs) were excluded from the domain of the home, the sphere within which womanhood and motherhood were defined. Without a "woman's sphere," both were rendered meaningless. Nevertheless, the narrative of Linda Brent's life stands as an exposition of her womanhood and motherhood contradicting and transforming an ideology that could not take account of her experience. The structure of Jacobs's narrative embodied the process through which the meaning of Linda Brent's and Jacobs's motherhood and womanhood were revealed. Jacobs, as author, confronted an ideology that denied her very existence as a black woman and as a mother, and, therefore, she had to formulate a set of meanings that implicitly and fundamentally questioned the basis of true womanhood. *Incidents* demystified a convention that appeared as the obvious, common-sense rules of behavior and revealed the concept of true womanhood to be an ideology, not a lived set of social relations as she exposed its inherent contradictions and inapplicability to her life.[14]

Jacobs rejected a patronizing offer by Harriet Beecher Stowe to incorporate her life story into the writing of *The Key to Uncle Tom's Cabin.* This incorporation would have meant that her history would have been circumscribed by the bounds of convention, and Jacobs responded that "it needed no romance." The suggestion that Stowe might write, and control, the story of Jacobs's life raised issues far greater than those which concerned the artistic and aesthetic merit of her narrative; Jacobs "felt denigrated as a mother, betrayed as a woman, and threatened as a writer by Stowe's action."[15] Jacobs knew that to gain her own public voice, as a writer, implicated her very existence as a mother and a woman; the three could not be separated. She also knew from experience, as did Prince and Wilson, that the white people of the North were not completely free from the power of the slaveholders, or from their racism. To be bound to the conventions of true womanhood was to be bound to a racist, ideological system.

Many slave authors changed the names of people and places in their narratives to protect those still subject to slavery. However, Jacobs's need for secrecy in the act of writing and her fear of scorn if discovered meant that her pseudonym, Linda Brent, functioned as a mechanism of self-protection. The creation of Linda Brent as a fictional narrator allowed Jacobs to manipulate a series of conventions that were not only literary in their effects but which also threatened the meaning of Jacobs's social existence. The construction of the history of Linda Brent was the terrain through which Jacobs had to journey in order to reconstruct the meaning of her own life as woman and mother. The journey provided an alternative path to the cult of true womanhood and challenged the readers of *Incidents* to interrogate the social and ideological structures in which they were implicated and to examine their own racism. Jacobs denied that she wrote to "excite sympathy" for her own "sufferings" but claimed that she wanted to "arouse the women of the North to a realizing sense of the condition of two millions of women at the South, still in bondage, suffering what I suffered, and most of them far worse" (xiv). Jacobs established that hers was the voice of a representative black female slave, and in a contemporary interpretation this appeal is defined as being an appeal to the sisterhood of all women:

> Seen from this angle of vision, Jacobs' book—reaching across the gulf separating black women from white, slave from free, poor from rich, reaching across the chasm separating "bad" women from "good"—represents an attempt to establish an American sisterhood and to activate that sisterhood in the public arena.[16]

However, these bonds of sisterhood are not easily or superficially evoked. "Sisterhood" between white and black women was realized rarely in the text of *Incidents*. Jacobs's appeal was to a potential rather than an actual bonding between white and black women. The use of the word *incidents* in the title of her narrative directs the reader to be aware of a consciously chosen selection of events in Jacobs's life.[17] Many of the relationships portrayed between Linda Brent and white women involve cruelty and betrayal and place white female readers in the position of having to realize their implication in the oppression of black women, prior to any actual realization of the bonds of "sisterhood."

The narrative was framed by Linda Brent's relationships to white mistresses. The relationship to Mrs. Willis with which the narrative concluded has already been discussed. The opening chapter, "Childhood," described Linda's early disillusion with a mistress whom she loved and trusted. Linda's early childhood was happy, and only on the death of her mother did Linda learn that she was a slave. *Sister* and *sisterhood* were made ambiguous terms for relationships which had dubious consequences for black women. Early in the text Linda referred to her mother and her mother's mistress as "foster sisters" because they were both fed at the breast of Linda's grandmother. This intimate "sisterhood" as babes was interrupted by the intervention of the starkly contrasting hierarchy of their social relationship. Linda's grandmother, the readers were told, had to wean her own daughter at three months old in order to provide sufficient food for her mistress's daughter. Although they played together as children, Linda's mother's slave status was reasserted when she had to become "a most faithful servant" to her "foster sister." At the side of the deathbed of Linda's mother, her mistress promised her that "her children [would] never suffer for anything" in the future. Linda described her subsequent childhood with this mistress as "happy," without "toilsome or disagreeable duties." A diligent slave, Linda felt "proud to labor for her as much as my young years would permit," and she maintained a heart "as free from care as that of any free born white child" (4-5).

Unlike Kate Drumgoold in *A Slave Girl's Story*, Linda Brent did not attempt to replace this mistress as surrogate mother. The phrase carefully chosen by Jacobs was "almost like a mother." The juxtaposition of the concepts of a carefree childhood with laboring registered an experience alien to that of the readership. This gentle disturbance to middle-class ideas of childhood moved toward a climactic shock at the death of the mistress, when Linda was bequeathed to the daughter of her mistress's sister. Linda and her community of friends had been convinced that she would be freed, but, with bitterness, Linda recalled the years of faithful servitude of her mother and her mistress's promise to her mother. In a passage that used a narrative strategy similar to that used by Prince in her *Life and Travels*, Jacobs's narrator indicted the behavior of her mistress according to conventional moral codes. Linda Brent reasserted the religious doctrine espoused by her mistress to condemn her action and reveal the hypocrisy of her beliefs:

> My mistress had taught me the precepts of God's word: "Thou shalt love thy neighbor as thyself." "Whatsoever ye would that men should do unto you, do ye even so unto them." But I was her slave, and I suppose she did not recognize me as her neighbor. (6)

The disparity between "almost a mother" and the lack of recognition as "neighbor" highlighted the intensity of Jacobs's sense of betrayal. Having taught her slave to read and spell, this mistress had contributed to the ability of Jacobs to tell her tale, but the story Jacobs told condemned the mistress, for it was her "act of injustice" that initiated the suffering in Linda Brent's life.

Because of the hierarchical nature of their social, as opposed to emotional, relationships, white mistresses in the text were placed in positions of power and influence over the course of the lives of slave women, an influence that was still being exerted at the close of the narrative after Linda's emancipation. Linda did not recount the actions of her mistress as if they were only an individual instance of betrayal but placed them within a history of acts of betrayal toward three generations of women in her family: herself, her mother, and her grandmother. Each served as faithful servant, each trusted to the honor of her mistress, and each was betrayed. The reconstruction of these acts through time and over generations was an attempt to assert their representative status within a historical perspective of dishonesty and hypocrisy.

The polarization between the lives of white sisters and black sisters was a recurring motif. The material differences in their lives that determined their futures and overwhelmed either biological relation or emotional attachment were continually stressed in the text. Linda Brent told the reader:

> I once saw two beautiful children playing together. One was a fair white child; the other was her slave, and also her sister. When I saw them embracing each other, and heard their joyous laughter, I turned sadly away from the lovely sight. I foresaw the inevitable blight that would fall on the little slave's heart. I knew how soon her laughter would be changed to sighs. The fair child grew up to be a still fairer woman. From childhood to womanhood her pathway was blooming with flowers. . . . How had those years dealt with her slave sister, the little playmate of her childhood? She was also very beautiful; but the flowers and sunshine of love were not for her. She drank the cup of sin, and shame,

and misery, whereof her persecuted race are compelled to drink. (28-29)

Any feminist history that seeks to establish the sisterhood of white and black women as allies in the struggle against the oppression of all women must also reveal the complexity of the social and economic differences between women. Feminist historiography and literary criticism also need to define the ways in which racist practices are gender-specific and sexual exploitation racialized. The dialectical nature of this process is reconstructed in the "incidents" that Jacobs reconstructed between the slave woman and her mistress.

Linda Brent described her second mistress, Mrs. Flint, in ways that utilized the conventions of an antebellum ideal of womanhood while exposing them as contradictory:

> Mrs. Flint, like many southern women, was totally deficient in energy. She had not strength to superintend her household affairs; but her nerves were so strong, that she could sit in her easy chair and see a woman whipped, till the blood trickled from every stroke of the lash. (10)

Mrs. Flint forced Linda Brent to walk barefoot through the snow because the "creaking" of her new shoes "grated harshly on her refined nerves" (17). In these and other passages the conventional figure of the plantation mistress is ironically undermined. The qualities of delicacy of constitution and heightened sensitivity, attributes of the Southern lady, appear as a corrupt and superficial veneer that covers an underlying strength and power in cruelty and brutality.

Linda Brent realized that because of Dr. Flint's overt sexual advances and intentions she represented an actual as well as potential threat to the dignity and pride of Mrs. Flint. Jacobs demonstrated the slave's capacity to analyze the grief and pain of her mistress; the slave, however, waited in vain for a reciprocal display of kindness or sympathy. The sisterhood of the two abused women could not be established, for Mrs. Flint, who "pitied herself as a martyr . . . was incapable of feeling for the condition of shame and misery in which her unfortunate, helpless slave was placed" (32).

In an attempt to appeal directly to the compassion of her white Northern readers, Jacobs contrasted the material conditions of black female slaves with their own lives:

> O, you happy free women, contrast *your* New Year's day with that of the poor bond-woman! With you it is a pleasant season, and the light of the day is blessed. . . . Children bring their little offerings, and raise their rosy lips for a caress. They are your own, and no hand but that of death can take them

from you. But to the slave mother New Year's day comes laden with peculiar sorrows. She sits on a cold cabin floor, watching the children who may all be torn from her the next morning; and often does she wish that she and they might die before the day dawns. (14)

Linda Brent was a demonstration of the consequences for motherhood of the social and economic relations of the institution of slavery. Jacobs recognized that plantation mistresses were subject to forms of patriarchal abuse and exploitation, but because they gave birth to the heirs of property they were also awarded a degree of patriarchal protection. Slave women gave birth to the capital of the South and were therefore, in Linda Brent's words, "considered of no value, unless they continually increase their owner's stock" (49). Upon this hierarchical differential in power relations an ideology was built which ensured that two opposing concepts of motherhood and womanhood were maintained. As Linda Brent argued, "that which commands admiration in the white woman only hastens the degradation of the female slave" (27). If a slave woman attempted to preserve her sexual autonomy, the economic system of slavery was threatened: "[I]t [was] deemed a crime in her to wish to be virtuous" (29).

The barriers to the establishment of the bonding of sisterhood were built in the space between the different economic, political, and social positions that black women and white women occupied in the social formation of slavery. Their hierarchical relationship was determined through a racial, not gendered, categorization. The ideology of true womanhood was as racialized a concept in relation to white women as it was in its exclusion of black womanhood. Ultimately, it was this racial factor that defined the source of power of white women over their slaves, for, in a position of dependence on the patriarchal system herself, the white mistress identified her interests with the maintenance of the status quo. Linda Brent concluded:

> No matter whether the slave girl be as black as ebony or as fair as her mistress. In either case, there is no shadow of law to protect her from insult, from violence, or even from death; all these are inflicted by friends who bear the shape of men. The mistress, who ought to protect the helpless victim, has no other feelings towards her but those of jealousy and rage. (26-27)

Jacobs thus identified that mistresses confirmed their own social position at the expense of denying the humanity of their slaves particularly when they were insecure in their own relation to patriarchal power: "I knew that the young wives of slaveholders often thought their authority and importance would be best established and maintained by cruelty" (94).

The Northern women who formed Jacobs's audience were implicated in the preservation of this oppression in two ways. In a passage that directly addressed the reader, Linda Brent accused Northerners of allowing themselves to be used as "bloodhounds" to hunt fugitives and return them to slavery (34-35). More subtly, Linda Brent also illustrated how Northerners were not immune to the effects of the slave system or to the influence of being able to wield a racist power when she described how, "when northerners go to the south to reside, they prove very apt scholars. They soon imbibe the sentiments and disposition of their neighbors, and generally go beyond their teachers. Of the two, they are proverbially the hardest masters" (44). *Incidents* also documented the numerous acts of racist oppression that Linda Brent had to suffer while in the Northern states. A major motive for her escape from the South was her determination to protect her daughter, Ellen, from the sexual exploitation she herself had experienced. However, Ellen was subject to sexual harassment in the household in which she lived and worked as a servant in New York, which made Linda Brent question the nature and extent of her freedom in the "free" states of the North. Described as being in a position of "servitude to the Anglo-Saxon race," Linda Brent urged the whole black community to defy the racism of Northerners, so that "eventually we shall cease to be trampled underfoot by our oppressors" (180-82).

This spirit of defiance characterized Jacobs's representations of all Linda Brent's encounters with her master. Conventional feminine qualities of submission and passivity were replaced by an active resistance. Although Flint had "power and law on his side," she "had a determined will," and "there was might in each." Her strength and resourcefulness to resist were not adopted from a reservoir of masculine attributes but were shown to have their source in her "woman's pride, and a mother's love for [her] children" (87). Thus, Jacobs developed an alternative set of definitions of womanhood and motherhood in the text which remained in tension with the cult of true womanhood.

The slave became the object of the jealousy and spite of her mistress; Jacobs wrote that Mrs. Flint even vented her anger on Linda Brent's grandmother for offering Linda and her children protective shelter: "She would not even speak to her in the street. This wounded my grandmother's feelings, for she could not retain ill will against the woman who she had nourished with her milk when a babe" (91). In an effective adaptation of convention it was Linda Brent's grandmother who was portrayed as a woman of genuine sensitivity. The two women were polarized: the grandmother exuded a "natural" warmth, but Mrs. Flint, as Jacobs's choice of name emphasized, displayed an unnatural, cold, and hard heart. For the grandmother, the act of nurturing gave rise to sustained feelings of intimacy; Mrs. Flint's rejection of this mothering relationship implied that she was an unnatural woman. Linda Brent stated that she was "indebted" to her grandmother for all her comforts, "spiritual or temporal" (9). It was the grandmother's labor that fed and clothed her when Mrs. Flint neglected her slave's material needs, and it was the grandmother who stood as the source of a strong moral code in the midst of an immoral system. In a considerable number of ways, Jacobs's figure of the grandmother embodied aspects of a *true* womanhood; she was represented as being pure and pious, a fountainhead of physical and spiritual sustenance for Linda, her whole family, and the wider black community. However, the quality of conventional womanhood that the grandmother did not possess was submissiveness, and Linda Brent was portrayed as having inherited her spirit. Her love for her grandmother was seen to be tempered by fear; she had been brought up to regard her with a respect that bordered on awe, and at the moment when Linda Brent needed the advice of another woman most desperately she feared to confide in her grandmother, who she knew would condemn her. Out of the moment of her most intense isolation Jacobs made her narrator forge her own rules of behavior and conduct of which even her grandmother would disapprove.

Dr. Flint was characterized by Jacobs as the epitome of corrupt white male power. He was a figure that was carefully dissected to reveal a lack of the conventional qualities of a gentleman. His lack of honor was established early in the text when he defrauded Linda Brent's grandmother. Presented as a representative slaveholder, Dr. Flint embodied the evil licentiousness that was the ultimate threat to virtue and purity. He whispered foul suggestions into Linda's ears when she was still an innocent girl and used his power to deny her the experience of romance, preventing her from marrying her first, true love. In the chapter entitled "The Lover," a freeborn black carpenter was described as possessing the qualities that were absent in Dr. Flint. Honor was posed against dishonor, respect for Linda's virtue against disrespect and insult. The lover Jacobs described as both "intelligent and religious," while Dr. Flint appeared as an animal watching a young girl as his prey. The "base proposals of a white man" were contrasted with the "honorable addresses of a respectable colored man" (40-41). But, despite the fact that Dr. Flint was the embodiment of the corruption of the slave system, as his prey Linda Brent was not corrupted by him, and her struggle was an aggressive refusal to be sexually used and compromised or to succumb to the will of the master.

Instead, hoping to gain a degree of protection from Dr. Flint, Linda Brent decided to become the lover of a white "gentleman," a Mr. Sands. She thought that in his fury Dr. Flint would sell her to her newly acquired lover and that it would be easier in the future to obtain her freedom from her lover than from her master. Linda's reasoning was shown to be motivated by consideration not only for her own welfare but also for improving the chances of survival for any children she might bear. From her experience she knew that Dr. Flint sold his offspring from slave women and hoped that if her children were fathered by Sands he could buy them and secure their future.

The struggle of Linda Brent to retain some control over her sexuality climaxed in a confession of her loss of virtue. It was at this point in the narrative that Jacobs most directly confronted conventional morality. In order to retain narrative authority and to preserve a public voice acceptable to an antebellum readership, Jacobs carefully negotiated the tension between satisfying moral expectations and challenging an ideology that would condemn her as immoral. Jacobs's confession was at once both conventional and unconventional in form and tone. The narrator declared in a direct address to her readers that the remembrance of this period in her "unhappy life" filled her with "sorrow and shame" and made no reference to sexual satisfaction, love, or passion, as such feelings were not meant to be experienced or encouraged outside of marriage and were rarely figured to exist within it.[18] Yet Jacobs refused to follow convention in significant ways. In contrast to the expected pattern of a confessional passage, which called for the unconditional acceptance of the judgment of readers, Linda Brent's act of sexual defiance was described as one of "deliberate calculation": the slave actively chose one fate as opposed to another. Jacobs attempted to deflect any judgmental response of moral condemnation through consistent narrative reminders to the reader that the material conditions of a slave woman's life were different from theirs. Readers were the "happy women" who had been "free to choose the objects of [their] affection." Jacobs, through Linda Brent, claimed the same right in her attempt to assert some control over the conditions of her existence: "It seems less degrading to give one's self, than to submit to compulsion. There is something akin to freedom in having a lover who has no control over you, except that which he gains by kindness and attachment" (55). Jacobs argued that the practice of conventional principles of morality was rendered impossible by the condition of the slave. Her own decision to take a lover was not described as immoral or amoral but as outside conventional ethical boundaries. In a key passage for understanding the extent to which Jacobs challenged ideologies of female sexuality, Linda Brent reflected, "in looking back, calmly, on the events of my life, I feel that the slave woman ought not to be judged by the same standard as others" (56). Within the series of "incidents" that Jacobs represented, this decision was pivotal to the structure of the text and to the development of an alternative discourse of womanhood. Previous events focused on the disruption to a normative journey through childhood, girlhood, and romantic youth; following incidents established the unconventional definitions of womanhood and motherhood that Jacobs, herself, tried to determine.

Linda Brent's decision as a slave, to survive through an act that resulted in her loss of virtue, placed her outside the parameters of the conventional heroine. Barbara Welter has described how heroines who were guilty of a loss of purity, in novels or magazines, were destined for death or madness.[19] According to the doctrine of true womanhood, death itself was preferable to a loss of innocence; Linda Brent not only survived in her "impure" state, but she also used her "illicit" liaison as an attempt to secure a future for herself and her children. Jacobs's narrative was unique in its subversion of a major narrative code of sentimental fiction: death, as preferable to loss of purity, was replaced by "Death is better than slavery" (63). *Incidents* entered the field of women's literature and history transforming and transcending the central paradigm of death versus virtue. The consequences of the loss of innocence, Linda Brent's (and Jacobs's) children, rather than being presented as the fruits of her shame, were her links to life and the motivating force of an additional determination to be free.

Linda Brent's second child was a girl, and the birth caused her to reflect on her daughter's possible future as a slave: "When they told me my new-born babe was a girl, my heart was heavier than it had ever been before. Slavery is terrible for men; but it is far more terrible for women. Superadded to the burden common to all, *they* have wrongs, and sufferings, and mortifications peculiarly their own" (79). The narrative that Jacobs wrote was assertively gender-specific and resonated against the dominant forms of the male slave narrative. But the sexual exploitation that Linda Brent confronted and feared for her daughter was, at the same moment, racially specific, disrupting conventional expectations of the attributes of a heroine. Death became the price that Linda Brent was prepared to pay to free her daughter from slavery: "I knew the doom that awaited my fair baby in slavery, and I determined to save her from it, or perish in the attempt." The slave mother made this vow by the graves of her parents, in the "burying-ground of the slaves," where "the prisoners rest together; they hear not the voice of the oppressor; the servant is free from his master" (92). Jacobs added the voice of her narrator to a history of slave rebels but at the same time completed a unique act. The transition from death as preferable to slavery to the stark polarity of freedom or death was made at this narrative moment. "As I passed the wreck of the old meeting house, where, before Nat Turner's time, the slaves had been allowed to meet for worship, I seemed to hear my father's voice come from it, bidding me not to tarry till I reached freedom or the grave" (93). Freedom replaced and transcended purity. Linda Brent's loss of innocence was a gain; she realized the necessity of struggling for the freedom of her children even more than for herself. Thus, the slave woman's motherhood was situated by Jacobs as the source of courage and determination.[20]

In order to save her children, Linda Brent apparently had to desert them. To precipitate a crisis and persuade Dr. Flint that he should sell the children to their father, Sands, Linda escaped and hid. The children were sold and returned to their great-grandmother's house to live, where, unknown to them, their mother was in hiding. However, Linda Brent's hopes for emancipation for her children were shattered when her daughter, Ellen, was "given" as a waiting maid to Sand's relatives in New York. After years in hiding, Linda escaped to New York and found employment. Her daughter was neglected, inadequately fed and clothed, and when Benjamin, her son, was finally sent north to join her, Linda realized that in order to protect her children she must own herself, freeing them all from the series of white people's broken promises that had framed her life.

Having obtained Ellen's freedom, Linda Brent confided her sexual history to her daughter as the one person whose forgiveness she desired. As opposed to the earlier confession, which was directly addressed to readers, Jacobs portrays Linda as in need of the unmediated judgment of Ellen. Ellen refused to condemn her mother and told her that she had been aware of her sexual relations with Sands, rejected her father as meaning nothing to her, and reserved her love for Linda. The motherhood that Jacobs defined and shaped in her narrative was vindicated through her own daughter, excluding the need for any approval from the readership. Jacobs bound the meaning and interpretation of her womanhood and motherhood to the internal structure of the text, making external validation unnecessary and unwarranted. Judgment was to be passed on the institution of slavery, not on deviations from conventions of true womanhood.

Jacobs gained her public voice and access to a sympathetic audience through the production of a slave narrative, a cultural form of expression supported and encouraged by the abolitionist movement. She primarily addressed the white Northern women whom she urged to advocate the abolition of the system of slavery. However, Jacobs's narrative problematized assumptions that dominated abolitionist literature in general and male slave narratives in particular, assumptions that linked slave women to illicit sexuality. Jacobs's attempt to develop a framework in which to discuss the social, political, and economic consequences of black womanhood prefigured the concerns of black women intellectuals after emancipation. For these intellectuals the progress of the race would be intimately tied to and measured by the progress of the black woman.

Black women writers would continue to adopt and adapt dominant literary conventions and to challenge racist sexual ideologies. Like Prince, Wilson, and Jacobs, they would explore a variety of narrative forms in the attempt to establish a public presence and continue to find ways to invent black heroines who could tran-

scend their negative comparison to the figure of the white heroine. The consequences of being a slave woman did not end with the abolition of slavery as an institution but haunted the texts of black women throughout the nineteenth century and into the twentieth. The transition from slave to free woman did not liberate the black heroine or the black woman from the political and ideological limits imposed on her sexuality. In the shift from slave narrative to fiction, I will concentrate on the ways in which the novel was seen by black women authors as a form of cultural and political intervention in the struggle for black liberation from oppression.

Notes

[1] Nancy Prince, *A Narrative of the Life and Travels of Mrs. Nancy Prince. Written by Herself* (Boston: by the author, 1850), preface. Page numbers will be given parenthetically in the text.

[2] See the recent edition of *The Life and Religious Experience of Jarena Lee; Memoirs of the Life, Religious Experience, Ministerial Travels and Labors of Mrs. Zilpha Elaw;* and *A Brand Plucked from the Fire: An Autobiographical Sketch by Mrs. Julia A. J. Foote,* in William L. Andrews, ed., *Sisters of the Spirit: Three Black Women's Autobiographies of the Nineteenth Century* (Bloomington: Indiana University Press, 1986).

[3] Harriet E. Wilson, *Our Nig; or, Sketches from the Life of a Free Black, in a Two-Story White House, North. Showing That Slavery's Shadows Fall Even There,* introduction by Henry Louis Gates, Jr. (Boston: by the author, 1859; reprint New York: Random House, 1983). References are to the 1983 edition; page numbers will be given parenthetically in the text.

[4] Harriet Jacobs, [Linda Brent], *Incidents in the Life of a Slave Girl, Written by Herself,* L. Maria Child, ed. (Boston: for the author, 1861). A paperback edition with an introduction by Walter Teller was published in New York by Harcourt Brace Jovanovich in 1973; the pages cited in parentheses are in this edition.

[5] John Blassingame, "Critical Essay on Sources," *The Slave Community: Plantation Life in the Antebellum South,* 2nd ed. (New York: Oxford University Press, 1979), pp. 367-82.

[6] Ibid., p. 373.

[7] Ibid., p. 367 (emphasis added).

[8] This evidence has focused on the discovery of a collection of Jacobs's letters to Amy Post held in the Post family papers at the University of Rochester library. See Dorothy Sterling, ed., *We Are Your Sisters: Black Women in the Nineteenth Century* (New York:

W. W. Norton, 1984); and Jean Yellin, "Written by Herself: Harriet Jacobs' Slave Narrative," *American Literature* 53 (November 1981): 479-86; "Texts and Contexts of Harriet Jacobs' Incidents in the Life of a Slave Girl: Written by Herself," in Charles T. Davis and Henry Louis Gates, Jr., eds., *The Slave's Narrative* (New York: Oxford University Press, 1985), pp. 262-82; and her introduction to a new annotated edition of *Incidents in the Life of a Slave Girl* (Cambridge: Harvard University Press, 1987). Yellin has also verified details of Jacobs's life in Edenton, North Carolina, and is preparing to write her biography.

[9] Harriet Jacobs, [Linda Brent], *The Deeper Wrong: Or, Incidents in the Life of a Slave Girl, Written by Herself,* L. Maria Child, ed. (London: W. Tweedie, 1862).

[10] For Jacobs on Willis, see Yellin, "Texts and Contexts," pp. 265, 279n.

[11] Jacobs to Post, May 18 and June 18 (1857?), cited in Yellin, "Written by Herself," pp. 485-86.

[12] Jacobs to Post, October 8 (1860?), in ibid., p. 483.

[13] Jacobs to Post, June 21 (1857?), cited in Yellin, "Texts and Contexts," p. 269.

[14] I am grateful to Jean Yellin for reading an earlier draft of this chapter and helping me clarify my ideas. Yellin argues that "Jacobs' narrator dramatizes the failure of her efforts to adhere to the sexual patterns she had been taught to endorse . . . and tentatively reaches toward an alternative moral code" ("Texts and Contexts," pp. 270-71). I am arguing that this alternative is the development of a discourse of black womanhood and that, far from being tentative, this movement away from the ideology of true womanhood is assertive.

[15] Yellin, "Written by Herself," p. 482.

[16] Yellin, "Texts and Contexts," p. 276.

[17] See the discussion of incidents in relation to plot in Nina Baym, *Novels, Readers and Reviewers: Responses to Fiction in Antebellum America* (Ithaca: Cornell University Press, 1984), pp. 75-79.

[18] Nina Baym's observations on morality in novels and reviews of novels are enlightening in any consideration of the extent to which writers could challenge convention. See *Novels, Readers and Reviewers,* pp. 173-89, where she makes the argument that female sexuality was consistently policed by reviewers: "Two basic Victorian assumptions about female character—that women do not experience sexual desire and that they are naturally suited to monogamous marriage where they are the servants of their husbands, their children, and society at large—are here exposed as cultural constrictions whose maintenance requires constant surveillance, even to the supervision of novel reading" (183).

[19] Barbara Welter, *Dimity Convictions: The American Woman in the Nineteenth Century* (Colombus: Ohio University Press, 1976), p. 23.

[20] Jacobs intended that this note of rebellion be repeated in her final chapter which was about John Brown, but at the suggestion of Lydia Maria Child the chapter was dropped. Had it been retained, it would have strengthened this interpretation of the importance of the linking of freedom and death.

Sarah Way Sherman (essay date 1990)

SOURCE: "Moral Experience in Harriet Jacobs's *Incidents in the Life of a Slave Girl*," in *NWSA Journal,* Vol. 2, No. 2, Spring, 1990, pp. 167-85.

[*In the following essay, Sherman pinpoints the source of the moral conflict and ambiguity in* Incidents *as the narrator's struggle with the exploitation and brutality of slavery and the idealized conception of "true womanhood." Furthermore, Sherman argues that the depiction of this conflict is the source of the work's strength.*]

"Slavery is terrible for men," Harriet Jacobs wrote in 1861, "but it is far more terrible for women." Citing this passage from **Incidents in the Life of a Slave Girl,** Jean Fagan Yellin argues that Jacobs's book was the first to address the sexual exploitation of women under slavery. But Yellin also notes the rhetorical strain of such outspokenness. Compared to the classic *Narrative of the Life of Frederick Douglass* (1845), Jacobs's narrative can appear weakened by conflict. As I hope to show, however, this important book's ambivalence and troubled voice point toward its strength.[1] While the thrust of **Incidents in the Life** comes from a unequivocal denunciation of an evil system, its tension comes from a painful confrontation with moral conflict and moral ambiguity. The pseudonymous narrator, Linda Brent, is caught between the brutal, exploitative bonds of slavery and the idealized, altruistic bonds of true womanhood.[2] The first she resists with great spirit and no ambivalence; the other she resists only with great pain and guilt, after deep disillusionment. Both systems denied her a selfhood; neither had words to authorize her choices.

Jacobs's story, now widely available, has found new readers, particularly in college courses where it is often read alongside Douglass's *Narrative.* The differences between the two are illuminating. I should say, however, that Douglass's text may not itself be a typical slave narrative. One reason he was assimilated into the American literary canon with relative ease may have been his brilliant deployment of white conventions, particularly the developmental drama of the self-made man. There are significant parallels between the trajectory of Benjamin Franklin's rise from obscurity to political office and Douglass's own emergence from slavery into the public forum.[3] One of the most important differences then between Jacobs and Douglass is gender. Gender directly shapes Jacobs's experience both as slave and free woman; moreover, gender shapes the conventions available for her interpretation of these experiences. The exemplary rise of a self-made woman was not a common literary plot. Before addressing gender differences, however, there is another key difference between Jacobs and Douglass: her early literacy and relatively privileged status as a slave.

The text opens with the lines, "I was born a slave, but I never knew it till six years of happy childhood had passed away." Linda and her brother, William, are raised by indulgent owners. Linda's mistress teaches her to read and treats her almost like a daughter. This woman had been herself nursed at the breast of Linda's grandmother; hence she is seen as the "foster sister" of Linda's own mother. Not only are the children taught to read, but they are raised within an intact black family which "fondly shields" them from the realities of slavery. Linda's father is a skilled carpenter. Her grandmother, Martha, has obtained her freedom, owns her own home, and supports herself through a lively business as a baker. This proud family holds Linda and William to the standards of middle-class behavior—the moral codes of free people—even though the two children cannot always fulfill them. The conflicts created by this situation appear early and are central to the text.

Linda, for example, describes how William is called by both his white mistress and his father. Whom should he obey? From an abstract, ideal perspective the moral claim of the father is obviously superior to that of the mistress. But in the fallen world of the slaveholding South, the father's claim is silenced. William assesses the context and goes to his mistress. For the time being, the greater good, greater even than goodness, is survival. But if William thereby escapes a whipping, or worse, he does not escape his father's wrath. He is held morally accountable and reprimanded for making the wrong choice.

The lesson that Linda and William must learn is excruciating. Although the dove of moral idealism may be beautiful, to act in a corrupt world it must learn a lesson from the serpent. Only a "fortunate fall" from innocence can develop a morality adequate to the complexity of human experience.[4] Thus while Douglass's narrative begins with a slave who does not know he is human; this one begins with a child who does not know she is a slave. If she is to survive, she must learn not to express her humanity but to hide it; not to find her tongue but to bite it. Powerless to fulfill the moral codes, one of white society, she develops a powerful critique of those codes that assesses moral action within its human context.

This lesson is complicated by Jacobs's other difference from Douglass—her gender. If "slavery was terrible" for men like William, it was, again in Linda Brent's words, "far more terrible for women." Slavery was acted out on male bodies but also within female ones. As "brood mare" or concubine, wet nurse or mammy, part of a slave woman's productive work was reproduction.[5] Slavery's threat was therefore even the more intimate and brutal. If slavery denied the female slave's selfhood, it tempted her master to monstrous selfishness, unfettered by recognition of their common humanity.

Not only was slavery's threat more sexual for women, but genteel codes for their behavior were more stringent. The standards of free people differed for men and women. With the example of her own mother's chaste courtship and marriage ever before her, Linda is carefully indoctrinated by her mistress and family into the cult of true womanhood. The ideology of woman's innate "piety, purity, submissiveness and domesticity" could be a significant weapon against male aggression, but it also opened new areas of vulnerability. As a model for human behavior, it had, as Linda discovers, serious flaws. "Angels in the house" might win self-respect and private influence but only by renouncing self-assertion and public power.[6]

While Linda's awareness of slavery begins at age six, with her mother's death, her moral education begins at twelve, with the death of her mistress, "almost a mother to her." She is not freed as she had come to expect but is "bequeathed" to her mistress's little niece, Emily Flint. This shock destroys whatever illusions Linda might have had about her actual condition. Not long after this first "fall," Emily's father, Dr. Flint, begins to make sexual advances. The story now takes on some qualities of a conventional seduction novel, a sentimental story of innocence pursued. Linda is not physically coerced, but she is, from puberty onward, relentlessly harassed by Flint, her master until Emily's majority. The language and plot of these sections led some critics, such as John Blassingame, to suspect that Jacobs's white editor, Lydia Maria Child influenced the text. Yellin's research, however, has shown that Jacobs herself was responsible for the text.[7] Its words and story are essentially her own. While the hesitations and expressions of shame associated with Linda's sexual history may be explained by her need to appease white middle-class readers, I believe they also result from Linda's own education in genteel codes of female behavior. Again, the source was from within her own family, particularly her freed grandmother, Martha.

Martha in many ways is a model of womanly strength and integrity. A capable, devout Christian, she has earned the respect of her community, black and white. After serving as wet nurse, cook, and mammy to Mrs. Flint's mother's household for many years, she gained her freedom to become mistress of her own home. This domestic space is not only a "haven in a heartless world" but literally a means to Linda's freedom when she later hides in its shed for seven years. (Confined to a tiny alcove, concealed even from her own children, she waits for a chance to escape to the North.) If her master Dr. Flint is the text's serpent, Linda's strong and kindly grandmother is its dove. Her memory remains with Linda like "light, fleecy clouds floating over a dark and troubled sea."[8] Yet that dark and troubled sea is the one which Linda has to cross.

As a young girl, Linda "had resolved that I would be virtuous, though I was but a slave. I had said, 'Let the storm beat! I will brave it till I die.' "[9] But the storm is ruthless. Not only does Dr. Flint batter her purity of mind with constant insinuations and harrassment, but he destroys any hopes for legitimate fulfillment by refusing to allow her to marry the free black man who loves her. Even if he had permitted it, the marriage would have had no legal existence because of her status as a slave. In Samuel Richardson's classic seducation novel *Pamela,* the chaste heroine triumphs when her employer and would-be seducer finally proposes marriage. But, as critic Valerie Smith points out, the happy endings of sentimental novels do not apply to a young slave girl's story. If legitimizing Flint's sexual advances were the only issue, racist laws alone would prevent him from marrying her.[10]

Of course, there is one conventional ending that could apply: martyrdom. Like Clarissa of Richardson's other seduction novel, Linda could choose to die rather than to live an "impure" life: a sullied blossom in a sullied world. As in the opening story of her brother William's choice, the constant question behind Linda's life and text is: when is your humanity worth dying for? At what moment, precisely, is survival as a compromised individual too painful? Her motto, Linda Brent says, is give me liberty or give me death, but the difficulty is knowing when that final choice has come. In this case she does not die in the storm but decides instead to take a free white man as a lover. The decision brings her into direct conflict not only with her master's will but also her grandmother's values. In the genteel code, virginity before marriage was equated with female self-worth and moral integrity. For the free, middle-class woman the choice of husband was *the* choice. Through this choice she exercised the majority of what control she had over her adult life. While agonizingly limited, the choice was, nevertheless, real. Denied this choice, Brent is forced to recognize that it is through the moral exercise of her right to choose that a woman gains moral integ-

rity, not through the physical virginity with which the choice is associated.

Thus, struggling to explain her history to white genteel readers, Brent says, "It seems less degrading to give one's self, than to submit to compulsion. There is something akin to freedom in having a lover who has no control over you, except that which he gains by kindness and attachment."[11] It is the quality of the relationship that marks it as moral or immoral, not its legal status: "A master may treat you as rudely as he pleases, and you dare not speak; moreover, the wrong does not seem so great with an unmarried man, as with one who has a wife to be made unhappy." At this point Brent seems aware of the radical turn her remarks are taking: "There may be sophistry in all this; but the condition of slavery confuses all principles of morality, and, in fact, renders the practice of them impossible."[12] What Brent seems reluctant to say, perhaps for fear of alienating her audience, is that if slavery renders the practice of morality impossible, far from confusing all principles of morality, it may actually clarify them. Under pressure, the genuinely ethical stands out from the merely conventional.

Linda, however, is not ready to dispense with womanly purity as an ideal. She never completely abandons her grandmother's values but argues that only those who are free to uphold them should be judged by them. Thus her voice moves between passionate idealism and calm realism: "I know I did wrong. No one can feel it more sensibly than I do. The painful and humiliating memory will haunt me to my dying day. Still, in looking back, calmly, on the events of my life, I feel that the slave woman ought not to be judged by the same standard as others."[13] In the same passage she bravely takes full responsibility for her choice: "I knew what I did, and I did it with deliberate calculation." But again, she asks her reader to read that confession within its context: "But, O, ye happy women, whose purity has been sheltered from childhood, who have been free to choose the objects of your affection, whose homes are protected by law, do not judge the poor desolate slave girl too severely."

In sum her grandmother's vision of the cult of true womanhood is "beautiful" but unattainable. If Linda had that choice in this world, she would take it. But she does not. Denied the innocence of the dove, she uses the wisdom of the serpent. She chooses survival: selfhood and self-determination. Through her liaison with Mr. Sands she gains some control over her body. If she cannot marry, she can at least choose with whom she will reproduce. Citing her birthright as a mother, she argues that, "Of a man who was not my master I could ask to have my children well supported; and in this case, I felt confident I should obtain the boon. I also felt quite sure that they would be made free."[14] Later she discovers that Sands is only apparently softer than Flint; both are made of the same slaveholding stuff although Sands is shiftier. Nevertheless, the central point remains; she says there is something akin to freedom in this choice, and she takes it.

But this is an understanding her grandmother does not share. She cannot contextualize her moral judgements. When Linda confesses her pregnancy, Martha's judgement is severe: " 'I had rather see you dead than to see you as you now are. You are a disgrace to your dead mother.' She tore from my fingers my mother's wedding ring and her silver thimble. 'Go away!' she exclaimed, 'and never come to my house again.' "[15] When Martha finally softens and goes to the terrified, despairing girl, she still does not give up her code: "She listened in silence. I told her I would bear any thing and do any thing, if in time I had hopes of obtaining her forgiveness. I begged of her to pity me, for my dead mother's sake. And she did pity me. She did not say, 'I forgive you'; but she looked at me lovingly, with her eyes full of tears. She laid her old hand gently on my head, and murmured, 'Poor child! Poor child!' "[16]

As the text clearly demonstrates, Linda has no ideology or language to justify her choice. After her escape she tells the people sheltering her that she is a mother but not a wife. Although they are understanding, they caution her against such honesty in the future; it could expose her to contempt. The "delicate silence of womanly sympathy" is the best that she can expect, but that is a lot. This silence does not demand the struggle to forge explanations. It acknowledges her history's context and forgives. Hence Jean Fagan Yellin and Hazel Carby read understanding in the silence of Linda's daughter, Ellen, who tells her mother there is nothing in her past she need explain. The daughter's understanding and acceptance heal the pain of the grandmother's first rejection, yet this silence means, again, that there is finally no language of justification.[17] Sexual purity remains an operative fiction: a value for that ideal world whose future possibility Linda is unwilling to give up—at the same time she must live with the reality of slavery in this one.

These issues of voice and virginity have been at the center of much critical discussion of this text. I believe, however, that Linda Brent's sexual initiation is only that, an initiation. The central experience of her mature morality is neither virginity nor its loss, but motherhood. The "moral mother" was a powerful image in Victorian ideology; one has only to think of how skillfully Harriet Beecher Stowe used it.[18] Thus, as Carby suggests, while Linda's fall from sexual innocence presented problems for her white readership, as well as for herself, her resultant motherhood conferred not only new knowledge but new power.[19] It is as a slave mother that Linda Brent addresses her reader; it is through this role that she claims authority to write.

The gift of motherhood, however, is also mixed, and Brent's description offers us another sobering critique. She shows how utterly inadequate the sentimental vision of selfless motherhood was to slave realities. Of her first child, Benjamin, Linda says: "The little vine was taking deep root in my existence, though its clinging fondness excited a mixture of love and pain. . . . I could never forget that he was a slave."[20] "Why," she asks, "does the slave ever love? Why allow the tendrils of the heart to twine around objects which may at any moment be wrenched away by the hand of violence?"[21] The imagery of twining vines and tendrils is a staple of Victorian sentimentalist fiction, but in this narrative the imagery of attachment lies close to the imagery of bondage. The chapter describing Benjamin's birth is "The New Tie to Life," and the one describing Ellen's, "Another Link to Life." These children give her reason to live, but the ties that bind her to motherhood can tighten her to slavery. When Flint suspects that Linda may escape, he threatens to bring Benny and Ellen to the plantation, thinking, she writes, "that my children's being there would fetter me to the spot." He knew "that my life was bound up in my children."[22]

As a slave mother, as in so many of her other roles, Linda must bear moral responsibility virtually without control, with only the slimmest margin of choice. Even before she hides in that tiny, cramped alcove, contingency hems her in at every side. At the Flint's plantation she lies down beside Ellen and "felt how much easier it would be to see her die than to see her master beat her." And earlier, looking on her newborn son, she states: "Sometimes I wished that he might die in infancy. . . . Death is better than slavery."[23] Death is the one choice she always has. While this subtext of infanticide becomes surface in Toni Morrison's *Beloved,* as well as *Uncle Tom's Cabin* (where Cassie gives her infant laudanum), in *Incidents in the Life of a Slave Girl* it is the constant, somber background, the desperate horizon.[24] The other direction from freedom is nevertheless an escape. Moreover, it is the final assertion of authority: in death her children would be hers to keep.

The complexities of Linda's situation appear in a passage describing Ellen's christening. Recognizing that Linda cannot give her child the baby's father's name, Linda's father's former mistress comes forward and offers the child her Christian name, to which Linda adds her own father's surname. But, she adds, her father "had himself no legal right to it; for my grandfather on the paternal side was a white gentleman. What tangled skeins are the genealogies of slavery!" Then, the white mistress, by way of a gift, "clasped a gold chain around my baby's neck. I thanked her for this kindness; but I did not like the emblem."[25]

At the close of a chapter entitled "Another Link to Life," this imagery is heavily loaded. William's initial dilemma has become more complex. He finds himself in a double-bind because he was doubly-bound: first by the legal chain of slavery, second by the reproductive chain of kinship. But now we see the two chains entwined, a tangled skein of black and white extending down through the generations. Because the chains themselves are deeply entwined, so are their moral claims. What if one's "owner" is also one's father?

The moral test, throughout the narrative, is love. When Sands takes his daughter Ellen with him to Washington, he does not bother to write her mother. Linda quietly comments: "The links of such relations as he had formed with me, are easily broken and cast away as rubbish." Later, when Linda attempts to tell Ellen about her father, Ellen stops her: " 'I am nothing to my father, and he is nothing to me. . . . I was with him five months in Washington, and he never cared for me. . . . I thought if he was my own father, he ought to love me. I was a little girl then, and didn't know any better.' "[26]

Brent repeatedly refers to Sands's fatherhood as "a parental relation," a relation which "takes slight hold of the hearts or consciences of slaveholders." Simple biological bonds are easily corrupted by power, greed, and sexuality; but most of all she laments, "how slavery perverted all the natural feelings of the human heart."[27] Sands treats his child as his slave, and therefore is not worthy of being her father, is *not* her father, and has no rightful authority over her. An umbilical cord is a "tie," but the only tie with moral authority is love.

Thus a third chain is a transcendent chain of affection, of motherly and fatherly, ultimately neighborly love. This chain transcends both slavery and biology; although it might have its roots in biological parenthood and kinship, it is not determined by them. This sacred chain, associated with the ethos of true womanhood and evangelical Christianity, presents Linda with her most painful moral dilemma: whether to run away or stay.

As Mary Helen Washington and Judith Fetterley, among others, point out, there are significant differences between the description of Linda Brent's escape and Frederick Douglass's.[28] Douglass opens by telling us how he was systematically denied the comforts of a mother and family life, then passes over his courtship of his wife-to-be in a few sentences. As in Benjamin Franklin's autobiography, the self which he presents is individual, strikingly outlined against the public sphere. His ultimate liberation is represented by a solitary self speaking in a voice unashamed and unconflicted before a public audience. The story of Douglass's escape from the bonds of slavery is central; the story of his loyalty to the bonds of love and friendship is peripheral.

The two stories, however, are deeply entwined in Linda Brent's narrative, and in many other male and female slave narratives. Indeed Eugene Genovese remarks that "almost every study of runaway slaves uncovers the importance of the family motive: thousands of slaves ran away to find children, parents, wives, or husbands from whom they had been separated by sale."[29] Other slaves, such as Henry Bibb, suffered agonies over the conflict between their desire for freedom and their responsibility to families.[30] Thus while resisting slavery presents no more ethical challenge to Linda Brent than it does to Frederick Douglass (she feels no moral responsibility to the Flints), leaving her children and grandmother presents a severe challenge. Honesty will not allow Linda to minimize the human consequences of this choice: her grandmother's suffering, her children's loneliness. She has defined a self, but she has defined it within the context of other selves. Bound by mutual love and responsibility, their identities are interdependent. If her obligation to her master is void, her obligation to this community is not.

When Martha first suspects Linda is planning to escape, "She looked earnestly at me, and said, 'Linda, do you want to kill your old grandmother? I am old now, and cannot do for your babies as I once did for you.' " Linda argues that only by fleeing can she keep Dr. Flint from using Benny and Ellen as a weapon to break her. In his absence he would have no reason to threaten them. Her desperate gamble is that she can work for her children's liberation from the North. Perhaps their father could buy them and set them free. But her grandmother is not so hopeful: " 'Stand by your own children,' " she says, " 'and suffer with them till death. Nobody respects a mother who forsakes her children; and if you leave them, you will never have a happy moment.' "[31]

Linda's conflicts, painful in themselves, are exacerbated by the ideology of true womanhood, represented once again by her grandmother. Both agree on the priority of Linda's duty to her children; how to fulfill that duty is the question. Linda accepts her responsibility to care for this community, but to do so she must care for herself. Her children's freedom depends upon her strength, her will, which must not be broken. despite her grandmother's fear and the genteel images of womanhood to which Linda might once have aspired. Ladylike martyrdom may be an option, but it is not the one Linda chooses. When Linda thinks of her daughter, and what she herself "had suffered in slavery at her age," her "heart was like a tiger's when a hunter tries to seize her young."[32] Moral action, and moral resistance, demand selfhood.

The choice, however, is still painful: "I remembered the grief this step would bring upon my dear old grandmother; and nothing less than the freedom of my children would have induced me to disregard her advice."[33] And her grandmother does not let her off easily: "Whenever the children climbed on my knee, or laid their heads on my lap, she would say, 'Poor little souls!

what would you do without a mother? She don't love you as I do.' "[34] Even though she knows the accusation is false and prompted by a human fear, Brent's narrative is haunted by guilt. In the midst of her first escape she imagines her grandmother saying, " 'Linda, you are killing me.' "

But if Linda does not obey her grandmother, neither does she judge her, for these feelings are ones she has shared. Early in the story, when her uncle Benjamin tells her about his plan to leave, Linda's first response is " 'Go . . . and break your mother's heart.' "[35] Though she immediately regrets the words, they are out. When her brother William makes his break, we see again that the heart's spontaneous reaction is not joy but grief: "If you had seen the tears, and heard the sobs, you would have thought the messenger had brought tidings of death instead of freedom."[36] These are people whose lives are bound up with those they love. Even when separation brings freedom, it brings pain. As her ship finally approaches Philadelphia and freedom, Linda sees what she calls not the City of Brotherly Love but "the city of strangers." She looks at her companion, also an escaping slave, "and the eyes of both were moistened with tears. We had escaped from slavery, and we supposed ourselves to be safe from the hunters. But we were alone in the world, and we had left dear ties behind us; ties cruelly sundered by the demon Slavery."[37]

Given the text's focus on mothering, the fact and imagery of nursing—both as physical breastfeeding and as emotional nurturing—are key throughout. If the perversion of human relations appears in the white father who sells his child into oppression; the ennobling of human relations appears in the black mother who nurtures the child of her oppressor. And this, of course, is Martha herself, who takes her own child off her breast in order to suckle the child of her beloved mistress. This white baby becomes in her eyes the "foster-sister" of her own child, Linda's mother. There is indeed a curious doubling in the text. Linda Brent's mother dies but is survived by a twin, Aunt Nancy.[38] The white foster daughter dies but leaves a sister. This sister becomes the revengeful Mrs. Flint, a frightening image of the slave-mistress.

Aunt Nancy's story is one of the most painful stories Brent tells. Nancy sleeps at the foot of Mrs. Flint's bed, undergoing a harrowing series of premature births and miscarriages while waiting on her foster sister, her white mistress. Mrs. Flint in turn gives birth to her own children, whom Nancy must raise. Nancy's fertility is literally sacrificed to her "sister's." When she finally dies, the letter describing her death—a letter probably written by Dr. Flint—blasphemously imitates the language of community: "Could you have seen us round her death bed, mingling our tears in one common stream, you would have thought the same heart-felt tie existed between a master and his servant, as between a mother and her child."[39] But of course the same heartfelt tie does not exist between a master and his servant. Not only is the servant forced to care for the master, but this care is not reciprocated. Mrs. Flint wants Nancy buried in their own plot as a sign of Nancy's devotion to her "family"; Linda's grandmother adamantly refuses. The true family is the one in which Nancy's care was returned. Aunt Martha claims ownership of her daughter's body at last.

But Martha's relationship to Mrs. Flint remains one of the most troubling in the book. This revengeful woman *is* her foster daughter, not just in name but in emotional reality. In extending her care to her owner's child, Martha blurred the boundaries between self and other, and with them, slave and master, white and black. According to racist ideology, a mother's milk cannot miscegenate. The merging of nurse and child was considered free from the taint of racial definition, and in this text its love is innocent: the milk of human kindness. The memory of this bond lays a claim on the old grandmother's loyalty. When Mrs. Flint won't speak to her former nurse, Linda writes, "This wounded my grandmother's feelings, for she could not retain ill will against the woman whom she had nourished with her milk as a babe." When Dr. Flint questions her, Martha simply says, " 'Your wife was my foster-child, Dr. Flint, the foster-sister of my poor Nancy, and you little know me if you think I can feel any thing but good will for her children.' " Martha's love for Mrs. Flint was, and remains, unconditional; she is indeed a dove. In a better world such goodness would confer moral authority. Linda admits that Dr. Flint was held at bay many times by her grandmother's reputation, but when Martha goes to Flint to plead for her granddaughter—reminding "him how long and how faithfully she had served in the family, and how she had taken her own baby from her breast to nourish his wife"—the doctor simply ignores her claims.[40] Here the ideology of true womanhood fails. Moral example alone is no match for positive evil.

One could argue, however, as Hazel Carby does, that Martha's behavior in this and other key instances is not submissive, but assertive. She is, Carby writes, "representative of a strong moral code in the midst of an immoral system."[41] She acts on behalf of the entire community of her care, black and white. The problem is that she has no power to enforce that code. By extending her love to a corrupt foster daughter, Martha endangers the other members of the community for whom she cares. By rejecting Mrs. Flint she would lose her Christ-like purity. The dove must learn a lesson from the serpent if it is to survive, and its peaceable kingdom come into this world, not just the next. Finally, even Martha is forced to agree that the greater good of Linda's escape justifies active resistance, including lies and deceit. She hides Linda in that womb-like, coffin-like space for seven years, caring for little Benjamin and Ellen all that time: a brave defiance of her own fear and honesty.[42]

Of course, Aunt Martha's love for her white foster children is not always the case in black literature. In Toni Morrison's *The Bluest Eye,* attachment to the oppressor's child appears as moral failure, a capitulation to white fantasies. In one excruciating scene Pauline rejects her own daughter in favor of the pretty white child who calls her Polly in the fancy house by the lake.[43] The implications and dangers of such nonreciprocal, powerless mothering are heightened in the horrifying violation of Sethe in *Beloved.* Forcibly taking milk meant for her child, the two white boys "with mossy teeth" pervert the sign of Sethe's womanly power and love freely given.[44] In Alice Walker's *The Color Purple* Sofia refuses to lie about loving *her* white "foster daughter's" child: "Some colored people so scared of whitefolks," she says, "they claim to love the cotton gin." Sofia does not deny she "feels something" for Eleanor Jane herself, "because out of all the people in your daddy's house you showed me some human kindness. But on the other hand, out of all the people in your daddy's house, I showed you some." Unlike Aunt Martha's, Sofia's love *is* conditional: "Kind feelings is what I offer you. I don't have nothing to offer your relatives but just what they offer me."[45]

In ***Incidents in the Life of a Slave Girl*** we see a black nursemaid who slaps the face of her dead mistress while the child she cares for, the child of the dead woman, looks on (the child tells and the nurse is sold). Here, however, as in *The Color Purple,* the white child before the corruption of consciousness *may* be worthy of love because that child may be capable of giving love. At the end of her long flight north, Linda Brent says she was so disillusioned that she was in danger of losing her compassion and hope. In the chapter called "A Home Found" she describes how Mary, her white employer's daughter, "thawed my heart, when it was freezing into cheerless distrust of all my fellow-beings." "I loved Mrs. Bruce's babe. When it laughed and crowed in my face, and twined its little tender arms confidingly about my neck . . . my wounded heart was soothed."[46]

The infant is not the source of the slave woman's exploitation. Although a black baby may be denied nourishment given to its white "sister," the demand is the slaveholder's, not the inarticulate child's. Brent reiterates her faith that "surely little children are true." In one parable-like story we see that truth uncorrupted: "I once saw two beautiful sisters playing together. One was a fair white child; the other was a slave, but also her sister. When I saw them embracing each other, and heard their joyous laughter, I turned sadly away from the lovely sight."[47] This Edenic moment is inevitably doomed. The serpent of slavery and white male sexuality insinuate themselves into the slave girl's innocence. She becomes aware of her difference, her enslavement, and her sexual vulnerability. Finally, she must drain "the cup of sin, and shame, and misery, whereof her persecuted race are compelled to drink."[48]

And what of her white sister? "From childhood to womanhood her pathway was blooming with flowers, and overarched by a sunny sky. Scarcely one day of her life had been clouded when the sun rose on her happy bridal morning."[49] But Brent stops at the bridal morning for good reason. If the serpent enters the slave girl's life at puberty, he enters her white sister's at marriage. Unchecked power and sexual exploitation make betrayal by her husband almost inevitable. Moral corruption blights her happiness and "ravages" her home, with its twining vines, "of all its loveliness."

This is the source, Brent implies, of Mrs. Flint's venom, the motivation behind her attack on the daughter of her foster sister and grandchild of her foster mother. Sexual jealousy, the "green-eyed monster," is personified in this woman's vindictiveness.[50] Brent is unsparing in her portrayal of that vindictiveness, but in an act of remarkable compassion, she writes, "Yet I, whom she detested so bitterly, had far more pity for her than he had, whose duty it was to make her life happy. I never wronged her, or wished to wrong her; and one word of kindness from her would have brought me to her feet."[51] Although deeply corrupted by slaveholding's unchecked power, Mrs. Flint persecutes Linda primarily out of helplessness and misery. The true source of her anger is her husband, but in a patriarchal world she too can be rendered powerless against him.

Linda Brent's story opens with the death of her white mistress. Her grief is real, "for she had been almost like a mother to me."[52] But this death brings another. When the will is read, Linda learns she has not been freed but "bequeathed" as a piece of property. "My mistress taught me the precepts of God's Word: 'thou shalt love thy neighbor as thyself.' 'Whatsoever ye would that men should do unto you, do ye even so unto them.' But I was her slave, and I suppose she did not recognize me as her neighbor."[53] This "one great wrong," emblem of slavery's moral blindness, cannot be forgotten or forgiven, but it is countered at the book's close by an act of neighborly love and courage.

After Linda's escape to the North she is employed by a Mr. and Mrs. Bruce as nursemaid for their daughter. Although the husband appears both obtuse and sympathetic to slaveholding, Mrs. Bruce is remarkable for her understanding and support. When Mrs. Bruce dies, the second wife proves even more remarkable. When Linda is threatened with capture by Mr. Dodge (her new master via his marriage to Emily Flint), the second Mrs. Bruce not only helps Linda escape once more but proposes she take Mrs. Bruce's own baby with her. If Linda is found, she reasons, the slavecatchers would be forced to return the white child to its mother before taking Linda south; Mrs. Bruce could then intervene on her behalf. Brent writes: "It was a comfort to me to have the child with me; for the heart is reluctant to be torn away from every object it loves. But how few mothers would have consented to have one of their own babies become a fugitive, for the sake of a poor, hunted nurse."[54] The sisterhood of that earlier Edenic image can be regained. Mrs. Bruce does recognize Linda as her neighbor. By risking her child, she assumes that neighbor's danger as her own.

But Linda's tale here also is "bittersweet," a word which reappears throughout the text. While Linda is in hiding with Mrs. Bruce's child, Mrs. Bruce writes that she intends to buy her from Mr. Dodge and end her persecution. Linda's response is sharply mixed. Although she is grateful, "The more my mind had become enlightened, the more difficult it was for me to consider myself an article of property; and to pay money to those who had so grievously oppressed me seemed like taking from my sufferings the glory of triumph." Linda writes to thank Mrs. Bruce but also to say "that being sold from one owner to another seemed too much like slavery; that such a great obligation could not be easily cancelled; and that I preferred to go to my brother in California."[55] She will take her stand on principle, uncompromised, passionate. Mary Helen Washington is correct in seeing this statement as Linda Brent's forthright assertion of selfhood, which is comparable to Frederick Douglass's rejection of *any* master, kind as well as cruel.[56]

Yet, here too, there is a difference; without Linda's knowledge, Mrs. Bruce goes ahead with the negotiations and purchases her friend's freedom. Again, Linda's response is deeply ambivalent. In her description of the bill of sale, the sentences themselves are split, pitting feeling against feeling: "I well know the value of that bit of paper; but much as I love freedom I do not like to look upon it. I am deeply grateful to the generous friend who procured it, but I despise the miscreant who demanded payment for what never rightfully belonged to him or his."[57] Despite her objections to the means, the end has been reached. Linda confesses that "when it was done I felt as if a heavy load had been lifted from my weary shoulders." She accepts the gift and does not judge Mrs. Bruce for dealing with slaveholders, any more than she judged her brother William for going to his mistress instead of his father, or her grandmother for preferring a living slave child to a lost free one. Mrs. Bruce has compromised a principle to gain Linda's freedom, and though Linda's bitterly resents the necessity, she forgives the act. After all, she has struck her own bargains with the devil.

"When I reached home, the arms of my benefactress were thrown round me, and our tears mingled." The imagery echoes the language of Dr. Flint's blasphemous letter at Nancy's death, but here the mutual identification is real. As Mrs. Bruce explains, "You wrote me as if you thought you were going to be transferred from one owner to another. But I did not buy you for your services. I should have done just the same if you were going to sail to California tomorrow. I should, at least, have the satisfaction of knowing that you left me a free woman."[58] Linda cannot help but remember how her father and grandmother had struggled to buy her freedom, and failed: "But God had raised me up a friend among strangers, who had bestowed on me the precious, long-desired boon." Mrs. Bruce, Brent writes, is her friend. "Friend! It is a common word, often lightly used. Like other good and beautiful things, it may be tarnished by careless handling; but when I speak of Mrs. Bruce as my friend, the word is sacred." As her narrative closes Linda Brent describes herself as "bound" to Mrs. Bruce's side, not by slavery and not only by economic circumstances but also by "love, duty, gratitude. . . ."[59]

"Reader, my story ends with freedom; not in the usual way, with marriage." The difference, however, goes even deeper. If her story does not end in the conventional feminine way, neither does it represent freedom in the conventional masculine way. Linda Brent's narrative ends, not with a solitary speaker, but with a woman gratefully acknowledging her bonds to her children and friends, bonds freely chosen. She has recovered her two children, Benjamin and Ellen. Although she still does not have a home of her own, her family is intact and free. The nineteenth-century vision of domesticity has become a kind of operative fiction: a Christian community of true sisterhood and brotherhood, based on mutual interdependence and identification, neighbor love. The power of this text, however, is its demonstration that moral action is not the work of pure, ego-less angels but of loving, self-determined women and men. The community of care cannot be sustained in a fallen, corrupted world merely through the innocence of the dove but requires the wisdom of the serpent to survive and prevail. Principled yet pragmatic, defiant and compassionate, Linda Brent's bittersweet voice is the voice of moral experience. Like Ralph Ellison's invisible man deep below his city's streets, she has emerged from her hiding place with a painful, healing knowledge. Ellison's hero closes by offering us that knowledge: "Who knows but that, on the lower frequencies, I speak for you."[60] Perhaps Linda Brent does too.

Notes

[1] See Jean Fagan Yellin, "Introduction," in Harriet A. Jacobs, *Incidents in the Life of a Slave Girl, Written by Herself*," ed. Jean Fagan Yellin (Cambridge, Mass.: Harvard University Press, 1987), xiii-xxxiv; also, Charles T. Davis and Henry Louis Gates, Jr., eds.,

"Text and Contexts of Harriet Jacobs' *Incidents in the Life of a Slave Girl: Written by Herself*," in *The Slave's Narrative* (New York: Oxford University Press, 1985), 262-82. For the text itself I have used the Yellin edition of Jacobs's work. In recognition of the fictional aspects of autobiography, I have referred to the author throughout as "Linda Brent." Finally, I would like to thank the anonymous readers of the *NWSA Journal* for their suggestions, as well as Patrocinio Schweickart and Lester A. Fisher for their encouragement and comments. This project was generously supported by a Faculty Summer Stipend from Dean Stuart Palmer and the College of Liberal Arts at the University of New Hampshire.

2 On the ideology of true womanhood see: Barbara Welter, "The Cult of True Womanhood," *American Quarterly,* 18 (Summer 1966): 151-74; Nancy Cott, *The Bonds of Womanhood: "Woman's Sphere" in New England, 1780-1835* (New Haven, Conn.: Yale University Press, 1977); Lucy Freibert and Barbara A. White, eds., *Hidden Hands: An Anthology of American Women Writers, 1790—1870* (New Brunswick, N.J.: Rutgers University Press, 1985); and Judith Fetterley, ed., *Provisions: A Reader from 19th-Century American Women* (Bloomington: Indiana University Press, 1985). For a discussion of nineteenth-century Afro-American women's responses to the cult of true womanhood, see Frances Smith Foster, "Adding Color and Contour to Early American Self-Portraitures: Autobiographical Writings of Afro-American Women," in *Conjuring: Black Women, Fiction, and Literary Tradition,* ed. Marjorie Pryse and Hortense J. Spillers (Bloomington: Indiana University Press, 1985), 25-38.

Recent key studies of Jacobs's text include: Mary Helen Washington, "Meditations on History: The Slave Woman's Voice," in *Invented Lives: Narratives of Black Women, 1860-1960,* ed. Mary Helen Washington (Garden City, N.J.: Doubleday Anchor, 1987), 3-15: Hazel Carby, *Reconstructing Womanhood: The Emergence of the Afro-American Woman Novelist* (New York: Oxford University Press, 1987), 40-61; Valerie Smith, *Self-Discovery and Authority in Afro-American Narrative* (Cambridge, Mass.: Harvard University Press, 1987), 28-43: and Yellin, "Introduction," in *Incidents,* xxvii-xi. Also, Thomas Doherty, "Harriet Jacobs' Narrative Strategies: *Incidents in the Life of a Slave Girl,*" *Southern Literary Journal* 19 (Fall 1986): 79-91.

3 For a discussion of the genre's conventions and Frederick Douglass's achievement within them see: Houston A. Baker, Jr., "Autobiographical Acts and the Voices of the Southern Slave"; and James Olney, " 'I Was Born': Slave Narratives, Their Status as Autobiography and as Literature," in *The Slave's Narrative,* 245-55; 148-75. On canon formation see: Henry Louis Gates, Jr., "Canon Formation, Literary History, and the Afro-American Tradition: From the Seen to the Told," in *Afro-American Literary Study in the 1990s,* ed. Houston A. Baker, Jr. and Patricia Redmond (Chicago: University of Chicago Press, 1989), 14-50; also Nina Baym, "Melodramas of Beset Manhood: How Theories of American Fiction Exclude Women Authors," *American Quarterly* 33 (Summer 1981): 123-39.

4 The themes of moral innocence and experience are, of course, central to many literatures in many cultures. This problem of the fortunate fall, however, was especially important to the fiction of Jacobs's better-known contemporaries, such as Nathaniel Hawthorne and Herman Melville. Hawthorne, in particular, provides an interesting parallel because, although a representative of elite culture, he worked within some of the same codes that Jacobs did, namely evangelical Protestantism and Victorian female ideology. *The Marble Faun* and *The Scarlet Letter* (that painted a sympathetic portrait of another mother who bears an illegitimate child and whose experience forces her to question conventional morality). Significantly, these texts, among the most valued in the Anglo-American canon, are known for their exploration of moral conflict and ambiguity. Like Linda Brent's, their narrative voices are complex.

5 On this history see Jacqueline Jones, *Labor of Love, Labor of Sorrow* (New York: Basic Books, 1985); Eugene D. Genovese, *Roll, Jordan, Roll: The World the Slaves Made* (New York: Vintage, 1972); Herbert C. Gutman, *The Black Family in Slavery and Freedom, 1750-1925* (New York: Random House, 1976).

6 Daniel Scott-Smith, "Family Limitation, Sexual Control, and Domestic Feminism in Victorian America," *Feminist Studies* 1 (Winter/Spring 1973): 40-57; Nancy F. Cott, "Passionlessness: An Interpretation of Victorian Sexual Ideology, 1790-1850," *Signs* 4 (Spring 1978), 219-36.

7 For the evidence behind this judgment see the "Introduction" and annotations to Yellin's edition of *Incidents,* as well as the appended letters by Harriet Jacobs herself. However, the issue has not been completely laid to rest. Yellin recently chaired a roundtable discussion of the issue, "The Ending of a White Novel? The Beginning of a Black Narrative? Authorship, Genre, and *Incidents in the Life of a Slave Girl,*" at the American Studies Association Convention in Toronto, Canada (3 November 1989). During the discussion panelist Alice Deck argued that Lydia Maria Child's editorial advice rendered the authorship of *Incidents* problematic, while fellow panelists Frances Smith Foster and Henry Louise Gates, Jr. affirmed Jacobs's ultimate authorship and authority. Here, as elsewhere, Jacobs deals with the constraints of her cultural context; here, as elsewhere, she exercises her power to choose.

For the relationship between *Incidents* and the classic seduction plot, see John Blassingame, "Critical Sources on Texts," in *The Slave Community: Plantation Life in the Antebellum South,* 2d ed. (New York: Oxford University Press, 1979), 367-82; John F. Bayliss, *Black Slave Narratives* (New York: MacMillan, 1970), 108; Frances Smith Foster, *Witnessing Slavery: The Development of the Ante-Bellum Slave Narrative* (Westport, Conn.: Greenwood Press, 1979), 58-59; Doherty, "Harriet Jacobs' Narrative," 83-91; Smith, *Self-Discovery,* 35-43; Carby, *Reconstructing Womanhood,* 45-48.

8 Jacobs, *Incidents,* 201.

9 Jacobs, *Incidents,* 56.

10 Smith, "Introduction," in *Narrative Authority,* 37.

11 Jacobs, *Incidents,* 55.

12 Jacobs, *Incidents,* 55.

13 Jacobs, *Incidents,* 55-56.

14 Jacobs, *Incidents,* 55. Mary Helen Washington discusses the slave woman's need for control over her sexuality and her life in *Invented Lives,* xxiii-xxiv. See also Smith, *Self-Discovery,* 33.

15 Jacobs, *Incidents,* 56-57. A comparison between the grandmother's response and mores among plantation slaves is revealing. According to historians Jacqueline Jones and Eugene Genovese, although the slave community highly valued marital fidelity, it generally tolerated pregnancy before marriage, even when the child's father was not the young woman's eventual husband. Jones, *Labor of Love,* 34-35; Genovese, *Roll, Jordan, Roll,* 458-75, esp. 465.

16 Jacobs, *Incidents,* 57.

17 For a discussion of Ellen's response to her mother's history, see: Yellin, "Introduction," in *Incidents,* xiv, and Carby, *Reconstructing Womanhood,* 60-61. For a discussion of the silences within this narrative, see Smith, *Self-Discovery,* 42-43.

18 Ruth Bloch, "American Feminine Ideals in Transition: The Rise of the Moral Mother, 1785-1815," *Feminist Studies* 4 (June 1978): 101-26; Elizabeth Ammons, "Stowe's Dream of the Mother Savior: *Uncle Tom's Cabin* and American Women Writers Before the 1920's," in *New Essays on Uncle Tom's Cabin,* ed. Eric J. Sundquist (New York: Cambridge University Press, 1986). Harriet Jacobs's relationship to Stowe, including Stowe's unneighborly treatment of Jacobs and her daughter, is documented in *Incidents,* see particularly, 232-36.

19 Carby, *Reconstructing Womanhood,* 60.

20 Jacobs, *Incidents,* 62.

21 Jacobs, *Incidents,* 37.

22 Jacobs, *Incidents,* 93, 101.

23 Jacobs, *Incidents,* 86-87, 62.

24 Toni Morrison, *Beloved* (New York: Knopf, 1987).

25 Jacobs, *Incidents,* 78, 79.

26 Jacobs, *Incidents,* 142, 189.

27 Jacobs, *Incidents,* 107, 142.

28 See Washington, "Mediations on History," in *Invented Lives, 8;* Fetterley, "Introduction to *Incidents in the Life of a Slave Girl,*" in *Provisions,* 279-85; and Smith, *Self-Discovery,* 27, 33-34.

29 Genovese, *Roll, Jordan, Roll,* 451.

30 Henry Bibb, "Narrative of the Life and Adventures of Henry Bibb, an American Slave," in *Puttin' On Ole Massa: The Significance of Slave Narratives,* ed. Gilbert Osofsky (New York: Harper & Row, 1969).

31 Jacobs, *Incidents,* 91.

32 Jacobs, *Incidents,* 199.

33 Jacobs, *Incidents,* 95.

34 Jacobs, *Incidents,* 92.

35 Jacobs, *Incidents,* 21.

36 Jacobs, *Incidents,* 134.

37 Jacobs, *Incidents,* 158.

38 Jacobs, *Incidents,* 281. According to Yellin, this is one of the few places in which Jacobs fictionalized her history, perhaps to make this moral point.

39 Jacobs, *Incidents,* 72.

40 Jacobs, *Incidents,* 85. Genovese's comments on the role and situation of black mammies are particularly helpful here: "That they loved the white children they raised—hardly astonishing for warm, sensitive, generous women—in no way proves that they loved their own children the less. Rather, their position in the Big House, including their close attention to the white children sometimes at the expense of their own, constituted the firmest protection they could have acquired

for themselves and their immediate families." But, as Genovese points out and as *Incidents* demonstrates, this protection was extremely limited, resting as it did solely on personal influence (Genovese, *Roll, Jordan, Roll,* 356-57).

⁴¹ Carby, *Reconstructing Womanhood,* 57.

⁴² Genovese in *Roll, Jordan, Roll,* 360-61, again illuminates the problems which Martha poses to her granddaughter: "More than any other slave, [the mammy] had absorbed the paternalistic ethos and accepted her place in a system of reciprocal obligations defined from above. In so doing she developed pride, resourcefulness, and a high sense of responsibility to white and black people alike, as conditioned by the prevalent systems of values and notions of duties. . . . Her tragedy lay, not in her abandonment of her own people but in her inability to offer her individual power and beauty to black people on terms they could accept without themselves sliding further into a system of paternalistic dependency."

⁴³ Toni Morrison, *The Bluest Eye* (New York: Washington Square Press, 1970), 87.

⁴⁴ Toni Morrison, *Beloved,* 70.

⁴⁵ Alice Walker, *The Color Purple* (New York: Washington Square Press, 1982), 233.

⁴⁶ Jacobs, *Incidents,* 190, 170.

⁴⁷ Jacobs, *Incidents,* 29.

⁴⁸ Jacobs, *Incidents,* 29.

⁴⁹ Jacobs, *Incidents,* 29.

⁵⁰ See Minrose C. Gwin, "Green-Eyed Monsters of the Slavocracy: Jealous Mistresses in Two Slave Narratives," in *Conjuring,* ed. Pryse and Spillers, 39-52.

⁵¹ Jacobs, *Incidents,* 32.

⁵² Jacobs, *Incidents,* 7.

⁵³ Jacobs, *Incidents,* 8.

⁵⁴ Jacobs, *Incidents,* 194.

⁵⁵ Jacobs, *Incidents,* 199.

⁵⁶ Washington, "Mediations on History," in *Invented Lives,* 11-12.

⁵⁷ Jacobs, *Incidents,* 200.

⁵⁸ Jacobs, *Incidents,* 200.

⁵⁹ Jacobs, *Incidents,* 201. A related pattern emerges in Sherley Anne Williams, *Dessa Rose* (New York: Berkley, 1986). Though more conflicted than the friendship of Linda Brent and Mrs. Bruce, the relationship of the escaped slave Dessa Rose and the white woman Miss Rufel is also rooted in the bonds of motherhood. Miss Rufel, raised by a beloved black nurse, gives her breast in turn to Dessa Rose's newborn child. If the white woman here becomes the mammy, in *Beloved* she becomes the midwife. In Denver's caring for the laboring Sethe we also see an unusual white woman able to resist the temptation of racist power. Like the Good Samaritan, she recognizes the other as her neighbor.

⁶⁰ Ralph Ellison, *The Invisible Man* (New York: Random House, 1947), 439.

Valerie Smith (essay date 1990)

SOURCE: " 'Loopholes of Retreat': Architecture and Ideology in Harriet Jacobs's *Incidents in the Life of a Slave Girl,*" in *Reading Black, Reading Feminist: A Critical Anthology,* edited by Henry Louis Gates, Jr., Meridian, 1990, pp. 212-26.

[*In the following essay, Smith examines the implications of the literal and figurative "structures of confinement" in* Incidents *(such as the attic crawlspace in which Jacobs lived for seven years and which she describes as a "loophole of retreat"). Smith argues that such periods of "apparent enclosure" serve to empower Jacobs to manipulate her destiny.*]

In *Incidents in the Life of a Slave Girl,* the account of her life as a slave and escape to freedom, Harriet Jacobs refers to the crawl space in which she concealed herself for seven years as a "loophole of retreat."¹ The phrase calls attention both to the closeness of her hiding place—three feet high, nine feet long, seven feet wide—and the passivity that even voluntary confinement imposes. For if the combined weight of racism and sexism already placed inexorable restrictions upon her as a black female slave in the antebellum South, her options seem even narrower after she conceals herself in the garret, where just to speak to her loved ones jeopardizes her own and their welfare.

And yet Jacobs's phrase, "the loophole of retreat," possesses an ambiguity of meaning that extends to the literal loophole as well. For if a loophole signifies for Jacobs a place of withdrawal, it signifies in common parlance an avenue of escape. Likewise, the garret, a place of confinement, also—perhaps more importantly—renders the narrator spiritually independent of her master, and makes possible her ultimate escape to freedom. It is thus hardly surprising that Jacobs finds her imprisonment, however uncomfortable, an improvement over "[her] lot as a slave" (117). As her statement implies, she dates her emancipation from the time she entered her loophole, even though she did not cross over into the free states until seven years later. Given the constraints that framed her ordinary life, even the act of choosing her own mode of confinement constituted an exercise of will, an indirect assault against her master's domination.[2]

The plot of Jacobs's narrative, her journey from slavery to freedom, is punctuated by a series of similar structures of confinement, both literal and figurative. Not only does she spend much of her time in tiny rooms (her grandmother's garret, closets in the homes of two friends), but she seems as well to have been hemmed in by the importunities of Dr. Flint, her master:

> My master met me at every turn, reminding me that I belonged to him, and swearing by heaven and earth that he would compel me to submit to him. If I went out for a breath of fresh air, after a day of unwearied toil, his footsteps dogged me. If I knelt by my mother's grave, his dark shadow fell on me even there (27).

Repeatedly, she escapes overwhelming persecutions only by choosing her own space of confinement: the stigma of unwed motherhood over sexual submission to her master; concealment in one friend's home, another friend's closet, and her grandmother's garret over her own and her children's enslavement on a plantation; Jim Crowism and the threat of the Fugitive Slave Law in the North over institutionalized slavery at home. As my discussion of *Incidents* will demonstrate, however, each moment of apparent enclosure actually empowers Jacobs to redirect her own and her children's destiny. To borrow Elaine Showalter's formulation, she inscribes a subversive plot of empowerment beneath the more orthodox, public plot of weakness and vulnerability.[3]

I would suggest further that these metaphoric loopholes provide a figure in terms of which we may read her relation to the literary forms that shape her story. Restricted by the conventions and rhetoric of the slave narrative—a genre that presupposes a range of options more available to men than to women—Jacobs borrows heavily from the rhetoric of the sentimental novel. This latter form imposed upon her restrictions of its own. Yet she seized authority over her literary restraints in much the same way that she seized power in life. From within her ellipses and ironies—linguistic narrow spaces—she expresses the complexity of her experience as a black woman.

It is not surprising that both literal and figurative enclosures proliferate in Jacobs's narrative. As a nineteenth-century black woman, former slave, and writer, she labored under myriad social and literary restrictions that shaped the art she produced. Feminist scholarship has shown that, in general, women's writing in the nineteenth and twentieth centuries has been strongly marked by imagery of confinement—a pattern of imagery that reflects the limited cultural options available to the authors because of their gender and chosen profession. Sandra Gilbert and Susan Gubar, for instance, describe the prodigious restraints imposed historically upon women that led to the recurrence of structures of concealment and evasion in their literature.[4] Not only were they denied access to the professions, civic responsibilities, and higher education, but their secular and religious instruction alike encouraged them from childhood in the "feminine," passive virtues of "submissiveness, modesty, self-lessness."[5] Taken to its extreme, such an idealization of female weakness and self-effacement contributed to what Ann Douglas has called a "domestication of death" characterized by the prevalence in literature of a hagiography of dying women and children, and the predilection in life for dietary, sartorial, and medical practices that led to actual or illusory weakness and illness.[6]

Literary women confronted additional restraints, given the widespread cultural identification of creativity with maleness. As Gubar argues elsewhere, "[our] culture is steeped in . . . myths of male primacy in theological, artistic, and scientific creativity," myths that image women as art objects perhaps, but never as creators.[7] These ideological restraints, made concrete by inhospitable editors, publishers, and reviewers, and by disapproving relatives and friends, have (as Gilbert and Gubar demonstrate) traditionally invaded women's literary undertakings with all manner of tensions. The most obvious sign of the nineteenth-century women writers' anxiety about their vocation (one which, however, might also be attributed to the demands of the literary marketplace) is the frequency with which they published either anonymously or under male pseudonyms. Their sense of engagement in an improper enterprise is evidenced as well by their tendency both to disparage their own accomplishments in autobiographical remarks, and to inscribe deprecations of women's creativity within their fictions. Moreover, they found themselves in a curious relation to the implements of their own craft. The literary conventions they received from genres dominated by male authors perpetuated reductive, destructive images of women that cried out to be revised. Yet the nature of the women writers' socialization precluded their confronting problematic stereotypes directly. Instead, as Patricia Spacks, Carolyn Heilbrun, and Catharine Stimpson, as well as Showalter, and Gilbert and Gubar, have shown, the most significant women writers secreted either within or behind the more accessible content of their work revisions of received plots and assumptions.[8]

Jacobs describes her escape as a progression from one small space to another. Indeed, as if to underscore her helplessness and vulnerability, she indicates that although she ran alone to her first friend's home, she left each of her hiding places only with the aid of someone else. In fact, when she goes to her second and third hiding places, she is entirely at the mercy of her companion, for she is kept ignorant of her destination. Yet each closet, while at one level a prison, is also a station on her journey to freedom. Moreover, from the garret of her seven-year imprisonment, she uses to her advantage all the power of the voyeur—the person who sees but remains herself unseen. When she learns that Sands is about to leave town, she descends from her hiding place and, partly because she catches him unawares, she secures his promise to free her children. In addition, she prevents her own capture not merely by remaining concealed, but more importantly, by embroiling her master in an elaborate plot that deflects his attention. Fearing that he suspects her whereabouts, she writes him letters that she then has postmarked in Boston and New York to send him off in hot pursuit in the wrong direction. Despite her grandmother's trepidation, Jacobs clearly delights in exerting some influence over the man who has tried to control her.

Indeed, I would argue that if the architectural close places are at once prisons and exists, then her relationship to Sands is both as well. She suggests that when she decides to take him as her lover, she's caught between Scylla and Charybdis. Forbidden to marry the freedman she loves, she knows that by becoming Sands's mistress she will compromise her virtue and reputation. But, she remarks, given that her alternative is the master she loathes, she has no choice but to have relations with Sands. As she writes: "It seems less degrading to give one's self, than to submit to compulsion. There is something akin to freedom in having a lover who has no control over you, except that which he gains by kindness and attachment (55)."

One might argue that Jacobs's dilemma encapsulates the slave woman's sexual victimization and vulnerability. But while I do not mean to impugn that reading, I would suggest that her relation to Sands provides her with a measure of power. Out of his consideration for her, he purchases her children and her brother from Flint. William, her brother, eventually escapes from slavery on his own, but Sands frees the children in accordance with their mother's wishes. In a system that allowed the buying and selling of people as if they were animals, Jacobs's influence is clearly minimal. Yet even at the moments when she seems most vulnerable, she manipulates some degree of control.

As the writer of a slave narrative, Jacobs's freedom to reconstruct her life was limited by a genre that suppressed subjective experience in favor of abolitionist polemics. But if slave narrators in general were restricted by the antislavery agenda, Jacobs was doubly bound by the form in which she wrote, for it contained a plot more compatible with received notions of mas-

Dr. James Norcom, in whose household Jacobs lived during her early teenage years.

culinity than with those of womanhood. Like the archetypal hero of the bildungsroman or the adventure tale, the representative hero of the slave narrative moves from the idyllic life of childhood ignorance in the country into a metaphoric wilderness, in this case the recognition of his status as a slave. His struggle for survival requires him to overcome numerous obstacles, but through his own talents (and some Providential assistance), he finds the Promised Land of a responsible social position, a job, and a wife. The slave narrative typically extols the hero's stalwart individuality. And the narratives of male slaves often link the escape to freedom to the act of physically subduing the master. Frederick Douglass writes, for example, that once he had overpowered the man whose job it was to break him, then he knew that he would soon be free.[9]

Like the prototypical bildungsroman plot, the plot of the slave narrative does not adequately accommodate differences in male and female development.[10] Jacobs's tale is not the classic story of the triumph of the individual will; rather, it is more a story of a triumphant self-in-relation.[11] With the notable exception of the narrative of William and Ellen Craft, most of the narratives by men represent the life in slavery and the escape as essentially solitary journeys. This is not to suggest that male slaves were more isolated than their female counterparts, but they were attempting to prove their equality, their manhood, in terms acceptable to their white, middle-class readers.

Under different, equally restrictive injunctions, Jacobs readily acknowledges the support and assistance she received, as the description of her escape makes clear. Not only does she diminish her own role in her escape, but she is quick to recognize the care and generosity of her family in the South and her friends in the North. The opening chapter of her account focuses not on the solitary "I" of so many narratives, but on Jacobs's relatives. And she associates her own desire for freedom with her desire to provide opportunities for her children.

By mythologizing rugged individuality, physical strength, and geographical mobility, the narratives enshrine cultural definitions of masculinity.[12] The plot of the standard narrative may thus be seen not only as the journey from slavery to freedom, but also as the journey from slavehood to manhood. Indeed, that rhetoric explicitly informs some of the best-known and most influential narratives. In the key scene in William Wells Brown's account, for example, a Quaker friend and supporter names the protagonist because, "Since thee has got out of slavery, thee has become a man, and men always have two names."[13] Douglass also explicitly contrasts slavehood and manhood, for he argues that learning to read made him a man, but being beaten made him a slave. Only by overpowering his overseer was he able to be a man—or free—again.

Simply by underscoring her reliance upon other people, Jacobs reveals another way that the story of slavery and escape might be written. But in at least one place in the narrative she makes obvious her problematic relation to the rhetoric she uses. The fourth chapter, "The Slave Who Dared to Feel Like a Man," bears a title reminiscent of one of the most familiar lines from Frederick Douglass's 1845 *Narrative*. Here, Jacobs links three anecdotes that illustrate the fact that independence of mind is incompatible with the demands of life as a slave. She begins with a scene in which her grandmother urges her family to content themselves with their lot as slaves, but her son and grandchildren, however, cannot help resenting her admonitions. The chapter then centers on the story of her Uncle Ben, a slave who retaliates when his master tries to beat him, and who eventually escapes to the North.

The chapter title thus refers explicitly to Ben, the slave who, by defending himself, dared to feel like a man. And yet, it might also refer to the other two stories included in the chapter. In the first, Jacobs's brother William refuses to capitulate to his master's authority. In the second, Jacobs describes her own earliest resolu-

tion to resist her master's advances. Although the situation does not yet require her to fight back, she does say that her young arm never felt half so strong. Like her uncle and brother, she determines to remain unconquered.

The chapter foregrounds Ben's story, then, but it indicates also that his niece and nephew resisted authority. Its title might therefore refer to either of them as well. As Jacobs suggests by indirection, as long as the rhetoric of the genre identifies the black man's freedom and independence of thought with manhood, it lacks a category for describing the achievements of the tenacious black woman.

As L. Maria Child's "Introduction," the author's "Preface," and the numerous asides in the narrative make clear, Jacobs wrote for an audience of northern white women, a readership that by mid-century had grown increasingly leisured, middle-class, and accustomed to the conventions of the novel of domestic sentiment. Under the auspices of Child, herself an editor and writer of sentimental fiction, Jacobs constructed the story of her life in terms that her reader would find familiar. Certainly Jacobs's *Incidents* contains conventional apostrophes that explicitly call attention to the interests she shares with her readers. But as an additional strategy for enlisting their sympathy, she couches her story in the rhetoric and structures of popular fiction.

As Annette Niemtzow has suggested, Jacobs may well have been drawn to the genre because it provided her with a way of talking about her vulnerability to the constant threat of rape.[14] Indeed, the details of the narrator's life that made her experience as a slave more comfortable than most are precisely those that render her story particularly amenable to the conventions and assumptions of the sentimental novel. Slave narratives often begin with an absence, the narrator announcing from the first that he has no idea where or when he was born, or who his parents were. But Jacobs was fortunate enough to have been born into a stable family at once nuclear and extended. Although both of her parents died young, she nurtures vivid, pleasant memories of them. Moreover, she remains close to her grandmother, an emancipated, self-supporting, property-owning black woman, and to her uncles and aunts, until she escapes to the North.

Jacobs's class affiliation, and the fact that she was subjected to relatively minor forms of abuse as a slave, enable her to locate a point of identification both with her readers and with the protagonists of sentimental fiction. Like them, she aspires to chastity and piety as consummate feminine virtues, and hopes that marriage and family would be her earthly reward. Her master, for some reason reluctant to force her to submit sexually, harasses, pleads with, and tries to bribe her into capitulating, in the manner of an importunate suitor like Richardson's seducer. He tells her, for example, that he would be within his right to kill her or have her imprisoned for resisting his advances, but he wishes to make her happy and thus will be lenient towards her. She likens his behavior to that of a jealous lover on the occasion that he becomes violent with her son. And he repeatedly offers to make a lady of her, volunteering to set her up in a cottage of her own where she can raise her children if she will grant him her favors.

By pointing up the similarities between her own story and those plots with which her readers would have been familiar, she could thus expect her readers to identify with her suffering. Moreover, this technique would enable them to appreciate the ways that slavery converts into liabilities the very qualities of virtue and beauty that women were taught to cultivate. This tactic has serious limitations, however. As is always the case when one attempts to universalize a specific political point, Jacobs here trivializes the complexity of her situation when she likens it to a familiar paradigm. Like Richardson's Pamela, Jacobs is servant to her pursuer. But Pamela is free to escape, if she chooses, to the refuge of her parents' home. As Dr. Flint's property, Jacobs's options are severely limited. Moreover, Mr. B., in the terms the novel constructs, can redeem his importunities by marrying Pamela and elevating her and their progeny to his position. No such possibility exists for Jacobs and her master. Indeed, the system of slavery, conflating as it does the categories of property and sexuality, ensures that her posterity will become his material possessions.

For other reasons as well, the genre seems inappropriate for Jacobs's purposes. As the prefatory documents imply, Jacobs's readers are accustomed to novels of propriety and circumlocution. In keeping with cultural injunctions against women's assertiveness and directness in speech, the literature they wrote and read tended to be "exercises in euphemism" that excluded certain subjects from the purview of fiction.[15] Jacobs's purpose, in contrast, is to celebrate her freedom to express what she has undergone, and to engender additional abolitionist support. Child and Jacobs both recognize that Jacobs's story may well violate the rules of decorum in the genre. Their opening statements express the tension between the content of the narrative and the form in which it appears.

Child's introduction performs the function conventional to the slave narrative of establishing the reliability of the accompanying narrative and the narrator's veracity. What is unusual about her introduction, however, is the basis of her authenticating statement; she establishes her faith in Jacobs's story upon the correctness and delicacy of the author's manner:

> The author of the following autobiography is personally known to me, and her conversation and manners inspire me with confidence. During the last

seventeen years, she has lived the greater part of the time with a distinguished family in New York, and has so deported herself as to be highly esteemed by them. This fact is sufficient, without further credentials of her character. I believe those who know her will not be disposed to doubt her veracity, though some incidents in her story are more romantic than fiction (xi).

This paragraph attempts to equate contradictory notions; Child implies not only that Jacobs is both truthful and a model of decorous behavior, but also that her propriety ensures her veracity. Child's assumption is troublesome, since ordinarily, decorousness connotes the opposite of candor—one equates propriety not with openness, but with concealment in the interest of taste.

Indeed, later in her introduction Child seems to recognize that an explicit political imperative may well be completely incompatible with bourgeois notions of propriety. While in the first paragraph she suggests that Jacobs's manner guarantees her veracity, by the last she has begun to ask if questions of delicacy have any place at all in discussions of human injustice. In the last paragraph, for example, she writes, "I am well aware that many will accuse me of indecorum for presenting these pages to the public." Here, rather than equating truthfulness with propriety, she acknowledges somewhat apologetically that candor about her chosen subject may well violate common rules of decorum. From this point, she proceeds tactfully but firmly to dismantle the usefulness of delicacy as a category where subjects of urgency are concerned. She remarks, for instance, that "the experiences of this intelligent and much-injured woman belong to a class which some call delicate subjects, and others indelicate." By pointing to the fact that one might identify Jacobs's story as either delicate or its opposite, she acknowledges the superfluity of this particular label.

In the third and fourth sentences of this paragraph, Child offers her most substantive critique of delicacy, for she suggests that it allows the reader an excuse for insensitivity and self-involvement. The third sentence reads as follows: "This peculiar phase of slavery has generally been kept veiled; but the public ought to be made acquainted with its monstrous features, and I willingly take the responsibility of presenting them with the veil withdrawn." Here, she invokes and reverses the traditional symbol of feminine modesty. A veil (read euphemism) is ordinarily understood to protect the wearer (read reader) from the ravages of a threatening world. Child suggests, however, that a veil (or euphemism) may also work the other way, to conceal the hideous countenance of truth from those who choose ignorance above discomfort.

In the fourth sentence, she pursues further the implication that considerations of decorum may well excuse the reader's self-involvement. She writes: "I do this for the sake of my sisters in bondage, who are suffering wrongs so foul, that our ears are too delicate to listen to them." The structure of this sentence is especially revealing, for it provides a figure for the narcissism of which she implicitly accuses the reader. A sentence that begins, as Child's does, "I do this for the sake of my sisters in bondage, who suffering wrongs so foul that . . ." would ordinarily conclude with some reference to the "sisters" or wrongs they endure. We would thus expect the sentence to read something like, "I do this for the sake of my sisters in bondage, who are suffering wrongs so foul that they must soon take up arms against their master," or "that they no longer believe in a moral order." Instead, Child's sentence rather awkwardly imposes the reader in the precise grammatical location where the slave woman ought to be. This usurpation of linguistic space parallels the potential for narcissism of which Child suggests her reader is guilty.

Child, the editor, the voice of form and convention in the narrative—the one who revised, condensed, and ordered the manuscript and "pruned [its] excrescences"—thus prepares the reader for its straightforwardness. Jacobs, whose life provides the narrative subject, in apparent contradiction of Child calls attention in her preface to her book's silences. Rather conventionally, she admits to concealing the names of places and people to protect those who aided in her escape. And, one might be tempted to say that rather conventionally she apologizes for the inadequacy of her literary skills. But in fact, when Jacobs asserts that her narrative is not fiction, that her adventures may seem incredible but they are nevertheless true, and that only experience can reveal the abomination of slavery, she underscores the inability of her form adequately to capture her experience.

Although Child and Jacobs are aware of the limitations of genre, the account often rings false. Characters speak like literate, middle-class workers out of a romance. Moreover, the form only allows Jacobs to talk about her sexual experiences when they are the result of her victimization. She becomes curiously silent about the fact that her relations with Sands continue even after Flint seems no longer a threat.

I would argue that its ideological assumptions are the most serious problem the form presents. Jacobs invokes a plot initiated by Richardson's *Pamela* and recapitulated in nineteenth-century American sentimental novels. In this plot, a persistent male of elevated social rank seeks to seduce a woman of a lower class. Through her resistance and piety, however, she educates her would-be seducer into an awareness of his own depravity and his capacity for true honorable love. In the manner of *Pamela*'s Mr. B., the reformed villain rewards the heroine's virtue by marrying her.

As is the case with popular literature generally, this paradigm affirms the dominant ideology, in this instance the power of patriarchy. As Tania Modleski and Janice Radway have shown, the seduction plot typically encodes pursuit or harassment as love, allowing the protagonist and reader alike to interpret the male's abusiveness as a sign of his inability to express his profound love for the heroine.[16] The problem is one that Ann Douglas attributes to sentimentalism as a mode of discourse, one that never challenges fundamental assumptions and structures:

> Sentimentalism is a complex phenomenon. It asserts that the values a society's activity denies are precisely the ones it cherishes; it attempts to deal with the phenomenon of cultural bifurcation by the manipulation of nostalgia. Sentimentalism provides a way to protest a power to which one has already in part capitulated.[17]

Capitulation is certainly not what Jacobs intends, especially since the patriarchy is, for her, synonymous with slavocracy. But to invoke that plot is, I would suggest, to invoke the clusters of associations and assumptions that surround it.

As Jacobs exercised authority over the limits of the male narrative, however, she triumphs as well over the limits of the sentimental novel, a genre more suited to the experience of her white, middle-class reader than it was to her own. From at least three narrative spaces, analogs to the garret in which she concealed herself, she displays her power over the forms at her disposal.

In the much-quoted line from the last paragraph of her account, she writes: "Reader, my story ends with freedom, not in the usual way, with marriage (207)." In this sentence, she calls attention to the space between the traditional happy ending of the novel of domestic sentiment and the ending of her story. She acknowledges that however much her story may resemble superficially the story of the sentimental heroine, as a black woman she plays for different stakes; marriage is not the ultimate reward she seeks.

Another gap occurs at the point when she announces her second pregnancy. She describes her initial involvement with Sands as a conundrum. The brutality of neighboring masters, the indifference of the legal system, and her own master's harassment force her to take a white man as her lover. Both in the way she leads up to this revelation, and in the explicit apostrophes to the reader, she presents it as a situation in which she has no choice. Her explanation for taking Sands as her lover is accompanied by the appropriate regret and chagrin, and then followed by two general chapters about slave religion and the local response to the Nat Turner rebellion. When we return to Jacobs's story, she remarks that Flint's harassment persists, and then announces her second pregnancy by saying simply, "When Dr. Flint learned that I was again to be a mother, he was exasperated beyond measure (79)." Her continued relations with Sands and her own response to her second pregnancy are submerged in the subtext of the two previous chapters and in the space between paragraphs. By consigning to the narrative silences those aspects of her own sexuality for which the genre does not allow, Jacobs points to an inadequacy in the form.

The third such gap occurs a bit later, just before she leaves the plantation. Her master's great-aunt, Miss Fanny, a kind-hearted, elderly woman who is a great favorite with Jacobs's grandmother, comes to visit. Jacobs is clearly fond of this woman, but as she tells the story she admits that she resents the old woman's attempts to sentimentalize her situation. As Jacobs tells it, Miss Fanny remarks at one point that she "wished that I and all my grandmother's family were at rest in our graves, for not until then should she feel any peace about us (91)." Jacobs then reflects privately that "The good old soul did not dream that I was planning to bestow peace upon her, with regard to myself and my children; not by death, but by securing our freedom." Here, Jacobs resists becoming the object of someone else's sentimentality, and calls attention to the inappropriateness of this response. Although she certainly draws on the conventions of sentimentalism when they suit her purposes, she is also capable of replacing the self-indulgent mythification of death with the more practical solution of freedom.

The work of Barbara Smith, Paula Giddings, Angela Davis, and Elizabeth Spelman has shown that the complex experience of the black woman has eluded analyses and theories that focus on any one of the variables of race, class, and gender alone.[18] As Barbara Smith has remarked, the effect of the multiple oppression of race, class, and gender is not merely arithmetic. That is, one cannot say only that in addition to racism, black women have had to confront the problem of sexism. Rather, we must recognize that issues of class and race alter one's experience of gender, just as gender alters one's experience of class and race. Whatever the limitations of her narrative, Jacobs anticipates these recent developments in class, race, and gender analysis. Her account indicates that the story of a black woman does not emerge from the superimposition of a slave narrative on a sentimental novel. Rather, in the ironies and silences and spaces of her book, she makes not-quite-adequate forms more truly her own.

Notes

[1] Linda Brent [Harriet Jacobs], *Incidents in the Life of a Slave Girl* (New York: Harcourt Brace Jovanovich, 1973), 117. Subsequent references will be to this edition.

[2] As I completed revisions of this discussion, I read Houston Baker's *Blues, Ideology, and Afro-American Literature* (Chicago: University of Chicago Press, 1984). He too considers the centrality of this image to Jacobs's account, but he focuses on Jacobs's ability to transform the economics of her oppression, while I concentrate on her use of received literary conventions.

[3] Elaine Showalter, "Review Essay," *Signs* 1 (1975), 435.

[4] Sandra M. Gilbert and Susan Gubar, *The Madwoman in the Attic* (New Haven: Yale University Press, 1979). 3-104 *passim.*

[5] Ibid., 23.

[6] Ann Douglas, *The Feminization of American Culture* (New York: Avon Books, 1977), 240-73 *passim.*

[7] Susan Gubar, " 'The Blank Page' and the Issues of Female Creativity," in Elizabeth Abel, ed., *Writing and Sexual Difference* (Chicago: University of Chicago Press, 1982), 74.

[8] See Showalter, Gilbert and Gubar, *op.cit.* See also Patricia Meyer Spacks, *The Female Imagination* (New York: Knopf, 1975), 317, and Carolyn Heilbrun and Catharine Stimpson, "Theories of Feminist Criticism: A Dialogue," in Josephine Donovan, ed., *Feminist Literary Criticism* (Lexington: University Press of Kentucky, 1975), 62.

[9] Frederick Douglass, *Narrative of the Life of Frederick Douglass, An American Slave, Written by Himself* (Cambridge: Harvard University Press, 1973), 104-105.

[10] See Elizabeth Abel, Marianne Hirsch, and Elizabeth Langland, eds., *The Voyage In: Fictions of Female Development* (University Press of New England, 1983), 3-19.

[11] I draw here on the vocabulary of recent feminist psychoanalytic theory that revises traditional accounts of female psychosexual development. See Jean Baker Miller, *Toward A New Psychology of Women* (Boston: Beacon Press, 1976); Nancy Chodorow, *The Reproduction of Mothering: Psychoanalysis and the Sociology of Gender* (Berkeley: University of California Press, 1978); Carol Gilligan, *In a Different Voice* (Cambridge: Harvard University Press, 1982).

[12] I acknowledge here my gratitude to Mary Helen Washington for helping me to recognize this characteristic of the narratives.

[13] William Wells Brown, *Narrative of William W. Brown* (Boston: The Anti-Slavery Office, 1847; New York: Arno Press, 1968), 105.

[14] Annette Niemtzow, "The Problematic of Self in Autobiography: The Example of the Slave Narrative," in *The Art of the Slave Narrative: Original Essays in Criticism and Theory*, ed. John Sekora and Darwin T. Turner (Macomb: Western Illinois University Press, 1982), 105-106.

[15] See Douglas, *op. cit*, 72.

[16] See Tania Modleski, *Loving With a Vengeance: Mass-Produced Fantasies for Women* (New York: Archon Books, 1982), 17; Janice Radway, *Reading the Romance: Women, Patriarchy, and Popular Literature* (Chapel Hill: University of North Carolina Press, 1984), 75.

[17] See Douglas, *op. cit.,* 12.

[18] See Barbara Smith, "Notes For Yet Another Paper on Black Feminism, Or Will the Real Enemy Please Stand Up," *Conditions 5*, 123-132.; Paula Giddings, *When And Where I Enter: The Impact of Black Women on Race and Sex in America* (New York: William Morrow and Company, 1984); Angela Davis, *Women, Race, and Class* (New York: Vintage Books, 1983); Elizabeth V. Spelman, "Theories of Race and Gender: The Erasure of Black Women," *Quest* 5 (1979), 36-62.

Bruce Mills (essay date 1992)

SOURCE: "Lydia Maria Child and the Endings to Harriet Jacobs's *Incidents in the Life of a Slave Girl*," in *American Literature*, Vol. 64, No. 2, June, 1992, pp. 255-72

[*In the essay that follows, Mills studies the influence of Lydia Maria Child (abolitionist and editor of* Incidents*) on Jacobs's writing and on the book's structure and content.*]

In a letter to Harriet Jacobs written prior to the publication of *Incidents in the Life of a Slave Girl*, Lydia Maria Child suggested a significant revision: "I think the last Chapter, about John Brown, had better be omitted. It does not naturally come into your story, and the M.S. is already too long. Nothing can be so appropriate to end with, as the death of your grandmother."[1] Child's advice is especially intriguing in light of her own involvement in the John Brown affair; just over a week after his capture on 18 October 1859, Child sent him a letter volunteering her aid: "I long to nurse you, to speak to you sisterly words of sympathy and consolation" (*CC*, 41/1123). Her abolitionist pamphlet entitled *Correspondence between Lydia Maria Child and Governor Wise and Mrs. Mason, of Virginia*, published in 1860, dealt sympathetically with John Brown and helped marshal Northern sentiment against the South immediately before the Civil War. Her recommendation to Jacobs, then, to delete the material on Brown initially seems surprising. After all, in her role as editor and promoter of the narrative Child certainly would have recognized that she had another unique opportunity to affect readers' perceptions of the Brown affair. Her concerns, however, seem more structural than political: she encourages Jacobs to omit the material because it does not "naturally" fit the story and because it is not as "appropriate" a conclusion as the grandmother's death. At the same time, it appears that Child felt something more than narrative unity was to be gained by turning readers' attention to the grandmother rather than to John Brown.

Child's letter raises important questions about her role in editing and shaping *Incidents.* Jean Fagan Yellin has summarized the lingering controversy over Child's involvement and has shown that she certainly did not ghost write Jacobs's narrative or transcribe it from conversations, but her editorial guidance nonetheless significantly affected the narrative's final shape (*Incidents,* xxii-xxv).[2] In addition to citing Child's advice regarding the ending, Yellin quotes a British reviewer who, having read Jacobs's story before its publication, notes that "the manuscript and the printed volume are substantially the same; whilst the narrative has been condensed and rendered more fluent and compact by the friendly assistance of Mrs. Child" (*Incidents,* xxii). Quite clearly, Child's editorial lens—a lens that made her see the John Brown chapter as an unnatural resolution—had a consequential effect upon the structure of the slave narrative.

I want to investigate here the ways in which Child's particular abolitionist views rendered Jacobs's story "more fluent and compact." Her advice to Jacobs underscores her conviction that a female slave narrative would be most forceful if it invoked the sanctity of motherhood. In choosing to emphasize the importance of the grandmother-granddaughter relationship throughout the text, both author and editor affirmed the role of domestic values in resolving the national crisis. In contrast to her own practice in the *Correspondence* pamphlet, Child indicated to Jacobs that a *story* about the incidents in the life of a slave girl would promote non-violent reform more effectively by appealing to eternal values than to passions engendered by contemporary events.

. . . . .

A look at the ending Child asked Jacobs to keep begins to reveal the cultural values that guided the sequencing of events and thematic structure.[3] Opening and closing the final chapter "Free at Last" are nostalgic references to the narrator's "good old grandmother." In fact, the section begins with part of a letter Linda Brent—Jacobs's pseudonym and the narrator in *Incidents*—receives from her grandmother, sometimes called Aunt Marthy by white Southern neighbors. This preoccupation with the grandmother is significant since the final chapter does not actually focus upon her. Instead, the drama concerns attempts by Brent's supposed master to capture her and, under the provisions of the Fugitive Slave Law, return her and her children to the South. Brent's employer, Mrs. Bruce, ultimately buys her freedom (199-200).

The final words of the chapter shift the emphasis away from Brent's abhorrence of the Fugitive Slave Law and her indignation at having her freedom purchased. Instead, we read of her hopes for a secure home and her memories of her grandmother. "The dream of my life," Jacobs laments, "is not yet realized. I do not sit with my children in a home of my own" (201). Jacobs's concluding paragraph encourages her readers to think of the redeeming power of maternal love: "It has been painful to me, in many ways, to recall the dreary years I passed in bondage. I would gladly forget them if I could. Yet the retrospection is not altogether without solace; for with those gloomy recollections come tender memories of my good old grandmother, like light, fleecy clouds floating over a dark and troubled sea" (201). The ending literally directs eyes heavenward; the grandmother figure seems a vision that allows Brent to transcend the worldly sufferings that she frames as increasingly distant occurrences. While the denouement is not marriage and thus, as Brent announces, does not resolve a female narrative "in the usual way," the reflections upon the potential joys of domestic life and upon her grandmother calm more than agitate.

This ending associates Christian values of self-sacrifice with female actions. To have concluded with a consideration of John Brown—even if his violent actions had been condemned—would not have done so. Rather than diverting readers' attention at the last moment away from these higher values, Child apparently encouraged Jacobs to embed her reactions to Brown's rebellion in an earlier chapter on Nat Turner's uprising. In the same letter that advised Jacobs to drop the Brown chapter, Child noted that her "object in writing at this time is to ask you to write what you can recollect of the outrages committed on the colored people, in Nat Turner's time. You say the reader would not believe what you saw 'inflicted on men, women, and children, without the slightest ground of suspicion against them' " (244). Child then asks questions concerning the aftermath of Turner's uprising, questions that Jacobs evidently used to develop the much earlier chapter "Fear of Insurrection." This chapter offered Jacobs the opportunity to comment upon Brown's rebellion obliquely and in a place that would not disrupt so dramatically the "natural" order of the story. Knowing that the events at Harper's Ferry would no doubt be in readers' minds, Jacobs counters negative reactions to them by detailing the way Southern society sanctions cruelty and lawlessness. The moral of Jacobs's chapter seems to be that while Turner's (and implicitly

Brown's) violence was isolated and transitory, the inhumanity in the South was institutional and ongoing.

Child must have feared that concluding *Incidents* with reflections on John Brown would have linked the narrative to precisely what would have most threatened Northern readers—the prospect of violence and disunion. Her recommendation to end with the original conclusion can be understood as an attempt to realign central elements of the story with other woman-centered antislavery narratives—both fictional and nonfictional—and thus to link the life of Linda Brent to immediate historical events only obliquely.[4]

Child's suggestion for the final chapter also works effectively because it brings the narrative full circle, back to the grandmother's role as a model for domestic values, a role first established in the opening chapters. In the first two the grandmother emerges as the moral center, the person most important to Linda Brent's rearing and protection. We discover that the grandmother has also suffered as a result of the machinations of Brent's antagonist Dr. Flint. Upon the death of his mother-in-law, Flint decides to sell Aunt Marthy instead of manumitting her. Because she serves the economic interests of the community by supplying families with her famous crackers and preserves, and because it is widely known that her mistress had intended to free her, Flint tries to convince the grandmother to submit to a private sale so that he may avoid public ridicule. She sees through his scheme and, demonstrating a defiance that Brent later shows in rejecting Flint's sexual advances, chooses to be sold on the auction block. In the end, her mistress's sister buys her and sets her free (11-12). Like Stowe's scenes with the senator's wife in *Uncle Tom's Cabin* and the scenes with Mrs. Bruce later in *Incidents,* Jacobs's early rendering of the grandmother illustrates that, although dependent on the arbitrary goodwill of slaveholders, women have a unique ability to influence and occasionally alter unchristian affairs.

But Aunt Marthy is not the only female slave upon the auction block. The experience of Brent's grandmother prefaces the story of a slave who bears Flint's child and who is sold off for the "crime" of making known her master's paternity. Clearly, the history of Aunt Marthy and the tale of her unnamed "sister" prepare the reader for Linda Brent's own ordeal. Before readers learn of Brent's sexual harassment, they know through these stories that to be a slave woman is to suffer the continual tearing asunder of mother and child.

Brent's relations with the white slaveholder Mr. Sands magnify the importance of the grandmother's emblematic roles.[5] Since Brent has two children by Sands, she cannot expect the sympathy readers reserved for the chaste heroines of women's fiction. Writing to Amy Post about the possibility of composing her life-story,

Jacobs privately agonizes over making public a personal history that violates sexual standards: "dear Amy if it was the life of a Heroine with no degradation associated with it far better to have been one of the starving poor of Ireland whose bones had to bleach on the highways than to have been a slave with the curse of slavery stamped upon yourself and Children . . ." (*Incidents,* 232). Because of the narrator/protagonist's "degraded" past, the grandmother must stand as the primary exemplar of and mediator for redemptive feminine virtue.[6]

The grandmother initially rebukes her granddaughter, but in forgiving Brent she enacts an understanding and compassion readers are meant to share. Both women's sufferings and their efforts to gain their children's freedom lead to hardship. In their striving, grandmother and granddaughter elevate the importance of domestic virtues and the role of women in confronting slavery. Although Brent's "sass"[7] affirms her independence and willfulness (and thus renders her a somewhat unconventional character), the grandmother's example positions the virtue of sacrifice as central to the resolution.

The opening and closing "grandmother" scenes, then, announce Martha's central role throughout the narrative. It is the grandmother who constantly asserts the importance of Brent's duty as a mother and thus champions the maternal power which gives Brent the strength to endure. When Martha hears that Linda is planning an escape, she reminds her that her first duty is to her children. Having been sent to Flint's plantation, Brent tries to convince her grandmother that if she could escape Mr. Sands could be persuaded to secure her children's freedom. But Martha will not be convinced: "Ah, my child, . . . don't trust too much to him. Stand by your own children, and suffer with them till death. Nobody respects a mother who forsakes her children; and if you leave them, you will never have a happy moment" (91). Martha's plea sets the condition for a proper run to freedom: in the end mother and children must reunite.

The grandmother's centrality is dramatized most powerfully during the period of Linda Brent's seven-year confinement in her grandmother's garret. Readers have consistently questioned the veracity of this episode, perhaps losing sight of the fact that Martha is once again providing a protective womb for Linda's birth to freedom. During this time, the grandmother and granddaughter both nurture Brent's son and daughter and arrange for their freedom. Brent's location also gives her an almost omniscient (*god*mother) position in the household and community. She hears and witnesses events which go unnoticed by others. Two significant incidents witnessed in her eavesdropping involve women—one a mother who despairs over the sale of her child and the other a woman who drowns herself to escape a whipping (121-22). In the end, it is the

grandmother who connects Brent to day-to-day life and with whom she discusses the children. During this seven-year imprisonment, Martha literally saves Brent from Flint's assaults and sustains her progress toward freedom.

. . . . .

In order to come to an even sharper sense of what Child and Jacobs intended in shaping *Incidents,* it is instructive to consider Child's own writing on John Brown. Seemingly contravening her own editorial advice to Jacobs, Child used the shocking incidents of Harper's Ferry as an occasion to advance abolitionist doctrine first in newspapers and then in pamphlets. Her own directness contrasts with the indirection she encouraged in *Incidents.*

On 26 October 1859, less than two weeks after Harper's Ferry, Child wrote Brown asking that she be allowed to help in his time of need. "I think of you night and day," she says, "bleeding in prison, surrounded by hostile faces, sustained only by trust in God and your own strong heart."[8] Child also sent a letter to Governor Henry A. Wise of Virginia, appealing to his "chivalrous sentiments" and urging him not to veto her "mission of humanity" (3).[9] Wise evidently allowed Child's letter and his response to it to become public. According to Child, a correspondent for the *New York Herald* got hold of her letter and published it on 12 November 1859 in Horace Greeley's *New York Tribune* (CC, 41/1131).[10] Not surprisingly, Southerners were outraged by her request to nurse Brown. Margaretta Mason, the wife of Senator James M. Mason, circulated one of the most notable replies in Virginia newspapers. (Senator Mason was infamous among abolitionists for having authored the 1850 Fugitive Slave Law, as well as for leading the questioning of Brown following his capture.) Child, having endured the unauthorized release of her letter and abuse from slaveholders, decided to embrace the controversy and turn Brown's actions into the stuff of martyrdom. By the summer and fall of 1860, the period of Child's editorial association with Jacobs, her role in the Brown affair had become well-known. First printed in the *Tribune* and *The Liberator,* her correspondence with Wise, Brown, and Mason was eventually published by the American Anti-Slavery Society in a pamphlet entitled *Correspondence between Lydia Maria Child and Governor Wise and Mrs. Mason, of Virginia.* The pamphlet sold over three hundred thousand copies and gained for Child the largest readership of her career (SL, 332-33).

Child did not condone John Brown's methods, as she made clear in all her letters. To Wise she announced that she believed in "peace principles" and could not sympathize with the use of violent means to "advance the cause of freedom" (*Correspondence,* 14). Not surprisingly, however, Wise used his response to forward, in Child's words, "lessons about the effects of abolition doctrines" (*CC*, 41/1131). Admitting that he did not have the right to stop Child's trip, he nonetheless questioned her judgment:

> I could not permit an insult even to woman in her walk of charity among us, though it be to one who whetted knives of butchery for our mothers, sisters, daughters and babes. We have no sympathy with your sentiments of sympathy with Brown, and are surprised that you were "taken by surprise when news came of Capt. Brown's recent attempt." His attempt was a natural consequence of your sympathy, and the errors of that sympathy ought to make you doubt its virtue from the effect on his conduct. (*Correspondence*, 5).

Wise's emphasis upon misdirected sympathy challenged more than abolitionist teachings. His words suggested that women's charity and sympathy could overreach their desired aim, that in fact such meddling in national affairs would ultimately be destructive. His subtle (and not-so-subtle) censure was therefore not without its cultural weight. Wise's rhetoric signaled an attempt to silence women's efforts to articulate the force of domestic values. For Wise, the inevitable outcome of bluestocking ideas was the real violence of misguided men.

Like Wise, Margaretta Mason undercut Child in ways the culture would have found persuasive, that is, with images of a domestic apocalypse: "*You* would soothe with sisterly and motherly care the hoary-headed murderer of Harper's Ferry! A man whose aim and intention was to incite the horrors of a servile war—to condemn women of your own race, ere death closed their eyes on their sufferings from violence and outrage, to see their husbands and fathers murdered, their children butchered, the ground strewed with the brains of their babes" (*Correspondence*, 16). Reflecting the common view that women abolitionists showed more compassion to the distant Negro than to their own poor, Mason offered a litany of rhetorical questions meant to condemn Child and her kind:

> *Do you* soften the pangs of maternity in those around you by all the care and comfort you can give? . . . Do *you* ever sit up until the "wee hours" to complete a dress for a motherless child, that she might appear on Christmas day in a new one, along with her more fortunate companions? *We* do these and more for our servants, and why? Because we endeavor *to do our duty in that state of life it has pleased God to place us.* (*Correspondence*, 17)

Child was not only forced to respond to another Southern explanation of proper "sympathy" but also called upon to defend Northern women's interpretation of their maternal role. In response to the "personal questions" Mason asked her, Child replied in the name of "all the

women of New England" and described the ways she and others attended to their domestic duties, adding: "I have never known an instance where the 'pangs of maternity' did not meet with requisite assistance; and here at the North, after we have helped the mothers, *we do not sell the babies*" (*Correspondence*, 26).

Throughout her letter to Mason, Child redirected her reader's attentions from images of white suffering to the realities of slave life. One of her most powerful condemnations of slavery was her direct assertion that women slaves served as breeding stock as well as objects of their masters' licentiousness. In other words, Margaretta Mason backed a system that dehumanized African Americans and through its internal slave trade destroyed the bond between mother and child as well as between white and black mothers. "The universal rule of the slave State," Child wrote, "is that 'the child follows the condition of its *mother*' " (*Correspondence*, 20). For Child and other abolitionists, this was an "index" to the way in which the "patriarchal institution" violated moral codes concerning marriage by exploiting laws and customs rendering "licentiousness a *profitable* vice" (*Correspondence*, 20). Jacobs would later agree in terms that had become common among abolitionists: " . . . for slaveholders have been cunning enough to enact that 'the child shall follow the condition of the *mother*,' not of the *father;* thus taking care that licentiousness shall not interfere with avarice" (***Incidents***, 76). Child's pamphlet argued that it was not Brown but the institution of slavery which threatened women and children and thus the domestic welfare of the nation.

. . . . .

For Child and Jacobs, the long history of defiled womanhood accounted for more than the isolated incidents at Harper's Ferry; however, because people like Wise and Mason effectively used images of violated women and murdered children to rouse fears of insurrection, abolitionist writers who did not promote violent resolution of the slavery question faced a dilemma. How could their works calm readers yet still persuade them to be morally outraged? How could the wrongs suffered by slaves be framed in a manner which alleviated fears, redirected sympathies, and encouraged an active but nonviolent response? Garrisonian abolitionists like Child had always struggled with such questions. By the time Jacobs solicited Child's help, however, the events of Harper's Ferry had heightened the importance of finding answers.

Jacob's need for Child was directly related to the publishers' initial concern with how readers would receive her slave narrative. Thayer and Eldridge directed Jacobs to Child because they felt the need for an introduction by "some one known to the public—to effect the sale of the Book" (***Incidents***, 246-47). Jacobs approached the well-known Child with some trepidation. This apprehension can be understood in light of Jacobs's earlier rebuff from another literary lion, Harriet Beecher Stowe.[11] The correspondence between Jacobs and Child, however, shows that the two understood each other quite well. "Mrs C is like your self a whole souled Woman—" Jacobs wrote to Amy Post—"we soon found the way to each others heart" (*Incidents,* 247). Child repeatedly spoke of Jacobs as a "highly intelligent and worthy colored woman" (*CC,* 47/1295).[12]

Child's letters to her acquaintances also indicate that Jacobs must have agreed to enlarge Child's role from author of an introduction to editor of her manuscript. On 8 August 1860, not long after she had met with Jacobs, Child described her role to Lucy Osgood:

> I also have been very busy for an interesting Fugitive Slave, who wanted advi[c]e and assistance about her Memoirs. I was desirous to aid her, because she tells her story in a very intelligent, spirited manner, and the details seem to me well calculated to advance the cause I have so deeply at heart. It involves the reading of a good many M.S. pages, and the writing of a good many; but to help the slave is about all my life is good for now. (*CC,* 46/1241)

At first, Child's admission that she is "writing a good many" pages seems to suggest that she might be composing part of the narrative. However, in her letter to Jacobs in the same week—the letter which contains her advice concerning the John Brown chapter—Child defined the nature of this writing: " . . . I am copying a great deal of [the manuscript], for the purpose of transposing sentences and pages, so as to bring the story into continuous *order,* and the remarks into *appropriate* places" (*Incidents,* 244). Within a month of its publication, Child further detailed her role when she told Lucy Searle that "I put the savage cruelties into one chapter, entitled 'Neighboring Planters,' in order that those who shrink from 'supping upon horrors,' might omit them, without interrupting the thread of the story. . . . I abridged, and struck out superfluous words sometimes; but I don't think I *altered* fifty words in the whole volume" (*CC,* 47/1282).

In promoting the book to figures such as John Greenleaf Whittier and Daniel Ricketson, Child echoed her words to Osgood, affirming that the book was "calculated to do great good to the Anti-Slavery cause" (*CC,* 47/1296, 47/1295). For Child, the sense of this "good" had been shaped by her belief in Garrisonian and Transcendental principles. She felt that the spiritual change necessary for lasting social change could be most effectively fostered through reform literature. This view emerged in part from her long association with William Lloyd Garrison (an association which preceded the initial publication of *The Liberator* on 1 January 1831) and in part from her connections with leading

Transcendentalists such as her brother Convers Francis, Margaret Fuller, and Ralph Waldo Emerson. Writing to William Lloyd Garrison and *The Liberator* in December 1859, Child tried to recast the actions of the "brave old martyr" Brown in terms consistent with the Garrisonian view that slavery was primarily a moral issue:

> Instead of blaming [Brown] for carrying out his own convictions by means we cannot sanction, it would be more profitable for us to inquire of ourselves whether we, who believe in a "more excellent way," have carried our convictions into practice, as faithfully as he did *his. We* believe in *moral influence* as a cure for the diseases of society. Have we exerted it as constantly and as strenuously as we ought against the giant wrong, that is making wreck of all the free institutions our fathers handed down to us as a sacred legacy? (*SL,* 336)

In Brown, as in Jacobs, Child saw uncompromising principle and ultimate self-sacrifice. The Brown that Child constructed became a man cleansed of violence and redeemed by an "honest heart" (*SL,* 337). Because citizens had failed in their duty to promote the "more excellent way," Child warned, "the end cometh by violence; because come it *must*" (*SL,* 337). But, though she may have come to see the inevitability of disunion and perhaps even of destructive insurrection, she never encouraged armed rebellion in her own writing and abolitionist work.

In contrast to the tale of Brown's actions at Harper's Ferry, Jacobs's narrative offered a nonviolent, matrilineal story of self-sacrifice and moral rebirth. Her story shows that the evil of slavery can be resolved by clinging to maternal values as steadfastly as Garrisonians adhered to their principles. As evidenced by the final shape of *Incidents,* both Child and Jacobs came to see that stressing domestic values would more powerfully promote Northern sympathy for the Linda Brents, encourage peace principles, and ease fears of racial conflict. Unlike Wise, both felt that such sympathy served the common good. *Incidents,* then, fit well within the continuum of Garrisonian abolitionism and served the cause well in the midst of the reaction to John Brown.

One later work by Child, *The Freedmen's Book,* provides additional insight into her editorial work with Jacobs's narrative and into the particular ideals she might have hoped *Incidents* would inculcate. *The Freedmen's Book* was published by Ticknor and Fields in 1865 and distributed to free blacks at Child's expense. This anthology contains biographies of famous black men and women—many written by Child herself—as well as poems, stories, and essays by black authors and other white abolitionists.[13] In a section entitled "The Good Grandmother," Child excerpted a portion of Jacobs's narrative. Significantly, only the descriptions of the grandmother which begin and end the book were included. Thus, the frame for Jacobs's life-story becomes another mini-narrative for freed slaves. In an editor's note following the selection, Child assures the reader that Jacobs's story is true and that the writer is an "esteemed friend"; she goes on to explain that she has included "this portion of her story here to illustrate the power of character over circumstances." In addition, she quotes part of a letter she had received from Jacobs: "I have lived to hear the Proclamation of Freedom for my suffering people. All my wrongs are forgiven. I am more than repaid for all I have endured. Glory to God in the highest!" (*The Freedmen's Book,* 218). As in the ending to *Incidents,* Child has Jacobs again direct the reader heavenward: the higher values will serve blacks in their search for equality just as they have served them in their quest for freedom.

Through such stories as "The Good Grandmother," *The Freedmen's Book* encouraged freed blacks to hope. This reassuring message guided the selection and tone of the entire text. In her closing "Advice from an Old Friend," Child made these intentions clear and, echoing her earlier postscript to "The Good Grandmother," explained that "I have made this book to encourage you to exertion by examples of what colored people are capable of doing. Such men and women as Toussaint l'Ouverture, Benjamin Banneker, Phillis Wheatley, Frederick Douglass, and William and Ellen Crafts, prove that the power of *character* can overcome all external disadvantages, even that most crushing of all advantages, Slavery" (*The Freedmen's Book,* 269). Child's words here expand upon sentiments expressed in a letter she received from Harriet Jacobs on 26 March 1864—a letter printed less than a month later in the *National Anti-Slavery Standard.* Observing the chaotic homes of newly-freed slaves, Jacobs lamented that "there was nothing about them to indicate the presence of a wifely wife, or a motherly mother. . . . The consciousness of working for themselves, and of having a character to gain, will inspire them with energy and enterprise, and a higher civilization will gradually come" (*CC,* 58/1552).

. . . . .

Child's public and private correspondence and her editorial work with *The Freedmen's Book* and *Incidents* show that literary reformers and abolitionists consciously used matriarchal plottings and emblems to exercise moral suasion. And when in these plottings the values of purity and sacrifice were violated, writers and editors were exploiting cultural expectations regarding women's domestic role. Having written fiction and nonfiction for the abolitionist cause since the late 1820s, Child knew the trade of literary reform. She had seen antislavery literature and its inevitable theme of violated domestic values germinate in colonization journals and blossom in antislavery pamphlets and narratives.[14]

Starting in *The African Repository,* one of the first and best-known colonization magazines, women of the North argued that mothers understood the immorality of slavery on an instinctual level and that slavery attacked the sanctity of the all-important calling to give birth to, protect, and educate the republic's children. In her address to the Hartford Female African Society on 5 July 1830, secretary Lydia Sigourney asserted that

> [s]ince the domestic sphere is our allotted province, it is natural that we should be deeply susceptible to whatever disturbs its tranquility, or destroys its honour. Has any form of evil been tolerated among mankind, which so effectually invaded its bounds, sundered its ties, wrecked its cherished joys, and obliterated its dearest hopes, as the Slave Trade?— Parents flying from their desolated abodes, children torn from arms unable to protect them, villages devoted to the flames . . . furnish combinations of misery, which, in this country of freedom and happiness, it is difficult to bring home to our hearts.[15]

To make her point more compelling, Sigourney appealed to "female sympathy" (153). She asked the mother who teaches "the little being whom she lulls upon her bosom, to breathe, ere he sinks in his cradle-slumbers, a prayer for the long-benighted, much-enduring Africa" (154).

Women abolitionists increasingly employed such powerful rhetoric in their appeals for immediate emancipation. Angelina Grimké laced *An Appeal to the Women of the Nominally Free States* (1837) with allusions to indignities suffered by women slaves and with explanations as to why and how women must fight for freedom. Central to her argument is the assumption that an attack upon the moral character of slavery and of slaveholders would most effectively sway public sentiment: "Have Northern women, then, nothing to do with slavery, when its demoralizing influence is polluting their domestic circles and blasting the fair characters of *their* sons and brothers?"[16] When Child wrote her historical novel *Philothea* (1836) and Stowe composed *Uncle Tom's Cabin,* both capitalized on their culture's belief that threats to the home were not a private concern but a national one. When the domestic sphere no longer provided a safe haven in which to raise children or a calm retreat from the harsh realities of worldly affairs, then the whole nation suffered. Only through domestic sympathies embodied in and engendered by such figures as Child's Transcendental heroine Philothea or Stowe's Eliza Harris, Mrs. Bird, and Rachel Halliday would domestic affairs be salvaged.

Two texts published closer in time to *Incidents* provide further evidence of contemporary views on the sanctity of motherhood: Eliza Follen's 1855 religious tract *To Mothers in the Free States* and the Reverend Hiram Mattison's *Louisa Picquet, The Octoroon: A Tale of Southern Slave Life,* published in 1861.[17] In a review of "Linda, the Slave Girl" in *The Liberator,* William C. Nell begins his praise of "Linda" by setting the narrative in a broader context: "The lamented Mrs. Follen, in her admirable tract, addressed to Mothers in the Free States, and with which that indefatigable colporteur, Miss Putnam, is doing so much good in her visits to families, seems to have anticipated just such a contribution to anti-slavery literature as this book, 'Linda.' "[18] Follen's antislavery tract opened with a simple, straightforward appeal to the mothers of the North; mothers, she asserted, are responsible for slavery. Follen thus seemed to have "anticipated" Jacob's slave narrative in her appeal to maternal sympathies. She asked her readers to imagine a daughter "exposed to the ill-usage, often cruelty, always to the lowest passions of humanity; her womanly feelings trampled upon,—if possible, obliterated; her pure affections laughed at and scorned . . ." (1). Initially encouraging empathy for those sons and daughters of slavery, Follen was soon describing the ways that Northern women could end such abuse of power: they would have to "take the subject to heart," make antislavery work their "soul's sincere desire," speak out when given the opportunity, and, most important, raise sons who would be faithful to higher laws (2-3). Such words resonated with Stowe's advice in the "Concluding Remarks" to *Uncle Tom's Cabin:* "There is one thing that every individual can do,—they can see to it [that] *they feel right.* An atmosphere of sympathetic influence encircles every human being; and the man or woman who *feels* strongly, healthily and justly, on the great interests of humanity, is a constant benefactor to the human race."[19] Clearly, *Incidents* fits in with this sort of advocacy. Jacobs believed that a moving representation of her afflictions and her grandmother's dedication to her children would encourage Northern women to "feel right" and to take their abolitionist duty to heart.

Mattison's *Louisa Picquet* was another woman-centered story promoting the antislavery cause. Unlike Jacobs, Picquet did not write the story herself but, as Jacobs had originally intended, had it written by a sympathetic listener, the Reverend Hiram Mattison. The "narrative" was largely Mattison's transcription of conversations with Louisa Picquet in May 1860 and was done to help the former slave raise money to purchase her mother. Many of Mattison's questions ask Picquet to reflect upon the peculiar degradation of female slaves and to describe her efforts to bring her mother North. Picquet's mother becomes especially important after the fourteen-year-old Louisa is sold to a New Orleans "gentleman" who intends to set her up as his mistress. Apparently touched by Picquet's descriptions of the parting at the auction block, Mattison interrupts a series of questions designed to elicit facts of slave life and offers the reflective and sympathetic query: "It seems like a dream, don't it?" Picquet responds: "No; it seems fresh in my memory when I think of it—no longer than yesterday. Mother was right on her knees, with her hands up, prayin' to the

Lord for me. She didn't care who saw her: the people all lookin' at her. I often thought her prayers followed me, for I never could forget her. Whenever I wanted any thing real bad after that, my mother was always sure to appear to me in a dream that night, and have plenty to give me, always" (18). Significantly, the mother is transformed into a transcendent figure who intercedes for her daughter in her continuous struggles. Like Jacobs's grandmother, Picquet's mother becomes as important for what she represents as for what she does.

Unlike *Incidents,* however, *Louisa Picquet* was not crafted with thematic coherence in mind. Whereas Jacobs and Child chose to make *Incidents* something of a romance, Mattison was guided more by the form of antislavery pamphlets. He was not as effective as Jacobs and Child at shaping the narrative in a way that would artfully enhance the emblematic importance of motherhood. Lamenting the separation between mother and daughter in chapter 25, Mattison offered a resolution similar to Jacobs's. In the two chapters which follow, however, he turned from the lives of Picquet and her mother to catalogue the barbarisms of slavery. Rather than stress the peculiar features of his female-centered story, Mattison chose to record other anecdotes of Southern cruelty. In doing so, he aligned his work more with Theodore and Angelina Grimké Weld's *American Slavery As It Is: Testimony of a Thousand Witnesses* (1839) and Child's *The Patriarchal Institution, as Described by Members of Its Own Family* than with a narrative such as *Incidents.*

For Child, slave narrative and antislavery fiction served important functions within the abolitionist movement. Unlike the antislavery propaganda of tracts and pamphlets, the narrative form elicited a more imaginative connection with the "characters" and shaped opinion by appealing to what Transcendentalists called the "God within."[20] Through plot and emblem, the stories of slave women became tales of national importance.

Child's antislavery pamphlets published in 1860 indicate that she made a significant distinction between slave narrative and antislavery tract—a distinction that Mattison, for instance, did not make.[21] Through her pamphlets she argued for legislative change and addressed specific misconceptions of slavery. The rules of debate dominated the form and style in these pamphlets, and her arguments usually depended upon a litany of facts to substantiate assertions. The narrative, however, was an art form which demanded different editorial and authorial choices. In narration, incidents could be used to argue political positions, yet they also could be sequenced and described so as to invoke spiritual laws. In other words, fiction could turn real events into parables of transcendence. If Child's pamphlets were designed to appeal to the mind, Jacobs's narrative was aimed at a higher Reason and thus was designed to nurture a more lasting reform.

Notes

¹ Harriet A. Jacobs, *Incidents in the Life of a Slave Girl, Written by Herself*, ed. Jean Fagan Yellin (Cambridge: Harvard Univ. Press, 1987), 244. Child's letter is also included in Lydia Maria Child, *The Collected Correspondence of Lydia Maria Child, 1817-1880*, ed. Patricia G. Holland and Milton Meltzer (Millwood, N.Y.: Kraus Microform, 1980), 46/1243; and Child, *Lydia Maria Child: Selected Letters, 1817-1880*, ed. Milton Meltzer, Patricia G. Holland, and Francine Krasno (Amherst: Univ. of Massachusetts Press, 1982), 357. All subsequent page citations from *Incidents* refer to Yellin's edition. Further references to Child's *Collected Correspondence* and *Selected Letters* will be included in the text and keyed to the abbreviations *CC* and *SL;* references to *CC* include both the microfiche card number and the letter number.

² Alice A. Deck makes a similar point in her look at the relationship between Jacobs and Child. See Deck, "Whose Book Is This?: Authorial Versus Editorial Control of Harriet Brent Jacobs' *Incidents in the Life of a Slave Girl: Written by Herself,*" *Women's Studies International Forum* 10 (1987): 33-40.

³ For other discussions of the role of Brent's grandmother in *Incidents,* see Jean Fagan Yellin, *Women & Sisters: Antislavery Feminists in American Culture* (New Haven: Yale Univ. Press, 1989), 89-93; and Joanne M. Braxton, *Black Women Writing Autobiography: A Tradition Within a Tradition* (Philadelphia: Temple Univ. Press, 1989), 18-38. Yellin also asserts the importance of motherhood to the text, writing that Linda Brent, the grandmother, and the grandmother's daughter Aunt Nancy "are all defined by the ways in which they respond to motherhood" (89). Braxton sees the grandmother as "the bearer of a system of values as well as the carrier of the female version of the black heroic archetype. [She] teaches and demonstrates the values and practical principles of sacrifice and survival . . ." (30).

⁴ The narrative's condemnation of the Fugitive Slave Law indicates that the author is not unconcerned with specific political matters. In the ending, however, Jacobs does not return to overtly political elements. For her most direct and extensive discussion of the Fugitive Slave Law, see chapter 40 of *Incidents.* Child's pamphlet *The Duty of Disobedience to the Fugitive Slave Act: An Appeal to the Legislators of Massachusetts* offers an interesting comparison with Jacobs's comments. See *The Duty of Disobedience* (Boston: American Anti-Slavery Society, 1860).

⁵ For a discussion of the ways in which Brent's actions and her reflections upon them are unique to slave narratives, see *Incidents,* xxix-xxxiv.

⁶ The grandmother's own history—like that of many slave women—also may not have suited the ideal of feminine virtue. However, Jacobs either did not know the father of Aunt Martha's (Molly Horniblow's) children or chose not to depict this part of her grandmother's past. At no time, however, did Jacobs indicate that the father of her grandmother's children was a slaveholder. Speaking of Benjamin, one of Aunt Martha's children, Jacobs wrote: "He was a bright, handsome lad, nearly white; for he inherited the complexion my grandmother had derived from Anglo-Saxon ancestors" (*Incidents,* 6).

⁷ See Braxton, 30-32.

⁸ Lydia Maria Child, *Correspondence between Lydia Maria Child and Gov. Wise and Mrs. Mason, of Virginia* (Boston: American Anti-Slavery Society, 1860), 14. Subsequent citations from the Child-Wise-Mason correspondence refer to this edition. Her letter to Brown is also included in *SL,* 324-25 and *CC,* 41/1123.

⁹ Child had included her letter to Brown in her correspondence to Governor Wise: "Relying upon these indications of honor and justice in your character, I venture to ask a favor of you. Enclosed is a letter to Capt. John Brown. Will you have the kindness, after reading it yourself, to transmit it to the prisoner?" (3). Wise and Brown replied within three weeks. Both discouraged Child from making the trip. Brown said he was being treated humanely and suggested that Child might instead arrange for the monetary relief of his family in North Elba, New York (15-16).

¹⁰ A *Herald* reporter had been present during Brown's questioning by Wise and Virginia senator James M. Mason on 18 October. See "A Conversation with Brown," in *John Brown,* ed. Richard Warch and Jonathan F. Fanton (Englewood Cliffs, N.J.: Prentice-Hall, 1973), 74-75.

¹¹ For a discussion of the relationship between Jacobs and Stowe, see *Incidents,* xviii-xix.

¹² Child's correspondence reveals that she and Jacobs maintained contact until after the Civil War. In November 1866, Child tried to solicit help for Jacobs's son from Rev. John Fraser. Jacobs had lost contact with him after he went out to Australia to search for gold (*CC,* 66/1746). For the Child-Jacobs correspondence, see also *CC,* 55/1474, 56/1508, 58/1552, 66/1748.

¹³ Lydia Maria Child, ed., *The Freedmen's Book* (Boston: Ticknor and Fields, 1865). Some of the more familiar writers include Frederick Douglass, William Lloyd Garrison, Frances E. W. Harper, Lydia Sigourney, Harriet Beecher Stowe, and Phillis Wheatley.

[14] Child's extensive reading of the period's literature is evident in her correspondence. Evidence of her reading may also be found in three additional places: records of her Boston Athenaeum borrowings from 14 January 1832 to 2 February 1835; a list of works posthumously donated to the Wayland, Massachusetts, public library; and a catalogue of books owned by Child and her brother Convers Francis put up for auction in 1887. The Boston Athenaeum houses the list of Child's borrowings. Records for her donated books are kept at the Beaman Memorial Public Library, West Boylston, Massachusetts. For the auction list, see Kenneth Walter Cameron, *American Transcendental Quarterly* no. 6, part two (Second Quarter 1970): 1-58.

As a member of the Nathaniel Parker Willis household, Jacobs also had access to an extensive collection of contemporary fiction. In addition, during her eighteen months in Rochester starting in March 1849, Jacobs worked in the antislavery reading room (*Incidents,* xvi).

[15] Lydia H. Sigourney, "Address to the 'Hartford Female African Society,' " *African Repository* 6 (July 1830): 152.

[16] Angelina Grimké, *An Appeal to the Women of the Nominally Free States, Issued by an Anti-Slavery Convention of American Women* (Boston: Isaac Knapp, 1838; rpt., Freeport: Books for Libraries, 1971), 15.

[17] See Eliza Lee (Cabot) Follen, *To Mothers in the Free States* (New York: American Anti-Slavery Society, 1855) and Hiram Mattison, *Louisa Picquet, The Octoroon: Or, Inside Views of Southern Domestic Life* (New York: Published by the Author, 1861). Mattison's book has been reprinted in *Collected Black Women's Narratives* (New York: Oxford Univ. Press, 1988). Subsequent references to *Louisa Picquet* refer to the reprinted text.

[18] William C. Nell, "Linda, The Slave Girl," *The Liberator,* 25 January 1861.

[19] Harriet Beecher Stowe, *Uncle Tom's Cabin: or, Life among the Lowly,* ed. Ann Douglas (New York: Penguin Books, 1981), 624.

[20] Child contributed significantly to the Transcendentalist movement of the 1830s and 1840s. Two of her major works of this period, *Philothea* (1836) and *Letters from New York, First and Second Series* (1843, 1845) show a unique blending of abolitionist and Transcendental thinking. (See Robert Streeter, "Mrs. Child's 'Philothea': A Transcendental Novel?" *New England Quarterly* 16 [December 1943]: 648-54.) In addition to these publications, Child's close relationship with her brother Convers Francis—the oldest among the group of men who first attended Bronson Alcott's "Symposeum" on 19 September 1836—and her atten-

dance at Emerson's lectures and Fuller's conversations guaranteed her ongoing participation in this dialogue of religious and social reform. For her synopsis of Transcendentalism, see "Letter XIII" in *Letters from New York, Second Series* (New York: C. S. Francis, 1845), 125-30. Here she argues that not all knowledge is received through the senses and that "the highest, and therefore most universal truths, are revealed within the soul, to a faculty *transcending* the understanding. This faculty they call pure Reason" (125-26). For Child, as for other Transcendentalists, literature provided the means to open the reader to a divine voice, the God within.

[21] Along with the *Correspondence* and *The Duty of Disobedience,* Child had two other pamphlets published by the American Anti-Slavery Society in 1860: *The Right Way, the Safe Way, Proved by Emancipation in the British West Indies, and Elsewhere* and *The Patriarchal Institution, as Described by Members of Its Own Family.*

Anne B. Dalton (essay date 1995)

SOURCE: "The Devil and the Virgin: Writing Sexual Abuse in *Incidents in the Life of a Slave Girl*," in *Violence, Silence, and Anger: Women's Writing as Transgression,* edited by Deirdre Lashgari, University Press of Virginia, 1995, pp. 38-61.

[*In the following essay, Dalton examines the "tensions between what [Jacobs] literally states and metaphorically suggests about sexual exploitation," pointing to the parallels between the way in which Jacobs, through Linda Brent, describes her sexual exploitation and twentieth-century studies on the effects of molestation on girls and women. Dalton suggests that through her language and imagery, Jacobs implies that greater sexual abuses occurred in her life than what Brent reports.*]

Harriet Jacobs confronted multiple binds as she attempted to render her experiences of sexual abuse and the systematic sexual exploitation of slave women. In her 1861 narrative, she grappled with the constraints of the literary conventions of the time, while also making use of them to keep her audience's sympathy and to rally support for the abolitionist cause. In her preface, Jacobs points to absences and silences in *Incidents in the Life of a Slave Girl.*[1] She writes that her "descriptions fall far short of the facts" (xiii) and that "it would have been more pleasant to [her] to have been silent about [her] own history" (xiv). Jacobs emphasizes that it is her desire to end the suffering of the enslaved that has made her "add [her] testimony" to that of others (xiv).

Introductory comments by the editor of *Incidents,* white abolitionist Lydia Maria Child, suggest why Jacobs's prose would demonstrate such conflict as she broaches the taboo subject of sexual exploitation.[2]

> I am well aware that many will accuse me of indecorum for presenting these pages to the public; for the experiences of this intelligent and much-injured woman belong to a class which some call delicate subjects, and others indelicate; but the public ought to be made acquainted with its monstrous features, and I willingly take the responsibility of presenting them with the veil withdrawn. I do this for the sake of my sisters in bondage, *who are suffering wrongs so foul, that our ears are too delicate to listen to them.* I do it with the hope of arousing conscientious and reflecting women at the North to a sense of their duty in the exertion of moral influence on the question of Slavery, on all possible occasions. (xii, emphasis added)

Child's description that Black women "are suffering wrongs so foul that our ears [white women's] are too delicate to listen to them" implies an obverse relation between Jacobs and her audience, one in which the *more* Jacobs tries to tell, the less she may be heard by those she feels she must persuade. To be politically effective, Jacobs needed to render the material relating to sexual exploitation in a "delicate" manner, so that she would not alienate her audience from listening, while still being graphic enough to be persuasive. By using metaphorical descriptions of "foulness" Jacobs could cope with the demands of such a bind; she would be telling all, but in such a way that "too delicate" ears would not find "plain" (see xii and xiv).

In *Incidents,* "Linda Brent" was Jacobs's pseudonym as protagonist and author, and the portrayal of Dr. Flint was based on Jacobs's former master, James Norcom, a prominent physician in Edenton, North Carolina.[3] Jacobs escaped to the North in 1842 and wrote her narrative between 1853 and 1858 under conditions of physical hardship, while working as a domestic servant. During this period, Jacobs sent letters to Amy Post, a founder of the women's rights movement and a member of the New York State Anti-Slave Society. These letters reveal that Jacobs felt she was placing herself at risk when she assumed the authorial role. In one letter, composed before completing her manuscript, Jacobs tells Post that she intends to write "the whole truth" of her experiences, even though she feels that her life has had "degradation associated with it."[4] However, in a later letter, Jacobs states that she has "left out" descriptions of some of the "cruel wrongs" she suffered. Her comment that "the world might believe that a slave woman was too willing" and her request to "be judged as a woman" both emphasize the sexual nature of what she has excluded.[5] Paradoxically, even Jacobs's desire to *conceal* seems to further her effort to expose the sexual victimization. Comments such as "descriptions fall short of the facts" signal to readers the need to examine her narrative carefully in order to discover what she "might have made plainer" (xiv).

The fact that Black women at this time were stereotyped as "innately super-sexed" may well have fueled Jacobs's anxiety as author.[6] Even the images presented by leading abolitionists often played on the association of Black women with the illicit. For example, defining the dialectic often reinforced by abolitionists, Hazel Carby argues that "Garrison's sexual metaphors for black women extended from passionate whore to hapless, cringing victim."[7] Jacobs's prose, especially her apologetic tone, suggests that she was influenced by the cultural edict against Black women "assuming the independence" to give public accounts of their experience.[8] For women in general, the act of making their experience public would itself be likely to be classed as "promiscuous" or "unnatural," regardless of specific content. Because Jacobs was an African-American woman writing about sexual abuse, her authorial position was far more precarious.

Jacobs's sense of her audience seems to have posed additional difficulties for her. At several points in *Incidents,* and notably in her preface, she addresses her remarks to white females. Angela Davis comments that "white women who joined the abolitionist movement were especially outraged by the sexual assaults on Black women" and that "activists in the female anti-slave societies often related stories of brutal rapes of slave women as they appealed to white women to defend their Black sisters."[9] Jacobs may have felt it politically effective to render an account of her sexual abuse, but as Davis implies, she also had reason to fear they might read about her suffering voyeuristically. As a woman who had been brutally betrayed by her Southern white mistresses during her childhood and young adulthood, Jacobs had many reasons to feel conflicted about relating the story of her sexual exploitation to even the most sympathetic white female audience she could imagine. Her persistent efforts to write in spite of these difficulties reveals her extraordinary commitment to speaking and being heard.

Although a number of feminist critics during the last five years have provided crucial biographical information about Jacobs as well as literary and historical analyses of *Incidents,* no one has yet examined the tensions between what she literally states and metaphorically suggests about sexual exploitation.[10] To understand the range of forces Jacobs confronted as a writer, it is instructive to look at the tension she creates by describing Dr. Flint's *verbal* sexual harassment of Linda Brent through imagery that implies that he was able to molest her physically.[11] This tension is connected with several issues: the psychology of survivors of sexual abuse, the thematics of slave narratives, Jacobs's status as a Black and female narrator, her relation to her audience, and nineteenth-century concepts of ladyhood. The recent research concerning the psychology of survivors of sexual abuse provides the key to my analysis, since the meaning of the gaps, negations, and displacements in Jacobs's narrative are linked directly to her position as an adult narrator describing trauma she experienced as a child and young woman.[12]

Jacobs may have felt compelled to use the pseudonym "Linda Brent" for her narrative's author and protagonist in order to protect herself, her family, and those who helped her escape. And yet, despite this conscious masking, the narrative's subtitle, "Written by Herself," stresses the authenticity of Jacobs's account. Such juxtaposed masking and assertion of authenticity marks the language of the narrative throughout. Although Jacobs might have used her own name if she had not feared reprisals, I am maintaining her distinction throughout my discussion. Even the most exacting and literal of autobiographers, in the process of writing, is creating a "fiction" about himself or herself. In maintaining the distinction Jacobs made, I am reminding the reader that her slave narrative is a constructed representation, while also attempting to respect her own delineations within the autobiography.[13]

In the range of critical interpretations that Jacobs's narrative has called forth, each one has stressed the degree to which Brent actively resisted Flint's abuse. Exploring the meaning of this resistance, Hazel Carby argues that although "Dr. Flint was the embodiment of the corruption of the slave system, as his prey Linda Brent was not corrupted by him, and her struggle was an aggressive refusal to be sexually used and compromised or to succumb to the will of the master."[14] Scrutinizing the conflicts between the literal and figurative meanings does not undercut the power of the resistance that Jacobs's narrative chronicles.[15] Instead, such analysis can reveal the ways in which Jacobs responded to her historical context to write " 'not the life of a heroine with no degradation associated with it,' but a woman's 'true and just account of [her] own life in slavery'."[16]

Revising Genesis: Writing the Best Kept Secret

Again and again, Jacobs shows Dr. Flint verbally harassing and following Linda Brent at all times of the day and night, as well as striking, shaking, and throwing her. She portrays his tremendous ability to violate Brent physically, but to suggest his sexual abuse she most often portrays him as a foul demon, fiend, or devil whispering in her ear. Through this imagery, which does not explicitly tell but metaphorically represents, Jacobs skillfully revises the thematics that nineteenth-century male slave narrators used, and she creates tropes through which she can tell the *female* slave's story.

In *The Best Kept Secret,* Florence Rush describes the extensive traffic in girls and women in Europe and America during the nineteenth century, Arguing that at the rare times when male abusers were prosecuted, the girls and women suffered from an equally abusive legal system and abusive publicity, Rush discusses how the widespread concept of "the sexually guilty female"—with Eve as the prototype—forced the abused female into shame and silence.[17] Jacobs's narrative suggests that she simultaneously internalized and resisted this concept.

In the opening pages of **Incidents,** Jacobs describes Brent's "fall into knowledge of evil."[18] But unlike the "falls" most male slave narrators described, which were into "the development of an awareness of what it means to be a slave," Brent's is a double one into a knowledge both of slavery and of sexual subjugation.[19] Jacobs expands the meaning of "fall," doubling it so that it relates to her position both as a slave and as a female slave. By drawing on the biblical imagery of temptation in Genesis and virgin insemination in the Gospels to show Brent's loss of her Edenic state of childhood innocence, Jacobs creates a striking counterpoint to many of the male slave narratives while also drawing on the parables and structures they often incorporated.

As male slave narrators portrayed the degradation of slavery, their role most often resembled that of an Adamic or Christ-like figure, who must "bear the slave's heavy cross."[20] In contrast to other narratives, Jacobs uses ear, demon, devil, and serpent imagery to show that Brent is parallel to both Eve and Mary. She is Eve-like because she is tempted by a foul devil, but also Mary-like as she strives desperately to resist Flint and maintain the purity that Mary personifies. It was more difficult for Jacobs to report Brent's "fall" than it was for a male narrator to portray the "fall" of an Adam-Christ figure, not only because of the Christian tradition of blaming the sexual and sexually abused woman, but also because of the strict nineteenth-century standards concerning female sexuality and respectability. In *The Madwoman in the Attic,* Sandra Gilbert and Susan Gubar analyze how nineteenth-century white women rewrote Miltonic myths, revising the story of Eve, as part of their effort to create themselves.[21] Like these women, Jacobs also revised patriarchal myths about women's sexuality, creativity, and status by telling her story from the position of an Eve figure.

Jacobs's portrayal of Dr. Flint as a demon violating Linda Brent by whispering in her ear is striking in several ways. While such imagery shows Dr. Flint's verbal sexual harassment, the image also suggests greater sexual abuse than the narrator literally reports. Jacobs first describes Flint's attempts to molest her in this passage: "But I now entered on my fifteenth year— a sad epoch in the life of a slave girl. My master began to whisper foul words in my ear. Young as I was, I could not remain ignorant of their import. I tried to treat them with indifference or contempt" (26).

There are several reasons why Jacobs might have implied the sexual abuse by describing Flint whispering in Brent's ear. In parables and folklore, the ear has traditionally been one site of the virginal woman's molestation and impregnation, as with the Christian Mary figure.[22] Also, by casting Flint as a devil-demon who whispers in Brent's ear, Jacobs retells the Genesis myth in which the serpent corrupts Eve; but in contrast to the biblical version, Jacobs's retelling emphasizes the abuser's guilt and the victim's innocence. Through this imagery, Jacobs can report what the young woman experienced while emphasizing her status as pure. Her representation of the ear as the site of sexual assault is also evocative of how a verbal attack can feel like a physical blow. Jacobs's imagery emphasizes the excruciating visceral effects that result from Flint's proximity and control: "For my master, whose restless, craving, vicious nature roved about day and night, seeking whom to devour, had just left me, with stinging, scathing words; words that scathed ear and brain like fire. O, how I despised him! I thought how glad I should be, if some day when he walked the earth, it would open and swallow him up and disencumber the world of a plague" (15-16).

With the severe injunctions women, and particularly slave women, experienced against speaking about sexual abuse, one might expect Jacobs to mask her descriptions of molestation. One such method is described by Hortense Spillers, who comments that Freud's notes articulate the "frequency with which sexual repression makes use of transpositions from a lower to an upper part of the body." She explains that Freud "specifically names the replacement of the genitals by the face as a dynamic in the symbolism of unconscious thinking."[23] Julia Kristeva, in "Stabat Mater," considers how in representations of the virginal body the ear becomes the site of the woman's sexual experience: "That the female sexual organ has become transformed into an innocent shell which serves only to receive sound may ultimately contribute to an eroticization of hearing and the voice, not to say of understanding. But by the same token sexuality is reduced to a mere implication. The female sexual experience is therefore anchored in the universality of sound."[24] Jacobs explored the correlation that Kristeva suggests among hearing, the voice, and sexuality. Her use of the woman's ear as the site of the attack is appropriate and evocative because the abused ear is parallel to the silenced mouth of the molested woman and what she cannot tell. Dr. Flint has the power to speak, but the sexually abused woman cannot name what he is "speaking," although she desperately wants to reveal the trauma: "In desperation I told him that I must and would apply to my grandmother for protection. He threatened me with death, and worse than

death, if I made any complaint to her" (30). In such passages, Jacobs demonstrates Flint's extreme power not only to control who speaks, but to render others silent. Jacobs's narrative is radical because she is able to speak through her imagery even while she portrays Brent as silenced.[25]

The following passage emphasizes Flint's demonic role as he alternately tries to tempt Brent gently or to abuse her ferociously. Jacobs's choice of the verb "peopled" in describing his attacks plays on the many meanings of the word (for example, to populate), suggesting that he has succeeded in forcing the girl to imagine "unclean images" and implying that he has attempted to impregnate her. The author's references to his violation of "the most sacred commandments of nature" again stress his demonic position as he creates the hellish atmosphere in which Brent was "compelled to live": "Sometimes he had stormy, terrific ways, that made his victims tremble; sometimes he assumed a gentleness that he thought must surely subdue. Of the two, I preferred his stormy moods, although they left me trembling. He tried his utmost to corrupt the pure principles my grandmother had instilled. He peopled my young mind with unclean images, such as only a vile monster could think of. I turned from him with disgust and hatred. But he was my master. I was compelled to live under the same roof with him—where I saw a man forty years my senior daily violating the most sacred commandments of nature" (26). Through her use of the Dr. Flint-demon association, Jacobs challenges and reverses the stereotypic descriptions of Black women as lascivious. Her imagery underscores this reversal, especially since in mythology it is the demons who are sexually insatiable.[26] Recounting his repeated assaults, Jacobs describes Flint as "a restless spirit from the pit" (79), likening him to a hellish demon from the underworld.

In chapter 6, "The Jealous Mistress," Jacobs shows how Flint's wife becomes an embodiment of his own lascivious behavior; like his familiar or a succubus, she acts out his abuse by standing over Brent's bed and accosting her when she believes she is asleep: "She now took me to sleep in a room adjoining her own. . . . Sometimes I woke up, and found her bending over me. At other times she whispered in my ear, as though it was her husband who was speaking to me, and listened to hear what I would answer. If she startled me, on such occasions, she would glide stealthily away; and the next morning she would tell me I had been talking in my sleep, and ask who I was talking to. At last, I began to be fearful for my life. It had been threatened; and you can imagine, better than I can describe, what an unpleasant sensation it must produce to wake up in the dead of night and find a jealous woman bending over you" (33). Jacobs's description contrasts ironically with stereotypic portrayals of the white mistress as "pure and morally uplifted." As if she were a demon like her husband, Mrs. Flint molests the victim of her husband's "vicious roving" while she sleeps by reenacting his molestation of her. By portraying the mistress as the defiling succubus, Jacobs reveals how the master's sexual abuses infect those around him, while also refuting definitions of slave women as "lasciviously sexual" and white women as "the model of virtue."

As male slave narrators did with their protagonists, Jacobs used the Christian imagery to stress the slave woman's humanity and refined nature while revealing the inhumanity of the master and mistress. She repeatedly emphasizes the pervasiveness of Dr. Flint's abuses by stating that through them he creates an "atmosphere of hell" (40). She also characterizes Flint as a representative of "the serpent of Slavery" who has "many and poisonous fangs" (63). She shows Flint, like Satan, attempting to entrap; however, unlike conventional Christian portrayals of Eve, Brent struggles continually against his efforts to control and molest her.

In one scene, Brent questions Flint's hypocrisy in joining the church for motives of social advancement, and challenges his statement that in acquiescing to his sexual advances she should be "as virtuous as" his wife:

> His voice became hoarse with rage. "How dare you preach to me about your infernal Bible!" he exclaimed. "What right have you, who are my negro, to talk to me about what you would like? I am your master and you shall obey me."
>
> No wonder slaves sing,—
> "Ole Satan's church is here below;
> Up to God's free church I have to go." (77)

Flint behaves satanically as he curses the Bible, sets himself up as a higher authority than the Christian God, and tries to compel Brent to abandon her moral principles. In this passage, he denies Brent the right to speak, threatening that she "shall obey" him. By ending the passage with the song's refrain, Jacobs shows the extent to which those within the slave community resisted their masters' injunctions against revealing their inhumanity. They used Christian metaphor to expose their masters' stifling of Christian teachings. Through the song, Jacobs manages to highlight the fact of mass resistance in the same passage in which Flint attempts to silence Brent.

Jacobs also stresses the importance of resistance within the Black community by stating that Brent might not have survived if she had been living on a plantation or in a less populated area throughout her years as a slave (33). But despite the fact that Brent's place within a larger community buffers her to some degree, many passages detail Flint's vast power: "My master met me at every turn, reminding me that I belonged to him, and swearing by heaven and earth that he would compel me to submit to him. If I went out for a breath of fresh air, after a day of unwearied toil, his footsteps dogged me. If I knelt by my mother's grave, his dark shadow fell on me even there" (27). The image of Brent being "dogged" by Flint's footsteps until "his dark shadow fell on [her]" emphasizes how his psychological and physical impingement reinforce each other.

In "A Perilous Passage in a Slave Girl's Life," Brent enters into a sexual relationship with Mr. Sands, a white slave-owning neighbor, in an attempt to protect herself from Flint's abuse in general and, specifically, to avoid becoming pregnant with a child fathered by Flint. But after the birth of her first, and then following the birth of her second child (both fathered, the narrator reports, by Sands), the intensity of Flint's "persecutions" increases. Jacobs writes that during the first time Brent was pregnant he was the only doctor who could be called to treat her (63) and that he attended during the birth of her child. Such details once again emphasize the numerous occasions Flint had to abuse Brent and the vast extent of his power to traumatize her. By indicating that the molester attended Brent as she gave birth, Jacobs poignantly depicts the degree of her vulnerability and danger.

What No Pen Could Describe: "The Plunge into the Abyss"

Jacobs tells her readers many times that she felt she could not describe all that she had witnessed and experienced about sexual abuse within slavery. She most often stresses that she cannot completely render her experience either before or just after a passage in which she metaphorically describes Flint's sexual exploitation of slave women. For example, while recounting Flint's attempts to make the fifteen-year-old Brent his concubine, Jacobs writes, "The degradation, the wrongs, the vices, that grow out of slavery, are more than I can describe. They are greater than you would willingly believe" (26). The passage reveals an important tension: the narrator claims she is unable to describe her experience fully, and then states that the reason for her silence is her audience's inability to accept the truth of that experience. At times, however, her phrasing reveals that she confronted other forces, besides her sense of audience, that limited what she could articulate: "He came every day; and *I was subjected to such insults as no pen can describe. I would not describe them if I could; they were too low, too revolting.* I tried to keep them from my grandmother's knowledge as much as I could. I knew she had enough to sadden her life, without having my troubles to bear" (79, emphasis added). That Brent "was subjected to such insults as no pen can describe" implies that Flint abused her more harshly than *anyone* could communicate. But the passage also suggests that the narrator recoiled from recalling the trauma of the past incidents because they were too disturbing for *her* to represent. Here, the ambivalence about disclosure and concealment that marks the passage is representative of accounts by girls and women who were molested.[27]

The cultural situation Jacobs portrays is, despite many parallels, a more extreme one than contemporary researchers of sexual abuse have studied. Jacobs stresses repeatedly that she grew up in a region in which white men sexually abused Black children and women extensively. She also makes clear that Linda Brent became aware of this systematic sexual abuse when she was eleven and that she became a victim of it by the age of fifteen at the latest. Researchers have found that girls feel extreme shame, guilt, and rage as a result of abuse and often respond by defining themselves as evil.[28] They relate that the early trauma, and especially the feeling of powerlessness and stigmatization, contribute to such feelings. Jacobs profoundly resists portraying Brent as the sexually guilty female, but one can infer from her narrative that, for the slave child, the feeling of powerlessness must have been extreme. Just as victims of child abuse are often trapped into silence and powerlessness by the authority figures in their lives, Brent is abused by Dr. Flint and then by the mistress of the household.[29] Jacobs describes Brent as threatened by Flint's vengeance *if she tells,* and as subject to the mistress's abuse if she tells, does not tell, or even if the mistress *suspects* that she was sexually abused (12). Commenting on similar dynamics, Diana Russell reports that girls who were disbelieved or blamed when they revealed that they had been sexually abused often suffered the most extreme aftereffects.[30] She emphasizes that, as adults, these women had the most difficulty disclosing the fact that they had been molested, and that they felt the most guilt.[31]

Incidents suggests that because the Flints assumed the role of master and mistress to Brent, she found the sexual assaults even more disturbing than if they had occurred in a different context. In contemporary America, guardians, stepfathers and foster fathers are the ones most likely to sexually abuse girls and young women.[32] Recent research shows that molestation by an older male in the position of guardian is typically more traumatic than that by a male who is not directly responsible for the girl's safety and well-being.[33] Brent's position differs from these contemporary dynamics in an important way; she repeatedly eschews Flint's attempts to cast himself in a paternal role, rejecting as repugnant his efforts, parallel to those of many slave owners, to cast himself as fictive kin to those he has enslaved. In spite of this distinction, Brent's experience of being sexually abused by one who has absolute authority and controls the basic material necessities of life clearly contributes to the difficulty of speaking about the molestation. Contemporary studies show that even when suffering incestuous abuse, a young

girl may realize that she will grow old enough to leave the household, and many girls who have been molested by a relative or acquaintance of the family leave the family at a very young age.[34] The situation of slave girls or women who suffered from the sexual abuse of white men was even more extreme because they knew that they had no legal recourse and little chance of escape, and that their status as possession was likely to be permanent. These women also had the added burden of knowing that any daughter they might bear could become subject to similar torture.

Jacobs reports that as a young child Brent learned about the doctor's power to whip and to sell slaves who spoke about his sexual abuse:

> Some said master accused him of stealing corn, others said the slave had quarrelled with his wife, in presence of the overseer, and had accused his master of being the father of her child. They were both Black and the child was very fair.

> I went into the work house next morning, and saw the cowhide still wet with blood, and the boards all covered with gore. The poor man lived, and continued to quarrel with his wife. A few months afterwards Dr. Flint handed them both over to a slave-trader. The guilty man put their value into his pocket, and had the satisfaction of knowing that they were out of sight and hearing. When the mother was delivered into the trader's hands, she said, "You *promised* to treat me well." To which he replied, "You have let your tongue run too far; damn you!" She had forgotten that it was a crime for a slave to tell who was the father of her child. (12)

Jacobs shows Brent's traumatic initiation, stressing that speaking about sexual abuse can destroy a slave family as well as subject individual men and women to physical torture. Early exposure to the fate of those who spoke out could have made Jacobs feel overwhelming pressure to be silent about sexual harassment and molestation during her childhood and young adulthood. The memory of such injunctions against speaking out could also have made it deeply painful for Jacobs, as a mature adult, to recall and write about her experiences in the Norcoms' household. Describing other traumatic incidents from Brent's childhood, Jacobs emphasizes that slave women who became pregnant by the white master were often greatly abused by the white mistress as well (see p. 12 for one example). Later in *Incidents* Brent confronts such a nexus of abuse when Mrs. Flint repeatedly threatens to kill her, believing she is a victim of her husband's sexual assaults.

The way in which Jacobs describes Mrs. Flint forcing Brent to recount what had "passed between" herself and her master clarifies the dynamics between the two women, while once again indicating how Jacobs's sense of her audience may have silenced her.

"If you have deceived me, beware! . . . Look me directly in the face, and tell me all that has passed between your master and you."

I did as she ordered. As I went on with my account her color changed frequently, she wept, and sometimes groaned . . . but she was incapable of feeling for the condition of shame and misery in which her unfortunate, helpless slave was placed. (32)

Jacobs portrays Mrs. Flint's command and reaction specifically, but does not begin to describe what Brent said to her, even though this would have been a logical point in the narrative at which to detail the sexual abuse Jacobs had briefly described in the previous chapter. By representing what Brent said to Mrs. Flint with the gap between the first and second sentences, Jacobs suggests that communicating Flint's actions to the threatening mistress traumatized Brent and that it may also have been traumatic for Jacobs to recall and write the scene for her readers. Although the passage shows that the abusive mistress violated Brent's privacy without any intention of protecting her from Flint, through her use of the lacuna in the scene Jacobs manages to shield Brent retroactively from the mistress's probing while also protecting herself from an audience she did not trust. At the same time, the lacuna once again signals that Flint's sexual abuse is so extreme that it cannot be represented. Even though Jacobs does not disclose to her readers what Brent said about Flint, by relating that Mrs. Flint "wept" and "sometimes groaned" in response, Jacobs indicates that Brent spoke of Flint's *sexual* abuse. Descriptions of the mistress's brutality early in the narrative establish that "her color" would not have "changed frequently" while hearing reports of the master's *physical* abuse of slaves.

Jacobs further delineates the forces that silenced Brent as she depicts Linda's relationship with her grandmother, exploring both why and what Linda cannot tell her about the sexual abuse she suffered within the Flints' household.

But Dr. Flint swore he would kill me, if I was not as silent as the grave. Then, although my grandmother was all in all to me, I feared her as well as loved her. I had been accustomed to look up to her with a respect bordering upon awe. I was very young, and felt shamefaced about telling her such impure things, especially as I knew her to be very strict on such subjects. Moreover, she was a woman of a high spirit. She was usually very quiet in her demeanor; but if her indignation was once roused, it was not very easily quelled. I had been told that she once chased a white gentleman with a loaded pistol, because he insulted one of her daughters. I dreaded the consequences of a violent outbreak; and both pride and fear kept me silent. (28)

Jacobs goes on to write that Brent "dare[d] not tell grandmother the worst," even though the grandmother had "long suspected that all was not right" (37), portraying Linda as a fifteen-year-old caught without recourse in a matrix of fear and shame. Linda fears the master will punish her family or herself if she tells all; she fears that her grandmother might endanger herself by trying to protect her, and she fears her "strict" grandmother's condemnation for revealing the "unpure" events that have transpired in the Flint household. Jacobs's phrase "I dreaded the consequences of a violent outbreak" recalls for her readers the scene she describes earlier, in which the slave man and woman who speak of the master's sexual transgressions are tortured and then separated and sold. Several contemporary theorists on child abuse indicate that molesters consciously choose victims who they feel have the least power to tell.[35] Dr. Flint's threat that he would kill Linda if she "was not as silent as the grave" emphasizes the extreme pressure slave women confronted not to disclose sexual abuse. By this point in the narrative Jacobs had already shown readers how brutally the doctor could enforce silence.

Later, Jacobs portrays the grandmother believing Mrs. Flint and repudiating Brent when she hears Mrs. Flint's false accusation that the girl has become pregnant with the doctor's child. The grandmother's harsh response makes Brent's earlier fear about disclosure understandable. "My grandmother . . . believed what she said. She exclaimed, 'O Linda! has it come to this? I had rather see you dead than to see you as you now are. You are a disgrace to your dear mother.' She tore from my fingers my mother's wedding ring and her silver thimble. 'Go away!' she exclaimed, 'and never come to my house, again' " (57). The extreme nature of the grandmother's reaction suggests that Jacobs may have felt pressured by literary conventions to portray the repudiation. Perhaps Jacobs showed her disapproval to emphasize the grandmother's "purity," so that the older woman would appear to the audience as a sympathetic and "morally uplifted" woman. As this chapter continues, Linda attempts to explain to her grandmother why she became pregnant; she tells her "all [she] had been bearing for *years*" (58; emphasis added). Although Jacobs's wording does not explicitly show that she is reporting the doctor's sexual abuse, the passage strongly suggests this, since Linda is attempting to explain why she felt compelled to become pregnant by Sands. The grandmother's initial harshness, her silence, and her eventual pity and tears dramatize the difficult position of the slave mother or grandmother; like the sexually abused daughter, she, too, is caught in a matrix of forces—knowing that if the daughter is not silent, she may face torture, that if she protests her daughter's molestation, the entire family could face severe reprisals, and that both the daughter and she lack the power to escape from the white abusers without suffering.

In the course of describing Brent's relationship with the slave owner Mr. Sands, and explaining why she decided to have children with him, Jacobs clarifies the nature of the dangers Linda faced within the Flint household. Notably, the passages that assert who is responsible for Brent's relationship with Sands directly contradict each other. At first Jacobs writes that Linda became sexually involved with him deliberately and without compulsion: "*I will not try to screen myself behind the plea of compulsion from a master; for it was not so.* Neither can I plead ignorance or thoughtlessness. For years my master had done his utmost to pollute my mind with foul images, and to destroy the pure principles inculcated by my grandmother, and the good mistress of my childhood. The influences of slavery had the same effect on me that they had on other young girls; they had made me prematurely knowing, concerning the evil way of the world. *I knew what I did, and I did it with deliberate calculation*" (54, emphasis added). A few pages later, however, Jacobs writes scathingly of Flint's moralizing against Linda's "sin," her pregnancy, telling the readers that Flint's "persecutions had been the cause" of it (59). Such contradictory passages suggest that Jacobs experienced a sense of splitting. Her letters and narrative emphasize that she felt she had to demonstrate respect for concepts of ladyhood, purity, and virtue as a white audience might expect, yet her own experience had taught her that "the practice" of such a morality was impossible for a slave woman:[36] "You never knew what it is to be a slave; to be entirely unprotected by law or custom. . . . You never exhausted your ingenuity in avoiding the snares and eluding the power of the hated tyrant; you never shuddered at the sound of his footsteps, and trembled within hearing of his voice" (56).

Jacobs addresses virtuous white women throughout the chapter, detailing how the lives of slave women contrast with their own and why they could not judge Brent's decision to become sexually involved with Sands. Jacobs reveals that Linda begins her sexual relationship with him in an effort to assert her identity and independence: "I knew nothing would enrage Dr. Flint so much as to know that I favored another; and it was something to triumph over my tyrant even in that small way" (56). But as Jacobs shows that Brent entered into the relationship with Sands as the most self-affirming choice from among her limited options, she also stresses Brent's grave danger.

The description of Brent's relationship with Sands demonstrates the extreme constraints slave women confronted in their efforts to control their own sexuality and protect themselves and their families. Jacobs relates that before Linda began the relationship, she felt a greater sense of doom than she ever had before. Historians relate that during the nineteenth century, the age of menarche was considerably later than it is today—on the average fifteen.[37] Although Jacobs is not explicit on this point, Linda's sense of impending disaster may have been related to the fact that this was the first year in which she was physically able to become pregnant.[38] Most obviously, Brent's feeling of doom stemmed from the fact that Flint was building an isolated house in which he planned to force her to live. The secluded setting would have given Flint much greater sexual access to her than he had had in the past, making it likely that Brent would become pregnant by him.[39] Not only does Jacobs make it clear that Brent is desperate to avoid such a pregnancy because she finds Flint repulsive, she also stresses that slave women who were owned by Flint, were subject to his sexual abuse, and gave birth to children he fathered, faced the gravest danger of being sold when "a new fancy took him" (see 56). In several places Jacobs reports that Flint separated such women and their offspring by selling them into the deep South.

Research concerning sexually abused girls consistently shows that, as a means of escape and of establishing an independent sexual identity, they will initiate sexual relationships at young ages. Many choose to initiate such relationships once they are capable of becoming pregnant, and do so to avoid becoming pregnant by the molester. Often, out of fear of discovery, the molester will cease to abuse a young woman when she begins another sexual relationship.[40] Jacobs does not describe Brent's sexual interactions with Sands after she "takes the plunge" and becomes pregnant. Beyond her statements about Linda's shame (which seem tailored to her "virtuous" audience), she does not detail how Linda felt about the experience (see 56). But she does show how pregnancy and motherhood at first buffers Brent to some degree from the Flints in that she is allowed to live with her grandmother after she becomes pregnant (mostly because Mrs. Flint threatens to kill her if she returns to that household).

Although Jacobs barely comments on the fact that Brent's relationship with Sands is an ongoing one, she does describe the danger she is in after she becomes pregnant by him for the second time. During this period, Flint visits the grandmother's house, attacks Linda, and searches each of the rooms at "all hours of the day and night" (62-78). Perhaps Jacobs represented Flint's continuing abuse to emphasize why Linda would need to become pregnant with another child: in order to avoid a worse pregnancy. The fact that she expresses many times the horror she felt about bearing a child who would be born into slavery suggests that she must have felt extremely compelled to have one child with Sands, let alone two. But since Jacobs barely describes the continuing relationship with Sands during this part of the narrative, one can only speculate on the events and dynamics.

Jacobs's decision to limit her descriptions of Brent's relationship with Sands was politically astute, since representing Brent's ongoing sexual involvement, which takes place outside marriage, and across race and class, would have seemed "indelicate" to many of her readers. Like other heroines of the period, such as Catherine Linton in *Wuthering Heights,* Brent has the sexual intercourse (which results in her second pregnancy) in the blank space between chapters. In one sense, Jacobs did not need to describe the sexual interactions with Sands graphically; the fact that both of Linda's children strongly resemble him adequately signifies the sexual and ongoing nature of their relationship. Because Brent does not become pregnant as a result of Flint's abuse, Jacobs needed to *signify* the molestation in another manner, as she does through her imagery.

Telling Every Slavewoman's Story and Her Own: Indicting the Hierarchy of Abusers

Shifts in focus and displacements punctuate Brent's history as Jacobs intersperses within it an almost ethnographic description of the fates of other sexually abused slave women. Many slave narrators grappled with what would be most effective politically: to focus on the experiences of the enslaved as a class, or on the heroic aspects of an individual slave, or on ways in which a particular slave's experience might represent that of many held in slavery. Discussing the development of slave narratives as a genre, Frances Foster argues: "The search for spiritual identity in the slave narratives was complicated by the desire to use incidents in the narrators' experiences as examples of the experience of many others like him. As a result, the slave narrator increasingly focused upon the effects of a dehumanizing environment upon his race rather than upon his own individuality."[41]

Jacobs seems to have had several motives for telling the story of "everywoman" who is a slave in the course of communicating her own experience; each of the stories exemplifies Angela Davis's assertion, "Slavery relied as much on routine sexual abuse as it relied on the whip and the lash."[42] Jacobs exposed the institutionalized practice of sexual abuse early in the narrative so that her readers would, from the outset, understand the slave woman's position as a sexual as well as racial commodity. She explicitly defines the vulnerable position of slave girls while describing the day her brother was sold: "He [the slave trader] said he would give any price if the handsome lad was a girl. We thanked God that he was not" (22). Also, by portraying a range of fates the abused slave women and their families might face, Jacobs charts the relation among slave women as a class. As part of this effort, Jacobs often compares Linda's position (as a skilled household manager and literate woman) with the position of the female field hand who is abused or with the position of the slave woman whom the master forcibly makes his concubine. Jacobs repeatedly shows how the white masters profit economically from the sale or labor of the children born to slave women—whom they, their white sons, or their overseers have raped—especially when the children are "too fair" (12). As Davis argues, "The right claimed by slaveowners and their agents over the bodies of female slaves was a direct expression of their presumed property rights over Black people as a whole. The license to rape emanated from and facilitated the ruthless economic domination that was the guesome hallmark of slavery."[43]

By describing the experiences of enslaved women as a class, Jacobs emphasizes the economic relation between rape and race oppression. However, Jacobs's technique of displacing her narration of the sexual abuse Brent suffered by presenting the stories of others also serves another crucial function. When she begins to describe Flint's sexual abuse of Brent, Jacobs frequently switches from first-person narration to a generalized, third-person story of what "slave girls" have or what "the slave girl" has suffered. Sometimes, after starting to describe Linda's experience, she abruptly switches to a more concrete description of what happened to another particular slave woman or girl. Significantly, after such tangential narration, Jacobs almost never returns to narrating the incident about Linda. Consider, for example, these rhetorical shifts:

> He told me that I was his property; that I must be subject to his will in all things. My soul revolted against the mean tyranny. But where could I turn for protection? No matter whether the slave girl be as black as ebony or as fair as her mistress. In either case, there is no shadow of law to protect her from insult, from violence or even from death; all these are inflicted by fiends who bear the shape of men. . . . The degradation, the wrongs, the vices that grow out of slavery are more than I can describe. . . . Even the little child, who is accustomed to wait on her mistress and her children, will learn before she is twelve years old, why it is that her mistress hates such and such among the slaves. . . . She will become prematurely knowing in evil things. Soon she will learn to tremble when she hears her master's footfall. She will be compelled to realize she is no longer a child. If God has bestowed beauty upon her, it will prove her greatest curse. That which commands admiration in the white woman only hastens the degradation of the female slave. . . . I cannot tell you how much I suffered in the presence of these wrongs, nor how I am still pained in retrospect. (26-27)

Jacobs's narrative technique of distancing herself from the trauma of sexual abuse is strongly reminiscent of the classic dissociation psychologists face when their clients mask their own problems as those of "a friend" or as problems faced by "everyone." Many survivors of sexual abuse experience some type of blocking that protects them from overwhelming memories, especially when first recalling what they suffered.[44] Jacobs's shifts to third person may have allowed her to report the molestation in masked form without actually recalling that she was the victim of molestation, or without being overwhelmed by affect that she could not endure.

Jacobs's first description of Flint's sexual abuse of Linda, tucked into a passage concerning her grandmother's kindness, the weather, and her brother's troubles, shows a similar pattern of displacement: "I was his [William's] confidant. He came to me with all his troubles. I remember one instance in particular. It was on a lovely spring morning, and when I marked the sunlight dancing here and there, its beauty seemed to mock my sadness. For my master, whose restless, craving, vicious nature roved about day and night, seeking whom to devour, had just left me, with stinging, scathing words; words that scathed ear and brain like fire. . . . So deeply was I absorbed in painful reflections afterwards, that I neither saw nor heard the entrance of any one, till the voice of William sounded close beside me" (16). The organization in this passage is striking because it suggests that Jacobs was trying to deflect attention from what is most horrifying within it. Her diction specifies that William's trials are the focus, even though the subsequent lines indicate that Linda's are more extreme than his at this point. When Jacobs writes soon after, "I remember one instance in particular," one would assume that she is referring to William's troubles, since that has been the focus in the preceding sentences. Instead, the passage digresses to reveal the young girl's anguish and danger, as if Jacobs had suddenly stopped in the middle of one thought to reveal a horrifying vision she could not repress.

In spite of the lacunae and displacements that mark the text, Jacobs reports on a wide range of sexual violence throughout *Incidents*. She indicts a hierarchy of white male sexual abusers as she describes the molestation of young girls, the rape of women, concubinage, and the sexual exploitation of male slaves by both white males and females. By stressing that slave-owning fathers corrupted their white sons, Jacobs highlighted the dynastic elements of these practices (see 51-52 for one example). Representing the dynastic reproduction of the class of sexual abusers served the political function of stressing for her readers that such oppression would continue long after her escape and after her book was published. Jacobs strove to communicate that slave women as a class had to cope with such trauma, and that even though she had suffered gravely, her position was less extreme than that of many other slave women who suffered from the "double burden" of gender and race oppressions.

In one of the saddest parts of *Incidents,* Jacobs demonstrated the on-going, institutionalized pattern of sexual abuse, using the same imagery of "pouring vile language" into the child's ear that she used earlier to portray Flint's molestation of Linda. But here, in the case of Brent's daughter, it would have been even less likely that what took place were mere "whisperings." Her daughter's position was even more vulnerable than her mother's had been; she was isolated from all her kin and in an unfamiliar Northern community. Jacobs again shows the tremendous difficulty the child has in speaking to her mother:

> She never made any complaint about her own inconveniences and troubles; but a mother's observing eye easily perceived that she was not happy. On the occasion of one of my visits I found her unusually serious. When I asked her what was the matter, she said nothing was the matter. But I insisted upon knowing what made her look so very grave. Finally I ascertained that she felt troubled about the dissipation that was continually going on in the house. She was sent to the store very often for rum and brandy. . . . She was always desirous not to add to my troubles more than she could help, and I did not discover till years afterwards that Mr. Thorne's intemperance was not the only annoyance she suffered from him. Though he professed too much gratitude to my grandmother to injure any of her descendants, he had poured vile language into the ears of her innocent great-grandchild. (183)

The dynamics in this scene replicate those earlier in the narrative in which Linda was unable to incriminate her abuser when her grandmother asked what was wrong. Similarly, Linda's daughter remains silent about what "made her look so grave."

Jacobs attributes the silence to the daughter's desire to spare her mother, recalling Linda's effort, as a child, to spare her grandmother. Even without detailing what the girl has suffered, Jacobs's repetition of the earlier imagery clearly conveys her meaning about sexual abuse. Through this passage, she further exposed the myth of the North as haven, showing that Linda could not prevent what she feared her daughter would experience when she was born. With crushing irony, the abuse has occurred in the "free" North where her daughter has been sent by her master-father to live as a slave.

Near the conclusion of the narrative, Linda speaks the taboo and tells her daughter of the abuses she experienced in childhood and young adulthood, overcoming the brutal silencing that both had suffered. Through phrasing that reverses the earlier images of Flint and the daughter's abuser "pour[ing] vile language" (183) into the young women's ears, Brent expresses with joy her daughter's understanding and acceptance of her story. She tells us, "my pent-up feelings had often longed to *pour themselves out to some one I could trust*" (93, emphasis added). Much as Alice Walker portrays her experience of a renewed self-love and acceptance through her daughter's vision of her mother and the world in "Beauty: When the Other Dancer is the Self," Jacobs, a hundred years earlier, portrayed

Linda experiencing a similar spiritual renewal through her daughter's insight and love. Perhaps finding greater self-acceptance through her daughter's support was part of what enabled Jacobs to express herself in writing.

Jacobs's legacy to her readers is a multilayered one. Already, her text has encouraged reexamination of such subjects as forms of slave resistance, relations between Black and white women in the old South and in the abolitionist movement, and concepts and practices of mothering within slavery. But scholars might further investigate how the psychodynamics within *Incidents* relate to other works, especially those that deal specifically with the subject of sexual exploitation. Nineteenth-century African American women writers textualized sexual abuse and sexual experience in general as they were constrained by, and yet transcended, images that historically defined them as sexually insatiable, primitive, and lascivious. Study of the psychodynamics, and especially the metaphors, lacunae, and displacements within these women's texts can help scholars to understand their complex responses to rigid cultural definitions of gender, sexuality, class, and race. Further critical examination would be especially timely since contemporary novelists such as Toni Morrison, Barbara Chase-Riboud, and Sherley Anne Williams are exploring the possible meanings of these lacunae and displacements in their fictional recreations of nineteenth-century African American women's experiences within and after slavery.

Much as Linda Brent could not, as a child, tell all to her grandmother, uncle, or brother, Jacobs emphasizes that she cannot tell all to her readers. However, one of Jacobs's final assertions, after she hears of Flint's death, demonstrates her skill as an author. She offers an indictment of Flint that functions as a powerful epitaph for him, inscribed in her text, that has proved more enduring than any inscription on his headstone would have been: "There are wrongs which even the grave does not bury. The man was odious to me while he lived and his memory is odious now" (201). Writing about the sexual abuse she suffered twenty years earlier, Jacobs exposed the man who strove to make her "as silent as the grave" and, in doing so, was able to write herself out of silence.

Notes

[1] Harriet Jacobs, *Incidents in the Life of a Slave Girl.* All page references in the text are to the 1973 edition.

[2] Minrose Gwin articulates the sense of splitting, schism, and doubleness that a Black woman was likely to feel as she wrote about her former enslavement. "In a literary remaking of her life as a slave, the black woman sees herself dually as an individual with a burgeoning sense of self and as a symbol of former powerlessness." See Minrose Gwin, *Black and White Women of the Old South,* 58-59.

[3] Dorothy Sterling, *We Are Your Sisters,* 20.

[4] Jean Fagin Yellin, "Text and Contexts of Harriet Jacobs' *Incidents in the Life of a Slave Girl*," 262.

[5] Ibid., 269.

[6] See Paula Giddings, *When and Where I Enter,* and Frances Foster, *Witnessing Slavery,* 131.

[7] Hazel Carby, *Reconstructing Womanhood,* 35. Many details in *Incidents* suggest that Jacobs was familiar with abolitionist texts. She had access to a wide range of these works during 1849-50 when she helped run the antislavery reading room above the offices of Frederick Douglass's *North Star.* See Jean Fagin Yellin's recent edition of Jacobs's *Incidents in the Life of a Slave Girl,* xvi.

[8] Angela Y. Davis, *Women, Race, and Class,* 41.

[9] Ibid., 27.

[10] Dorothy Sterling, in *We Are Your Sisters,* and Jean Fagin Yellin, in her new edition of *Incidents,* have provided much needed biographical information about Jacobs that documents the factual nature of her narrative. In *Self-Discovery and Authority in Afro-American Narrative,* Valerie Smith discusses how "both literal and figurative enclosures proliferate" within the text (30); she also points to several "narrative silences" in *Incidents* and relates them to "those aspects of her [Jacobs's] own sexuality for which the genre does not allow" (42). Hazel Carby in *Reconstructing Womanhood* focuses on the female slave narrators' responses to "the general terrain of images and stereotypes produced by antebellum sexual ideologies," and assesses how "the ideology of true womanhood . . . determined the shape of the public voice of black women writers" (40). In addition to these literary scholars, Elizabeth Fox-Genovese and Minrose Gwin have, through their merging of literary and historical methods, made valuable contributions to assessing the relations between Black and white women in the old South.

[11] In her commentary on *Incidents,* Sterling characterizes Jacobs's relation to her former master by writing, "Fifteen-year-old Harriet Jacobs and Louisa Picquet fought off their masters only to say 'yes' to the next white men who approached them" (22). Gwin (in a discussion like Sterling's that conflates the author, Harriet Jacobs, and her fictionalized self-representative, Linda Brent) only comments briefly on descriptions of Flint's abuse: "At fifteen Harriet Jacobs became the mistress of a white man [Sands] quite simply to escape the clutches of her lecherous master" (57). Yellin ("Texts and Contexts," 270), the most explicit in her commentary on Flint's abuse, writes that Brent "prevents her master from raping her." Smith seems to

agree with Yellin: "Her master, for some reason reluctant to force her to submit sexually, harassed her, pleaded with her, and tried to bribe her into capitulating in the manner of an importunate suitor" (*Narrative*, 36). From a substantially different point of view, Fox-Genovese makes a suggestion that can serve as a starting point for my analysis: "It stretches the limits of all credulity that Linda Brent actually eluded her master's sexual advances." See *Within the Plantation Household*, 392.

[12] Throughout my consideration of Jacobs's descriptions of sexual exploitation, I use the terms "sexual abuse" and "molestation" to define a range of practices, including "any kind of exploitative sexual contact," especially that which had to be kept secret. See Diana Russell, *The Secret Trauma*, 59. Judith Lewis Herman comments: "From the psychological point of view, especially from the child's [or young adult's] point of view, the sexual motivation of the contact, and the fact that it must be kept secret, are far more significant than the exact nature of the act itself." See Judith Lewis Herman with Lisa Hirshman, *Father-Daughter Incest*, 70. In order to distinguish physical from nonphysical assault, when I refer to sexual "harassment" I am referring solely to verbal sexual abuse.

[13] The degree to which Jacobs may or may not be portraying literal details and events is not the central issue in my analysis; rather, my primary focus is on the ways in which Jacobs has constructed her literary representation of her experiences and the ways in which this representation relates to her position as a Black woman writing about sexuality and sexual abuse.

[14] Carby, *Reconstructing Womanhood*, 57. Several historical sources emphasize the profound levels of the slave women's resistance to sexual exploitation. See Davis, *Women, Race, and Class*, and bell hooks, *Ain't I a Woman?*

[15] Several critics have argued that Jacobs was reticent about writing because she had had a sexual relationship outside marriage and had borne children as a result. Analyzing the descriptions of Brent's relationship with Sands accounts for some of the ambivalence about disclosure in the narrative. I offer the analysis of Flint's sexual abuse of Brent as an additional explanation of Jacobs's ambivalence about disclosure, rather than as a strictly alternative one. See Yellin, Fox-Genovese, and Carby for discussions of Brent's relationship with Sands.

[16] Yellin, "Text and Contexts," p. 277.

[17] Florence Rush, *The Best Kept Secret*, 63.

[18] Foster, *Witnessing Slavery*, 84.

[19] Ibid., 85.

[20] Ibid., 83-84.

[21] Sandra Gilbert and Susan Gubar, *The Madwoman in the Attic*.

[22] In similar terms, seventy years later, W. B. Yeats described the sexual assault on the Virgin Mary's ear in his poem "The Mother of God": "The threefold terror of love; a fallen flare / Through the hollow of an ear; / Wings beating about the room; / The terror of all terrors that I bore / The Heavens in my womb." See *The Selected Poems and Two Plays of William Butler Yeats*, ed. M. L. Rosenthal, 133. The contemporary idiom of protecting or not offending the "virgin ears" of a young female listener also characterizes the ear as a sexualized orifice.

[23] Hortense Spillers, "Interstices," 97. Jacobs's portrayal of the abused ear also recalls the imagery in *Hamlet* when the ghost describes his brother as a "serpent" who "rankly abused" him by pouring poison in his ear while he was "sleeping in [his] orchard." Thus Claudius murdered the king and "won to his shameful lust / the will of [the] most seeming-virtuous queen" (1.5.35-75). The description links images of virtue, corrupt sexuality, references to Genesis, and demonic abuse with poison administered through the ear.

[24] Julia Kristeva, "Stabat Mater," 142.

[25] Other Black women found it difficult to describe the sexual abuse they suffered. Mary Prince's (1831) narrative was one of the earliest to portray the sexual abuse of Black women by slave owners. See *The History of Mary Prince, a West African Slave*, in Henry Louis Gates, Jr., ed., *The Classic Slave Narrative*. Elizabeth Keckley describes four years of sexual abuse in two sentences, concluding, "I do not care to dwell upon this subject because it is one that is fraught with pain." See Elizabeth Keckley, *Behind the Scenes*, 50.

[26] See Barbara G. Walker, *The Woman's Encyclopedia of Myths and Secrets*, 431-33.

[27] See Ellen Bass and Laura Davis, *The Courage to Heal*.

[28] Ibid., 104-10.

[29] See ibid., 92-103.

[30] Russell, *The Secret Trauma*, 128.

[31] Ibid., 33-35.

[32] Ibid., pp. 256-59.

[33] Herman, *Father-Daughter Incest*, 28-29; and Russell, *The Secret Trauma*, 256-59.

[34] Herman, *Father-Daughter Incest,* 116-19.

[35] Ibid., 131-35.

[36] See Yellin, "Text and Contexts," 271, 273-74.

[37] See Rush, *The Best Kept Secret,* 62-65.

[38] At the time of her first pregnancy, Linda is sixteen, and Jacobs portrays Flint's sexual abuse beginning when she was fifteen. However, by referring to "all [she] had been bearing for *years*" (58, emphasis added), Jacobs implies that the doctor may have been molesting Brent for a longer period of time than she chronicles in the narrative.

[39] Comparing the way Brent resists her master's plan to make her his concubine with the idealized portrayal of concubinage in Lydia Maria Child's story "The Quadroons" (1847) reveals the radical nature of *Incidents.* By incorporating much of Child's story in the various versions of *Clotel* (1853), William Wells Brown reinforced definitions of the slave concubine as a passive and tragic beauty with a "high poetic nature." See "The Quadroons," by Lydia Maria Child, in Child, *Fact and Fiction,* and Brown, *Clotel or, The President's Daughter.*

[40] See Russell, *The Secret Trauma,* 166-67; and Herman, *Father-Daughter Incest,* 100. Much of the recent research on sexual abuse focuses on incest and the way in which an older family member's molestation constitutes a betrayal of a dependent child's trust; but for the slave girl who was molested by a white man, the dynamics relating to dependency and betrayal would be quite different. More sociological and psychological research is needed on the way in which race oppression changes the dynamics and effects of sexual abuse. In contrast to the lack of social science research, contemporary novelists such as Gayle Jones, Toni Morrison, Sherley Anne Williams, and Barbara Chase-Riboud have been exploring the effects of white male sexual exploitation of African American women within slavery; Jones's *Corregidora* is especially powerful because it explores the complex effects of both incestuous and transgenerational sexual abuse.

[41] Foster, *Witnessing Slavery,* 5.

[42] Davis, *Women, Race, and Class,* 175.

[43] Ibid., 175.

[44] For some examples, see Bass and Davis, *The Courage to Heal,* 54-93.

Works Cited

Bass, Ellen, and Laura Davis. *The Courage to Heal: A Guide for Women Survivors of Child Sexual Abuse.* New York: Harper & Row, 1988.

Brown, William Wells. *Clotel or, The President's Daughter.* 1853. Rpt. New York: Carol Publishing Group, 1969.

Carby, Hazel. *Reconstructing Womanhood: The Emergence of the Afro-American Woman Novelist.* New York: Oxford Univ. Press, 1987.

Child, Lydia Maria. *Fact and Fiction: A Collection of Stories.* New York, 1847.

[Davis, Angela Y.] *Women, Race, and Class.* New York: Vintage Books, 1981.

Foster, Frances. *Witnessing Slavery: The Development of Ante-Bellum Slave Narratives.* Westport, Conn.: Greenwood Press, 1979.

Fox-Genovese, Elizabeth. *Within the Plantation Household: Black and White Women of the Old South.* Chapel Hill: Univ. of North Carolina Press, 1988.

Giddings, Paula. *When and Where I Enter: The Impact of Black Women on Race and Sex in America.* New York: Bantam Books, 1985.

Gilbert, Sandra M., and Susan Gubar. *The Madwoman in the Attic: The Woman Writer and the Nineteenth-Century Literary Imagination.* New Haven, Conn.: Yale Univ. Press, 1979.

Gwin, Minrose. *Black and White Women of the Old South.* Knoxville: Univ. of Tennessee Press, 1985.

[Herman, Judith Lewis, with Lisa Hirshman.] *Father-Daughter Incest.* Cambridge: Harvard Univ. Press, 1981.

Jacobs, Harriet. *Incidents in the Life of a Slave Girl.* New York: Harcourt Brace Jovanovich, 1973. Ed. Jean Fagin Yellin. Cambridge: Harvard Univ. Press, 1987. Orig. ed. Maria Lydia Child, 1861.

Jones, Gayl. *Corregidora.* New York: Random House, 1975.

Keckley, Elizabeth. *Behind the Scenes; or, Thirty Years a Slave and Four in the White House.* New York: Arno, 1968 (1868).

Kristeva, Julia. "Stabat Mater." *Poetics Today* 6, no. 1-2 (1985): 133-52. Trans. Toril Moi. Rpt. in *The Kristeva Reader,* 160-86. New York: Columbia Univ. Press, 1986.

Morrison, Toni. *Beloved.* New York: Knopf, 1987.

———. *The Bluest Eye.* New York: Simon & Schuster, 1970.

———. "Unspeakable Things Unspoken: The Afro-American Presence in American Literature." In *Toni*

Morrison (Modern Critical Views series), ed. Harold Bloom, 201-30. New York: Chelsea House, 1990.

Prince, Mary. *The History of Mary Prince, A West African Slave.* 1831. Rpt. in *The Classic Slave Narrative,* ed. Henry Louis Gates, Jr., 183-242. New York: Mentor, 1987.

Rush, Florence. *The Best Kept Secret: Sexual Abuse of Children.* Englewood Cliffs, N.J.: Prentice Hall, 1980.

Russell, Diana. *The Secret Trauma.* New York: Basic Books, 1986.

Smith, Valerie. *Self-Discovery and Authority in Afro-American Narrative.* Cambridge: Harvard Univ. Press, 1987.

Spillers, Hortense J. "Interstices: A Small Drama of Words." In *Pleasure and Danger: Exploring Female Sexuality,* ed. Carole S. Vance, 73-100. Boston: Routledge and Kegan Paul, 1984.

Sterling, Dorothy. *We Are Your Sisters.* New York: Norton, 1984.

Walker, Barbara G. *The Woman's Encyclopedia of Myths and Secrets.* San Francisco: Harper & Row, 1983.

Williams, Sherley Anne. *Dessa Rose.* New York: Berkley, 1987.

———. *Give Birth to Brightness: A Thematic Study in Neo-Black Literature.* New York: Dial, 1972.

———. "Meditations on History." In *Midnight Birds: Stories by Contemporary Black Women Writers,* ed. Mary Helen Washington, 200-248. Garden City, N.Y.: Anchor, 1980.

———. *The Peacock Poems.* Hanover, N.H.: Univ. Press of New England, 1975.

———. "Returning to the Blues: Esther Phillips and Contemporary Blues Culture." *Callaloo* 14 (1991): 816-28.

———. *Someone Sweet Angel Chile.* New York: Morrow, 1982.

Yeats, William Butler. "The Mother of God." In *The Selected Poems and Two Plays of William Butler Yeats,* ed. M. L. Rosenthal, 133. New York: Collier Books, 1962.

Yellin, Jean Fagin. "Text and Contexts of Harriet Jacobs' *Incidents in the Life of a Slave Girl: Written by Herself.*" In *The Slave's Narrative,* ed. Charles Davis and Henry Louis Gates, Jr., 262-82. New York: Oxford Univ. Press, 1985.

Carolyn Sorisio (essay date 1996)

SOURCE: " 'There is might in Each': Conceptions of Self in Harriet Jacobs's *Incidents in the Life of a Slave Girl, Written by Herself,*" in *Legacy,* Vol. 13, No. 1, 1996, pp. 1-18.

[*In the following essay, Sorisio discusses the influence of Romanticism and Transcendentalism on the nineteenth-century's—and on Jacobs's—perception of "self," arguing that Linda Brent's sense of self encompasses both an individual and a collective identity. Additionally, Sorisio examines Jacobs's exploitation of sentimental conventions.*]

In 1992, archaeologists discovered an eighteenth-century slave burial ground in lower Manhattan, sparking controversy over the fate of the skeletal remains. Then-mayor David Dinkens called for construction on the site to halt, dismayed by the "highly inappropriate and insensitive" handling of the bones. However, the chief archaeologist praised the excavation: "We're picking up the pages from an 18th-century primary document and dusting them off, but as of yet, we haven't read them." The archaeologist's comparison of the bones to text underscores the intricate question of how we read the remains of a past that systematically denied people dignity in both their lives and their deaths. Some saw the bones as individuals, while others viewed them as part of a cultural text, sacred not for their own identity, but rather for what they could collectively contribute to African-American history.[1]

A similar debate frames readings of Harriet Jacobs's 1861 narrative ***Incidents in the Life of a Slave Girl, Written by Herself.*** As scholars continue to unearth and reexamine America's literature and history, Jacobs's text, which has gained considerable attention since Jean Fagan Yellin's 1987 edition, serves a pivotal role. Like the graveyard, it is a rare find. Although more than one hundred book-length pre-emancipation narratives and thousands more post-emancipation memoirs endure, few ante-bellum narratives were written by women. Within the scarcity of the slave woman's word, we find Jacobs's text—powerfully written, wonderfully articulated, and enormously complex. Yet like the fragile bones, people have trouble determining the proper way to handle what remains of Harriet Jacobs.[2]

To some, her document stands as the historical record of an individual slave woman, evidencing a unified "self" who recorded her life for future generations. This interpretation is supported by the tradition of the slave narrative genre, in which African Americans "proved" their full humanity and potential for citizenship through their command of literacy. As Charles T. Davis and Henry Louis Gates, Jr., remind us, "The slave narrative represents the attempts of blacks to *write themselves into being*" (xxiii). So why should we be surprised when critics and historians read *Incidents* as a primary historical document, the remains of a "self" whose presence is intentionally translated into text?[3]

By contrast, some critics read Jacobs's work as a textual presentation designed to gratify the aesthetic and ideological expectations of white Northern Christian women. Rather than finding Jacobs in the text, they see a reflection only of bourgeois values. For example, Elizabeth Fox-Genovese views Jacobs's work as primarily persona, a performance designed to please her audience. She doubts that Jacobs's master did not rape her, and that she spent seven years in an attic space (374-92). Likewise, some critics impose contemporary critical paradigms onto Jacobs's text without paying sufficient attention to historical findings. In her otherwise excellent essay, Sidonie Smith refers to the role of the text's editor, Lydia Maria Child, as "editorial colonization," wording that suggests Jacobs had little control over her text (98). In such a framework, it is hard to find the "person" of Jacobs at all.

When taken to extremes, the interpretation of Jacobs's text as some type of mask to please her audience disturbingly echoes the doubt over authenticity that surrounded the publication of slave narratives in their times. For years, many erroneously assumed that *Incidents* was either fiction or an account written or drastically altered by Child. However, Yellin's meticulous excavation of historical archives demonstrates that Jacobs was not only a real person, but that the facts of her life are, as she claimed in her preface, "strictly true." Also, Child's biographer, Carolyn L. Karcher, indicates that Child did not unduly influence the text.[4] The fact that Yellin published her research prior to both Fox-Genovese's and Smith's work is troublesome, as it points to a lingering tendency to deny Jacobs the same authority given to many of her contemporaries.

Part of the challenge in handling the remains of Jacobs is reconsidering the critical binaries we establish between a "true" or "core" self and a "masked" or "presentational" one. Like archaeologists, careful readers should look to Jacobs both for the remains of an individual self and for an indication of collective cultural stories. But, also like the scientists who dig, readers encounter various strata. Rather than assume the layers we unearth are somehow "false" and that a "true" Jacobs lies buried in the text, we can understand them as exhibiting competing and contradictory ideologies of self in the nineteenth century. Although Jacobs's narrative functions as an abolitionist text, it also participates in heated philosophical debates over the nature of identity that were prevalent during her time. Jacobs challenges notions of a corporeal "essential" self, and revises concepts of a transcendental or metaphysical one to include African-American women. Doing so, she carves an unprecedented space for African-American women in the philosophical, literary, and political spheres. Uncovering Jacobs leads us not only to her story, but also to an alternative record of "the American self" in the nineteenth century.

. . . . .

One of the nineteenth century's most devastating legacies to our own is the understanding of gender and race as natural and innate. In an effort in part to justify slavery in the New Republic, American ethnologists were the first to develop a theory of polygenesis, the assertion that various races were created as permanent and separate species. American scientists were obsessed with finding physiological justification for race and gender hierarchy in a nation that upheld a democratic ideal.[5] As one of its founders defined it, ethnology was invented to investigate "the mental and physical differences of mankind, and the organic laws upon which they depend" in order to determine the "principles" of "social existence" (Nott 49).

However, despite—or perhaps because of—the increasing prevalence of scientific essentialism, many people also upheld a belief in identity as transcendent and disembodied, a concept that coincided with both Romanticism and Spiritualism.[6] Sidonie Smith traces the general rise in the eighteenth and nineteenth century of a metaphysical self both disembodied and dissociated from communal roles (76). The metaphysical self was based heavily upon Enlightenment faith in reason, and rested on both the "I" and the "eye" of the individual:

> Then through the lens of a coherent self-knowledge, this "self" that "sees" turns toward the world and elaborates through reason that "transcends all situation, context and perspective," a universalizing, unifying vision characterized as "impartial." (77)[7]

Many Romantics could take this I/eye for granted, a privilege that was ironically obtained through their embodied status in society. For writers and philosophers such as Ralph Waldo Emerson and Henry David Thoreau, the I/eye was the primary vantage point, and the self was able to transcend both nature and the body. Emerson states in his 1836 essay "Nature,"

> Strictly speaking, therefore, all that is separate from us, all which Philosophy distinguishes as the NOT ME, that is, both nature and art, all other men and my own body, must be ranked under this name, NATURE. (1: 8)

For many Romantics, philosophy could create an escape from corporeality. Yet, Smith argues, this "self of essences" usually relied on the construction of both women and non-Caucasian races as not only embodied, but also encumbered and defined by biology. It legitimized its transcendent existence, in part, through the examination of the "natural" world, and considered women and "other" races phenomena to be studied. In this sense, although the Romantic self offered transcendence in an age that increasingly tended toward scientific essentialism, it nonetheless rested on a similar dynamic as the scientific paradigm. Both entailed scrutinizing others as objects to authorize the status of subject. In the case of both gender and race, Jacobs would "naturally" fall under the category of object.

At times, Romanticism's emphasis on a transcendent self could result in an aversion to the political sphere and a zealous faith in individual rather than communal identity. It remains one of the greatest paradoxes of the time that writers such as Thoreau and Emerson, although intellectually opposed to slavery, nonetheless encouraged a retreat from communal solutions to political problems by defining them as individual questions of ethics. Twelve years before the publication of *Incidents,* Thoreau asserts in "Resistance to Civil Government,"

> I came into this world, not chiefly to make this a good place to live in, but to live in it, be it good or bad. A man has not everything to do, but something; and because he cannot do *everything,* it is not necessary that he should do *something* wrong. It is not my business to be petitioning the Governor or the Legislature any more than it is theirs to petition me; and if they should not hear my petition, what should I do then? (92-93)

For Thoreau, the best response to atrocities such as the Mexican War and slavery was to withdraw support from the state and personally refrain from participating in evil. His night in prison serves as an epiphany, from which he learns to privilege solitude: "The people among whom I lived . . . their friendship was for summer weather only" (99). Punished by the state, exiled by his moral code, Thoreau is primed to become a "majority of one."

Like Thoreau's essay, Emerson's "Self-Reliance" serves as the quintessential call to individualism. Two decades before the publication of Jacobs's narrative, Emerson defines the conspiracy of society against the manhood of its members, and, in a passage that becomes very telling when juxtaposed with Jacobs, insists that the individual self must transcend even familial bonds to search for an intangible truth:

> Live no longer to the expectation of these deceived and deceiving people with whom we converse. Say to them, O father, O mother, O wife, O brother, O friend, I have lived with you after appearances hitherto. Henceforward I am the truth's. (2: 41-42)

Thoreau and Emerson withdraw from community and retreat to a self that transcends both their bodies and their surroundings. This shift distanced them from the rhetoric of the late eighteenth century, which was of-

ten accompanied by Enlightenment faith in the communal actions of rational beings. Eric Sundquist argues that revolutionary rhetoric—rather than disappearing in ante-bellum America as some critics claim—surfaces in the writings of African Americans (36). To write oneself into a person, or more specifically into a man, the former slave needed to articulate himself as an individual in the Enlightenment sense. As Joanne M. Braxton notes, critics have defined the "primary Afro-American archetype as that of the articulate hero who discovers the links among freedom, literacy, and struggle" (19). Thus, Frederick Douglass's 1845 *Narrative of the Life of Frederick Douglass, an American Slave,* marks Douglass as a man not only by his climactic fight with his overseer Covey, but also through his mastery of literacy. In this way, Douglass depicts himself as Emersonian in his self-reliance, but revolutionary in his faith in the communal and active citizenship signified by his participation in the "Republic of Letters."

How strange Jacobs appears when compared to these men. Prison is not an overnight stay, which translates into an apt metaphor or lesson in solitude, but a seven-year reality that leaves her physically handicapped the remainder of her life. A "thicket of bushes" concealing poisonous snakes replaces Thoreau's refuge at Walden pond. Jacobs's embodied experiences as a slave woman taught her to question Emerson's and Thoreau's transcendental individualism. She knew that part of her identity was determined by the body, which she could not presume to label "not me."

However, Jacobs was also aware of the scientific debates surrounding the nature of the "Negro" and "mulatto" and did not want to assert an identity based solely on corporeal experience. In chapter 8, she dismisses polygenesis as a "libel upon the heavenly Father, who 'made of one blood all nations of men!' " (44). Jacobs's challenge as an author, then, was to write the knowledge that came through her embodied experience without reifying scientific essentialism. She does so by writing about her life while at the same time asserting an amorphous and transcendent will that exists outside her slave's body. By insisting so firmly on a noncorporeal will, Jacobs can, like Emerson, assert a "me" that is "not me," breaking the binary of metaphysical self/embodied other. She can also reaffirm the ideal of an American as a race and gender neutral citizen, and reaffirm the Revolutionary rhetoric from which many Romantics retreated.

Throughout her narrative, Jacobs—via her persona, Linda Brent—echoes both revolutionary rhetoric and "Self-Reliance" by emphasizing her natural drive to be a free individual.[8] When her relatives urge her to turn herself in after she flees, she reminds herself that she previously resolved that there would be "no turning back. 'Give me liberty, or give me death,' was my motto" (99). She resembles not only Patrick Henry in privileging liberty over life, but also Emerson in her determination to listen to her self rather than her family or community. However, although self-reliance clearly appeals to Linda, it nonetheless is a model which cannot completely fit her experience. Repeatedly, Linda regrets that she is not a sole individual, that so many lives are caught up in a common destiny with hers. She agonizes for her friends and family who risk their lives to help her and laments, "It seemed as if I were born to bring sorrow on all who befriended me, and that was the bitterest drop in the bitter cup of my life" (104).

Linda's collective identity and destiny is not atypical for female slaves. Braxton indicates that the dominant definition of self, prevalent in male narratives, was not satisfactory for female slaves. Rather, the heroine "celebrates her liberation and her children's as the fruit of a collective effort, not an individual one" (20). Valerie Smith also suggests, "Jacobs's tale is not the classic story of the triumph of the individual will; rather, it is more a story of a triumphant self-in-relation" (216-17). Linda exhibits an interdependence with other characters, and has to balance her revolutionary and transcendent impulses with the reality of her historically constructed roles—heavily influenced by gender and race—as a female slave and mother.

It is appropriate, then, that Jacobs chooses to use the discourse of sentimental fiction, a genre which, according to Jane Tompkins, "represents a monumental effort to reorganize culture from the woman's point of view" (83). Sentimental discourse, besides privileging a Christian ideology that is significant to Jacobs and her readers, also demonstrates a far more relational self, as it accentuates motherhood and family, areas in which individualism must be radically redefined. Linda's early childhood experience can hardly be overestimated in importance. She introduces herself via her family, which consists of hard-working slaves dating back to the Revolutionary War; she begins, "I was born a slave; but I never knew it till six years of happy childhood had passed away" (5). Rather than seeing herself as the dominant society saw her—as chattel—Linda identifies herself primarily in relation to her family.

The tension between societal views of Linda and her own identity is highlighted in the second chapter, when Linda's brother, called by both his father and mistress, answers his mistress first. His father tells him, "You are *my* child . . . and when I call you, you should come immediately, if you have to pass through fire and water" (9). As this incident suggests, Linda's family privileges collective respect of each other over the rules of slavery. As we will see, the family functions as a source of strength for Linda, but, paradoxically, it also stands as a substantial roadblock on her journey to freedom.

Because Linda is a self-in-relation, she cannot gain her freedom by escaping alone, as did her Uncle Benjamin; she has to consider her allegiance to her children and grandmother, bonds that are primarily defined by gender.

Linda considers her grandmother, Aunt Martha, "a great treasure," but her love for her is not without complications. After the death of Linda's mother, her grandmother serves as both a surrogate mother and a strong grandmother. However, Aunt Martha's love for her family forces her into preferring that they remain slaves rather than escape North, which she believes would end either in permanent separation or in death. When Linda resolves to run away, Aunt Martha asks, "Linda, do you want to kill your old grandmother?" Not content to rely on Linda's responsibilities as a granddaughter, she continues, "Do you mean to leave your little helpless children?" Linda's response is telling: "My courage failed me, in view of the sorrow I should bring on that faithful, loving old heart" (91). Aunt Martha symbolizes the woman who would forfeit freedom for family. She can be read in relation to the text's Northern audience, many of whom may have felt they surrendered personal liberty to maintain the family, and asked their daughters for a similar sacrifice. However, Linda shows that such a price for familial stability—especially under patriarchal and slave-holding terms—is too high to pay. Like Emerson, she resolves to follow her own notion of truth and longs to be free. However, she cannot and will not allow this goal to overpower her responsibilities to, and love for, her family. Her story becomes the quest to obtain both family and freedom.

Consequently, the most important decisions in Linda's life stem not from what she wants as an individual, but rather from what is best for her family; she balances the emotions of all family members and strives for the collective best solution. She states,

> I could have made my escape alone; but it was more for my helpless children than for myself that I longed for freedom. Though the boon would have been precious to me, above all price, I would not have taken it at the expense of leaving them in slavery. (89)

Unlike the archetypal American hero who can emerge from his place of confinement and seek freedom as an individual, Linda must be concerned with how her decisions affect others. When her master, Flint, gives her a choice between moving into a private house (with the expectation of concubinage) or going to the plantation (a serious threat as its remoteness allowed for uncensured abuse of slaves), Linda calls his offer a "snare" and decides that, if accepted, "escape would be impossible." So, despite the serious threat of sexual assault from Flint's son, she goes to the plantation, resolving "I would foil my master and save my children, or I would perish in the attempt" (84). Linda's final decision to escape is motivated by the news that her children are to be sent permanently to the plantation, which she fears will result in the sexual abuse of her daughter and the demotion of her son to the status of field laborer. Distress for her children gives Linda the strength to defy her grandmother, a move she does not accomplish without significant guilt.

Society, as Emerson suggests, is "a joint-stock company" in conspiracy against her, but Linda cannot opt to be a majority of one. The rest of her narrative becomes a lesson in courage through compromise. At all points in the journey, Linda is prompted primarily by concern for her children, such as when she crawls down from her hiding space to plead with her children's father for their freedom. Consequently, one of Flint's tactics to trap Linda is to punish her family; her brother William and children are jailed after she escapes. Although Linda's first impulse is to turn herself in, her brother sends her a note to stay away. Encouraged, she remains hidden and further schemes for her children.

Linda's experiences repeatedly demonstrate the complex role she plays in relation to her family. Perhaps the most poignant example of the self-in-relation is the life-long guilt, and simultaneous denial of that guilt, that accompanies Linda's decision to enter into a sexual liaison with Sands, a prominent white citizen, in order to avoid being raped by Flint. In one of the most complex chapters of her narrative, Linda describes her choice to her audience. Although she begins by saying "I knew what I did, and I did it with deliberate calculation," she undercuts her claim in the next paragraph, declaring, "I was forsaken by God and man . . . and I became reckless in my despair." Linda continues throughout her story to apologize for her "fall" while simultaneously arguing that "the slave woman ought not to be judged by the same standard as others" (54-56).

Her dilemma comes in part from her attempt to explain herself to readers who may universally apply bourgeois standards of chastity to all women and harbor notions of the black woman as an innately sexual Jezebel.[9] When Linda wants to tell of the abusive sexual language Flint thrusts upon her, she cannot utter his words to her grandmother. Her inability to speak about the wrongs she suffers indicates the devastating effects of True Womanhood. Just as the young Linda is afraid to speak about sexuality, many women, represented by Aunt Martha, may consider themselves too genteel to listen. Child attempts to address this paradox in her introduction to Jacobs's text, stating that she hopes the Northern readers' ears are not "too delicate to listen" to the "foul" wrongs the bond women suffer (4).

Although Linda's contradictory impulses result in part from her intricate relationship with her audience, they also derive from Aunt Martha, who insists that her female relatives maintain a standard of chastity in both their language and action despite the brutal reality of their position as slaves. When Aunt Martha learns of Linda's pregnancy, she enacts the sentimental gestures of ripping off Linda's mother's wedding band from Linda's hand, casting her out of the home, and speaking in the prose of sentimental fiction: "I had rather see you dead than to see you as you now are. You are a disgrace to your dead mother." Although she later allows Linda to return home, she refuses to forgive her verbally (56-57). In part, Linda's ambivalence about her sexual actions can be read as evidence of her internalization of the nineteenth-century ideals of womanhood and sexual purity that she learns from Aunt Martha. Although these ideals pose as the norm, they are in fact attainable only to an elite minority of women.[10]

Historically, the majority of fugitives were men, most of whom made their escape alone. Although women did run away, many attempted to take their children with them, and many more remained enslaved rather than leave their children behind to an uncertain future. In this sense, the slave system "rewarded" those who could harden themselves against their family to hazard escape. However, the price to pay for freedom was often life-long anxiety and guilt over loved ones left behind.[11] For Jacobs to separate herself from her family and community allows the institution to prevail, as she would be removed from the sources of her strength. The only solution to this dilemma in her life and text is to turn the self-in-relation into a source of power.

The Mask of Presentation: Mastering the Sentimental

In his discussion of modern African-American literary strategies, Houston Baker describes the "mastery of form." Marking Booker T. Washington as a primary example, Baker argues that by "stepping inside of the white world's nonsense syllables," Washington is able to achieve his economic and social goals (25). In some respects, Jacobs can also be read as a master of form, who "conceals, disguises, floats like a trickster butterfly in order to sting like a bee" (Baker 50). In part, she wears the mask of nineteenth-century sentimental conventions to present herself to her immediate audience. According to Frances Smith Foster, unlike other African-American women of her time, Jacobs "identifies white women as a significant portion of her readership" and "attempts to write across the color line, to mediate between the races and if not to resuscitate their former coalition then at least to establish that they did have mutual concerns" (96). The process of working with Child and communicating with Amy Post about the text shows that Jacobs understands her audience. Yet this awareness should not be confused with editorial pandering. The manipulation of sentimental conventions displays a doubleness of self that is central to African-American texts and is a historical feature of slave women's lives.[12] As Deborah White points out, the camouflaging of emotions was common for slave women:

> It is unfortunate, but so much of what we would like to know about slave women can never be known because they masked their thoughts and personalities in order to protect valued parts of their lives from white and male invasion. (24)

Although Jacobs creates a mask, she simultaneously confronts the reader with a recognition of the guise, thus hinting at—but never fully revealing—a self that the spectator recognizes as a paradoxically intangible presence.

Because the anti-slavery genre attempted to contain radically discordant elements, it was available for the skillful manipulation of writers such as Jacobs, who could use the genre both to contain the doubleness inherent in her story and to introduce a powerful subtext into a "polite" text. Karcher points to the incongruities found in anti-slavery writing:

> It was an enterprise fraught with contradictions: the conventions of romance must serve to dispel readers' romantic illusions about slavery; a language shorn of ugly details must convey the violence of the institution to an audience convinced that abolitionists exaggerated its cruelty; a code of gentility that did not protect slave women against rape or white women against their husbands' philandering must govern fictional treatment of sexuality. ("Rape, Murder, and Revenge" 63)

The genteel tradition did influence depictions of slavery; however, as Karcher indicates, writers could manipulate the conventions and speak—at least partially—the previously unutterable. Jacobs exploits the genre's tensions to fit her needs and tell her story. However, before investigating Jacobs's subversion of the genre, we must first understand how she stocks her narrative with sentimental language and tropes.

Consistent with her position as a self-in-relation, Jacobs continually portrays herself as a mother who would sacrifice everything for the lives and freedom of her children. Such determination would certainly have been admired in the nineteenth century, when the Cult of Motherhood was ideologically entrenched and a standard ingredient in sentimental works. However, Jacobs goes even further, appealing to the ideal of home throughout her narrative. As Fox-Genovese demonstrates, the Doctrine of Separate Spheres in which men dealt with the marketplace while women triumphed over the home did not apply to many Southern households, as they were sites of both production and consumption (61-66). *Incidents* can be read as the move-

ment from a Southern household, represented both by Flint's house and the plantation, to a Northern ideal of home separated from the marketplace.

Describing her early life, Linda stresses that she comes from a home shared by loving and hard-working parents: "They lived together in a comfortable home; and, though we were all slaves, I was so fondly shielded that I never dreamed I was a piece of merchandise" (5). Her childhood home guards her from a harsh reality of the nondomestic sphere, and protects her from the knowledge that she is capital. After her parents' deaths, Aunt Martha's home, stocked with the white linen, silver and other items that mark it as a nineteenth-century haven, serves as Linda's place of comfort. What Northern woman would not have shuddered when Linda describes "lower-class" white men invading the sacred sphere in retaliation for Nat Turner's rebellion:

> The door was rudely pushed open; and in they tumbled, like a pack of hungry wolves. They snatched at every thing within their reach. Every box, trunk, closet, and corner underwent a thorough examination. (64)

The language here connotes rape, as "hungry wolves" leave nothing untouched. The home has been assaulted by men, who, speaking in non-standard English, have none of the genteel sensibilities of Linda and her readers. At the end of her narrative, what Linda expresses as most missing in her life is not a marriage, but a home: "The dream of my life is not yet realized. I do not sit with my children in a home of my own" (201). Part of Linda's appeal—part of her mask—is to appear to want exactly what all Northern white women have been taught to long for, the ideal home in which the feminine power of maternal love could reign supreme.

In addition to privileging motherhood and home, Jacobs also introduces the seduction plot of sentimental romance into her narrative. She portrays Flint as an evil seducer, someone who uses twisted versions of the conventional love letter to tempt her to fall. In describing why she chose Sands over Flint, Linda models Sands as a pursuing lover, as someone who "has no control over you, except that which he gains by kindness and attachment" (55). The reader of *Incidents* who was already accustomed through sentimental romance conventions both to judge and to sympathize with the fallen woman would certainly have identified with Linda's dismay, when after depicting Sands as caring and sympathetic, she goes on to declare, "He was an educated and eloquent gentleman; too eloquent, alas, for the poor slave girl who trusted in him" (54).[13] Additionally, as if to ease any secret fears white women may have had of slave women (and free African-American women) "invading" their homes with their sexuality, Linda continues by telling her readers that she also chose Sands because he was unmarried, and she remains silent as to their continuing sexual relationship.

Jacobs's use of sentimental conventions permeates her text. She fills her narrative with flowery language, often stopping to solicit directly emotional responses. Standard sentimental tropes, such as visits to the graveyard, are incorporated into the work. But as we shall see, this aspect of mask, although presentational, is also a ceremonial marking of difference between the performer and her audience, between Jacobs and her reader. For even as Jacobs creates her mask, she hints that it is only one possible manifestation of herself by gesturing to gaps in her narrative, to spaces that we as readers can never fill. In her preface, she begins by stressing not what she has to relate, but rather what she cannot or will not tell: "My descriptions fall far short of the facts. I have concealed the names of places, and given persons fictitious names" (1). Although we often refer to her story as a narrative due to its connections with the slave narrative genre, she in fact titles it *Incidents,* which implies not a complete linear story, but rather a series of episodes, with spaces and silences between the various events.[14]

As we read *Incidents,* we become increasingly curious about the silences, and Jacobs repeatedly reminds readers of the distance between them and her through direct appeals such as: "O you happy free women, contrast *your* New Year's day with that of the poor bondwoman!" (16). Perhaps the most startling example of wedging space between herself and her readers comes at the end of the narrative, when the reader has been finessed into thinking that the mask we have been viewing is in fact Jacobs. Here, she stops readers short and claims, "Reader, my story ends with freedom; not in the usual way, with marriage" (201). In this one sentence, Jacobs has mastered an important trick; she teaches her readers not to presume too much about the story of her life, about how it unfolds and how it should end. Although she has used the genre that so appeals to her audience, she has also subtly revised that genre. She will not close her book with either the death of the fallen woman or with the marriage her readers may expect. Rather, she suggests that the stories of slave women cannot fit into the genres she has used.[15] By writing a text that contains the contradictions Karcher describes, Jacobs revises the genre of sentimental fiction to challenge her audience's assumptions. Through her absence, she signifies her presence. Through her persona, she tricks us into viewing her as a person.

The Person of Jacobs: Claiming the Voice of an Individual

Jacobs's text radically undercuts conceptions of an individual self by presenting a self-in-relation and a manipulative persona. Yet to read Jacobs only in relation to others is to overlook the disembodied will she forcefully presents, and to deny much of the text's

"might." Ultimately, what makes Jacobs so remarkable is her ability to present simultaneously herself as an individual deserving of legal and moral respect, while not denying the power of the self-in-relation and the presentational self. Doing so, Jacobs revises not only sentimental fiction, but also the mostly male discourse of the slave narrative, both genres that were culturally vital in the nineteenth century. The political stakes of claims toward individualism, if persuasive, were high by 1861 when *Incidents* was published, as the nation debated what rights black men would have if emancipated and the women's movement agitated for political rights. To represent oneself as a person was to establish potential access to citizenship.

We have seen that Linda's role as a family member often impedes her move toward freedom. However, her family also provides her with collective pride in her own individualism. In many respects, her grandmother's story is allegorical not only for her family, but also for all slaves. Emancipated during the Revolutionary War by her master, she is nonetheless captured and sold back into slavery. Therefore, she is "freed" by the Revolution, but held immorally by the slave system, and her entire family inherits her sense of innate liberty. Linda's father, a carpenter, "had more of the feelings of a freeman than is common among slaves" (9), and both the young Linda and her Uncle Benjamin reason, as did the Revolutionary forefathers, that God wills them to be free (17).

Linda links herself to her family's innate determination most directly in chapter 4, "The Slave Who Dared to Feel Like a Man," which, although purportedly written about her Uncle Benjamin, is also about Linda. In this chapter we learn that both William and Uncle Benjamin are "spirited" young men who refuse to accept society's definition of themselves as slaves. Both fight with their masters, in descriptions reminiscent of Douglass's confrontation with Covey. True, she has no similar physical encounter, but Jacobs (who has been lamenting Flint's treatment of her) makes her first resolution to defy Flint: "The war of my life had begun; and though one of God's most powerless creatures, I resolved never to be conquered" (19). The parallels are striking. Although Linda cannot use her body in the same manner as her male relatives to resist slavery, she has inherited their sense of pride and strength. So, determined not to be conquered—not to be raped by Flint, not to think herself a slave, not to allow her identity to be defined solely by her body—Linda begins her path of resistance. Through this chapter, Linda not only shows herself as an individual, but also indicates that the means of declaring selfhood are necessarily different based on gender. However, the impulse for selfhood is the same, and it is possible that it is Linda who *dares to feel like a man,* by exhibiting a fierce need for liberty that is not included in the ideology of True Womanhood.

Besides claiming her courage through her family, Linda also empowers her individual actions through her role as a mother. Braxton argues that the "outraged mother" can be read as an archetype in women's slave narratives: "Implied in all her actions and fueling her heroic ones is abuse of her people and her person" (21). Although Linda's children represent relational ties that could hinder her movement toward freedom, they actually motivate her to all of her most daring and dangerous actions. Even the titles of the chapters that portray their births, "The New Tie to Life" and "Another Link to Life," indicate the fortitude they provide for her. Far more than just an appeal to an audience familiar with the Cult of Motherhood, Linda's actions as an "outraged mother" also write her into womanhood, into humanity. Angela Davis reminds us, "Ideological exaltation of motherhood, as popular as it was during the nineteenth century, did not extend to slaves" (7). To show maternal strength was to claim herself as a person while also expanding the mid-nineteenth-century definition of motherhood to include active and heroic deeds on the part of slave women.

Perhaps the most complicated aspect of professing her personhood comes through Linda's difficult negotiation of the politics of body and her decision to enter into a sexual liaison with Sands rather than submit to Flint. As White indicates, many slave women "willingly" entered into a sexual relationship to secure certain benefits: "There was no reason for them to believe that even freedom could not be bought for the price of their bodies" (34). Yet Linda's decision indicates more than her terrible personal dilemma. For, in the slave system, Davis argues, "Rape was a weapon of determination, a weapon of repression, whose covert goal was to extinguish slave women's will to resist" (23-24). In this context, rape works on a symbolic, as well as literal, level. For Flint, Linda reminds us, loves power more than anything, even more than money. Accordingly, Flint's desire to rape Linda is far more sinister than his need to increase his stock in slaves or to gratify his sexual desire. Flint seeks Linda's submission to and approval of both the physical brutality of slavery and the racism and sexism that attempted to justify it. He needs her to accept cheerfully her "natural" role as a sexual being whose duty is to fulfill the white man's needs. For Linda, then, to choose Sands is an act not only of economic defiance (as she gives to Sands the body that "belongs" to Flint) but of resistance to the racist and sexist ideologies that "legitimized" the economics of slavery. Her decision to give her body to Sands, however riddled with the painful contradictions of her oppression, is also a mark of her control of the politics of body, her declaration of personhood.

However, Linda's discussion of sexuality does not dominate the narrative. Rather than with her body, Linda wins her freedom through words.[16] Emphasizing the power of literacy was not unique to Jacobs, as the slave narrative genre often links literacy with freedom. Because Linda is taught relatively early to read and write, her narrative does not incorporate the story of becoming literate as primary. Nonetheless, she shows the power words provide for defense and escape. Thus, in her own way, Jacobs connects the conventions of the slave narrative to the genre of sentimental fiction, whose more timid readers might approve of nonviolent resistance even if they did not dare—as Linda challenges them to—to feel like "men" and accept aggression and physical resistance. If they cannot use the strength of their bodies, Linda suggests, her readers certainly can learn to deploy two powers—their voices and their pens—to free themselves and their country from oppression.

Linda's early acts of defiance come through the oral, rather than the written, word. Braxton defines Jacobs's "sass," which she identifies as a word of "West African derivation that is associated with the female aspect of the trickster." She continues, "Whenever Linda is under sexual attack, she uses sass as a weapon of self-defense" (31). Braxton's reading is highly insightful, as language is one of Flint's most powerful tools. He is described in serpent-like images, whispering obscene language into Linda's ear to harass and dominate her. Unlike Eve, Linda defeats the serpent by talking back to him. At one of their most intense moments of confrontation, instead of hitting Flint, Linda reacts with words: "You have struck me for answering you honestly. How I despise you!" (39). After becoming pregnant with Sands's child, Linda most looks forward to the "thought of telling" Flint (56). Flint often holds a razor to Linda's throat, symbolically underscoring both his hatred of her voice and her determination to use it despite the violence of slavery.

Once Linda escapes from Flint, her primary weapon becomes the letter. Repeatedly, she allegedly sends letters from the North, when she is actually in Flint's neighborhood. Part of the deadly game that Linda plays rests on who has the knowledge to best read the various letters. Linda's family must recognize Flint's letters as falsified. Often, they communicate through code, "knowing" that part of a letter indirectly applies to Linda. When she goes North, this contest continues, and Linda regularly searches the newspapers for news of visitors from the South, and continues to correspond with the Flints, trying to negotiate her freedom. Throughout all of these scenes, Linda proves to be a very astute reader of letters and people. She detects fraudulent promises, and mocks Flint's conspicuous attempts to lure her back under false pretenses. "Verily," Linda says of Flint when reading one of his letters, "he relied too much on 'the stupidity of the African race'" (172).

Throughout her story, Linda repeatedly talks back to Flint, insisting that she has an identity outside the one that slavery forces upon her. When Flint refuses to allow her marriage, Linda tells him that she despises him. Flint, infuriated, responds: "Do you know that I have a right to do as I like with you,—that I can kill you, if I please?" Linda answers: "You have tried to kill me, and I wish you had; but you have no right to do as you like with me" (39). By saying that Flint can kill her, Linda condescends to Southern practice that gives a master absolute control over the body of his slave woman. However, by adding that "you have no right to do as you like with me," she suggests that there is a noncorporeal part of her that he cannot touch, be it spirit, soul, or will. At the end of her story, Linda once again reiterates the relationship between the mind and the body, but hints that the mind must take precedence for her whole self to be free. She comments on her ambivalence about having her freedom bought by her employer/friend, Mrs. Bruce:

> The more my mind had become enlightened, the more difficult it was for me to consider myself an article of property; and to pay money to those who had so grievously oppressed me seemed like taking from my sufferings the glory of triumph. (199)

For Linda, the mind has a quality of its own, not linked to one's corporeal status.

As these examples indicate, Jacobs depicts a dialectical relationship between the mind and the body throughout her narrative, keeping transcendent individualism firmly in check through her embodied experience. However, beginning with chapter 15, one can detect a subtle shift in the emphasis of the story, and the representation of the corporeal wrongs of slavery gives way to a depiction of a disembodied will. Chapter 15 centers around Flint's offer to Linda to be his concubine. Linda determines that she will "fight" her "battle alone," and once again juxtaposes a sense of will with the objective facts of her existence: "My master had power and law on his side; I had a determined will. There is might in each" (85).

From that moment, Linda will begin what she calls in the title of chapter 25 a "competition in cunning." Matching herself against Flint—wit to wit, pen to pen, and will to will—she masters him, and therefore becomes her own master. Ironically, she first asserts her will forcefully when she is imprisoned in her garret space. From her garret, she not only learns how to survey Southern society, but also uses the power of literacy—the same power she deploys to avoid recapture when she is in the North and when she writes her autobiography—to secure her freedom. The spoken and written word are represented as noncorporeal, and therefore as spaces where Linda can compete on more equal terms with Flint.

Jacobs's emphasis on literacy can be interpreted as creating a space in which she is not viewed solely in terms of her body. She suggests that—while certainly not color blind—the "Republic of Letters" offers a "competition in cunning" that is at least on fairer ground. As more African Americans and women published in the nineteenth century, the territory of the written word was fertile soil on which to set her sights. However, she is hardly naive. As a writer who was also a former slave, she knew full well the power that more influential figures could attempt to exert on her text, and although she did everything she could to gain control, she understood that her life, and work, would continue to be a struggle.[17]

By asserting her transcendent individualism, Jacobs breaks the binary between a Romantic metaphysical self and the "other" phenomena upon which it rested. Philosophically, she carves a space for herself and other women of color in her era's debates over the nature of identity. In literary terms, her claim to a disembodied will also grants her access to the genre of autobiography, for, as Sidonie Smith argues, "Autobiography itself functioned as guarantor of 'metaphysical selfhood' " (79). Politically, her individualism challenges the ideologies that sustained slavery and discrimination, and also disrupts True Womanhood by daring women to *feel like men* and seek liberty. Yellin demonstrates how through writing herself as a literary subject, Jacobs revises the primary emblem of the antislavery feminists, in which the "activity of the white female emancipator renders the black woman passive" (*Women and Sisters* 95-96). Jacobs refuses to portray or accept any such powerlessness.

However, Jacobs's individualism is not without qualifications. Although she depicts a self-reliant hero who pursues her own version of truth and freedom at great peril, she also shows how historical realities complicate her quest. Her narrative both extends the privilege of a Romantic self to African-American women and checks its optimistic transcendence through embodied experience. Jacobs's text stands as a powerful juxtaposition to conceptions of self made seemingly natural by the canonization of Thoreau and Emerson. It provokes us to reexamine our own narratives about the development of an "American self" from the nineteenth-century ideal of a transcendent Romantic ego to a twentieth-century conception of fragmented modern consciousness.

The process of reading the "remains" of Jacobs, then, neither results in the uncovering of a core self, nor relegates the text to the space of persona. Rather, Jacobs's text dares us to reconsider the binary nature of the formulation. Is it not possible, she questions, to situate one's identity in relation to—and apart from—others? Can one, although "fallen," also remain pure in thought, true to her own moral code? Can the most "powerless creature" win her freedom? Can we have identity both of and out of the body? Jacobs teaches us that every version of self has room for subversion, and that there is "might in each."

Notes

¹ For information on reaction to the excavation, see Maykuth and Rotenstein.

² White reminds us that material "on the general nature of slavery exists in abundance, but it is very difficult to find source material about slave women in particular" (23).

³ For example, White uses *Incidents* as a primary historical text throughout *Ar'n't I a Woman? Female Slaves in the Plantation South.*

⁴ Yellin discusses the doubt surrounding Jacobs's authenticity in her introduction (xxii-xxiii). For information on the relationship between Jacobs and Child, see Karcher, *The First Woman in the Republic* (435-37).

⁵ For a discussion of the creation of the theory of polygenesis, see Gould. For information on the increasing tendency in the nineteenth-century to reduce women's identity solely to their reproductive functions, see Smith-Rosenberg (182-216).

⁶ Braude explores the complex relationship between the body, power, and Spiritualism in *Radical Spirits.* See, in particular, chapters 4-6 (82-161).

⁷ The citation from Smith quotes from Iris Marion Young, "Impartiality and the Civic Public: Some Implications of Feminist Critiques of Moral and Political Theory," in *Feminism as Critique: On the Politics of Gender,* Ed. Seyla Behnabib and Drucilla Cornell (Minneapolis: U of Minnesota P, 1987), 57-76. She also draws upon the work of Jane Flax, "Postmodernism and Gender Relations in Feminist Theory," *Signs: Journal of Women in Culture and Society* 12 (1987): 621-43.

⁸ Because of Jacobs's use of a persona, discussion of *Incidents* can become confusing. Although I do not want to imply that any author has complete control of her text, I nonetheless use "Jacobs" when referring to overall aspects of the narrative that are determined by the author and refer to "Linda" when discussing specifics of the life depicted in the text.

⁹ White reminds us that "one of the most prevalent images of black women in ante-bellum America was of a person governed almost entirely by her libido, a Jezebel character. In every way Jezebel was the counterimage of the mid-nineteenth-century ideal of the Victorian lady" (28-29).

¹⁰ Linda's internalization of the ideals of True Womanhood and Aunt Martha's initial reactions to her pregnancy seem to contradict White's overall findings regarding the sexuality of slave women. White argues that, despite efforts by their mothers to veil them from sex, slave girls in their teen years may have had "a degree of sexual freedom unknown to Southern white girls" (97). Also, generally, "Slaves seemed to have understood what slave mothers did for the individual slave and for the slave community, and therefore did not condemn motherhood out of wedlock" (109).

¹¹ White reviews the statistics of fugitives and concludes that "Women would probably have escaped more often if they could have done so with their husbands and offspring but children, in particular, made the journey more difficult than it already was and increased the chance of capture" (71).

¹² In *To Tell a Free Story,* Andrews aptly summarizes the paradox faced by the slave narrative author in reference to doubleness: "The reception of his narrative as truth depended on the degree to which his artfulness could hide his art" (3).

¹³ By the time of Jacobs's publication, female readers' relationship to the sentimental heroine was firmly entrenched, if complicated. See Davidson's discussion of the sentimental novel in the early Republic (110-50).

¹⁴ Yellin also notes the contradictions contained in *Incidents*'s title and preface in her introduction to the 1987 edition: "But this title is unusual in announcing that its narrator is female, and that her book is not the narrative of a life but of incidents in a life. The Preface, while claiming the truthfulness of her tale, reports that she has written pseudonymously and hidden the identities of people and places" (xxvi).

¹⁵ In *Writing beyond the Ending,* Rachel Blau DuPlessis argues that the primary mode of resolution in nineteenth-century fictive plots dealing with women is an ending in which "quest or *Bildung,* is set aside or repressed, whether by marriage or by death" (3-4). The novelist's task was to write beyond the Romance plot that "muffles the main female character, represses quest, valorizes heterosexual as opposed to homosexual ties," and "incorporates individuals within couples as a sign of their personal and narrative success" (5). By ending her story with "freedom," not "marriage," Jacobs breaks the Romance plot and begins to forge a new cultural ending to women's stories.

¹⁶ In this respect, my interpretation differs from that of Sanchez-Eppler, who reads Jacobs's text as describing slavery "primarily in terms of sexual experience" (83-84).

¹⁷ In her introduction to *Incidents,* Yellin documents Jacobs's effort to maintain her autonomy as an author (xviii-xix). See also Hedrick's discussion of Harriet Beecher Stowe's relationship with Jacobs in *Harriet Beecher Stowe: A Life* (248-49).

Works Cited

Andrews, William L. *To Tell a Free Story: The First Century of Afro-American Autobiography, 1760-1865.* Chicago: U of Illinois P, 1986.

Baker, Houston. *Modernism & the Harlem Renaissance.* Chicago: U of Chicago P, 1987.

Braude, Ann. *Radical Spirits: Spiritualism and Women's Rights in Nineteenth-Century America.* Boston: Beacon, 1989.

Braxton, Joanne M. *Black Women Writing Autobiography: A Tradition within a Tradition.* Philadelphia: Temple UP, 1989.

Davidson, Cathy N. *Revolution and the Word: The Rise of the Novel in America.* New York: Oxford UP, 1986.

Davis, Angela. *Women, Race & Class.* New York: Random, 1981.

Davis, Charles T, and Henry Louis Gates, Jr. "Introduction: The Language of Slavery." *The Slave's Narrative.* New York: Oxford UP, 1985. xi-xxxiv.

DuPlessis, Rachel Blau. *Writing beyond the Ending: Narrative Strategies of Twentieth-Century Women Writers.* Bloomington: Indiana UP, 1985.

Emerson, Ralph Waldo. *The Collected Works of Ralph Waldo Emerson.* 5 vols. Ed. Alfred R. Ferguson. Cambridge: Belknap-Harvard UP, 1971.

Foster, Frances Smith. *Written by Herself: Literary Production by African American Women, 1746-1892.* Bloomington: Indiana UP, 1993.

Fox-Genovese, Elizabeth. *Within the Plantation Household: Black and White Women of the Old South.* Chapel Hill: U of North Carolina P, 1988.

Gould, Stephen Jay. "American Polygeny and Craniometry before Darwin: Blacks and Indians as Separate, Inferior Species." *The "Racial" Economy of Science.* Ed. Sandra Harding. Bloomington: Indiana UP, 1993. 84-115.

Hedrick, Joan D. *Harriet Beecher Stowe: A Life.* New York: Oxford UP, 1994.

Jacobs, Harriet. *Incidents in the Life of a Slave Girl, Written by Herself.* 1861. Ed. Jean Fagan Yellin. Cambridge: Harvard UP, 1987.

Karcher, Carolyn L. "Rape, Murder, and Revenge in 'Slavery's Pleasant Homes': Lydia Maria Child's Antislavery Fiction and the Limits of the Genre." *The Culture of Sentiment: Race, Gender & Sentimentality in Nineteenth-Century America.* Ed. Shirley Samuels. Oxford: Oxford UP, 1992. 58-72.

———. *The First Woman in the Republic: A Cultural Biography of Lydia Maria Child.* Durham: Duke UP, 1994.

Maykuth, Andrew. "Grave Injustice?" *Philadelphia Inquirer* 29 July 1992, final ed.: C01.

———. "Work is Halted at N.Y. Burial Ground." *Philadelphia Inquirer* 30 July 1992, final ed.: A02.

Nott, J. C., and George R. Gliddon. *Types of Mankind: or Ethnological Researches based upon the Ancient Monuments, Paintings, Sculptures, and Crania of Races, and upon their Natural, Geographical, Philological, and Biblical History.* Philadelphia: Lippincott, Grambo, 1854.

Rotenstein, David. "Let those in African Graveyards Rest in Peace." *Philadelphia Inquirer* 4 Aug. 1992, final ed.: A09.

Sánchez-Eppler, Karen. *Touching Liberty: Abolition, Feminism, and the Politics of the Body.* Berkeley: U of California P, 1993.

Smith-Rosenberg, Carroll. *Disorderly Conduct: Visions of Gender in Victorian America.* New York: Oxford UP, 1985.

Smith, Sidonie. "Resisting the Gaze of Embodiment: Women's Autobiography in the Nineteenth Century." *American Women's Autobiography: Fea(s)ts of Memory.* Ed. Margo Culley. Madison: U of Wisconsin P, 1992. 75-110.

Smith, Valerie. " 'Loopholes of Retreat': Architecture and Ideology in Harriet Jacobs's *Incidents in the Life of a Slave Girl.*" *Reading Black, Reading Feminist: A Critical Anthology.* Ed. Henry Louis Gates, Jr. New York: Penguin, 1990. 212-26.

Sundquist, Eric J. *To Wake the Nations: Race in the Making of American Literature.* Cambridge: Belknap-Harvard UP, 1993.

Thoreau, Henry David. *Walden and Other Writings.* Ed. Joseph Wood Krutch. New York: Bantam, 1962.

Tompkins, Jane. "Sentimental Power: *Uncle Tom's Cabin* and the Politics of Literary History." *The New Feminist Criticism: Essays on Women, Literature & Theory.* Ed. Elaine Showalter. New York: Pantheon, 1985. 81-104.

White, Deborah Gray. *Ar'n't I a Woman? Female Slaves in the Plantation South.* New York: Norton, 1985.

Yellin, Jean Fagan. *Women and Sisters: The Antislavery Feminists in American Culture.* New Haven: Yale UP, 1989.

————. Introduction. *Incidents in the Life of a Slave Girl, Written by Herself.* By Harriet Jacobs. Ed. Yellin. Cambridge: Harvard UP, 1987. xiii-xxiii.

FURTHER READING

Biography

Yellin, Jean Fagan. "Harriet Jacobs's Family History." *American Literature* 66, No. 4 (December 1994): 765-67.

Corrects an error in her 1987 edition of Jacobs's *Incidents in the Life of a Slave Girl: Written by Herself*, published by Harvard University Press. Yellin discusses the earlier misinformation she provided regarding the identity of Jacobs's father, and the impact of the new, correct information on the understanding of Jacobs's family history.

————. "*Legacy* Profile: Harriet Ann Jacobs." *Legacy* 5, No. 2 (Fall 1988): 55-61.
Offers an overview of Jacobs's life and her work, *Incidents in the Life of a Slave Girl.*

Criticism

Bartholomaus, Craig. "'What Would You Be?' Racial Myths and Cultural Sameness in *Incidents in the Life of a Slave Girl.*" *CLA Journal* XXXIX, No. 2 (December 1995): 179-94.

Examines the use of "true womanhood" as well as other textual elements in *Incidents* "against the backdrop of nineteenth-century racial science," in order to demonstrate the ways in which the text refutes the negative stereotypes advanced by that science.

Becker, Elizabeth C. "Harriet Jacobs's Search for Home." *CLA Journal* XXXV, No. 4 (June 1992): 411-21.
Analyzes the effect of the "cult of true womanhood" on Jacobs as a black woman, arguing that the "cult," in its emphasis on the home as "the locus of all female purpose" influences every aspect of Jacobs's narrative.

Braxton, Joanne M. "Harriet Jacobs' *Incidents in the Life of a Slave Girl*: The Re-Definition of the Slave Narrative Genre." *The Massachusetts Review* 27, No. 2 (Summer 1986): 379-87.
Uses *Incidents*, among other works, to explore the impact of the female slave narrative on the male-dominated genre.

Braxton, Joanne M. and Sharon Zuber. "Silences in Harriet 'Linda Brent' Jacobs's *Incidents in the Life of a Slave Girl.*" In *Listening to Silences: New Essays in Feminist Criticism*, edited by Elaine Hedges and Shelley Fisher Fishkin, pp. 146-55. New York: Oxford University Press, 1994.
Discusses the ways in which Jacobs transcends the "silences imposed upon her as a slave, a woman, and a mother" and the manner through which, as an author, Jacobs uses silence as a means of empowering *Incidents* and the narrator, Linda Brent.

Hedin, Raymond. "Strategies of Form in the American Slave Narrative." In *The Art of Slave Narrative: Original Essays in Criticism and Theory*, edited by John Sekora and Darwin T. Turner, pp. 25-35. Western Illinois University, 1982.
Discusses two aspects of the slave narrative form: the use of well-established, traditional genres, such as the sentimental novel, and the varying techniques regarding the use of "closure."

Kaplan, Carla. "Narrative Contracts and Emancipatory Readers: *Incidents in the Life of a Slave Girl.*" *Yale Journal of Criticism* 6, No. 1 (Spring 1993): 93-119.
Argues that Jacobs "seeks to create a new black narrative position," one that rejects aspects of both the slave narrative genre and the romance genre and that avoids "being drawn into narrative contracts which can neither grant her [Jacobs's] freedom nor change her status."

MacKethan, Lucinda H. "Mother Wit: Humor in Afro-American Women's Autobiography." *Studies in American Humor* 4, Nos. 1 and 2 (Spring/Summer 1985): 51-81.
Explores the use of humor in *Incidents*, among other works, arguing that a particular brand of humor is "the verbal weapon of survival that informs the experience in these works and makes them . . . assertions of identity, proclamations of the beauty and mastery of circumstance that simply being Black and a woman can affirm."

Morgan, Winifred. "Gender-Related Difference in the Slave Narratives of Harriet Jacobs and Frederick Douglass." *American Studies* 35, No. 2 (Fall 1994): 73-94.
Contrasts the male and female slave narratives, specifically the "strategies of coping and resistance" found in each, using Jacobs's *Incidents* and Douglass's *Narrative* as representatives of the genre. Morgan argues that male narrators emphasize their "*right* to autonomy in a political democracy" whereas female narrators emphasize "womanliness" and tell their stories "in terms of relationships."

Nudelman, Franny. "Harriet Jacobs and the Sentimental Politics of Female Suffering." *ELH* 59, No. 4 (Winter 1992): 939-64.
Recounts the ways in which both Jacobs's use of the conventions of the sentimental novel and the influence of the "cult of true womanhood" have been analyzed

by critics. Nudelman argues that the political impact of the novel is best understood "not by overlooking or excusing its conventionality, but by examining the sources and consequences of its conventionality."

Sánchez-Eppler, Karen. "Righting Slavery and Writing Sex: The Erotics of Narration in Harriet Jacobs's *Incidents*." In *Touching Liberty: Abolition, Feminism, and the Politics of the Body*, pp. 83-104. Berkeley: University of California Press, 1993.

> Examines the relationship between slavery and the act of writing for Jacobs, arguing that for Jacobs, writing was "affiliated alternately with both self-mastery and enslavement."

Tanner, Laura E. "Self-Conscious Representation in the Slave Narrative." *Black American Literature Forum* 21, no. 4 (Winter 1987): 415-24.

Studies Jacobs's depiction of her narrator's relationship with Mr. Sands in order to identify the "externally imposed consciousness" that interrupts the "self-conscious representation" which is typical of autobiography. Tanner further explores the problems related to the slave narrative "as a means of self-conscious representation for the black former slave."

Warhol, Robyn R. " 'Reader, Can You Imagine? No, You Cannot': The Narratee as Other in Harriet Jacobs's Text." *Narrative* 3, No. 1 (January 1995): 57-72.

> Examines *Incidents* as a "reconstruction" of the codes that the textual conventions of domestic, sentimental, and Gothic literature promoted in the nineteenth-century, and argues that through the study of Jacobs's narrative, one can discover "how an author like Harriet Jacobs is engaged in changing the world."

Immanuel Kant

1724-1804

German philosopher.

For additional information on Kant's life and works, see *NCLC*, Volume 27.

INTRODUCTION

Considered one of the most important and influential figures in Western philosophy, Kant developed a comprehensive philosophical system in which he analyzed the foundations of metaphysics, ethics, and aesthetics. The most important exposition of his ideas can be found in his *Kritik der reinen Vernunft* (1781; *Critique of Pure Reason*), *Kritik der praktischen Vernunft* (1788; *Critique of Practical Reason*), and *Kritik der Urteilskraft* (1790; *Critique of Judgment*). In the *Critique of Pure Reason*, Kant decisively altered the development of modern philosophy by insisting on a separation of the "sensible" and "intelligible" worlds, that which can be perceived by the senses and that which can be ascertained only by the intellect. He applied this distinction to the ethical realm in the *Critique of Practical Reason*, wherein he argued that an individual's moral decisions are based on rational precepts that are independent of experience in the world and therefore display the exercise of free will. In his study of the basis of aesthetic discrimination, the *Critique of Judgment*, Kant continued this line of thinking, suggesting that nature, like humanity, has an ideal purpose—a moral end that is revealed by the overall "fitness of things." While Kant is best known for these three central works, his writings on history, politics, and religion are also considered vital contributions to the development of Western thought.

Biographical Information

Kant was born in Königsberg in East Prussia in 1724. His family belonged to the Pietist branch of the Lutheran church, a sect that placed great emphasis on austerity and virtue. Kant's father, a saddler, was of modest means, but through the influence of a local pastor, Kant acquired an excellent formal education. From 1732 to 1740 Kant studied at the local Gymnasium, a Pietist school offering intensive study in Latin. Thereafter he entered the University of Königsberg, where he studied philosophy, mathematics, and the natural sciences under a young instructor named Martin Knutzen, who first introduced him to the philosophy of Gottfried Wilhelm Leibniz and Christian von

Wolff. Kant's father died in 1746, leaving him without income. Kant found employment as a private tutor for the children of distinguished families, which enabled him to acquire the social graces expected of men of letters at that time. During this period, he published an impressive series of papers on natural history, beginning with *Gedanken von der wahren Schätzung der lebendigen Kräfte* (1746; *Thoughts on the True Estimation of Living Forces*), a study of kinetic forces. After completion of his degree in 1755, he spent fifteen years as a non-salaried lecturer, his income derived entirely from modest student fees, and he continued to write prolifically on scientific subjects. In 1764 he published *Untersuchung über die Deutlichkeit der Grundsätze der natürlichen Theologie und der Moral*, a critique of traditional metaphysics as defined by Leibniz, which is considered his most important work of this formative period.

Kant was appointed to the chair of logic and metaphysics at the University of Königsberg in 1770. His inaugural thesis, *De mundi sensibilis atque intelligibilis forma et principiis dissertatio* (*Dissertation on the Form and Principles of the Sensible and Intelligible Worlds*), published the same year, is important for its distinction between sense and understanding, a key concept in his philosophical system. Kant published little while he composed his *Critique of Pure Reason*, which appeared in 1781, initiating the series of extraordinary works that ultimately brought him widespread recognition for his Critical Philosophy. For the next twenty years, Kant's reputation as a leading spokesman of Enlightenment thought increased as he continued to write prolifically on philosophy, religion, and political theory. A treatise on theology, *Die Religion innerhalb der Grenzen der blossen Vernunft* (1793; *Religion within the Limits of Reason Alone*), which denied the supernatural elements of Christianity, resulted in a government ban on future writings by Kant on religious subjects. Around 1800, Kant's health, which had always been precarious, began to deteriorate. After relinquishing his university position in November 1801, Kant rarely left his house and experienced increasing difficulty in following his customary work habits. He died in 1804.

Major Works

Kant's major philosophical principles are contained in the three *Critiques*. While the first of these works, *Critique of Pure Reason*, has often been criticized for the density of its style, attributed by scholars to Kant's reliance on the scholastic jargon of Wolff and his followers, the clarity and originality of the philosophical concepts articulated in the treatise are universally acknowledged. In *Critique of Pure Reason*, Kant systematically analyzed the foundations of human knowledge. The majority of the book is devoted to a "Transcendental Doctrine of Elements," wherein Kant elaborates his epistemology; this is followed by a much shorter "Transcendental Doctrine of Method," which outlines the proper application of "pure reason." The *Critique*'s first part is divided into the "Transcendental Aesthetic," the "Transcendental Analytic," and the "Transcendental Dialectic," which examine the foundations of mathematics, the physical sciences, and metaphysics, respectively. In all three areas Kant sought to determine if it was possible to prove the validity of "*a priori* synthetic statements," that is, philosophical propositions that are not only true without reference to experience, but which also expand our knowledge. In the process, Kant effected what he called a "Copernican revolution" in philosophy: whereas formerly philosophers had considered the mind a passive agent whose judgments conformed to objects in the world, Kant believed that there were epistemic constraints on what could constitute objects of possible knowledge, and that experience is constituted both by sensible intuitions and concepts.

Like the first *Critique*, Kant's second major treatise, *Critique of Practical Reason*, is subdivided into a table of "Elements" and a "Methodology." While theoretical reason is concerned with the basis of experience, practical reason is concerned with the ethical significance of free action. In *Critique of Pure Reason*, Kant distinguishes between phenomenal and noumenal reality—that which appears to us through the senses and that which lies behind appearances. In the second *Critique*, he draws a similar distinction. On a purely phenomenal level, Kant explains, individuals are conditioned by the law of causality, which states that every effect has a predetermined cause. Practically speaking, this would destroy the possibility of freedom. Kant also suggests, however, that the individual is aware of himself as a purely rational, intelligible being. As such, an individual's actions may be conditioned by sensuous motives or grounded in the moral law, the "categorical imperative," which requires us to "act only on that maxim through which you can at the same time will that it should become a universal law." Kant also asserts, in concluding his arguments about freedom, that the concepts of God and immortality, while entertained as a mere possibility for theoretical reason, are necessary for practical reason.

In *Critique of Judgment*, Kant discusses judgments of taste and purposiveness in nature. The work is divided into a "Critique of Aesthetic Judgment" and a "Critique of Teleological Judgment." The first section is devoted to aesthetic judgments of the beautiful, which for Kant are subjective but universally valid. In the contemplation of a beautiful object, Kant explains, the person experiences a free play of the understanding and the imagination. In the second part of *Critique of Judgment*, Kant rejects the then fashionable mechanistic argument as an explanation for the harmony of parts in organisms, as well as the theological argument that it is the product of an intelligent design. Rather, purposiveness in nature must be adopted as a methodological assumption in any scientific explanation.

Critical Reception

Kant's Copernican turn in philosophy marks a revolution in philosophical methodology that spawned a whole generation of followers, critics, and disagreeing interpreters of his thought. Kant greatly influenced Johann Gottlieb Fichte's (1762-1814) idealism, which along with a fuller appreciation of the third *Critique* fueled German Romanticism, especially Friedrich Schelling (1775-1854) and Johann Christoph Friedrich von Schiller (1759-1805). Later philosophers, such as Arthur Schopenhauer (1788-1860) and Georg Wilhelm Friedrich Hegel (1770-1831), developed particular aspects of Kant's thought in their own philosophies, as did other idealists such as Josiah Royce (1855-1916). While Kant has been criticized for his abstruse style and overuse of technical vocabulary, his philosophical works continue to be intensely scrutinized by scholars throughout the world. In ethics, metaphysics, mathematics, and aesthetics, philosophers since Kant have had to address his thought in developing their own, upholding Kant's legacy as possibly the most influential philosopher of the modern era.

PRINCIPAL WORKS

Gedanken von der wahren Schätzung der lebendigen Kräfte (essay) 1746
[*Thoughts on the True Estimation of Living Forces* (partial translation) published in *Kant's Inaugural Dissertation, and Early Writings on Space*, 1929]
Allgemeine Naturgeschichte und Theorie des Himmels (philosophical prose) 1755
[*Kant's Cosmology*, 1900; also published as *Universal Natural History and Theory of the Heavens*, 1968]
Prolegomena zu einer jeden künftigen Metaphysik die als Wissenschaft auftreten können (philosophical prose) 1764
[*Prolegomena to Every Future Metaphysik, Which Can Appear as a Science,* 1819; also published as *Prolegomena to Future Metaphysics* in *Metaphysical Works of the Celebrated Immanuel Kant*, 1836, and *Prolegomena to Any Future Metaphysics*, 1902]
Untersuchung über die Deutlichkeit der Grundsätze der natürlichen Theologie und der Moral (philosophical prose) 1764
Beobachtungen über das Gefühl des Schönen und Erhabenen (philosophical prose) 1765
[*Observations on the Feeling of the Beautiful and Sublime*, 1965]
Träume eines Geistersehers, erläutert durch Träume der Metaphysik (philosophical prose) 1766
[*Dreams of a Spirit-Seer*, 1900]
De mundi sensibilis atque intelligibilis forma et principiis dissertatio (dissertation) 1770
[*Dissertation on the Form and Principles of the Sensible and Intelligible Worlds* published in *Kant's Inaugural Dissertation, and Early Writings on Space*, 1929]
Kritik der reinen Vernunft (philosophical prose) 1781
[*Critique of Pure Reason*, 1838]
Beantwortung der Frage: Was ist Aufklärung? (essay) 1784
[*What Is Enlightenment?* published in *Kant's Critique of Practical Reason, and Other Writings in Moral Philosophy*, 1949]
Idee zu einer allgemeinen Geschichte in weltbürgerlicher Absicht (essay) 1784
[*Idea for a Universal History from a Cosmopolitan Point of View* published in *Kant On History*, 1963]
Grundlegung zur Metaphysik der Sitten (philosophical prose) 1785
[*Fundamental Principles of the Metaphysic of Morals* published in *Kant's Critique of Practical Reason, and Other Works on the Theory of Ethics*, 1873; *Groundwork of the Metaphysic of Morals*, 1948;

Foundations of the Metaphysics of Morals in *Critique of Practical Reason and Other Writings in Moral Philosophy*, 1949; *The Metaphysical Principles of Virtue*, 1964; *The Metaphysics of Morals*, 1965; and *Foundations of the Metaphysics of Morals*, 1990]
Metaphysische Anfangsgrunde der Naturwissenschaft (philosophical prose) 1786
[*Metaphysical Foundations of Natural Science* published in *Kant's Prolegomena and Metaphysical Foundations of Natural Science*, 1883]
Kritik der praktischen Vernunft (philosophical prose) 1788
[*Critique of Practical Reason* published in *Kant's Critique of Practical Reason and Other Writings on the Theory of Ethics*, 1873]
Kritik der Urteilskraft (philosophical prose) 1790
[*Critique of Judgment*, 1892; also published as *Critique of Aesthetic Judgment*, 1911]
Die Religion innerhalb der Grenzen der blossen Vernunft (philosophical prose) 1793
[*Religion within the Sphere of Naked Reason* published in *Essays and Treatises on Moral, Political, and Various Philosophical Subjects*, 1798; also published as *Religion within the Boundary of Pure Reason*, 1838; and *Religion within the Limits of Reason Alone*, 1960]
Zum ewigen Frieden: Ein philosophischer Entwurf (philosophical prose) 1795
[*A Philosophical Treatise on Perpetual Peace*, 1948; also published as *Inevitable Peace*, 1948, and *Perpetual Peace* in *Critique of Practical Reason, and Other Writings in Moral Philosophy*, 1949]
Die Metaphysik der Sitten (philosophical prose) 1797
[*The Metaphysik of Morals, Divided into Metaphysical Elements of Law and of Ethics*, 1799]
Anthropologie in pragmatischer Hinsicht (philosophical prose) 1798
[*Anthropology from a Pragmatic Point of View*, 1974]
Gesammelte Schriften. 23 vols. (philosophical prose, essays, notes, and letters) 1902-55
Eine Vorlesung über Ethik (lectures) 1924
[*Lectures on Ethics*, 1930]
Kant On History (essays) 1963
Kant: Philosophical Correspondence, 1759-99 (letters) 1967
Opus Postumum (notes) 1996

*This collection publishes for the first time Kant's philosophical notes, the *Opus Postumum*.

CRITICISM

Friedrich Paulsen (essay date 1902)

SOURCE: An introduction, and "The Practical Philosophy," in *Immanuel Kant: His Life and Doctrine,* translated by J. E. Creighton and Albert LeFevre, Charles Scribner's Sons, 1902, pp. 1-21, 294-342.

[*In the following excerpt from his* Immanuel Kant: His Life and Doctrine *(1902), Paulsen discusses the sources and historical importance of Kant's philosophy and outlines the central tenets of his practical philosophy.*]

Introduction

I. Kant's Significance in the General History of Thought

There are three attitudes of the mind towards reality which lay claim to truth,—Religion, Philosophy, and Science. Although sprung from a single root, they become differentiated in the higher stages of mental life, reunite, and again stand opposed to one another in a variety of ways, receiving their characteristic stamp through the manner in which this process takes place. Especially is it true that every philosophy is essentially determined through the attitude which it adopts towards religion and science.

In general, philosophy occupies an intermediate place between science and religion. If one adopts the figure of Bacon which represents the mental world as a ball (*globus intellectualis*), similar to the *globus materialis* by means of which the mediæval cosmology pictured the external world, then one might divide the world into three concentric spheres, corresponding to the three spheres of the cosmos. The outermost sphere of this ball, corresponding to the region of the fixed stars, would represent science; the inner kernel, corresponding to the earth, would represent religion; while philosophy finally would occupy the middle or planetary sphere.

Science holds the peripheral position in the mental life. In this field the thinking and calculating understanding gives rise to a system of concepts and formulas by means of which it externally comprehends and rules over nature. Religion forms the inner kernel of our view of the world; its goal is the interpretation of the meaning of things. Science makes the world conceivable, but does not render it intelligible. Conformity to law is not its meaning. All religion claims certainly to possess the meaning of life and of the world, and to reveal this in concrete examples of the good and the perfect. Philosophy occupies an intermediate position between the two,—relating itself on the one hand to science, and on the other to religion. It seeks not only to conceive the world, but also to understand it. The history of philosophy shows that its task consists simply in mediating between science and religion. It seeks to unite knowledge and faith, and in this way to restore the unity of the mental life. It performs this task both for the individual and for society. As in the case of the individual, it mediates between the head and the heart, so in society it prevents science and religion from becoming entirely strange and indifferent to each other, and hinders also the mental life of the people from being split up into a faith-hating science and a science-hating faith or superstition.

It follows from what has been said that the character of a philosophy is essentially determined through the manner in which it performs this historical task. From this standpoint we may distinguish two fundamental forms of philosophy: I shall name them with Kant the *dogmatic* and the *critical*. The essence of dogmatic philosophy consists in the fact that it undertakes to found faith upon knowledge; it seeks to demonstrate what is to be believed. It produces as a variation of itself its own contradictory, that is, the *sceptical* philosophy. For when the latter tests the demonstrations and perceives their inadequacy, it comes at last to discard faith itself as a delusion, and to maintain that knowledge through scientific concepts constitutes the only form of truth. The critical philosophy comes forward in opposition to this. Its real nature is seen in the fact that it makes clear the essential difference between the functions of knowing and of believing, between conceiving things through a system of laws, and understanding their significance; and through a strict division of the field it shows how an agreement may be reached. Matters of faith cannot be demonstrated by the understanding, as dogmatism undertakes to do, because they are not derived from the understanding. But just for this reason they cannot be overthrown by the understanding, as scepticism tries to show.

I shall indicate the way in which this conceptual schema is borne out by the historical development.

The original form of positive dogmatism in the Western world is the *idealistic* philosophy of the Greeks; the original form of negative dogmatism is found in their *materialistic* philosophy. Plato and his successor Aristotle set out from the fundamental principle that the world is the realization of ideas. The cosmic order manifested through mathematically formulated laws is objective reason. Every living being is the realization of a purposive idea, while man, as the highest living creature, as knowing his own end and the purpose of the universe, is the self-realization of reason. The real function that philosophy has to perform, then, is to make known the meaning of the world in the form of a scientific system.

The same view of the nature of the world and of philosophy is dominant in the systems of the middle ages, which retained their place as the accepted school-philosophy until the beginning of the eighteenth century. It was also an assumption of the natural theology that after the time of Locke and Leibniz superseded scholasticism. The purpose of this natural theology is to furnish scientific demonstrations of the truth of what is held through faith, at least in its main principles, or to discover the divine purpose in nature and in history. Apart from the dependence of Christian philosophy upon external authority, it is distinguished from Greek philosophy mainly by the fact that it adopts a teleological philosophy of history, while Greek speculation limits itself to a teleology of nature.

Along with positive dogmatism, we have, as the obverse, negative dogmatism. In the ancient world, we meet this in the Epicurean philosophy, which knows only bodies and uniform natural laws, and refuses to recognize ideas and purposes in the real world. Although this point of view disappears almost completely during the middle ages, it emerges again as soon as pure scientific thought, which first showed itself in mathematics and the sciences of nature, found freer expression. In the second half of the eighteenth century, this philosophy was at the same time both the prohibited and the prevailing form of thought. This was especially the case in France.

Now, the real purpose of the critical philosophy, the philosophy of Kant, is to overcome the opposition which has extended through the entire history of human thought. Kant undertakes with positive dogmatism to restore the agreement between faith and knowledge. In the last resort, however, he establishes this agreement by means of a philosophy of morals, not by means of a philosophy of nature. In this way, he is able to grant to negative dogmatism its right to a free, unprejudiced investigation of the entire world of phenomena.

In his theoretical philosophy, Kant overthrows at one blow both positive and negative dogmatism. With materialism, he asserts that science leads only to a knowledge of the uniform connection of things according to law, not to a recognition of their meaning; it is mechanical, not teleological. A teleology of nature and of history is impossible from the scientific standpoint, and consequently it is impossible to have a science of natural theology. But a scientific knowledge of the world, which construes all things, from the formation of the cosmos to the origin of life on the earth, and the course of human history, as the necessary effects of given causes, is possible. On the other hand, Kant holds with idealism that there is a meaning in things, and that we can become certain of this meaning. Life has a real significance. With immediate certainty we affirm moral good as the real purpose of life. We do this, not by means of the understanding or scientific thinking, but through the will, or, as Kant says, the practical reason. In the fact that the will, which alone judges things as 'good' or 'bad,' determines morality as that which has absolute worth, we have the point of departure for the interpretation of life. It is through the will, not through the understanding, that we interpret history; such persons and events as, *e.g.,* Jesus and his life and death, are the historical facts of supreme importance. Thus arise all the historical religions. And in the fact that the entire world is referred to this fixed point, the religious view of the world has its origin; nature is interpreted as a means for the fulfilment of that purpose. Faith is convinced that God has made the world in order to realize in it his salvation toward men. All dogmas of every religion are the diverse expressions of the conviction that the world exists for the

sake of the good, and that nature and history find their explanation in the purposes of God.

But how now is it possible to bring together in a unitary view of the world these two independent ways of regarding things,—the scientific explanation and the religious interpretation? Kant's answer is, by means of the distinction between a sensible and a super-sensible world. The world which constitutes the object of mathematico-scientific knowledge is not reality as such, but only the appearance of reality to our sensibility. The world of religious conviction, on the contrary, is the supersensuous reality itself. This can never become the object of scientific knowledge, on account of the nature of human cognition, which presupposes perception. Regarding it we can know only that it exists; that is the ultimate point to which knowledge attains. In reflecting critically on its own nature and limits, the understanding recognizes that there is an absolute reality beyond the world of sense. And now the spirit (which is something more than understanding) claims, as a moral being, to be a member of this absolute reality, and defines the nature of this reality through its own essence. This is Kant's doctrine of the primacy of the practical reason over the theoretical.

In this way the critical philosophy solves the old problem of the relation of knowledge and faith. Kant is convinced that by properly fixing the limits of each he has succeeded in furnishing a basis for an honorable and enduring peace between them. Indeed, the significance and vitality of his philosophy will rest principally upon this. Although in the details of this philosophy there may be much that is not agreeable to us, it is its enduring merit to have drawn for the first time, with a firm hand and in clear outline, the dividing line between knowledge and faith. This gives to knowledge what belongs to it,—the entire world of phenomena for free investigation; it conserves, on the other hand, to faith its eternal right to the interpretation of life and of the world from the standpoint of value.

There is indeed no doubt that the great influence which Kant exerted upon his age was due just to the fact that he appeared as a deliverer from unendurable suspense. The old view regarding the claims of the feelings and the understanding on reality had been more and more called in question during the second half of the eighteenth century. Voltaire and Hume had not written in vain. Science seemed to demand the renunciation of the old faith. On the other hand, the heart still clung to it. Pietism had increased the sincerity and earnestness of religion, and given it a new and firm root in the affections of the German people. At this point Kant showed a way of escape from the dilemma. His philosophy made it possible to be at once a candid thinker and an honest man of faith. For that, thousands of hearts have thanked him with passionate devotion. It was a deliverance similar to that which the Reformation had brought to the German spirit a century or two earlier. Indeed, one may in a certain sense regard Kant as the finisher of what Luther had begun. The original purpose of the Reformation was to make faith independent of knowledge, and conscience free from external authority. It was the confusion of religion and science in scholastic philosophy against which Luther first revolted. That faith had been transformed into a philosophical body of doctrines, that *fides* had been changed to *credo,* seemed to him to be the root of all evil. To substitute for belief in a human dogma the immediate certainty of the heart in a gracious God reconciled through Christ, to emphasize the importance of the inner disposition, as opposed to outer acts, was the soul of his work. Kant was the first who definitely destroyed the scholastic philosophy. By banishing religion from the field of science, and science from the sphere of religion, he afforded freedom and independence to both. And at the same time he placed morality on a Protestant basis,—not works, but the disposition of the heart.

To this interpretation and evaluation of the Kantian philosophy there are opposed two other views. Criticism is combated by two forms of dogmatism. Though opposed to each other, they agree in their unfavorable opinion of Kant. Negative dogmatism accuses him of treachery to knowledge; positive dogmatism, of yielding the rights of faith. The latter reproaches him as the destroyer of religion and of the philosophy which was well disposed towards it; the former despises him for his subservience to traditional modes of thought and to the pretended necessities of the heart,—a weakness which at most can be forgiven only in view of his other services.[1]

I shall not further discuss negative dogmatism and the judgment which it passes on Kant. At the present day it plays no great rôle. Materialism does not nowadays speak the final word. The representatives of science for the most part occupy the Kantian position. So much the more frequent and vigorous are the attacks from the other side. Revived scholasticism, in particular, directs its attacks at Kant as the champion of the hostile philosophy. With Thomism, as the fundamental form of constructive idealism, is contrasted criticism, as the type of subjective, false, and destructive idealism. Thus it has been pictured by Otto Willmann in his three-volume *History of Idealism.* He represents the history of philosophy according to the following schema. First, the ascending branch. From Plato to St. Thomas we have the ever richer and fuller unfolding of pure idealism, which posits the ideas as objective, constitutive principles of reality. With Thomas the highest point is reached. Then with Nominalism begins the downward course; the disaster of the Reformation followed, and this in logical train led to the Illumination and the Revolution. In Kant's philosophy the spirit of denial has found its completest expression.

It is at the very opposite pole from Thomism. In it false idealism has attained to its final consequence— the reduction of all ideal principles to subjectivism. In this system, the subject, with boundless self-conceit, claims to be the bearer of all reality, the creator of both the laws of nature and of morals. The autonomy of reason is the real nerve of Kant's philosophizing. Kant is the absolutely free thinker, "an advocate for the overthrow of faith, morals, and science." "The idea that he is a pure German philosopher is quite preposterous. Kant is a cosmopolite: he follows the English, is an enthusiastic admirer of Rousseau, and raves about the French Revolution. To German honesty (*Treue*) Kant's destructive sophistic is in direct opposition."[2]

There can be no doubt that this condemnatory judgment regarding Kant is a direct consequence of the Catholic principle. The autonomy of reason and the infallibility of the dogma are evidently irreconcilably opposed. It is also a matter of course that for the adherent of the absolute philosophy, sanctioned by the authority of the Pope, there only exist outside his own standpoint various forms of error, over whose differences it is scarcely worth while to linger. *Philosophia cœlestis* has only one opposite, the *philosophia terrena,* unless one should oppose to it a *philosophia infernalis,* which, moreover, also stands in the same relation. Both are sisters born of arrogance and disobedience.

What attitude would Kant have taken towards such criticism? I think he would have accepted unconditionally the characterization *philosophia terrena.* He recognizes that he is a man placed in this world; his standing-place is the earth. It is not strange, then, that the result of an attempt to orient himself in the world should be an earthly and not a heavenly philosophy. To be sure, it will not escape the man who devotes a more careful scrutiny to Kant's thoughts that his standpoint does not at all seek absolute satisfaction in the things of this earth; he rather points everywhere beyond the *mundus sensibilis* to a *mundus intelligibilis.* But his modesty, or rather his critical reflection upon man's position in the world, prevented him from taking this intelligible world as his standpoint and building his system upon it. He sees that he does not enjoy the privilege of dwelling in that world beyond, or of receiving his inspiration from it. So he is compelled to leave the heavenly philosophy to those who are more favorably situated in this respect. There are two considerations which enable him more easily to endure the arrogance of such people. The first is that the alleged heavenly philosophy has as yet accomplished little or nothing for the advancement of human knowledge. It is only since the earthly standpoint has been adopted that the sciences have gained a sure method of advance. The other is that the lauded service of the pretended heavenly philosophy on behalf of religion and idealism becomes very questionable on unprejudiced historical investigation. It seems rather to Kant that the

Catholic church and school philosophy, which was derived directly from Thomism, is so far from affording support to religious faith at the end of the eighteenth century that the latter is rather hopelessly compromised, and has been brought into suspicion through its connection with the dead body of Thomism. It is the critical philosophy which has again restored to life the faith of the spirit in itself, and as a result of this has revived faith in spirit in general and its creative power in the world. Only through it has an idealistic philosophy which believes in itself become possible.

Indeed it is a remarkable coincidence that in the same year, 1770, there appeared in Catholic France the *Système de la nature,* in Protestant Germany Kant's treatise **De mundi sensibilis et intelligibilis forma ac principiis**—an end and a beginning: the former work an end,—the final and consistent formulation of the materialistic point of view, to which French thought had long tended under the impulse of the scholastic systems which were protected and fostered in the universities; the latter a beginning,—the first outline of an idealistic philosophy of a new kind, the point of departure, even to our own day, for a long series of idealistic systems. On the other hand also an end,—namely, the definitive end of materialism, if we are to accept the authority of the historian F. A. Lange.

At the same time we will also say what is to be thought of the other boast of the Catholic school-philosophy, that it is the *philosophia perennis.* At the end of last century it was as dead as out-worn system ever was. If that system at present is experiencing a kind of revival in the school of Catholicism, this is due not so much to its own inner vitality as to its supposed fitness to serve an ecclesiastical political system which through the favor of circumstances—*patientia Dei et stultitia hominum,* an old Lutheran would say—has attained again in our time to unexpected power. Moreover, there still remains the question whether continuance of existence is in general something of which a philosophy can boast. Perhaps fruitfulness is a better characteristic, and this the Kantian philosophy shows; it still gives rise to new systems of thought. Thomism, on the contrary, though of course a great achievement for its own time, yields to-day nothing except unfruitful repetitions. It does not set free the spirit, it enslaves it, which of course is just its intention.

But, finally, in regard to the doctrine of the autonomy of reason, with its groundless subjectivism and its immanent tendency to revolution, it is naturally impossible to discuss these matters with those who are not open to conviction. Whoever is determined to subject his reason to ecclesiastical, which now means papist, authority, cannot be hindered. And it would be just as vain to maintain against such a one the right of reason to independent judgment. He would in all circumstances see in this defence arrogance and culpable insubordi-

nation. To what purpose has he subjected himself if others may venture to make exceptions and go their own way?

But for those who are not yet so firmly convinced, the remark may be added that the grounding of the certainty of knowledge of morals and of faith upon the inner certainty of the individual is the firmest foundation which is possible in human matters. This is the very foundation that Kant has laid (at least in intention). He thought that he had proved that reason makes explicit its own essence in the laws of nature and of morals, and in rational faith; and that, therefore, so soon as it has knowledge of the real circumstances, it cannot refrain from recognizing this law. Of course, Kant's doctrine is not universally accepted. Nevertheless, in this respect no external authority has an advantage over it, not even that of the chair of Peter. Indeed, one can say that it lies in the nature of reason to react with inner hostility against every external authority that demands absolute subjection in spiritual and moral things. The history of Catholic lands does not permit us to doubt that absolutism brings as its opposite intellectual and even moral and political anarchism.

II. Kant's Position in the Thought of His Own Time

If we wish to describe Kant's position in a single formula we may say that he is at once the finisher and conqueror of the Illumination.

Kant's early training falls in the period when the two opposing tendencies of pietism and rationalism were influencing the minds of men. The period of his personal activity is the age of the illumination. The spread of his philosophy towards the end of the century coincides with the decline of the illumination and the appearance of the new humanism. By the turn of the century, which Kant as an old man lived to see, the critical philosophy in connection with modern classical literature had victoriously completed the great spiritual revolution in Germany, which ran parallel with the politico-social revolution in France. A new view of the world and a new ideal of culture had gained predominance.

I shall attempt to characterize in a few words the general tendencies and the leaders in this movement.

Pietism and rationalism both begin to find their way into Protestant Germany from the Netherlands and France in the second half of the seventeenth century. Although mutually antagonistic, they coöperate in overturning the theologico-dogmatic mode of thought that had prevailed since the generation in which the reformed doctrines had been fixed.

Pietism is, in its origin, a popular religious movement. Its object is to make Christianity—which in the state churches had degenerated into a subject of dispute for theological scholars, and a tool for obtaining the mastery on the part of the scheming politicians—what it originally sought to be, the great personal concern of the individual. This explains the insistence on conversion. Connection with a church is of no avail; everything depends on the personal turning to God in Christ. There is in this something of the original impulse of the Reformation. The subjective religious life asserts itself against the religion objectified in church doctrine and ordinance,—Luther rebels against Lutheranism.

If pietism is the renewing of the original and most fundamental tendencies of the Reformation, rationalism may be characterized as the continuance of the Renaissance. Like the latter, it proceeds from a worldly aristocratic impulse toward culture; the soil in which it grows is independent investigation that has been emancipated from authority. The new sciences, cosmology and physics, united with mathematics, and also that critical historical investigation which, since the days of Valla and Erasmus, had rent the veil which lay over the past, have given to reason confidence in itself. In the great philosophical systems of Descartes, Hobbes, Spinoza, and Leibniz, it sets itself the task of constructing on the basis of all the modern sciences a world-system of a purely rational character. Rationalism, in the most general sense, is nothing else than the confidence that reason must succeed, without any other presuppositions than those which scientific investigation and necessary thinking afford, in producing an all-embracing system of demonstrable truths in which God and nature, life and history, will be included without any unexplained remainder.

Pietism and rationalism, in spite of their intrinsic opposition, seem, on their first appearance, to be connected just as the Reformation and the Renaissance formerly were. They have a common foe in the dominant system, and a common characteristic in their endeavor after freedom, after the realization of the personal life. In the university which had just been founded at Halle (1694), they met in the persons of two of their most important representatives, August Hermann Francke (1662-1727), and Christian Thomasius (1665-1727). Both had been expelled from the land of pure Lutheranism, the old conservative Saxony, and its university at Leipzig, and both found the sphere of their permanent and wide-reaching influence in the young university of the energetic Prussian State. The theologian and the jurist were soon joined by a third, the philosopher, Christian Wolff (1679-1754). His importance consists in the fact that he reduced modern philosophy to an inclusive system that could be taught and learned in the universities, and by this means banished the Aristotelian school-philosophy from the German universities. The modern sciences, mathematics and mathematical physics, form the basis of his system. Like Leibniz and Descartes, Hobbes and Spinoza,

Wolff sets out from these sciences, in which he had already worked as a teacher and writer. From their point of view he writes his logic and metaphysic, his ethics and psychology. The motto of his philosophy, "nothing without sufficient reason," denotes its strong rationalistic character; nothing happens and nothing is true without a sufficient reason.

As the political friendship between the Renaissance and the Reformation was broken so soon as the common enemy, scholasticism, had been overcome, so the intrinsic opposition between pietism and rationalism passed into open hostility as soon as the old orthodoxy had lost its dominant position. Even in Halle it came to a bitter fight, which ended with the well-known disaster, the expulsion of Wolff (1723). But the joy of his pietistical opponents was too hasty; the power of the illumination was already too strong. Persecution heightened Wolff's fame and increased his influence. In the year 1740, immediately after the accession of Frederick the Great, he was recalled with fullest honors and held his triumph as victor in Halle.

From the year 1740 we may date the undisputed dominance of the illumination in Germany. It lasted until about the death of its great representatives on the German thrones, Friedrich and Joseph. If we wish to define its character in a formula we may say: It was the period of the peaceful and universally recognized sway of reason upon the earth, attained after long combat and final victory. Confidence in reason was universal and unconditioned,—reason in things and reason in men. Now, reason undertakes to arrange all things according to their principles. The institutions and arrangements of life are examined with a critical glance, and ordered anew according to rational concepts. In like manner, knowledge is rationalized. Reason explains all things as due to reason. God, the world-reason, has formed nature in accordance with rational thoughts. The task of the philosopher is to discover these rational thoughts in things and to re-think them. The historical world, too, is explained from rational thoughts and purposes. Here is human reason itself, which creates its own world. Language and religion, law and the State, are means invented by the reason for the attainment of rational ends. And alongside this rationalistic philosophy of history stands a rationalistic æsthetic that explains art and poetry from rational principles, and affords guidance for rational production. Gottsched's critical art of poetry is the type of this æsthetic. Thus reason has become the all-prevailing principle—both formal and material—of philosophy. All things are made by reason and are intelligible through reason.

In the second half of the eighteenth century there appeared, at first imperceptibly, then more openly, a reaction against the universal sovereignty of reason, which finally led to the direct opposite of the illumination,—

to Romanticism. Among the foreign influences which gave rise to this movement we may mention in the first place Voltaire, Rousseau, and the English philosophers. All these stand on the ground of the illumination, but they undermine its foundation. Voltaire directs his sarcasm against the perfection of the world as the optimistic rationalism of Leibniz had represented it. Rousseau champions the cause of the heart against the head; he emphasizes the importance of nature, and of the unconscious, as opposed to conscious reason; he praises innocent simplicity and good will above the arrogance of the culture of the understanding. English empiricism combats rationalism in epistemology and metaphysics. When carried to its extreme form by Hume, it denies the possibility of metaphysics or of natural theology in general. It asserts that there is no absolute knowledge of the world, that reality does not manifest itself to human reason. A metaphysical theory of the world, according to the view to which Hume's *Dialogues on Natural Religion* leads, is based rather on the disposition of the heart than upon reason and demonstration. It possesses the subjective necessity of faith, not the objective necessity of knowledge.

Similar transformations in the German world of thought are connected with the names of Winckelmann, Lessing, Hamann, Herder, Goethe, and Schiller. To this group also belongs Kant. These men all grew up in the school of the illumination, but they all transcend the conceptions of the illumination. For they abandon strict rationalism and advance to the historico-genetic standpoint, which asserts that things are not fashioned according to fixed plans, they develop and grow. Neither the great works of art and literature, nor the great historical achievements like language and religion, nor even nature and her products have been contrived as means for the realization of ends. Organic growth became the dominant concept, superseding the notion of mechanical creation. The view of the world which belongs to this type of thought is evolutionary pantheism. This displaced the metaphysic of the illumination, anthropomorphic theism.

A transformation in our attitude towards life, and in our general view of the world always shows itself first in the æsthetic field. We find, therefore, that this is the case here. Klopstock, Winckelmann, and Lessing shake men's faith in the rationalistic æsthetic, and in the art and poetry whose expression it is, or which has been framed according to its rules. Klopstock turns from the French to the English, from art to nature, and from what is foreign to what is domestic and national. Gottsched and the poetry formed after the rules of classic verse are despised. Winckelmann proclaimed the degradation of the court academy art in the midst of its own territory. He accused it of being a product of arbitrary choice, and of pandering to the vulgar taste for what is fashionable and exaggerated. In this he contrasts it with the simplicity and calm nobility of the art of the Greeks. Their works of art are not imitative products, fashioned according to the rules of academic art for the satisfaction of vanity or for the purpose of entertaining the fashionable world, but they have proceeded by uniform development from the national life itself. Lessing, the hero who rejoiced in conflict, begins his great war against everything which is canonical and conventional, against the dogmas of the old æsthetics and poetics, as well as against the dogmas of the orthodox or new-fashioned rational theology. He is the first who sees Spinoza's thoughts shining through Leibniz's system, the first who ventured to follow up Spinoza's thought of the . . . doctrine of the All-One.

When Lessing in the summer of 1780 carried on those conversations with F. H. Jacobi about Spinoza in Gleim's garden-house, he did not know that the work was already thought out which should give the death blow to the metaphysics of the illumination. This work was the *Critique of Pure Reason.* Kant showed that the world is in no respect such a transparent thought-product as the illumination assumed; indeed, that reality in general cannot be apprehended by our thought, that it necessarily transcends the standpoint of knowledge. And from this there followed for him the further consequences that religion cannot be derived from or demonstrated by reason, as the illumination attempted. Its roots lie deeper, they are to be sought in the will. The will, the practical side of our nature, determines the fundamental direction of our view of the world, as it determines the value of human life. Kant himself did not complete the transition from the intellectualistic to the voluntaristic metaphysics and psychology. He still possessed, even to the end, too great confidence in the power of reason. But he started the movement which was fully carried out by Schopenhauer.

Kant's younger countryman, Hamann, the "magician of the North," had many points of contact with him. In Hamann, the pietistic sceptic, the reaction against rationalism is almost transformed into a hostility towards reason. He will allow almost no merit to reason except that it leads men to a knowledge of its inevitable shortcomings. In so far as Hume and Kant (whom he once called the Prussian Hume) effect this, he recognizes in them the true philosophy. He was especially concerned with the problem of the origin of language and poetry, and finds its source, not in the reason, where the philosophers of the illumination had sought it, but in the dispositions and passions through which nature works. Hamann is the prophet of those inclined to mysticism among the devout of both confessions who at the beginning of the nineteenth century introduced the great revival of the emotional religiosity which clings fast to mysteries.

A pupil of Kant and Hamann is Herder, though both of them regard him as influenced by Hume and Rousseau. His importance in the development of the German intellectual life consists in the fact that he destroyed rationalism in the philosophy of history. Language, poetry, religion, are not manufactured products, but natural growths, which are produced by the different peoples with the same inner necessity with which the various regions produce different forms of plant and animal life. With this is connected Herder's fondness for the original form of poetry, the popular ballads. This is genuine poetry, which cannot be said of the manufactured verses of the professors of poetics and their pupils. And the same is true of religion. Religion is originally poetry, the great world-poem which the spirit of the people produces in its struggle with reality, and in which are reflected its own nature and destiny. It is said that religion is the manifestation of God. That is certainly true, but the manifestation of God through human nature, in the same sense that Homer is a manifestation of God, or the Zeus of Phidias, or the Madonna of Raphael. This point of view overthrows the old doctrine of special inspiration. It also destroys rationalistic theology, which explains religion as the invention of priests and religious societies, and seeks to purify it, by critical endeavors, of what is false and unessential. The final postulate of the new point of view is here again pantheistic metaphysics: the entire world is the manifestation of God. Herder too found in Spinoza his philosopher.

Goethe's thought, which was enriched by Herder, moved in the same path. Pantheism, poetically apprehended through feeling, is his faith,—Spinoza's philosophy and Rousseau's sensibility to nature united. His first great poetical works, *Werther, Faust, Prometheus,* are entirely filled with this spirit. He despised the conventional philosophy and science of the schools; he scorned the understanding which works designedly and according to rule,—*encheiresin natuæ,* so chemistry names it! Feeling and intuition are everything; name and concept are only the external appearance. This is the doctrine that he proclaims with youthful vehemence. But even in the scientific form of his later thought, there remains the opposition to the mechanico-rational view. This shows itself in his color theory, as aversion towards Newton; in his geological and biological views as dislike for the Plutonian hypothesis, and as belief in the gradual growth and development of natural forms. It is the idea of organic development which gave direction to his scientific thinking. Development, organic increase, is also the form of his personal life and practical activity. To both is the idea foreign of producing according to set plan. In his own person the wonderful richness of his nature unfolded itself in unbroken continuity throughout his long life without the haste and commotion of voluntarily setting about to produce it. And in the same way his great poetical works took form in an organic way from his own inner experience. Thus Goethe is in his own person the living refutation of the old, narrow, rationalistic view of the nature of poetry, and of life, and of reality in general. Schiller also was impreg-

nated with the doctrines of Spinoza and Rousseau before he found his world-formula in the Kantian philosophy; but neither in his practical nor in his theoretical philosophy did the influences of his early mode of thought disappear.

To sum up: In the half-century which followed the death of Christian Wolff a mighty transformation had occurred. The intellectual theology of reason which took the form of anthropomorphic theism had been replaced by a poetic, naturalistic pantheism as the fundamental form of its view of the world. God is the All-One who manifests his nature both in the world and in the process of organic development. The highest revelation of his nature for us is found in the spiritual life of man in society. Dogmatic anthropomorphism, such as rational theology tried to construct, is impossible; but a symbolic anthropomorphism may perhaps be allowed. If the nature of the All-One manifests itself in man, man may represent God after his own image, not with the intention of thereby adequately defining the nature of God, but perhaps with the conviction that what is best and deepest in human nature is not foreign to the nature of God; indeed that it forms the essence of his nature.

To have cleared the ground and pointed the way to these thoughts, which have become dominant in the poetry and philosophy of the German people, is the imperishable service of Kant.

Notes

[1] H. Heine, in his essay on "Religion and Philosophy in Germany," has characterized, or rather caricatured, Kant's relation to religion as follows: After Kant, in the *Critique of Pure Reason,* had destroyed deism, or the old Jehovah himself, the tragedy was followed by a farce. Behind the dreadful critic stands, carrying an umbrella, his old servant Lampe, tears and drops of anguish upon his face. "Then Immanuel Kant has compassion and shows that he is not only a great philosopher, but also a good man, and, half kindly, half ironically, he speaks: 'Old Lampe must have a God or else he cannot be happy, says the practical reason; for my part, the practical reason may, then, guarantee the existence of God.' "

[2] III., pp. 503, 528.—In an essay on this book by Commer, the editor of the Catholic *Jahrbücher für Philos. und spekul. Theologie* (1896), we find the following statements: There are two species of philosophy, the true and the false—*philosophia cælestis* and *philosophia terrena.* These correspond to the two kingdoms of reality, as St. Augustine has distinguished them,—the *civitas Dei* and the *civitas terrena.* The one philosophy has its roots in love to God; the other, in self-love. On the one side stands St. Thomas, the rep-

resentative of divine and true philosophy; and on the other, stand Materialism, Anarchism, Pantheism, Atheism, Agnosticism, and in the midst, Criticism, as the most dangerous foe of God and of religion.—I have made some criticisms of Willmann's book in an essay entitled, "The Most Recent Inquisition on Modern Philosophy," in the *Deutsche Rundschau,* August, 1898.

. . . . .

Second Book

The Practical Philosophy

The central principle of Kant's practical philosophy is the *idea of freedom,* not in the technical sense of the system, but in the general acceptation of *spontaneous self-activity.* In epistemology, Kant opposes sensationalism by making knowledge the product of the mind's activity. And in the same way, he combats hedonism by basing ethics entirely on spontaneous activity. The value of man's life depends solely on what he does, not on what happens to him. And the same notion forms the leading principle of the subordinate disciplines. In the philosophy of the State and of Law, the constitution and laws of a state have value only when they are based upon the freedom and spontaneous activity of citizens who are regarded as the end. An autocratic form of government may, under certain circumstances, be very conducive to the peace and wellbeing of its subjects; but it is as much inferior to a republican, or representative form of government as a machine is to an organism. The same principle runs through the philosophy of Religion. Religion is believing in God and fulfilling his commands—the moral law—freely. Thus the church is nothing but the voluntary association, formed to fight against evil, of all the righteous and true believers. With the true church there is contrasted the priestly church, which degrades the people into passive laity, for whom the priest makes the creed and performs divine service. Finally, in the pedagogical works true education is distinguished from mere training by the fact that it has in view the self-activity and the freely acting good-will of the pupil.

First Section

The Moral Philosophy

Literature: Among the precritical writings, the *Beobachtungen über das Gefühl des Schönen und Erhabenen* (1764) is of special importance for Kant's ethical views, and contains contributions for a moral characterology. After hints of a change in his theory of morals in the *Dissertation* and the *Kritik der reinen Vernunft,* Kant published the *Grundlegung zur Metaphysik der Sitten* (1785), the first systematic exposition of his ethical views. It contains preliminary sketches that were subsequently omitted, and, above

all, the important notion of a kingdom of ends. The *Kritik der practischen Vernunft* adds, in particular, the moral theology, and the *Kritik der Urteilskraft* [Eng. trans. by J. H. Bernard, 1892] contributes to the same subject. The systematic exposition of the ethics, according to the principles laid down in these writings, is contained in a work that belongs to his old age, *Anfangsgründe der Tugendlehre.* In the Anthropology there is much that concerns moral dietetics. Interesting fragments of earlier attempts at construction are contained in Reicke's *Lose Blätter.* [J. G. Schurman, *Kantian Ethics and the Ethics of Evolution;* 1881; Noah Porter, *Kant's Ethics* (Griggs Philos. Classics), 1886.] For the development of Kant's ethical views, *cf.* F. W. Förster, *Der Entwickelungsgang der Kantischen Ethik bis 1781* (1893), and P. Menzer, in Vaihinger's *Kantstudien,* II., pp. 290 ff., III., pp. 41 ff. Also, A. Hegler, *Die Psychologie in Kants Ethik* (1891); A. Cresson, *La morale de Kant* (1897). [T. K. Abbott's volume, entitled *Kant's Theory of Ethics* (1883), contains English translations of the *Grundlegung zur Metaphysik der Sitten (Fundamental Principles of the Metaphysic of Morals),* the *Kritik der pract. Vernunft (Critique of Practical Reason),* the general Introduction to the *Metaphysische Anfangsgründe der Sittenlehre (Metaphysical Principles of the Science of Morals),* and the preface and Introduction to the *Metaphysische Anfangsgründe der Tugendlehre (Metaphysical Principles of the Doctrine of Virtue).*]

I. The General Character of Kant's Moral Philosophy

The character and position of moral philosophy in Kant's system is described by the name which he gives it, "metaphysic of morals." By means of this title, it is paralleled with the "metaphysic of nature." Like the latter, it is a system of pure rational laws, valid *a priori,* applying, not to the realm of nature, but to that of freedom. But, on the other hand, the name implies a contrast with the "physics of morals." It is not to be a theoretical science of the origin, importance, and effect of subjective and objective morality in the life of human experience, but a system of pure *a priori* valid formulæ, without any relation to the guidance of life according to the teachings of experience. The pure concepts of the understanding are absolutely indifferent to any particular content of experience, but are valid *a priori* for every possible experience. And, in the same way, the moral law is completely unconcerned with life and particular circumstances. It is valid *a priori* for every rational being, quite irrespective of what the conditions of life may be. The concepts of the understanding do indeed require for their objective validity confirmation through experience; for otherwise they are only empty thought-forms. But, for the moral law, it is not essential that it shall be obeyed anywhere in the real world. It does not determine what is, but what ought to be, what abides, even if what is actual everywhere follows a different course. In truth, there is no way of demonstrating that the moral law anywhere determines the nature of the real. Morality, as an act of freedom, can never be found as a fact in the empirical world. The metaphysic of morals has nothing at all to do with actual occurrences, with life and history as empirical facts. These things belong to the "physics of morals."

As this point is of great importance in understanding and estimating the value of Kant's moral philosophy, it will be well to consider it at somewhat greater length.

One may give the title of "physics of morals" to the theoretical consideration of morality as empirical facts of ordinary life. As an empirical living being, man belongs to nature, and all theoretical knowledge of his character and development forms a part of natural science in its broader sense. That is as true of psychical anthropology, including the philosophy of history, as of physical. All these disciplines consider man purely as a natural product, just in the same way as the zoölogist considers any other species of animal. Investigation into the history of his development may show how the species man has differentiated itself into various races in adapting itself to different conditions of life in different quarters of the globe. In the brief essays *On the Various Races of Mankind* (1775), and *Determination of the Concept of a Race of Men* (1785), Kant pointed out the way to this mode of treatment. If this procedure were ever able to show how mankind originally had evolved from an earlier form of life, Kant would have nothing to object. Then, too, sociology and philosophy of history consider man as a social being. The former may show how in a common life certain uniform relations necessarily grow up, and how these become, through the specific character of man, who differs from other gregarious animals in possessing higher intelligence and more strongly marked individuality, rational usages, consciously adopted and maintained, in distinction from the social instincts of animals. Again, it may go on to show how these usages assume different forms among different peoples, corresponding to the various conditions and ends of life, but how they everywhere have the tendency to promote life in the sense of preserving and raising the historical type. Finally, the philosophy of history may attempt to gain an insight into the unity of all the data presented by empirical history, and to discover in them progress towards a final purpose, perhaps the complete development of all the natural powers of humanity. In doing this it may represent the moral and legal usages as essential conditions of progress toward this goal.—All these would be purely theoretical sciences, investigating the uniform connection of given facts according to the law of causality.

And to the same sphere belong also disciplines like politics or pedagogy that deal with the problems of some special department of life, and even those that profess to furnish guidance for life in general, like morality in the popular sense of the word. These are all technical disciplines that really belong, as far as content is concerned, to the theoretical sciences. They convert into a rule that which theory expresses as a law. Medicine is nothing but the sum of the applications of the knowledge that physical anthropology possesses. It may be connected with the latter as a mere corollary. In like manner, the ordinary laws of morality, as a set of practical or technical precepts, might be added or annexed to general anthropology, as "pragmatic" anthropology. Kant has himself furnished an example of this in his *Anthropology with a Pragmatic Purpose.* All this belongs to the "physics of morals."

Now, a "metaphysic of morals" is entirely different from all this. It is not at all concerned with what happens, but only with that which should happen, whether it now is taking place anywhere or not. It sets up a law for the realm of Freedom. This is something that lies entirely outside the realm of nature, that is, outside of the real world in so far as the latter is known as an object. It lies in the intelligible world. Since obedience to the moral law is an intelligible act of free will, it does not belong at all to the observable facts of empirical reality. Real occurrences, which are objects of knowledge, belong entirely to the phenomenal world, and are to be explained according to the law of causality. The only thing that is evident as a fact is the consciousness of the unconditional obligation of a law that commands categorically. The effects and purposes of the action do not enter at all into this consciousness. In like manner, it is altogether free from inclinations and conditions of the possibility of the action. It contains only the form of a universal law by means of which all action is to be determined. Now, this law is the sole object of practical philosophy in the true sense, as opposed to pragmatic and technical disciplines that have wrongly assumed the name of practical, when really they are only offshoots of the theoretical sciences.[1]

Thus Kant's practical philosophy, or the "metaphysic of morals," is in principle completely divorced from empirical reality, from the life of the individual, and from the historical life of humanity. It is not at home on the earth among men, but in the transcendental world of purely rational beings. It is the natural law of the *mundus intelligibilis.* The moral law is suspended over life merely as a norm for passing judgments upon the will. It does not have its origin in life, and from the very nature of the case no knowledge of its effectiveness in life is possible.—It is another question whether Kant always remained true to this fundamental conception in elaborating it in detail. Probably such a purely transcendent morality cannot always be carried through. So soon as we attempt to deal with concrete norms, over and above the mere demands of formal accordance with the law, the special empirically given content of life will necessarily claim recognition. "Thou shalt not lie," is not a rule for purely rational beings as such, but for those who communicate their thoughts by speech and other symbols. "Thou shalt not mutilate, destroy, or defile thy body," is a rule only for those rational beings who have a body with the organs in question. In a pure "metaphysic of morals" there should really be no mention of any of these things. Of course the content of such a 'science' would be very scant.

II. *The Elaboration of the System*

The system of the "metaphysics of morals" was long delayed, although Kant had intended, as early as 1785, to undertake at once its complete elaboration.[2] First there appeared as a prolegomenon the *Fundamental Principles* (*Grundlegung*), which, according to the preface,[3] was intended to represent the *Critique*. Then followed still another *"Critique" of Practical Reason,*—in reality quite an unsuitable title, as Kant himself recognized: the practical reason requires no critique. The theoretical reason, or the understanding, requires criticism because it has a tendency to overstep its limits. But the practical reason is not subject to any criticism, to a judicial sentence before any other court as to its claims. It is itself the final court of appeal regarding all human affairs. Instead of a "Critique" we might have expected an "apology," or rather an "apotheosis" of the practical reason. But after the *Critique of Pure Reason,* it seemed to Kant that this doctrine, too, must have a critique as a prolegomenon. And when the critique was written, in this case also the doctrine was long in following. Not until 1797 did it appear, and then not as a "system," but under the apparently stereotyped titles, *Metaphysical Principles of Doctrine of Virtue,* and *Metaphysical Principles of Right.* It was not until the second edition (1798) that the two works received the common title, *Metaphysic of Morals.* These works exhibit Kant's tendency to undertake all sorts of preliminary discussions, which developed into a kind of dislike to give a final exposition of the real question itself. They also show his ever-increasing tendency towards schematic uniformity in the construction of his system, the pernicious effects of which Adickes has traced throughout Kant's entire period of authorship in his acute investigation, entitled *Kant's Schematic Tendency as a Factor in the Construction of his System.* To this latter tendency in particular is to be ascribed the fact that the working out of the system (the doctrinal part, as Kant says) is lacking, or remains in the form of "Critiques." The elaboration of the *Critique of Pure Reason* had left such deep traces on Kant's mind that his thought always fell again into this groove. This is the limitation of the human understanding that we so often meet with. If one has once happily solved a problem by means of a certain method, one tries to solve all the problems of the world in the same way.

The *Critique of Practical Reason,* which therefore remained the chief work on moral philosophy, follows the *Critique of Pure Reason* step by step, not only in its intrinsic method, as the *Fundamental Principles* does, but also in its external divisions. We have the same statement of the problem regarding the possibility of synthetic judgments *a priori;* the same divisions into a Doctrine of Elements and a Doctrine of Method, into Analytic and Dialectic, with a table of categories and antinomies. If the schema was not adapted to the epistemological investigation, it is here still more ill-fitting. Kant's thought had become enslaved by the schema: it looks more at the fixed form of the system than at the facts. He is not troubled by the fact that his ideas suffer from this fixed arrangement, that necessary investigations are lacking, and empty, formal notions find place. He rejoices in the thorough-going analogy, and finds in this an important confirmation of the truth of his system. In what follows, I propose to treat merely the fundamental conceptions, without following in detail the schematic execution.

(1) *The Form of Morality*

The form of morality is determined by the essential character of the critical philosophy, formal rationalism. This element comes out so clearly just at this point that no one can mistake it and find the main purpose in something else, *e. g.,* in phenomenalism or the determination of limits. The undertaking is to show that the practical reason, like the theoretical, is *a priori* legislative. Moral philosophy, as metaphysics in the *Critique of Pure Reason,* is traced back to a transcendental logic: the moral law is a purely logical law of action.

The point of departure for the investigation is here, as in his theoretical work, the division of human nature into two sides, sensibility and reason, which are related to each other as matter and form. In the *Critique of Pure Reason,* we have the understanding as spontaneity opposed to sensibility as the receptivity for impressions. It is the function of the understanding to bring the manifold of sensation to a unity subject to laws. In the *Critique of Practical Reason,* sensibility has the form of a plurality of impulses that by means of objects are stimulated into a variety of desires. Impulses aim at satisfaction. The satisfaction of all the impulses, posited as the common goal of sensibility, is called *happiness.* Also here we have reason as the formal principle opposed to sensibility. As in the theoretical sphere reason is the origin of the laws of nature, so here it assigns a law to the realm of voluntary action. This is the moral law. The moral laws correspond in the sphere of the will to the pure concepts of the understanding in the realm of intellect. Like the latter they possess universality and necessity, and in a two-fold sense. That is, they are valid for all rational beings, and they admit of absolutely no exceptions. Here as in the theoretical field their *a priori* character is established by means of these marks.

Of course the difference that we already described, that in the theoretical field the universality refers to what is, and in the practical to what ought to be, shows itself here. Natural phenomena correspond without exception to natural laws; but, on the contrary, action is not invariably controlled by the moral law. It should be so controlled, but it is not. But that the universality of obligation is not merely an empty and arbitrary demand, perhaps on the part of the moral philosophers, but rests upon a real law of reason, is shown by the fact that all men know and recognize it, if not in act, at least in passing moral judgments. In estimating the worth of our own actions and those of others, there is always presupposed an underlying standard. This is the moral law, and just in this way is its universal validity recognized.

It is noteworthy, as a further parallel, that the characteristic position of man, both in a theoretical and practical regard, rests upon this union of sensibility and reason. The nature of human knowledge is determined by the fact that there must enter into it both perception and understanding. Understanding without sensibility is a description of the divine intelligence, while sensibility without understanding is the condition of the brutes. In like manner, the human will is characterized by the fact that reason and sensibility are always united in action, the former determining the form of the will, and the latter furnishing the object of desire. Reason without sensibility characterizes the divine will, whose nature is expressed in the moral law, which alone determines its activity. Sensible impulses without reason result in the animal will, made up of lawless and accidental desires, subject to the natural course of events.

Now, just on this point rests the characteristic nature of morality, which is *action out of respect for a law.* Among beings above and below the human race there is no obligation and no morality, but only the act of will. The divine will corresponds completely with the divine reason: it is holy, not moral. The will of the lower animal is made up of passive excitations of impulse: it does not act, but is passive as a part of nature, and consequently is entirely without moral quality. In the case of man, morality rests upon the control of the sense impulses by the reason. Through the fact that man as a rational being prescribes a law to himself as a sensible being, obligation first arises. Here we have a volition that contains a moment of negation,—even of contradiction.

The point of departure and the basis for moral philosophy are found in the analysis of the moral consciousness. This reveals just that consciousness of the opposition of duty and inclination, the consciousness of

obligation, as the original phenomenon in the field of morality in general. The interpretation of these facts is the first problem of moral philosophy. Kant solves it, as we have indicated, by tracing it back to the opposition of reason and sensibility. The inclinations are all derived ultimately from sense impulses, while the consciousness of duty proceeds from reason, as is evident from the fact that obligation presupposes a universal law as norm. Every system of moral philosophy that does not recognize the absolute nature of this opposition, that attempts, like eudæmonism, to explain obligation by some indirect derivation from the inclinations, destroys, according to Kant, the very essence of morality. For this reason he constantly treats eudæmonism not only as a false theory, but as a moral perversity. He sympathizes, however, with the morality of the common man, who finds as unconditionally given in his conscience the opposition of duty and inclination. One can at once say that Kant's system of morality is the restoration of the common morality of conscience with its absolute imperative, as opposed to philosophical theories of morality, which all undertake some explanation of that imperative.

The second point that results from an analysis of the moral consciousness is the fundamental form of moral judgments of value. A will is morally good when it is determined solely by duty, or the moral law. In so far as the will is determined by inclinations, whether these are bodily or mental, coarse or refined, its actions can have no moral value. They may in such cases correspond with the moral law. But legality is not morality. The latter rests solely upon the form of the determination of the will. It is only when duty is done out of respect for the law, without any reference to the results of the act for the inclinations, that we have the habit of will that alone possesses moral value. The ordinary reason always makes these distinctions with complete certainty. It distinguishes what is morally good from what is useful and agreeable, and also from what is merely in accordance with law and duty.

The content of the general moral consciousness may consequently be expressed as follows, in the form of a demand: Let the moral law be the sole determining ground of thy will. It has the form of a categorical imperative: Thou shalt do what the law prescribes, unconditionally, whatever consequences may result. Impulses that seek happiness, and the dictates of prudence speak in hypothetical imperatives: If you would obtain this or that, if you wish to consult your advantage, you must do this or that, or leave them undone. You must not be intemperate if you would not injure your health or your good name, and so act contrary to your happiness. The pure practical reason may command the same line of action. But by means of its form as unconditional imperative it can unmistakably be distinguished from all such prudential rules. Even if no injury could ever result to one from lying, or from a dishonorable act, the imperative retains its force. This is the mandate of the reason, the expression of its nature. Universality and necessity, not comparative and conditional, but absolute and unconditional, constitute the essence of all rationality.

For this very reason, universality is the touchstone through which the rational origin of the will's motives may be infallibly recognized. If the maxim of the will cannot be represented as a universal law, it is not derived from reason, but from sensibility, and the resulting act is without moral value, or non-moral. One may accordingly express the categorical imperative also in the formula: Act so that thy maxim may be capable of becoming the universal natural law of all rational beings. If it is from its very nature incapable of this extension, then it proceeds from the arbitrariness of sensibility, and not from reason. For example, the question may arise whether it is right for me to tell a lie to rescue myself or some one else from a difficulty. The maxim of the decision of the will might be: If by a lie or by a promise that I do not intend to keep I can obtain an advantage that is greater than any disadvantage for myself or others that may result, then I regard it as allowable, and will act accordingly. Now attempt to represent this maxim as a universal natural law of willing and acting. One sees at once that it is impossible: it would destroy itself. If every one constantly acted in accordance with this maxim, no one would ever believe the statements or promises of another, and accordingly there would be an end to statements and promises themselves. Lies and dishonesty are self-contradictory: they are possible only on the condition that they do not become universal natural laws of speech and conduct. The liar and deceiver wills at the same time that there shall not be lying and deceit; for he does not wish others to deceive him. The reason in him, therefore, is opposed to the sensible nature, which regards merely its momentary advantage.

And just in this fact lies the real ground for rejecting such a condition. Reason and sensibility are related as higher and lower. If one lies, he follows the lower faculty of desire; he permits the animal in him to rule, following his desires and fears. He divorces himself from his character as a rational being and renounces his humanity. The worth of man rests on the fact that reason rules in his life and is not subordinated to the impulses of sense. In virtue of his reason, man belongs to a higher order of things, an intelligible and divine world. As a sensible being he is a product of nature. How shameful and degrading it would be to subject his divine part to the animal nature, to renounce his citizenship in the kingdom of rational beings, and content himself with merely an animal existence. It is an absolute inversion of things to subject the reason, which from its very nature is its own absolute purpose, to the sensibility that it is naturally intended to serve. Justice . . . , to use Plato's phraseology to express

Kant's thought, consists for man in every part of his soul performing its proper function. It is necessary that reason, the part that is divine in nature and in origin, shall rule, and that the will shall obey its commands and make them the law of its action, and that the system of sensory and animal impulses shall provide for the preservation of the bodily life in strict subjection to reason, and without causing the mind disquiet and disturbance.

We here touch upon the deepest side of the Kantian theory of morals, where it passes over at once into religious feeling. To this we shall return immediately. But first I wish to consider another of the fundamental notions of the system, that of freedom.

Freedom is the postulate of morality as something internally consistent. A being without freedom, a being whose activities are determined by causes either outside him or in him, is never the subject of a moral judgment. And it makes no difference whether this causality is mechanical or mediated through ideas. An *automaton spirituale* is not less an automaton than a bodily one. Freedom therefore signifies absolute spontaneity, the ability to act unconditionally, and not as determined by causes. The possibility of this notion was shown in the *Critique of Pure Reason.* There it was proved that empirical causality is valid in the world of phenomena, not in the intelligible world. It is therefore thinkable that the same being stands under the law of causality as a member of the phenomenal world, but as a *noumenon,* possesses causality according to the concept of freedom. This notion, which remains problematical from the speculative standpoint, is rendered certain by means of the practical reason. The moral law commands unconditionally. Its fulfilment must therefore be possible. In other words, there must be a will that is not determined by sense solicitation, but that determines itself merely through the idea of the law. That is a free will. Freedom, or the capacity to make the moral law the absolute ground of determination of the will, without regard to all the solicitations of inclination or to the influence of fixed habits, education, natural disposition and temperament, is directly posited in the recognition of the moral law itself. Although the understanding may not be able to explain it, the absolute validity of the notion is not less certain. Thou canst, for thou oughtst—common-sense recognizes at once the necessity of the connection.

With the concept of freedom that of autonomy is closely connected. The moral is not a law imposed by some external authority, but the essential expression of reason itself. The theological theory of morality, that derives the law from the arbitrary will of God, and finds its sanction in the power of the Almighty to punish and reward, is refuted by the notion of autonomy. There is no being except I myself that can say "thou shalt," to me. Another will can say "thou must," but that is a hypothetical imperative that always has some external sanction—if you would avoid or obtain this or that. That is heteronomy, and a will that is determined in this way never has any moral value. It is true the moral law is God's will; but God's will and the will of the rational being harmonize spontaneously, as being both expressions of the nature of reason itself. It is not binding as an arbitrarily imposed command that might even have been different.

And now I return to the point already mentioned: the moral law is the law or natural order of the intelligible world. The intelligible world is the kingdom of rational beings, of which God is the sovereign. In this world every rational being has full citizen rights and is a constituent member, furnishing from his own will the law that here obtains. In Rousseau's republic every citizen is subject and yields obedience only to laws that he assents to as a part of the legislative body. In the republic of spirits a similar autonomy prevails. There, no one is determined by means of causes external to himself, as takes place in nature where external conditioning is the rule, but there is nothing except free self-determination, which is at the same time in harmonious agreement with the reason of others.

In this way the moral law receives at Kant's hands a metaphysical and cosmical character. It is the natural order of what is actually real, of the intelligible world, while the law of causality is merely the natural order of the phenomenal world. It is for this reason that he so earnestly tries to show that the moral law is not merely the law for all men, but for all rational beings in general. It is a law of transcendent import, the most intimate law of the universe itself. In so far as man realizes this law in his life, he belongs directly to a different order of things from that of nature. During the earthly life this relation is concealed. Our faculty of ideas is limited by sensibility, and can conceive only what takes place in space and time. It cannot conceive freedom and eternity. Nevertheless, as moral beings, we are immediately certain that we are not merely natural beings belonging to the phenomenal world, but that as rational beings we belong to a truly real, a spiritual and divine universe. Is the earthly and temporal life merely one phase of our existence? If so we may suppose that when we put off the body we shall be free from the obscuring of consciousness by sensibility, and that the mind will then completely and with full consciousness recognize itself as a member of that real world, which it already knows through action and faith, though not through sight. Eternal life would be life as a purely rational being, without the trouble and limitation of the life of sense.

It is Kant's Platonism that is here evident as the fundamental form of his ontology. The *Critique of Pure Reason* and the *Critique of Practical Reason* unite for the purpose of establishing an ethical and religious view of the world on the basis of objective idealism,—a mode of thought that in its essential features is older than the critical philosophy. We found it already in the *Dreams of a Ghost-Seer* as the serious background to the humorous representation of Swedenborgianism. Criticism, looked at as a whole, appears even from the beginning as the new method of establishing a Platonic system of metaphysics.

These are the fundamental concepts of Kant's moral philosophy. They form, as we have already said, the most complete contrast to the empirical and eudæmonistic point of view. This latter appeared to Kant not merely false and superficial, but also perverse and profane. It reduces morality to self-love. Enlightened self-interest demands virtuous conduct, though in moderation, and as a means which best conduces to happiness. It makes reason subservient to the sensuous desires, and denies the possibility of a disinterested action, and thereby of any genuine morality whatever. In so far as it has any influence on action, it poisons morality at the root. Moreover, it is nothing but weak sophistry that "can exist only in the confusing speculations of schools which are bold enough to close their ears against the heavenly voice (of reason) in order to maintain a theory which does not cost much racking of the brain." The ordinary man of unsophisticated understanding, with the "wise simplicity" of Rousseau, dismisses at once these shallow arguments. He holds fast to the clear distinction between actions performed from a sense of duty and from inclination, and maintains its absolute significance for moral judgments of value.

Not only eudæmonism, the morality of enlightened self-interest, but the morality of feeling is abhorrent to Kant. He especially condemns the sentimental and rhetorical form that seeks to furnish moral stimulus by dressing up moral heroes, and by representations of actions that lie beyond the limits of duty. The morality of reason alone, with its fixed principles, affords a permanent basis for the moral will. The sentimental procedure produces merely momentary emotions that soon evaporate, and in doing so render the heart dry and dead.

It is worthy of note that also in these points the critical philosophy represents a reaction against Kant's past. The writings of the sixties show everywhere traces of the mode of thought that he now so decidedly rejects— the eudæmonistic morality of perfection,[4] and the English ethics of feeling. And also in this field the change dates from the revolution of 1769. In 1785 (in the announcement of his lectures),[5] he spoke of Shaftesbury, Hutcheson, and Hume as his predecessors whom he followed in investigations in the field of moral philosophy. But, in a remark in the *Dissertation* of 1770[6], he dismisses Shaftesbury and his followers with contempt. Pure reason alone is to be considered. As contrasted with it all empirical principles are "impure."

(2) *The Material of The Will*

Up to this point Kant's thought is on the whole simple and clear. The difficulties and vacillations begin with the problem of finding an object and end of action for the will that is only formally determined. Two ends are possible, happiness and perfection. The adoption of the one or the other of these constitutes the difference between the systems of moral philosophy to which one can apply the names Hedonism and Energism.

The former finds the ultimate end in pleasure, the latter in complete development of character and activity. Even Kant takes account of these two ends. He hesitated long, however, in deciding regarding their relation to morality proper, even after the critical point of view had been discovered. I shall deal first with happiness and its relation to morality.

The analogy of the practical with the theoretical seems to demand that the matter of the will should be furnished by sensibility. The impulses of sense all aim at satisfaction; in the last resort they may together be said to seek happiness. This accordingly would be the goal of natural volition and action. The moral law, according to the same analogy, would have to be represented as a condition of the possibility of this end, perhaps because it would harmonize the various desires and bring unity into the actions of the many persons whose actions have influence on one another's happiness. From this standpoint, happiness would be the effect, but not the motive of the will. This is determined *a priori* by reason, not *a posteriori* by the results to be expected, just as the pure concepts find their application and illustration in experience, although they do not originate in experience, but are necessary to its possibility.[7]

Another mode of establishing a necessary relation between virtue and happiness is by making the consciousness of virtue the source of happiness. This was the position of the Stoics, for whom the wise man as such is happy, whatever his external conditions of life. Internal happiness. . . is not dependent upon external fortune. . . , but is derived entirely from the individual's own will and the consciousness of his personal power and worth. Spinoza is a representative of the same standpoint.

This combination, too, is not unknown to Kant. A long and interesting sketch, published by Reicke in the *Loose Leaves*,[8] contains, among other things, the following thoughts:[9] "The material of happiness is sensible, but the form is intellectual. Now, this is not possible except as freedom under *a priori* laws of its agreement with itself, and this not to make happiness actual, but to render its idea possible. For happiness consists just in well-being in so far as this is not externally accidental, or even empirically dependent, but as based upon our volition. This must be active, and not dependent

upon the determination of nature. . . . It is true that virtue has the advantage that it carries with it the greatest happiness in the use of natural endowments. But its higher value does not consist in the fact that it serves as it were as a means. Its real value consists in the fact that it is we who creatively produce it, irrespective of its empirical conditions, which can furnish only particular rules of life, and that it brings with it self-sufficiency. . . . There is a certain stock of contentment necessary and indispensable, and without which no happiness is possible; what is over and above this is non-essential. This is self-sufficiency,—as it were, *apperceptio jucunda primitiva.*"[10]

This in essence was the Stoic solution of the relation between virtue and happiness. Kant found it nearer home in Shaftesbury and Pope. It is at bottom the view of Aristotle and Plato. Not pleasure, but virtue, is the highest good and final purpose. Or the exercise of the specifically human powers and capacities is what gives an absolute meaning and value to life. Since, however, the possession of this good is directly connected with the consciousness of one's own worth, one can say: Virtue insures at the same time happiness. But this name does not, of course, imply the satisfaction of all the desires of sense, but just the consciousness of possessing that which alone has absolute worth.

In the later expositions these positions are abandoned. In the *Fundamental Principles* the notion of happiness plays no part whatever. The concept of a kingdom of ends is introduced, but even this finds no further extension and application. The formal determination of the will by the law is here the only dominating conception. On this depends the worth of man. As a rational being, he belongs to the higher order of things. In the second half (Dialectic) of the *Critique of Practical Reason,* on the other hand, after the first part has repeated the formal determinations of the *Fundamental Principles,* pleasure appears prominently as a necessary element of practical philosophy. It is here combined with virtue (as the worthiness of happiness) into the concept of the highest good, and in this form serves as basis or moving principle of moral theology. The "postulates"—God and immortality, together with the complete adjustment of happiness and worthiness—are founded on this notion. In the end, all natural connection between virtue and happiness is rejected. Kant now emphatically denies the view of the ancient philosophers that there is any natural connection between the two. For him the connection is now "synthetic," not "analytic." Entirely reprehensible is the position of the Epicureans that makes virtue an external means to happiness. But the Stoic view is also untenable, that the consciousness of virtue is itself at once happiness. Obedience to the law, he explains here, is motived by "reverence,"—a feeling that has absolutely no kinship with the pathological feeling of pleasure. The truth is rather that man, as a sensible being, feels oppressed by the moral law which restrains his self-love and lowers his self-conceit by the demand for obedience that it makes. Obedience to the law also brings with it, indeed, a feeling of exaltation and self-respect, but neither have these the character of pleasure. "Contentment" (*Selbszufriedenheit*) really signifies only a negative pleasure in its existence.[11]

Nevertheless, happiness is an essential object of the rational will. Virtue is indeed the highest good (*bonum supremum*); but it is not therefore the complete and perfected good (*bonum consummatum*), as an object of desire for finite, rational beings. For that purpose happiness is an essential condition. And this is true not only from the partial standpoint of the man who makes himself his own end, but even in the judgment of impartial reason, which regards happiness in general as itself an end in the universe. For to desire happiness, and also to be worthy of it, and yet not to share in it, is a condition of things that cannot at all accord with the perfect volition of a rational being.[12] Since, now, the connection of the two elements is not analytic, "in accordance with the rule of identity," but synthetic, the question how the highest good is practically possible requires a transcendental solution.

The key to this transcendental solution is again naturally found in the distinction between the sensible and the intelligible world. In the sense-world, happiness is not proportionate to worthiness, and so the adjustment is postponed to the future life. The practical reason ensures the possibility of the highest good by means of the two postulates, immortality of the soul and the existence of God. Immortality, or rather life beyond the grave, makes possible an indefinitely prolonged advance towards moral perfection, consequently towards worthiness for happiness. The existence of God, as an all-powerful and holy will, and at the same time the author of nature, guarantees the second element of the highest good, happiness in proportion to worthiness. Further, since to bring the highest good into existence through free volition is a requirement that is *a priori* necessary, the possibility of doing this must be a necessary postulate of practical reason. Or, in other words, the truth of the existence of God and of the life beyond the grave is apprehended by a necessary act of rational faith. It is not the object of theoretical knowledge. For this, perception would be necessary, and this is impossible for us who are limited to sense perception in space and time. Moreover, it is not the object of a command, imposed either internally or externally; for that is impossible. But it is guaranteed by an inextinguishable conviction that is posited along with my rational nature itself. The rightly constituted person can say: "I will God's existence, and that my existence in this world shall include, over and above the life of nature, membership in an intelligible world. Finally, I will my own immortality. I hold fast to these beliefs, and do not allow them to be taken from me.

This is the single case where it is inevitable that my interest should determine my judgment, since I am not permitted to renounce any of its demands."

Moral theology is thus based on the lack of natural connection between virtue and happiness. The desire of the human will, which is unable to unite in this world the two indispensable elements, morality and happiness, by means of necessary concepts, becomes an imperative demand to pass to the region of the intelligible for what is necessary to complete our theory. Without God and immortality, without a transcendental world-order, the realization of the highest good, which is enjoined by the moral law, would not be possible.

In the form in which these thoughts are presented in the ***Critique of Practical Reason,*** there are many sides open to criticism. It reminds one somewhat too much of the police argument for God's existence: if one does not receive reward or punishment here, he will find it laid up for him in the next world. And Schopenhauer's gibe is not entirely unjustified, that Kant's virtue, which at first bore itself so bravely towards happiness, afterwards holds out its hand to receive a tip. Even formally the combination of the two factors is open to criticism. Happiness for Kant is the satisfaction of the inclinations of sense. Now, are there still inclinations of this kind in the other world? We are supposed to be in an intelligible world where sensibility is entirely lacking. And how does the matter stand with regard to the infinite progress towards moral perfection? In the other world is there still time in which change and progress can take place? And how is moral progress itself possible for a being without sensibility? The *noumenon* is "a purely rational being," "an intelligible character." In what, then, can its progress consist? It appears as if Kant would have to postulate indefinite continuance in time in the form of sensible existence in order to render progress and compensation possible. It would be necessary for him to adopt something like the East Indian notion of rebirth and transmigrations of souls.

Nevertheless, if one disregards the somewhat wooden form of exposition, and holds fast what is essential in Kant's thought, one will estimate the doctrine differently. We may say that Kant here really touches upon a strong, if not the strongest, motive of religious faith. The unsatisfactory nature of the present world, the conflict of the natural order of events with the irrelinquishable demands of the spirit, is the strongest motive to transcend the visible order and to seek an invisible one. The fact that in the natural course of events, as observation shows, the good and great are often oppressed and perish, while the vulgar and the wicked triumph, is the goad that drives us to deny the absolute reality of nature. It is and remains the final and indestructible axiom of the will that reality cannot be absolutely indifferent to good and evil. If, then, nature is indifferent, it cannot be the true reality. Then only behind or above nature, as mere phenomenon, can the true world be discovered, and in it the good is absolutely real; *i.e.,* in God who is the absolutely real and the absolutely good. It was Plato who first united the notions of the absolutely real and the absolutely good in the concept of God. And since that time philosophy has never abandoned this thought, and it is this that constitutes the essential element in Kant's thought. This point of view would have been attainable without using happiness as the vehicle of the postulate. Kant really does happiness too much honor in making it, or the lack of correspondence between it and virtue in the empirical world, the copingstone of his entire system. If he had set out from the notion of a kingdom of ends, his road would have been shorter and smoother. He who wills the kingdom of ends believes in the possibility of its realization. He who lives for the kingdom of God, and is ready to die for it, believes in God.

At this point we return to the second definition of the object of volition—perfection as the end of the will. If Kant had given, as he intended, an exposition of his system about the middle of the eighties, this notion might perhaps have played an important rôle. As it is, it occupies an unimportant place in the *Metaphysical Principles of the Doctrine of Virtue,* as an end of the will that is necessary in addition to happiness. As the two ends which duty prescribes, although they must not be motives of will, Kant here names our own perfection, and the happiness of others. Under the head of our own perfection, the cultivation of all our powers and talents, bodily, mental, and moral, is enjoined. To promote these with all our strength is a duty. On the other hand, it is never one's duty to promote one's own happiness, "since every one inevitably does that spontaneously." Nevertheless, it may even become a duty to promote one's own happiness as a means, although not as an end, since disappointment, pains, and want furnish great temptations to transgression of duty. On the other hand, it is not a duty to promote the perfection of others—that is their own business—but to work for their happiness. In doing this, one performs a grateful service if one simply makes concessions to their inclinations, but undertakes a thankless task if one regards their real advantage, although they themselves do not recognize it as such.

Here, just as little as in the *Critique of Practical Reason,* is any attempt made to unite in an organic way the "necessary purposes" and the formal law. In the former work, happiness, both for ourselves and others, is without any mediation declared to be a necessary object of desire for the practical reason. Here Kant takes the same position with regard to perfection. If Kant had not been so hardened in formal rationalism, if he had not so blindly maintained in the sphere of the

will the absolute separation of form and matter that in the *Critique of Pure Reason* determined the form of his critical philosophy, if he had been able for a moment to lay aside the axiom that the good will is that which is determined solely by the form of the law, and that all determination of the will by the matter of volition proceeds from sensibility and renders it "impure," he would necessarily have arrived at a different system of ideas from the concept of perfection as the end of the will. He would have seen that man as a rational being aims at the establishment and enlargement of a kingdom of reason, of a kingdom of humanity, of a kingdom of God upon the earth. The moral law is the natural law of this kingdom in the sense that its enlargement depends upon obedience to the law. Transgression against the law, on the other hand, has, as a natural effect, disorder and destruction.

This line of thought is not entirely foreign to Kant. He employed it in the concept of "end in itself," which he ascribed to rational beings as a distinguishing characteristic, in the related notion of a "kingdom of ends" or a "kingdom of God" in contrast with the kingdom of nature, as he speaks of it in the *Critique of Pure Reason* in Leibniz's phrase. The notion is also the foundation of his philosophy of history (in the *Idea of a Universal History*). It recurs in the *Fundamental Principles* in the following passage: "The kingdom of ends would actually come into existence by means of maxims whose rule the categorical imperative prescribes to all rational beings if these maxims were universally followed."[13] But it is not employed seriously. The horror of rendering the determination of the will "impure" by any matter of volition prevented Kant from following up this thought. In the *Critique of Practical Reason* it no longer played any part. Here nothing but formalism prevails. This work begins at once with the propositions:[14] "All practical principles which presuppose an object (matter) of the faculty of desire as the ground of determination of the will are empirical and can furnish no practical laws." "All material practical principles are as such of one and the same kind, and come under the general principle of self-love or personal happiness." With these "propositions" the notion of purpose is *a priori* debarred from entrance into the practical philosophy, at least from any influence on its main problem. At a later point, in the Dialectic, we have not the concept of "perfection" or of a "kingdom of rational beings," but that of happiness suddenly reappearing from some unknown quarter, and presenting itself, after having been previously rejected as derived from sensibility, as an *a priori* necessary element of the complete good, and one that reason has to recognize in addition to virtue.

One must say that anything so internally inconsistent as the *Critique of Practical Reason,* with its two parts, the Analytic and the Dialectic, with the form and the matter of the will, the law and happiness, is perhaps not to be met with again in the history of philosophical thought. Kant, however, is so certain of his *a priori* procedure that he unhesitatingly rejects, as forming a single *massa perditionis,* all previous forms of moral philosophy, Epicurus and the Stoics, Shaftesbury, Wolff, and Crusius, since they all have started with material grounds of determination. The critical metaphysic of morals is the first and only true system of moral philosophy.

If Kant had taken the concept of a kingdom of ends as his starting-point, and if, instead of forming his ethics after the pattern of his epistemology, he had elaborated it as a practical discipline, establishing or maintaining its natural connection with anthropology and philosophy of history, his thought might have attained something like the following form, which seems to me more felicitous.

The vocation of man, the purpose that God or nature has prescribed to him, and whose accomplishment is the business of the historical life, is the development from animality to humanity through the employment of his own reason. Education, civilization, and moralization, are the three parts of the process of humanizing. The final goal of the process of development is to form a united and harmonious kingdom of rational beings in which the moral law, as a natural law, shall determine volition and action, or in religious language to build up the kingdom of God upon the earth.

Man stands in a twofold relation in regard to this vocation. The sensuous impulses that he shares with the animals (the lower desiderative faculty) resist it, because in the process they suffer loss. The sense impulses are restrained by the advance of culture. On this point Kant shares Rousseau's conviction. But man has also a "higher desiderative faculty," practical reason, and this has as its end nothing else than the enforcement of its own demands. From this view-point the explanation of the essential concepts of moral philosophy would be as follows:

Morality is the constant resolution of the will of a being who is at once sensuous and rational to follow reason as opposed to the impulses of sense. It gives to action the form of universal conformity to law, instead of the accidental and arbitrary character that belongs to sensible impulses. Moral laws are universal laws of conduct, that, in so far as they determine the will, direct its activity towards the ultimate end. Duty in the objective sense is the obligation to determine action by reference to the moral law. Freedom is the corresponding capacity to determine conduct in independence of the incitations of sense, and in accordance with the moral law. The moral worth of the individual depends upon his disposition. Conscientious performance of duty carries with it moral worth and dignity, irrespective of the amount and extent of what is accomplished. For

the latter is not dependent on the will alone, but also upon fortune.

Happiness is used in a double sense, and corresponding to this its relation to sensibility is different. In so far as the word denotes the satisfaction of the sense impulses, virtue is not a means of promoting one's own happiness. But in so far as the realization of the higher desiderative faculty (the practical reason) is accompanied by the feeling of satisfaction, one may even say, if one likes to name this feeling happiness, that virtue is the only means of attaining the true happiness, which, in the case of a rational being, depends before everything else upon self-respect, and is inseparable from morality and the maintenance of the dignity proper to man.—Complete humanizing and moralizing, together with the happiness that is their result, constitute the highest good. This is a mere idea to which there can be no corresponding object in the sense-world. The significance of the idea consists in the fact that it sets a goal for empirical reality as manifested in the historical life, to which the human race is required to approximate through constant stages of progress.

Belief in God is the moral certainty that the highest good is the ground and goal of all things. Perfect divine service is a life spent for the honor of God, and in the service of the highest good.

In this way we might have all of Kant's essential thoughts without the formalism.

III. Criticism of the Moral Philosophy

In what has been said we have already indicated the standpoint from which Kant's moral philosophy is to be criticised. According to my opinion, it is just that which Kant regarded as his special service that constitutes his fundamental error. This is the expulsion of teleological considerations from ethics. I shall attempt to show this in describing the place of teleology in the historical development of philosophy. In undertaking this, I emphasize the fact that the criticism has reference only to Kant's moral *theory,* not to his moral *views.* These are better than his theory, and I shall return to them in the next section.

All philosophical reflection upon the nature of morality sets out from two points: (1) from the fact of moral judgment, (2) from the fact that the will is directed towards some end. From the first point of view, one reaches the problem regarding the final standard in passing judgments of value upon human actions. From the second standpoint, the question regarding the ultimate end or the highest good presents itself. In this way, arise the two types of moral philosophy,—the ethics of duty, and the ethics of the good. The original form of the ethics of duty is to be found in religious theories of morals: the law of God is the final standard of judgment and of value. Theological ethics, Christian and Jewish alike, declare that an action is morally good when it agrees with the command of God, and that a man is morally good when he makes the Divine command the law of his own will.

Philosophical ethics is inclined to the form of the ethics of the good. Greek ethics is entirely dominated by the question regarding the final end of all volition and action. Two tendencies manifest themselves at this point: that toward hedonism, and that toward energism. The former places the highest good in a state of feeling, pleasure; the latter, in an objective condition of character and realization of purposes: the complete development of all the human powers and capacities, and their complete realization is the highest good. Aristippus and Epicurus belong to the first side, Plato, Aristotle, and the Stoics to the second. The two tendencies approach each other in so far as the first asserts that a happy life can be attained only by virtue and ability, and the other concedes that virtue and ability has happiness as its necessary though not intentional result.

Modern ethics begins in the seventeenth century with the abandonment of the theological form of the ethics of duty prevailing in the school philosophy. An immanent basis for ethics was sought, instead of the transcendent foundation in the will of God as expressed in the ten commandments. This is gained in the same way as in Greek ethics. For the distinctions of value in what is good and what is evil are based on the recognition of a highest good, and on the relation of will and conduct to it. This highest good was defined as self-preservation, realization of the complete character, human perfection, complete development of humanity (in the systems of Hobbes, Spinoza, Leibniz and Wolff, and Shaftesbury). Then a volition or action whose natural result is in harmony with this end is declared to be good. At the same time, egoistic hedonism, which makes the individual's own advantage the absolute ground for the determination of the will, made its appearance. The distinction between good and evil is then reduced to the difference between greater or less certainty and cleverness in attaining this end. On the other hand, the theological form of moral philosophy also perpetuated itself. Kant takes Crusius as its representative.

The fundamental distinction between the chief types is that the theological ethics of duty is formal, the philosophical ethics of the good, teleological. The latter derives the distinctions of value in human conduct and relations in a last resort from the effects in relation to an ultimate end. The former has regard merely to the formal agreement of the will with the law, or to the formal character of the will's determination by means of the law: the moral good is absolutely good, not good for something.

Now, Kant's position was determined in this way. Originally he occupied the standpoint of the Wolffian morality of perfection. To this was added in the sixties, by way of a basis and complement, the English morality of feeling with its anthropological tendencies. The critical philosophy brought a complete reversal: Kant went over to the side of formal moral philosophy; only, the pure reason takes the place of God as the autonomous source of the law. Henceforth he rejects the teleological conception, not merely as false, but as dangerous for morality itself. A will is good solely on account of its formal determination by the law, not on account of what it wills or what is effected through it.

I am unable to convince myself either of the dangerous character of teleological ethics, or of the tenability of this purely formalistic theory of morals. The latter sees only what stands nearest, and leaves entirely unsolved the problem of a general theory of life and of conduct.[15]

If one attempts, as is reasonable, to find a reconciliation, one may take as a basis the distinction between two kinds of judgments regarding the value of human volition and conduct, the subjective-formal and the objective-material. The first refers entirely to the disposition, to the relation of the will to the moral judgment of the person acting. And since we name an action good in so far as it results from a consciousness of its moral necessity, the content may be what it will. The Arab, as an avenger of blood, the fanatic who persecutes the enemies of his God, acting, not from personal hatred, but perhaps overcoming personal inclination or universal sympathy for his kind, and following the "categorical imperative" in his breast, acts morally. And his moral maxim would perhaps stand the test that Kant demands—act in such a way that thou canst will that thy maxim should become a universal law of conduct. "Certainly I will this," he might say, and even Kant could not prove the logical impossibility of this maxim prevailing as a law of nature.

But, we should now add, this is not the end of the matter. A second and quite independent question is whether avenging blood, and persecuting those of a different faith, are good when considered objectively. Our moral sense condemns both. Why? Evidently because they are in contradiction with our idea of a peaceful and equitable common life, with our conception of the value of freedom in our intellectual life, and of the worthlessness of forced convictions, and with our experience regarding the injurious influence of repression and protection in the spiritual life. Or, in a word, because the objective results of such ways of acting do not tend to promote, but to disturb and destroy the highest good, quite irrespective of what are the subjective motives of the person acting, whether he kills or persecutes from inclination or from a sense of duty.

And now we would go on to assert that the real problem of moral philosophy does not consist in discovering the subjective moral value of the actions of the individual. It has done all that it can do in this connection when it has established the principle that one acts morally, from a subjective point of view, when one acts from a feeling of duty, out of reverence for the absolute command. But the problem is rather to determine the objective value of actions and relations, or to explain the different moral evaluation placed upon them (varying among different peoples and at different times). Ethics will seek to determine why lying, stealing, killing, adultery, etc., are condemned, and truth, honesty, friendliness, and faithfulness in the marriage relation are good. In this investigation, it will find that actions of the sort first mentioned tend to disturb and to destroy man's social life, and thereby to undermine the foundations upon which all healthy human life must rest. Lying is not evil because it cannot be posited as universal without destroying itself, but because, so far as in it lies, it destroys an essential good, namely, the confidence that is the fundamental condition of all social life among men. And in like manner, thieving, and adultery, and impurity, are reprehensible because they destroy goods, like property, the material basis of all human culture, and the family life, the medium in which the spiritual life of man is maintained and handed down. In general, vices are objectively bad because they are destructive forces; virtues are objectively valuable because they act as forces to preserve and promote the kingdom of reason and of humanity. The capacity for logical universalization, however, is a useful means of discovering the result of any kind of action. It is difficult to say how a single action may result in any particular case. But it becomes clear what its nature is, what general tendency it possesses, as soon as one asks what the result would be if every man always acted in this way.

Finally, teleological ethics is able to derive from its own principle what is valuable in the purely subjective morality. It shows that the habit of determining one's actions from a sense of duty, which we call conscientiousness, has the tendency to preserve the content of human life. What actually determines the will in this case is uniformly the objective morality of the community and the time. Custom and law, however, usually tend to preserve this community life: a people whose custom and law tended towards disintegration would be incapable of living, and would perish. In so far, then, as conscience has objective morality as its content, it has the tendency to determine the conduct of the individual in the direction of the preservation of the community, and also to influence his actions as a member of the community.

Thus the teleological moral philosophy attains a unitary view of the moral world. It is able to derive both the form and the matter of the will, to speak in Kant's phrase, from a single principle. The will that is directed towards the highest good, wills at the same time its own determination by the moral law, as the norm upon whose maintenance the possibility of its realization depends. In this it may, of course, happen that this or that particular impulse sometimes determines the volition in a direction opposite to the norm. We have in this all the valuable elements of the Kantian ethics. We have the autonomy of the will in a twofold sense. As independent of external authority, the moral rational will wills the highest good, and in doing so gives itself the law. And, as independent of sensibility, the rational will, not the lawless impulses of sense, furnishes the motives of life. In like manner, we have freedom from hedonism and egoism. The rational will does not will pleasure as the absolute good, but an objective state of things. And the object of its will is not merely itself, or its own existence and advantage, but the preservation and development of the spiritual and moral life of the community, and of itself as a member of the community. And so we say with Kant that the worth and significance of a life depends entirely upon the good that man does, not upon the good or evil that he suffers.

On all these points, the Kantian morality is significant of an exceedingly healthy reaction against sensualistic and egoistic eudæmonism, which was then to some extent in vogue, especially in the polite world. Think, for example, of La Mettrie and Helvétius. It is the reaction of the sound morality of the people against the sophistical view of the court and the gentry. On the other hand, as a philosophical theory of morality, it is just as untenable as the old theological view. Above all, it is unable to discover the unity of form and matter of the formal and real motives of the will. As in the old theological moral philosophy, so also in Kant, the content of what is morally good is in the last resort given by command of God, and the end of the will, eternal blessedness, is only accidentally connected with morality by means of the will of God. Moreover, he brings in, as matter of the will, happiness or even perfection in addition; but he cannot find the natural connection of these with the moral law and so takes refuge in a supernatural connection. He had really before him all the elements for a teleological interpretation,—the concept of a kingdom of ends, the unity of rational beings, perfection and happiness as necessary objects of volition, the moral law as the natural law in the domain of freedom,—but as if by some fatality they were held apart. More than once, it seems as if he must reach a proper synthesis, especially in the second section of the ***Fundamental Principles,*** as, *e. g.,* in the remark:[16] "Teleology considers nature as a kingdom of ends, morality views a possible kingdom of ends as a kingdom of nature." But he does not draw the conclusion that the moral law is the natural law of the kingdom of ends, in the sense that on its realization depends the maintenance and actualization of that kingdom. He had the analogy that the laws of the state are the natural laws of civic society, in the sense that the preservation of the state as a social unit depends on the maintenance of the legal order. Nevertheless, he does not discover the formula of solution. He is so intent on the pure law of reason and its logical universality, so much in love with the purity of the pure will that is determined solely by means of the law, that he turned away in horror from the derivation of its validity from the matter of volition as from a sacrilegious defilement of morality.

Instead of this, he toiled over the absolutely vain attempt to squeeze a "matter" of volition out of the "pure" law of the logical universality of the motive of the will—*ex aqua pumicem,* one might say, inverting his quotation. Lying and suicide are morally impossible actions, for when made universal, they destroy their own possibility. Suicide would destroy life, and in this negate itself, and so with lying. These things, therefore, can occur only as irregular exceptions, and are thus contrary to reason and its logic. If in the case of these negative commands there is still a certain significance in this rule of universality—the same which belongs to the universal validity of legal commands— the positive duties resist most decidedly every attempt at an investigation of this kind. Consider the attempts to derive the duty of cultivating our own talents, and the duty of charity: "As a rational being man necessarily wills that all his powers should be developed because they are useful and given to him for all kinds of possible purposes." And: Even if absolute egoism could exist as a natural law, yet no one could will it, "since many cases might occur when he would require the love and sympathy of others." It is evident that Kant here drops his formula and falls back on the matter of volition, even appealing to egoistic motives. Thus the facts of the case emphatically reject his theory. Nevertheless he does not abandon it, but clings to it on principle: all derivation of duties from ends is empirical, false, and ruinous.

The cause of all this difficulty lies in the mysterious prominence that epistemology had won in his thought. It hindered the free, spontaneous development of Kant's ethics, as it did also of his metaphysics. It determined both the problems and the form of their solution. Above all it is responsible for the unfortunate theory that makes the human will a union of practical reason which merely sets up a law, and sensible impulses that merely clamor for egoistic satisfaction. Thus arises the empty concept of a pure will as the complement to "pure" perception and thought. And the mysterious over-estimation of "pure" thinking then led to the clearly untenable assumption that the "pure" will is the good will. And from this there resulted, as a further consequence, the denial of any moral difference whatsoever between the material grounds that determine the will. In principle, it is quite indifferent for the moral value of the action

whether the satisfaction of sense desires, the love of fame, the good of a people, the salvation of a people from the bonds of injustice and falsehood, is the end that determines the will, in so far as they are all material principles of determination. At least, between the moral theories that adopt material principles, between egoistic hedonism and the Aristotelian and Stoic ethics of perfection, there is said to be no difference. According to Kant, they all reduce in the last resort to Epicureanism. Epicurus alone had the courage of his convictions. One may well say that the consequences of a false principle cannot be carried further.

And with this unfortunate theory of the will is connected the tendency of Kant's moral philosophy that from the first does violence to feeling. It is commonly called rigorism, but I should rather name it negativism. To act morally is to do what one does not want to do. Of course, according to Kant the natural and sensuous will always aims at the satisfaction of its desires. Duty, however, commands unconditionally that we shall allow nothing but the law to determine our will. Even the virtuous man might really always prefer to follow his sensuous inclinations to luxury, ease, etc. But the "idea of the law," with its "thou shalt not" or "thou shalt" interposes. And so, practising the hard virtue of repression, he does what he does not want to do. Greek moral philosophy, on the other hand, with its sound theory of the will, regards virtue as a joyous, positive mode of action, as the attraction of the will by a noble and beautiful purpose. In "perfection of character" and "completion of will," the human being attains that which his deepest nature seeks. To be sure, Kant at bottom holds to this also; he defends himself against Schiller's reproach, he struggles with his own negativism, but vainly. For he held fast to the principle that a will is only good when it is determined solely by the "idea of the law," and that all material determinations are reducible to happiness. And, as a consequence, duty remains that which one does not want to do, and virtue abstinence from that which one really desires.

I refrain from showing how this fanaticism for "purity," or fixed formalism, is connected with the inability of Kant's moral philosophy to account for important facts of the moral life as they exist, as, *e. g.,* the conflict of duties, a doubtful or erring conscience, the moral necessity of a white lie, etc. Kant made shift as one usually does in such cases: he denied the possibility of that which could not be derived from his theory, or did not agree with it, and in this way he was led to deny the reality of the most evident facts.

However, let this suffice for criticism. We propose now to consider Kant's philosophy from another and a more pleasing side.

IV. Kant's Moral Perceptions as based in his personality

The moral perceptions of a man are not the result of his moral theory, but arise from his personal character. The theory is an attempt at their explanation, and is also partially determined by other influence of all sorts. Thus, in Kant's case, his moral perceptions have their root in his personality, while their exposition in his moral philosophy is very greatly influenced and perverted by his epistemology. I shall attempt to give an account of these perceptions themselves. It is to them that the Kantian morality owes the influence which it has exercised, and still continues to exert.

Into Kant's moral personality, or personal character, two moments, as we have already intimated, entered as determining factors.[17] He had a strong will, but not a vigorous or even an amiable nature. He had formed his character through his will, and was a self-made man in the moral sense. And it was his pride that his moral quality was not a natural endowment, but the work of his own will. From the Essay, ***On the Power of the Spirit to Control its Morbid Feelings by mere Resolution,*** which he added as the third essay to that collection of essays called ***The Controversy of the Faculties,*** we learn how he brought his weak body into subjection by means of discipline that was continued even until his old age. The universal principle of his Dietetics reads: "Dietetics must not tend towards luxurious ease, for indulgence of one's powers and feelings is coddling, and results in weakness." His inner life was regulated according to similar principles. In the same passage he reports how by discipline of his ideas and feelings he had gained the mastery over the tendency to hypochondria, and had attained peace and cheerfulness, though in earlier life it had rendered his life almost unbearable. This self-control "also enabled him to express himself deliberately and naturally in society, and not according to the mood of the moment." Thus from a character naturally weak and retiring he developed the bold self-sufficiency that lies in the blood of bolder and more self-assertive natures. In like manner, the active sympathy that he showed for those about him appears to have been grounded in the moral consciousness of duty rather than to spring from a warm heart. It seems not improbable that he was thinking of himself when speaking of a man "in whose heart nature has placed little sympathy, who is naturally cold and indifferent to the sufferings of others; perhaps, being endowed with great patience and endurance, he makes little of his own pains, and presupposes or even demands that every other person should do the same." When such a person does good to others merely from a sense of duty, and without any promptings of inclination, his act has a much higher value than if it were the result of a "kind-hearted disposition."[18] At least, one gets the impression from his biography that he did not possess a heart that was naturally very sensitive to what happened to others. Thus his interest in his sisters and their families, for whom he did much, had not the directness and heartiness of a lovable nature. One might almost say that there was an excess of rationality about it. He puts a low estimate on enjoyment—it is only activity that is valuable and gives worth to man—and likewise condemns the soft, tender, "moving" feelings. Only the "vigorous" emotions (*animus strenuus*) find favor in his eyes. Stoic apathy, independence of things and mastery over them is his personal ideal. It is obvious how strong an influence this exercised upon his moral theory.

A second point where his ethics was in close touch with his personality is found in his democratic feeling for the people, which always made him sympathize with the common man against the social pretensions of the aristocracy. This feeling is not unconnected with his own descent. Rosseau, his favorite author, even at that time a famous writer, and much affected in the polite world, knew how to understand and sympathize with the artisans, peasants, and shepherds, with whom he had shared bed and board in his youth. And in the same way Kant always remained faithful in his moral feelings to the circle of humble people from whom he had sprung. He is not at all inclined to grant that the advantage which the rich and polite claim to have in culture and manners is a real advantage. Their advantage consists more in what they enjoy than in what they do. He does not even recognize any merit in their charities. "The ability to give to charity," he says, not without a certain harshness, "is usually the result of the advantage given to various men by the injustice of the government. This brings about an inequality of fortune that renders charity to others necessary. Under these circumstances does the help that the rich may vouchsafe to those suffering from want deserve the name of charity, which one is so ready to apply to it in priding one's self on it as a virtue?"[19]

Not to the rich and the noble do we owe thanks, but to the laboring and productive masses. He called them once "the people most worthy of respect,"[20] who have borne the pains and cost of our culture, without enjoying the fruit that usually belong to endurance and self-denial, in order that the few might have freedom and abundance.

These sentiments show that Kant belongs to the great movement which took place about the middle of the century, in which sympathy for the life of the people burst through the aristocratic ideas of rank that had hitherto prevailed in society. He thus belongs to the group of great writers who not merely created a new literary epoch, but founded a new epoch in the life of the German people. It is the period when the people, the long unnoticed masses, and their spiritual life were again discovered. Möser, Hamann, Herder, Goethe, and Pestalozzi had a share in bringing it about. Goethe, for example, in a letter to Frau von Stein (Dec. 4, 1777) says: "How much that dark journey (to the Harz in winter) taught me in the way of love for those who are called the lower classes, but who certainly are the highest in God's estimation. There we find all the virtues united: limitation, contentment, straightforwardness, fidelity, joy in the most moderate fortune, innocence, patience, patience—endurance in the face of privation."

One can say at once that Kant's morality is that of humble folk, the morality that he had learned in his parents' home. Conscientious and faithful performance of moral demands without thought of reward, with hard work and often severe self-denial, was the mode of life and of thought in which he grew up. With this corresponded a mood, not gloomy but somewhat austere, that was only slightly modified by the consciousness that they were living as God had willed it, and by the hope of a better life beyond the grave, in which the powers and natural talents that here lie under the pressure of necessity, will have opened up to them a freer field for their activity. That is essentially the mode of life and the attitude towards it that Kant has before him as a moral philosopher. His morality is not that of the ruling classes, or not that of the artist or poet, but the plain morality of the common man. The morality of the ruling classes (*Herrenmoral*), of which one hears so much talk nowadays in Germany, is individualistic and egoistic. Its philosophy is to live the life of the impulses, giving them free vent without any thought of a law, and without reference to others, or even at the cost of others, of the herd of humanity who are produced wholesale by nature for the service and enjoyment of the ruling class. The "artistic" morality is equally individualistic and egoistic. It also claims for itself a special standard, a morality of its own, which leaves room for the free development of the natural talents, and the elevation of the imagination above the common things of every-day reality. As opposed to a morality of this kind that claims to be for distinguished persons, the morality that flourished at the court at Versailles and perhaps also at Potsdam, and again at every seat of a petty *grand-seigneur* in Prussia, where sophists and court philosophers retailed "enlightenment" in the form of egoistic eudæmonism,—in opposition to morality with exemptions for the privileged classes, Kant sets up his account of morality, the simple morality of the common people. It has no exemptions for the gods or demigods of this earth, but its laws possess strict universality. It did not address itself to "volunteers" of morality, but preached simple obedience; it knew nothing of meritorious conduct, but only of obligation. In opposition to the tendency of the upper classes to estimate the worth of life from its accidental filling, to make the social judgment of a man's importance the final standard of evaluation, he took as the foundation of his morality the principle: "It is not possible to think of anything anywhere in the world, or even outside it, that can be regarded as good without any limitation except only a good will." The will, however, is not good through what it achieves, but

good in and for itself, because it is determined only through the feeling of duty, and not through inclination. Whether you rule states and win battles, whether you render humanity richer by miracles of art or science, whether with weary feet you tread the furrows as a ploughboy, or on the remotest outskirts of the city you make harness or patch shoes,—none of these things have any significance at all for your moral worth. For this standard it matters not what external fortune or natural gifts you may possess, but all depends upon the disposition and faithfulness with which you perform your duty. If you do not follow your own inclinations and moods, but obey the moral law within, you will rise to a plane of grandeur and dignity that will always remain far from those who follow after happiness, or guide their actions merely according to maxims of prudence. You belong then, whatever your place in this earthly existence, to the kingdom of freedom; you are a citizen of the intelligible world, citizen of the kingdom of God.

Kant here stands in close connection with the Christian view of life and attitude toward it. I do not mean with the worldly, courtier Christianity of fashionable people, of the cavalier type, who rejoice in duels, but with the original spirit of true Christianity. Its depreciation of the world and its pomps and glories, its indifference to all external distinctions of culture and education, the absolute value that it places upon the good will, the fidelity with which one serves God and his neighbor, its insistence on the equality of all men before God,—these are all characteristic of Kant's view of life. He stood quite outside Christianity in its ecclesiastical form, where under the protection of the state it forces on people its doctrines and creeds; but to the Christianity of the heart and the will, as it was and still is practised among the common people, his relation was close and intimate. Indeed, one may say that his morality is nothing but the translation of this Christianity from the religious language to the language of reflection: in place of God we have pure reason, instead of the ten commandments the moral law, and in place of heaven the intelligible world.

It is only when we take this standpoint, then, that we gain a real understanding of Kant's moral philosophy. But it seems to me that here lies also the secret of the influence that it has exerted. This has not been due to the form of conceptual construction that it employs, but to the perceptions upon which this construction is based. These moral views corresponded to the temper of the period, which in Germany enthusiastically honored Rousseau as the true pioneer and guide. The thoughts through which Kant expresses the strongest sentiments of his time are contained in propositions like these: "Every man is to be respected as an absolute end in himself, and it is a crime against the dignity that belongs to him as a human being to use him as a mere means for some external purpose" (think, *e.g.,* of bond-service and traffic in soldiers), and: "In the moral world the worth and dignity of each man has nothing at all to do with his position in society." The truth of these ideas is limited to no particular period, and they possess a very real significance for our time that has perhaps grown somewhat insensible to their force.

Even the first point, the emphasis on the power of the will as opposed to natural disposition, has its permanent value. It is the fashion to say that Kant aroused the generation of the illumination who were sunken in weak and selfish sentimentalism. His doctrine of the categorical imperative is supposed to have tempered the race of freedom's warriors. I do not know whether or not the voice of a philosopher is able to accomplish so much. In that great conflict there were perhaps stronger influences at work than the feeling of duty. I do not know either whether the age of the illumination deserves all the hard names that have been provided for it by a later time. We can at any rate say that on the whole it was a time of unusually hearty and vigorous effort in the cause of truth and right, for freedom and education and all that makes for the progress of humanity, and also especially for the elevation of the backward and oppressed classes. The present age has scarcely cause to pride itself as contrasted with that generation. But there is no doubt that the appeal to the will to assert itself in the face of natural impulses has its justification and its necessity in every age. The fundamental form of all moral teaching is as follows: You do not really will when you are moved by the impulses of sense; your real self, your true will, is directed toward a higher goal. And your proper moral dignity rests upon the fact that you are ruler of nature, not merely of what is external to yourself, but of what is in you, and that you fashion your life according to your own volition. An animal is a natural product, and just for this reason it has no real moral value, however beautiful and admirable it may be. This highest and absolute value you can bestow on yourself, even if you have received little from nature or from society. You cannot attain happiness by the unaided efforts of your will; that depends also on the natural course of events. But something that is higher than happiness, you and you alone can gain for yourself, *i.e.,* personal dignity, which includes worthiness to be happy. It is indeed possible that you may be unfortunate, but you can never be miserable: the consciousness of personal worth will provide you with strength to bear the hardships of fate.

In conclusion, I may add a word regarding the coping-stone of the Kantian philosophy, the doctrine of the primacy of the practical reason. This also is closely connected with Kant's personal feelings. It is a protest against attaching too much importance to science, and estimating too highly its importance for life, as had been the fashion since the days of the revival of learning. For three hundred years the maxim of the Renaissance that education is the presupposition of morality,

had been accepted. Then Rousseau entered his emphatic protest. This came closely home to Kant; he felt the truth to which the prevailing opinion had hitherto rendered him blind. And his entire system of philosophy became for him a means for the confirmation of this truth. The critical philosophy degrades scientific knowledge to a technical means of orientation in the world of phenomena. It follows, of course, that the possession of such a technique, however valuable it may be as a means for all purposes of culture, cannot decide regarding the personal worth of a man. So long as one believed that through science and philosophy it was possible to obtain absolute insight into the nature of things, and the being of God, these things appeared to have some part in constituting the dignity of man. Now Kant declares that knowledge of this kind is absolutely impossible, and in its place he set *practical faith,* which rests solely on the good will, not on knowledge and demonstration. And this faith is the only way of approach to the supersensible world, which through it stands open to all alike, to all, that is, of good will. Learning of the schools, theology, and metaphysics are of no advantage here.

This point also was doubtless of essential importance in helping the Kantian philosophy to find an entrance. Belief in metaphysics and dogmas was in process of vanishing, and natural theology was losing its credit. To many it seemed that science had perhaps spoken its last word in the *Système de la nature.* Then Kant brought faith back to a place of honor. Science can afford us no final philosophy. Its certainty always rests upon the faith that has its deepest roots in the will.

It is my deepest conviction that in this doctrine Kant teaches us definitive truth.

Notes

[1] *Cf.* especially the first preface to the *Critique of Judgment* (VII., pp. 377 ff.).

[2] *Cf.* the letter to Schütz, of Sept. 13, 1785.

[3] IV., p. 239.

[4] *Cf.* II., p. 307.

[5] II., p. 319.

[6] § 9.

[7] Pölitz, *Kants Vorlesungen über Metaphysik,* p. 321: "Worthiness for happiness consists in the practical agreement of our actions with the idea of universal happiness. When we act in such a way that there would result, if every one acted in the same way, the greatest amount of happiness, then our conduct has rendered us worthy of happiness.—Good conduct is the condition of universal happiness."

[8] I., pp. 9 ff.

[9] Förster and Höffding (*Archiv f. Gesch. der Philos.,* VII., p. 461, Vaihinger's *Kantstudien,* II., pp. 11 ff.) place this sketch, perhaps rightly, in the seventies. Reicke, from external evidence, is inclined to fix the date in the eighties. Even this does not appear to me impossible. It is only certain that it is to be placed before the *Grundlegung.*

[10] I add a few more sentences: "Happiness is not really the greatest sum of enjoyment, but pleasure arising from the consciousness of one's own ability to be contented,—at least this is the essential and formal condition of happiness, though still other material conditions are necessary."—"Morality (as freedom under universal laws) renders happiness as such possible. Though it does not depend upon it as its purpose, it is the original form of happiness, which, when one possesses, one can dispense entirely with pleasures, and bear many evils of life without any loss of contentment,—indeed even with a heightening of it."—"Morality is the idea of freedom as a principle of happiness (a regulative principle of happiness *a priori*). Accordingly, the laws of freedom must contain *a priori* the formal conditions of our own happiness without any direct reference to it."—"Freedom is in itself a power independent of empirical grounds for acting or refraining to act.—I am free, but only from the compelling forces of sense, not also from the limiting laws of reason.—That 'freedom of indifference' by means of which I can will what is contrary to my will, and which allows me no certain ground for counting on myself, would necessarily be in the highest degree unsatisfactory to me. It is essential, then, to recognize as *a priori* necessary a law according to which freedom may be limited to conditions that render the will self-consistent. To this law I can bring no objection, for it alone can establish, according to principles, the practical unity of the will."

[11] V., p. 123.

[12] V., p. 116.

[13] IV., p. 286.

[14] § § 2, 3.

[15] A detailed account of the controversy between teleological and formalistic moral philosophy is given in my *System der Ethik* (4th ed. 1896), I., pp. 201 ff., 314 ff. [English translation by F. Thilly, pp. 222 ff., 340 ff.].

[16] IV., p. 284. Footnote.

[17] p. 54.

[18] IV., p. 246; V., p. 284.

[19] *Tugendlehre,* § 31; *cf. Kr. d. r. V.,* Doctine of Method, p. 161.

[20] Preface to the 2d edition of the *Kritik der pract. Vernunft.*

John Rawls (essay date 1980)

SOURCE: "Kantian Constructivism in Moral Theory," in *The Journal of Philosophy,* Vol. LXXVII, No. 9, September, 1980, pp. 515-72.

[*In this essay, originally presented as three lectures at Columbia University in April, 1980, Rawls explores Kantian constructivism in moral theory (as illustrated by justice as fairness and adopted in* A Theory of Justice, *by which objectivity is established through "a suitably constructed social point of view."*]

Rational and Full Autonomy

In these lectures I examine the notion of a constructivist moral conception, or, more exactly, since there are different kinds of constructivism, one Kantian variant of this notion. The variant I discuss is that of justice as fairness, which is presented in my book *A Theory of Justice.*[1] I have two reasons for doing this: one is that it offers me the opportunity to consider certain aspects of the conception of justice as fairness which I have not previously emphasized and to set out more clearly the Kantian roots of that conception. The other reason is that the Kantian form of constructivism is much less well understood than other familiar traditional moral conceptions, such as utilitarianism, perfectionism, and intuitionism. I believe that this situation impedes the advance of moral theory. Therefore, it may prove useful simply to explain the distinctive features of Kantian constructivism, to say what it is, as illustrated by justice as fairness, without being concerned to defend it. To a degree that it is hard for me to estimate, my discussion assumes some acquaintance with *A Theory of Justice,* but I hope that, for the most part, a bare familiarity with its main intuitive ideas will suffice; and what these are I note as we proceed.

I would like to think that John Dewey, in whose honor these lectures are given, would find their topic hospitable to his concerns. We tend to think of him as the founder of a characteristically American and instrumental naturalism and, thus, to lose sight of the fact that Dewey started his philosophical life, as many did in the late nineteenth century, greatly influenced by Hegel; and his genius was to adapt much that is valuable in Hegel's idealism to a form of naturalism congenial to our culture. It was one of Hegel's aims to overcome the many dualisms which he thought disfigured Kant's transcendental idealism, and Dewey shared this emphasis throughout his work, often stressing the continuity between things that Kant had sharply separated. This theme is present particularly in Dewey's early writings, where the historical origins of his thought are more in evidence.[2] In elaborating his moral theory along somewhat Hegelian lines, Dewey opposes Kant, sometimes quite explicitly, and often at the same places at which justice as fairness also departs from Kant. Thus there are a number of affinities between justice as fairness and Dewey's moral theory which are explained by the common aim of overcoming the dualisms in Kant's doctrine.

I

What distinguishes the Kantian form of constructivism is essentially this: it specifies a particular conception of the person as an element in a reasonable procedure of construction, the outcome of which determines the content of the first principles of justice. Expressed another way: this kind of view sets up a certain procedure of construction which answers to certain reasonable requirements, and within this procedure persons characterized as rational agents of construction specify, through their agreements, the first principles of justice. (I use 'reasonable' and 'rational' to express different notions throughout, notions which will be explained below, in section v, 528-530.) The leading idea is to establish a suitable connection between a particular conception of the person and first principles of justice, by means of a procedure of construction. In a Kantian view the conception of the person, the procedure, and the first principles must be related in a certain manner—which, of course, admits of a number of variations. Justice as fairness is not, plainly, Kant's view, strictly speaking; it departs from his text at many points. But the adjective 'Kantian' expresses analogy and not identity; it means roughly that a doctrine sufficiently resembles Kant's in enough fundamental respects so that it is far closer to his view than to the other traditional moral conceptions that are appropriate for use as benchmarks of comparison.

On the Kantian view that I shall present, conditions for justifying a conception of justice hold only when a basis is established for political reasoning and understanding within a public culture. The social role of a conception of justice is to enable all members of society to make mutually acceptable to one another their shared institutions and basic arrangements, by citing what are publicly recognized as sufficient reasons, as identified by that conception. To succeed in doing this, a conception must specify admissible social institutions and their possible arrangements into one system, so that they can be justified to all citizens, whatever their social position or more particular interests. Thus, whenever a sufficient basis for agreement among citizens is not presently known, or recognized, the task of justifying a conception of justice becomes: how can people settle on a conception of justice, to serve this social role, that is (most) reasonable for them in virtue

of how they conceive of their persons and construe the general features of social cooperation among persons so regarded?

Pursuing this idea of justification, we take our examination of the Kantian conception of justice as addressed to an impasse in our recent political history; the course of democratic thought over the past two centuries, say, shows that there is no agreement on the way basic social institutions should be arranged if they are to conform to the freedom and equality of citizens as moral persons. The requisite understanding of freedom and equality, which is implicit in the public culture of a democratic society, and the most suitable way to balance the claims of these notions, have not been expressed so as to meet general approval. Now a Kantian conception of justice tries to dispel the conflict between the different understandings of freedom and equality by asking: which traditionally recognized principles of freedom and equality, or which natural variations thereof, would free and equal moral persons themselves agree upon, if they were fairly represented solely as such persons and thought of themselves as citizens living a complete life in an on-going society? Their agreement, assuming an agreement would be reached, is conjectured to single out the most appropriate principles of freedom and equality and, therefore, to specify the principles of justice.

An immediate consequence of taking our inquiry as focused on the apparent conflict between freedom and equality in a democratic society is that we are not trying to find a conception of justice suitable for all societies regardless of their particular social or historical circumstances. We want to settle a fundamental disagreement over the just form of basic institutions within a democratic society under modern conditions. We look to ourselves and to our future, and reflect upon our disputes since, let's say, the Declaration of Independence. How far the conclusions we reach are of interest in a wider context is a separate question.

Hence, we should like to achieve among ourselves a practicable and working understanding on first principles of justice. Our hope is that there is a common desire for agreement, as well as a sufficient sharing of certain underlying notions and implicitly held principles, so that the effort to reach an understanding has some foothold. The aim of political philosophy, when it presents itself in the public culture of a democratic society, is to articulate and to make explicit those shared notions and principles thought to be already latent in common sense; or, as is often the case, if common sense is hesitant and uncertain, and doesn't know what to think, to propose to it certain conceptions and principles congenial to its most essential convictions and historical traditions. To justify a Kantian conception within a democratic society is not merely to reason correctly from given premises, or even from publicly shared and mutually recognized premises. The real task is to discover and formulate the deeper bases of agreement which one hopes are embedded in common sense, or even to originate and fashion starting points for common understanding by expressing in a new form the convictions found in the historical tradition by connecting them with a wide range of people's considered convictions: those which stand up to critical reflection. Now, as I have said, a Kantian doctrine joins the content of justice with a certain conception of the person; and this conception regards persons as both free and equal, as capable of acting both reasonably and rationally, and therefore as capable of taking part in social cooperation among persons so conceived. In addressing the public culture of a democratic society, Kantian constructivism hopes to invoke a conception of the person implicitly affirmed in that culture, or else one that would prove acceptable to citizens once it was properly presented and explained.

I should emphasize that what I have called the "real task" of justifying a conception of justice is not primarily an epistemological problem. The search for reasonable grounds for reaching agreement rooted in our conception of ourselves and in our relation to society replaces the search for moral truth interpreted as fixed by a prior and independent order of objects and relations, whether natural or divine, an order apart and distinct from how we conceive of ourselves. The task is to articulate a public conception of justice that all can live with who regard their person and their relation to society in a certain way. And though doing this may involve settling theoretical difficulties, the practical social task is primary. What justifies a conception of justice is not its being true to an order antecedent to and given to us, but its congruence with our deeper understanding of ourselves and our aspirations, and our realization that, given our history and the traditions embedded in our public life, it is the most reasonable doctrine for us. We can find no better basic charter for our social world. Kantian constructivism holds that moral objectivity is to be understood in terms of a suitably constructed social point of view that all can accept. Apart from the procedure of constructing the principles of justice, there are no moral facts. Whether certain facts are to be recognized as reasons of right and justice, or how much they are to count, can be ascertained only from within the constructive procedure, that is, from the undertakings of rational agents of construction when suitably represented as free and equal moral persons. (The points noted in this paragraph will be discussed in more detail in the third lecture.)

II

These first remarks were introductory and intended merely to suggest the themes of my discussion. To proceed, let's specify more exactly the above-mentioned

impasse in our political culture as follows, namely, as a conflict between two traditions of democratic thought, one associated with Locke, the other with Rousseau. Using the distinction drawn by Benjamin Constant between the liberties of the moderns and the liberties of the ancients, the tradition derived from Locke gives pride of place to the former, that is, to the liberties of civic life, especially freedom of thought and conscience, certain basic rights of the person, and of property and association; while the tradition descending from Rousseau assigns priority to the equal political liberties and values of public life, and views the civic liberties as subordinate. Of course, this contrast is in many respects artificial and historically inaccurate; yet it serves to fix ideas and enables us to see that a mere splitting of the difference between these two traditions (even if we should agree on a favored interpretation of each) would be unsatisfactory. Somehow we must find a suitable rendering of freedom and equality, and of their relative priority, rooted in the more fundamental notions of our political life and congenial to our conception of the person.

But how are we to achieve this? Justice as fairness tries to uncover the fundamental ideas (latent in common sense) of freedom and equality, of ideal social cooperation and of the person, by formulating what I shall call "model-conceptions." We then reason within the framework of these conceptions, which need be defined only sharply enough to yield an acceptable public understanding of freedom and equality. Whether the doctrine that eventually results fulfills its purpose is then decided by how it works out: once stated, it must articulate a suitable conception of ourselves and of our relation to society, and connect this conception with workable first principles of justice, so that, after due consideration, we can acknowledge the doctrine proposed.

Now the two basic model-conceptions of justice as fairness are those of a *well-ordered society* and of a *moral person*. Their general purpose is to single out the essential aspects of our conception of ourselves as moral persons and of our relation to society as free and equal citizens. They depict certain general features of what a society would look like if its members publicly viewed themselves and their social ties with one another in a certain way. The *original position* is a third and mediating model-conception: its role is to establish the connection between the model-conception of a moral person and the principles of justice that characterize the relations of citizens in the model-conception of a well-ordered society. It serves this role by modeling the way in which the citizens in a well-ordered society, viewed as moral persons, would ideally select first principles of justice for their society. The constraints imposed on the parties in the original position, and the manner in which the parties are described, are to represent the freedom and equality of moral persons as understood in such a society. If certain principles of justice would indeed be agreed to (or if they would belong to a certain restricted family of principles), then the aim of Kantian constructivism to connect definite principles with a particular conception of the person is achieved.

For the present, however, I am concerned with the parties in the original position only as rationally autonomous agents of construction who (as such agents) represent the aspect of rationality, which is part of the conception of a moral person affirmed by citizens in a well-ordered society. The rational autonomy of the parties in the original position contrasts with the full autonomy of citizens in society. Thus *rational* autonomy is that of the parties as agents of construction: it is a relatively narrow notion, and roughly parallels Kant's notion of hypothetical imperatives (or the notion of rationality found in neo-classical economics); *full* autonomy is that of citizens in everyday life who think of themselves in a certain way and affirm and act from the first principles of justice that would be agreed to. In section v, I shall discuss the constraints imposed on the parties which enable the original position to represent the essential elements of full autonomy.

Let us briefly recall the features of a well-ordered society most relevant here.[3] First, such a society is effectively regulated by a public conception of justice; that is, it is a society in which every one accepts, and knows that others likewise accept, the same first principles of right and justice. It is also the case that the basic structure of society, the arrangement of its main institutions into one social scheme, actually satisfies, and is believed by all on good grounds to satisfy, these principles. Finally, the public principles of justice are themselves founded on reasonable beliefs as established by the society's generally accepted methods of inquiry; and the same is true of the application of these principles to judge social institutions.

Second, the members of a well-ordered society are, and view themselves and one another in their political and social relations (so far as these are relevant to questions of justice) as, free and equal moral persons. Here there are three distinct notions, specified independently: freedom, equality, and moral (as applied to) person. The members of a well-ordered society are moral persons in that, once they have reached the age of reason, each has, and views the others as having, an effective sense of justice, as well as an understanding of a conception of their good. Citizens are equal in that they regard one another as having an equal right to determine, and to assess upon due reflection, the first principles of justice by which the basic structure of their society is to be governed. Finally, the members of a well-ordered society are free in that they think they are entitled to make claims on the design of their common institutions in the name of their own

fundamental aims and highest-order interests. At the same time, as free persons, they think of themselves not as inevitably tied to the pursuit of the particular final ends they have at any given time, but rather as capable of revising and changing these ends on reasonable and rational grounds.

There are other features of a well-ordered society, such as its stability with respect to its sense of justice, its existing under the circumstances of justice, and so on. But these matters can be left aside. The essential thing is that, when we formulate the model-conception of the original position, we must view the parties as selecting principles of justice which are to serve as effective public principles of justice in a well-ordered society, and hence for social cooperation among persons who conceive of themselves as free and equal moral persons. Although this description of a well-ordered society is formal, in that its elements taken alone do not imply a specific content for the principles of justice, the description does impose various conditions on how the original position can be set up. In particular, the conception of moral persons as free and equal, and the distinction between rational and full autonomy, must be appropriately reflected in its description. Otherwise the original position cannot fulfill its mediating role to connect a certain conception of the person with definite first principles by means of a procedure in which the parties, as rationally autonomous agents of construction, adopt principles of justice, the public affirmation of which by citizens of a well-ordered society in every-day life enables them to be fully autonomous.

III

Let us descend from these abstractions, at least a bit, and turn to a summary account of the original position. As I have said, justice as fairness begins from the idea that the most appropriate conception of justice for the basic structure of a democratic society is one that its citizens would adopt in a situation that is fair between them and in which they are represented solely as free and equal moral persons. This situation is the original position: we conjecture that the fairness of the circumstances under which agreement is reached transfers to the principles of justice agreed to; since the original position situates free and equal moral persons fairly with respect to one another, any conception of justice they adopt is likewise fair. Thus the name: 'justice as fairness'.

In order to ensure that the original position is fair between individuals regarded solely as free and equal moral persons, we require that, when adopting principles for the basic structure, the parties be deprived of certain information; that is, they are behind what I shall call a "veil of ignorance." For example, they do not know their place in society, their class position, or social status, nor do they know their fortune in the distribution of natural talents and abilities. It is assumed also that they do not know their conception of the good, that is, their particular final ends; nor finally, their own distinctive psychological dispositions and propensities, and the like. Excluding this information is required if no one is to be advantaged or disadvantaged by natural contingencies or social chance in the adoption of principles. Otherwise the parties would have disparate bargaining advantages that would affect the agreement reached. The original position would represent the parties not solely as free and equal moral persons, but instead as persons also affected by social fortune and natural accident. Thus, these and other limitations on information are necessary to establish fairness between the parties as free and equal moral persons and, therefore, to guarantee that it is as such persons that they agree to society's basic principles of justice.

Now the original position, as described, incorporates pure procedural justice at the highest level. This means that whatever principles the parties select from the list of alternative conceptions presented to them are just. Put another way, the outcome of the original position defines, let us say, the appropriate principles of justice. This contrasts with perfect procedural justice, where there is an independent and already given criterion of what is just (or fair) and where a procedure exists to ensure a result that satisfies this standard. This is illustrated by the familiar example of dividing a cake: if equal division is taken as fair, then we simply require the person who cuts it to have the last piece. (I forego the assumptions necessary to make the example airtight.) The essential feature of pure procedural justice, as opposed to perfect procedural justice, is that there exists no independent criterion of justice; what is just is defined by the outcome of the procedure itself.

One reason for describing the original position as incorporating pure procedural justice is that it enables us to explain how the parties, as the rational agents of construction, are also autonomous (as such agents). For the use of pure procedural justice implies that the principles of justice themselves are to be constructed by a process of deliberation, a process visualized as being carried out by the parties in the original position. The appropriate weight of considerations for and against various principles is given by the force of these considerations for the parties, and the force of all reasons on balance is expressed by the agreement made. Pure procedural justice in the original position allows that in their deliberations the parties are not required to apply, nor are they bound by, any antecedently given principles of right and justice. Or, put another way, there exists no standpoint external to the parties' own perspective from which they are constrained by prior and independent principles in questions of justice that arise among them as members of one society.

I call your attention to the following: I have said above that there is no standpoint external to the parties' own perspective from which they are bound in questions of justice that arise between them. Here the phrase 'between them' is significant. It signals the fact that I am leaving aside two important matters: questions of justice between societies (the law of nations), and our relations to the order of nature and to other living things. Both these questions are of first importance and immensely difficult; except in a few special cases, no attempt was made in *A Theory of Justice* to discuss these questions.[4] I shall simply proceed on the idea that we may reasonably begin with the basic structure of one society as a closed and self-sufficient system of cooperation. Should we find a suitable conception for this case, we can then work both inward to principles for associations and practices, and outward to the law of nations and order of nature itself. How far this can be done, and to what extent the conception of justice for the basic structure will have to be revised in the process, cannot be foreseen in advance. Here I merely wish to register these limitations of my discussion.

So far the autonomy of the parties is expressed by their being at liberty to agree to any conception of justice available to them as prompted by their rational assessment of which alternative is most likely to advance their interests. In their deliberations they are not required to apply, or to be guided by, any principles of right and justice, but are to decide as principles of rationality dictate, given their situation. But the propriety of the term 'autonomy' as applied to the parties also depends on what their interests are and on the nature of constraints to which they are subject. So let's review these matters.

IV

Recall that the parties are to adopt principles to serve as the effective public conception of justice for a well-ordered society. Now the citizens of such a society regard themselves as moral persons and as having a conception of the good (an ordered scheme of final ends) for the sake of which they think it proper to make claims on the design of their common institutions. So in the original position we may describe the parties either as the representatives (or trustees) of persons with certain interests or as themselves moved by these interests. It makes no difference either way, although the latter is simpler and I shall usually speak in this vein.

To continue: we take moral persons to be characterized by two moral powers and by two corresponding highest-order interests in realizing and exercising these powers. The first power is the capacity for an effective sense of justice, that is, the capacity to understand, to apply and to act from (and not merely in accordance with) the principles of justice. The second moral power is the capacity to form, to revise, and rationally to pursue a conception of the good. Corresponding to the moral powers, moral persons are said to be moved by two highest-order interests to realize and exercise these powers. By calling these interests "highest-order" interests, I mean that, as the model-conception of a moral person is specified, these interests are supremely regulative as well as effective. This implies that, whenever circumstances are relevant to their fulfillment, these interests govern deliberation and conduct. Since the parties represent moral persons, they are likewise moved by these interests to secure the development and exercise of the moral powers.

In addition, I assume that the parties represent developed moral persons, that is, persons who have, at any given time, a determinate scheme of final ends, a particular conception of the good. Thus the model-conception defines moral persons as also determinate persons, although from the standpoint of the original position, the parties do not know the content of their conception of the good: its final ends. This conception yields a third interest that moves the parties: a higher-order interest in protecting and advancing their conception of the good as best they can, whatever it may be. The reason this is but a higher-order and not a highest-order interest is that, as we shall see later, it is in essential respects subordinate to the highest-order interests.

Now in view of these three regulative interests, the veil of ignorance poses a problem: how are we to set up the original position so that the parties, as representatives of persons with these interests, can make a rational agreement? It is at this point that the account of primary goods is introduced: by stipulating that the parties evaluate conceptions of justice by a preference for these goods, we endow them, as agents of construction, with sufficiently specific desires so that their rational deliberations reach a definite result. We look for social background conditions and general all-purpose means normally necessary for developing and exercising the two moral powers and for effectively pursuing a conception of the good. Thus a very brief explanation of the parties' preference for the primary goods enumerated in *A Theory of Justice* is this:[5]

(i) The basic liberties (freedom of thought and liberty of conscience, etc.) are the background institutions necessary for the development and exercise of the capacity to decide upon and revise, and rationally to pursue, a conception of the good. Similarly, these liberties allow for the development and exercise of the sense of right and justice under social conditions that are free.

(ii) Freedom of movement and free choice of occupation against a background of diverse opportunities are required for the pursuit of final ends, as well as to give effect to a decision to revise and change them, if one so desires.

(iii) Powers and prerogatives of offices and positions of responsibility are needed to give scope to various self-governing and social capacities of the self.

(iv) Income and wealth, understood broadly as they must be, are all-purpose means (having an exchange value) for achieving directly or indirectly almost any of our ends, whatever they happen to be.

(v) The social bases of self-respect are those aspects of basic institutions which are normally essential if individuals are to have a lively sense of their own worth as moral persons and to be able to realize their higher-order interests and advance their ends with zest and self-confidence.

Granted the correctness of these observations, the parties' preference for primary goods is rational. (I shall assume that in this context our intuitive notion of rationality suffices for our purposes here, and so I shan't discuss it until the next section.)

There are many points about primary goods which need to be examined. Here I mention only the leading idea, namely, that primary goods are singled out by asking which things are generally necessary as social conditions and all-purpose means to enable human beings to realize and exercise their moral powers and to pursue their final ends (assumed to lie within certain limits). Here we must look to social requirements and the normal circumstances of human life in a democratic society. Now note that the conception of moral persons as having certain specified highest-order interests selects what is to count as primary goods within the framework of the model-conceptions. Thus these goods are not to be understood as general means essential for achieving whatever final ends a comprehensive empirical or historical survey might show people usually or normally to have in common under all social conditions. There may be few if any such ends; and those there are may not serve the purpose of constructing a conception of justice reasonable for us. The list of primary goods does not rest on that kind of general fact, although it does rely on general social facts, once the conception of the person and its highest-order interests are fixed. (Here I should comment that, by making the account of primary goods rest upon a particular conception of the person, I am revising the suggestions in *A Theory of Justice,* since there it can seem as if the list of primary goods is regarded as the outcome of a purely psychological, statistical, or historical inquiry.)[6]

What bearing do these remarks about primary goods have on our original question about rational autonomy? We observed that this autonomy surely depends in part upon the interests that move the parties and not solely on their being bound by no prior and independent principles of right. Were the parties moved solely by lower-order impulses, say for food and drink, or by certain particular affections for this or that group of persons, association, or community, we might think of them as heteronomous and not as autonomous. But at the basis of the desire for primary goods are the highest-order interests of moral personality and the need to secure one's conception of the good (whatever it is). Thus the parties are simply trying to guarantee and to advance the requisite conditions for exercising the powers that characterize them as moral persons. Certainly this motivation is neither heteronomous nor self-centered: we expect and indeed want people to care about their liberties and opportunities in order to realize these powers, and we think they show a lack of self-respect and weakness of character in not doing so. Thus the assumption that the parties are mutually disinterested and, hence, concerned to ensure their own highest-order interests (or those of the persons they represent) should not be confused with egoism.

In conclusion, then, the parties as rational agents of construction are described in the original position as autonomous in two respects: first, in their deliberations they are not required to apply, or to be guided by, any prior and antecedent principles of right and justice. This is expressed by the use of pure procedural justice. Second, they are said to be moved solely by the highest-order interests in their moral powers and by their concern to advance their determinate but unknown final ends. The account of primary goods and its derivation convey this side of autonomy. Given the veil of ignorance, the parties can be prompted only by these highest-order interests, which they must, in turn, render specific by the preference for primary goods.

V

So much for the notion of rational autonomy of the parties as agents of construction. I now turn to the notion of full autonomy; although this notion is realized only by the citizens of a well-ordered society in the course of their daily lives, the essential features of it must nevertheless be represented in a suitable manner in the original position. For it is by affirming the first principles that would be adopted in this situation and by publicly recognizing the way in which they would be agreed to, as well as by acting from these principles as their sense of justice dictates, that citizens' full autonomy is achieved. We must ask, then, how the original position incorporates the requisite elements of full autonomy.

Now these elements are not expressed by how the parties' deliberations and motivation are described. The parties are merely artificial agents, and are presented not as fully but only as rationally autonomous. To explain full autonomy, let us note two elements of any notion of social cooperation. The first is a conception of the *fair terms of cooperation,* that is, terms each participant may reasonably be expected to accept, provided that everyone else likewise accepts them. Fair terms of cooperation articulate an idea of reciprocity and mutuality: all who cooperate must benefit, or share in common burdens, in some appropriate fashion as judged by a suitable benchmark of comparison. This element in social cooperation I call the *Reasonable.* The other element corresponds to the *Rational:* it expresses a conception of each participant's rational advantage, what, as individuals, they are trying to advance. As we have seen, the rational is interpreted by the original position in reference to the desire of persons to realize and to exercise their moral powers and to secure the advancement of their conception of the good. Given a specification of the parties' highest-order interests, they are rational in their deliberations to the extent that sensible principles of rational choice guide their decisions. Familiar examples of such principles are: the adoption of effective means to ends; the balancing of final ends by their significance for our plan of life as a whole and by the extent to which these ends cohere with and support each other; and finally, the assigning of a greater weight to the more likely consequences; and so on. Although there seems to be no one best interpretation of rationality, the difficulties in explaining Kantian constructivism do not lie here. Thus I ignore these matters, and focus on the more obscure notion of the Reasonable and how it is represented in the original position.

This representing is done essentially by the nature of the constraints within which the parties' deliberations take place and which define their circumstances with respect to one another. The Reasonable is incorporated into the background setup of the original position which frames the discussions of the parties and situates them symmetrically. More specifically, in addition to various familiar formal conditions on first principles, such as generality and universality, ordering and finality, the parties are required to adopt a public conception of justice and must assess its first principles with this condition in mind. (I shall say more about the publicity condition in the next lecture.)

Again, the veil of ignorance implies that persons are represented solely as moral persons and not as persons advantaged or disadvantaged by the contingencies of their social position, the distribution of natural abilities, or by luck and historical accident over the course of their lives. As a result they are situated equally as moral persons, and in this sense fairly. Here I appeal to the idea that, in establishing the truly basic terms of social cooperation, the possession of the minimum adequate powers of moral personality (the powers that equip us to be normally cooperating members of society over a complete life) is the sole relevant characteristic. This presumption, plus the precept that equals in all relevant respects are to be represented equally, ensures that the original position is fair.

The last constraint I shall mention here is this: the stipulation that the first subject of justice is the basic structure of society, that is, the main social institutions and how they cohere together into one system, supports situating the parties equally and restricting their information by the veil of ignorance. For this stipulation requires the parties to assess alternative conceptions as providing first principles of what we may call *background justice:* it is only if the basic structure satisfies the requirements of background justice that a society treats its members as equal moral persons. Otherwise, its fundamental regulative arrangements do not answer to principles its citizens would adopt when fairly represented solely as such persons.

Let us pull together these remarks as follows: the Reasonable presupposes and subordinates the Rational. It defines the fair terms of cooperation acceptable to all within some group of separately identifiable persons, each of whom possesses and can exercise the two moral powers. All have a conception of their good which defines their rational advantage, and everyone has a normally effective sense of justice: a capacity to honor the fair terms of cooperation. The Reasonable presupposes the Rational, because, without conceptions of the good that move members of the group, there is no point to social cooperation nor to notions of right and justice, even though such cooperation realizes values that go beyond what conceptions of the good specify taken alone. The Reasonable subordinates the Rational because its principles limit, and in a Kantian doctrine limit absolutely, the final ends that can be pursued.

Thus, in the original position we view the Reasonable as expressed by the framework of constraints within which the deliberations of the parties (as rationally autonomous agents of construction) take place. Representative of these constraints are the condition of publicity, the veil of ignorance and the symmetry of the parties' situation with respect to one another, and the stipulation that the basic structure is the first subject of justice. Familiar principles of justice are examples of reasonable principles, and familiar principles of rational choice are examples of rational principles. The way the Reasonable is represented in the original position leads to the two principles of justice. These principles are constructed by justice as fairness as the content of the Reasonable for the basic structure of a well-ordered society.

VI

This concludes my account of the distinction between Rational and Full Autonomy and explains how these notions are expressed in the original position. In certain respects, however, the contrast between the Reasonable and the Rational, as drawn in the last two paragraphs, is too stark and may give a misleading impression of how these notions are to be understood. By way of clarification, I consider an objection which parallels the criticism Schopenhauer made against Kant's doctrine of the Categorical Imperative.[7] You will recall that Schopenhauer maintained that, in arguing for the duty of mutual aid in situations of distress (the fourth example in the *Grundlegung*), Kant appeals to what rational agents, as finite beings with needs, can consistently will to be universal law. In view of our need for love and sympathy, on at least some occasions, we cannot will a social world in which others are always indifferent to our pleas in such cases. From this Schopenhauer claimed that Kant's view is at bottom egoistic, from which it follows that it is but a disguised form of heteronomy after all.

Here I am concerned not to defend Kant against this criticism but to point out why the parallel objection to justice as fairness is incorrect. To this end, observe that there are, offhand, two things that prompt Schopenhauer's objection. First, he believes that Kant asks us to test maxims in the light of their general consequences for our natural inclinations and needs, when these maxims are made universal laws, and that these inclinations and needs are viewed egoistically. Second, the rules that define the procedure for testing maxims Schopenhauer interprets as external constraints, imposed so to speak from the outside by the limitations of our situation, which we should like to surmount, and not derived from the essential features of ourselves as moral persons. These two considerations lead Schopenhauer to say that the categorical imperative is a principle of reciprocity which egoism cunningly accepts as a compromise; as such a principle, it may be appropriate for a confederation of nation states but not as a moral principle.

Now consider the parallel criticism of justice as fairness in regard to these two points. Concerning the first, though it is indeed true that the parties in the original position are mutually disinterested and evaluate principles of justice in terms of primary goods, they are moved in the first instance by their highest-order interests in developing and exercising their moral powers; and the list of primary goods, and the index of these goods, is to be explained so far as possible by reference to these interests. Since these interests may be taken to specify their needs as moral persons, the parties' aims are not egoistic, but entirely fitting and proper. It accords with the conception of free personality held in a democratic society that citizens should secure the conditions for realizing and exercising their moral powers, as well as the social bases and means of their self-respect. This contrasts with Schopenhauer's presumption that in Kant's doctrine maxims are tested by their consequences for the fulfillment of the agent's natural inclinations and needs.

Turning to the second point, what I have called "the constraints imposed on the parties in the original position" are indeed external to the parties as rational agents of construction. Nevertheless, these constraints express the Reasonable and, therefore, the formal conditions implicit in the moral powers of the members of a well-ordered society, whom the parties represent. This contrasts with Schopenhauer's second presumption that the constraints of the categorical imperative derive from the limitations of our finite nature, which, prompted by our natural inclinations, we should like to overcome. In justice as fairness, the Reasonable frames the Rational and is derived from a conception of moral persons as free and equal. Once this is understood, the constraints of the original position are no longer external. Thus neither basis for Schopenhauer's objection applies.

Finally, the way in which the Reasonable frames the Rational in the original position represents a feature of the unity of practical reason. In Kant's terms, empirical practical reason is represented by the rational deliberations of the parties; pure practical reason is represented by the constraints within which these deliberations take place. The unity of practical reason is expressed by defining the Reasonable to frame the Rational and to subordinate it absolutely; that is, the principles of justice that are agreed to are lexically prior in their application in a well-ordered society to claims of the good. This means, among other things, that the principles of justice and the rights and liberties they define cannot, in such a society, be overridden by considerations of efficiency and a greater net balance of social well-being. This illustrates one feature of the unity of reason: the Reasonable and the Rational are unified within one scheme of practical reasoning which establishes the strict priority of the Reasonable with respect to the Rational. This priority of the right over the good is characteristic of Kantian constructivism.

Now in a well-ordered society we stipulate that the justification of the principles of justice as the outcome of the original position is publicly understood. So not only do citizens have a highest-order desire, their sense of justice, to act from the principles of justice, but they understand these principles as issuing from a construction in which their conception of themselves as free and equal moral persons who are both reasonable and rational is adequately represented. By acting from these principles, and affirming them in public life, as so derived, they express their full autonomy. The rational autonomy of the parties is merely that of artificial agents who inhabit a construction designed to model this more inclusive conception. It is the inclusive conception which expresses the ideal to be realized in our social world.

It is natural to reply that, all the same, fully autonomous citizens in a well-ordered society act from some desire, and so are still heteronomous, since they are not moved by reason alone.[8] To this the answer is that a Kantian view does not deny that we act from some desire. What is of moment is the kinds of desires from which we act and how they are ordered; that is, how these desires originate within and are related to the self, and the way their structure and priority are determined by principles of justice connected with the conception of the person we affirm. The mediating conception of the original position enables us to connect certain definite principles of justice with a certain conception of free and equal moral persons. Given this connection, an effective sense of justice, the desire to act from the principles of justice, is not a desire on the same footing with natural inclinations; it is an executive and regulative highest-order desire to act from certain principles of justice in view of their connection with a conception of the person as free and equal. And that desire is not heteronomous: for whether a desire is heteronomous is settled by its mode of origin and role within the self and by what it is a desire for. In this case the desire is to be a certain kind of person specified by the conception of fully autonomous citizens of a well-ordered society.

VII

I conclude with a few observations which may help to keep in focus the discussion so far. First, it is important to distingush three points of view: that of the parties in the original position, that of citizens in a well-ordered society, and finally, that of ourselves—you and me who are examining justice as fairness as a basis for a conception of justice that may yield a suitable understanding of freedom and equality.

The first two points of view occur within the doctrine of justice as parts of two of its model-conceptions. Whereas the conceptions of a well-ordered society and of moral persons are fundamental, the original position is the mediating conception once we stipulate that the parties as rational agents of construction are subject to reasonable constraints and are to view themselves as adopting principles to serve as the public conception of justice for a well-ordered society. The intent of justice as fairness is badly misunderstood if the deliberations of the parties and their rational autonomy are confused with full autonomy. Full autonomy is a moral ideal and part of the more comprehensive ideal of a well-ordered society. Rational autonomy is not, as such, an ideal at all, but a device of representation used to connect the conception of the person with definite principles of justice. (Of course, this is not to deny that rational deliberation, suitably circumscribed, is an aspect of the ideal of full autonomy.)

The third point of view—that of you and me—is that from which justice as fairness, and indeed any other doctrine, is to be assessed. Here the test is that of general and wide reflective equilibrium, that is, how well the view as a whole meshes with and articulates our more firm considered convictions, at all levels of generality, after due examination, once all adjustments and revisions that seem compelling have been made. A doctrine that meets this criterion is the doctrine that, so far as we can now ascertain, is the most reasonable for us.

A final observation: it is also useful to distinguish between the roles of a conception of the person and of a theory of human nature.[9] In justice as fairness these ideas are distinct elements and enter at different places. For one thing, the conception of the person is a companion moral ideal paired with that of a well-ordered society. Like any other ideal, it must be possible for people to honor it sufficiently closely; and hence the feasible ideals of the person are limited by the capacities of human nature and the requirements of social life. To this extent such an ideal presupposes a theory of human nature, and social theory generally, but the task of a moral doctrine is to specify an appropriate conception of the person that general facts about human nature and society allow. Starting from the assumption that full autonomy is a feasible ideal for political life, we represent its various aspects in the original position under the headings of the Reasonable and the Rational. Thus this ideal is mirrored in how this position is set up.

A theory of human nature, by contrast, appears in the general facts available to the parties for them to use in assessing the consequences of the various principles of justice and so in deciding which principles are best able to secure their highest-order interests and to lead to a well-ordered society that is stable with respect to its public conception of justice. When we formulate justice as fairness from the third point of view, we supply the parties with the requisite general facts that we take to be true, or true enough, given the state of public knowledge in our society. The agreement of the parties is relative, then, to these beliefs. There is no other way to proceed, since we must start from where we are. But, leaving this aside, the point is that a theory of human nature is not part of the framework of the original position, except as such theories limit the feasibility of the ideals of person and society embedded in that framework. Rather, a theory of human nature is an element to be filled in, depending upon the general facts about human beings and the workings of society which we allow to the parties in their deliberations.

In this lecture I have focused on the distinction between rational and full autonomy and have said very little about the notions of the freedom and equality of persons, and even less about how these notions are represented in the original position. These matters I consider in the next lecture.

Representation of Freedom and Equality

In the last lecture, I focused largely on the distinction between rational and full autonomy. Rational autonomy is expressed in the deliberations of the parties as artificial agents of construction within the original position. Full autonomy is the more comprehensive notion and expresses an ideal of the person affirmed by the citizens of a well-ordered society in their social life. But although I described the parties as representatives of free and equal moral persons, I indicated only briefly what freedom and equality mean and how these features of the person are represented in the original position. Nor did I say very much about the formal condition of publicity, which is a distinctive element of a Kantian view. Exploring these matters will help to fill in the account of the original position and show how justice as fairness is an illustration of Kantian constructivism in moral theory.

I

I shall begin with some further remarks about the model-conception of a well-ordered society. You will recall that I said last time that there are various forms of constructivism. A number of views not usually thought of as constructivist can be presented in this way.[10] This suggests that the three main model-conceptions of justice as fairness—those of a well-ordered society, the conception of the person, and the original position—are all special renderings of more general notions. What characterizes a Kantian doctrine is the particular way in which it interprets these three model-conceptions; especially characteristic, of course, is its conception of the person as reasonable and rational, and fully autonomous. I shall not examine here what these more general model-notions are or how they might be defined; I mention these questions only to remind us that the model-conceptions I discuss are special cases that define a particular moral doctrine.

To continue: recall that a well-ordered society is conceived as an on-going society, a self-sufficient association of human beings which, like a nation-state, controls a connected territory. Its members view their common polity as extending backward and forward in time over generations, and they strive to reproduce themselves, and their cultural and social life in perpetuity, practically speaking; that is, they would envisage any final date at which they were to wind up their affairs as inadmissible and foreign to their conception of their association. Finally, a well-ordered society is a closed system; there are no significant relations to other societies, and no one enters from without, for all are born into it to lead a complete life.

Next, we assume that, as an on-going society, the scheme of social and economic activities set up and framed by the basic structure is productive and fruitful. This implies, for example, that a well-ordered society does not have a manna economy, nor are its economic arrangements a zero-sum game in which none can gain unless others lose. Yet it does exist under circumstances of justice, of which there are two kinds: first, the objective circumstances of moderate scarcity; and, second, the subjective circumstances, namely, that persons and associations have contrary conceptions of the good as well as of how to realize them, and these differences set them at odds, and lead them to make conflicting claims on their institutions. They hold opposing religious and philosophical beliefs, and affirm not only diverse moral and political doctrines, but also conflicting ways of evaluating arguments and evidence when they try to reconcile these oppositions. In view of the circumstances of justice, the members of a well-ordered society are not indifferent to how the fruits of their social cooperation are distributed, and, for their society to be stable, the distribution that results and is expected in the future must be seen to be (sufficiently) just.

Thus, as we noted last time, the stability of a well-ordered society is not founded merely on a perceived balance of social forces the upshot of which all accept since none can do better for themselves. To the contrary, citizens affirm their existing institutions in part because they reasonably believe them to satisfy their public and effective conception of justice. Now the notion of publicity has three levels, which may be distinguished as follows:[11]

The first was mentioned last time: it means that society is effectively regulated by public principles of justice; that is, everyone accepts and knows that the others likewise accept the same principles, and this knowledge in turn is publicly recognized. Also, the institutions that constitute the basic structure of society actually satisfy these principles of justice, and everyone with reason acknowledges this on the basis of commonly shared beliefs confirmed by methods of inquiry and ways of reasoning agreed to be appropriate for questions of social justice.

The second level of publicity concerns the general beliefs in the light of which first principles of justice themselves can be accepted, that is, the theory of human nature and of social institutions generally. Citizens in a well-ordered society roughly agree on these beliefs because they can be supported (as at the first level) by publicly shared methods of inquiry and ways of reasoning thought to be appropriate for this case. These methods and ways of reasoning I assume to be familiar from common sense and to include the procedures and conclusions of science, when these are well established and not controversial. Keep in mind that we aim to find a conception of justice for a democratic society under modern conditions; so we may properly assume that in its public culture the methods and con-

clusions of science play an influential role. It is precisely these general beliefs, which reflect the current public views in a well-ordered society, that we allow to the parties in the original position for the purpose of assessing alternative principles of justice.

The third and last level of publicity has to do with the complete justification of the public conception of justice as it would be presented in its own terms. This justification includes everything that we would say—you and me—when we set up justice as fairness, and reflect why we do this one way rather than another. At the third level I suppose this full justification also to be publicly known or, better, at least publicly available; this weaker condition allows for the possibility that some will not want to carry moral reflection so far, and certainly they are not required to do so. But if they wish to, the justification is present in public culture, reflected in law and political institutions, and in the philosophical and historical traditions of their interpretation. More specifically, the full justification includes connecting the moral doctrine's model-conceptions with the society's particular conception of the person and of social co-operation. This conception is shown in how citizens think of themselves as members of a democratic polity when they examine the doctrine as a whole and find after due reflection that it matches their considered judgments at all levels of generality.

A well-ordered society satisfies what I shall call the *full publicity condition* when all three levels are exemplified. (I reserve the adjective 'full' for the elements of the complete and full rendering of the conception of a well-ordered society.) Now this full condition may seem excessively strong; so let's ask why it is adopted. One reason is that the model-conception of a well-ordered society is to incorporate various formal moral notions into an ideal of social cooperation between persons regarded in a certain way. This ideal is to hold for free and equal moral persons, and views social cooperation not simply as productive and socially coordinated activity, but as fulfilling a notion of fair terms of cooperation and of mutual advantage, as expressed by the distinction between the Reasonable and the Rational. So we should like to find a conception of justice that answers to the full condition; it seems bound to define more specific constraints on conceptions of justice and, hence, is more likely to provide a sharper basis for deciding among conflicting understandings of freedom and equality and for determining how their claims are to be balanced against one another. Recall that this conflict of understandings sets the present practical task of political philosophy.

Another reason for the full publicity condition (and indeed for any of its levels) is that is seems particularly appropriate for a conception of political and social justice. No doubt, publicity is less compelling for other moral notions. But the principles of justice apply to the political constitution and the basic institutions of society, which normally include, even under favorable conditions, some machinery of legal coercion, if only to guarantee the stability of social cooperation.[12] Moreover, these institutions can have decisive long-term social effects and importantly shape the character and aims of the members of society, the kinds of persons they are and want to be. It seems fitting, then, that the fundamental terms of social cooperation between free and equal moral persons should answer to the requirements of full publicity. For if institutions rely on coercive sanctions, however seldom necessary and however scrupulously applied, and influence people's deepest aspirations, the grounds and tendency of these institutions should stand up to public scrutiny. When political principles satisfy the full publicity condition, and social arrangements and individual actions are similarly justifiable, the citizens can fully account for their beliefs and conduct to everyone else with assurance that this avowed reckoning itself will strengthen and not weaken the public understanding. The maintenance of the social order does not depend on historically accidental or institutionalized delusions, or other mistaken beliefs about how its institutions work. Publicity ensures, so far as the feasible design of institutions can allow, that free and equal persons are in a position to know and to accept the background social influences that shape their conception of themselves as persons, as well as their character and conception of their good. Being in this position is a precondition of freedom; it means that nothing is or need be hidden.[13]

Thus, given the circumstances of justice, the full publicity condition applies only to the principles of political and social justice and not to all moral notions. Now, although moderate scarcity may possibly be overcome or largely mitigated, justice as fairness assumes that deep and pervasive differences of religious, philosophical, and ethical doctrine remain. For many philosophical and moral notions public agreement cannot be reached; the consensus to which publicity applies is limited in scope to the public moral constitution and the fundamental terms of social cooperation. That citizens in a well-ordered society can agree before one another on principles of justice and recognize their institutions to be just means that they have also agreed that, for certain parts of their common life, considerations of justice are to have a special place. Other reasons are taken not to be appropriate, although elsewhere they may have a governing role, say, within the life of associations. In public questions, ways of reasoning and rules of evidence for reaching true general beliefs that help settle whether institutions are just should be of a kind that everyone can recognize. Although, in a democratic society under modern conditions, these norms are the shared principles and practices of common sense and science (when not controversial), to apply them to other convictions is a different matter.

To conclude: the conception of a well-ordered society includes and generalizes the idea of religious liberty; it assigns to people's conception of the good a public status analogous to that of religion. Although a well-ordered society is divided and pluralistic, its citizens have nevertheless reached an understanding on principles to regulate their basic institutions. While they cannot achieve agreement in all things, the public agreement on questions of political and social justice supports ties of civic friendship and secures the bonds of association.

II

I now consider how the publicity condition is represented in the original position and examine some queries by way of clarification. Actually, the representation of publicity (at any level) is quite straightforward: we simply require the parties as agents of construction to assess conceptions of justice, subject to the constraint that the principles they agree to must serve as a public conception of justice in the stipulated sense. Principles which might work quite well provided they were not publicly acknowledged (as defined at the first level) or provided the general beliefs upon which they are founded are not commonly understood, or which would be recognized as fallacious (as defined by the second level) are to be rejected. Thus the parties must evaluate the social and psychological consequences of various kinds of public knowledge against a certain background of common beliefs, and these consequences will affect which conception of justice they adopt, all things considered.

Since the representation of publicity seems simple enough, it is more instructive to take up a few points that naturally arise. To begin with, even the first level of publicity cannot be satisfied in society unless the parties also agree upon rules of evidence and forms of reasoning to be used in deciding whether existing institutions fulfill the principles of justice. An agreement on a conception of justice is fruitless in the absence of an understanding about the application of its principles. Now, given the subjective circumstances of justice (the existence of deep and pervasive religious and philosophical differences, and the like), the admissible grounds for holding institutions just or unjust must be limited to those allowed by forms of reasoning accepted by common sense, including the procedures of science when generally accepted. Otherwise no effective undertaking has been made. In a well-ordered society citizens' judgments of their basic institutions in questions of justice rest on common knowledge and on shared practices of inquiry. As I have noted, these restrictions apply only to political and social justice. On philosophical or religious or other grounds people may, of course, think certain institutions and policies wrong, but when their beliefs are not commonly based (in the sense defined), they refrain from urging these considerations. The claims of justice have priority and are accepted as decisive in questions concerning the design of the basic structure. The parties recognize, then, that the agreement in the original position has two parts: first, an agreement on principles of justice and, second, a companion agreement on ways of reasoning and rules for weighing evidence which govern the application of those principles. The subjective circumstances of justice limit this companion agreement to the shared beliefs and the recognized procedures of science and common sense.

These remarks are connected with the restrictions contained in the veil of ignorance, as follows. The second level of full publicity is that the general beliefs of social theory and moral psychology relied on by the parties in order to rank conceptions of justice must also be publicly known. Citizens in a well-ordered society know what beliefs are thought to support the recognized principles of justice and belong, therefore, to their complete public justification. This presupposes that, when the original position is set up, we stipulate that the parties must reason only from general beliefs that are suitably common. Thus, the question arises: what is the reason for limiting the parties to these beliefs and not allowing them to take into account all true beliefs? Surely some religious and philosophical doctrines must be true, even if they merely deny other false or incoherent doctrines. Why isn't the most reasonable conception that which is founded on the whole truth and not simply on a part of it, much less on merely commonly based beliefs that happen to be publicly accepted at any given time, for these presumably contain at least some error?

A fully adequate answer to this question involves a number of matters that I cannot go into here. Therefore I restrict my reply to the practical answer implicit in what has already been said.[14] In view of the practical task of political philosophy, it would be a mistake to dismiss this answer as merely practical. But to proceed: as I shall note in the last lecture, Kantian constructivism allows us to say that the (or a) most reasonable conception of justice (should one or more exist) is the conception that the parties would adopt were they to know all the relevant and true beliefs concerning human nature and social theory. This conception of justice has a natural preeminence. It is essential to see, however, that not even this conception is accepted on the basis of the whole truth, if the whole truth is to include the truths of religion and philosophy and of moral and political doctrine. By assumption, in a well-ordered democratic society under modern conditions, there is no settled and enduring agreement on these matters; this stipulation is contained in the subjective circumstances of justice. If we ask why these circumstances are assumed, the reply is that, unlike the objective circumstances of moderate scarcity, which might be overcome, the subjective circumstances seem

bound to obtain in the absence of a sustained and coercive use of state power that aims to enforce the requisite unanimity. There is no alternative, then, to founding a conception of justice suitable for a well-ordered democratic society on but a part of the truth, and not the whole, or, more specifically, on our present commonly based and shared beliefs, as above defined.

It is important to observe that this practical answer does not imply either skepticism or indifference about religious, philosophical, or moral doctrines. We do not say that they are all doubtful or false, or address questions to which truth and falsehood do not apply. Instead, long historical experience suggests, and many plausible reflections confirm, that on such doctrines reasoned and uncoerced agreement is not to be expected. Religious and philosophical views express outlooks toward the world and our life with one another, severally and collectively, as a whole. Our individual and associative points of view, intellectual affinities and affective attachments, are too diverse, especially in a free democratic society, to allow of lasting and reasoned agreement. Many conceptions of the world can plausibly be constructed from different standpoints. Diversity naturally arises from our limited powers and distinct perspectives; it is unrealistic to suppose that all our differences are rooted solely in ignorance and perversity, or else in the rivalries that result from scarcity. Justice as fairness tries to construct a conception of justice that takes deep and unresolvable differences on matters of fundamental significance as a permanent condition of human life. Indeed, this condition may have its good side, if only we can delineate the character of social arrangements that enable us to appreciate its possible benefits.

One final comment: in order to explain why the veil of ignorance excludes certain kinds of beliefs, even when we as individuals are convinced they are true, I have cited the public role that a conception of justice has in a well-ordered society. Because its principles are to serve as a shared point of view among citizens with opposing religions, philosophical and moral convictions, as well as diverse conceptions of the good, this point of view needs to be appropriately impartial among those differences. Now this brings out in striking fashion the practical purposes and social role that a conception of social justice must fulfill. The very content of the first principles of justice, in contrast with the content of derivative standards and precepts, is determined in part by the practical task of political philosophy. We are accustomed to the idea that secondary norms and working criteria, by which our moral views are applied, must be adjusted to the normal requirements of social life as well as to the limited capacities of human reasoning, and the like. But we tend to regard these adjustments as made in the light of various first principles, or a single such principle. First principles themselves are not widely regarded as affected by practical limitations and social requirements. In Kantian constructivism at least, the situation is different, as we shall see next time: the first principles of justice are thought to depend on such practical considerations.

III

Let us now turn to freedom and equality. I have said that citizens in a well-ordered society regard themselves as free and equal moral persons. Last time we took up the notion of moral persons as characterized by two moral powers: the capacity to act from a sense of justice, and a capacity to form and rationally to pursue a conception of the good. Moral persons are moved by two corresponding highest-order interests to develop and to exercise these powers. We surveyed how moral personality is represented in the original position by elements falling under the Reasonable and the Rational and how in turn this distinction connects with the contrast between Rational and Full Autonomy.

I begin with freedom: I said that citizens in a well-ordered society view themselves as free in two ways. First of all, they hold themselves entitled to make claims on the design of social institutions in the name of their highest-order interests and final ends, when these ends lie within certain limits. We can elaborate this by saying: citizens think of themselves as self-originating sources of valid claims. Provided their final ends are not things directly contrary to the public principles of justice, these ends along with their highest-order interests support such claims, the weight of which may depend, of course, on particular circumstances. People are self-originating sources of claims in the sense that their claims carry weight on their own without being derived from prior duties or obligations owed to society or to other persons, or, finally, as derived from, or assigned to, their particular social role. Claims that are said to be founded on duties to self, if some hold that there are such duties, are counted as self-originating for the purposes of a conception of social justice.

Thus, one aspect of freedom is that of the person as a self-originating source of claims. We can see this by contrasting this basis of claims with one derived from our social role, for example, that of claims implied by the duties we must discharge in certain positions of authority, or of those which result from obligations we have assumed. Again, people who act as agents for others have rights and powers dependent upon the rights and intentions of those who have authorized them as their agents. To take the extreme case, slaves are human beings who are not counted as self-originating sources of claims at all; any such claims originate with their owners or in the rights of a certain class in society. Of course, this extreme condition is usually mitigated to some degree, but even when the legal system allows slaves to originate claims, the explanation may rest not on claims that slaves have as moral persons

but on the recognition of the unhappy consequences for the rest of society of an extreme institution of slavery. The contrast with slavery makes clear why counting moral personality itself as a source of claims is an aspect of freedom.

A second aspect of freedom, as I described it last time, is that, as free persons, citizens recognize one another as having the moral power to have a conception of the good. This means that they do not view themselves as inevitably tied to the pursuit of the particular conception of the good and its final ends which they espouse at any given time.[15] Instead, as citizens, they are regarded as, in general, capable of revising and changing this conception on reasonable and rational grounds. Thus it is held to be permissible for citizens to stand apart from conceptions of the good and to survey and assess their various final ends; indeed this must be done whenever these ends conflict with the principles of justice, for in that case they must be revised. And here I should explain that by a conception of the good is meant not merely a system of final ends but also a view about one's relation to others and to the world which makes these ends appropriate.

In sum, then, citizens as free persons have the right to view their persons as independent and not identified with any particular system of ends. Given their moral power to form, to revise, and rationally to pursue a conception of the good, their public identity as a moral person and a self-originating source of claims is not affected by changes over time in their conceptions of the good, at least so long as these changes are in certain ways continuous and have suitable explanations. These remarks are unhappily extremely vague; their only purpose, however, is to indicate the conception of the person connected with the public conception of justice in a well-ordered society, and so with the principles of justice that apply to its basic institutions. By contrast, citizens in their personal affairs, or within the internal life of associations, may regard their ends and aspirations differently. They may have attachments and loves that they believe they would not, or could not, stand apart from; and they might regard it as unthinkable for them to view themselves without certain religious and philosophical convictions and commitments. But none of this need affect the conception of the person connected with society's public conception of justice and its ideal of social cooperation. Within different contexts we can assume diverse points of view toward our person without contradiction so long as these points of view cohere together when circumstances require. As always, our focus here is on the public conception that underlies the principles of social justice.[16]

A third aspect of freedom I shall only mention here: namely, as responsibility for ends. Very roughly, this means that, given just background institutions and the provision for all of a fair index of primary goods (as required by the principles of justice), citizens are capable of adjusting their aims and ambitions in the light of what they can reasonably expect and of restricting their claims in matters of justice to certain kinds of things. They recognize that the weight of their claims is not given by the strength or intensity of their wants and desires, even when these are rational. But to explain these matters here would take us too far afield.[17] I shall consider only two aspects of freedom: one as self-originating source of claims, the other as independence.

I have yet to state the sense in which citizens in a well-ordered society are equal moral persons. But before I do this, let's introduce a further idealization of the notion of a well-ordered society. Our aim is to ascertain the conception of justice most appropriate for a democratic society in which citizens conceive of themselves in a certain way. So let's add that all citizens are fully cooperating members of society over the course of a complete life. This means that everyone has sufficient intellectual powers to play a normal part in society, and no one suffers from unusual needs that are especially difficult to fulfill, for example, unusual and costly medical requirements. Of course, care for those with such requirements is a pressing practical question. But at this initial stage, the fundamental problem of social justice arises between those who are full and active and morally conscientious participants in society, and directly or indirectly associated together throughout a complete life. Therefore, it is sensible to lay aside certain difficult complications. If we can work out a theory that covers the fundamental case, we can try to extend it to other cases later. Plainly a theory that fails for the fundamental case is of no use at all.

To return to equality, we say: everyone is equally capable of understanding and complying with the public conception of justice; therefore all are capable of honoring the principles of justice and of being full participants in social cooperation throughout their lives. On this basis, together with each person's being a self-originating source of valid claims, all view themselves as equally worthy of being represented in any procedure that is to determine the principles of justice that are to regulate the basic institutions of their society. This conception of equal worth is founded on the equally sufficient capacity (which I assume to be realized) to understand and to act from the public conception of social cooperation.

Now some citizens have a deeper understanding of justice than others, and a greater facility in applying its principles and making reasonable decisions, especially in hard cases. The judicial virtues depend upon special gifts and acquired wisdom. Equality means that, although these virtues may render some better qualified than others for certain more demanding offices and positions (those of a judicial kind, for example), nevertheless, given people's actual place in just institutions, including the status all have as equal citizens, everyone's sense of justice is equally sufficient relative to what is asked of them. This suffices for everyone to be equally worthy of representation in a procedure that is to settle the fundamental terms of social cooperation, given that all are able to be fully co-operating members of society over a complete life.

Finally, citizens in a well-ordered society are in their conduct (more or less) above reproach. Whatever their actions, all conform to the acknowledged requirements of justice for the most part. This follows from the assumption that everyone has an equally effective sense of justice. The usual differences in the degree to which people are open to censure in matters of justice do not obtain. Nevertheless, certain social and economic inequalities presumably exist, but, whatever their explanation, they do not match differences in the degree to which people comply with just arrangements. Since justice regulates these inequalities, the public conception, whatever it is, cannot read: to persons according to their moral worth. This much follows from the general description of a well-ordered society.

IV

It remains to consider the representation of freedom and equality in the original position. I observe first, however, that the two powers of moral persons are represented in a purely formal way. Thus while the parties as agents of construction are assumed to have an effective sense of justice, this is taken to mean that they have a capacity to understand and apply the various principles of justice that are under discussion, as well as a sufficiently strong desire to act upon whatever principles are eventually adopted. Since these principles are not yet agreed to, the parties' sense of justice lacks content. Their formal sense of justice simply ensures that, as members of society, they can follow the most reasonable conception of justice, everything taken into account. The original agreement meets this condition on a bona fide undertaking.

The second capacity of moral personality is likewise represented in a formal fashion. Although the parties have the power to develop, revise, and pursue rationally a conception of the good, they do not know its particular final ends. The capacity for such a conception is assumed to be realized in society, and indeed to have some determinate content. These restrictions on information, which are consequences of the veil of ignorance, require us to characterize the parties' moral powers in a formal way.

To prevent misunderstanding, I reiterate what I said last time: that the motivation of the parties is appropriate to the representation of moral persons. Once such persons are characterized by the moral powers, it is

Engraving of Kant.

proper that they should strive to realize and exercise these capacities, and be moved by what I have called their "highest-order" interests. This leads us to say that the parties are mutually disinterested, that is, that they aim to secure the interests of their moral personality and to try to guarantee the objective social conditions that enable them rationally to assess their final ends and to do their part in cooperating with others in fair social arrangements to produce the all-purpose means to achieve them. Since the parties are determinate persons, they also try to ensure their own ability to pursue their particular aims and to protect the objects of their affections, whatever these are. Given the limits on information, they settle an index of primary goods as the most effective way of achieving these objectives.

Now the freedom of persons as self-originating sources of claims is represented by not requiring the parties to justify the claims they wish to make. Whether they are citizens acting as deputies for themselves or whether they are trustees, they are free to act in the best interests of whomever they represent within the framework of reasonable constraints embedded in the original position. It belongs to the parties' rational autonomy that there are no given antecedent principles external to their point of view to which they are bound. The interests they try to advance need not be derived from some prior duty or obligation, either to other persons

or to society. Nor do the parties recognize certain intrinsic values as known by rational intuition, for example, the perfectionist values of human excellence or of truth and beauty. This is how freedom as originating claims is represented. Although some or all in society may recognize these values, their acceptance is, from the standpoint of political and social justice, self-imposed, or else a consequence of the principles of justice still to be adopted.

Freedom as independence is represented in how the parties are moved to give priority to guaranteeing the social conditions for realizing their highest-order interests, and in their having grounds for agreement despite the severe restrictions on information implied by the veil of ignorance. To explain this, consider the objection that, since these restrictions exclude knowledge of final ends, no rational agreement is possible. The reply to this objection is that it ties the aspirations of the person too closely to the particular conception of the good that is being pursued at any given time. As free persons have been characterized, rational deliberation is still possible even when the final ends of this conception are unknown. The explanation is that free persons have a regulative and effective desire to be a certain kind of person, so that the veil of ignorance does not eliminate all bases for deliberation. For if it did, the parties would lack the highest-order interests in guaranteeing the objective social conditions for developing and exercising their moral powers and in securing the normally essential all-purpose means for advancing their plan of life.

In a Kantian constructivist view, then, it is a feature attributed to persons (for the purposes of a conception of social justice) that they can stand above and critically survey their own final ends by reference to a notion of the Reasonable and the Rational. In this sense, they are independent from and moved by considerations other than those given by their particular conception of the good. The veil of ignorance forces the parties to do something analogous, but on a more abstract level: since they are ignorant of their final ends and of much else, they must try to work out which conception of justice is most likely to secure the social conditions and all-purpose means necessary to realize their highest-order interests and determinate but unknown conception of the good.

A further feature of a Kantian doctrine is that it aims at the thickest possible veil of ignorance.[18] This may be explained as follows: there are two distinct rationales for excluding information, and one leads to a thicker veil of ignorance than the other. The rationale drawn from Hume's "judicious spectator" is designed to prevent the parties from reasoning according to the principle: to persons according to their threat advantage. By denying everyone a knowledge of these contingencies, a kind of impartiality is achieved. We begin by allowing the parties all information about themselves: their social position, realized natural assets, their ends and aims, and so on. Enough information is then ruled out to achieve impartiality in the sense of the elimination of threat advantage. The veil of ignorance is thin, because no more knowledge is excluded than is necessary to secure this result; the parties still know the general configuration of society, its political structure and economic organization, and so on. So long as the relevant particular facts are unknown, the influence of threat advantage is eliminated.

The Kantian rationale proceeds in the opposite direction: it starts by allowing the parties no information and then adds just enough so that they can make a rational agreement. The first principles of justice should be those of rationally autonomous agents moved to secure the conditions for the development and exercise of their moral powers, and their determinate (but unknown) final ends. It does not suffice that they are impartial in the sense of being unable to take advantage of their superior position (if such they have). The parties are not to be influenced by any particular information that is not part of their representation as free and equal moral persons with a determinate (but unknown) conception of the good, unless this information is necessary for a rational agreement to be reached. And so the veil of ignorance is presumably thicker: the Humean rationale will not exclude certain particular information; the Kantian will not include it. Even if these different restrictions led to the same principles, the thicker veil of ignorance would still be preferable, since these principles are then connected more clearly to the conception of free and equal moral persons. Were we to allow knowledge of the general institutional features of society, we would permit particular information about the outcome of society's history to obscure how intimately the principles adopted are tied to the conception of the person. And should this information yield different principles, it would do so on inappropriate grounds. In either case it should be excluded in order to have a lucid representation of the notion of freedom that characterizes a Kantian view.

V

The representation of equality is an easy matter: we simply describe all the parties in the same way and situate them equally, that is, symmetrically with respect to one another. Everyone has the same rights and powers in the procedure for reaching agreement. Now it is essential to justice as fairness that the original position be fair between equal moral persons so that this fairness can transfer to the principles adopted. Let's recall, then, why the original position is said to be fair.

To begin with, we take the basic structure of society as the first subject of justice. Next, we say that to determine first principles for this subject, the only relevant feature of human beings is their having the minimum sufficient capacity for moral personality (as expressed by the two moral powers), given that, as I suppose, all are fully capable of being fully cooperating members of society over a complete life. Finally, we assume that persons equal in all relevant respects are to be represented equally. These presumptions ensure that the original position is fair between equal moral persons and, therefore, that it correctly represents how the members of a well-ordered society regard one another. Doubts about the fairness of the original position are perhaps best dealt with by defense against various objections.

For example, it is sometimes said that the original position is unfair to those with superior natural endowments, since, by excluding knowledge of such gifts, it precludes them from affecting the outcome. Again, justice as fairness is said to be unfair to those who have conscientiously acquired certain skills in the expectation of benefiting from them. But these objections fail, I think, to allow for the special features of the problem of background justice. Keep in mind that we seek principles to regulate the basic structure into which we are born to lead a complete life. The thesis is that the only relevant feature in connection with these principles is the capacity for moral personality in the sense defined. The way in which we think about fairness in everyday life ill prepares us for the great shift in perspective required for considering the justice of the basic structure itself.

Once this is understood, we must distinguish between features of persons relevant for the justice of the basic structure and features relevant for the fairness of the actual distributions of benefits that come about within this structure as a result of the particular decisions and activities of individuals and associations. These distributions arise from the honoring of legitimate expectations and are, of course, affected by what people actually decide to do, given their knowledge of existing institutional rules, as well as by the various realized skills and talents of individuals. A further essential distinction is between the unequal distribution of natural assets, which is simply a natural fact and neither just nor unjust, and the way the basic structure of society makes use of these natural differences and permits them to affect the social fortune of citizens, their opportunities in life, and the actual terms of cooperation between them. Plainly it is the way that social institutions use natural differences, and allow accident and chance to operate, which defines the problem of social justice.[19]

Now the original position is seen to be fair between equal moral persons once we grant that the natural distribution of abilities does not support a claim, grounded solely on an individual person's place in this distribution, to any particular scheme of background institutions, to a scheme that would favor that person's special endowments over the special endowments of others. This seems perfectly obvious. The veil of ignorance reflects this idea by excluding all knowledge of these matters in the original position. Neither the more nor the less fortunate as such has a claim to be especially favored. The basic structure, and the entitlements it generates and the legitimate expectations it honors, are to be governed by principles of justice that the parties adopt as representatives of free and equal moral persons.

In justice as fairness, then, there is no prior and independent notion of desert, perfectionist or intuitionist, that could override or restrict the agreement of the parties as agents of construction. To suppose that there is such a notion would violate the equality and autonomy of free and equal moral persons, which the rational autonomy of the parties in part represents. Thus citizens come to deserve this or that by their actual decisions and efforts within an on-going background system of cooperation with publicly announced rules that support legitimate expectations and acquired claims.[20] The only available notion of desert for judging this background system is derivative from the principles agreed to by the parties. Once this is recognized, the original position is seen as fair—or more accurately, as fair within a Kantian view, given its conception of free and equal persons, and of their autonomy.

VI

As I did in the first lecture, I conclude with a few general remarks. First, the guiding idea in representing persons is that, so far as possible, the parties in the original position as agents of construction should be constrained or influenced in the adoption of principles solely by features that fall under the Reasonable and the Rational and reflect the freedom and equality of moral persons. The original position thereby serves to connect, in the most explicit possible manner, the way the members of a well-ordered society view themselves as citizens with the content of their public conception of justice.

Another observation is that, although I regard justice as fairness as a Kantian view, it differs from Kant's doctrine in important respects. Here I note that justice as fairness assigns a certain primacy to the social; that is, the first subject of justice is the basic structure of society, and citizens must arrive at a public understanding on a conception of justice for this subject first. This understanding is interpreted via the unanimous agreement of the parties in the original position. By contrast, Kant's account of the Categorical Imperative applies to the personal maxims of sincere and conscientious individuals in everyday life. To be sure, in the course of testing such maxims we are to com-

pare social worlds, that is, the social world that results when everyone follows the proposed maxim, as if by a law of nature, with the social world in which the contradictory maxim is followed. But this comparison of social worlds is undertaken singly by each person and for the purpose of judging a given personal maxim. Thus Kant proceeds from the particular, even personal, case of everyday life; he assumed that this process carried out correctly would eventually yield a coherent and sufficiently complete system of principles, including principles of social justice. Justice as fairness moves in quite the reverse fashion: its construction starts from a unanimous collective agreement regulating the basic structure of society within which all personal and associational decisions are to be made in conformity with this prior undertaking.

Finally, I have stressed the full publicity condition and its consequences for a conception of justice. Now this condition is related to the wide, as opposed to the narrow, view of the social role of morality.[21] The narrow view restricts this role to achieving the more or less minimum conditions of effective social cooperation, for example, by specifying standards to settle competing claims and setting up rules for coordinating and stabilizing social arrangements. Moral norms are regarded as inhibiting self- or group-centered tendencies, and aimed at encouraging less limited sympathies. Any moral doctrine accepts these requirements in some form, but they do not involve the full publicity condition. Once this condition is imposed, a moral conception assumes a wide role as part of public culture. Not only are its first principles embodied in political and social institutions and public traditions of their interpretation, but the derivation of citizens' rights, liberties, and opportunities invokes a certain conception of their person. In this way citizens are made aware of and educated to this conception. They are presented with a way of regarding themselves that otherwise they would most likely never have been able to entertain. Thus the realization of the full publicity condition provides the social milieu within which the notion of full autonomy can be understood and within which its ideal of the person can elicit an effective desire to be that kind of person. This educative role of the moral conception defines the wide view.

Now Kant often notes the publicity requirement in some form, but he seems to think that the conception of ourselves as fully autonomous is already given to us by the Fact of Reason, that is, by our recognition that the moral law is supremely authoritative for us as reasonable and rational beings.[22] Thus this conception of ourselves is implicit in individual moral consciousness, and the background social conditions for its realization are not emphasized or made part of the moral doctrine itself. Justice as fairness departs from Kant, then, both in the primacy it assigns to the social and in the further aspect of this primacy contained in the full publicity condition. I believe these departures enable justice as fairness to avoid some of the faults that Dewey found in Kant's view.

Construction and Objectivity

In the preceding lectures I sketched the main idea of Kantian constructivism, which is to establish a connection between the first principles of justice and the conception of moral persons as free and equal. These first principles are used to settle the appropriate understanding of freedom and equality for a modern democratic society. The requisite connection is provided by a procedure of construction in which rationally autonomous agents subject to reasonable conditions agree to public principles of justice. With the sketch of these ideas behind us, I consider in this final lecture how a Kantian doctrine interprets the notion of objectivity in terms of a suitably constructed social point of view that is authoritative with respect to all individual and associational points of view. This rendering of objectivity implies that, rather than think of the principles of justice as true, it is better to say that they are the principles most reasonable for us, given our conception of persons as free and equal, and fully cooperating members of a democratic society. [Here 'reasonable' is used, as explained later (569/70), in contrast with 'true' as understood in rational intuitionism, and not, as previously (528-530), with 'rational', as in the notion of rational autonomy.]

I

To fix ideas, let's look back roughly a hundred years to Henry Sidgwick. *The Methods of Ethics* (first edition 1874) is, I believe, the outstanding achievement in modern moral theory.[23] By "moral theory" I mean the systematic and comparative study of moral conceptions, starting with those which historically and by current estimation seem to be the most important. Moral philosophy includes moral theory, but takes as its main question justification and how it is to be conceived and resolved; for example, whether it is to be conceived as an epistemological problem (as in rational intuitionism) or as a practical problem (as in Kantian constructivism). Sidgwick's *Methods* is the first truly academic work in moral theory, modern in both method and spirit. Treating ethics as a discipline to be studied like any other branch of knowledge, it defines and carries out in exemplary fashion, if not for the first time, some of the comprehensive comparisons that constitute moral theory. By pulling together the work of previous writers, and through its influence on G. E. Moore and others, this work defined much of the framework of subsequent moral philosophy. Sidgwick's originality lies in his conception and mode of presentation of the subject and in his recognition of the significance of moral theory for moral philosophy.

It is natural, then, that the limitations of *Methods* have been as important as its merits. Of these limitations I wish to mention two. First, Sidgwick gives relatively little attention to the conception of the person and the social role of morality as main parts of a moral doctrine. He starts with the idea of a method of ethics as a method specified by certain first principles, principles by which we are to arrive at a judgment about what we ought to do. He takes for granted that these methods aim at reaching true judgments that hold for all rational minds. Of course, he thinks it is best to approach the problem of justification only when a broad understanding of moral theory has been achieved. In the preface of the first edition of *Methods* he explains that he wants to resist the natural urgency to discover the true method of ascertaining what it is right to do. He wishes instead to expound, from a neutral position and as impartially as possible, the different methods found in the moral consciousness of humankind and worked into familiar historical systems.[24] But these detailed expositions—necessary as they are—are merely preparation for comparing the various methods and evaluating them by criteria that any rational method that aims at truth must satisfy.

But a consequence of starting with methods of ethics defined as methods that seek truth is not only that it interprets justification as an epistemological problem, but also that it is likely to restrict attention to the first principles of moral conceptions and how they can be known. First principles are however only one element of a moral conception; of equal importance are its conception of the person and its view of the social role of morality. Until these other elements are clearly recognized, the ingredients of a constructivist doctrine are not at hand. It is characteristic of Sidgwick's *Methods* that the social role of morality and the conception of the person receive little notice. And so the possibility of constructivism was closed to him.

Sidgwick overlooked this possibility because of a second limitation: he failed to recognize that Kant's doctrine (and perfectionism also for that matter) is a distinctive method of ethics. He regarded the categorical imperative as a purely formal principle, or what he called "the principle of equity": whatever is right for one person is right for all similar persons in relevantly similar circumstances. This principle Sidgwick accepts, but, since it is plainly not a sufficient basis for a moral view, Kant's doctrine could not be counted a substantive method (209/10). This formal reading of Kant, together with the dismissal of perfectionism, led Sidgwick to reduce the traditional moral conceptions essentially to three main methods: rational egoism, (pluralistic) intuitionism, and classical utilitarianism. Surely he was right to restrict himself to a few conceptions so that each could be explored in considerable detail. Only in this way can depth of understanding be achieved. But rational egoism, which he accepted as a method of ethics, is really not a moral conception at all, but rather a challenge to all such conceptions, although no less interesting for that. Left with only (pluralistic) intuitionism and classical utilitarianism as methods of ethics in the usual sense, it is no surprise that utilitarianism seemed superior to Sidgwick, given his desire for unity and system in a moral doctrine.

Since Kant's view is the leading historical example of a constructivist doctrine, the result once again is that constructivism finds no place in *Methods*. Nor is the situation altered if we include another leading representative work, F. H. Bradley's *Ethical Studies* (first edition 1876); following Hegel, Bradley likewise regarded Kant's ethics as purely formal and lacking in content and, therefore, to be assigned to an early stage of the dialectic as an inadequate view.[25] The result of these formal interpretations of Kant is that constructivism was not recognized as a moral conception to be studied and assimilated into moral theory. Nor was this lack made good in the first half of this century; for in this period, beginning with Moore's *Principia Ethica* (1903), interest centered mainly on philosophical analysis and its bearing on justification regarded as an epistemological problem and on the question whether its conclusions support or deny the notion of moral truth. During this time, however, utilitarianism and intuitionism made important advances. A proper understanding of Kantian constructivism, on a par with our grasp of these views, is still to be achieved.

II

Let us now try to deepen our understanding of Kantian constructivism by contrasting it with what I shall call *rational intuitionism.* This doctrine has, of course, been expressed in various ways; but in one form or another it dominated moral philosophy from Plato and Aristotle onwards until it was challenged by Hobbes and Hume, and, I believe, in a very different way by Kant. To simplify matters, I take rational intuitionism to be the view exemplified in the English tradition by Clarke and Price, Sidgwick and Moore, and formulated in its minimum essentials by W. D. Ross.[26] With qualifications, it was accepted by Leibniz and Wolff in the guise of perfectionism, and Kant knows of it in this form.

For our purposes here, rational intuitionism may be summed up by two theses: first, the basic moral concepts of the right and the good, and the moral worth of persons, are not analyzable in terms of nonmoral concepts (although possibly analyzable in terms of one another); and, second, first principles of morals (whether one or many), when correctly stated, are self-evident propositions about what kinds of considerations are good grounds for applying one of the three basic moral concepts, that is, for asserting that something is (intrinsically) good, or that a certain action is the right

thing to do, or that a certain trait of character has moral worth. These two theses imply that the agreement in judgment which is so essential for an effective public conception of justice is founded on the recognition of self-evident truths about good reasons. And what these reasons are is fixed by a moral order that is prior to and independent of our conception of the person and the social role of morality. This order is given by the nature of things and is known, not by sense, but by rational intuition. It is with this idea of moral truth that the idea of first principles as reasonable will be contrasted.

It should be observed that rational intuitionism is compatible with a variety of contents for the first principles of a moral conception. Even classical utilitarianism, which Sidgwick was strongly inclined to favor (although he could not see how to eliminate rational egoism as a rival) was sometimes viewed by him as following from three principles each self-evident in its own right.[27] In brief, these three propositions were: the principle of equity so-called: that it cannot be right to treat two different persons differently merely on the ground of their being numerically different individuals; a principle of rational prudence: that mere difference of position in time is not by itself a reasonable ground for giving more regard to well-being at one moment than to well-being at another; and a principle of rational benevolence: the good of one person is of no more importance from the point of view of the universe than the good of any other person. These three principles, when combined with the principle that, as reasonable beings, we are bound to aim at good generally and not at any particular part of it, Sidgwick thought yielded the principle of utility: namely, to maximize the net balance of happiness. And this principle, like those from which it followed, he was tempted to hold as self-evident.

Of all recent versions of rational intuitionism, the appeal to self-evidence is perhaps most striking in Moore's so-called "ideal utilitarianism" in *Principia Ethica* (1903). A consequence of Moore's principle of organic unity is that his view is extremely pluralistic; there are few if any useful first principles, and distinct kinds of cases are to be decided by intuition as they arise. Moore held a kind of Platonic atomism:[28] moral concepts (along with other concepts) are subsisting and independent entities grasped by the mind. That pleasure and beauty are good, and that different combinations of them alone or together with other good things are also good, and to what degree, are truths known by intuition: by seeing with the mind's eye how these separate and distinct objects (universals) are (timelessly) related. This picture is even more vivid in the early philosophy of mathematics of Bertrand Russell, who talks of searching for the indefinable concepts of mathematics with a mental telescope (as one might look for a planet).[29]

Now my aim in recalling these matters is to point out that rational intuitionism, as illustrated by Sidgwick, Moore, and Ross, is sharply opposed to a constructivist conception along Kantian lines. That Kant would have rejected Hume's psychological naturalism as heteronomous is clear.[30] I believe that the contrast with rational intuitionism, no matter what the content of the view (whether utilitarian, perfectionist, or pluralist) is even more instructive. It is less obvious that for Kant rational intuitionism is also heteronomous. The reason is that from the first thesis of rational intuitionism, the basic moral concepts are conceptually independent of natural concepts, and first principles are independent of the natural world and, as grasped by rational intuition, are regarded as synthetic a priori. This may seem to make these principles not heteronomous. Yet it suffices for heteronomy that these principles obtain in virtue of relations among objects the nature of which is not affected or determined by the conception of the person. Kant's idea of autonomy requires that there exist no such order of given objects determining the first principles of right and justice among free and equal moral persons. Heteronomy obtains not only when first principles are fixed by the special psychological constitution of human nature, as in Hume, but also when they are fixed by an order of universals or concepts grasped by rational intuition, as in Plato's realm of forms or in Leibniz's hierarchy of perfections.[31] Perhaps I should add, to prevent misunderstanding, that a Kantian doctrine of autonomy need not deny that the procedures by which first principles are selected are synthetic a priori. This thesis, however, must be properly interpreted. The essential idea is that such procedures must be suitably founded on practical reason, or, more exactly, on notions which characterize persons as reasonable and rational and which are incorporated into the way in which, as such persons, they represent to themselves their free and equal moral personality. Put another way, first principles of justice must issue from a conception of the person through a suitable representation of that conception as illustrated by the procedure of construction in justice as fairness.

Thus in a Kantian doctrine a relatively complex conception of the person plays a central role. By contrast, rational intuitionism requires but a sparse notion of the person, founded on the self as knower. This is because the content of first principles is already fixed, and the only requirements on the self are to be able to know what these principles are and to be moved by this knowledge. A basic assumption is that the recognition of first principles as true and self-evident gives rise, in a being capable of rationally intuiting these principles, to a desire to act from them for their own sake. Moral motivation is defined by reference to desires that have a special kind of cause, namely, the intuitive grasp of first principles.[32] This sparse conception of the person joined with its moral psychology characterizes the rational intuitionism of Sidgwick, Moore, and Ross, al-

though there is nothing that forces rational intuitionism to so thin a notion. The point is rather that, in rational intuitionism in contrast to a Kantian view, since the content of first principles is already given, a more complex conception of the person, of a kind adequate to determine the content of these principles, together with a suitable moral psychology, is simply unnecessary.

III

Having contrasted Kantian constructivism to rational intuitionism with respect to the idea of a moral order that is prior to and independent from our conception of the person, I now consider a second contrast, namely, how each regards the inevitable limitations that constrain our moral deliberations. The constructionist view accepts from the start that a moral conception can establish but a loose framework for deliberation which must rely very considerably on our powers of reflection and judgment. These powers are not fixed once and for all, but are developed by a shared public culture and hence shaped by that culture. In justice as fairness this means that the principles adopted by the parties in the original position are designed by them to achieve a public and workable agreement on matters of social justice which suffices for effective and fair social cooperation. From the standpoint of the parties as agents of construction, the first principles of justice are not thought to represent, or to be true of, an already given moral order, as rational intuitionism supposes. The essential point is that a conception of justice fulfills its social role provided that citizens equally conscientious and sharing roughly the same beliefs find that, by affirming the framework of deliberation set up by it, they are normally led to a sufficient convergence of opinion. Thus a conception of justice is framed to meet the practical requirements of social life and to yield a public basis in the light of which citizens can justify to one another their common institutions. Such a conception need be only precise enough to achieve this result.

On the constructivist view, the limitations that constrain our moral deliberations affect the requirements of publicity and support the use of priority rules. These limitations also lead us to take the basic structure of a well-ordered society as the first subject of justice and to adopt the primary goods as the basis of interpersonal comparisons. To begin with publicity: at the end of the preceding lecture I mentioned why in a constructivist view first principles are to satisfy the requirements of publicity. The moral conception is to have a wide social role as a part of public culture and is to enable citizens to appreciate and accept the conception of the person as free and equal. Now if it is to play this wide role, a conception's first principles cannot be so complex that they cannot be generally understood and followed in the more important cases. Thus, it is desirable that knowing whether these principles are satisfied, at least with reference to fundamental liberties and basic institutions, should not depend on information difficult to obtain or hard to evaluate. To incorporate these desiderata in a constructivist view, the parties are assumed to take these considerations into account and to prefer (other things equal) principles that are easy to understand and simple to apply. The gain in compliance and willing acceptance by citizens more than makes up for the rough and ready nature of the guiding framework that results and its neglect of certain distinctions and differences. In effect, the parties agree to rule out certain facts as irrelevant in questions of justice concerning the basic structure, even though they recognize that in regard to other cases it may be appropriate to appeal to them. From the standpoint of the original position, eliminating these facts as reasons of social justice sufficiently increases the capacity of the conception to fulfill its social role. Of course, we should keep in mind that the exclusion of such facts as reasons of social justice does not alone entail that they are not reasons in other kinds of situation where different moral notions apply. Indeed, it is not even ruled out that the account of some notions should be constructivist, whereas the account of others is not.

It is evident, then, why a constructivist view such as justice as fairness incorporates into the framework of moral deliberation a number of schematic and practical distinctions as ways that enable us to deal with the inevitable limitations of our moral capacities and the complexity of our social circumstances. The need for such distinctions supports and helps to account for the use of certain priority rules to settle the relative weight of particular kinds of grounds in extremely important cases. Two such rules in justice as fairness are: first, the priority of justice over efficiency (in the sense of Pareto) and the net balance of advantages (summed over all individuals in society), and, second, the priority of the principle of equal liberty (understood in terms of certain enumerated basic liberties) over the second principle of justice.[33] These rules are introduced to handle the complexity of the many prima facie reasons we are ready to cite in everyday life; and their plausibility depends in large part on the first principles to which they are adjoined. But although these rules are intended to narrow the scope of judgment in certain fundamental questions of justice, this scope can never be entirely eliminated, and for many other questions sharp and definite conclusions cannot usually be derived. Sharp and definite conclusions are not needed, however, if sufficient agreement is still forthcoming (TJ 44/5).

Similar considerations apply in beginning with the basic structure of a well-ordered society as the first subject of justice and trying to develop a conception of justice for this case alone. The idea is that this structure plays a very special role in society by establishing what we

may call *background justice;* and if we can find suitable first principles of background justice, we may be able to exclude enough other considerations as irrelevant for this case, so as to develop a reasonably simple and workable conception of justice for the basic structure. The further complexities of everyday cases that cannot be ignored in a more complete moral conception may be dealt with later in the less general situations that occur within the various associations regulated by the basic structure, and in that sense subordinate to it.[34]

Finally, parallel observations hold in finding a feasible basis for interpersonal comparisons of well-being relevant for questions of justice that arise in regard to the basic structure. These comparisons are to be made in terms of primary goods (as defined in the first lecture), which are, so far as possible, certain public features of social institutions and of people's situations with respect to them, such as their rights, liberties, and opportunities, and their income and wealth, broadly understood. This has the consequence that the comparison of citizens' shares in the benefits of social cooperation is greatly simplified and put on a footing less open to dispute.

Thus the reason why a constructivist view uses the schematic or practical distinctions we have just noted is that such distinctions are necessary if a workable conception of justice is to be achieved. These distinctions are incorporated into justice as fairness through the description of the parties as agents of construction and the account of how they are to deliberate. Charged with the task of agreeing to a workable conception of justice designed to achieve a sufficient convergence of opinion, the parties can find no better way in which to carry out this task. They accept the limitations of human life and recognize that at best a conception of justice can establish but a guiding framework for deliberation.

A comparison with classical utilitarianism will highlight what is involved here. On that view, whether stated as a form of rational intuitionism (Sidgwick) or as a form of naturalism (Bentham), every question of right and justice has an answer: whether an institution or action is right depends upon whether it will produce the greatest net balance of satisfaction. We may never be in a position to know the answer, or even to come very near to it, but, granting that a suitable measure of satisfaction exists, there is an answer: a fact of the matter. Of course, utilitarianism recognizes the needs of practice: working precepts and secondary rules are necessary to guide deliberation and coordinate our actions. These norms may be thought of as devised to bring our actions as close as possible to those which would maximize utility, so far as this is feasible. But of course, such rules and precepts are not first principles; they are at best directives that when followed make the results of our conduct approximate to what the principle of utility enjoins. In this sense, our working norms are approximations to something given.

By contrast, justice as fairness, as a constructivist view, holds that not all the moral questions we are prompted to ask in everyday life have answers. Indeed, perhaps only a few of them can be settled by any moral conception that we can understand and apply. Practical limitations impose a more modest aim upon a reasonable conception of justice, namely, to identify the most fundamental questions of justice that can be dealt with, in the hope that, once this is done and just basic institutions established, the remaining conflicts of opinion will not be so deep or widespread that they cannot be compromised. To accept the basic structure as the first subject of justice together with the account of primary goods is a step toward achieving this more modest goal. But in addition, the idea of approximating to moral truth has no place in a constructivist doctrine: the parties in the original position do not recognize any principles of justice as true or correct and so as antecedently given; their aim is simply to select the conception most rational for them, given their circumstances. This conception is not regarded as a workable approximation to the moral facts: there are no such moral facts to which the principles adopted could approximate.

As we have just seen, the differences between constructivism and classical utilitarianism are especially sharp in view of the content of the principle of utility: it always yields an answer that we can at least verbally describe. With the rational (pluralistic) intuitionism of Ross, however, the contrast is less obvious, since Ross's list of self-evident prima facie principles that identify good reasons also specifies but a loose guiding framework of moral deliberation which shares a number of the features of the framework provided by constructivism. But though these resemblances are real, the underlying idea of Ross's view is still essentially different from constructivism. His pluralistic intuitionism rejects utilitarianism (even an ideal utilitarianism) as oversimplifying the given moral facts, especially those concerning the correct weight of special duties and obligations. The complexity of the moral facts in particular kinds of cases is said to force us to recognize that no family of first principles that we can formulate characterizes these facts sufficiently accurately to lead to a definite conclusion. Decision and judgment are almost always to some degree uncertain and must rest with "perception,"[35] that is, with our intuitive estimate of where the greatest balance of prima facie reasons lies in each kind of case. And this perception is that of a balance of reasons each of which is given by an independent moral order known by intuition. The essential contrast with constructivism remains.

IV

Having examined several contrasts between Kantian constructivism and rational intuitionism, we are now in a position to take up a fundamental point suggested by the discussion so far: an essential feature of a constructivist view, as illustrated by justice as fairness, is that its first principles single out what facts citizens in a well-ordered society are to count as reasons of justice. Apart from the procedure of constructing these principles, there are no reasons of justice. Put in another way, whether certain facts are to count as reasons of justice and what their relative force is to be can be ascertained only on the basis of the principles that result from the construction. This connects with the use of pure procedural justice at the highest level. It is, therefore, up to the parties in the original position to decide how simple or complex the moral facts are to be, that is, to decide on the number and complexity of the principles that identify which facts are to be accepted as reasons of justice by citizens in society (see TJ 45). There is nothing parallel to this in rational intuitionism.

This essential feature of constructivism may be obscured by the fact that in justice as fairness the first principles of justice depend upon those general beliefs about human nature and how society works which are allowed to the parties in the original position. First principles are not, in a constructivist view, independent of such beliefs, nor, as some forms of rational intuitionism hold, true in all possible worlds. In particular, they depend on the rather specific features and limitations of human life that give rise to the circumstances of justice.[36] Now, given the way the original position is set up, we can allow, in theory, that, as the relevant general beliefs change, the beliefs we attribute to the parties likewise change, and conceivably also the first principles that would be agreed to. We can say, if we like that *the* (most reasonable) principles of justice are those which would be adopted if the parties possessed all relevant general information and if they were properly to take account of all the practical desiderata required for a workable public conception of justice. Though these principles have a certain preeminence, they are still the outcome of construction. Furthermore, it is important to notice here that no assumptions have been made about a theory of truth. A constructivist view does not require an idealist or a verificationist, as opposed to a realist, account of truth. Whatever the nature of truth in the case of general beliefs about human nature and how society works, a constructivist moral doctrine requires a distinct procedure of construction to identify the first principles of justice. To the extent that Kant's moral doctrine depends upon what to some may appear to be a constructivist account of truth in the ***First Critique*** (I don't mean to imply that such an interpretation is correct), justice as fairness departs from that aspect of Kant's view and seeks to preserve the over-all structure of his moral conception apart from that background.

In the preceding paragraph I said that the way justice as fairness is set up allows the possibility that, as the general beliefs ascribed to the parties in the original position change, the first principles of justice may also change. But I regard this as a mere possibility noted in order to explain the nature of a constructivist view. To elaborate: at the end of the first lecture I distinguished between the roles of a conception of the person and of a theory of human nature, and I remarked that in justice as fairness these are distinct elements and enter at different places. I said that a conception of the person is a companion moral ideal paired with the ideal of a well-ordered society. A theory of human nature and a view of the requirements of social life tell us whether these ideals are feasible, whether it is possible to realize them under normally favorable conditions of human life. Changes in the theory of human nature or in social theory generally which do not affect the feasibility of the ideals of the person and of a well-ordered society do not affect the agreement of the parties in the original position. It is hard to imagine realistically any new knowledge that should convince us that these ideals are not feasible, given what we know about the general nature of the world, as opposed to our particular social and historical circumstances. In fact, the relevant information on these matters must go back a long time and is available to the common sense of any thoughtful and reflective person. Thus such advances in our knowledge of human nature and society as may take place do not affect our moral conception, but rather may be used to implement the application of its first principles of justice and suggest to us institutions and policies better designed to realize them in practice.[37]

In justice as fairness, then, the main ideals of the conception of justice are embedded in the two model-conceptions of the person and of a well-ordered society. And, granting that these ideals are allowed by the theory of human nature and so in that sense feasible, the first principles of justice to which they lead, via the constructivist procedure of the original position, determine the long-term aim of social change. These principles are not, as in rational intuitionism, given by a moral order prior to and independent from our conception of the person and the social role of morality; nor are they, as in some naturalist doctrines, to be derived from the truths of science and adjusted in accordance with advances in human psychology and social theory. (These remarks are admittedly too brief, but we must return to the main line of discussion.)

V

The rational intuitionist may object that an essential feature of constructivism—the view that the facts to count as reasons of justice are singled out by the parties in the original position as agents of construction and that, apart from such construction, there are no reasons of justice—is simply incoherent.[38] This view is incompatible not only with the notion of truth as given by a prior and independent moral order, but also with the notions of reasonableness and objectivity, neither of which refer to what can be settled simply by agreement, much less by choice. A constructivist view, the objection continues, depends on the idea of adopting or choosing first principles, and such principles are not the kind of thing concerning which it makes sense to say that their status depends on their being chosen or adopted. We cannot "choose" them; what we can do is choose whether to follow them in our actions or to be guided by them in our reasoning, just as we can choose whether to honor our duties, but not what our duties are.

In reply, one must distinguish the three points of view that we noted at the end of the first lecture (in section VII, 533/4): that of the parties in the original position, that of the citizens in a well-ordered society, and that of you and me who are examining justice as fairness to serve as a basis for a conception that may yield a suitable understanding of freedom and equality. It is, of course, the parties in the original position whose agreement singles out the facts to count as reasons. But their agreement is subject to all the conditions of the original position which represent the Reasonable and the Rational. And the facts singled out by the first principles count as reasons not for the parties, since they are moved by their highest-order interests, but for the citizens of a well-ordered society in matters of social justice. As citizens in society we are indeed bound by first principles and by what our duties are, and must act in the light of reasons of justice. Constructivism is certain to seem incoherent unless we carefully distinguish these points of view.

The parties in the original position do not agree on what the moral facts are, as if there already were such facts. It is not that, being situated impartially, they have a clear and undistorted view of a prior and independent moral order. Rather (for constructivism), there is no such order, and therefore no such facts apart from the procedure of construction as a whole; the facts are identified by the principles that result. Thus the rational intuitionists' objection, properly expressed, must be that no hypothetical agreement by rationally autonomous agents, no matter how circumscribed by reasonable conditions in a procedure of construction, can determine the reasons that settle what we as citizens should consider just and unjust; right and wrong are not, even in that way, constructed. But this is merely to deny what constructivism asserts. If, on the other hand, such a construction does yield the first principles of a conception of justice that matches more accurately than other views our considered convictions in general and wide reflective equilibrium, then constructivism would seem to provide a suitable basis for objectivity.

The agreement of the parties in the original position is not a so-called "radical" choice: that is, a choice not based on reasons, a choice that simply fixes, by sheer fiat, as it were, the scheme of reasons that we, as citizens, are to recognize, at least until another such choice is made. The notion of radical choice, commonly associated with Nietzsche and the existentialists, finds no place in justice as fairness. The parties in the original position are moved by their preference for primary goods, which preference in turn is rooted in their highest-order interests in developing and exercising their moral powers. Moreover, the agreement of the parties takes place subject to constraints that express reasonable conditions.

In the model-conception of a well-ordered society, citizens affirm their public conception of justice because it matches their considered convictions and coheres with the kind of persons they, on due reflection, want to be. Again, this affirmation is not radical choice. The ideals of the person and of social cooperation embedded in the two model-conceptions mediated by the original position are not ideals that, at some moment in life, citizens are said simply to choose. One is to imagine that, for the most part, they find on examination that they hold these ideals, that they have taken them in part from the culture of their society.

The preceding paragraph ties in with what I said at the beginning of the first lecture, except that there I was talking about us and not about a well-ordered society. Recall that a Kantian view, in addressing the public culture of a democratic society, hopes to bring to awareness a conception of the person and of social cooperation conjectured to be implicit in that culture, or at least congenial to its deepest tendencies when properly expressed and presented. Our society is not well-ordered: the public conception of justice and its understanding of freedom and equality are in dispute. Therefore, for us—you and me—a basis of public justification is still to be achieved. In considering the conception of justice as fairness we have to ask whether the ideals embedded in its model-conceptions are sufficiently congenial to our considered convictions to be affirmed as a practicable basis of public justification. Such an affirmation would not be radical choice (if choice at all); nor should it be confused with the adoption of principles of justice by the parties in the original position. To the contrary, it would be rooted in the fact that this Kantian doctrine as a whole, more fully than other views available to us, organized our considered convictions.

Given the various contrasts between Kantian constructivism and rational intuitionism, it seems better to say that in constructivism first principles are reasonable (or unreasonable) than that they are true (or false)—better still, that they are most reasonable for those who conceive of their person as it is represented in the procedure of construction. And here 'reasonable' is used instead of 'true' not because of some alternative theory of truth, but simply in order to keep to terms that indicate the constructivist standpoint as opposed to rational intuitionism. This usage, however, does not imply that there are no natural uses for the notion of truth in moral reasoning. To the contrary, for example, particular judgments and secondary norms may be considered true when they follow from, or are sound applications of, reasonable first principles. These first principles may be said to be true in the sense that they would be agreed to if the parties in the original position were provided with all the relevant true general beliefs.

Nor does justice as fairness exclude the possibility of there being a fact of the matter as to whether there is a single most reasonable conception. For it seems quite likely that there are only a few viable conceptions of the person both sufficiently general to be part of a moral doctrine and congruent with the ways in which people are to regard themselves in a democratic society. And only one of these conceptions may have a representation in a procedure of construction that issues in acceptable and workable principles, given the relevant general beliefs.[39] Of course, this is conjecture, intended only to indicate that constructivism is compatible with there being, in fact, only one most reasonable conception of justice, and therefore that constructivism is compatible with objectivism in this sense. However, constructivism does not presuppose that this is the case, and it may turn out that, for us, there exists no reasonable and workable conception of justice at all. This would mean that the practical task of political philosophy is doomed to failure.

VI

My account of Kantian constructivism in moral theory (as illustrated by justice as fairness) is now concluded. I should stress, however, that for all I have said it is still open to the rational intuitionist to reply that I have not shown that rational intuitionism is false or that it is not a possible basis for the necessary agreement in our judgments of justice. It has been my intention to describe constructivism by contrast and not to defend it, much less to argue that rational intuitionism is mistaken. In any case, Kantian constructivism, as I would state it, aims to establish only that the rational intuitionist notion of objectivity is unnecessary for objectivity. Of course, it is always possible to say, if we ever do reach general and wide reflective equilibrium, that now at last we intuit the moral truths fixed by a given moral order; but the constructivist will say instead that our conception of justice, by all the criteria we can think of to apply, is now the most reasonable for us.

We have arrived at the idea that objectivity is not given by "the point of view of the universe," to use Sidgwick's phrase. Objectivity is to be understood by reference to a suitably constructed social point of view, an example of which is the framework provided by the procedure of the original position. This point of view is social in several respects. It is the publicly shared point of view of citizens in a well-ordered society, and the principles that issue from it are accepted by them as authoritative with regard to the claims of individuals and associations. Moreover, these principles regulate the basic structure of society within which the activities of individuals and associations take place. Finally, by representing the person as a free and equal citizen of a well-ordered society, the constructivist procedure yields principles that further everyone's highest-order interests and define the fair terms of social cooperation among persons so understood. When citizens invoke these principles they speak as members of a political community and appeal to its shared point of view either in their own behalf or in that of others. Thus, the essential agreement in judgments of justice arises not from the recognition of a prior and independent moral order, but from everyone's affirmation of the same authoritative social perspective.

The central place of the conception of the person in these lectures prompts me to conclude with a note of warning, addressed as much to me as to anyone else: ever since the notion of the person assumed a central place in moral philosophy in the latter part of the eighteenth century, as seen in Rousseau and Kant and the philosophy of idealism, its use has suffered from excessive vagueness and ambiguity. And so it is essential to devise an approach that disciplines our thought and suitably limits these defects. I view the three model-conception that underlie justice as fairness as having this purpose.

To elucidate: suppose we define the concept of a person as that of a human being capable of taking full part in social cooperation, honoring its ties and relationships over a complete life. There are plainly many specifications of this capacity, depending, for example, on how social cooperation or a complete life is understood; and each such specification yields another conception of the person falling under the concept. Moreover, such conceptions must be distinguished from specifications of the concept of the self as knower, used in epistemology and metaphysics, or the concept of the self as the continuant carrier of psychological states: the self as substance, or soul. These are prima facie distinct notions, and questions of identity, say, may well be different for each; for these notions arise in connection with different problems. This much is perhaps obvious. The consequence is that there are numerous conceptions of the person as the basic unit of agency and responsibility in social life, and of its requisite intellectual, moral, and active powers. The specification of these conceptions by philosophical analysis alone, apart from any background theoretical structure or general requirements, is likely to prove fruitless. In isolation these notions play no role that fixes or limits their use, and so their features remain vague and indeterminate.

One purpose of a model-conception like that of the original position is that, by setting up a definite framework within which a binding agreement on principles must be made, it serves to fix ideas. We are faced with a specific problem that must be solved, and we are forced to describe the parties and their mutual relations in the process of construction so that appropriate principles of justice result. The context of the problem guides us in removing vagueness and ambiguity in the conception of the person, and tells us how precise we need to be. There is no such thing as absolute clarity or exactness; we have to be only clear or exact enough for the task at hand. Thus the structure defined by the original position may enable us to crystallize our otherwise amorphous notion of the person and to identify with sufficient sharpness the appropriate characterization of free and equal moral personality.

The constructivist view also enables us to exploit the flexibility and power of the idea of rational choice subject to appropriate constraints. The rational deliberations of the parties in the original position serve as a way to select among traditional or other promising conceptions of justice. So understood, the original position is not an axiomatic (or deductive) basis from which principles are derived but a procedure for singling out principles most fitting to the conception of the person most likely to be held, at least implicitly, in a modern democratic society. To exaggerate, we compute via the deliberations of the parties and in this way hope to achieve sufficient rigor and clarity in moral theory. Indeed, it is hard to see how there could be any more direct connection between the conception of free and equal moral persons and first principles of justice than this construction allows. For here persons so conceived and moved by their highest-order interests are themselves, in their rationally autonomous deliberations, the agents who select the principles that are to govern the basic structure of their social life. What connection could be more intimate than this?

Finally, if we ask, what is clarity and exactness enough? the answer is: enough to find an understanding of freedom and equality that achieves workable public agreement on the weight of their respective claims. With this we return to the current impasse in the understanding of freedom and equality which troubles our democratic tradition and from which we started. Finding a way out of this impasse defines the immediate practical task of political philosophy. Having come full circle, I bring these lectures to a close.

Notes

Presented as three lectures, on Kantian Constructivism in Moral Theory, given at Columbia University in April,

1980; the first, "Rational and Full Autonomy," on April 14; the second, "Representation of Freedom and Equality," on April 15; the third, "Construction and Objectivity," on April 16. These lectures constitute the fourth series of John Dewey Lectures, which were established in 1967 to honor the late John Dewey, who had been from 1905 to 1930 a professor of philosophy at Columbia.

In revising these lectures for publication I should like to thank Burton Dreben for helpful discussion which has led to numerous improvements and clarifications, and also Joshua Cohen and Samuel Scheffler for valuable criticisms of an earlier version of material included in lectures I and III, originally prepared for the Howison Lecture at Berkeley in May 1979. As always, I am indebted, at many points, to Joshua Rabinowitz.

[1] Cambridge, Mass.: Harvard University Press, 1971. Hereafter referred to as TJ.

[2] See, for example, Dewey's *Outlines of a Critical Theory of Ethics* (1891) and *The Study of Ethics: A Syllabus* (1894) reprinted in *John Dewey: The Early Works, 1882-1898* (Carbondale: Southern Illinois University Press, 1971), in volumes 3 and 4, respectively. From Dewey's critique of Kant in *Outlines*, pp. 290-300, and his statement of his own form of the self-realization doctrine, pp. 300-327, Dewey's debt to idealism is plain enough.

[3] These features were not conveniently stated at any one place in TJ. In this and the next lectures I try to give a clearer and more systematic account of this notion and to indicate its basic role as a model-conception.

[4] See TJ, § 58, where several cases of conscientious refusal are considered in connection with the problem of just war. As for our relations with the order of nature, note the last paragraph of § 77.

[5] A fuller discussion can be found in Allen Buchanan, "Revisability and Rational Choice," *Canadian Journal of Philosophy*, v, 3 (November 1975): 395-408. For a more general account of which the use of primary goods is a special case, see T. M. Scanlon, "Preference and Urgency," this JOURNAL, LXXII, 19 (Nov. 6, 1975): 655-669.

[6] See, for example, § 15, pp. 92 ff, where primary goods are first discussed at some length; and also pp. 142 f, 253, 260, and 433 f. The question whether the account of primary goods is a matter for social theory, or depends essentially on a conception of the person, is not discussed. I am grateful to Joshua Cohen, Joshua Rabinowitz, T. M. Scanlon, and Michael Teitelman for helpful criticism and clarification on this important point.

[7] See *On the Basis of Ethics* (1840), Part II, § 7, E. F. J. Payne, trans. (New York: Liberal Arts Press, 1965), pp. 89-92. I am indebted to Joshua Cohen for pointing out to me that my previous reply to this criticism misses the force of Schopenhauer's objection. See TJ, pp. 147 f. Thanks to him, I believe the reply in the text is better and connects with the revised account of primary goods. I am indebted also to Stephen Darwall's "A Defense of the Kantian Interpretation," *Ethics*, LXXXVI, 2 (January 1976): 164-170.

[8] This seems to be the view of Oliver A. Johnson in his reply to Darwall, see fn 7 above. See *Ethics*, LXXXVII, 3 (April 1977): 251-259, p. 253 f.

[9] I am indebted to Norman Daniels for clarification of this point.

[10] Thus, for example, average utilitarianism might be presented as a kind of constructivism. See TJ, § 27.

[11] I am indebted to Joshua Rabinowitz for clarification concerning these distinctions.

[12] Here I should explain that in a well-ordered society coercive sanctions are rather rarely, if ever, actually applied (since offences are presumably infrequent), nor need severe sanctions be legally permitted. Stability means that institutional rules are generally complied with, and the role of the machinery of sanctions is to support citizens' mutual expectations of one another's settled intention to follow these norms. See TJ, pp. 269 f, 336, 576 f.

[13] Put in a different way: a well-ordered society does not require an ideology in order to achieve stability, understanding 'ideology' (in Marx's sense) as some form of false consciousness or delusory scheme of public beliefs.

[14] I am indebted to Thomas Nagel, Derek Parfit, and T. M. Scanlon for instructive discussion on this and related points.

[15] I should like to thank Sidney Morgenbesser for improvements in this and the next paragraph.

[16] The remarks in this paragraph indicate part of the basis for a reply that I believe can be made to some of the objections raised by Bernard Williams to a Kantian view. See his paper "Persons, Character and Morality," in A. O. Rorty, ed., *The Identities of Persons* (Berkeley: University of California Press, 1976), pp. 197-216.

[17] For a brief account, see "Fairness to Goodness," *Philosophical Review*, LXXXIV, 4 (October 1975): 536-554, pp. 551-554.

[18] I am indebted to Joshua Rabinowitz for the distinction between a thick and a thin veil of ignorance as stated in this and the next paragraph.

[19] For a discussion of the basic structure as the first subject of justice, see "The Basic Structure as Subject," in A. I. Goldman and Jaegwon Kim, eds., *Values and Morals* (Boston: Reidel, 1978), pp. 47-72.

[20] See TJ, § 48, and pp. 88 f.

[21] These terms are suggested by a similar distinction drawn by J. L. Mackie, *Ethics* (New York: Penguin Books, 1977), pp. 106 f, 134 ff.

[22] It is in some such fashion that I am inclined to interpret the important although difficult passages in the *Second Critique* where the Fact of Reason enters in.

[23] On Sidgwick now, see the comprehensive work by J. B. Schneewind, *Sidgwick's Ethics and Modern Victorian Moral Philosophy* (New York: Oxford, 1977).

[24] *The Methods of Ethics* (London: Macmillan 1907), 7th ed., pp. v-vi; parenthetical page references to Sidgwick are to this book, this edition.

[25] See Essay IV: "Duty for Duty's Sake," 2nd ed. (New York: Oxford, 1927).

[26] See *The Right and the Good* (Oxford: The Clarendon Press, 1930), esp. chs. 1-2. I shall adopt Ross's characterization of rational intuitionism, adjusted to allow for any number of first principles and, thus, as fitting either single-principle or pluralistic intuitionism. I should add that, for my purposes here, I interpret Aristotle's view as combining teleological and metaphysical perfectionism. Although this may not be a sound interpretation in the light of contemporary scholarship, it suits well enough how Aristotle was interpreted up to Kant's time.

[27] *Methods,* Book III, ch. 13, pp. 379-389. See Schneewind's discussion, ch. 10, pp. 286-309.

[28] I borrow this expression from Peter Hylton's discussion, *The Origins of Analytic Philosophy,* ch. 3 (Dissertation: Harvard University, 1978).

[29] See *The Principles of Mathematics* (London: Allen & Unwin, 1937), 2nd ed. (1st ed. 1903), pp. xv-xvi. The analogy of the mental telescope is Russell's.

[30] Because it formulates definitions of the basic moral concepts in terms of nonmoral concepts, this being the mode of identifying those facts which are to count as good reasons in applying the basic moral concepts, naturalism is a form of heteronomy from the Kantian standpoint. The various definitions, presumably arrived at by the analysis of concepts, convert moral judgments into statements about the world on all fours with those of science and common sense. Therefore, these definitions, combined with the natural order itself, now come to constitute the moral order, which is prior to and independent from our conception of ourselves as free and equal moral persons. If time permitted, this could be substantiated by setting out, for example, the details of Hume's view (as often interpreted) and of Bentham's hedonistic utilitarianism, at least once these views are expressed in the requisite naturalistic format. (Rational intuitionism tries to secure a kind of independence of the moral order from the order of nature.)

[31] This fundamental contention is unfortunately obscured by the fact that although in the *Grundlegung* Kant classifies the view of Leibniz and Wolff as a form of heteronomy, his criticism of it is that it is circular and therefore empty. See Academy Edition, p. 443. Much the same happens in the *Second Critique,* Academy Edition, p. 41, where Kant argues that the notion of perfection in practical reasoning means fitness for any given ends and therefore is again empty until these ends are specified independently. These arguments give the erroneous impression that, if perfectionism had sufficient content, it would be compatible with autonomy.

[32] See, for example, *Methods,* pp. 23-28, 34-37, 39 f, read together with the discussion of the self-evident basis of the principle of utility, cited in fn 5 above.

[33] For a statement of these principles and priority rules, see TJ, pp. 60-62, 250, 302/3.

[34] See "The Basic Structure as Subject," in A. I. Goldman and Jaegwon Kim, eds., *Values and Morals* (Boston: Reidel, 1978), especially secs. IV-V, pp. 52-57.

[35] See *The Right and the Good,* pp. 41/2. Ross refers to Aristotle's remark: "The decision rests with perception" (*Nicomachean Ethics* 1109 b 23, 1126 b 4).

[36] See Lecture II, section I.

[37] Therefore these advances in our knowledge of human psychology and social theory might be relevant at the constitutional, legislative, and judicial stages in the application of the principles of justice, as opposed to the adoption of principles in the original position. For a brief account of these stages, see TJ, § 31.

[38] For this and other objections to what I call "constructivism" in this lecture, see the review of TJ by Marcus Singer, *Philosophy of Science,* XLIV, 4 (December 1977): 594-618, pp. 612-615. I am grateful to him for raising this objection, which I here try to meet. Singer's criticism starts from the passage on page

45 of TJ (also referred to above, 564/5). It should not be assumed that Singer's own position is that of rational intuitionism. I simply suppose that a rational intuitionist would make this objection.

[39] I am indebted to Samuel Scheffler for valuable discussion on this point.

Christine Korsgaard (essay date 1985)

SOURCE: "Kant's Formula of Universal Law," in *Pacific Philosophical Quarterly*, Vol. 66, 1985, pp. 24-47.

[*In the following essay, Korsgaard evaluates different interpretations regarding the kind of contradiction referred to in Kant's first formulation of the Categorical Imperative.*]

Kant's first formulation of the Categorical Imperative, the Formula of Universal Law, runs:

> Act only according to that maxim by which you can at the same time will that it should become a universal law. (G 421/39)[1]

A few lines later, Kant says that this is equivalent to acting as though your maxim were by your will to become a law of nature, and he uses this latter formulation in his examples of how the imperative is to be applied. Elsewhere, Kant specifies that the test is whether you could will the universalization for a system of nature "of which you yourself were a part" (C$_2$ 69/72); and in one place he characterizes the moral agent as asking "what sort of world he would create under the guidance of practical reason, . . . a world into which, moreover, he would place himself as a member."[2] But how do you determine whether or not you can will a given maxim as a law of nature? Since the will is practical reason, and since everyone must arrive at the same conclusions in matters of duty, it cannot be the case that what you are able to will is a matter of personal taste, or relative to your individual desires. Rather, the question of what you can will is a question of what you can will *without contradiction*.

According to Kant, willing universalized maxims may give rise to contradictions in two ways:

> Some actions are of such a nature that their maxim cannot even be *thought* as a universal law of nature without contradiction, far from it being possible that one could will that it should be such. In others this internal impossibility is not found, though it is still impossible to *will* that their maxim should be raised to the universality of a law of nature, because such a will would contradict itself. We easily see that the former maxim conflicts with the stricter or narrower (imprescriptible) duty, the latter with broader (meritorious) duty. (G 424/41-42)

The first sort of contradiction is usually called a contradiction in conception, and the second a contradiction in the will.

In this paper I am concerned with identifying the sense in which there is a "contradiction" in willing the universalization of an immoral maxim, and especially with the sense in which the universalization of such a maxim can be said to have a contradiction *in* it—that is, with the idea of a contradiction in conception. There are three different interpretations of the kind of contradiction Kant has (or ought to have) in mind found in the literature.[3] They are:

i) The Logical Contradiction Interpretation. On this interpretation, there is something like a logical impossibility in the universalization of the maxim, or in the system of nature in which the maxim is a natural law: if the maxim were universalized, the action or policy that it proposes would be inconceivable.

ii) The Teleological Contradiction Interpretation. On this interpretation, it would be contradictory to will your maxim as a law for a system of nature teleologically conceived: either you are acting against some natural purpose, or your maxim could not be a teleological law. The maxim is inconsistent with a systematic harmony of purposes, or with the principle that any organ, instinct, or action-type has a natural purpose for which it must be the one best suited.

iii) The Practical Contradiction Interpretation. On this interpretation, the contradiction is that your maxim would be self-defeating if universalized: your action would become ineffectual for the achievement of your purpose if everyone (tried to) use it for that purpose. Since you propose to use that action for that purpose at the same time as you propose to universalize the maxim, you in effect will the thwarting of your own purpose.

In trying to determine which of these views is correct, it is important to remember that it is not just because of the contradiction in the universalized maxim that immoral action is irrational. Kant is not claiming that immoral conduct is contradictory—if he were, the moral law would be analytic rather than synthetic. In any event, a contradiction in the universalization of your maxim would not prove that there is a contradiction in your maxim, for these are different. The Formula of Universal Law is a test of the sufficiency of the reasons for action and choice which are embodied in our maxims. The idea the universalizability is a test for sufficiency ("what if everybody did that?") is a familiar one, and shows in an intuitive way why it is rational to attend to a universalizability requirement. But the claim that universalizability is a test for a reason sufficient to motivate a rational being cannot be fully defended at this stage of the argument, for the full defense requires the connection to autonomy. Kant's critical ethical project is to prove that perfect rationality includes conformity to the categorical imperative: but in the **Foundations** this project is not directly taken up until the Third Section.[4] The Second Section, where the Formula of Universal Law appears, is devoted to showing us what the content of the categorical imperative will be *if there is one*. The question of contradictions arises not in the context of determining *why* you must conform your conduct to the categorical imperative, but of *how* you do so.

Yet in trying to come to an understanding of how the Formula of Universal Law is to be applied, we must not lose sight of this further goal. Any view of how the Formula of Universal Law is applied must presuppose some view of what rational willing is. The problem is most obviously pressing for the case of contradictions in the will, for it seems impossible to say what contradicts a rational will until we know what a rational will is, or what is necessarily contains. There is a contradiction in one's beliefs if one believes both x and not-x, or things that imply both x and not-x. There is a contradiction in one's will if one wills both x and not-x, or things that imply both x and not-x. But until one knows what things are involved in or implied by "willing x," one will not know how to discover these contradictions. So in determining which maxims can be willed as universal law without contradiction, we will have to employ some notion of what rational willing is. Some of the interpretations of the contradiction in conception test also rely on particular views of what rational willing is. This is why we must keep in view Kant's eventual aim of showing that moral conduct is rational conduct. Whatever view of the nature of rational willing is used in determining how the formula is to be applied must also be used in determining why it is rational to act as the formula prescribes.

One constraint this places on interpretations of the test is this: it must not employ a notion of rational willing that already has moral content. An example will show what I mean. John Stuart Mill says of Kant:

> But when he begins to deduce from this precept any of the actual duties of morality, he fails, almost grotesquely, to show that there would be any contradiction, any logical (not to say physical) impossibility, in the adoption by all rational beings of the most outrageously immoral rules of conduct. All he shows is that the consequences of their universal adoption would be such as no one would choose to incur.[5]

Mill thinks that Kant's view really amounts to an appeal to utility, to what we would now call rule-utilitarianism. A rule-utilitarian interpretation of the Formula of Universal Law gives, as Mill points out, no sense to Kant's use of the word "contradiction" in this context. Yet, we could give it sense by claiming that a rational being is *by definition* opposed to undesirable consequences, and therefore cannot, without contradiction, will the universalization of any maxim if that universalization would have undesirable consequences. But roughly this kind of connection between a rational will and a moral will is what Kant is trying to *establish,* and therefore to use such a definition in explaining the contradiction test would make the Kantian argument circular. For if we use this definition we are already presupposing a morality-laden conception of what it is to be rational: we are assuming the sort of connection between moral goodness and rationality that Kant is preparing to demonstrate. So although the contradiction tests by themselves do not show us why immoral action is irrational, the notion of rational willing which they presuppose must be one that can be used at the later stage of the argument.

My question is which of the three "kinds" of contradiction we should expect to find in the universalized version of an immoral maxim, and my aim is to defend the third answer, that it is a practical contradiction. I should say from the outset that although there is one important piece of textual evidence for this answer, it is my view that no interpretation can be based on textual considerations alone. Language supporting all of them can be found in Kant's texts, and it seems possible that he was not aware of the differences among them. My defense of the practical contradiction interpretation will therefore be based primarily on philosophical considerations. For each interpretation I will ask (i) what kinds of cases it can handle, (ii) whether it can meet some standard objections, (iii) what sort of distinction between the contradiction in conception test and the contradiction in the will test is implied by it, and, most importantly, (iv) what presuppositions about rationality it makes and so what kind of case it will allow Kant to make when he turns to the critical project of showing that morality *is* pure rationality.

I. The Logical Contradiction Interpretation

Some of Kant's defenders have tried to identify a contradiction of just the sort Mill denies can be found. Versions of a Logical Contradiction Interpretation have been defended by Dietrichson, Kemp, and Wood,[6] among others. I suppose hardly any of this interpretation's proponents have held it in the pure form that Mill describes: what they have looked for is something very like a logical or physical impossibility. Part of the reason for this is that it is clear that nothing like a logical contradiction can be found for the contradiction in the will test, since we are explicitly told that maxims that fail that test are conceivable. But there is no question that much of Kant's language favors a Logical Contradiction Interpretation for the contradiction in conception test. He says that universalizations of immoral maxims destroy themselves (G 403/19), annihilate themselves (C$_2$ 27/27), are inconceivable or cannot be thought, and so on. The example that fits this view best is the false promising example. A man in financial difficulties considers "borrowing" money which he knows he can never repay. Kant explains how this fails the contradiction in conception test this way:

> ...the universality of a law which says that anyone who believes himself to be in need could promise what he pleased with the intention of not fulfilling it would make the promise itself and the end to be accomplished by it impossible; no one would believe what was promised to him but would only laugh at any such assertion as vain pretense. (G 422/40)

Proponents of the Logical Contradiction Interpretation tend to focus on the remark that the promise itself would be impossible, as this seems to be where a logical inconceivability would lie. Kant tells us that promises would be impossible if this maxim were universalized because no one would believe them. There are various ways to find a contradiction here. One could say that the contradiction is that we are trying to conceive a world in which the agent (and everyone with his purpose) is making a certain sort of false promise, but at the same time we are necessarily conceiving a world in which no one can be making this sort of promise, since you cannot make a promise (of this sort) to someone who will not accept it. Perhaps the clearest way to bring out a logical contradiction is to say that there would be no such thing as a promise (or anyway a repayment-promise) in the world of the universalized maxim. The practice of offering and accepting promises would have died out under stress of too many violations. Thus we are imagining a world in which the agent and everyone with his purpose is making a certain sort of promise, but also a world in which there is no such thing. And this is logically inconceivable. If universalizing a maxim makes the action proposed inconceivable, then, we can get a logical contradiction.

A Problem About Violence

The difficulty in taking this line shows up in a problem that Dietrichson describes in "Kant's Criteria of Universalizability." He considers the case of a woman who has decided to consider the maxim "if I give birth to a baby weighing less than six pounds, I shall do everything in my power to kill it."[7] Dietrichson points out that it is certainly possible to conceive the idea of every mother behaving according to this rule. In my view, Dietrichson's example is not a properly formulated maxim, since it does not mention the mother's reason for killing the child. The child's weighting less than six pounds is not by itself recognizable as a *prima facie* reason for killing it. Since the Formula of Universal Law is a test of the sufficiency of reasons, the

maxim must include them. But this is not the problem brought out by Dietrichson's example. We can make the maxim one of killing children that tend to cry at night more than average, in order to get enough sleep. Either Dietrichson's maxim or mine could clearly be a universal law without a logical contradiction. There could in fact be worlds where these things happen. They could happen in our world.

Dietrichson's solution is to appeal to the second contradiction test, and to place this among the maxims whose universalizations cannot be willed although they can be conceived. But this will not work. Different ways of deriving duties lead to different kinds of duty, with different moral and legal consequences. In the *Foundations,* Kant associates the contradiction in the will test with wide, meritorious duties (G 424/42), and the duty not to kill a child is obviously not of that kind.

Since Kant's account of the division of duties changes it is worth noting that even the later views will not permit Dietrichson's solution. The examples in the *Foundations* are divided in the text into perfect duties to self, perfect duties to others, imperfect duties to self and imperfect duties to others. A footnote warns us, however, that Kant will make his own division of duties in the *Metaphysics of Morals.* (G 421/39) That work is divided into duties of justice and of virtue. Now it might seem tempting to simply identify duties of justice, narrow duties, perfect duties, and negative duties with one another and similarly to suppose that duties of virtue, wide duties, imperfect duties, and positive duties are the same. But this would be an oversimplification: Kant's categorizations are more intricate than that.[8] For although the duties of virtue are said to be broad or wide duties, there are perfect and negative duties that appear in this category: the duty not to commit suicide (one of Kant's *Foundations* examples) being an important instance. The perfect duties of virtue are the duties not to abuse your own moral and physical person and duties of respect (as opposed of those of love) to others. (MM 464/130, § 41)

There is room for controversy about exactly what effect this complex categorization has on the derivation of the relevant duties. In the *Foundations,* Kant's view seems to be that all perfect duties, whether of virtue or of justice, are to be derived from the contradiction in conception test. At least, this is how he tries to derive the duty not to commit suicide. Later, I will explain why I think that the derivation of this duty given by Kant under the Formula of Universal Law in the *Foundations* does not work. My own opinion is that this is because the perfect duties of virtue require a more complex derivation than Kant gives them in the *Foundations.* Perfect duties of virtue spring from the fact that there are ends against which we must not act, and ends cannot be assigned to us by the contradiction in the conception test, although they can by the contradiction in the will test. Kant's own texts do not give us direct guidance here, for in spelling out the duties of virtue in the *Metaphysics of Morals* he for the most part uses the concepts and casuistical methods of the Formula of Humanity rather than that of Universal Law. But if one holds that all duties of virtue, perfect or imperfect, depend on obligatory ends, one might be tempted to use the contradiction in the will test, which now can identify some perfect duties, for cases like Dietrichson's.

But this move could not solve the problem because even if this is a way to derive some perfect duties they are still only duties of virtue if they are arrived at in this way. Like the imperfect duties of virtue that assign ends we are to promote, they are externally unenforceable because the law cannot make us hold an end. (MM 379-385/36-43) Imperfect duties of virtue are wide duties because the law does not prescribe exactly what and how much you must do to promote the obligatory ends. Perfect duties of virtue are wide for the somewhat different reason that acting for the sake of these ends is something we must work towards—we cannot, in our "phenomenal" lives, just decide to act for the sake of these ends. (MM 392/51 and § 22, 446/110-111) You can decide to treat someone with outward respect, but you cannot *just* decide to treat them so out of real respect. The attitudes involved are ones that you must cultivate, a sort of internal labor that ethics assigns to us, and how much and what you can do may depend on the circumstances of your life and perhaps the temperamental obstacles you have to overcome. But the murder of a child does not merely show the mother's failure to value it as an end in itself (although it does do that). This means only that the mother lacks virtues that she ought to have. The murder is also an injustice, a violation of right, and the duty not to commit murder is—as duties of virtue are not—rightfully enforceable. (MM 218-221/17-20 and 383-384/40-41) This puts it into the category of duties of justice, which are enforceable. We need the contradiction in conception test to identify this *kind* of immorality.[9]

Natural and Conventional Actions

The problem that is demonstrated by Dietrichson's example springs from the fact that the action contemplated is one of natural violence. In the promising case we were able to generate a logical contradiction because the practice of promising was, under stress of universal violation, ushered off the scene. There would no longer be such a thing as promising. No such analysis is available here, because killing cannot be ushered off the scene by the way it is employed. The reason is obvious. Promising is, in the sense developed by Rawls in "Two Concepts of Rules,"[10] a practice. Both the possibility and the efficacy of actions performed within a convention such as promising—such as making, ac-

cepting, and keeping promises—depend on the existence, by conventional establishment, of the practice. The practice is comprised of certain rules, and its existence (where it is not embodied in an institution with sanctions) consists in the general acknowledgement and following of those rules. Now it is perhaps difficult to say exactly under what conditions a practice exists. We know that practices can exist if their rules are violated sometimes, for they do. But they cannot exist if their rules are universally violated. One may generate the contradiction by saying that when this happens the practice has new rules and becomes a different practice, but this is somewhat obscure. The clearer thing to say is this: a practice has a standard purpose, and if its rules are universally violated it ceases to be efficacious for this purpose, and so ceases to exist. People find some other way to achieve it, and the practice simply goes out of business. This is what happens in Kant's false promising example. Repayment promises, because they are never accepted, become nonexistent. People either make no loans or find another way to ensure repayment. For this reason, all actions which could not intelligibly exist or would not be efficacious without the existence of practices, and yet violate the rules of those practices, are easily handled by both the Logical and the Practical Interpretations of the contradiction test. Willing universal violation creates an inconsistency by making the action-type that it universalizes a non-existent one, and *ipso facto,* ineffectual.

But in Dietrichson's case there is no practice. The action is killing, and no amount or kind of use of the action of killing is going to make it impossible. And this is because the existence of this kind of action and its efficacy depend only on the laws of nature, not on any conventional practice. For shorthand, I am going to call actions like promising "conventional actions" and actions like killing "natural actions." The Logical Contradiction interpretation works well for immoral conventional actions, but it is not very clear how it can handle immoral natural actions. When an action's possibility depends only on the laws of nature it cannot become inconceivable through universal practice.

Two Hegelian Objections

In my view, it is the difficulty about natural actions which is most damaging to the Logical Contradiction Interpretation. Before I turn to the other views, however, I should mention some objections that are usually taken to be its most serious problem. I will call these the Hegelian objections, since they were originally put forward by Hegel and promulgated by Bradley and others.[11] One of the Hegelian objections is that universal law test is empty. I will borrow the formulation used by H. B. Action, discussing Kant's *Critique of Practical Reason* example of a man who is considering not returning a deposit (C₂ 27-28/26-27):

In an essay entitled *On the Scientific Treatment of Natural Law* (1803), Hegel says that all Kant's argument shows is that a system without deposits is contradicted by a system with deposits, but not that there is any contradiction in a system without deposits. Kant makes there seem to be a contradiction in a system without deposits because he assumes that everyone would want there to be deposits, and this, says Hegel, shows that Kant was assuming the system of property and was arguing that if everyone kept what belongs to others then there would be no system of property. The interesting question, Hegel goes on, is just why there should be property, and about this Kant says nothing.[12]

This objection as it stands does not hold. On the Logical Contradiction Interpretation, the contradiction lies not in envisioning a society in which there are no deposits, but in envisioning a society in which the agent and others with his purpose are making use of the deposit system even though there is no such thing. The contradiction is generated when the agent tries to will his maxim and the universalization of his maxim *at the same time,* or tries to will it for a system of which he is to be a part. The non-existence of the practice that results from universalization is contradicted by the existence of it presupposed in the individual maxim.

The other Hegelian objection pulls in the opposite direction: instead of showing the test to be empty, it shows it to be too strong. Bradley describes it this way:

> 'Steal property' is a contradiction, for it destroys property, and with it possibility of theft.

> We have no need here to push further a metaphysical argument against this view, for it supplies us at once with a crushing instance against itself. The essence of morality was a similar contradiction. . . . Morality is . . . as inconsistent as theft. 'Succor the poor' both negates and presupposes (hence posits) poverty: as Blake comically says:

> > Pity would be no more,
> > If we did not make somebody poor.

> If you are to love your enemies, you must never be without them; and yet you try to get rid of them. Is that consistent? In short, every duty which presupposes something to be negated is no duty; it is an immoral rule, because self-contradictory,[13]

It is true that we cannot imagine a world in which people give to the poor and there are no poor. Since there is no one to give to, it is an impossible state of affairs. But the advocate of Logical Contradiction Interpretation can handle the objection. He can say that Bradley has misstated the maxim. The maxim is to succor those who need it, and this maxim can be consistently held (and in a degenerate sense acted on) in a world where no one needs help. The policy of succoring those who need it when no one does is not inconceivable. It merely gives one nothing to do.

II. The Teleological Contradiction Interpretation

According to the Teleological Contradiction interpretation, when we test our maxim by the two contradiction tests under the Formula of the Law of Nature, we are to consider whether we could will the universalized maxim as a possible law in a teleologically organized system of nature. There are two versions of this view. The first, which I will call the simple view, is usually understood this way: the contradiction emerges when an action or instinct is used in a way that is inconsistent with its natural purpose, or is not used in a way that its natural purpose calls for. A problem with this view as I have just stated it is that it makes no real use of universalization. Yet, there is some textual support for this interpretation: Kant does not scruple to use teleological language, and there are five arguments in the published ethical writings in which Kant's reasoning is explicitly teleological. One is the argument about the function of practical reasoning in the first section of the *Foundations.* (G 395-396/11-12) That argument is certainly teleological—Kant indeed carefully sets forth its teleological basis—but it is not a derivation of duty. Of the other four, two appear in the *Foundations,* in connection with the first set of examples: in deriving the duty not to commit suicide (G 421-422/39-40) and in deriving the duty of self-cultivation. (G 423/41) The other two are in the *Metaphysics of Morals,* where lying is said to violate the natural purpose of the power of communication (MM 429/91) and carnal self-defilement is denounced by appeal to the natural purpose of the sexual instincts. (MM 424-425/85-87)

The second version of this view is that of H. J. Paton, spelled out in Chapter XV of *The Categorical Imperative.*[14] Paton is the major proponent of the Teleological Contradiction Interpretation and Beck partly endorses Paton's view. Aune also believes that Kant relies on a teleological conception in applying the Law of Nature formulation.[15] Paton thinks that it is clear that the laws of nature Kant had in mind were teleological rather than causal, and that the test is whether "a will which aimed at a systematic harmony of purposes in human nature could consistently will this particular maxim as a law of human nature."[16] Paton's view differs from the simple view in that he thinks that a teleological system serves as the *type* of the moral law, rather than thinking that our actions must not contradict actual natural purposes. However, in his account of the examples he takes Kant's explicitly teleological language as evidence for his interpretation, although that language suits the simple view.[17] The difference matters more than Paton seems to realize, for the presuppositions about rationality are different. On his own view the claim must be that a rational being as such values a systematic harmony of human purposes, whereas on the simple view we must claim that a rational being as such values natural purposes. In what follows I will consider both versions.

As I mentioned, the usual understanding of the teleological view is that we find some way to assign natural purposes to various instincts and types of actions and then find the contradiction when universalized maxims involve uses of those instincts and actions that defeat the natural purpose or perhaps are merely deviant. The best evidence that Kant understood the contradiction test this way is the suicide example,[18] and it can be made to fit this pattern.

In the first teleological argument in the **Foundations,** Kant offers this as a general principle of teleological judgment: "we assume as an axiom that no organ will be found for any purpose which is not the fittest and best adapted to that purpose." (G 395/11) We can use this regulative principle to assign natural purposes to action-types as well as to organs, instincts, and other organic arrangements. Kant uses it to establish that the attainment of happiness is not the natural purpose of practical reason—the argument being that since instinct would be a better guide to happiness than reason is, reason is not the fittest and best adapted thing for that purpose. So let us say that there is a teleological contradiction if we propose as a universal law that a certain organ, instinct, or action-type be used in a way that makes it less than the fittest and best device for achieving its natural purpose. For example, we will say that the "natural purpose" of promising is to establish trust and confidence and the cooperation which they make possible. False promising on a universal scale makes promising less than the best device for this natural purpose. The suicide case will work this way: self-love is for the natural purpose of self-preservation; in the system of nature that results from universalizing the maxim of committing suicide out of self-love, self-love would not be the instinct fittest and best adapted to the purpose of self-preservation. As Kant says, "One sees immediately a contradiction in a system of nature whose law would be to destroy life by the feeling whose special office is to impel the improvement of life." (G 422/40) So the standard set by the regulative principle of teleological judgment is not met.

An attraction of the Teleological Contradiction Interpretation is that it looks at first as if it is going to resolve the most difficult problem faced by the Logical Contradiction Interpretation, that of natural actions. Suicide, after all, is such an action. The reason that it is not hard to find a contradiction in willing the universal violation of a practice is that the practice has a standard purpose: universal violation causes people to find some other way to carry out this purpose, and that

is why the practice is abandoned. The Teleological view promises to allow us to treat natural actions in a similar way, for it assigns these actions or the instincts that prompt them standard purposes like the ones practices have—namely natural purposes. Of course it is true that a natural action or instinct, unlike a practice, will survive its universal abuse. But this is not a problem for the Teleological Contradiction Interpretation, for the defender of this view can say that the action or instinct will not, if universally misused, be best fitted for its purpose. That, not the existence of the action-type or instinct, is his criterion for establishing the contradiction.

But there is a difficulty with this solution to the problem of natural actions and with the proposed reading of the suicide case generally. It is that the suicide *himself* is not supposed to be able to will the teleological system based on the universalization of his maxim. Now it may be said that the suicide certainly cannot will the teleological system resulting from the universalization of his maxim, since, *qua* teleological system, it has a contradiction in it (an instinct not best adapted to its purpose). But this is a curiously abstract way to make a case against suicide. The contradiction in the teleological system is, after all, that a mechanism designed for the protection of life is malfunctioning. But the suicide doesn't want the mechanism to function well in his own case, and he may be indifferent about other cases. So neither his own purpose nor anything else commits him to the purpose. So if Kant's point were that the suicide cannot will the teleological system in question because *qua* teleological system it has a contradiction in it, Kant would simply be committed to the view that a rational being as such wills a well-functioning teleological system, regardless of whether he wills the purposes that it serves. But then it is hard to see how the argument can go through. This instinct would be malfunctioning with regard to *this* purpose, but nothing prevents the suicide from willing that both the instinct and its purpose be scrapped. The problem is that of the first Hegelian objection: just in the same way that Hegel says that there is no contradiction in willing away deposits because the world does not require them, so the suicide will say that the world does not require a self-preservation instinct (or any other teleological device) to make people go on living unless one supposes that it is better that people go on living. But this is what a suicide undertakes not to suppose. And we cannot use the answer to that objection that we used before. In the false promising case we said, using the Logical Contradiction view, that the man who is unable to will the universalization of the maxim of false promising does envision promising going on. *He* is going to make a promise. But the suicide's intention does not require him either to will or to envision the well-functioning of the self-preservation instincts. He does not plan to use them, or care whether they exist.

This objection does not apply in the same way to Paton's view. On Paton's view, the order of nature is a typic for the systematic harmony of human purposes. He supposes that a rational agent is committed to *this* harmony. One might object that this has the same problem as the utilitarian view: it presupposes a morality-laden view of reason. But Paton can counter this objection. He cites as evidence Kant's argument in the **Critique of Practical Reason** that self-love cannot be the basis of morality because it does not produce a harmony of purposes. (C$_2$ 28/27-28)[19] And he might also cite as evidence the **Critique of Pure Reason** view that a harmony of purposes is the highest formal unity of pure reason.[20] These things may be taken to imply that Kant thinks that rationality commits us to a harmony of purposes. Of course, this conclusion does not necessarily imply that when we reason morally we reason *from* such a harmony—it might instead be that this is a harmony that morality teaches us how to achieve. However that may be, the idea that a rational being is committed to a harmony of purposes will only help us with the Formula of Universal Law if we can somehow establish that the proposed natural purpose of the action-type is one needed for the systematic harmony of all human purposes and therefore is one that the agent must will.

The problem shows up in Paton's analysis of the false promising case. He reads the Teleological Contradiction Interpretation into the promising case by suggesting that the purpose of promises is to produce trust and mutual confidence; false promises destroy trust and therefore universalization makes the purpose of promising impossible. Paton comments:

> What Kant says is true enough so far as it goes, but it does not offer a satisfactory basis for moral judgment unless we make the further assumption that the keeping of such promises and the mutual confidence thereby aroused are essential factors in the systematic harmony of human purposes.[21]

That is, we have to presuppose that the teleological system needs promises. Again, we get a problem like that of the first Hegelian objection.

On either Paton's or the simple view, the teleological analysis requires a commitment to specific purposes: either purposes of nature (like the preservation of life in the suicide example) or purposes required for the systematic harmony of human purposes. The trouble with bringing in teleological considerations in order to assign these purposes to natural as well as conventional actions is that such purposes may have nothing to do with what the agent wants or ought rationally to want, or even with what any human being wants. Unless we can show that the agent is committed to the purpose, it is possible to say that the system can do without the teleological arrangement because it can do without the purpose.

The Practical Contradiction Interpretation, which appeals to thwarting of the agent's *own* purpose in formulating the maxim in the first place, will solve this problem.

III. The Practical Contradiction Interpretation

According to the Practical Contradiction Interpretation[22] of the contradiction in conception test, the contradiction that is involved in the universalization of an immoral maxim is that the agent would be unable to act on the maxim in a world in which it were universalized so as to achieve his own purpose—that is, the purpose that is specified in the maxim. Since he wills to act on his maxim, this means that his purpose will be frustrated. If this interpretation is correct, then it is essential that in testing maxims of actions the purpose always be included in the formulation of the maxim. It is what happens to the purpose that is the key to the contradiction.

The test is carried out by imagining, in effect, that the action you propose to perform in order to carry out your purpose is the standard procedure for carrying out that purpose.[23] What the test shows to be forbidden are just those actions whose efficacy in achieving their purposes depends upon their being exceptional. If the action no longer works as a way of achieving the purpose in question when it is universalized, then it is an action of this kind. Intuitively speaking, the test reveals unfairness, deception, and cheating. For instance, in the false promising case, the difficulty is that the man's end—getting the money—cannot be achieved by his means—making a false promise—in the world of the universalized maxim. The efficacy of the false promise as a means of securing the money depends on the fact that not everyone uses promises this way. Promises are efficacious in securing loans only because they are believed, and they are believed only if they are normally true. Since promising is the means he proposes to use, his end would not be achieved at all, but frustrated. In willing the world of the universalized maxim and—as Kant says—*at the same time*—willing the maxim itself, the man wills the frustration of his own end. As Kant says, the man "would make the promise itself and the end to be accomplished by it impossible." (G 422/40) This way of looking at the test also shows us one sense in which violations of the universal law test imply that you are using others as mere means. If you do something that only works because most people do not do it, their actions are making your action work. In the false promising case, other people's honesty makes your deceit effective.

Practical Contradictions

Even proponents of this view, or versions of it, sometimes describe a practical contradiction as being a contradiction in a weaker sense than a theoretical one.[24]

This is not correct. Kant's ethics is based on the idea that there is a specifically practical employment of reason, which is not the same as an application of theoretical reason. It includes a specifically practical sense of "contradiction." The argument that shows this seems to me to be an almost decisive one in favor of this interpretation.

After laying out the three kinds of imperatives, Kant tells us that hypothetical imperatives are analytic. This means, ordinarily, two things: the relation expressed is one of conceptual containment, and the opposite or denial is a flat contradiction. Intuitively, we can see why failing to conform your conduct to relevant hypothetical imperatives, and thus frustrating your own purposes, is contradictory. Someone who wills an end, knows that it will be brought about by a certain necessary and available means, has no extraneous reason not to use that means, and yet is utterly unmoved to take it, is irrational in a way that does seem to amount to contradiction.[25] We might capture the sense that there is a contradiction here by saying that such a person is acting as if she both did and didn't will the end. But Kant can do better than that, for he also explains the containment relation that makes the hypothetical imperative analytic:

> Whoever wills the end, so far as reason has decisive influence on his action, wills also the indispensably necessary means to it that lie in his power. This proposition, in what concerns the will, is analytical; for, in willing the object as my effect, my causality as an acting cause, i.e., the use of means, is already thought, and the imperative derives the concept of necessary actions to this end from the concept of willing this end. (G 417/34-35)

The argument is based on an idea that plays a central role in Kant's ethics generally, namely that willing is regarding yourself as a cause: that the will is, as Kant says in the opening argument of Section Three of the **Foundations,** "a causality of living beings insofar as they are rational." (G 446/64) It is because we must regard ourselves not only as a cause but as a free cause or a first cause that it turns out rationality requires autonomy, and this is the basis of moral obligation. In the argument above, Kant's point is this: willing is regarding yourself as the cause of the end in question—as the one who will bring it about. This distinguishes willing from mere wanting or wishing or desiring. Conceiving yourself as a cause of the end is conceiving yourself as setting off a causal chain that will result in the production of the end. It is conceiving yourself as using the available causal connections. But the available causal connections are, by definition, "means." So, willing the end contains, or insofar as you are rational is already, willing the means. It is because this is a "containment" relation—in the logic of practical reason—that acting against the hypotheti-

cal imperative is contradictory. This gives us a sense of practical contradiction—of contradiction in the will—which is different from but not weaker than "theoretical" contradiction.

Since this is the sort of contradiction implied by the analyticity of hypothetical imperatives, it is reasonable to think that this will be the sort of contradiction employed in the categorical imperative tests. On the Practical Contradiction Interpretation, such a contradiction in the universalization of an immoral maxim is exactly what the test shows. In the world of the universalized maxim, the *hypothetical* imperative from which the false promiser constructs his maxim is no longer true. It was "if you want some ready cash, you ought to make a false promise." But at the same time that he employs this hypothetical imperative in constructing his maxim, he wills its falsification, by willing a state of affairs (the world of the universalized maxim) in which it will be false. In that world, false promising is not a means to getting ready cash. Kant, therefore, not only has a specifically practical sense of "contradiction," but should be seen as employing it in his contradiction tests.

The Hegelian Objections

Like the Logical Contradiction Interpretation, the Practical Contradiction Interpretation enables us to answer the Hegelian objections, and it shows even more clearly why those objections miss the *moral* point of a universalization test. The first Hegelian objection is that the universalization test is empty. There is no contradiction in a system without such practices as deposits or promises. The proponent of the Logical Contradiction view replies that the contradiction is not merely in a system without these practices but in an agent engaging in these practices in a system without them. On the Practical Contradiction Interpretation the answer we shall give is still better. The person who tries to will the universalization of this maxim is not only thereby willing a situation in which practices like deposits and promises do not exist. He is also willing that they do exist, precisely because he is willing to *use* them to achieve his ends. The man who wills the universalization of the false promise, for example, is also willing to use a false promise to get the money. But he cannot rationally will to use a promise to achieve his end at the same time that he wills a situation in which promises will not be accepted, because if his promise is not accepted it is not a means to achieving his end. Thus the Practical Contradiction Interpretation's answer to this Hegelian objection is that Kant need not be assuming that everyone wants there to be deposits. The man in the example wants there to be a system of deposits, because he proposes to use that system as the means to his end. In a clear sense he is unfair.

The second objection was that the test is too strong. You cannot universalize "succor the poor," since if everyone did this poverty would be eliminated and there would be no one to succor. The Practical Contradiction Interpretation answers this objection both readily and, in an obvious way, correctly. One's purpose in succoring the poor is to give them relief. The world of the universalized maxim only contradicts one's will if it thwarts one's purpose. A world without poverty does not contradict this purpose, but rather satisfies it another (better) way, and no contradiction arises.[26]

Contradictions in Conception and in the Will

Another advantage of this view is that it should enable us to employ the same sense of contradiction in interpreting the two contradiction tests, and yet still to distinguish between them. Consider what the other two interpretations say about this question. The Logical Contradiction Interpretation forces us to look for a different sort of contradiction altogether for the contradiction in the will test, since Kant is explicit about the fact that no logical inconceivability is involved there. The Logical Contradiction Interpretation seems initially to have the virtue that it involves no presuppositions about rationality that are not completely uncontroversial. The contradiction it identifies in universalizing immoral maxims is of a familiar kind. But this advantage is lost if we must use different presuppositions in order to understand the contradiction in the will test. Often, proponents of the Logical Contradiction Interpretation for contradictions in conception end up with something like a utilitarian or a teleological view about contradictions in the will. But the utilitarian reading has the same problem for the second test as it does for the first: it presupposes a morality-laden conception of rationality. The Teleological Contradiction Interpretation, on the other hand, does not seem to allow for a very well-defined distinction between the two tests. I suppose one may say that in the case of a contradiction in conception, some specific instinct or action is found not to be best adapted to its particular purpose; and in the case of a contradiction in the will, we lose some positive good needed for a teleological system, or for the systematic harmony of human purposes. But it is not really obvious that these are distinct. Recall that Paton could not find a contradiction in the false promising case without assuming that promises are needed for the harmony of human purposes. This problem tends to collapse the two tests.

Now consider the Practical Contradiction Interpretation. If a thwarted purpose is a practical contradiction, we must understand the contradiction in the will test this way: we must find some purpose or purposes which belong essentially to the will, and in the world where maxims that fail these tests are universal law, these essential purposes will be thwarted, because the means of achieving them will be unavailable. Examples of purposes that might be thought to be essential to the will are its general effectiveness in the pursuit of its ends, and its freedom to adopt and pursue new ends. The arguments for self-development and mutual aid will then be that without the development of human talents and powers and the resources of mutual cooperation, the will's effectiveness and freedom would be thwarted. This is of course just a sketch. Exactly which purposes are essential to the will and how they can be shown to be so is a topic in its own right, which I will not pursue further here. The point is that the Practical Contradiction Interpretation gives a better account of the relation between the two tests than either of the others. The difference between the two tests will not lie in the use of a different kind of contradiction, as it does in the Logical Contradiction Interpretation. And yet there will be a difference. The purpose thwarted in the case of a maxim that fails the contradiction in the conception test is *the one in the maxim itself,* and so the contradiction can be said to be *in* the universalized maxim. The purpose thwarted in the case of the contradiction in the will test is not one that is in the maxim,[27] but one that is essential to the will.

The Problem of Natural Actions

The Practical Contradiction Interpretation, like the Logical, works especially well with respect to wrong actions which are conventional. But the reason why it works is slightly different. On the Logical Contradiction Interpretation, the contradiction arises because the agent wills to engage in a conventional action, but he also wills a state of affairs in which that kind of action will no longer *exist*. On the Practical Contradiction Interpretation, the contradiction arises because the agent wills to engage in a conventional action, but he also wills a state of affairs in which that action will no longer *work*. When we are dealing with an action that falls under a practice, the two views are readily confused, because the reason the action no longer works is *because* it no longer exists. But on the Practical Contradiction Interpretation it is the failure of efficacy, not the non-existence, that really matters.

This gives rise to the possibility that with the Practical Contradiction Interpretation we will be able to derive at least some of our duties of omission with respect to natural actions. Natural actions are not going to cease to exist if used wrongly, but their efficacy for some purposes may depend on their exceptional use. A great deal depends here on what the purpose is taken to be and how it is described. One case that is borderline between natural and conventional is stealing. That might seem wholly conventional, since property is a practice, but it is difficult to imagine an economic system in which the means of production and action were not guaranteed to the use of particular persons at particular times.[28] And any violation of these guaranteed assignments would be "stealing." Now if the purpose of stealing is to acquire something for your personal use or possession—to get something you want when you want it—and you imagine that anyone in your situation—anyone who wants something not assigned to him—steals it, as a standard procedure—then you see that under these conditions it is quite impossible to acquire something for your use or possession, to have it when you want it. The idea here is that what the thief really wants is to make something his property, to have some *guarantee* that he will have it when he wants it. His purpose is therefore thwarted if his maxim is universalized.

That case is borderline, but a similar analysis might apply to wholly natural acts. Here is a silly example. Suppose you are second in line for a job, and are considering murder as a way of dealing with your more successful rival. Can this be universalized? Killing is a natural act, not a conventional one. We cannot say that if this sort of action is abused the practice will die out, for that makes no sense whatever. Nor can we say that any amount or kind of use of killing will destroy its efficacy in achieving its purpose *if* we specify that purpose simply as that of getting someone dead. So here the test will only work if the purpose is specified differently. We must say that the purpose is that of securing a job, and we must emphasize the fact that if anyone else wants this job, or any job you hold, universalization makes you the victim. Now, it may seem that the purpose that is thwarted by universalization—that of staying alive—is not the same as the purpose in your maxim—that of securing the job. This would be bad. It is the fact that it is the purpose in the maxim that gets thwarted in the world of the universalized maxim that enables us to carry out the test without any extraneous information about the agent's desires and purposes. If it is some other, contingent, purpose that gets thwarted, then it looks as if the test (i) requires empirical information about what other purposes people have and (ii) functions idiosyncratically, giving different results to people with different desires. These are both conclusions the Kantian wants to avoid. We shall avoid them here by pointing out that this is not a case of an extraneous end being thwarted. Staying alive matters in this example because it is a necessary condition of having the job.

That might seem like a silly thing to say in this case, but it is an application of a point which is not in general silly at all. In *Utilitarianism*, Mill argues that justice is specifically concerned with a special object of human interest—that of security. Security is not merely one good thing among others, but to put it in Kantian language, a condition of the goodness of anything else:

> . . . but security no human being can possibly do without; on it we depend for all our immunity from evil, and for the whole value of all and every good, beyond the passing moment, since nothing but the gratification of the instant could be of any worth to

us, if we could be deprived of anything the next instant by whoever was momentarily stronger than ourselves.[29]

The Kantian may avail himself of this insight. To want something is to want to be secure in the possession of it. The use of violent natural means for achieving ends cannot be universalized because that would leave us insecure in the possession of these goods, and without that security these goods are no good to us at all. So, if we include as part of the purpose that the agent wants to be secure in the possession of the end, we can get a practical contradiction in the universalization of violent methods. And in fact, Kant's argument in the *Metaphysical Elements of Justice* about why there must be proprietary rights is not very different from Mill's: it is that we need to be secure in the possession of certain sorts of goods in order to successfully make use of them. (MM 246ff/52ff)

The method of dealing with natural acts which I have just suggested focuses on the question whether you could really achieve your purpose—with everything that purpose involves (i.e., security in its possession) in a world where your action was the universal method of achieving that purpose. Another way to approach this problem is to consider whether the social conditions that allow violence to work as a method of achieving this purpose would exist if it were the universal method. It is true that natural laws are all that is needed to make violent methods yield their natural effects, but more is needed to make them yield their social effects. For example, the simplest way of making the argument against cheating on an entrance examination is to point out that if everyone did this the entrance examination would cease to be used as a criterion for selection. Since a lot of incompetent people would get in, it would be found impracticable and some other method would be chosen. ("Everyone would laugh at entrance examinations as vain pretenses.") Placing people in jobs is like this: it is something for which there must be a method, and if one method were universally abused, another, not liable to that abuse, would be found. Now if murder to get a job were universally practiced, the best candidates would not get the jobs. So whatever it is about the old selection process that makes this possible would be changed. Perhaps no one would be told who the candidates were, or people would even keep it a secret what jobs they held. Again, the argument sounds silly in this case but is meant to bring out something that is not silly. Cheating could not be the first or standard procedure for getting into an educational program. It is essentially parasitic on the existence of another method. Violence, in many cases, also has this parasitic nature when it is a way of achieving a purpose in society.

The Practical Contradiction Interpretation can therefore handle some cases of natural actions. A harder kind of case would be something like killing for revenge, or out of hatred. In these cases it is not some enduring condition that the agent wants to achieve—he wants the immediate result—so the security consideration will not help us here.[30] These grim kinds of cases are managed without difficulty when using the Formula of Humanity, but it will be difficult to find any contradiction of the sort needed here. And this problem applies to the suicide case as well. On the Practical Contradiction Interpretation we cannot get an analysis of that case, for the suicide's purpose, if it is release from his own misery, will not be thwarted by universal practice. There is an important parallel to this problem. Kant's theory is least helpful and least plausible when one is dealing with a case where other people around the agent have already introduced evil into the situation. His debate with Benjamin Constant about whether you may lie to the murderer whose victim is hidden in your house, and his insistence that there is never a right to revolution, are infamous examples of cases in which his view seems to forbid us to try to prevent or to set right the wrongs committed by others. I believe that there is a similar sort of difficulty in making out what Kant is to say about cases where something has gone wrong inside, where the problem is not the selfish pursuit of an ordinary purpose, but a diseased purpose. I do not say that Kant is unable to give us an account of these cases. But the kind of case around which the view is framed, and which it handles best, is the temptation to make oneself an exception: selfishness, meanness, advantage-taking, and disregard for the rights of others. It is this sort of thing, not violent crimes born of despair or illness, that serves as Kant's model of immoral conduct. I do not think we can fault him on this, for this and not the other is the sort of evil that most people are tempted by in their everyday lives.

Conclusion

It is conceivable that Kant did not perceive the differences among these three readings, and that this is why language supporting all of them can be found in his texts. In a certain kind of case, the three readings are very close. Where the immoral action involves the abuse of a practice, the Logical Contradiction Interpretation says you cannot universalize because the practice will not exist and the action will be inconceivable; the Teleological Contradiction Interpretation says you cannot universalize because the practice will then not be best suited for what in a teleological system would be its natural purpose; and the Practical Contradiction Interpretation says you cannot universalize because if the practice disappears it will of course no longer be efficacious in producing your purpose. These three analyses are very close, and for this kind of case the differences are insignificant. It is only when we begin to consider the problems created by natural actions,

the Hegelian objections, and the need to extend our analysis in the right way to the contradiction in the will test that differences emerge. In my view, the Practical Contradiction Interpretation deals with these problems better than the other two, although not always with complete success.

The best argument for it, however, is that it employs the sense of contradiction which Kant identifies in his analysis of the hypothetical imperative. Each interpretation must presuppose some notion of rationality in determining whether a rational being can will the universalization of a maxim at the same time as that maxim without contradiction. The Logical Contradiction view works with a notion of contradiction indistinguishable from that of theoretical rationality and this is a great advantage. But this advantage is lost when we turn to contradictions in the will, which then require another interpretation. The Teleological Contradiction view works with a rather rich notion of rationality as aiming at a harmony of purposes. I think on Kant's view pure reason does aim at a harmony of purposes, but that only morality tells us how that is to be achieved. We cannot reason morally from that idea. The Practical Contradiction view uses a specifically practical notion of rationality and of contradiction which springs from the notion of the will as a causality. This is not a morality-laden notion of rationality, for on Kant's view this notion is needed to explain *instrumental* rationality.

Yet the same notion will also be employed in explaining why the moral law applies to us. The Practical Contradiction Interpretation allows us to sketch an explanation, in terms of autonomy, of why the conformity to the Formula of Universal Law is a requirement of reason. Start with a parallel to theoretical reasoning: as a rational being, you may take the connection between two events to be a causal one. But this connection must always hold—must hold universally—if the cause you have identified is indeed *sufficient* to produce that effect. Only in this case is what you have identified a law. The rational will, regarding itself as a causality, models its conception of a law on a causal law. As a rational being you may take the connection between a purpose you hold and an action that would promote it to be a reason for you to perform the action. But this connection must be universalizable *if the reason is sufficient.* Only in this case have you identified a law. If universalization would destroy the connection between action and purpose, the purpose is not a sufficient reason for the action. This is how, on the Practical Contradiction Interpretation, the contradiction in conception test shows an immoral maxim to be unfit to be an objective practical law. As an autonomous rational being, you must act on your conception of a law. This is why autonomy requires comformity to the Formula of Universal Law.[31]

Notes

[1] References to Kant's ethical works will be given in the text, using the abbreviations below. In each case, the first number represents the page in the relevant volume of the Prussian Academy of Sciences edition of Kant's works, and the second the page number in the translation listed.

G *Foundations of the Metaphysics of Morals.* Translated by Lewis White Beck. Library of Liberal Arts, 1959.

C₂ *Critique of Practical Reason.* Translated by Lewis White Beck. Library of Liberal Arts, 1956.

MM *The Metaphysics of Morals.* For the Preface and General Introduction, and for the *Metaphysical Principles of Virtue,* I have used the translation by James Ellington in *Immanuel Kant: Ethical Philosophy.* Hackett, 1983. For the *Metaphysical Elements of Justice,* see the translation by John Ladd, Library of Liberal Arts, 1965.

[2] Immanuel Kant, *Religion Within the Limits of Reason Alone,* translated by Theodore M. Greene and Hoyt H. Hudson. Harper Torchbooks, 1960, p. 5.

[3] Of course, these are general categories and fitting everyone's views into them would involve distortion; there are many slight differences in interpretation. I think, however, that they represent the main kinds of reading, and will indicate how I am classifying some important commentators as I present the views.

[4] See the last paragraph of Section Two, G 444-445/ 63-64; also the last full paragraph on G 420/38.

[5] John Stuart Mill, *Utilitarianism,* in *Mill: Utilitarianism with Critical Essays,* edited by Samuel Gorovitz, Bobbs-Merrill Text and Commentary Series, p. 15.

[6] See Paul Dietrichson, "Kant's Criteria of Universalizability" in *Kant: Foundations of the Metaphysics of Morals: Text and Critical Essays,* edited by Robert Paul Wolff. Bobbs-Merrill, 1969. This essay is based on Dietrichson's "When is a Maxim Fully Universalizable?" *Kant-Studien,* Band 55, 1964. For Kemp's views, see J. Kemp, "Kant's Examples of the Categorical Imperative" *The Philosophical Quarterly,* Vol. 8 No. 30, 1958, also reprinted in *Kant: Foundations of the Metaphysics of Morals: Text and Critical Essays.* I attribute this view to Allen Wood on the basis of his paper "Kant on False Promises" in *Proceedings of the Third International Kant Conference,* edited by Lewis White Beck. Dordrecht Holland: D. Reidel, 1972.

[7] Dietrichson, "Kant's Criteria of Universalizability" in *Kant: Foundations of the Metaphysics of Morals: Text and Critical Essays,* p. 188.

[8] For a good discussion of this issue, see Onora Nell (O'Neill), *Acting on Principle: An Essay on Kantian Ethics.* Columbia University Press, 1975. Although I do not agree with this work on every point, it will be obvious to anyone who knows the book that I owe a great deal to it.

[9] Kant does not use the Formula of Universal Law to derive the duties of justice in the *Metaphysics of Morals.* Instead he uses the Universal Principle of Justice, which tells us that our actions should be consistent with universalizable external freedom. (MM 230-231/ 35) But in the *Foundations,* Kant suggests that violations of right are wrong in the same way as false promising (G 430/48), and this suggests that they should be derivable from the contradiction in conception test. Furthermore, it is reasonable to think that if injustices are by definition inconsistent with universalizable external freedom, their universalizations should display contradictions in conception if anything does.

[10] John Rawls, "Two Concepts of Rules," *Philosophical Review* 64, 1955.

[11] Obviously, this discussion is not intended as a complete treatment of Hegel's criticisms of Kant's ethical philosophy. I mean only to cover some objections that recur in the literature and are usually referred to Hegel.

[12] H. B. Acton, *Kant's Moral Philosophy.* Macmillan, St. Martin's Press, 1970, pp. 24-25.

[13] F. H. Bradley, "Duty for Duty's Sake," Essay IV in *Ethical Studies.* (1876), Oxford, 1970, p. 155.

[14] H. J. Paton, *The Categorical Imperative.* (1947), University of Pennsylvania Press, 1971, pp. 146-157.

[15] See Lewis White Beck, *A Commentary on Kant's Critique of Practical Reason.* Chicago, 1960, pp. 159-163; and Bruce Aune, *Kant's Theory of Morals.* Princeton, 1979, pp. 59ff.

[16] Paton, *The Categorical Imperative,* p. 151.

[17] This emerges when Paton, in discussing one of Kant's direct uses of teleological language, says that in this case " . . . Kant is on stronger ground. Here his teleology is more explicit . . . " See *The Categorical Imperative,* p. 155.

[18] This is contrary to the view of Paton, who thinks this example is the best evidence that Kant intended the typic to be ordinary causal laws, and also that it is not a good example. See *The Categorical Imperative,* p. 148.

[19] Paton, *The Categorical Imperative,* p. 140.

[20] Immanuel Kant, *Critique of Pure Reason* (1781 and 1787), translated by Norman Kemp Smith, Macmillan, St. Martin's Press, 1965, p. 560, (A 686-687; B 714-715).

[21] Paton, *The Categorical Imperative,* p. 153.

[22] This view is supported by Marcus Singer in *Generalization in Ethics* and a version of it is supported in Onora Nell (O'Neill), *Acting on Principle: An Essay on Kantian Ethics.*

[23] The test works most smoothly where the hypothetical reasoning behind the maxim to be tested is purely instrumental. The problem of universalizing maxims like that of becoming a doctor in order to make one's living (the objection being that not everyone could do this) arises because the reasoning is constitutive. Being a doctor is an *instance* of a profession with certain features which the agent wants. The more we can specify these features, the closer we will come to the testable reasons that should be embodied in the maxim.

[24] See for instance Singer, *Generalization in Ethics,* p. 259. Although Nell's version of the test is like the Practical Contradiction Interpretation in that she emphasizes the impossibility of acting on the maxim in the world of the universalized maxim, she supposes that Kant appeals to the Law of Nature formulation because applying the notions of self-defeat or self-frustration is not as clear as applying that of contradiction. See *Acting on Principle,* p. 63. Although she notes that Kant thinks that hypothetical imperatives are analytic, she thinks this is in a loose sense. (p. 70n)

[25] Perhaps you will be tempted to say that this case does not occur. There would always be some extraneous reason for such a person not to take the means. This temptation is one to be resisted. Kant thinks that we are imperfectly rational: and one thing this means is that we will not always have *reasons* for being uninfluenced by reasons. It may be that there is always a cause of irrationality. Perhaps someone does not take the means to an end because she is depressed. This can be forced into the mold of a reason ("I feel so tired it would not be worth it to me right now"), and the agent herself will feel inclined to treat it that way. But it may not be the best way to describe what is really going on to say she has a reason not to take the means. If we think she would be better off taking the means even though she feels lethargic, we will find it better to say the depression is a cause of irrationality rather than that it changes the structure of the available reasons.

[26] See the discussion in Singer, *Generalization in Ethics,* (1961) Atheneum, 1971, pp. 279-292.

[27] In Kant's first set of examples of the contradiction in the will test in the *Foundations,* there is no purpose given in the maxim. But even if we assigned purposes to the agents who adopt these maxims the point will hold. The man who does not develop his talents and powers presumably has the purpose of taking his ease. But the purpose that is thwarted is the development of his rational nature.

[28] I do not mean that there has to be property in the thick Lockean sense of complete control of an object and absolute right to do anything with it. I only mean that there could not be a society in which persons did not have rights of use with respect to objects for certain durations—say the way you "own" the furniture in your office. An editor has pointed out to me that a system without something like promises may be just as hard to imagine, in which case those too will be a borderline case.

[29] Mill, *Utilitarianism,* in *Mill: Utilitarianism, Text and Critical Essays,* p. 50.

[30] Here is something we cannot do. We cannot get something like the security condition by saying that the vengeful killer wants to kill and get away with it—he wants not to be killed in turn himself, so he cannot universalize his vengeful maxim. We cannot say this because we don't know it. The security argument works only if we can say that security in the possession of a good or the continuance of a situation is really a condition of achieving that good or situation at all. It must not be a separate end. But wanting to get away with it is a separate end; getting away with it is not a condition of getting revenge. For notice that if we tried to make this our argument a vengeful killer would be morally all right if he did not mind paying the price.

[31] I would like to thank an editor for comments which have enabled me to make this paper much clearer.

Andrews Reath (essay date 1989)

SOURCE: "The Categorical Imperative and Kant's Conception of Practical Rationality," in *The Monist,* Vol. 72, No. 3, July, 1989, pp. 384-410.

[*In this essay, Reath traces Kant's derivation of the moral law from his conception of practical rationality.*]

1. Introduction

The primary concern of this paper is to outline an explanation of how Kant derives morality from reason. We all know that Kant thought that morality comprises a set of demands that are unconditionally and universally valid (valid for all rational beings). In addition, he thought that to support this understanding of moral principles, one must show that they originate in reason *a priori,* rather than in contingent facts about human psychology, or the circumstances of human life.[1] But do we really understand how he tries to establish that moral principles originate in reason? In at least two passages in the second section of the **Groundwork,** Kant insists upon the importance of grounding the moral law in practical reason *a priori,* and subsequently states a conception of practical reason from which he appears to extract a formulation of the Categorical Imperative.[2] The reasoning employed in these passages would appear to be of central importance to the overall argument of the **Groundwork,** but in each case the route travelled from the definition of practical reason to the ensuing formulation of the moral law is obscure. My goal is to work out a plausible reconstruction of this portion of Kant's argument. At the very least, I hope that my interpretation will illuminate the distinctive structure of the Kantian approach to questions of justification in ethics. What I understand of Kant's view leads me to believe that its aims and overall shape are different in important respects from what is often assumed. It also represents an approach to foundational issues in ethics, which provides an alternative to many contemporary attempts to ground morality in reason.

I will be limiting myself to a small part of this very large question. Theories of this sort, Kant's included, tend to address two separate questions of justification. The first is that of justifying one substantive moral conception as opposed to another. This is primarily a concern with *content:* which moral principles should we adopt, given the fact that we are going to adopt some? The second is that of giving some account of why moral reasons make valid claims on agents, or why we should adhere to them (whatever they may involve). This is a concern with the reasons that one has for acting morally, or with the justification of the moral life. In part this is a question of identifying, or producing, the motivation for adhering to moral principles, but I shall refer to it less specifically as a concern with their *validity.* I will be examining Kant's approach to the first issue—how he derives the outline of a substantive moral conception from a concept of practical reason.[3] Here I shall be particularly concerned to identify the conception of practical rationality that Kant draws on, and to explain how it functions in his derivation of morality.

Contemporary attempts to derive morality from reason often seek an independent foundation for morality in a more basic conception of rationality. As David Wiggins has put it, such a theory supposes that one can "construct an *a priori* theory of rationality or prudence such that . . . rationality is definable both independently of morality and ideals of agency and in such a way as to have independent leverage in these ancient disputes."[4] In other words, it seeks a comprehensive and morally neutral definition of practical rationality that is universally valid, from which a set of moral principles can be derived. In this way, one would have provided a jus-

tification for a set of moral principles, and shown that adherence to them is a basic requirement of rationality on conduct, which has authority for any agent regardless of professed desires and motives.

It is often assumed that Kant's theory fits this pattern, by attempting to provide a foundation for morality that is morally neutral, and thus, in Bernard Williams's phrase, to construct morality "from the ground up."[5] I will argue that this is not the case. While the conception of practical rationality which Kant assumes is *a priori* and has a claim to universal validity, it is not empty of substantive ideals. Indeed it is a distinguishing feature of a Kantian view that it does not attempt to derive morality from a morally neutral starting point. Its general structure is that it ties the content of a moral conception to a more general set of ideals—of the person, of agency, or of rationality—which, while applying widely, and providing some kind of independent perspective on morality, need not be empty of moral content. The validity of the moral conception for us is established by the fundamental character of these ideals and the reasonableness of applying them to ourselves, and the motivation to act from it comes ultimately from an understanding of the ideals in question, and of how they are expressed in the actions which it singles out.

If this is the case, Kant's account is not aimed at showing that bad conduct is irrational, or inconsistent with principles to which one is committed qua rational, as that is often understood, where the sense of irrationality is explained solely in terms of prudential or instrumental rationality plus logical consistency. More generally, Kant clearly did not think that any form of instrumental rationality (rationality as the effective pursuit of one's ends, or as consistency among desires, beliefs and actions) is sufficient by itself to yield a moral conception. For it is fundamental to his moral view that we recognize different forms of practical reasoning, that moral evaluation is distinct from prudential and involves a set of concerns not reducible to something more primitive.[6] The Hypothetical Imperative and the Categorical Imperative, or what Kant also calls empirical practical reason and pure practical reason, represent different kinds of normative standards and patterns of evaluation. Indeed it is a major aim of the **Critique of Practical Reason** to show that the "empirically conditioned use of reason" does not exhaust the use of reason in the practical sphere, and that there is such a thing as pure practical reason. [*KpV* 15/15]

We may distinguish these two forms of rationality provisionally as follows. The Hypothetical Imperative is the principle underlying the empirically conditioned use of reason. It states that if one wills an end, then one ought to will the means needed to achieve it insofar as they are in one's power (or else give up the end). It assesses the rationality of actions relative to the ends which one desires or has adopted, and thus yields specific judgments about what an individual ought to do only in conjunction with information about her ends.[7] What makes this use of reason "empirically conditioned" is that it assesses actions relative to given desires or ends, and yields judgments whose application is conditional on one's desires or ends. The Hypothetical Imperative is often thought to apply primarily to the pursuit of one's own happiness, but in fact it applies to the pursuit of any end that an agent can adopt, including moral ends. In contrast, pure practical reason will address questions of evaluation that are beyond the scope of empirical practical reason. It will introduce standards for evaluating actions and ends that are non-instrumental, and apply independently of given desires and ends—principles which ground judgments of intrinsic goodness or acceptability to anyone, which for Kant are the basis of justification to others. There are grounds for thinking, in addition, that pure practical reason will be concerned with the evaluation and choice of ends for their own sake (in contrast to the choice of actions as means to ends). This will include the capacity to elect aims and goals viewed as intrinsically good or worthy of choice, which can initiate actions and structure larger practical pursuits.[8]

Any account of how Kant derives the content of the moral law from reason must be consistent with the existence of these distinct forms of rationality. But then the question arises of how a derivation of the moral law from reason can actually be carried out. The moral law cannot be derived from any notion of empirical practical reason, and a derivation from pure practical reason would seem to lack independent force, since it already contains the concerns essential to morality. In a sense this is right. On the interpretation that I develop, something like moral ideals are embedded in the conception of choice and the ordinary use of practical reason from the start. But the way to explain Kant's view is to show how moral choice builds on features present in any form of choice, and thus to trace morality to features of rationality found in all forms of conduct. The fact that moral rationality cannot be derived from a more primitive (non-moral) basis need not imply that it is not found in less developed forms.

The key here is that Kant thought that *both* forms of reasoning inform *all* rational choice, including choice of actions that we might not think of as morally motivated. Even in the pursuit of purely personal ends, the rational agent is not concerned solely to make her actions rational relative to her desires. She will also view at least some of her ends as good in themselves, and as providing reasons for her actions whose justifying force extends to the point of view of others. Thus the concern with justifying reasons and with the goodness of ends that define pure practical reason is

found, in some form, in all choice; indeed, comprises the essential element in choice.

If moral reasoning represents a distinct form of rationality found in all forms of choice, then Kant's derivation of the moral law from reason should be understood along the following lines: moral choice represents the most complete realization of an ideal of rationality found in all forms of choice. All choice meets certain conditions, which, in moral choice, are extended to their limit, or completed—so that the conditions that define moral choice are built into the ordinary notion of rational choice.

To explain: we think of choice as guided by reasons, or normative considerations that the agent takes to provide some justification for an action. The reasons that guide agents' choices lead them to view their actions as good in some respect (and this is the source of their motivating force). They also have normative force from the point of view of others. They may be cited to explain or justify an action to others; and even if such explanations do not get others to accept or approve, they may provide a partial justification by enabling others to see why the agent took the action to be a good thing to do. In addition, Kant assumes, not implausibly, that as rational agents we take some of our reasons to be final or ultimate. The particular reasons for action that we may cite are in turn supported by more general reasons or principles, which give the particular reasons their normative force. Thus it would appear to be a structural feature of practical reason that some reasons function as final or ultimate reasons: they are viewed (by an agent) as good per se, and as conferring support on more specific concerns from which we act. What different agents take to provide final reasons may be quite varied. They could include specific ends or activities, such as a successful career, a personal relationship, or involvement in a social cause; or more general aims—e.g., happiness, or leading an honorable life. They might also be values such as honesty, fairness, or protecting one's own interests. Furthermore, an agent's final reasons may be more or less admirable. Some, properly cited, may be sufficient to get others to accept or approve of the resulting actions; others may fall short of this, rendering an action intelligible without fully justifying it.

This characterization of rational choice allows us to see the way in which moral choice might be viewed as the most complete realization of an ideal of rationality found in all forms of choice. Morally good choices are those which are fully justified in that the agent acts from reasons which are final and universally valid. What happens in moral choice is that the normative force characteristic of any reason has been extended along certain dimensions, as it were. In particular the justifying force which they have for the agent is universal and extends to the point of view of any agent—

so that it is sufficient to lead anyone to accept the action as good. In short, all rational choice is guided by normative considerations (reasons with normative force for the agent). In moral choice, the reasons from which the agent acts are in fact sufficient to justify the action to anyone.

I will now argue that such a view underlies Kant's derivation of the Categorical Imperative, and offers the best understanding of the connection that he draws between moral principles and the nature of practical reason. To do so I will offer a reconstruction of the derivation of the Formula of Universal Law in the first two sections of the *Groundwork.* Section 2 of the paper is an overview of the argument of *Groundwork,* I, which explains how Kant thinks that the concept of morality implicit in ordinary thought leads to the Formula of Universal Law. Sections 3 through 5 explain, respectively, what leads Kant to undertake another derivation of the Formula of Universal Law in *Groundwork,* II—this time one that traces it to the nature of practical reason; his conception of practical reason; and how it is most fully expressed by the Categorical Imperative.

2. The Aims of *Groundwork, I*

The *Groundwork* offers a foundational account of a concept of morality that Kant takes to be well-established in ordinary thought and practice; indeed he takes it to be *the* concept of morality. His concern is to provide an account that preserves and grounds its essential features. The initial aim of the First Section is to articulate the defining features of this concept of morality through an examination of ordinary moral consciousness—that is, through examples and attention to our concept of a "duty." What has received most attention are Kant's theses about moral worth—that an action has moral worth when done from the motive of duty, and that its moral worth is determined by its underlying principle, rather than its results or intended consequences.[9] While important Kantian doctrines, they ought to be viewed as intermediate conclusions on the way to the larger objective of a formulation of the Categorical Imperative. Kant uses his discussion of when an action displays a good will (has moral worth) to get at the principle of right conduct which a good will uses in assessing actions and deciding how to act. [*Gl* 392, 403-404][10]

I would argue that Kant's examination of ordinary moral consciousness in *Groundwork,* I, produces two results of primary importance. First, it reveals the special authority that (it is part of our concept of morality that) moral reasons and value have in practical deliberation. In more general terms, it reveals the formal features of moral reasons which are definitive of our concept of morality—the necessity and univerality with which they are thought to apply. Second, from this

concept of morality Kant derives the moral principle implicit in ordinary thought. He attempts to move from the formal features of moral reasons to the principle that allows us to determine what moral reasons there are in a given situation. This principle will turn out to be a representation of the general form of reasoning implicit in actual instances of moral deliberation.[11] The movement of the argument here is from form towards content, or more accurately, from formal considerations to a principle that, with suitable input, may be used to construct a substantive moral conception. Argumentation of this sort is characteristic of Kant's moral theory, and this same move is repeated in *Groundwork,* II. Here Kant argues that the very concept of a categorical imperative provides the only principle that can be a categorical imperative. An imperative that commands categorically (whatever its content) specifies an action as unconditionally and absolutely good, and thus applies with the necessity of a practical law.[12] Kant thinks that these concepts lead to the Formula of Universal Law, as a principle that expresses the concept of a practical law, or states the form of an unconditional requirement on action. Ultimately Kant will argue that the "form of volition in general" yields a principle by which one may guide one's particular volitions and choices. [Cf. *Gl* 444.] Here we see an important aspect of his claim that morality must rest on the principle of autonomy: the very nature of the will yields the principle from which the standards we recognize as moral are derived.

In the text, the notion of respect for the moral law provides the bridge between the claims about moral worth and the statement of the moral law, by focussing our attention on the overriding authority that moral concerns have in our thought.[13] Kant's examples have shown that the agent who exhibits the exemplary moral attitude is motivated simply by the recognition that his action is right—that is, by respect for the moral law. The motive of respect "excludes the influence of inclination," but also "outweighs it." [*Gl* 400, 401] It is a response to a kind of intrinsic value that is not mediated by an agent's desires. But more importantly, it is the recognition of a value that overrides other forms of value. To show respect for the moral law is to give the reasons which it yields an absolute weight in practical deliberation. [*Gl* 401n, 403] In this way, the attitude of respect for the law shows us that we take moral reasons to apply with *necessity* (do not presuppose any particular desires on the part of the agent and are independent of ways in which individuals tend to act) and to have *absolute priority* over other kinds of reasons (i.e., are overriding relative to the reasons given by an agent's desires). Their application must also be *universally valid,* since it is independent of contingent features of the self and motives an agent could lack.[14] They represent reasons that would hold for anyone in the relevant situation, and reasons that anyone can recognize as valid and authoritative. Necessity, absolute priority and universal validity are formal features in that they can be attributed to moral reasons without specifying the particular actions which such reasons pick out, and they may be taken as definitive of morality.[15] It is simply part of our concept of morality that, whatever moral reasons there turn out to be, they will apply to us in this way.

Otherwise put, reflection on the attitude of respect shows that we take moral principles and reasons to have the status of *law*. As the recognition of an order of value that limits the authority of other forms of value, respect is the proper attitude towards a law as such. Thus it shows that the idea of a practical law is central to our concept of morality. Here it is important to note that a practical law is not just a principle which makes claims about how anyone should act in a kind of situation, or one whose validity anyone can recognize—i.e., one which is universal in form. A practical law, in addition, provides reasons of special weight. Its application to an agent's circumstances yields determinate reasons for acting that apply with necessity and take priority over other kinds of reasons.[16] By noting how the conditions of necessity and universality function together, we can see that a practical law also grounds a kind of justification, which will be equally central to our concept of morality. The absolute weight that moral reasons possess must itself be one of the features that is universally applicable. Thus, the application of a practical law yields reasons for acting that *anyone* can recognize as *overriding* in that situation. That would seem to be the strongest kind of reason that there is, and one which justifies completely.

This suggests a way of understanding Kant's final move to the statement of the Formula of Universal Law in **Groundwork,** I. When moved by respect for the law, one is concerned with the "universal conformity of [one's] action to law as such." [*Gl* 402] That is, one wants one's action to be supported by reasons that are necessary and universally valid (unconditionally valid), and thus sufficient to justify the action fully to anyone. The following would seem to be a principle that expresses the practical implications of these concepts, and as such a candidate for the "supreme principle of morality":

> P: Let your reasons for performing an action at the same time suffice to justify your action fully to anyone no matter how situated (give anyone reason to accept what you do).

It is a plausible expression of the requirement that the agent's maxim have the "form of a practical law" (meet the formal criteria of necessity and universality implied by the concept of a practical law), and one who acts from this principle would be realizing the ideals central to the concept of morality. The principle that Kant in fact states is:

> FUL: Act only on a maxim which you can at the same time will should hold as a universal law.

Thus, Kant must take the idea of acting from maxims that you could act on while willing that everyone act on them to be equivalent to, or to express, the idea of acting from reasons that are necessary and universally valid. The argument needs supplementation to see why the idea of necessity and universal validity gets cashed out in terms of universalisability. If these principles are equivalent, it is because the Formula of Universal Law provides a procedure for determining whether one's reasons are unconditionally valid. As I interpret it, the key idea is that of reasons sufficient to justify one's action fully to anyone. Since this ideal is quite abstract, we need a way to determine when a maxim satisfies it. This must be the intent of the Formula of Universal Law: asking whether your maxim is one you can at the same time will as a universal law should be construed as the way of determining whether you are acting from reasons that anyone can accept.[17]

3. Why Moral Principles Must Originate in Reason

Early in **Groundwork,** II, Kant stresses at several points that moral principles must originate in reason *a priori,* and at least two of these passages are preparatory to another derivation of the Formula of Universal Law.[18] It is evident that Kant now seeks a deeper grounding for the concept of morality articulated thus far, by connecting it directly with the nature of practical reason. Why? His primary motivation must be that a grounding of this sort is needed to explain and to preserve the necessity and universality which have emerged as definitive of moral reasons in ordinary thought. If substantive moral reasons do have the unconditional validity that we take them to have, they must come from a principle that originates in reason *a priori,* since only reason yields principles that apply in this way. A theory that seeks the origin of moral principles elsewhere, such as an empiricist theory, cannot account for their standing as practical laws. Thus, Kant's insistence on the importance of deriving moral principles from reason is in part a rejection of alternative accounts as inadequate, in being unable to ground what he has identified as the features essential to our concept of morality.

To get clear about the problem that Kant is addressing, we ought to note that the first section of the **Groundwork** simply assumes the ordinary concept of morality, and that Kant thinks that mere clarification of what this concept implies leaves open the possibility that it involves a kind of delusion, or is an empty idea.[19] Perhaps the considerations that we recognize as moral do not really have the authority that we accord them. We may take certain substantive principles such as truth-telling, refraining from manipulation and coercion of others, helping others, etc, when properly applied, to yield unconditional reasons for acting. But our taking them in this way may reflect nothing more than a process of social conditioning for which no further justification can be given. Or the validity of these principles may depend on desires that one could lack, so that an agent without these desires could claim exemption from the principle. Perhaps there are no unconditional reasons for acting, and the concept of morality, defined as the set of such reasons (or the set of practical laws), while perfectly coherent, is empty and contains nothing. At issue here for Kant is whether there is such a thing as "morality" in the sense of that term implicit in ordinary practice. If morality is what it claims to be, it consists of practical laws; but principles with the character of law must originate in reason.

Kant's account is not directed towards individuals who claim that the authority of moral concerns is illusory, but rather toward those whose understanding of morality threatens to make it an illusion, or to undermine its central features.[20] These include both agents whose moral practice implicitly fails to acknowledge that moral principles have the status of law, and theorists whose account of morality is unable to explain how moral conclusions can have this status. Regarding the first, one of the major obstacles to good conduct in Kant's eyes is not the explicit denial of moral claims, but the tendency to exempt oneself from moral requirements through various forms of rationalization.[21] We often weaken principles we otherwise accept by making exceptions for ourselves, or by interpreting them so as not apply to the situation in which one is acting. This is to act as though the claims of self-interest are on a par with, or even limit, moral claims, and is equivalent in practice to denying that moral requirements have the status of law. What is needed to counter this tendency is an unambiguous recognition of the authority of moral claims and a story that explains where it comes from. In this respect, moral theory plays a particular practical role for Kant: a proper understanding of the nature and status of moral claims is integral to producing the moral disposition.

Second, Kant's insistence on deriving morality from reason is a rejection of influential empiricist theories that ground moral obligation in empirical facts about human beings, including both psychological facts and facts about the needs of human society and the structure of social interaction. The empiricist may assume some principles of prudential rationality; but he will avoid *a priori* principles or normative standards whose motivation cannot be supplied by desires and behavioural tendencies people are generally observed to have. Kant's general criticism is that by deriving moral principles from empirically given desires, such theories are unable to ground the notion of a practical law. If the validity of a principle depends on the presence of a desire or interest that one may lack, then there may be agents without that motive, to whom the

principle would not apply. Such an agent could only be subject to criticism for lacking the motive which the principle presupposes. But that is to depart from the empiricist viewpoint, by introducing an *a priori* normative standard to which an individual's desires ought to conform.

Kant wishes to provide an understanding of moral requirements that supports their unconditional validity, and his alternative to empiricism is to derive the moral law from a conception of practical reason which is given *a priori*. Since Kant is concerned both with content and validity, he must first give a characterization of rational agency that yields this principle and, in addition, guides its application.[22] The best way to understand the connection is to say that the principle as stated expresses the conception of rational agency. This is to say that it is a principle of choice that an agent defined by that conception of rational agency would choose as his fundamental maxim, in which his practical rationality is most fully realized. Second, Kant must establish the validity of the principle for us by showing that we are rational beings in the required sense, or have reason to view ourselves in that way. Though this involves a separate and further step, which is not without its complications, it must to some extent depend on how the first step is carried out. Much of the issue of validity hinges on showing that the principle does express the conception of rational agency, or is the appropriate principle for a being with this nature to act on.

4. Kant's Conception of Practical Rationality

At the core of Kant's conception of rational agency is the idea that rational action is guided by considerations that the agent takes to provide justifications for acting in a certain way. We find this view in the following well-known and very important passage:

> Everything in nature works in accordance with laws. Only a rational being has the power to act according to the conception of laws, i.e., according to principles. This capacity is will [*Wille*]. Since reason is required for the derivation of actions from laws, will is nothing else than practical reason . . . the will is a faculty of choosing only that which reason, independently of inclination, recognizes as practically necessary, i.e., as good [*Gl* 412.]

The features of rationality cited are quite general, in that in addition to action, they apply to the formation of belief, the carrying out of a proof, and so on. Rational agency is defined here as the capacity to guide one's actions by normative standards that are generally applicable, such that one's understanding, acceptance and application of these standards to one's circumstances of action figure in the origination of actions. This section will take up the most significant assertions made in the passage, which amount to an ideal of practical rationality. (1) First, it makes claims about the way in which rational conduct originates in the conscious activity of the agent. (2) In addition, it proposes a distinctive view about the nature of practical reasoning and the structure of justification, in which general normative principles play a central role. (3) What emerges is that for Kant, practical reason is in the business of evaluation and justification, and that its essential role is to produce judgments about the goodness of actions. Rational conduct is motivated by the recognition of an action as good in some respect, where the goodness of the action consists in the fact that it follows from a general normative principle, or is justified by reasons whose force can be recognized by others. This will be a property of anything we can recognize as a choice.

First, regarding the origin of actions, Thomas Nagel interprets the passage as pointing out that rational action requires a certain form of explanation. He writes:

> Kant observed that rational motivation is unique among systems of causation because any explanation of action in terms of the theory refers essentially to the application of its principles by individuals to themselves in the determination of their actions.[23]

An agent's understanding of principles and reasons, and the resulting evaluative judgments, are the determining features of the causal process by which an action originates, and this must be reflected in any appropriate explanation of why the action occurred.[24]

To see how Kant understands the structure of practical reasoning, we should unpack his remarks that rational agency involves the ability to act "according to the conception of laws, i.e., according to principles." Kant is viewing practical rationality as the capacity to act from "objective practical principles."[25] These are normative principles, general in form, which state how an agent ought to act in a specified kind of situation.[26] As normative, they correct against distortions in one's judgment about how to act that come from inclinations, or other subjective factors such as lack of information, limited foresight, and so on. Their objectivity consists in the fact that they yield results valid for anyone, and this will have two sides. When properly applied to a situation, they will yield a conclusion about action that will have motivating force for anyone in that situation. In addition, the force which these conclusions have for the agent (in the relevant situation) can be understood by anyone, including by agents not in the relevant situation, for whom they are not reasons to act.[27] It is important to note that under objective practical principles Kant includes both principles that are conditionally valid as well as those that are unconditionally valid—in other words hypothetical as well as categorical imperatives.[28] A principle may make

claims about how one ought to act given the fact that one desires certain ends. It would be objective because it states how anyone with certain desires has (some kind of) reason to act in the kind of situation covered. Properly applied, it will yield conclusions about action that have force for anyone in that situation with the relevant desires; and the force of these conclusions can be understood by anyone, including those for whom they are not reasons to act (because they are not in that situation, because they lack or even disapprove of the assumed desires, etc.). In short, an objective practical principle translates facts about one's situation, and possibly one's ends and desires, into conclusions about how to act whose force can be understood by anyone.

By conceiving of practical reason, or will, as the ability to derive actions from principles, Kant suggests a model in which one arrives at a maxim or course of action by determining whether it is the correct instantiation of a normative principle judged to cover the situation in question. Deliberation proceeds by finding a principle covering the circumstances, and then determining what it requires in that situation. This process is open-ended in that the more general principles themselves may be evaluated by the same pattern of reasoning until one reaches an ultimate principle, which neither needs nor is susceptible to further evaluation. Though somewhat awkward as a picture of decision making, this conception does establish a plausible pattern for evaluating proposed actions: an intention already formulated can be assessed by seeing if it is the correct application of a general principle with justifying force for that kind of situation. Moreover, this is the pattern of reasoning that an agent might engage in when explaining why he did a certain action (either to others, or to himself viewing his action from a detached perspective).[29]

There are several points to note here. The first is that this conception locates choice within a thoroughly normative context, in that it sees it as motivated by what the agent takes to be a reason for acting. In this regard, practical reasoning should not be reduced to a kind of calculation or deduction (as might be suggested by one reading of "deriving actions from principles"). It does not simply select actions by deducing them from habitually followed rules, but is rather the ability to choose an action by seeing that it instantiates a normative principle taken to have justifying force. Practical reason evaluates according to normative principles. Second, since this pattern of reasoning may be carried out at higher and higher levels, the structure of practical reasoning leaves room for and creates a push towards ultimate principles that are a source of final reasons. This provides one ground for reading into the text the assumption that rational conduct is guided by some high level principles or ends. A rational agent will have a set of priorities and final ends that provide reasons for action in specific situations, as well as setting limits on the actions there are reasons to perform.

Third, because of their objectivity, the principles that figure in practical reasoning can ground justifications to others; indeed that is the primary impetus of objectivity in the practical sphere. To provide a justification for an action is just to support it with reasons whose force extends beyond the point of view of the agent for whom they are reasons to act. This one does by connecting an action (or maxim) with a general principle stating how anyone ought to act in a certain kind of situation. This provides support for the action which may potentially lead others to accept it (or may lead the agent to accept his own action when viewing it impartially, or from a later point in time). Kant expresses this by saying that objective practical principles issue in judgments of goodness of one sort or another (conditional or unconditional). To call an action or an end good in some respect is just to support it with reasons whose force can be understood by anyone—in other words to provide a justification, by bringing it under an appropriate principle. The goodness of a particular action is a function of the objectivity of the grounding normative principles.[30]

Fourth, these points make it plain that one pattern of reasoning serves the dual role of both guiding decision, and of justifying to others. It is distinctive of the Kantian view of rationality that there is a deep connection between motivation and justification: the same considerations by which an agent is motivated also provide some justification of the action to others. The rationality of choice lies in the fact that it is motivated by considerations whose force can be understood by anyone. In this respect it is built into the concept of a rational choice that it proceeds from the recognition of justifying reasons that can be stated in general form, or from judgments of goodness, and that these supply its motivation. It is in this sense that practical reason, as conceived by Kant, is essentially in the business of evaluation and justification.

To make this discussion less schematic and abstract, it may help to give some examples of principles from which an agent might act, which might figure in practical reasoning. Such principles might be formal, such as Kant's Hypothetical Imperative, or the standard principles of rational choice. But of greater interest are agents' substantive principles, which they take to state good ways of acting (to be objectively valid). These are principles accepted by an agent which are sources of reasons for the agent in particular situations, and which they might cite to others to justify their actions. Here some categories are needed, through their boundaries must remain approximate and inexact. One might first distinguish principles taken to represent objective, desire-independent values, e.g.:

(a) One should always be truthful, except when dishonesty is needed to resist manipulation or coercion against yourself, or harm to another.

(b) When someone on the street asks you for money, give what you can if they appear truly destitute, but not otherwise.

(c) Never respond to those Publisher's Clearing House mass mailings (since that simply plays into the crass commercialism of our society which ought to be resisted).

Some desire-dependent principles state generally reliable ways of satisfying desires that most people have, or might come to have at some point. These fit what Kant terms "counsels of prudence":

(d) Honesty is the best policy.

(e) Always respond to those Publishers Clearing House mass mailings; it takes little time and energy to fill out the form and you never know when you might win.

(f) Never give a sucker a break. (Since a sucker is an easy target, that is a generally effective way of furthering your ends.)

Other desire-dependent principles depend more openly on desires peculiar to specific individuals:

(g) When you see someone who is about to ask you for money, cross the street right away (so that you won't feel pressured to give, can avoid a disgusting sight).

(h) What is important above all else is leading a life of luxury and ease.

A principle that an agent accepts as objectively valid may or may not have the status that he or she takes it to have. A principle such as (c) might be viewed by the agent as unconditionally valid; but it might turn out to be no more than an expression of a value or a desire peculiar to the agent not universally supportable, and thus only conditionally valid. A principle such as (d) might simply be false if, in the circumstances intended by the agent, honesty is not the best way of furthering one's interests. (In that case, as stated, it would only be a subjective principle—a principle from which the agent acts, through not objectively valid.)

The last group do not appear to have much normative force; they seem more like characteristic principles of specific individuals, rather than principles that make claims about how people in general ought to act. But they may be viewed as (elliptical) hypothetical imperatives directed to individuals with certain desires (those undone by the sight of destitute people, or those who detest hard work, uncertainty and anxiety, etc.). If they in fact stated effective means of satisfying certain desires, and thus conformed to the Hypothetical Imperative, they would be objective practical principles. And they might have derivative normative force if they were instantiations for an individual of a higher level principle taken to have final justifying force, which (following Kant) could be termed the Principle of Happiness:

> (PH) Act so as to maximize over time the satisfaction of your own desires, whatever they may be.

I include these latter examples to show that the justifying force of some conditional principles might be quite minimal. The reasons derived from a principle may at most render an action intelligible, and fall far short of giving others reason to accept or approve of the actions that fall under it. In cases of this sort, objectivity may amount to nothing more than an appropriate connection between an action and given desires and aims of an individual in a particular situation, that anyone can discern. For example, if your guiding aim is to lead a life of luxury and ease, that will be a source of reasons for you in specific circumstances, even if not good reasons. I, who favor penury and struggle (or perhaps as someone in great need), can appreciate that you have a reason not to be generous in some situation given this general aim, even though I may reject the aim from which these reasons get their force, and the actions to which they lead.

This passage stresses the ability to act from normative principles, but that does not exhaust Kant's understanding of practical rationality. Elsewhere in the **Groundwork** Kant articulates other aspects of his conception of rational agency, which appear to be implicit in the fundamental notion.[31] In a second important passage preceding the introduction of the Formula of Humanity, Kant writes:

> The will is thought of as a faculty determining itself to action in accordance with the representation of certain laws, and such a faculty can only be found in rational beings. Now what serves the will as the objective ground of its determination is an end. . . . [*G*] 427]

What this passage and the ensuing discussion add is that rational agency also involves the ability to set and pursue ends. In light of the preceding account of practical reason, this capacity must be understood as a responsiveness to objective value. The rational agent does not simply act so as to satisfy given preferences, but adopts ends (including objects of its preferences) for reasons which have force from the point of view of others. Thus, it involves the capacity to select ends

viewed as good or worthy of choice, or to recognize or place a value on a state of affairs. To say that an end is adopted by being regarded as good or of value implies several things. An agent adopts an end because it instantiates a higher level end or value taken to be good per se (in which case the value of the end is derivative), or because it is taken to be good in itself. Once adopted, the end becomes a source of reasons for the agent which give it a degree of priority relative to one's other desires and ends. These reasons are desire independent to the extent that their force can remain constant despite fluctuations in the strengths of one's desires, and can override desires that may interfere with the pursuit of the end. They are sufficient both to initiate courses of action, as well as restrict other actions and pursuits that are inconsistent with an end. In addition, the agent's reasons for adopting an end should allow other agents to see why he takes it to be worthy of choice. Presumably its value to the agent can be recognized by others, and gives them a reason to respect the agent's pursuit of the end (though one that can be overriden in various ways).[32]

5. Practical Reason and Complete Justification

To understand how Kant locates the origin of moral principles in reason, we must consider how the above conception of practical rationality leads to a statement of the moral law. The view that I want to attribute to Kant is that the idea of a practical law is implicit in the nature of practical reason as a faculty that evaluates according to normative principles and constructs justifications. If so, the arguments of **Groundwork** I and II discussed earlier would give Kant what he needs. Recall his view that the idea of a practical law, or equivalently, the concept of a categorical imperative, yields a formulation of the only principle that can be a categorical imperative—that is, the idea of a practical law yields the Categorical Imperative.[33] If this argument holds, and if the idea of a practical law may be derived from the nature of practical reason (as understood by Kant), then the Categorical Imperative would have been traced to the nature of practical reason. What we want to see here is how the Categorical Imperative can be viewed as the principle in which this conception of practical rationality is most fully expressed—say, as the principle by which the business of practical reason is most fully carried out or completed. Roughly, it is because movement towards the unconditional is built into the process of evaluation and justification, and it is by finding justifications that are unconditionally valid that the process is completed. But justifications of this sort require grounding in a practical law. Since the Categorical Imperative states the form that any practical law will have, it is the principle by which the business of practical reason is completed. In this way, the characteristics of moral evaluation are tied to the nature of practical reason, and shown to be expressed in the Categorical Imperative.

To develop this point, let us consider what is needed to arrive at justifications that are complete. The discussion of the last section shows that objective practical principles, and the justifications which they ground, need only be conditionally valid. The objectivity of a practical principle requires only that its application yield conclusions about action that have force for anyone in the relevant situation, and that their force can be understood by anyone. This allows that an objective principle may show that an action is a good thing to do, or that there are reasons to perform it, given certain further conditions (the agent desires certain ends, accepts certain values, etc.). Justifications of this sort are partial or incomplete, and the ways in which they are conditioned lay out directions in which development towards completion is possible. Complete justification is achieved by extending the normative force of reasons as far as possible in these directions.

We may distinguish two different dimensions along which justification must move to achieve completion. The first is the direction of finality. You may judge that an action is good as a means to an end, or relative to certain desires. In that case, there is reason to perform the action only if there is reason to pursue the end, or if the desires in question are good ones to act on. Or, you might judge that an action or an end is good in itself, but that there is reason to pursue it only if certain limiting conditions are satisfied. It is good "other things being equal"—i.e., if it is consistent with your other priorities, violates no prior obligations, etc. Such judgments lead one to look for further reasons beyond those initially advanced in support of the action—either to seek reasons for the end, in the first case, or to determine whether the limiting conditions are satisfied, as in the second case. In both cases a search is initiated for final reasons not in need of further support, which either provide positive support for the action, or show that it is fully consistent with other considerations that have priority.

The other direction is towards universal validity. What you take to be a sufficient reason for acting may fall short of giving others reason to accept what you do. You intend to do X because it promotes a life of luxury and ease, which is for you a final aim of overriding importance. (It will give you happiness, and after all, what else is there?) I can see why X is a good thing for you given your aims, but since I do not place the same value on the aim as you, I am not moved by your explanation. (Besides, X shows a disregard for my person.) Here your justification is shown to be conditional on an assumption that is not universally acceptable; specifically, I have no reason to accept it. Justification is complete in this direction when the objectivity of reasons has been pushed towards universal validity. That is, in addition to leading others to see why you take the action to be a good thing to do, your reasons lead them to see it as good and to accept it. In

this case, an agent's reasons for acting are at the same time sufficient to give anyone reason to accept what he does.

One has travelled as far as one can in each direction when one arrives at reasons whose finality is universally valid. Such reasons are necessary, universal and take priority over others; that is, have the status of a practical law. They complete the process of justification in that they are sufficient to justify an action fully to anyone. This represents the most complete exercise of practical rationality, in that the normative features present in any reason are found in their most complete form, and the normal function of practical reason is carried out to a maximal degree.

I hope to have shown how, in Kant's view, moral choice builds on and extends a concern for justification and evaluation present in all forms of reasoning and choice. A strength of this interpretation is that it reveals a continuity between moral and non-moral choice that we tend to overlook due to various of Kant's dichotomies. It suggests, for example, that the psychology needed to explain how we can care about and act from the moral law is provided by the capacities constitutive of rational agency. Moral conduct requires no fundamentally different abilities or motives beyond those that go into the reasoned choice of actions and ends in ordinary contexts. What makes this possible, of course, is that Kant's conception of practical rationality already incorporates substantive ideals with a recognizably moral component. But that should not trouble us as long as the ideals are sufficiently fundamental to our way of viewing ourselves. Kant's project, as I have said, is not to derive the moral law from a morally neutral starting point, but to connect it with basic features of reasoning and choice, and to show how deeply embedded the elements of morality are in all forms of deliberation.

This paper has focused on the Formula of Universal Law. Since Kant derives three principal formulations of what he thinks is a single imperative, to complete the account begun here would require showing that the framework which it adopts may be extended to the other formulas and their equivalence. I will conclude with a suggestion about how this may be done, which I can only sketch here. It is that the alternate formulations of the Categorical Imperative express different aspects of a single conception of rational agency, and that we look to the relationships between these aspects of rationality to throw light on the equivalence of the formulas. We have seen that the core notion of practical rationality is the capacity to act from general normative principles which may be used to justify one's actions to others. The Formula of Universal Law may be regarded as the principle by which this capacity is most completely expressed, in that it embodies the ideal of acting from reasons that are unconditionally valid.

In representing the general form of a practical law, it states the ideal of complete justification. Rational agency also involves the ability to set and pursue ends, which in this context should be understood as the capacity to adopt ends viewed as good or of value. This aspect of practical rationality is most fully expressed in the Formula of Humanity, which states the requirement of guiding one's conduct by the recognition of an end of absolute value, that conditions the value of any end. Finally, the ideas of freedom and self-determination are built into this conception of practical rationality. The actions of a rational agent are self-determined in that they result from the agent's understanding and application to herself of reasons and principles that she accepts. The capacity to be guided by normative considerations makes one free by giving one the ability to choose actions other than those that would result from the balance of existing desires; you can do what you ought to do, regardless of what you desire. This aspect of practical rationality underlies the Formula of Autonomy. That the Formula of Autonomy follows directly from the Formula of Universal Law [G] 431-433] shows that autonomy is the foundation of morality—that moral principles must be such that we can regard ourselves as their authors and subject to them for that reason, and that when we act from the moral law we act with full autonomy. The latter point in particular must rest on the idea that in acting from reasons that are unconditionally valid, one's actions are most completely guided by one's capacity to act from reasons, and thus most completely self-determined. Thus the powers of freedom and self-determination implicit in all rational choice are most fully realized in morally good conduct. Kant thinks that the form of a practical law is identical with the form of volition in general, or the general structure of what it is to act from will.[34]

Here is a way of relating the different formulas by showing that each is the full expression of a different aspect of a single ideal of rational agency. It offers support for the contention that they are just different versions of the same Idea. One of the more remarkable features of Kant's theory is its attempt to demonstrate the deep connections between these ideals, and to weld them together into a single moral conception.[35]

Notes

[1] Cf., e.g., *Gl* 389. References to the *Groundwork of the Metaphysic of Morals* will be to the pagination in the Prussian Academy edition of Kant's *Gesammelte Schriften,* and are included in the body of the paper where possible. (Though I prefer Paton's title, the translation used is that of James Ellington.) Citations to other works of Kant give the page in translation, followed by the page in the Prussian Academy edition. The abbreviations and translations used are as follows:

Gl Grounding of the Metaphysics of Morals, tr. James W. Ellington, in *Kant's Ethical Philosophy* (Indianapolis, IN: Hackett Publishing Company, 1983).

KpV Critique of Practical Reason, tr. Lewis White Beck (Indianapolis, IN: Bobbs-Merrill, 1956).

KU Critique of Judgment, tr. James Meredith (Oxford: Clarendon Press, 1952).

MdS The Doctrine of Virtue: Part II of the Metaphysic of Morals, tr. Mary J. Gregor (University of Pennsylvania Press, 1964)

Rel Religion Within the Limits of Reason Alone, tr. T. M. Greene and H. H. Hudson (New York: Harper & Row, 1960)

[2] Cf. *Gl* 412ff and 426ff, which precede, respectively, the statements of the first two formulations of the Categorical Imperative. In the first Kant writes that "the principles should be derived from the universal concept of a rational being in general, since moral laws should hold for every rational being as such." He then says that to carry this out, he will "present the practical faculty of reason from its universal rules of determination to the point where the concept of duty springs from it." In the second, Kant says that the moral law "must be connected (completely *a priori*) with the concept of the will of a rational being as such." The discovery of this connection requires a "step into metaphysics" and an investigation into the possibility of reason determining conduct *a priori.*

[3] In the Preface, Kant writes that "the present Groundwork . . . is nothing more than the seeking out and establishment of the supreme principle of morality. . . ." (*Gl* 392) The "seeking out" of the supreme principle occupies the first two sections of the *Groundwork;* their concern is the proper formulation of the moral law (the content) and they leave open the question of its validity. For Kant, the latter is the question of whether the demands contained in our ordinary concept of morality are indeed valid and real: do they really bind us? (For different statements of the question of validity see *Gl* 426, 445, and especially 449ff: "But why should I subject myself as a rational being . . . to this law?" Why must "the universal validity of our maxim as a law be the restricting condition of our action"?) The moral law is not "established" until the third section, when this issue is addressed. My discussion will be limited to the arguments of the first two sections of the *Groundwork.*

Recent commentators concerned with Kant's derivation of morality from reason have tended to take the validity of the moral law to be the main issue, and have thus focused on the third section, and related arguments in the *Critique of Practical Reason.* See, e.g., Thomas E. Hill, "Kant's Argument for the Rationality of Moral Conduct," *Pacific Philosophical Quarterly* 66, nos. 1 & 2 (Jan/April 1985); Henry E. Allison, "Morality and Freedom: Kant's Reciprocity Thesis," *The Philosophical Review* 95, no. 3 (July 1986); and Christine M. Korsgaard, "Morality as Freedom" (forthcoming in *Kant's Practical Philosophy Reconsidered*, the proceedings of the 7th Jerusalem Philosophy Encounter). (But see also her "Kant's Formula of Humanity" (*Kant-Studien* 77, no. 2, 1986), which includes an account of how the Formula of Humanity is derived from practical reason.) However it is equally important to see how Kant derives the content of the moral law from a conception of practical reason. Indeed, the answer to this question may largely determine how the later issue ought to be treated.

4 "Truth, Invention and the Meaning of Life," in *Proceedings of the British Academy,* LXII (1976), p. 364n. For a recent discussion and response to Wiggins's critique of this project see David Gauthier, "The Unity of Reason: A Subversive Reinterpretation of Kant," in *Ethics* 96 (October, 1985): 83-86.

5 See *Ethics and the Limits of Philosophy* (Cambridge, MA: Harvard University Press, 1985), p. 28. Williams's discussion of Kant by and large assumes that Kant's conception of practical reason is morally neutral; see ch. 4. Gauthier also makes this assumption (see work cited above, p. 84).

6 Here note Kant's distinction between the "predisposition to humanity in man, taken as a living and at the same time a rational being" and the "predisposition to personality in man, taken as a rational and an accountable being." [*Rel* 21ff/26ff] The former is a conception of instrumental rationality in that it involves, among other things, the ability to set and pursue ends on the basis of their contribution to one's overall happiness, understood to involve the maximally harmonious satisfaction of given desires. The predisposition to personality is the basis of morality, and Kant stresses that it is a "special predisposition" not included in the first. I am indebted to Stephen Engstrom for discussion of this passage and related issues.

7 This point is made by Thomas E. Hill, Jr., "The Hypothetical Imperative," *The Philosophical Review* 82 (1973): 443, whose account I follow in this paragraph.

8 For textual evidence of this interpretation see *MdS* 56/395; while in the Introduction to the *Metaphysic of Morals* pure practical reason had been described as a "power of principles" [*MdS* 10/214], here it is called "a power of ends as such." See also the "Conjectural Beginning of Human History" where reason is viewed as the power to set ends beyond those given by instinct and inclination (and which can create new desires), as well as the power to make provision for future ends

one may have; in *On History,* ed. Lewis White Beck (Indianapolis, IN: Bobbs-Merrill, 1975), 55/111-59/115. Though the uses of reason referred to here are not "pure," it is worth noting its independence from inclination, as well as the continuity between these uses of reason and the form of moral reasoning referred to at the end of the passage.

9 Cf. *Gl* 393-94, 397-401.

10 There is some ambiguity throughout the *Groundwork* as to whether Kant's primary focus is moral worth or moral rightness. I take it to be the latter, despite Kant's constant attention to acting from the motive of duty. Thus, I view the discussion of moral worth in the First Section as a step on the way towards a statement of the principle of right conduct. One aspect of Kant's theory that may promote this ambiguity is that the principle of right, in addition to outlining a procedure for evaluating actions, also determines the weight that moral reasons have relative to other kinds of reasons. Since moral worth is achieved by recognizing the priority of moral reasons and being motivated accordingly, considerations of right conduct lead naturally to considerations of moral worth.

11 In other words, moral deliberation will generally be about actions under descriptions, in which agents bring certain kinds of substantive considerations to bear on a situation (honesty, fairness, etc.). The Categorical Imperative is the schematic rendering of the reasoning implicitly used, which states its underlying form.

12 As he says, the "mere concept of a categorical imperative . . . [may] supply us with the formula containing the proposition that can alone be a categorical imperative"; and that "if I think of a categorical imperative, I know immediately what it contains." [*Gl* 420] I comment on this argument in n33 below.

13 Here see Kant's "third proposition" [*Gl* 400]: "Duty is the necessity of an action executed from respect for the law." While much is packed into this statement, I take the main idea to be that the concept of duty represents the special weight that those actions have which are done from the recognition that they are morally right. Thus Kant focuses on the "necessity" of actions selected by the balance of moral reasons—the fact that they ought to be done no matter what one desires most strongly, no matter how people tend to act in such situations, whether or not the action is sanctioned by existing social practices, etc.

In this passage Kant focuses on the motivational state which is the appropriate response to (full recognition of) moral reasons as a way of bringing out their defining features. But he could also have looked simply at what is implied by the concept of a duty, insofar as the necessity and universality of particular duties are a part of their content. This Kant does, I believe, in the Preface [389], when he says that "the common idea of duty" must carry with it "absolute necessity." Kant's preference for the "subjective route" (through attention to the characteristic motivational attitude) might be explained by the fact that much of the First Section works through an appeal to moral experience. The defining features of morality are not just described; Kant wishes to elicit through examples a recognition of them that has motivating force.

[14] That is, "conditions only contingently related to the will," or "contingent subjective conditions that differentiate one rational being from another." See *KpV* 18f./20f.

[15] I am calling necessity and absolute priority what I take to be slightly different features contained in Kant's usage of "necessity" [*Notwendigkeit*]. For brevity, I will generally refer (as he does) simply to the necessity and universality of moral reasons, or to their unconditional validity.

[16] Any practical principle is going to be universal in that it applies to anyone who satisfies its conditions. Universality in this sense is, of course, not sufficient to make a practical principle a law. (In fact, this is better called its "generality".) Here it is worth noting that the distinction between principles and ends is not important in the derivation of a practical law. To show that there is an end which has an intrinsic and absolute value (i.e., one which takes priority over and limits other forms of value) is to have established the existence of a practical law. This, of course, is what Kant does in his derivation of the Formula of Humanity, and it explains in part why the first two formulas are equivalent. What is crucial to the concept of a practical law is the notion of absolute value, and this can be expressed equally in a principle that yields determinate prescriptions with overriding weight, or in the idea of an end of absolute value.

[17] Here I suggest that we need to complete Kant's argument by showing how the idea of unconditional validity leads to the universality tests that he adopts in various texts. This involves determining the implications of the Moral Law when applied to the general circumstances of human life. One would proceed by showing how universality tests might be derivable from the idea of reasons that justify one's actions fully to anyone in conjunction with general facts about human beings and human social existence. Attention to general human needs, to the fact that we live in the society of others and are dependent on certain forms of social cooperation, to the ways in which social practices operate and to social interaction in general, and so on, might make it plain why the Formula of Universal Law is required by the idea of unconditional validity. For example, facts about how social practices deliver

the benefits that they do, and about the degree of adherence that is required for them to operate, might explain where the Contradiction in Conception test comes from, or why fairness is required by full justifiability to anyone. In addition, the primary concepts may have implications for the construction of universality tests; we want forms of reasoning that are aimed at uncovering reasons that anyone can accept.

[18] Cf. *Gl* 408-09, 411-12, 425-27; see also 389-90.

[19] Kant raises the possibility that the concept of morality might lack objective reality, though not always in the same sense, at *Gl* 402, 405, 407-08, 421, 425, and 445. He writes that "mere conformity to law as such" must be the principle of the will "if duty is not to be an empty delusion [*ein leerer Wahn*] and a chimerical idea [*chimärischer Begriff*] [402]; and that the objective of the step into practical philosophy in the Second Section is to "obtain information and clear instruction regarding the source of its own principle and the correct determination of this principle in its opposition to maxims based on need and inclination, so that reason . . . may avoid the risk of losing all genuine moral principles through the ambiguity into which it easily falls." [405] Here his point is that our concept of duty requires that we treat moral considerations as unconditionally valid, which presupposes that they originate in reason *a priori*. (Somewhat optimistically he thinks that clarity about the fact that moral requirements originate in reason is enough to get us to accept the practical impact of their having the status of law.) See in particular 408: " . . . unless we want to deny to the concept of morality all truth and reference to a possible object, we cannot but admit that the moral law . . . [holds] for all rational beings generally, and that it must be valid not merely under coningent conditions and with exceptions, but must be absolutely necessary."

It seems that different questions about the "reality" of the moral law are left open at different stages of the argument, and that both *Groundwork* II and III address a question of whether the moral law might only be an empty idea. The First Section articulates some of the essential features of moral claims, as we understand them; but they would still be illusory unless they originate in reason. The Second Section is a more detailed analysis of the concept of morality that shows that duties must be expressed in categorical imperatives [*Gl* 425] and that the autonomy of the will must be the foundation of morality [*Gl* 445], and gives the proper formulation of the moral law. It addresses the issue left open by the First Section by tracing the Categorical Imperative to the nature of practical reason [*Gl* 412-16, 420ff], but stops short of establishing the validity of its requirements for us. [*Gl* 425, 440-45] That requires a "synthetical use" of reason, presumably one which shows that we have the rational nature presupposed by the moral law, and is the subject of the Third Section.

[20] Here I am in agreement with Thomas Hill, who argues that Kant is not addressing the moral skeptic, but rather an audience with ordinary moral concerns "whose moral commitment is liable to be called into question by philosophical accounts of practical reason which imply that morality could not be grounded in reason." See "Kant on the Rationality of Moral Conduct," *Pacific Philosophical Quarterly* 66 (1985): 4.

I might add that, if Kant is not addressing an audience which is initially indifferent to moral concerns, then his conception of reason need not be devoid of substantive ideas (of the person, or of agency). Indeed a theory that does proceed from such a starting point is likely to obscure the way of viewing persons to which Kant thinks that moral thought provides access.

[21] This is the "natural dialectic" within practical reason which Kant describes as "a propensity to quibble with these strict laws of duty, to throw doubt upon their validity or at least upon their purity and strictness, and to make them, where possible, more compatible with our wishes and inclinations. . . ." [*Gl* 405; see also *Gl* 424f. and *KpV* 16/16.]

[22] Ideally the notion of rational agency will be a foundation that really supports and animates the structure. That is, it does not just yield the basic principle; it will also figure in the application of the principle to concrete situation, and thus hold a substantive role in the moral conception which it grounds. The conception of rational agency should be an ideal that we can plausibly apply to ourselves and others in normal social interactions, which will have implications for how individuals are appropriately treated. (Certain ways of treating others recognize their rationality in the relevant sense, and an understanding of the conception of rational agency should guide one's judgments, and make one better at applying the principle.)

[23] *The Possibility of Altruism* (Princeton, NJ: Princeton University Press, 1970, 1978), p. 22. See also Thomas E. Hill's discussion in, "Kant's Argument for the Rationality of Moral Conduct," pp. 8-9. He notes that a rational agent is able

> to make things happen in such a way that the appropriate explanation is reference to the principles, laws, or reasons on which the person acted. Principles, even laws, enter into the explanation of why a rational agent did something . . . as the agent's guiding "ideas" or rationale, not as empirically observable regularities among types of events.

Cf. also H. J. Paton, in *The Categorical Imperative* (University of Pennsylvania Press, 1971), pp. 81-82.

[24] Of course, other forms of explanation are possible, but they no longer view the causality as rational. Many people would agree that such explanations are incomplete because they ignore aspects of an agent's perspective on his or her conduct, which are central to the agent's self-conception. For a discussion of this point in a different context, see H. L. A. Hart on the "internal aspect of rules," and his argument that certain positivist accounts of law fail by ignoring it: *The Concept of Law* (Oxford: Oxford University Press, 1972) pp. 55-57, 81-82, 86-88, 99-102. See also Nagel's recent discussion in *The View From Nowhere* (Oxford: Oxford University Press, 1986) pp. 141-43, 150-52.

[25] The text is made somewhat unclear by a terminological slide from "objective laws" to "objective principles," or "imperatives." He may appear to define rational agency as the capacity to act from practical laws (i.e., categorical imperatives), but the context makes it clear that he intends the weaker definition as the capacity to act from objective practical principles, which, as I explain, include both hypothetical and categorical imperatives. (The first interpretation would make rational agency a moral capacity by definition.) A similar ambiguity is seen in the definition of practical principles early in the second *Critique*. (*KpV* 17ff/19ff) Here Kant begins by distinguishing practical laws from maxims, or subjective principles of action—i.e., those actually adopted by an agent. But it becomes clear that the distinction in which he is interested is between subjective principles of action and objective practical principles valid for any rational being, including both practical laws and valid prudential precepts.

How Kant distinguishes subjective and objective principles has been the source of a certain amount of confusion. See, e.g., Bruno Bauch, *Immanuel Kant* (Berlin und Leipzig: De Gruyter, 1921), pp. 304-08.

[26] Thus, a practical principle does not simply state a characteristic way of acting, or a rule to which an agent's behaviour conforms. That would assimiliate practical laws to the model of laws of nature. Rational conduct presupposes not just that behaviour conform to a principle, but that it be guided by an awareness or acceptance of that principle. It provides a description of the behaviour that the agent would apply to himself, which could be used to state his intentions, or would be accepted as relevant to evaluation of the action.

[27] Here I draw on Nagel's discussions of objectivity; see *The View From Nowhere,* pp. 152-54.

[28] Hypothetical Imperatives are objectively valid, in that they embody claims about the means needed to achieve a given end that are true for anyone. However they give reasons conditionally, in that they lead to determinate prescriptions only in conjunction with facts

about an individual's desires. Thus, hypothetical imperatives are practical principles that are objectively, but conditionally valid, stated in imperative form for finite rational beings. For discussion, see Thomas E. Hill, "The Hypothetical Imperative," *The Philosophical Review* 82 (1973): 440 ff; and Henry E. Allison, "Morality and Freedom: Kant's Reciprocity Thesis," *The Philosophical Review* 95 (1986): 399-400.

[29] It is implausible to think that an agent must consciously go through such a process in deciding how to act, but that need not be Kant's view. Rather, a structure of this sort may be implicit in practical reasoning, and presupposed by what agents offer as justifications for their actions. Thus I would argue that Kant views a maxim (first person principle stating an agent's underlying intention) as providing a *prima facie* justification for an action. But since it must instantiate a general principle stating how anyone ought to act in order to function in this way, some such principle is presupposed in the background. It is enough for Kant's purposes that this structure be brought into play in assessing proposed alternatives; it need not describe how an agent arrives at these alternatives.

[30] Thus Kant writes:

> That is practically good which determines the will by means of representations of reason and hence not by subjective causes, but, objectively, i.e., on grounds valid for every rational being as such. [*Gl* 413]

What is good is also "practically necessary"—an action supported by an ought-judgment of some kind. Cf. *Gl* 412. See also *KpV* 60ff/58ff, esp. 62/60: "What we call good must be, in the judgment of every reasonable man, an object of the faculty of desire . . . ;" and *KU* § 4.

[31] See also *Gl* 448:

> Now we cannot possibly think of a reason that consciously lets itself be directed from outside as regards its judgments; for in that case the subject would ascribe the determination of his faculty of judgment, not to his reason, but to an impulse. Reason must regard itself as the author of its principles independent of foreign influences.

Here Kant views rationality as a power of self-determination.

[32] In support of this interpretation of the attitude of rational agents towards their ends, note that when Kant discusses the adoption of ends he standardly refers to their value or worth [*Wert*]. He asks whether it is conditional, relative or absolute [*Gl* 428ff]; he also refers to the question of whether an end is "reasonable and good" and comments on the importance of "judgments regarding the worth of things which might be chosen as ends." [*Gl* 415]

For a more complete discussion of this passage than I am able to provide here, see Christine Korsgaard, "Kant's Formula of Humanity," secs. III-V. One of her aims is to clarify how the traits of rational nature (what she terms its power to "confer value") are the source of its unconditional value. Briefly, the argument (as I understand it) is that rational nature is an end of absolute value because it is a precondition of the existence of any ends. Without the ability to pursue ends for reasons and to confer value on the objects of our desires, there could be no valuable ends. Since rational nature is an end of absolute value, it imposes limiting conditions on choice which must always be respected.

[33] This argument would appear to begin by defining a categorical imperative as one that states an unconditionally valid requirement on action. Kant writes:

> For since, besides the law, the imperative contains only the necessity that the maxim should conform with this law, while the law contains no condition to restrict it, there remains nothing but the universality of law as such with which the maxim of the action should conform. This conformity alone is represented as necessary by the imperative. [*Gl* 420-21]

I gloss this passage as follows. A categorical imperative will contain a law—that is, a substantive requirement on action that applies without restriction to anyone. In addition, it specifies the priority which this requirement has with respect to one's desires and ends: it states the *necessity* of acting consistently with this particular law. The Categorical Imperative—as the principle underlying all particular categorical imperatives, which states their general form—can only contain the necessity for conformity to law as such. It states the requirement of acting from reasons that satisfy the criteria of necessity and universality, or are sufficient to justify one's action fully to anyone. So the supreme practical law says: act from maxims that have the form of law.

[34] In these remarks about autonomy I simply summarize the directions that Kant's thought takes. I intend to examine them more critically in another paper.

[35] I received support for this paper from a National Endowment for the Humanities Summer Stipend (# FT-29143-87). I am also indebted to Stephen Engstrom, Hannah Ginsberg, and Christine Korsgaard for discussion of various topics within Kant's philosophy during the writing of this paper, which have no doubt influenced its present form.

J. B. Schneewind (essay date 1992)

SOURCE: "Autonomy, Obligation, and Virtue: An Overview of Kant's Moral Philosophy," in *The Cambridge Companion to Kant,* edited by Paul Guyer, Cambridge University Press, 1992, pp. 309-41.

[*In the following essay, Schneewind discusses Kant's conception of autonomy and the moral agent, and the ground of his obligation to the moral law.*]

Kant invented a new way of understanding morality and ourselves as moral agents. The originality and profundity of his moral philosophy have long been recognized. It was widely discussed during his own lifetime, and there has been an almost continuous stream of explanation and criticism of it ever since. Its importance has not diminished with time. The quality and variety of current defenses and developments of his basic outlook and the sophistication and range of criticism of it give it a central place in contemporary ethics.[1] In the present essay I offer a general survey of the main features of Kant's moral philosophy. Many different interpretations of it have been given, and his published works show that his views changed in important ways. Nonetheless there is a distinctive Kantian position about morality, and most commentators are agreed on its main outlines.[2]

I

At the center of Kant's ethical theory is the claim that normal adults are capable of being fully self-governing in moral matters. In Kant's terminology, we are "autonomous." Autonomy involves two components. The first is that no authority external to ourselves is needed to constitute or inform us of the demands of morality. We can each know without being told what we ought to do because moral requirements are requirements we impose on ourselves. The second is that in self-government we can effectively control ourselves. The obligations we impose upon ourselves override all other calls for action, and frequently run counter to our desires. We nonetheless always have a sufficient motive to act as we ought. Hence no external source of motivation is needed for our self-legislation to be effective in controlling our behavior.

Kant thinks that autonomy has basic social and political implications. Although no one can lose the autonomy that is a part of the nature of rational agents,[3] social arrangements and the actions of others can encourage lapses into governance by our desires, or heteronomy. Kant, as we shall see, found it difficult to explain just how this could happen; but he always held that the moral need for our autonomy to express itself was incompatible with certain kinds of social regulation. There is no place for others to tell us what morality requires, nor has anyone the authority to do so—

not our neighbors, not the magistrates and their laws, not even those who speak in the name of God. Because we are autonomous, each of us must be allowed a social space within which we may freely determine our own action. This freedom cannot be limited to members of some privileged class. The structure of society must reflect and express the common and equal moral capacity of its members.

Kant's interest in the social and political implications of autonomy is shown in many places. In the short essay "What is enlightenment?" Kant urges each of us to refuse to remain under the tutelage of others. I do not need to rely on "a book which understands for me, a pastor who has a conscience for me." We must think and decide for ourselves. To foster this, public freedom of discussion is necessary, particularly in connection with religion. An enlightened ruler will allow such discussion to flourish, knowing he has nothing to fear from it (7:35, 40ff / H 3-4, 8ff). Later in "Perpetual Peace" Kant expressed the hope that eventually all states will be organized as republics, in which every citizen can express his moral freedom[4] publicly in political action (7:349ff / H 93ff).

What stands out in Kant's vision of the morality through which we govern ourselves is that there are some actions we simply have to do. We impose a moral law on ourselves, and the law gives rise to obligation, to a necessity to act in certain ways. Kant does not see morality as springing from virtuous dispositions that make us want to help others. He sees it as always a struggle. Virtue itself is defined in terms of struggle: It is "moral strength of will" in overcoming temptations to transgress the law (*Morals,* 7:405 / 66-7). Law is prior to virtue, and must control desires to help others as well as desires to harm.

It has sometimes been thought that the salience of law and obedience in Kant's view shows that he had an authoritarian cast of mind. Some unpublished early notes show quite clearly that the moral stance behind his emphasis on obligation was very different. "In our condition," he wrote around 1764,

> when universal injustice stands firm, the natural rights of the lowly cease. They are therefore only debtors; the superiors owe them nothing. Therefore these superiors are called gracious lords. He who needs nothing from them but justice and can hold them to their debts does not need this submissiveness.[5]

A society built around the virtues of benevolence and kindness is for Kant a society requiring not only inequality[6] but servility as well. If nothing is properly mine except what someone graciously gives me, I am forever dependent on how the donor feels toward me. My independence as an autonomous being is threatened. Only if I can claim that the others *have to* give me what is mine by right can this be avoided. Kant makes the point even more plainly in a comment written a few years later:

> Many people may take pleasure in doing good actions but consequently do not want to stand under obligations toward others. If one only comes to them submissively they will do everything; they do not want to subject themselves to the rights of people, but to view them simply as objects of their magnanimity. It is not all one under what title I get something. What properly belongs to me must not be accorded to me merely as something I ask for.[7]

Kant did not deny the moral importance of beneficent action, but his theoretical emphasis on the importance of obligation or moral necessity reflects his rejection of benevolent paternalism and the servility that goes with it,[8] just as the centrality of autonomy in his theory shows his aim of limiting religious and political control of our lives.

II

Kant's attribution of autonomy to every normal adult was a radical break with prevailing views of the moral capacity of ordinary people. The natural law theorists whose work was influential through the seventeenth and much of the eighteenth centuries did not on the whole think that most people could know, without being told, everything that morality requires of them. The lawyers were willing to admit that God had given everyone the ability to know the most basic principles of morality. But they held that the many are unable to see all the moral requirements implicit in the principles and often cannot grasp by themselves what is required in particular cases. Like Kant later, the natural lawyers thought of morality as centering on obligations imposed by law. For them, however, God is the legislator of moral law, and humans his unruly subjects. Most people are unwilling to obey the laws of nature, and must be made to do so through the threat of punishment for noncompliance. This view was built into the concept of obligation as the natural lawyers understood it. They held that obligation could only be explained as necessity imposed by a law backed by threats of punishment for disobedience. They would accordingly have thought Kant's view that we can make and motivate ourselves to obey the moral law not only blasphemous but foolish.[9] They would also have wondered what kind of account of moral necessity Kant could give, once he refused to appeal to an external lawgiver or to sanctions.

A number of philosophers before Kant had begun to reject the natural lawyers' low estimate of human moral capacity, and to present theories in which a greater ability for self-governance is attributed to people. A brief look at the philosophers whom Kant himself has told us were important in his development will help us see how far beyond them he went.[10]

In deliberate opposition to natural law views, the British philosophers Shaftesbury and Hutcheson portrayed virtue rather than law and obligation as central to morality.[11] They argued that to be virtuous we have only to act regularly and deliberately from benevolent motives that we naturally approve. Because approval is naturally felt by everyone, and because we all have benevolent motives, we can all equally see and do what morality calls for, without need of external guidance or of sanctions. Christian Wolff, whose philosophy dominated German universities when Kant was a student, tried to reach a similar conclusion by a different route.[12] He argued that we can be self-governed because we can see for ourselves what the consequences of our actions will be, and can tell which action will bring about the greatest amount of perfection. Since we are always drawn to act so as to bring about what we believe is the greatest amount of perfection, Wolff says we are bound or necessitated to do what we think will be for the best. And this seems to him to explain the necessity we call "moral," or our moral obligation. In political matters we are obligated or obliged to act by sanctions imposed by a political ruler; but in morality we oblige ourselves to act through our perception of perfection. Hence in morality we are self-governed. We need no sanctions to move us to act for the best.[13]

Kant came to hold that neither of these kinds of moral theory was acceptable. They imply that the only necessity involved in morality is the necessity of using a means to an end you desire. If you do not want the end, there is no need for you to do the act that leads to it. But Kant thinks it is just a contingent empirical fact that you have the desires you have.[14] If so, then on these views it is a matter of happenstance whether or not someone is bound by any moral necessity. Obligation becomes a matter of what one wants to do. But true moral necessity, Kant held, would make an act necessary regardless of what the agent wants.

One philosopher prior to Kant, the Lutheran pastor C. A. Crusius,[15] had taken moral necessity to be independent of our contingent ends. There are, Crusius said, obligations of prudence, which arise from the need to act in a certain way to attain one's end. But there are also obligations of virtue, or moral obligations, and these make it necessary to act in certain ways regardless of any of one's own ends. Both the knowledge of these requirements and the motive to comply with them are available to everyone alike because certain laws are incorporated in the structure of our will, and carry their own impetus to action. Because everyone has a will, everyone can always know what morality requires; and when we act accordingly we are determining ourselves to action. Crusius thus explains the idea of moral obligation in terms of an unconditional necessity, and claims that because this necessity binds our will by its own nature we need no external guidance or stimulus to be moral. Crusius's aim in asserting our high moral capacity was in fact to show that we are fully responsible for our actions before God. He took the laws structuring our will to obligate us because they are God's commands; and he believed that obedience is our highest virtue. If Crusius provided Kant with some of the tools he used to work out his idea of autonomy, he was not the inspiration for that idea.

It took a radical critic of society, Jean-Jacques Rousseau, to suggest the idea. Rousseau convinced Kant that everyone must have the capacity to be a self-governing moral agent, and that it is this characteristic that gives each person a special kind of value or dignity.[16] Culture in its present corrupt state conceals this capacity of ours, Rousseau thought, and society must be changed to let it show and be effective. In the *Social Contract* he called for the construction of a community in which everyone agrees to be governed by the dictates of the "general will," a will representing each individual's truest and deepest aims and directed always at the good of the whole. The general will would have to be able to override the passing desires each of us feels for private goods. But, Rousseau said, "the impulse of appetite alone is slavery, and obedience to the law one has prescribed for oneself is freedom."[17] Previous thinkers had frequently used the metaphor of slavery to describe the condition in which we are controlled by our passions, but for them the alternative was to follow laws that God or nature prescribe. Rousseau held that we make our own law and in doing so create the foundation for a free and just social order. This thought became central to Kant's understanding of morality.

III

The problem Kant faced was to show how such law-making is possible. In particular he had to explain how we can impose a necessity upon ourselves. If my obligations arise simply through my own will, how can there be any real constraints on my action? Can't I excuse myself from any obligations I alone impose? Rousseau had nothing to suggest beyond the thought that conscience is a sentiment that moves us without regard for our own interest; and we have already seen why Kant could not accept that suggestion. Someone might not have conscientious sentiments, or might get rid of them. Then on such a view no obligations bind her. Moral necessity could not be explained on that basis. Kant eventually found an explanation by comparing moral necessity to the necessity involved in the laws governing the physical universe. Kant was a Newtonian. He held that the sequence of events in the world is necessary. But its laws involve no commands and no sanctions. Morality, however, is not science. Science shows us how the world has to be. Morality

tells us how it ought to be. How can the model of scientific laws help us understand morality?

Kant had read Rousseau and rethought morality before he came to the breakthrough that led to the critical philosophy.[18] In developing his new view of morality he used the tools the critical standpoint gave him. In the *Critique of Pure Reason* he argued that perceptual experience of the world shows only what *does* happen. Since laws say what *has to* happen they must involve a nonexperiential, or *a priori,* aspect, and it must be this that explains the necessity they impart. How is this nonexperiential aspect of lawfulness to be explained? The mind, Kant answered, involves the activity of imposing different forms of order on the perceptual material that its passive receptivity gives it. The forms of order are not externally imposed on the mind. They are an aspect of itself, the aspect through which it makes experience lawful. And they are "pure" or devoid of any empirical content in themselves. Their constitution is independent of their actual forming of perceptions into lawfully ordered sequences.

The question then is whether there is an aspect of the mind that does for action what the mental activities revealed in the first *Critique* do for experience. Thinking in terms of separate faculties of the mind, Kant attributes the initiation of action to the will, responding to desires. Desires, he assumes, are not rational as such. They arise in us because we are finite beings, with bodily and other needs. If there is to be rationality in action, the will must be its source. Kant therefore equates the will with practical reason. Does the faculty of practical reason have an inherent structure in the way that the faculty of pure reason does? If it does, and if it imposes form on the givens we feel as desires, then we have a clue to an explanation of exactly how and why we are autonomous. Taking the activity of practical reason as the source of the necessities that we impose on our willed behaviour would show that these necessities are no more escapable than those that give structure to the physical world. They could therefore constitute our morality.

IV

To translate this idea into a moral theory, Kant had to show that the main concepts of morality can be explained in terms of a self-imposed necessity. We can begin to see how he does this by examining the way he relates three ideas central to morality: the ideas of the moral worth of an agent, of the rightness of an action, and of the goodness of the states of affairs that are the goals or outcomes of action.

One way of relating these ideas is to take as basic the goodness of states of affairs that can be brought about by human action. We consider, say, that being happy, or having fully developed talents, is intrinsically good.

Then a right act can be defined as one that brings about good states of affairs, or brings them about to the greatest extent possible; and a good agent is one who habitually and deliberately does right acts. In such a scheme, right acts will have only an instrumental value, and we can and indeed must know what is good before we can make justifiable claims about what acts are right. Such a scheme is common feature of the work of Kant's predecessors. Kant rejected it.

He rejected it because it makes autonomy in his sense impossible. Suppose that a kind of state of affairs is intrinsically good because of the very nature of that kind of state of affairs. Then the goodness occurs independently of the will of any finite moral agent, and if she must will to pursue it, she is not self-legislating. Suppose the goodness of states of affairs comes from their conformity to some standard. Then the standard itself is either the outcome of someone's will—say, God's—or it is self-subsistent and eternal. In either case, conformity to it is not autonomy.[19] Conformity would be what Kant calls heteronomy.

An alternative way of relating the three moral concepts became available to Kant through the idea that moral necessity, as embedded in the laws of morality, might have a pure *a priori* status akin to that of the necessity characterizing Newton's gravitational laws. While the mind imposes necessity in both cases, in morality the relevant aspect of mind is the rational will. This leads Kant to take the concept of the good agent as basic. Think of the good agent as one whose will is wholly determined *a priori,* and think of the pattern of that determination as the moral law.[20] Then we can say that it is necessarily true that whatever acts such an agent does are right acts; and whatever states of affairs such an agent deliberately brings about through those acts are good states of affairs. Kant makes it clear in the second *Critique* that this is his position:

> the concept of good and evil is not defined prior to the moral law, to which, it would seem, the former would have to serve as foundation; rather the concept of good and evil must be defined after and by means of the law.

> (*Practical Reason* 5:62-3 / 65)

For Kant then the rightness of acts is prior to the goodness of states of affairs, because only outcomes of right acts can count as good states of affairs. We do not discover what is right by first finding out what is good. Indeed we cannot determine what states of affairs are good without first knowing what is right. In order to know what is right all we need to know is what the perfectly good agent would do. Then whenever there is an act that a perfectly good agent could not omit, it is an act anyone in those circumstances has to do.[21]

Kant thinks one more step must be taken before we can obtain a full account of the moral concepts. So far we have considered a will completely determined by its own inner lawfulness. Because this law is a law constituting practical reason, such a will—unlike ours—would be perfectly rational. We finite beings do not have what Kant calls a "holy will," a will so fully determined by its inner lawful constitution that it acts spontaneously and without struggle. Our desires clamor for satisfaction whether they are rational or not. Hence for us the operation of the law in our rational will is not automatic. We feel its operation within us as a constraint, because it must act against the pull of desire. In finite beings, Kant says, the moral law "necessitates," rather than acting necessarily (*Groundwork,* 4:413-14 / 81). The terminology is not helpful, but Kant's thought here is familiar. If you were perfectly reasonable, you would go to the dentist to have that aching tooth looked at; and if you don't go because you fear dentists, you will find yourself thinking that you really ought to go. This is a prudential illustration of something that holds in the purely moral realm as well. When we see a compelling reason to do an act we are reluctant to do, we may not do it; but we admit we ought to.

The term "ought" is central to our moral vocabulary because the tension between reason and desire is central to our moral experience. "Ought" can be defined, on Kant's view, by saying that whatever a holy will, or perfectly rational will, necessarily *would* do is what we imperfectly rational agents *ought* to do (*Groundwork,* 4:413-14 / 81; *Practical Reason,* 325: / 32-3; *Morals,* 6:394-5 / 54-5). When we speak of our obligation to do something, we are referring to the necessity of a given act, without specifying which act is necessary; and to call an act a duty is to say that it is an action that is obligatory. It is Kant's belief in the importance of struggle in the moral life that leads him to his view that virtue cannot be defined as a settled habit or disposition. God, Kant thinks, necessarily acts morally and for that reason cannot have virtue. Only beings who find morality difficult and who develop persistence in struggling against the temptations can be virtuous. We finite beings will never get to the point at which we do not need the strength to resist desire. We are neither angels nor animals. Virtue is our proper station in the universe (*Morals,* 6:405-9 / 66-71).

V

If we grant Kant his account of the central moral concepts, we want next to know what the moral law is, and how and to what extent it can serve as a principle for showing us what we ought to do. Many critics, from Hegel to the present, have argued that Kant's principle cannot yield any results at all, because it is a formal principle.[22] Are they right?

I have tried to explain why, in order to assure the autonomy of the moral agent, the moral law must be pure and *a priori*. This means, Kant insists, that the law must be *formal*. Like the logical law of contradiction, which rules out any proposition of the form 'P and not-P', the moral law must not itself contain any "matter" or content. Nonetheless Kant thinks form without content in morality is as empty as he thinks it would be in our experience of nature. There must be content, Kant holds, but it can only come from outside the will—from desires and needs, shaped by our awareness of the world in which we live into specific urges to act or plans for action. Our finitude makes the needy aspect of the self as essential to our particular mode of being as is the free will. It takes the two working together to produce morality. But all that the moral law can do is to provide the form for matter that comes from our desires.

Our urges to act come to the will through what Kant calls "maxims." A maxim is a personal or subjective plan of action, incorporating the agent's reasons for acting as well as a sufficient indication of what act the reasons call for. When we are fully rational, we act, knowing our circumstances, in order to obtain a definite end, and aware that under some conditions we are prepared to alter our plans. Because circumstances and desires recur, a maxim is general. It is like a private rule. A maxim might look like this: If it's raining, take an umbrella in order to stay dry, unless I can get a ride. We often don't think explicitly about the circumstances or the contingencies when we are acting, and Kant does not always include them in his examples of maxims. Sometimes we don't even think of the purpose or goal of an action, only of what we are intent on doing. But if we are rational our action always has a purpose, and we are responsive to the surroundings in which we act. A full maxim simply makes all this explicit. A rational agent tests her maxims before acting on them. To do so she uses the laws of rational willing.

Kant thinks there are two basic laws of rational willing. One governs goal-oriented action generally, and is easily stated:

> Who wills the end, wills (so far as reason has decisive influence on his actions) also the means which are indispensably necessary and in his power.
>
> (*Groundwork*, 4:417 / 84-85)

This simply says that when a rational agent is genuinely in pursuit of a goal, she must and will do whatever is needed to get it. Otherwise she is not really pursuing the goal. Now whenever there is a law determining a perfectly rational being to action, there is a counterpart, couched in terms of "ought," governing the actions of imperfectly rational beings such as ourselves. Kant calls such "ought" counterparts of the laws

of rational willing "imperatives." He uses this term because the laws of rational willing appear as constraining us in the way that commands do. The "ought" counterpart of the law of goal-oriented willing is easily stated:

> Whoever wills an end ought to will the means.

Kant calls it the "hypothetical" imperative. It is hypothetical because the necessity of action that it imposes is conditional. You ought to do a certain act *if* you will a certain end.[23]

Given Kant's claim that means-ends necessity is inadequate for morality, it is plain that he must think there is another law of rational willing, and so another kind of "ought" or imperative. The kind of "ought" that does not depend on the agent's ends arises from the moral law; and Kant calls the imperative version of that law "the categorical imperative." The moral law itself, Kant holds, can only be the form of lawfulness itself, because nothing else is left once all content has been rejected. The moral law can therefore be stated as follows:

> A perfectly rational will acts only through maxims which it could also will to be universal law.

When this appears to us in the form of the categorical imperative, it says:

> Act only according to that maxim through which you can at the same time will that it should become a universal law.
>
> (*Groundwork*, 4:421 / 88)

We might think of Kant as recommending a two-stage testing of maxims. First test a maxim by the hypothetical imperative. Does the proposed act effectively bring about a desired end? If not, reject it; and if it does, test it by the categorical imperative. If it passes this test, you may act on it, but if it does not, you must reject it. It is not hard to see how to apply the test of prudential rationality. The question is whether the test of morality, the categorical imperative, actually enables us to decide whether or not we may act on a maxim.

Kant gives us a formulation of the categorical imperative that he thinks is easier to use than the one I have already cited:

> Act as if the maxim of your action were to become through your will a universal law of nature.
>
> (*Groundwork*, 4:421 / 89)

Now suppose you need money. You think of getting some by asking a friend to lend it to you, but you have no intention of ever repaying him. You plan to make a false promise to repay. Your maxim (omitting circumstances and conditions) is something like this: Use a lying promise to get money I want. Suppose this passes the prudential test. You then consider whether your maxim could be a universal law of nature, whether there could be a world in which everyone was moved, as by a law of nature, to make lying promises to get what they want. It would have to be a world in which it is prudentially rational to make a lying promise to get money. Well, if everyone made lying promises it would be pretty obvious, and people would stop believing promises. But in a world where no promises are trusted, it cannot be rational to try to use a promise in this way. Thus you cannot coherently think a world for which your maxim is a law of nature. You are therefore not permitted to act on it (*Groundwork,* 4:422 / 89-90).

Another example shows a different way in which the categorical imperative works. I pass someone collapsed on the street, and decide not to help him. My maxim is something like this: Ignore people in need of help, in order not to interfere with my plans. Kant says that I can coherently *conceive* of a world of people indifferent to one another's distress. But he believes that I cannot *will* the existence of such a world. Look at it this way. As a rational agent I necessarily will the means to any of my ends. The help of others is often a means I need for my own ends. So it would be irrational to will to exclude the help of others as a possible means when I need it. But if I universalize my maxim, I will to make it a law of nature that no one helps others in need. I would therefore be willing both that others help me when I need it and that no one help others when they need it. This is incoherent willing. Hence I may not act on my maxim (*Groundwork,* 4:423 / 90-91).[24]

When we use the categorical imperative in these cases we suppose that we are examining a maxim embodying the agent's genuine reasons for proposing the action, rather than irrelevancies (such as that the act will be done by a gray-bearded man) that might let it get by the categorical imperative. A vocabulary for formulating our plans is also presupposed (though that vocabulary itself might be called into question, as when we reject racist language).[25] Given these assumptions, the examples show that if maxims of the kind they involve are what the categorical imperative is to test, then the moral law is not empty. There are at least some cases in which we can assess the moral permissibility of a plan simply by considering its rationality, without basing our conclusion on the goodness or badness of its consequences. The Kantian position is a real option for understanding morality.

VI

The categorical imperative can be formulated in several ways. Kant thinks they are all equivalent, and

insists that the first formulation, the one we have been considering, is basic. Though the others bring out various aspects of the moral law, they cannot tell us more than the first formula does. It concentrates on the agent's point of view. The second formulation draws our attention to those affected by our action:

> Act in such a way that you always treat humanity, whether in your own person or in the person of another, never simply as a means, but always at the same time as an end.
>
> (*Groundwork,* 4:429 / 96)

Kant is saying that the ends of others—if morally permissible—set limits to the ends we ourselves may pursue. We must respect the permissible ends of others, and we may make others serve our own purposes only when they as moral agents assent to such use, as when someone willingly takes a job working for another. Thus we may not pursue our own ends if they impermissibly conflict with the ends of others.[26] We are also to forward the ends of others, a point to which I will shortly return.

The third formulation instructs us to look at agent and recipient of action together in a community as we legislate through our maxims:

> All maxims as proceeding from our own law-making ought to harmonize with a possible kingdom of ends as a kingdom of nature.
>
> (*Groundwork,* 4:436 / 104)

Here we are told always to think of ourselves as members of a society of beings whose permissible ends are to be respected, and to test our maxims by asking whether, supposing the maxims were natural laws, there would be a society of that kind.[27]

Because the richer formulations of the categorical imperative can take us no further than the formula requiring us to test our maxims by asking if they could be universal laws, we must ask how well that principle can serve to show us the way through all of our relations with one another.

The categorical imperative clearly requires a kind of impartiality in our behavior. We are not permitted to make exceptions for ourselves, or to do what we would not rationally permit others to do. But it would be a mistake to suppose that Kantian morality allows for nothing but impartiality in personal relations. The maxim "If it is my child's birthday, give her a party, to show I love her" is thinkable and willable as a law of nature, as are some maxims of helping family members and friends rather than helping others. Of course our actions for those we prefer must be within rationally allowable limits, but within those limits Kantian ethics has nothing to say against the working of human affection.

A broader point is involved here. Although the categorical imperative operates most directly by vetoing proposed maxims of action, it is a mistake to suppose that it does nothing more. It is usually true that from its prohibitions alone no positive directives follow. Whatever is not forbidden is simply permitted. Sometimes, however, a veto forces a requirement on us. Where what is forbidden is *not* doing something—for instance, not paying my taxes—the veto requires me to do something, to pay my taxes, because it is not permitted not to do so. Beyond this, the categorical imperative can set requirements that are not so specifically tied to prohibitions. Kant gives us more detail on this in the ***Metaphysics of Morals.***

He there divides morality into two domains, one of law or right (*Recht*), and one of virtue (***Morals,*** 6:218-21 / 16-19). The domain of law, which extends to civil law, arises from maxims that are vetoed because they cannot even be thought coherently when universalized. The rejection of such maxims turns out to provide a counterpart to the recognition of the strict rights of others. We may not interfere with their legitimate projects, may not take their property, and so on. The domain of virtue involves maxims that can be thought but not willed as universal laws. Most of what morality requires as action rather than abstention is a requirement of virtue.

We have already seen why Kant thinks we cannot will a maxim of universal neglect of the needs of others, even though such a maxim is thinkable as a law of nature. Now the denial of this vetoed maxim is not the maxim "Always help everyone." It is rather the maxim "Help some others at some times." Kant thinks that further argument from this point will show that it is morally required that one of our own ends be to forward the ends of others. He thinks it can be shown in similar fashion that we must make the perfection of our moral character and of our abilities one of our ends (***Morals,*** 6:384-8 / 43-7).

The differences between the domain of law and that of virtue are significant. To be virtuous, I must be acting for the sake of the good of another, or for my own perfection, and viewing these ends as morally required. In the domain of law it does not matter why I do what I do, so long as I abstain from violating the rights of others. Because the motive does not matter in legal affairs, if I do not perform as I ought, I can rightly be compelled to do so. I obtain no moral merit for carrying out legal duties. I simply keep my slate clean. In the domain of virtue, by contrast, there is nothing to which I can be compelled, because what is required is that I have certain ends, and ends must be freely adopted (***Morals,*** 6:381 / 39). Moreover in the realm of virtue there are no requirements about specific actions. It is up to me to decide which of my talents to improve, where my worst moral failings are, and how, when,

and how much to help others. Of course I may only do what is permissible within the limits of my legal duties. But the more I make the required ends mine, the more I will do. In the realm of virtue, moreover, I can become entitled to moral praise through my efforts for others. My merit increases as I make their goals my own.

Kant thus makes a place for a concern for human well-being as well as for negative respect for rights.[28] What is to be noted is that he does not base the requirement of concern for others on the goodness of the results virtue brings about. And he does not require us to bring about as much happiness (or as much of our own perfection) as we possibly can. He allows that we will have permissible ends that will compete for time and resources with the morally required ends. Morality does not tell us how to decide between them. It only tells us that we must pursue the required as well as the personal ends, staying always within the limits of justice.

How adequate, then, is the categorical imperative as a moral guide? One might wish to reject the whole vocabulary of law and obligation, and with it Kant's principle, on the grounds that it gives a skewed and harmful portrayal of human relations.[29] But even if one does not wish thus to set aside or subordinate the moral concerns that led Kant to make that vocabulary central, one must allow that there are problems with Kant's claims for the categorical imperative. I note only two.

First, Kant held that his principle leads to certain conclusions that many sensible people do not accept, such as that lying, suicide, and political revolution are always prohibited. If his inferences to these moral conclusions are valid, then his principle is questionable. If he is not right, then a question must be raised about his claim that his principle is so easy to apply that an ordinary person, "with this compass in hand, is well able to distinguish, in all cases that present themselves, what is good or evil, right or wrong. . . ." (***Groundwork,*** 4:404 / 71-2). It is not clear that any single principle can do all that Kant claims for the categorical imperative.

Second, if the adequacy of the categorical imperative for cases involving only relations between two people is hard to determine, its adequacy for helping settle large-scale social issues is even more so. Kant thought that individual decision making would be able to guide people to coordinated action on matters of general concern. This seems extremely doubtful. It does not follow, however, that there is no way of revising the Kantian principle so that it might handle such issues in a way that preserves the intent of Kant's own formulation.[30]

VII

Kant held that the proper way to proceed in moral philosophy is to start with what we all know about morality and see what principle underlies it. The

Groundwork accordingly begins with an examination of commonsense opinion. From it Kant extracts the motive that is central to morality as well as the basic principle of decision making.

He begins with the claim that we all recognize a kind of goodness different from the goodness of wealth, power, talent, and intellect, and even different from the goodness of kindly or generous dispositions. Under certain conditions any of these might turn out not to be good. But there is another kind of goodness that stays good under any conditions. This is the special kind of goodness a person can have. It is shown most clearly, Kant thinks, when someone does what she believes right or obligatory, and does it just because she thinks it so. Someone lacking kindly feelings, pity, or generosity, and not even caring about her own interest any more, may nonetheless do what she thinks right. The special sort of merit we attribute to this person is the goodness central to morality. It is best thought of as the goodness of a good will (*Groundwork,* 4:393-4 / 61-2).

Reflection on the agent of good will brings out an important point. Her value does not depend on her actual accomplishments. And because she is moved by a desire to do the act or to bring about its results, her value cannot depend on the results she intended either. Her value must depend, Kant says, "solely on the *principle of volition*" from which she acted. And the only principle available, because she is not moved by the content of her action, must be formal. The agent of good will must therefore be moved by the bare lawfulness of the act. Kant puts it by saying that she is moved by respect or reverence (*Achtung*) for the moral law (*Groundwork,* 4:400 / 68).

Commonsense beliefs about the moral goodness of the good agent show us, Kant thinks, that the categorical imperative is the principle behind sound moral judgment. Kant also thinks he obtains from beliefs about the good agent his view about the motivation proper to morality. Historically the latter was as revolutionary as the former, and systematically the two aspects of the theory are inseparably linked. But the motivational view leads to some new problems for Kant.

The psychological doctrine prevalent in Kant's time held that what motivates us in voluntary rational action is desire for good and aversion to evil. Granting that people often fail to pursue the good either through mistake or through perversity, the view implies that if we do not act from a desire for some perceived good, we are acting wrongly or at least irrationally. Of course it was allowed that people sometimes do their duty just because they ought to. But since doing one's duty was understood to be productive of good—the good of the community—even conscientious action was seen as motivated by desire for the good.[31]

Kant sitting at a desk to work.

Crusius broke with this tradition when he said that we could obey God's laws simply because they are ordained by him.[32] Kant's assertion that in obeying the dictates of the categorical imperative we could be motivated by what he called respect for the law accepts this decisive break with the older view. Respect, as we have seen, is a concern not for the ends or goods of action, but for the form. So when we are moved by it, we are not pursuing good. But neither are we acting wrongly or irrationally. The central moral motive therefore does not fit the standard pattern.

Respect is unlike other motives in two further ways. First, it is a feeling that arises solely from our awareness of the moral law as the categorical imperative. And it always arises from such awareness. While other motives may or may not be present in everyone at all times, every rational agent always has available this motive, which is sufficient to move her to do what the categorical imperative bids. Second, other motives, such as fear of punishment, greed, love, or pity, can lead us to act rightly. But it is merely contingent if they do. Love, like greed or hatred, can lead one to act immorally. The sole motive that necessarily moves us to act rightly is respect, because it alone is only activated by the dictates of the categorical imperative.

It is easy to see the place of respect in Kant's portrayal of autonomy. Respect provides an answer to the claim, made famous by Hume but probably known to Kant through work by Hume's influential predecessor Francis Hutcheson,[33] that reason cannot motivate us. On the contrary, Kant replies: Practical reason generates its own unique motive. External sanctions, of the sort the natural law theorists thought indispensable to give obligation its motivating power, are unnecessary, at least in principle, because we all have within ourselves an adequate motive for compliance. Respect also makes up for the inequities of nature. Some people are naturally loving, friendly, and thoughtful. Nature has not been so generous to others. If only natural motives were available to move us to do what morality requires, then some, through no fault of their own, would be unable to comply with it. Kant's doctrine implies that no one need be prevented by the niggardliness of nature from attaining moral worth.

If the attractions of the doctrine of respect are plain, it nonetheless gets Kant into difficulties. It leads him to think along the following lines. If I act from any motive other than respect, I am simply doing something I find myself wanting to do. My action may be right, but if so that is merely contingent. Even if it is, I show no special concern for morality when I am moved by my desire. All that is shown by a right act done from a nonmoral motive is that morality and my interest here coincide. Consequently I deserve no praise unless I act from respect. Action from respect is the only kind of action that shows true concern for morality. No other motivation entitles me to count as a virtuous agent.

As critics have frequently pointed out, this seems a paradoxical position.[34] It seems to make almost every aspect of character unimportant to morality, because it denies any moral worth to actions springing entirely from feelings of love, loyalty, friendship, pity, or generosity, and seems to rule out mixed motives as sources of moral worth.[35] Worse, it suggests that kind or loving feelings can get in the way of our achieving moral merit. If merit accrues only when we act from a sense of duty, it seems that human relations must be either unduly chilly or else without moral worth. Did Kant really hold this view? There are passages that suggest he did,[36] and others where he asserts a much more humane view.[37] The most plausible alternative to the extreme position is one that allows conditional mixed motives: I may have merit when moved by the motive of pity, say, if I allow pity to operate only on condition that in moving me it leads me to nothing the categorical imperative forbids, and if respect is strong enough in me to move me were pity to fail. Because the texts show a change of mind, the best interpretation depends on systematic considerations, of which not the least is whether one accepts Kant's belief that there is a unique and supremely important kind of merit or worthiness, the moral kind.

VIII

So far I have tried to explain the principle Kant takes to be central to morality and the motivation he thinks is unique to it. I have said nothing about the justification he thinks he can give for claiming that the principle really holds. We are thus at the point Kant reaches toward the end of the second part of the *Groundwork.* He there says that so far all he has done is to show what ordinary moral consciousness takes morality to involve if there is such a thing. But is there? A parallel question about prudential rationality would be easy to answer. The law of prudence is true by definition, or analytic. To say someone is a "perfectly rational agent" simply means (in part) that she "uses the means needed to attain her goals." But the moral law is not analytic. The concepts "completely good will" or "perfectly rational agent" do not include "acts only through universalizable maxims." And we cannot base the moral law on experience. It is a necessary proposition, and experience alone never grounds such propositions. What basis then is there for the moral law?[38]

The problem as Kant sees it is to discover something through which we can join the subject of the moral law—"perfectly rational agent"—and its predicate—"acts only through universalizable maxims." He sees a possible solution in the idea of freedom of the will. Freedom has a negative aspect: If we are free, we are not determined solely by our desires and needs. But freedom is more than the absence of determination. A will wholly undetermined would be random and chaotic. It would not allow for responsibility, nor consequently for praise and blame.[39] The only viable way to think of a free will, Kant holds, is to think of it as a will whose choices are determined by a law that is internal to its nature. Such a will is determined only by itself, and is therefore free. But we have already seen that the only self-determined actions are actions done because of the universalizability of the agent's maxim. So if we could show that a rational will must be free, we would have shown that a rational will acts only on universalizable maxims.[40] We would have proven the first principle of morality.

Given Kant's Newtonian model of the physical world, a strong claim about freedom of the will raises problems. Our bodies as physical objects are subject to Newton's laws of motion. If they are moved by our natural desires, this is unproblematic, because desires themselves arise in accordance with deterministic laws (as yet undiscovered). Morality, however, requires the possibility of action from a wholly nonempirical motive. We never know whether real moral merit is attained, but if it is, the motive of respect must move us to bodily action, regardless of the strength of our desires. Is this possible?

In the first *Critique* Kant argued that no theoretical proof (or disproof) of free will can be given. In the *Groundwork* Kant thinks he can give at least indirect support to the claim that we are free. When we as rational beings act, he says, we must take ourselves to be free. He means that whenever we deliberate or choose we are presupposing freedom, even if we are unaware of the presupposition or consciously doubtful of it. More broadly, whenever we take ourselves to be thinking rationally (even about purely theoretical matters) we must take ourselves to be free, because we cannot knowingly accept judgments determined by external sources as judgments we ourselves have made. Now anything that would follow about us if we were really free still follows for practical purposes if we have to think of ourselves as free. Because freedom entails the moral law, we must think of ourselves as bound by it (*Groundwork,* 4:447-8 / 115-16).[41]

Can we both take ourselves to be free and believe theoretically in a deterministic universe? Kant's answer appeals to his first *Critique.* Theoretical knowledge has limits: It applies only to the world as we experience it, the phenomenal world. We cannot say that the determinism holding in the realm of phenomena holds beyond it as well, in the noumenal world. If we think of ourselves as belonging to the noumenal as well as the phenomenal world, then we can see how in one respect we may be beings bound in a web of mechanistic determination, while in another respect we are the free rational agents morality supposes us to be. Our theoretical beliefs and our practical presupposition of freedom do not come into any conflict.

There are many difficulties with this argument. One of them is this. The argument seems to suppose that we are free just when we are acting rationally. But then if we act irrationally, we are not free. Immoral action is, however, irrational. So it seems to follow that we are responsible only when acting as the moral law requires, and not responsible when we do something wicked. Kant might have had a reply to this objection, but if so he did not give it. In his later writings, he introduced a distinction between the will and the power of choice (*Wille* and *Willkür*), which was meant to remove the problem.[42] He held that the will is simply identical with practical rationality and is therefore the home of the moral law, but that we have in addition a power of choice, whose task is to choose between the promptings of desire and the imperatives stemming from the will. It is in the power of choice that our freedom, properly speaking, resides. The will itself is neither free nor unfree.

Kant not only developed his view of free will considerably; he changed his mind about how to argue in

support of it.[43] In the *Critique of Practical Reason* Kant continued to hold his earlier view that if we are free we are under the moral law, and if we are under the moral law we are free. But he now argues that what he calls "the fact (*Faktum*) of reason" is what shows us that we are free. There is considerable difficulty in clarifying just what Kant supposes the fact of reason be be.[44] One possible interpretation starts with Kant's claim that the fact of reason is revealed to us through our moral awareness that we are bound by unconditional obligations. Because we know we are bound by such obligations, we know also that we can do what we are obligated to do. This means that we can do it, no matter what the circumstances and no matter what has gone on before. In other words awareness of categorical obligation contains awareness of freedom. But it is awareness of freedom as it expresses itself in imperfectly rational beings. The fact of reason, we might take it, is pure rationality displaying itself as immediately as it can in imperfectly rational beings.[45]

In the *Critique,* therefore, Kant treats freedom as the ground of our *having* moral obligations, and our awareness of categorical imperatives as the ground of our *knowledge* that we are free. He thus gives up the one attempt he made to support the principle of morals by appeal to something other than itself—rationality in general—and he uses our awareness of morality as a foundation from which we can extend our understanding of ourselves and our place in the universe.[46]

Kant is not here retracting the claims he made in the first *Critique* about the limits of knowledge. Our justified assurance that we are free is not theoretical knowledge. While we are entitled to that assurance for practical purposes, we cannot infer from it anything of pertinence to our theoretical understanding of the world. Indeed Kant thinks that without the positions established in the theoretical *Critique* the moral outlook he aims to defend would be impossible. Unless we see that knowledge is limited, we will think that the kind of theoretical knowledge science gives us is all the knowledge there can be. Then a theoretical understanding of our own behavior will become inevitable. Kant held that if we think of ourselves solely in empirical and deterministic terms we will necessarily think of ourselves as heteronomous, as moved by our desires for this or that, and never solely by respect for law. This thought would be debilitating to our effort to be moral.[47] But the first *Critique* showed that the deterministic stance of theoretical reason is valid only within the bounds of experience. Theoretical reason has no jurisdiction over the beliefs morality requires us to hold.

IX

Kant calls this the primacy of practical reason (*Practical Reason,* 5:119-21 / 124-6). If the categorical imperative requires us to think of ourselves and the world in certain ways, then the limitations on speculative reason cannot be used to deny that we have any warrant for those beliefs. Our nature as rational agents thus dominates our nature as rational knowers. There are two matters, other than freedom, on which practical reason requires us to accept beliefs that can be neither proven nor disproven theoretically. One concerns our hopes for our own private futures, the other concerns our hopes for the future of humanity. In one case we are led by morality to have certain religious beliefs; in the other, to have certain views about history and progress.

In the second *Critique* Kant argues not only that we must think of ourselves as free moral agents but also that we must see ourselves as immortal, and as living in a universe governed by a providential intelligence through whose intervention in the course of nature the virtuous are rewarded and the vicious punished. We must have these beliefs, Kant holds, because morality requires each of us to make ourselves perfectly virtuous—to give ourselves a character in which the dictates of the categorical imperative are never thwarted by the passions and desires. And it also requires that happiness be distributed in accordance with virtue.[48] The former cannot be done in a finite amount of time, so we must believe that we each have something like an infinite amount of time available for carrying out the task, or at least for approaching closer and closer to completion. The latter is not possible if the mechanisms of nature are the sole ordering force in the universe, nature being indifferent to virtue and vice. Hence we must believe that there is some nonnatural ordering force that will intervene to bring about what morality requires (*Practical Reason,* 5:122-32 / 126-36).

In his essays on history[49] Kant argues that theoretical reason can never determine whether mankind is progressing or not. War and the innumerable ghastly ways in which people mistreat one another seem sometimes to be waning, sometimes to be increasing, sometimes simply to go through an endless see-saw of more and less. But morality requires us to try to bring it about that there is peace in the world, and that the standing form of government is everywhere one in which individual autonomy is publicly acknowledged and respected. We must therefore believe that it is possible to bring this about, and we must see history as moving, however slowly, and at whatever cost to innumerable individuals throughout countless generations, in this direction. Thus within the world constituted by theoretical reason, practical reason directs us to form a moral world by imposing moral order on the whole of human society as well as on our individual desires.

Kant is not saying that moral agents come to believe these propositions about religion and history through arguments. He is saying rather that each moral agent will find herself acting as if she saw the world as Kant's propositions portray it. Morality, as Kant understands it, makes sense only if certain background conditions are met. Unless these conditions hold, a form of *pointlessness* threatens action dictated by the categorical imperative; and the rational agent cannot act while thinking her action pointless. The belief in freedom is needed first of all, because otherwise we would lack the assurance that we can do what the categorical imperative requires. The other morally required beliefs ward off a different kind of pointlessness.

What is evident in all of these other beliefs to which we are led on practical grounds alone is a concern for human happiness. Kant is often thought to hold that happiness is not valuable, and even to have ignored it wholly in his ethics. This is a serious mistake. It is true that for Kant moral worth is the supreme good, but by itself it is not the perfect or complete good.[50] To be virtuous, for Kant, is to be worthy of happiness: And the perfect good requires that happiness be distributed in accordance with virtue (*Practical Reason,* 5:110-11/114-15). Happiness, or the sum of satisfaction of desires, is a conditional good. It is good only if it results from the satisfaction of morally permissible desires. But it is intrinsically valuable nonetheless. It is valued by a rational agent for itself, and not instrumentally.[51]

Atheism and meaninglessness in history threaten to make morality pointless. A holy will necessarily aims at the perfect good, and we imperfect beings therefore ought to do what we can to bring it about. But it seems simply irrational to devote serious effort to bringing about a goal that one believes cannot be brought about. If reason showed the perfect good to be a required but unattainable goal, reason would be at odds with itself. The moral agent, knowing herself required to act in ways that make sense only if certain ends can be achieved, finds herself simply taking it that the world must allow the possibility of success. Since this attitude is not translatable into theoretical knowledge, the agent cannot have any details about *how* her effort will help bring about the ends. All that is needed is the confidence that it will. Philosophy helps, Kant thinks, by showing that nothing can prove the attitude unwarranted.[52]

Notes

[1] Contemporary English-language study of Kant's ethics owes a great deal to the important commentaries of H. J. Paton, *The Categorical Imperative* (London: Hutchinson, 1946), and Lewis White Beck, *A Commentary to Kant's Critique of Practical Reason* (Chicago: University of Chicago Press, 1960), both of which helped stimulate German scholarship as well. John Rawls's widely read *A Theory of Justice* (Cambridge, Mass.: Harvard University Press, 1971) showed one direction in which Kantianism could be revised, and was a major impetus to the use of Kantian insights in

developing general ethical theory and in handling concrete current issues.

[2] Although Kant did a great deal of thinking about ethics during his early years, he wrote little about it before the publication of the first *Critique*. That *Critique* contains some discussion of moral philosophy, but the major works are the following:

Groundwork of the Metaphysics of Morals (1785), reference to *Akademie* edition volume and page followed by the page number of the translation by H. J. Paton, *The Moral Law* (London: Hutchinson, 1948).

Critique of Practical Reason (1788), references followed by page numbers of the translation by Lewis White Beck (Indianapolis: Bobbs-Merrill, 1956).

Metaphysics of Morals, in two parts, known as the *Doctrine of Right* and the *Doctrine of Virtue,* which were published separately in 1797; references when quotations are from the *Doctrine of Virtue* followed by the page number of the translation by Mary Gregor (Philadelphia: University of Pennsylvania Press, 1964).

Religion within the Limits of Reason Alone (1793), references followed by the page number of the translation by Theodore M. Greene and Hoyt H. Hudson (1934; 2d ed., New York: Harper & Row, 1960).

Kant's essays on history and politics are important sources as well. There are two useful collections: Lewis White Beck et al., *Kant on History* (Indianapolis: Bobbs-Merrill, 1963), and Ted Humphrey, *Perpetual Peace and Other Essays* (Indianapolis: Hackett, 1983). References are followed by "H" and page number from the Beck translation.

Volumes 27 and 29 of the *Akademie* edition of *Kants gesammelte Schriften* contain over a thousand pages of student notes on Kant's classes on ethics, which he taught between twenty and thirty times from 1756-7 to 1793-4 (see Emil Arnoldt, *Gesammelte Schriften* [Berlin: 1909], Vol. V, p. 335). The earliest notes come from 1763-4, the latest from 1793-4. Notes taken in 1780-1 are available in English: *Lectures on Ethics,* trans. Louis Infield (originally 1930) (New York: Harper & Row, 1963).

The student notes offer many insights into Kant's ethical thought, but they also pose several new interpretative problems. In this essay I concentrate on the published works.

[3] Not only humans: Kant thinks any rational agents would be autonomous.

[4] The term "his" is used advisedly here: Kant had unfortunate views about women. He also thought servants were not sufficiently independent to be entitled to full political status.

[5] This is from marginal notes Kant jotted down as he was reading Rousseau's *Social Contract* and *Emile* during 1763-4 (20:140-1; I have added some punctuation). It is largely from these notes that we know of the considerable impact that Rousseau had on Kant.

[6] 20:36, "kindnesses occur only through inequality."

[7] *R* 6736, 19:145.

[8] See Kant's late remarks on servility in *Morals,* 6:434-6; 99-101; see also Thomas E. Hill, Jr., "Servility and Self-Respect," *Monist* 57 (1973): 87-104.

[9] In the essay "On the Common Saying: 'That may be true in theory but it does not work in practice'," Kant says that in connection with our moral self-legislation "man thinks of himself according to an analogy with the divinity" (8:280 n.). The essay is translated in Hans Reiss, ed., *Kant's Political Writings* (Cambridge: Cambridge University Press, 1970).

[10] The standard work on the development of Kant's ethics is Josef Schmucker, *Die Ursprünge der Ethik Kants* (Meisenheim am Glan: Anton Hain, 1961). There is no reliable study of the subject in English.

[11] For selections from Shaftesbury and Hutcheson, see. D. D. Raphael, *The British Moralists,* 2 vols. (Oxford: Oxford University Press, 1969), and J. B. Schneewind, *Moral Philosophy from Montaigne to Kant,* 2 vols. (Cambridge: Cambridge University Press, 1990). Their works were available in German, and Kant owned the translations of Hutcheson's most important writings.

[12] There are no studies of Wolff in English, and little of his work has been translated. Lewis White Beck, *Early German Philosophy* (Cambridge, Mass.: Harvard University Press, 1969) discusses his general philosophy but says little about his ethics. For an excellent study of the early German enlightenment and Wolff's place in it, see Hans M. Wolff, *Die Weltanschauung der deutschen Aufklärung* (Bern, 1949). For selections in English of his ethics, see Schneewind, *Moral Philosophy from Montaigne to Kant,* Vol. I.

[13] These views are compendiously presented in Christian Wolff, *Vernünftige Gedancken von der Menschen Thun und Lassen* (1720).

[14] Kant holds that it is necessarily true that each of us desires his or her own happiness, and he sometimes equates happiness with the satisfaction of the totality of our desires. But no single desire is a necessary feature of any particular individual. This is a point on which many of Kant's recent critics, particularly those

sympathetic to Aristotle, disagree with him. They would argue that some desires or motives or active dispositions are essential to the individual identity of the person. See, e.g., Jonathan Lear, *Aristotle: The Desire to Understand* (Cambridge: Cambridge University Press, 1988), p. 189. Kant would think that if you must have some specific effective desire then you are not free with respect to it. Kant does not think, as some of his critics believe, that the free will constitutes the whole identity of each individual. But he does think that whatever constitutes individual identity does so only contingently.

[15] Crusius was a leader of the anti-Wolffian movement. His moral philosophy is contained in his *Anweisung, vernünftig zu leben* (1744). There is good discussion of his general position in Beck, *Early German Philosophy.* For translated selections, see Schneewind, *Moral Philosophy from Montaigne to Kant,* Vol. II.

[16] There is considerable difficulty in interpreting Rousseau's influence on Kant. As indicated above, the most important evidence comes from the notes Kant made when he first read *Emile* and the *Social Contract* during 1763-4 (20:1-192). One of the most frequently quoted notes compares Rousseau's clarification of the hidden aspects of human nature to Newton's uncovering of the hidden aspects of physical nature (20:58-9). Another is more personal: "I am myself a researcher by inclination. I feel the whole thirst for knowledge and the eager unrest to move further on into it, also satisfaction with each acquisition. There was a time when I thought this alone could constitute the honor of humanity and I despised the know-nothing rabble. Rousseau set me straight. This delusory superiority vanishes, I learn to honor men, and I would find myself more useless than a common laborer if I did not believe this observation could give everyone a value which restores the rights of humanity" (20:44).

[17] *Social Contract,* I.viii.§ 4, in *On the Social Contract,* ed. Roger D. Masters, trans. Judith R. Masters (New York: St. Martin's Press, 1978), p. 56.

[18] In the 1763-4 notes (see note 5 in this chapter) there are several attempts to formulate the principle behind what Kant later called the categorical imperative. There are also clear indications both of the distinction between it and the hypothetical imperative and of the idea that the former is central to morality.

[19] Those who insisted that God laid down the laws of morality by absolute fiat argued that unless that were true, God would be limited by something external to himself. They thought that even eternal moral standards would be an intolerable constraint on God's absolute freedom.

[20] Pure theoretical reason is an activity determined *a priori,* and one might think of one of its patterns of activity as embodying the "causal law." The causal law, in this sense, explains why every event must have a cause, but does not alone tell us what event causes what other event; to obtain this knowledge we need data of experience in addition. Similarly, as I explain later, the moral law does not by itself tell us which specific acts are obligatory; we must use it to test maxims in order to learn what we ought to do.

[21] Some theorists have taken the rightness of acts as basic, defining a good agent as one who has a conscious habit of doing such acts, and good states of affairs as those intended to be the outcome of right acts. This view tends to go along with intuitionist explanations of how we know what is right. Thomas Reid's *Essays on the Active Powers of Man* (1788) offers one theory of this kind.

[22] A brilliant account of Hegelian objections of this kind, as well as other criticisms, is given in F. H. Bradley, *Ethical Studies* (1876; 2d ed., Oxford: Clarendon Press, 1927), ch. 2. The literature on the subject is extensive. The best book in English is Onora (O'Neill) Nell, *Acting on Principle: An Essay on Kantian Ethics* (New York: Columbia University Press, 1975), to which I am much indebted. For a sample of other criticisms of Kant see C. D. Broad, *Five Types of Ethical Theory* (London, 1930), ch. 5. See also the articles by Jonathan Harrison, "Kant's Examples of the First Formulation of the Categorical Imperative," *Philosophical Quarterly* 7 (1957); Julius Ebbinghaus, "Interpretation and Misinterpretation of the Categorical Imperative" (1959), reprinted in Robert Paul Wolff, ed., *Kant: A Collection of Critical Essays* (Garden City, N.Y.: Anchor/Doubleday, 1967), pp. 211-27; Jonathan Kemp, "Kant's Examples of the Categorical Imperative," *Philosophical Quarterly* 8: 63-71 (1958); Nelson Potter, "Paton on the Application of the Categorical Imperative," *Kant-Studien* 64 (1973): 411-22; Ottfried Höffe, "Kants kategorischer Imperativ als Kriterium des Sittlichen," *Zeitschrift für philosophische Forschung* 31 (1977): 354-84; and the following books: Paton, *The Categorical Imperative;* Marcus G. Singer, *Generalization in Ethics* (New York: Alfred A. Knopf, 1961); Bruce Aune, *Kant's Theory of Morals* (Princeton, N.J.: Princeton University Press, 1979); and John Atwell, *Ends and Principles in Kant's Moral Thought* (Dordrecht: D. Reidel, 1986).

[23] The formula given indicates the essential form underlying all particular hypothetical imperatives ("If you want to preserve your health, you ought to go to the dentist"). What makes an imperative hypothetical is not the appearance of an "if" clause in its formulation. Such clauses might appear in categorical imperatives: "If you are asked a question, you ought to answer truthfully." And they need not appear in hypothetical imperatives: "Eat whenever you are hungry." The sole defining feature of a hypothetical imperative is that it

obligates the agent to an action only on condition that the agent has desire for something that the action would bring about. For an excellent discussion, see Thomas E. Hill, Jr., "The Hypothetical Imperative," *Philosophical Review* 82 (1973): 429-50.

[24] There are many other views about how universalizability or the application of the formula of universal law should be understood. For an excellent discussion, see Christine Korsgaard, "Kant's Formula of Universal Law," *Pacific Philosophical Quarterly* 66 (1985): 24-47.

[25] See Barbara Herman, "The Practice of Moral Judgment," *Journal of Philosophy* 82 (1985): 414-35.

[26] See Christine Korsgaard, "Kant's Formula of Humanity," *Kant-Studien* 77 (1986): 183-202.

[27] Kant seems to assume that those who apply the categorical imperative to their maxims will come out with answers that agree when the maxims tested are alike.

[28] He also shows how the basic principles of morality can be extended to handle cases where agents do not comply with the moral requirement of acting from respect for the law. The treatment even of those who are indifferent to morality falls under an extension of the moral law.

[29] For strong representations of this point of view, see Alasdair MacIntyre, *After Virtue* (Notre Dame, Ind.: Notre Dame University Press, 1981), and Bernard Williams, *Ethics and the Limits of Philosophy* (Cambridge, Mass.: Harvard University Press, 1985).

[30] For an excellent example of an attempt to use the Kantian thinking to deal with a major social issue, see Onora O'Neill, *Faces of Hunger* (Oxford: Basil Blackwell, 1986).

[31] If you obey the natural law only because of fear of God's sanctions, you are still motivated by desire for good—the good of avoiding punishment.

[32] There are unclear and wavering anticipations of the Kantian move in Pufendorf and Samuel Clarke, but Crusius was the first to make the point central to his moral psychology.

[33] See Dieter Henrich, "Hutcheson und Kant," *Kant-Studien* 49 (1957-8): 49-69, and "Über Kants früheste Ethik," *Kant-Studien* 54 (1963): 404-31.

[34] The poet Schiller first made this kind of criticism. Schiller's and related objections are discussed at length in Hans Reiner, *Duty and Inclination* (The Hague: Martinus Nijhoff, 1983). A considerable literature has grown up on the subject. For recent discussion of it, see Michael Stocker, "The Schizophrenia of Modern Ethical Theories," *Journal of Philosophy* 73 (1976): 453-66; Richard Henson, "What Kant Might Have Said: Moral Worth and the Overdetermination of Dutiful Action," *Philosophical Review* 88 (1979): 39-54; Barbara Herman, "On the Value of Acting from the Motive of Duty," *Philosophical Review* 90 (1981): 359-82; Marcia Baron, "The Alleged Moral Repugnance of Acting from Duty," *Journal of Philosophy* 81 (1984): 197-220; Judith Baker, "Do One's Motives Have to be Pure?" in Richard Grandy and Richard Warner, eds., *Philosophical Grounds of Rationality* (Oxford: Oxford University Press, 1986), pp. 457-74; and Tom Sorrell, "Kant's Good Will," *Kant-Studien* 78 (1987): 87-101.

[35] Kant says that action from any of these desires is heteronomous. This is not because he thinks the desires are not part of the self. It is because through these desires action is governed by something other than the self. In these desires the self pursues good and avoids ill. It is therefore governed by the features of things that make them objects of desire or aversion, and these features are, of course, independent of our wills. Thus in describing heteronomy Kant speaks of the object determining the will "by means of" inclination (*vermittelst der Neigung*) (*Groundwork,* 4:444 / 111).

[36] He rejects the feeling of love as a proper moral motive (*Groundwork,* 4:399 / 67); he usually treats the passions and desires as if their aim is always the agent's own pleasure or good (e.g., *Groundwork,* 4:407 / 75); and at one point he says it must be the wish of every rational person to be free of desire (*Groundwork,* 4:428 / 955-6).

[37] This is particularly evident in the *Religion.* See 6:28 / 23, where the natural dispositions in human nature leading us to sexual activity and to strive for social superiority are said to be dispositions for good, though they can be misused; and 6:58 / 51: "Natural inclinations, *considered in themselves,* are *good,* that is not a matter of reproach, and it is not only futile to want to extirpate them but to do so would also be harmful and blameworthy."

[38] Kant here raises the questions of whether a transcendental deduction of the moral law is possible. The problem differs from that involved in constructing a transcendental argument for, say, the principle that every event must have a cause. We experience a spatiotemporal world of stable and interacting objects, and can therefore ask under what conditions such experience is possible. But we are so far from experiencing a stable moral world that we cannot point with certainty, Kant thinks, to even one case where someone was motivated by respect alone.

[39] Freedom of that kind, Kant thinks, would be terrifying, not something to cherish. See 20:91 ff., 27:258, 1320, and 1482.

[40] On the thesis that a free will and a will governed by the moral law are one and the same, see Henry E. Allison, "Morality and Freedom: Kant's Reciprocity Thesis," *Philosophical Review* 95 (1986): 393-425, and, more fully, the same author's *Kant's Theory of Freedom* (Cambridge: Cambridge University Press, 1990).

[41] For an attempt to unpack this difficult argument, see Thomas E. Hill, Jr., "Kant's Argument for the Rationality of Moral Conduct," *Pacific Philosophical Quarterly* 66 (1985): 3-23; and Allison, *Kant's Theory of Freedom,* ch. 12.

[42] See *Religion,* 6:21-6 / 16-21; *Morals,* 6:213-14 / 10-11; 6:225 / 25.

[43] For discussion, see Karl Ameriks, *Kant's Theory of Mind* (Oxford: Oxford University Press, 1982), ch. 6.

[44] For valuable assistance, see John Rawls, "Themes in Kant's Moral Philosophy," in Eckart Förster, ed., *Kant's Transcendental Deductions: The Three "Critiques" and the "Opus postumum"* (Stanford, Calif.: Stanford University Press, 1989), pp. 81-113; Henry E. Allison, "Justification and Freedom in the *Critique of Practical Reason,"* ibid., pp. 114-30; and the discussion of both papers by Barbara Herman, ibid., pp. 131-41.

[45] See Dieter Henrich, "Der Begriff der sittlichen Einsicht und Kants Lehre vom Faktum der Vernunft," in *Die Gegenwart der Griechen im neueren Denken,* ed. Dieter Henrich et al. (Tübingen: J. C. B. Mohr Paul Siebeck, 1960), pp. 77-115; and "Die Deduktion des Sittengesetzes," in *Denken im Schatten des Nihilismus,* ed. Alexander Schwann (Darmstadt: Wissenschaftliche Buchgesellschaft, 1975), pp. 55-112.

[46] Whether this marks the failure of an attempt to ground morality or a wise realization that morality needs no grounds beyond itself is of course a matter of considerable philosophical disagreement. For extended discussion, see Gerold Prauss, *Kant über Freiheit als Autonomie* (Frankfurt am Main: Vittorio Klostermann, 1983).

[47] The second *Critique* is a critique of practical reason generally, and not only of *pure* practical reason, because it examines, among other things, the claim of empirical practical reason—means/end reasoning—to be the only practical reason there is. The establishment through the fact of reason of pure practical reason disproves this claim.

[48] "The proposition: Make the highest good possible in the world your own final end! is a synthetical proposition *a priori,* which is introduced by the moral law itself" (*Religion,* 6:7 n. / 7 n.). Kant's argument for this is to say the least unclear. For further discussion see the essay by Allen Wood in the present book.

[49] In addition to the collections cited in note 2, see the important essay "An Old Question Raised Again: Is the Human Race Constantly Progressing?" in the *Streit der Fakultäten* (7:77-94); a translation is included in the Beck collection and in *The Conflict of the Faculties,* trans. Mary Gregor (New York: Abaris Books, 1979).

[50] Kant repeatedly criticizes the Stoics for making the mistake of thinking virtue the perfect good. The Epicureans, he held, made just the opposite mistake, taking happiness to be the complete good. His view synthesizes the two in the proper way (*Practical Reason,* 5:111-13 / 115-17).

[51] A basically virtuous person takes as her fundamental maxim to pursue her own good only on condition that doing so meets the requirements of morality. A basically vicious person reverses the order, and takes as fundamental the maxim of doing what morality requires only if it is not in conflict with the pursuit of her own good. See the discussion in *Religion,* 6:36-7 / 31-2 and 6:42-4 / 37-9.

[52] I should like to thank Richard Rorty, David Sachs, Larry Krasnoff, Paul Guyer, Fred Beiser, and Richard Flathman, who read this essay at various stages of its development and made helpful suggestions.

FURTHER READING

Acton, H. B. *New Studies in Ethics: Kant's Moral Philosophy.* London: Macmillan and Co., 1970, 71 p.
    Critical and historical assessment of Kant's ethical philosophy.

Allison, Henry E. *Kant's Theory of Freedom.* Cambridge: Cambridge University Press, 1990, 304 p.
    Interprets Kant's concept of freedom as it functions in his ethics and moral psychology, and surveys the secondary literature of the subject.

————. "Morality and Freedom: Kant's Reciprocity Thesis." *The Philosophical Review* 95, No. 3 (July 1986): 393-425.
    Explores Kant's view that freedom of the will and the moral law are reciprocal concepts.

Beck, Lewis White. *A Commentary on Kant's "Critique of Practical Reason."* Chicago: University of Chicago Press, 1960, 308 p.
    Study of Kant's second *Critique,* placing the treatise in its historical context and assessing "the contents of this work on their philosophical merits."

Buchanan, Allen. "Categorical Imperatives and Moral Principles." *Philosophical Studies* 31, No. 4 (April 1977): 249-60.

Attempts to render compatible seemingly inconsistent statements by Kant regarding the uniqueness and *a priori* of the categorical imperative.

Jones, Hardy E. *Kant's Principle of Personality.* Madison: University of Wisconsin Press, 1971, 163 p.

Inquiry into Kant's ethical doctrines, emphasizing the importance of the categorical imperative.

Korsgaard, Christine. "Kant." In *Ethics in the History of Western Philosophy*, edited by Robert J. Cavalier, James Gouinlock, and James P. Sterba, pp. 201-43. New York: St. Martin's Press, 1989.

Overviews Kant's life and work and places his moral philosophy in the context of his larger transcendental philosophy.

Louden, Robert B. "Kant's Virtue Ethics." *Philosophy* 61, No. 238 (Oct. 1986): 473-89.

Advances a picture of Kant's moral theory that tempers interpretations of it as an extreme rule of ethics.

McCarty, Richard. "The Limits of Kantian Duty, and Beyond." *American Philosophical Quarterly* 26, No. 1 (Jan. 1989): 43-52.

Addresses the possibility of a Kantian approach to morality accounting for supererogation.

O'Neill, Onora. *Constructions of Reason: Explorations of Kant's Practical Philosophy.* Cambridge: Cambridge University Press, 1989, 249 p.

Defends an antifoundationalist, constructivist picture of Kant's moral philosophy against recent objections and would-be Kantian positions.

Paton, H. J. *The Categorical Imperative.* Chicago: University of Chicago Press, 1948, 283 p.

Elucidates the complex structure of Kant's moral philosophy, focusing on *The Metaphysics of Morals*.

Reich, Klaus. "Kant and Greek Ethics." Trans. W. H. Walsh. *Mind* 48, No. 192 (Oct. 1939): 338-54, 446-63.

Explores the legacy of Greek thought (especially Stoicism) in Kant's moral philosophy, particularly as it was disseminated through the Wolffians.

Ross, Sir David. *Kant's Ethical Theory: A Commentary on the "Grundlegung zur Metaphysik der Sitten."* Oxford: Oxford University Press, 1954, 96 p.

Clarifies the main points of Kant's moral philosophy.

Sedgwick, Sally. "Can Kant's Ethics Survive the Feminist Critique?" *Pacific Philosophical Quarterly* 71, No. 1 (March 1990): 60-79.

Surveys and evaluates common feminist objections to Kant's groundwork for a metaphysics of morals.

Ward, Keith. *The Development of Kant's View of Ethics.* Oxford: Basil Blackwell, 1972, 184 p.

Study of Kant's moral philosophy that aims to "put the well-known doctrines in the overall context of Kant's developing philosophy."

Wolff, Robert P. *The Autonomy of Reason: A Commentary on Kant's "Groundwork of the Metaphysic of Morals."* New York: Harper & Row, 1973, 228 p.

Detailed technical analysis of the argument of the *Groundwork*.

Additional coverage of Kant's life and career is contained in the following sources published by Gale Research: *Dictionary of Literary Biography,* Vol. 94.

Gérard de Nerval

1808-1855

(Born Gérard Labrunie) French poet, short story writer, dramatist, translator, novelist, essayist, and critic.

For additional information on Nerval's life and works, see *NCLC*, Volume 1.

INTRODUCTION

Widely regarded as a precursor of the Symbolists and the Surrealists, Nerval was one of the first writers to explore the subconscious in fiction and poetry. Noted for his vivid delineation of hallucination and dreaming and for the far-reaching influence of his artistic vision, Nerval presented images in his works that originate from such diverse sources as art, mythology, religion, fantasy, and the occult. Plagued by mental illness for much of his life, Nerval is said to have derived his greatest creative energy from his madness, while the themes of his most highly esteemed works, notably *Les chiméres* (1854; *The Chimeras*) and *Sylvie* (1854; *Sylvie: Recollections of Valois*), are thought to have been directed by his several persistent personal obsessions.

Biographical Information

Nerval was a small child when his mother died. He was raised by a great-uncle in the Valois, a rural region of France that appears in *Sylvie* and other works as an idyllic landscape. At age twenty he published a translation of Goethe's *Faust*, which Goethe himself acclaimed. Nerval became a member of the *Jeune-France*, a group of Romantic artists and writers who challenged the established classical school with radical artistic theories, flamboyant dress, and eccentric behavior. But Nerval's carefree bohemian life became troubled as increasingly severe money problems and mental difficulties befell him. Biographers suggest that Nerval's premature separation from his mother led to intense infatuations with women later in life; in his writing, women are depicted in various guises as unattainable embodiments of ideal femininity. The most enduring of these unrequited passions was for an actress named Jenny Colon, whose aloofness and early death hastened the deterioration of Nerval's mental health. Soon after her death, Nerval embarked on an extended journey through Egypt, Turkey, and Lebanon. This trip excited his imagination with mystical and exotic motifs and provided material for *Voyage en Orient* (1851; *Journey to the Orient*). Ironically, the

madness that afflicted Nerval also heightened his artistic sensibility, and it was in his final, most painful years that he produced his greatest works. Nerval committed suicide by hanging himself from a railing in a Paris alley at the age of forty-six.

Major Works

Nerval's first literary success came with his *Journey to the Orient*, a book of travel essays interjected with fictional elements. In 1854 Nerval published his first generally acclaimed masterwork, a compilation of short stories and poetry titled *Les filles du feu* (*Daughters of Fire*). Many of the minor narratives in this collection feature elements of fantasy and autobiography, as well as accounts of hallucinations, dreams, humor, and a treatment of the doppelgänger theme. The work also contains the story *Sylvie*. Merging fantasy with reality, the narrativ's protagonist, Gérard, struggles with his love for an imaginary, idealized woman, Aurelie-Adrienne, as well as the real Sylvie. Obsessed with the fantastic images of ideal women he fabricates in his mind, Gérard eventually destroys his chances of forming a relationship with the real woman. Also published as part of *Les filles du feu*, the sonnet sequence *Les chiméres* is considered by most critics to be Nerval's greatest poetic accomplishment. Each of the twelve sonnets is imbued with mythological and religious imagery, as well as themes derived from Nerval's own life. The poems of *Les chiméres* are interwoven, with recurring characters and allusions that parallel religious history and the alchemist's process of turning base metals into gold. The author's last published work, *Aurélia* (1855) suggests that each person lives a second life through his or her dreams. This story features a narrator who, after falling into a hallucinatory state, begins to see his doppelgänger. Using the figure of his double, Nerval in *Aurélia* presented his impressions of his own mental deterioration in a narrative he described as a symbolic "descent into hell."

Critical Reception

Criticism of Nerval since his death has generally focused on the visionary quality of his writings and his influence on later writers. Charles Baudelaire and the Symbolists were inspired by his use of cryptic symbols and his fascination with hallucinatory states. The Surrealists celebrated Nerval as a spiritual ancestor, a courageous pioneer in the exploration of the subconscious. Also, Nerval's recreation of scenes from memory and reverie bears similarities to later stream-of-consciousness writing and prefigures the work of Marcel Proust, who called Nerval Aassuredly one of the three or four greatest writers of the nineteenth century. In recent years, scholars have begun to look more closely at Nerval's texts, particularly *Sylvie*, *Les chiméres*, and *Aurélia,* all of which were written during periods of madness. In these works critics commend Nerval's innovative use of dreams and visions, the semiotic qualities of his language, his copious references to mythology and religion, and the incorporation of events and people from his own life.

PRINCIPAL WORKS

Faust de Göthe [translator] (poetry) 1828
Léo Burckart (drama) 1839
Voyage en Orient [*Journey to the Orient*] (travel essays) 1851
Les illuminés (sketches) 1852
Lorely: souvenirs d'Allemagne (travel essays) 1852
*Les filles du feu [*Daughters of Fire*] (short stories and poetry) 1854
†*La rêve et la vie* [*Dreams and Life*] (poetry and short stories) 1855
Selected Writings (poetry and short stories) 1957

Œuvres complètes. 10 vols. 1926-32
Œuvres. 2 vols. 1960-61

*Includes the short story *Sylvie* (translated as *Sylvie: Recollections of Valois* in 1887) and the collection of poems titled *Les chiméres* (translated as *The Chimeras* in 1933).

†Includes the short story *Aurélia* (translated as *Aurelia* in 1932).

CRITICISM

Geoffrey Wagner (essay date 1957)

SOURCE: Introduction to *Selected Writings of Gérard de Nerval, translated and with a Critical Introduction and Notes by Geoffrey Wagner,* Grove Press, 1957, pp. 5-46.

[*In the following excerpt, Wagner offers a survey of Nerval's works and a summary of his influence.*]

> Il n'y a qu'un problème philosophique vraiment sérieux: c'est le suicide. Juger que la vie vaut ou ne vaut pas la peine d'être vécue, c'est répondre à la question fondamentale de la philosophie.
>
> Albert Camus, *Le Mythe de Sisyphe*

More than most writers Gérard de Nerval has suffered from failing to fall into any very definite period or genre. His influence has been wider than his appeal and he has not always come off well in the rather arid region of literary history for his work, like the work of any mystic poet, resists classification. André Gide, of all writers, has lately been referred to as a mystic and in the sense that his work was always concerned with spiritual values this surprising judgment is just enough. But if Nerval is anything, he is that rarity, a natural French mystic poet, and it was this aspect of his genius that demanded from him that withdrawal from what we call the social ego, that attempt to mount higher "pour nous isoler de la foule," as he put it, which has meant much to the surrealist writers of our century.

Although a poet like Yeats refers to Nerval with the obvious affection of affinity, he has too often been handicapped by the stereotype of him as the gentle dreamer, which developed in the latter half of the last century. In his own time he meant a great deal. Baudelaire, we believe, was introduced to both Petrus Borel and Nerval by Edouard Ourliac;[1] he paid tribute to Nerval in his article on Hégésippe Moreau[2] and borrowed his well-known gibbet image in "Un Voyage à Cythère" from Nerval's ***Voyage en Orient.*** Beyond this Nerval's translations from Goethe, Bürger, and other German authors, persuaded many French scholars and writers to further efforts in this field and he himself was one of the first major French poets to assimilate fully into his work the influence of the *blaue Blume* school of poetry. His whole erotic orientation is deeply indebted to Hoffmann. His appreciation of Ronsard, Du Bellay, and their contemporaries, considerably affected his successors, while his work on the legends of the Valois, which he loved so much, awakened a living interest in the literature of the French provinces. Nerval seems to have been read consistently in France throughout the Symbolist movement and his influence there to have been pervasive. But if for Henri de Régnier his voice was like a silver bell, it is more to the somber notes of *Aurélia* that our century has responded. There have been, of course, notable exceptions. Even Jean-Paul Sartre has confessed to being seduced by *Sylvie,* the "divine Sylvie" as Maurice Barrès called it. Proust, in whom we find perhaps the happiest and most confident elaboration of the implications of Nerval's work, referred to *Sylvie* in *Le Temps Retrouvé* as one of the masterpieces of French literature and likened its method of involuntary memory to his own.

But it has been Nerval's visions, particularly those of *Aurélia,* that have chiefly fascinated our century, especially in the attempt of surrealism to find a new freedom in the casuistry of the dream.

. . . . .

Nerval's first poems, published when he was still in his teens, were political verses after the style of Delavigne, rather exaggerated for contemporary taste, but interesting as showing the young "revolutionary" poet looking back to the heroism of a warlike France, a France now left "malheureuse et trahie." These *Élégies Nationales* were quickly followed by the translation of the first part of *Faust* which drew such praise from Goethe. To Eckermann, Goethe added that he thought the work a prodigy of style and that Nerval would become one of the purest and most elegant writers in France. Gretchen's song at her spinning wheel, *"Chambre de Marguerite,"* resembling the later cries of Nerval's own heart, is put into French with a simplicity that makes it a poem in its own right, and Nerval indeed printed it separately on occasion.

Content to remain for the moment a translator, and a scrupulously careful one (he produced, for instance, five versions of a ballad by Bürger between 1829 and 1835), Nerval published French versions of selections from Klopstock, Schiller, Heine, and others. He then edited a volume containing work by Ronsard, Du Bellay, and their contemporaries, whose style so influenced his own. In his comments on these writers in *La Bohème Galante,* called **"Les Poëtes du XVIᵉ Siècle,"** however, he is by no means uncritical and sees them, in Ben Jonson's words of the ancients, "as guides, not commanders." Referring to the "école de Ronsard" in particular, he laments "l'espèce de despotisme qu'elle a introduit en littérature."

After 1830 Nerval began writing his first plays, as was only natural for a young author who had that year witnessed the *bataille d'Hernani,* and his work became more original. His **Odelettes,** deliberately modelled on Ronsard, began appearing in various periodicals and attracted attention chiefly for their classical adherence to conventions of form, which were at that time so out of fashion among the young. However at this point, as we know, Nerval's interests were unfortunately returned to drama by Jenny Colon, and shortly after she left him, his only success came out, **Léo Burckart.**

This political piece of young Germany of the *Sturm und Drang* era, reminiscent of the early Schiller, once again shows the "revolutionary" Nerval. There are some excellent scenes, particularly where the student's court passes sentence of death on Léo, who is actually among them behind a mask, and there is a powerful finale where the fanatical student idealist, Frantz Lewald, sent in to kill Léo, is driven to take his own life. The character of Léo himself is well drawn—the theoretical revolutionary who is offered, and forced to accept, the task of putting his theories into practice, only to find the pitfalls of politics too much for him; while Frantz, torn between love for Marguerite, Léo's wife, and his revolutionary ideals, though perhaps an over-romanticized character, can still arouse our sympathy.

After his first bout of insanity and subsequent trip to the Middle East, Nerval published his **Scènes de la Vie Orientale,** re-edited in 1851 as **Voyage en Orient,** a work Gautier called, in a typical phrase, "ce livre adorable, plein d'amour, d'azur et de lumière." Apart from its interest in connection with contemporary travel, mentioned above, it contains, in some of Nerval's best prose, much of his deepest thinking on nature and esoteric religions, on Swedenborg and the Cabala "qui lie les mondes" and in the heavenly correspondences of things on earth.

His poems began appearing more frequently now, and a collection came out at about the same time as **La Bohème Galante** which, apart from its critical section referred to, is an account of his life in Paris, in the same way that **Lorely, Souvenirs d'Allemagne,** dedicated to Janin and published in 1852, was an account of his experiences in Germany.

On August 15th, 1853, Nerval's first really important work, **Sylvie,** appeared in the *Revue des Deux Mondes.* This enchanting work is a frame-story with its roots in literary pastoralism. One thinks of d'Urfé's Sylvie in what is perhaps a consummate instance of pastoral romance, and one recalls that *l'Astrée* was, like Nerval's work, both an autobiographical compilation and a *roman à clef* with an obdurate shepherdess and that "chagrin d'amour" which must have drawn Heine to Nerval, and vice versa. Both works, *l'Astrée* and **Sylvie,** reacted against prevalent philosophies of materialism, both are covered in a patina of nostalgic reverie, with the longing of late afternoon and with a desire for the golden age. Meanwhile, the idyllic moment on an island, which we find in so many romantics, including once again Rousseau, lends itself readily to various interpretations; *The Tempest* is perhaps a supreme example of this literature which the Jungian symbolism fits so well, with the fortunate island (personality) set in the turbulent sea (unconscious).

The main theme of *Sylvie* is formed by a series of utterly simple anecdotes of the author's youth at his uncle's home in the Valois. By its sense of unusual intimacy, by the pathos of Sylvie's position objectively conveyed, and by its derangement of time in the interests of the life of the psyche rather than in those of normal chronology, the work would alone rank high among autobiographies of adolescence. But it is in manner that it is almost perfect, for here the purity of Nerval's heart was clearly reflected in the luminosity of his style.

Of course the reader must remember that the element of distortion, present here in the purposeful confusion Nerval makes of the three women, Sylvie, Adrienne, and Aurélia, was due to the fact that memories of all three were entwined in his own mind around that central conception of womanhood which stylized his amatory writing from now on. The round dance, with which the work begins, is essentially a round of his erotic trinity, Sylvie and Adrienne surmounted by Aurélia, the Blessed Virgin.

In a sense *Sylvie* is one of our last and most lovely pastorals, a lament for a vanished and vanishing world, not only, Rousseau-like, for the rural life yielding to increasing urbanization, but also for the past world of the author's own soul. *Sylvie* is singularly touching when Nerval interjects moments of humor that show us how well he understood himself. This, then, is conscious nostalgia. It is devoid of self-pity. It is a laurel wreath Nerval places on the passing of time, and its permanent appeal, especially its appeal to Proust, shows how harmoniously conceived, how deceptively well controlled, and how beautifully balanced in its antiphonal refrains from section to section, this little masterpiece is. In the light of his whole work its pantheism balances the Christianity of the last part of *Aurélia,* unorthodox as this may be.

In 1854 *Sylvie* was put together with other stories, including *"Emilie,"* a narrative of the Revolution in Alsace, one of Nerval's finest, if least typical, stories, and published as *Les Filles du Feu,* together with an important dedicatory letter to Dumas. *"Emilie,"* which is equal to the best of Merimée or Maupassant, shows another side of Nerval's genius, one that should not be overlooked, and it is as well to balance any large weight of his autobiographical writings with a plain story like this in which he showed admirable technical ability. It is not surprising that the author of this tale was the son of an Army surgeon, but it is pleasant to see Nerval fully in control of a form of writing of his day, and it is only in the old Abbé's descriptions of the countryside that Nerval here relinquished a fairly taut, direct narrative style. Again, suicide haunts the story.

Nerval's most significant prose work, *Aurélia,* did not appear complete in his lifetime. In a phrase, Gautier called the work "la Folie se racontant elle-même" and so indeed it is. It is not difficult to find Freudian symbolism, in our enlightened age, in these hallucinations. Nerval, however, warns us against the vulgarity of the purely scientific method of approach. Yet L.-H. Sebillotte has not had to be perversely ingenious to find an Oedipus complex in *Aurélia.*[12] Almost everything, ranging from Mariolatry to Orphism, could be, and has been, worked out of Nerval's hallucinations, but presumably only Dr. Blanche will ever know which of these manifestations were the outstanding signs and signals of Nerval's illness.

The basis of the book is Nerval's unrequited passion for Aurélia, or Jenny Colon, and his spiritual pilgrimage through a disordered world to this goal. The central figure is a composite abstraction of womanhood, an *Ewig-Weibliche* invested with Nerval's omnivorous reading in the Cabala, the Zohar, Egyptian religions, the medieval schoolmen, and the magnetic scientists, like Gilbert, of the early Seventeenth Century, sources which have been skilfully detailed by Jean Richer.[13] Adjusting time in a Proustian way, Nerval presents this central figure as his cryptic trinity, in the main consisting of Sylvie and Adrienne surmounted by Aurélia. Octavie is only a passing flame—did not Anthony leave Octavia for Egypt?—while Pandora, Marie Pleyel, leads this Faust to his Helen, as we read at the beginning.

Aurélia herself is essentially a Beatrice, rather than a Gretchen; she is a Schekhina, the woman, like Spenser's Sapience, with the attributes of pure good who alone leads to the Godhead. She is the Blessed Virgin and the eternal mother, in short, the vision who tells the protagonist:

> Je suis la même que Marie, la même que ta mère, la même aussi que sous toutes les formes tu as toujours aimée. A chacune de tes épreuves j'ai quitté l'un des masques dont je voile mes traits, et bientôt tu me verras telle que je suis.

Around this composite creation unites a conflagration of dream and reality. On the physical level there is the woman who played such a special erotic role in Nerval's life: on the spiritual, we have the transformation— "l'actrice Jenny Colon, Aurélia, devient la Médiatrice,

Isis, la Vierge," as Béguin puts it. As with other mystical writers, like Hoffmann, for example, with whom Nerval has such close affinity, occult or pseudo-occult ideas become direct emotional stimulants to the artist. Nerval's hallucinations are sanctified in his sight by the imagination, they are *pure* vision, unlimited by the conscious, and for this reason he sees it his duty to give them to posterity:

> Je croirai avoir fait quelque chose de bon et d'utile en énonçant naïvement la succession des idées par lesquelles j'ai retrouvé le repos et une force nouvelle à opposer aux malheurs futurs de la vie.

This method of awakening memory, then, opened the way for the vision that so triumphantly greets us in the work of Marcel Proust; it hints directly at Proust's method of involuntary memory, a method which, as Justin O'Brien puts it, "repose sur une de ces expériences où la mémoire affective agit sans qu'intervienne la volonté."

Nerval's love attitude, as we have seen, involved the phantasy that Jenny was with him always; this idea, like the doctrine of *noblesse oblige* in literature (in which our ancestors are always looking over our shoulders), surely enhances the exhibitionist factor. For under the surveillance of what we like to call the ego ideal there is little privacy. Consequently you must put all on paper, you are forced to confessional literature, of which *Aurélia* is an outstanding example.

At the same time Jenny-Aurélia, like Beatrice for Dante, was his "étoile" (*"El Desdichado"*): the poet is astrophel, guided (like the magi) by the star, which plays a moral role. There is here, as under different circumstances to Dante, a proximate relationship between ritual and myth. To be a lover in this world is to be a poet, and to be a poet is to love. Like Beatrice, too, Jenny-Aurélia exists on four levels: she is a beautiful girl, she is a living symbol of God's beauty, she is an incitement to virtuous behavior in this life (the moral meaning), and, lastly, on the anagogical level, she is the fortress of heaven itself. This longing for union, coupled with the mission of poet as prophet (*vates*), Nerval saw as his highest aspiration; contemplation of his "étoile" was the function of his work.

Aurélia is outstanding, one has to confess, more for its subject-matter than for its style. It is not one of Nerval's best-written works; marred too often by the fulsome phrasing of its period, its last pages show his artistic discrimination at its lowest ebb. The picture of individual man horribly alone, walking through a lost world where the stones shout out at him and bodiless voices shriek from the shadows, is, however, like a nerve-end of our consciousness contracting in advance. Just as it is impossible to read the city poems of Baudelaire and Verlaine today without feeling that they contain an extraordinary significance for our time, so it is hard to hear Nerval calling out from his asylum without a tremor of sympathy, and perhaps also fear at the apparently uncontrollable progress of materialism that can make a poet write:

> les visions qui s'étaient succédé pendant mon sommeil m'avaient réduit à un tel désespoir que je pouvais à peine parler . . .
>
> Je me levai plein de terreur . . .
> le sentiment qui résulta pour moi de ces visions . . . était si triste, queje me sentais comme perdu . . .
>
> je n'ai jamais éprouvé que le sommeil fut un repos . . .

Yet if we take a cosmic view of this suffering, we must remember that Nerval did not. For him it was simply a hellish dualism—"dualisme chronique," as Baudelaire is thought to have called it—and a "descente aux enfers" to bring back what he thought was truth. He would have agreed with Gauguin that God belongs to the dream, but this does not mean that he treated insanity as an escape.

"Tendre fol," he has been called, "le pauvre Gérard," "gentil Nerval," "doux rêveur,"[14] but there is something stronger about this man who, while writing to Deschamps in 1854 "je travaille et j'enfante désormais dans la douleur," could produce this epitaph on his own life, not as a plea for leniency, but as the picture of a world that he thought would help others. In some ways the words of the document Hermann Hesse's Steppenwolf left behind him in his bourgeois boarding-house fit *Aurélia* also:

> These records, however much or however little of real life may lie at the back of them, are not an attempt to disguise or to palliate this widespread sickness of our times. They are an attempt to present the sickness itself in its actual manifestation. They mean, literally, a journey through hell, a sometimes fearful, sometimes courageous journey through the chaos of a world whose souls dwell in darkness, a journey undertaken with the determination to go through hell from one end to the other, to give battle to chaos, and to suffer torture to the full.

. . . . .

Nerval's poetry was only posthumously assembled, the collection of 1877 being the first to enable a true appreciation of his value as a poet, and to show how the three ages of the poet, of which he wrote in *Petits Châteaux de Bohème,* bear a direct relation to his work.

First, there come what he called the poems written "par enthousiasme de jeunesse." These include the early political poems, imitations of Delavigne, Béranger, and others, the best of which concern the Grande Armée in

Russia, perhaps owing to his mother's death and his father's wound in these campaigns.

Second, there are the poems "faits par amour," the *Odelettes,* translations of German ballads, popular songs, and personal anecdotes.

Third, we have the poems written "par désespoir" or in a *"supernaturaliste"* state of mind—Nerval himself italicized this word, adding "comme diraient les Allemands," and he used it to describe the poems of his later years, when he was mad, the verse counterpart, in fact, of *Aurélia.*

The poems of the first group are generally unoriginal. Those of the second are largely reminiscent of his own life. Exquisitely expressed and perfectly formal they are little cameos of experience which, though less sentimental than Coppée, remind one more of him, or of Jammes, than of Baudelaire and his successors. *"Une Allée du Luxembourg,"* for instance, should be set beside Baudelaire's *"A Une Passante"* (which is said to be indebted to it) to see the essential difference between the two poets. Nerval is chiefly out to capture the atmosphere of Parisian spring, and his verse is accordingly light:

> Elle a passé, la jeune fille
> Vive et preste comme un oiseau:
> A la main une fleur qui brille,
> A la bouche un refrain nouveau.

At the end comes the poet's comment, in this case a spiritual nostalgia that is typically *nervalien:* and here the metre slows.

> Mais non,—ma jeunesse est finie. . . .
> Adieu, doux rayon qui m'as lui,—
> Parfum, jeune fille, harmonie . . .
> Le bonheur passait,—il a fui!

The poem, *"Avril,"* too, is so perfect that it might well have come fresh from the Pléiade, simple as an act of faith. In this sort of work Nerval is not trying to produce original matter, so much as to give "What oft was thought but ne'er so well expressed." His emphasis is on manner. In *"Les Cydalises,"* with its delightful opening stanza, we have a characteristic instance of Nerval's use of a word to symbolize a meaning. Who are these "cydalises"? They were female camp-followers, as it were, of the *jeunesse dorée* or bohemian set of the day, and they include as their number one Camille Rogier's girl friend who, apparently unusually beautiful, was fêted by several poets of her day and caught Nerval's eye on more than one occasion. Like Jenny she died young and in the full flower of her beauty. So Nerval, in company with Ourliac, used her as a symbol of all youthful, but transient, beauty, the type of the *jeunes-France.* He mentions her several times, in several contexts, but he deliberately confuses her with Jenny Colon when he writes, in *La Bohème Galante,* "Ma Cydalise à moi, perdue, à jamais perdue!"

Here we have, then, a typical example of Nerval's cypher-like use of that personal mythology which is to fill his last poems and make some of them almost impossibly obscure. Again, in *"Épitaphe,"* we have another enigmatic reference to one of these word-symbols—"rêveur comme un triste Clitandre." Clitandre was a common stage name in Seventeenth-Century French drama. Molière's Clitandre is the sham doctor of *Amour médicin* who is called to attend Sganarelle's daughter but contents himself, on the basis of sympathy between father and daughter, with taking Sganarelle's own pulse, a sort of Dr. Knock in advance. Corneille's *Clitandre* has, as its sub-title, *l'Innocence delivrée,* which is surely not the explanation for her sadness in Nerval's poem. There are many theories put forward by exegetes on these tempting obscurities, but it is as well to remember perhaps that *"Les Cydalises,"* so Nerval told Arsène Houssaye, "est venue malgré moi sous forme de chant." Although later than the other *Odelettes,* and somewhat chimeric in content, it belongs to the early collection by style and language, and is a glance back from the terror of his present to the happier days of his past, again to be found in *"La Cousine."*

In *Lyrisme et Vers d'Opéra* we have more poems written "par amour," with the same facility as the *Odelettes.* *"La Sérénade,"* an imitation of Uhland's *"Ständchen,"* is an excellent example of the sort of standard for which Nerval was always striving in work of this kind.

It is in *Les Chimères* and *Autres Chimères* that we reach the third period, the *"supernaturaliste"* poems which, Nerval wrote, "perdraient de leur charme à être expliqués, si la chose était possible." These poems are filled with just those mysterious references that beset the reader of *Aurélia.* The poetry is again formal and direct, if more rhetorical in style, with none of the syntactical obscurity to be found in French poetry later in the century. The language is lucid, but the message is, as even Béguin has to confess, "à la fois d'une essence religieuse, proprement ineffable, et de nature très subjective."

Of this group, *"El Desdichado"*—"ce blason de haute noblesse lyrique et de destin accablé," as Henri Strentz calls it—has always attracted most comment, and T. S. Eliot borrowed from it for *The Waste Land.* It presents typical complexities which have been studied in detail by specialist scholars like Paul Gautier, Jeanine Moulin, Pierre Audiat, André Rousseaux, and Fernand Verhesen. But it is not hard for the general reader to see at once that the poet himself is the "desdichado," the unfortunate one, the outcast. He it is who is "le ténébreux," "le veuf" (because of Jenny), and he is inconsolable because the image of Aurélia, the memory of whom saturates the poem, evades him. When "el desdichado" cries out, "Ma seule étoile est morte," it is Nerval himself mourning the loss of Jenny and his ideal of womanhood. In line 4, he makes one of his numerous references to Dürer's engraving *Melancolia I* which gradually came to personify the grief by which he was haunted, and which attracted criticism from both Baudelaire and Michelet. In line 9 we have another memory of his childhood, for in *Sylvie* we read how at the village festival he kissed, and was kissed by, the Queen of the Festival—Adrienne. Caught in the round dance, in the orbit of desire, the poet illides the laws of physics and those of the psyche.

Finally, in the last triplet, Nerval recalls his own tragedy. Twice he himself had made a "descente aux enfers," and twice he had recovered and returned to normal life, while "les soupirs de la sainte" refer to Adrienne, the childhood love who became a nun, according to his suppositions, and died in a convent. "Les cris de la fée" point to Jenny who, as we know from *Aurélia,* appeared several times to Nerval after her death in the guise of a fairy or goddess. Most of Nerval's femininity conceptions are in this poem, in fact, from "la reine de Saba" to the blonde English girl, Octavie, whom he usually associated with Pausilippus, or Posilipo, where he took her and where, possibly, he learnt of her crippled husband. Nearly all Nerval's poetry has this autobiographical level; in another "chimère," *"Le Christ aux Oliviers,"* he makes a Christ in his own image, an "insensé sublime," an "Icare oublié qui remontait les cieux," this Christ-identification polarizing the now frequently expressed dislike of Jehovah, "le dieu vainqueur" and force of inhibition, the super-ego.

The exhibitionist quality of the neurotic is indeed very evident in this transference of the Rousseauian "good life" of the instincts to Christ: the erotic pressure behind the poems, meanwhile, forces the rhetorical apostrophes on the poet. He knows he is guilty, damned, he challenges God, and attempts to dramatize the virginity of the instincts. He associates himself with heroic rebels, as in the poem *"A Madame Ida Dumas."* There is nothing very new in another Manfred struggling to liberate his potentialities against the fabric of society—Nerval's *"Pensée de Byron"* recognizes this fellow spirit—but Nerval's attitude to his material in *Les Chimères* is extraordinary. Owing to his insanity he can push further than the romantic hero. He shatters the microcosm-macrocosm relationship in these poems, he *is* the universe, and at the end of *Aurélia* he rides beside Christ to the new Jerusalem and learns "le secret du monde des mondes."

The remainder of Nerval's poems fall more happily into place if we will concede his method in this period,

epitomized in *"El Desdichado."* Thus *"Myrtho,"* *"Horus,"* and the other poems of this group, are all experiences of different visions, while *"Vers Dorés"* recalls another central theme of *Aurélia,* the Pythagorean premise of the transmigration of souls. In this poem we see Nerval's longing for a synthesis of religions and that sense of the one behind the many which tends to categorize him as a mystic poet:

Respecte dans la bête un esprit agissant:
Chaque fleur est une âme à la Nature éclose;
Un mystère d'amour dans le métal repose;
'Tout est sensible!' Et tout sur ton être
   est puissant.

The poems of *Autres Chimères* are in many cases merely rewritten versions of *Les Chimères: "A J. Y. Colonna"* is a repetition, with amendments, of the earlier *"Delfica."* None of the poems of *Autres Chimères,* either new or rewritten, were published in Nerval's lifetime. But it was to these poems that he developed in technical ability; one can scarcely compare the youthful enthusiasm and intransigeance of *"La Mort de l'Exilé,"* which appeared in 1826, with the beautiful *"Une Femme est l'Amour,"* which came out just after his death in 1855, and in which the gratitude to woman is doubly impressive in the light of Nerval's own life. *"Après Ma Journée Faite"* is one of the old songs of the Valois which Nerval collected and put on paper for the first time. It is impossible to tell how much of what he recorded in these poems belonged to oral tradition and how much came from himself, but many of these songs had never been printed before. We owe a debt to Nerval—for better or for worse—every time we hear Jean Sablon sing *"Sur le Pont d'Avignon."*

Finally, we have the brave *"Épitaphe,"* found among the poet's papers after his death, but not published until 1897. In it we can once again, and for the last time, appreciate Nerval's courageous attitude to his own fate. Here is a man who lived in constant dread of madness overtaking him permanently, who had for the past fifteen years known nothing but misfortune, bidding farewell to life without a trace of bitterness. Throughout all this poetry, even the most obscure of it, Nerval takes us by his side and invites us to be his intimate. Devoid of the slightest pretentiousness he is a poet who will surely live as one of the most likeable figures in recent literature. And it was for this very kindness of nature that he paid so dearly. As Kléber Haedens has put it, "L'excès des vertus les plus estimables peut décider des faiblesses malheureuses, et l'être le plus simple et le plus généreux qui ait jamais paru ne fut pas épargné."

. . . . .

In conclusion, a word should be said as to Nerval's influence. If we may say that the Renaissance witnessed in Europe a change in phantasy, a shift in li-bido, from the invisible to the visible, so we may say that the Symbolist movement evinced a similar shift in libido, this time from the visible to the invisible, from the material to the spiritual world. So Baudelaire, who worked towards what for us is the matrix of modern letters, saw photography, in his celebrated *"Salon de 1859,"* as the spirit of progress revenging itself on the masses, and Daguerre its dreadful Messiah.

Baudelaire, in his art criticism which anticipated that of Worringer and T. E. Hulme, denied the external world validity as a source of art, it was only of significance in that it contained hidden analogies with the spiritual world. Hence, in his article "Morale du Joujou,"[15] Baudelaire championed the child's approach to nature as a new method for the artist. The child used nature, Baudelaire presciently observed, as "pure excitation," as a point of departure for the presentation of an inner state, suppressing all detail and going to the essence of the thing—as when it destroyed a toy to reach its heart.

So Baudelaire realized that art had to recapture innocence, if it was to live, and to do this it was necessary to free the imagination. Nature unexplained, he wrote in "Le Gouvernement de l'Imagination," an article backed by his delightful letter on vegetables to Desnoyers in 1855, unsifted by the imagination, only presented a spectacle of general abasement. Art, as in a woman's make-up, refined and civilized the chaotic nature of her normal face. One need but add to this Samuel Cramer's comment in Baudelaire's novel, *La Fanfarlo,* that reproduction was the vice of love, and we are already in the climate of Wilde and Beardsley.

In another article, "Puisque Rélisme il ya a," Baudelaire defended what he called Poe's drunkenness as "une méthode de travail," and in this he theoretically approaches Nerval. Again and again Baudelaire attacked false nature, and upheld artists, like Delacroix, who worked, not from the detail outwards, like Meissonier, not from nature to spirit, but from inner spirit to a corresponding nature. Baudelaire, and the symbolists who succeeded him, saw in the photographic realism of their day only an indolence of spirit which deprived the exterior world of all significance. By leaning heavily on memory-sensation as a source of analogy, by using what De Quincey had called the "palimpsest" of the brain for the recording of images, and then inviting the imagination to arrange these at will, Baudelaire paved the way for Proust. Naturally, then, didacticism was for Baudelaire a prime heresy in art. Spiritual values alone were worth seeking, for all human systematologies, including those of ethics, were fallible.

Nerval takes his place in this literary movement which was, to some extent, the rationalization of an aesthetic

dilemma, for it gave the artist, whose position in the social organism was being threatened, a new and privileged position in mankind. The poet became an intercessor and he carried priest-like qualities. Baudelaire put the poet in heaven in his *"Bénédiction,"* a supreme accolade to be conferred on the poet again by Stefan George in his lovely poem, *"Ich forschte bleichen eifers nach dem horte."* That this led to art-for-art's sake and to the justification of the emotional state as valid per se, was no fault of Baudelaire's, who had always argued that any wealth of imagination should be met with a similar effloration of discipline.

For Nerval also, who more than anyone was responsible for the phrase "ivory tower," and who was equally born into a society where the artist's position was undefined, the material world was fallible and utility the negative of art. Like Baudelaire, and somewhat like Hart Crane in America, Nerval wrote in the teeth of the utilitarian concept of the universe, and all these men died, like Cyrano, fencing with their shadows, their invisible, yet deadly enemy "la Sottise," and exclaiming "c'est bien plus beau lorsque c'est inutile."

This frustration, that of the pure poet, reached a height perhaps in the théâtre de l'Oeuvre of the eighteen nineties but, as Dada was to show, to be positivized the movement had to be accompanied by that sublimation of desire which leads to letters. Axel, the symbolist hero par excellence, has all the seeds of Dada in his make-up. "Vivre?" he cries to Sara at the end of the play, "les serviteurs feront cela pour nous . . . J'ai trop pensé pour daigner agir!" How close we are here to that monstrous caricature of the modern intellectual given us in M. Teste!

Villiers' Baron Bathybius Bottom with his fantastic "machine à gloire," his Edison longing to create a beautiful woman with spare parts in *L'Eve Future* (like Apollinaire's hero creating children from old newspapers), we have here all the elements from which Dada was to construct itself in its early demonstrations, some of them, significantly, at the théâtre de l'Oeuvre. But Tzara's two monocles, the antics of Cocteau, Picabia, and others of this time, are essentially based on the same antagonism to utilitarianism; so a typical Dada exhibit would be a flat-iron with spikes in its base, a tea-cup lined with fur, an inverted urinal.

Now Nerval never envisaged his theories (or, rather, the way he wrote, for he never pretended to be a literary theoretician) being carried as far as this, but it is in his interest to mention briefly how he has been taken up by contemporary surrealists.

Guillaume Apollinaire's *Les Mamelles de Tirésias,* first put on in 1917, carried with it a preface, supposedly written in 1903, in which he claims to have forged the adjective surrealist to define a new tendency in art.

Since then, it has been confessedly that the Twentieth-Century surrealists have looked to the spirit of *Aurélia.* Here, they seem to have felt, was a work that would set them free. So, in the *Premier Manifeste du Surréalisme* of 1924, André Breton writes:

> nous désignâmes sous le nom de SURRÉALISME le nouveau mode d'expression pure que nous tenions à notre disposition . . . à plus juste titre encore, sans doute aurions-nous dû nous emparer du mot SUPERNATURALISME, employé par Gérard de Nerval dans la dédicace des *Filles du Feu.*

Both Breton and Eluard (the owner, while he lived, of the most important extant Nerval manuscripts) have confessed to their dialectical insistence on dreams and insanity in art; Breton and Aragon signed an essay terming hysteria a new means of expression. Desnos, Tzara, Soupault, all at one time moved with their painter colleagues in what has been called a belief in "hallucinatory intuition." It was, as Georges Lemaître has written, by a "voluntary recourse to simulated insanity," that the surrealists hoped to beat down the barriers of inhibition in the conscious and reap where Nerval had sowed. For them, madness was the rubric of our agony. Sensing what they felt to be the insanity or chaos of our material life, they craved the formalism of the wholly private world. "Le surréalisme vous introduira dans la mort," writes Breton, "qui est une société secrète." The idea of madness being vision is not something new, of course; the conjunction of seer and madman we meet in the ancient Hebrew mind, the ecstatic emoter, is eventually reproved by Hosea ("the spiritual man is mad"— IX, 7). Lautréamont's Maldoror was in some respects the "fol délicieux," which Nerval has been called, taken to desperate conclusion. The danger, however, is to read into Nerval a sponsoring, or tolerance, of surrealist doctrine which he did not own. Whereas the surrealists were to interpret the insane world as a prolongation of our experience in the sane, Nerval saw a clear line between his normal and abnormal lives. While, then, it is true that he suffered the madness of the "immediate" man, in Kierkegaard's sense in *Either/Or,* that of the artist or lover indifferent to life, the trauma, in other words, of adolescence introduced by an urban civilization, yet he himself always saw the two levels of experience as separate. The subtitle of *Aurélia* is *Le Rêve et la Vie,* not *ou la Vie.* Moreover, does he not begin with the sentence, "Le rêve est une seconde vie," meaning *another* life?[16]

Although Rimbaud's famous statement, "Je est un autre," has been variously explicated, in general critics have taken it to mean that the visionary is separate from his everyday self. Nerval would have found exactly this separation in Rousseau's *Dialogues.* And Anna Balakian, in her admirable study of the origins of surrealism, has pointed out how Nerval always introduces his dreams with some such comment as "je

fis un rêve." Moreover, the idea of the double, or "sosie," occurs constantly throughout Nerval's whole work.

Miss Balakian has demonstrated what is virtually a misreading of Nerval for their own purposes by certain surrealist writers, not to mention an apparent mistranslation of Achim von Arnim's *Die Majorats-Herren* which Breton used in the same interests. The surrealists found an intellectual respectability in Nerval and they read the *Aurélia* as a narcissistic reverie, whereas in fact the moments of narcissism in the work are moments of horrified self-recognition—"O terreur! ô colère! c'était mon visage . . ." Nerval emerges from this re-reading as something he never posed as; Norman Cohn has called *Aurélia* "Dali in words" in *Horizon,* and Dali writes, "I register without choice and with all possible exactitude the dictates of my subconscious, my dreams," a statement fortunately belied by the intricately careful conscious composition of his pictures. It was the method of *Aurélia* which attracted the surrealists, the hint in Nerval's work of that possession by a force outside oneself which drove men like Jarry, Hart Crane, Modigliani, and others, to stifle their conscious in alcohol in the belief that they became more "free" if the psyche could ejaculate directly. This attitude is debatable, but to say that Nerval advocated it is not—he never did.

> A Surrealist writer is not supposed to make any effort to express and organize his sentiments or thoughts. He must be content to listen to the voice of his subconsciousness.

So writes Lemaître. How different this is from Nerval's terror—"Je n'ai pu percer sans frémir ces portes d'ivoire ou de corne qui nous séparent du monde visible."

The world of *Aurélia* is a world of lost happiness, of inharmonious nature, and of conscious spiritual pilgrimage. An act of atonement and redemption, it was his *Vita Nuova,* to which he never lived to add a *Commedia.* Nerval frequently refers to Dante's autobiography of adolescence and the XXIII Canzone of the *Vita Nuova,* structurally the highest, and the closest to Guido Guinizelli, bears remarkable resemblance to *Aurélia* with its visions which Dante said came to him when out of his mind. But the *Vita Nuova* is a consciously shaped phantasy, as its strict architecture shows, and we should not valuably pursue this comparison.

The surrealists purposefully broke away from the tradition of the artistic presentation of private emotions to synthesize with the public emotions of an audience. Since the artist's private consciousness is molded willy-nilly by the public world, is it not, they argued, important even in its total retreat? Further, is there not a common "I" in any dream, a "collective unconscious" with its store of "archetypes" or "primordial images?" It is hard not to find theories like these more than

excuses for spiritual fatigue. For, as has often been remarked, poetry may be a dream but a dream is not
necessarily poetry. Coleridge allows us, for instance, to
be his privileged dreamer for a while. Le douanier
Rousseau's painting *Le Rêve* of 1910 is more permanent
than the equally "surnaturel" *Dans le Rêve,* say, of Odilon
Redon not because there are more "archetypes" in it but
because through conscious control it affects us commu-
nally more than does Redon's picture.

In this sense Nerval does comprise within his life and
work the whole of the surrealist movement. Indeed
many of his dreams are in danger, unlike *"Kubla
Khan,"* of being non-affective for in many of them it
is hard to share in either subject or object. At its worst,
in the last leaves of *Aurélia* perhaps, his phantasy obeys
only the laws of the dreamed object, to which his
conscious talent becomes a slave, in the same way that
his common-sense life became enslaved to the dream
state and we find a multiplicity of examples of him
obeying chance happenings as "fate." Here indeed is
the secret society of the dead.

Fortunately, of course, Nerval controlled the majority
of his writings by traditional techniques, which are
what make them vital today, just as Dali's work may
last not for its phantasy—there is little of this in a Dali
painting—but for the more formal gifts demonstrated.
Those of Nerval's contemporaries, for instance, who
did not control their work by conscious technique are
not known now. Borel will remain a lesser figure than
Nerval. Charles Coligny is today forgotten, although
his life and interests were similar to Nerval's. The
Jungian theory of the "collective unconscious," brought
to us from the pre-Socratics (with the exception of
Heraclitus), endangered art for only a short while,
however; phantasy was poured into art by the surrealists and all too often poetry ceased to act, its life was
atrophied to magic. For Nerval the dream was not
something that should deprive the poet of artistic liberty; he knew too well, hence his dread, that the laws
of the dream are ineluctable and coerce the dreamer.
For him the dream, separate from common-sense life,
was an aspect of behavior, one previously unexplored,
and thus a part of humanity to be revealed to all.

It is, finally, possible to push this conception to Nerval's
detriment. Antonin Artaud, writing of van Gogh,
claimed that the authentic lunatic is a man strangled by
society because he utters unbearable truths, a man who
prefers to be incarcerated rather than forfeit a superior
idea of human honor. Cyril Connolly tells us that
Nerval's madness "contributed more to the community
than many another's sanity." There is a grain of truth,
a disturbing grain of truth, in these lively speculations,
but Artaud's is on the whole a romantic conception.
Competent studies of insanity remind us that the de-
ranged try pathetically to conform, rather than exploit
the chaos of their condition. It is one thing to think of

Nerval as the first surrealist, it is quite another to hold
him responsible for the vulgarizations of surrealism in
our day. The whole erotic sensibility of the *Aurélia,*
for example, is now reduced to the pornography of
Breton and Eluard's *L'Immaculée Conception.*

The difficulty our society seems to find in accomodating
genius turns it so often over the hairline—for the two
are physiologically close—into madness. Genius is a
kind of madnes in our midst, but madness is not genius. Aside, then, from this rather obvious relevance to
our time, and aside from what is rapidly becoming a
curio interest in connection with surrealism, Nerval's
work is principally valuable to us today for its form,
its harmony, and good taste, when such are at a discount. As Baudelaire accepted the challenge of
Malherbe, Nerval won the artistic freedom he knew in
Sylvie from a complete mastery of technique. "Chose
étrange," writes Paul de Saint-Victor, "au milieu du
désordre intellectuel qui l'envahissait, son talent resta
net, intact, accompli." It must never be said that Nerval
indulged in lunacy.

One cannot conclude on a harsh note to a man who
saw his padded cell as an Oriental pavilion. Like us,
Nerval was born "dans les jours de révolutions et
d'orage, où toutes les croyances ont été brisées," but
the first thing we sense in his work is a feeling of
immediacy and friendliness, that kind of innate kindness which starts out from the portrait of the poet by
his friend (and enthusiastic balloonist), Nadar. Heine,
who saw himself in Nerval, wrote of him:

> C'était vraiment plutôt une âme qu'un homme, je
> dis une âme d'ange . . . Cette âme était
> essentiellement sympathique. Et c'était un grand
> artiste . . . il était tout candeur enfantine; il était
> d'une délicatesse de sensitive; il était bon . . .

Such was "le bon Gérard;" continually good-natured,
he presupposed in others the same felicitous freedom
from all bitterness inherent in himself, and he was
rewarded by a circle of devoted friends. His lovable
sincerity, the perfect pellucidity of his language coupled
with his unaffectedly limpid style, these qualities have
even been called banal—there could be no sadder commentary on our century. Nerval's letter to the young
Princesse de Solms, on January 2nd, 1853, is a masterpiece of compassion that sums up his character completely; he had just given his all, he writes, to a poor
family he had found by chance living in misery in the
rue Saint-Jacques. Go to them, he begs Mme de Solms,[17]
and help them, and—put on your best clothes, for I
have promised them that a Princess is coming.

The search into the mind for a new myth, and an historically non-recognizable myth, which surrealism represents, seemed at first to offer a limitless potential.
Yet now even Henry Miller, "the American Céline" as

he has been called, admits that surrealism is "a confession of intellectual and spiritual bankruptcy." This is, however, not something to gloat over. When we hear Nerval cry from the asylum, we are aware of our own disaster, of which our art is an aspect.

In Canto 3 of *Childe Harold's Pilgrimage,* when he comes to mention the heroine of *La Nouvelle Héloïse* and Rousseau's unrequited love for the Comtesse d'Houdetot, Byron writes that Jean-Jacques knew "how to make madness beautiful." Nerval, too, was Lord Pilgrim in truth. Adrienne was the spirit who celebrated Christ the conqueror of hell. Aurélia was the divine intercessor for whom he was prepared to die. Such was the twist he gave to Hoffmann's vampire. Nerval's lot was to suffer human experience intensified to a personal purgatory, and we must see that his influence, however it may have been taken up and interpreted, yet evinces that painstaking evolution which is the progress of art. Like Kit Smart, like Hölderlin, van Gogh, and the rest of the "great abnormals" increasing in our midst, Nerval voiced a convulsion of humanity in advance. He was under the same accusation with his Savior, for they said He is beside Himself.

Notes

1 Charles Baudelaire, "Réflexions sur mes contemporains," *l'Art Romantique, Oeuvres Complètes,* Pléiade, II, p. 518.

2 Baudelaire, *OC,* II, pp. 562 ff.

12 L.-H. Sebillotte, *La Vie Secrète de Gérard de Nerval,* Paris, Corti, 1948.

13 Jean Richer, *Gérard de Nerval et les doctrines ésotériques,* Paris, Griffon d'Or, 1947.

14 This persistent phrase, used in almost any context (and out of it) with Nerval, appears to be infectious. Thus, in Jean-Jacques Bernard's *Le Secret d'Arvers,* we find Nodier talking of Michelet as a "doux rêveur," and are not surprised to hear that Nerval has been invited for the evening a few lines later.

15 *Le Monde Littéraire,* April 17th, 1853.

16 The ivory or horned gates of dream with which Nerval opens the *Aurélia* are explained by Penelope in Book XIX of *The Odyssey;* Nerval is clearly aware of her distinction throughout.

17 Another extraordinary lady involved on the fringe of Nerval's life and aspirations, Marie Laetitia Studolmine Wyse, Princesse de Solms, and later Contessa Rattazzi, was the daughter of an English M.P., Sir Thomas Wyse. After her marriage to Frédéric de Solms, she became a sort of Madame de Staël of the Second Empire. Shortly after Nerval wrote her this appeal she was expelled from France by Napoleon III and led a checkered career in Italy. However, she obtained permission to return to France and, her husband having died in America, married Count Rattazzi who was involved in the Cavour-Castiglione affair and whom she obliged to fight a number of duels on her behalf. She herself wrote several books, painted, dabbled dangerously in politics, and edited a review. The Princess Caroline Murat pays a long tribute to her in her memoirs. It is interesting, if not coincidental, that in the inventory of her tastes given by Frederic Loliée her favorite book should appear as *La Nouvelle Héloïse.* She died in Paris in 1902, having first published Nerval's hitherto unknown poem *"Épitaphe."*

The Times Literary Supplement (review date 1958)

SOURCE: "World of a Visionary," in *The Times Literary Supplement,* No. 2933, May 16, 1958, pp. 261-62.

[*In the following excerpt from an anonymous review of* The Selected Writings of Gérard de Nerval, *the critic comments on the wide appeal that Nerval's work has held for readers and critics over time.*]

Gérard de Nerval's quasi-canonical status, attained in recent years, depends on a bewildering variety of appeals, exercised at different times and in different ways: the erotic pastoral of the tales associated with the scenery of the Île de France; the Bohemian note that attracted Andrew Lang; the blander landscapes of Giraudoux's "Théocrite d'outre-terre"; the dream images that caught the eye of Éluard and Breton; the esoteric hints and gestures, always sure of a small following; the pathetic witness to the power of repentance which Albert Béguin so persuasively (and so influentially) presents—the list is not exhaustive. Each decade of the present century has added to it, bringing into new focus one of the ten or so principal titles (*Sylvie, Les Nuits du Ramazan, Les Chiméres, Aurélia* . . .) and forming round it new perspectives. If we accept all these claims, then Nerval is a very considerable writer; if we challenge some, Nerval adepts have still much to rejoice over.

To his contemporaries, Gérard was simply a delightful journalist, half-successful playwright, first-nighter, librettist, and odd-job man: precocious translator of *Faust* and Hoffmann, editor and imitator of Ronsard, light-hearted associate of Théophile Gautier, friend of Heine, leading light of the *jeunesse dorée,* author of travel diaries full of sentimental adventures involving pretty actresses and English tourists in Naples, with desultory parentheses about the places visited (mostly filled out from equally desultory reading). He was the cheerfullest man alive, in a modest, even diffident, infinitely courteous way, and there is no lack of gaiety in his copy. Nor of worth: Nerval's style, even in letters to Cabinet Ministers, has a limpidity, a purity, that in his time was only to be matched by Maurice de Guérin, and a lightness and ease that remain unequalled. "Candeur enfantine," said Heine.

A phase opens halfway through his short life, heralded by a banal sentimental disappointment with one of the little actresses, but in reality involving much else. Fourteen years were spent under the growing shadow of a mental derangement which presented symptoms of both obsessional melancholia and mild schizophrenia. In a career as scattered as Nerval's, it is not easy to chart the stages of serious decline. There were plenty of commissions, always; but among the commissions it is disquieting to see how much of what he undertook was in collaboration with Dumas, or Auguste Maquet, or other less butterfly-minded, more tenacious writers. From 1851 to his suicide four years later, between more and more frequent collapses and visits to the padded cell, he struggled pathetically to prepare a collected edition of what was by then a sizable mass of dispersed writings.

In these dark years he wrote—or assembled or revised—all his best work. His creative powers were in most respects unimpaired, but he was producing little new material; his mind was largely turning in a groove, along lines covered and re-covered several times already. **"Pandora,"** a late story, attempts to be sprightly and gaily ironical, but the tone is strained, even painful; both there and elsewhere the groove is an autobiographical one, the circle narrowing more and more to sentimental misfortune and its cosmological import, round and round the same hallowed sets of memories and obsessions. At the centre of the spiral stand *Les Chiméres* and *Aurélia:* the pure lyrical fusion and the autobiographical tangle.

In his by now classical period study Arthur Symons stated that it was "not necessary to exaggerate the importance of the half-dozen volumes which make up the works of Nerval. . . . He was not a great writer, he had moments of greatness." There is truth in this statement, though it needs qualification. Symons was writing at a time when patient scholarly exegesis had not yet unravelled all—or even many of—the threads of Gérard's private mythology; at a time when Henri de Régnier could speak of the "incomplete meaning" of the Sonnets. Today, with the whole picture before us, we tend to go to the other extreme and (on the strength of recurrent images and themes) carry over into minor and dispersed works the valuations which properly belong only to the "moments of greatness."

Certainly it would be a serious mistake to isolate the lonely and tragic figure of the two late works from the Nerval of earlier, happier times. There is a particular Nerval landscape and climate (brilliantly explored by

M. J.-P. Richard): it took shape early and was constantly revisited. In a famous sonnet, the line "mon front est rouge encore du baiser de la reine" echoes the myth of Balkis in the *Voyage en Orient,* and Balkis goes back at least to a libretto on *The Queen of Sheba* written for Meyerbeer in 1832. Goethe's Helena, recaptured from the underworld and lost a second time, pointed across fifteen years towards *Aurélia.* Hoffmann's *Doppelgänger* haunted and threatened his dreams persistently. Nerval proclaimed himself one of those "who cannot invent without identifying themselves with the figures of their imagination." The identifications stuck, and over a lifetime each of these crucial mythical encounters, once recognized, remained a powerful shaping force in the mind of a man whose grasp of the "real world" was half-hearted and precarious. By a process common to not a few visionary poets the images grew and possessed him until he came to be more at home in their subterranean world than on more prosaic surfaces; at the end he surrendered wholly to them (*Les Chimères*) or followed their paths out to the broken cliffs of apparently confessional writing.

To do him justice, Nerval avoids being a bore when he is talking about his myths and hobby-lorses. He is always engaging—"here I am, I must talk about something, so I shall tell you of my deep convictions and meditations"—but there is a precautionary smile. He believes privately, with deep seriousness, that the "human imagination has invented nothing that is not true, either in this world or in the next," and in so doing joins hands on the one side with Giordano Bruno, on the other with André Breton: but putting this intuition to account for the readers of a light-hearted annual, *Le Diable à Paris,* he assumes his most irresponsible manner to show that the most farfetched hoax or *canard* "always" turns out to be true—imaginary dragons are vindicated by the discovery of the pterodactyl, the sirens of ancient belief can be seen to-day pickled in museums. . . . Cowardice? Uncertainty? Double-take? Some of each, no doubt. Only in the poems and in *Aurélia* is this conscious irony laid aside.

Of the two slender works on which Nerval's greatness is poised, *Les Chimères* are poems whose character and status are not in doubt. The same is unfortunately not true of *Aurélia.* Ever since the well-intentioned efforts of Théophile Gautier endless irrelevancies have been strung together, through the fact of the proofs of its Second Part being discovered on the corpse of the suicide; an altogether much too naively romantic approach survives in the largest standard biography (that of A. Marie); while eminent apologists, reacting to-day against Gautier and all he stood for, have regrettably confused problematic religious messages with uncertain literary evaluations in a text still considered somehow as a last testament.

What is *Aurélia* exactly? Evidently it presents something more than a casual reportage such as for example Nerval's other "descent into hell" or pub-crawl round Paris, *Les Nuits d'octobre* (written only two years earlier). Though it sets out as a narrative of some vague period in the life of the author, this is stated to be a *Vita Nuova;* it begins and ends with—for once—entirely serious assertions about the use and significance of dreams and visions. *Aurélia* is made to look like a personal confession through the circumstantial detail of scraps of narrative here and there, and the intended inclusion of part of Nerval's correspondence with Jenny Colon; above all, the narrative makes use of key situations and themes already familiar through *Les Filles du Feu* and *"Pandora"*: notably the identification of various feminine faces with the lost features of the heroine. Is *Aurélia* then, at the lowest estimate, a naive attempt from a full heart to record a harrowing set of private experiences, a kind of apologia? One wonders, if so, why Nerval should borrow scenes and visions not only from himself but from other writers. . . .

Again, it has been often assumed that the narrative tells of a victorious personal struggle against neurotic despair, obsession, guilt. But in fact the despair was not exorcised; in spite of his avowed aim in describing how he escaped from the desperate longing to commit suicide, no one doubts that Nerval hanged himself during a pitiable (but non-violent) recurrence of his disorder. Nerval's generation was brought up to believe that confessional novels were hygienically useful as sentimental purgatives. *Werther* was the grand example. If *Aurélia* was ever envisaged in this way, it is clear it is a failure. But a *Vita Nuova* is more than a confession, it is the record of a profound religious event. Can such a record be found here?

Aurélia is, in part, a restrained, almost detached account of how, beset by the fear that the "dilecta" is dead and lost to him, Nerval succumbs to intense nervous worry, finds the visions of his sleeping hours invading the waking day, falls seriously ill on frequent occasions, is shut up, and then after various recoveries and relapses, emerges finally apparently cured. But the bulk of the work consists in a careful description of the visions and dreams themselves which have stolen his mind away. They are *not* analysed in their relation to the progress of the disease and its cure. The "cure" story ends when the cycle of *memorabilia* is brought to its conclusion; but there is no clear connexion between the two sets of events.

The dreams and hallucinations are, at the beginning, agreeable and instructive. From them Nerval gains belief in a future existence, in which he will find satisfaction for his various mystic longings, perhaps even be reunited to Aurélia. The visions, and the conduct they promote, have already caused him to be shut up, but he is unconcerned, lives only for the encounters of his consoling dreamworld. Suddenly, however, there come terrible intimations: Aurélia is dead; and presently, by reason of some trivial long-forgotten fault, she is to be allotted in the spirit-world not to him but to his Double (a Double who is also a king of glory, and his judge). Powerless, he attempts a Promethean enchantment, which only aggravates his fault; waking, he realizes he is cursed.

After this he enters the circle of hell, or despair. The visions are briefer, more capricious, erupt out of everyday things as he wanders brooding in the street or leaps along the passages and staircases of mental homes. Familiarity with despair breeds compassion for others, sometimes lachrymose, sometimes disdainful: at the Jardin des Plantes it begins to rain; he throws his hat to the hippopotamus and feels a huge pity for mankind about to undergo extinction in the Flood—and is shut up again. Now, however, hope filters strangely back, a hope which failed to come in answer to prayer and penitence. He turns to the goddess Isis, begins to see more reassuring signs around him; his anxieties are calmed, partly, perhaps, by treatment, partly by the goddess—it is not clear. Aurélia visits him in dreams, to announce pardon, to him and all mankind, even to Thor and Balder, enemies of Christian charity. He rides between the Messiah and Jenny-Sophia-Isis-Aurélia across the firmament to the gates of the mystic city; the message of hope is repeated in a variety of *memorabilia.* At the same time his concern for another madman entrusted to his care has borne some fruit—Saturnin (as he has decided to call him) reveals that he had thought himself dead and buried, but knows now he is simply in purgatory:

> Such are the strange ideas which illness of this sort provokes; I realized within myself that I too had come very near this odd conviction. The attentions I had received had already helped me back to the affection of my family and my friends, and I could now pass saner judgement on the world of illusions that I had passed through. Yet even so *I am the happier for the beliefs I have acquired,* and I compare the cycle of trials I have been through with all that, for the ancients, was implied by the idea of a descent into hell.

These smooth and beautiful closing lines exemplify the pitfalls of a much misunderstood work. Nerval has, for example, been credited with writing (in his own way) a fundamentally Christian account of his salvation after a divinely ordained expiation. This, however carefully qualified, is hard to make plausible. What, to begin with, were the "trials" imposed on him by Isis? Incarceration at the height of his disorder in mental homes? Then the trials would be his attempt to help in curing himself, in returning to "what other men call reason" (his own ominous formulation). Yet at the very moment Nerval becomes aware of being on trial, the moment hope enters to check his suicidal urges, a new "invincible force" or delirium seizes him, nature speaks secret words to him, his fellow-inmates' remarks disclose hidden meanings. The visions persist, though stripped of terror now. Again, either the "trials" must consist of difficulties to be surmounted (but there is no mention of any such) or they must at least present the choice of good or bad conduct (and his behaviour is effortlessly blameless). In fact, there is no recognizable trial: only the sense of one. And this is so of the salvation. Nerval distinguishes—confusedly but doggedly—the return to reason from the gaining of forgiveness. Moreover, salvation is offered *before* the charitable act of sympathy with a fellow-patient which might be supposed to bring the three levels together (clinical cure, moral regeneration, mystic salvation). Isis-Aurélia holds out forgiveness presumably as the reward of trials successfully accomplished: but the one is as inexplicable as the other. *Aurélia* contains no pattern pointing to an organized design for a *Vita Nuova*.

Nerval the man has been adequately excused for founding his faith on private visions instead of on Scripture: in his last months he was hardly capable of disciplined thought. And we have no means of doubting that he considered his salvation "proved," and that he believed his proofs to have come to him in moments of what others even so would call madness. But we are concerned with the book, not the man. We cannot but take note of the concluding words of *Aurélia,* and of the passage immediately preceding them:

> Who knows but that there is some link between these two existences [waking and sleeping] and that our souls might perhaps effect the link here and now? At once I applied my mind to seeking the meaning of my dreams. . . . I thought I understood there to be a link between the inner and the outer world, that only inattentiveness or disorderly thinking upset the evident relationships—and that this explained the strangeness of certain pictures, which resemble the distorted reflections of real objects seen in troubled water.

The intuition is expressed tentatively; what does it mean? Possibly that the dreams related are to be taken as having yielded up their meaning in the narrative itself; at the very least, though, Nerval expresses confidence in the visions from which he has been cured by the doctors—visions among which there are some even which Isis has allowed him to see are "illusory," while the others determine the sense and perspective of his explanation.

Crudely, it is impossible to say whether *Aurélia* is the statement of a neurotic or of a psychotic. These pages, read as a whole, are intensely moving, earnest, urgent even—yet in the last analysis they cannot be pinned down to a clear message. They describe a set of experiences which furnish the standards and purposes now accepted by the narrator, yet at the same time the experiences in question provide the narrator, back from hell, with the means of exorcising them. The paradox is inescapable, and less easily resolved than the paradox of the liar. (In this case the *orders* of statements can be sorted out, in a wider context, by appeal to psychiatric models; but that recourse is not open to strict analysis of *Aurélia,* any more than the romantic biographical approach of Gautier, or the apologetics of Béguin.) When this ambiguity is fully perceived, *Aurélia's* impeccable surface, its tragic restraint and moving simplicity, take on quite a new quality. Attentively read, it must rank as one of the most invulnerably *ironic* masterpieces ever to be committed. Unconsciously ironic, certainly: since perhaps by definition irony in such a case can only be in the eye of the beholder—therefore in no way comparable to the mere flippancy which a writer whom we identify as the same Nerval put into *Le Diable à Paris*. In a sense, the positions of the two major works are thus reversed: *Les Chimères* are obscure, but not hermetic, since their multiple allusions, exhaustively elucidated, are unambiguous; *Aurélia* is the hermetic, because ironic, testament, and if it is to be justified and confirmed in its very special status, this peculiarity must one day be seriously analysed.

Alison Fairlie (essay date 1961)

SOURCE: "An Approach to Nerval," in *Imagination and Language: Collected Essays on Constant, Baudelaire, Nerval and Flaubert,* Cambridge University Press, 1981, pp. 271-87.

[*In the following essay, originally published in 1961, Fairlie discusses the prevailing themes and images in Nerval's* Les Chimeres *and* Sylvie.]

The immensely increasing volume of detailed and often valuable research on Nerval has made it difficult for any but the most impenitent specialist to pretend to an understanding or an appreciation of his works. A generation ago it was easier to enjoy him with a clear conscience, and he was no recognized part of academic studies. Since then he has made a triumphal progress from log cabin to White House, and academic consecration was reached when he became a set author for the Agrégation. Even then, the Sorbonne seemed unhappy about how he might best be approached, for to their list of recommended reading they added the unusual, suggestive and badly-needed cautionary footnote: 'De valeur très inégale.'

When affectionate condescension for the charming minor romantic with a touching love-life and engaging eccentricities gave way to apotheosis, the results were at first chaotic and often unfortunate. The Nerval of the 1940s was often seen as a seer, communicating a gospel of transcendental value. Instead of his lobster on a blue ribbon he now held as obligatory attribute the cross of saints and martyrs, the lore-book of the illuminist, the alchemist's retort or the pack of tarot cards, when he was not reclining on the psychoanalyst's couch. Albert Béguin[1] would have wished to make him a Catholic 'sans le savoir'; Jean Richer[2] in his earlier investigations found a mystical revelation based on occult traditions compounded of neo-platonism, cabbalism, free-masonry, arithmology and even astrology. Under Sébillotte's promising title *Le Secret de Nerval*[3] lay the the conclusion that the real secret was sexual inadequacy. G. Le Breton's discovery[4] of allusions to alchemy and tarot cards forced on *nervaliens* an important 'crise de conscience' which was not always adequately faced: annotators tended simply to allow the possibility that this or that detail might have these associations rather than discussing the consequences to central meaning and value in such a range of reference.

An Étiemble might well have written 'Le Mythe de Nerval'. Myths die hard, but recent criticism has discarded most of the extravagances of pseudo-biographical[5] and occult approach, is trying to appreciate not the man or the seer, but the artist, and is moving away from the position which Jean Prévost so aptly attacked when he wrote: 'Beaucoup adorent en Nerval son mystère plus que son génie; c'est un prétexte à majuscules plutôt qu'un objet d'examen.'[6]

But the first stages in making him an 'objet d'examen' have added to the difficulties of appreciation. The Pléiade edition has amassed some three thousand pages of his writings and is far from complete; the first of seven projected volumes of *Œuvres complémentaires*[7] has appeared. The cross-currents of allusion from one work to another are probably more important in Nerval than in any other author, and the most minor articles he wrote can suddenly illuminate central problems. Yet this new interest brings a new danger. Already a kind of spiritual snobbery, or an honest attachment to the object of much toil, had tended to surround the most 'difficult' works with an aura of suspect supremacy; now it is the hitherto neglected ones which are sometimes given an inflated value. To say, for instance, that the *'Histoire de la Reine du Matin'* is 'un des sommets de l'œuvre de Nerval, sa véritable expression' is, I think, to confuse representative with artistic value.

Thanks to many patient studies, we now know much more of Nerval's wildly heterogeneous reading and of his affinities with those authors he has 'convertis en sang et nourriture': Goethe, Hoffmann, Apuleius, Rousseau, Rétif de la Bretonne, Scarron, Cazotte and many more. These are not just material for source-grubbing: the resonances Nerval draws from them are an essential part of his meaning.

Precisely because of this abundance of material, the problem of the nature and value of Nerval's art involves a severe 'examen de conscience', an 'examen de conscience' that is perhaps particularly painful for those whose business, or whose pleasure, it is to introduce students to his work. It is not surprising that G. Rouger shudders at the vision of a slender text smothered under a 'débauche d'herméneutique' and retreats as many have done to the suggestion: 'Qu'il nous suffise d'écouter les vers des *Chimères* avec délices, comme de la musique.'[8] Have things come to the stage where Nerval can be appreciated only by two extremes: the dilettante content to let the poem make a lovely sound, or the specialist with a lifetime to give to one author?

The impenitent enjoyers have to find a way out. I should like here, while very conscious of the dangers of oversimplification, and knowing that I shall touch on points which other critics have been aware of in slightly different contexts,[9] to suggest a method of approach to what I consider Nerval's central works: *Les Chimères* and *Sylvie.* For I think it essential, in any honest approach, to see how far, when these works are read closely, in themselves and without apparatus of notes, there emerge a worth-while meaning and an art, a meaning and an art which make Nerval neither just the poet of the music-makers nor the delight of the juggler with cryptograms and crossword-puzzles. After, but only after, this initial impact, the further allusions which research has discovered or has still to discover come to enrich and to underline something which should make its central effect unaided.

First, *Les Chimères.* The challenge of this strange form with its apparently random, dissociated and unelucidated images, and the processes gone through by the reader's mind as he attempts gradually to sort them out, are an essential part of the meaning. The form is not just one way of expressing sense, but forces a re-enactment of that process about which the *Chimères* are written.

Their first impact conveys two impressions: music and dissociated images. The music does not lull or jingle; it has a particular quality (shared perhaps only by Mallarmé and Valéry), rich, closely-knit and haunting, which imprints lines and stanzas in the memory before they have been understood and without conscious learning-by-heart. This, surely, is a first absolute essential for 'obscure' poetry. Why otherwise, unless just as puzzle-solving, idle curiosity or academic habit, should one go further? It is only when the poem has bitten itself inescapably into the mind and become an incantation that it forces conscious intellect and subconscious faculties to follow up its suggestions. Mallarmé's *Le Démon de l'Analogie* offers an allegory of how this kind of poetry works: it is because the musical and apparently meaningless phrase 'la pénultième est morte' echoes infuriatingly in his mind that he is forced to search dictionary meanings, musical associations, imaginative links and elaborations of all kinds until a pattern forms. The search into the allusions of 'obscure' poetry should be neither dutiful nor gratuitous, but simply inescapable because of its echo in the mind and the sensibility, and only a particularly obsessive music can ensure this.

The music of the *Chimères* has not yet been as fully analyzed as it deserves. To mention only one most obvious point, no-one has discussed the astonishing variations on the 'rime riche' and their echoes within the lines; and that no-one has done so is significant. For usually the 'rime riche' makes blatant calls on the attention by its sheer virtuosity or by contrast with the flat or contorted line used to lead up to it. In Nerval the density and suggestiveness of both sound and allusion throughout the sonnets are such that the rhyme passes almost unnoticed as a fitting part of the whole. The delicacy, subtlety and precision of the musical effects in a form so demanding as the sonnet are in themselves a guarantee that Nerval is not the dreamer in a state of automatism but is consciously and lucidly shaping his material.[10]

The first effect is an obsessive incantation; the second the kaleidoscopic shift and play of dissociated images. There have been many efforts to find 'La Clef des Chimères'; I should suggest that one important key not only to their meaning but to their form is to be found not outside but within them, at its clearest in the sequence of five sonnets *'Le Christ aux Oliviers.'* Vigny's poem on the same subject and taken from the same source is set within the bounds of a human, 'realistic' scene; his Christ takes for granted that a plan exists behind the universe and the reproach is that the Creator has not revealed it. Nerval evokes at its utmost the cosmic terror of being hurled through fantastic spaces to find only purposelessness and chaos. The full meaning of the fourth sonnet which follows has not, I think, been looked at closely. Unable to find God, the absolute good, Christ turns to Judas: His terror of chaos is such that He would be reassured by the existence of absolute evil, for this at least would provide a purpose and a pattern behind things. But that absolute too crumbles: Judas is no mighty criminal but a mere mercenary disgusted with his petty reward, and already beginning to experience bitter remorse. It is no plan which brings about Christ's death: Pilate 'sentant quelque pitié, se tourna *par hasard*'. Nerval has pushed to its pitch the anguished fear of a blind chance ruling a wheeling chaos. Then comes the last sonnet, with its triumphant answer. Christ is yet another in a sequence of sacrificed victims, struggling, cast down and resuscitated in turn. Icarus, Phaeton, Atys, each succeeds the other and the ritual is endlessly repeated. I should stress as vital that the answer is rationally inexplicit. There is no reply to the questions, no logically exposed philosophy and no defined faith; simply the ter-

ror of chaos gives way to ordered pattern as the repeated sacrifice—*oublié, perdu, meurtri*—is followed by the rebirth—*remontait, ranime*. After the total disintegration of the universe, the horror of chance and chaos, the one elemental security of an ordered pattern emerges.

'Le Christ aux Oliviers' is more discursive, more dilute and more explicit than the rest of the *Chimères.* In the others, the form itself is part of the working of the central meaning. Their first impression is of dissociation and mystery; slowly, as they lie in the mind, associations make links and take shape. Constantly the evocation of the random and the chaotic works out into the satisfaction and reassurance of recognizing parallel and repeated patterns. One remembers Valéry's phrase: 'Créer une angoisse pour la résoudre.' The detailed intellectual or associative meanings of the final pattern are secondary. The shift of mood from chaos to pattern, from terror to consolation, is the core of what Nerval has to convey (and he is always lucid and modest enough not to confuse consolation with truth). The content of the pattern may matter less than the fact of its triumphant appearance out of chaos and the new kind of expression given to this basic human need.

Behind the shaping of ritual repetitions in the *Chimères* there are, of course, and are meant to be, many levels of association with their own parallel meanings. Meanings personal to Nerval in his struggles through illusion to lucidity. Meanings that are partly political and run parallel with those of the Parnassians under the Second Empire: the spirit of opposition constantly repressed and constantly about to rise, though the time is not yet ripe. Meanings that call up the central myths of humanity on the hero's descent into hell and the eternal return, on the rebirth of the Golden Age, or Nature myths on the cycle of Spring reborn after Winter. Constancy echoes again and again in the obsessive *encor* and *toujours,* and the verbs press home their reiteration: *rends-moi, rouvert, ressème, recommence, reconnais, reviendront, ramener, se releva, rapporte, reparais . . .*

Even if *'El Desdichado'* is the best known, it is perhaps worth looking at it as if one had never seen it before, and discovering how it can simply in itself convey a meaning and a value which detailed research does thoroughly enrich but does not alter. Its first effect is deliberately one of dreamlike, unconnected and unelucidated images. But one thing is utterly clear: the syntax. By contrast with Mallarmé, certain simple verbal phrases give a time-sequence and a general sense which works its way out regardless of detailed allusions. '*Je suis* le ténébreux' (present sorrow); '*Toi qui m'as consolé*' (past comfort); '*Rends-moi*' (desire for renewal); '*Suis-je* Amour ou Phébus?' (hesitation over the nature of self); 'mon front *est rouge encor* du baiser' (persistence of past joy); finally the climax of repeated victories in '*J'ai deux fois* vainqueur . . . Modulant sur la lyre . . .' . Loss, hesitation, fugitive and strange beauty, renewed consolation and final victory through a song gradually emerge before any detailed elucidation.

Another kind of pattern forms from images showing light suddenly plunged into darkness, darkness giving way miraculously to light. The struggle between despair and ecstasy, the pause in the half-light of dream and hesitation, the reiterated victory are given through the sensuous effect of the intensely rapid shift and play of light and dark.

Many of the images or proper names have general associations that begin to make parallel suggestions. A medieval Prince has lost his kingdom; a lute-player sings of the deprivations of courtly love. His lute is decked with the star that is the symbol of his lady; then it becomes the lyre of Orpheus who descended into the underworld to find a lost love and lost her yet again; Orpheus whose singing magically vanquished the whole world; Orpheus whose lute in legend became a constellation. Lusignan, if less familiar to English ears, would in France call up the legend of the fairy Mélusine, half-woman, half-serpent, so linking with the mermaid in the cavern; an enchantress lost through her lover's own fault; giving strange cries in the night around her castle: all this begins to fit with the theme of the elusive and enchanting—the mermaid, the lost Eurydice, the 'cris de la fée'.

There will be many details which ask for something further, but without any complex apparatus of notes, reiterated themes keep forming: a sequence of loss and consolation; doubt and hesitation shot through by memories of ecstasy; a sense of being alternately consecrated and bewitched, and the repeated conquest by the poet who has shaped a triumphant song out of loss and longing. Jean Richer, looking for an astrological enigma, speaks of this as a poem 'dénué de sens apparent'. One might go to the opposite extreme and see in it two of the best-known themes of the nineteenth century: the pursuit of the 'idéal insaisissable' and the assertion that memory and art triumph over time, change and death. But instead of anecdotal pathos or explicit argument, Nerval has found a form which involves all the reader's perceptions in following the shift from apparently random chaos to reiterated pattern.

Round this theme there are many other undertones. Names and images take on a fuller range of association when we can pick up their echoes from other works of Nerval. A network of reminiscences enriches the suggestive value, but constantly leads back to the same central theme.

The same is true of alchemy and the tarot cards. G. Le Breton has suggestively shown how in Dom Pernetty, whom Nerval read and mentioned in other works,

expressions such as *Le ténébreux, le veuf, la nuit du tombeau, la Mer d'Italie, la grotte, la sirène, Achéron* and *Orphée* all stand for terms in the alchemical experiment. One might irreverently remark that if Pernetty could show in detail how Virgil's descent into the underworld was intended as an alchemical treatise, it is perhaps possible *après-coup* to force any literary work into the alchemical retort. Moreover the system of symbols among alchemists is so wildly varied and shifting that at times it seems as if anything may justifiably stand for anything. Yet, though I might disagree on some points of detail in M. Le Breton's analysis, the weight of the evidence certainly does go to show that Nerval is consciously recalling the alchemists. The essential point here is that alchemical symbolism, far from changing the meaning and intention, is simply a parallel way of enriching what I have suggested as the central preoccupation of the **Chimères.** In a sequence of repeated ritual stages the alchemist is seeking to refine crude undifferentiated matter, whose first state he often calls the chaotic, into gold or the elixir of life. He is concerned with the shaping of chaos, and with the struggle between the volatile and the fixed (echoing Nerval's evocation of the elusive and the permanent) and after each failure he sets out again and again on his experiment. To be able to trace in the poem the colour-sequences and the detailed references of alchemy brings a parallel set of suggestive associations to the same central theme: form emerging from chaos; the struggle between the shifting and the constant.

So too for the tarot cards. At the beginning of **'El Desdichado'** the fifteenth, sixteenth and seventeenth of the symbolic pictures of the fortune-telling pack are perhaps being laid in order before us. If so, and if we recognize them, the associations will again be with chance and hazard moving into some strange order (and we may remember how T. S. Eliot later uses the tarot pack to call up the conflict between the random and the patterned).

In Nerval's world a theme or an image has value perhaps less in itself than because it echoes, catches up and forms parallels and patterns with other themes and other images round the same centre. He is playing on two delights of the human mind—the half-magical and half-mathematical pleasure in the coinciding of patterns, which becomes richer as we recognize more of them. In **'El Desdichado'** the medieval lute-player, Orpheus, Lusignan the alchemist, Nerval the poet, all take up the same ritual sequence of human experience. **'Delfica,'** prophesying the rebirth of the past, beats out a variation on the famous prophecy of the Sybil in Virgil: 'Jam redit et Virgo, redeunt Saturnia regna', and weaves through it Goethe's *'Kennst du das Land.'* When the oppressors become the avengers in **'A Madame Ida Dumas,'** the figures of archangels, the Goths and Huns at the fall of the Roman Empire, the rebels in Nerval's own century and the poet himself are all associated in the greatest of the songs of the exiles, the Psalm *'Super flumina Babylonis.'*

To present the sonnets as, for example, a convinced statement of faith in positive religious syncretism, as is often done, is, I think, to simplify and falsify them. It is the sheer pattern of rebirth and not the content of what is reborn which matters to Nerval. And this is where he differs from the Parnassians who also present the succession of religions and the avenger in revolt. Leconte de Lisle and Ménard define explicitly and describe in detail the abstract and the historical qualities of the lost world they recall. In Nerval there rise again 'ces Dieux que tu pleures toujours' and 'l'ordre des anciens jours', but we know no more of them than that. We are made to experience intensely the fascination, consolation and confidence of seeing the traditions of the ages shape to the same ritual. This elemental experience evokes three main moods: timeless persistence, revolt and rebirth, and, in several sonnets, the pause of expectancy, a stilled motionless waiting, for the time is not yet ripe.

The tone of these concise and suggestive poems fuses in a new way the epic and the intimate, the cosmic and the personal. A litany of revolt calls up the avengers of the ages—Antaeus, Cain, Baal . . . —but it starts with a line that is bare, piercing and personal: 'Tu demandes pourquoi j'ai tant de rage au cœur.' In the briefest space the wheeling worlds, the ashes falling round vast horizons after volcanic eruption, the gods and heroes of Egypt, India, Greece or Phoenicia, the races and dynasties of the middle ages, form a background to something gently and almost conversationally intimate: 'Je pense à toi', 'Je sais pourquoi', 'Tu demandes pourquoi', 'Toi qui m'as consolé', 'La connais-tu?', 'protégeant tout seul ma mère', 'ces dieux que tu pleures toujours'. The imagery brings out the contrast and fusion of the elusive and the permanent, the frail and the firm, the tenuous and the solid. Against the immense still dignity of colonnades and arches in *'Delfica'* ('péristyle immense', 'sévère portique', 'arc de Constantin') are set the most delicate and graceful flowers and shrubs, slight and slender ('l'olivier, le myrte et les saules tremblants'), while past the motionless architecture winds the thread of a song, the lightest song of all, an 'ancienne romance'. The central figures unite implacability with delicacy, tenderness with ferocity, hesitation with persistence as in the graceful and biting line of *'A téros'*: 'Et sur un col flexible une tête indomptée.' The conquest of chaos is wrought from human frailty as well as human force.

There are many details of the *Chimères* which have been illuminated by research; many remain mysterious and a challenge. The sense of an unelucidated and private range of reference is perhaps one of the deliberate threads of which the poems are woven; a cosmic

and a private fate are being worked out at once, and of the private sense we may be given only glimpses. Some images will have too wide a range of possible associations, others too personal an interpretation to mean much without the most careful elucidation. But, between narrowing and rigidifying interpretations by pseudo-biography or literal belief in syncretism, and the defeatism that abandons everything to incantation, there is, I think, a body of meaning and value to be found in even the most obscure.

I have suggested that to Nerval it is less things in themselves that count than the fascination of echoes and parallels between things. The individual moment matters not for its uniqueness but for its place in a pattern of half-magical coincidence and reassuring permanence. The most basic activity of the human mind in general is of course the search for valid relationships between isolated objects. 'Rapports' is probably the key-word in Nerval's personal writings. In his daily experience the search for connections takes on an obsessional force and omens are read into the slightest event. But he is constantly aware of the dividing line, so difficult to draw, between the rational and the superstitious 'rapport'. The very instinctive and obsessive effect of certain patterns provokes in him an utterly lucid mistrust.[11] His mind tends to work in four stages. First, the bewilderment at the random and the chaotic; second, the weaving of patterns that are haunting but perhaps fallacious (absolute good and absolute evil in *'Le Christ aux Oliviers'*; the echo of the ideal between Adrienne and Aurélie in *Sylvie*); third, a lucid questioning and a gentle mockery directed at these fallacious patterns, and finally, when they have been undone, the discovery of a persuasive ritual cycle of human experience; a reconciliation with the relative and faulty, but lovely and persistent, nature of things.

The poetry is less concerned with the direct questioning of fallacious patterns (it gives merely the moments of hesitation); the more leisurely prose of *Sylvie* has space for the weaving and undoing of the obsession before the final discovery. Here the obsession is seen as an obsession, not as a truth; the utter lucidity behind the evoking and destroying of a dream is one of the main values of *Sylvie*.

Sylvie used to be read as a delightful country idyll. Reaction set in and it became 'le poème de la fin du monde', a 'bilan de la faillite'—'Sylvie s'achève en débâcle'. Here I disagree, and think that the undertones of the last chapter have been overlooked, and with them some of the use of themes and form throughout the story.

The outline is simple: the narrator had pursued in the actress Aurélie the reflection of the 'idéal sublime' once seen in the child Adrienne; not only had this reflection of the ideal proved illusory but in its pursuit he had let slip Sylvie, 'la douce réalité'. Summarized in this form, it sounds like an obvious temptation to various kinds of insufferable romanticization: it might either glorify the ideal as a metaphysical super-reality, or twist round to give an equally spurious glorification to the lost Sylvie, or finally exalt loss, anguish and hankering after the impossible as superior values in themselves. And the story is often presented as if Nerval were doing one or other or all of these. Quite the contrary. The obsession by Adrienne and Aurélie is worked out not in supernatural but in human terms, and every detail of background is made to suggest that it is as fallacious as it is gripping and lovely. The narrator is neither psychopath nor prophet; he analyses lucidly the conditions which cause sensitive minds in his generation to set woman on a pedestal and fear to approach her, since feelings have been distorted in the moulds both of inherited idealism and of inherited cynicism.[12] Then, though Adrienne deliberately suggests the archetypal figures of Queen and Saint, Aurélie the Enchantress and the Siren, and Sylvie the strange Fairy, yet the sense of dream and illusion that surrounds them is woven from the live details of an everyday world with its children's games and folk-songs, its plays in the convent or on the Paris stage. The hero is haunted by the idea that Aurélie strangely recalls Adrienne, but the echoes between them are called up in terms of the real world, by suggestive sense-impressions of the two kinds most evocative in Nerval: play of light and modulations of voice. Aurélie sings on the stage as Adrienne had in the garden or the convent play; the stage lighting casts a circle round her head as the moon in the garden or the halo in the mystery-play had done for Adrienne. And constantly the illusory nature of his worship is suggested. From the first sentence he mocks gently at his passion as he sits every night in the theatre 'en grande tenue de soupirant', among a thinly-scattered audience in frumpish clothes, watching his idol in a second-rate play. Adrienne is made mysterious by the half-light of sunset or moonrise, and wreathed in swirls of evening mist; in the convent play her halo is of gilded cardboard. Lucidly and consciously the dream is presented as lovely but a mere imagining: the narrator punctures it with 'Reprenons pied sur le réel', Aurélie with her pointed 'Vous cherchez un drame, voilà tout', and Sylvie, questioned as to any strange connection between Adrienne and Aurélie, with a burst of gay laughter at the very idea.

The pursuit of the ideal proved illusory, and because of it he has lost Sylvie. Here was the opportunity for the large-scale disillusion in romantic terms: Nerval has delicately avoided it. There is no psychological analysis, simply the tiny details of everyday life which the reader must juxtapose with the past: the Sylvie who had never heard of Rousseau now reads *La Nouvelle Héloïse* and sees the countryside in terms of Walter Scott; instead of sitting with her green cushion

and lace-bobbins she works in a glove-factory; in her bedroom the old-fashioned 'trumeau' has given place to something more modern; instead of folk-songs she sings fashionable operas in sophisticated style. She had seemed the opposite of Aurélie, but she has followed the same pattern: Aurélie will marry the devoted and useful 'jeune premier ridé' and Sylvie too realizes that 'il faut songer au solide' so is engaged to the village baker. Yet he does not erect her into a lost ideal in her turn: when he reflects on what he might have had it is in the form: 'Là était le bonheur *peut-être, cependant* . . . '

Nerval has refused to inflate either dream or reality, or to confuse the two. His particular sense of irony is vital; an irony quite without bitterness. When the narrator comes back to beg Sylvie to save him from his obsessions, at the key point we have what might have been seen as the Interruption of Fate. But here it is no large-scale incident or dramatic lamentation: simply Sylvie's brother and the baker in a benevolent state of post-ball fuddledness blundering their wavering course through the undergrowth at daybreak, and without recriminations all go home together. When he returns to the scenes of his childhood, there is the dangerous opportunity for the obligatory romantic set-piece. But the two things which survive from the past are not the lofty emotions: they are the intellectual and the touchingly comic. Through the eighteenth-century characters who decked the countryside with their maxims now so out of date comes the realization that '*la soif de connaître* restera éternelle'. And childhood memories are evoked not through lofty symbols but from the odd bits and pieces dug up by the amateur archaeologist, and most of all from a stuffed dog and an ancient parrot who 'me regarda de cet œil rond, bordé d'une peau chargée de rides, qui fait penser au regard expérimenté des vieillards.' The theme of loss and persistence finds an individual dimension in that live comic glance of ancient and friendly irony.

Then there comes, in the last chapter, the very opposite of a 'bilan de la faillite.' As always, Nerval's method is not to analyze feeling or to sum up explicitly (though one sentence, with a graceful apology, brings home the value of experience, even with its bitterness). What he does is to take a series of tiny details, each of which is deliberately directed to calling up something almost unnoticed from earlier in the story, and through both details and tone to convey the rebirth of all that seemed lost, in a cycle of repetitive and satisfying pattern. It is some years later, and now, time after time, the narrator sets out from Paris for the old country inn, arriving in the evening. In his inn room he finds the 'trumeau au-dessus de la glace'. There is no statement, but we must recognize it as that same old-fashioned object which had decked Sylvie's room in childhood and been banished as she grew sophisticated. The odd collection of 'bric-à-brac' recalls that in his own room at the beginning of the story, later given up. He wakes in the morning and sees round the inn window the same flowers that grew round Sylvie's in childhood; looks out over the same countryside with its memories of eighteenth-century thinkers and lovers. Every word contributes not to a sense of failure but to the joy and renewal of a fresh country morning: 'Après avoir rempli mes poumons de l'air si pur, je descends gaiement . . . ' His foster-brother greets him with the familiar nicknames of childhood. Sylvie's children play round the ruins of the castle, the 'tours de brique' recalling the background where he first saw Adrienne; they practise for the archery festival which had been part of his own memories at the beginning and was linked with druidical traditions from a further past. The cycle of repetitive pattern has caught up in the present all that seemed to have disappeared. He and Sylvie read together old tales now out of date. Again the tone mixes loveliness with gentle mockery: he and Sylvie are part of a permanent human experience but one that will not take itself melodramatically: 'Je l'appelle quelquefois Lolotte et elle me trouve un peu de ressemblance avec Werther, moins les pistolets, qui ne sont plus de mode.' Nostalgia and mockery have achieved a gentle reconciliation with the world as it is, and out of the elusive, the fallacious, the fragmentary or the lost, has come, as in the **Chimères,** the persistent ritual of human traditions.

Again form as well as theme deliberately evokes a play of opposites, a setting of the elusive and the chaotic against the patterned and the permanent. Memories apparently evoked at random are in fact grouped round a meticulous time-sequence and complex echoes of detail. There is a deliberate sense of inconsequentiality: events which would normally be prepared, stressed and led up to seem to flicker past almost unimportantly; then there come the sudden transformation scenes where we stand outside time and the characters become exemplars: a hushed circle listens to Adrienne singing and 'nous pensions être en Paradis'; or the boy and girl stand dressed up in the old wedding-clothes: 'Nous étions l'époux et l'épouse pour tout un beau matin d'été.'

The whole story has of course created the palimpsest of the past beneath the present. To pick out the extraordinary tissue of allusions to different ages is to make it sound an artificial and strange amalgam: Herculaneum, the Queen of Trebizond, Apuleius, Dante, the neo-platonists and the druids, Virgil and Rousseau, the Tiburtine Sybil and the Song of Solomon, the Carolingian, Valois and Medici monarchs—but all are intimately and relevantly evoked by a fresh and real countryside and a personal experience. If the air of the story is given to the elusive and the fugitive, the accompaniment constantly and irresistibly suggests a timeless world where the present catches up the echoes of the past.

Sylvie obviously takes on a new richness when the reader knows Nerval's other works and Nerval's reading. The theme of the 'double' (here the foster-brother) has all kinds of undertones. Nerval has worked fascinating coincidences between themes suggested by works and authors as startlingly different as the *Pastor Fido*[13] and Rétif de la Bretonne, the *Roman Comique,* the *Songe de Poliphile* and *Wilhelm Meister.* To recognize them is to be brought back once again to the coincidence of experience across the ages, the weaving of parallel patterns out of disparate elements.

There is one particular tone that I should suggest is distinctively Nervalian in the world of **Sylvie.** What he has specially picked out from the past are those traditions that stand outside the accepted line of greatness. Sainte-Beuve and Baudelaire had talked of how all the 'great' subjects had already been monopolized, and how beauty must now be drawn from the prosaic, the horrible or the bizarre. Nerval quietly turns to more neglected material. The themes he takes up have stood outside the margin of the great tradition for two opposite reasons: some because they were too mannered and artificial, others for their naivety, simplicity and halting clumsiness. From the outmoded and the neglected Nerval brings a gentle mockery at whatever is odd or stiff or strange, and a sense of the permanent human value so particular in its loveliness and its oddity. So he consciously chooses the note of the Gessner pastoral, the ancient idyll, or the countryside of the pre-romantics with its elaborately natural parks and its deliberately constructed ruins, its sentimental moral maxims carved on temples and trees, its delightful conventionalizing of the ceremonies of antiquity in the stylized engravings of the *'Voyage du Jeune Anacharsis,'* and all its delicate formality: 'les traces fugitives d'une époque où le naturel était affecté.' And on the other hand the folk-songs attract him because they are limping and irregular, sung by young voices haltingly imitating the quavers of old age. Elsewhere he loves them because they are 'ces mélodies d'un style *suranné*', and even 'des airs anciens *d'un mauvais goût sublime*'.

Loveliness is evoked through the *suranné* and what is outside accepted taste, and is the more penetrating for that. Aurélie shines out from a second-rate play, in a dowdy theatre; Adrienne enchants as a mechanically propelled angel with a cardboard halo; Sylvie dressed up as a bride is all the more charming for the outmoded sleeves, the material yellowed with age, the faded ribbons and tinsel, the 'deux éventails de nacre un peu cassés', and the whole gentle air of the ridiculous of a Greuze village wedding. In the background of this scene stand the portraits of the old aunt and her husband, perhaps the most Nervalian touch of all. No great paintings: the local artist has done his doubtful best in the charming and half-ridiculous conventions of his day, with their mixed stiffness and grace; but through this laborious and well-meant art, and the necessary pose with the obligatory bird on curved finger, there shines the personality of the gay mischievous girl, now a bent old woman, beside the self-consciously pink-and-white martial air of her husband the gamekeeper, and the two come alive again in the boy and girl who borrow their clothes, while the naive, halting country songs the old aunt remembers from her pompous village wedding seem to go back to the tradition of the Song of Solomon. From both the limpingly natural and the elaborately formalized Nerval weaves his sense of tenderness, irony and final persistence.

Nerval wrote of Goethe, 'Le génie n'aperçoit pas un chaos sans qu'il lui prenne envie d'en faire un monde.' The world he himself creates exercises a hallucinatory fascination as the reader moves further into the intertwining suggestions of age-long traditions, whether familiar or strange. The present article has deliberately concentrated on one or two simple points. The reader who has once been captured by Nerval will sooner or later find himself both deeply grateful for the recent research which has made possible the understanding of so many details, and impelled, deliberately or instinctively, to look further at the allusions that have not yet been elucidated.

Notes

[1] *Gérard de Nerval,* Corti, 1945.

[2] In *Gérard de Nerval et les doctrines ésotériques,* Editions du Griffon d'or, 1947, and in many articles on points of detail. Béguin and Richer produced jointly the Pléiade edition, and the introduction to Vol. 1, 1952, shows how each has modified his earlier point of view. (See p. 12: it would be wrong to 'l'annexer à n'importe quelle doctrine occulte' or to 'supposer chez lui une adhésion chrétienne'.)

[3] Corti, 1948. This work is criticized even from the point of view of the psychiatrist by Ch. Mauron, *Cahiers du Sud,* 293, 1949. In so far as biography is relevant, discussions of Nerval's 'ambivalent' relationship with his father do not seem to have considered two more obvious points. No term has yet been invented for the strain imposed on the 'infant prodigy' who is expected to keep up his early dazzling successes. Nerval seemed brilliant at an early age and earned an outstanding reputation in youth for his translation of *Faust.* He is determined to make a name in literature, yet until well on into his life he produces only plans, works in collaboration, the occasional short story or light poem, and the miscellanea of journalism; there is nothing on which a great reputation can be founded. The underlying fear of the loss of the power to write can already be seen in the Preface to the 1840 *Faust.* Like Baudelaire's mother, Nerval's father would

have wished for his son a career leading to conventional success and stability. The effort to justify, as about to bring fame and fortune, a career which has all too visibly as yet produced neither gives to the letters of both Baudelaire and Nerval at times the same note of submerged appeal, bursts of pride, and naive evaluation of prospects. Nerval's letters seem to show abundantly that this desire to justify in the eyes of a loved and practical parent a hand-to-mouth literary career, and the fear of being unable to fulfil early promise, are a very large cause of the tension and the sense of guilt (Letters of 18/9/38; 26/11/39; 30/1/40; 5/3/41; 31/5/54; 19/7/54, etc.).

[4] *Fontaine,* 44-5, 1945. Two essential and penetrating articles.

[5] The tendency to confuse the prose tales with biography and to 'explain' the *Chimères* in the light of this mixture has been pervasive; as late as 1955 the Hachette selection *Le Rêve et la Vie* opens with a preface where the confusion is pushed to an extraordinary degree. The often quoted: 'Je suis du nombre des écrivains dont la vie tient intimement aux ouvrages qui les ont fait connaître' requires to be set against its neglected counter-statement from a letter where, speaking of the falsity of a contemporary biography, Nerval remarks: 'ce qui prouve que j'ai bien fait de mettre à part ma vie poétique et ma vie réelle.' One welcomes the opening to L. Cellier's *Gérard de Nerval:* 'Imagine-t-on un biographe de Proust retraçant avec une émotion discrète les amours de Marcel et d'Albertine? C'est ce spectacle déconcertant que, toutes proportions gardées, ont donné et donnent encore maints biographes de Nerval, qui, ne sachant pas ce qu'est un roman, ont pris argent comptant de fausses confidences.' Biographers have still not picked out how central in Nerval is the struggle to create and to prove his worth by his writings. (See Pléiade edition, 1, 754, 985, 1029, 1034, 1070, etc.)

[6] *Baudelaire,* Mercure de France, 1953, p. 11.

[7] *Œuvres Complémentaires de Gérard de Nerval,* I, *La Vie des Lettres,* textes recueillis et présentés par Jean Richer, Lettres Modernes, 1959.

[8] *Cahiers du Sud,* 292, 1948: 'En marge des *Chimères.*'

[9] The most stimulating from among many books and articles have, to my mind, been: G. Poulet, 'Sylvie et la pensée de Nerval', *Cahiers du Sud,* October 1938; O. Nadal, 'Poétique et Poésie des *Chimères*', *Mercure de France,* 1/11/55; M. J. Durry, *Gérard de Nerval et le Mythe,* Flammarion, 1955; L. Cellier, *Gérard de Nerval, l'homme et l'œuvre,* Hatier-Boivin, 1956; J. Gaulmier, *Gérard de Nerval et les Filles du Feu,* Nizet, 1956. The nature and scope of the present article obviously does not allow detailed discussion of the points where I should differ in interpretation and evaluation.

Jeanine Moulin's annotated edition of the *Chimères,* Droz, 1949, would require further discussion both of what it takes for granted and of many of its 'explanations'.

[10] In an article in the *Revue des Sciences Humaines,* July-September 1958 (see below pp. 304-7), I have examined his use of Richelet's rhyming dictionary. This shows both his lucid consciousness as a craftsman and his use of still another means of stimulating wide and rich associations.

[11] See for example Pléiade edition, II, 354. The questioning of fallacious but obsessive patterns is the centre of many other works. Hashish is made a means of evoking them in *Le Calife Hakem,* and *Aurélia* is the study of patterns of significance which intensely seem, yet in the real world are not held to be, truths.

[12] Some passages at the beginning of *Sylvie* distinctly recall Constant's *Adolphe.* From several remarks in Nerval's personal writings it is obvious that *Adolphe* made a deep impression on his mind. I hope briefly to investigate this subject on another occasion (See above, pp. 88-90).

[13] The *Pastor Fido* is mentioned by Nerval himself as one of the works which had an early influence on him.

Dennis G. Sullivan (essay date 1965)

SOURCE: "The Function of the Theater in the Work of Nerval," *Modern Language Notes,* Vol. 80, 1965, pp. 610-17.

[*In the following essay, Sullivan examines Nerval's use of the theater as a religious and metaphysical image in his writing.*]

Nerval is obsessed by the theatre. As if reflected in the pieces of a shattered mirror, the theater's every aspect—the stage, the actress, the play, the idea of the play—casts its particular image. The poet's attraction to the theater and his pervasive use of theatrical imagery have been related to biographical sources as various as these aspects of the theater themselves. The unsuccessful dramatist, the drama critic, and the "seigneur poète" of *Sylvie* stand well accounted for, and Nerval's impossible love for Jenny Colon must be a cornerstone for any interpretation of his work. But discussions of the theater in Nerval have stopped at this point; the mirror has remained shattered and the theater has been read as an abstract and disparate symbolism. On the assumption that the significance of the theater terminates in the psychological complex which forms it, a major Nervalian theme has passed unrecognized.

For Nerval, any symbol, any image, is incarnate; any symbol, any image performs a function in the poet's

existential quest for salvation and possesses a basic unity in relation to that function. The theater fully partakes of this pattern. Its significance is metaphysical and its function is that of a spiritual instrument which is concretely employed in this quest. Nerval defines this instrument in *Aurélia.* The resolution of his dream is dependent upon the affective realization of the identity of the temporal and the eternal, the real and the ideal. Only through such a realization may he be assured that his is a destiny common to all humanity, which in turn will give assurance of both his own immortality and that of the persons he has loved. When he moves towards such an assurance through the experience of the "épanchement du songe dans la vie réelle," the image of the theater appears as the comprehensible formulation which this identity assumes. It is an instrument which defines the correspondence between the two worlds which are affectively one:

> La terre où nous avons vécu est toujours le théâtre où se nouent et se dénouent nos destinées. . . .

> C'est ainsi que je croyais percevoir les rapports du monde réel avec le monde des esprits. La terre, ses habitants et leur histoire étaient le théâtre où venaient s'accomplir les actions physiques qui préparaient l'existence et la situation des êtres immortels attachés à sa destinée. . . .

The employment of the image of the theater to join the two realms of Nerval's experience is neither spontaneous nor simply metaphorical. Its components may be seen to exist throughout the body of his work. For Nerval, any aspect of human experience which embodies a certain ritualistic purity, which explicitly passes beyond itself to a more universal mode of existence, is desperately grasped as proof of the identification of the temporal and the eternal. The dramatic performance, presenting life as a microcosm stripped of contingencies, lends itself perfectly to this pattern. When Proust says, "Mais la vie me paraissait agréable! l'insignifiance de celle que je menais n'avait aucune importance, pas plus que les moments où on s'habille, où se prépare pour sortir, puisque au-delà existait, d'une facon absolue, bonnes et difficiles à approcher, impossibles à posséder tout entières, ces réalités plus solides, *Phèdre,* la manière dont disait la Berma," he is expressing, and probably consciously, the source of Nerval's attraction. It is this personal modification of the baroque theme of the theater of the world which renders this theme a constant obsession for Nerval. As early as his Gothic novel, *Le Prince des Sots,* the real will take this form for him:

> Le comédien offrit la main au moine pour l'aider à descendre de la scène où l'un et l'autre venaient de répéter un rôle devant se jouer sur le grand théâtre du monde, où chacun de nous fait sa partie, sujet principal ou comparse . . . c'est une vérité triste mais réelle. . . . Nous jouons tous la comédie, dit Shakespeare.

Of similar duration is the association of the theater with the idea of the fundamental identity of mankind, with the idea that Nerval's destiny and salvation are those of all men. Paralleling the motivation for his studies of religion, mythology, and history, his early theoretical writings on the theater function only to affirm this identity. The poet proposes the standard oppositions of classic-romantic, tragédie-drame, in a manner which illuminates the fundamental lack of difference between them—"mœurs" may change, as may genres and styles, but the fundamental human situations which they adorn remain always the same. Man is everywhere and at all times the same, and Oedipus is identified with Hamlet just as Gérard is identified with Francesco Colonna, with Lusignan, Biron. For Nerval, the modern dramatist need not even differ in subject matter from the ancients:

> Ne reprochons donc pas aux poètes modernes de traiter des sujets vieux comme le monde: c'est le monde qui se repète, c'est l'homme qui tourne dans le cercle abstrait indiqué par Vico. . . .

Years later in *Aurélia* this theme will be expressed in conjunction with that of the theater of the world. The pervasiveness of both themes, however, and their final expression in a formula which expresses so well Nerval's entire aspiration, suggests that they may be affectively unified throughout the poet's total experience. That they are so unified at least by the time of *Sylvie,* is shown by the full presence in that work of the "theater of the world" of *Aurélia,* a presence which proves that the conception itself is in no way metaphorical, but represents a vibrant reality for the poet. In *Sylvie* the theater which establishes a correspondence between this world and the beyond is not expressed, it is lived. It is reflected in various associations which possess a common center: as it is used to bridge the temporal and eternal in *Aurélia,* it is used to bridge the incarnation of these terms, the real and the ideal woman, in *Sylvie.*

The basic structures of these two works are identical, and the "folie" of the author of *Aurélia* differs from that of *Sylvie* only in intensity. In each Nerval will attempt to achieve the assurance of immortality and a vindication of his temporal existence through an experience that will permit the unity upon which a solution must be based to be *felt* as a reality. In *Sylvie* this attempt is portrayed in terms of Nerval's desire for earthly love and the impossibility of its attainment without the sacrifice of his dream of eternal love. To possess the real woman would be to sacrifice the ideal; yet for Nerval the ideal woman *is* the real woman, she is composed of the real women he has lost, who become ideal precisely because they cannot be possessed. Just as the correspondence between the temporal and the eternal must take the form of the immanence of the eternal in the temporal, there must be no division between the women real and ideal. Yet there is such a division. Sylvie and Aurélia are the same, yet Sylvie cannot be possessed without the loss of Aurélia, who in turn cannot be possessed apart from Sylvie. This is the tormenting paradox which Nerval must seek to overcome. He will initially attempt to do so through a Platonic conception which, because it affirms a division between real and ideal, can in no way be satisfactory. Gérard and Sylvie are everywhere identified with Francesco Colonna and Lucretia Polia de Trévisse, whose situation, as it is described in the *Voyage en Orient,* is a counterpart to Gérard's conception of his own:

> Dès lors, imitant les chastes amours des croyants de Vénus-Uranie, il se promirent de vivre séparés pendant la vie pour être unis après la mort. . . .

They are further identified with Polia and Polyphile who will seal this Platonic conception with the religious consecration of Venus. Gérard and Sylvie will parallel this consecration through the form of Christian marriage, and the "corbeille" and the "cygne" which partake in the pagan ritual of the *Voyage* significantly reappear at the festival that presages the trip to the house of Sylvie's aunt. If earthly love were possible for Nerval it would be possible precisely through the form of marriage, an intermediary between carnal and divine love. But it is not possible, and marriage with Sylvie is out of the question. If a Platonic division between the real and the ideal were possible, he would be able simply to withdraw from the real and from the ideal of marriage. But this too is impossible, because a withdrawal from the real would simultaneously be a withdrawal from the ideal. The solution to this paradox lies in the concept of the theater as a spiritual instrument. Nerval will both accept and reject the real: he will *simulate* the real; he will *act out* the marriage with Sylvie which is both necessary and impossible. For if, as he is assured in *Aurélia,* the real may be conceived as a theater in which all actions correspond to the eternal, the simulation is in itself meaningful. It may provide the accomplishment in eternity of that which slips away simultaneously in the realm of the terrestrial, and thereby may satisfy the paradox which tortures him. What appears to be the real, the loss of Sylvie, the succession of earthly failures, need have no sense of finality. The theatrical nature of the "mariage des enfants" and the underlying idea of the theater of *Aurélia* provide the key to *Sylvie.* The structure of the work, which proceeds from the actress-ideal, transcendant behind the footlights, to Sylvie, who incarnates her in reality and is lost, to the final vindictive evocation of Adrienne, is incomprehensible apart from this concept. Each progressive realization of the loss of Sylvie, each step away from the idyllic Valois in which she might have been possessed, is vindicated by a theatrical association. When the brutality of the present threatens and he realizes that she is no longer a peasant, he immediately thinks of the simulated marriage:

. . . mais je n'osais lui rappeler cette opinion d'un temps si ancien. Je ne sais pourquoi ma pensée se porta sur les habits de noces que nous avions revêtus chez la vieille tante à Othys. . . .

When he discovers that she no longer sings the songs of the Valois, he has her repeat the words that Adrienne has spoken in the passion play. When the thought of seducing Sylvie brings near the terrestrial in its most dangerous form, Nerval immediately turns to the theater, to Aurélia:

Sylvie, que j'avais vue grandir, était pour moi comme une soeur. Je ne pouvais tenter une séduction. . . . Une tout autre idée vint traverser mon esprit.—A cette heure-ci, me dis-je, je serais au théâtre. . . . Qu'est-ce qu'Aurélia (c'etait le nom de l'actrice) doit donc jouer ce soir?

Behind the stage upon which Aurélia plays nightly lies a greater stage which Gérard embraces as a vindication of the loss of Sylvie. But these two theaters cannot simply become one for Nerval, just as the real and ideal cannot totally be reconciled apart from the affective identification of "le rêve" and "la vie" in *Aurélia.* The poet is, at his own admission, "le fils déshérité d'illusions qui a besoin de toucher pour croire." Doubt is the generative power of his quest, and until *Aurélia* he will strive for objective proof to validate the identification of his dream of immortality and the ideologies which sustain it. It is thus that the death and rebirth of the gods becomes dependent upon the eternal perpetuation of their formal manifestation, religion; not simply in the abstract sense of religious syncretism, but in the equation of the disappearance of concrete religious structures, the ruins of churches, "portes ouvertes sur le néant," with the disappearance of the absolute itself. If the marriage with Sylvie is to be more real than a real marriage, if the underlying concept of the theater of the world as it is finally expressed in *Aurélia* is to be accepted as true, objective proof, analogous to the physical presence of a church, is needed. For Nerval there is only one manner in which this proof might be provided: the theater must be identified with religion. The establishment of this identification is a constant and pervasive theme. It may be seen in *Sylvie,* where the "comédienne" and the "religieuse" must be identified, where Gérard must demand that Aurélia herself state that this is so. As early as *Le Prince des Sots,* the quest and the frustration derived from it are the same. Here the "confrères de la Passion," "exerçant leur art pour la gloire de Dieu," play upon a medieval stage which represents the world, and the "moine ménétrier" complains:

Ah! qu'est devenu le temps où nous représentions le Mystère de la Passion dans toute sa splendeur, Mystère de quarante (et) un mille vers . . . , imitant du geste et de la voix les saints, les évangelistes, les

apôtres, les juges, les bourreaux, les soldats. . . . Ah! Notre profession était alors vénérée, tout à l'égal des gens d'église: mais cela n'a duré qu'un temps. Les bourgeois des villes se sont mis à jouer des Mystères eux-mêmes. . . . Et Dieu sait comme!

Here, as with Adrienne, the play as well as the actor is identified with religion, and in *La Pâques Dramatique,* Nerval will demand that the entire dramatic function be recognized as religious:

L'Eglise a-t-elle oublié que c'est elle-même qui institua les premiers théâtres en France et qui répandait le goût du spectacle parmi nos simples aïeux? Le vaste répertoire des moralités et des mystères défraya, pendant deux siècles, les premiers tréteaux de Paris et de la province, et l'opéra, le drame, ainsi que la comédie, ont puisé là les elements de leur existence actuelle.

This desire for an objective identification of the theater with religion corresponds to a subjective identification which may serve to clarify the relationship of the theater of the world to the broader structures of Nerval's work. When the poet makes his descent into hell in *Aurélia* he receives a warning from his uncle at the very same time that the image of the theater assures him of the realization of his desire for love and immortality:

Ne te hâte pas, dit-il, de te réjouir, car tu appartiens encore au monde d'en haut et tu as à supporter de rudes années d'épreuves. Le séjour qui t'enchante a lui-même ses douleurs, ses luttes, et ses dangers. . . .

The earth is not only a theater, it is also a place of "épreuve," and it is in terms of an "épreuve" that Nerval conceives of the theater throughout his work. An entire aspect of his quest resonates in this word. It evokes the conception that his earthly experience is itself a penance which he must undergo to merit immortality. It transforms the loss of Sylvie into a purposeful ascesis which he must endure to regain her. At a deeper level of intensity, at a darker point of Nerval's journey, it assumes an explicitly religious connotation: "je compare cette série d'épreuves que j'ai traversées à ce qui, pour les anciens, représentait l'idée d'une descente aux enfers." It is no coincidence that the structure of the Nervalien "descente aux enfers," as it appears in *Les Nuits D'Octobre* and *Aurélia,* is identical to that of the theatrical presentation of *Le Prince des Sots,* whose hero, Nerval's earliest Caïnite double, descends into hell upon the stage and returns, "revenu peu à peu du monde fantastique où l'avait poussé la Gueule d'Enfer, au monde réel." Nor is it coincidental that the company has sold all of its settings but that of hell. For the "épreuve" represented by the theatre and that represented by the "descente aux enfers" are basically the same. The "descente aux enfers" of *Aurélia* is the "épanchement du songe dans la vie réelle" which permits Nerval to pass beyond the bonds of reason, his "désordre d'esprit," and to *passively experience* what had before been an abstract ideology for him. It permits him to say that "la certitude de l'immortalité et de la coexistence de toutes les personnes que j'avais aimées *m'était arrivée matériellement* pour ainsi dire." The theater performs this same function at a lesser level of intensity. The vision of the stage, the footlights, and the actress somehow evokes in Nerval the same inexplicable experience which later shall need no such stimulus, and the theater in *Sylvie* is really an oracle of the whole of *Aurelia*:

> Que dire maintenant qui ne soit l'histoire de tant d'autres? J'ai passé par tous les cercles de ces lieux d'épreuves qu'on appelle théâtres. "J'ai mangé du tambour et bu de la cymbale," comme dit la phrase dénuée de sens apparent des initiés d'Éleusis.—Elle signifie sans doute qu'il faut au besoin passer les bornes du nonsens et de l'absurdité: la raison pour moi, c'était de conquérir et de fixer mon idéal.

It is this experience which causes Nerval to transform the world itself into a theater, and to make his salvation dependent upon this transformation.

Phyllis Zuckerman (essay date 1974)

SOURCE: "Comedy, Tragedy, and Madness in Nerval's *Roman Tragique*," *Modern Language Notes*, Vol. 89, No. 4, May, 1974, pp. 600-13.

[*In the following essay, Zuckerman analyzes Nerval's difficulty with presenting a tragic vision in his novel* Roman Tragique.]

Nerval presents the *Roman tragique* within the introduction to *Les Filles du Feu* as an illustration of his inability to write a novel from a comic perspective. The unfinished state of the *Roman tragique,* however, indicates that for Nerval writing a novel from a tragic perspective is equally problematic. In fact, the tragic novel continually puts its own structure into question, suggesting that for Nerval the language of the novel and a tragic vision of the world are in some sense incompatible.

The narrator of the *Roman tragique* begins his story by showing ways in which he is different from Destin, a character in Scarron's *Roman comique;* he concludes by showing ways in which he is different from Racine's tragic heroes. The problematic relationship between these two perspectives, and the narrator's inability to govern his passage from one to the other, provide the basic framework for the story. While the narrator describes himself as a comedian for whom comedy has

disappeared, he is equally unable to identify with the position of the tragic hero. The language by means of which he describes his tragic nature subverts the assumptions upon which his tragic vision of the world is based. In this sense, the *Roman tragique* functions as a critique of its own desire to remain completely tragic. Without ever becoming a comic novel, the tragic novel nonetheless operates by means of a process of negation which resembles irony. The *Roman tragique* thematizes the ability of tragedy to turn itself without warning into its opposite.

We can see how the novel provides a critique of its own tragic structure by examining the narrator's statements concerning tragedy and comedy, real and symbolic violence, and self and other. In each of these contexts, the narrator sees the world in terms of an unequivocal dichotomy between truth and fiction. Yet the very manner in which he states this dichotomy tends to dissolve it in the eyes of the reader. While Brisacier claims that truth and fiction are opposed to one another, he reacts to them as if they were identical. Without realizing what he is doing, the narrator provides a perspective within his story which completely undermines the clear oppositions he is trying to establish. Brisacier reveals the circularity of the distinction between truth and fiction upon which all of his other terms are based.

We can see this circularity in the narrator's definition of himself as a tragic hero. Brisacier describes himself as an actor for whom comic roles have become difficult to play because he has been abandoned by the actress L'Etoile opposite whom he once played, because his identity has been distorted by the pseudonym imposed upon him by the other comedians, and because a mask has been permanently attached to his face. The actor considers his situation to be tragic because there are no signs which represent his true identity, and because he cannot negate the false signs of his identity which have been imposed upon him by others:

> Ma bonne mine, défigurée d'un vaste emplâtre, n'a servi même qu'à me perdre plus sûrement. L'hôte, séduit par les discours de La Rancune, a bien voulu se contenter de tenir en gage le propre fils du grand khan de Crimée envoyé ici pour faire ses études, et avantageusement connu dans toute l'Europe sous le pseudonyme de Brisacier. Encore si ce misérable, si cet intrigant suranné m'eût laissé quelques vieux louis, quelques carolus, ou même une pauvre montre entourée de faux brillants, j'eusse pu sans doute imposer le respect à mes accusateurs et éviter la triste péripétie d'une aussi sotte combinaison. Bien mieux, vous ne m'aviez laissé pour tout costume qu'une méchante souquenille puce, un justaucorps rayé de noir et de bleu, et des chausses d'une conservation équivoque. Si bien qu'en soulevant ma valise après votre départ, l'aubergiste inquiet a

soupçonné une partie de la triste vérité, et m'est venu
dire tout net que j'étais *un prince de contrebande.*[1]

In order to insist upon the tragic nature of his situation, the narrator explains that he cannot commit suicide because the only means at his disposal is a comic
sword. He implies that the logical consequence of his
tragic experience of the world would be to kill himself, and yet he considers the theater to be a false sign
which would distort or attenuate the tragic nature he is
trying to represent. Committing suicide on the stage
with a theatrical prop would turn the tragic hero into
a parody of the fictional heroes of novels. The tragic
hero cannot commit suicide because he must be true,
in opposition to heroes of novels and comic heroes
whose actions can take place symbolically, as fictions:

> A ces mots, j'ai voulu sauter sur mon épée, mais La
> Rancune l'avait enlevée, prétextant qu'il fallait
> m'empêcher de m'en percer le coeur sous les yeux
> de l'ingrate qui m'avait trahi! Cette dernière
> supposition était inutile, ô La Rancune! on ne se
> perce pas le coeur avec une épée de comédie, on
> n'imite pas le cuisinier Vatel, on n'essaie pas de
> parodier les héros de roman, quand on est un héros
> de tragédie: et je prends tous nos camarades à témoin
> qu'un tel trépas est impossible à mettre en scène un
> peu noblement. (I, 152)

The narrator's refusal to commit an action which might
place him in danger of becoming a parody of a comic
hero suggests that the tragic and the comic are not as
distant from one another as he considers them to be.
The vehemence of the narrator's avoidance of parody
unwittingly places the hero of the novel and the comic
hero in the position of the serious or original literary
form, in relation to which the tragic hero is on the verge
of becoming an imitation or derivation. While the
narrator's intention is to show that the tragic hero is
superior to comic or romanesque heroes, his use of the
term "parody" undermines the very superiority of tragedy which he seeks to establish. His opposition between
the comic and the tragic suggests that his own actions
are but a caricature of the actions of heroes in comic
novels, that he is less true than the comic hero rather
than more so. The narrator's intolerance for the possible
presence of fiction in his actions prevents him from
achieving the unequivocally tragic identity he desires.

On the one hand, Brisacier cannot commit suicide
because the comic sword would detract from the truth
and seriousness of his tragic action. On the other hand,
he refuses suicide because he is a religious comedian.
A theatrical death is unacceptable because it is not
"real" enough, while death outside of the theater is
equally impossible, because it is too real. The narrator
is unable to fulfill his image of himself as a tragic hero
because his actions are inhibited on one side by the
possible presence of fiction, and on the other side by
the presence of reality:

> La fenêtre est d'ailleurs assez ouverte et assez haute
> sur la rue pour qu'il soit loisible à tout désespoir
> tragique de terminer par là son cours. Mais . . .
> mais, je vous l'ai dit mille fois, je suis un comédien
> qui a de la religion. (I, 152)

The narrator sees himself in terms of an unequivocal
dichotomy between truth and fiction, but the way in
which he defines this opposition reverses itself from
one sentence to the next. In one context, the actor
places himself in the position of reality with respect
to the theater, while in another, he places himself
within the theater, as an actor on a stage, in opposition to religion, which occupies the position of reality. These reversals reveal that the opposition between
truth and fiction has no specific content apart from its
limiting function within his language. The narrator
thinks that the terms "truth" and "fiction" define a
hierarchy of values upon which his identity can rest,
but in terms of their limiting function within his language, the comic sword and religion are identical.
Both truth and fiction violate the actor's tragic nature
and prevent him from corresponding to his image of
himself as a tragic hero.

This reversal suggests that the narrator is tragic for
another reason than the ones he explicitly states. He is
tragic in that he is unaware of the possibility of parody
inherent in his own language. His statements suggest
both what he intends for them to say and the opposite.
This process of negation unwittingly subverts the unambiguous vision of the world he seeks to present. His
inability to see his own language at work is one of the
reasons for the disappearance of wit. The narrator sees
himself as a tragic actor but does not explicitly refer to
the fact that he is also the narrator of a novel.

We might say that the distinction between truth and
fiction that governs Brisacier's tragic vision functions
to prevent him from coming into contact with his own
death. While he speaks of suicide and murder throughout the story, he nonetheless considers himself to be a
spontaneous, unmediated hero. He refuses to recognize that his actions are governed by rivalry with other
actors and that he is not only invaded by the violence
of others, but desires the other's death.

We can understand this problem more clearly if we
examine the narrator's statements concerning real and
symbolic violence. He describes a series of attempts to
move beyond theatrical violence to violence outside of
the theater that would be unmediated, spontaneous, and
real. When he plays Achilles, he imagines killing
Agamemnon and his court:

> Moi, je m'indignais parfois d'avoir à débiter de si
> longues tirades dans une cause aussi limpide et
> devant un auditoire aisément convaincu de mon
> droit. J'étais tenté de sabrer, pour en finir, toute la

cour imbécile du roi des rois, avec son espalier de figurants endormis! (I, 153)

He denies desiring to kill I phigenia, yet speculates that her death is necessary because she is a sacrificial figure:

> La tuer? elle! qui donc y songe? Grands dieux! personne peutêtre? . . . Au contraire; chacun s'est dit déjà qu'il fallait qu'elle mourût pour tous, plutôt que de vivre pour un seul; (. . .). (I, 153-4)

As Nero, the actor imagines burning down the theater and the audience along with it in order to defeat his rival Britannicus. His desire for violence goes along with his intense identification with the role of the tyrant. He must kill the other, as well as the theater in general, in order to gain absolute possession of the actress:

> j'ai eu un moment l'idée, l'idée sublime, et digne de César luimême, l'idée que cette fois nul n'aurait osé mettre au-dessous de celle du grand Racine, l'idée auguste enfin de brûler le théâtre et le public, et vous tous! et de l'emporter seule à travers les flammes, échevelée, à demi nue, selon son rôle, ou du moins selon le récit classique de Burrhus. Et soyez sûrs alors que rien n'aurait pu me la ravir, depuis cet instant jusqu'à l'échafaud! et de là dans l'éternité! (I, 155)

The conclusion that one can draw from these attempts to encounter unmediated violence is that the actor experiences violence as a reality only when it is symbolic. As in the case of suicide, he reverses his statements concerning the real and the theatrical. Death within the theater is unacceptable because it is not "real" enough, and yet death outside of the theater is equally impossible because it is the presence of mediation itself which the actor experiences as death. He claims that real and symbolic violence are opposed to one another, and yet in terms of his actions in the roles he plays, the real and the symbolic are identical.

We can see this reversal when the actor plays the hero Achilles. He first imagines killing his rival, then decides that the words of the play and the time necessary to say them are inseparable from the experience of violence they represent. In order to commit a "real" act of murder, he must remain within the limits of the play:

> Le public en eût été charmé; mais il aurait fini par trouver la pièce trop courte, et par réfléchir qu'il lui faut le temps de voir souffrir une princesse, un amant et une reine; de les voir pleurer, s'emporter et répandre un torrent d'injures harmonieuses contre la vieille autorité du prêtre et du souverain. Tout cela vaut bien cinq actes et deux heures d'attente, et le public ne se contenterait pas à moins; il lui

faut sa revanche de cet éclat d'une famille unique, pompeusement assise sur le trône de la Grèce, et devant laquelle Achille lui-même ne peut s'emporter qu'en paroles; il faut qu'il sache tout ce qu'il y a de misères sous cette pourpre, et pourtant d'irrésistible majesté! (I, 153)

A similar reversal can be seen with reference to Iphigenia. It is the sacrifical nature of her death that the actor experiences as a compelling necessity, not a death which takes place apart from a symbolic context. His desire to burn down the theater when he plays the role of Nero even more clearly emphasizes this idea. As before, he sees the theater in terms of a dichotomy between truth and fiction and as before, he reveals that truth and fiction are inseparable from one another. He cannot murder the theater in general in the same way that he can murder another character in a play. Violence directed against the theater is the most theatrical violence of all, since burning down the theater is a gesture which is significant only insofar as it is symbolic. Burning down the theater appears to Brisacier to be a way of eliminating mediation from his experience, yet he finds that in destroying the theater he gives theatrical roles more power than ever within the framework of his imagination. Once he imagines burning down the theater, he speaks of the play as if it were a circus game in which there is nothing to mediate a violent struggle between two identical rivals:

> Mes amis! comprenez surtout qu'il ne s'agissait pas pour moi d'une froide traduction de paroles compassées; mais d'une scène où tout vivait, où trois coeurs luttaient à chances égales, où comme au jeu du cirque, c'était peut-être du vrai sang qui allait couler! (I, 156)

Yet this experience of the theater as an encounter with unmediated violence is brought about by his total identification with a theatrical role. The role has absolute power to determine his actions precisely because he sees himself as a spontaneous hero who has eliminated all forms of mediation. Burning down the theater brings about an identification in which the actor is at once himself and his rival, innocent victim of the other's violence and an unjust tyrant at the origin of violence:

> Oui, depuis cette soirée, ma folie est de me croire un Romain, un empereur; mon rôle s'est identifié à moi-même, et la tunique de Néron s'est collée à mes membres qu'elle brûle, comme celle du centaure dévorait Hercule expirant. Ne jouons plus avec les choses saintes, même d'un peuple et d'un âge éteints depuis si longtemps, car il y a peut-être quelque flamme encore sous les cendres des dieux de Rome! . . . (I, 156)

The actor's relationship to the theater parallels the narrator's relationship to his language. In both cases, the narrator claims that there is no correspondence between signs and his true identity, and yet at both levels, he is entirely mediated by a fictional role in a play. We can understand the problem of mediation more clearly if we examine the narrator's statements concerning self and other. These statements explain why the actor experiences all forms of mediation—the mask, the role, and the theater in general—as his own death.

The tragic structure of the roles with which the actor identifies depends upon an inequality between the positions of self and other. This inequality is the basis for a law which distinguishes between the hero and the unjust father, or between the hero and the unjust tyrant. The tragic hero might be defined as the one who occupies the symbolic position of the son in a self/other relationship where the father's law is experienced as arbitrary and thus as a form of violence. Briasacier occupies this same position with respect to the other comedians. His narrative is on the side of truth and justice, while the language of others is a form of hostility, a distortion whose aim is to dominate and imprison:

> c'est bien assez de se laisser clouer ce masque au visage dans les endroits où l'on ne peut faire autrement. Mais, moi, que vais-je dire, et comment me dépêtrer de l'infernal réseau d'intrigues où les récits de La Rancune viennent de m'engager? Le grand couplet du *Menteur* de Corneille lui a servi assurément à composer son histoire, car la conception d'un faquin tel que lui ne pouvait s'élever si haut. Imaginez . . . Mais que vais-je vous dire que vous ne sachiez de reste et que vous n'ayez comploté ensemble pour me perdre? L'ingrate qui est cause de mes malheurs n'y aura-t-elle pas mélangé tous les fils de satin les plus inextricables que ses doigts d'Arachné auront pu tendre autour d'une pauvre victime? . . . (I, 157)

It is significant that Nerval underlines the continuity between Greek sacrifice and ritual, religion, tragedy, and the tragic vision of the narrator of an autobiographical novel. This continuity lies in the fact that identification is brought about by an inequality between self and other. There is one position and one position only in which the actor, narrator, or reader sees himself reflected, the position of the hero, defined in opposition to a figure whose authority is unjust and who therefore must be killed. The inequality between two rivals is based on a fantasy that derives from the desire to kill the father.

What is interesting in Nerval's **Roman tragique** is that the actor's total identification with the figure of the tyrant tends to undermine his tragic vision of the world and to make him consider himself to be identical to his rival. Beneath what might appear to be an Oedipal myth, the actor discovers a symmetrical structure where both are equally just and equally criminal.[2] To the extent

that he renounces a position of absolute difference from the other, Brisacier fails to coincide with his image of himself as a tragic hero. His rival, too, is a victim of the violence of the other. In the beginning of the story, Brisacier considers himself unable to be completely tragic because he is so different from the others, while at the end, he is unable to remain tragic because he and the other too closely resemble one another:

> Ah! le débutant d'amour savait son métier . . . mais il n'avait rien à craindre, car je suis trop juste pour faire un crime à quelqu'un d'aimer comme moi, et c'est en quoi je m'éloigne du monstre idéal rêvé par le poète Racine: je ferais brûler Rome sans hésiter, mais en sauvant Junie, je sauverais aussi mon frère Britannicus. (I, 156)

Brisacier's encounter with unmediated violence is also an encounter with the absolute power of mediation in his imagination. Insofar as he refuses to recognize his desire to occupy the position of the tyrannical other, he is obsessed with violence and domination. Once he occupies that position he discovers the degree to which his own language and his own desire constitute violence with respect to the other. When the story begins, violence is entirely on the side of the other; at its conclusion, violence lies on the side of the narrator himself. Thus he asks to be taken back into the troupe of comedians so that he may play the role of the monster. The excluded term is no longer opposed to the world of the theater. The exclusion of the monster lies within the framework of the theater. This exclusion is based on a myth of difference which makes the actor's identity outside of the theater identical to his identity within it:

> Hé bien! je suis pris, je l'avoue; je cède, je demande grâce. Vous pouvez me reprendre avec vous sans crainte, et, si les rapides chaises de poste qui vous emportèrent sur la route de Flandre, il y a près de trois mois, ont déjà fait place à l'humble charrette de nos premières équipées, daignez me recevoir au moins en qualité de monstre, de phénomène, de *calot* propre à faire amasser la foule, et je réponds de m'acquitter de ces divers emplois de manière à contenter les amateurs les plus sévères des provinces . . . (I, 157-8)

Brisacier's relationships to others are based on an unchanging pattern of identification in which he sees himself consistently as the victim, the son, or the excluded term. Yet in the role of Nero he witnesses his ability to become the monster he considers to be the other. He is at once the master and the slave. His refusal to recognize himself in the role of the master leads to a return of the repressed in which this role has the power of long-dead gods or of something sacred. The tyrannical nature of the actor's desire stems from the fact that he cannot see himself reflected in the figure of the tyrant, even though it is this figure, and not the actress, who is the object of his desire. It is his denial that he is both terms of a master-slave relation that leads to violent actions and to a process of unconscious negation in his language. The sacred character of the role of Nero indicates that the role exceeds the actor's conscious image of himself, that it corresponds to a desire which he can recognize only in disguised form, by means of negation.

It is in the role of Nero that the actor comes into direct contact with the symbolic system that governs his imaginary identifications. He loses his previous identity, based on an innocent self-image and while mad, gains a certain distance from himself. Madness serves as a point of reversal in his relationship to the other. Madness leads to a lifting of repression which renders the master-slave relation once again theatrical.

While Brisacier's narrative undermines the unambiguous dichotomies that form his tragic vision of the world, tragedy never transforms itself into comedy. The presence of the sacred marks the place of an invisible illusion, a gap in Brisacier's awareness of himself, a level of repression which renders a fully comic novel impossible. Brisacier cannot tell his story from the tragic perspective of a Racinian character, nor can he adopt the comic perspective of the characters in Scarron's novel. Yet both the tragic and the comic are fundamental elements of his conception of himself. The *Roman tragique* thematizes the extent to which it can understand itself neither as an arbitrary fiction, based on a mythical difference between self and other, nor as an unmediated truth, where the master-slave relation and the Oedipal conflict constitute an unchangeable reality. The novel presents itself as inherently schizophrenic, moving from a comic structure to a tragic one, and back again.

Nerval's allusions to Scarron and Racine indicate that one of the themes of the *Roman tragique* is a historical change that has taken place in the relationship between the writer, the reader, and literature. Our discussion has, until now, emphasized ways in which Brisacier is unable to sustain the perspective of a tragic hero. We have suggested that this difficulty is related to the problem of mediation. We can understand this problem more fully if we examine Brisacier's difficulty sustaining a comic perspective.

Scarron, like Nerval, associates the theater with violence and the law of the father. Scarron treats theatrical roles and masks as mediating terms which protect individuals from the violence of the other. Le Destin wears a plaster mask attached to his face in order to disguise himself from his enemies. The mask is not imposed upon him by hostile others. Quite the contrary, it enables him to escape from their hostility:

> La Rappinière demanda à Destin pourquoi il se déguisoit le visage d'un emplâtre: il lui dit qu'il en avait sujet; et que se voyant travesti par accident, il avait voulu ôter aussi la connaissance de son visage à quelques ennemis qu'il avoit.[3]

The narrator's attitude toward his own language parallels Le Destin's view of the mask and theatrical roles. The narrator does not claim that his own language is true, in opposition to the lies of the characters in the story. He refers to himself as a hypocrite and a liar. The "sot" is any reader who is scandalized by lies, and who fails to recognize his own folly in the foolishness of the characters. From this perspective, madness is a form of stupidity or blindness in which one assumes a position of illusory superiority with respect to others. For Scarron, a comic perspective depends upon the idea that author, reader, and characters are fundamentally identical to one another:

> Scache le sot qui s'en scandalise, que tout homme est sot en ce bas monde, aussi-bien que menteur; les uns plus, les autres moins; et moi qui vous parle, peut-être plus sot que les autres, quoique j'aye plus de franchise à l'avouer, et que mon livre n'étant qu'un ramas de sottises, j'espère que chaque sot y trouvera un petit caractère de ce qu'il est, s'il n'est trop aveugle de l'amour-propre.[4]

This view of the world functions well as the justification for a rising bourgeoisie that desires to assert its equality with the nobility above it. While tragedy emphasizes struggles among heroic and noble characters, the comic novel presents the view that no one is inherently more noble than anyone else. We can see this same view of the world in Diderot, Stendhal, and Flaubert, where the tragic hero is shown to be mystified in his belief that he is superior to those around him.

Within this framework, Scarron accepts the idea that relationships in society are based on disguise and deception. Churches serve as a pretext for flirtatious encounters. Disguises always make relatives or lovers unrecognizable to one another, as well as to their enemies:

> Ce jour-là Dom-Carlos s'habilla le mieux qu'il put, et se trouva avec quantité d'autres tirans des coeurs dans l'église de la galanterie. On profane les églises en ce pais-là aussi bien qu'au nôtre, et le temple de dieu sert de rendez-vous aux godelureaux, et aux coquettes, à la honte de ceux qui ont l'ambition d'achalander leurs églises, et de s'ôter la pratique les uns aux autres.[5]

The violence that governs the world goes along with its patriarchal character. A taboo on virginity makes wives and daughters into sacred possessions. Intrigues are based upon theft of lovers, wives, and daughters, upon the violation of this private property.

The disappearance of a comic perspective in Nerval's story might be explained as a change in this patriarchal structure of society. Brisacier's identifications with theatrical roles are disturbing because they place him immediately in the position of the tyrant. While Scarron protects his characters from the other's violence by means of the mask, Nerval treats the mask as an unchangeable structure of identification, as a fixed way of experiencing the relationship between self and other. The mask is a myth of inequality which the individual cannot separate from his experience of himself, that is, from what he considers to be his real identity. What Scarron treats as an attenuation of violence, Nerval treats as violence itself.

We can better understand this contrast if we look briefly at the relationship between the mask and negation. For the psychoanalyst O. Mannoni, the mask operates by means of a process of negation. The mask and roles in the theater allow the spectator to come into contact with that which has been repressed in the form of its negation. Not only the mask, but the distance between spectator and spectacle serve to negate the spectator's identification with a fictional role. Thus the theater allows the spectator to see himself as a tyrant because he is able at the same time to negate this identification by his knowledge that there is a clear separation between what takes place in the theater and his identity outside of the theater:

> la nature de l'illusion théâtrale ne peut pas du tout être comprise en référence à un problème de *croyance*. L'expression "croire aux masques" n'aurait aucun sens si cela voulait dire que nous croyons aux masques comme à quelque chose de vrai ou à quelque chose de réel. Par exemple, que nous prendrions les masques pour de vrais visages. (. . .) Le masque ne se donne pas pour autre qu'il n'est, mais il a le pouvoir d'évoquer les images de la fantaisie. (. . .) les effets de masque et ceux de théâtre sont possibles en partie grâce à la présence de processus qui s'apparentent à ceux de la négation. (. . .) Le théâtre joue un rôle proprement symbolique. Il serait tout entier comme la grande négation, le symbole de négation, qui rend possible le retour du refoulé sous sa forme niée. (. . .) l'illusion est loin d'être la présentation d'un faux réel. Cette illusion n'est au théâtre jamais la nôtre, mais toujours assez bizarrement celle d'un autre spectateur que nous ne savons où situer.[6]

We have seen that the theater no longer functions in this way for Nerval's mad comedian. By the same token, the mask no longer serves as a defense against the other's violence. The mask and the theatrical role engender a process of repression which the actor cannot consciously undo. The theater does not create pleasure and laughter, but pain and the experience of one's own death.

In Mannoni's analysis, the process of negation that operates in the theater upholds the institutions of society, the law, and the normal ego. The theater makes possible a momentary lifting of repression because the basis for this repression is not in itself put into question. Thus Mannoni distinguishes between the normal ego's experience of the theater and that of the neurotic, for whom the theater is the occasion for an identification with a false image of oneself:

> si je suis un simple spectateur du théâtre, je ne suis pas acteur, je ne suis pas roi, ici encore c'est un autre qui peut l'être, et si le théâtre met d'une certaine façon en mouvement mes capacités d'identification et les libère, en même temps, par ses conventions, et par son institutionalisation, il renforce les protections et les défenses.[7]

For the neurotic, the theater serves "à soutenir désespérérément une image de soi donnée mensongèrement à soi et aux autres, comme vraie, ou réelle."[8]

In terms of our previous analysis, Brisacier's madness functions as a moment of enlightenment in his narrative, for it is at this point that he gains a slight distance from the self/other relation from which he suffers. Madness is not an entirely tragic experience in that it undermines the duality between truth and fiction which has previously governed his vision and reveals that this duality is the source of mystification, as well as of violence with respect to others.

With this view of madness in mind, we could say that Brisacier cannot experience the theater as the return of the repressed in negated form, as Mannoni suggests, without also experiencing the arbitrary nature of the cultural tradition that has brought about this repression. Brisacier's madness is a critique of the inequality between father and son which serves as the basis for the Oedipal myth, and a critique, as well, of the normal ego that constitutes itself as an identity by internalizing a process of negation. Brisacier refuses an original repression which serves as the basis for the lifting of repression in the theater.

For similar reasons, Brisacier cannot experience the mask as a defense or displacement of aggression. The breakdown of a hierarchy in which truth is superior to fiction implies the breakdown of the superego, ego, id hierarchy in the individual.

We could regard the breakdown of comedy in Nerval's **Roman tragique** as the disintegration of the vision of the world which brought the bourgeoisie to power. It is no longer possible to regard the mask as external to the individual. The mask is a process of mediation which has been internalized, a place of authority which continues to dominate the individual's imagination even when the concrete figures that once filled that place, the gods or the state, have disappeared. The mask marks a cultural tradition which repeats itself from generation to generation and which has a tendency to erase itself, to be experienced not as myth or as fiction, but as one's own spontaneous nature.

We might also regard the ***Roman tragique*** as an excellent example of the character structure that made it possible for the bourgeoisie to rise to a position of power. If we assume that psychoanalysis describes the family structure of the bourgeoisie, and that upon this family structure Freud projects a continuity between his time and Greek culture, that is, between the prehistorical past of the Oedipal myth and the historical events of the present, we might see Freud's emphasis on the figure of the father as the justification for presenting the individual of a particular class, at a particular moment in history, as a universal example of human nature. If this is the case, then Nerval's story can be situated simultaneously within two different frameworks. Within a psychoanalytical framework, the story reveals the power of the law of the father in the individual's imagination and his subsequent inability to lift repression. Within a Marxist framework, the story reveals the ideology of the bourgeoisie which considers its own language to be true, universal, and to correspond to an eternally existing nature. The narrator's lack of awareness of his own language would indicate a progressive mystification on the part of the bourgeoisie, a progressive identification with the master's illusion of autonomy and a forgetting of the fact that the slave's revolutionary energy derives from his awareness of himself as being entirely mediated by the other.

Notes

1 Gérard de Nerval, "A Alexandre Dumas," *Oeuvres Complètes* (Paris: Bibliothèque de la Pléiade, 1966), I, 152. All quotations from Nerval's work refer to this edition and will be referenced in parentheses in the text.

2 Cf. René Girard, *Mensonge romantique et vérité romanesque* (Paris: Bernard Grasset, 1962). It is interesting that critics often speak of the tragic structure of the nineteenth-century novel and that this tragic structure depends upon an implicit myth of inequality between the positions of self and other. Writers who move from tragic to comic novels, Stendhal and Flaubert, for example, tend to replace this inequality with identical doubles.

3 Paul Scarron, *Le Roman comique, Oeuvres de Scarron,* Nouvelle Edition (Paris: Chez Jean-François Bastien, 1786), II, 11.

4 *Ibid.,* p. 29.

5 *Ibid.,* p. 28.

6 Octave Mannoni, "Le théâtre du point de vue de l'imaginaire," *La Psychanalyse,* 5 (1951), 198-199. See also Gilles Deleuze and Félix Guattari, *L'Anti-Oedipe* (Paris: Minuit, "Collection Critique," 1972), p. 264.

7 Mannoni, *op. cit.,* p. 207.

8 *Ibid.,* p. 208.

Victor Brombert (essay date 1978)

SOURCE: "Nerval's Privileged Enclosures," in *The Romantic Prison: The French Tradition*, Princeton University Press, 1978, pp. 120-32.

[*In the following essay, Brombert investigates "motifs of enclosure, escape, and freedom" in Nerval's work.*]

Facetious Prisons?

"Politique (1831)," originally entitled "Cour de prison," is one of the most graceful poems of ***Petits Châteaux de Bohème.*** Its wistful sadness and flexible workmanship bring to mind Verlaine.

> *Dans Sainte-Pélagie,*
> *Sous ce règne élargie,*
> *Où, rêveur et pensif,*
> *Je vis captif,*
>
> *Pas une herbe ne pousse*
> *Et pas un brin de mousse*
> *Le long des murs grillés*
> *Et frais taillés!*
>
> *Oiseau qui fends l'espace . . .*
> *Et toi, brise, qui passe*
> *Sur l'étroit horizon*
> *De la prison,*
>
> *Dans votre vol superbe,*
> *Apportez-moi quelque herbe,*
> *Quelque gramen, mouvant*
> *Sa tête au vent!*
>
> *Qu'à mes pieds tourbillonne*
> *Une feuille d'automne*
> *Peinte de cent couleurs*
> *Comme les fleurs!*

The combination of a masculine rhyme and a four-syllable verse at the end of each stanza conveys the impression of broken movement, of interrupted flight. The meter serves irony. The six-syllable lines lead to the claudication of the briefer verse. We are far indeed from André Chenier's famous *Iambes* which also describe a prison experience, but in the register of indignation.

Le messager de mort, noir recruteur des ombres,

  Escorté d'infâmes soldats
Ebranlant de [son] nom ces longs corridors sombres.

To be sure, Nerval's poem draws on stereotypes of prison poetry: the wall, the bird, the wind, the glimpsed or remembered space. Yet in spite of the imagery and the literal meaning, the rhythmic pattern maintains an atmosphere of ease.[1]

The motif of the facetious prison, blending parody and melancholy, recurs in Nerval's work. **"Sainte-Pélagie en 1832,"** first published in 1841 in *L'Artiste,* is a humorous text. The narrator, arrested for disturbing the peace, explains that he will never be a Silvio Pellico, but that he has known a real cell and seen the pale light of dawn filtered through barred windows. Waiting for daybreak and food, he and his dissolute companions evoke legendary prisoners who overcame their suffering by growing a flower or taming a spider. Then, feeling the pangs of appetite, they remember the tortures of Dante's Ugolino. But all ends well: they dine together gaily. Prison has in fact become so pleasant that the narrator requests to remain until the next day. The request is, however, not granted: he is set free, and not even allowed to finish his meal. Nerval concludes playfully: "I was about to give the spectacle of a prisoner forcefully thrown out of his jail."[2] This text, ironizing on a literary tradition, develops in its own self-conscious way the theme of the happy prison.

A similarly humorous imprisonment is described in the last three chapters of **Les Nuits d'Octobre,** where the travelling narrator, in search of *realism,* finds himself arrested and jailed in Crespy-en-Valois for having forgotten his passport in Meaux. The dream he has in his cell is filled with images explicitly attributed to Poe, Dickens, and Ainsworth. Masters of that "realism" he ironically wishes to emulate, they are all creators of scenes of incarceration. Once again, de-mystifying parody seems to take over. The narrator claims to be disappointed because the vault, which goes back to the time of the Crusades, has been patched up with concrete. "I was offended by this luxury; I would have liked to raise rats and to tame spiders." And there are other disappointments: the vault is not oozing humidity, the feather bed is equipped with a comfortable quilt.

But the reader must beware. An unspoken anguish underlies these apparently smiling pages. The irrational arrest corresponds to a no less irrational sense of guilt. *Vagabondage, essayisme, réalisme, troubadourisme exagéré*—these are snatches of sentences formulated in the indictment. In his dream, the narrator appears in court, facing a tribunal cut out against a background of "deep shadows." It is a liter-ary guilt, perhaps a more secret guilt also, barely hinted at. The adventurous excursion ends in good fun, to the accompaniment of the gendarme's surly but fundamentally good-natured voice.

Nerval's smile often resembles a grimace of anguish. Ever since his earliest writings, dark humor presides over images of captivity. In **La Main enchantée** (1832), Eustache Bouteroue, locked up in a cell of the Châtelet for having slapped a judge, exercises his wit by metaphorizing the jail into a *vêtement de roc.* Here too, significantly, the narration turns around an absurd guilt, or rather an undemonstrable innocence. When the protagonist loudly proclaims that he is innocent, the jailor gently but firmly replies, in a tone calculated to calm down excitable inmates: "By golly . . . where do you think you are? We have only that kind here."[3] The answer is doubly ironic: it pretends to agree with the prisoner, while affirming ambiguously the essential innocence of any man in jail.

The prison motif haunts Nerval. Historic jails seem to charm him as they did other romantic lovers of local color and picturesque effects. He too was a reader of Latude and Casanova. The 12th letter of **Angélique** evokes, in tourist manner, Abélard's tower, as well as the underground cells and the prison where Louis the Debonnair was held captive by his children. The end of the chapter mentions the purchase of a book about the abbé de Bucquoy, with its title facing an engraving of the Bastille, the inscription "The Hell of the Living" (*L'Enfer des vivants*), and a quotation from the *Aeneid: Facilis descensus Averni* (sic). In a later addition to this passage, Nerval quotes André Chénier's famous lines on the hell of the Bastille and "holy liberty."

The book is in fact already mentioned at the beginning of **Angélique,** and for a good reason: the story of the abbé comte de Bucquoy had been fully developed in the text of the *Faux Saulniers* (1850), of which **Angélique** was an integral part before being detached and made into a separate story of **Les Filles du Feu.** This **"Histoire de l'Abbé de Bucquoy"** is almost entirely set in prison (at the For l'Evêque, in Soissons, in the Bastille) and shows that Nerval had been a most attentive reader of various so-called documentary texts on state prisons published during the Revolutionary years, in particular *La Bastille dévoilée* (1789) and probably also the *Mémoires Historiques et Authentiques sur la Bastille.* All the commonplaces of this kind of literature reappear: the eight towers of the Bastille, the oubliettes, the cruelty of the jailors (a governor's nephew tries to rape one of the prisoners and drives her to suicide), the ingenious efforts to make contact with the other captives or with the outside world (letter codes by means of knocks, pens and ink fabricated with pigeon bones and diluted soot)—nothing is left out, not even the macabre descriptions of the putrid corpse reminiscent of Pétrus Borel's collection of horrors in *Madame Putiphar*. As for the planned, aborted, and successful escapes (complete with ropes made from bed sheets and chair wicker, filed bars, drilled walls, crossings of moats filled with water and mud), they are no doubt inspired, as were so many adventures of this kind in 19th-century literature, by the famous exploits told in Latude's *Mémoires*. Romantic literature plays endless variations on this escape heroism.

The "Fantastique Sérieux"

Much of this might appear as a peculiarity of literary history, were it not for the tight link existing, throughout Nerval's work, between the motifs of enclosure, escape, and freedom. Personal experiences more significant than being arrested for disturbing the peace left their scar. The fear of madness and of commitment are echoed in his work: Hakem's stay in the Moristan insane asylum, Raoul Spifame's imprisonment in Bicêtre, the narrator's descent into the private hell of *Aurélia*, which proposes to describe a sickness that occurred entirely in the "mysteries of [his] mind." Nerval's taste for travel and aimless wandering is the psychological obverse of his claustrophobia. Enclosure and vagrancy remain simultaneous temptations.

Variants of close confinement constitute metaphoric avatars of the prison theme. Grim prisons, joyful prisons: Nerval's privileged fortresses suggest either an impossible search for a lost reality, or a dream-promise of the superior bliss of freedom. The *chateau périssable* of projected ideals or of past innocence remains, however, fundamentally disquieting. Seen from a distance, Beit-Eddin, the ancient residence of emirs in *"Druses et Maronites,"* resembles a fairy-tale castle. From close up, the only inhabited part of the ruins turns out to be a jail (II, 473-474).[4] Terrifying castles and dungeons—the indispensable features of the *fantastique sérieux* he discusses in his essay on Cazotte—continue to tempt him.

Labyrinths, corridors, the network of narrow city streets—places of quest and perdition—exercise an even stronger attraction. A revealing transfer of images occurs early in *Les Nuits d'Octobre,* in the chapter entitled "Capharnaum":

> Corridors—endless corridors! Stairs—stairs one climbs up and down, and up again, whose lower part always dips into a black water perturbed by wheels, under huge arches of a bridge . . . through inextricable constructs! To climb up, down, or to wander through the corridors—and this during several eternities— could this be the punishment to which I am condemned for my faults? (Chapter XVII.)

This passage, whose key terms (corridors, stairs, climbing up and down, tangled constructs, eternity, condemnation, mysterious guilt) suggest a Piranesi-like incar-

ceration, follows hard on the evocation of an urban landscape of which the *arches de pont* are a logical dream extension. The city-labyrinth and the city-hell are obsessive images in Nerval. Through contamination and analogy, they confer on apparently trivial episodes a thematic and structural weight that a first reading does not always reveal. The exploratory drive (*fureur d'investigation*) that propels the narrator through the streets of Vienna at the beginning of *Voyage en Orient* should not be attributed to frivolous tourism. The compulsive roaming is directly related to the obscure joy of being led to the "most tangled part of the city," to the need to lose himself in the private myth of a maze (II, 131). Yet this sense of loss is in itself illusory, theatrical. Parisian hell in *Les Nuits d'Octobre* (Chapter X) proposes Dantesque visions of La Pia and Francesca. But the secret of Paris, as Nerval confides in one of his notebooks, is that captivity itself is an appearance, that the prison-city provides numerous openings for escape (I, 863).

Nerval's work refers to many enclosures that are not walled up, to prisons that are not truly locked. The pyramids, with their low vaultings and mysterious galleries, appear to him as the ideal setting for an initiatory performance of *The Magic Flute*. The underground palace Soliman built in the Kaf mountain, so that after death he would escape the laws of decomposition, remains accessible to the humble mite. The microscopic arachnid undermines the pillar of the throne, making it collapse and thereby liberating the humiliated spirits (II, 674-676). The subterranean world in the *"Nuits de Ramazan"* is both a figuration of hell and a privileged place for the fiercely independent sect of Adoniram. In this inner topography, volcanoes and grottoes are places of both terror and hospitality. Princess Setalmulc, sister of Caliph Hakem, sits in her labyrinthine dwelling, in the remotest corner of a room whose wrought ceiling imitates a stalactite grotto (II, 414). Nature and artifice end up by resembling each other; they blend in an atmosphere of a Thousand and One Nights. A disquieting correspondence is established between dissimilar places. The convent whose walls lock up the inaccessible woman in *Sylvie*; Madame Carlès' "pension," a place shut off on all sides from "external nature" (*"Druses et Maronites,"* II, 381); the seraglio, in *"Nuits de Ramazan,"* the setting for a dangerous escape adventure—all these enclosures allow for a characteristic blending of a sense of mystery, the joy of discovery, the dream of a secret loophole. Walls, as well as thresholds, veils, and barriers, are essential to Nerval's mental landscape.[5]

It is, however, the theater that provides the most suggestive recurrent image, linking together notions of encincture and flight, barriers and openings, pleasure and anxiety, veils and rendings of delicately woven textures. In *Sylvie,* the theater is indeed the point of departure of reverie and unrest. The prefatory dedication of *Les Filles du Feu* evokes the actor Brisacier, who wound up identifying with the roles he played. A letter to Alexandre Dumas shows us Nerval at Baden Baden, imagining that he is on a make-believe opera stage, looking at the set and the props (28 August 1838). Theater metaphors pervade landscape descriptions. In *Voyage en Orient,* Lausanne offers an "opera perspective"; the Munich square resembles those "unlikely sets" (*décors impossibles*) that theaters sometimes venture; Syra displays to the traveller-spectator a décor that is equally "impossible"; the row of houses along the river Nile looks like a *décoration de théâtre;* Constantinople, another *décoration de théâtre,* should be admired without visiting the wings (II, 16, 27, 93, 279, 694). The theater represents for Nerval a temporal and spatial experience embracing, within the same privileged locus, a diversity of moments within a singular duration. The narrator, in *Sylvie,* sits in the stage boxes of the same theater "every night." At regular hours he participates in a repeated ritual. The same moments are played over, immobilized in the ceremonial of art. The actress, true "apparition," is compared to the "Heures divines" standing out against the background of the Herculaneum frescoes (I, 589-590). On the one hand, the theater creates the illusion of distance, making the close-by seem unrealizable; on the other, the theatrical experience is the threshold to the unreal, nourishing dreams, conflating illusion and reality, suggesting an eventual *passage.* In these rites, distance is transformed into immediacy. In *"Les Femmes du Caire,"* Nerval observes that the theater is unique in providing the illusion of possessing the feminine unknown: " . . . *il vous donne l'illusion de connaître parfaitement une inconnue*" (II, 210). The true exit of the enclosed theatrical space opens unto the ideal.

The Escape Within

These metaphors are interesting not because they betray fixations but because they are marshalled thematically. Proust saw Nerval's work as a model of sickly obsessiveness (*hantise maladive*).[6] But the model is of course a structured *literary* mediation of haunting private motifs. Enclosures and walled-in landscapes function at a number of levels. They suggest latent apprehension, anxiety in the face of the so-called "real" world. Imagination, symbolically captive in a miserable dwelling, knocks against the windows of its hovel "like an imprisoned insect" (II, 151). There is anxiety in the face of the to-be-discovered secret. The city again functions symbolically, revealing gradually its hidden districts to the visitor, in particular the unknown Oriental city, with its walled streets and veiled women. But it is the theater, with its curtain and illusionist sets, that provides Nerval with the metaphors most suggestive of the exhilaration and ache of an illusive presence. The restless teasing of the riddle is in fact the sign of a more radical interrogation of identities. Caliph Hakem, in the Moristan prison asylum, wondering whether he is God or simply caliph, has great difficulty assembling the "scattered fragments" of his thoughts (II, 424). In *Aurélia,* this fragmentation, symptom of a long illness affecting the recesses of the mind, logically calls for images of subterranean corridors. These obsessional motifs confirm the link between theatrical and claustral images.

The condemnation to a sense of perpetual wandering in dark, indeterminate, Daedalian spaces reflects Nerval's anguished fascination as he confronts his madness—an anguish and a fascination intensified by mirror effects that compel him to *see himself* in the act of wandering. Nerval indulges in his alienation: the image of the mental labyrinth becomes the privileged figuration of his private hell. In *Aurélia,* he compares the entrance of the underground realm of Fire to the veins and vessels "that meander in the lobes of the brain" (I, 765). The metaphor, by inversion, reconverts the image into a clinical reality. As for the notion of hell, it is explicitly stated. In the preface to *Les Filles du Feu,* dedicated to Alexandre Dumas, the substance of *Aurélia* is unmistakably announced: "Some day I shall write the story of this 'descent to hell' " (I, 502).

Yet the fantasy world of Nerval, so hemmed in and oppressive, also appears reassuring. Enclosure is protective. Weakness calls for a refuge, just as alienation seems to seek an asylum. Georges Poulet defines Nerval's nostalgia for the singular, yet repeated moment: "He sees himself surrounded by himself. His past dances the round about him."[7] The fact is that Nerval wishes to step within the circle; he yearns to penetrate into the enclosed space—prison, asylum, or underground labyrinth—to find a shelter or stronghold that might restitute his lost vigor. He dreams of a breakthrough, of an escape *within.* At the very outset of *Aurélia* he speaks indeed of "breaking through" (*percer*) the gates of ivory and of horn which separate him from the invisible world. But the early signal of a transcendental flight is quickly followed, in the same paragraph, by the image of a shady underground world (*souterrain vague*—I, 753).

Nerval's labyrinths are not necessarily malefic.[8] Places of confinement and of secrecy, they also protect against the erosive workings of time. Behind the yellow façade of the uncle's house in *Sylvie,* behind the closed green shutters and the locked door, the ancient furniture is perfectly "preserved." The old prints, the antiquated engravings, the stuffed dog—all the objects in this scene suggest a comforting fixity (I, 612). In *Aurélia,* there is talk of very old necromancer-kings whom powerful cabbalists "locked up" in "well kept" sepulchers to preserve them from the ravages of death, while the treasures that were to protect them against the anger of the gods were buried in *vastes souterrains* (I, 777-778). Similarly, Tubal-Kaïn explains to Adoniram that he had long galleries dug to serve as "retreats" for his tribe, that the stones of the protective pyramid were cemented with "impenetrable" bitumen, and that he personally "sealed" the little door of the narrow passageway which was its only opening. According to Nervalian logic, the image of these underground dwellings, where water itself is "imprisoned," corresponds to the supreme instinct of preservation that impels Tubal-Kaïn to seek reentrance into the pyramid (II, 629-630).

These places of conservation also confer strength and freedom. Against the granitic fortresses and inaccessible caverns of Kaïn's descendants, even Adonaï's tyrannical might remains inoperative. The immunity is of a spiritual nature. The fear of death, made manifest through dreams of regenerative survival and magic confinement, implies the release of the soul. The inaccessible palace within the Kaf mountain is destined to protect Soliman against decomposition. It is also to rejuvenate his exiled spirit. If Soliman does not succeed in his quest for immortality, this has to do with the limitations of his character. Tubal-Kaïn, however, succeeds. And this success, in the context of his inner, subterranean world, means that his "soul [is] freed" (II, 630). The parallel between the survival of Tubal-Kaïn and the rebirth of the necromancer-kings in their well-guarded sepulchers is obvious. The underlying unity of Nerval's work is indeed unmistakable if one grants the relation between an image such as the stuffed dog in the uncle's house (*Sylvie,* Chapter IX) and the buried talismans in the underground passages in *Aurélia.* Magic hollows and secret chambers correspond to the same temporal anguish and the same dream of an escape through closure.

This notion of a salvational confinement, of a metaphoric prison escape, casts light on Nerval's symbolic descent to the nether regions. His *descentes aux enfers* are quests aimed at transmuting disaster into victory. Hence his taste for stories of incarceration and feats of escape (the abbé de Bucquoy, Raoul Spifame), as well as his fascination for accounts of inner liberations. The powers of the imagination seem multiplied in any state of detention and oppression. Real imprisonment, just as confinement within one's own madness, brings about a *multiplication* of the personality. The Nervalian "double" manifests itself by preference in a circumscribed and restricted intimacy. The paradox of a spiritual freedom attained within prison walls is confirmed by a teasing observation jotted down in a text entitled "Sur un Carnet": "The jailor is another kind of captive.—Is the jailor jealous of his prisoner's dreams?" (I, 866.)

Nerval's mental itinerary, though it implies a negation of what is not at the center, quickly becomes centrifugal. The imaginary monk's cell opens onto space; it is the threshold to transcendence. Francesco and Lucrèce, in *"Le Songe de Polyphile,"* escape from their convent and monastery to meet in a mythological otherworldliness: " . . . in their double dream, they crossed the immensity of space and time" (II, 79). Yousouf, in *"Histoire du Calife Hakem,"* similarly experiences temporal and spatial release: " . . . the spirit, delivered from the body, its weighty jailor, escapes like a prisoner whose keeper falls asleep, leaving the key in the cell's door." Hakem's *double* describes the joys of a flight, in a state of spiritual inebriation, through "atmospheres of unutterable bliss" (II, 404). The image—an old one—is that of the soul freed of its worldly frame.

Man's mortal condition thus assumes for Nerval the form of a captivity that must de denied. Spiritual correspondences, allowing glimpses of the mystery of things, derive from the awareness of limits. "Presently a captive on this earth, I converse with the choir of stars participating in my joys and sorrows!" This sentence in *Aurélia* (I, 810) sums up a cosmic dialogue entirely founded on the double notion of bounds and liberation. Madness itself is projected through the dual image of the cell and of its negation. A "strip-tease" of insanity illustrates this escape through the hell of consciousness-turned-jailor: the narrator, while walking and singing, takes off his "terrestrial clothes," waits for the soul to leave the body, and has a vision of the "unveiling" of the sky (I, 760-761). Madness, the cause of a literal and metaphoric seclusion, remains throughout Nerval's work the symbol of a liberating immurement. Raoul Spifame, within the triple walls of Bicêtre, is convinced that his dreams are his life, and that his prison is but a dream (I, 85-86).

This text, ironically entitled *"Le Roi de Bicêtre,"* is of central importance. Raoul Spifame, "a suzerain without seigniory," bears an uncanny resemblance to his king Henri II. He commits such weird acts that his family decides to have him committed. The one who takes himself for the king is locked up in a madhouse, locked up with a fanatic who takes himself for the king of poets. Nerval's authorship of this text has been questioned. Yet the themes are so unmistakably his own that any doubt seems unwarranted. Spifame's jail is a reality from which he escapes, not by loosening the bars (though a brief episode does exploit this romantic cliché), but through the illusion of happiness which metamorphoses his prison into a palace, his rags into brilliant finery, his miserable meals into opulent feasts. The end of the story is not only ironic, but logical and deeply meaningful. Spifame has been caught again after a successful escape. The king, however, touched by the gentle madness of this unhappy nobleman, refuses to have him sent back to the madhouse. He gives orders instead that Spifame be "kept" in one of his "pleasure castles." The place of internment and the place of contentment ultimately become indistinguishable.

The ironic treatment of the prison theme leads us back to texts such as **"Sainte-Pélagie en 1832"** and the Crespy-en-Valois episode in *Les Nuits d'Octobre.* Only in the major texts, the irony cannot be read as a frivolous literary exercise or as facile parody. The recurrent prison metaphors, combining self-punishment and self-justification, linking the search for a secret to the anxiety of dreams and to the fear of insanity, suggest an ambivalent state of captivity. Escape itself is fraught with insecurity. Nerval thus assumes a special status in the literary tradition of escapism. His prisons are essentially happy prisons. But, unlike Stendhal, in whose work the notion of freedom is elaborated within the four walls of a cell, where love and the inner life are discovered inside the symbolic Farnese Tower, Nerval grants himself only intuitions of freedom and velleities of escape. It is a freedom that cannot be attained, an ineffective freedom, always to be questioned. Nerval's prisons themselves are in the last analysis unstable, and their images interchangeable. That is surely why Nerval's jailor is not jealous of his prisoner, but of his propensity to dream.

Notes

[1] Gianni Mombello, speaking of a literary tradition parallel to the one that was inaugurated by Silvio Pellico's *Le Mie Prigioni,* points out the metrical resemblance of certain poems by Musset, Nerval, and Verlaine. ("Breve nota su 'Mes Prisons' de Verlaine," in *Studi Francesi,* 17, May-August 1962, pp. 292-293.)

[2] Gerard de Nerval, *Œuvres,* Pléiade, 1956, I, 85.

[3] *Ibid.,* I, 513.

[4] The numbers in parentheses refer to the Garnier edition of Nervals *Œuvres* (ed. H. Lemaître), 2 vols., 1958.

[5] See J.-P. Richard, "Géographie magique de Nerval," in *Poésie et Profondeur,* Seuil, 1955, pp. 20-22.

[6] "Gérard de Nerval," in *Contre Sainte-Beuve,* Gallimard, 1954, p. 165.

[7] "Nerval," in *Les Métamorphoses du cercle,* Plon, 1961, p. 248.

[8] The obsession with barriers, limits, and the "curse of the crust," has been excellently discussed by Jean-Pierre Richard in "Géographie magique de Nerval," in *Poésie et Profondeur,* Seuil, 1955.

Claire Gilbert (essay date 1979)

SOURCE: "Hakem," *in Nerval's Double: A Structural Study,"* Romance Monographs, 1979, pp. 46-58.

[In the following essay, Gilbert analyzes the figure of the double in Nerval's story "L'Histoire du Calife Hakem."]

Two Nervalian heroes, Hakem and Spifame, were confined to an asylum for insanity, apparently as victims of a type of schizophrenia. They both have autoscopic experiences, a hallucinatory perception of one's own body image projected into external space.[1] For both, there exist historical models which Nerval altered to fit his own experience. In providing the details of their speech and life, with obvious sympathy, Nerval invites his reader to examine these figures as projections of his own existential dilemma.

Hakem's story presents the most explicit treatment of the double, or autoscopic experience, in Nerval's writings; it forms the core model whose transformations can be traced in his other works. **"L'Histoire du Calife Hakem,"** first published in 1847, appears in the *Voyage en Orient.* It was written six years after Nerval's first psychotic crisis in 1841, and was based on his 1843 trip to Egypt, Libya, and Turkey.

The historical Hakem was the ruler, or calife, of Cairo in the medieval period (993-1021). Besides his secular powers, he claimed godhood. The religion which became the Druse sect was founded to worship him (1017) by Darazi (hence the name) and by Hamza, who gave the Hakem cult its definitive Druze form.[2] The Druzes today survive as a minority sect, combining Moslem and Christian elements in their worship. Hakem is revered now merely as a prophet, not as a god. Hakem's reign was notable for religious fanaticism, great cruelty, resultant rebellions, and many eccentricities, verging on madness.[3]

Nerval's Hakem differs in many ways from the historical figure. He jeopardizes his royal status by frequently disguising himself as a beggar, whereas the real Hakem had himself carried openly about by servants. The fictional calife wishes to mingle with the common people and to learn better how to govern his realm. This is, of course, a classical theme. It figures prominently in the tradition of the Oriental tale and in French authors, such as Montesquieu, working within that tradition.

In this novella, the disguise theme is vitalized by its relevance to the life of Nerval. Within the context given, this disguise has the power to destroy the authentic royalty that it clothes; madness and death will result from the counterfeit costume, which at first appears to be a banal plot device.

Hakem is introduced during an argument in a Cairo café, the very locale in which Nerval claims to have heard this story during his travels. Hakem violently refuses to attend a religious service, and declares "avec une puissance de blasphème incroyable" that "Mahomet et Jésus sont des imposteurs" (Pl. II, p. 364).[4] At the very beginning, he has a vocabulary of imposters and usurpation, a central theme here. He goes on: "Je n'adore personne, puisque je suis Dieu moi-même! le seul, le vrai, l'unique Dieu, dont les autres ne sont que les ombres" (Pl. II, p. 365).

This declaration is greeted by a violent attack upon the disguised calife; Hakem must be rescued by a new friend, Yousouf, who is unaware of his true status. At this point, the reader cannot tell if the assertion is a literal one; indeed, the ambiguity over Hakem's divinity will continue throughout the narrative. If Hakem executes power on the levels of both calife and God, as two separate functions, then at least one role would seem to be unnecessary. This is not a case of a divine right to rule a secular kingdom, but a demand for dual recognition on earthly and on cosmic levels.

Nerval has further added to the ambiguity by placing this scene in a hashish house. Hakem has been asked to partake of the "pâte verdâtre" and has been assured that it contains (for Moslems) "le paradis promis par ton prophète à ses croyants" (Pl. II, p. 360). The narrative implies that when the Calife Hakem forbad the consumption of alcohol, he opened the way for the adoption of other ways to alter consciousness. In fact, the historical Hakem was very unpopular for his repeated bans on wine.

After some protests against this illegal drug, Hakem agrees to experience hashish for the first time. Nerval then gives a rather unrealistic description of the speed of the effects of this drug, which might lead to a conclusion that Nerval lacked first-hand experience with it:

> Il paraissait en proie à une exaltation extraordinaire; des essaims de pensées nouvelles, inouïes, inconcevables, traversaient son âme en tourbillons de feu. (Pl. II, p. 360)

An explanation of the effects of this drug would seem to vitiate the claims of his hero to divinity: "Le hachich rend pareil à Dieu," as Hakem explains. This recalls the ironic introduction to the story, which promised to tell the story of "Hakem, que les historiens ont peint comme un fou furieux" (Pl. II, p. 337).

Yet the irony is overtaken by a tragic tone as the narrative progresses. The prison theme is introduced into the account of Hakem's delirium, foreshadowing his tragic asylum experience. The question of the author's conscious manipulation of key image structures is certainly worth posing in this context; they do work to unify the narrative:

> L'ivresse, en troublant les yeux du corps, éclaircit ceux de l'âme; l'esprit dégagé du corps, son pesant *geôlier*, s'enfuit comme un *prisonnier* dont le

gardien s'est endormi, laissant la clef à la porte du *cachot*. Il erre joyeux et libre dans l'espace et la lumière . . . (Pl. II, p. 361; italics added)

The longing for freedom takes on here a neoplatonic coloration, and presents the interior duality as the real problem before Hakem is subjected to the external prison experience, which will in turn alter his perception of the internal conflicts.

The aesthetic distance that Nerval had established between himself and his hero is diminished. Here is a portrait of Hakem as he returns that night to his adored sister, Sétalmulc, in the royal palace:

> Hakem semblait n'être pas animé par la vie terrestre. Son teint pâle reflétait la lumière d'un autre monde. C'était bien la forme du calife, mais éclairée d'un autre esprit et d'*une autre âme*. Ses gestes étaient des gestes de *fantôme*, et il avait l'air de *son propre spectre*. (Pl. II, pp. 371-372; italics added)

This passage is meant to reflect the fact that two paragraphs later Hakem fell into his bed "vaincu par le hachich." The drug is not the real problem; this passage points clearly to a diagnosis of a type of schizophrenia. During, or just prior to, autoscopic experience, the subject often feels that his own reality is diminished, or ghostly.[5] The devaluation of his own "real" person in favor of a supposedly more authentic, denser other self is the beginning of the loss of self that schizophrenia entails.[6]

More importantly, it also establishes Hakem as a double of Nerval, endowed with some of the most disturbing of his own experiences.

Nerval too felt that he was his own ghost. In a touching letter to a friend, he agonized over a portrait of himself engraved by Gervais, used by booksellers at Strasbourg and elsewhere as an advertisement for Nerval's works:

> Dites donc, je tremble ici de rencontrer aux étalages un certain portrait pour lequel on m'a fait poser lorsque j'étais malade . . . L'artiste est un homme de talent, . . . mais, . . . *il fait trop vrai!*
>
> Dites partout que c'est mon portrait ressemblant, mais *posthume,*—ou bien encore que Mercure avait pris les traits de Sosie et posé à ma place.
>
> Je veux me débarbouiller avec de l'ambroisie, si les dieux m'en accordent un demi-verre seulement.
>
> Infâme daguerréotype! (Pl. I, pp. 1114-1115; L. 311; May 31, 1854; original italics)

In rejecting a portrait of himself which he feels is unflattering, Nerval introduced precisely the same themes of imposture and of ghostly possession as in the description of Hakem. He seems far more depressed and irritated than the circumstance of an unflattering portrait would warrant. He refers to the Sosie figure, from the Molière play discussed above, in a doomed attempt at humour. This hateful Sosie, the rejected double of himself, is "trop vrai," because it forecasts his death.

A letter written the next day to Dr. Blanche, the son of Dr. Esprit Blanche who cared for Nerval during his psychotic crises from 1841 until 1852, repeats the same theme. He begs the doctor to apologize to those who ate with him at the clinic:

> Expliquez-leur que l'être pensif qu'elles ont vu se traîner, inquiet et morose, dans le salon, dans le jardin, ou le long de votre table hospitalière, n'était pas moi-même assurément. De l'autre bord du Rhin, je renie le sycophante qui m'avait pris mon nom et peut-être mon visage. (Pl. I, p. 1118; L. 312)

Nerval feels his own life slipping away from him, and already feels his life is being usurped. He is as eager as Hakem to deny the ghostly imposter.

Through this transformation into a victim, the calife has become one of the most touching of the fictional doubles of Nerval; Hakem fails to establish control over his own identity or over others. The historical Hakem was undeniably the ruler of Cairo, although his bizarre and contradictory behavior troubled his subjects. His godhead, presented here with disturbing ambiguity, was accepted by some members of the Druze cult during his lifetime.

The way in which Nerval adapts the historical model here demonstrates central aspects of the way his personal accretions of meaning build up throughout his writing.[7] This double must violate laws, and must display hubris, so that he can be punished. Since he is already royal, mere assertion of his legitimate power will not suffice. He must exaggerate his claims to power in order to invite defeat; Hakem must win attention, even at tremendous cost.

Hakem commands his sister, Sétalmulc, to marry him. This royal command is a function of his own belief in his divinity; it is the fatal act of greed, the transgression of taboos, that will precipitate his downfall. Hakem claims to be a god, when the calife's power should suffice; and he insists on an incestuous marriage when a harem full of women should be enough.

When an evil vizir is sent by Sétalmulc to arrest Hakem at a hashish house, he is in his commoner disguise, and so cannot prevent the arrest. His protests are all met with disbelief. They now will earn him an added condemnation, as a royal usurper. The vizir sends him to Moristan, the royal prison of which a part was "consacrée aux foux furieux."

Hakem accosts the doctor who comes to visit the psychotic wing of the prison. Doubles abound; the doctor's title is "hekim." The calife protests his true identity:

> O toi qui me vois ici, tel qu'autrefois Aissé (Jésus), abandonné sous cette forme et dans mon impuissance humaine aux entreprises de *l'enfer, doublement méconnu* comme calife et comme Dieu, songe qu'il convient que je sorte au plus tôt de cette indigne situation. (Pl. II, p. 378; original parentheses; italics added)

Hakem calls his confusion "l'enfer," just as Nerval termed his psychotic experiences and autoscopic projections recounted in *Aurélia* "une descente aux enfers." The mistake here is double, because Hakem claims the functions of temporal ruler and of god to be two separate roles. The desperate pleading for help does not correspond very well to the accents to be expected from a ruler to a hereditary throne, accustomed to power from an early age. But it does correspond to Nerval's feelings when he was interned for his mental crises.

A letter to a friend during his first internment gives a sentiment often expressed by Nerval, that he is not mad at all. He tries to gloss over his fright at the loss of liberty:

> . . . j'ai le malheur de m'être cru toujours dans mon bon sens. J'ai peur d'être dans une maison de sages et que les fous soient au dehors. (Pl. I, p. 898; L. 85 bis; April 27, 1841)

During a later internment paranoia and panic at being imprisoned are given in a letter to his father:

> [j'ai] été ramené ici dans des circonstances singulières et par des gens qui me sont suspects. . . . j'ai des papiers que je ne voudrais pas voir entre toutes les mains: nous vivons dans une époque de complots et je me méfie de tous. . . . (Pl. I, p. 1063; L. 253; Oct. 7, 1853)

Although this letter was written several years after the publication of Hakem's story, there is another letter from the same month, written October 21, 1853, which reveals that the fate of Hakem was very much in his mind during this period. After addressing his father, M. Labrunie, by his title "Ancien Médecin en Chef militaire," Nerval relates:

> Je ne puis persuader à personne ici que je suis un peu médecin . . . On ne veut pas croire que j'ai soigné des malades pendant le choléra et que j'ai fait alors une centaine de visites avec ou sans toi. . . . j'ai quelque droit à donner mon opinion et à me dire *hakim.* (Pl. I, pp. 1067-1068; L. 257; original italics)

This is the title of "hekim," meaning doctor, which was used in the 1847 Hakem story; the spelling has been contaminated by the name of this hero, with whom Nerval identified himself so intensely.

When he has established the self-defeating pattern for his hero, Nerval must continue to lead his calife into despair through repeated inconsistencies. Hakem confuses his real station as the calife of all Egypt with the risky claim to be God. These actions contradict the earlier Hakem who had admitted that the drug hashish could impart a feeling of divinity. Both that calmer version of Hakem and the voice of desperation correspond to the variations of tone that Nerval uses to discuss his own case.

Hakem is thrown into a radical doubt of his very existence after a visit by the royal doctors, who have been instructed by his sister to pronounce him mad; he doubts that he is a god, or even that he is the calife (Pl. II, p. 379). He is then led into conversations with other inmates, much as Nerval himself in the clinic of Dr. Blanche took an interest in the other patients, and fancied that he could help to cure them. Hakem watches the other inmates of Moristan who fancy that they are divine spirits or rulers; their roles of emperor, demigod, or titan are completed by a toy crown which is passed around or disputed.

This is a theatre in which the hero passes from actor to spectator, from agent to critic. Now Hakem, who was so confused in his own role, finds comfort in this jousting with a crown; "il provoquait même" these conversations when they lag. Nerval feels obliged to explain that Hakem is "seul maître de sa raison au milieu de ces intelligences égarées" (Pl. II, p. 380). Just above, Hakem was terrified of his own fate; now he is the shining light of sanity. The other patients recognize this quality in him, and turn to him "comme les plantes . . . vers la lumière." Inside this radically transformed system, Hakem seems to prove that perhaps "les sages" are inside the hospital, and the outsiders are "les fous," as Nerval's letter had proclaimed. He seems to briefly reach the status of prophet of Cairo that was denied in the "real" world outside.

Now that he is restored to some degree of effectiveness, his self-doubt is on a nobler plane:

> Hakem arrivait par instants à douter de lui-même, comme le Fils de l'homme au mont des Oliviers . . . ce qui surtout frappait . . . c'était l'idée que sa divinité lui avait été d'abord révélée dans les extases du hachich. (Pl. II, p. 380)

This vocabulary recalls Nerval's poem **"Le Christ aux Oliviers"** which concludes with pity for "ce fou, cet insensé sublime" who must be sacrificed by a cruel and distant God.[8] It would be difficult to establish here that Hakem is a Christ figure; but it would be rather logical to show that Christ, in the works of Nerval, is a Hakem figure.

When Hakem realizes that an imposter has been placed upon his throne while he is imprisoned, he protests against this "fantôme qui me ressemble et qui tient ma place" (Pl. II, p. 381). The political usurpation is brought into the imagery of supernatural events again for him.

When he escapes to address a large crowd, he seems to have recovered his divine status:

> Un éclat surhumain environnait sa face. . . . Était-ce comme souverain, était-ce comme dieu que le calife s'adressait ainsi à la foule? Certainement il avait en lui cette raison suprême qui est au-dessus de la justice ordinaire. (Pl. II, pp. 384-385)

There seems to be no irony in Nerval's presentation of him here, which makes this superhuman exercise of powers hard to reconcile with his earlier doubts.

This awesome figure now leads the burning and sacking of Cairo, which brings about the downfall of the evil vizir and restores Hakem to power. This incident is based on one of the most cruel acts of the historical Hakem. In 1020, he burned down the town of al-Fustat as a punishment for protests against his proclaimed divinity; his troops plundered the town and committed atrocities, and finally had to be restrained when foreign powers tried to defend the homeless citizens of the town.[9]

Nerval does not condemn this, but seems to praise the burning as a worthy act. By wielding this dangerous element, and seeming to profit from it, Hakem becomes what might be termed a "Fils du Feu," part of a select group of Nervalian heroes who can rise above the means of ordinary mortals to gain their ends.

In the midst of the burning of Cairo, his greatest triumph, Hakem is assailed by doubt. He hears that his pretensions to divinity echo the illusions once held by his grandfather; this apparent reference to inherited mental instability throws him into melancholy reflection (Pl. II, p. 387).

After this diabolic success, Nerval's Hakem institutes religious tolerance for Christians and Jews in his Moslem city, while regretting the poor acceptance of his own cult (Pl. II, p. 387). The historical Hakem was highly intolerant, repeatedly sacking churches and forcing Christians and Jews to wear special clothes and signs of their religion.[10] Again, Nerval wishes to sustain sympathy for his hero, changing the historical record for his own fictional purposes.

Hakem swings back to belief in his own divinity upon hearing about bad predictions from the positions of the stars; like God, he knows that he is eternal (Pl. II, p. 388). Then, he will pass from being serene to being mortally helpless, in a crucial scene that must be examined in some detail.

Upon returning to the palace late at night, he is surprised to see the palace lit up for a celebration. Crowds of servants bear sweetmeats, and dancing girls perform, while guests crowd everywhere. As in a dream, he seems to be invisible in his commoner disguise.

This demonstrates the extent to which Nerval invests theatre and costuming with existential density. The calife is not recognized by anyone in his own palace, after he changes clothes. And even the most malevolent vizir dare not arrest him when Hakem is playing the official role of calife, in the appropriate costume.

Hakem is especially disturbed at this noise, for he had planned to marry his sister Sétalmulc in a quiet private ceremony. He is alarmed to see a man covered with jewels seated on the throne next to his sister. The confrontation with this imposter is truly terrifying to Hakem:

> Cette vision lui semblait un avertissement céleste, et son trouble augmenta encore lorsqu'il reconnut ou crut reconnaître ses propres traits dans ceux de l'homme assis près de sa sœur. Il crut que c'était *son ferouer ou son double,* et, pour les Orientaux, voir *son propre spectre* est un signe du plus mauvais augure. L'ombre force le corps à la suivre dans le délai d'un jour. (Pl. II, pp. 389-390; italics added except for ferouer)

Nerval thus brings his hero into a long tradition of the threatening appearance of a double, or "Doppelgänger," that brings death in its wake. This concept, discussed earlier, was used ironically and tragically by the German romantics as a way to externalize their own internal anxieties, and has its roots in the primitive folklore of many different cultures.[11] The myth of the double is part of a complex of beliefs that add up to an "overkill" of explanations for death; in primitive beliefs, all deaths are caused by agents or circumstances that can be named. There are no accidental deaths, or those resulting from simple old age. This redundant causality for death will be seen in Nerval's conclusion.

The double also arouses terror by his usurpation of the project of marriage to Sétalmulc. This seems to Hakem a "symbole mystérieux et terrible" of "quelque divinité jalouse" who seeks to usurp the very heavens from him (Pl. II, p. 390).

In seeking to understand this event as a sign of divine vengeance, Hakem reminds us that this marriage was to have established irrevocably his divine status. Only the divine dare, or must, marry their siblings, to keep royal blood pure (Pl. II, p. 372). This act would have linked Hakem to the great pharaohs of ancient Egypt, who freely married siblings, or who conferred the title of brother or sister upon their spouses after the marriage.[12]

The "ferouer," or double, has thus threatened Hakem on several levels: sexually, politically, and metaphysically. Like the victim of a nightmare, Hakem slips around unobserved at the edges of this ceremony; he does not cry out in protest, or utter the special words of command that a calife would know. Instead, he is curiously passive, and makes his way to a palace exit to wait for the imposter to leave.

When the imposter leaves the palace and meets Hakem outside, it is Yousouf, his friend who had introduced him to hashish; this experience caused his arrest. Yousouf, still not realizing his companion is the calife, compares the ceremony to a dream sequence. Hakem is struck by the resemblance between them which he had not noticed before; they then establish that their parents come from the same remote province (Pl. II, p. 391). This revelation has been prepared throughout the story, since they have addressed each other as "frère."

Hakem shifts back to being secure in his divinity, which inspires "cette immense affection paternelle qu'un dieu doit ressentir" (Pl II, p. 394). He therefore decides to forgive and to bless this imposter's marriage. He then revisits his observatory, to see for himself the "funeste signe" of his tragic destiny.

As he descends into town, three men attack him with drawn knives. One recognizes the calife and dies fighting at his side, with "O mon frère!" on his lips (Pl. II, p. 395). For it is the double, Yousouf, who kills Hakem, on orders from Sétalmulc.[13] And Hakem is responsible for his brother's death because of this recognition at the edge of death; Hakem acted the role of the fatal "ferouer" for Yousouf as well. The assassin (a word derived from hashish) is bound to Hakem by ties of blood, of friendship, of mutual hashish experiences, and by mutual love for the beautiful and treacherous Sétalmulc.

She is a sibling figure to both of the heroes, as well as the only female interest throughout the story. She acts here the part of Lilith, the ageless temptress who is the consort of Satan. Nerval had traced a part of Lilith's career throughout the ages in several of his works, notably in the plays *Les Monténégrins* and *L'Imagier de Harlem.* She fascinates, meddles with, attracts, and ultimately kills the unfortunate men who fall into her sphere. She fulfills her function by promising Eros and delivering Thanatos.

Nerval has transformed Calife Hakem's life into a fatal struggle between a man and his own double, and thus narrates Hakem's death with redundant causality. The political facts, of religious wars, of his own disputed divinity, and of rivalry with his sister's ministers, do not suffice to explain the tragic ending:

> Il est probable que dans ce récit, fait au point de vue particulier des Druses, on assiste à une de ces luttes millénaires entre les bons et les mauvais esprits incarnés dans une forme humaine, dont nous avons donné un aperçu. (Pl. II, p. 396)

Now he has given an abstract, allegorical explanation of this story that seemed touching through its very human presentation of frailty. This Manichean explanation would pit good and evil forces against each other for eternity, since they are evenly matched. This approach seems inappropriate here. It seems to correspond more to Nerval's deep need for a meaningful pattern in his own life than to a real statement on any version of Hakem, the historical one or the one that has been presented in this work. The inconsistent behavior of Hakem has caused harsh criticism of the literary value of this story; yet these logical problems appear to point clearly to parallels with Nerval's own problems.

Yousouf is not a bad spirit; he seems to share the passive, dreamy psychology of Hakem, although by acting in the royal charade of marriage he appears to escape punishment for his hashish experiences. Yousouf seems to be an agent of doom in accidental fashion; what might have been presented as inevitable destiny for Hakem has been softened by the style of the narrative to a rather arbitrary murder. The real tragedy of Hakem's life is constituted not by one flaw in his character from which the action flows, but by the essential dualism of his life, which is exteriorized as the threat of his double. The inconsistency of Hakem's divinity in the narrative makes it difficult to take this aspect as the central one; it is variously presented as authentic, or the result of madness, or the result of his drug experience.

The strongest and most disturbing part of the narrative is the loss of selfhood which Hakem experiences progressively throughout the story. His drug experience, then his incarceration, are accompanied by a diminution of his own reality for himself, so that his eventual death by exterior force is preceded by a psychic suicide. Paradoxically, his assertions of divinity do not strengthen or unify his personality, but serve to fatally weaken Hakem's divided self, and thus to precipitate his failure.

Notes

1. N. Lukianowicz, "Autoscopic Phenomena," *A.M.A. Arch. Neurol. Psychiat.*, LXXX (1958), pp. 199-220.

2. M. G. S. Hodgson, "Duruz," in: *Encyclopedia of Islam*, III, 2nd ed. (1974), pp. 631-634. Nerval's source, which he mentions (Pl. II, p. 396), was the monumental and still authoritative work of Silvestre de Sacy, *Exposé de la religion des Druzes* (Paris, 1838).

3. M. Canard, "al-Hakim Bi-Amr Allah" in: *Encyclopedia of Islam*, above edition, pp. 76-82.

4. Most of the citations from Nerval are taken from the edition of his works in the Bibliothèque de la Pléiade: Gérard de Nerval, *Œuvres*, t. I (1960), t. II (1961), ed. par Albert Béguin et Jean Richer, Paris. References are given as Pl. I and Pl. II for the two volumes. Works of Nerval cited that are not in this edition will be identified as used. See Brief Bibliography for further information.

5. Lukianowicz, p. 205.

6. R. D. Laing, *The Divided Self* (London, 1961).

7. For a discussion of this syncretic process in relation to feminine archetypes, cf. Georges Poulet, *Trois essais de mythologie romantique* (Paris, 1971).

8. This poem, which is adapted from the German poet Jean-Paul, was published in *Les Chimères* in 1844, three years before Hakem's story.

9. Canard, p. 79.

10. Canard, p. 77; this wave of intolerance included the destruction of the famous Church of the Holy Sepulchre in Jerusalem.

11. Otto Rank, *The Double: A Psychoanalytical Study* (Chapel Hill, 1971); a translation of "Der Doppelgänger" (1914 and 1925).

12. Sigmund Freud discusses the relation of incest and royal status in *Moses and Monotheism* (New York, 1939), pp. 154-155:

> What is reputed to offend our feelings used to be a general custom—one might say, a sacred tradition—in the ruling families of the ancient Egyptians and other peoples. It went without saying that each Pharaoh found his first and foremost wife in his sister. . . . So far we seem to discern that incest—in this case between brother and sister—was a prerogative forbidden to ordinary mortals and reserved for kings who represented the gods on earth.

13. Canard, p. 80. The historical Hakem disappeared while out on a mountaintop overlooking the city. His body was never found, although his clothes pierced with dagger holes were found five days later. It is probable that his sister ordered him killed, although

there are several other plausible theories; no killer was ever found or punished.

Lillian Feder (essay date 1980)

SOURCE: "The Aesthetics of Madness," in *Madness in Literature,* Princeton University Press, 1980, pp. 247-78.

[*In the following excerpt, Feder explicates* Aurélia *as a work depicting madness as a process of self-creation and discovery for Nerval.*]

The Aesthetics of Madness

The extremes of Gérard de Nerval's individual transformation of certain Romantic modes, like Nietzsche's, make his work, especially his prose, anomalous within its literary and historical period. Except for this characteristic, which seems a peculiar modernism, the two writers are utterly different, even in their visionary grandiosity. Despite the narcissistic isolation to which Nietzsche considers himself consigned as the last adherent of instinctual release in a repressive and decadent society, his concept of Dionysiac frenzy is a social one, a reformer's vision. But the madness that Nerval describes as his own experience has little to do with social or psychic reformation; it is an interpretation of the self within the cosmos through dreams and hallucinations. In *Aurélia* [citations from the Société D'Edition D'Enseignement Supérieor edition, 1971], the work in which his madness is his subject, he employs the primitivism, mysticism, and exoticism characteristic of much Romantic literature to develop a metamorphic style that recreates the processes of mental pathology, particularly schizophrenia. Through this fluidity of language, structure, and tone, Nerval depicts the ever-shifting moods, images, feelings, withdrawals, and remarkable sudden insights that constitute the self as he experiences it.

In the first two paragraphs of *Aurélia* (p. 23), Nerval presents his basic material: "dreams" and the "long sickness that took place entirely within the secrets of my soul." Explaining his view of dreams as "a second life," he says that the "first moments of sleep" are an "image of death." In the "hazy numbness" which "seizes our thought" at this time, "we cannot determine the precise moment when the I, under another form, continues the work of existence." The "œuvre" that "le moi" continues in its dream life in *Aurélia* is remarkably similar to what Freud was later to describe as "the dream work," the reversals and condensations of thoughts transformed into images, the distortion of "existence" into apparent absurdities that disclose something of the "mystères" the dreamer approaches.

The hallucinations Nerval recounts are similar in the fluidity of their form and sometimes in contents to his dreams. His symptoms of madness, like his dreams, provide him with the material for a study of the human soul. He does not know, he says, why he refers to his periods of insanity as a "maladie," since he was then physically well, at times even extraordinarily energetic. Furthermore, he seemed, during these periods, "to know everything, to comprehend everything; my imagination supplied me infinite delight," and he wonders whether, "in recovering what men call reason," he has not "to regret having lost" such satisfactions (p. 23). Nerval's account of his madness records his depression and terror as well as times of manic joy, but he makes no distinction between these moods as avenues of discovery, and they are often alternating responses to the continual metamorphoses of his symbolizations.

The soul that Nerval professes to study in *Aurélia* is, of course, his own, but he suggests that his is a paradigm of the self released in dreams and in the hallucinations that he describes as "the overflowing of dream into real life" (p. 28). These states constitute a *"Vita nuova"* (p. 24) and, like Dante, who is one of his models (p. 23), Nerval centers his quest upon an ideal woman who symbolizes the merging of sexual desire, religious purity, and mystical yearnings. But Dante's visions of Beatrice in the *Vita nuova,* his fantasies of his death and hers, his feelings of being confused and possessed by his imaginings, serve Nerval only as allusive extensions in time and space of his own emotional fixations. Actually, the differences between Nerval and this "model" are more important than the similarities. Most crucial is Nerval's almost total divergence from Dante's method of representation, which he explicates (*Vita nuova* xxv) in distinguishing between the nature of affective experience and its reification through the rhetorical devices of metaphor or simile. For Nerval the visions centered around his idealized love are substantial; his method of fusing probable events with fantastic ones, the ancient past with the present and the future, is designed to convey the reality of dreams and hallucinations as superseding the generally accepted limits of time and space.

The question of whether Nerval wrote from memory of his own hallucinatory experience, the accounts of others, his own imaginary reconstructions combined with literary associations, or, as is probable, all three, is actually irrelevant to his method of conveying his accommodation to a continually shifting conception of existence. This he does by depicting fragmentation as a process of self-creation and discovery, which are one in *Aurélia.* Nerval uses his panic, his projections of his desires on beneficent forces and his anger on hostile ones, his paranoia, the splitting of his ego, his grandiosity, and other schizophrenic symptoms as means of communicating his perception and assimilation of experience.

In one hallucination in which "everything changed its form around me," the spirit who had been instructing him is transformed into a youth whom he now teaches. Frightened by his assumption of a dominant role and by his own recurrent Faustian "obscure and dangerous" questioning, the narrator immediately transforms himself into a wanderer in a more placid environment, "a populous, unknown city," in which he discovers a primitive race from the primordial past continuing to maintain its integrity and influence under modern urban conditions. He participates in this merging of past and present by feeling his feet "sinking into successive layers of buildings of different epochs" and by first observing and then being welcomed by and responding affectionately to the "primitive, heavenly family" the archaic race has now become. But these forms soon melt away, leaving only grief and confusion. Having concluded his account of this "vision," Nerval comments, without transition, on the "cataleptic state in which [he] had been for several days" and disparages the "scientific" explanation for it that he was given (pp. 34-37). The sinking feet, the ideal harmonious family, the merging time and shifting forms, the melting faces, the tears shed at "the memory of a lost paradise" are all the "moi" who has withdrawn from a reality that cannot fulfill its cravings or assuage its guilt, an explanation more "logical" than the "scientific" one he rejects.

Another hallucination recreates the world from its beginnings, the narrator struggling with monsters in the "chaos of nature." Even his own body is "as strange as theirs." Within this monstrous combat with nature there appears "a singular harmony" that "reverberates through our solitude," and suddenly the "confused cries, the roaring and hissing" of the primitive creatures assumes "this divine melody." There follow "infinite variations" and "metamorphoses" in the cosmos and in the earth and its inhabitants as they respond to this celestial influence. The miracle, of course, has been performed by a "radiant goddess" (pp. 42-43), one of the many versions of the image of the all-loving mother, the goal in the fragmentation of madness and, paradoxically, the potential source of integration. This image incorporates all the metamorphoses of mood and tone, of scene and episode of which the dreams and hallucinations are composed. No sooner does it appear than its other aspect—the hostile and denying—emerges, producing blood and groaning, years of "captivity" (pp. 44-45), and infinite recurrences of the monstrous in varied metamorphoses of the self. But in the second part of *Aurélia,* this "goddess" appears to the narrator in a dream vision and explains her role: "I am the same as Mary, the same as your mother, the same one whom in every form you have loved. In each of your trials, I have laid aside one of the masks by which I hide my features and soon you will see me as I am" (p. 69).

This moment of illumination occurs in a paradisaical atmosphere, which denies the mundane reality of the insight, and the narrator emerges from the dream with the delusion that he is Napoleon, inspired to accomplish "great things." Incorporating the real world into his delusional system, he believes that everyone in the galleries of the Palais-Royal is staring at him. Although he makes no overt connection, this delusion seems related to those he next alludes to—his "persistent idea that there were no more dead" and that he "had committed a sin" to be discovered by "consulting his memory" which was "that of Napoleon." His delusions grow more grandiose as, installed in an asylum, he imagines that he has the power of a god (pp. 69-70).

From this point on, the narrator almost consciously decides to use his delusions to reestablish a more stable identity. In another asylum, observing the "insane," he understands that "everthing had been an illusion for [him] up to then." Nevertheless, he submits to a "series of trials" which he feels he owes to the goddess Isis (p. 70). These are delusions centered on his own "role" in reestablishing "universal harmony" by Cabbalistic arts and other occult powers (p. 72). The most dreaded of his projections, the "magnetic rays emanating from [himself] or others," can serve as means not only of domination but of communication with all of the created universe (p. 73). He emerges from a hallucination of decapitation and dismemberment—which he himself recognizes as symbols of fragmentation (p. 77)—to offer friendship to another patient with whom he feels "united" by "a certain magnetism" (p. 78).

Near the end of *Aurélia,* the narrator asks himself if it is possible to "dominate his sensations instead of submitting to them, . . . to master this fascinating and terrible chimera, to impose order on these spirits of the night which play with our reason." His answer lies in discovering the meaning of his dreams and in the "link between the external and the internal worlds." He is now convinced of his own immortality and of the "coexistence of all the people [he] has loved" (p. 84). Through Nerval's very method of narration, in which a few factual details serve to link dream, hallucination, and delusion, he creates "le moi" he seeks in every image, every idealized figure, every fantastic episode, and every metamorphosis that represents what Freud calls "unconscious mental acts." The timelessness of the unconscious becomes for the narrator of *Aurélia* evidence of his own immortality and the continuous existence of those he loves. Through condensation, displacement, and reversal, he fuses elements of his fragmented identity, investing conflicting feelings in symbols of eternal unification, a fragile defense against the "void," the image of "nothingness" (p. 74) that he fears may be the definition of his own soul.

Bettina L. Knapp (essay date 1980)

SOURCE: "Angelique" and "Sylvie," in *Gérard de Nerval: The Mystic's Dilemma*, University of Alabama Press, 1980, pp. 203-11; 211-25

[*In the following excerpt, Knapp interprets the myths that Nerval created in* Angelique *and* Sylvie, *relating them to Nerval's own psychological states.*]

> *Love that moves the sun and the other stars . . .*
> Dante, *Divine Comedy, Paradise.*

The Daughters of Fire,[1] a remarkable work, includes a veritable metaphysics of fire, which takes on mythical and philosophical ramifications. The heroines of the tales in this volume—Angélique, Sylvie, Octavie, Isis, Corilla, Emilie—are all fire spirits, descendants of "that cursed race."

Fire is associated with solar symbolism and heroes: Helios or Phoebus Apollo; the worshippers of Mithra who looked upon the Sun as a conqueror: *Sol Invictus.* Because of the sun's daily rise and fall, it came to represent death and resurrection of the hero—the eternal repetition of life. The sun is a heroic force, synonymous with vital heat, creative energy, and a guide to man in his daily ventures. Heraclitus considered it a "mediator" between the created and the uncreated.[2] Its energy (both spiritual and animal) makes it a catalyzing force capable of "transmuting" people and things, melting metals and chemicals. Paracelsus drew an analogy between fire and life, both of them elements being necessary for growth and production.

Being so powerful and aggressive, and an illuminating principle connected with intelligence, the sun has been endowed with masculine qualities. Its positive attributes include growth, fecundation, vital heat, and the like. But it can also burn, blind, scorch, and cause sterility. Empedocles felt this dichotomy so acutely that he could no longer bear the conflict and threw himself into Mt. Etna.

For Nerval, fire meant heroism and suffering. Prometheus, Cain, Adoniram, Tubal-Cain—all had helped mankind bring in new attitudes, and all, therefore, had been compelled to suffer the fate of the hero who acts against the status quo, against God. Such creative types are so blinded by the fire within them that they overlook the dangers involved in accomplishing their goals; they are determined to brave the rigid circumscribed world. But in so doing, they earn the wrath of the forces they seek to annihilate and are tormented. Their reward, if any, will come to them only in some remote future.

The suffering heroes with whom Nerval identified may be looked upon as fallen angels. Eblis, according to

Mohammedan tradition, represents evil; he is a fallen angel who refused to adore Adam as God had commanded. Eblis argued that since he and his friends had been formed from fire and not from a lesser material, earth, as Adam was, they would not be subservient to him. The Persian poet Esfahani expressed the idea as follows: "Fire, which is the origin of nature and of Ibba's pride, will be the instrument of his punishment."[3]

Prometheus, Cain, Tubal-Cain, Adoniram, Sheba, Eblis, Lucifer[4]—all belonged to the "red race" and were doomed to eternal martyrdom for having been "light bringers"—for having refused to adhere to certain fixed and immutable laws promulgated by God in his attempt, they believed, to enslave man.

The Illuminists, such as Martinès de Pasqually, had written at length about these fire beings, that is, those responsible for the discovery of the molten metals that saved man from virtual annihilation after the flood. Romantic poets such as Byron, de Vigny, and Hugo identified with Cain and Prometheus and viewed themselves as Messiah types, as inventors of new literary credoes and techniques—and as victims of society's callous attitudes. Nerval, more than the others, bore the mark of Cain because his suffering had been more intense than theirs: he had been incarcerated and they had not; he had not won the admiration nor achieved their popularity. Nerval, like Cain, was prepared to endure his agony. He was truly of the "red race," and to prove his lineage he merely had to point to his name: "Labrunie," which means "the one who seizes thunder," and the word "*brunnir*, "*brennen*," to burn, indicating the presence of the dynamic fire principle.[5]

Angélique

Nerval chose the name Angélique for the heroine of his story very deliberately.[6] The semidivine "angels," composed of fire, water, or both, and "divinely harmonized," were looked upon as agents capable of encompassing both celestial and earthly spheres—messengers (as the word "*angelos*" in Greek and "*malakh*," the Hebrew word, indicate). Angels are of all types: destroyers (II Samuel, 24, 16); interpreters of God's message (Job, 32, 23), protectors as in Exodus, prognosticators as described in the Gospels. Angels may assume any form, according to their particular function.[7]

Angélique is a messenger, the harbinger of a new way. Like her illustrious predecessors, the fire-people, she braves conventions and, because of her rebellious spirit, must suffer the punishment meted out to transgressors. Because she is pure in heart and irreproachably honest, Angélique may be used by the others to their advantage—bringing destruction both upon herself and those surrounding her.

Nerval's *Angélique* is a quest, an odyssey with mythic grandeur. It is a search for the treasure hard to attain— a symbolical expression of an inner drama, a numinous or sacred experience. Nerval may have chosen the mythic form because, in a sense, it "takes" man back to past times, which then become part of present reality. Fabulous and miraculous adventures may be integrated into the world of actuality. The teller of the myth divests himself of chronological time and lives in a "transfigured" realm, surrounded by supernatural beings or peoples. Myths may also "solidify" beliefs previously considered incredible, or they may justify new situations.[8]

Nerval declared in his preface that he had "seized the series of all of his anterior existences"; that "it was no more difficult for me to consider myself to have been a prince, a king, a magus, a genie and even God."[9] *Angélique* might thus be the vehicle that permitted him to fuse a mythological and limitless past with his mortal existence. In so doing, he became part of an eternal life cycle.

Because a myth narrates an original or religious experience—because, that is, it "relates back to the past" or to some nebulous precognitive realm—Nerval could use such a literary device as a stepping-stone toward the discovery of what he considered to be his own fabulous origins. Was he not the descendant of Nerva? Was his secret name not Roma?

A longing to establish oneself in some time long past reveals an intense dissatisfaction with present conditions. Yet a return (or a regression) into a spaceless and timeless mythical past may constellate new ideas and principles, and may even pave the way for a new orientation *if* such a retreat is fully understood. Nerval's *regressus ad uterum,* as delineated in *Angélique,* so autobiographical a tale, may be looked upon as a symptom of his urgent need to reimmerse himself in the "waters of life," in the "earth's womb," and so to free himself from guilt and sin.

Nerval's myth takes us on a quest for a book. He is looking for a volume that describes the exploits of a historical figure, the abbé Bucquoy. He first explores the libraries in Frankfurt and then pursues his labors in the libraries and book shops of Paris and the Valois region. Clues appear in each episode; digressions and asides associated with the abbé are inserted at regular intervals, enlarging the story's dimensions. Finally, Nerval discovers a volume in the Compiègne library describing the life of one Angélique de Longueval, the abbé's grandaunt, and he sets out for Paris coincidentally on the day that this town commemorates the dead. Nerval looks upon this solemn occasion with awe, and upon his walk with the village folk as a pilgrimage in respect to the memory of Angélique, whose life he now begins to narrate.

Myths are filled with special objects, even sacred ones—*hierophanies,* that their heroes are forever retrieving either from the hands of enemies or from loss: the Chalice in the Grail Legend, the word that must be recovered in Masonic mysteries, the philosopher's stone in alchemy. The volume relating the life of the abbé Bucquoy is a hierophany; it enables Nerval to make forays into the past, to revive a world long since dead— and to write a work of art.

Secrecy is usually attendant upon a quest. As Goethe wrote: "A very deep meaning lies in that notion, that a man in search of buried treasure must work in utter silence; [that he] must speak not a word, whatever appearance, either terrific or delightful, may present itself."[10] For philosophical reasons, Nerval made excellent use of secrecy in his narration, but secrecy also served to enhance the literary values, to intensify the suspense, and to increase the pace and excitement of his tale.

Nerval's quest begins in a world he knows well: the cerebral realm of the library, the written world— specifically, the Arsenal in Paris, with all its wonderful memories for Nerval. This had been the home of one of the finest story tellers of them all, Charles Nodier, and here Nerval had often met his friends Gautier, Balzac, Dumas, Lamartine, Musset, and others. Now, like so many phantoms from the past, these figures would intrude upon his present: in *Angélique,* each time Nerval describes a library he visits, or its entourage, he associates his friends with historical or literary figures, linking specific incidents to objective situations—and thus making use of another myth-making device.

Nerval surely identified with Angélique, the daughter of a wealthy nobleman. Her character coincided with his in so many ways. She was angelic, pure in heart, a victim of injustice; she was also a dreamer who dwelled in another world, frequently in the dominion of death.

> Ever since the age of thirteen, Angélique de Longueval, whose character was sad and dreamy, neither enjoyed, as she said, costly precious stones, beautiful tapestries, nor beautiful clothes; she aspired only for death to cure her spirit.[11]

As the story progresses, Nerval's identification grows more intense. When he tells of the love the young man bore for Angélique (and who because of his passion had been so cruelly murdered by her father's orders), he talks of the excoriating pain experienced by the one left behind: "The tearing apart which she experienced with this death revealed her love."[12] Angélique first knew love in relation to a loss.[13] Before his death she had been unaware of the meaning of affection and, like Adam and Eve, had been living in a paradisiac state; after his demise, which we may equate with Adam and Eve's fall into matter, she began her worldly existence.

The letter Angélique's suitor wrote her before being killed was premonitory—a warning such as that found in many myths. He described his passion for her in terms of contrasting colors: dawn, light, circle of darkness, shadow—always underscoring an essential duality, the great separation in store for them. The color symbolism also implied that he would be the victim of some overpowering force—some black and evil principle—that would make him incapable of breaking out of the circle of doom into the clarity of celestial spheres. Other dichotomies are also implicit in the letter: the impact of a spiritual and ethereal love based on illumination (golden hues) and the dark forces of his instinctual self (the more sombre and lugubrious tonalities).[14]

Angélique, like Nerval, associated her love with death. Unlike Nerval, after two years of mourning, she found a substitute to "take the place of this eternally dead being."[15] Another young man in her father's employ, La Corbinière, develops a passion for her. After innumerable trysts, Angélique flees with him, but not without taking some of her parents' silverware to ensure their immediate financial security. The couple goes to Italy, where La Corbinière joins the army, on to Germany, and then back to Italy. In the course of all this, La Corbinière begins leading a dissolute life. The silverware money is soon spent and both he and Angélique are reduced to penury. After much suffering, he dies. Angélique returns to France to live out her life in solitude and poverty.

Some authors, Nerval wrote, "cannot invent without identifying with their imaginary characters" to such an extent that their lives are sometimes fashioned upon one's own; their "ambitions" and "loves" become the author's.[16] The same can be said of Nerval in his Angélique tale—not the actual events that were experienced, but the manner in which they were lived, and the make-up of the protagonist's personality and temperament.

More important, perhaps, were the autobiographical events that Nerval wove into this subjective tale. To commemorate the pain that Angélique had experienced during her lifetime (and, by association, Nerval's own pain), he set out on a pilgrimage, together with the people on the day reserved to commemorate the dead. As he began, he felt as if he were entering consecrated territory, penetrating a mystery, a secret *rite de passage*. Each person, tree, lake, house, event, the scenery itself, took on a mystical aura and was transformed into a series of hierophanies.[17]

Pilgrimages link one's own past with that of another. Both Nerval and Angélique would be merged in the fluidity of time, and Nerval would succeed in abolishing the present temporal reality.

To enter an atemporal (or mythological) realm is to lose one's own individuality, at least temporarily. Such a journey can be accomplished through a double-memory technique (objective and subjective), which Nerval uses with felicity. The objective memory, when recounting Angélique's life, is used to recall or examine specific historical dates and personal reminiscences. The subjective memory filters through the subliminal realms, recreating anterior existences and, concomitantly, the feelings, sensations, and ideations appropriate to the eras involved. To be capable of reentering the past, as Nerval had done in this tale, is to master a formidable weapon. It gives one the ability to reshape one's life, divest oneself of the negative Karma that had predominated until this moment.[18] Nerval had always felt himself to be the victim of some negative astral or divine force that was bent upon destroying him, and he longed, therefore, to reenter time and to recast his life.

Nerval's return to the past via the double-memory technique required a sacrifice: the loss of his identity. According to Plato, waters from the fountain of Lethe were given to each person before he was reborn and returned to earth. Proper use of one's memory implies the recollection of ideas that have been forgotten—of transpersonal and eternal truths that were lost through "forgetfulness" before one's birth.[19] One's subjective memory was designed to restore, as best it could, the experiences of past existences that had been washed away before one's "return" to earth. To discover one's past, Plato intimated, was to experience one's previous life. Accordingly, Nerval questioned the meaning of "imagination" at the very outset of his story. "To invent, really is to remember," Nerval wrote, quoting both Plato and Pythagoras.

Nerval achieved his goal. He recaptured the use of his subjective memory when walking through the melancholy autumnal landscape, which he continually personified and termed "the most beautiful and the saddest."[20] He was again in the land of his ancestors. In this almost transparent atmosphere of foggy climes, reddish hues, and denuded trees, which he compared to the colors that the Flemish painters splashed onto their canvases, he felt a certain *reverie*. Through his return to the past, to his ancestors, he gathered new strength. "I feel strengthened on this maternal soil."[21]

Through *Angélique* Nerval was able to create a veritable cult out of *reverie* or *souvenir*.

> Whatever one may have to say philosophically speaking, we are bound to the earth by many bonds. One does not carry the ashes of one's ancestors on the soles of one's shoes, and the poorest guardian

recalls a sacred souvenir which brings to mind those who loved him. Religion or philosophy, everything proves to man the importance of the eternal cult of souvenir.[22]

As Nerval walked further into the country, other associations came to mind with an ever-increasing circular effect. The countryside echoed the Watteau painting *The Embarkation for Cythera,* with its fragile delineations, its medley of delicate harmonies. As peasants came into view, Nerval stopped and listened to their chatter. He was receptive to the musicality of their language, their rhythms and intonations. They spoke, he observed, as their ancestors had spoken centuries earlier. Their language had remained untouched by outside influences and each word was uncontaminated and "rose to heaven as does the song of a skylark."[23] It was as if time had stopped and Nerval were entering still further the remote regions of the myth.

It is no wonder that Nerval was moved by this visual and aural spectacle. Scholars such as Richer have pointed out that ***Angélique*** was constructed in the manner of a concerto with its prelude, its main and secondary themes, each winding in and out of the piece, a first movement.[24] Nerval had always loved ancient ballads, the lyrical stanzas that the bards and troubadours of France had sung in medieval times and during the Renaissance—songs commemorating a variety of occasions: a wife complaining of her husband's infidelities, a beautiful shepherdess fending off a nobleman, a nun lamenting her vocation, a knight riding to meet his lady love—political songs, weaving songs, satirical verse.[25] Nerval knew the songs of William of Poitiers (1071-1127), Jaufre Rudel (1147), Bernard de Ventadour (1150-1170). He had made a study of certain songs of the Valois region, which he published in magazines and included in ***The Daughters of Fire.***

Music not only had a hypnotic effect upon Nerval, but acted as a stimulant to his subjective memory. When he listened to the peasant boys and girls singing their village songs, sections of his past were reintegrated into the present; "a melody with which I had been cradled" emerged before him.[26] More than ever, he realized how precious his childhood had been—the few days spent with his Uncle Boucher at Mortefontaine before his father had intruded upon his existence and taken him back to Paris. And there were the wonderful but all-too-short summer vacations. Now, all those he had loved were dead—as was his youth. "The souvenirs of childhood revivify when one has reached the half-way mark in life. It's like a palimpsest the lines of which one is able to bring to view with certain chemical procedures."[27]

The visual image came into sharper focus now. Nerval saw the little peasant girls dancing about so merrily and it was as if he were witnessing a magical ritual—

like Shiva creating the world through his dancing; like some divine spirits emanating from the world beyond. The girls were like hieroglyphics weaving arabesques in outer space. They became potent factors in his mind—constellating sacred powers, forces that succeeded in conjuring up time past. They were no longer individual little girls, but had taken on mythical proportions; they had been depersonalized, transformed into archetypal figures.

Like Angélique these maidens must have been made of both water and fire—they too had the power of angels, of restoring chunks of past life into present reality. Their dance, like those of the Greek girls Nerval had seen on one of his trips, took on circular patterns, created serpentine effects, encouraged a hypnotic reverie—enabling him to wander still further back into the past.[28]

Nerval's associations grew firmer, more detailed. They centered around a mystery play he had seen as a child. He recalled a particular scene: Christ's descent into hell. A beautiful blond girl had starred in the play. She was dressed in white, with pearls interwoven in her hair, a nimbus surrounding her head; she held a golden sword.[29]

Nerval's objective memory had aroused his subjective faculty of recall by moving from the immediate object (the young girls) to an incident he had experienced before (the mystery play). In unifying these dual memory functions, he encouraged an even more remote past to emerge; the historical time in which the medieval mystery play had been written and Christ's era.[30] To these two epochs was added the image of the ideal female principle: the blond girl dressed in white, associated with the Virgin Mary or with Sophia (the representative of divine wisdom).

Christ's descent into hell is of particular interest in these scenes as it may be equated with two other journeys into the underworld: that of Orpheus when he tried to claim his beautiful Eurydice, and that of Osiris when he retired to the underworld after his dismemberment.

By associating Christ and Orpheus (and Osiris) with his own descent into the past, Nerval was in effect experiencing an *imitatio dei,* a desire to return to the primordial unity, the center of the "Earth's Umbilicus," the self or the beginning. To reenter the *axis mundi,* where opposites no longer exist, a timeless and spaceless area, is to identify with the eternal and universal principle—with God. Aristotle called this central point that of the "unmoved mover" because it is at the center that creation starts and extends outward, frequently in circular fashion. In most mythologies, the cardinal points emerge or are born from the center. (In many cathedrals and temples, the altars are placed in the center.) Nerval's desire to reach the focal point, the center of his problem, indicates an obsessive desire to relive his life. To experience the center necessitates a *rite de passage* that enables the initiate to go from the transitory to the eternal, from the profane to the sacred, from life to death.

Nerval's fusion with his personal (subjective reminiscences) and collective (historical, Angélique) past, using the Abbé Bucquoy as the vehicle for his quest, lends further credence to his own need to escape from his present condition, to his desire to regress into some past existence or anterior world.

Angélique has been considered Nerval's double. She slipped through life from misfortune to misfortune, always buoyed by her dreams and reveries. While she represents the negative, shadowy side of Nerval, the little girls with their freshness, vigor and spontaneity, stand for his positive attributes. They also represent the collective image of life as it bursts into song and dance—as it burgeons each spring and fecundates the earth, when all avenues are open, all possibilities still available.

Angélique, an archetypal image, represents a fire principle—that of the young girl who loves too naïvely, too blindly, and whose life is consumed by these very forces. Because she lacked wisdom and insight—that burning force within her, which scorched rather than illuminated—she was forced to suffer and live in exile until her husband's death, and then in penury in her own land. Yet, because of the beauty of her passion, she succeeded in living life thoroughly, fully, totally, not as a superficial joyride but as a *rite de passage,* enabling her eventually to earn rebirth in another domain—that of the myth.

. . . . .

He is not disquieted by the moon that he sees every night, till it comes bodily to him, sleeping or waking, draws near and charms him with silent movements, or fascinates him with the evil or sweetness of its touch. He does not retain from this the visual representation, say, of the wandering orb of light, or of a demonic being that somehow belongs to it, but at first he has in him only the dynamic, stirring image of the moon's effect, streaming through his body. Out of this the image of the moon personally achieving the effect only gradually emerges. Only now, that is to say, does the memory of the unknown that is nightly taken into his being begin to kindle and take shape as the doer and bringer of the effect. Thus it makes possible the transformation of the unknown into an object, a He or a She out of a Thou that could not originally be experienced, but simply suffered.

Martin Buber, *I and Thou.*

Sylvie, one of the most exquisite prose works in French literature, is considered by men of letters a superb example of French "clarity of expression." Paradoxically, it was written at a time when Nerval was a victim of schizophrenia.[1] Its language is limpid, musical, and delicate; its images, which serve to delineate individual protagonists and situate events, also encourage Nerval's optical meanderings, which frequently take on circular or cyclical contours.

Sylvie is a myth because the experiences revealed in it are both personal (they depict events experienced by Nerval during the walking trips he had been permitted to take to the Valois region while in and out of rest homes) and transcendental because they are associated with events and people in his own "fabulous" and remote past—when he was a child in Ermenonville, Loisy, Châalis, and Senlis. In the early years of primitive times, life seemed beautiful and was filled with infinite possibilities; each time he returned to it—either through the dream or reveries—he felt refreshed, renewed, cleansed. It was as if he had undergone a baptism, a purification ceremony.

Because the narrator felt reborn with each foray into the past—particularly the early ones—*Sylvie* may be looked upon as a creation myth. When dwelling upon his youth, he experienced an obliteration of chronological time and a resurgence of cyclical or sacred time. Past events became contemporaneous, lending a sense of eternity to the narrative. The entire scene assumes extratemporal dimensions, since it is no longer subject to the ravages of chronological time. The protagonists who make up the narrator's world, endowed with almost prehuman or superhuman personality traits, assume mythical grandeur and enjoy divine powers: the ability to appear and disappear in the story, as had the goddesses of old. Because they are such fleeting forces, they remain mysterious, evanescent, intangible, and abstract. Their power over the narrator is immeasurable.

At the outset of the tale, the narrator lives in Paris and goes to the theatre nightly to admire from afar his beloved stage star Aurélie, whom he has not yet met. One evening, after a performance, the narrator thumbs through a newspaper and notices an article concerning a celebration to be held at Loisy, a district not far from Paris where he had spent his childhood. A whole series of impressions invades his conscious mind: his entire life passes in review before him. The creation myth takes root as he plunges back to the past: he is a young lad at Loisy and in love with Sylvie, a beautiful country girl with black eyes, regular features, and a most ingratiating and outgoing personality. He sees himself dancing a round on a beautiful lawn in front of a castle dating from the time of Henri IV of France. The rules of the dance oblige him to kiss Adrienne, the girl who finds herself in the inner circle with him. As her "golden hair brushed against his cheek,"[2] he is overcome with feelings of a "strange uneasiness." He listens to Adrienne sing an old French romance, then places a crown of laurel leaves on her head and kisses her, while Sylvie's eyes brim with tears.

Some years later, the narrator returns to Loisy for the celebration of another national holiday. He renews his friendship with Sylvie and with her brother, and learns that Adrienne has become a nun. As they walk in the woods, chatting and reminiscing, they experience a revival of times past.

On another occasion, the narrator and Sylvie visit her Aunt Othys. They disguise themselves (as children often do) in the aunt's wedding dress and her husband's uniform—a visualization of their unconscious desires.

Now older, the narrator experiences conflicting sensations. He ponders his relationship with Sylvie. She is good for him, he reasons; she represents earthiness, health, and life. But he cannot forget that celestial vision of Adrienne, which returns to haunt him. Nor can he obliterate the image of Aurélie, the actress. The three female images blur in his mind, and he wishes desperately that they were one. Conflict and indecisiveness have entered his life. He is no longer living in a carefree child's world—in an Eden-like paradise.

In Paris, he meets Aurélie, writes a play for her, then tours with her and her troupe in the Valois region. When he tells her of his feelings for Adrienne, she realizes that he is not in love with her. She marries the manager of her troupe, who offers her love with a workable relationship. When the narrator sees Sylvie again he knows now that for her own well-being she must live in the world of reality, even though he cannot. She marries a hard-working young man, Le Grand Frisé. The narrator learns that Adrienne had died many years earlier, in 1832, when in the convent.

The narrator, who had attempted to recreate himself by returning to his origins, is aware of his failure to achieve his goal, but he cannot adjust to the world of reality in which he is forced to live. He opts for escape in travel.

The three female protagonists around whom Nerval's tale focuses—Aurélie, Sylvie, and Adrienne—are all archetypal figures, aspects of the Eternal Feminine or the Great Mother. The narrator's goal is to unify what is divided, to create one person out of the three, to incorporate the characteristics and qualities of each in the others, thus creating a complete or total being who for him represents the ideal.

If such a *coniunctio* were possible, the narrator could render the infinite finite, the abstract concrete. In his perpetual attempt to create unity, he is bringing forth a prismatic world, forever seeing aspects of Adrienne in Sylvie, Adrienne in Aurélie, differentiating still further what he seeks to bind together. Only in a state of reverie or dream can he reshuffle his emotions and coalesce the three women.

Aurélie, Sylvie, and Adrienne—three deities—are not fecundating forces for the narrator because he experiences their powers as an observer: he is a sterile receiver, not an activator. The forces these deities arouse within his psyche serve only to stir his feelings, but never sufficiently to make him act overtly; so he slips in and out of their lives as he does his own reverie. Nothing has changed in his situation—except that at the end he realizes the impossibility of changing three into one and thus of changing his own life's course.

Because the three female figures are archetypal they take on eternal significance—enter the realm of the divine. Aurélie, Adrienne, and Sylvie are representatives of the triunal aspects of the Magna Mater as viewed in Venus in her celestial, terrestrial and infernal manifestations; in the Moon goddess called Selene during the full moon; Artemis with the waxing moon and Hecate when the moon is dark; in the Virgin Mary as saint (the mother of Christ), in her earthly guise as the mother of the other children she had by Joseph; as sinner in Mary the Harlot.

1. Aurélie

Venus (Infernal): Hecate (Dark Moon): Mary the Harlot (Sinner)

Because Aurélie is an actress and represents the world of illusion, which glows only when artificially lit, she stands for Venus in her infernal aspects. Like Venus, she has the power to lure men to her fold, to compel them to fall victim to her power, to incorporate them into her since she is a deity, a transpersonal force. She is an infernal Venus such as had been worshipped in ancient Assyria and Babylonia: goddesses of sensual love and immorality. In Eastern lands such women became sacred prostitutes, consecrating their bodies to the earthly representatives of certain deities.[3]

The narrator is obsessed with his vision of Aurélie and "indifferent" to everything except for this "one well known apparition which illuminated the empty space, infused life with one breath and one word, into those faces which surrounded me."[4] She embodies his ideal and because she injects life into him, he believes her to be a creative force in his life. In reality, he responds passively to her—as a votary before a goddess. He worships her from afar.

> I felt myself living in her and she lived for me alone. Her smile filled me with infinite beatitude; the vibration of her voice, so tender and yet whose timber was strong, made me shudder with joy and love. She possessed, for me, all the perfections, she answered all my bursts of enthusiasm, all my

caprices, beautiful like the day when illuminated by the stage lights which shone on her from below, pale like the night, when the stage lights were dimmed, letting the rays from the chandelier above shine on her, showing her in a more natural manner, glittering in the shadow from her beauty alone, like the Divine Hours, with a star on their forehead, sculptured on the brown background of the frescoes at Herculaneum![5]

The Divine Hours to which Nerval referred were goddesses, in the service of Venus, representing time: years, hours, minutes, seconds—all united and linking all generations together. By associating Aurélie with these Divine Hours, he infuses her with an eternal quality (cyclical time) and since they are in Venus' employ, with love. By adding the city of Herculaneum to the image, he gives historical credence to what was merely a fantasy before and, by the same token, endows Aurélie with a real, ideal, and eternal existence—thereby fixing time. But Herculaneum has its negative side. It was destroyed by volcanic eruption—and the narrator's vision of perfection in Aurélie could also be shattered. To prevent such an outcome, he refrains from approaching her, and signs the notes he hides in the bouquets he sends her, "from a stranger."

Ideals—such as his vision of Aurélie—cannot remain potent forces in terrestrial relationships; they cannot be nurtured on earthly contact. Since Nerval's ideals are anima figures, they feed in unconscious and dark realms; the light of consciousness causes them to vanish, to shrivel: "It's an image that I am pursuing, nothing more."[6] The narrator stays aloof. He avoids coming into contact with Aurélie, rationalizing "that actresses were not women," that "nature had forgotten to give them a heart," that they were cold, elusive, beautiful, unfeeling, hypnotic in their ways. Unconsciously, he must feel that familiarity breeds contempt.

> Love, alas! vague forms, rose and blue hues, metaphysical phantoms! Seen from close, the real woman would revolt our ingenuity; she had to appear as queen or goddess, and under no circumstances should one approach her.[7]

To contact Aurélie would be to demythify her by humanizing her. Distance is essential for worship. Perfection incarnate exists only as an abstraction, a creation of the mind; it can be kept alive only when experienced in some remote realm—illuminated on stage by an artificial light, functioning as an illusion, wearing a mask. Yet the fear of losing or destroying the image he has of her comes into sharper focus: "I was afraid of troubling the magic mirror which reflected her image."[8] To stare as he had at Aurélie or at a "magic mirror" (or any mirror at all) is to become narcissistic, and this limits any kind of development and leads to death. Gazing into one's own reflection is comparable to an incarceration; it is a fixing, immobilizing agent. If his idealization of Aurélie is not in some way altered, it will not only remain unproductive but will become an agent of self-destruction.

Because of the way Aurélie is illuminated on stage and comes to life only at night in the creation of a world of illusion, she is comparable to the moon goddess Hecate in her blackened phase.

By worshipping the moon, as the narrator does through Aurélie, he is returning to a matriarchal social structure, to even more remote periods in the world, antedating patriarchal sun worship. The "unseen powers of the spirit world," as manifested in the moon's "mysterious qualities," held the narrator spellbound, lulled him into unconsciousness and perhaps even death.[9] So long as he remained in the theatre, he stated, he was happy; the minute he left and his image vanished, he was invaded with melancholy, "the bitter sadness which remains after the disappearance of a dream."[10]

Only at night, in the darkened realms, did the narrator come to life. The Hecate aspect of the night deity, the goddess of the darkened moon who reigned over the lower world, tantalizes the narrator. In ancient times she was worshipped as a goddess of ghosts and magic; she haunted crossways and graves, accompanied the dogs of the Styx and the shadow of departed specters. Aurélie, in her "glorious" and "terrible" aspects—her "nonhuman" way of life—mesmerized the narrator,[11] and engendered beauty, mystery, and excitement within his psyche.

Because she is a representative of infernal love, the passion she inspires is dark, Hecate-like, mysterious, frightening, and perhaps even fatal. Like Hecate, Aurélie causes confusion, chaos.[12] The epithet *phosphorous* has been associated with Hecate, who is frequently pictured as carrying a torch. She is a "light bringer," not of purification but of consciousness.[13]

The light illuminating her on stage brings out her sensuality, her volatile nature; it shimmers, underlining an erotic and passionate side. In this respect, Aurélie may be likened to Mary the Harlot (or Mary the Egyptian) before her redemption.

Mary the Harlot represented the infernal side of this triunal figure, the debauched individual who remained so until her conversion. This "infernal" Mary prostituted her way to the Holy Land, and then lived as an anchorite in the desert. Along with Mary Magdalene, this infernal Virgin is frequently depicted in sculptures and paintings as black. In Einsiedeln, Switzerland, the black Virgin "stands on the moon" and works miracles for cripples and invalids. In Chartres, the statue of the Black Virgin bears a dark face. At Notre Dame de la Recourance (Orléans), the statue of the Black Virgin, highly prized, is supposed to possess great powers.[14] Aurélie also shines "in the shadow of her beauty alone"—and returns to darkness, as does the moon, when not lighted by some external force.

When the narrator listens to her recite Schiller's verses, he is enraptured by the "sublime" manner in which she brings them to life. He sends her a note, then leaves for Germany. He wants this image to remain with him eternally: "That's something fixed for the future." To alter his relationship with her would be to personalize it and to bring it down to earth, to debase his love by putting her on a footing with other "vulgar ones."[15]

When the narrator returns to Paris, she agrees to act in his play; then he goes on tour with Aurélie and her troupe, and the ideals begin to slip as the world of reality takes possession of him. The narrator invites her to lunch at the castle of the "white queen," and as she rides over the fields in her riding habit, her blond hair floats in the wind, reminding him of "a queen of yesteryear," a goddess. Even the peasants stop, astounded, and look at her. He takes her to the place where he had first seen Adrienne, and tells her of his love for this beautiful girl. Aurélie understands, and says, "You don't love me! You are waiting for me to tell you that the actress is the same person as the nun; you are searching for a drama and the ending escapes you . . ."[16] Dismayed, he questions: "Then it wasn't love after all?"

The illusion has vanished. The attempted fusion of Aurélie (the symbol of all that is infernal, dark, and sinful) and Adrienne (the world of the spirit) cannot take place in the domain of reality. Now Aurélie flows out of narrator's life back to some remote past, some fabulous era—a fantasmagoria.

2. Adrienne

Venus (Celestial), Moon Goddess Selene (Full Moon), Virgin Mary (Saint)

Adrienne is the most elusive and haunting figure in **Sylvie**. She may be linked to Venus in her celestial aspects and called "the Heavenly" one who represented pure and idealistic love. Many temples to honor her were built on mountains and citadels in Greece and Asia Minor. As a goddess and celestial figure, she inspired mystery and awe, which rendered her even more captivating than Aurélie with whom he could come into contact at will.

Adrienne is first described dancing around with the little girls from the ancient province of Valois. The reddened stone façade, the pointed slate-covered roof, the varied carvings on the castle that stood at the far side of the lawn—all injected an outer-worldly atmosphere onto the scene. Adrienne began singing as "the

setting sun pierced through the leaves with its flaming rays" and he heard an ancient French romance which filled him with "melancholia and love."[17]

The coloring and hues used by Nerval to describe Adrienne attest to her spirituality and purity: "heavenly" blends of pastel tones, blond curls, the whiteness of her skin and countenance. All these stand in sharp contrast wih the surrounding tonalities. And because of these hues, she is associated with one of the triunal aspects of the moon goddess, Selene, who was worshipped in East Asia and Syria, as a celestial figure depicted in subdued light. She was a beautiful woman with long wings who wore a golden diadem. When her great love, Endymion, died, Zeus bestowed on him eternal youth, which could only be experienced in a sleeping state. It was believed that Selene came down from the heavens nightly to embrace her beloved in his grotto.

Adrienne also possessed spiritual and reflective qualities. As she began her song, the moon became visible in the distance, its diaphanous and ethereal hues invaded the entire scene, "the shadow descended along the great trees and the moon light thus being born shed itself on her alone, isolated from our circle. . . ." It was as if her "divine" essence were being illuminated, all blending so exquisitely with the beauty of her song, the stillness of the evening, and the intensity of the emotion she had aroused in the narrator. The narrator, believing himself to be "in paradise," kissed Adrienne, as was the custom, and she became a "sacred" object for him.[18]

Adrienne was the same type of evanescent human being as the Vestal Virgins of old who performed their religious rituals in natural surroundings, exuding spirituality and implanted in a diaphanous setting: the grass "was covered with condensation which gave off feeble vapors which unrolled their white flakes on the tips of the grass. . . ." It was as if all the elements—the universe united—had come into play in this image: water, fire, earth, air.

As the image comes into sharper focus, Adrienne represents the celestial aspects of the Virgin Mary: the mother of Christ, the heavenly, saintly, immaculate and perfect side of the triunal great mother archetype. She is surrounded with "the shining leaves on her blond hair dazzling when illuminated by the pale rays of the moon. . . ."[19] Like many statues, paintings, and descriptions of the celestial Venus, Selene and the Virgin Mary, Adrienne's face was bathed in an ethereal and spiritual light. A halo encircled her head—not brilliant or brash, but "pale," representing the internal or reflective qualities in a human being. Because of the dreamy atmosphere, the narrator considers her to be semidivine—like Dante's Beatrice—a soul in all of its beauty and purity.

The fusion of Adrienne as a moon deity and as the celestial Virgin Mary is even more apparent when recalling the sculptures in medieval art, when the Virgin Mary was featured "enthroned" on the moon and called by Catholic church fathers "The Moon of the Church, or Moon, the Spiritual Moon, the Perfect and Eternal Moon."[20] As Adrienne stood on the lawn singing her ancient romance, the rays of the moon filtered through the surrounding trees and shrubs, lighting up her countenance, infusing it with a mysterious power.

In antiquity the moon goddess, believed to be the "actual fire of the moon," was depicted carrying a torch and wearing a moon crescent. The festival of candles (or torches), celebrated in her honor in pagan times on August 15, was carried into Christian tradition to mark the day the Virgin Mary ascended to heaven, "when the course of her earthly life was run" and she "assumed in body and in soul to heavenly glory." (This belief became doctrine by papal decree in 1950.)

Some years later the narrator returns to Valois region and learns that Adrienne had become a nun. He goes to Châalis, a town with monuments dating from the Renaissance. With Sylvie's brother, he enters an ancient abbey and watches a medieval mystery play that depicts Christ's descent into Hell. Adrienne suddenly appears to him in the role of the Virgin Mary.

> A spirit was rising from the abyss, holding a flaming sword in its hand calling the others to come and admire the glory of Christ vanquisher of Hades. This spirit was Adrienne transfigured by her costume, as she already had been by her vocation. The golden colored cardboard nimbus which surrounded her angelic head appeared to us quite naturally a circle of light: her voice had increased in force and in dimension.[21]

After the performance, the narrator and Sylvie's brother go to the guardhouse where they see an ancient coat of arms on the door: a swan with outspread wings.[22] The swan, an animal close to the narrator's heart, is known to sing out his beautiful song just before he is to die.[23] An ominous tone seems to be injected into the narrative at this juncture—a premonition of death.

But Adrienne was already dead to him; she had become a nun and departed from the world of the living to enter the realm of God. His image of her singing on the lawn as a young girl had not grown dim; on the contrary, it became more powerful in his mind's eye in an idealized and divine form. Her portrayal of the Virgin Mary seemed, therefore, to corroborate his own inner feelings: she had really entered the world of the divine—as a swan she had eclipsed herself from his life.

The narrator is told only at the end of the tale that Adrienne had died in 1832 at the convent of Saint S. . . .[24] Death, however, was not an end to life for the narrator and was considered merely as a temporary change. According to certain ancient sects, including the Pythagoreans, the dead went to the moon for three nights (when the moon was not visible). On the fourth night, when the moon could again be seen, it was believed that the individuals who had departed from the earth had been reborn in light and in joy. Pythagoras spoke of the "Isle of the Blessed," a celestial plane located on the sun, the moon and the Milky Way. Plutarch believed that after death the spirit went to the sun; the body remained in the earth and the soul was purified in the moon. It is understandable that the narrator associated the divine Adrienne with the celestial aspects of the moon.

Throughout the tale the narrator attempted to unify what had been severed, to fuse the celestial and infernal aspects—Adrienne, Aurélie. Aurélie, who held the narrator's attention nightly was a theatrical performer: an entertainer, a seductress, a sinner, a Mary the Harlot type, an incarnation of the sensual Venus (infernal) of the Hecate Moon figure. Men succumbed to this type of woman, to her wiles; Zagreus, Pentheus, Orpheus had all, passively, bowed to her ways.

Yet the memory of the celestial Adrienne invaded his very being—"the flower of night as it emerges, pink and rose phantom slipping onto the green grass half bathed in white vapors."[25] He could think only of her.

Unable to capture what was evanescent, to unite what was divided, the narrator's feelings forever oscillate. Aurélie incorporates his being. "I felt myself live in her."[26] Then he recalls Adrienne as she sang, as she entertained, and perhaps, they were one and the same person: saint and sinner. "To love a nun under the guise of an actress. . . . It's enough to drive one insane!"[27]

Mythologically, the narrator's desire to incorporate the differentiated aspects of the Magna Mater archetype is perfectly valid but can only happen in a nondifferentiated realm—either in the unconscious, in the cosmic pleroma, in death, or in the religious cult. During these moments, each aspect inhabits the other; just as the maiden becomes the future woman and the woman once again the maiden, the two become one. In the Eleusinian mysteries, the initiate celebrated and worshipped Demeter as both girl and woman—and in this very unification the mystery was buried.[28] It was neither unusual nor contradictory to unite opposites in ancient religious and philosophical thought. The moon goddess promoted fertility but she also destroyed life. In Christian tradition, God in Christ cannot be both good and evil, fertile and destructive. He is one or the other. The other then is either the Devil or the Anti-Christ. Moon worshippers expressed the duality of their divinity in terms of the brightness or darkness of the moon: the full or celestial moon was interpreted as spreading goodness; the smaller the crescent, the greater the dimness and darkness in the heavens and, therefore, the possibility of evil.[29]

As the narrator attempts to fuse the saint and sinner in his tale, his visualizations grow increasingly mysterious, blurred. What he seeks cannot exist in the clear, rational, differentiated world of reality. Only in his dream could the memories of Adrienne and Aurélie coalesce; then, engulfed by their presences, he sensed "a fatal attraction toward the unknown, like the firefly escaping into the rushes on stagnant waters. . . . "[30]

3. Sylvie

Venus (Earthly), Moon Goddess Artemis (Waxing Moon), Virgin Mary (Terrestrial).

Sylvie is the only feminine figure with whom the narrator establishes a direct and relatively continuous relationship. She represents all that is normal, healthy, beautiful, fresh, pleasant, and natural.

Sylvie stands for the earthly Venus, as manifested in ancient times in her appearance in groves, gardens, spring time; she is fructifying and creative. Sylvie belongs to the country; she is in harmony with nature and featured always in pastoral scenes.

Because Sylvie is described as the most "beautiful" girl at Loisy, "good and pure in heart," she may be likened to Artemis and to the Virgin Mary. Artemis was a fertilizing force; she helped seeds to germinate, plants to grow, affected tides, and was instrumental in the evolution of plants and animals. She was also looked upon as the luminous god of the day. She is portrayed as a huntress chasing wild animals; a joyful maiden dancing, bathing with her friends; she is revered as a virgin goddess, instrumental in the healthy development of childbirth, though not necessarily marriage. Like the terrestrial Virgin Mary—the mother who gave birth to her other children with Joseph—Sylvie too will become a mother and wife at the end of the tale. That Sylvie may be associated with the virgin goddess Artemis as well as with the Virgin Mary becomes clear when analyzing the word *parthenos* associated with the great moon goddesses of antiquity. *Parthenos,* in ancient times, meant "unmarried," but not necessarily chaste as it came to mean with regard to Mary. When Isaiah wrote "and a virgin shall be with child" he meant simply that an unmarried woman would give birth.[31] The virgin goddesses of antiquity differed from the Christian Mary in that the latter had been chaste when giving birth to her firstborn; the other children she bore with Joseph in a natural manner.[31]

Because she is an earth principle and represents the human side of Venus, the moon, and the Virgin Mary,

Sylvie stands for balance and relatedness—the wife, maiden, and mother archetype all in one. She was a positive force for the narrator because she brought him down to earth, focusing, orienting and stabilizing him as best she could. She possessed everything he lacked.[32]

Sylvie also comes to represent chronological, irreversible time. When the narrator focuses his attention on Loisy and Sylvie, he asks himself: "What time is it?"[33] and wonders what she is doing at this very moment. Though he has no watch, he looks at a rococo clock wih the figures of time encrusted on it and with "the historical Diana" leaning on her stag and "depicted in bas relief under the face of the clock."[34] By associating mythological time (Diana-Artemis) with chronological time (the clock), he injects eternity as well as earthbound aspects into his image.

Time plays an important part in this tale with respect to Sylvie, as it had with Aurélie (when he noticed the Divine Hours depicted on the frescoes of Herculaneum).[35] When young and enjoying Sylvie's company at Loisy, he had no notion of time; it was as meaningless as it had been for primitive man. Youth stands for activity, growth, and futurity; it cannot be viewed objectively. Only with age, when distinctions came into existence (past, present, future) does the narrator become aware of the destructive nature of time and equate it with loss of youth and death. When the narrator looks back at his adolescent years, he realizes that time is his arch enemy, propelling the days, seasons, years. Only by plunging back into his youth (through the dream or reverie) can he avoid the negative time factor.

Both cosmic and historical time are brought in during the national holiday celebrated in the "land of old families," in "castles lost in the forest," domains hidden from civilization. In part, the festivities consist in crossing a small pond that takes the guests onto a tiny island on which an unfinished temple stands, once dedicated to Urania, the muse of astronomy represented with a globe and compass. As a representative of the cosmic world (astronomy, astrology) she gives orientation and focus to her ideations by means of the globe and compass, making order out of chaos. The maidens, as they frolicked on this tiny island, reminded the narrator of beautiful Greek girls celebrating their festivities centuries back. The entire scene is likened to Watteau's painting *Embarking for Cythera,* the island on which Venus had once been worshipped and where Francesco Colonna experienced beatitude with his love. The image is not flawless: modern times intrude in the form of the up-to-date clothes worn by the guests. Once again he realizes that he is unable to experience either complete reimmersion in the past or perfection in reality.

Before and during the feast, "toward the last rays of the sun,"[36] the narrator notices a change in Sylvie: she is more seductive, more irresistible than his last image of her. Her smile has transformed her into a Greek statue: the symmetry of her features has become exquisite, her hands, delicate and white, "worthy of antique art" and "during the night hour" she becomes even more captivating and enchanting.[37] The narrator and Sylvie chat of their "childhood souvenirs," which, with the lapse of time, have become sacred to them; the past has been transformed into a hierophany. As their reverie deepens, so nature descriptions acquire new dimensions, uniting in their imagination both celestial and earthly spheres: images of trees that reach up toward heaven and bury their roots deeply into the ground follow; "their shadows are cast" on the waters, and such seemingly disparate forces as sky and earth are linked.[38]

During the festivities, a wild swan, hidden in a basket under the garlands and crowns of flowers, flies forth toward the "dying sun" and in its flight displaces the garlands that the guests grab for themselves. The narrator avails himself of one, places it on Sylvie's head, kisses her as he had Adrienne so many years before, obliterating in her mind the pain he had caused her as a child.

In Adrienne's case, the swan image had been associated with death. With Sylvie, it represents womanliness—and a union of opposites or, for the alchemist, the hermaphrodite. The swan's body is female in its rounded contours but its elongated neck, associated with the phallus, symbolizes the male. The fact that Nerval's swan flies toward the sun, dropping the garlands of flowers on it way, stresses the dual aspect of the image—man (earth) and spirit (as it rises upward and drops the floral or female components that fall to earth, thereby returning them to mother nature).

In Wagner's *Lohengrin* (1846-48), the knight of the Holy Grail is led by a swan to rescue the Princess Elsa of Brabant, whom he marries. Upon learning of her violation of a pledge (she was not supposed to ask him his name or details of his life) he departs on the back of the swan to the Grail castle forever. The implication of the Wagnerian motif is that it is best to remain aloof from others, best to refrain from delving too deeply into relationships, because if one does so, love vanishes. To become intimate is to kill love, an emotion that is enhanced by distance and imagination.

The image of the swan as a composite of opposites and as used in *Lohengrin* may be a visualization of the course of the narrator's relationship with Sylvie.

Because of the narrator's desperate need to unite what is disparate, Adrienne's image intrudes upon certain scenes. When he walks through the country drenched in Rousseau-like atmosphere, he approaches a convent where he thinks Adrienne may have lived: "the moon hid from time to time behind the clouds, hardly lighting the dark grey rocks." These rocks, dating from Roman times, lend a sense of mystery to the atmosphere; they are also mirrorlike, reflecting a vague, clouded vision of ancient periods. As the narrator walks, his conscious mind is focused on Sylvie, yet he is invaded with Adrienne's presence. Both Sylvie and Adrienne seem to come to life in the spectacle of nature before him. He lies down on the grass, attempts to take in the entire cosmos in his embrace, falls asleep and reawakens the following morning to the sound of church bells. He is tempted to climb the convent wall before his departure but refrains from doing so because he feels it would be a "profanation" of Adrienne's image. The word *profanation* implies that Adrienne is a goddess; to approach divinity would be to demythify her and render her powerless.

Sylvie's earth-bound nature becomes all the more evident with the passing of years. Yet some quality remaining within her infuses her with extratemporal characteristics. She is a maker of fine lace now, and as she worked with agility a "divine smile" seemed to radiate from her face, elevating her; she is not a remote deity but an earthly and breathtakingly beautiful goddess. Later, as the two walk through the forests and meadows, listening to the birds, the sound of the flowing water, the entire vision is impregnated with flowers, trees and grass—a fitting background for this maiden, who draws her real strength from the ground.

Water images, used throughout the tale, link and unify what is disparate. The water is always "calm," describing most succinctly the soothing nature of Sylvie's attitude toward life; when walking, "the reflections of heaven cast their shadows on the waters," indicating the narrator's desire to encapsulate the world through her. He says: "I saw the distant ponds etched out like mirrors on a foggy plain." This suggests the muddiness and ambiguity of the narrator's attitude toward life, his constant dissatisfaction with the world of reality in its differentiated form. A puddle "formed a little lake in the middle of gladiolas and irises"—underscoring the fluid, mysterious and dreamy aspect of his relationship with Sylvie, as well as its terrestrial side.[39]

Without water, life could not exist. It is a creative element, just as Botticcelli's painting *The Birth of Venus Emerging from the Waters* depicted it. The flowing, calm and serene waters in the early sections of *Sylvie* are transformed little by little into dead or stagnant waters, or coexist, as in the following image.

> The Thève flowed to our left, leaving at its bends eddies of stagnant water where yellow and white lilies grew, where, daisies like the frail embroidery of starfish burst forth. The fields were covered with bundles and stacks of hay, the odor of which went

to my head without making me drunk, as the fresh odor of the woods and thickets with flowery thorns had formerly.[40]

The stagnant waters in which the lilies grow symbolize the narrator's narcissism, his desire to fix things and to prevent any kind of change, his longing to live permanently in a world of beauty, idealism, abstraction. The immobility of this image is present in the very motility of waters: its continuous metamorphosis, its ceaseless activity. Its transitory nature is endless and, therefore, eternal. The lilies that have grown from the depths of these waters represent a fertile and positive force, but they also usher in moods of melancholia because they are rooted in dead waters—notions that have never evolved.[41] Yet even narcissistic meditation and obsessions may have their positive results: they may produce a work of art (flowers)—in the narrator's case, the story itself. The piles of wheat in the distance also have value: they nourish and activate, and they indicate life's desire to cope with the forces that may hamper it. Wheat, as the "staff of life," encourages earth-bound nature to grow and pursue its course. Wheat suggests Sylvie, the earth-being; the stagnant waters, the narrator or poet. They are poles apart at this juncture, and it is fitting that he now realize Sylvie no longer loves him.

Sylvie, who has entered womanhood, is no longer satisfied with the tenuous, imaginative, poetic world that the narrator offers her. She must have more tangible things: a husband, children. She affirms life. When he realizes that he has been rejected from her world, he throws himself at her feet. "I confessed while weeping." He promises to change his ways. Just "Save me" he pleads. But both know that for Sylvie to enter the narrator's domain would be as fatal as for him to become part of her world.[42]

When the narrator learns that Sylvie is to marry another childhood friend, the hard-working down-to-earth Grand Frisé, who is to become a baker, the Sylvie he had once idealized as Artemis, as the earthly Venus, as the sublime Virgin, is transformed into the prosaic country bourgeoise. "Illusions fall, one after another, like the skin from fruit and the fruit, is experience. Its taste is bitter, yet there is a bitterness about it which strengthens."[43]

The narrator's pain is lessened when he remembers that her husband-to-be was his *frère de lait;* in a remote way they are related, so he is still bound to Sylvie. More important, Le Grand Frisé, who once saved him from drowning when he was a young boy, represents the steady, heroic force in life: the swimmer, the conqueror of the elements. By marrying Sylvie, he prevents another death—hers, which would have been inevitable if she had married the narrator.

Later, the narrator understands the meaning of his "lost star" of the loves he had experienced when a youth "which glistened with double power . . . two halves of a single love." Adrienne was the "sublime ideal," and Sylvie, the "tender reality."[44]

The love the narrator felt for the three feminine deities in their triunal aspects—Adrienne, Aurélie, Sylvie—is a deep-seated death wish. By projecting onto them so continuously he had become completely passive, seldom reacting overtly in any way—rarely, except in the case of Sylvie, establishing any relationship with them. He experienced their force as a votary, a sacrificial agent. Unlike the aggressive heroes he so admired—Prometheus, Cain, Tubal-Cain, Adoniram—the narrator's sacrifice was in vain. He found no true love and could never concretize his ideal vision because he was himself incapable of loving either of the three protagonists as they were, on their terms. He could only love those characteristics he projected on to them, those aspects of himself or those he saw in them at certain periods in his life. As such, "they became a function of his own psyche,"[45] and when they could not conform to his standard, he experienced dejection and alienation. He was forever imprisoning Adrienne, Sylvie, and Aurélie in his own limited vision of them, viewing them always in terms of himself.[46] Because he was unaware of what was happening to him, he was incapable of judging, analyzing, or assessing their personalities objectively. He was dominated by his own inner world and what it saw in the three archetypal figures involved. No mediating function between the image he had of the three young girls and reality ever emerged. Only further disparity between the ideal and the real could possibly ensue—and with it, increased tendencies toward self-destruction or emotional castration.[47]

Rosanna Warren (essay date 1983)

SOURCE: "The 'Last Madness' of Gérard de Nerval," *The Georgia Review,* Vol. XXXVII, No. 1, Spring, 1983, pp. 131-38.

[*In the following essay, Warren surveys prominent themes and images in Nerval's poetry and fiction.*]

When Gérard de Nerval hanged himself on the night of 25 January 1855 in Rue de la Vieille Lanterne, a sordid Parisian alley, he inscribed himself into an already hackneyed romantic mythology which mingles poetry with death in a peculiar eros. In life he had already demonstrated himself picturesquely mad, walking his pet lobster on a blue ribbon in the park of the Palais-Royal; his death by hanging from the Queen of Sheba's garter (an old apron string), was more fantastic still. His contemporaries were not slow to respond to the event. In that year Gustave Doré created his famous lithograph depicting the slightly paunchy poet dangling from a grille fence while his female soul, of Rubenesque proportions, leans lovingly over him; a trumpet-playing skeleton pulls her up out of the shadows into what appears to be a cataract of heavenly ladies in negligé whooshing from a Gothic cathedral. So Nerval entered the ranks of the romantically insane, the martyrs to art. Years later, it was this stereotypical image of the poet that the young Mallarmé exorcised in "Le Guignon," in which the romantic poets, after a life of insult and torment, "ridiculously hang themselves from lamp posts." And it was as a charming madman that Nerval appealed to the sentimentality of André Breton, Paul Eluard, and other twentieth-century Surrealists enamored of the unconscious.

Nerval was a mystic, and a learned one, although he dreaded rather than encouraged his fits of madness. Yet it was not only the romanticization of his insanity and death that obscured the real nature of his work for so long. For one thing, his close friends in writing of him tended to pass over the horror of his crises as well as the courage and clarity with which he made them into art. In *L'Histoire du Romantisme,* the poet Théophile Gautier, Nerval's friend from schooldays and a veteran with him of the 1830 theater battles over Victor Hugo's *Hernani,* depicts only the charm of his comrade's divagations. Alexandre Dumas, the novelist and playwright, also a close friend of Nerval, is similarly delicate in treating his insanity. In these affectionate writings Nerval appears as a sort of angelic and witty will-o'-the-wisp, but not, certainly, as the enduring poet and prose-writer he has turned out to be-in the words of Marcel Proust, "surely one of the three or four great writers of the nineteenth century."[1]

A later barrier to appreciation of Nerval's worth took the form, curiously enough, of misplaced appreciation. It required his kindred spirit Proust to point this out more than half a century after his death. For if Nerval was noted at all by critics after Sainte-Beuve had called him the traveling salesman between Munich and Paris, it was as the prose restorer of traditional French qualities of balance and moderation, notably in the story *Sylvie.* Such a characterization not only ignored the poetic achievement of his sonnets, *Les Chimères,* but distorted the nature of his fiction, which, as Proust showed, was so far from being a demonstration of rationality that it depended for its very method on an intrinsic madness. Proust called *Sylvie* "the dream of a dream," and it was precisely its intense subjectivity and its bizarre narrative transitions incited by memory and obsession that so appealed to him.[2]

The modern reader finds still another barrier in much twentieth-century criticism of Nerval. In looking up the sources of that mysterious poem **"El Desdichado"** (a fragment of which found its way into *The Waste Land*), one is plunged into a stew of occult erudition which includes Apuleius, alchemy, the mysteries of Eleusis, the Rosicrucians, Freemasonry, Pythagorean mysticism, eighteenth-century Illuminists, the Tarot, and Swedenborg. Although most of this information is eventually useful in understanding Nerval's myth-making, it provides only the beginning, not the conclusion, of the investigation. All too often his devotees only manage to present him as a crazed packrat of esoteric lore.

Who, then, is Gérard de Nerval? The question leads into the heart of his work. Baptized Gérard Labrunie, he used pseudonyms obsessively, writing as "Lord Pilgrim," "Ex," "Cadet Roussel," and others until settling in 1844 on "de Nerval" from a property of his uncle's. Across his own portrait by Nadar he scrawled, *"Je suis l'autre"* (I am the other). His attempt to define a self beyond the bounds of space and time animates the entire *oeuvre,* in drama, fiction, poetry, and journalism, and leads as well to a nightmare doubling of identity as the finite, "real" self opposes the infinite longings of the spirit. Nerval uses a doubled self, often personified, as in the novella *Aurélia,* as the *doppelgänger,* to explore the boundaries of conscious and unconscious life and to evolve poetic and fictional techniques that seem to dissolve time and space. In so doing he places himself, as heir to Rousseau, in the main line of the Romantic enterprise, but of all his contemporaries of the heyday of French Romanticism of 1830, he survives not as a period piece but as a peculiarly modern artist.

The modernity pertains as much to the use of the unconscious as a theme as to the literary techniques devised to register it. Nerval remained lucid to an extraordinary degree during his attacks and felt it his duty to transcribe these journeys to the land of the dead, as he regarded his crises. Again and again the myth of the Descent to Hell recurs in his work, as in **"El Desdichado" ("The Disinherited")**, which concludes with the Orphic poet singing a woman of dangerously double nature:

> *Et j'ai deux fois vainqueur traversé l'Achéron*
> *Modulant tour à tour sur la lyre d'Orphée*
> *Les soupirs de la sainte et les cris de la fée.*

> (And twice, triumphant, I crossed Acheron:
> modulating in turn on the Orphean lyre
> the sighs of the saint and the fairy's wild cry.)

But the most poignant expression of the Descent to Hell appears in *Aurélia,* his last work, whose epigraph is "Eurydice! Eurydice!" Nerval's *Vita Nuova,* it is both an account of madness and a spiritual diary, begun just after his first breakdown in 1841, continued in 1853 as the attacks intensified, and finished in 1854. Part I came out in "La Revue de Paris," 1 January 1855, just before Nerval's death; Part II was published post-humously from uncorrected proofs apparently found on his corpse. In those last years he lived wretchedly in and out of clinics, and yet it is from that feverish period that his major works date: *Voyage en Orient* coming out in its definitive version in 1851; *Lorely, Souvenirs d'Allemagne, Les Nuits d'Octobre, Les Illuminés, La Bohème galante,* and *Contes et facéties*—all in 1852; and, finally, the monuments of *Les Filles du Feu* (stories), *Les Chimères* (poems), and *Aurélia.* It was also in this period that Nerval met another version of his Orphic self, a poor, mad soldier in the clinic who, when asked why he would not eat, replied, "It's because I'm dead. I was buried in such and such a cemetery, at such and such a place . . ."— "And where do you think you are now?" Gérard asked him.—"In Purgatory. I'm working out my expiation."[3]

Aurélia unites two dominant themes of Nerval's work: the Orphic descent and the pursuit of the Eternal Feminine—a figure he idealized in various works as Aurélia (a name taken from stories of his adored E. T. A. Hoffmann, another artist of the Double). Aurélia is a composite of his mother, dead in his infancy; the Baroness Sophie Dawes, whose image haunted his childhood and who died shortly before his first breakdown; and the actress Jenny Colon, dead in 1842. The madness described in *Aurélia* is an attempt to transcend his temporal identity in order to join the spirits of the beloved dead, but from another level of detachment the narrator observes his own visionary labor as it proceeds through memories, dreams, and hallucinations. So Nerval appears as a "doubled" figure in the very structure of his work: "If I did not feel that the mission of a writer is to analyze sincerely what he feels in the most serious circumstances of life, and if I were not setting myself a goal I consider useful, I would stop here, and wouldn't attempt to describe what I went on to experience in a series of visions, perhaps mad, or vulgarly morbid . . ." (p. 16).

For Nerval, as for Proust's narrator, true perception requires a dissolution of the normal logics of time and identity. Only then can the fundamental patterns within experience be revealed. It is significant that most of his protagonists are wanderers whose watches have stopped and who are propelled only by their own psychic fluctuations. Memory and dream, then, because they permit that double transcendence (of sequential time and of the ego-bound identity), function as laboratories of the spirit. In their radically disordering capacity they are paradigms of death. And a ritual death is required, in Nerval's conception, both for the reintegration of the individual soul into the world soul,[4] and for the creation of a work of art. Hence, all through his work there is a strong attraction to death, often personified as a seductive woman (as in the story . . ."Octavie")— particularly after the literal death of Jenny Colon in 1842.

For Nerval, the reality underlying the world of contingency and appearance is an order both spiritual and

outside of time, and it is in that order that his protagonists try to move. In the preface to the third edition of his translation of Goethe's *Faust* he writes, "It would be consoling to think that nothing dies which has struck the human intelligence, and that eternity preserves in its breast a kind of universal history, visible to the eye of the soul, a divine synchronicity which would allow us someday to share in the knowledge of him who sees all future and all past in a single glance."[5] And it is in *Faust,* which he translated at eighteen and for which Goethe complimented him, that he found already dramatized the themes of transcendence of time and the pursuit of the Eternal Feminine (Helen), as well as the Descent to the Underworld, which he would make his own and live out so tragically in trying to possess Jenny as Faust tries to possess Helen.

In Nerval's work, as in Proust's, memory presides over the soul's voyages, a memory both personal and collective. In the **"Letter to Dumas"** introducing *Les Filles du Feu,* Nerval writes, "To invent is, ultimately, to re-remember. . . ."[6] His characters, delving into their own childhoods, are brought back by geographical, musical, genealogical, and etymological clues into pre-Christian Antiquity, both Druidic and classical, and experience the past as a living and present force. Concurrently, the world perceived as spirit entails a constant transmigration of souls, so that the type is always visible behind the particular. Just as Orpheus and Dante, voyagers to Hell, stand in shadowy lineaments behind the crazed soldier in *Aurélia,* so the merged figures of Isis, Venus, and the Virgin Mary stand behind Aurélia; Aurélia and Adrienne of the story *Sylvie;* the queens and saints of the sonnets; and the actress, the Bohemian girl, and Octavie of **"Octavie."** As the Great Goddess herself says, when she appears to Gérard in a dream in *Aurélia:* "I am the same as Mary, the same as your mother, the same as you have always loved, under all forms . . ." (p. 90). Each story, therefore, becomes a structure of mirroring identities.

These identities migrate not only within the frame of each tale or poem, but throughout Nerval's whole *oeuvre.* The same types keep reappearing in different incarnations; the sonnets can be read as glosses of the stories, and vice versa. But where the flux of identities becomes terrifying is in Nerval's own conception of himself; the fanciful pseudonymic games lead eventually to *Aurélia,* in which the narrator is haunted by a mystic double who appears at times as a hostile usurper, at times a guide and brother. In the **"Letter to Dumas"** . . ., Nerval tries to explain another, but related, form of what is in essence radical self-doubt: the process of imaginative identification with a fictional character. Here the prose enacts the process of doubling by "doubling" a rhetorical image. In the first section, written in the author's voice, Nerval tells how a writer can "incarnate himself within his imaginative hero" so that he "burns with the factitious flames of his ambitions and his loves." The middle section is written in the voice of the fictional hero in whom Nerval-author is thus smoldering. The hero is an actor, playing the part of Nero—a role, he says, "that identified itself with me, and Nero's tunic stuck to my scorching limbs like the centaur's cloak which devoured the dying Hercules" (p. 28). Author and character are united in the flame of fictitious identification, in the introduction to a book which is itself defined by fire, *Les Filles du Feu* (*The Daughters of Fire*).

Nerval's Faustian attempts to surpass a selfhood contained in space and time take form, in his fiction, as challenges to conventions and genre, plot, and sustained illusion. Travelogues shade unexpectedly into romances, journalism into novellas, novellas into confessions and letters. The confusion of modes results partly from the pressure of debts which forced Nerval to compose hastily for piecemeal publication, but in a much more significant sense it derives from his refusal to accept boundaries, in literary form as well as in life, and from his desire to break through the surface of conventionally perceived reality to the Spirit World beyond. The story **"Angélique,"** for instance, purports not to be a work of fiction at all but an account of scholarly research. The narrator—invoking Diderot, Sterne, Swift, Rabelais, and the supposedly original Homer—leads us on a scramble through historical documents and wild fantasies, involving us somewhat in the adventures of the maiden Angélique but more in the adventure of composition itself.

These dramas of illusion and disillusion, peculiarly modern in their attention to the act of fiction-making, call for a great range of style, from bald narration of facts to the most impassioned and lyrical outcries, with elegant flicks of the pen all along the way. Action follows hard upon action; time is continually disrupted by flashbacks, detours, authorial reflections, and prefigurations. Within any particular frame of time, actions erupt mysteriously into the text and disappear without explanation after a single sentence. It is a poetic and elliptical juxtaposition of images that is at work here, not the discursive linking of events the fictional form has led us to expect. Both structure and style are designed to annihilate time.

Reality and hallucination melt together terrifyingly, as in the scene in *Aurélia* in which the narrator, who has been conversing with a star, is picked up by the night watch and spends the night on an army cot hovering between two worlds as short phrases like "lying on an army cot" hover between extravagant passages of supernatural description. Nerval's visions are potent because one very observant eye never loses sight of *this* world. The Bohemian girl who appears in **"Octavie"** is a poor little seamstress *and* Isis; as for Aurélia, the star both of theater and sky, Nerval acknowledges, "What madness, I told myself, to love a woman pla-

tonically who doesn't love you. My reading is to blame for this: I took the poets' inventions seriously, and made myself up a Laura or a Beatrice out of an ordinary little person of our century . . ." (p. 17).

Proust later defined Nerval's madness as essentially literary. In *Aurélia,* the narrator asserts, "However it may be, I believe the human imagination has invented nothing that isn't true, in this world or in others, and I could not doubt what I had *seen* so distinctly" (p. 50). He had a Keatsian faith in the imagination, refusing to distinguish not only genre from genre but his life from his creations. Of Nerval it can truly be said that his biography lies in his works. Finally, it appears, his visions overtook him, and he could no longer contain himself in his mortal time and body. But through the disorder and suffering he remained faithful to his vocation, and it was only in his third month out of the sanatorium, when he was wandering from one flophouse room to another and his poverty and sense of abandonment grew so great that he could no longer write, that he succumbed to the temptation to join his mother and his various long-dead loves. For all his fantastic scrambling of identities, he essentially knew himself, as the letter to Dumas reveals, just a year before his death: "The last madness I'll persist in is believing myself a poet."[7] Not only his sonnets, but his stories as well, have proved him right.

Notes

[1] À propos du style de Flaubert," in *Contre Sainte-Beuve* (Paris: Gallimard, 1971), p. 596.

[2] Such close affinities link Proust to Nerval that it seems the first paragraph of *Aurélia* could almost have opened *Combray*: "Dreaming is a second life. . . . The first moments of sleep are the very image of death: a nebulous torpor seizes our thought, and we can't determine the exact moment in which the 'I', transformed, continues the work of existence. . . ." Both Marcel and Gérard suffer a strange metempsychosis as they hover between sleep and waking. It is not hard to see why Proust felt compelled to come to terms with Nerval's "excessive subjectivity" in his *Contre Sainte-Beuve,* that embryonic version of *À la recherche du temps perdu.* He sees Nerval's as an essentially literary madness, an intensification of the writer's explorations in dream, memory, and personal sensation. Proust, so disposed to that same research, was driven to define Nerval's case and distance him so that he could place his own exceedingly subjective fictional character Marcel within the corrective context of the social and dramatic world of the novel. The essay is a fascinating exorcism.

[3] Gérard de Nerval, *Aurélia* (Paris: Le Divan, 1928), p. 117.

[4] Nerval studied occult initiation rites for years: Free Mason, Rosicrucian, the rites of Isis, the Mysteries of

Eleusis . . . One of his principal sources was the *Traité de la Réintégration des Êtres* by the Illuminist Martines de Pasqually, who had founded the order of the Elues Coëns. The *Traité* was circulating in manuscript during Nerval's lifetime and was introduced to him by a friend, but it was not published until 1899.

[5] Quoted by Jean Richer, *Gérard de Nerval et les doctrines ésotériques* (Paris: Editions Griffon d'Or, 1947), p. 163.

[6] Gérard de Nerval, *Les Filles du Feu* (Paris: Garnier Flammarion, 1965), p. 21.

[7] I am responsible for all quotations translated in the introductory essay. As far as I know, English translations of the "Letter to Dumas" and "Octavie" have not been available to contemporary readers until now, although Geoffrey Wagner's excellent *Gérard de Nerval: Selected Writings* (Ann Arbor: Univ. of Michigan Press, 1970) contains many of the other works mentioned here: "Sylvie" and "Émilie" from *Les Filles du Feu,* as well as *Aurélia* and some selected poems.

John W. Kneller (essay date 1986)

SOURCE: "Nerval's 'Artemis,' " in *Textual Analysis: Some Readers Reading,* edited by Mary Ann Caws, The Modern Language Association of America, 1986, pp. 26-32.

[In the following essay, Kneller studies the language, imagery, and literary devices used in "Artemis."]

The approaches to *Les chimères* of Gérard de Nerval have followed rather than anticipated the successive stages of literary criticism in France, Great Britian, and the United States. In brief, they have been extrinsic, intrinsic, and structural. For current purposes, extrinsic method will be synonymous with projection; intrinsic procedure will also go by the name of explication or commentary; and structural system will include not only structuralism but also semiotics and theories of reading.

After the thunderous silence of late nineteenth- and early twentieth-century Lansonian literary historians, who hardly mentioned Nerval in their manuals, practitioners of extrinsic methods prevailed after World War II and took two different courses. Some applied techniques of other fields, such as psychiatry, biography, astrology, and alchemy. Others attempted to use texts or parts of texts as a means of obtaining access to obscure parts of the poet's life. The first group, in their procrustean determination to make the evidence fit the theory, often stretched the text to death or cut off its head and feet. The second, by resolving a word, phrase, or sentence into an antecedent person, object, or event, fell into the genetic fallacy.

In the fifties, following the centennial of Nerval's death, intrinsic approaches took over and summoned their practitioners to eschew genetic, affective, intentional, and historical fallacies, to affirm the interiority of the text, and to illuminate its meaning and form. Projection was clearly put to rout by explication and structuralism. In 1960, I characterized **"El Desdichado"** as "a coherent, unified statement of an experience. . . . {It} is complete in itself; it contains its own meaning" ["The Poet and His Moira: 'El Desdichado,' " *PMLA* 75]. Three years later, studying the same sonnet, Albert S. Gérard wrote: "le poème, pour être valable, doit contenir une signification perceptible sans références excessives à autre chose qu'à lui-même" ["Images, structure et thèmes dans 'El Desdichado,' " *Modern Language Review* 58 (1963)]. Eight years after the 1963 study by Jakobson and Lévi-Strauss of Baudelaire's "Les chats," Jacques Geninasca, inspired by Jakobson, published his *Analyse structurale des "Chimères" de Nerval.* For Geninasca, analyzing a text meant dismantling its system to expose its literary devices, while respecting the specific character of its poetic language and symbolic thought. His ultimate goal was to arrive at the author's total system through the properties of literary discourse uncovered in the process. Thanks to him and to other structuralists and semioticians, it was no longer necessary to plead for the validity and value of detailed poetic analysis.

Today everyone treats projection with the neglect it deserves. Two generations of Americans schooled in the methodology of the New Criticism and many more generations of French reared on explications de texte have seen to that. Some Nervalists now prefer structural approaches; others continue to practice explication. When most successful, the former have shown that it is possible to be systematic without being totally scientific, and the latter have demonstrated their ability to be interpretive without being utterly intuitive. All, let us presume, would agree that no one can really appreciate a work of art without understanding its form and its matter. For my part, I am willing to be called eclectic. Like explicators and semioticians, I am swayed most of all by the imperatives of the text itself, but I would insist that these imperatives include not only careful analysis of each word or symbol but a respect for the order in which they were written.

Since **"Artémis,"** like the other sonnets of *Les chimères,* is a coherent, ordered statement, I shall try to elucidate its words, images, and devices in the order set forth by the poet. Beginning with the circumstances surrounding its publication, I propose to discuss the title and then take the poem from top to bottom, the way it was written.

Artémis

> La Treizième revient . . . C'est encore la
>   première;

Et c'est toujours la seule,—ou c'est le
  seul moment:
Car es-tu reine, o toi! la première ou dernière?
Es-tu roi, toi le seul ou le dernier amant? . . .

Aimez qui vous aima du berceau dans la bière;
Celle que j'aimai seul m'aime encore tendrement:
C'est la mort—ou la morte . . . O délice! o
  tourment!
La rose qu'elle tient, c'est la *Rose trémière*.

Sainte napolitaine aux mains pleines de feux,
Rose au coeur violet, fleur de sainte Gudule:
As-tu trouvé ta croix dans le désert des cieux?

Roses blanches, tombez! vous insultez nos
  dieux:
Tombez fantômes blanches de votre ciel qui
  brûle:
—La sainte de l'abîme est plus sainte à
  mes yeux.

"Artémis" was first published, with other sonnets, in *Les filles du feu,* in 1854, while the poet was still alive. Although the manuscript of this version has not come to light, the text, as it appeared, was undoubtedly reviewed by Nerval and is therefore definitive.

The original title of *Aurélia* was *Artémis ou le rêve et la vie.* This datum not only invites us to link the sonnet with the récit but also eliminates any remote possibility that "Artémis" could be an invented masculine form of "Artémise." True, the speaker of **"El Desdichado"** thinks of himself as a widower ("Je suis le ténébreux, le veuf . . ."). True, the gloss "olim mausole" appears in the margin of the Eluard manuscript next to the word "veuf" of that sonnet. But even if El Desdichado's widowerhood could be compared, mutatis mutandis, to that of Artemisia—the widow of Mausoleus, in whose memory she erected the mausoleum of Halicarnassus, one of the seven wonders of the ancient world—there can be no question about the sex of Artemis or Aurelia. This Artemis is an avatar of the moon deity, a new being whose identity and essential qualities are determined not by classical antiquity but by the sonnet that bears her name. She is "La Treizième" and "la première" of the first line; "la seule" of the second; "la première ou dernière" of the third. She is the one that the speaker loves and "la morte" of the second quatrain. She is, above all, "la sainte de l'abîme" of the last line.

The Thirteenth One returns . . . once more she
  is the first;
And she is still the only one—or this is the
  only moment:
For are you queen, oh you! the first or last?
Are you king, the sole or last lover? . . .

The Eluard manuscript bears a reference near "Treizième" to a note in Nerval's own handwriting: "La XIIIe heure (pivotale)." It is tempting to let this note be an exclusive identification of the "Thirteenth One." Doing so, however, would rob the poem of its inherent richness and complexity. **"La Treizième"** unfolds the major themes of the sonnet—love, time, number, death, and religion—all at once. The ordinary language of analysis will force us to take them up seriatim, but this simultaneity is fundamental, not only here but elsewhere in the text.

"La Treizième" calls forth a woman. Obviously not anybody's thirteenth mistress, she is the heroine of this poem, already named in the title. She is thirteenth because she is "unique" and "fated." She is endowed, further on, with the common love superlatives "first," "last," "always," and "only": Nerval used these superlatives in the ninth letter to Jenny Colon and in the third chapter of *Sylvie,* and he repeats them here as a kind of exorcism to bring back together the myriad aspects of love that have disintegrated in the inexorable course of time.

Since adjectival nouns in French are more effective in presenting poetic ambiguity than is any possible English equivalent, "La Treizième" not only evokes the goddess and queen but also introduces the "thirteenth hour," because time and love are considered indissoluble. Science easily relates time to space; poetry can, as it does here, relate time to love. Instructive in this matter are two passages in Nerval's *Sylvie.* In this récit, the speaker pauses in the third chapter to describe a tortoiseshell Renaissance clock, whose gilded dome is topped by the figure of Time. On the face of this clock, in bas-relief, Diana, leaning on her stag, is surrounded by the enameled figures of the hours. The clock has not been rewound for two centuries and was not acquired to tell the time. In the first chapter of *Sylvie,* the speaker, describing the actress with whom he is infatuated, extols her perfections and compares her to the "divine Hours, which stand out so clearly, with stars on their foreheads, against the brown backgrounds of the Herculaneum frescoes." If we bear in mind that **"Artémis"** was published in the same volume as *Sylvie,* we cannot doubt that Nerval was preoccupied with the reckoning of time and that he associated it with the goddess Artemis when he wrote this poem.

The Lombard manuscript of **"Artémis"** bears the title "Ballet des heures." This fact makes some examination of the word *heures* essential. The Greek and Latin *Horae* were divinities of the seasons; only by an improper translation from Latin to French have they come to be confused with the hours of the day. The Hours, as they appear in art and the dance, may depict the seasons, the day, or parts of the day: they do not depict any particular hour. In Ponchielli's *La gioconda,* for example, the Hours portray the first faint glimmerings of dawn, then high noon, twilight, and finally night; victory goes to the Hours representing light over the Hours representing darkness. Nerval could well have been unaware of the etymology of this word; he was no scholar. He certainly did not know Ponchielli's opera, which was first performed at La Scala in Milan in 1876, long after his death. But as an enthusiastic and informed devotee of music, dance, and theater, he could not have ignored the meaning of the Hours for the arts. Nor should we.

If the Thirteenth One is nobody's mistress, it is certainly not one o'clock in the afternoon. Rather, it is the pivotal hour, season, or year. Like the small hand on the old Renaissance clock or the shadow on a sundial, time completes one span at a certain instant, then passes on to the next. Depending on whether it is seen ending a cycle or beginning a new one, it is the thirteenth hour or the first—or both.

In the history of humanity, time has been reckoned on the basis of either the solar or the lunar cycle. As early as the fifth millenium BC, in matriarchal Sumer, time was based on lunations, or lunar months—the time from one full moon to another. This period was approximately twenty-eight days. Analogies with the menstrual cycle are inescapable. There were thirteen lunations, or thirteen times twenty-eight days, in a year. To that total was added the extra day between the thirteenth and first month—a unique day that was both the end and the beginning. In the ancient lunar calendar, thirteen was the number of the sun's death month, when the days are the shortest of the year. As a result, it has always had ominous overtones for the superstitious. In fortune-telling tarots, thirteen is the death card. This pivotal, fated, and mysterious number is central in importance and function in **"Artémis"**; the symbols and themes revolve around it, as the planets revolve around the sun.

The exact meaning of "ou," which appears three times in the first stanza and once in the second, invites scrutiny. It does not indicate an alternative between different or unlike things (the only moment, but not the only woman). It indicates, rather, the synonymous, equivalent, and substitutive character of two ideas (the only woman *is* the only moment). "Ou" enriches the polysemous nature of the entire sonnet. For the thirteenth woman is also the first, as the thirteenth hour is the first. First and thirteenth merge with last and, with the help of "encore" and "toujours," introduce the themes of cyclic movement, recurrence, and permanence.

The suspension points after "revient" and "amant" ask the reader to pause and wonder what is left out, signaling a change of thought. They emphasize the importance of the Thirteenth One, relate her or it to the title, and invite us to ponder all the resonances of meaning

that this woman, this period in time, and this number beget. Time fades in the third and fourth lines, as love takes over again. Opposite this "queen"—the multiple Artemis of the poem—the speaker looks at a projection of himself and asks whether he is "king," the first, the last, the unique love, the hero of this drama.

Paradoxically, these complex ideas are expressed in simple language. The stanza contains only two verbs: "revenir," which, followed by the suspension points, evokes cyclic movement, and "être," which appears five times, expressing permanence and essential being. The rhyme scheme (abab) departs from the traditional sonnet form (abba) and emphasizes the oscillation of themes in this quatrain.

> Love the one who loved you from the cradle
>   to the grave;
> The one I alone loved still loves me tenderly;
> She is death—or the dead one. . . . Oh
>   delight! Oh torment!
> The rose that she holds is the *Rose mallow.*

In the first line of the second stanza, taking an aphoristic tone, the speaker tells all living beings to love the unique woman of many names and attributes who figures in this sonnet. To the boldness of simplicity and repetition in the first stanza is added the temerity of the cliché in the first line of the second. The time-worn locution "from the cradle to the grave" relates the apparent polarities of "first" and "last" to human existence, as the speaker strives to resolve them into eternal principles.

This unique woman resides in the realm of the dead. She is the personification of death ("la mort") or the incarnation of death ("la morte"). This juxtaposition is matched by another ("délice" and "tourment"), and the pairs can be shuffled: "La mort-tourment" may be death without expectation of survival of soul; "la morte-délice" may portray the deceased beloved who, as in *Aurélia,* will guide the speaker through a series of trials to salvation. The pair "mort-délice" bespeaks physical death, a joy, with certainty of afterlife; "mort-tourment," physical death, an intense suffering, if not perceived as a transition to another life. Pervading all the couplings is the painful uncertainty concerning death.

This woman, whether death itself, or the deceased beloved, appears in line 8 holding a flower in her hand. The flower she holds is the very one held by Aurélia in the garden scene of the récit that bears her name. Coming at the end in italics, *"Rose trémière"* recalls "bière," with which it forms a rich rhyme—as well as with "première" and "dernière" in the first stanza. Unlike many saints in Christian iconography and many heroines in German romanticism, the bearer of this flower must be associated with the multiple Artemis of this poem, who opposes them. That is the significance of *"Rose trémière."* Standing midway in the sonnet, the one who holds it embodies the themes presented in the first part and those that will appear in the second.

A frequent attribute of saints in Christian iconography, "rose" appears four times in the sonnet: twice here; once in line 10; once, in the plural, in line 12. By metonymy, it is manipulated to stand for Artemis, for saints who oppose her, and ultimately for the opposing religions that those saints embrace.

> Neapolitan saint with hands full of fires,
> Violet-hearted rose, flower of Saint Gudula:
> Have you found your cross in the wilderness
>   of heaven?

In Nerval's sonnets, the first two lines of the sestet often contain the key to the entire poem. These two are perhaps the most famous that he ever wrote. Maurice Barrès supposedly took delight in repeating them; Tristan Derême honored them with a poetic "garland"; François Constans considered them to be at the heart of Nerval's thought. The repetition of vowel sounds ("*sain*te-m*ain*s," "napolit*ain*e-pl*ein*es") explains some of that charm, but to appreciate the verses fully, one must read them in context.

The "Neapolitan saint" cannot possibly be the one who holds the rose mallow in line 8, nor can she be the saint of the abyss in the last line. On the Eluard manuscript—which, let us recall, is not the basis for the final version of this poem—the name "Rosalie" appears next to "la sainte de l'abîme" of line 14, leading some commentators to assume that the Neapolitan saint, the saint of the abyss, and Saint Rosalie were all one and the same. Such an interpretation pushes poetic ambiguity to the brink of chaos. The memories that might have gone into the making of these tercets are legion. Rosalie (in reality a Sicilian saint) appears in works that Nerval read, as well as in works that he wrote. But even if my approach did not exclude extrinsic matters of this sort, except where they are essential to an understanding of the text itself, I could not avoid the observation that if Nerval had wanted Rosalie in this poem, he would not have taken such pains to keep her out.

The Neapolitan saint is, on the contrary, a person consecrated in this poem to arouse devotional memories or feelings of holiness. Instead of bearing a flower, as one might expect, she holds a lantern, or lights. This is a nice twist, because Gudula, patron saint of Brussels, is usually represented with a lantern. According to tradition, this lantern, symbolizing the faith, went out and was then miraculously relit by Gudula's prayer. On the Lombard manuscript, Nerval originally wrote "soeur de Sainte Gudule." By replacing "soeur" with "fleur," he not only avoided sibilant cacophony but

also achieved a synthesis of the two saints, the Latin and the Nordic. This new saint stands in opposition to the Artémis of this poem.

The eleventh line completes the apostrophe. The speaker asks the combined saint of the previous two lines whether she has found her cross (her salvation), in the wilderness of heaven. Has she been as fortunate, for example, as Saint Helena, mother of Constantine I, who, according to tradition, found a relic of the true cross near Calvary in 326 (an event usually called the invention of the cross)? Obviously not, since the heavens are empty. The ironic tone here recalls the defiance of Nerval's **"Antéros,"** the despair of his **"Le Christ aux oliviers,"** and Musset's 1842 satire, "Sur la paresse": "Et, pour qui joint les mains, pour qui lève les yeux, / Une croix en poussière et le désert aux cieux. . . ."

Nerval originally wrote, "l'abîme des cieux." Let's be grateful for the change, for the ambiguity of associating "abîme" with a saint of heaven as well as with the saint of the last line would have been sloppy rather than poetic.

> White roses fall! You insult our gods:
> Fall, white phantoms, from your burning heaven:
> The saint of the abyss is saintlier in my eyes!

Falling roses constitute a familiar symbol of the victory of Christian faith over death. When Saint Rosalie died, cherubs are said to have rained roses upon her body. In the denouement of Goethe's *Faust,* part 2, after the death of the hero, Mephistopheles speaks ironically of his disciple's fate. The angels answer with hymns, and a shower of roses falls on the ground, signifying that Faust, who has repented at the last moment of his life, will be saved. Even Mephistopheles is moved by the scene and, for a moment, begins to doubt his own denial of faith. The sense of this sonnet is, however, quite different. The speaker doubts the efficacy of forgiveness symbolized by falling roses. For him they are "white ghosts" ("fantômes blancs"), and they insult his gods—that is, the gods who preceded monotheism. It is Artemis, the saint of the abyss, who is holier in his eyes, for she has twofold saintliness: she is the symbol of pre-Christian, polytheistic faith and the embodiment of an eternal beloved woman.

Some of Nerval's works lie close to the events that he witnessed, encountered, underwent, or lived through as he wrote them, but this poem does not. **"Artémis"** is not the transcript of a particular poetic experience, nor is it a "song without words" or "pure poetry," as some readers have suggested. It is a profound meditation on time, love, faith, life, and death. Not a word in it is haphazard or empty of meaning. In my view, it is the most ambitious, the most carefully elaborated, and the most beautiful of this great poet's writings.

Kari Lokke (essay date 1987)

SOURCE: "Woman: The Other as Sister,"in *Gérard de Nerval: The Poet as Social Visionary,* French Forum Publishers, 1987, pp. 65-103.

[*In the following excerpt, Lokke discusses Nerval's social, psychological, and mythological portrayal of women in his prose.*]

One glance at the titles of Nerval's major works shows women to be the heart, the center, of his fictional and poetic universe: *Les Filles du feu (Angélique, Sylvie, Jemmy, Octavie, Isis, Corilla, Emilie), Pandora, Aurélia, Les Chimères* ("Myrtho," "Delfica," "Artémis"). Even the *Voyage en Orient* seems less a travelogue than an attempt to come to terms with the feminine beauties of Austria in **"Les Amours de Vienne,"** with Egyptian marriage customs in **"Les Femmes du Caire"** and with the problematics of love triangles in the tales of Hakem and of Solomon, Sheba and Adoniram.

This poet, who never knew his mother, who never married, who seemed most at ease with women when separated from them by the costumes, theatrical makeup and footlights of the stage, compensated for their absence in his life by granting them overwhelming power and presence in his art. The contemporary critic, inevitably looking at Nerval through the lens of current psychological and feminist theory, cannot help responding to such an obviously compensatory effort with a certain skepticism. Such an artist, one assumes, must be telling us much more about himself, his own fears, needs and projections, than about the reality of 19th-century womanhood.

Nevertheless, the almost preternatural sensitivity to the plight of victims of economic, political and religious persecution reflected in so many of Nerval's works suggests that he might be equally sensitive to the oppression of women as a social injustice in need of commentary and correction. And in fact, as an artist, Nerval, like Blake, seems to have been endowed with a visionary imagination so subjective that, following the laws of Hegel's dialectic, it becomes objective and impersonal as well as concrete and historical. A careful look at Nerval's fictional portrayal of the social roles imposed upon women by patriarchal society reveals a remarkably modern critique of marriage and the bourgeois family as vehicles for entrapping, taming and breaking the female spirit. Once again, just as Nerval understood and elucidated the role played by ideological and political repression in the creation of mental illness, so his works consistently portray women, both in their strengths and in their vulnerabilities, as pitted against the constraints of patriarchal society.

Yet Nerval is certainly not first and foremost a conscious social theorist or critic, and perhaps the most striking feature of his poetic presentation of woman is his mythification of the feminine. Woman is daughter, wife, mother, mistress and worker for Nerval, but she is also saint, victim, goddess, siren, courtesan, amazon and witch. How does one reconcile these seemingly opposing impulses—a clear and explicit sympathy with women as victims of societal oppression and an even more powerful urge to view women through the strictures of age-old archetypes, perhaps even misogynistic stereotypes?

This tension between a progressive historical view of woman's evolving social roles and an apparently conservative mythological presentation of her seemingly ahistorical essence characterizes Nerval's portrayal of woman from beginning to end of his œuvre. In fact the relationship between social and mythological woman in Nerval's work is one of interpenetration and creative complementarity. It is in the socially determined and accepted roles of mother, wife and daughter that Nerval shows women to be oppressed and unnecessarily limited. And, paradoxically, it is his seemingly restrictive stereotypes of witch, siren, queen and saint that in fact release and celebrate the power of women.

This conception of the role of myth in cultural imagination follows the lead of Nina Auerbach's eloquent study of 19th-century British images of womanhood, *Woman and the Demon: The Life of a Victorian Myth* Auerbach asserts that the process of understanding and demystifying male myths of womanhood should include the task of searching those same archetypes for the subversive and emancipatory power they enclose. She suggests that feminist criticism should move beyond its earlier simplistic condemnation of myths of womanhood to a rediscovery of myth as a source of contemporary strength: "Woman's freedom is no longer simple initiation into historical integrity, but the rebirth of mythic potential. The mythologies of the past as well have become stronger endowments than oppressions."[1] Interpretative revaluation of myth can act as a corrective to what Auerbach terms the "sleek complacency" of modernist formalism, as well as to the lack of imaginative spirit and promise in behaviorist and empiricist research:

> The allegiance of feminism in the early 1970's was to the social sciences, whose demographic charts and statistics affirmed the reality of our half-life in society—and nothing else. But lives are inspired by beliefs before they are immortalized in statistics. It may be time for feminists to circle back to those "images" of angels and demons, nuns and whores, whom it seemed so easy and so liberating to kill, in order to retrieve a less tangible, but also less restricting, facet of woman's history than the social sciences can encompass. (p. 3)

Nerval's obsessive fascination with the enigma of the feminine creates in his poetry a kind of ideal repository of 19th-century myths of woman. The archetypes of mother, saint, amazon, courtesan, siren—protean, self-transformatory images that recur incessantly, blend into and flow out of one another—form the heart of all of Nerval's major works. It is almost as if the absence of close relationships with women in his personal life allowed Nerval the distance needed to present a kind of panoramic view of 19th-century woman's social and mythic essence. The complementary relationship between Nerval's mythic and social representations of women can perhaps best be demonstrated by showing that for Nerval mythic woman often has precisely those powers denied or repressed by her social roles of daughter, wife and worker. Finally, what is of ultimate interest, as Mary Harper suggests in an excellent study of the *Voyage en Orient,* is not "any simple opposition between myth and 'reality'," but rather "the blurring of the boundaries between them—not as a seamless narrative but rather as a tangled web of attitudes which need to be explored."[2] My discussion will seek to render evident the connections between Nerval's criticism of patriarchy and his mythification of women by proceeding from those texts—*Angélique* and the *Voyage en Orient*—which deal explicitly with women as victims of societal oppression to *Aurélia, Octavie* and *Pandora,* narratives that embody a mythic vision of women. Even that most misogynistic of myths, the tale of Pandora, can in Nerval's hands become an expression of women's emancipatory power.

Nerval's most important collection of fiction is entitled *Les Filles du feu,* daughters of fire. Before Nerval's women are mothers or lovers, they are daughters, not of earthly men and women, but of the creative, active and rebellious Promethean element of fire. Yet they are daughters of earthly parents as well, parents who represent the demands of social order and hierarchy against the demands of the free spirit. Thus it is the figure of Iphigenia under the knives of her father Agamemnon and the priest Calchas, Iphigenia sacrificed to "la vieille autorité du prêtre et du souverain" (I, 153), to the demands of war and nationalism, who stands as central symbol of woman in Nerval's introduction to this series of novellas. In his dedication to Alexandre Dumas, Nerval creates a narrative persona, one of his many fictional doubles, who is an actor imagining himself in the role of Achilles. Achilles, as lover of Iphigenia, is trying to save her from martyrdom. Yet the modern ironic self-consciousness of Nerval's actor prevents him from taking his own role seriously, though he presents Iphigenia's plight with empathy and intensity of feeling:

> J'entrais comme la foudre au milieu de cette action forcée et cruelle; je rendais l'espérance aux mères et le courage aux pauvres filles, sacrifiées toujours à un devoir, à un Dieu, à la vengeance d'un peuple, à l'honneur ou au profit d'une famille! . . . car on comprenait bien partout que c'était là l'histoire

> éternelle des mariages humains. Toujours le père livrera sa fille par ambition, et toujours la mère la vendra avec avidité; mais l'amant ne sera pas toujours cet honnête Achille, si beau, si bien armé, si galant et si terrible, quoiqu'un peu rhéteur pour un homme d'épée! (I, 153)

Yet despite—or in fact precisely because of—the beauty and superiority of these lovers, both the Greek witnesses and the French audiences, Nerval suggests, are desirous of the sacrifice of Iphigenia as scapegoat: "Chacun s'est dit déjà qu'il fallait qu'elle mourût pour tous, plutôt que de vivre pour un seul; chacun a trouvé Achille trop beau, trop grand, trop superbe!" (I, 154). Daughters, then, like the archetypal son in Nerval's "Christ aux Oliviers" and like the victims of religious and political persecution described in Chapter I, are scapegoats of a cruel and authoritarian social order.

The first of *Les Filles du feu* is *Angélique,* written in 1850 and originally published together with the story of l'abbé de Bucquoy in *Le National.* In his search for "les Bucquoy sous toutes les formes" (p. 178) Nerval discovers the diary of Angélique de Longueval, his elusive abbé's great aunt who, in disobedience to her father, eloped with a servant to embark on a life of exile, hardship and brutalization at the hands of her husband. Because Nerval's aims are primarily esthetic and spiritual rather than political, his depiction of women as an oppressed social group often seems more a product of unconscious sympathy and sensitivity than one of a conscious commitment to the emancipation of women. With *Angélique* it is almost as if Nerval had unconsciously asked himself a question analogous to Virginia Woolf's "What if Shakespeare had been a woman?" For in the life of Angélique de Longueval Nerval shows how the courage, determination and will to freedom characteristic of "Les Bucquoys" manifested themselves in a woman unable to move about in society on her own, bound to the "protection" of a husband or a father. Angélique, Nerval writes, represents "l'opposition même en cotte hardie" (I, 207). As Ross Chambers suggests, she shares with her descendant l'abbé de Bucquoy "l'hérédité valoise, grande source de rebelles et de ligueurs de tous camps" (p. 168).

Angélique tells her story in her own voice as Nerval quotes long passages from her diary. Nerval mirrors her naïve, straightforward and unflinching style in his own restrained, almost matter-of-fact narration of her profoundly tragic life story. Thus he resurrects the historical voice of a woman whose name had been effaced from the genealogical records of her family. As he states ironically, "Angélique n'était pas en odeur de sainteté dans sa famille, et cela paraît en ce fait qu'elle n'a pas même été nommée dans la généalogie de sa famille" (I, 214). Although all her brothers are listed, "on ne parle pas de la fille."

Angélique, Nerval suggests, is an exceptional human being, "d'un caractère triste et rêveur" (I, 180), an early victim of Romantic melancholy. Before she had reached twenty years of age, two men had been murdered as punishment for their passion for her, uniting in truly Nervalian fashion love, death and sorrow in a seemingly indissoluble whole. It is almost easier to see Angélique as a fictional creation, an angel-anima, rather than as a historical personage. She is in fact clearly Nerval's sister soul—note the relationship of equality—a personage, like so many of Nerval's fictional characters, with whom Nerval cannot help identifying. The line between fact and fiction, between historical and imaginative reality, is never clear for Nerval. In one of his letters to Jenny Colon Nerval admits that he conceives of his life "comme un roman" (I, 758), and he makes the following confession in the dedication of *Les Filles du feu* to Alexandre Dumas:

> Il est, vous le savez, certains conteurs qui ne peuvent inventer sans s'identifier aux personnages de leur imagination [. . . .] l'on arrive pour ainsi dire à s'incarner dans le héros de son imagination, si bien que sa vie devienne la vôtre et qu'on brûle des flammes factices de ses ambitions et de ses amours! (I, 150)

As much as Nerval emphasizes that Angélique's passionate and dreamy character creates her fate, he also makes it clear that the restrictions placed on her as a woman and daughter force a person of such passionate determination to rebel. Once again, with Nerval sympathetic identification produces acute insight into the realities of political and social oppression. For Nerval Angélique is like the heroine of the folk song he records in the seventh letter of the text, a brave heroine who refuses to reject her poor lover and is, therefore, sentenced by her father to confinement in a tower that will become a tomb:

> —Ma fille, il faut changer d'amour . . .
> Ou vous resterez dans la tour.
> —J'aime mieux rester dans la tour,
> Mon père, que de changer d'amour!

After the death of her first lover at the hands of her father, Angélique had begged him to introduce her into the world in the hopes that she would find someone to free her from the memory of "ce mort éternel" (I, 181), as Nerval calls him. It appears that the count ignored her wishes, as her later attempts to forget her love for La Corbinière, her father's servant, are frustrated by the lack of any occupation or company worthy of her. She cannot be satisfied with the concerns traditionally assumed to be the province of women. Thus when La Corbinière is forced to spend a year in Paris, she succumbs to depression and melancholy, distracted only by their exchange of letters. She writes, "Je n'avais pas d'autre divertissement, [. . .] car les belles pierres,

ni les belles tapisseries et beaux habits, sans la conversation des honnêtes gens, ne me pouvaient plaire . . ." (I, 184).

Angélique finally resolves to leave the prison of her father's castle with his servant, her lover. Love seeks to invalidate class distinctions here, just as it does in the *"Histoire du Calife Hakem"* and just as it seeks to transcend international warfare and hatred in *"Emilie."* Love, no matter how strong, is not all-powerful, for Angélique, a victim of a societal and familial repetition compulsion, chooses a husband who is every bit as insensitive and tyrannical as her father. Her search for freedom only subjugates her more deeply to an oppressive and tragic fate.

Her account of their life together reveals her husband's nightmarish brutality and stupidity. After escaping with the family silver, she quickly changes into men's clothing so as to avoid detection and capture. One evening when they are resting at an inn, La Corbinière is questioned about the "demoiselle vêtue en homme" who is accompanying him. Nerval isolates his proprietary response and records it with condemnatory silence: "Ouida, Monsieur . . . Pourquoi avez-vous quelque chose à dire là-dessus? Ne suis-je pas maître de faire habiller ma femme comme il me plaît?" (I, 201). Similarly, there seems to be a kind of silent horror behind Nerval's matter-of-fact quoting of the passage in Angélique's diary where she records her lover's "cavalier" response to having accidentally shot her: "Il dit seulement à ceux qui le blâmaient de son imprudence: 'C'est un malheur qui m'est arrivé . . . je puis dire à moi-même, puisque c'est ma femme' " (I, 202).

The fleeing couple, exhausted, sick and nearly starving, finally reach Italy, where they are married. As a woman exiled from family and home, Angélique is subjected to the advances and propositions of a number of men, but she remains true to her husband, even following him when he is forced by their poverty to join the Austrian army. La Corbinière falls critically ill with a fever, and Angélique nearly dies of the combined effects of a miscarriage and exposure. Doubtless Nerval associates Angélique with his own mother, who followed her husband, an army surgeon, into battle six months after Nerval was born, and died two years later in Silesia, never having seen her infant again. It is, however, Angélique, rather than her husband, who appears to have the greater physical endurance, for she nurses him back to health, obtains a pardon for him when he is detained for desertion and eventually leads him back to Verona. In Verona they set up a home, but are soon forced by his debauchery and profligacy to open up a tavern.

All of Angélique's love and devotion are rewarded by murderous brutality on her husband's part. After witnessing her exchange greetings with a passing army officer, La Corbinière tries to strangle her, nearly kicks her to death and feels justified in threatening to eviscerate her if she ever speaks to the man again. Beginning with this event, her story is no longer recounted in her own voice. Angélique has been silenced, perhaps by shame and misery. Her diary stops here, and the sparse facts of her last years are known through the manuscript of her cousin, a Celestine monk to whom she appealed for help in her last years. When Angélique finally receives a pardon from her mother and wishes to return to France, her husband refuses, fearing that he will be executed there. Finally, after the death of both her parents they return to France, where La Corbinière dies and Angélique lives out the rest of her life in ignominy and the most abject poverty.

Angélique is Nerval's portrait of a lady, his tribute to a woman who, once she had committed herself to a husband, never complained and never wavered: "en constatant quelques malheureuses dispositions de celui qu'elle ne nomme jamais, elle n'en dit pas de mal un instant. Elle se borne à constater les faits,—et l'aime toujours, en épouse platonicienne et soumise à son sort par le raisonnement" (I, 207-08). As mythic vision, the appropriately named Angélique is a strange melding of scandalous fallen woman and self-sacrificing saint, revealing to the careful reader the proximity of these two dialectically opposed images. These stereotypes in fact both contain and reveal her strength of will and endurance of spirit. She refuses to succumb to the tyranny and brutality of either her father or her husband, remaining true to her conception of love and outliving both men, refusing the traditional escape of death, suicide or seclusion in a convent usually reserved for the fictional fallen woman/saint.

Yet there is something Brechtian as well, perhaps unconsciously so, in Nerval's portrait of this "good woman." Like Brecht's Shen Te, she does not want to "count the cost" of going with the man she loves. During all her hardships her constant refrain is a simple "Voyez [. . .] ce que c'est de l'amour" (I, 202). This heart-rending exclamation cannot but frustrate and even anger a modern reader who wishes in vain for Angélique that she wake up to a consciousness of her right to personal freedom and dignity and that she leave her brutish husband. This discrepancy between character and reader consciousness, as in Brecht's plays, is a highly effective tool of social criticism. *Angélique* stands as an implicit critique of a social and familial structure that made it almost impossible for her to give serious consideration to leaving her husband even after his debauchery and cruelty had reduced her to utter misery.

The institution of marriage comes under a different kind of scrutiny in Nerval's *Voyage en Orient*. This text, a strange mixture of fact, fiction and borrowings from orientalist readings and studies, much of which was written before Nerval ever left Europe for the Middle East, is more a travelogue of an inner, subjective journey than the record of actual physical wanderings: "C'est une assez triste litanie de mésaventures, c'est une bien pauvre description à faire, un tableau sans horizon, sans paysage" (II, 3), he announces in the opening lines of the text. Similarly, he writes early on in his stay in Cairo: "Avant tout, il faut songer encore à constituer mon intérieur" (II, 140). The process of understanding and creating his own inner world, his inner self, means above all else coming to terms with the relationship between the realm of the dream and the outer physical world. In the *Voyage en Orient* this tension between inner and outer realities is embodied most intensely in the opposition Nerval creates between woman as social being, as spouse and physical mate, and woman as ideal mythic vision, soul mate and spiritual guide.

In the first chapter to focus almost exclusively on women, "Les Amours de Vienne," woman is at first a sexual and esthetic object, the goal of the conqueror's quest for sensual pleasure. This chapter, originally published in 1841, was written before the death of Nerval's beloved Jenny Colon had impelled him to embark upon his Middle Eastern voyage. As self-styled Don Juan, Nerval describes women with the predatory distance of the jaded connoisseur and seducer:

> Mon ami! imagine que c'est une beauté de celles que nous avons tant de fois rêvées,—la femme idéale des tableaux de l'école italienne, la Vénitienne de Gozzi; bionda et grassota, la voilà trouvée! [. . .] Figure-toi une tête ravissante, blonde, blanche, une peau incroyable [. . .]; les traits les plus nobles, le nez aquilin, le front haut, la bouche en cerise; puis un col de pigeon gros et gras, arrêté par un collier de perles; puis des épaules blanches et fermes, où il y a de la force d'Hercule et de la faiblesse et du charme de l'enfant de deux ans. (II, 33)

Gérard's attitude here seems a reflection of the Viennese atmosphere of free and open sensuality without coquetry on the part of women. In contrast to Parisian women, Viennese beauties seem a part of nature, as Gérard suggests in a rather paternalistic fashion: "Ici les femmes font très peu de cas d'elles-mêmes et de leurs charmes, car il est évident que cela est commun comme les belles fleurs, les beaux animaux, les beaux oiseaux, qui, en effet, sont très communs si l'on a soin de les cultiver ou de les bien nourrir" (ll, 39). These "natural" beauties find him as an unmarried man particularly charming:[3]

> Les dames ont parmi eux des maris et des amants avoués, connus; mais tu sais que les amants passent en général à l'état de maris, c'est-à-dire ne comptent plus comme individualité masculine. Cette remarque est très forte, songes-y bien. (II, 58)

Marriage, Nerval emphasizes, reduces one to the status of social category, strips one of individuality as a sexual being, whether one is male or female, for according to his observations, the husbands and their wives are equally bored with one another. The charm of Vienna, then, is the atmosphere of sensual love, outside marriage, open and free of hypocrisy:

> Cette atmosphère de beauté, de grâce, d'amour, a quelque chose d'enivrant: on perd le tête, on soupire, on est amoureux fou, non d'une, mais de toutes ces femmes à la fois. L'odor di femina est partout dans l'air, et on l'aspire de loin comme don Juan. (II, 39)

Yet there is something ethereal, evasive and idealized in this "profumo di donna" as experienced and described by the poet-voyager. He makes a strikingly unconvincing Casanova, as he is first to admit. His self-consciousness and sense of self-irony are simply too strong: "Hélas! mon ami, nous sommes de bien pâles don Juan. J'ai essayé la séduction la plus noire, rien n'y a fait" (II, 34). Hence, his efforts at seduction often take a comic turn, foiled by the nonchalance and utter naturalness of the Viennese women. Gérard presents himself as clumsy, almost weak in relation to the full-bodied beauties of Vienna. His attempts to seduce the Bohemian Vhaby are frustrated first by an ugly black dog which, in typically obsessive Nervalian fashion, calls to mind Faust's poodle, and then later by the presence of a sick man—the hunter—who foils the narrator's neat attempts at categorization:

> Voilà un joli rendez-vous qu'on m'a donné là. Je salue le chasseur en lui souhaitant une meilleure santé, et je repasse dans l'autre pièce. Ah, çà! dis-je à la jeune Bohême, ce monsieur malade est-il votre mari?—Non.—Votre frère?—Non.—Votre amoureux?—Non.—Qu'est-ce qu'il est donc?—Il est chasseur. Voilà tout. (II, 47)

Ultimately, then, Nerval is no Don Juan. His account of his amatory adventures becomes a kind of anti-narrative, with little completed action, no dénouement, a fragmentary search for something Vienna cannot provide. "Les Amours de Vienne" represents a typical Nervalian pattern—the unfinished episode, the anti-climax—with Gérard leaving a strong, seductive, appealing woman to travel into an unknown future. There is, however, in the place of glorification of the wandering male almost a sense of envy for female happiness, strength and stability. There is even something forced in his attempt to console himself and justify himself: "Et d'ailleurs, qu'importe après tout? . . . nous ne vivons pas, nous n'aimons pas. Nous étudions la vie, nous analysons l'amour, nous sommes des philosophes, pardieu!" (II, 57). Thus he is attracted to the type "bionda et grassota" as art connoisseur rather than as womanizer, for she represents the ideal of the Venetian school of Gozzi. And unfortunately, Gérard

notes in a tone of self-mockery, communication of this fact to La Kathy is hardly an effective tool for seduction: "J'ai expliqué à cette beauté qu'elle me plaisait, surtout-parce qu'elle [. . .] réalisait en elle seule le Saint-Empire romain, ce qui a paru peu la toucher" (II, 33).

Already, in Vienna, Gérard, self-reflective as ever, presents his idealization of women as in conflict with their sensuous and natural reality. After Vienna the *Voyage* moves by way of the Adriatic to Cairo. In fact, as Richer and Beguin's notes point out, Nerval never saw Cythera, the focal point of his fictive journey from Europe to Egypt.[4] Cythera, though desecrated by English occupation, is nevertheless above all else the island dedicated to the worship of Venus. The description of Cythera, gateway to the Orient, provides a key to the symbolic significance of the entire Middle Eastern voyage. The reign of the Eternal Feminine begins as soon as one reaches Greece:

> Le principe féminin, et, comme dit Goethe, le féminin céleste, régnera toujours sur ce rivage. La Diane sombre et cruelle du Bosphore, la Minerve prudente d'Athènes, la Vénus armée de Sparte, telles étaient leurs plus sincères religions: la Grèce d'aujourd'hui remplace par une seule vierge tous ces types de vierges saintes, et compte pour bien peu de chose la trinité masculine et tous les saints de la légende. (II, 78)

In homage to the feminine, Nerval's pen expresses itself in a seemingly uncontrollable proliferation of Venuses: Aphrodite, la Vénus Panagia, la Vénus Pontia, la Vénus Calva, la Vénus Apostrophia, la Vénus Péristéria.

This flux and flow of female divinities is divided by Nerval into three separate, but interdependent images, all of which, he suggests, were at one time worshipped by the Greeks: the celestial Venus, "Vénus-Uranie"; the popular Venus, or terrestrial Venus, Aphrodite; and the demonic, devouring subterranean Venus. It is of course the celestial Venus who attracts Gérard. The earthly Venus, "plus riante, plus humaine," is the patroness of most poets and painters, presiding over their "fantaisies galantes" (II, 74). This "Vénus frivole des poètes, la mère des Amours, l'épouse légère du boiteux Vulcain" (II, 1309), is clearly also the Venus Gérard left behind in Vienna. The subterranean Venus, on the other hand, is a dark woman of dreams and death, an avatar of Nemesis, a sister spirit of Pluto and Morpheus.

Vénus-Uranie is also the patron goddess of the ideal Nervalian lovers, Polyphile and Polia of Francesco Colonna's *Songe de Polyphile*. Subversive beyond the powers of Aphrodite, Vénus-Uranie inspires a love the exclusivity and concentrated power of which gives the human will the courage to threaten social hierarchy and class distinctions, as Colonna, a poor painter, falls in love with Lucrétia Polia, a wealthy princess who learns of his love for her on a carnival night, a night of liberty and transcendence of social restrictions and barriers. They vow to serve Vénus-Uranie as monk and priestess in order to meet in dreams on Cythera, far from "la loi d'un Dieu sévère" (II, 69). It is this patriarchal God of the Church of Rome who has forbidden them marriage at the altar of Christ: "La distance des conditions rendait le mariage impossible; l'autel du Christ . . . du Dieu de l'égalité! . . . leur était interdit; ils rêvèrent celui de dieux plus indulgents [. . .]" (II, 68).

The easy sensuality of the earthly Venus worshipped in Vienna is, on the other hand, harmless to the political powers that be, as witnessed by the amused, accepting response by the Viennese police censor—once again the ubiquitous, subtly oppressive and invasive police presence in Nerval's œuvre—to Gérard's reports of his attempts at womanizing in the letters inspected by the police (II, 51-53). For Nerval, as for the Surrealists, erotic freedom is primarily imaginative rather than sensuous. It is, as Paz writes of the Surrealist vision of Provençal poetry, "subversive in the face of bourgeois morality because of its exaltation of adultery, and subversive in the face of modern promiscuity for its celebration of exclusive love" (p. 132).

Without doubt it is the celestial Venus whom Gérard worships, "divinité sévère, au symbole complexe, au sexe douteux" (II, 74), "la Vénus austère, idéale et mystique, que les néo-platoniciens d'Alexandrie purent opposer, sans honte, à la Vierge des chrétiens" (II, 77). This powerful, mysterious Venus is associated, in her specific iconography, with the essence of the Orient itself:

> Le symbole qui la distinguait des autres déesses était le croissant surmonté d'une étoile à huit rayons; ce signe, brodé sur la pourpre, règne sur l'Orient, mais c'est bien chez ceux qui l'arborent que Vénus a toujours le voile sur la tête et les chaînes aux pieds. (II, 1309-10)

This image—Venus crowned by a crescent and star, yet veiled and chained—might stand as a kind of microstructure of the entire *Voyage en Orient.* Venus becomes a religious symbol and an embodiment of sublimated, transfigured androgynous sexuality; at the same time she is a profoundly political symbol as well. Turkish and Moslem power is associated in Nerval's mind with a preeminently feminine iconography: the crescent moon and the star. This symbolism, particularly that of the star—l'Etoile, the seventeenth arcana of the Tarot—recurs with obsessive frequency in Nerval's œuvre as the icon of womanhood.

The Orient, then, presents an explicit contradiction in its attitude towards women: while seeming to acknowledge and even glorify the real power of the feminine, it veils and enslaves that power. One is reminded of the passage Nina Auerbach adopts from Maxine Hong Kingston's *The Woman Warrior* as motto for her *Woman and the Demon*: "Perhaps women were once so powerful they had to have their feet bound." It could be that the myth of the origins of Vénus-Uranie provides a clue to the fear she inspires in men, for she was born of the genitals of Uranus after he had been castrated by his child Saturn (II, 1310).

Both polarities of this self-contradictory vision of woman are dramatized in Gérard's narrative of his personal pilgrimage to the East. The *Voyage en Orient* represents a kind of dialectical inner journey in which Nerval as 19th-century male writer attempts to come to terms with his own conflicting reactions to women through the opposition between his perception of the realities of Eastern women as wives and slaves and his vision of the East as a land of the powerful, mysteriously veiled goddess Isis. Although this same dichotomy exists in his perception of European women, the exotic and unknown world of the East allows his imagination freer reign than would the familiar Western world.

Edward Said writes in his *Orientalism* that all the 19th-century French poets and writers who made personal pilgrimages to the Middle East associated it with sexual fantasy and with sexual experience unobtainable in Europe. This is certainly true of Nerval. Whereas most writers like Flaubert associated the East with "the freedom of licentious sex," with "a different type of sexuality, perhaps more libertine and less guilt-ridden"[5] than in Europe, Nerval, true to his idealizing and platonizing temperament, sees the Orient as the locus of sublimated, spiritualized sexuality. As Said emphasizes, the Middle East for Nerval is a screen upon which he projects his imaginative and esthetic vision, at the same time giving expression to his own sublimated sexual needs.

The chapters dealing with Egypt are gathered together under the title "Les Femmes du Caire," once again emphasizing the centrality of women in Nerval's representation of the Orient. The first of these chapters, entitled "Le Masque et le voile" and "Une Noce aux flambeaux," are meditations on Egyptian marriage as a mysterious, mystical union. "Les Femmes du Caire" opens with Gérard recognizing only the spiritual and imaginative implications of Egypt's veiled feminity: "Le Caire est la ville du Levant où les femmes sont encore le plus hermétiquement voilées. [. . .] Arrêtonsnous, et cherchons à soulever un coin du voile austère de la déesse de Saïs" (II, 90). This veil is a suggestive stimulus to the imagination, lending reality the allure of the work of art. The market place takes on the aspect of a masked ball, the gracefully draped women appearing as statues from antiquity. Thus the veils enveloping "la plus intéressante moitié du peuple d'Orient" reinforce Nerval's vision of Egypt as "le pays des rêves et de l'illusion" (II, 92) where it becomes almost impossible to distinguish past from present, dream from reality.

Nerval's narrator awakens from his first night's sleep in Cairo to the hauntingly repetitive music of a marriage procession moving through the streets. This ceremonial music creates an atmosphere that blends "gaieté patriarchale" and "tristesse mythologique" as Gérard creates and experiences a netherworld of dream and illusion. The bride, the focal point of the entire procession, is "un fantôme rouge"—an image of fiery intensity—crowned by a tiara of precious gems and surrounded by an entourage bearing torches and huge candelabra. Here, then, Gérard imagines, is a people for whom marriage has true significance, "un peuple pour qui le mariage est une grande chose" (II, 99) and not simply an embodiment of bourgeois materialism and stultification.

This popular marriage festival has, in Gérard's eyes, an egalitarian, emancipatory aspect similar to that described by Bakhtin as the essence of the medieval folk festival: "Où chercher ailleurs une égalité plus réelle?" he asks.[6] There is no need of wealth, for the bride's elaborate costume and opulent gown are borrowed, the musicians, dancers and clowns are friends and relatives. For one night an ideal, utopian vision is created that will in fact influence the reality of their married life together, as the young bride is transfigured into "l'antique déesse du Nil."

Myth and ritual clearly do not exist for Nerval in a social vacuum. Thus his narrative persona moves in the realm of fantasy to an understanding of the imbalance of power implied in this polygamous marriage system. Identifying with the male, Gérard seems to glory in the fantasy of the proprietary rights granted this bridegroom:

> Un seul homme aura le secret de cette beauté ou de cette grâce ignorée; un seul peut tout le jour poursuivre en paix son idéal et se croire le favori d'une sultane ou d'une fée; le désappointement même, laisse à couvert son amour-propre; et d'ailleurs tout homme n'a-t-il pas le droit, dans cet heureux pays, de renouveler plus d'une fois cette journée de triomphe et d'illusion? (II, 100)

Nerval, however, is too honest, too sensitive to the rights of others to identify for long, even in fantasy, with a position of oppressive power. Throughout the rest of the *Voyage* his narrator seems caught between his attraction to the privileges of male power over women and his sympathy for the women who are victims of this unfair distribution of power. The text becomes a kind of narrative meditation of the social, sexual and spiritual relations between man and woman

in which Nerval, perhaps unconsciously, works towards an evening out of the balance of power between the sexes in the fictive world he creates.

When Gérard moves from the dream-like marriage ceremony to the reality of daily life in a foreign country, the first difficulty he describes is the Egyptian cultural opposition to his bachelorhood. He is nearly forced to abandon the apartment he has rented because his social status as a single man scandalizes the neighborhood. Like the details of the marriage ceremony, this presumably autobiographical incident from Nerval's own travels is in fact borrowed from William Lane's *An Account of the Manners and Customs of the Modern Egyptians Written in Egypt During the Years 1833, 1834, 1835* (II, 1318). The narrative structure of the rest of the *Voyage*—from the first chapter to the tales of Hakem and Adoniram—is built around Gérard's attempts to come to terms with this fictive dilemma of his bachelorhood. This choice of narrative thread lends a strange veneer of coherence to the rather chaotic compilation of travelogue, dreamscape and borrowings from orientalist and occultist readings that is the *Voyage en Orient.* It also allows Nerval to focus upon women, "la plus intéressante moitié du peuple d'Orient." Perhaps ultimately, like Kafka with his stories involving F.B. and his obsessive lists of the advantages and disadvantages of the married state, Nerval, through the vehicle of geographical and imaginative displacement, is attempting to come to terms with his own choice to remain unmarried. As Gautier emphasized, the platonic love of Jenny Colon was the ideal love relationship for his eternally restless, otherworldly friend:

> C'était une nature ailée, voltigeante, que l'ombre d'un lien effrayait, et qui papillonnait au-dessus de la réalité dans un rayon de soleil ou de clair de lune, au gré de la fantaisie, sans se poser nulle part.—Le mariage, même le plus heureux, eût été pour Gérard un horrible supplice.—Son esprit, de plus en plus détaché de la vie pratique et perdu dans l'infini du rêve, ne pouvait plus s'astreindre à des rapports humains. La sollicitude même de l'amitié lui pesait. Il fallait l'accepter quand il venait, mais ne pas lui demander de commerce suivi, comme l'hirondelle, il entrait lorsqu'il voyait la fenêtre ouverte et faisait deux ou trois fois le tour de la chambre avec de petits cris joyeux; mais c'eût été effaroucher son indépendance que de fermer la croisée.[7]

Contemplation of an exotic, imaginary marriage allows Nerval both social analysis and compulsive, perhaps even therapeutic self-analysis. In the name of art and social commentary, the ethereal Gérard confronts the extremely awkward, difficult situation of the Westerner seeking a Coptic or Moslem bride. The process is essentially a business transaction in which a go-between presents him to the parents of marriageable girls so that a financial agreement can be arranged. There are four varieties of marriage from which he can choose, ranging from the easily dissolved "Turkish" union to the solid European marriage that would obligate him to take his bride with him when he left Egypt. This, then, is the reality of marriage in the homeland of the mythological Isis!

Presented to a number of young girls, Gérard is disturbed by their servility, charmed by their beauty, embarrassed by his own position in relation to them. He recognizes the seductive allure as well as the danger of assuming the role of husband to a girl still a child: "ne serait-il pas charmant de voir grandir et se développer près de soi l'épouse que l'on s'est choisie, de remplacer quelque temps le père avant d'être l'amant! . . . Mais pour le mari quel danger!" (II, 130). He cannot, however, abandon his European "religious prejudice" and sense of morality:

> Faire un mariage à la cophte, [. . .] ce n'est rien que de fort simple; mais le faire avec une toute jeune enfant, qu'on vous livre pour ainsi dire, et qui contracte un lien illusoire pour vous-même, c'est une grave responsabilité morale assurément. (II, 130)

These "sentiments délicats" are interrupted by the go-between's arrival and his announcement that the dowry demanded by the parents is 5000 francs! The final word in marriage settlements, then, is money, and he simply cannot afford this bride. Once again, as in the introduction to *Les Filles du feu,* Nerval reveals marriage to be anything but an affair of the heart or a contract protecting the rights of the bride; it is first and foremost a business matter transacted in the social and financial interests of the family.

Appropriately, the answer to Gérard's quandary is the bazaar, where women are available for little money as slaves, where his dragoman tells him he can find a bargain. The purchase of the Javanese slave Zeynab has produced a fascinating legacy of critical commentary. In reality, Nerval never bought a slave; it was his traveling companion Le Fonfrède who, Nerval writes Gautier, was stupid enough to do so.[8] Yet Gautier cannot resist perpetuating his own sexual fantasy of his close friend Gérard with a Javanese mistress.[9] Similarly, Geoffrey Wagner, a modern translator of Nerval into English, does not question the story. Even the author of one of the most recent studies of Nerval, Bettina Knapp, is too disturbed by the idea to get the facts straight: "Nerval did take a Javanese slave girl to live with him, but their relations must have been asexual," she tells us.[10] Jean Richer, however, sets the record straight: "Rappelons une fois pour toutes que c'est en réalité son compagnon Fonfrède [. . .] qui avait acheté l'esclave."[11]

This confusion is the result perhaps less of carelessness than of the fascination which the sexuality of Eastern women seems to hold for the Western observer. It is possible that Nerval's original intent was to exploit this fascination in an effort to hold the reader's interest throughout the somewhat labyrinthian *Voyage* with the tale of Zeynab. What in fact occurs with this narrative device is anything but a tale of exotic sexual adventure. From the first visit to the slave market Nerval's traveler is caught in an impossible position between his liberal European horror at the buying and selling of human beings and his liberal commitment to cultural relativism, his desire to refrain from judging a foreign culture, to refrain from imposing his ideas and values upon a way of life he knows only from the outside. The end result is subtle social criticism and ironic self-analysis in which Nerval exposes both the intrusive, imperialist impulses of Western culture and the inevitable tendency of racism and sexism in any culture to enslave both the oppressed and the oppressor.

Notes

[1] Nina Auerbach, *Woman and the Demon: The Life of a Victorian Myth* (Cambridge, MA: Harvard Univ. Press, 1982), 12.

[2] Mary Harper, "Recovering the Other: Women and the Orient in the Writings of Early Nineteenth-Century France," *Critical Matrix,* 1, No. 3 (1985), 24.

[3] This observation is emphasized through its reappearance in *Pandora, Œuvres,* I, 352.

[4] Nerval, *Œuvres,* II, 1307-17.

[5] Edward Said, *Orientalism* (New York: Vintage, 1979), 190.

[6] See Mikhail Bakhtin, *L'Œuvre de François Rabelais et la culture populaire au moyen-âge et sous la Renaissance,* trans. Andrée Robel (Paris: Gallimard, 1970).

[7] Jean Richer, *Nerval par les témoins de sa vie,* 16-17.

[8] Nerval, *Œuvres,* II, 924.

[9] Richer, *Nerval par les témoins de sa vie,* 15.

[10] Bettina Knapp, *Gérard de Nerval: The Mystic's Dilemma* (University: Univ. of Alabama Press, 1980), 117.

[11] Jean Richer, *Nerval par les témoins de sa vie,* 29.

Scott Carpenter (essay date 1996)

SOURCE: "Traveling from the Orient to *Aurélia*: Nerval Looks for the Words," in *Acts of Fiction: Resistance and Resolution from Sade to Baudelaire,* Pennsylvania State University Press, 1996, pp. 101-24.

[In the following excerpt, Carpenter draws a connection between translation, language, and madness in Nerval's works, focusing on "Aurélia."]

Nerval was sensitive to the limitations inherent in translation even before he undertook to introduce his readers to the world of delirium in which he often sojourned. Entering the literary scene in 1828 with a new rendering of *Faust,* he prefaced his version of the epic with comments pertaining to the ultimate *impossibility* of translation: "Here is a third translation of *Faust;* and what is certain is that none of the three can say, '*Faust* is translated!' It is not that I wish to cast any aspersions on the work of my predecessors, the better to conceal the weaknesses of my own, but rather that I consider a satisfactory translation of this stunning work to be impossible" (preface to *Faust,* 1).

"Impossible" presumably because of the idiosyncrasies of language: German is not simply a code of French, and its idioms are idiomatic precisely to the extent that they can be said to resist translation. What is "lost" in translation is the "German-ness" of the original; or, if not lost, it is at least "exchanged" (in an essentially metaphoric transaction) for French nonequivalents.[12]

The fact that Nerval knew translation to be irremediably flawed did not keep him from pursuing his interest in it, nor from enlarging its scope in his own work. He did not content himself with the translation of language per se (although he did continue with it, translating Heine, for example, through the 1840s); he was even to expand his role as interpreter into the various domains of culture, history, society, and, of course, mental states. In a sense, translation could be considered the overarching image of his work. From the ***Chansons et légendes du Valois*** (1854) to ***Les Illuminés*** (1852), from the ***Voyage en Orient*** (1848-51) to *Aurélia* (1855), Nerval sought to communicate to his readers special knowledge to which he alone was privy.

Certainly, the same could to some extent be said of every author, for narrators always mediate between reader and story. Nerval, however, does not introduce the reader to an otherness he has viewed from the outside, but to an intimate circle of which he is an initiate. He can thus mediate in good faith precisely because of the privileged status of the translator, who straddles the boundary between sameness and difference. Nerval can appreciate the difficulties of translation because he speaks *both* German *and* French (*Faust*), because he is in some sense a product of *both* the eighteenth *and* the nineteenth centuries (*Les Illuminés*),[13] because he is *both* pagan *and* Christian ("**Isis**"),[14] because he has been *both* sane *and* mad (*Aurélia*).

The difference between inside and outside perspectives might best be illustrated in the case of the Ro-

mantic travelogue, and one might usefully compare Chateaubriand's *Itinéraire de Paris à Jérusalem* (1811) to Nerval's ***Voyage en Orient*** (***Trip to the Orient,*** 1851 [definitive edition]). Chateaubriand allegedly undertakes his journey in order to *confirm* preconceived ideas: "I had determined the structure of *Les Martyrs.* Most of the volumes of this book had already been sketched out; I thought I should not put the finishing touches on them before seeing the country where my story takes place" (5, 109). Thus Chateaubriand's travels are marked by the desire to see what he already knows, especially structures or landscapes referred to in books he has read—or previously written. Traveling with an escort and maintaining the profile of a *grand seigneur,*[15] he represents a pocket of Frenchness while abroad. As such, he is sensitized primarily to that with which he can identify:

> I enjoyed happening upon the vestiges of French honor, beginning with my first steps in the true fatherland of glory and in the country of a people which had recognized true merit. But where does one not find these vestiges! In Constantinople, in Rhodes, in Syria, in Egypt, in Carthage; everywhere I landed I was shown the French camp, the French tower, the French castle; the Arab showed me the tombs of our soldiers under the sycamores of Cairo, as the Seminole [showed me those] under the poplars of Florida. (5: 125)[16]

Chateaubriand is also supremely untroubled by the question of language: his narrative incorporates almost no record of local tongues (foreign language in the *Itinéraire* consists principally of Italian and Latin, which are used only ornamentally), and Chateaubriand proceeds almost as if the *drogman,* or translator, were neither present nor necessary.

Nerval, on the other hand, takes a different tack. For one thing, he dispenses with the monumental descriptions that had become a convention of the genre. Moreover, attempting to shed his identity as a Frenchman, he moves increasingly throughout the narrative toward a direct experience of the otherness of Middle Eastern life. In the lingo of modern anthropologists, he takes a step toward "going native." He thus rejects the French hotels in favor of a home in a comfortable Arab neighborhood of Cairo, conforms to local custom by adding a woman slave to his household, and much later will successfully disguise himself as a Persian in order to take up quarters in Istanbul during Ramadan[17]. Yet in spite of his assimilation, language remains a barrier. Unlike Chateaubriand's *Itinéraire,* the ***Voyage*** presents translation, incarnated in the form of the narrator's *drogman,* as *the* central problem of Nerval's experience of otherness, and it is one Nerval elaborates thematically. Relying at first on international *bonhomie,* the narrator is soon alerted to the dangers of translation by Youssef, a casual acquaintance:

"I heard," he told me, "that they made you buy a slave; I'm quite upset about it."

"Why is that?"

"Because they have certainly cheated or robbed you: the *drogmans* are always in cahoots with the slave trader. . . . Abdallah will have received at least one purse for himself." (*OC,* 2: 349)

The narrator's realization that his interpreter—indeed, that translation as a whole—is unreliable and inadequate, leads him to dismiss Abdallah, and to take the only course of action left open. Immediately following the interpreter's departure comes the chapter, "First Lessons in Arabic" (*OC,* 2: 353), and the text is hereafter liberally sprinkled with transcriptions of words from a variety of tongues, principally Arabic and Turkish. In addition to producing the first occurrence in French literature of such words as *baklava* (*OC,* 2: 638), the narrator's entrance into oriental languages (much more successful, in fact, than Nerval's own) signals an important shift in perspective. Unwilling to remain at the mercy of his *drogman,* he works to *replace* him, to move himself into the privileged position of translator that Nerval's narrators customarily occupy. Although he occasionally has recourse to such intermediaries as Mme Bonhomme and other displaced Europeans, the narrator eventually achieves a degree of self-sufficiency. It is thanks to this straddling of languages and cultures that he is able, during the *fête du Ramadan* to steal into Istanbul, where "no Christian has the right to reside." (*OC,* 2: 636). Here, in the longest and last narration of the book, he himself will fulfill for the reader the role of *drogman,* providing a translation of the legend of Adoniram.

In the *Voyage en Orient* Nerval took steps to resolve the problem of how to "get at" foreignness, and his solution consisted of dismissing mediation, of confronting otherness directly, and of learning its logic. However, he did not address the issue of how to communicate this foreignness directly to his reader. Just as the narrator of the *Voyage* is originally at the mercy of his *drogman,* so the reader finds himself entirely dependent on the mediation of the narrative voice. Of course, Nerval's accounts and translations are no less transparent than those of the scheming Abdallah. The interpreter lost his job for failing to translate neutrally, that is, for fabricating, for entering into *fiction.* Nerval, whose true itinerary strayed significantly from that of his narrative, and whose "legend" of Adoniram was less translated than fabricated, was guilty of as much.

Nevertheless, the *Voyage en Orient* can be seen as an essential step toward the achievement of Nerval's other objective: the presentation of the ultimate otherness of madness *in its fullness.*[18] The *Voyage* suggests that although translation betrays, the translator himself enjoys unmediated interaction with foreignness, a foreignness he will nevertheless be unable to render. Introducing one's readers to a direct experience of otherness would entail allowing *them* to accede to the position of translator. They must, in a sense, repeat the narrator's usurpation of the place of Abdallah; this time, however, the reader would supplant the narrator himself. It is for this reason that, in *Aurélia,* when he tries to introduce readers to the extreme otherness of madness, Nerval surrenders the model of translation for that of language acquisition. To understand madness, the reader needs to learn how to speak it.

It is not insignificant that a similar approach to the study of madness was being advocated in the clinic. As we saw earlier, figures such as Moreau de Tours and Maury had adopted a model of mental illness that likened it to foreign language. Yet it remained unclear what the clinical applications of this model might be.

Surprisingly, what might be considered an unrecognized breakthrough in this respect came from the practice of a rather retrograde clinician, François Leuret. In 1846 Leuret published a slender manual for practicing psychiatrists, entitled *Des indications à suivre dans le traitement moral de la folie.* Although a student of Esquirol, Leuret's methods tended toward those of pre-Pinelian psychiatry, relying heavily on intimidation and on such characteristically eighteenth-century therapies as the *bain de surprise.* What is the most revealing in the series of cases outlined in *Des indications à suivre* is the occasional account of Leuret's irascibility. One such account occurs in the report on a certain Mme Louise, who was plagued and terrified by visions of communion hosts. When the young woman failed to respond to therapy, Leuret succumbed to a petty desire to vent his frustration on his patient. But how could he obtain satisfaction from a person who was not responsive to his professional terrorism? In a moment of inspired malice, Leuret called for a box of sealing wax, the white disks of which resemble the host; the doctor then threatened to scatter them about the room, much to Mme Louise's horror (Leuret, 15-32).[19]

Leuret illustrated, albeit unwittingly, a radical and enlightening departure from standard clinical practice. Despairing of his chances for making his patient adopt the language of "reason," he entered into the alienated discourse of Mme Louise. Linking "getting mad" to "going mad," Leuret interacted and communicated with his patient *on her own terms.* Indeed, he seemed to have learned her logic so well that an outsider happening upon the scene of a man hurling wafer-shaped pieces of wax at a cowering victim might well have been hard-pressed to determine which figure represented the cause of science and which the face of insanity.

Nerval's bouts with mental illness were perfectly contemporaneous with Leuret's fiascoes and with the development of the linguistic model of madness, a model increasingly sanctioned by the medical community, and with which Nerval's own views can be shown to be entirely consonant.

His strategies for communicating otherness did not, then, form in a vacuum. In the same year that Maury's article on the "secret links" of delirious discourse appeared in the *Annales Médico-psychologiques* (1853), Nerval began serious work on *Aurélia* (published in *La Revue de Paris* in the beginning of 1855, the second part appearing shortly after the author took his own life). The narrator of this work—closely associated with Nerval himself—undertakes to describe his encounters with madness. He also relates what is often understood as his "cure": at the end of the novel the main character emerges from the sanitarium with a newfound control over language. As the character becomes the narrator of his own story, a series of oppositions pitting narrator against hero, sanity against madness, and past against present, seem to end in resolution.

However, Nerval explicitly rejects the notion that *Aurélia* is the story of a cure, resisting from the outset the analogy of illness: "I am going to try . . . to transcribe the impressions of a long illness which took place entirely within the mysteries of my mind; and I do not know why I use the term illness, for never, as far as I am concerned, have I felt myself to be in better health" (*O,* 1: 359).[20]

Moreover, the final lines of the novella assert the positive nature of the narrator's experiences: "Nevertheless, I am happy for the beliefs I have acquired, and I compare this series of trials that I have undergone to what the Ancients saw in a descent into Hell" (*O,* 1: 414).

Aurélia thus figures as a kind of *roman d'éducation,* although not in the traditional sense, for it is not the protagonist who is in need of schooling. He already possesses the special knowledge he hopes to relate; the implied "student" of the educational narrative is none other than the reader.

Nerval then undertakes, in the manner of Alfred Maury, to illustrate the "secret links," the hidden logic of madness. He explicitly strives to "transcribe" the impressions of his so-called illness (*O,* 1: 359). The word "transcribe" would seem to suggest that Nerval intends to record elements of his experience without resorting to mediation. Yet it quickly becomes apparent that this record—at least at the outset—will come with a commentary. The narrator positions himself as the *translator* of the hieroglyphic language of dream and madness. That some form of translation or interpretation is needed becomes evident in the inaugural line: "Le Rêve est une seconde vie" (Dreams are a second life). Not only does this assertion suggest a mysterious articulation between sleeping and waking states, but the

capitalization of "Rêve," as Ross Chambers has shown, elevates dream to the level of allegory, one that virtually begs for interpretation ("Récits d'aliénés," 78-79).

The narrator bolsters the view of himself as interpreter, *drogman* if you will, by allusions to earlier texts that serve as models for his own enterprise: Virgil's *Aeneid,* Swedenborg's *Memorabilia,* Apuleius's *Golden Ass,* and Dante's *Divine Comedy* and *Vita nuova.* Significantly, all these texts are linked to problems of interpretation: each written in a language foreign to Nerval and each depicting a world so laden with mysterious analogies that they require the assistance of a guide or commentator.

Just as the poet of the *Vita nuova* explains the structures and images of his verse, so Nerval's narrator sets about interpreting "the invisible world" (*O,* 1: 359), "the world of illusion in which I sojourned for some while" (*O,* 1: 414). Thus when he crosses paths with Aurélia in another city, the narrator links her greeting to a divine pardon that transforms his "profane" love, inscribing it with a new sign:

> How was I to interpret this action and the deep, sad gaze which she added to her greeting? I thought I saw in it the pardon of the past; the divine accent of pity made those simple words she spoke to me inexpressibly dear, as if something religious were blending with the sweetness of a love heretofore profane, and *imprinting* upon it *the character* of eternity. (*O,* 1: 361)

The narrator intervenes regularly as a commentator to assist us (insofar as he is able) in our reading, particularly in the deciphering of dreams. "One perceives fairly easily in the father and mother the analogy of the electric forces of nature," he interprets after the dream of chapter 4, "but how can one see the individual centers emanating from them, from which they emanate, as a collective animistic *figure*?" (*O,* 1: 369, emphasis in original). Or, after a particularly perplexing dream: "What did it mean? I did not know until later. Aurélia was dead" (*O,* 1: 374).

These visions can be understood by the reader precisely because of the narrator's position as polyglot, fluent in the various discourses of reason and madness. The linguistic analogy is one he himself invokes: in his attempt to synthesize a history of the world, he tries to incorporate "a thousand figures accompanied by stories, verses, and inscriptions in all known languages" (*O,* 1: 375). Similarly, in his dreams he recognizes meaning in what appears to be the mere "confused chattering" of birds (*O,* 1: 379), and seems even to divine meaning: "Such were the words, more or less, that were either spoken to me, or whose meaning I thought I had grasped" (*O,* 1: 383).

Such passages clearly partake of the mode of translation; yet the function of translation in *Aurélia* is not that of rendering madness totally transparent, of forcing it to imitate the language of reason. In order not to betray the essential difference of the discourse of madness, Nerval retains elements of his dreams in his prose, principally those indicating discontinuity and juxtaposition. Part 1 is thus marked by a certain number of ellipses and parataxes (Chambers "Récits d'aliénés," 79), as well as by a repeated expression of the untranslatability of certain ideas:

> The divine accent of pity made her words . . . *inexpressibly* dear. (*O*, 1: 361)

> While walking I sang a mysterious hymn . . . which filled me with an *ineffable* joy. (*O*, 1: 363)

> *I cannot convey* the feeling I had amidst those charming beings. (*O*, 1: 371)

> *I do not know how to explain* that, to my mind, earthly events could coincide with the those of the supernatural world. (*O*, 1: 380)

The problem of the ineffable situates Nerval squarely within the parameters of Romantic discourse, a discourse scarred by the collapse of what we have called the classical imagination. The question then becomes how, given the newfound indeterminacy and mutability of language, the Romantic is ever to express meaning. Certainly not by means of conventional discourse, whose steady disintegration *Aurélia* chronicles. Indeed, at the final stage of this disintegration, and as if to punctuate it, the narrator refers to his library as nothing more than "the Tower of Babel in two hundred volumes" (*O*, 1: 406).

Tellingly, the narrator's conclusion that language has failed him coincides with the erruption of conflict within his dream world, and this conflict results in the abandoning of translation. The crisis occurs at the end of part 1, when the parallel worlds between which Nerval's narrator divides his time suddenly turn incompatible. The inability of Nerval's language to translate, to transparently *figure* his supernatural experience, manifests itself in the narrator's incompatibility with the figure who parallels his own existence: his double. "*The other* is my enemy," he says of his mystical brother (*O*, 1: 381). Later, "I know he has already struck me with his weapons, but I await him without fear, and I know the sign which is to vanquish him" (*O*, 1: 384).

The clash signals the disintegration of parallelism between what the narrator cells the "internal" and "external" worlds: "What had I done? I had upset the harmony of the magic universe which gave my soul the assurance of immortal existence" (*O*, 1: 385). As his position disintegrates, the narrator becomes less and less capable of expressing the meanings of his other world, a difference that will necessarily elude conventional discourse. The very language that was to have been the vehicle of translation reveals itself to be fundamentally flawed: "The magical alphabet, the mysterious hieroglyph come to us incomplete and distorted either by time, or by those who have an interest in our ignorance" (*O*, 1: 387). To repair this imperfection, the narrator hopes to "recover the lost letter [*la lettre perdue*] or the erased sign" (*O*, 1: 387), thus restoring the ability of language to render the meaning of his altered states. However, his hopes are not realized: "The dream became confused" (*O*, 1: 392), and the only sense the narrator vaguely deciphers consists of a reprimand: "All this was done in order to teach you the secret of life, and you have not understood. Religions and fables, saints and poets all came together to explain the fatal enigma, *and you interpreted wrong*" (*O*, 1: 392).

The ability of language to convey meaning, to translate adequately, appears to have collapsed. In this respect, Nerval's plight is not unrelated to Balzac's; both are troubled by upheavals in the world of signs. Unlike the novelist, however, Nerval does not deny the seriousness of the rupture between signs and meanings, nor does he cling, as did Balzac, to the shreds of a language that seemed to have lost its fullness. Nerval's disillusionment with language is more profound than Balzac's. . . . Nerval finds himself in a desperate situation: the disintegration of sign systems, or at least of Nerval's ability to manipulate them, undermines all his attempts at symbolic resolution. Indeed, Nerval's plight is that he now needs to resolve the problem (at least symbolically) of the inadequacy of symbolic resolutions. He will do so by a powerful act of fiction. Unable to abide the insanity of a language cut adrift from meaning, he works in the mode of reconstruction, foring a new discourse. This new discourse will always be full for Nerval, but only because it will be full *of* Nerval. For the insane irony of conventional language Nerval will substitute the personal idiolect of madness. In so doing, he relies implicitly on the current medical analogies, which (as we have seen) validated the legitimacy of such "personal" languages.[21]

Giving himself over to *one* language, that of plenitude, Nerval sidesteps the problems of mediating between two discourses, of translating. Accordingly, interpretation cases within the text. In part 2 of *Aurélia,* the narrative commentary, which had previously translated the dream discourse, all but disappears. These chapters are marked by many discursive gaps; interjections, ruptures, or changes of narrative perspective are framed merely by blank lines, or by ellipses. Distinctions regularly made in part 1 between past and present, between narrator and protagonist, often vanish. Both thematically and graphically the language of "sanity" begins to falter: the narrator loses his record of the location of Aurélia's tomb; the letters to her that he announces are missing; words themselves begin to disintegrate, "Aurélia" turning into the letter "A" followed by three asterisks, and finally shrinking merely to the three asterisks. With the effacement of the narrator and the predominance of a new semantics, the textual discourse begins to resemble the source language more than the target language, and the reader must fend for himself.

What has happened is that the novella has tried to move from the interpretation of madness to its presentation, from the *translation* of madness to its *transcription*. The narrative commentary of part 1, having served as a primer to the otherness of madness, now fades, forcing the reader to confront this otherness without mediation; that is, to accede to the role of translator himself, and to read the secret links. Thus the fading of Aurélia's name might be read as a representation obeying a different logic: associated earlier with the narrator's *star* of destiny, she is now reduced to asterisks, which, as the Greek root *aster* implies, are but "little *stars*."

That one must read *Aurélia* in such a "perverse" fashion (not just rhetorically, but hieroglyphically) is the crux of the matter. It is in the dicey indeterminacy of rhetoric that Nerval formulates a grammar, whose "secret links" can only occasionally be gleaned.[22] The reader's instruction in this new language has two components: the first part of the novella constitutes a sort of language primer, one that outlines the rudiments of the hero's "insane" grammar; next, the near disappearance of the narrator in part 2 of *Aurélia* corresponds to the narrative plan of the *Voyage en Orient*. That is to say, the *drogman*—here the narrator himself—has been dismissed. After the brief lesson of part 1, the reader, able to straddle discourses, is left to step into the role of translator.

The fact that one is able to decipher any of part 2 at all is a credit to the apprenticeship given earlier; indeed, generations of critics have tossed up their hands at the difficulty of the end of *Aurélia.*[23] But part 1 has shown that the language of Nerval's madness is to be read allegorically, or iconographically, or even hieroglyphically. Thus the narrator's aimless peregrinations through Paris, related in chapter 4 of part 2 (*O,* 1: 396-98), might be construed as corresponding to the disorder of his mind, as well as to the wandering of various signifiers: Notre-Dame changes into Notre-Dame de Lorette and Notre-Dame-des-Victoires; the candles in the church reappear in the night sky; the inscription "Allah! Mohamed! Ali!" is echoed in the choral repetition "Christe! Christe! Christe!"; and the priest ("l'abbé Dubois") becomes the psychiatrist ("they took me to the Dubois clinic [*la maison Dubois*]"). Lunacy itself is inscribed in the narrator's vision of the "moons streaming across the sky," and the textual divagations resemble the narrator's sense that "the earth was drifting in the firmament like a dismasted vessel."

That a concentrated allegorical logic is also at work in this passage is evidenced by the narrator's self-destructive impulse when he reaches the Place de la Concorde: "Having arrived at the place de la Concorde, my thoughts turned to suicide." The Concorde can be established as the intersection—or the point of concordance—of various levels of reading. It is significant not only because of its intertextuality (the image of the obelisk evoking one of René's images from a similar peregrination: "Sometimes a tall column appeared standing alone in a desert, just as a great thought rises . . . in a ravaged soul" [Chateaubriand, *Oeuvres romanesques,* 1: 122]), but also because the square is, from the time of the Revolution, associated with death. (During the Revolution the place de la Concorde had been renamed the place de la Révolution, and was the principal site for public executions.) Furthermore, the place de la Concorde marks the beginning of the Champs-Elysées (the narrator's original destination), the other end of which is defined, in Parisian toponymy, by the place de l'Etoile. The mention of the Champs-Elysées, the "Elysian Fields," recalls the Virgilian descent into hell evoked at the beginning of the text, as well as the descent of Orpheus, referred to in the epigraph of part 2. Both of these classical allusions serve as metaphors for Nerval's descent into madness: he later remarks that "I compare this series of trials . . . to what the Ancients saw in a descent into Hell" (*O,* 1: 414). For the Ancients such descents were positive encounters (leading to knowledge for Aeneas and to a glimpse of Eurydice for Orpheus), and Nerval clearly views such a descent as a possibility to recover what has been lost. So, in the passage in question, the fact that the Champs-Elysées should lead to l'Etoile suggests that the narrator sees a descent into the Elysian Fields of the dead—presumably achieved through suicide—as the only possibility of reaching l'Etoile, that little star, the asterisk that Aurélia has become.

One finds similar complexity in the hero's encounter with "Saturnin," the fellow-patient in the asylum (*O,* 1: 407-8). The apparently arbitrarily selected name ("I don't know why it occurred to me that his name was Saturnin" [*O,* 1: 408]), is a near anagram of the adjective the narrator has used to describe him: taciturn. On another register, the resonance "Saturn" calls to mind the mythological Golden Age, the *aureas aetas,* an original utopia ruled by Saturn, and one in which Astraea, the "Star-maiden" (later to be associated with the constellation Virgo, thus joining the Nervalian fascinations of the star and the Virgin) watched over mankind. Saturnin is thus linked to Aurélia, "the golden one,"[24] and Nerval continues with the references to a mythological scene when he calls his companion "indefinable" and compares him to a sphinx. The notion of the sphinx implicitly ties Saturnin to the "fatal enigma" (*O,* 1: 392) used to describe the dream discourse. Moreover, the narrator's coaxing of Saturnin into speech corresponds to the process of language acquisition practiced upon the taciturn reader of *Aurélia;* Saturnin is in fact emblematic of a reader confronted with a discourse he must learn (or relearn) in order to speak (Chambers, *Maneuver,* 131-40). Indeed, he represents everything to which the narrator has tried to give voice: dreams, images, hallucinations, and Aurélia herself.

The reader who begins to understand this textual logic, to "acquire" this language, can begin to appreciate the otherness and fullness of Nerval's alternative discourse. Indeed, the sense of resolution pervading the end of the story, in contrast to the frustration so prevalent earlier, seems to derive from a sense that communication has finally been achieved *without* the distortions of translation.

Yet, for all of its ingenuity, Nerval's shift from a model of translation to one of language acquisition is not altogether unproblematic.[25] Although the fading of the narrator serves to allow the reader into the position of translator, this effacement can never be complete. Furthermore, the success of *Aurélia* in representing Nerval's delusions depends on the validity of the linguistic analogy of madness, which is itself perhaps only one more translating metaphor by which a discourse of otherness is appropriated into a dominant vocabulary. Moreover, even if the new language Nerval proposes is in some sense "hieroglyphic"—and therefore akin to the supposedly pictorial, figurative origin attributed to language by eighteenth-century linguistics—Nerval can never quite escape language completely. He may, at best, attenuate its effects. However, the *reduction* of distortion does not imply its *elimination,* and Nerval cannot transcend the basic properties of a language—"insane" or otherwise—that will necessarily distort experience while structuring it in terms of linguistic logic. Avoiding translation removes only one of the layers of mediation in language.

Nerval is not oblivious to these problems. Although it seems clear that for him concerns of language and reason overlap considerably, and that his particular world is indeed susceptible to the linguistic analogy of madness, he nevertheless suggests that he has grasped incompletely the link between "the internal and external worlds" (*O,* 1: 413). The internal world remains just beyond his reach.[26] This is not because something has been lost *in* translation, an activity the narrator has avoided, but because something was lost *before* translation, even before language: Aurélia herself. This loss that exists outside of language (indeed, that Nerval's language, in all its contortions, attempts to fill), remains irremediably beyond the experience of the reader. The narrator's series of losses, of Aurélia once and even "a second time" (*O,* 1: 385), of her correspondence, of the very tomb that marks her absence, makes

of Aurélia a version of that *lettre perdue,* that if found, would provide fullness. Indeed, in her disintegration from a proper noun to "A***" and finally "***," Aurélia becomes the *lettre qui se perd.* Vanishing even as a letter, Aurélia thus eludes language, and it is this loss that Nerval will never be able to render.

The ambivalence of the conclusion of *Aurélia,* where the narrator oscillates between a fondness for and the abandonment of his delirium, and where the narrative straddles its end and its beginning, evokes the equivocation of the reader. Having acceded to the position of translator, the reader is able to enter into another language; in so doing, however, he glimpses the inadequacy of language (and fiction) as a whole, as it never does more than camouflage in various vocabularies the losses it cannot fill.

Nerval's strategy of reconstruction, of attempting to lay a foundation for a new language, one that might recover the integrity of a mythical primitive tongue, leads to the most dreadful of discoveries. He struggles to escape the opposition pitting the literal against the figurative, and hopes to invent a form of representation that is neither one nor the other. Yet that way lies madness, and far from providing an oasis of meaningfulness in an otherwise desolate world, madness reveals itself to be the abyss of irony Nerval had sought to avoid. The meaningfulness madness has promised is always *almost*; it is always an illusion concealing an absence, always a disappointment. Meaning, it turns out, rather than being that which representation represents, resides in representation itself. When Nerval lifts the veils of representation in order to *see* truth without mediation, *nothing is there.* In the end, madness reveals the endless *peregrination* of meaning within representation, an aimlessness that for Nerval was cause for despair.

Notes

[12] Nor is French a code for English: my (English) translation of Nerval's (French) assertions about the untranslatability of the (German) original would seem to compound the problem. . . .

[13] Nerval comments repeatedly on his education in eighteenth-century literature through his uncle, as well as on his uncle's peculiar library. His affinity for the earlier century is especially clear in the similarities evident between Rétif de la Bretonne and Nerval in "M. Nicolas," in *Les Illuminés.*

[14] "Isis" (1845) is essentially a story of the transformation, or translation, of pagan images into Christian ones, specifically of Isis into the Virgin Mary.

[15] See Claude Pichois' *Notice* to the *Voyage en Orient,* in Gérard de Nerval, *Oeuvres complètes,* 2: 1377.

[16] One is reminded of Levi-Strauss' travelers who, when brought to New York, judge it according to European cities, the terms of their own existence (*Tristes tropiques,* 85). The reverse side of this experience is Flaubert, who, years later, complains that he cannot escape France in the Orient. The passage is commented on in Richard Terdiman's *Discourse/Counter-Discourse* (240-41). The cultural collision between the East and the West resulted in, one might say, a serious occident.

[17] *Oeuvres complétes,* 2: 637. All further reference to the *Voyage en Orient* will be to this edition, hereafter cited as *OC.*

[18] For Nerval, the otherness of the Orient was in some ways analogous to that of madness. Thus, in *Aurélia,* when the narrator heads into delirium, he proclaims to a friend that he is headed "for the Orient." For other links between the *Voyage en Orient* and *Aurélia,* see Jeanneret, "Sur le *Voyage en Orient* de Nerval."

[19] It is interesting to note that Nerval's own doctor, Esprit-Sylvestre Blanche, had earlier decried Leuret's methods, which touted "the desirable effects of *intimidation* in the treatment of madness" (Blanche, 5-6). On Nerval's relationship with his doctors, especially Blanche and his son, see Peter Dayan, *Nerval.*

[20] At the time of this writing, the volume containing *Aurélia* in the new Pichois edition had not yet appeared. All citations from *Aurélia* thus refer to the Béguin and Richer edition (*Oeuvres,* [Paris: Gallimard, 1974]); hereafter cited as *O.*

[21] Ross Chambers has shown how even before this shift in the text the narrator has recruited a sympathetic reader by grafting the "insane" discourse on other medical analogies, especially that of the dream (*Room for Maneuver,* 131-32).

[22] Evidence that one can indeed learn aspects of Nerval's language can be seen in Christopher Prendergast's reading of "Sylvie" (*The Order of Mimesis,* 148-79).

[23] Two readings have helped immensely in penetrating this part of the text. See Jean Richer, *Gérard de Nerval et les doctrines ésotériques,* esp. the discussion of tarot and numerology. Frank Paul Bowman fills in many of the gaps and offers a brilliant reading of the historical allusions in the *Mémorables* (*French Romanticism,* 167-81).

[24] For further discussion of the importance of the Golden Age in *Aurélia,* see Françoise Gaillard, "Aurélia ou la question du nom," 240, 245.

[25] The majority of readings have viewed *Aurélia* as a clinical "success" story (see Jeanneret's influential reading in *La Lettre perdue,* 170); some have sensed the incompleteness of the adventure of *Aurélia* (see esp. Lynne Huffer, 39-50).

[26] "I thought I understood that there existed between the internal and external worlds a link; that inattention or mental disturbances distorted only the superficial bonds between them" (1: 413).

FURTHER READING

Bibliography

Villas, James. *Gérard de Nerval: A Critical Bibliography, 1900 to 1967.* Columbia: University of Missouri Press, 1968, 118 p.

Annotated bibliography of criticism on Nerval published from 1900 to 1967.

Biography

Hearn, Lafcadio. "A Mad Romantic." In *Essays in European and Oriental Literature*, pp. 43-54. New York: Dodd, Mead and Company, 1923.

Characterizes Nerval as "an insane man" who nevertheless produced "literary work of the very best quality."

Quennell, Peter. "Gérard de Nerval." In *The Singular Preference: Portraits & Essays*, pp. 18-24. London: Collins, 1952.

Brief biographical sketch that calls Nerval "the founder of the Symbolist movement."

Rhodes, S. A. *Gérard de Nerval, 1808-1855: Poet, Traveler, Dreamer.* New York: Philosophical Library, 1951, 416 p.

The only full-length English biography of Nerval. The author presents critical commentary in addition to biographical information.

Symons, Arthur. "Gérard de Nerval." In *The Symbolist Movement in Literature*, pp. 10-36. New York: E. P. Dutton, 1908.

Surveys Nerval's life and writings and describes the author's role in the Symbolist movement.

Criticism

Bales, Richard. "A Poetics of Modesty: The Art of Deflection in Nerval's *Sylvie.*" *Essays in French Literature* 27 (November 1990): 11-27.

Analyzes *Sylvie* as an unstable text that ultimately disperses the focus of the reader.

Beauchamp, William. *The Style of Nerval's 'Aurélia.'* The Hague: Mouton Publishers, 1976, 108 p.

A detailed semiotic discussion of *Aurélia.*

Carpenter, Scott D. "Figures of Interpretation in Nerval's *Aurélia*." *Nineteenth-Century French Studies* 17, No. 1 (Fall 1988): 152-60.

Explores various interpretations of madness portrayed in *Aurélia*.

Chambers, Ross. "Speed and Delay in Nerval." *Australian Journal of French Studies* 1, No. 1 (1964): 40-57.

Perceives a connection in Nerval's works between travel and escape from the "time-bound life of reality."

Dunn, Susan. "Nerval: Transgression and the *amendement Riancey*." *Nineteenth-Century French Studies* 12, Nos. 1 and 2 (Fall-Winter 1983): 86-95.

Comments on how Nerval's writings are affected by his fear of transgression, a phobia exacerbated by the formation of the 1851 censorship law *amendement Riancey*.

————. "Nerval and Money: The Currency of Dreams." *Nineteenth-Century French Studies* 19, No. 1 (Fall 1990): 54-64.

Discusses the role of money in Nerval's life and works.

Fairlie, Alison. "Aspects of Suggestion in Nerval." In *Imagination and Language: Collected Essays on Constant, Baudelaire, Nerval and Flaubert*, pp. 288-303. Cambridge: Cambridge University Press, 1961.

Probes Nerval's interest in the problems of expressing experience; literary tradition; and themes of the double, disillusionment, and the quest for the ideal.

Felman, Shoshana. "Gérard de Nerval: Writing, Living, or Madness as Autobiography." In *Writing and Madness*, translated by Martha Noel Evans, Shoshana Felman, and Brian Massumi, pp. 59-77. Ithaca: N. Y.: Cornell University Press, 1985.

Presents Nerval's view of madness and expounds on the antithetical relationship between rationality and insanity in *Aurélia*.

Jones, Robert Emmet. *Gérard de Nerval*. New York: Twayne Publishers, 1974, 188 p.

Critical study that emphasizes Nerval's development from a minor to a major poet.

Lowe, Catherine. "The *Roman tragique* and the Discourse of Nervalian Madness." In *Pre-Text Text Context: Essays on Nineteenth-Century French Literature*, edited by Robert

L. Mitchell, pp. 37-50. Columbus: Ohio State University Press, 1980.

Investigates the "textual coincidence of madness and artistic creation" dramatized in Nerval's *Roman tragique*.

MacLennan, George. "Gérard de Nerval (1): Romanticism, Medicine and Madness" and "Gérard de Nerval (2): 'Madness Tells Her Story'." In *Lucid Interval: Subjective Writing and Madness in History*, pp. 153-95. Rutherford, N. J.: Fairleigh Dickinson University Press, 1992.

Studies Nerval's madness and its manifestation in his work.

Newmark, Kevin. "The Forgotten Figures of Symbolism: Nerval's *Sylvie*." *Yale French Studies*, No. 74 (1988): 207-29.

Discusses the historic and linguistic components of symbolism in Nerval's writing.

Radcliff-Umstead, Douglas. "Cainism and Gérard de Nerval." *Philological Quarterly* XLV, No. 2 (April 1966): 395-408.

Examines Nerval's literary "exalt[ation] of Cain as a wronged hero."

Raitt, A. W. "Time and Instability in Nerval's *Sylvie*." *The Modern Language Review* 83, No. 4 (October 1988): 843-51.

Comments on "warping" and "dissonances" in *Sylvie*. According to Raitt, the reader is intentionally disoriented and "made to share the narrator's anguish at his inability to find a stable point amid the endlessly moving planes of time."

Sieburth, Richard. "Nerval's *Lorely*, or the Lure of Origin." *Studies in Romanticism* 22, No. 2 (Summer 1983): 199-239.

Detailed symbolic analysis of Nerval's German travelogue *Lorely*.

Whitridge, Arnold. "Gérard de Nerval." In *Critical Ventures in Modern French Literature*, pp. 45-64. New York: Charles Scribner's Sons, 1924.

Largely biographical essay offering brief critical commentary.

Winston, Phyllis Jane. *Nerval's Magic Alphabet*. New York: Peter Lang, 1989, 135 p.

Considers the depiction of madness in Nerval's works.

Additional coverage of Nerval's life and career is contained in the following sources published by Gale Research: *Poetry Criticism*, Vol. 13, and *Short Story Criticism*, Vol. 18.

Nineteenth-Century Literature Criticism

Cumulative Indexes
Volumes 1-67

How to Use This Index

The main references

> **Calvino, Italo**
> 1923-1985.....CLC 5, 8, 11, 22, 33, 39,
>   73; SSC 3

list all author entries in the following Gale Literary Criticism series:

BLC = Black Literature Criticism
CLC = Contemporary Literary Criticism
CLR = Children's Literature Review
CMLC = Classical and Medieval Literature Criticism
DA = DISCovering Authors
DC = Drama Criticism
HLC = Hispanic Literature Criticism
LC = Literature Criticism from 1400 to 1800
NCLC = Nineteenth-Century Literature Criticism
PC = Poetry Criticism
SSC = Short Story Criticism
TCLC = Twentieth-Century Literary Criticism
WLC = World Literature Criticism, 1500 to the Present

The cross-references

> See also CANR 23; CA 85-88;
>   obituary CA 116

list all author entries in the following Gale biographical and literary sources:

AAYA = Authors & Artists for Young Adults
AITN = Authors in the News
BEST = Bestsellers
BW = Black Writers
CA = Contemporary Authors
CAAS = Contemporary Authors Autobiography Series
CABS = Contemporary Authors Bibliographical Series
CANR = Contemporary Authors New Revision Series
CAP = Contemporary Authors Permanent Series
CDALB = Concise Dictionary of American Literary Biography
CDBLB = Concise Dictionary of British Literary Biography
DLB = Dictionary of Literary Biography
DLBD = Dictionary of Literary Biography Documentary Series
DLBY = Dictionary of Literary Biography Yearbook
HW = Hispanic Writers
JRDA = Junior DISCovering Authors
MAICYA = Major Authors and Illustrators for Children and Young Adults
MTCW = Major 20th-Century Writers
NNAL = Native North American Literature
SAAS = Something about the Author Autobiography Series
SATA = Something about the Author
YABC = Yesterday's Authors of Books for Children

Literary Criticism Series
Cumulative Author Index

Abasiyanik, Sait Faik 1906-1954
See Sait Faik
See also CA 123

Abbey, Edward 1927-1989 ...... **CLC 36, 59**
See also CA 45-48; 128; CANR 2, 41

Abbott, Lee K(ittredge) 1947- ...... **CLC 48**
See also CA 124; CANR 51; DLB 130

Abe, Kobo
1924-1993 .... **CLC 8, 22, 53, 81;
DAM NOV**
See also CA 65-68; 140; CANR 24, 60;
DLB 182; MTCW

Abelard, Peter c. 1079-c. 1142 ... **CMLC 11**
See also DLB 115

Abell, Kjeld 1901-1961 .... **CLC 15**
See also CA 111

Abish, Walter 1931- .... **CLC 22**
See also CA 101; CANR 37; DLB 130

Abrahams, Peter (Henry) 1919- ..... **CLC 4**
See also BW 1; CA 57-60; CANR 26;
DLB 117; MTCW

Abrams, M(eyer) H(oward) 1912-... **CLC 24**
See also CA 57-60; CANR 13, 33; DLB 67

Abse, Dannie
1923- ... **CLC 7, 29; DAB; DAM POET**
See also CA 53-56; CAAS 1; CANR 4, 46;
DLB 27

Achebe, (Albert) Chinua(lumogu)
1930- ..... **CLC 1, 3, 5, 7, 11, 26, 51, 75;
BLC; DA; DAB; DAC; DAM MST,
MULT, NOV; WLC**
See also AAYA 15; BW 2; CA 1-4R;
CANR 6, 26, 47; CLR 20; DLB 117;
MAICYA; MTCW; SATA 40;
SATA-Brief 38

Acker, Kathy 1948- .... **CLC 45**
See also CA 117; 122; CANR 55

Ackroyd, Peter 1949- .... **CLC 34, 52**
See also CA 123; 127; CANR 51; DLB 155;
INT 127

Acorn, Milton 1923- .... **CLC 15; DAC**
See also CA 103; DLB 53; INT 103

Adamov, Arthur
1908-1970 .... **CLC 4, 25; DAM DRAM**
See also CA 17-18; 25-28R; CAP 2; MTCW

Adams, Alice (Boyd)
1926- .... **CLC 6, 13, 46; SSC 24**
See also CA 81-84; CANR 26, 53;
DLBY 86; INT CANR-26; MTCW

Adams, Andy 1859-1935........ **TCLC 56**
See also YABC 1

Adams, Douglas (Noel)
1952- .... **CLC 27, 60; DAM POP**
See also AAYA 4; BEST 89:3; CA 106;
CANR 34; DLBY 83; JRDA

Adams, Francis 1862-1893....... **NCLC 33**

Adams, Henry (Brooks)
1838-1918 ...... **TCLC 4, 52; DA; DAB;
DAC; DAM MST**
See also CA 104; 133; DLB 12, 47

Adams, Richard (George)
1920- .... **CLC 4, 5, 18; DAM NOV**
See also AAYA 16; AITN 1, 2; CA 49-52;
CANR 3, 35; CLR 20; JRDA; MAICYA;
MTCW; SATA 7, 69

Adamson, Joy(-Friederike Victoria)
1910-1980 .... **CLC 17**
See also CA 69-72; 93-96; CANR 22;
MTCW; SATA 11; SATA-Obit 22

Adcock, Fleur 1934- .... **CLC 41**
See also CA 25-28R; CAAS 23; CANR 11,
34; DLB 40

Addams, Charles (Samuel)
1912-1988 .... **CLC 30**
See also CA 61-64; 126; CANR 12

Addams, Jane 1860-1935......... **TCLC 76**

Addison, Joseph 1672-1719 .... **LC 18**
See also CDBLB 1660-1789; DLB 101

Adler, Alfred (F.) 1870-1937 ...... **TCLC 61**
See also CA 119; 159

Adler, C(arole) S(chwerdtfeger)
1932- .... **CLC 35**
See also AAYA 4; CA 89-92; CANR 19,
40; JRDA; MAICYA; SAAS 15;
SATA 26, 63

Adler, Renata 1938- .... **CLC 8, 31**
See also CA 49-52; CANR 5, 22, 52;
MTCW

Ady, Endre 1877-1919 .... **TCLC 11**
See also CA 107

A.E. 1867-1935 .... **TCLC 3, 10**
See also Russell, George William

Aeschylus
525B.C.-456B.C........ **CMLC 11; DA;
DAB; DAC; DAM DRAM, MST; DC 8;
WLCS**
See also DLB 176

Africa, Ben
See Bosman, Herman Charles

Afton, Effie
See Harper, Frances Ellen Watkins

Agapida, Fray Antonio
See Irving, Washington

Agee, James (Rufus)
1909-1955 .... **TCLC 1, 19; DAM NOV**
See also AITN 1; CA 108; 148;
CDALB 1941-1968; DLB 2, 26, 152

Aghill, Gordon
See Silverberg, Robert

Agnon, S(hmuel) Y(osef Halevi)
1888-1970 .... **CLC 4, 8, 14; SSC 29**
See also CA 17-18; 25-28R; CANR 60;
CAP 2; MTCW

Agrippa von Nettesheim, Henry Cornelius
1486-1535 .... **LC 27**

Aherne, Owen
See Cassill, R(onald) V(erlin)

Ai 1947- .... **CLC 4, 14, 69**
See also CA 85-88; CAAS 13; DLB 120

Aickman, Robert (Fordyce)
1914-1981 .... **CLC 57**
See also CA 5-8R; CANR 3

Aiken, Conrad (Potter)
1889-1973 .... **CLC 1, 3, 5, 10, 52;
DAM NOV, POET; SSC 9**
See also CA 5-8R; 45-48; CANR 4, 60;
CDALB 1929-1941; DLB 9, 45, 102;
MTCW; SATA 3, 30

Aiken, Joan (Delano) 1924-........ **CLC 35**
See also AAYA 1; CA 9-12R; CANR 4, 23,
34; CLR 1, 19; DLB 161; JRDA;
MAICYA; MTCW; SAAS 1; SATA 2,
30, 73

Ainsworth, William Harrison
1805-1882 .... **NCLC 13**
See also DLB 21; SATA 24

Aitmatov, Chingiz (Torekulovich)
1928- .... **CLC 71**
See also CA 103; CANR 38; MTCW;
SATA 56

Akers, Floyd
See Baum, L(yman) Frank

Akhmadulina, Bella Akhatovna
1937- .... **CLC 53; DAM POET**
See also CA 65-68

Akhmatova, Anna
1888-1966 .... **CLC 11, 25, 64;
DAM POET; PC 2**
See also CA 19-20; 25-28R; CANR 35;
CAP 1; MTCW

Aksakov, Sergei Timofeyvich
1791-1859 .... **NCLC 2**

Aksenov, Vassily
See Aksyonov, Vassily (Pavlovich)

Aksyonov, Vassily (Pavlovich)
1932- .... **CLC 22, 37, 101**
See also CA 53-56; CANR 12, 48

Akutagawa, Ryunosuke
1892-1927 .... **TCLC 16**
See also CA 117; 154

Alain 1868-1951 .... **TCLC 41**

Alain-Fournier.................... TCLC 6
See also Fournier, Henri Alban
See also DLB 65

Alarcon, Pedro Antonio de
1833-1891 .... **NCLC 1**

Alas (y Urena), Leopoldo (Enrique Garcia)
1852-1901 .... **TCLC 29**
See also CA 113; 131; HW

Albee, Edward (Franklin III)
1928- ...... **CLC 1, 2, 3, 5, 9, 11, 13, 25, 53, 86; DA; DAB; DAC; DAM DRAM, MST; WLC**
See also AITN 1; CA 5-8R; CABS 3; CANR 8, 54; CDALB 1941-1968; DLB 7; INT CANR-8; MTCW

Alberti, Rafael 1902- .... **CLC 7**
See also CA 85-88; DLB 108

Albert the Great 1200(?)-1280.... **CMLC 16**
See also DLB 115

Alcala-Galiano, Juan Valera y
See Valera y Alcala-Galiano, Juan

Alcott, Amos Bronson 1799-1888 .. **NCLC 1**
See also DLB 1

Alcott, Louisa May
1832-1888 ..... **NCLC 6, 58; DA; DAB; DAC; DAM MST, NOV; SSC 27; WLC**
See also AAYA 20; CDALB 1865-1917; CLR 1, 38; DLB 1, 42, 79; DLBD 14; JRDA; MAICYA; YABC 1

Aldanov, M. A.
See Aldanov, Mark (Alexandrovich)

Aldanov, Mark (Alexandrovich)
1886(?)-1957 .... **TCLC 23**
See also CA 118

Aldington, Richard 1892-1962 ...... **CLC 49**
See also CA 85-88; CANR 45; DLB 20, 36, 100, 149

Aldiss, Brian W(ilson)
1925- .... **CLC 5, 14, 40; DAM NOV**
See also CA 5-8R; CAAS 2; CANR 5, 28; DLB 14; MTCW; SATA 34

Alegria, Claribel
1924- .... **CLC 75; DAM MULT**
See also CA 131; CAAS 15; DLB 145; HW

Alegria, Fernando 1918- .... **CLC 57**
See also CA 9-12R; CANR 5, 32; HW

Aleichem, Sholom .... **TCLC 1, 35**
See also Rabinovitch, Sholem

Aleixandre, Vicente
1898-1984 .... **CLC 9, 36; DAM POET; PC 15**
See also CA 85-88; 114; CANR 26; DLB 108; HW; MTCW

Alepoudelis, Odysseus
See Elytis, Odysseus

Aleshkovsky, Joseph 1929-
See Aleshkovsky, Yuz
See also CA 121; 128

Aleshkovsky, Yuz .... **CLC 44**
See also Aleshkovsky, Joseph

Alexander, Lloyd (Chudley) 1924- .. **CLC 35**
See also AAYA 1; CA 1-4R; CANR 1, 24, 38, 55; CLR 1, 5, 48; DLB 52; JRDA; MAICYA; MTCW; SAAS 19; SATA 3, 49, 81

Alexander, Samuel 1859-1938 ..... **TCLC 77**

Alexie, Sherman (Joseph, Jr.)
1966- .... **CLC 96; DAM MULT**
See also CA 138; DLB 175; NNAL

Alfau, Felipe 1902- .... **CLC 66**
See also CA 137

Alger, Horatio, Jr. 1832-1899 ..... **NCLC 8**
See also DLB 42; SATA 16

Algren, Nelson 1909-1981 .... **CLC 4, 10, 33**
See also CA 13-16R; 103; CANR 20, 61; CDALB 1941-1968; DLB 9; DLBY 81, 82; MTCW

Ali, Ahmed 1910- .... **CLC 69**
See also CA 25-28R; CANR 15, 34

Alighieri, Dante
1265-1321 .... **CMLC 3, 18; WLCS**

Allan, John B.
See Westlake, Donald E(dwin)

Allan, Sidney
See Hartmann, Sadakichi

Allan, Sydney
See Hartmann, Sadakichi

Allen, Edward 1948- .... **CLC 59**

Allen, Paula Gunn
1939- .... **CLC 84; DAM MULT**
See also CA 112; 143; DLB 175; NNAL

Allen, Roland
See Ayckbourn, Alan

Allen, Sarah A.
See Hopkins, Pauline Elizabeth

Allen, Sidney H.
See Hartmann, Sadakichi

Allen, Woody
1935- .... **CLC 16, 52; DAM POP**
See also AAYA 10; CA 33-36R; CANR 27, 38; DLB 44; MTCW

Allende, Isabel
1942- .... **CLC 39, 57, 97; DAM MULT, NOV; HLC; WLCS**
See also AAYA 18; CA 125; 130; CANR 51; DLB 145; HW; INT 130; MTCW

Alleyn, Ellen
See Rossetti, Christina (Georgina)

Allingham, Margery (Louise)
1904-1966 .... **CLC 19**
See also CA 5-8R; 25-28R; CANR 4, 58; DLB 77; MTCW

Allingham, William 1824-1889 ... **NCLC 25**
See also DLB 35

Allison, Dorothy E. 1949- .... **CLC 78**
See also CA 140

Allston, Washington 1779-1843.... **NCLC 2**
See also DLB 1

Almedingen, E. M. .... **CLC 12**
See also Almedingen, Martha Edith von
See also SATA 3

Almedingen, Martha Edith von 1898-1971
See Almedingen, E. M.
See also CA 1-4R; CANR 1

Almqvist, Carl Jonas Love
1793-1866 .... **NCLC 42**

Alonso, Damaso 1898-1990 .... **CLC 14**
See also CA 110; 131; 130; DLB 108; HW

Alov
See Gogol, Nikolai (Vasilyevich)

Alta 1942- .... **CLC 19**
See also CA 57-60

Alter, Robert B(ernard) 1935- ...... **CLC 34**
See also CA 49-52; CANR 1, 47

Alther, Lisa 1944-................ **CLC 7, 41**
See also CA 65-68; CANR 12, 30, 51; MTCW

Althusser, L.
See Althusser, Louis

Althusser, Louis 1918-1990 .... **CLC 106**
See also CA 131; 132

Altman, Robert 1925-............. **CLC 16**
See also CA 73-76; CANR 43

Alvarez, A(lfred) 1929-.......... **CLC 5, 13**
See also CA 1-4R; CANR 3, 33; DLB 14, 40

Alvarez, Alejandro Rodriguez 1903-1965
See Casona, Alejandro
See also CA 131; 93-96; HW

Alvarez, Julia 1950-.............. **CLC 93**
See also CA 147

Alvaro, Corrado 1896-1956 .... **TCLC 60**

Amado, Jorge
1912-.............. **CLC 13, 40, 106; DAM MULT, NOV; HLC**
See also CA 77-80; CANR 35; DLB 113; MTCW

Ambler, Eric 1909-............. **CLC 4, 6, 9**
See also CA 9-12R; CANR 7, 38; DLB 77; MTCW

Amichai, Yehuda 1924- ...... **CLC 9, 22, 57**
See also CA 85-88; CANR 46, 60; MTCW

Amichai, Yehudah
See Amichai, Yehuda

Amiel, Henri Frederic 1821-1881 .. **NCLC 4**

Amis, Kingsley (William)
1922-1995 ..... **CLC 1, 2, 3, 5, 8, 13, 40, 44; DA; DAB; DAC; DAM MST, NOV**
See also AITN 2; CA 9-12R; 150; CANR 8, 28, 54; CDBLB 1945-1960; DLB 15, 27, 100, 139; DLBY 96; INT CANR-8; MTCW

Amis, Martin (Louis)
1949- .... **CLC 4, 9, 38, 62, 101**
See also BEST 90:3; CA 65-68; CANR 8, 27, 54; DLB 14; INT CANR-27

Ammons, A(rchie) R(andolph)
1926- .... **CLC 2, 3, 5, 8, 9, 25, 57; DAM POET; PC 16**
See also AITN 1; CA 9-12R; CANR 6, 36, 51; DLB 5, 165; MTCW

Amo, Tauraatua i
See Adams, Henry (Brooks)

Anand, Mulk Raj
1905- .... **CLC 23, 93; DAM NOV**
See also CA 65-68; CANR 32; MTCW

Anatol
See Schnitzler, Arthur

Anaximander
c. 610B.C.-c. 546B.C......... **CMLC 22**

Anaya, Rudolfo A(lfonso)
1937- .... **CLC 23; DAM MULT, NOV; HLC**
See also AAYA 20; CA 45-48; CAAS 4; CANR 1, 32, 51; DLB 82; HW 1; MTCW

Andersen, Hans Christian
1805-1875 .... **NCLC 7; DA; DAB; DAC; DAM MST, POP; SSC 6; WLC**
See also CLR 6; MAICYA; YABC 1

Arnold, Matthew
1822-1888 ..... **NCLC 6, 29; DA; DAB;
DAC; DAM MST, POET; PC 5; WLC**
See also CDBLB 1832-1890; DLB 32, 57

Arnold, Thomas 1795-1842 ...... **NCLC 18**
See also DLB 55

Arnow, Harriette (Louisa) Simpson
1908-1986 .... **CLC 2, 7, 18**
See also CA 9-12R; 118; CANR 14; DLB 6;
MTCW; SATA 42; SATA-Obit 47

Arp, Hans
See Arp, Jean

Arp, Jean 1887-1966............... **CLC 5**
See also CA 81-84; 25-28R; CANR 42

Arrabal
See Arrabal, Fernando

Arrabal, Fernando 1932- ... **CLC 2, 9, 18, 58**
See also CA 9-12R; CANR 15

Arrick, Fran...................... **CLC 30**
See also Gaberman, Judie Angell

Artaud, Antonin (Marie Joseph)
1896-1948 ... **TCLC 3, 36; DAM DRAM**
See also CA 104; 149

Arthur, Ruth M(abel) 1905-1979.... **CLC 12**
See also CA 9-12R; 85-88; CANR 4;
SATA 7, 26

Artsybashev, Mikhail (Petrovich)
1878-1927 .... **TCLC 31**

Arundel, Honor (Morfydd)
1919-1973 .... **CLC 17**
See also CA 21-22; 41-44R; CAP 2;
CLR 35; SATA 4; SATA-Obit 24

Arzner, Dorothy 1897-1979........ **CLC 98**

Asch, Sholem 1880-1957 .... **TCLC 3**
See also CA 105

Ash, Shalom
See Asch, Sholem

Ashbery, John (Lawrence)
1927- ...... **CLC 2, 3, 4, 6, 9, 13, 15, 25,
41, 77; DAM POET**
See also CA 5-8R; CANR 9, 37; DLB 5,
165; DLBY 81; INT CANR-9; MTCW

Ashdown, Clifford
See Freeman, R(ichard) Austin

Ashe, Gordon
See Creasey, John

Ashton-Warner, Sylvia (Constance)
1908-1984 .... **CLC 19**
See also CA 69-72; 112; CANR 29; MTCW

Asimov, Isaac
1920-1992 ...... **CLC 1, 3, 9, 19, 26, 76,
92; DAM POP**
See also AAYA 13; BEST 90:2; CA 1-4R;
137; CANR 2, 19, 36, 60; CLR 12;
DLB 8; DLBY 92; INT CANR-19;
JRDA; MAICYA; MTCW; SATA 1, 26,
74

Assis, Joaquim Maria Machado de
See Machado de Assis, Joaquim Maria

Astley, Thea (Beatrice May)
1925- .... **CLC 41**
See also CA 65-68; CANR 11, 43

Aston, James
See White, T(erence) H(anbury)

Asturias, Miguel Angel
1899-1974 .... **CLC 3, 8, 13;
DAM MULT, NOV; HLC**
See also CA 25-28; 49-52; CANR 32;
CAP 2; DLB 113; HW; MTCW

Atares, Carlos Saura
See Saura (Atares), Carlos

Atheling, William
See Pound, Ezra (Weston Loomis)

Atheling, William, Jr.
See Blish, James (Benjamin)

Atherton, Gertrude (Franklin Horn)
1857-1948 .... **TCLC 2**
See also CA 104; 155; DLB 9, 78, 186

Atherton, Lucius
See Masters, Edgar Lee

Atkins, Jack
See Harris, Mark

Atkinson, Kate.................... **CLC 99**

Attaway, William (Alexander)
1911-1986 .... **CLC 92; BLC;
DAM MULT**
See also BW 2; CA 143; DLB 76

Atticus
See Fleming, Ian (Lancaster)

Atwood, Margaret (Eleanor)
1939- ..... **CLC 2, 3, 4, 8, 13, 15, 25, 44,
84; DA; DAB; DAC; DAM MST, NOV,
POET; PC 8; SSC 2; WLC**
See also AAYA 12; BEST 89:2; CA 49-52;
CANR 3, 24, 33, 59; DLB 53;
INT CANR-24; MTCW; SATA 50

Aubigny, Pierre d'
See Mencken, H(enry) L(ouis)

Aubin, Penelope 1685-1731(?)........ **LC 9**
See also DLB 39

Auchincloss, Louis (Stanton)
1917- .... **CLC 4, 6, 9, 18, 45;
DAM NOV; SSC 22**
See also CA 1-4R; CANR 6, 29, 55; DLB 2;
DLBY 80; INT CANR-29; MTCW

Auden, W(ystan) H(ugh)
1907-1973 ...... **CLC 1, 2, 3, 4, 6, 9, 11,
14, 43; DA; DAB; DAC; DAM DRAM,
MST, POET; PC 1; WLC**
See also AAYA 18; CA 9-12R; 45-48;
CANR 5, 61; CDBLB 1914-1945;
DLB 10, 20; MTCW

Audiberti, Jacques
1900-1965 ...... **CLC 38; DAM DRAM**
See also CA 25-28R

Audubon, John James
1785-1851 .... **NCLC 47**

Auel, Jean M(arie)
1936- .... **CLC 31; DAM POP**
See also AAYA 7; BEST 90:4; CA 103;
CANR 21; INT CANR-21; SATA 91

Auerbach, Erich 1892-1957 .... **TCLC 43**
See also CA 118; 155

Augier, Emile 1820-1889 .... **NCLC 31**

August, John
See De Voto, Bernard (Augustine)

Augustine, St. 354-430 ...... **CMLC 6; DAB**

Aurelius
See Bourne, Randolph S(illiman)

Aurobindo, Sri 1872-1950 .... **TCLC 63**

Austen, Jane
1775-1817 ..... **NCLC 1, 13, 19, 33, 51;
DA; DAB; DAC; DAM MST, NOV;
WLC**
See also AAYA 19; CDBLB 1789-1832;
DLB 116

Auster, Paul 1947- .... **CLC 47**
See also CA 69-72; CANR 23, 52

Austin, Frank
See Faust, Frederick (Schiller)

Austin, Mary (Hunter)
1868-1934 .... **TCLC 25**
See also CA 109; DLB 9, 78

Autran Dourado, Waldomiro
See Dourado, (Waldomiro Freitas) Autran

Averroes 1126-1198 .... **CMLC 7**
See also DLB 115

Avicenna 980-1037 .... **CMLC 16**
See also DLB 115

Avison, Margaret
1918- .... **CLC 2, 4, 97; DAC;
DAM POET**
See also CA 17-20R; DLB 53; MTCW

Axton, David
See Koontz, Dean R(ay)

Ayckbourn, Alan
1939- ...... **CLC 5, 8, 18, 33, 74; DAB;
DAM DRAM**
See also CA 21-24R; CANR 31, 59;
DLB 13; MTCW

Aydy, Catherine
See Tennant, Emma (Christina)

Ayme, Marcel (Andre) 1902-1967... **CLC 11**
See also CA 89-92; CLR 25; DLB 72;
SATA 91

Ayrton, Michael 1921-1975......... **CLC 7**
See also CA 5-8R; 61-64; CANR 9, 21

Azorin........................... **CLC 11**
See also Martinez Ruiz, Jose

Azuela, Mariano
1873-1952 ..... **TCLC 3; DAM MULT;
HLC**
See also CA 104; 131; HW; MTCW

Baastad, Babbis Friis
See Friis-Baastad, Babbis Ellinor

Bab
See Gilbert, W(illiam) S(chwenck)

Babbis, Eleanor
See Friis-Baastad, Babbis Ellinor

Babel, Isaac
See Babel, Isaak (Emmanuilovich)

Babel, Isaak (Emmanuilovich)
1894-1941(?) ...... **TCLC 2, 13; SSC 16**
See also CA 104; 155

Babits, Mihaly 1883-1941 .... **TCLC 14**
See also CA 114

Babur 1483-1530.................. **LC 18**

Bacchelli, Riccardo 1891-1985 ..... **CLC 19**
See also CA 29-32R; 117

Bach, Richard (David)
1936- ...... **CLC 14; DAM NOV, POP**
See also AITN 1; BEST 89:2; CA 9-12R;
CANR 18; MTCW; SATA 13

Bachman, Richard
  See King, Stephen (Edwin)

Bachmann, Ingeborg 1926-1973. . . . . **CLC 69**
  See also CA 93-96; 45-48; DLB 85

Bacon, Francis 1561-1626 . . . . . . **LC 18, 32**
  See also CDBLB Before 1660; DLB 151

Bacon, Roger 1214(?)-1292 . . . . . . **CMLC 14**
  See also DLB 115

Bacovia, George. . . . . **TCLC 24**
  See also Vasiliu, Gheorghe

Badanes, Jerome 1937-. . . . . **CLC 59**

Bagehot, Walter 1826-1877 . . . . . . **NCLC 10**
  See also DLB 55

Bagnold, Enid
  1889-1981 . . . . . . **CLC 25; DAM DRAM**
  See also CA 5-8R; 103; CANR 5, 40;
  DLB 13, 160; MAICYA; SATA 1, 25

Bagritsky, Eduard 1895-1934 . . . . . **TCLC 60**

Bagrjana, Elisaveta
  See Belcheva, Elisaveta

Bagryana, Elisaveta. . . . . **CLC 10**
  See also Belcheva, Elisaveta
  See also DLB 147

Bailey, Paul 1937- . . . . **CLC 45**
  See also CA 21-24R; CANR 16, 62;
  DLB 14

Baillie, Joanna 1762-1851 . . . . **NCLC 2**
  See also DLB 93

Bainbridge, Beryl (Margaret)
  1933- . . . . **CLC 4, 5, 8, 10, 14, 18, 22, 62;**
                                        DAM NOV
  See also CA 21-24R; CANR 24, 55;
  DLB 14; MTCW

Baker, Elliott 1922- . . . . **CLC 8**
  See also CA 45-48; CANR 2

Baker, Jean H. . . . . **TCLC 3, 10**
  See also Russell, George William

Baker, Nicholson
  1957- . . . . **CLC 61; DAM POP**
  See also CA 135

Baker, Ray Stannard 1870-1946 . . . **TCLC 47**
  See also CA 118

Baker, Russell (Wayne) 1925-. . . . . . **CLC 31**
  See also BEST 89:4; CA 57-60; CANR 11,
  41, 59; MTCW

Bakhtin, M.
  See Bakhtin, Mikhail Mikhailovich

Bakhtin, M. M.
  See Bakhtin, Mikhail Mikhailovich

Bakhtin, Mikhail
  See Bakhtin, Mikhail Mikhailovich

Bakhtin, Mikhail Mikhailovich
  1895-1975 . . . . **CLC 83**
  See also CA 128; 113

Bakshi, Ralph 1938(?)-. . . . . **CLC 26**
  See also CA 112; 138

Bakunin, Mikhail (Alexandrovich)
  1814-1876 . . . . **NCLC 25, 58**

Baldwin, James (Arthur)
  1924-1987 . . . . . **CLC 1, 2, 3, 4, 5, 8, 13,**
    15, 17, 42, 50, 67, 90; BLC; DA; DAB;
    DAC; DAM MST, MULT, NOV, POP;
                              DC 1; SSC 10; WLC
  See also AAYA 4; BW 1; CA 1-4R; 124;
    CABS 1; CANR 3, 24;
    CDALB 1941-1968; DLB 2, 7, 33;
    DLBY 87; MTCW; SATA 9;
    SATA-Obit 54

Ballard, J(ames) G(raham)
  1930- . . . . **CLC 3, 6, 14, 36; DAM NOV,**
                                        POP; SSC 1
  See also AAYA 3; CA 5-8R; CANR 15, 39;
  DLB 14; MTCW; SATA 93

Balmont, Konstantin (Dmitriyevich)
  1867-1943 . . . . **TCLC 11**
  See also CA 109; 155

Balzac, Honore de
  1799-1850 . . . . **NCLC 5, 35, 53; DA;**
    DAB; DAC; DAM MST, NOV; SSC 5;
                                             WLC
  See also DLB 119

Bambara, Toni Cade
  1939-1995 . . . . . . **CLC 19, 88; BLC; DA;**
    DAC; DAM MST, MULT; WLCS
  See also AAYA 5; BW 2; CA 29-32R; 150;
  CANR 24, 49; DLB 38; MTCW

Bamdad, A.
  See Shamlu, Ahmad

Banat, D. R.
  See Bradbury, Ray (Douglas)

Bancroft, Laura
  See Baum, L(yman) Frank

Banim, John 1798-1842 . . . . **NCLC 13**
  See also DLB 116, 158, 159

Banim, Michael 1796-1874 . . . . . . **NCLC 13**
  See also DLB 158, 159

Banjo, The
  See Paterson, A(ndrew) B(arton)

Banks, Iain
  See Banks, Iain M(enzies)

Banks, Iain M(enzies) 1954- . . . . **CLC 34**
  See also CA 123; 128; CANR 61; INT 128

Banks, Lynne Reid . . . . **CLC 23**
  See also Reid Banks, Lynne
  See also AAYA 6

Banks, Russell 1940- . . . . **CLC 37, 72**
  See also CA 65-68; CAAS 15; CANR 19,
  52; DLB 130

Banville, John 1945-. . . . . **CLC 46**
  See also CA 117; 128; DLB 14; INT 128

Banville, Theodore (Faullain) de
  1832-1891 . . . . **NCLC 9**

Baraka, Amiri
  1934- . . . . **CLC 1, 2, 3, 5, 10, 14, 33;**
    BLC; DA; DAC; DAM MST, MULT,
    POET, POP; DC 6; PC 4; WLCS
  See also Jones, LeRoi
  See also BW 2; CA 21-24R; CABS 3;
    CANR 27, 38, 61; CDALB 1941-1968;
    DLB 5, 7, 16, 38; DLBD 8; MTCW

Barbauld, Anna Laetitia
  1743-1825 . . . . **NCLC 50**
  See also DLB 107, 109, 142, 158

Barbellion, W. N. P. . . . . **TCLC 24**
  See also Cummings, Bruce F(rederick)

Barbera, Jack (Vincent) 1945-. . . . . . **CLC 44**
  See also CA 110; CANR 45

Barbey d'Aurevilly, Jules Amedee
  1808-1889 . . . . **NCLC 1; SSC 17**
  See also DLB 119

Barbusse, Henri 1873-1935 . . . . **TCLC 5**
  See also CA 105; 154; DLB 65

Barclay, Bill
  See Moorcock, Michael (John)

Barclay, William Ewert
  See Moorcock, Michael (John)

Barea, Arturo 1897-1957 . . . . **TCLC 14**
  See also CA 111

Barfoot, Joan 1946- . . . . **CLC 18**
  See also CA 105

Baring, Maurice 1874-1945 . . . . **TCLC 8**
  See also CA 105; DLB 34

Barker, Clive 1952- . . . **CLC 52; DAM POP**
  See also AAYA 10; BEST 90:3; CA 121;
  129; INT 129; MTCW

Barker, George Granville
  1913-1991 . . . . . **CLC 8, 48; DAM POET**
  See also CA 9-12R; 135; CANR 7, 38;
  DLB 20; MTCW

Barker, Harley Granville
  See Granville-Barker, Harley
  See also DLB 10

Barker, Howard 1946-. . . . . **CLC 37**
  See also CA 102; DLB 13

Barker, Pat(ricia) 1943-. . . . . . . **CLC 32, 94**
  See also CA 117; 122; CANR 50; INT 122

Barlow, Joel 1754-1812 . . . . **NCLC 23**
  See also DLB 37

Barnard, Mary (Ethel) 1909-. . . . . . **CLC 48**
  See also CA 21-22; CAP 2

Barnes, Djuna
  1892-1982 . . . **CLC 3, 4, 8, 11, 29; SSC 3**
  See also CA 9-12R; 107; CANR 16, 55;
  DLB 4, 9, 45; MTCW

Barnes, Julian (Patrick)
  1946-. . . . . **CLC 42; DAB**
  See also CA 102; CANR 19, 54; DLBY 93

Barnes, Peter 1931-. . . . . **CLC 5, 56**
  See also CA 65-68; CAAS 12; CANR 33,
  34; DLB 13; MTCW

Baroja (y Nessi), Pio
  1872-1956 . . . . **TCLC 8; HLC**
  See also CA 104

Baron, David
  See Pinter, Harold

Baron Corvo
  See Rolfe, Frederick (William Serafino
  Austin Lewis Mary)

Barondess, Sue K(aufman)
  1926-1977 . . . . **CLC 8**
  See also Kaufman, Sue
  See also CA 1-4R; 69-72; CANR 1

Baron de Teive
  See Pessoa, Fernando (Antonio Nogueira)

Barres, Maurice 1862-1923 . . . . **TCLC 47**
  See also DLB 123

Berrigan, Ted. CLC 37
See also Berrigan, Edmund Joseph Michael,
Jr.
See also DLB 5, 169

Berry, Charles Edward Anderson   1931-
See Berry, Chuck
See also CA 115

Berry, Chuck. . . . . CLC 17
See also Berry, Charles Edward Anderson

Berry, Jonas
See Ashbery, John (Lawrence)

Berry, Wendell (Erdman)
1934- . . . . CLC 4, 6, 8, 27, 46;
DAM POET
See also AITN 1; CA 73-76; CANR 50;
DLB 5, 6

Berryman, John
1914-1972 . . . . . . CLC 1, 2, 3, 4, 6, 8, 10,
13, 25, 62; DAM POET
See also CA 13-16; 33-36R; CABS 2;
CANR 35; CAP 1; CDALB 1941-1968;
DLB 48; MTCW

Bertolucci, Bernardo   1940- . . . . CLC 16
See also CA 106

Berton, Pierre (Francis De Marigny)
1920- . . . . CLC 104
See also CA 1-4R; CANR 2, 56; DLB 68

Bertrand, Aloysius   1807-1841 . . . . NCLC 31

Bertran de Born   c. 1140-1215 . . . . . CMLC 5

Besant, Annie (Wood)   1847-1933 . . . TCLC 9
See also CA 105

Bessie, Alvah   1904-1985. . . . . CLC 23
See also CA 5-8R; 116; CANR 2; DLB 26

Bethlen, T. D.
See Silverberg, Robert

Beti, Mongo. . . . CLC 27; BLC; DAM MULT
See also Biyidi, Alexandre

Betjeman, John
1906-1984 . . . . CLC 2, 6, 10, 34, 43;
DAB; DAM MST, POET
See also CA 9-12R; 112; CANR 33, 56;
CDBLB 1945-1960; DLB 20; DLBY 84;
MTCW

Bettelheim, Bruno   1903-1990 . . . . . . CLC 79
See also CA 81-84; 131; CANR 23, 61;
MTCW

Betti, Ugo   1892-1953 . . . . TCLC 5
See also CA 104; 155

Betts, Doris (Waugh)   1932-. . . . CLC 3, 6, 28
See also CA 13-16R; CANR 9; DLBY 82;
INT CANR-9

Bevan, Alistair
See Roberts, Keith (John Kingston)

Bialik, Chaim Nachman
1873-1934 . . . . TCLC 25

Bickerstaff, Isaac
See Swift, Jonathan

Bidart, Frank   1939- . . . . CLC 33
See also CA 140

Bienek, Horst   1930- . . . . CLC 7, 11
See also CA 73-76; DLB 75

Bierce, Ambrose (Gwinett)
1842-1914(?) . . . . . . TCLC 1, 7, 44; DA;
DAC; DAM MST; SSC 9; WLC
See also CA 104; 139; CDALB 1865-1917;
DLB 11, 12, 23, 71, 74, 186

Biggers, Earl Derr   1884-1933 . . . . . TCLC 65
See also CA 108; 153

Billings, Josh
See Shaw, Henry Wheeler

Billington, (Lady) Rachel (Mary)
1942- . . . . CLC 43
See also AITN 2; CA 33-36R; CANR 44

Binyon, T(imothy) J(ohn)   1936- . . . . CLC 34
See also CA 111; CANR 28

Bioy Casares, Adolfo
1914- . . . . CLC 4, 8, 13, 88;
DAM MULT; HLC; SSC 17
See also CA 29-32R; CANR 19, 43;
DLB 113; HW; MTCW

Bird, Cordwainer
See Ellison, Harlan (Jay)

Bird, Robert Montgomery
1806-1854 . . . . NCLC 1

Birney, (Alfred) Earle
1904- . . . . CLC 1, 4, 6, 11; DAC;
DAM MST, POET
See also CA 1-4R; CANR 5, 20; DLB 88;
MTCW

Bishop, Elizabeth
1911-1979 . . . . . . CLC 1, 4, 9, 13, 15, 32;
DA; DAC; DAM MST, POET; PC 3
See also CA 5-8R; 89-92; CABS 2;
CANR 26, 61; CDALB 1968-1988;
DLB 5, 169; MTCW; SATA-Obit 24

Bishop, John   1935- . . . . CLC 10
See also CA 105

Bissett, Bill   1939- . . . . CLC 18; PC 14
See also CA 69-72; CAAS 19; CANR 15;
DLB 53; MTCW

Bitov, Andrei (Georgievich)   1937-. . . CLC 57
See also CA 142

Biyidi, Alexandre   1932-
See Beti, Mongo
See also BW 1; CA 114; 124; MTCW

Bjarme, Brynjolf
See Ibsen, Henrik (Johan)

Bjornson, Bjornstjerne (Martinius)
1832-1910 . . . . TCLC 7, 37
See also CA 104

Black, Robert
See Holdstock, Robert P.

Blackburn, Paul   1926-1971 . . . . . . CLC 9, 43
See also CA 81-84; 33-36R; CANR 34;
DLB 16; DLBY 81

Black Elk
1863-1950 . . . . . TCLC 33; DAM MULT
See also CA 144; NNAL

Black Hobart
See Sanders, (James) Ed(ward)

Blacklin, Malcolm
See Chambers, Aidan

Blackmore, R(ichard) D(oddridge)
1825-1900 . . . . TCLC 27
See also CA 120; DLB 18

Blackmur, R(ichard) P(almer)
1904-1965 . . . . CLC 2, 24
See also CA 11-12; 25-28R; CAP 1; DLB 63

Black Tarantula
See Acker, Kathy

Blackwood, Algernon (Henry)
1869-1951 . . . . TCLC 5
See also CA 105; 150; DLB 153, 156, 178

Blackwood, Caroline
1931-1996 . . . . CLC 6, 9, 100
See also CA 85-88; 151; CANR 32, 61;
DLB 14; MTCW

Blade, Alexander
See Hamilton, Edmond; Silverberg, Robert

Blaga, Lucian   1895-1961 . . . . CLC 75

Blair, Eric (Arthur)   1903-1950
See Orwell, George
See also CA 104; 132; DA; DAB; DAC;
DAM MST, NOV; MTCW; SATA 29

Blais, Marie-Claire
1939- . . . . CLC 2, 4, 6, 13, 22; DAC;
DAM MST
See also CA 21-24R; CAAS 4; CANR 38;
DLB 53; MTCW

Blaise, Clark   1940-. . . . . CLC 29
See also AITN 2; CA 53-56; CAAS 3;
CANR 5; DLB 53

Blake, Fairley
See De Voto, Bernard (Augustine)

Blake, Nicholas
See Day Lewis, C(ecil)
See also DLB 77

Blake, William
1757-1827 . . . . NCLC 13, 37, 57; DA;
DAB; DAC; DAM MST, POET; PC 12;
WLC
See also CDBLB 1789-1832; DLB 93, 163;
MAICYA; SATA 30

Blasco Ibanez, Vicente
1867-1928 . . . . TCLC 12; DAM NOV
See also CA 110; 131; HW; MTCW

Blatty, William Peter
1928- . . . . CLC 2; DAM POP
See also CA 5-8R; CANR 9

Bleeck, Oliver
See Thomas, Ross (Elmore)

Blessing, Lee   1949-. . . . . CLC 54

Blish, James (Benjamin)
1921-1975 . . . . CLC 14
See also CA 1-4R; 57-60; CANR 3; DLB 8;
MTCW; SATA 66

Bliss, Reginald
See Wells, H(erbert) G(eorge)

Blixen, Karen (Christentze Dinesen)
1885-1962
See Dinesen, Isak
See also CA 25-28; CANR 22, 50; CAP 2;
MTCW; SATA 44

Bloch, Robert (Albert)   1917-1994 . . . CLC 33
See also CA 5-8R; 146; CAAS 20; CANR 5;
DLB 44; INT CANR-5; SATA 12;
SATA-Obit 82

Blok, Alexander (Alexandrovich)
1880-1921 . . . . TCLC 5
See also CA 104

Blom, Jan
See Breytenbach, Breyten

Bloom, Harold 1930- . . . . **CLC 24, 103**
See also CA 13-16R; CANR 39; DLB 67

Bloomfield, Aurelius
See Bourne, Randolph S(illiman)

Blount, Roy (Alton), Jr. 1941- . . . . . **CLC 38**
See also CA 53-56; CANR 10, 28, 61;
INT CANR-28; MTCW

Bloy, Leon 1846-1917. . . . . **TCLC 22**
See also CA 121; DLB 123

Blume, Judy (Sussman)
1938- . . . **CLC 12, 30; DAM NOV, POP**
See also AAYA 3; CA 29-32R; CANR 13,
37; CLR 2, 15; DLB 52; JRDA;
MAICYA; MTCW; SATA 2, 31, 79

Blunden, Edmund (Charles)
1896-1974 . . . . **CLC 2, 56**
See also CA 17-18; 45-48; CANR 54;
CAP 2; DLB 20, 100, 155; MTCW

Bly, Robert (Elwood)
1926- . . . . **CLC 1, 2, 5, 10, 15, 38;**
DAM POET
See also CA 5-8R; CANR 41; DLB 5;
MTCW

Boas, Franz 1858-1942. . . . . **TCLC 56**
See also CA 115

Bobette
See Simenon, Georges (Jacques Christian)

Boccaccio, Giovanni
1313-1375 . . . . **CMLC 13; SSC 10**

Bochco, Steven 1943- . . . . **CLC 35**
See also AAYA 11; CA 124; 138

Bodenheim, Maxwell 1892-1954 . . . **TCLC 44**
See also CA 110; DLB 9, 45

Bodker, Cecil 1927- . . . . **CLC 21**
See also CA 73-76; CANR 13, 44; CLR 23;
MAICYA; SATA 14

Boell, Heinrich (Theodor)
1917-1985 . . . . **CLC 2, 3, 6, 9, 11, 15, 27,**
32, 72; DA; DAB; DAC; DAM MST,
NOV; SSC 23; WLC
See also CA 21-24R; 116; CANR 24;
DLB 69; DLBY 85; MTCW

Boerne, Alfred
See Doeblin, Alfred

Boethius 480(?)-524(?) . . . . **CMLC 15**
See also DLB 115

Bogan, Louise
1897-1970 . . . . **CLC 4, 39, 46, 93;**
DAM POET; PC 12
See also CA 73-76; 25-28R; CANR 33;
DLB 45, 169; MTCW

Bogarde, Dirk . . . . **CLC 19**
See also Van Den Bogarde, Derek Jules
Gaspard Ulric Niven
See also DLB 14

Bogosian, Eric 1953- . . . . **CLC 45**
See also CA 138

Bograd, Larry 1953- . . . . **CLC 35**
See also CA 93-96; CANR 57; SAAS 21;
SATA 33, 89

Boiardo, Matteo Maria 1441-1494 . . . . **LC 6**

Boileau-Despreaux, Nicolas
1636-1711 . . . . **LC 3**

Bojer, Johan 1872-1959 . . . . **TCLC 64**

Boland, Eavan (Aisling)
1944- . . . . **CLC 40, 67; DAM POET**
See also CA 143; CANR 61; DLB 40

Bolt, Lee
See Faust, Frederick (Schiller)

Bolt, Robert (Oxton)
1924-1995 . . . . . . **CLC 14; DAM DRAM**
See also CA 17-20R; 147; CANR 35;
DLB 13; MTCW

Bombet, Louis-Alexandre-Cesar
See Stendhal

Bomkauf
See Kaufman, Bob (Garnell)

Bonaventura. . . . . **NCLC 35**
See also DLB 90

Bond, Edward
1934- . . . **CLC 4, 6, 13, 23; DAM DRAM**
See also CA 25-28R; CANR 38; DLB 13;
MTCW

Bonham, Frank 1914-1989. . . . . **CLC 12**
See also AAYA 1; CA 9-12R; CANR 4, 36;
JRDA; MAICYA; SAAS 3; SATA 1, 49;
SATA-Obit 62

Bonnefoy, Yves
1923- . . . . . . **CLC 9, 15, 58; DAM MST,**
POET
See also CA 85-88; CANR 33; MTCW

Bontemps, Arna(ud Wendell)
1902-1973 . . . . **CLC 1, 18; BLC;**
DAM MULT, NOV, POET
See also BW 1; CA 1-4R; 41-44R; CANR 4,
35; CLR 6; DLB 48, 51; JRDA;
MAICYA; MTCW; SATA 2, 44;
SATA-Obit 24

Booth, Martin 1944- . . . . **CLC 13**
See also CA 93-96; CAAS 2

Booth, Philip 1925- . . . . **CLC 23**
See also CA 5-8R; CANR 5; DLBY 82

Booth, Wayne C(layson) 1921- . . . . . **CLC 24**
See also CA 1-4R; CAAS 5; CANR 3, 43;
DLB 67

Borchert, Wolfgang 1921-1947 . . . . . **TCLC 5**
See also CA 104; DLB 69, 124

Borel, Petrus 1809-1859. . . . . **NCLC 41**

Borges, Jorge Luis
1899-1986 . . . **CLC 1, 2, 3, 4, 6, 8, 9, 10,**
13, 19, 44, 48, 83; DA; DAB; DAC;
DAM MST, MULT; HLC; SSC 4; WLC
See also AAYA 19; CA 21-24R; CANR 19,
33; DLB 113; DLBY 86; HW; MTCW

Borowski, Tadeusz 1922-1951 . . . . . . **TCLC 9**
See also CA 106; 154

Borrow, George (Henry)
1803-1881 . . . . **NCLC 9**
See also DLB 21, 55, 166

Bosman, Herman Charles
1905-1951 . . . . **TCLC 49**
See also Malan, Herman
See also CA 160

Bosschere, Jean de 1878(?)-1953 . . . **TCLC 19**
See also CA 115

Boswell, James
1740-1795 . . . . . . **LC 4; DA; DAB; DAC;**
DAM MST; WLC
See also CDBLB 1660-1789; DLB 104, 142

Bottoms, David 1949- . . . . **CLC 53**
See also CA 105; CANR 22; DLB 120;
DLBY 83

Boucicault, Dion 1820-1890 . . . . . . **NCLC 41**

Boucolon, Maryse 1937(?)-
See Conde, Maryse
See also CA 110; CANR 30, 53

Bourget, Paul (Charles Joseph)
1852-1935 . . . . **TCLC 12**
See also CA 107; DLB 123

Bourjaily, Vance (Nye) 1922- . . . . **CLC 8, 62**
See also CA 1-4R; CAAS 1; CANR 2;
DLB 2, 143

Bourne, Randolph S(illiman)
1886-1918 . . . . **TCLC 16**
See also CA 117; 155; DLB 63

Bova, Ben(jamin William) 1932- . . . . **CLC 45**
See also AAYA 16; CA 5-8R; CAAS 18;
CANR 11, 56; CLR 3; DLBY 81;
INT CANR-11; MAICYA; MTCW;
SATA 6, 68

Bowen, Elizabeth (Dorothea Cole)
1899-1973 . . . . . . **CLC 1, 3, 6, 11, 15, 22;**
DAM NOV; SSC 3, 28
See also CA 17-18; 41-44R; CANR 35;
CAP 2; CDBLB 1945-1960; DLB 15, 162;
MTCW

Bowering, George 1935- . . . . **CLC 15, 47**
See also CA 21-24R; CAAS 16; CANR 10;
DLB 53

Bowering, Marilyn R(uthe) 1949- . . . **CLC 32**
See also CA 101; CANR 49

Bowers, Edgar 1924- . . . . **CLC 9**
See also CA 5-8R; CANR 24; DLB 5

Bowie, David . . . . **CLC 17**
See also Jones, David Robert

Bowles, Jane (Sydney)
1917-1973 . . . . **CLC 3, 68**
See also CA 19-20; 41-44R; CAP 2

Bowles, Paul (Frederick)
1910- . . . . **CLC 1, 2, 19, 53; SSC 3**
See also CA 1-4R; CAAS 1; CANR 1, 19,
50; DLB 5, 6; MTCW

Box, Edgar
See Vidal, Gore

Boyd, Nancy
See Millay, Edna St. Vincent

Boyd, William 1952- . . . . **CLC 28, 53, 70**
See also CA 114; 120; CANR 51

Boyle, Kay
1902-1992 . . . . . **CLC 1, 5, 19, 58; SSC 5**
See also CA 13-16R; 140; CAAS 1;
CANR 29, 61; DLB 4, 9, 48, 86;
DLBY 93; MTCW

Boyle, Mark
See Kienzle, William X(avier)

Boyle, Patrick 1905-1982. . . . . **CLC 19**
See also CA 127

Boyle, T. C. 1948-
See Boyle, T(homas) Coraghessan

Brooke, Rupert (Chawner)
 1887-1915 .... TCLC 2, 7; DA; DAB;
  DAC; DAM MST, POET; WLC
 See also CA 104; 132; CANR 61;
  CDBLB 1914-1945; DLB 19; MTCW

Brooke-Haven, P.
 See Wodehouse, P(elham) G(renville)

Brooke-Rose, Christine 1926(?)- .... CLC 40
 See also CA 13-16R; CANR 58; DLB 14

Brookner, Anita
 1928- .... CLC 32, 34, 51; DAB;
  DAM POP
 See also CA 114; 120; CANR 37, 56;
  DLBY 87; MTCW

Brooks, Cleanth 1906-1994 ..... CLC 24, 86
 See also CA 17-20R; 145; CANR 33, 35;
  DLB 63; DLBY 94; INT CANR-35;
  MTCW

Brooks, George
 See Baum, L(yman) Frank

Brooks, Gwendolyn
 1917- ...... CLC 1, 2, 4, 5, 15, 49; BLC;
  DA; DAC; DAM MST, MULT, POET;
  PC 7; WLC
 See also AAYA 20; AITN 1; BW 2;
  CA 1-4R; CANR 1, 27, 52;
  CDALB 1941-1968; CLR 27; DLB 5, 76,
  165; MTCW; SATA 6

Brooks, Mel .... CLC 12
 See also Kaminsky, Melvin
 See also AAYA 13; DLB 26

Brooks, Peter 1938- .... CLC 34
 See also CA 45-48; CANR 1

Brooks, Van Wyck 1886-1963 ...... CLC 29
 See also CA 1-4R; CANR 6; DLB 45, 63,
  103

Brophy, Brigid (Antonia)
 1929-1995 .... CLC 6, 11, 29, 105
 See also CA 5-8R; 149; CAAS 4; CANR 25,
  53; DLB 14; MTCW

Brosman, Catharine Savage 1934- .... CLC 9
 See also CA 61-64; CANR 21, 46

Brother Antoninus
 See Everson, William (Oliver)

Broughton, T(homas) Alan 1936- ... CLC 19
 See also CA 45-48; CANR 2, 23, 48

Broumas, Olga 1949- .... CLC 10, 73
 See also CA 85-88; CANR 20

Brown, Alan 1951- .... CLC 99

Brown, Charles Brockden
 1771-1810 .... NCLC 22
 See also CDALB 1640-1865; DLB 37, 59,
  73

Brown, Christy 1932-1981 .... CLC 63
 See also CA 105; 104; DLB 14

Brown, Claude
 1937- ..... CLC 30; BLC; DAM MULT
 See also AAYA 7; BW 1; CA 73-76

Brown, Dee (Alexander)
 1908- .... CLC 18, 47; DAM POP
 See also CA 13-16R; CAAS 6; CANR 11,
  45, 60; DLBY 80; MTCW; SATA 5

Brown, George
 See Wertmueller, Lina

Brown, George Douglas
 1869-1902 .... TCLC 28

Brown, George Mackay
 1921-1996 .... CLC 5, 48, 100
 See also CA 21-24R; 151; CAAS 6;
  CANR 12, 37, 62; DLB 14, 27, 139;
  MTCW; SATA 35

Brown, (William) Larry 1951- ...... CLC 73
 See also CA 130; 134; INT 133

Brown, Moses
 See Barrett, William (Christopher)

Brown, Rita Mae
 1944- ..... CLC 18, 43, 79; DAM NOV,
  POP
 See also CA 45-48; CANR 2, 11, 35, 62;
  INT CANR-11; MTCW

Brown, Roderick (Langmere) Haig-
 See Haig-Brown, Roderick (Langmere)

Brown, Rosellen 1939- .... CLC 32
 See also CA 77-80; CAAS 10; CANR 14, 44

Brown, Sterling Allen
 1901-1989 .... CLC 1, 23, 59; BLC;
  DAM MULT, POET
 See also BW 1; CA 85-88; 127; CANR 26;
  DLB 48, 51, 63; MTCW

Brown, Will
 See Ainsworth, William Harrison

Brown, William Wells
 1813-1884 .... NCLC 2; BLC;
  DAM MULT; DC 1
 See also DLB 3, 50

Browne, (Clyde) Jackson 1948(?)- ... CLC 21
 See also CA 120

Browning, Elizabeth Barrett
 1806-1861 .... NCLC 1, 16, 61, 66; DA;
  DAB; DAC; DAM MST, POET; PC 6;
  WLC
 See also CDBLB 1832-1890; DLB 32

Browning, Robert
 1812-1889 .... NCLC 19; DA; DAB;
  DAC; DAM MST, POET; PC 2; WLCS
 See also CDBLB 1832-1890; DLB 32, 163;
  YABC 1

Browning, Tod 1882-1962 .... CLC 16
 See also CA 141; 117

Brownson, Orestes (Augustus)
 1803-1876 .... NCLC 50

Bruccoli, Matthew J(oseph) 1931- .. CLC 34
 See also CA 9-12R; CANR 7; DLB 103

Bruce, Lenny .... CLC 21
 See also Schneider, Leonard Alfred

Bruin, John
 See Brutus, Dennis

Brulard, Henri
 See Stendhal

Brulls, Christian
 See Simenon, Georges (Jacques Christian)

Brunner, John (Kilian Houston)
 1934-1995 ...... CLC 8, 10; DAM POP
 See also CA 1-4R; 149; CAAS 8; CANR 2,
  37; MTCW

Bruno, Giordano 1548-1600 .... LC 27

Brutus, Dennis
 1924- ..... CLC 43; BLC; DAM MULT,
  POET
 See also BW 2; CA 49-52; CAAS 14;
  CANR 2, 27, 42; DLB 117

Bryan, C(ourtlandt) D(ixon) B(arnes)
 1936- .... CLC 29
 See also CA 73-76; CANR 13;
  INT CANR-13

Bryan, Michael
 See Moore, Brian

Bryant, William Cullen
 1794-1878 ..... NCLC 6, 46; DA; DAB;
  DAC; DAM MST, POET; PC 20
 See also CDALB 1640-1865; DLB 3, 43, 59

Bryusov, Valery Yakovlevich
 1873-1924 .... TCLC 10
 See also CA 107; 155

Buchan, John
 1875-1940 .... TCLC 41; DAB;
  DAM POP
 See also CA 108; 145; DLB 34, 70, 156;
  YABC 2

Buchanan, George 1506-1582 .... LC 4

Buchheim, Lothar-Guenther 1918- ... CLC 6
 See also CA 85-88

Buchner, (Karl) Georg
 1813-1837 .... NCLC 26

Buchwald, Art(hur) 1925- .... CLC 33
 See also AITN 1; CA 5-8R; CANR 21;
  MTCW; SATA 10

Buck, Pearl S(ydenstricker)
 1892-1973 .... CLC 7, 11, 18; DA; DAB;
  DAC; DAM MST, NOV
 See also AITN 1; CA 1-4R; 41-44R;
  CANR 1, 34; DLB 9, 102; MTCW;
  SATA 1, 25

Buckler, Ernest
 1908-1984 .. CLC 13; DAC; DAM MST
 See also CA 11-12; 114; CAP 1; DLB 68;
  SATA 47

Buckley, Vincent (Thomas)
 1925-1988 .... CLC 57
 See also CA 101

Buckley, William F(rank), Jr.
 1925- .... CLC 7, 18, 37; DAM POP
 See also AITN 1; CA 1-4R; CANR 1, 24,
  53; DLB 137; DLBY 80; INT CANR-24;
  MTCW

Buechner, (Carl) Frederick
 1926- ...... CLC 2, 4, 6, 9; DAM NOV
 See also CA 13-16R; CANR 11, 39;
  DLBY 80; INT CANR-11; MTCW

Buell, John (Edward) 1927- .... CLC 10
 See also CA 1-4R; DLB 53

Buero Vallejo, Antonio 1916- ... CLC 15, 46
 See also CA 106; CANR 24, 49; HW;
  MTCW

Bufalino, Gesualdo 1920(?)- .... CLC 74

Bugayev, Boris Nikolayevich 1880-1934
 See Bely, Andrey
 See also CA 104

Bukowski, Charles
1920-1994 . . . . CLC 2, 5, 9, 41, 82;
DAM NOV, POET; PC 18
See also CA 17-20R; 144; CANR 40, 62;
DLB 5, 130, 169; MTCW

Bulgakov, Mikhail (Afanas'evich)
1891-1940 . . . . TCLC 2, 16;
DAM DRAM, NOV; SSC 18
See also CA 105; 152

Bulgya, Alexander Alexandrovich
1901-1956 . . . . TCLC 53
See also Fadeyev, Alexander
See also CA 117

Bullins, Ed
1935- . . . . CLC 1, 5, 7; BLC;
DAM DRAM, MULT; DC 6
See also BW 2; CA 49-52; CAAS 16;
CANR 24, 46; DLB 7, 38; MTCW

Bulwer-Lytton, Edward (George Earle Lytton)
1803-1873 . . . . NCLC 1, 45
See also DLB 21

Bunin, Ivan Alexeyevich
1870-1953 . . . . TCLC 6; SSC 5
See also CA 104

Bunting, Basil
1900-1985 . . . . CLC 10, 39, 47;
DAM POET
See also CA 53-56; 115; CANR 7; DLB 20

Bunuel, Luis
1900-1983 . . . . CLC 16, 80;
DAM MULT; HLC
See also CA 101; 110; CANR 32; HW

Bunyan, John
1628-1688 . . . . . . LC 4; DA; DAB; DAC;
DAM MST; WLC
See also CDBLB 1660-1789; DLB 39

Burckhardt, Jacob (Christoph)
1818-1897 . . . . NCLC 49

Burford, Eleanor
See Hibbert, Eleanor Alice Burford

Burgess, Anthony
. CLC 1, 2, 4, 5, 8, 10, 13, 15, 22, 40, 62,
81, 94; DAB
See also Wilson, John (Anthony) Burgess
See also AITN 1; CDBLB 1960 to Present;
DLB 14

Burke, Edmund
1729(?)-1797 . . . . . . LC 7, 36; DA; DAB;
DAC; DAM MST; WLC
See also DLB 104

Burke, Kenneth (Duva)
1897-1993 . . . . CLC 2, 24
See also CA 5-8R; 143; CANR 39; DLB 45,
63; MTCW

Burke, Leda
See Garnett, David

Burke, Ralph
See Silverberg, Robert

Burke, Thomas 1886-1945 . . . . TCLC 63
See also CA 113; 155

Burney, Fanny 1752-1840 . . . . NCLC 12, 54
See also DLB 39

Burns, Robert 1759-1796 . . . . PC 6
See also CDBLB 1789-1832; DA; DAB;
DAC; DAM MST, POET; DLB 109;
WLC

Burns, Tex
See L'Amour, Louis (Dearborn)

Burnshaw, Stanley 1906- . . . . . CLC 3, 13, 44
See also CA 9-12R; DLB 48

Burr, Anne 1937- . . . . CLC 6
See also CA 25-28R

Burroughs, Edgar Rice
1875-1950 . . . . TCLC 2, 32; DAM NOV
See also AAYA 11; CA 104; 132; DLB 8;
MTCW; SATA 41

Burroughs, William S(eward)
1914-1997 . . . . . . CLC 1, 2, 5, 15, 22, 42,
75; DA; DAB; DAC; DAM MST, NOV,
POP; WLC
See also AITN 2; CA 9-12R; 160;
CANR 20, 52; DLB 2, 8, 16, 152;
DLBY 81; MTCW

Burton, Richard F. 1821-1890 . . . . NCLC 42
See also DLB 55, 184

Busch, Frederick 1941- . . . CLC 7, 10, 18, 47
See also CA 33-36R; CAAS 1; CANR 45;
DLB 6

Bush, Ronald 1946- . . . . CLC 34
See also CA 136

Bustos, F(rancisco)
See Borges, Jorge Luis

Bustos Domecq, H(onorio)
See Bioy Casares, Adolfo; Borges, Jorge
Luis

Butler, Octavia E(stelle)
1947- . . . . . CLC 38; DAM MULT, POP
See also AAYA 18; BW 2; CA 73-76;
CANR 12, 24, 38; DLB 33; MTCW;
SATA 84

Butler, Robert Olen (Jr.)
1945- . . . . CLC 81; DAM POP
See also CA 112; DLB 173; INT 112

Butler, Samuel 1612-1680 . . . . LC 16
See also DLB 101, 126

Butler, Samuel
1835-1902 . . . . . . TCLC 1, 33; DA; DAB;
DAC; DAM MST, NOV; WLC
See also CA 143; CDBLB 1890-1914;
DLB 18, 57, 174

Butler, Walter C.
See Faust, Frederick (Schiller)

Butor, Michel (Marie Francois)
1926- . . . . CLC 1, 3, 8, 11, 15
See also CA 9-12R; CANR 33; DLB 83;
MTCW

Butts, Mary 1892(?)-1937 . . . . TCLC 77
See also CA 148

Buzo, Alexander (John) 1944- . . . . . . CLC 61
See also CA 97-100; CANR 17, 39

Buzzati, Dino 1906-1972 . . . . CLC 36
See also CA 160; 33-36R; DLB 177

Byars, Betsy (Cromer) 1928- . . . . CLC 35
See also AAYA 19; CA 33-36R; CANR 18,
36, 57; CLR 1, 16; DLB 52;
INT CANR-18; JRDA; MAICYA;
MTCW; SAAS 1; SATA 4, 46, 80

Byatt, A(ntonia) S(usan Drabble)
1936- . . . CLC 19, 65; DAM NOV, POP
See also CA 13-16R; CANR 13, 33, 50;
DLB 14; MTCW

Byrne, David 1952- . . . . CLC 26
See also CA 127

Byrne, John Keyes 1926-
See Leonard, Hugh
See also CA 102; INT 102

Byron, George Gordon (Noel)
1788-1824 . . . . . NCLC 2, 12; DA; DAB;
DAC; DAM MST, POET; PC 16; WLC
See also CDBLB 1789-1832; DLB 96, 110

Byron, Robert 1905-1941 . . . . TCLC 67
See also CA 160

C. 3. 3.
See Wilde, Oscar (Fingal O'Flahertie Wills)

Caballero, Fernan 1796-1877 . . . . . NCLC 10

Cabell, Branch
See Cabell, James Branch

Cabell, James Branch 1879-1958 . . . TCLC 6
See also CA 105; 152; DLB 9, 78

Cable, George Washington
1844-1925 . . . . TCLC 4; SSC 4
See also CA 104; 155; DLB 12, 74;
DLBD 13

Cabral de Melo Neto, Joao
1920- . . . . CLC 76; DAM MULT
See also CA 151

Cabrera Infante, G(uillermo)
1929- . . . . . CLC 5, 25, 45; DAM MULT;
HLC
See also CA 85-88; CANR 29; DLB 113;
HW; MTCW

Cade, Toni
See Bambara, Toni Cade

Cadmus and Harmonia
See Buchan, John

Caedmon fl. 658-680 . . . . CMLC 7
See also DLB 146

Caeiro, Alberto
See Pessoa, Fernando (Antonio Nogueira)

Cage, John (Milton, Jr.) 1912- . . . . . CLC 41
See also CA 13-16R; CANR 9;
INT CANR-9

Cahan, Abraham 1860-1951 . . . . . . TCLC 71
See also CA 108; 154; DLB 9, 25, 28

Cain, G.
See Cabrera Infante, G(uillermo)

Cain, Guillermo
See Cabrera Infante, G(uillermo)

Cain, James M(allahan)
1892-1977 . . . . CLC 3, 11, 28
See also AITN 1; CA 17-20R; 73-76;
CANR 8, 34, 61; MTCW

Caine, Mark
See Raphael, Frederic (Michael)

Calasso, Roberto 1941- . . . . CLC 81
See also CA 143

Calderon de la Barca, Pedro
1600-1681 . . . . LC 23; DC 3

Caldwell, Erskine (Preston)
1903-1987 . . . . CLC 1, 8, 14, 50, 60;
DAM NOV; SSC 19
See also AITN 1; CA 1-4R; 121; CAAS 1;
CANR 2, 33; DLB 9, 86; MTCW

Author Index

Cary, (Arthur) Joyce (Lunel)
1888-1957 .... **TCLC 1, 29**
See also CA 104; CDBLB 1914-1945;
DLB 15, 100

Casanova de Seingalt, Giovanni Jacopo
1725-1798 .... **LC 13**

Casares, Adolfo Bioy
See Bioy Casares, Adolfo

Casely-Hayford, J(oseph) E(phraim)
1866-1930 .... **TCLC 24; BLC;**
DAM MULT
See also BW 2; CA 123; 152

Casey, John (Dudley) 1939- .... **CLC 59**
See also BEST 90:2; CA 69-72; CANR 23

Casey, Michael 1947- .... **CLC 2**
See also CA 65-68; DLB 5

Casey, Patrick
See Thurman, Wallace (Henry)

Casey, Warren (Peter) 1935-1988 ... **CLC 12**
See also CA 101; 127; INT 101

Casona, Alejandro .... **CLC 49**
See also Alvarez, Alejandro Rodriguez

Cassavetes, John 1929-1989 .... **CLC 20**
See also CA 85-88; 127

Cassian, Nina 1924- .... **PC 17**

Cassill, R(onald) V(erlin) 1919- ... **CLC 4, 23**
See also CA 9-12R; CAAS 1; CANR 7, 45;
DLB 6

Cassirer, Ernst 1874-1945 .... **TCLC 61**
See also CA 157

Cassity, (Allen) Turner 1929- .... **CLC 6, 42**
See also CA 17-20R; CAAS 8; CANR 11;
DLB 105

Castaneda, Carlos 1931(?)- .... **CLC 12**
See also CA 25-28R; CANR 32; HW;
MTCW

Castedo, Elena 1937- .... **CLC 65**
See also CA 132

Castedo-Ellerman, Elena
See Castedo, Elena

Castellanos, Rosario
1925-1974 ...... **CLC 66; DAM MULT;**
HLC
See also CA 131; 53-56; CANR 58;
DLB 113; HW

Castelvetro, Lodovico 1505-1571 ..... **LC 12**

Castiglione, Baldassare 1478-1529 ... **LC 12**

Castle, Robert
See Hamilton, Edmond

Castro, Guillen de 1569-1631 .... **LC 19**

Castro, Rosalia de
1837-1885 ...... **NCLC 3; DAM MULT**

Cather, Willa
See Cather, Willa Sibert

Cather, Willa Sibert
1873-1947 .... **TCLC 1, 11, 31; DA;**
DAB; DAC; DAM MST, NOV; SSC 2;
WLC
See also CA 104; 128; CDALB 1865-1917;
DLB 9, 54, 78; DLBD 1; MTCW;
SATA 30

Cato, Marcus Porcius
234B.C.-149B.C. .... **CMLC 21**

Catton, (Charles) Bruce
1899-1978 .... **CLC 35**
See also AITN 1; CA 5-8R; 81-84;
CANR 7; DLB 17; SATA 2;
SATA-Obit 24

Catullus c. 84B.C.-c. 54B.C. ..... **CMLC 18**

Cauldwell, Frank
See King, Francis (Henry)

Caunitz, William J. 1933-1996 ..... **CLC 34**
See also BEST 89:3; CA 125; 130; 152;
INT 130

Causley, Charles (Stanley) 1917- ..... **CLC 7**
See also CA 9-12R; CANR 5, 35; CLR 30;
DLB 27; MTCW; SATA 3, 66

Caute, David 1936- .... **CLC 29; DAM NOV**
See also CA 1-4R; CAAS 4; CANR 1, 33;
DLB 14

Cavafy, C(onstantine) P(eter)
1863-1933 .... **TCLC 2, 7; DAM POET**
See also Kavafis, Konstantinos Petrou
See also CA 148

Cavallo, Evelyn
See Spark, Muriel (Sarah)

Cavanna, Betty .... **CLC 12**
See also Harrison, Elizabeth Cavanna
See also JRDA; MAICYA; SAAS 4;
SATA 1, 30

Cavendish, Margaret Lucas
1623-1673 .... **LC 30**
See also DLB 131

Caxton, William 1421(?)-1491(?)..... **LC 17**
See also DLB 170

Cayrol, Jean 1911- .... **CLC 11**
See also CA 89-92; DLB 83

Cela, Camilo Jose
1916- ..... **CLC 4, 13, 59; DAM MULT;**
HLC
See also BEST 90:2; CA 21-24R; CAAS 10;
CANR 21, 32; DLBY 89; HW; MTCW

Celan, Paul ...... **CLC 10, 19, 53, 82; PC 10**
See also Antschel, Paul
See also DLB 69

Celine, Louis-Ferdinand
.... **CLC 1, 3, 4, 7, 9, 15, 47**
See also Destouches, Louis-Ferdinand
See also DLB 72

Cellini, Benvenuto 1500-1571 .... **LC 7**

Cendrars, Blaise 1887-1961 .... **CLC 18, 106**
See also Sauser-Hall, Frederic

Cernuda (y Bidon), Luis
1902-1963 .... **CLC 54; DAM POET**
See also CA 131; 89-92; DLB 134; HW

Cervantes (Saavedra), Miguel de
1547-1616 .... **LC 6, 23; DA; DAB;**
DAC; DAM MST, NOV; SSC 12; WLC

Cesaire, Aime (Fernand)
1913- .... **CLC 19, 32; BLC;**
DAM MULT, POET
See also BW 2; CA 65-68; CANR 24, 43;
MTCW

Chabon, Michael 1963- .... **CLC 55**
See also CA 139; CANR 57

Chabrol, Claude 1930- .... **CLC 16**
See also CA 110

Challans, Mary 1905-1983
See Renault, Mary
See also CA 81-84; 111; SATA 23;
SATA-Obit 36

Challis, George
See Faust, Frederick (Schiller)

Chambers, Aidan 1934- .... **CLC 35**
See also CA 25-28R; CANR 12, 31, 58;
JRDA; MAICYA; SAAS 12; SATA 1, 69

Chambers, James 1948-
See Cliff, Jimmy
See also CA 124

Chambers, Jessie
See Lawrence, D(avid) H(erbert Richards)

Chambers, Robert W. 1865-1933... **TCLC 41**

Chandler, Raymond (Thornton)
1888-1959 .... **TCLC 1, 7; SSC 23**
See also CA 104; 129; CANR 60;
CDALB 1929-1941; DLBD 6; MTCW

Chang, Eileen 1921- .... **SSC 28**

Chang, Jung 1952- .... **CLC 71**
See also CA 142

Channing, William Ellery
1780-1842 .... **NCLC 17**
See also DLB 1, 59

Chaplin, Charles Spencer
1889-1977 .... **CLC 16**
See also Chaplin, Charlie
See also CA 81-84; 73-76

Chaplin, Charlie
See Chaplin, Charles Spencer
See also DLB 44

Chapman, George
1559(?)-1634 ..... **LC 22; DAM DRAM**
See also DLB 62, 121

Chapman, Graham 1941-1989 ...... **CLC 21**
See also Monty Python
See also CA 116; 129; CANR 35

Chapman, John Jay 1862-1933 ..... **TCLC 7**
See also CA 104

Chapman, Lee
See Bradley, Marion Zimmer

Chapman, Walker
See Silverberg, Robert

Chappell, Fred (Davis) 1936- .... **CLC 40, 78**
See also CA 5-8R; CAAS 4; CANR 8, 33;
DLB 6, 105

Char, Rene(-Emile)
1907-1988 .... **CLC 9, 11, 14, 55;**
DAM POET
See also CA 13-16R; 124; CANR 32;
MTCW

Charby, Jay
See Ellison, Harlan (Jay)

Chardin, Pierre Teilhard de
See Teilhard de Chardin, (Marie Joseph)
Pierre

Charles I 1600-1649 .... **LC 13**

Charriere, Isabelle de 1740-1805 .. **NCLC 66**

Charyn, Jerome 1937- .... **CLC 5, 8, 18**
See also CA 5-8R; CAAS 1; CANR 7, 61;
DLBY 83; MTCW

Chase, Mary (Coyle) 1907-1981 . . . . . . **DC 1**
See also CA 77-80; 105; SATA 17;
SATA-Obit 29

Chase, Mary Ellen 1887-1973 . . . . **CLC 2**
See also CA 13-16; 41-44R; CAP 1;
SATA 10

Chase, Nicholas
See Hyde, Anthony

Chateaubriand, Francois Rene de
1768-1848 . . . . **NCLC 3**
See also DLB 119

Chatterje, Sarat Chandra 1876-1936(?)
See Chatterji, Saratchandra
See also CA 109

Chatterji, Bankim Chandra
1838-1894 . . . . **NCLC 19**

Chatterji, Saratchandra . . . . **TCLC 13**
See also Chatterje, Sarat Chandra

Chatterton, Thomas
1752-1770 . . . . **LC 3; DAM POET**
See also DLB 109

Chatwin, (Charles) Bruce
1940-1989 . . **CLC 28, 57, 59; DAM POP**
See also AAYA 4; BEST 90:1; CA 85-88;
127

Chaucer, Daniel
See Ford, Ford Madox

Chaucer, Geoffrey
1340(?)-1400 . . . . **LC 17; DA; DAB;**
DAC; DAM MST, POET; PC 19; WLCS
See also CDBLB Before 1660; DLB 146

Chaviaras, Strates 1935-
See Haviaras, Stratis
See also CA 105

Chayefsky, Paddy . . . . **CLC 23**
See also Chayefsky, Sidney
See also DLB 7, 44; DLBY 81

Chayefsky, Sidney 1923-1981
See Chayefsky, Paddy
See also CA 9-12R; 104; CANR 18;
DAM DRAM

Chedid, Andree 1920- . . . . **CLC 47**
See also CA 145

Cheever, John
1912-1982 . . . . . . **CLC 3, 7, 8, 11, 15, 25,**
64; DA; DAB; DAC; DAM MST, NOV,
POP; SSC 1; WLC
See also CA 5-8R; 106; CABS 1; CANR 5,
27; CDALB 1941-1968; DLB 2, 102;
DLBY 80, 82; INT CANR-5; MTCW

Cheever, Susan 1943- . . . . **CLC 18, 48**
See also CA 103; CANR 27, 51; DLBY 82;
INT CANR-27

Chekhonte, Antosha
See Chekhov, Anton (Pavlovich)

Chekhov, Anton (Pavlovich)
1860-1904 . . . . . **TCLC 3, 10, 31, 55; DA;**
DAB; DAC; DAM DRAM, MST; SSC 2,
28; WLC
See also CA 104; 124; SATA 90

Chernyshevsky, Nikolay Gavrilovich
1828-1889 . . . . **NCLC 1**

Cherry, Carolyn Janice 1942-
See Cherryh, C. J.
See also CA 65-68; CANR 10

Cherryh, C. J. . . . . **CLC 35**
See also Cherry, Carolyn Janice
See also DLBY 80; SATA 93

Chesnutt, Charles W(addell)
1858-1932 . . . . **TCLC 5, 39; BLC;**
DAM MULT; SSC 7
See also BW 1; CA 106; 125; DLB 12, 50,
78; MTCW

Chester, Alfred 1929(?)-1971 . . . . . . **CLC 49**
See also CA 33-36R; DLB 130

Chesterton, G(ilbert) K(eith)
1874-1936 . . . . **TCLC 1, 6, 64;**
DAM NOV, POET; SSC 1
See also CA 104; 132; CDBLB 1914-1945;
DLB 10, 19, 34, 70, 98, 149, 178; MTCW;
SATA 27

Chiang Pin-chin 1904-1986
See Ding Ling
See also CA 118

Ch'ien Chung-shu 1910- . . . . **CLC 22**
See also CA 130; MTCW

Child, L. Maria
See Child, Lydia Maria

Child, Lydia Maria 1802-1880 . . . . **NCLC 6**
See also DLB 1, 74; SATA 67

Child, Mrs.
See Child, Lydia Maria

Child, Philip 1898-1978 . . . . **CLC 19, 68**
See also CA 13-14; CAP 1; SATA 47

Childers, (Robert) Erskine
1870-1922 . . . . **TCLC 65**
See also CA 113; 153; DLB 70

Childress, Alice
1920-1994 . . . . **CLC 12, 15, 86, 96; BLC;**
DAM DRAM, MULT, NOV; DC 4
See also AAYA 8; BW 2; CA 45-48; 146;
CANR 3, 27, 50; CLR 14; DLB 7, 38;
JRDA; MAICYA; MTCW; SATA 7, 48,
81

Chin, Frank (Chew, Jr.) 1940- . . . . **DC 7**
See also CA 33-36R; DAM MULT

Chislett, (Margaret) Anne 1943- . . . . **CLC 34**
See also CA 151

Chitty, Thomas Willes 1926- . . . . **CLC 11**
See also Hinde, Thomas
See also CA 5-8R

Chivers, Thomas Holley
1809-1858 . . . . **NCLC 49**
See also DLB 3

Chomette, Rene Lucien 1898-1981
See Clair, Rene
See also CA 103

Chopin, Kate
. . **TCLC 5, 14; DA; DAB; SSC 8; WLCS**
See also Chopin, Katherine
See also CDALB 1865-1917; DLB 12, 78

Chopin, Katherine 1851-1904
See Chopin, Kate
See also CA 104; 122; DAC; DAM MST,
NOV

Chretien de Troyes
c. 12th cent. - . . . . **CMLC 10**

Christie
See Ichikawa, Kon

Christie, Agatha (Mary Clarissa)
1890-1976 . . . . . . **CLC 1, 6, 8, 12, 39, 48;**
DAB; DAC; DAM NOV
See also AAYA 9; AITN 1, 2; CA 17-20R;
61-64; CANR 10, 37; CDBLB 1914-1945;
DLB 13, 77; MTCW; SATA 36

Christie, (Ann) Philippa
See Pearce, Philippa
See also CA 5-8R; CANR 4

Christine de Pizan 1365(?)-1431(?) . . . . **LC 9**

Chubb, Elmer
See Masters, Edgar Lee

Chulkov, Mikhail Dmitrievich
1743-1792 . . . . **LC 2**
See also DLB 150

Churchill, Caryl 1938- . . . **CLC 31, 55; DC 5**
See also CA 102; CANR 22, 46; DLB 13;
MTCW

Churchill, Charles 1731-1764 . . . . **LC 3**
See also DLB 109

Chute, Carolyn 1947- . . . . **CLC 39**
See also CA 123

Ciardi, John (Anthony)
1916-1986 . . . . **CLC 10, 40, 44;**
DAM POET
See also CA 5-8R; 118; CAAS 2; CANR 5,
33; CLR 19; DLB 5; DLBY 86;
INT CANR-5; MAICYA; MTCW;
SATA 1, 65; SATA-Obit 46

Cicero, Marcus Tullius
106B.C.-43B.C. . . . . **CMLC 3**

Cimino, Michael 1943- . . . . **CLC 16**
See also CA 105

Cioran, E(mil) M. 1911-1995 . . . . **CLC 64**
See also CA 25-28R; 149

Cisneros, Sandra
1954- . . . . . **CLC 69; DAM MULT; HLC**
See also AAYA 9; CA 131; DLB 122, 152;
HW

Cixous, Helene 1937- . . . . **CLC 92**
See also CA 126; CANR 55; DLB 83;
MTCW

Clair, Rene . . . . **CLC 20**
See also Chomette, Rene Lucien

Clampitt, Amy 1920-1994 . . . **CLC 32; PC 19**
See also CA 110; 146; CANR 29; DLB 105

Clancy, Thomas L., Jr. 1947-
See Clancy, Tom
See also CA 125; 131; CANR 62; INT 131;
MTCW

Clancy, Tom . . . . . **CLC 45; DAM NOV, POP**
See also Clancy, Thomas L., Jr.
See also AAYA 9; BEST 89:1, 90:1

Clare, John
1793-1864 . . . . **NCLC 9; DAB;**
DAM POET
See also DLB 55, 96

Clarin
See Alas (y Urena), Leopoldo (Enrique
Garcia)

Clark, Al C.
See Goines, Donald

Clark, (Robert) Brian 1932- . . . . **CLC 29**
See also CA 41-44R

Clark, Curt
See Westlake, Donald E(dwin)

Clark, Eleanor   1913-1996 . . . . **CLC 5, 19**
See also CA 9-12R; 151; CANR 41; DLB 6

Clark, J. P.
See Clark, John Pepper
See also DLB 117

Clark, John Pepper
1935- . . . . **CLC 38; BLC; DAM DRAM,
MULT; DC 5**
See also Clark, J. P.
See also BW 1; CA 65-68; CANR 16

Clark, M. R.
See Clark, Mavis Thorpe

Clark, Mavis Thorpe   1909- . . . . **CLC 12**
See also CA 57-60; CANR 8, 37; CLR 30;
MAICYA; SAAS 5; SATA 8, 74

Clark, Walter Van Tilburg
1909-1971 . . . . **CLC 28**
See also CA 9-12R; 33-36R; DLB 9;
SATA 8

Clarke, Arthur C(harles)
1917- . . . . **CLC 1, 4, 13, 18, 35;
DAM POP; SSC 3**
See also AAYA 4; CA 1-4R; CANR 2, 28,
55; JRDA; MAICYA; MTCW; SATA 13,
70

Clarke, Austin
1896-1974 . . . . . . **CLC 6, 9; DAM POET**
See also CA 29-32; 49-52; CAP 2; DLB 10,
20

Clarke, Austin C(hesterfield)
1934- . . . . **CLC 8, 53; BLC; DAC;
DAM MULT**
See also BW 1; CA 25-28R; CAAS 16;
CANR 14, 32; DLB 53, 125

Clarke, Gillian   1937- . . . . **CLC 61**
See also CA 106; DLB 40

Clarke, Marcus (Andrew Hislop)
1846-1881 . . . . **NCLC 19**

Clarke, Shirley   1925- . . . . **CLC 16**

Clash, The
See Headon, (Nicky) Topper; Jones, Mick;
Simonon, Paul; Strummer, Joe

Claudel, Paul (Louis Charles Marie)
1868-1955 . . . . **TCLC 2, 10**
See also CA 104

Clavell, James (duMaresq)
1925-1994 . . . . **CLC 6, 25, 87;
DAM NOV, POP**
See also CA 25-28R; 146; CANR 26, 48;
MTCW

Cleaver, (Leroy) Eldridge
1935- . . . . . **CLC 30; BLC; DAM MULT**
See also BW 1; CA 21-24R; CANR 16

Cleese, John (Marwood)   1939- . . . . . **CLC 21**
See also Monty Python
See also CA 112; 116; CANR 35; MTCW

Cleishbotham, Jebediah
See Scott, Walter

Cleland, John   1710-1789 . . . . **LC 2**
See also DLB 39

Clemens, Samuel Langhorne   1835-1910
See Twain, Mark
See also CA 104; 135; CDALB 1865-1917;
DA; DAB; DAC; DAM MST, NOV;
DLB 11, 12, 23, 64, 74, 186; JRDA;
MAICYA; YABC 2

Cleophil
See Congreve, William

Clerihew, E.
See Bentley, E(dmund) C(lerihew)

Clerk, N. W.
See Lewis, C(live) S(taples)

Cliff, Jimmy. . . . . **CLC 21**
See also Chambers, James

Clifton, (Thelma) Lucille
1936- . . . . **CLC 19, 66; BLC;
DAM MULT, POET; PC 17**
See also BW 2; CA 49-52; CANR 2, 24, 42;
CLR 5; DLB 5, 41; MAICYA; MTCW;
SATA 20, 69

Clinton, Dirk
See Silverberg, Robert

Clough, Arthur Hugh   1819-1861. . **NCLC 27**
See also DLB 32

Clutha, Janet Paterson Frame   1924-
See Frame, Janet
See also CA 1-4R; CANR 2, 36; MTCW

Clyne, Terence
See Blatty, William Peter

Cobalt, Martin
See Mayne, William (James Carter)

Cobb, Irvin S.   1876-1944. . . . . **TCLC 77**
See also DLB 11, 25, 86

Cobbett, William   1763-1835 . . . . . **NCLC 49**
See also DLB 43, 107, 158

Coburn, D(onald) L(ee)   1938- . . . . . . **CLC 10**
See also CA 89-92

Cocteau, Jean (Maurice Eugene Clement)
1889-1963 . . . . **CLC 1, 8, 15, 16, 43; DA;
DAB; DAC; DAM DRAM, MST, NOV;
WLC**
See also CA 25-28; CANR 40; CAP 2;
DLB 65; MTCW

Codrescu, Andrei
1946- . . . . **CLC 46; DAM POET**
See also CA 33-36R; CAAS 19; CANR 13,
34, 53

Coe, Max
See Bourne, Randolph S(illiman)

Coe, Tucker
See Westlake, Donald E(dwin)

Coetzee, J(ohn) M(ichael)
1940- . . . . . . **CLC 23, 33, 66; DAM NOV**
See also CA 77-80; CANR 41, 54; MTCW

Coffey, Brian
See Koontz, Dean R(ay)

Cohan, George M(ichael)
1878-1942 . . . . **TCLC 60**
See also CA 157

Cohen, Arthur A(llen)
1928-1986 . . . . **CLC 7, 31**
See also CA 1-4R; 120; CANR 1, 17, 42;
DLB 28

Cohen, Leonard (Norman)
1934- . . . . **CLC 3, 38; DAC; DAM MST**
See also CA 21-24R; CANR 14; DLB 53;
MTCW

Cohen, Matt   1942- . . . . **CLC 19; DAC**
See also CA 61-64; CAAS 18; CANR 40;
DLB 53

Cohen-Solal, Annie   19(?)- . . . . **CLC 50**

Colegate, Isabel   1931- . . . . **CLC 36**
See also CA 17-20R; CANR 8, 22; DLB 14;
INT CANR-22; MTCW

Coleman, Emmett
See Reed, Ishmael

Coleridge, M. E.
See Coleridge, Mary E(lizabeth)

Coleridge, Mary E(lizabeth)
1861-1907 . . . . **TCLC 73**
See also CA 116; DLB 19, 98

Coleridge, Samuel Taylor
1772-1834 . . . . . **NCLC 9, 54; DA; DAB;
DAC; DAM MST, POET; PC 11; WLC**
See also CDBLB 1789-1832; DLB 93, 107

Coleridge, Sara   1802-1852. . . . . . . **NCLC 31**

Coles, Don   1928- . . . . **CLC 46**
See also CA 115; CANR 38

Colette, (Sidonie-Gabrielle)
1873-1954 . . . . **TCLC 1, 5, 16;
DAM NOV; SSC 10**
See also CA 104; 131; DLB 65; MTCW

Collett, (Jacobine) Camilla (Wergeland)
1813-1895 . . . . **NCLC 22**

Collier, Christopher   1930- . . . . **CLC 30**
See also AAYA 13; CA 33-36R; CANR 13,
33; JRDA; MAICYA; SATA 16, 70

Collier, James L(incoln)
1928- . . . . **CLC 30; DAM POP**
See also AAYA 13; CA 9-12R; CANR 4,
33, 60; CLR 3; JRDA; MAICYA;
SAAS 21; SATA 8, 70

Collier, Jeremy   1650-1726. . . . . **LC 6**

Collier, John   1901-1980. . . . . **SSC 19**
See also CA 65-68; 97-100; CANR 10;
DLB 77

Collingwood, R(obin) G(eorge)
1889(?)-1943 . . . . **TCLC 67**
See also CA 117; 155

Collins, Hunt
See Hunter, Evan

Collins, Linda   1931- . . . . **CLC 44**
See also CA 125

Collins, (William) Wilkie
1824-1889 . . . . **NCLC 1, 18**
See also CDBLB 1832-1890; DLB 18, 70,
159

Collins, William
1721-1759 . . . . . . **LC 4, 40; DAM POET**
See also DLB 109

Collodi, Carlo   1826-1890. . . . . **NCLC 54**
See also Lorenzini, Carlo
See also CLR 5

Colman, George
See Glassco, John

Colt, Winchester Remington
See Hubbard, L(afayette) Ron(ald)

Colter, Cyrus 1910- .... **CLC 58**
See also BW 1; CA 65-68; CANR 10;
DLB 33

Colton, James
See Hansen, Joseph

Colum, Padraic 1881-1972........ **CLC 28**
See also CA 73-76; 33-36R; CANR 35;
CLR 36; MAICYA; MTCW; SATA 15

Colvin, James
See Moorcock, Michael (John)

Colwin, Laurie (E.)
1944-1992 .... **CLC 5, 13, 23, 84**
See also CA 89-92; 139; CANR 20, 46;
DLBY 80; MTCW

Comfort, Alex(ander)
1920- .... **CLC 7; DAM POP**
See also CA 1-4R; CANR 1, 45

Comfort, Montgomery
See Campbell, (John) Ramsey

Compton-Burnett, I(vy)
1884(?)-1969 ...... **CLC 1, 3, 10, 15, 34;**
DAM NOV
See also CA 1-4R; 25-28R; CANR 4;
DLB 36; MTCW

Comstock, Anthony 1844-1915 .... **TCLC 13**
See also CA 110

Comte, Auguste 1798-1857....... **NCLC 54**

Conan Doyle, Arthur
See Doyle, Arthur Conan

Conde, Maryse
1937- .... **CLC 52, 92; DAM MULT**
See also Boucolon, Maryse
See also BW 2

Condillac, Etienne Bonnot de
1714-1780 .... **LC 26**

Condon, Richard (Thomas)
1915-1996 ..... **CLC 4, 6, 8, 10, 45, 100;**
DAM NOV
See also BEST 90:3; CA 1-4R; 151;
CAAS 1; CANR 2, 23; INT CANR-23;
MTCW

Confucius
551B.C.-479B.C....... **CMLC 19; DA;**
DAB; DAC; DAM MST; WLCS

Congreve, William
1670-1729 .... **LC 5, 21; DA; DAB;**
DAC; DAM DRAM, MST, POET;
DC 2; WLC
See also CDBLB 1660-1789; DLB 39, 84

Connell, Evan S(helby), Jr.
1924- .... **CLC 4, 6, 45; DAM NOV**
See also AAYA 7; CA 1-4R; CAAS 2;
CANR 2, 39; DLB 2; DLBY 81; MTCW

Connelly, Marc(us Cook)
1890-1980 .... **CLC 7**
See also CA 85-88; 102; CANR 30; DLB 7;
DLBY 80; SATA-Obit 25

Connor, Ralph .... **TCLC 31**
See also Gordon, Charles William
See also DLB 92

Conrad, Joseph
1857-1924 .... **TCLC 1, 6, 13, 25, 43, 57;**
DA; DAB; DAC; DAM MST, NOV;
SSC 9; WLC
See also CA 104; 131; CANR 60;
CDBLB 1890-1914; DLB 10, 34, 98, 156;
MTCW; SATA 27

Conrad, Robert Arnold
See Hart, Moss

Conroy, Donald Pat(rick)
1945- ... **CLC 30, 74; DAM NOV, POP**
See also AAYA 8; AITN 1; CA 85-88;
CANR 24, 53; DLB 6; MTCW

Constant (de Rebecque), (Henri) Benjamin
1767-1830 .... **NCLC 6**
See also DLB 119

Conybeare, Charles Augustus
See Eliot, T(homas) S(tearns)

Cook, Michael 1933- .... **CLC 58**
See also CA 93-96; DLB 53

Cook, Robin 1940- .... **CLC 14; DAM POP**
See also BEST 90:2; CA 108; 111;
CANR 41; INT 111

Cook, Roy
See Silverberg, Robert

Cooke, Elizabeth 1948- .... **CLC 55**
See also CA 129

Cooke, John Esten 1830-1886..... **NCLC 5**
See also DLB 3

Cooke, John Estes
See Baum, L(yman) Frank

Cooke, M. E.
See Creasey, John

Cooke, Margaret
See Creasey, John

Cook-Lynn, Elizabeth
1930- .... **CLC 93; DAM MULT**
See also CA 133; DLB 175; NNAL

Cooney, Ray .... **CLC 62**

Cooper, Douglas 1960-........... **CLC 86**

Cooper, Henry St. John
See Creasey, John

Cooper, J(oan) California
.... **CLC 56; DAM MULT**
See also AAYA 12; BW 1; CA 125;
CANR 55

Cooper, James Fenimore
1789-1851 .... **NCLC 1, 27, 54**
See also AAYA 22; CDALB 1640-1865;
DLB 3; SATA 19

Coover, Robert (Lowell)
1932- .... **CLC 3, 7, 15, 32, 46, 87;**
DAM NOV; SSC 15
See also CA 45-48; CANR 3, 37, 58;
DLB 2; DLBY 81; MTCW

Copeland, Stewart (Armstrong)
1952- .... **CLC 26**

Coppard, A(lfred) E(dgar)
1878-1957 .... **TCLC 5; SSC 21**
See also CA 114; DLB 162; YABC 1

Coppee, Francois 1842-1908 ...... **TCLC 25**

Coppola, Francis Ford 1939-....... **CLC 16**
See also CA 77-80; CANR 40; DLB 44

Corbiere, Tristan 1845-1875 ..... **NCLC 43**

Corcoran, Barbara 1911-......... **CLC 17**
See also AAYA 14; CA 21-24R; CAAS 2;
CANR 11, 28, 48; DLB 52; JRDA;
SAAS 20; SATA 3, 77

Cordelier, Maurice
See Giraudoux, (Hippolyte) Jean

Corelli, Marie 1855-1924........ **TCLC 51**
See also Mackay, Mary
See also DLB 34, 156

Corman, Cid.................... **CLC 9**
See also Corman, Sidney
See also CAAS 2; DLB 5

Corman, Sidney 1924-
See Corman, Cid
See also CA 85-88; CANR 44; DAM POET

Cormier, Robert (Edmund)
1925- .... **CLC 12, 30; DA; DAB; DAC;**
DAM MST, NOV
See also AAYA 3, 19; CA 1-4R; CANR 5,
23; CDALB 1968-1988; CLR 12; DLB 52;
INT CANR-23; JRDA; MAICYA;
MTCW; SATA 10, 45, 83

Corn, Alfred (DeWitt III) 1943-.... **CLC 33**
See also CA 104; CAAS 25; CANR 44;
DLB 120; DLBY 80

Corneille, Pierre
1606-1684 .... **LC 28; DAB; DAM MST**

Cornwell, David (John Moore)
1931- .... **CLC 9, 15; DAM POP**
See also le Carre, John
See also CA 5-8R; CANR 13, 33, 59;
MTCW

Corso, (Nunzio) Gregory 1930-... **CLC 1, 11**
See also CA 5-8R; CANR 41; DLB 5, 16;
MTCW

Cortazar, Julio
1914-1984 ...... **CLC 2, 3, 5, 10, 13, 15,**
33, 34, 92; DAM MULT, NOV; HLC;
SSC 7
See also CA 21-24R; CANR 12, 32;
DLB 113; HW; MTCW

CORTES, HERNAN 1484-1547..... **LC 31**

Corwin, Cecil
See Kornbluth, C(yril) M.

Cosic, Dobrica 1921- .... **CLC 14**
See also CA 122; 138; DLB 181

Costain, Thomas B(ertram)
1885-1965 .... **CLC 30**
See also CA 5-8R; 25-28R; DLB 9

Costantini, Humberto
1924(?)-1987 .... **CLC 49**
See also CA 131; 122; HW

Costello, Elvis 1955-............. **CLC 21**

Cotes, Cecil V.
See Duncan, Sara Jeannette

Cotter, Joseph Seamon Sr.
1861-1949 .... **TCLC 28; BLC;**
DAM MULT
See also BW 1; CA 124; DLB 50

Couch, Arthur Thomas Quiller
See Quiller-Couch, Arthur Thomas

Coulton, James
See Hansen, Joseph

Cunha, Euclides (Rodrigues Pimenta) da
1866-1909 .... **TCLC 24**
See also CA 123

Cunningham, E. V.
See Fast, Howard (Melvin)

Cunningham, J(ames) V(incent)
1911-1985 .... **CLC 3, 31**
See also CA 1-4R; 115; CANR 1; DLB 5

Cunningham, Julia (Woolfolk)
1916- .... **CLC 12**
See also CA 9-12R; CANR 4, 19, 36;
JRDA; MAICYA; SAAS 2; SATA 1, 26

Cunningham, Michael 1952- .... **CLC 34**
See also·CA 136

Cunninghame Graham, R(obert) B(ontine)
1852-1936 .... **TCLC 19**
See also Graham, R(obert) B(ontine)
Cunninghame
See also CA 119; DLB 98

Currie, Ellen 19(?)- .... **CLC 44**

Curtin, Philip
See Lowndes, Marie Adelaide (Belloc)

Curtis, Price
See Ellison, Harlan (Jay)

Cutrate, Joe
See Spiegelman, Art

Cynewulf c. 770-c. 840 .... **CMLC 23**

Czaczkes, Shmuel Yosef
See Agnon, S(hmuel) Y(osef Halevi)

Dabrowska, Maria (Szumska)
1889-1965 .... **CLC 15**
See also CA 106

Dabydeen, David 1955- .... **CLC 34**
See also BW 1; CA 125; CANR 56

Dacey, Philip 1939- .... **CLC 51**
See also CA 37-40R; CAAS 17; CANR 14,
32; DLB 105

Dagerman, Stig (Halvard)
1923-1954 .... **TCLC 17**
See also CA 117; 155

Dahl, Roald
1916-1990 ...... **CLC 1, 6, 18, 79; DAB;**
DAC; DAM MST, NOV, POP
See also AAYA 15; CA 1-4R; 133;
CANR 6, 32, 37, 62; CLR 1, 7, 41;
DLB 139; JRDA; MAICYA; MTCW;
SATA 1, 26, 73; SATA-Obit 65

Dahlberg, Edward 1900-1977 ... **CLC 1, 7, 14**
See also CA 9-12R; 69-72; CANR 31, 62;
DLB 48; MTCW

Daitch, Susan 1954- .... **CLC 103**
See also CA 161

Dale, Colin .... **TCLC 18**
See also Lawrence, T(homas) E(dward)

Dale, George E.
See Asimov, Isaac

Daly, Elizabeth 1878-1967 .... **CLC 52**
See also CA 23-24; 25-28R; CANR 60;
CAP 2

Daly, Maureen 1921- .... **CLC 17**
See also AAYA 5; CANR 37; JRDA;
MAICYA; SAAS 1; SATA 2

Damas, Leon-Gontran 1912-1978 ... **CLC 84**
See also BW 1; CA 125; 73-76

Dana, Richard Henry Sr.
1787-1879 .... **NCLC 53**

Daniel, Samuel 1562(?)-1619 .... **LC 24**
See also DLB 62

Daniels, Brett
See Adler, Renata

Dannay, Frederic
1905-1982 .... **CLC 11; DAM POP**
See also Queen, Ellery
See also CA 1-4R; 107; CANR 1, 39;
DLB 137; MTCW

D'Annunzio, Gabriele
1863-1938 .... **TCLC 6, 40**
See also CA 104; 155

Danois, N. le
See Gourmont, Remy (-Marie-Charles) de

d'Antibes, Germain
See Simenon, Georges (Jacques Christian)

Danticat, Edwidge 1969- .... **CLC 94**
See also CA 152

Danvers, Dennis 1947- .... **CLC 70**

Danziger, Paula 1944- .... **CLC 21**
See also AAYA 4; CA 112; 115; CANR 37;
CLR 20; JRDA; MAICYA; SATA 36,
63; SATA-Brief 30

Da Ponte, Lorenzo 1749-1838 .... **NCLC 50**

Dario, Ruben
1867-1916 ..... **TCLC 4; DAM MULT;**
HLC; PC 15
See also CA 131; HW; MTCW

Darley, George 1795-1846 .... **NCLC 2**
See also DLB 96

Darwin, Charles 1809-1882 ...... **NCLC 57**
See also DLB 57, 166

Daryush, Elizabeth 1887-1977 .... **CLC 6, 19**
See also CA 49-52; CANR 3; DLB 20

Dashwood, Edmee Elizabeth Monica de la
Pasture 1890-1943
See Delafield, E. M.
See also CA 119; 154

Daudet, (Louis Marie) Alphonse
1840-1897 .... **NCLC 1**
See also DLB 123

Daumal, Rene 1908-1944 .... **TCLC 14**
See also CA 114

Davenport, Guy (Mattison, Jr.)
1927- .... **CLC 6, 14, 38; SSC 16**
See also CA 33-36R; CANR 23; DLB 130

Davidson, Avram 1923-
See Queen, Ellery
See also CA 101; CANR 26; DLB 8

Davidson, Donald (Grady)
1893-1968 .... **CLC 2, 13, 19**
See also CA 5-8R; 25-28R; CANR 4;
DLB 45

Davidson, Hugh
See Hamilton, Edmond

Davidson, John 1857-1909 .... **TCLC 24**
See also CA 118; DLB 19

Davidson, Sara 1943- .... **CLC 9**
See also CA 81-84; CANR 44

Davie, Donald (Alfred)
1922-1995 .... **CLC 5, 8, 10, 31**
See also CA 1-4R; 149; CAAS 3; CANR 1,
44; DLB 27; MTCW

Davies, Ray(mond Douglas) 1944- .. **CLC 21**
See also CA 116; 146

Davies, Rhys 1903-1978 .... **CLC 23**
See also CA 9-12R; 81-84; CANR 4;
DLB 139

Davies, (William) Robertson
1913-1995 ..... **CLC 2, 7, 13, 25, 42, 75,**
91; DA; DAB; DAC; DAM MST, NOV,
POP; WLC
See also BEST 89:2; CA 33-36R; 150;
CANR 17, 42; DLB 68; INT CANR-17;
MTCW

Davies, W(illiam) H(enry)
1871-1940 .... **TCLC 5**
See also CA 104; DLB 19, 174

Davies, Walter C.
See Kornbluth, C(yril) M.

Davis, Angela (Yvonne)
1944- .... **CLC 77; DAM MULT**
See also BW 2; CA 57-60; CANR 10

Davis, B. Lynch
See Bioy Casares, Adolfo; Borges, Jorge
Luis

Davis, Gordon
See Hunt, E(verette) Howard, (Jr.)

Davis, Harold Lenoir 1896-1960 .... **CLC 49**
See also CA 89-92; DLB 9

Davis, Rebecca (Blaine) Harding
1831-1910 .... **TCLC 6**
See also CA 104; DLB 74

Davis, Richard Harding
1864-1916 .... **TCLC 24**
See also CA 114; DLB 12, 23, 78, 79;
DLBD 13

Davison, Frank Dalby 1893-1970 ... **CLC 15**
See also CA 116

Davison, Lawrence H.
See Lawrence, D(avid) H(erbert Richards)

Davison, Peter (Hubert) 1928- ..... **CLC 28**
See also CA 9-12R; CAAS 4; CANR 3, 43;
DLB 5

Davys, Mary 1674-1732............. **LC 1**
See also DLB 39

Dawson, Fielding 1930- .... **CLC 6**
See also CA 85-88; DLB 130

Dawson, Peter
See Faust, Frederick (Schiller)

Day, Clarence (Shepard, Jr.)
1874-1935 .... **TCLC 25**
See also CA 108; DLB 11

Day, Thomas 1748-1789............ **LC 1**
See also DLB 39; YABC 1

Day Lewis, C(ecil)
1904-1972 .... **CLC 1, 6, 10;**
DAM POET; PC 11
See also Blake, Nicholas
See also CA 13-16; 33-36R; CANR 34;
CAP 1; DLB 15, 20; MTCW

Dazai, Osamu .... **TCLC 11**
See also Tsushima, Shuji
See also DLB 182

Devkota, Laxmiprasad
1909-1959 . . . . **TCLC 23**
See also CA 123

De Voto, Bernard (Augustine)
1897-1955 . . . . **TCLC 29**
See also CA 113; 160; DLB 9

De Vries, Peter
1910-1993 . . . . **CLC 1, 2, 3, 7, 10, 28, 46;**
DAM NOV
See also CA 17-20R; 142; CANR 41;
DLB 6; DLBY 82; MTCW

Dexter, John
See Bradley, Marion Zimmer

Dexter, Martin
See Faust, Frederick (Schiller)

Dexter, Pete
1943- . . . . **CLC 34, 55; DAM POP**
See also BEST 89:2; CA 127; 131; INT 131;
MTCW

Diamano, Silmang
See Senghor, Leopold Sedar

Diamond, Neil 1941- . . . . **CLC 30**
See also CA 108

Diaz del Castillo, Bernal 1496-1584 . . **LC 31**

di Bassetto, Corno
See Shaw, George Bernard

Dick, Philip K(indred)
1928-1982 . . . . **CLC 10, 30, 72;**
DAM NOV, POP
See also CA 49-52; 106; CANR 2, 16;
DLB 8; MTCW

Dickens, Charles (John Huffam)
1812-1870 . . . . . . **NCLC 3, 8, 18, 26, 37,**
50; DA; DAB; DAC; DAM MST, NOV;
SSC 17; WLC
See also CDBLB 1832-1890; DLB 21, 55,
70, 159, 166; JRDA; MAICYA; SATA 15

Dickey, James (Lafayette)
1923-1997 . . . . **CLC 1, 2, 4, 7, 10, 15, 47;**
DAM NOV, POET, POP
See also AITN 1, 2; CA 9-12R; 156;
CABS 2; CANR 10, 48, 61;
CDALB 1968-1988; DLB 5; DLBD 7;
DLBY 82, 93, 96; INT CANR-10;
MTCW

Dickey, William 1928-1994 . . . . . . **CLC 3, 28**
See also CA 9-12R; 145; CANR 24; DLB 5

Dickinson, Charles 1951- . . . . **CLC 49**
See also CA 128

Dickinson, Emily (Elizabeth)
1830-1886 . . . . **NCLC 21; DA; DAB;**
DAC; DAM MST, POET; PC 1; WLC
See also AAYA 22; CDALB 1865-1917;
DLB 1; SATA 29

Dickinson, Peter (Malcolm)
1927- . . . . **CLC 12, 35**
See also AAYA 9; CA 41-44R; CANR 31,
58; CLR 29; DLB 87, 161; JRDA;
MAICYA; SATA 5, 62, 95

Dickson, Carr
See Carr, John Dickson

Dickson, Carter
See Carr, John Dickson

Diderot, Denis 1713-1784 . . . . **LC 26**

Didion, Joan
1934- . . **CLC 1, 3, 8, 14, 32; DAM NOV**
See also AITN 1; CA 5-8R; CANR 14, 52;
CDALB 1968-1988; DLB 2, 173;
DLBY 81, 86; MTCW

Dietrich, Robert
See Hunt, E(verette) Howard, (Jr.)

Dillard, Annie
1945- . . . . **CLC 9, 60; DAM NOV**
See also AAYA 6; CA 49-52; CANR 3, 43,
62; DLBY 80; MTCW; SATA 10

Dillard, R(ichard) H(enry) W(ilde)
1937- . . . . **CLC 5**
See also CA 21-24R; CAAS 7; CANR 10;
DLB 5

Dillon, Eilis 1920-1994 . . . . **CLC 17**
See also CA 9-12R; 147; CAAS 3; CANR 4,
38; CLR 26; MAICYA; SATA 2, 74;
SATA-Obit 83

Dimont, Penelope
See Mortimer, Penelope (Ruth)

Dinesen, Isak . . . . **CLC 10, 29, 95; SSC 7**
See also Blixen, Karen (Christentze
Dinesen)

Ding Ling . . . . **CLC 68**
See also Chiang Pin-chin

Disch, Thomas M(ichael) 1940- . . . **CLC 7, 36**
See also AAYA 17; CA 21-24R; CAAS 4;
CANR 17, 36, 54; CLR 18; DLB 8;
MAICYA; MTCW; SAAS 15; SATA 92

Disch, Tom
See Disch, Thomas M(ichael)

d'Isly, Georges
See Simenon, Georges (Jacques Christian)

Disraeli, Benjamin 1804-1881 . . **NCLC 2, 39**
See also DLB 21, 55

Ditcum, Steve
See Crumb, R(obert)

Dixon, Paige
See Corcoran, Barbara

Dixon, Stephen 1936- . . . . . **CLC 52; SSC 16**
See also CA 89-92; CANR 17, 40, 54;
DLB 130

Doak, Annie
See Dillard, Annie

Dobell, Sydney Thompson
1824-1874 . . . . **NCLC 43**
See also DLB 32

Doblin, Alfred . . . . **TCLC 13**
See also Doeblin, Alfred

Dobrolyubov, Nikolai Alexandrovich
1836-1861 . . . . **NCLC 5**

Dobyns, Stephen 1941- . . . . **CLC 37**
See also CA 45-48; CANR 2, 18

Doctorow, E(dgar) L(aurence)
1931- . . . . . **CLC 6, 11, 15, 18, 37, 44, 65;**
DAM NOV, POP
See also AAYA 22; AITN 2; BEST 89:3;
CA 45-48; CANR 2, 33, 51;
CDALB 1968-1988; DLB 2, 28, 173;
DLBY 80; MTCW

Dodgson, Charles Lutwidge 1832-1898
See Carroll, Lewis
See also CLR 2; DA; DAB; DAC;
DAM MST, NOV, POET; MAICYA;
YABC 2

Dodson, Owen (Vincent)
1914-1983 . . . . **CLC 79; BLC;**
DAM MULT
See also BW 1; CA 65-68; 110; CANR 24;
DLB 76

Doeblin, Alfred 1878-1957 . . . . **TCLC 13**
See also Doblin, Alfred
See also CA 110; 141; DLB 66

Doerr, Harriet 1910- . . . . **CLC 34**
See also CA 117; 122; CANR 47; INT 122

Domecq, H(onorio) Bustos
See Bioy Casares, Adolfo; Borges, Jorge
Luis

Domini, Rey
See Lorde, Audre (Geraldine)

Dominique
See Proust, (Valentin-Louis-George-Eugene-)
Marcel

Don, A
See Stephen, Leslie

Donaldson, Stephen R.
1947- . . . . **CLC 46; DAM POP**
See also CA 89-92; CANR 13, 55;
INT CANR-13

Donleavy, J(ames) P(atrick)
1926- . . . . **CLC 1, 4, 6, 10, 45**
See also AITN 2; CA 9-12R; CANR 24, 49,
62; DLB 6, 173; INT CANR-24; MTCW

Donne, John
1572-1631 . . . . **LC 10, 24; DA; DAB;**
DAC; DAM MST, POET; PC 1
See also CDBLB Before 1660; DLB 121,
151

Donnell, David 1939(?)- . . . . **CLC 34**

Donoghue, P. S.
See Hunt, E(verette) Howard, (Jr.)

Donoso (Yanez), Jose
1924-1996 . . . . **CLC 4, 8, 11, 32, 99;**
DAM MULT; HLC
See also CA 81-84; 155; CANR 32;
DLB 113; HW; MTCW

Donovan, John 1928-1992 . . . . **CLC 35**
See also AAYA 20; CA 97-100; 137;
CLR 3; MAICYA; SATA 72;
SATA-Brief 29

Don Roberto
See Cunninghame Graham, R(obert)
B(ontine)

Doolittle, Hilda
1886-1961 . . . . . **CLC 3, 8, 14, 31, 34, 73;**
DA; DAC; DAM MST, POET; PC 5;
WLC
See also H. D.
See also CA 97-100; CANR 35; DLB 4, 45;
MTCW

Dorfman, Ariel
1942- . . . . **CLC 48, 77; DAM MULT;**
HLC
See also CA 124; 130; HW; INT 130

Dunbar, William 1460(?)-1530(?) .... **LC 20**
See also DLB 132, 146

Duncan, Dora Angela
See Duncan, Isadora

Duncan, Isadora 1877(?)-1927..... **TCLC 68**
See also CA 118; 149

Duncan, Lois 1934-............... **CLC 26**
See also AAYA 4; CA 1-4R; CANR 2, 23,
36; CLR 29; JRDA; MAICYA; SAAS 2;
SATA 1, 36, 75

Duncan, Robert (Edward)
1919-1988 .... **CLC 1, 2, 4, 7, 15, 41, 55;**
                                DAM POET; PC 2
See also CA 9-12R; 124; CANR 28, 62;
DLB 5, 16; MTCW

Duncan, Sara Jeannette
1861-1922 .... **TCLC 60**
See also CA 157; DLB 92

Dunlap, William 1766-1839....... **NCLC 2**
See also DLB 30, 37, 59

Dunn, Douglas (Eaglesham)
1942-..................... **CLC 6, 40**
See also CA 45-48; CANR 2, 33; DLB 40;
MTCW

Dunn, Katherine (Karen) 1945-..... **CLC 71**
See also CA 33-36R

Dunn, Stephen 1939-............. **CLC 36**
See also CA 33-36R; CANR 12, 48, 53;
DLB 105

Dunne, Finley Peter 1867-1936.... **TCLC 28**
See also CA 108; DLB 11, 23

Dunne, John Gregory 1932-........ **CLC 28**
See also CA 25-28R; CANR 14, 50;
DLBY 80

Dunsany, Edward John Moreton Drax
    Plunkett 1878-1957
See Dunsany, Lord
See also CA 104; 148; DLB 10

Dunsany, Lord................. **TCLC 2, 59**
See also Dunsany, Edward John Moreton
Drax Plunkett
See also DLB 77, 153, 156

du Perry, Jean
See Simenon, Georges (Jacques Christian)

Durang, Christopher (Ferdinand)
1949-..................... **CLC 27, 38**
See also CA 105; CANR 50

Duras, Marguerite
1914-1996 ..... **CLC 3, 6, 11, 20, 34, 40,**
                                        68, 100
See also CA 25-28R; 151; CANR 50;
DLB 83; MTCW

Durban, (Rosa) Pam 1947-........ **CLC 39**
See also CA 123

Durcan, Paul
1944-........ **CLC 43, 70; DAM POET**
See also CA 134

Durkheim, Emile 1858-1917 ...... **TCLC 55**

Durrell, Lawrence (George)
1912-1990 .... **CLC 1, 4, 6, 8, 13, 27, 41;**
                                        DAM NOV
See also CA 9-12R; 132; CANR 40;
CDBLB 1945-1960; DLB 15, 27;
DLBY 90; MTCW

Durrenmatt, Friedrich
See Duerrenmatt, Friedrich

Dutt, Toru 1856-1877........... **NCLC 29**

Dwight, Timothy 1752-1817...... **NCLC 13**
See also DLB 37

Dworkin, Andrea 1946-.......... **CLC 43**
See also CA 77-80; CAAS 21; CANR 16,
39; INT CANR-16; MTCW

Dwyer, Deanna
See Koontz, Dean R(ay)

Dwyer, K. R.
See Koontz, Dean R(ay)

Dye, Richard
See De Voto, Bernard (Augustine)

Dylan, Bob 1941-...... **CLC 3, 4, 6, 12, 77**
See also CA 41-44R; DLB 16

Eagleton, Terence (Francis) 1943-
See Eagleton, Terry
See also CA 57-60; CANR 7, 23; MTCW

Eagleton, Terry.................. **CLC 63**
See also Eagleton, Terence (Francis)

Early, Jack
See Scoppettone, Sandra

East, Michael
See West, Morris L(anglo)

Eastaway, Edward
See Thomas, (Philip) Edward

Eastlake, William (Derry)
1917-1997 .... **CLC 8**
See also CA 5-8R; 158; CAAS 1; CANR 5;
DLB 6; INT CANR-5

Eastman, Charles A(lexander)
1858-1939 ..... **TCLC 55; DAM MULT**
See also DLB 175; NNAL; YABC 1

Eberhart, Richard (Ghormley)
1904-.. **CLC 3, 11, 19, 56; DAM POET**
See also CA 1-4R; CANR 2;
CDALB 1941-1968; DLB 48; MTCW

Eberstadt, Fernanda 1960-......... **CLC 39**
See also CA 136

Echegaray (y Eizaguirre), Jose (Maria Waldo)
1832-1916 .... **TCLC 4**
See also CA 104; CANR 32; HW; MTCW

Echeverria, (Jose) Esteban (Antonino)
1805-1851 .... **NCLC 18**

Echo
See Proust, (Valentin-Louis-George-Eugene-)
Marcel

Eckert, Allan W. 1931-........... **CLC 17**
See also AAYA 18; CA 13-16R; CANR 14,
45; INT CANR-14; SAAS 21; SATA 29,
91; SATA-Brief 27

Eckhart, Meister 1260(?)-1328(?) .. **CMLC 9**
See also DLB 115

Eckmar, F. R.
See de Hartog, Jan

Eco, Umberto
1932-... **CLC 28, 60; DAM NOV, POP**
See also BEST 90:1; CA 77-80; CANR 12,
33, 55; MTCW

Eddison, E(ric) R(ucker)
1882-1945 .... **TCLC 15**
See also CA 109; 156

Eddy, Mary (Morse) Baker
1821-1910 .... **TCLC 71**
See also CA 113

Edel, (Joseph) Leon
1907-1997 .... **CLC 29, 34**
See also CA 1-4R; 161; CANR 1, 22;
DLB 103; INT CANR-22

Eden, Emily 1797-1869 .... **NCLC 10**

Edgar, David
1948-.......... **CLC 42; DAM DRAM**
See also CA 57-60; CANR 12, 61; DLB 13;
MTCW

Edgerton, Clyde (Carlyle) 1944-.... **CLC 39**
See also AAYA 17; CA 118; 134; INT 134

Edgeworth, Maria 1768-1849... **NCLC 1, 51**
See also DLB 116, 159, 163; SATA 21

Edmonds, Paul
See Kuttner, Henry

Edmonds, Walter D(umaux) 1903-.. **CLC 35**
See also CA 5-8R; CANR 2; DLB 9;
MAICYA; SAAS 4; SATA 1, 27

Edmondson, Wallace
See Ellison, Harlan (Jay)

Edson, Russell.................... **CLC 13**
See also CA 33-36R

Edwards, Bronwen Elizabeth
See Rose, Wendy

Edwards, G(erald) B(asil)
1899-1976 .... **CLC 25**
See also CA 110

Edwards, Gus 1939-.............. **CLC 43**
See also CA 108; INT 108

Edwards, Jonathan
1703-1758 .... **LC 7; DA; DAC;**
                                        DAM MST
See also DLB 24

Efron, Marina Ivanovna Tsvetaeva
See Tsvetaeva (Efron), Marina (Ivanovna)

Ehle, John (Marsden, Jr.) 1925-.... **CLC 27**
See also CA 9-12R

Ehrenbourg, Ilya (Grigoryevich)
See Ehrenburg, Ilya (Grigoryevich)

Ehrenburg, Ilya (Grigoryevich)
1891-1967 .... **CLC 18, 34, 62**
See also CA 102; 25-28R

Ehrenburg, Ilyo (Grigoryevich)
See Ehrenburg, Ilya (Grigoryevich)

Eich, Guenter 1907-1972 .... **CLC 15**
See also CA 111; 93-96; DLB 69, 124

Eichendorff, Joseph Freiherr von
1788-1857 .... **NCLC 8**
See also DLB 90

Eigner, Larry..................... **CLC 9**
See also Eigner, Laurence (Joel)
See also CAAS 23; DLB 5

Eigner, Laurence (Joel) 1927-1996
See Eigner, Larry
See also CA 9-12R; 151; CANR 6

Einstein, Albert 1879-1955 .... **TCLC 65**
See also CA 121; 133; MTCW

Eiseley, Loren Corey 1907-1977 ..... **CLC 7**
See also AAYA 5; CA 1-4R; 73-76;
CANR 6

Ericson, Walter
   See Fast, Howard (Melvin)

Eriksson, Buntel
   See Bergman, (Ernst) Ingmar

Ernaux, Annie 1940- .... **CLC 88**
   See also CA 147

Eschenbach, Wolfram von
   See Wolfram von Eschenbach

Eseki, Bruno
   See Mphahlele, Ezekiel

Esenin, Sergei (Alexandrovich)
   1895-1925 .... **TCLC 4**
   See also CA 104

Eshleman, Clayton 1935- .... **CLC 7**
   See also CA 33-36R; CAAS 6; DLB 5

Espriella, Don Manuel Alvarez
   See Southey, Robert

Espriu, Salvador 1913-1985........ **CLC 9**
   See also CA 154; 115; DLB 134

Espronceda, Jose de 1808-1842... **NCLC 39**

Esse, James
   See Stephens, James

Esterbrook, Tom
   See Hubbard, L(afayette) Ron(ald)

Estleman, Loren D.
   1952- ...... **CLC 48; DAM NOV, POP**
   See also CA 85-88; CANR 27;
   INT CANR-27; MTCW

Eugenides, Jeffrey 1960(?)- .... **CLC 81**
   See also CA 144

Euripides
   c. 485B.C.-406B.C...... **CMLC 23; DA;**
   DAB; DAC; DAM DRAM, MST; DC 4;
   WLCS
   See also DLB 176

Evan, Evin
   See Faust, Frederick (Schiller)

Evans, Evan
   See Faust, Frederick (Schiller)

Evans, Marian
   See Eliot, George

Evans, Mary Ann
   See Eliot, George

Evarts, Esther
   See Benson, Sally

Everett, Percival L. 1956- .... **CLC 57**
   See also BW 2; CA 129

Everson, R(onald) G(ilmour)
   1903- .... **CLC 27**
   See also CA 17-20R; DLB 88

Everson, William (Oliver)
   1912-1994 .... **CLC 1, 5, 14**
   See also CA 9-12R; 145; CANR 20; DLB 5,
   16; MTCW

Evtushenko, Evgenii Aleksandrovich
   See Yevtushenko, Yevgeny (Alexandrovich)

Ewart, Gavin (Buchanan)
   1916-1995 .... **CLC 13, 46**
   See also CA 89-92; 150; CANR 17, 46;
   DLB 40; MTCW

Ewers, Hanns Heinz 1871-1943 ... **TCLC 12**
   See also CA 109; 149

Ewing, Frederick R.
   See Sturgeon, Theodore (Hamilton)

Exley, Frederick (Earl)
   1929-1992 .... **CLC 6, 11**
   See also AITN 2; CA 81-84; 138; DLB 143;
   DLBY 81

Eynhardt, Guillermo
   See Quiroga, Horacio (Sylvestre)

Ezekiel, Nissim 1924-............. **CLC 61**
   See also CA 61-64

Ezekiel, Tish O'Dowd 1943- .... **CLC 34**
   See also CA 129

Fadeyev, A.
   See Bulgya, Alexander Alexandrovich

Fadeyev, Alexander.............. **TCLC 53**
   See also Bulgya, Alexander Alexandrovich

Fagen, Donald 1948-............. **CLC 26**

Fainzilberg, Ilya Arnoldovich 1897-1937
   See Ilf, Ilya
   See also CA 120

Fair, Ronald L. 1932-............. **CLC 18**
   See also BW 1; CA 69-72; CANR 25;
   DLB 33

Fairbairn, Roger
   See Carr, John Dickson

Fairbairns, Zoe (Ann) 1948- .... **CLC 32**
   See also CA 103; CANR 21

Falco, Gian
   See Papini, Giovanni

Falconer, James
   See Kirkup, James

Falconer, Kenneth
   See Kornbluth, C(yril) M.

Falkland, Samuel
   See Heijermans, Herman

Fallaci, Oriana 1930-............. **CLC 11**
   See also CA 77-80; CANR 15, 58; MTCW

Faludy, George 1913-............. **CLC 42**
   See also CA 21-24R

Faludy, Gyoergy
   See Faludy, George

Fanon, Frantz
   1925-1961 .... **CLC 74; BLC;**
   DAM MULT
   See also BW 1; CA 116; 89-92

Fanshawe, Ann 1625-1680 .... **LC 11**

Fante, John (Thomas) 1911-1983 ... **CLC 60**
   See also CA 69-72; 109; CANR 23;
   DLB 130; DLBY 83

Farah, Nuruddin
   1945- ..... **CLC 53; BLC; DAM MULT**
   See also BW 2; CA 106; DLB 125

Fargue, Leon-Paul 1876(?)-1947 ... **TCLC 11**
   See also CA 109

Farigoule, Louis
   See Romains, Jules

Farina, Richard 1936(?)-1966 .... **CLC 9**
   See also CA 81-84; 25-28R

Farley, Walter (Lorimer)
   1915-1989 .... **CLC 17**
   See also CA 17-20R; CANR 8, 29; DLB 22;
   JRDA; MAICYA; SATA 2, 43

Farmer, Philip Jose 1918-....... **CLC 1, 19**
   See also CA 1-4R; CANR 4, 35; DLB 8;
   MTCW; SATA 93

Farquhar, George
   1677-1707 .... **LC 21; DAM DRAM**
   See also DLB 84

Farrell, J(ames) G(ordon)
   1935-1979 .... **CLC 6**
   See also CA 73-76; 89-92; CANR 36;
   DLB 14; MTCW

Farrell, James T(homas)
   1904-1979 .. **CLC 1, 4, 8, 11, 66; SSC 28**
   See also CA 5-8R; 89-92; CANR 9, 61;
   DLB 4, 9, 86; DLBD 2; MTCW

Farren, Richard J.
   See Betjeman, John

Farren, Richard M.
   See Betjeman, John

Fassbinder, Rainer Werner
   1946-1982 .... **CLC 20**
   See also CA 93-96; 106; CANR 31

Fast, Howard (Melvin)
   1914- .... **CLC 23; DAM NOV**
   See also AAYA 16; CA 1-4R; CAAS 18;
   CANR 1, 33, 54; DLB 9; INT CANR-33;
   SATA 7

Faulcon, Robert
   See Holdstock, Robert P.

Faulkner, William (Cuthbert)
   1897-1962 ..... **CLC 1, 3, 6, 8, 9, 11, 14,**
   18, 28, 52, 68; DA; DAB; DAC;
   DAM MST, NOV; SSC 1; WLC
   See also AAYA 7; CA 81-84; CANR 33;
   CDALB 1929-1941; DLB 9, 11, 44, 102;
   DLBD 2; DLBY 86; MTCW

Fauset, Jessie Redmon
   1884(?)-1961 .... **CLC 19, 54; BLC;**
   DAM MULT
   See also BW 1; CA 109; DLB 51

Faust, Frederick (Schiller)
   1892-1944(?) ..... **TCLC 49; DAM POP**
   See also CA 108; 152

Faust, Irvin 1924-................. **CLC 8**
   See also CA 33-36R; CANR 28; DLB 2, 28;
   DLBY 80

Fawkes, Guy
   See Benchley, Robert (Charles)

Fearing, Kenneth (Flexner)
   1902-1961 .... **CLC 51**
   See also CA 93-96; CANR 59; DLB 9

Fecamps, Elise
   See Creasey, John

Federman, Raymond 1928- ...... **CLC 6, 47**
   See also CA 17-20R; CAAS 8; CANR 10,
   43; DLBY 80

Federspiel, J(uerg) F. 1931-........ **CLC 42**
   See also CA 146

Feiffer, Jules (Ralph)
   1929- ...... **CLC 2, 8, 64; DAM DRAM**
   See also AAYA 3; CA 17-20R; CANR 30,
   59; DLB 7, 44; INT CANR-30; MTCW;
   SATA 8, 61

Feige, Hermann Albert Otto Maximilian
   See Traven, B.

Feinberg, David B. 1956-1994...... **CLC 59**
   See also CA 135; 147

Feinstein, Elaine 1930-............ **CLC 36**
   See also CA 69-72; CAAS 1; CANR 31;
   DLB 14, 40; MTCW

Feldman, Irving (Mordecai) 1928-.... **CLC 7**
See also CA 1-4R; CANR 1; DLB 169

Felix-Tchicaya, Gerald
See Tchicaya, Gerald Felix

Fellini, Federico 1920-1993 ..... **CLC 16, 85**
See also CA 65-68; 143; CANR 33

Felsen, Henry Gregor 1916- .... **CLC 17**
See also CA 1-4R; CANR 1; SAAS 2;
SATA 1

Fenton, James Martin 1949-....... **CLC 32**
See also CA 102; DLB 40

Ferber, Edna 1887-1968....... **CLC 18, 93**
See also AITN 1; CA 5-8R; 25-28R; DLB 9,
28, 86; MTCW; SATA 7

Ferguson, Helen
See Kavan, Anna

Ferguson, Samuel 1810-1886 ..... **NCLC 33**
See also DLB 32

Fergusson, Robert 1750-1774 .... **LC 29**
See also DLB 109

Ferling, Lawrence
See Ferlinghetti, Lawrence (Monsanto)

Ferlinghetti, Lawrence (Monsanto)
1919(?)-............ **CLC 2, 6, 10, 27;
DAM POET; PC 1**
See also CA 5-8R; CANR 3, 41;
CDALB 1941-1968; DLB 5, 16; MTCW

Fernandez, Vicente Garcia Huidobro
See Huidobro Fernandez, Vicente Garcia

Ferrer, Gabriel (Francisco Victor) Miro
See Miro (Ferrer), Gabriel (Francisco
Victor)

Ferrier, Susan (Edmonstone)
1782-1854 .... **NCLC 8**
See also DLB 116

Ferrigno, Robert 1948(?)-......... **CLC 65**
See also CA 140

Ferron, Jacques 1921-1985 ... **CLC 94; DAC**
See also CA 117; 129; DLB 60

Feuchtwanger, Lion 1884-1958 ..... **TCLC 3**
See also CA 104; DLB 66

Feuillet, Octave 1821-1890 ...... **NCLC 45**

Feydeau, Georges (Leon Jules Marie)
1862-1921 ..... **TCLC 22; DAM DRAM**
See also CA 113; 152

Fichte, Johann Gottlieb
1762-1814 .... **NCLC 62**
See also DLB 90

Ficino, Marsilio 1433-1499 .... **LC 12**

Fiedeler, Hans
See Doeblin, Alfred

Fiedler, Leslie A(aron)
1917- .... **CLC 4, 13, 24**
See also CA 9-12R; CANR 7; DLB 28, 67;
MTCW

Field, Andrew 1938-.............. **CLC 44**
See also CA 97-100; CANR 25

Field, Eugene 1850-1895 .... **NCLC 3**
See also DLB 23, 42, 140; DLBD 13;
MAICYA; SATA 16

Field, Gans T.
See Wellman, Manly Wade

Field, Michael .... **TCLC 43**

Field, Peter
See Hobson, Laura Z(ametkin)

Fielding, Henry
1707-1754 ...... **LC 1; DA; DAB; DAC;
DAM DRAM, MST, NOV; WLC**
See also CDBLB 1660-1789; DLB 39, 84,
101

Fielding, Sarah 1710-1768 .... **LC 1**
See also DLB 39

Fierstein, Harvey (Forbes)
1954- ..... **CLC 33; DAM DRAM, POP**
See also CA 123; 129

Figes, Eva 1932-................ **CLC 31**
See also CA 53-56; CANR 4, 44; DLB 14

Finch, Robert (Duer Claydon)
1900- .... **CLC 18**
See also CA 57-60; CANR 9, 24, 49;
DLB 88

Findley, Timothy
1930-.. **CLC 27, 102; DAC; DAM MST**
See also CA 25-28R; CANR 12, 42;
DLB 53

Fink, William
See Mencken, H(enry) L(ouis)

Firbank, Louis 1942-
See Reed, Lou
See also CA 117

Firbank, (Arthur Annesley) Ronald
1886-1926 .... **TCLC 1**
See also CA 104; DLB 36

Fisher, M(ary) F(rances) K(ennedy)
1908-1992 .... **CLC 76, 87**
See also CA 77-80; 138; CANR 44

Fisher, Roy 1930-................ **CLC 25**
See also CA 81-84; CAAS 10; CANR 16;
DLB 40

Fisher, Rudolph
1897-1934 .... **TCLC 11; BLC;
DAM MULT; SSC 25**
See also BW 1; CA 107; 124; DLB 51, 102

Fisher, Vardis (Alvero) 1895-1968.... **CLC 7**
See also CA 5-8R; 25-28R; DLB 9

Fiske, Tarleton
See Bloch, Robert (Albert)

Fitch, Clarke
See Sinclair, Upton (Beall)

Fitch, John IV
See Cormier, Robert (Edmund)

Fitzgerald, Captain Hugh
See Baum, L(yman) Frank

FitzGerald, Edward 1809-1883 .... **NCLC 9**
See also DLB 32

Fitzgerald, F(rancis) Scott (Key)
1896-1940 ..... **TCLC 1, 6, 14, 28, 55;
DA; DAB; DAC; DAM MST, NOV;
SSC 6; WLC**
See also AITN 1; CA 110; 123;
CDALB 1917-1929; DLB 4, 9, 86;
DLBD 1, 15, 16; DLBY 81, 96; MTCW

Fitzgerald, Penelope 1916-... **CLC 19, 51, 61**
See also CA 85-88; CAAS 10; CANR 56;
DLB 14

Fitzgerald, Robert (Stuart)
1910-1985 .... **CLC 39**
See also CA 1-4R; 114; CANR 1; DLBY 80

FitzGerald, Robert D(avid)
1902-1987 .... **CLC 19**
See also CA 17-20R

Fitzgerald, Zelda (Sayre)
1900-1948 .... **TCLC 52**
See also CA 117; 126; DLBY 84

Flanagan, Thomas (James Bonner)
1923- .... **CLC 25, 52**
See also CA 108; CANR 55; DLBY 80;
INT 108; MTCW

Flaubert, Gustave
1821-1880 ..... **NCLC 2, 10, 19, 62, 66;
DA; DAB; DAC; DAM MST, NOV;
SSC 11; WLC**
See also DLB 119

Flecker, Herman Elroy
See Flecker, (Herman) James Elroy

Flecker, (Herman) James Elroy
1884-1915 .... **TCLC 43**
See also CA 109; 150; DLB 10, 19

Fleming, Ian (Lancaster)
1908-1964 ...... **CLC 3, 30; DAM POP**
See also CA 5-8R; CANR 59;
CDBLB 1945-1960; DLB 87; MTCW;
SATA 9

Fleming, Thomas (James) 1927- .... **CLC 37**
See also CA 5-8R; CANR 10;
INT CANR-10; SATA 8

Fletcher, John 1579-1625...... **LC 33; DC 6**
See also CDBLB Before 1660; DLB 58

Fletcher, John Gould 1886-1950 ... **TCLC 35**
See also CA 107; DLB 4, 45

Fleur, Paul
See Pohl, Frederik

Flooglebuckle, Al
See Spiegelman, Art

Flying Officer X
See Bates, H(erbert) E(rnest)

Fo, Dario 1926-..... **CLC 32; DAM DRAM**
See also CA 116; 128; MTCW

Fogarty, Jonathan Titulescu Esq.
See Farrell, James T(homas)

Folke, Will
See Bloch, Robert (Albert)

Follett, Ken(neth Martin)
1949- ...... **CLC 18; DAM NOV, POP**
See also AAYA 6; BEST 89:4; CA 81-84;
CANR 13, 33, 54; DLB 87; DLBY 81;
INT CANR-33; MTCW

Fontane, Theodor 1819-1898 ..... **NCLC 26**
See also DLB 129

Foote, Horton
1916- .... **CLC 51, 91; DAM DRAM**
See also CA 73-76; CANR 34, 51; DLB 26;
INT CANR-34

Foote, Shelby
1916- .... **CLC 75; DAM NOV, POP**
See also CA 5-8R; CANR 3, 45; DLB 2, 17

Forbes, Esther 1891-1967.......... **CLC 12**
See also AAYA 17; CA 13-14; 25-28R;
CAP 1; CLR 27; DLB 22; JRDA;
MAICYA; SATA 2

Forche, Carolyn (Louise)
1950- .... **CLC 25, 83, 86; DAM POET;**
PC 10
See also CA 109; 117; CANR 50; DLB 5;
INT 117

Ford, Elbur
See Hibbert, Eleanor Alice Burford

Ford, Ford Madox
1873-1939 .... **TCLC 1, 15, 39, 57;**
DAM NOV
See also CA 104; 132; CDBLB 1914-1945;
DLB 162; MTCW

Ford, Henry 1863-1947 .... **TCLC 73**
See also CA 115; 148

Ford, John 1586-(?) .... **DC 8**
See also CDBLB Before 1660;
DAM DRAM; DLB 58

Ford, John 1895-1973.............. **CLC 16**
See also CA 45-48

Ford, Richard .... **CLC 99**

Ford, Richard 1944-.............. **CLC 46**
See also CA 69-72; CANR 11, 47

Ford, Webster
See Masters, Edgar Lee

Foreman, Richard 1937-.......... **CLC 50**
See also CA 65-68; CANR 32

Forester, C(ecil) S(cott)
1899-1966 .... **CLC 35**
See also CA 73-76; 25-28R; SATA 13

Forez
See Mauriac, Francois (Charles)

Forman, James Douglas 1932-...... **CLC 21**
See also AAYA 17; CA 9-12R; CANR 4,
19, 42; JRDA; MAICYA; SATA 8, 70

Fornes, Maria Irene 1930-...... **CLC 39, 61**
See also CA 25-28R; CANR 28; DLB 7;
HW; INT CANR-28; MTCW

Forrest, Leon 1937- .... **CLC 4**
See also BW 2; CA 89-92; CAAS 7;
CANR 25, 52; DLB 33

Forster, E(dward) M(organ)
1879-1970 ..... **CLC 1, 2, 3, 4, 9, 10, 13,**
15, 22, 45, 77; DA; DAB; DAC;
DAM MST, NOV; SSC 27; WLC
See also AAYA 2; CA 13-14; 25-28R;
CANR 45; CAP 1; CDBLB 1914-1945;
DLB 34, 98, 162, 178; DLBD 10; MTCW;
SATA 57

Forster, John 1812-1876 .... **NCLC 11**
See also DLB 144, 184

Forsyth, Frederick
1938- .. **CLC 2, 5, 36; DAM NOV, POP**
See also BEST 89:4; CA 85-88; CANR 38,
62; DLB 87; MTCW

Forten, Charlotte L. .... **TCLC 16; BLC**
See also Grimke, Charlotte L(ottie) Forten
See also DLB 50

Foscolo, Ugo 1778-1827.......... **NCLC 8**

Fosse, Bob .... **CLC 20**
See also Fosse, Robert Louis

Fosse, Robert Louis 1927-1987
See Fosse, Bob
See also CA 110; 123

Foster, Stephen Collins
1826-1864 .... **NCLC 26**

Foucault, Michel
1926-1984 .... **CLC 31, 34, 69**
See also CA 105; 113; CANR 34; MTCW

Fouque, Friedrich (Heinrich Karl) de la Motte
1777-1843 .... **NCLC 2**
See also DLB 90

Fourier, Charles 1772-1837 ...... **NCLC 51**

Fournier, Henri Alban 1886-1914
See Alain-Fournier
See also CA 104

Fournier, Pierre 1916- .... **CLC 11**
See also Gascar, Pierre
See also CA 89-92; CANR 16, 40

Fowles, John
1926- ...... **CLC 1, 2, 3, 4, 6, 9, 10, 15,**
33, 87; DAB; DAC; DAM MST
See also CA 5-8R; CANR 25; CDBLB 1960
to Present; DLB 14, 139; MTCW;
SATA 22

Fox, Paula 1923-................ **CLC 2, 8**
See also AAYA 3; CA 73-76; CANR 20,
36, 62; CLR 1, 44; DLB 52; JRDA;
MAICYA; MTCW; SATA 17, 60

Fox, William Price (Jr.) 1926- ..... **CLC 22**
See also CA 17-20R; CAAS 19; CANR 11;
DLB 2; DLBY 81

Foxe, John 1516(?)-1587 .... **LC 14**

Frame, Janet
1924- ... **CLC 2, 3, 6, 22, 66, 96; SSC 29**
See also Clutha, Janet Paterson Frame

France, Anatole .... **TCLC 9**
See also Thibault, Jacques Anatole Francois
See also DLB 123

Francis, Claude 19(?)- .... **CLC 50**

Francis, Dick
1920- ... **CLC 2, 22, 42, 102; DAM POP**
See also AAYA 5, 21; BEST 89:3; CA 5-8R;
CANR 9, 42; CDBLB 1960 to Present;
DLB 87; INT CANR-9; MTCW

Francis, Robert (Churchill)
1901-1987 .... **CLC 15**
See also CA 1-4R; 123; CANR 1

Frank, Anne(lies Marie)
1929-1945 .... **TCLC 17; DA; DAB;**
DAC; DAM MST; WLC
See also AAYA 12; CA 113; 133; MTCW;
SATA 87; SATA-Brief 42

Frank, Elizabeth 1945-............ **CLC 39**
See also CA 121; 126; INT 126

Frankl, Viktor E(mil) 1905-1997.... **CLC 93**
See also CA 65-68; 161

Franklin, Benjamin
See Hasek, Jaroslav (Matej Frantisek)

Franklin, Benjamin
1706-1790 ..... **LC 25; DA; DAB; DAC;**
DAM MST; WLCS
See also CDALB 1640-1865; DLB 24, 43,
73

Franklin, (Stella Maraia Sarah) Miles
1879-1954 .... **TCLC 7**
See also CA 104

Fraser, (Lady) Antonia (Pakenham)
1932- .... **CLC 32**
See also CA 85-88; CANR 44; MTCW;
SATA-Brief 32

Fraser, George MacDonald 1925-.... **CLC 7**
See also CA 45-48; CANR 2, 48

Fraser, Sylvia 1935-.............. **CLC 64**
See also CA 45-48; CANR 1, 16, 60

Frayn, Michael
1933- .... **CLC 3, 7, 31, 47;**
DAM DRAM, NOV
See also CA 5-8R; CANR 30; DLB 13, 14;
MTCW

Fraze, Candida (Merrill) 1945-..... **CLC 50**
See also CA 126

Frazer, J(ames) G(eorge)
1854-1941 .... **TCLC 32**
See also CA 118

Frazer, Robert Caine
See Creasey, John

Frazer, Sir James George
See Frazer, J(ames) G(eorge)

Frazier, Ian 1951-................. **CLC 46**
See also CA 130; CANR 54

Frederic, Harold 1856-1898...... **NCLC 10**
See also DLB 12, 23; DLBD 13

Frederick, John
See Faust, Frederick (Schiller)

Frederick the Great 1712-1786...... **LC 14**

Fredro, Aleksander 1793-1876..... **NCLC 8**

Freeling, Nicolas 1927- .... **CLC 38**
See also CA 49-52; CAAS 12; CANR 1, 17,
50; DLB 87

Freeman, Douglas Southall
1886-1953 .... **TCLC 11**
See also CA 109; DLB 17

Freeman, Judith 1946-............ **CLC 55**
See also CA 148

Freeman, Mary Eleanor Wilkins
1852-1930 .... **TCLC 9; SSC 1**
See also CA 106; DLB 12, 78

Freeman, R(ichard) Austin
1862-1943 .... **TCLC 21**
See also CA 113; DLB 70

French, Albert 1943- .... **CLC 86**

French, Marilyn
1929- .... **CLC 10, 18, 60;**
DAM DRAM, NOV, POP
See also CA 69-72; CANR 3, 31;
INT CANR-31; MTCW

French, Paul
See Asimov, Isaac

Freneau, Philip Morin 1752-1832 .. **NCLC 1**
See also DLB 37, 43

Freud, Sigmund 1856-1939 .... **TCLC 52**
See also CA 115; 133; MTCW

Friedan, Betty (Naomi) 1921-...... **CLC 74**
See also CA 65-68; CANR 18, 45; MTCW

Friedlander, Saul 1932-........... **CLC 90**
See also CA 117; 130

Friedman, B(ernard) H(arper)
1926-...................... **CLC 7**
See also CA 1-4R; CANR 3, 48

Friedman, Bruce Jay 1930-.... **CLC 3, 5, 56**
See also CA 9-12R; CANR 25, 52; DLB 2,
28; INT CANR-25

Friel, Brian   1929-..... **CLC 5, 42, 59; DC 8**
See also CA 21-24R; CANR 33; DLB 13;
MTCW

Friis-Baastad, Babbis Ellinor
1921-1970 .... **CLC 12**
See also CA 17-20R; 134; SATA 7

Frisch, Max (Rudolf)
1911-1991 ..... **CLC 3, 9, 14, 18, 32, 44;**
DAM DRAM, NOV
See also CA 85-88; 134; CANR 32;
DLB 69, 124; MTCW

Fromentin, Eugene (Samuel Auguste)
1820-1876 .... **NCLC 10**
See also DLB 123

Frost, Frederick
See Faust, Frederick (Schiller)

Frost, Robert (Lee)
1874-1963 .... **CLC 1, 3, 4, 9, 10, 13, 15,**
26, 34, 44; DA; DAB; DAC; DAM MST,
POET; PC 1; WLC
See also AAYA 21; CA 89-92; CANR 33;
CDALB 1917-1929; DLB 54; DLBD 7;
MTCW; SATA 14

Froude, James Anthony
1818-1894 .... **NCLC 43**
See also DLB 18, 57, 144

Froy, Herald
See Waterhouse, Keith (Spencer)

Fry, Christopher
1907- ..... **CLC 2, 10, 14; DAM DRAM**
See also CA 17-20R; CAAS 23; CANR 9,
30; DLB 13; MTCW; SATA 66

Frye, (Herman) Northrop
1912-1991 .... **CLC 24, 70**
See also CA 5-8R; 133; CANR 8, 37;
DLB 67, 68; MTCW

Fuchs, Daniel   1909-1993 .... **CLC 8, 22**
See also CA 81-84; 142; CAAS 5;
CANR 40; DLB 9, 26, 28; DLBY 93

Fuchs, Daniel   1934-.............. **CLC 34**
See also CA 37-40R; CANR 14, 48

Fuentes, Carlos
1928-...... **CLC 3, 8, 10, 13, 22, 41, 60;**
DA; DAB; DAC; DAM MST, MULT,
NOV; HLC; SSC 24; WLC
See also AAYA 4; AITN 2; CA 69-72;
CANR 10, 32; DLB 113; HW; MTCW

Fuentes, Gregorio Lopez y
See Lopez y Fuentes, Gregorio

Fugard, (Harold) Athol
1932- .... **CLC 5, 9, 14, 25, 40, 80;**
DAM DRAM; DC 3
See also AAYA 17; CA 85-88; CANR 32,
54; MTCW

Fugard, Sheila   1932- .... **CLC 48**
See also CA 125

Fuller, Charles (H., Jr.)
1939- .... **CLC 25; BLC; DAM DRAM,**
MULT; DC 1
See also BW 2; CA 108; 112; DLB 38;
INT 112; MTCW

Fuller, John (Leopold)   1937-....... **CLC 62**
See also CA 21-24R; CANR 9, 44; DLB 40

Fuller, Margaret .... **NCLC 5, 50**
See also Ossoli, Sarah Margaret (Fuller
marchesa d')

Fuller, Roy (Broadbent)
1912-1991 .:............. **CLC 4, 28**
See also CA 5-8R; 135; CAAS 10;
CANR 53; DLB 15, 20; SATA 87

Fulton, Alice   1952-.............. **CLC 52**
See also CA 116; CANR 57

Furphy, Joseph   1843-1912........ **TCLC 25**

Fussell, Paul   1924-.............. **CLC 74**
See also BEST 90:1; CA 17-20R; CANR 8,
21, 35; INT CANR-21; MTCW

Futabatei, Shimei   1864-1909 ...... **TCLC 44**
See also DLB 180

Futrelle, Jacques   1875-1912 ...... **TCLC 19**
See also CA 113; 155

Gaboriau, Emile   1835-1873 ...... **NCLC 14**

Gadda, Carlo Emilio   1893-1973 .... **CLC 11**
See also CA 89-92; DLB 177

Gaddis, William
1922- ..... **CLC 1, 3, 6, 8, 10, 19, 43, 86**
See also CA 17-20R; CANR 21, 48; DLB 2;
MTCW

Gage, Walter
See Inge, William (Motter)

Gaines, Ernest J(ames)
1933- .... **CLC 3, 11, 18, 86; BLC;**
DAM MULT
See also AAYA 18; AITN 1; BW 2;
CA 9-12R; CANR 6, 24, 42;
CDALB 1968-1988; DLB 2, 33, 152;
DLBY 80; MTCW; SATA 86

Gaitskill, Mary   1954-............. **CLC 69**
See also CA 128; CANR 61

Galdos, Benito Perez
See Perez Galdos, Benito

Gale, Zona
1874-1938 ...... **TCLC 7; DAM DRAM**
See also CA 105; 153; DLB 9, 78

Galeano, Eduardo (Hughes)   1940-... **CLC 72**
See also CA 29-32R; CANR 13, 32; HW

Galiano, Juan Valera y Alcala
See Valera y Alcala-Galiano, Juan

Gallagher, Tess
1943-.. **CLC 18, 63; DAM POET; PC 9**
See also CA 106; DLB 120

Gallant, Mavis
1922-...:........ **CLC 7, 18, 38; DAC;**
DAM MST; SSC 5
See also CA 69-72; CANR 29; DLB 53;
MTCW

Gallant, Roy A(rthur)   1924- .... **CLC 17**
See also CA 5-8R; CANR 4, 29, 54;
CLR 30; MAICYA; SATA 4, 68

Gallico, Paul (William)   1897-1976 ... **CLC 2**
See also AITN 1; CA 5-8R; 69-72;
CANR 23; DLB 9, 171; MAICYA;
SATA 13

Gallo, Max Louis   1932-........... **CLC 95**
See also CA 85-88

Gallois, Lucien
See Desnos, Robert

Gallup, Ralph
See Whitemore, Hugh (John)

Galsworthy, John
1867-1933 ...... **TCLC 1, 45; DA; DAB;**
DAC; DAM DRAM, MST, NOV;
SSC 22; WLC 2
See also CA 104; 141; CDBLB 1890-1914;
DLB 10, 34, 98, 162; DLBD 16

Galt, John   1779-1839 .... **NCLC 1**
See also DLB 99, 116, 159

Galvin, James   1951-............... **CLC 38**
See also CA 108; CANR 26

Gamboa, Federico   1864-1939...... **TCLC 36**

Gandhi, M. K.
See Gandhi, Mohandas Karamchand

Gandhi, Mahatma
See Gandhi, Mohandas Karamchand

Gandhi, Mohandas Karamchand
1869-1948 ..... **TCLC 59; DAM MULT**
See also CA 121; 132; MTCW

Gann, Ernest Kellogg   1910-1991.... **CLC 23**
See also AITN 1; CA 1-4R; 136; CANR 1

Garcia, Cristina   1958- .... **CLC 76**
See also CA 141

Garcia Lorca, Federico
1898-1936 ... **TCLC 1, 7, 49; DA; DAB;**
DAC; DAM DRAM, MST, MULT,
POET; DC 2; HLC; PC 3; WLC
See also CA 104; 131; DLB 108; HW;
MTCW

Garcia Marquez, Gabriel (Jose)
1928- .... **CLC 2, 3, 8, 10, 15, 27, 47, 55,**
68; DA; DAB; DAC; DAM MST,
NOV, POP; HLC; SSC 8; WLC
See also AAYA 3; BEST 89:1, 90:4;
CA 33-36R; CANR 10, 28, 50; DLB 113;
HW; MTCW

Gard, Janice
See Latham, Jean Lee

Gard, Roger Martin du
See Martin du Gard, Roger

Gardam, Jane   1928-.............. **CLC 43**
See also CA 49-52; CANR 2, 18, 33, 54;
CLR 12; DLB 14, 161; MAICYA;
MTCW; SAAS 9; SATA 39, 76;
SATA-Brief 28

Gardner, Herb(ert)   1934-.......... **CLC 44**
See also CA 149

Gardner, John (Champlin), Jr.
1933-1982 ..... **CLC 2, 3, 5, 7, 8, 10, 18,**
28, 34; DAM NOV, POP; SSC 7
See also AITN 1; CA 65-68; 107;
CANR 33; DLB 2; DLBY 82; MTCW;
SATA 40; SATA-Obit 31

Gardner, John (Edmund)
1926- .... **CLC 30; DAM POP**
See also CA 103; CANR 15; MTCW

Gardner, Miriam
See Bradley, Marion Zimmer

Gardner, Noel
See Kuttner, Henry

Gardons, S. S.
See Snodgrass, W(illiam) D(e Witt)

Garfield, Leon   1921-1996......... **CLC 12**
See also AAYA 8; CA 17-20R; 152;
CANR 38, 41; CLR 21; DLB 161; JRDA;
MAICYA; SATA 1, 32, 76;
SATA-Obit 90

Garland, (Hannibal) Hamlin
1860-1940 .... **TCLC 3; SSC 18**
See also CA 104; DLB 12, 71, 78

Garneau, (Hector de) Saint-Denys
1912-1943 .... **TCLC 13**
See also CA 111; DLB 88

Garner, Alan
1934- .... **CLC 17; DAB; DAM POP**
See also AAYA 18; CA 73-76; CANR 15;
CLR 20; DLB 161; MAICYA; MTCW;
SATA 18, 69

Garner, Hugh   1913-1979 .... **CLC 13**
See also CA 69-72; CANR 31; DLB 68

Garnett, David   1892-1981 .... **CLC 3**
See also CA 5-8R; 103; CANR 17; DLB 34

Garos, Stephanie
See Katz, Steve

Garrett, George (Palmer)
1929- .... **CLC 3, 11, 51**
See also CA 1-4R; CAAS 5; CANR 1, 42;
DLB 2, 5, 130, 152; DLBY 83

Garrick, David
1717-1779 ...... **LC 15; DAM DRAM**
See also DLB 84

Garrigue, Jean   1914-1972 .... **CLC 2, 8**
See also CA 5-8R; 37-40R; CANR 20

Garrison, Frederick
See Sinclair, Upton (Beall)

Garth, Will
See Hamilton, Edmond; Kuttner, Henry

Garvey, Marcus (Moziah, Jr.)
1887-1940 .... **TCLC 41; BLC;**
DAM MULT
See also BW 1; CA 120; 124

Gary, Romain .... **CLC 25**
See also Kacew, Romain
See also DLB 83

Gascar, Pierre .... **CLC 11**
See also Fournier, Pierre

Gascoyne, David (Emery)   1916- .... **CLC 45**
See also CA 65-68; CANR 10, 28, 54;
DLB 20; MTCW

Gaskell, Elizabeth Cleghorn
1810-1865 .... **NCLC 5; DAB;**
DAM MST; SSC 25
See also CDBLB 1832-1890; DLB 21, 144,
159

Gass, William H(oward)
1924- ... **CLC 1, 2, 8, 11, 15, 39; SSC 12**
See also CA 17-20R; CANR 30; DLB 2;
MTCW

Gasset, Jose Ortega y
See Ortega y Gasset, Jose

Gates, Henry Louis, Jr.
1950- .... **CLC 65; DAM MULT**
See also BW 2; CA 109; CANR 25, 53;
DLB 67

Gautier, Theophile
1811-1872 .... **NCLC 1, 59;**
DAM POET; PC 18; SSC 20
See also DLB 119

Gawsworth, John
See Bates, H(erbert) E(rnest)

Gay, Oliver
See Gogarty, Oliver St. John

Gaye, Marvin (Penze)   1939-1984 ... **CLC 26**
See also CA 112

Gebler, Carlo (Ernest)   1954- .... **CLC 39**
See also CA 119; 133

Gee, Maggie (Mary)   1948- .... **CLC 57**
See also CA 130

Gee, Maurice (Gough)   1931- .... **CLC 29**
See also CA 97-100; SATA 46

Gelbart, Larry (Simon)   1923- ... **CLC 21, 61**
See also CA 73-76; CANR 45

Gelber, Jack   1932- .... **CLC 1, 6, 14, 79**
See also CA 1-4R; CANR 2; DLB 7

Gellhorn, Martha (Ellis)   1908- .. **CLC 14, 60**
See also CA 77-80; CANR 44; DLBY 82

Genet, Jean
1910-1986 ...... **CLC 1, 2, 5, 10, 14, 44,**
46; DAM DRAM
See also CA 13-16R; CANR 18; DLB 72;
DLBY 86; MTCW

Gent, Peter   1942- .... **CLC 29**
See also AITN 1; CA 89-92; DLBY 82

Gentlewoman in New England, A
See Bradstreet, Anne

Gentlewoman in Those Parts, A
See Bradstreet, Anne

George, Jean Craighead   1919- ...... **CLC 35**
See also AAYA 8; CA 5-8R; CANR 25;
CLR 1; DLB 52; JRDA; MAICYA;
SATA 2, 68

George, Stefan (Anton)
1868-1933 .... **TCLC 2, 14**
See also CA 104

Georges, Georges Martin
See Simenon, Georges (Jacques Christian)

Gerhardi, William Alexander
See Gerhardie, William Alexander

Gerhardie, William Alexander
1895-1977 .... **CLC 5**
See also CA 25-28R; 73-76; CANR 18;
DLB 36

Gerstler, Amy   1956- .... **CLC 70**
See also CA 146

Gertler, T. .... **CLC 34**
See also CA 116; 121; INT 121

Ghalib........................ **NCLC 39**
See also Ghalib, Hsadullah Khan

Ghalib, Hsadullah Khan   1797-1869
See Ghalib
See also DAM POET

Ghelderode, Michel de
1898-1962 .... **CLC 6, 11; DAM DRAM**
See also CA 85-88; CANR 40

Ghiselin, Brewster   1903- .... **CLC 23**
See also CA 13-16R; CAAS 10; CANR 13

Ghose, Zulfikar   1935- .... **CLC 42**
See also CA 65-68

Ghosh, Amitav   1956- .... **CLC 44**
See also CA 147

Giacosa, Giuseppe   1847-1906 ...... **TCLC 7**
See also CA 104

Gibb, Lee
See Waterhouse, Keith (Spencer)

Gibbon, Lewis Grassic .... **TCLC 4**
See also Mitchell, James Leslie

Gibbons, Kaye
1960- .... **CLC 50, 88; DAM POP**
See also CA 151

Gibran, Kahlil
1883-1931 .... **TCLC 1, 9; DAM POET,**
POP; PC 9
See also CA 104; 150

Gibran, Khalil
See Gibran, Kahlil

Gibson, William
1914- .... **CLC 23; DA; DAB; DAC;**
DAM DRAM, MST
See also CA 9-12R; CANR 9, 42; DLB 7;
SATA 66

Gibson, William (Ford)
1948- .... **CLC 39, 63; DAM POP**
See also AAYA 12; CA 126; 133; CANR 52

Gide, Andre (Paul Guillaume)
1869-1951 .... **TCLC 5, 12, 36; DA;**
DAB; DAC; DAM MST, NOV; SSC 13;
WLC
See also CA 104; 124; DLB 65; MTCW

Gifford, Barry (Colby)   1946- .... **CLC 34**
See also CA 65-68; CANR 9, 30, 40

Gilbert, Frank
See De Voto, Bernard (Augustine)

Gilbert, W(illiam) S(chwenck)
1836-1911 ..... **TCLC 3; DAM DRAM,**
POET
See also CA 104; SATA 36

Gilbreth, Frank B., Jr.   1911- .... **CLC 17**
See also CA 9-12R; SATA 2

Gilchrist, Ellen
1935- .... **CLC 34, 48; DAM POP;**
SSC 14
See also CA 113; 116; CANR 41, 61;
DLB 130; MTCW

Giles, Molly   1942- .... **CLC 39**
See also CA 126

Gill, Patrick
See Creasey, John

Gilliam, Terry (Vance)   1940- .... **CLC 21**
See also Monty Python
See also AAYA 19; CA 108; 113;
CANR 35; INT 113

Gillian, Jerry
See Gilliam, Terry (Vance)

Gilliatt, Penelope (Ann Douglass)
1932-1993 .... **CLC 2, 10, 13, 53**
See also AITN 2; CA 13-16R; 141;
CANR 49; DLB 14

Gilman, Charlotte (Anna) Perkins (Stetson)
1860-1935 .... **TCLC 9, 37; SSC 13**
See also CA 106; 150

Gilmour, David   1949- .... **CLC 35**
See also CA 138, 147

Gilpin, William   1724-1804 .... **NCLC 30**

Gilray, J. D.
See Mencken, H(enry) L(ouis)

Gilroy, Frank D(aniel)   1925- .... **CLC 2**
See also CA 81-84; CANR 32; DLB 7

Gilstrap, John   1957(?)- .... **CLC 99**
See also CA 160

Gordon, Mary (Catherine)
1949- .... CLC **13, 22**
See also CA 102; CANR 44; DLB 6;
DLBY 81; INT 102; MTCW

Gordon, N. J.
See Bosman, Herman Charles

Gordon, Sol 1923-............... CLC **26**
See also CA 53-56; CANR 4; SATA 11

Gordone, Charles
1925-1995 .... CLC **1, 4; DAM DRAM;
DC 8**
See also BW 1; CA 93-96; 150; CANR 55;
DLB 7; INT 93-96; MTCW

Gore, Catherine 1800-1861 ...... NCLC **65**
See also DLB 116

Gorenko, Anna Andreevna
See Akhmatova, Anna

Gorky, Maxim
1868-1936 ..... TCLC **8; DAB; SSC 28;
WLC**

See also Peshkov, Alexei Maximovich

Goryan, Sirak
See Saroyan, William

Gosse, Edmund (William)
1849-1928 .... TCLC **28**
See also CA 117; DLB 57, 144, 184

Gotlieb, Phyllis Fay (Bloom)
1926- .... CLC **18**
See also CA 13-16R; CANR 7; DLB 88

Gottesman, S. D.
See Kornbluth, C(yril) M.; Pohl, Frederik

Gottfried von Strassburg
fl. c. 1210-................ CMLC **10**
See also DLB 138

Gould, Lois .... CLC **4, 10**
See also CA 77-80; CANR 29; MTCW

Gourmont, Remy (-Marie-Charles) de
1858-1915 .... TCLC **17**
See also CA 109; 150

Govier, Katherine 1948-.......... CLC **51**
See also CA 101; CANR 18, 40

Goyen, (Charles) William
1915-1983 .... CLC **5, 8, 14, 40**
See also AITN 2; CA 5-8R; 110; CANR 6;
DLB 2; DLBY 83; INT CANR-6

Goytisolo, Juan
1931- ..... CLC **5, 10, 23; DAM MULT;
HLC**
See also CA 85-88; CANR 32, 61; HW;
MTCW

Gozzano, Guido 1883-1916 .... PC **10**
See also CA 154; DLB 114

Gozzi, (Conte) Carlo 1720-1806 .. NCLC **23**

Grabbe, Christian Dietrich
1801-1836 .... NCLC **2**
See also DLB 133

Grace, Patricia 1937-............ CLC **56**

Gracian y Morales, Baltasar
1601-1658 .... LC **15**

Gracq, Julien.................. CLC **11, 48**
See also Poirier, Louis
See also DLB 83

Grade, Chaim 1910-1982 .... CLC **10**
See also CA 93-96; 107

Graduate of Oxford, A
See Ruskin, John

Grafton, Garth
See Duncan, Sara Jeannette

Graham, John
See Phillips, David Graham

Graham, Jorie 1951-.............. CLC **48**
See also CA 111; DLB 120

Graham, R(obert) B(ontine) Cunninghame
See Cunninghame Graham, R(obert)
B(ontine)
See also DLB 98, 135, 174

Graham, Robert
See Haldeman, Joe (William)

Graham, Tom
See Lewis, (Harry) Sinclair

Graham, W(illiam) S(ydney)
1918-1986 .... CLC **29**
See also CA 73-76; 118; DLB 20

Graham, Winston (Mawdsley)
1910- .... CLC **23**
See also CA 49-52; CANR 2, 22, 45;
DLB 77

Grahame, Kenneth
1859-1932 .... TCLC **64; DAB**
See also CA 108; 136; CLR 5; DLB 34, 141,
178; MAICYA; YABC 1

Grant, Skeeter
See Spiegelman, Art

Granville-Barker, Harley
1877-1946 ...... TCLC **2; DAM DRAM**
See also Barker, Harley Granville
See also CA 104

Grass, Guenter (Wilhelm)
1927- ..... CLC **1, 2, 4, 6, 11, 15, 22, 32,
49, 88; DA; DAB; DAC; DAM MST,
NOV; WLC**
See also CA 13-16R; CANR 20; DLB 75,
124; MTCW

Gratton, Thomas
See Hulme, T(homas) E(rnest)

Grau, Shirley Ann
1929- .... CLC **4, 9; SSC 15**
See also CA 89-92; CANR 22; DLB 2;
INT CANR-22; MTCW

Gravel, Fern
See Hall, James Norman

Graver, Elizabeth 1964-.......... CLC **70**
See also CA 135

Graves, Richard Perceval 1945- .... CLC **44**
See also CA 65-68; CANR 9, 26, 51

Graves, Robert (von Ranke)
1895-1985 ...... CLC **1, 2, 6, 11, 39, 44,
45; DAB; DAC; DAM MST, POET;
PC 6**
See also CA 5-8R; 117; CANR 5, 36;
CDBLB 1914-1945; DLB 20, 100;
DLBY 85; MTCW; SATA 45

Graves, Valerie
See Bradley, Marion Zimmer

Gray, Alasdair (James) 1934- ...... CLC **41**
See also CA 126; CANR 47; INT 126;
MTCW

Gray, Amlin 1946- .... CLC **29**
See also CA 138

Gray, Francine du Plessix
1930- .... CLC **22; DAM NOV**
See also BEST 90:3; CA 61-64; CAAS 2;
CANR 11, 33; INT CANR-11; MTCW

Gray, John (Henry) 1866-1934 .... TCLC **19**
See also CA 119

Gray, Simon (James Holliday)
1936- .... CLC **9, 14, 36**
See also AITN 1; CA 21-24R; CAAS 3;
CANR 32; DLB 13; MTCW

Gray, Spalding
1941- ...... CLC **49; DAM POP; DC 7**
See also CA 128

Gray, Thomas
1716-1771 .... LC **4, 40; DA; DAB;
DAC; DAM MST; PC 2; WLC**
See also CDBLB 1660-1789; DLB 109

Grayson, David
See Baker, Ray Stannard

Grayson, Richard (A.) 1951- .... CLC **38**
See also CA 85-88; CANR 14, 31, 57

Greeley, Andrew M(oran)
1928- .... CLC **28; DAM POP**
See also CA 5-8R; CAAS 7; CANR 7, 43;
MTCW

Green, Anna Katharine
1846-1935 .... TCLC **63**
See also CA 112; 159

Green, Brian
See Card, Orson Scott

Green, Hannah
See Greenberg, Joanne (Goldenberg)

Green, Hannah 1927(?)-1996........ CLC **3**
See also CA 73-76; CANR 59

Green, Henry 1905-1973 ..... CLC **2, 13, 97**
See also Yorke, Henry Vincent
See also DLB 15

Green, Julian (Hartridge) 1900-
See Green, Julien
See also CA 21-24R; CANR 33; DLB 4, 72;
MTCW

Green, Julien................ CLC **3, 11, 77**
See also Green, Julian (Hartridge)

Green, Paul (Eliot)
1894-1981 ...... CLC **25; DAM DRAM**
See also AITN 1; CA 5-8R; 103; CANR 3;
DLB 7, 9; DLBY 81

Greenberg, Ivan 1908-1973
See Rahv, Philip
See also CA 85-88

Greenberg, Joanne (Goldenberg)
1932- .... CLC **7, 30**
See also AAYA 12; CA 5-8R; CANR 14,
32; SATA 25

Greenberg, Richard 1959(?)- .... CLC **57**
See also CA 138

Greene, Bette 1934- .... CLC **30**
See also AAYA 7; CA 53-56; CANR 4;
CLR 2; JRDA; MAICYA; SAAS 16;
SATA 8

Greene, Gael .... CLC **8**
See also CA 13-16R; CANR 10

Guthrie, Isobel
See Grieve, C(hristopher) M(urray)

Guthrie, Woodrow Wilson 1912-1967
See Guthrie, Woody
See also CA 113; 93-96

Guthrie, Woody . . . . **CLC 35**
See also Guthrie, Woodrow Wilson

Guy, Rosa (Cuthbert) 1928- . . . . **CLC 26**
See also AAYA 4; BW 2; CA 17-20R;
CANR 14, 34; CLR 13; DLB 33; JRDA;
MAICYA; SATA 14, 62

Gwendolyn
See Bennett, (Enoch) Arnold

H. D. . . . . **CLC 3, 8, 14, 31, 34, 73; PC 5**
See also Doolittle, Hilda

H. de V.
See Buchan, John

Haavikko, Paavo Juhani
1931- . . . . **CLC 18, 34**
See also CA 106

Habbema, Koos
See Heijermans, Herman

Habermas, Juergen 1929- . . . . **CLC 104**
See also CA 109

Habermas, Jurgen
See Habermas, Juergen

Hacker, Marilyn
1942- . . . . **CLC 5, 9, 23, 72, 91;**
DAM POET
See also CA 77-80; DLB 120

Haggard, H(enry) Rider
1856-1925 . . . . **TCLC 11**
See also CA 108; 148; DLB 70, 156, 174,
178; SATA 16

Hagiosy, L.
See Larbaud, Valery (Nicolas)

Hagiwara Sakutaro
1886-1942 . . . . **TCLC 60; PC 18**

Haig, Fenil
See Ford, Ford Madox

Haig-Brown, Roderick (Langmere)
1908-1976 . . . . **CLC 21**
See also CA 5-8R; 69-72; CANR 4, 38;
CLR 31; DLB 88; MAICYA; SATA 12

Hailey, Arthur
1920- . . . . **CLC 5; DAM NOV, POP**
See also AITN 2; BEST 90:3; CA 1-4R;
CANR 2, 36; DLB 88; DLBY 82; MTCW

Hailey, Elizabeth Forsythe 1938- . . . **CLC 40**
See also CA 93-96; CAAS 1; CANR 15, 48;
INT CANR-15

Haines, John (Meade) 1924- . . . . **CLC 58**
See also CA 17-20R; CANR 13, 34; DLB 5

Hakluyt, Richard 1552-1616 . . . . **LC 31**

Haldeman, Joe (William) 1943- . . . . . **CLC 61**
See also CA 53-56; CAAS 25; CANR 6;
DLB 8; INT CANR-6

Haley, Alex(ander Murray Palmer)
1921-1992 . . . . **CLC 8, 12, 76; BLC; DA;**
DAB; DAC; DAM MST, MULT, POP
See also BW 2; CA 77-80; 136; CANR 61;
DLB 38; MTCW

Haliburton, Thomas Chandler
1796-1865 . . . . **NCLC 15**
See also DLB 11, 99

Hall, Donald (Andrew, Jr.)
1928- . . **CLC 1, 13, 37, 59; DAM POET**
See also CA 5-8R; CAAS 7; CANR 2, 44;
DLB 5; SATA 23

Hall, Frederic Sauser
See Sauser-Hall, Frederic

Hall, James
See Kuttner, Henry

Hall, James Norman 1887-1951 . . . **TCLC 23**
See also CA 123; SATA 21

Hall, (Marguerite) Radclyffe
1886-1943 . . . . **TCLC 12**
See also CA 110; 150

Hall, Rodney 1935- . . . . **CLC 51**
See also CA 109

Halleck, Fitz-Greene 1790-1867 . . **NCLC 47**
See also DLB 3

Halliday, Michael
See Creasey, John

Halpern, Daniel 1945- . . . . **CLC 14**
See also CA 33-36R

Hamburger, Michael (Peter Leopold)
1924- . . . . **CLC 5, 14**
See also CA 5-8R; CAAS 4; CANR 2, 47;
DLB 27

Hamill, Pete 1935- . . . . **CLC 10**
See also CA 25-28R; CANR 18

Hamilton, Alexander
1755(?)-1804 . . . . **NCLC 49**
See also DLB 37

Hamilton, Clive
See Lewis, C(live) S(taples)

Hamilton, Edmond 1904-1977 . . . . . . **CLC 1**
See also CA 1-4R; CANR 3; DLB 8

Hamilton, Eugene (Jacob) Lee
See Lee-Hamilton, Eugene (Jacob)

Hamilton, Franklin
See Silverberg, Robert

Hamilton, Gail
See Corcoran, Barbara

Hamilton, Mollie
See Kaye, M(ary) M(argaret)

Hamilton, (Anthony Walter) Patrick
1904-1962 . . . . **CLC 51**
See also CA 113; DLB 10

Hamilton, Virginia
1936- . . . . **CLC 26; DAM MULT**
See also AAYA 2, 21; BW 2; CA 25-28R;
CANR 20, 37; CLR 1, 11, 40; DLB 33,
52; INT CANR-20; JRDA; MAICYA;
MTCW; SATA 4, 56, 79

Hammett, (Samuel) Dashiell
1894-1961 . . . . **CLC 3, 5, 10, 19, 47;**
SSC 17
See also AITN 1; CA 81-84; CANR 42;
CDALB 1929-1941; DLBD 6; DLBY 96;
MTCW

Hammon, Jupiter
1711(?)-1800(?) . . . . **NCLC 5; BLC;**
DAM MULT, POET; PC 16
See also DLB 31, 50

Hammond, Keith
See Kuttner, Henry

Hamner, Earl (Henry), Jr. 1923- . . . **CLC 12**
See also AITN 2; CA 73-76; DLB 6

Hampton, Christopher (James)
1946- . . . . **CLC 4**
See also CA 25-28R; DLB 13; MTCW

Hamsun, Knut . . . . **TCLC 2, 14, 49**
See also Pedersen, Knut

Handke, Peter
1942- . . . . **CLC 5, 8, 10, 15, 38;**
DAM DRAM, NOV
See also CA 77-80; CANR 33; DLB 85,
124; MTCW

Hanley, James 1901-1985 . . . **CLC 3, 5, 8, 13**
See also CA 73-76; 117; CANR 36; MTCW

Hannah, Barry 1942- . . . . **CLC 23, 38, 90**
See also CA 108; 110; CANR 43; DLB 6;
INT 110; MTCW

Hannon, Ezra
See Hunter, Evan

Hansberry, Lorraine (Vivian)
1930-1965 . . . . . . **CLC 17, 62; BLC; DA;**
DAB; DAC; DAM DRAM, MST,
MULT; DC 2
See also BW 1; CA 109; 25-28R; CABS 3;
CANR 58; CDALB 1941-1968; DLB 7,
38; MTCW

Hansen, Joseph 1923- . . . . **CLC 38**
See also CA 29-32R; CAAS 17; CANR 16,
44; INT CANR-16

Hansen, Martin A. 1909-1955 . . . . . **TCLC 32**

Hanson, Kenneth O(stlin) 1922- . . . . **CLC 13**
See also CA 53-56; CANR 7

Hardwick, Elizabeth
1916- . . . . **CLC 13; DAM NOV**
See also CA 5-8R; CANR 3, 32; DLB 6;
MTCW

Hardy, Thomas
1840-1928 . . . . . . **TCLC 4, 10, 18, 32, 48,**
53, 72; DA; DAB; DAC; DAM MST,
NOV, POET; PC 8; SSC 2; WLC
See also CA 104; 123; CDBLB 1890-1914;
DLB 18, 19, 135; MTCW

Hare, David 1947- . . . . **CLC 29, 58**
See also CA 97-100; CANR 39; DLB 13;
MTCW

Harewood, John
See Van Druten, John (William)

Harford, Henry
See Hudson, W(illiam) H(enry)

Hargrave, Leonie
See Disch, Thomas M(ichael)

Harjo, Joy 1951- . . . **CLC 83; DAM MULT**
See also CA 114; CANR 35; DLB 120, 175;
NNAL

Harlan, Louis R(udolph) 1922- . . . . . **CLC 34**
See also CA 21-24R; CANR 25, 55

Harling, Robert 1951(?)- . . . . **CLC 53**
See also CA 147

Harmon, William (Ruth) 1938- . . . . . **CLC 38**
See also CA 33-36R; CANR 14, 32, 35;
SATA 65

Harper, F. E. W.
See Harper, Frances Ellen Watkins

Harper, Frances E. W.
See Harper, Frances Ellen Watkins

Harper, Frances E. Watkins
See Harper, Frances Ellen Watkins

Harper, Frances Ellen
See Harper, Frances Ellen Watkins

Harper, Frances Ellen Watkins
1825-1911 . . . . **TCLC 14; BLC;
DAM MULT, POET**
See also BW 1; CA 111; 125; DLB 50

Harper, Michael S(teven) 1938- . . **CLC 7, 22**
See also BW 1; CA 33-36R; CANR 24;
DLB 41

Harper, Mrs. F. E. W.
See Harper, Frances Ellen Watkins

Harris, Christie (Lucy) Irwin
1907- . . . . **CLC 12**
See also CA 5-8R; CANR 6; CLR 47;
DLB 88; JRDA; MAICYA; SAAS 10;
SATA 6, 74

Harris, Frank 1856-1931 . . . . **TCLC 24**
See also CA 109; 150; DLB 156

Harris, George Washington
1814-1869 . . . . **NCLC 23**
See also DLB 3, 11

Harris, Joel Chandler
1848-1908 . . . . **TCLC 2; SSC 19**
See also CA 104; 137; DLB 11, 23, 42, 78,
91; MAICYA; YABC 1

Harris, John (Wyndham Parkes Lucas)
Beynon 1903-1969
See Wyndham, John
See also CA 102; 89-92

Harris, MacDonald . . . . **CLC 9**
See also Heiney, Donald (William)

Harris, Mark 1922- . . . . **CLC 19**
See also CA 5-8R; CAAS 3; CANR 2, 55;
DLB 2; DLBY 80

Harris, (Theodore) Wilson 1921- . . . . **CLC 25**
See also BW 2; CA 65-68; CAAS 16;
CANR 11, 27; DLB 117; MTCW

Harrison, Elizabeth Cavanna 1909-
See Cavanna, Betty
See also CA 9-12R; CANR 6, 27

Harrison, Harry (Max) 1925- . . . . . . **CLC 42**
See also CA 1-4R; CANR 5, 21; DLB 8;
SATA 4

Harrison, James (Thomas)
1937- . . . . **CLC 6, 14, 33, 66; SSC 19**
See also CA 13-16R; CANR 8, 51;
DLBY 82; INT CANR-8

Harrison, Jim
See Harrison, James (Thomas)

Harrison, Kathryn 1961- . . . . **CLC 70**
See also CA 144

Harrison, Tony 1937- . . . . **CLC 43**
See also CA 65-68; CANR 44; DLB 40;
MTCW

Harriss, Will(ard Irvin) 1922- . . . . . . **CLC 34**
See also CA 111

Harson, Sley
See Ellison, Harlan (Jay)

Hart, Ellis
See Ellison, Harlan (Jay)

Hart, Josephine
1942(?)- . . . . **CLC 70; DAM POP**
See also CA 138

Hart, Moss
1904-1961 . . . . . . **CLC 66; DAM DRAM**
See also CA 109; 89-92; DLB 7

Harte, (Francis) Bret(t)
1836(?)-1902 . . . . **TCLC 1, 25; DA; DAC;
DAM MST; SSC 8; WLC**
See also CA 104; 140; CDALB 1865-1917;
DLB 12, 64, 74, 79; SATA 26

Hartley, L(eslie) P(oles)
1895-1972 . . . . **CLC 2, 22**
See also CA 45-48; 37-40R; CANR 33;
DLB 15, 139; MTCW

Hartman, Geoffrey H. 1929- . . . . **CLC 27**
See also CA 117; 125; DLB 67

Hartmann, Sadakichi 1867-1944 . . . **TCLC 73**
See also CA 157; DLB 54

Hartmann von Aue
c. 1160-c. 1205 . . . . **CMLC 15**
See also DLB 138

Hartmann von Aue 1170-1210 . . . . **CMLC 15**

Haruf, Kent 1943- . . . . **CLC 34**
See also CA 149

Harwood, Ronald
1934- . . . . **CLC 32; DAM DRAM, MST**
See also CA 1-4R; CANR 4, 55; DLB 13

Hasek, Jaroslav (Matej Frantisek)
1883-1923 . . . . **TCLC 4**
See also CA 104; 129; MTCW

Hass, Robert
1941- . . . . **CLC 18, 39, 99; PC 16**
See also CA 111; CANR 30, 50; DLB 105;
SATA 94

Hastings, Hudson
See Kuttner, Henry

Hastings, Selina . . . . **CLC 44**

Hathorne, John 1641-1717 . . . . **LC 38**

Hatteras, Amelia
See Mencken, H(enry) L(ouis)

Hatteras, Owen . . . . **TCLC 18**
See also Mencken, H(enry) L(ouis); Nathan,
George Jean

Hauptmann, Gerhart (Johann Robert)
1862-1946 . . . . . . **TCLC 4; DAM DRAM**
See also CA 104; 153; DLB 66, 118

Havel, Vaclav
1936- . . . . **CLC 25, 58, 65;
DAM DRAM; DC 6**
See also CA 104; CANR 36; MTCW

Haviaras, Stratis . . . . **CLC 33**
See also Chaviaras, Strates

Hawes, Stephen 1475(?)-1523(?) . . . . . **LC 17**

Hawkes, John (Clendennin Burne, Jr.)
1925- . . . . . . **CLC 1, 2, 3, 4, 7, 9, 14, 15,
27, 49**
See also CA 1-4R; CANR 2, 47; DLB 2, 7;
DLBY 80; MTCW

Hawking, S. W.
See Hawking, Stephen W(illiam)

Hawking, Stephen W(illiam)
1942- . . . . **CLC 63, 105**
See also AAYA 13; BEST 89:1; CA 126;
129; CANR 48

Hawthorne, Julian 1846-1934 . . . . . **TCLC 25**

Hawthorne, Nathaniel
1804-1864 . . . . **NCLC 39; DA; DAB;
DAC; DAM MST, NOV; SSC 29; WLC**
See also AAYA 18; CDALB 1640-1865;
DLB 1, 74; YABC 2

Haxton, Josephine Ayres 1921-
See Douglas, Ellen
See also CA 115; CANR 41

Hayaseca y Eizaguirre, Jorge
See Echegaray (y Eizaguirre), Jose (Maria
Waldo)

Hayashi Fumiko 1904-1951 . . . . **TCLC 27**
See also CA 161; DLB 180

Haycraft, Anna
See Ellis, Alice Thomas
See also CA 122

Hayden, Robert E(arl)
1913-1980 . . . . . **CLC 5, 9, 14, 37; BLC;
DA; DAC; DAM MST, MULT, POET;
PC 6**
See also BW 1; CA 69-72; 97-100; CABS 2;
CANR 24; CDALB 1941-1968; DLB 5,
76; MTCW; SATA 19; SATA-Obit 26

Hayford, J(oseph) E(phraim) Casely
See Casely-Hayford, J(oseph) E(phraim)

Hayman, Ronald 1932- . . . . **CLC 44**
See also CA 25-28R; CANR 18, 50;
DLB 155

Haywood, Eliza (Fowler)
1693(?)-1756 . . . . **LC 1**

Hazlitt, William 1778-1830 . . . . . . **NCLC 29**
See also DLB 110, 158

Hazzard, Shirley 1931- . . . . **CLC 18**
See also CA 9-12R; CANR 4; DLBY 82;
MTCW

Head, Bessie
1937-1986 . . . . **CLC 25, 67; BLC;
DAM MULT**
See also BW 2; CA 29-32R; 119; CANR 25;
DLB 117; MTCW

Headon, (Nicky) Topper 1956(?)- . . . . **CLC 30**

Heaney, Seamus (Justin)
1939- . . . . . . **CLC 5, 7, 14, 25, 37, 74, 91;
DAB; DAM POET; PC 18; WLCS**
See also CA 85-88; CANR 25, 48;
CDBLB 1960 to Present; DLB 40;
DLBY 95; MTCW

Hearn, (Patricio) Lafcadio (Tessima Carlos)
1850-1904 . . . . **TCLC 9**
See also CA 105; DLB 12, 78

Hearne, Vicki 1946- . . . . **CLC 56**
See also CA 139

Hearon, Shelby 1931- . . . . **CLC 63**
See also AITN 2; CA 25-28R; CANR 18,
48

Heat-Moon, William Least . . . . **CLC 29**
See also Trogdon, William (Lewis)
See also AAYA 9

Hebbel, Friedrich
1813-1863 . . . . **NCLC 43; DAM DRAM**
See also DLB 129

Hebert, Anne
1916- . . . . **CLC 4, 13, 29; DAC;
DAM MST, POET**
See also CA 85-88; DLB 68; MTCW

Hecht, Anthony (Evan)
1923- ...... CLC **8, 13, 19; DAM POET**
See also CA 9-12R; CANR 6; DLB 5, 169

Hecht, Ben 1894-1964 .... **CLC 8**
See also CA 85-88; DLB 7, 9, 25, 26, 28, 86

Hedayat, Sadeq 1903-1951....... **TCLC 21**
See also CA 120

Hegel, Georg Wilhelm Friedrich
1770-1831 .... **NCLC 46**
See also DLB 90

Heidegger, Martin 1889-1976 ...... **CLC 24**
See also CA 81-84; 65-68; CANR 34;
MTCW

Heidenstam, (Carl Gustaf) Verner von
1859-1940 .... **TCLC 5**
See also CA 104

Heifner, Jack 1946- .... **CLC 11**
See also CA 105; CANR 47

Heijermans, Herman 1864-1924 ... **TCLC 24**
See also CA 123

Heilbrun, Carolyn G(old) 1926-..... **CLC 25**
See also CA 45-48; CANR 1, 28, 58

Heine, Heinrich 1797-1856 .... **NCLC 4, 54**
See also DLB 90

Heinemann, Larry (Curtiss) 1944- .. **CLC 50**
See also CA 110; CAAS 21; CANR 31;
DLBD 9; INT CANR-31

Heiney, Donald (William) 1921-1993
See Harris, MacDonald
See also CA 1-4R; 142; CANR 3, 58

Heinlein, Robert A(nson)
1907-1988 ...... CLC **1, 3, 8, 14, 26, 55;**
DAM POP
See also AAYA 17; CA 1-4R; 125;
CANR 1, 20, 53; DLB 8; JRDA;
MAICYA; MTCW; SATA 9, 69;
SATA-Obit 56

Helforth, John
See Doolittle, Hilda

Hellenhofferu, Vojtech Kapristian z
See Hasek, Jaroslav (Matej Frantisek)

Heller, Joseph
1923- .... CLC **1, 3, 5, 8, 11, 36, 63; DA;**
DAB; DAC; DAM MST, NOV, POP;
WLC
See also AITN 1; CA 5-8R; CABS 1;
CANR 8, 42; DLB 2, 28; DLBY 80;
INT CANR-8; MTCW

Hellman, Lillian (Florence)
1906-1984 ...... CLC **2, 4, 8, 14, 18, 34,**
44, 52; DAM DRAM; DC 1
See also AITN 1, 2; CA 13-16R; 112;
CANR 33; DLB 7; DLBY 84; MTCW

Helprin, Mark
1947- .... CLC **7, 10, 22, 32;**
DAM NOV, POP
See also CA 81-84; CANR 47; DLBY 85;
MTCW

Helvetius, Claude-Adrien
1715-1771 .... **LC 26**

Helyar, Jane Penelope Josephine 1933-
See Poole, Josephine
See also CA 21-24R; CANR 10, 26;
SATA 82

Hemans, Felicia 1793-1835 ...... **NCLC 29**
See also DLB 96

Hemingway, Ernest (Miller)
1899-1961 .... CLC **1, 3, 6, 8, 10, 13, 19,**
30, 34, 39, 41, 44, 50, 61, 80; DA; DAB;
DAC; DAM MST, NOV; SSC 25; WLC
See also AAYA 19; CA 77-80; CANR 34;
CDALB 1917-1929; DLB 4, 9, 102;
DLBD 1, 15, 16; DLBY 81, 87, 96;
MTCW

Hempel, Amy 1951- .... **CLC 39**
See also CA 118; 137

Henderson, F. C.
See Mencken, H(enry) L(ouis)

Henderson, Sylvia
See Ashton-Warner, Sylvia (Constance)

Henderson, Zenna (Chlarson)
1917-1983 .... **SSC 29**
See also CA 1-4R; 133; CANR 1; DLB 8;
SATA 5

Henley, Beth .... CLC **23; DC 6**
See also Henley, Elizabeth Becker
See also CABS 3; DLBY 86

Henley, Elizabeth Becker 1952-
See Henley, Beth
See also CA 107; CANR 32; DAM DRAM,
MST; MTCW

Henley, William Ernest
1849-1903 .... **TCLC 8**
See also CA 105; DLB 19

Hennissart, Martha
See Lathen, Emma
See also CA 85-88

Henry, O. .... TCLC **1, 19; SSC 5; WLC**
See also Porter, William Sydney

Henry, Patrick 1736-1799 .... **LC 25**

Henryson, Robert 1430(?)-1506(?).... **LC 20**
See also DLB 146

Henry VIII 1491-1547 .... **LC 10**

Henschke, Alfred
See Klabund

Hentoff, Nat(han Irving) 1925-..... **CLC 26**
See also AAYA 4; CA 1-4R; CAAS 6;
CANR 5, 25; CLR 1; INT CANR-25;
JRDA; MAICYA; SATA 42, 69;
SATA-Brief 27

Heppenstall, (John) Rayner
1911-1981 .... **CLC 10**
See also CA 1-4R; 103; CANR 29

Heraclitus
c. 540B.C.-c. 450B.C......... **CMLC 22**
See also DLB 176

Herbert, Frank (Patrick)
1920-1986 ...... CLC **12, 23, 35, 44, 85;**
DAM POP
See also AAYA 21; CA 53-56; 118;
CANR 5, 43; DLB 8; INT CANR-5;
MTCW; SATA 9, 37; SATA-Obit 47

Herbert, George
1593-1633 .... LC **24; DAB;**
DAM POET; PC 4
See also CDBLB Before 1660; DLB 126

Herbert, Zbigniew
1924- .... CLC **9, 43; DAM POET**
See also CA 89-92; CANR 36; MTCW

Herbst, Josephine (Frey)
1897-1969 .... **CLC 34**
See also CA 5-8R; 25-28R; DLB 9

Hergesheimer, Joseph
1880-1954 .... **TCLC 11**
See also CA 109; DLB 102, 9

Herlihy, James Leo 1927-1993 ...... **CLC 6**
See also CA 1-4R; 143; CANR 2

Hermogenes fl. c. 175- .... **CMLC 6**

Hernandez, Jose 1834-1886 ...... **NCLC 17**

Herodotus c. 484B.C.-429B.C..... **CMLC 17**
See also DLB 176

Herrick, Robert
1591-1674 ..... LC **13; DA; DAB; DAC;**
DAM MST, POP; PC 9
See also DLB 126

Herring, Guilles
See Somerville, Edith

Herriot, James
1916-1995 .... CLC **12; DAM POP**
See also Wight, James Alfred
See also AAYA 1; CA 148; CANR 40;
SATA 86

Herrmann, Dorothy 1941-......... **CLC 44**
See also CA 107

Herrmann, Taffy
See Herrmann, Dorothy

Hersey, John (Richard)
1914-1993 .... CLC **1, 2, 7, 9, 40, 81, 97;**
DAM POP
See also CA 17-20R; 140; CANR 33;
DLB 6; MTCW; SATA 25;
SATA-Obit 76

Herzen, Aleksandr Ivanovich
1812-1870 .... **NCLC 10, 61**

Herzl, Theodor 1860-1904....... **TCLC 36**

Herzog, Werner 1942- .... **CLC 16**
See also CA 89-92

Hesiod c. 8th cent. B.C.-......... **CMLC 5**
See also DLB 176

Hesse, Hermann
1877-1962 .... CLC **1, 2, 3, 6, 11, 17, 25,**
69; DA; DAB; DAC; DAM MST, NOV;
SSC 9; WLC
See also CA 17-18; CAP 2; DLB 66;
MTCW; SATA 50

Hewes, Cady
See De Voto, Bernard (Augustine)

Heyen, William 1940- .... CLC **13, 18**
See also CA 33-36R; CAAS 9; DLB 5

Heyerdahl, Thor 1914- .... **CLC 26**
See also CA 5-8R; CANR 5, 22; MTCW;
SATA 2, 52

Heym, Georg (Theodor Franz Arthur)
1887-1912 .... **TCLC 9**
See also CA 106

Heym, Stefan 1913- .... **CLC 41**
See also CA 9-12R; CANR 4; DLB 69

Heyse, Paul (Johann Ludwig von)
1830-1914 .... **TCLC 8**
See also CA 104; DLB 129

Heyward, (Edwin) DuBose
1885-1940 .... **TCLC 59**
See also CA 108; 157; DLB 7, 9, 45;
SATA 21

Hibbert, Eleanor Alice Burford
1906-1993 . . . . CLC 7; DAM POP
See also BEST 90:4; CA 17-20R; 140;
CANR 9, 28, 59; SATA 2; SATA-Obit 74

Higgins, George V(incent)
1939- . . . . CLC 4, 7, 10, 18
See also CA 77-80; CAAS 5; CANR 17, 51;
DLB 2; DLBY 81; INT CANR-17;
MTCW

Higginson, Thomas Wentworth
1823-1911 . . . . TCLC 36
See also DLB 1, 64

Highet, Helen
See MacInnes, Helen (Clark)

Highsmith, (Mary) Patricia
1921-1995 . . . . CLC 2, 4, 14, 42, 102;
DAM NOV, POP
See also CA 1-4R; 147; CANR 1, 20, 48,
62; MTCW

Highwater, Jamake (Mamake)
1942(?)- . . . . CLC 12
See also AAYA 7; CA 65-68; CAAS 7;
CANR 10, 34; CLR 17; DLB 52;
DLBY 85; JRDA; MAICYA; SATA 32,
69; SATA-Brief 30

Highway, Tomson
1951- . . . . . CLC 92; DAC; DAM MULT
See also CA 151; NNAL

Higuchi, Ichiyo 1872-1896. . . . . . NCLC 49

Hijuelos, Oscar
1951- . . . . CLC 65; DAM MULT, POP;
HLC
See also BEST 90:1; CA 123; CANR 50;
DLB 145; HW

Hikmet, Nazim 1902(?)-1963. . . . . . CLC 40
See also CA 141; 93-96

Hildegard von Bingen
1098-1179 . . . . CMLC 20
See also DLB 148

Hildesheimer, Wolfgang
1916-1991 . . . . CLC 49
See also CA 101; 135; DLB 69, 124

Hill, Geoffrey (William)
1932- . . . CLC 5, 8, 18, 45; DAM POET
See also CA 81-84; CANR 21;
CDBLB 1960 to Present; DLB 40;
MTCW

Hill, George Roy 1921- . . . . CLC 26
See also CA 110; 122

Hill, John
See Koontz, Dean R(ay)

Hill, Susan (Elizabeth)
1942- . . CLC 4; DAB; DAM MST, NOV
See also CA 33-36R; CANR 29; DLB 14,
139; MTCW

Hillerman, Tony
1925- . . . . CLC 62; DAM POP
See also AAYA 6; BEST 89:1; CA 29-32R;
CANR 21, 42; SATA 6

Hillesum, Etty 1914-1943 . . . . TCLC 49
See also CA 137

Hilliard, Noel (Harvey) 1929- . . . . . . CLC 15
See also CA 9-12R; CANR 7

Hillis, Rick 1956- . . . . CLC 66
See also CA 134

Hilton, James 1900-1954 . . . . TCLC 21
See also CA 108; DLB 34, 77; SATA 34

Himes, Chester (Bomar)
1909-1984 . . . . CLC 2, 4, 7, 18, 58; BLC;
DAM MULT
See also BW 2; CA 25-28R; 114; CANR 22;
DLB 2, 76, 143; MTCW

Hinde, Thomas . . . . CLC 6, 11
See also Chitty, Thomas Willes

Hindin, Nathan
See Bloch, Robert (Albert)

Hine, (William) Daryl 1936- . . . . CLC 15
See also CA 1-4R; CAAS 15; CANR 1, 20;
DLB 60

Hinkson, Katharine Tynan
See Tynan, Katharine

Hinton, S(usan) E(loise)
1950- . . . . CLC 30; DA; DAB; DAC;
DAM MST, NOV
See also AAYA 2; CA 81-84; CANR 32,
62; CLR 3, 23; JRDA; MAICYA;
MTCW; SATA 19, 58

Hippius, Zinaida . . . . TCLC 9
See also Gippius, Zinaida (Nikolayevna)

Hiraoka, Kimitake 1925-1970
See Mishima, Yukio
See also CA 97-100; 29-32R; DAM DRAM;
MTCW

Hirsch, E(ric) D(onald), Jr. 1928- . . . CLC 79
See also CA 25-28R; CANR 27, 51;
DLB 67; INT CANR-27; MTCW

Hirsch, Edward 1950- . . . . CLC 31, 50
See also CA 104; CANR 20, 42; DLB 120

Hitchcock, Alfred (Joseph)
1899-1980 . . . . CLC 16
See also AAYA 22; CA 159; 97-100;
SATA 27; SATA-Obit 24

Hitler, Adolf 1889-1945 . . . . TCLC 53
See also CA 117; 147

Hoagland, Edward 1932- . . . . CLC 28
See also CA 1-4R; CANR 2, 31, 57; DLB 6;
SATA 51

Hoban, Russell (Conwell)
1925- . . . . CLC 7, 25; DAM NOV
See also CA 5-8R; CANR 23, 37; CLR 3;
DLB 52; MAICYA; MTCW; SATA 1,
40, 78

Hobbes, Thomas 1588-1679 . . . . LC 36
See also DLB 151

Hobbs, Perry
See Blackmur, R(ichard) P(almer)

Hobson, Laura Z(ametkin)
1900-1986 . . . . CLC 7, 25
See also CA 17-20R; 118; CANR 55;
DLB 28; SATA 52

Hochhuth, Rolf
1931- . . . . . CLC 4, 11, 18; DAM DRAM
See also CA 5-8R; CANR 33; DLB 124;
MTCW

Hochman, Sandra 1936- . . . . CLC 3, 8
See also CA 5-8R; DLB 5

Hochwaelder, Fritz
1911-1986 . . . . . . CLC 36; DAM DRAM
See also CA 29-32R; 120; CANR 42;
MTCW

Hochwalder, Fritz
See Hochwaelder, Fritz

Hocking, Mary (Eunice) 1921- . . . . . CLC 13
See also CA 101; CANR 18, 40

Hodgins, Jack 1938- . . . . CLC 23
See also CA 93-96; DLB 60

Hodgson, William Hope
1877(?)-1918 . . . . TCLC 13
See also CA 111; DLB 70, 153, 156, 178

Hoeg, Peter 1957-. . . . . CLC 95
See also CA 151

Hoffman, Alice
1952- . . . . CLC 51; DAM NOV
See also CA 77-80; CANR 34; MTCW

Hoffman, Daniel (Gerard)
1923- . . . . CLC 6, 13, 23
See also CA 1-4R; CANR 4; DLB 5

Hoffman, Stanley 1944- . . . . CLC 5
See also CA 77-80

Hoffman, William M(oses) 1939- . . . CLC 40
See also CA 57-60; CANR 11

Hoffmann, E(rnst) T(heodor) A(madeus)
1776-1822 . . . . NCLC 2; SSC 13
See also DLB 90; SATA 27

Hofmann, Gert 1931-. . . . . CLC 54
See also CA 128

Hofmannsthal, Hugo von
1874-1929 . . . . TCLC 11; DAM DRAM;
DC 4
See also CA 106; 153; DLB 81, 118

Hogan, Linda
1947- . . . . CLC 73; DAM MULT
See also CA 120; CANR 45; DLB 175;
NNAL

Hogarth, Charles
See Creasey, John

Hogarth, Emmett
See Polonsky, Abraham (Lincoln)

Hogg, James 1770-1835. . . . . NCLC 4
See also DLB 93, 116, 159

Holbach, Paul Henri Thiry Baron
1723-1789 . . . . LC 14

Holberg, Ludvig 1684-1754 . . . . LC 6

Holden, Ursula 1921-. . . . . CLC 18
See also CA 101; CAAS 8; CANR 22

Holderlin, (Johann Christian) Friedrich
1770-1843 . . . . NCLC 16; PC 4

Holdstock, Robert
See Holdstock, Robert P.

Holdstock, Robert P. 1948-. . . . . CLC 39
See also CA 131

Holland, Isabelle 1920- . . . . CLC 21
See also AAYA 11; CA 21-24R; CANR 10,
25, 47; JRDA; MAICYA; SATA 8, 70

Holland, Marcus
See Caldwell, (Janet Miriam) Taylor
(Holland)

Hollander, John 1929-. . . . . . CLC 2, 5, 8, 14
See also CA 1-4R; CANR 1, 52; DLB 5;
SATA 13

Hollander, Paul
See Silverberg, Robert

Holleran, Andrew 1943(?)-. . . . . CLC 38
See also CA 144

Hughes, Richard (Arthur Warren)
   1900-1976 . . . . . . CLC **1, 11; DAM NOV**
   See also CA 5-8R; 65-68; CANR 4;
   DLB 15, 161; MTCW; SATA 8;
   SATA-Obit 25

Hughes, Ted
   1930- . . . . CLC **2, 4, 9, 14, 37; DAB;
                              DAC; PC 7**
   See also Hughes, Edward James
   See also CA 1-4R; CANR 1, 33; CLR 3;
   DLB 40, 161; MAICYA; MTCW;
   SATA 49; SATA-Brief 27

Hugo, Richard F(ranklin)
   1923-1982 . . . . CLC **6, 18, 32;
                                      DAM POET**
   See also CA 49-52; 108; CANR 3; DLB 5

Hugo, Victor (Marie)
   1802-1885 . . . . NCLC **3, 10, 21; DA;
      DAB; DAC; DAM DRAM, MST, NOV,
                        POET; PC 17; WLC**
   See also DLB 119; SATA 47

Huidobro, Vicente
   See Huidobro Fernandez, Vicente Garcia

Huidobro Fernandez, Vicente Garcia
   1893-1948 . . . . TCLC **31**
   See also CA 131; HW

Hulme, Keri   1947- . . . . CLC **39**
   See also CA 125; INT 125

Hulme, T(homas) E(rnest)
   1883-1917 . . . . TCLC **21**
   See also CA 117; DLB 19

Hume, David   1711-1776 . . . . LC **7**
   See also DLB 104

Humphrey, William   1924-1997 . . . . . CLC **45**
   See also CA 77-80; 160; DLB 6

Humphreys, Emyr Owen   1919- . . . . . CLC **47**
   See also CA 5-8R; CANR 3, 24; DLB 15

Humphreys, Josephine   1945- . . . . CLC **34, 57**
   See also CA 121; 127; INT 127

Huneker, James Gibbons
   1857-1921 . . . . TCLC **65**
   See also DLB 71

Hungerford, Pixie
   See Brinsmead, H(esba) F(ay)

Hunt, E(verette) Howard, (Jr.)
   1918- . . . . CLC **3**
   See also AITN 1; CA 45-48; CANR 2, 47

Hunt, Kyle
   See Creasey, John

Hunt, (James Henry) Leigh
   1784-1859 . . . . . . NCLC **1; DAM POET**

Hunt, Marsha   1946- . . . . CLC **70**
   See also BW 2; CA 143

Hunt, Violet   1866-1942 . . . . TCLC **53**
   See also DLB 162

Hunter, E. Waldo
   See Sturgeon, Theodore (Hamilton)

Hunter, Evan
   1926- . . . . CLC **11, 31; DAM POP**
   See also CA 5-8R; CANR 5, 38, 62;
   DLBY 82; INT CANR-5; MTCW;
   SATA 25

Hunter, Kristin (Eggleston)   1931-. . . CLC **35**
   See also AITN 1; BW 1; CA 13-16R;
   CANR 13; CLR 3; DLB 33;
   INT CANR-13; MAICYA; SAAS 10;
   SATA 12

Hunter, Mollie   1922- . . . . CLC **21**
   See also McIlwraith, Maureen Mollie
   Hunter
   See also AAYA 13; CANR 37; CLR 25;
   DLB 161; JRDA; MAICYA; SAAS 7;
   SATA 54

Hunter, Robert   (?)-1734 . . . . LC **7**

Hurston, Zora Neale
   1903-1960 . . . . CLC **7, 30, 61; BLC; DA;
      DAC; DAM MST, MULT, NOV; SSC 4;
                                            WLCS**
   See also AAYA 15; BW 1; CA 85-88;
   CANR 61; DLB 51, 86; MTCW

Huston, John (Marcellus)
   1906-1987 . . . . CLC **20**
   See also CA 73-76; 123; CANR 34; DLB 26

Hustvedt, Siri   1955- . . . . CLC **76**
   See also CA 137

Hutten, Ulrich von   1488-1523 . . . . LC **16**
   See also DLB 179

Huxley, Aldous (Leonard)
   1894-1963 . . . . . CLC **1, 3, 4, 5, 8, 11, 18,
      35, 79; DA; DAB; DAC; DAM MST,
                                  NOV; WLC**
   See also AAYA 11; CA 85-88; CANR 44;
   CDBLB 1914-1945; DLB 36, 100, 162;
   MTCW; SATA 63

Huysmans, Charles Marie Georges
   1848-1907
   See Huysmans, Joris-Karl
   See also CA 104

Huysmans, Joris-Karl . . . . TCLC **7, 69**
   See also Huysmans, Charles Marie Georges
   See also DLB 123

Hwang, David Henry
   1957- . . . . CLC **55; DAM DRAM; DC 4**
   See also CA 127; 132; INT 132

Hyde, Anthony   1946- . . . . CLC **42**
   See also CA 136

Hyde, Margaret O(ldroyd)   1917- . . . CLC **21**
   See also CA 1-4R; CANR 1, 36; CLR 23;
   JRDA; MAICYA; SAAS 8; SATA 1, 42,
   76

Hynes, James   1956(?)- . . . . CLC **65**

Ian, Janis   1951- . . . . CLC **21**
   See also CA 105

Ibanez, Vicente Blasco
   See Blasco Ibanez, Vicente

Ibarguengoitia, Jorge   1928-1983 . . . . CLC **37**
   See also CA 124; 113; HW

Ibsen, Henrik (Johan)
   1828-1906 . . . . TCLC **2, 8, 16, 37, 52;
      DA; DAB; DAC; DAM DRAM, MST;
                                        DC 2; WLC**
   See also CA 104; 141

Ibuse Masuji   1898-1993 . . . . CLC **22**
   See also CA 127; 141; DLB 180

Ichikawa, Kon   1915- . . . . CLC **20**
   See also CA 121

Idle, Eric   1943- . . . . CLC **21**
   See also Monty Python
   See also CA 116; CANR 35

Ignatow, David   1914- . . . . . . CLC **4, 7, 14, 40**
   See also CA 9-12R; CAAS 3; CANR 31, 57;
   DLB 5

Ihimaera, Witi   1944- . . . . CLC **46**
   See also CA 77-80

Ilf, Ilya . . . . TCLC **21**
   See also Fainzilberg, Ilya Arnoldovich

Illyes, Gyula   1902-1983 . . . . PC **16**
   See also CA 114; 109

Immermann, Karl (Lebrecht)
   1796-1840 . . . . NCLC **4, 49**
   See also DLB 133

Inchbald, Elizabeth   1753-1821 . . . NCLC **62**
   See also DLB 39, 89

Inclan, Ramon (Maria) del Valle
   See Valle-Inclan, Ramon (Maria) del

Infante, G(uillermo) Cabrera
   See Cabrera Infante, G(uillermo)

Ingalls, Rachel (Holmes)   1940- . . . . . CLC **42**
   See also CA 123; 127

Ingamells, Rex   1913-1955 . . . . TCLC **35**

Inge, William (Motter)
   1913-1973 . . CLC **1, 8, 19; DAM DRAM**
   See also CA 9-12R; CDALB 1941-1968;
   DLB 7; MTCW

Ingelow, Jean   1820-1897 . . . . NCLC **39**
   See also DLB 35, 163; SATA 33

Ingram, Willis J.
   See Harris, Mark

Innaurato, Albert (F.)   1948(?)- . . CLC **21, 60**
   See also CA 115; 122; INT 122

Innes, Michael
   See Stewart, J(ohn) I(nnes) M(ackintosh)

Innis, Harold Adams   1894-1952 . . . TCLC **77**
   See also DLB 88

Ionesco, Eugene
   1909-1994 . . . . CLC **1, 4, 6, 9, 11, 15, 41,
      86; DA; DAB; DAC; DAM DRAM,
                                  MST; WLC**
   See also CA 9-12R; 144; CANR 55;
   MTCW; SATA 7; SATA-Obit 79

Iqbal, Muhammad   1873-1938 . . . . . TCLC **28**

Ireland, Patrick
   See O'Doherty, Brian

Iron, Ralph
   See Schreiner, Olive (Emilie Albertina)

Irving, John (Winslow)
   1942- . . . . . CLC **13, 23, 38; DAM NOV,
                                          POP**
   See also AAYA 8; BEST 89:3; CA 25-28R;
   CANR 28; DLB 6; DLBY 82; MTCW

Irving, Washington
   1783-1859 . . . . . NCLC **2, 19; DA; DAB;
      DAM MST; SSC 2; WLC**
   See also CDALB 1640-1865; DLB 3, 11, 30,
   59, 73, 74; YABC 2

Irwin, P. K.
   See Page, P(atricia) K(athleen)

Isaacs, Susan   1943- . . . CLC **32; DAM POP**
   See also BEST 89:1; CA 89-92; CANR 20,
   41; INT CANR-20; MTCW

Kafka, Franz
    1883-1924 .... **TCLC 2, 6, 13, 29, 47, 53;**
      DA; DAB; DAC; DAM MST, NOV;
               SSC 29; WLC
    See also CA 105; 126; DLB 81; MTCW

Kahanovitsch, Pinkhes
    See Der Nister

Kahn, Roger 1927- .... **CLC 30**
    See also CA 25-28R; CANR 44; DLB 171;
    SATA 37

Kain, Saul
    See Sassoon, Siegfried (Lorraine)

Kaiser, Georg 1878-1945 .... **TCLC 9**
    See also CA 106; DLB 124

Kaletski, Alexander 1946- .... **CLC 39**
    See also CA 118; 143

Kalidasa fl. c. 400- .... **CMLC 9**

Kallman, Chester (Simon)
    1921-1975 .... **CLC 2**
    See also CA 45-48; 53-56; CANR 3

Kaminsky, Melvin 1926-
    See Brooks, Mel
    See also CA 65-68; CANR 16

Kaminsky, Stuart M(elvin) 1934- ... **CLC 59**
    See also CA 73-76; CANR 29, 53

Kane, Francis
    See Robbins, Harold

Kane, Paul
    See Simon, Paul (Frederick)

Kane, Wilson
    See Bloch, Robert (Albert)

Kanin, Garson 1912- .... **CLC 22**
    See also AITN 1; CA 5-8R; CANR 7;
    DLB 7

Kaniuk, Yoram 1930- .... **CLC 19**
    See also CA 134

Kant, Immanuel 1724-1804 ...... **NCLC 27**
    See also DLB 94

Kantor, MacKinlay 1904-1977 ...... **CLC 7**
    See also CA 61-64; 73-76; CANR 60;
    DLB 9, 102

Kaplan, David Michael 1946- ...... **CLC 50**

Kaplan, James 1951- .... **CLC 59**
    See also CA 135

Karageorge, Michael
    See Anderson, Poul (William)

Karamzin, Nikolai Mikhailovich
    1766-1826 .... **NCLC 3**
    See also DLB 150

Karapanou, Margarita 1946- .... **CLC 13**
    See also CA 101

Karinthy, Frigyes 1887-1938 ...... **TCLC 47**

Karl, Frederick R(obert) 1927- ..... **CLC 34**
    See also CA 5-8R; CANR 3, 44

Kastel, Warren
    See Silverberg, Robert

Kataev, Evgeny Petrovich 1903-1942
    See Petrov, Evgeny
    See also CA 120

Kataphusin
    See Ruskin, John

Katz, Steve 1935- .... **CLC 47**
    See also CA 25-28R; CAAS 14; CANR 12;
    DLBY 83

Kauffman, Janet 1945- .... **CLC 42**
    See also CA 117; CANR 43; DLBY 86

Kaufman, Bob (Garnell)
    1925-1986 .... **CLC 49**
    See also BW 1; CA 41-44R; 118; CANR 22;
    DLB 16, 41

Kaufman, George S.
    1889-1961 .... **CLC 38; DAM DRAM**
    See also CA 108; 93-96; DLB 7; INT 108

Kaufman, Sue .... **CLC 3, 8**
    See also Barondess, Sue K(aufman)

Kavafis, Konstantinos Petrou 1863-1933
    See Cavafy, C(onstantine) P(eter)
    See also CA 104

Kavan, Anna 1901-1968 ...... **CLC 5, 13, 82**
    See also CA 5-8R; CANR 6, 57; MTCW

Kavanagh, Dan
    See Barnes, Julian (Patrick)

Kavanagh, Patrick (Joseph)
    1904-1967 .... **CLC 22**
    See also CA 123; 25-28R; DLB 15, 20;
    MTCW

Kawabata, Yasunari
    1899-1972 .... **CLC 2, 5, 9, 18;**
             DAM MULT; SSC 17
    See also CA 93-96; 33-36R; DLB 180

Kaye, M(ary) M(argaret) 1909- ..... **CLC 28**
    See also CA 89-92; CANR 24, 60; MTCW;
    SATA 62

Kaye, Mollie
    See Kaye, M(ary) M(argaret)

Kaye-Smith, Sheila 1887-1956 ..... **TCLC 20**
    See also CA 118; DLB 36

Kaymor, Patrice Maguilene
    See Senghor, Leopold Sedar

Kazan, Elia 1909- .... **CLC 6, 16, 63**
    See also CA 21-24R; CANR 32

Kazantzakis, Nikos
    1883(?)-1957 .... **TCLC 2, 5, 33**
    See also CA 105; 132; MTCW

Kazin, Alfred 1915- .... **CLC 34, 38**
    See also CA 1-4R; CAAS 7; CANR 1, 45;
    DLB 67

Keane, Mary Nesta (Skrine) 1904-1996
    See Keane, Molly
    See also CA 108; 114; 151

Keane, Molly .... **CLC 31**
    See also Keane, Mary Nesta (Skrine)
    See also INT 114

Keates, Jonathan 19(?)- .... **CLC 34**

Keaton, Buster 1895-1966 .... **CLC 20**

Keats, John
    1795-1821 .... **NCLC 8; DA; DAB;**
      DAC; DAM MST, POET; PC 1; WLC
    See also CDBLB 1789-1832; DLB 96, 110

Keene, Donald 1922- .... **CLC 34**
    See also CA 1-4R; CANR 5

Keillor, Garrison .... **CLC 40**
    See also Keillor, Gary (Edward)
    See also AAYA 2; BEST 89:3; DLBY 87;
    SATA 58

Keillor, Gary (Edward) 1942-
    See Keillor, Garrison
    See also CA 111; 117; CANR 36, 59;
    DAM POP; MTCW

Keith, Michael
    See Hubbard, L(afayette) Ron(ald)

Keller, Gottfried
    1819-1890 .... **NCLC 2; SSC 26**
    See also DLB 129

Kellerman, Jonathan
    1949- .... **CLC 44; DAM POP**
    See also BEST 90:1; CA 106; CANR 29, 51;
    INT CANR-29

Kelley, William Melvin 1937- ...... **CLC 22**
    See also BW 1; CA 77-80; CANR 27;
    DLB 33

Kellogg, Marjorie 1922- .... **CLC 2**
    See also CA 81-84

Kellow, Kathleen
    See Hibbert, Eleanor Alice Burford

Kelly, M(ilton) T(erry) 1947- .... **CLC 55**
    See also CA 97-100; CAAS 22; CANR 19,
    43

Kelman, James 1946- .... **CLC 58, 86**
    See also CA 148

Kemal, Yashar 1923- .... **CLC 14, 29**
    See also CA 89-92; CANR 44

Kemble, Fanny 1809-1893 .... **NCLC 18**
    See also DLB 32

Kemelman, Harry 1908-1996 .... **CLC 2**
    See also AITN 1; CA 9-12R; 155; CANR 6;
    DLB 28

Kempe, Margery 1373(?)-1440(?) ..... **LC 6**
    See also DLB 146

Kempis, Thomas a 1380-1471 .... **LC 11**

Kendall, Henry 1839-1882 .... **NCLC 12**

Keneally, Thomas (Michael)
    1935- ...... **CLC 5, 8, 10, 14, 19, 27, 43;**
                   DAM NOV
    See also CA 85-88; CANR 10, 50; MTCW

Kennedy, Adrienne (Lita)
    1931- ..... **CLC 66; BLC; DAM MULT;**
                       DC 5
    See also BW 2; CA 103; CAAS 20; CABS 3;
    CANR 26, 53; DLB 38

Kennedy, John Pendleton
    1795-1870 .... **NCLC 2**
    See also DLB 3

Kennedy, Joseph Charles 1929-
    See Kennedy, X. J.
    See also CA 1-4R; CANR 4, 30, 40;
    SATA 14, 86

Kennedy, William
    1928- ... **CLC 6, 28, 34, 53; DAM NOV**
    See also AAYA 1; CA 85-88; CANR 14,
    31; DLB 143; DLBY 85; INT CANR-31;
    MTCW; SATA 57

Kennedy, X. J. .... **CLC 8, 42**
    See also Kennedy, Joseph Charles
    See also CAAS 9; CLR 27; DLB 5;
    SAAS 22

Kenny, Maurice (Francis)
    1929- .... **CLC 87; DAM MULT**
    See also CA 144; CAAS 22; DLB 175;
    NNAL

Klopstock, Friedrich Gottlieb
1724-1803 . . . . **NCLC 11**
See also DLB 97

Knapp, Caroline 1959- . . . . **CLC 99**
See also CA 154

Knebel, Fletcher 1911-1993 . . . . **CLC 14**
See also AITN 1; CA 1-4R; 140; CAAS 3;
CANR 1, 36; SATA 36; SATA-Obit 75

Knickerbocker, Diedrich
See Irving, Washington

Knight, Etheridge
1931-1991 . . . . **CLC 40; BLC;**
DAM POET; PC 14
See also BW 1; CA 21-24R; 133; CANR 23;
DLB 41

Knight, Sarah Kemble 1666-1727 . . . . . **LC 7**
See also DLB 24

Knister, Raymond 1899-1932 . . . . . . **TCLC 56**
See also DLB 68

Knowles, John
1926- . . . . . . **CLC 1, 4, 10, 26; DA; DAC;**
DAM MST, NOV
See also AAYA 10; CA 17-20R; CANR 40;
CDALB 1968-1988; DLB 6; MTCW;
SATA 8, 89

Knox, Calvin M.
See Silverberg, Robert

Knox, John c. 1505-1572 . . . . **LC 37**
See also DLB 132

Knye, Cassandra
See Disch, Thomas M(ichael)

Koch, C(hristopher) J(ohn) 1932- . . . **CLC 42**
See also CA 127

Koch, Christopher
See Koch, C(hristopher) J(ohn)

Koch, Kenneth
1925- . . . . **CLC 5, 8, 44; DAM POET**
See also CA 1-4R; CANR 6, 36, 57; DLB 5;
INT CANR-36; SATA 65

Kochanowski, Jan 1530-1584 . . . . **LC 10**

Kock, Charles Paul de
1794-1871 . . . . **NCLC 16**

Koda Shigeyuki 1867-1947
See Rohan, Koda
See also CA 121

Koestler, Arthur
1905-1983 . . . . **CLC 1, 3, 6, 8, 15, 33**
See also CA 1-4R; 109; CANR 1, 33;
CDBLB 1945-1960; DLBY 83; MTCW

Kogawa, Joy Nozomi
1935- . . . . . . **CLC 78; DAC; DAM MST,**
MULT
See also CA 101; CANR 19, 62

Kohout, Pavel 1928- . . . . **CLC 13**
See also CA 45-48; CANR 3

Koizumi, Yakumo
See Hearn, (Patricio) Lafcadio (Tessima
Carlos)

Kolmar, Gertrud 1894-1943 . . . . . . **TCLC 40**

Komunyakaa, Yusef 1947- . . . . . . **CLC 86, 94**
See also CA 147; DLB 120

Konrad, George
See Konrad, Gyoergy

Konrad, Gyoergy 1933- . . . . . . **CLC 4, 10, 73**
See also CA 85-88

Konwicki, Tadeusz 1926- . . . . . **CLC 8, 28, 54**
See also CA 101; CAAS 9; CANR 39, 59;
MTCW

Koontz, Dean R(ay)
1945- . . . . . . **CLC 78; DAM NOV, POP**
See also AAYA 9; BEST 89:3, 90:2;
CA 108; CANR 19, 36, 52; MTCW;
SATA 92

Kopit, Arthur (Lee)
1937- . . . . . **CLC 1, 18, 33; DAM DRAM**
See also AITN 1; CA 81-84; CABS 3;
DLB 7; MTCW

Kops, Bernard 1926- . . . . **CLC 4**
See also CA 5-8R; DLB 13

Kornbluth, C(yril) M. 1923-1958 . . . . **TCLC 8**
See also CA 105; 160; DLB 8

Korolenko, V. G.
See Korolenko, Vladimir Galaktionovich

Korolenko, Vladimir
See Korolenko, Vladimir Galaktionovich

Korolenko, Vladimir G.
See Korolenko, Vladimir Galaktionovich

Korolenko, Vladimir Galaktionovich
1853-1921 . . . . **TCLC 22**
See also CA 121

Korzybski, Alfred (Habdank Skarbek)
1879-1950 . . . . **TCLC 61**
See also CA 123; 160

Kosinski, Jerzy (Nikodem)
1933-1991 . . . . **CLC 1, 2, 3, 6, 10, 15, 53,**
70; DAM NOV
See also CA 17-20R; 134; CANR 9, 46;
DLB 2; DLBY 82; MTCW

Kostelanetz, Richard (Cory) 1940- . . . **CLC 28**
See also CA 13-16R; CAAS 8; CANR 38

Kostrowitzki, Wilhelm Apollinaris de
1880-1918
See Apollinaire, Guillaume
See also CA 104

Kotlowitz, Robert 1924- . . . . **CLC 4**
See also CA 33-36R; CANR 36

Kotzebue, August (Friedrich Ferdinand) von
1761-1819 . . . . **NCLC 25**
See also DLB 94

Kotzwinkle, William 1938- . . . **CLC 5, 14, 35**
See also CA 45-48; CANR 3, 44; CLR 6;
DLB 173; MAICYA; SATA 24, 70

Kowna, Stancy
See Szymborska, Wislawa

Kozol, Jonathan 1936- . . . . **CLC 17**
See also CA 61-64; CANR 16, 45

Kozoll, Michael 1940(?)- . . . . **CLC 35**

Kramer, Kathryn 19(?)- . . . . **CLC 34**

Kramer, Larry
1935- . . . . . . **CLC 42; DAM POP; DC 8**
See also CA 124; 126; CANR 60

Krasicki, Ignacy 1735-1801 . . . . **NCLC 8**

Krasinski, Zygmunt 1812-1859 . . . . **NCLC 4**

Kraus, Karl 1874-1936 . . . . **TCLC 5**
See also CA 104; DLB 118

Kreve (Mickevicius), Vincas
1882-1954 . . . . **TCLC 27**

Kristeva, Julia 1941- . . . . **CLC 77**
See also CA 154

Kristofferson, Kris 1936- . . . . **CLC 26**
See also CA 104

Krizanc, John 1956- . . . . **CLC 57**

Krleza, Miroslav 1893-1981 . . . . **CLC 8**
See also CA 97-100; 105; CANR 50;
DLB 147

Kroetsch, Robert
1927- . . . . **CLC 5, 23, 57; DAC;**
DAM POET
See also CA 17-20R; CANR 8, 38; DLB 53;
MTCW

Kroetz, Franz
See Kroetz, Franz Xaver

Kroetz, Franz Xaver 1946- . . . . **CLC 41**
See also CA 130

Kroker, Arthur (W.) 1945- . . . . **CLC 77**
See also CA 161

Kropotkin, Peter (Aleksieevich)
1842-1921 . . . . **TCLC 36**
See also CA 119

Krotkov, Yuri 1917- . . . . **CLC 19**
See also CA 102

Krumb
See Crumb, R(obert)

Krumgold, Joseph (Quincy)
1908-1980 . . . . **CLC 12**
See also CA 9-12R; 101; CANR 7;
MAICYA; SATA 1, 48; SATA-Obit 23

Krumwitz
See Crumb, R(obert)

Krutch, Joseph Wood 1893-1970 . . . . **CLC 24**
See also CA 1-4R; 25-28R; CANR 4;
DLB 63

Krutzch, Gus
See Eliot, T(homas) S(tearns)

Krylov, Ivan Andreevich
1768(?)-1844 . . . . **NCLC 1**
See also DLB 150

Kubin, Alfred (Leopold Isidor)
1877-1959 . . . . **TCLC 23**
See also CA 112; 149; DLB 81

Kubrick, Stanley 1928- . . . . **CLC 16**
See also CA 81-84; CANR 33; DLB 26

Kumin, Maxine (Winokur)
1925- . . . . . **CLC 5, 13, 28; DAM POET;**
PC 15
See also AITN 2; CA 1-4R; CAAS 8;
CANR 1, 21; DLB 5; MTCW; SATA 12

Kundera, Milan
1929- . . . . **CLC 4, 9, 19, 32, 68;**
DAM NOV; SSC 24
See also AAYA 2; CA 85-88; CANR 19,
52; MTCW

Kunene, Mazisi (Raymond) 1930- . . . **CLC 85**
See also BW 1; CA 125; DLB 117

Kunitz, Stanley (Jasspon)
1905- . . . . **CLC 6, 11, 14; PC 19**
See also CA 41-44R; CANR 26, 57;
DLB 48; INT CANR-26; MTCW

Kunze, Reiner 1933- . . . . **CLC 10**
See also CA 93-96; DLB 75

Lathen, Emma . . . . **CLC 2**
See also Hennissart, Martha; Latsis, Mary J(ane)

Lathrop, Francis
See Leiber, Fritz (Reuter, Jr.)

Latsis, Mary J(ane)
See Lathen, Emma
See also CA 85-88

Lattimore, Richmond (Alexander)
1906-1984 . . . . **CLC 3**
See also CA 1-4R; 112; CANR 1

Laughlin, James 1914- . . . . **CLC 49**
See also CA 21-24R; CAAS 22; CANR 9, 47; DLB 48; DLBY 96

Laurence, (Jean) Margaret (Wemyss)
1926-1987 . . . . CLC 3, 6, 13, 50, 62;
DAC; DAM MST; SSC 7
See also CA 5-8R; 121; CANR 33; DLB 53; MTCW; SATA-Obit 50

Laurent, Antoine 1952- . . . . **CLC 50**

Lauscher, Hermann
See Hesse, Hermann

Lautreamont, Comte de
1846-1870 . . . . **NCLC 12; SSC 14**

Laverty, Donald
See Blish, James (Benjamin)

Lavin, Mary
1912-1996 . . . . . . **CLC 4, 18, 99; SSC 4**
See also CA 9-12R; 151; CANR 33; DLB 15; MTCW

Lavond, Paul Dennis
See Kornbluth, C(yril) M.; Pohl, Frederik

Lawler, Raymond Evenor 1922- . . . . **CLC 58**
See also CA 103

Lawrence, D(avid) H(erbert Richards)
1885-1930 . . . . TCLC 2, 9, 16, 33, 48, 61;
DA; DAB; DAC; DAM MST, NOV,
POET; SSC 4, 19; WLC
See also CA 104; 121; CDBLB 1914-1945; DLB 10, 19, 36, 98, 162; MTCW

Lawrence, T(homas) E(dward)
1888-1935 . . . . **TCLC 18**
See also Dale, Colin
See also CA 115

Lawrence of Arabia
See Lawrence, T(homas) E(dward)

Lawson, Henry (Archibald Hertzberg)
1867-1922 . . . . **TCLC 27; SSC 18**
See also CA 120

Lawton, Dennis
See Faust, Frederick (Schiller)

Laxness, Halldor . . . . **CLC 25**
See also Gudjonsson, Halldor Kiljan

Layamon fl. c. 1200- . . . . **CMLC 10**
See also DLB 146

Laye, Camara
1928-1980 . . . . **CLC 4, 38; BLC;
DAM MULT**
See also BW 1; CA 85-88; 97-100; CANR 25; MTCW

Layton, Irving (Peter)
1912- . . . . **CLC 2, 15; DAC; DAM MST,
POET**
See also CA 1-4R; CANR 2, 33, 43; DLB 88; MTCW

Lazarus, Emma 1849-1887 . . . . **NCLC 8**

Lazarus, Felix
See Cable, George Washington

Lazarus, Henry
See Slavitt, David R(ytman)

Lea, Joan
See Neufeld, John (Arthur)

Leacock, Stephen (Butler)
1869-1944 . . **TCLC 2; DAC; DAM MST**
See also CA 104; 141; DLB 92

Lear, Edward 1812-1888 . . . . **NCLC 3**
See also CLR 1; DLB 32, 163, 166; MAICYA; SATA 18

Lear, Norman (Milton) 1922- . . . . . . **CLC 12**
See also CA 73-76

Leavis, F(rank) R(aymond)
1895-1978 . . . . **CLC 24**
See also CA 21-24R; 77-80; CANR 44; MTCW

Leavitt, David 1961- . . . **CLC 34; DAM POP**
See also CA 116; 122; CANR 50, 62; DLB 130; INT 122

Leblanc, Maurice (Marie Emile)
1864-1941 . . . . **TCLC 49**
See also CA 110

Lebowitz, Fran(ces Ann)
1951(?)- . . . . **CLC 11, 36**
See also CA 81-84; CANR 14, 60; INT CANR-14; MTCW

Lebrecht, Peter
See Tieck, (Johann) Ludwig

le Carre, John . . . . **CLC 3, 5, 9, 15, 28**
See also Cornwell, David (John Moore)
See also BEST 89:4; CDBLB 1960 to Present; DLB 87

Le Clezio, J(ean) M(arie) G(ustave)
1940- . . . . **CLC 31**
See also CA 116; 128; DLB 83

Leconte de Lisle, Charles-Marie-Rene
1818-1894 . . . . **NCLC 29**

Le Coq, Monsieur
See Simenon, Georges (Jacques Christian)

Leduc, Violette 1907-1972 . . . . **CLC 22**
See also CA 13-14; 33-36R; CAP 1

Ledwidge, Francis 1887(?)-1917 . . . **TCLC 23**
See also CA 123; DLB 20

Lee, Andrea
1953- . . . . . **CLC 36; BLC; DAM MULT**
See also BW 1; CA 125

Lee, Andrew
See Auchincloss, Louis (Stanton)

Lee, Chang-rae 1965- . . . . **CLC 91**
See also CA 148

Lee, Don L. . . . . **CLC 2**
See also Madhubuti, Haki R.

Lee, George W(ashington)
1894-1976 . . . . **CLC 52; BLC;
DAM MULT**
See also BW 1; CA 125; DLB 51

Lee, (Nelle) Harper
1926- . . . . **CLC 12, 60; DA; DAB; DAC;
DAM MST, NOV; WLC**
See also AAYA 13; CA 13-16R; CANR 51; CDALB 1941-1968; DLB 6; MTCW; SATA 11

Lee, Helen Elaine 1959(?)- . . . . **CLC 86**
See also CA 148

Lee, Julian
See Latham, Jean Lee

Lee, Larry
See Lee, Lawrence

Lee, Laurie
1914-1997 . . . **CLC 90; DAB; DAM POP**
See also CA 77-80; 158; CANR 33; DLB 27; MTCW

Lee, Lawrence 1941-1990 . . . . **CLC 34**
See also CA 131; CANR 43

Lee, Manfred B(ennington)
1905-1971 . . . . **CLC 11**
See also Queen, Ellery
See also CA 1-4R; 29-32R; CANR 2; DLB 137

Lee, Shelton Jackson
1957(?)- . . . . **CLC 105; DAM MULT**
See also Lee, Spike
See also BW 2; CA 125; CANR 42

Lee, Spike
See Lee, Shelton Jackson
See also AAYA 4

Lee, Stan 1922- . . . . **CLC 17**
See also AAYA 5; CA 108; 111; INT 111

Lee, Tanith 1947- . . . . **CLC 46**
See also AAYA 15; CA 37-40R; CANR 53; SATA 8, 88

Lee, Vernon . . . . **TCLC 5**
See also Paget, Violet
See also DLB 57, 153, 156, 174, 178

Lee, William
See Burroughs, William S(eward)

Lee, Willy
See Burroughs, William S(eward)

Lee-Hamilton, Eugene (Jacob)
1845-1907 . . . . **TCLC 22**
See also CA 117

Leet, Judith 1935- . . . . **CLC 11**

Le Fanu, Joseph Sheridan
1814-1873 . . . . **NCLC 9, 58; DAM POP;
SSC 14**
See also DLB 21, 70, 159, 178

Leffland, Ella 1931- . . . . **CLC 19**
See also CA 29-32R; CANR 35; DLBY 84; INT CANR-35; SATA 65

Leger, Alexis
See Leger, (Marie-Rene Auguste) Alexis Saint-Leger

Leger, (Marie-Rene Auguste) Alexis
Saint-Leger
1887-1975 . . . . **CLC 11; DAM POET**
See also Perse, St.-John
See also CA 13-16R; 61-64; CANR 43; MTCW

Leger, Saintleger
See Leger, (Marie-Rene Auguste) Alexis Saint-Leger

Le Guin, Ursula K(roeber)
1929- . . . . . . **CLC 8, 13, 22, 45, 71; DAB;
DAC; DAM MST, POP; SSC 12**
See also AAYA 9; AITN 1; CA 21-24R; CANR 9, 32, 52; CDALB 1968-1988; CLR 3, 28; DLB 8, 52; INT CANR-32; JRDA; MAICYA; MTCW; SATA 4, 52

Li Fei-kan 1904-
See Pa Chin
See also CA 105

Lifton, Robert Jay 1926-......... **CLC 67**
See also CA 17-20R; CANR 27;
INT CANR-27; SATA 66

Lightfoot, Gordon 1938-.......... **CLC 26**
See also CA 109

Lightman, Alan P. 1948- .... **CLC 81**
See also CA 141

Ligotti, Thomas (Robert)
1953- .... **CLC 44; SSC 16**
See also CA 123; CANR 49

Li Ho 791-817..................... **PC 13**

Liliencron, (Friedrich Adolf Axel) Detlev von
1844-1909 .... **TCLC 18**
See also CA 117

Lilly, William 1602-1681.......... **LC 27**

Lima, Jose Lezama
See Lezama Lima, Jose

Lima Barreto, Afonso Henrique de
1881-1922 ....**TCLC 23**
See also CA 117

Limonov, Edward 1944-.......... **CLC 67**
See also CA 137

Lin, Frank
See Atherton, Gertrude (Franklin Horn)

Lincoln, Abraham 1809-1865..... **NCLC 18**

Lind, Jakov .... **CLC 1, 2, 4, 27, 82**
See also Landwirth, Heinz
See also CAAS 4

Lindbergh, Anne (Spencer) Morrow
1906- .... **CLC 82; DAM NOV**
See also CA 17-20R; CANR 16; MTCW;
SATA 33

Lindsay, David 1878-1945 ....**TCLC 15**
See also CA 113

Lindsay, (Nicholas) Vachel
1879-1931 .... **TCLC 17; DA; DAC;
DAM MST, POET; WLC**
See also CA 114; 135; CDALB 1865-1917;
DLB 54; SATA 40

Linke-Poot
See Doeblin, Alfred

Linney, Romulus 1930- .... **CLC 51**
See also CA 1-4R; CANR 40, 44

Linton, Eliza Lynn 1822-1898.... **NCLC 41**
See also DLB 18

Li Po 701-763................... **CMLC 2**

Lipsius, Justus 1547-1606 .... **LC 16**

Lipsyte, Robert (Michael)
1938- .... **CLC 21; DA; DAC;
DAM MST, NOV**
See also AAYA 7; CA 17-20R; CANR 8,
57; CLR 23; JRDA; MAICYA; SATA 5,
68

Lish, Gordon (Jay) 1934-.. **CLC 45; SSC 18**
See also CA 113; 117; DLB 130; INT 117

Lispector, Clarice 1925-1977...... **CLC 43**
See also CA 139; 116; DLB 113

Littell, Robert 1935(?)- .... **CLC 42**
See also CA 109; 112

Little, Malcolm 1925-1965
See Malcolm X
See also BW 1; CA 125; 111; DA; DAB;
DAC; DAM MST, MULT; MTCW

Littlewit, Humphrey Gent.
See Lovecraft, H(oward) P(hillips)

Litwos
See Sienkiewicz, Henryk (Adam Alexander
Pius)

Liu E 1857-1909............... **TCLC 15**
See also CA 115

Lively, Penelope (Margaret)
1933- .... **CLC 32, 50; DAM NOV**
See also CA 41-44R; CANR 29; CLR 7;
DLB 14, 161; JRDA; MAICYA; MTCW;
SATA 7, 60

Livesay, Dorothy (Kathleen)
1909- .... **CLC 4, 15, 79; DAC;
DAM MST, POET**
See also AITN 2; CA 25-28R; CAAS 8;
CANR 36; DLB 68; MTCW

Livy c. 59B.C.-c. 17 .... **CMLC 11**

Lizardi, Jose Joaquin Fernandez de
1776-1827 .... **NCLC 30**

Llewellyn, Richard
See Llewellyn Lloyd, Richard Dafydd
Vivian
See also DLB 15

Llewellyn Lloyd, Richard Dafydd Vivian
1906-1983 .... **CLC 7, 80**
See Llewellyn, Richard
See also CA 53-56; 111; CANR 7;
SATA 11; SATA-Obit 37

Llosa, (Jorge) Mario (Pedro) Vargas
See Vargas Llosa, (Jorge) Mario (Pedro)

Lloyd Webber, Andrew 1948-
See Webber, Andrew Lloyd
See also AAYA 1; CA 116; 149;
DAM DRAM; SATA 56

Llull, Ramon c. 1235-c. 1316..... **CMLC 12**

Locke, Alain (Le Roy)
1886-1954 .... **TCLC 43**
See also BW 1; CA 106; 124; DLB 51

Locke, John 1632-1704 .... **LC 7, 35**
See also DLB 101

Locke-Elliott, Sumner
See Elliott, Sumner Locke

Lockhart, John Gibson
1794-1854 .... **NCLC 6**
See also DLB 110, 116, 144

Lodge, David (John)
1935- .... **CLC 36; DAM POP**
See also BEST 90:1; CA 17-20R; CANR 19,
53; DLB 14; INT CANR-19; MTCW

Loennbohm, Armas Eino Leopold 1878-1926
See Leino, Eino
See also CA 123

Loewinsohn, Ron(ald William)
1937- .... **CLC 52**
See also CA 25-28R

Logan, Jake
See Smith, Martin Cruz

Logan, John (Burton) 1923-1987..... **CLC 5**
See also CA 77-80; 124; CANR 45; DLB 5

Lo Kuan-chung 1330(?)-1400(?)...... **LC 12**

Lombard, Nap
See Johnson, Pamela Hansford

London, Jack.. **TCLC 9, 15, 39; SSC 4; WLC**
See also London, John Griffith
See also AAYA 13; AITN 2;
CDALB 1865-1917; DLB 8, 12, 78;
SATA 18

London, John Griffith 1876-1916
See London, Jack
See also CA 110; 119; DA; DAB; DAC;
DAM MST, NOV; JRDA; MAICYA;
MTCW

Long, Emmett
See Leonard, Elmore (John, Jr.)

Longbaugh, Harry
See Goldman, William (W.)

Longfellow, Henry Wadsworth
1807-1882 ..... **NCLC 2, 45; DA; DAB;
DAC; DAM MST, POET; WLCS**
See also CDALB 1640-1865; DLB 1, 59;
SATA 19

Longley, Michael 1939-.......... **CLC 29**
See also CA 102; DLB 40

Longus fl. c. 2nd cent. -.......... **CMLC 7**

Longway, A. Hugh
See Lang, Andrew

Lonnrot, Elias 1802-1884........ **NCLC 53**

Lopate, Phillip 1943- .... **CLC 29**
See also CA 97-100; DLBY 80; INT 97-100

Lopez Portillo (y Pacheco), Jose
1920- .... **CLC 46**
See also CA 129; HW

Lopez y Fuentes, Gregorio
1897(?)-1966 .... **CLC 32**
See also CA 131; HW

Lorca, Federico Garcia
See Garcia Lorca, Federico

Lord, Bette Bao 1938-............ **CLC 23**
See also BEST 90:3; CA 107; CANR 41;
INT 107; SATA 58

Lord Auch
See Bataille, Georges

Lord Byron
See Byron, George Gordon (Noel)

Lorde, Audre (Geraldine)
1934-1992 .... **CLC 18, 71; BLC;
DAM MULT, POET; PC 12**
See also BW 1; CA 25-28R; 142; CANR 16,
26, 46; DLB 41; MTCW

Lord Houghton
See Milnes, Richard Monckton

Lord Jeffrey
See Jeffrey, Francis

Lorenzini, Carlo 1826-1890
See Collodi, Carlo
See also MAICYA; SATA 29

Lorenzo, Heberto Padilla
See Padilla (Lorenzo), Heberto

Loris
See Hofmannsthal, Hugo von

Loti, Pierre .... **TCLC 11**
See also Viaud, (Louis Marie) Julien
See also DLB 123

Mackenzie, Compton (Edward Montague)
1883-1972 .... CLC **18**
See also CA 21-22; 37-40R; CAP 2;
DLB 34, 100

Mackenzie, Henry 1745-1831 .... NCLC **41**
See also DLB 39

Mackintosh, Elizabeth 1896(?)-1952
See Tey, Josephine
See also CA 110

MacLaren, James
See Grieve, C(hristopher) M(urray)

Mac Laverty, Bernard 1942-....... CLC **31**
See also CA 116; 118; CANR 43; INT 118

MacLean, Alistair (Stuart)
1922(?)-1987 .... CLC **3, 13, 50, 63;**
DAM POP
See also CA 57-60; 121; CANR 28, 61;
MTCW; SATA 23; SATA-Obit 50

Maclean, Norman (Fitzroy)
1902-1990 .... CLC **78; DAM POP;**
SSC 13
See also CA 102; 132; CANR 49

MacLeish, Archibald
1892-1982 .... CLC **3, 8, 14, 68;**
DAM POET
See also CA 9-12R; 106; CANR 33; DLB 4,
7, 45; DLBY 82; MTCW

MacLennan, (John) Hugh
1907-1990 .... CLC **2, 14, 92; DAC;**
DAM MST
See also CA 5-8R; 142; CANR 33; DLB 68;
MTCW

MacLeod, Alistair
1936- ...... CLC **56; DAC; DAM MST**
See also CA 123; DLB 60

Macleod, Fiona
See Sharp, William

MacNeice, (Frederick) Louis
1907-1963 ...... CLC **1, 4, 10, 53; DAB;**
DAM POET
See also CA 85-88; CANR 61; DLB 10, 20;
MTCW

MacNeill, Dand
See Fraser, George MacDonald

Macpherson, James 1736-1796 ...... LC **29**
See also DLB 109

Macpherson, (Jean) Jay 1931-...... CLC **14**
See also CA 5-8R; DLB 53

MacShane, Frank 1927-.......... CLC **39**
See also CA 9-12R; CANR 3, 33; DLB 111

Macumber, Mari
See Sandoz, Mari(e Susette)

Madach, Imre 1823-1864 .... NCLC **19**

Madden, (Jerry) David 1933- .... CLC **5, 15**
See also CA 1-4R; CAAS 3; CANR 4, 45;
DLB 6; MTCW

Maddern, Al(an)
See Ellison, Harlan (Jay)

Madhubuti, Haki R.
1942-.............. CLC **6, 73; BLC;**
DAM MULT, POET; PC 5
See also Lee, Don L.
See also BW 2; CA 73-76; CANR 24, 51;
DLB 5, 41; DLBD 8

Maepenn, Hugh
See Kuttner, Henry

Maepenn, K. H.
See Kuttner, Henry

Maeterlinck, Maurice
1862-1949 ...... TCLC **3; DAM DRAM**
See also CA 104; 136; SATA 66

Maginn, William 1794-1842....... NCLC **8**
See also DLB 110, 159

Mahapatra, Jayanta
1928- .... CLC **33; DAM MULT**
See also CA 73-76; CAAS 9; CANR 15, 33

Mahfouz, Naguib (Abdel Aziz Al-Sabilgi)
1911(?)-
See Mahfuz, Najib
See also BEST 89:2; CA 128; CANR 55;
DAM NOV; MTCW

Mahfuz, Najib .... CLC **52, 55**
See also Mahfouz, Naguib (Abdel Aziz
Al-Sabilgi)
See also DLBY 88

Mahon, Derek 1941-............. CLC **27**
See also CA 113; 128; DLB 40

Mailer, Norman
1923- ...... CLC **1, 2, 3, 4, 5, 8, 11, 14,**
28, 39, 74; DA; DAB; DAC; DAM MST,
NOV, POP
See also AITN 2; CA 9-12R; CABS 1;
CANR 28; CDALB 1968-1988; DLB 2,
16, 28; DLBD 3; DLBY 80, 83; MTCW

Maillet, Antonine 1929-...... CLC **54; DAC**
See also CA 115; 120; CANR 46; DLB 60;
INT 120

Mais, Roger 1905-1955 .... TCLC **8**
See also BW 1; CA 105; 124; DLB 125;
MTCW

Maistre, Joseph de 1753-1821 .... NCLC **37**

Maitland, Frederic 1850-1906 ..... TCLC **65**

Maitland, Sara (Louise) 1950-...... CLC **49**
See also CA 69-72; CANR 13, 59

Major, Clarence
1936- .... CLC **3, 19, 48; BLC;**
DAM MULT
See also BW 2; CA 21-24R; CAAS 6;
CANR 13, 25, 53; DLB 33

Major, Kevin (Gerald)
1949-................. CLC **26; DAC**
See also AAYA 16; CA 97-100; CANR 21,
38; CLR 11; DLB 60; INT CANR-21;
JRDA; MAICYA; SATA 32, 82

Maki, James
See Ozu, Yasujiro

Malabaila, Damiano
See Levi, Primo

Malamud, Bernard
1914-1986 ...... CLC **1, 2, 3, 5, 8, 9, 11,**
18, 27, 44, 78, 85; DA; DAB; DAC;
DAM MST, NOV, POP; SSC 15; WLC
See also AAYA 16; CA 5-8R; 118; CABS 1;
CANR 28, 62; CDALB 1941-1968;
DLB 2, 28, 152; DLBY 80, 86; MTCW

Malan, Herman
See Bosman, Herman Charles; Bosman,
Herman Charles

Malaparte, Curzio 1898-1957 ..... TCLC **52**

Malcolm, Dan
See Silverberg, Robert

Malcolm X .... CLC **82; BLC; WLCS**
See also Little, Malcolm

Malherbe, Francois de 1555-1628..... LC **5**

Mallarme, Stephane
1842-1898 .... NCLC **4, 41;**
DAM POET; PC 4

Mallet-Joris, Francoise 1930-...... CLC **11**
See also CA 65-68; CANR 17; DLB 83

Malley, Ern
See McAuley, James Phillip

Mallowan, Agatha Christie
See Christie, Agatha (Mary Clarissa)

Maloff, Saul 1922- .... CLC **5**
See also CA 33-36R

Malone, Louis
See MacNeice, (Frederick) Louis

Malone, Michael (Christopher)
1942- .... CLC **43**
See also CA 77-80; CANR 14, 32, 57

Malory, (Sir) Thomas
1410(?)-1471(?) ...... LC **11; DA; DAB;**
DAC; DAM MST; WLCS
See also CDBLB Before 1660; DLB 146;
SATA 59; SATA-Brief 33

Malouf, (George Joseph) David
1934- .... CLC **28, 86**
See also CA 124; CANR 50

Malraux, (Georges-)Andre
1901-1976 ...... CLC **1, 4, 9, 13, 15, 57;**
DAM NOV
See also CA 21-22; 69-72; CANR 34, 58;
CAP 2; DLB 72; MTCW

Malzberg, Barry N(athaniel) 1939-... CLC **7**
See also CA 61-64; CAAS 4; CANR 16;
DLB 8

Mamet, David (Alan)
1947- .... CLC **9, 15, 34, 46, 91;**
DAM DRAM; DC 4
See also AAYA 3; CA 81-84; CABS 3;
CANR 15, 41; DLB 7; MTCW

Mamoulian, Rouben (Zachary)
1897-1987 .... CLC **16**
See also CA 25-28R; 124

Mandelstam, Osip (Emilievich)
1891(?)-1938(?) ...... TCLC **2, 6; PC 14**
See also CA 104; 150

Mander, (Mary) Jane 1877-1949... TCLC **31**

Mandeville, John fl. 1350-....... CMLC **19**
See also DLB 146

Mandiargues, Andre Pieyre de....... CLC **41**
See also Pieyre de Mandiargues, Andre
See also DLB 83

Mandrake, Ethel Belle
See Thurman, Wallace (Henry)

Mangan, James Clarence
1803-1849 .... NCLC **27**

Maniere, J.-E.
See Giraudoux, (Hippolyte) Jean

Manley, (Mary) Delariviere
1672(?)-1724 .... LC **1**
See also DLB 39, 80

Masefield, John (Edward)
1878-1967 .... **CLC 11, 47; DAM POET**
See also CA 19-20; 25-28R; CANR 33;
CAP 2; CDBLB 1890-1914; DLB 10, 19,
153, 160; MTCW; SATA 19

Maso, Carole 19(?)- .... **CLC 44**

Mason, Bobbie Ann
1940- .... **CLC 28, 43, 82; SSC 4**
See also AAYA 5; CA 53-56; CANR 11,
31, 58; DLB 173; DLBY 87;
INT CANR-31; MTCW

Mason, Ernst
See Pohl, Frederik

Mason, Lee W.
See Malzberg, Barry N(athaniel)

Mason, Nick 1945-............... **CLC 35**

Mason, Tally
See Derleth, August (William)

Mass, William
See Gibson, William

Masters, Edgar Lee
1868-1950 ...... **TCLC 2, 25; DA; DAC;**
DAM MST, POET; PC 1; WLCS
See also CA 104; 133; CDALB 1865-1917;
DLB 54; MTCW

Masters, Hilary 1928-............ **CLC 48**
See also CA 25-28R; CANR 13, 47

Mastrosimone, William 19(?)-...... **CLC 36**

Mathe, Albert
See Camus, Albert

Mather, Cotton 1663-1728.......... **LC 38**
See also CDALB 1640-1865; DLB 24, 30,
140

Mather, Increase 1639-1723 .... **LC 38**
See also DLB 24

Matheson, Richard Burton 1926- ... **CLC 37**
See also CA 97-100; DLB 8, 44; INT 97-100

Mathews, Harry 1930-......... **CLC 6, 52**
See also CA 21-24R; CAAS 6; CANR 18,
40

Mathews, John Joseph
1894-1979 ...... **CLC 84; DAM MULT**
See also CA 19-20; 142; CANR 45; CAP 2;
DLB 175; NNAL

Mathias, Roland (Glyn) 1915-...... **CLC 45**
See also CA 97-100; CANR 19, 41; DLB 27

Matsuo Basho 1644-1694............ **PC 3**
See also DAM POET

Mattheson, Rodney
See Creasey, John

Matthews, Greg 1949- .... **CLC 45**
See also CA 135

Matthews, William 1942-.......... **CLC 40**
See also CA 29-32R; CAAS 18; CANR 12,
57; DLB 5

Matthias, John (Edward) 1941-...... **CLC 9**
See also CA 33-36R; CANR 56

Matthiessen, Peter
1927- .... **CLC 5, 7, 11, 32, 64;**
DAM NOV
See also AAYA 6; BEST 90:4; CA 9-12R;
CANR 21, 50; DLB 6, 173; MTCW;
SATA 27

Maturin, Charles Robert
1780(?)-1824 .... **NCLC 6**
See also DLB 178

Matute (Ausejo), Ana Maria
1925-..................... **CLC 11**
See also CA 89-92; MTCW

Maugham, W. S.
See Maugham, W(illiam) Somerset

Maugham, W(illiam) Somerset
1874-1965 .... **CLC 1, 11, 15, 67, 93;**
DA; DAB; DAC; DAM DRAM, MST,
NOV; SSC 8; WLC
See also CA 5-8R; 25-28R; CANR 40;
CDBLB 1914-1945; DLB 10, 36, 77, 100,
162; MTCW; SATA 54

Maugham, William Somerset
See Maugham, W(illiam) Somerset

Maupassant, (Henri Rene Albert) Guy de
1850-1893 ..... **NCLC 1, 42; DA; DAB;**
DAC; DAM MST; SSC 1; WLC
See also DLB 123

Maupin, Armistead
1944- .... **CLC 95; DAM POP**
See also CA 125; 130; CANR 58; INT 130

Maurhut, Richard
See Traven, B.

Mauriac, Claude 1914-1996........ **CLC 9**
See also CA 89-92; 152; DLB 83

Mauriac, Francois (Charles)
1885-1970 .... **CLC 4, 9, 56; SSC 24**
See also CA 25-28; CAP 2; DLB 65;
MTCW

Mavor, Osborne Henry 1888-1951
See Bridie, James
See also CA 104

Maxwell, William (Keepers, Jr.)
1908- .... **CLC 19**
See also CA 93-96; CANR 54; DLBY 80;
INT 93-96

May, Elaine 1932- .... **CLC 16**
See also CA 124; 142; DLB 44

Mayakovski, Vladimir (Vladimirovich)
1893-1930 .... **TCLC 4, 18**
See also CA 104; 158

Mayhew, Henry 1812-1887 ...... **NCLC 31**
See also DLB 18, 55

Mayle, Peter 1939(?)-............ **CLC 89**
See also CA 139

Maynard, Joyce 1953-............ **CLC 23**
See also CA 111; 129

Mayne, William (James Carter)
1928- .... **CLC 12**
See also AAYA 20; CA 9-12R; CANR 37;
CLR 25; JRDA; MAICYA; SAAS 11;
SATA 6, 68

Mayo, Jim
See L'Amour, Louis (Dearborn)

Maysles, Albert 1926- .... **CLC 16**
See also CA 29-32R

Maysles, David 1932-............ **CLC 16**

Mazer, Norma Fox 1931- .... **CLC 26**
See also AAYA 5; CA 69-72; CANR 12,
32; CLR 23; JRDA; MAICYA; SAAS 1;
SATA 24, 67

Mazzini, Guiseppe 1805-1872 .... **NCLC 34**

McAuley, James Phillip
1917-1976 .... **CLC 45**
See also CA 97-100

McBain, Ed
See Hunter, Evan

McBrien, William Augustine
1930-..................... **CLC 44**
See also CA 107

McCaffrey, Anne (Inez)
1926- ...... **CLC 17; DAM NOV, POP**
See also AAYA 6; AITN 2; BEST 89:2;
CA 25-28R; CANR 15, 35, 55; DLB 8;
JRDA; MAICYA; MTCW; SAAS 11;
SATA 8, 70

McCall, Nathan 1955(?)-.......... **CLC 86**
See also CA 146

McCann, Arthur
See Campbell, John W(ood, Jr.)

McCann, Edson
See Pohl, Frederik

McCarthy, Charles, Jr. 1933-
See McCarthy, Cormac
See also CANR 42; DAM POP

McCarthy, Cormac
1933-............. **CLC 4, 57, 59, 101**
See also McCarthy, Charles, Jr.
See also DLB 6, 143

McCarthy, Mary (Therese)
1912-1989 ...... **CLC 1, 3, 5, 14, 24, 39,**
59; SSC 24
See also CA 5-8R; 129; CANR 16, 50;
DLB 2; DLBY 81; INT CANR-16;
MTCW

McCartney, (James) Paul
1942-.................... **CLC 12, 35**
See also CA 146

McCauley, Stephen (D.) 1955- ..... **CLC 50**
See also CA 141

McClure, Michael (Thomas)
1932-..................... **CLC 6, 10**
See also CA 21-24R; CANR 17, 46;
DLB 16

McCorkle, Jill (Collins) 1958-...... **CLC 51**
See also CA 121; DLBY 87

McCourt, James 1941-............. **CLC 5**
See also CA 57-60

McCoy, Horace (Stanley)
1897-1955 .... **TCLC 28**
See also CA 108; 155; DLB 9

McCrae, John 1872-1918........ **TCLC 12**
See also CA 109; DLB 92

McCreigh, James
See Pohl, Frederik

McCullers, (Lula) Carson (Smith)
1917-1967 ...... **CLC 1, 4, 10, 12, 48, 100;**
DA; DAB; DAC; DAM MST, NOV;
SSC 9, 24; WLC
See also AAYA 21; CA 5-8R; 25-28R;
CABS 1, 3; CANR 18;
CDALB 1941-1968; DLB 2, 7, 173;
MTCW; SATA 27

McCulloch, John Tyler
See Burroughs, Edgar Rice

McCullough, Colleen
1938(?)- .... **CLC 27; DAM NOV, POP**
See also CA 81-84; CANR 17, 46; MTCW

Metcalf, John 1938- .... **CLC 37**
See also CA 113; DLB 60

Metcalf, Suzanne
See Baum, L(yman) Frank

Mew, Charlotte (Mary)
1870-1928 .... **TCLC 8**
See also CA 105; DLB 19, 135

Mewshaw, Michael 1943- .... **CLC 9**
See also CA 53-56; CANR 7, 47; DLBY 80

Meyer, June
See Jordan, June

Meyer, Lynn
See Slavitt, David R(ytman)

Meyer-Meyrink, Gustav 1868-1932
See Meyrink, Gustav
See also CA 117

Meyers, Jeffrey 1939- .... **CLC 39**
See also CA 73-76; CANR 54; DLB 111

Meynell, Alice (Christina Gertrude Thompson)
1847-1922 .... **TCLC 6**
See also CA 104; DLB 19, 98

Meyrink, Gustav .... **TCLC 21**
See also Meyer-Meyrink, Gustav
See also DLB 81

Michaels, Leonard
1933- .... **CLC 6, 25; SSC 16**
See also CA 61-64; CANR 21, 62;
DLB 130; MTCW

Michaux, Henri 1899-1984 ...... **CLC 8, 19**
See also CA 85-88; 114

Micheaux, Oscar 1884-1951 ...... **TCLC 76**
See also DLB 50

Michelangelo 1475-1564 .... **LC 12**

Michelet, Jules 1798-1874 ...... **NCLC 31**

Michener, James A(lbert)
1907(?)-1997 ...... **CLC 1, 5, 11, 29, 60;**
DAM NOV, POP
See also AITN 1; BEST 90:1; CA 5-8R;
161; CANR 21, 45; DLB 6; MTCW

Mickiewicz, Adam 1798-1855 ..... **NCLC 3**

Middleton, Christopher 1926- ...... **CLC 13**
See also CA 13-16R; CANR 29, 54;
DLB 40

Middleton, Richard (Barham)
1882-1911 .... **TCLC 56**
See also DLB 156

Middleton, Stanley 1919- .... **CLC 7, 38**
See also CA 25-28R; CAAS 23; CANR 21,
46; DLB 14

Middleton, Thomas
1580-1627 .... **LC 33; DAM DRAM,**
MST; DC 5
See also DLB 58

Migueis, Jose Rodrigues 1901- ..... **CLC 10**

Mikszath, Kalman 1847-1910 ..... **TCLC 31**

Miles, Jack .... **CLC 100**

Miles, Josephine (Louise)
1911-1985 .... **CLC 1, 2, 14, 34, 39;**
DAM POET
See also CA 1-4R; 116; CANR 2, 55;
DLB 48

Militant
See Sandburg, Carl (August)

Mill, John Stuart 1806-1873 .. **NCLC 11, 58**
See also CDBLB 1832-1890; DLB 55

Millar, Kenneth
1915-1983 .... **CLC 14; DAM POP**
See also Macdonald, Ross
See also CA 9-12R; 110; CANR 16; DLB 2;
DLBD 6; DLBY 83; MTCW

Millay, E. Vincent
See Millay, Edna St. Vincent

Millay, Edna St. Vincent
1892-1950 ...... **TCLC 4, 49; DA; DAB;**
DAC; DAM MST, POET; PC 6; WLCS
See also CA 104; 130; CDALB 1917-1929;
DLB 45; MTCW

Miller, Arthur
1915- .... **CLC 1, 2, 6, 10, 15, 26, 47, 78;**
DA; DAB; DAC; DAM DRAM, MST;
DC 1; WLC
See also AAYA 15; AITN 1; CA 1-4R;
CABS 3; CANR 2, 30, 54;
CDALB 1941-1968; DLB 7; MTCW

Miller, Henry (Valentine)
1891-1980 .... **CLC 1, 2, 4, 9, 14, 43, 84;**
DA; DAB; DAC; DAM MST, NOV;
WLC
See also CA 9-12R; 97-100; CANR 33;
CDALB 1929-1941; DLB 4, 9; DLBY 80;
MTCW

Miller, Jason 1939(?)- .... **CLC 2**
See also AITN 1; CA 73-76; DLB 7

Miller, Sue 1943- ..... **CLC 44; DAM POP**
See also BEST 90:3; CA 139; CANR 59;
DLB 143

Miller, Walter M(ichael, Jr.)
1923- .... **CLC 4, 30**
See also CA 85-88; DLB 8

Millett, Kate 1934- .... **CLC 67**
See also AITN 1; CA 73-76; CANR 32, 53;
MTCW

Millhauser, Steven 1943- .... **CLC 21, 54**
See also CA 110; 111; DLB 2; INT 111

Millin, Sarah Gertrude 1889-1968 .. **CLC 49**
See also CA 102; 93-96

Milne, A(lan) A(lexander)
1882-1956 .... **TCLC 6; DAB; DAC;**
DAM MST
See also CA 104; 133; CLR 1, 26; DLB 10,
77, 100, 160; MAICYA; MTCW;
YABC 1

Milner, Ron(ald)
1938- ..... **CLC 56; BLC; DAM MULT**
See also AITN 1; BW 1; CA 73-76;
CANR 24; DLB 38; MTCW

Milnes, Richard Monckton
1809-1885 .... **NCLC 61**
See also DLB 32, 184

Milosz, Czeslaw
1911- .... **CLC 5, 11, 22, 31, 56, 82;**
DAM MST, POET; PC 8; WLCS
See also CA 81-84; CANR 23, 51; MTCW

Milton, John
1608-1674 ...... **LC 9; DA; DAB; DAC;**
DAM MST, POET; PC 19; WLC
See also CDBLB 1660-1789; DLB 131, 151

Min, Anchee 1957- .... **CLC 86**
See also CA 146

Minehaha, Cornelius
See Wedekind, (Benjamin) Frank(lin)

Miner, Valerie 1947- .... **CLC 40**
See also CA 97-100; CANR 59

Minimo, Duca
See D'Annunzio, Gabriele

Minot, Susan 1956- .... **CLC 44**
See also CA 134

Minus, Ed 1938- .... **CLC 39**

Miranda, Javier
See Bioy Casares, Adolfo

Mirbeau, Octave 1848-1917 ...... **TCLC 55**
See also DLB 123

Miro (Ferrer), Gabriel (Francisco Victor)
1879-1930 .... **TCLC 5**
See also CA 104

Mishima, Yukio
1925-1970 .... **CLC 2, 4, 6, 9, 27; DC 1;**
SSC 4
See also Hiraoka, Kimitake
See also DLB 182

Mistral, Frederic 1830-1914 ...... **TCLC 51**
See also CA 122

Mistral, Gabriela .... **TCLC 2; HLC**
See also Godoy Alcayaga, Lucila

Mistry, Rohinton 1952- ...... **CLC 71; DAC**
See also CA 141

Mitchell, Clyde
See Ellison, Harlan (Jay); Silverberg, Robert

Mitchell, James Leslie 1901-1935
See Gibbon, Lewis Grassic
See also CA 104; DLB 15

Mitchell, Joni 1943- .... **CLC 12**
See also CA 112

Mitchell, Joseph (Quincy)
1908-1996 .... **CLC 98**
See also CA 77-80; 152; DLBY 96

Mitchell, Margaret (Munnerlyn)
1900-1949 ...... **TCLC 11; DAM NOV,**
POP
See also CA 109; 125; CANR 55; DLB 9;
MTCW

Mitchell, Peggy
See Mitchell, Margaret (Munnerlyn)

Mitchell, S(ilas) Weir 1829-1914 .. **TCLC 36**

Mitchell, W(illiam) O(rmond)
1914- ...... **CLC 25; DAC; DAM MST**
See also CA 77-80; CANR 15, 43; DLB 88

Mitford, Mary Russell 1787-1855 .. **NCLC 4**
See also DLB 110, 116

Mitford, Nancy 1904-1973 .... **CLC 44**
See also CA 9-12R

Miyamoto, Yuriko 1899-1951 ..... **TCLC 37**
See also DLB 180

Miyazawa Kenji 1896-1933 ...... **TCLC 76**
See also CA 157

Mizoguchi, Kenji 1898-1956 ...... **TCLC 72**

Mo, Timothy (Peter) 1950(?)- ...... **CLC 46**
See also CA 117; MTCW

Modarressi, Taghi (M.) 1931- ...... **CLC 44**
See also CA 121; 134; INT 134

Modiano, Patrick (Jean) 1945- ..... **CLC 18**
See also CA 85-88; CANR 17, 40; DLB 83

Moerck, Paal
See Roelvaag, O(le) E(dvart)

Mofolo, Thomas (Mokopu)
1875(?)-1948 . . . . **TCLC 22; BLC;**
DAM MULT
See also CA 121; 153

Mohr, Nicholasa
1935- . . . . . **CLC 12; DAM MULT; HLC**
See also AAYA 8; CA 49-52; CANR 1, 32;
CLR 22; DLB 145; HW; JRDA; SAAS 8;
SATA 8

Mojtabai, A(nn) G(race)
1938- . . . . **CLC 5, 9, 15, 29**
See also CA 85-88

Moliere
1622-1673 . . . . . **LC 28; DA; DAB; DAC;**
DAM DRAM, MST; WLC

Molin, Charles
See Mayne, William (James Carter)

Molnar, Ferenc
1878-1952 . . . . . **TCLC 20; DAM DRAM**
See also CA 109; 153

Momaday, N(avarre) Scott
1934- . . . . . **CLC 2, 19, 85, 95; DA; DAB;**
DAC; DAM MST, MULT, NOV, POP;
WLCS
See also AAYA 11; CA 25-28R; CANR 14,
34; DLB 143, 175; INT CANR-14;
MTCW; NNAL; SATA 48;
SATA-Brief 30

Monette, Paul 1945-1995 . . . . **CLC 82**
See also CA 139; 147

Monroe, Harriet 1860-1936 . . . . . . **TCLC 12**
See also CA 109; DLB 54, 91

Monroe, Lyle
See Heinlein, Robert A(nson)

Montagu, Elizabeth 1917- . . . . **NCLC 7**
See also CA 9-12R

Montagu, Mary (Pierrepont) Wortley
1689-1762 . . . . **LC 9; PC 16**
See also DLB 95, 101

Montagu, W. H.
See Coleridge, Samuel Taylor

Montague, John (Patrick)
1929- . . . . **CLC 13, 46**
See also CA 9-12R; CANR 9; DLB 40;
MTCW

Montaigne, Michel (Eyquem) de
1533-1592 . . . . . **LC 8; DA; DAB; DAC;**
DAM MST; WLC

Montale, Eugenio
1896-1981 . . . . **CLC 7, 9, 18; PC 13**
See also CA 17-20R; 104; CANR 30;
DLB 114; MTCW

Montesquieu, Charles-Louis de Secondat
1689-1755 . . . . **LC 7**

Montgomery, (Robert) Bruce 1921-1978
See Crispin, Edmund
See also CA 104

Montgomery, L(ucy) M(aud)
1874-1942 . . . . **TCLC 51; DAC;**
DAM MST
See also AAYA 12; CA 108; 137; CLR 8;
DLB 92; DLBD 14; JRDA; MAICYA;
YABC 1

Montgomery, Marion H., Jr. 1925- . . **CLC 7**
See also AITN 1; CA 1-4R; CANR 3, 48;
DLB 6

Montgomery, Max
See Davenport, Guy (Mattison, Jr.)

Montherlant, Henry (Milon) de
1896-1972 . . . . **CLC 8, 19; DAM DRAM**
See also CA 85-88; 37-40R; DLB 72;
MTCW

Monty Python
See Chapman, Graham; Cleese, John
(Marwood); Gilliam, Terry (Vance); Idle,
Eric; Jones, Terence Graham Parry; Palin,
Michael (Edward)
See also AAYA 7

Moodie, Susanna (Strickland)
1803-1885 . . . . **NCLC 14**
See also DLB 99

Mooney, Edward 1951-
See Mooney, Ted
See also CA 130

Mooney, Ted . . . . **CLC 25**
See also Mooney, Edward

Moorcock, Michael (John)
1939- . . . . **CLC 5, 27, 58**
See also CA 45-48; CAAS 5; CANR 2, 17,
38; DLB 14; MTCW; SATA 93

Moore, Brian
1921- . . . . . . **CLC 1, 3, 5, 7, 8, 19, 32, 90;**
DAB; DAC; DAM MST
See also CA 1-4R; CANR 1, 25, 42; MTCW

Moore, Edward
See Muir, Edwin

Moore, George Augustus
1852-1933 . . . . **TCLC 7; SSC 19**
See also CA 104; DLB 10, 18, 57, 135

Moore, Lorrie . . . . **CLC 39, 45, 68**
See also Moore, Marie Lorena

Moore, Marianne (Craig)
1887-1972 . . . . **CLC 1, 2, 4, 8, 10, 13, 19,**
47; DA; DAB; DAC; DAM MST, POET;
PC 4; WLCS
See also CA 1-4R; 33-36R; CANR 3, 61;
CDALB 1929-1941; DLB 45; DLBD 7;
MTCW; SATA 20

Moore, Marie Lorena 1957-
See Moore, Lorrie
See also CA 116; CANR 39

Moore, Thomas 1779-1852 . . . . **NCLC 6**
See also DLB 96, 144

Morand, Paul 1888-1976 . . **CLC 41; SSC 22**
See also CA 69-72; DLB 65

Morante, Elsa 1918-1985 . . . . **CLC 8, 47**
See also CA 85-88; 117; CANR 35;
DLB 177; MTCW

Moravia, Alberto
1907-1990 . . . . **CLC 2, 7, 11, 27, 46;**
SSC 26
See also Pincherle, Alberto
See also DLB 177

More, Hannah 1745-1833 . . . . **NCLC 27**
See also DLB 107, 109, 116, 158

More, Henry 1614-1687 . . . . **LC 9**
See also DLB 126

More, Sir Thomas 1478-1535 . . . . **LC 10, 32**

Moreas, Jean . . . . **TCLC 18**
See also Papadiamantopoulos, Johannes

Morgan, Berry 1919- . . . . **CLC 6**
See also CA 49-52; DLB 6

Morgan, Claire
See Highsmith, (Mary) Patricia

Morgan, Edwin (George) 1920- . . . . . **CLC 31**
See also CA 5-8R; CANR 3, 43; DLB 27

Morgan, (George) Frederick
1922- . . . . **CLC 23**
See also CA 17-20R; CANR 21

Morgan, Harriet
See Mencken, H(enry) L(ouis)

Morgan, Jane
See Cooper, James Fenimore

Morgan, Janet 1945- . . . . **CLC 39**
See also CA 65-68

Morgan, Lady 1776(?)-1859 . . . . . . **NCLC 29**
See also DLB 116, 158

Morgan, Robin 1941- . . . . **CLC 2**
See also CA 69-72; CANR 29; MTCW;
SATA 80

Morgan, Scott
See Kuttner, Henry

Morgan, Seth 1949(?)-1990 . . . . **CLC 65**
See also CA 132

Morgenstern, Christian
1871-1914 . . . . **TCLC 8**
See also CA 105

Morgenstern, S.
See Goldman, William (W.)

Moricz, Zsigmond 1879-1942 . . . . . **TCLC 33**

Morike, Eduard (Friedrich)
1804-1875 . . . . **NCLC 10**
See also DLB 133

Mori Ogai . . . . **TCLC 14**
See also Mori Rintaro

Mori Rintaro 1862-1922
See Mori Ogai
See also CA 110

Moritz, Karl Philipp 1756-1793 . . . . . . **LC 2**
See also DLB 94

Morland, Peter Henry
See Faust, Frederick (Schiller)

Morren, Theophil
See Hofmannsthal, Hugo von

Morris, Bill 1952- . . . . **CLC 76**

Morris, Julian
See West, Morris L(anglo)

Morris, Steveland Judkins 1950(?)-
See Wonder, Stevie
See also CA 111

Morris, William 1834-1896 . . . . **NCLC 4**
See also CDBLB 1832-1890; DLB 18, 35,
57, 156, 178, 184

Morris, Wright 1910- . . . **CLC 1, 3, 7, 18, 37**
See also CA 9-12R; CANR 21; DLB 2;
DLBY 81; MTCW

Morrison, Arthur 1863-1945 . . . . . . **TCLC 72**
See also CA 120; 157; DLB 70, 135

Morrison, Chloe Anthony Wofford
See Morrison, Toni

Morrison, James Douglas 1943-1971
See Morrison, Jim
See also CA 73-76; CANR 40

Morrison, Jim . . . . **CLC 17**
See also Morrison, James Douglas

Morrison, Toni
1931- . . . . **CLC 4, 10, 22, 55, 81, 87;**
BLC; DA; DAB; DAC; DAM MST,
MULT, NOV, POP
See also AAYA 1, 22; BW 2; CA 29-32R;
CANR 27, 42; CDALB 1968-1988;
DLB 6, 33, 143; DLBY 81; MTCW;
SATA 57

Morrison, Van 1945- . . . . **CLC 21**
See also CA 116

Morrissy, Mary 1958- . . . . **CLC 99**

Mortimer, John (Clifford)
1923- . . . . . . **CLC 28, 43; DAM DRAM,**
POP
See also CA 13-16R; CANR 21;
CDBLB 1960 to Present; DLB 13;
INT CANR-21; MTCW

Mortimer, Penelope (Ruth) 1918-. . . . **CLC 5**
See also CA 57-60; CANR 45

Morton, Anthony
See Creasey, John

Mosca, Gaetano 1858-1941 . . . . . . **TCLC 75**

Mosher, Howard Frank 1943-. . . . . . **CLC 62**
See also CA 139

Mosley, Nicholas 1923-. . . . . **CLC 43, 70**
See also CA 69-72; CANR 41, 60; DLB 14

Mosley, Walter
1952- . . . . . **CLC 97; DAM MULT, POP**
See also AAYA 17; BW 2; CA 142;
CANR 57

Moss, Howard
1922-1987 . . . . **CLC 7, 14, 45, 50;**
DAM POET
See also CA 1-4R; 123; CANR 1, 44;
DLB 5

Mossgiel, Rab
See Burns, Robert

Motion, Andrew (Peter) 1952-. . . . . . **CLC 47**
See also CA 146; DLB 40

Motley, Willard (Francis)
1909-1965 . . . . **CLC 18**
See also BW 1; CA 117; 106; DLB 76, 143

Motoori, Norinaga 1730-1801 . . . . **NCLC 45**

Mott, Michael (Charles Alston)
1930- . . . . **CLC 15, 34**
See also CA 5-8R; CAAS 7; CANR 7, 29

Mountain Wolf Woman
1884-1960 . . . . **CLC 92**
See also CA 144; NNAL

Moure, Erin 1955- . . . . **CLC 88**
See also CA 113; DLB 60

Mowat, Farley (McGill)
1921- . . . . . . **CLC 26; DAC; DAM MST**
See also AAYA 1; CA 1-4R; CANR 4, 24,
42; CLR 20; DLB 68; INT CANR-24;
JRDA; MAICYA; MTCW; SATA 3, 55

Moyers, Bill 1934- . . . . **CLC 74**
See also AITN 2; CA 61-64; CANR 31, 52

Mphahlele, Es'kia
See Mphahlele, Ezekiel
See also DLB 125

Mphahlele, Ezekiel
1919- . . . . . **CLC 25; BLC; DAM MULT**
See also Mphahlele, Es'kia
See also BW 2; CA 81-84; CANR 26

Mqhayi, S(amuel) E(dward) K(rune Loliwe)
1875-1945 . . . . **TCLC 25; BLC;**
DAM MULT
See also CA 153

Mrozek, Slawomir 1930- . . . . **CLC 3, 13**
See also CA 13-16R; CAAS 10; CANR 29;
MTCW

Mrs. Belloc-Lowndes
See Lowndes, Marie Adelaide (Belloc)

Mtwa, Percy (?)-. . . . . **CLC 47**

Mueller, Lisel 1924-. . . . . **CLC 13, 51**
See also CA 93-96; DLB 105

Muir, Edwin 1887-1959 . . . . **TCLC 2**
See also CA 104; DLB 20, 100

Muir, John 1838-1914 . . . . **TCLC 28**

Mujica Lainez, Manuel
1910-1984 . . . . **CLC 31**
See also Lainez, Manuel Mujica
See also CA 81-84; 112; CANR 32; HW

Mukherjee, Bharati
1940- . . . . **CLC 53; DAM NOV**
See also BEST 89:2; CA 107; CANR 45;
DLB 60; MTCW

Muldoon, Paul
1951- . . . . **CLC 32, 72; DAM POET**
See also CA 113; 129; CANR 52; DLB 40;
INT 129

Mulisch, Harry 1927-. . . . . **CLC 42**
See also CA 9-12R; CANR 6, 26, 56

Mull, Martin 1943-. . . . . **CLC 17**
See also CA 105

Mulock, Dinah Maria
See Craik, Dinah Maria (Mulock)

Munford, Robert 1737(?)-1783 . . . . **LC 5**
See also DLB 31

Mungo, Raymond 1946-. . . . . **CLC 72**
See also CA 49-52; CANR 2

Munro, Alice
1931- . . . . . . **CLC 6, 10, 19, 50, 95; DAC;**
DAM MST, NOV; SSC 3; WLCS
See also AITN 2; CA 33-36R; CANR 33,
53; DLB 53; MTCW; SATA 29

Munro, H(ector) H(ugh) 1870-1916
See Saki
See also CA 104; 130; CDBLB 1890-1914;
DA; DAB; DAC; DAM MST, NOV;
DLB 34, 162; MTCW; WLC

Murasaki, Lady. . . . . **CMLC 1**

Murdoch, (Jean) Iris
1919- . . . . . . **CLC 1, 2, 3, 4, 6, 8, 11, 15,**
22, 31, 51; DAB; DAC; DAM MST,
NOV
See also CA 13-16R; CANR 8, 43;
CDBLB 1960 to Present; DLB 14;
INT CANR-8; MTCW

Murfree, Mary Noailles
1850-1922 . . . . **SSC 22**
See also CA 122; DLB 12, 74

Murnau, Friedrich Wilhelm
See Plumpe, Friedrich Wilhelm

Murphy, Richard 1927- . . . . **CLC 41**
See also CA 29-32R; DLB 40

Murphy, Sylvia 1937-. . . . . **CLC 34**
See also CA 121

Murphy, Thomas (Bernard) 1935-. . . **CLC 51**
See also CA 101

Murray, Albert L. 1916- . . . . **CLC 73**
See also BW 2; CA 49-52; CANR 26, 52;
DLB 38

Murray, Judith Sargent
1751-1820 . . . . **NCLC 63**
See also DLB 37

Murray, Les(lie) A(llan)
1938- . . . . **CLC 40; DAM POET**
See also CA 21-24R; CANR 11, 27, 56

Murry, J. Middleton
See Murry, John Middleton

Murry, John Middleton
1889-1957 . . . . **TCLC 16**
See also CA 118; DLB 149

Musgrave, Susan 1951- . . . . **CLC 13, 54**
See also CA 69-72; CANR 45

Musil, Robert (Edler von)
1880-1942 . . . . **TCLC 12, 68; SSC 18**
See also CA 109; CANR 55; DLB 81, 124

Muske, Carol 1945- . . . . **CLC 90**
See also Muske-Dukes, Carol (Anne)

Muske-Dukes, Carol (Anne) 1945-
See Muske, Carol
See also CA 65-68; CANR 32

Musset, (Louis Charles) Alfred de
1810-1857 . . . . **NCLC 7**

My Brother's Brother
See Chekhov, Anton (Pavlovich)

Myers, L(eopold) H(amilton)
1881-1944 . . . . **TCLC 59**
See also CA 157; DLB 15

Myers, Walter Dean
1937- . . . . . **CLC 35; BLC; DAM MULT,**
NOV
See also AAYA 4; BW 2; CA 33-36R;
CANR 20, 42; CLR 4, 16, 35; DLB 33;
INT CANR-20; JRDA; MAICYA;
SAAS 2; SATA 41, 71; SATA-Brief 27

Myers, Walter M.
See Myers, Walter Dean

Myles, Symon
See Follett, Ken(neth Martin)

Nabokov, Vladimir (Vladimirovich)
1899-1977 . . . . . **CLC 1, 2, 3, 6, 8, 11, 15,**
23, 44, 46, 64; DA; DAB; DAC;
DAM MST, NOV; SSC 11; WLC
See also CA 5-8R; 69-72; CANR 20;
CDALB 1941-1968; DLB 2; DLBD 3;
DLBY 80, 91; MTCW

Nagai Kafu 1879-1959 . . . . **TCLC 51**
See also Nagai Sokichi
See also DLB 180

Nagai Sokichi 1879-1959
See Nagai Kafu
See also CA 117

Nagy, Laszlo 1925-1978. . . . . **CLC 7**
See also CA 129; 112

North, Andrew
  See Norton, Andre

North, Anthony
  See Koontz, Dean R(ay)

North, Captain George
  See Stevenson, Robert Louis (Balfour)

North, Milou
  See Erdrich, Louise

Northrup, B. A.
  See Hubbard, L(afayette) Ron(ald)

North Staffs
  See Hulme, T(homas) E(rnest)

Norton, Alice Mary
  See Norton, Andre
  See also MAICYA; SATA 1, 43

Norton, Andre 1912- .... CLC 12
  See also Norton, Alice Mary
  See also AAYA 14; CA 1-4R; CANR 2, 31;
  DLB 8, 52; JRDA; MTCW; SATA 91

Norton, Caroline 1808-1877...... NCLC 47
  See also DLB 21, 159

Norway, Nevil Shute 1899-1960
  See Shute, Nevil
  See also CA 102; 93-96

Norwid, Cyprian Kamil
  1821-1883 .... NCLC 17

Nosille, Nabrah
  See Ellison, Harlan (Jay)

Nossack, Hans Erich 1901-1978 ..... CLC 6
  See also CA 93-96; 85-88; DLB 69

Nostradamus 1503-1566 .... LC 27

Nosu, Chuji
  See Ozu, Yasujiro

Notenburg, Eleanora (Genrikhovna) von
  See Guro, Elena

Nova, Craig 1945-............. CLC 7, 31
  See also CA 45-48; CANR 2, 53

Novak, Joseph
  See Kosinski, Jerzy (Nikodem)

Novalis 1772-1801 .... NCLC 13
  See also DLB 90

Novis, Emile
  See Weil, Simone (Adolphine)

Nowlan, Alden (Albert)
  1933-1983 .. CLC 15; DAC; DAM MST
  See also CA 9-12R; CANR 5; DLB 53

Noyes, Alfred 1880-1958 .... TCLC 7
  See also CA 104; DLB 20

Nunn, Kem...................... CLC 34
  See also CA 159

Nye, Robert
  1939- .... CLC 13, 42; DAM NOV
  See also CA 33-36R; CANR 29; DLB 14;
  MTCW; SATA 6

Nyro, Laura 1947- .... CLC 17

Oates, Joyce Carol
  1938-...... CLC 1, 2, 3, 6, 9, 11, 15, 19,
    33, 52; DA; DAB; DAC; DAM MST,
    NOV, POP; SSC 6; WLC
  See also AAYA 15; AITN 1; BEST 89:2;
  CA 5-8R; CANR 25, 45;
  CDALB 1968-1988; DLB 2, 5, 130;
  DLBY 81; INT CANR-25; MTCW

O'Brien, Darcy 1939-............. CLC 11
  See also CA 21-24R; CANR 8, 59

O'Brien, E. G.
  See Clarke, Arthur C(harles)

O'Brien, Edna
  1936- .... CLC 3, 5, 8, 13, 36, 65;
    DAM NOV; SSC 10
  See also CA 1-4R; CANR 6, 41;
  CDBLB 1960 to Present; DLB 14;
  MTCW

O'Brien, Fitz-James 1828-1862... NCLC 21
  See also DLB 74

O'Brien, Flann....... CLC 1, 4, 5, 7, 10, 47
  See also O Nuallain, Brian

O'Brien, Richard 1942- .... CLC 17
  See also CA 124

O'Brien, (William) Tim(othy)
  1946- ... CLC 7, 19, 40, 103; DAM POP
  See also AAYA 16; CA 85-88; CANR 40,
  58; DLB 152; DLBD 9; DLBY 80

Obstfelder, Sigbjoern 1866-1900 ... TCLC 23
  See also CA 123

O'Casey, Sean
  1880-1964 ...... CLC 1, 5, 9, 11, 15, 88;
    DAB; DAC; DAM DRAM, MST; WLCS
  See also CA 89-92; CANR 62;
  CDBLB 1914-1945; DLB 10; MTCW

O'Cathasaigh, Sean
  See O'Casey, Sean

Ochs, Phil 1940-1976............. CLC 17
  See also CA 65-68

O'Connor, Edwin (Greene)
  1918-1968 .... CLC 14
  See also CA 93-96; 25-28R

O'Connor, (Mary) Flannery
  1925-1964 .... CLC 1, 2, 3, 6, 10, 13, 15,
    21, 66, 104; DA; DAB; DAC;
    DAM MST, NOV; SSC 1, 23; WLC
  See also AAYA 7; CA 1-4R; CANR 3, 41;
  CDALB 1941-1968; DLB 2, 152;
  DLBD 12; DLBY 80; MTCW

O'Connor, Frank........... CLC 23; SSC 5
  See also O'Donovan, Michael John
  See also DLB 162

O'Dell, Scott 1898-1989........... CLC 30
  See also AAYA 3; CA 61-64; 129;
  CANR 12, 30; CLR 1, 16; DLB 52;
  JRDA; MAICYA; SATA 12, 60

Odets, Clifford
  1906-1963 .... CLC 2, 28, 98;
    DAM DRAM; DC 6
  See also CA 85-88; CANR 62; DLB 7, 26;
  MTCW

O'Doherty, Brian 1934-........... CLC 76
  See also CA 105

O'Donnell, K. M.
  See Malzberg, Barry N(athaniel)

O'Donnell, Lawrence
  See Kuttner, Henry

O'Donovan, Michael John
  1903-1966 .... CLC 14
  See also O'Connor, Frank
  See also CA 93-96

Oe, Kenzaburo
  1935- ..... CLC 10, 36, 86; DAM NOV;
    SSC 20
  See also CA 97-100; CANR 36, 50;
  DLB 182; DLBY 94; MTCW

O'Faolain, Julia 1932-........ CLC 6, 19, 47
  See also CA 81-84; CAAS 2; CANR 12, 61;
  DLB 14; MTCW

O'Faolain, Sean
  1900-1991 .... CLC 1, 7, 14, 32, 70;
    SSC 13
  See also CA 61-64; 134; CANR 12;
  DLB 15, 162; MTCW

O'Flaherty, Liam
  1896-1984 .... CLC 5, 34; SSC 6
  See also CA 101; 113; CANR 35; DLB 36,
  162; DLBY 84; MTCW

Ogilvy, Gavin
  See Barrie, J(ames) M(atthew)

O'Grady, Standish (James)
  1846-1928 .... TCLC 5
  See also CA 104; 157

O'Grady, Timothy 1951- .... CLC 59
  See also CA 138

O'Hara, Frank
  1926-1966 .... CLC 2, 5, 13, 78;
    DAM POET
  See also CA 9-12R; 25-28R; CANR 33;
  DLB 5, 16; MTCW

O'Hara, John (Henry)
  1905-1970 .... CLC 1, 2, 3, 6, 11, 42;
    DAM NOV; SSC 15
  See also CA 5-8R; 25-28R; CANR 31, 60;
  CDALB 1929-1941; DLB 9, 86; DLBD 2;
  MTCW

O Hehir, Diana 1922- .... CLC 41
  See also CA 93-96

Okigbo, Christopher (Ifenayichukwu)
  1932-1967 .... CLC 25, 84; BLC;
    DAM MULT, POET; PC 7
  See also BW 1; CA 77-80; DLB 125;
  MTCW

Okri, Ben 1959- .... CLC 87
  See also BW 2; CA 130; 138; DLB 157;
  INT 138

Olds, Sharon
  1942-.... CLC 32, 39, 85; DAM POET
  See also CA 101; CANR 18, 41; DLB 120

Oldstyle, Jonathan
  See Irving, Washington

Olesha, Yuri (Karlovich)
  1899-1960 .... CLC 8
  See also CA 85-88

Oliphant, Laurence
  1829(?)-1888 .... NCLC 47
  See also DLB 18, 166

Oliphant, Margaret (Oliphant Wilson)
  1828-1897 .... NCLC 11, 61; SSC 25
  See also DLB 18, 159

Oliver, Mary 1935-........ CLC 19, 34, 98
  See also CA 21-24R; CANR 9, 43; DLB 5

Olivier, Laurence (Kerr)
  1907-1989 .... CLC 20
  See also CA 111; 150; 129

Paracelsus 1493-1541 . . . . **LC 14**
See also DLB 179

Parasol, Peter
See Stevens, Wallace

Pareto, Vilfredo 1848-1923 . . . . **TCLC 69**

Parfenie, Maria
See Codrescu, Andrei

Parini, Jay (Lee) 1948- . . . . **CLC 54**
See also CA 97-100; CAAS 16; CANR 32

Park, Jordan
See Kornbluth, C(yril) M.; Pohl, Frederik

Park, Robert E(zra) 1864-1944 . . . . **TCLC 73**
See also CA 122

Parker, Bert
See Ellison, Harlan (Jay)

Parker, Dorothy (Rothschild)
1893-1967 . . . . **CLC 15, 68;**
DAM POET; SSC 2
See also CA 19-20; 25-28R; CAP 2;
DLB 11, 45, 86; MTCW

Parker, Robert B(rown)
1932- . . . . . . **CLC 27; DAM NOV, POP**
See also BEST 89:4; CA 49-52; CANR 1,
26, 52; INT CANR-26; MTCW

Parkin, Frank 1940- . . . . **CLC 43**
See also CA 147

Parkman, Francis, Jr.
1823-1893 . . . . **NCLC 12**
See also DLB 1, 30

Parks, Gordon (Alexander Buchanan)
1912- . . . **CLC 1, 16; BLC; DAM MULT**
See also AITN 2; BW 2; CA 41-44R;
CANR 26; DLB 33; SATA 8

Parmenides
c. 515B.C.-c. 450B.C. . . . . **CMLC 22**
See also DLB 176

Parnell, Thomas 1679-1718 . . . . **LC 3**
See also DLB 94

Parra, Nicanor
1914- . . . . **CLC 2, 102; DAM MULT;**
HLC
See also CA 85-88; CANR 32; HW; MTCW

Parrish, Mary Frances
See Fisher, M(ary) F(rances) K(ennedy)

Parson
See Coleridge, Samuel Taylor

Parson Lot
See Kingsley, Charles

Partridge, Anthony
See Oppenheim, E(dward) Phillips

Pascal, Blaise 1623-1662 . . . . **LC 35**

Pascoli, Giovanni 1855-1912 . . . . . **TCLC 45**

Pasolini, Pier Paolo
1922-1975 . . . . . **CLC 20, 37, 106; PC 17**
See also CA 93-96; 61-64; DLB 128, 177;
MTCW

Pasquini
See Silone, Ignazio

Pastan, Linda (Olenik)
1932- . . . . **CLC 27; DAM POET**
See also CA 61-64; CANR 18, 40, 61;
DLB 5

Pasternak, Boris (Leonidovich)
1890-1960 . . . . . . **CLC 7, 10, 18, 63; DA;**
DAB; DAC; DAM MST, NOV, POET;
PC 6; WLC
See also CA 127; 116; MTCW

Patchen, Kenneth
1911-1972 . . . **CLC 1, 2, 18; DAM POET**
See also CA 1-4R; 33-36R; CANR 3, 35;
DLB 16, 48; MTCW

Pater, Walter (Horatio)
1839-1894 . . . . **NCLC 7**
See also CDBLB 1832-1890; DLB 57, 156

Paterson, A(ndrew) B(arton)
1864-1941 . . . . **TCLC 32**
See also CA 155

Paterson, Katherine (Womeldorf)
1932- . . . . **CLC 12, 30**
See also AAYA 1; CA 21-24R; CANR 28,
59; CLR 7; DLB 52; JRDA; MAICYA;
MTCW; SATA 13, 53, 92

Patmore, Coventry Kersey Dighton
1823-1896 . . . . **NCLC 9**
See also DLB 35, 98

Paton, Alan (Stewart)
1903-1988 . . . . . . **CLC 4, 10, 25, 55, 106;**
DA; DAB; DAC; DAM MST, NOV;
WLC
See also CA 13-16; 125; CANR 22; CAP 1;
MTCW; SATA 11; SATA-Obit 56

Paton Walsh, Gillian 1937-
See Walsh, Jill Paton
See also CANR 38; JRDA; MAICYA;
SAAS 3; SATA 4, 72

Paulding, James Kirke 1778-1860 . . **NCLC 2**
See also DLB 3, 59, 74

Paulin, Thomas Neilson 1949-
See Paulin, Tom
See also CA 123; 128

Paulin, Tom . . . . **CLC 37**
See also Paulin, Thomas Neilson
See also DLB 40

Paustovsky, Konstantin (Georgievich)
1892-1968 . . . . **CLC 40**
See also CA 93-96; 25-28R

Pavese, Cesare
1908-1950 . . . . . **TCLC 3; PC 13; SSC 19**
See also CA 104; DLB 128, 177

Pavic, Milorad 1929- . . . . **CLC 60**
See also CA 136; DLB 181

Payne, Alan
See Jakes, John (William)

Paz, Gil
See Lugones, Leopoldo

Paz, Octavio
1914- . . . . **CLC 3, 4, 6, 10, 19, 51, 65;**
DA; DAB; DAC; DAM MST, MULT,
POET; HLC; PC 1; WLC
See also CA 73-76; CANR 32; DLBY 90;
HW; MTCW

p'Bitek, Okot
1931-1982 . . . . **CLC 96; BLC;**
DAM MULT
See also BW 2; CA 124; 107; DLB 125;
MTCW

Peacock, Molly 1947- . . . . **CLC 60**
See also CA 103; CAAS 21; CANR 52;
DLB 120

Peacock, Thomas Love
1785-1866 . . . . **NCLC 22**
See also DLB 96, 116

Peake, Mervyn 1911-1968 . . . . **CLC 7, 54**
See also CA 5-8R; 25-28R; CANR 3;
DLB 15, 160; MTCW; SATA 23

Pearce, Philippa . . . . **CLC 21**
See also Christie, (Ann) Philippa
See also CLR 9; DLB 161; MAICYA;
SATA 1, 67

Pearl, Eric
See Elman, Richard

Pearson, T(homas) R(eid) 1956- . . . . **CLC 39**
See also CA 120; 130; INT 130

Peck, Dale 1967- . . . . **CLC 81**
See also CA 146

Peck, John 1941- . . . . **CLC 3**
See also CA 49-52; CANR 3

Peck, Richard (Wayne) 1934- . . . . . . **CLC 21**
See also AAYA 1; CA 85-88; CANR 19,
38; CLR 15; INT CANR-19; JRDA;
MAICYA; SAAS 2; SATA 18, 55

Peck, Robert Newton
1928- . . . **CLC 17; DA; DAC; DAM MST**
See also AAYA 3; CA 81-84; CANR 31;
CLR 45; JRDA; MAICYA; SAAS 1;
SATA 21, 62

Peckinpah, (David) Sam(uel)
1925-1984 . . . . **CLC 20**
See also CA 109; 114

Pedersen, Knut 1859-1952
See Hamsun, Knut
See also CA 104; 119; MTCW

Peeslake, Gaffer
See Durrell, Lawrence (George)

Peguy, Charles Pierre
1873-1914 . . . . **TCLC 10**
See also CA 107

Pena, Ramon del Valle y
See Valle-Inclan, Ramon (Maria) del

Pendennis, Arthur Esquir
See Thackeray, William Makepeace

Penn, William 1644-1718 . . . . **LC 25**
See also DLB 24

PEPECE
See Prado (Calvo), Pedro

Pepys, Samuel
1633-1703 . . . . . **LC 11; DA; DAB; DAC;**
DAM MST; WLC
See also CDBLB 1660-1789; DLB 101

Percy, Walker
1916-1990 . . . . **CLC 2, 3, 6, 8, 14, 18, 47,**
65; DAM NOV, POP
See also CA 1-4R; 131; CANR 1, 23;
DLB 2; DLBY 80, 90; MTCW

Perec, Georges 1936-1982 . . . . **CLC 56**
See also CA 141; DLB 83

Pereda (y Sanchez de Porrua), Jose Maria de
1833-1906 . . . . **TCLC 16**
See also CA 117

Raleigh, Sir Walter
    1554(?)-1618 .... **LC 31, 39**
    See also CDBLB Before 1660; DLB 172

Rallentando, H. P.
    See Sayers, Dorothy L(eigh)

Ramal, Walter
    See de la Mare, Walter (John)

Ramon, Juan
    See Jimenez (Mantecon), Juan Ramon

Ramos, Graciliano 1892-1953 ..... **TCLC 32**

Rampersad, Arnold 1941-......... **CLC 44**
    See also BW 2; CA 127; 133; DLB 111;
    INT 133

Rampling, Anne
    See Rice, Anne

Ramsay, Allan 1684(?)-1758 .... **LC 29**
    See also DLB 95

Ramuz, Charles-Ferdinand
    1878-1947 .... **TCLC 33**

Rand, Ayn
    1905-1982 ...... **CLC 3, 30, 44, 79; DA;**
        DAC; DAM MST, NOV, POP; WLC
    See also AAYA 10; CA 13-16R; 105;
    CANR 27; MTCW

Randall, Dudley (Felker)
    1914- ...... **CLC 1; BLC; DAM MULT**
    See also BW 1; CA 25-28R; CANR 23;
    DLB 41

Randall, Robert
    See Silverberg, Robert

Ranger, Ken
    See Creasey, John

Ransom, John Crowe
    1888-1974 .... **CLC 2, 4, 5, 11, 24;**
        DAM POET
    See also CA 5-8R; 49-52; CANR 6, 34;
    DLB 45, 63; MTCW

Rao, Raja 1909- ... **CLC 25, 56; DAM NOV**
    See also CA 73-76; CANR 51; MTCW

Raphael, Frederic (Michael)
    1931- .... **CLC 2, 14**
    See also CA 1-4R; CANR 1; DLB 14

Ratcliffe, James P.
    See Mencken, H(enry) L(ouis)

Rathbone, Julian 1935- .... **CLC 41**
    See also CA 101; CANR 34

Rattigan, Terence (Mervyn)
    1911-1977 .... **CLC 7; DAM DRAM**
    See also CA 85-88; 73-76;
    CDBLB 1945-1960; DLB 13; MTCW

Ratushinskaya, Irina 1954-........ **CLC 54**
    See also CA 129

Raven, Simon (Arthur Noel)
    1927- .... **CLC 14**
    See also CA 81-84

Rawley, Callman 1903-
    See Rakosi, Carl
    See also CA 21-24R; CANR 12, 32

Rawlings, Marjorie Kinnan
    1896-1953 .... **TCLC 4**
    See also AAYA 20; CA 104; 137; DLB 9,
    22, 102; JRDA; MAICYA; YABC 1

Ray, Satyajit
    1921-1992 ... **CLC 16, 76; DAM MULT**
    See also CA 114; 137

Read, Herbert Edward 1893-1968.... **CLC 4**
    See also CA 85-88; 25-28R; DLB 20, 149

Read, Piers Paul 1941- ...... **CLC 4, 10, 25**
    See also CA 21-24R; CANR 38; DLB 14;
    SATA 21

Reade, Charles 1814-1884 .... **NCLC 2**
    See also DLB 21

Reade, Hamish
    See Gray, Simon (James Holliday)

Reading, Peter 1946- .... **CLC 47**
    See also CA 103; CANR 46; DLB 40

Reaney, James
    1926- ...... **CLC 13; DAC; DAM MST**
    See also CA 41-44R; CAAS 15; CANR 42;
    DLB 68; SATA 43

Rebreanu, Liviu 1885-1944 ...... **TCLC 28**

Rechy, John (Francisco)
    1934- .... **CLC 1, 7, 14, 18;**
        DAM MULT; HLC
    See also CA 5-8R; CAAS 4; CANR 6, 32;
    DLB 122; DLBY 82; HW; INT CANR-6

Redcam, Tom 1870-1933 .... **TCLC 25**

Reddin, Keith.................... **CLC 67**

Redgrove, Peter (William)
    1932- .... **CLC 6, 41**
    See also CA 1-4R; CANR 3, 39; DLB 40

Redmon, Anne................... **CLC 22**
    See also Nightingale, Anne Redmon
    See also DLBY 86

Reed, Eliot
    See Ambler, Eric

Reed, Ishmael
    1938- .... **CLC 2, 3, 5, 6, 13, 32, 60;**
        BLC; DAM MULT
    See also BW 2; CA 21-24R; CANR 25, 48;
    DLB 2, 5, 33, 169; DLBD 8; MTCW

Reed, John (Silas) 1887-1920 ...... **TCLC 9**
    See also CA 106

Reed, Lou.................... **CLC 21**
    See also Firbank, Louis

Reeve, Clara 1729-1807 .... **NCLC 19**
    See also DLB 39

Reich, Wilhelm 1897-1957....... **TCLC 57**

Reid, Christopher (John) 1949-..... **CLC 33**
    See also CA 140; DLB 40

Reid, Desmond
    See Moorcock, Michael (John)

Reid Banks, Lynne 1929-
    See Banks, Lynne Reid
    See also CA 1-4R; CANR 6, 22, 38;
    CLR 24; JRDA; MAICYA; SATA 22, 75

Reilly, William K.
    See Creasey, John

Reiner, Max
    See Caldwell, (Janet Miriam) Taylor
    (Holland)

Reis, Ricardo
    See Pessoa, Fernando (Antonio Nogueira)

Remarque, Erich Maria
    1898-1970 .... **CLC 21; DA; DAB; DAC;**
        DAM MST, NOV
    See also CA 77-80; 29-32R; DLB 56;
    MTCW

Remizov, A.
    See Remizov, Aleksei (Mikhailovich)

Remizov, A. M.
    See Remizov, Aleksei (Mikhailovich)

Remizov, Aleksei (Mikhailovich)
    1877-1957 .... **TCLC 27**
    See also CA 125; 133

Renan, Joseph Ernest
    1823-1892 .... **NCLC 26**

Renard, Jules 1864-1910 .... **TCLC 17**
    See also CA 117

Renault, Mary................ **CLC 3, 11, 17**
    See also Challans, Mary
    See also DLBY 83

Rendell, Ruth (Barbara)
    1930- .... **CLC 28, 48; DAM POP**
    See also Vine, Barbara
    See also CA 109; CANR 32, 52; DLB 87;
    INT CANR-32; MTCW

Renoir, Jean 1894-1979 .... **CLC 20**
    See also CA 129; 85-88

Resnais, Alain 1922-.............. **CLC 16**

Reverdy, Pierre 1889-1960 .... **CLC 53**
    See also CA 97-100; 89-92

Rexroth, Kenneth
    1905-1982 ...... **CLC 1, 2, 6, 11, 22, 49;**
        DAM POET; PC 20
    See also CA 5-8R; 107; CANR 14, 34;
    CDALB 1941-1968; DLB 16, 48, 165;
    DLBY 82; INT CANR-14; MTCW

Reyes, Alfonso 1889-1959 .... **TCLC 33**
    See also CA 131; HW

Reyes y Basoalto, Ricardo Eliecer Neftali
    See Neruda, Pablo

Reymont, Wladyslaw (Stanislaw)
    1868(?)-1925 .... **TCLC 5**
    See also CA 104

Reynolds, Jonathan 1942- .... **CLC 6, 38**
    See also CA 65-68; CANR 28

Reynolds, Joshua 1723-1792........ **LC 15**
    See also DLB 104

Reynolds, Michael Shane 1937- .... **CLC 44**
    See also CA 65-68; CANR 9

Reznikoff, Charles 1894-1976 .... **CLC 9**
    See also CA 33-36; 61-64; CAP 2; DLB 28,
    45

Rezzori (d'Arezzo), Gregor von
    1914- .... **CLC 25**
    See also CA 122; 136

Rhine, Richard
    See Silverstein, Alvin

Rhodes, Eugene Manlove
    1869-1934 .... **TCLC 53**

R'hoone
    See Balzac, Honore de

Rhys, Jean
    1890(?)-1979 .... **CLC 2, 4, 6, 14, 19, 51;**
        DAM NOV; SSC 21
    See also CA 25-28R; 85-88; CANR 35, 62;
    CDBLB 1945-1960; DLB 36, 117, 162;
    MTCW

Ribeiro, Darcy 1922-1997 .... **CLC 34**
    See also CA 33-36R; 156

Ribeiro, Joao Ubaldo (Osorio Pimentel)
1941- .... **CLC 10, 67**
See also CA 81-84

Ribman, Ronald (Burt) 1932- .... **CLC 7**
See also CA 21-24R; CANR 46

Ricci, Nino 1959- .... **CLC 70**
See also CA 137

Rice, Anne 1941- ..... **CLC 41; DAM POP**
See also AAYA 9; BEST 89:2; CA 65-68;
CANR 12, 36, 53

Rice, Elmer (Leopold)
1892-1967 .... **CLC 7, 49; DAM DRAM**
See also CA 21-22; 25-28R; CAP 2; DLB 4,
7; MTCW

Rice, Tim(othy Miles Bindon)
1944- .... **CLC 21**
See also CA 103; CANR 46

Rich, Adrienne (Cecile)
1929- .... **CLC 3, 6, 7, 11, 18, 36, 73, 76;**
DAM POET; PC 5
See also CA 9-12R; CANR 20, 53; DLB 5,
67; MTCW

Rich, Barbara
See Graves, Robert (von Ranke)

Rich, Robert
See Trumbo, Dalton

Richard, Keith.................... **CLC 17**
See also Richards, Keith

Richards, David Adams
1950- .... **CLC 59; DAC**
See also CA 93-96; CANR 60; DLB 53

Richards, I(vor) A(rmstrong)
1893-1979 .... **CLC 14, 24**
See also CA 41-44R; 89-92; CANR 34;
DLB 27

Richards, Keith 1943-
See Richard, Keith
See also CA 107

Richardson, Anne
See Roiphe, Anne (Richardson)

Richardson, Dorothy Miller
1873-1957 .... **TCLC 3**
See also CA 104; DLB 36

Richardson, Ethel Florence (Lindesay)
1870-1946
See Richardson, Henry Handel
See also CA 105

Richardson, Henry Handel......... **TCLC 4**
See also Richardson, Ethel Florence
(Lindesay)

Richardson, John
1796-1852 .... **NCLC 55; DAC**
See also DLB 99

Richardson, Samuel
1689-1761 ...... **LC 1; DA; DAB; DAC;**
DAM MST, NOV; WLC
See also CDBLB 1660-1789; DLB 39

Richler, Mordecai
1931- .... **CLC 3, 5, 9, 13, 18, 46, 70;**
DAC; DAM MST, NOV
See also AITN 1; CA 65-68; CANR 31, 62;
CLR 17; DLB 53; MAICYA; MTCW;
SATA 44; SATA-Brief 27

Richter, Conrad (Michael)
1890-1968 .... **CLC 30**
See also AAYA 21; CA 5-8R; 25-28R;
CANR 23; DLB 9; MTCW; SATA 3

Ricostranza, Tom
See Ellis, Trey

Riddell, J. H. 1832-1906 .... **TCLC 40**

Riding, Laura................... **CLC 3, 7**
See also Jackson, Laura (Riding)

Riefenstahl, Berta Helene Amalia 1902-
See Riefenstahl, Leni
See also CA 108

Riefenstahl, Leni................ **CLC 16**
See also Riefenstahl, Berta Helene Amalia

Riffe, Ernest
See Bergman, (Ernst) Ingmar

Riggs, (Rolla) Lynn
1899-1954 ..... **TCLC 56; DAM MULT**
See also CA 144; DLB 175; NNAL

Riley, James Whitcomb
1849-1916 ...... **TCLC 51; DAM POET**
See also CA 118; 137; MAICYA; SATA 17

Riley, Tex
See Creasey, John

Rilke, Rainer Maria
1875-1926 .... **TCLC 1, 6, 19;**
DAM POET; PC 2
See also CA 104; 132; CANR 62; DLB 81;
MTCW

Rimbaud, (Jean Nicolas) Arthur
1854-1891 ..... **NCLC 4, 35; DA; DAB;**
DAC; DAM MST, POET; PC 3; WLC

Rinehart, Mary Roberts
1876-1958 .... **TCLC 52**
See also CA 108

Ringmaster, The
See Mencken, H(enry) L(ouis)

Ringwood, Gwen(dolyn Margaret) Pharis
1910-1984 .... **CLC 48**
See also CA 148; 112; DLB 88

Rio, Michel 19(?)-................ **CLC 43**

Ritsos, Giannes
See Ritsos, Yannis

Ritsos, Yannis 1909-1990..... **CLC 6, 13, 31**
See also CA 77-80; 133; CANR 39, 61;
MTCW

Ritter, Erika 1948(?)-............. **CLC 52**

Rivera, Jose Eustasio 1889-1928... **TCLC 35**
See also HW

Rivers, Conrad Kent 1933-1968...... **CLC 1**
See also BW 1; CA 85-88; DLB 41

Rivers, Elfrida
See Bradley, Marion Zimmer

Riverside, John
See Heinlein, Robert A(nson)

Rizal, Jose 1861-1896.......... **NCLC 27**

Roa Bastos, Augusto (Antonio)
1917- ..... **CLC 45; DAM MULT; HLC**
See also CA 131; DLB 113; HW

Robbe-Grillet, Alain
1922- ...... **CLC 1, 2, 4, 6, 8, 10, 14, 43**
See also CA 9-12R; CANR 33; DLB 83;
MTCW

Robbins, Harold
1916- .... **CLC 5; DAM NOV**
See also CA 73-76; CANR 26, 54; MTCW

Robbins, Thomas Eugene 1936-
See Robbins, Tom
See also CA 81-84; CANR 29, 59;
DAM NOV, POP; MTCW

Robbins, Tom................ **CLC 9, 32, 64**
See also Robbins, Thomas Eugene
See also BEST 90:3; DLBY 80

Robbins, Trina 1938- .... **CLC 21**
See also CA 128

Roberts, Charles G(eorge) D(ouglas)
1860-1943.................. **TCLC 8**
See also CA 105; CLR 33; DLB 92;
SATA 88; SATA-Brief 29

Roberts, Elizabeth Madox
1886-1941 .... **TCLC 68**
See also CA 111; DLB 9, 54, 102;
SATA 33; SATA-Brief 27

Roberts, Kate 1891-1985 .... **CLC 15**
See also CA 107; 116

Roberts, Keith (John Kingston)
1935- .... **CLC 14**
See also CA 25-28R; CANR 46

Roberts, Kenneth (Lewis)
1885-1957 .... **TCLC 23**
See also CA 109; DLB 9

Roberts, Michele (B.) 1949-........ **CLC 48**
See also CA 115; CANR 58

Robertson, Ellis
See Ellison, Harlan (Jay); Silverberg, Robert

Robertson, Thomas William
1829-1871 .... **NCLC 35; DAM DRAM**

Robeson, Kenneth
See Dent, Lester

Robinson, Edwin Arlington
1869-1935 .... **TCLC 5; DA; DAC;**
DAM MST, POET; PC 1
See also CA 104; 133; CDALB 1865-1917;
DLB 54; MTCW

Robinson, Henry Crabb
1775-1867 .... **NCLC 15**
See also DLB 107

Robinson, Jill 1936-.............. **CLC 10**
See also CA 102; INT 102

Robinson, Kim Stanley 1952- ...... **CLC 34**
See also CA 126

Robinson, Lloyd
See Silverberg, Robert

Robinson, Marilynne 1944-........ **CLC 25**
See also CA 116

Robinson, Smokey................ **CLC 21**
See also Robinson, William, Jr.

Robinson, William, Jr. 1940-
See Robinson, Smokey
See also CA 116

Robison, Mary 1949-.......... **CLC 42, 98**
See also CA 113; 116; DLB 130; INT 116

Rod, Edouard 1857-1910 .... **TCLC 52**

Roddenberry, Eugene Wesley 1921-1991
See Roddenberry, Gene
See also CA 110; 135; CANR 37; SATA 45;
SATA-Obit 69

Roddenberry, Gene . . . . CLC 17
See also Roddenberry, Eugene Wesley
See also AAYA 5; SATA-Obit 69

Rodgers, Mary   1931- . . . . CLC 12
See also CA 49-52; CANR 8, 55; CLR 20;
INT CANR-8; JRDA; MAICYA;
SATA 8

Rodgers, W(illiam) R(obert)
1909-1969 . . . . CLC 7
See also CA 85-88; DLB 20

Rodman, Eric
See Silverberg, Robert

Rodman, Howard   1920(?)-1985 . . . . . CLC 65
See also CA 118

Rodman, Maia
See Wojciechowska, Maia (Teresa)

Rodriguez, Claudio   1934- . . . . CLC 10
See also DLB 134

Roelvaag, O(le) E(dvart)
1876-1931 . . . . TCLC 17
See also CA 117; DLB 9

Roethke, Theodore (Huebner)
1908-1963 . . . . . . CLC 1, 3, 8, 11, 19, 46,
101; DAM POET; PC 15
See also CA 81-84; CABS 2;
CDALB 1941-1968; DLB 5; MTCW

Rogers, Thomas Hunton   1927- . . . . . CLC 57
See also CA 89-92; INT 89-92

Rogers, Will(iam Penn Adair)
1879-1935 . . . TCLC 8, 71; DAM MULT
See also CA 105; 144; DLB 11; NNAL

Rogin, Gilbert   1929- . . . . CLC 18
See also CA 65-68; CANR 15

Rohan, Koda . . . . TCLC 22
See also Koda Shigeyuki

Rohlfs, Anna Katharine Green
See Green, Anna Katharine

Rohmer, Eric . . . . CLC 16
See also Scherer, Jean-Marie Maurice

Rohmer, Sax . . . . TCLC 28
See also Ward, Arthur Henry Sarsfield
See also DLB 70

Roiphe, Anne (Richardson)
1935- . . . . CLC 3, 9
See also CA 89-92; CANR 45; DLBY 80;
INT 89-92

Rojas, Fernando de   1465-1541 . . . . . . LC 23

Rolfe, Frederick (William Serafino Austin
Lewis Mary)   1860-1913 . . . . . . TCLC 12
See also CA 107; DLB 34, 156

Rolland, Romain   1866-1944 . . . . . . TCLC 23
See also CA 118; DLB 65

Rolle, Richard   c. 1300-c. 1349 . . . CMLC 21
See also DLB 146

Rolvaag, O(le) E(dvart)
See Roelvaag, O(le) E(dvart)

Romain Arnaud, Saint
See Aragon, Louis

Romains, Jules   1885-1972 . . . . CLC 7
See also CA 85-88; CANR 34; DLB 65;
MTCW

Romero, Jose Ruben   1890-1952 . . . TCLC 14
See also CA 114; 131; HW

Ronsard, Pierre de
1524-1585 . . . . LC 6; PC 11

Rooke, Leon
1934- . . . . CLC 25, 34; DAM POP
See also CA 25-28R; CANR 23, 53

Roosevelt, Theodore   1858-1919 . . . . TCLC 69
See also CA 115; DLB 47

Roper, William   1498-1578 . . . . LC 10

Roquelaure, A. N.
See Rice, Anne

Rosa, Joao Guimaraes   1908-1967 . . . CLC 23
See also CA 89-92; DLB 113

Rose, Wendy
1948- . . . . CLC 85; DAM MULT; PC 13
See also CA 53-56; CANR 5, 51; DLB 175;
NNAL; SATA 12

Rosen, R. D.
See Rosen, Richard (Dean)

Rosen, Richard (Dean)   1949- . . . . CLC 39
See also CA 77-80; CANR 62;
INT CANR-30

Rosenberg, Isaac   1890-1918 . . . . . . TCLC 12
See also CA 107; DLB 20

Rosenblatt, Joe . . . . CLC 15
See also Rosenblatt, Joseph

Rosenblatt, Joseph   1933-
See Rosenblatt, Joe
See also CA 89-92; INT 89-92

Rosenfeld, Samuel   1896-1963
See Tzara, Tristan
See also CA 89-92

Rosenstock, Sami
See Tzara, Tristan

Rosenstock, Samuel
See Tzara, Tristan

Rosenthal, M(acha) L(ouis)
1917-1996 . . . . CLC 28
See also CA 1-4R; 152; CAAS 6; CANR 4,
51; DLB 5; SATA 59

Ross, Barnaby
See Dannay, Frederic

Ross, Bernard L.
See Follett, Ken(neth Martin)

Ross, J. H.
See Lawrence, T(homas) E(dward)

Ross, Martin
See Martin, Violet Florence
See also DLB 135

Ross, (James) Sinclair
1908- . . . . . . CLC 13; DAC; DAM MST;
SSC 24
See also CA 73-76; DLB 88

Rossetti, Christina (Georgina)
1830-1894 . . . . NCLC 2, 50, 66; DA;
DAB; DAC; DAM MST, POET; PC 7;
WLC
See also DLB 35, 163; MAICYA; SATA 20

Rossetti, Dante Gabriel
1828-1882 . . . . NCLC 4; DA; DAB;
DAC; DAM MST, POET; WLC
See also CDBLB 1832-1890; DLB 35

Rossner, Judith (Perelman)
1935- . . . . CLC 6, 9, 29
See also AITN 2; BEST 90:3; CA 17-20R;
CANR 18, 51; DLB 6; INT CANR-18;
MTCW

Rostand, Edmond (Eugene Alexis)
1868-1918 . . . . . . TCLC 6, 37; DA; DAB;
DAC; DAM DRAM, MST
See also CA 104; 126; MTCW

Roth, Henry   1906-1995 . . . CLC 2, 6, 11, 104
See also CA 11-12; 149; CANR 38; CAP 1;
DLB 28; MTCW

Roth, Philip (Milton)
1933- . . . . . . CLC 1, 2, 3, 4, 6, 9, 15, 22,
31, 47, 66, 86; DA; DAB; DAC;
DAM MST, NOV, POP; SSC 26; WLC
See also BEST 90:3; CA 1-4R; CANR 1, 22,
36, 55; CDALB 1968-1988; DLB 2, 28,
173; DLBY 82; MTCW

Rothenberg, Jerome   1931- . . . . CLC 6, 57
See also CA 45-48; CANR 1; DLB 5

Roumain, Jacques (Jean Baptiste)
1907-1944 . . . . TCLC 19; BLC;
DAM MULT
See also BW 1; CA 117; 125

Rourke, Constance (Mayfield)
1885-1941 . . . . TCLC 12
See also CA 107; YABC 1

Rousseau, Jean-Baptiste   1671-1741 . . . LC 9

Rousseau, Jean-Jacques
1712-1778 . . . . LC 14, 36; DA; DAB;
DAC; DAM MST; WLC

Roussel, Raymond   1877-1933 . . . . . TCLC 20
See also CA 117

Rovit, Earl (Herbert)   1927- . . . . CLC 7
See also CA 5-8R; CANR 12

Rowe, Nicholas   1674-1718 . . . . LC 8
See also DLB 84

Rowley, Ames Dorrance
See Lovecraft, H(oward) P(hillips)

Rowson, Susanna Haswell
1762(?)-1824 . . . . NCLC 5
See also DLB 37

Roy, Gabrielle
1909-1983 . . . . CLC 10, 14; DAB; DAC;
DAM MST
See also CA 53-56; 110; CANR 5, 61;
DLB 68; MTCW

Rozewicz, Tadeusz
1921- . . . . CLC 9, 23; DAM POET
See also CA 108; CANR 36; MTCW

Ruark, Gibbons   1941- . . . . CLC 3
See also CA 33-36R; CAAS 23; CANR 14,
31, 57; DLB 120

Rubens, Bernice (Ruth)   1923- . . . CLC 19, 31
See also CA 25-28R; CANR 33; DLB 14;
MTCW

Rubin, Harold
See Robbins, Harold

Rudkin, (James) David   1936- . . . . . . CLC 14
See also CA 89-92; DLB 13

Rudnik, Raphael   1933- . . . . CLC 7
See also CA 29-32R

Ruffian, M.
See Hasek, Jaroslav (Matej Frantisek)

Ruiz, Jose Martinez . . . . CLC 11
See also Martinez Ruiz, Jose

Rukeyser, Muriel
1913-1980 . . . . **CLC 6, 10, 15, 27;**
DAM POET; PC 12
See also CA 5-8R; 93-96; CANR 26, 60;
DLB 48; MTCW; SATA-Obit 22

Rule, Jane (Vance) 1931- . . . . CLC 27
See also CA 25-28R; CAAS 18; CANR 12;
DLB 60

Rulfo, Juan
1918-1986 . . . . **CLC 8, 80; DAM MULT;**
HLC; SSC 25
See also CA 85-88; 118; CANR 26;
DLB 113; HW; MTCW

Rumi, Jalal al-Din 1297-1373 . . . . **CMLC 20**

Runeberg, Johan 1804-1877 . . . . . . **NCLC 41**

Runyon, (Alfred) Damon
1884(?)-1946 . . . . **TCLC 10**
See also CA 107; DLB 11, 86, 171

Rush, Norman 1933- . . . . CLC 44
See also CA 121; 126; INT 126

Rushdie, (Ahmed) Salman
1947- . . . . **CLC 23, 31, 55, 100; DAB;**
DAC; DAM MST, NOV, POP; WLCS
See also BEST 89:3; CA 108; 111;
CANR 33, 56; INT 111; MTCW

Rushforth, Peter (Scott) 1945- . . . . . CLC 19
See also CA 101

Ruskin, John 1819-1900 . . . . TCLC 63
See also CA 114; 129; CDBLB 1832-1890;
DLB 55, 163; SATA 24

Russ, Joanna 1937- . . . . CLC 15
See also CA 25-28R; CANR 11, 31; DLB 8;
MTCW

Russell, George William 1867-1935
See Baker, Jean H.
See also CA 104; 153; CDBLB 1890-1914;
DAM POET

Russell, (Henry) Ken(neth Alfred)
1927- . . . . CLC 16
See also CA 105

Russell, Willy 1947- . . . . CLC 60

Rutherford, Mark . . . . TCLC 25
See also White, William Hale
See also DLB 18

Ruyslinck, Ward 1929- . . . . CLC 14
See also Belser, Reimond Karel Maria de

Ryan, Cornelius (John) 1920-1974 . . . CLC 7
See also CA 69-72; 53-56; CANR 38

Ryan, Michael 1946- . . . . CLC 65
See also CA 49-52; DLBY 82

Ryan, Tim
See Dent, Lester

Rybakov, Anatoli (Naumovich)
1911- . . . . CLC 23, 53
See also CA 126; 135; SATA 79

Ryder, Jonathan
See Ludlum, Robert

Ryga, George
1932-1987 . . **CLC 14; DAC; DAM MST**
See also CA 101; 124; CANR 43; DLB 60

S. H.
See Hartmann, Sadakichi

S. S.
See Sassoon, Siegfried (Lorraine)

Saba, Umberto 1883-1957 . . . . TCLC 33
See also CA 144; DLB 114

Sabatini, Rafael 1875-1950 . . . . TCLC 47

Sabato, Ernesto (R.)
1911- . . . . **CLC 10, 23; DAM MULT;**
HLC
See also CA 97-100; CANR 32; DLB 145;
HW; MTCW

Sacastru, Martin
See Bioy Casares, Adolfo

Sacher-Masoch, Leopold von
1836(?)-1895 . . . . **NCLC 31**

Sachs, Marilyn (Stickle) 1927- . . . . . CLC 35
See also AAYA 2; CA 17-20R; CANR 13,
47; CLR 2; JRDA; MAICYA; SAAS 2;
SATA 3, 68

Sachs, Nelly 1891-1970 . . . . CLC 14, 98
See also CA 17-18; 25-28R; CAP 2

Sackler, Howard (Oliver)
1929-1982 . . . . CLC 14
See also CA 61-64; 108; CANR 30; DLB 7

Sacks, Oliver (Wolf) 1933- . . . . CLC 67
See also CA 53-56; CANR 28, 50;
INT CANR-28; MTCW

Sadakichi
See Hartmann, Sadakichi

Sade, Donatien Alphonse Francois Comte
1740-1814 . . . . **NCLC 47**

Sadoff, Ira 1945- . . . . CLC 9
See also CA 53-56; CANR 5, 21; DLB 120

Saetone
See Camus, Albert

Safire, William 1929- . . . . CLC 10
See also CA 17-20R; CANR 31, 54

Sagan, Carl (Edward) 1934-1996 . . . . CLC 30
See also AAYA 2; CA 25-28R; 155;
CANR 11, 36; MTCW; SATA 58;
SATA-Obit 94

Sagan, Francoise . . . . CLC 3, 6, 9, 17, 36
See also Quoirez, Francoise
See also DLB 83

Sahgal, Nayantara (Pandit) 1927- . . . CLC 41
See also CA 9-12R; CANR 11

Saint, H(arry) F. 1941- . . . . CLC 50
See also CA 127

St. Aubin de Teran, Lisa 1953-
See Teran, Lisa St. Aubin de
See also CA 118; 126; INT 126

Saint Birgitta of Sweden
c. 1303-1373 . . . . **CMLC 24**

Sainte-Beuve, Charles Augustin
1804-1869 . . . . **NCLC 5**

Saint-Exupery, Antoine (Jean Baptiste Marie
Roger) de
1900-1944 . . . . **TCLC 2, 56; DAM NOV;**
WLC
See also CA 108; 132; CLR 10; DLB 72;
MAICYA; MTCW; SATA 20

St. John, David
See Hunt, E(verette) Howard, (Jr.)

Saint-John Perse
See Leger, (Marie-Rene Auguste) Alexis
Saint-Leger

Saintsbury, George (Edward Bateman)
1845-1933 . . . . TCLC 31
See also CA 160; DLB 57, 149

Sait Faik . . . . TCLC 23
See also Abasiyanik, Sait Faik

Saki . . . . TCLC 3; SSC 12
See also Munro, H(ector) H(ugh)

Sala, George Augustus . . . . NCLC 46

Salama, Hannu 1936- . . . . CLC 18

Salamanca, J(ack) R(ichard)
1922- . . . . CLC 4, 15
See also CA 25-28R

Sale, J. Kirkpatrick
See Sale, Kirkpatrick

Sale, Kirkpatrick 1937- . . . . CLC 68
See also CA 13-16R; CANR 10

Salinas, Luis Omar
1937- . . . . . **CLC 90; DAM MULT; HLC**
See also CA 131; DLB 82; HW

Salinas (y Serrano), Pedro
1891(?)-1951 . . . . TCLC 17
See also CA 117; DLB 134

Salinger, J(erome) D(avid)
1919- . . . . . . **CLC 1, 3, 8, 12, 55, 56; DA;**
DAB; DAC; DAM MST, NOV, POP;
SSC 2, 28; WLC
See also AAYA 2; CA 5-8R; CANR 39;
CDALB 1941-1968; CLR 18; DLB 2, 102,
173; MAICYA; MTCW; SATA 67

Salisbury, John
See Caute, David

Salter, James 1925- . . . . CLC 7, 52, 59
See also CA 73-76; DLB 130

Saltus, Edgar (Everton)
1855-1921 . . . . TCLC 8
See also CA 105

Saltykov, Mikhail Evgrafovich
1826-1889 . . . . **NCLC 16**

Samarakis, Antonis 1919- . . . . CLC 5
See also CA 25-28R; CAAS 16; CANR 36

Sanchez, Florencio 1875-1910 . . . . . TCLC 37
See also CA 153; HW

Sanchez, Luis Rafael 1936- . . . . CLC 23
See also CA 128; DLB 145; HW

Sanchez, Sonia
1934- . . . . . . **CLC 5; BLC; DAM MULT;**
PC 9
See also BW 2; CA 33-36R; CANR 24, 49;
CLR 18; DLB 41; DLBD 8; MAICYA;
MTCW; SATA 22

Sand, George
1804-1876 . . . . **NCLC 2, 42, 57; DA;**
DAB; DAC; DAM MST, NOV; WLC
See also DLB 119

Sandburg, Carl (August)
1878-1967 . . . . **CLC 1, 4, 10, 15, 35; DA;**
DAB; DAC; DAM MST, POET; PC 2;
WLC
See also CA 5-8R; 25-28R; CANR 35;
CDALB 1865-1917; DLB 17, 54;
MAICYA; MTCW; SATA 8

Sandburg, Charles
　See Sandburg, Carl (August)

Sandburg, Charles A.
　See Sandburg, Carl (August)

Sanders, (James) Ed(ward)　1939- . . .　**CLC 53**
　See also CA 13-16R; CAAS 21; CANR 13,
　44; DLB 16

Sanders, Lawrence
　1920- . . . .　**CLC 41; DAM POP**
　See also BEST 89:4; CA 81-84; CANR 33,
　62; MTCW

Sanders, Noah
　See Blount, Roy (Alton), Jr.

Sanders, Winston P.
　See Anderson, Poul (William)

Sandoz, Mari(e Susette)
　1896-1966 . . . .　**CLC 28**
　See also CA 1-4R; 25-28R; CANR 17;
　DLB 9; MTCW; SATA 5

Saner, Reg(inald Anthony)　1931- . . . .　**CLC 9**
　See also CA 65-68

Sannazaro, Jacopo　1456(?)-1530 . . . . . .　**LC 8**

Sansom, William
　1912-1976 . . . . . .　**CLC 2, 6; DAM NOV;**
　　　　　　　　　　　　　　　　　　　　SSC 21
　See also CA 5-8R; 65-68; CANR 42;
　DLB 139; MTCW

Santayana, George　1863-1952 . . . . .　**TCLC 40**
　See also CA 115; DLB 54, 71; DLBD 13

Santiago, Danny . . . .　**CLC 33**
　See also James, Daniel (Lewis)
　See also DLB 122

Santmyer, Helen Hoover
　1895-1986 . . . .　**CLC 33**
　See also CA 1-4R; 118; CANR 15, 33;
　DLBY 84; MTCW

Santoka, Taneda　1882-1940 . . . . . .　**TCLC 72**

Santos, Bienvenido N(uqui)
　1911-1996 . . . . . .　**CLC 22; DAM MULT**
　See also CA 101; 151; CANR 19, 46

Sapper . . . .　**TCLC 44**
　See also McNeile, Herman Cyril

Sapphire　1950- . . . .　**CLC 99**

Sappho
　fl. 6th cent. B.C.- . . . .　**CMLC 3;**
　　　　　　　　　　　　　　　　DAM POET; PC 5
　See also DLB 176

Sarduy, Severo　1937-1993 . . . .　**CLC 6, 97**
　See also CA 89-92; 142; CANR 58;
　DLB 113; HW

Sargeson, Frank　1903-1982 . . . .　**CLC 31**
　See also CA 25-28R; 106; CANR 38

Sarmiento, Felix Ruben Garcia
　See Dario, Ruben

Saroyan, William
　1908-1981 . . . . .　**CLC 1, 8, 10, 29, 34, 56;**
　　　　　　　DA; DAB; DAC; DAM DRAM, MST,
　　　　　　　　　　　　　　NOV; SSC 21; WLC
　See also CA 5-8R; 103; CANR 30; DLB 7,
　9, 86; DLBY 81; MTCW; SATA 23;
　SATA-Obit 24

Sarraute, Nathalie
　1900- . . . .　**CLC 1, 2, 4, 8, 10, 31, 80**
　See also CA 9-12R; CANR 23; DLB 83;
　MTCW

Sarton, (Eleanor) May
　1912-1995 . . . .　**CLC 4, 14, 49, 91;**
　　　　　　　　　　　　　　　　　　　　DAM POET
　See also CA 1-4R; 149; CANR 34, 55;
　DLB 48; DLBY 81; INT CANR-34;
　MTCW; SATA 36; SATA-Obit 86

Sartre, Jean-Paul
　1905-1980 . . . .　**CLC 1, 4, 7, 9, 13, 18, 24,**
　　　　　　　44, 50, 52; DA; DAB; DAC;
　　　　　　　DAM DRAM, MST, NOV; DC 3; WLC
　See also CA 9-12R; 97-100; CANR 21;
　DLB 72; MTCW

Sassoon, Siegfried (Lorraine)
　1886-1967 . . . .　**CLC 36; DAB;**
　　　　　　　　　DAM MST, NOV, POET; PC 12
　See also CA 104; 25-28R; CANR 36;
　DLB 20; MTCW

Satterfield, Charles
　See Pohl, Frederik

Saul, John (W. III)
　1942- . . . . . .　**CLC 46; DAM NOV, POP**
　See also AAYA 10; BEST 90:4; CA 81-84;
　CANR 16, 40

Saunders, Caleb
　See Heinlein, Robert A(nson)

Saura (Atares), Carlos　1932- . . . .　**CLC 20**
　See also CA 114; 131; HW

Sauser-Hall, Frederic　1887-1961 . . . .　**CLC 18**
　See also Cendrars, Blaise
　See also CA 102; 93-96; CANR 36, 62;
　MTCW

Saussure, Ferdinand de
　1857-1913 . . . .　**TCLC 49**

Savage, Catharine
　See Brosman, Catharine Savage

Savage, Thomas　1915- . . . .　**CLC 40**
　See also CA 126; 132; CAAS 15; INT 132

Savan, Glenn　19(?)- . . . .　**CLC 50**

Sayers, Dorothy L(eigh)
　1893-1957 . . . . .　**TCLC 2, 15; DAM POP**
　See also CA 104; 119; CANR 60;
　CDBLB 1914-1945; DLB 10, 36, 77, 100;
　MTCW

Sayers, Valerie　1952- . . . .　**CLC 50**
　See also CA 134; CANR 61

Sayles, John (Thomas)
　1950- . . . .　**CLC 7, 10, 14**
　See also CA 57-60; CANR 41; DLB 44

Scammell, Michael　1935- . . . .　**CLC 34**
　See also CA 156

Scannell, Vernon　1922- . . . .　**CLC 49**
　See also CA 5-8R; CANR 8, 24, 57;
　DLB 27; SATA 59

Scarlett, Susan
　See Streatfeild, (Mary) Noel

Schaeffer, Susan Fromberg
　1941- . . . .　**CLC 6, 11, 22**
　See also CA 49-52; CANR 18; DLB 28;
　MTCW; SATA 22

Schary, Jill
　See Robinson, Jill

Schell, Jonathan　1943- . . . .　**CLC 35**
　See also CA 73-76; CANR 12

Schelling, Friedrich Wilhelm Joseph von
　1775-1854 . . . .　**NCLC 30**
　See also DLB 90

Schendel, Arthur van　1874-1946 . . .　**TCLC 56**

Scherer, Jean-Marie Maurice　1920-
　See Rohmer, Eric
　See also CA 110

Schevill, James (Erwin)　1920- . . . .　**CLC 7**
　See also CA 5-8R; CAAS 12

Schiller, Friedrich
　1759-1805 . . . .　**NCLC 39; DAM DRAM**
　See also DLB 94

Schisgal, Murray (Joseph)　1926- . . . . .　**CLC 6**
　See also CA 21-24R; CANR 48

Schlee, Ann　1934- . . . .　**CLC 35**
　See also CA 101; CANR 29; SATA 44;
　SATA-Brief 36

Schlegel, August Wilhelm von
　1767-1845 . . . .　**NCLC 15**
　See also DLB 94

Schlegel, Friedrich　1772-1829 . . . .　**NCLC 45**
　See also DLB 90

Schlegel, Johann Elias (von)
　1719(?)-1749 . . . .　**LC 5**

Schlesinger, Arthur M(eier), Jr.
　1917- . . . .　**CLC 84**
　See also AITN 1; CA 1-4R; CANR 1, 28,
　58; DLB 17; INT CANR-28; MTCW;
　SATA 61

Schmidt, Arno (Otto)　1914-1979 . . . .　**CLC 56**
　See also CA 128; 109; DLB 69

Schmitz, Aron Hector　1861-1928
　See Svevo, Italo
　See also CA 104; 122; MTCW

Schnackenberg, Gjertrud　1953- . . . . .　**CLC 40**
　See also CA 116; DLB 120

Schneider, Leonard Alfred　1925-1966
　See Bruce, Lenny
　See also CA 89-92

Schnitzler, Arthur
　1862-1931 . . . .　**TCLC 4; SSC 15**
　See also CA 104; DLB 81, 118

Schoenberg, Arnold　1874-1951 . . . .　**TCLC 75**
　See also CA 109

Schonberg, Arnold
　See Schoenberg, Arnold

Schopenhauer, Arthur
　1788-1860 . . . .　**NCLC 51**
　See also DLB 90

Schor, Sandra (M.)　1932(?)-1990 . . .　**CLC 65**
　See also CA 132

Schorer, Mark　1908-1977 . . . .　**CLC 9**
　See also CA 5-8R; 73-76; CANR 7;
　DLB 103

Schrader, Paul (Joseph)　1946- . . . . . .　**CLC 26**
　See also CA 37-40R; CANR 41; DLB 44

Schreiner, Olive (Emilie Albertina)
　1855-1920 . . . .　**TCLC 9**
　See also CA 105; DLB 18, 156

Schulberg, Budd (Wilson)
　1914- . . . .　**CLC 7, 48**
　See also CA 25-28R; CANR 19; DLB 6, 26,
　28; DLBY 81

Schulz, Bruno
1892-1942 . . . . **TCLC 5, 51; SSC 13**
See also CA 115; 123

Schulz, Charles M(onroe) 1922- . . . . **CLC 12**
See also CA 9-12R; CANR 6;
INT CANR-6; SATA 10

Schumacher, E(rnst) F(riedrich)
1911-1977 . . . . **CLC 80**
See also CA 81-84; 73-76; CANR 34

Schuyler, James Marcus
1923-1991 . . . . . **CLC 5, 23; DAM POET**
See also CA 101; 134; DLB 5, 169; INT 101

Schwartz, Delmore (David)
1913-1966 . . . **CLC 2, 4, 10, 45, 87; PC 8**
See also CA 17-18; 25-28R; CANR 35;
CAP 2; DLB 28, 48; MTCW

Schwartz, Ernst
See Ozu, Yasujiro

Schwartz, John Burnham 1965- . . . . **CLC 59**
See also CA 132

Schwartz, Lynne Sharon 1939- . . . . . **CLC 31**
See also CA 103; CANR 44

Schwartz, Muriel A.
See Eliot, T(homas) S(tearns)

Schwarz-Bart, Andre 1928- . . . . **CLC 2, 4**
See also CA 89-92

Schwarz-Bart, Simone 1938- . . . . **CLC 7**
See also BW 2; CA 97-100

Schwob, (Mayer Andre) Marcel
1867-1905 . . . . **TCLC 20**
See also CA 117; DLB 123

Sciascia, Leonardo
1921-1989 . . . . **CLC 8, 9, 41**
See also CA 85-88; 130; CANR 35;
DLB 177; MTCW

Scoppettone, Sandra 1936- . . . . **CLC 26**
See also AAYA 11; CA 5-8R; CANR 41;
SATA 9, 92

Scorsese, Martin 1942- . . . . **CLC 20, 89**
See also CA 110; 114; CANR 46

Scotland, Jay
See Jakes, John (William)

Scott, Duncan Campbell
1862-1947 . . . . **TCLC 6; DAC**
See also CA 104; 153; DLB 92

Scott, Evelyn 1893-1963 . . . . **CLC 43**
See also CA 104; 112; DLB 9, 48

Scott, F(rancis) R(eginald)
1899-1985 . . . . **CLC 22**
See also CA 101; 114; DLB 88; INT 101

Scott, Frank
See Scott, F(rancis) R(eginald)

Scott, Joanna 1960- . . . . **CLC 50**
See also CA 126; CANR 53

Scott, Paul (Mark) 1920-1978 . . . . **CLC 9, 60**
See also CA 81-84; 77-80; CANR 33;
DLB 14; MTCW

Scott, Walter
1771-1832 . . . . **NCLC 15; DA; DAB;**
DAC; DAM MST, NOV, POET; PC 13;
WLC
See also AAYA 22; CDBLB 1789-1832;
DLB 93, 107, 116, 144, 159; YABC 2

Scribe, (Augustin) Eugene
1791-1861 . . . . **NCLC 16; DAM DRAM;**
DC 5

Scrum, R.
See Crumb, R(obert)

Scudery, Madeleine de 1607-1701 . . . . . **LC 2**

Scum
See Crumb, R(obert)

Scumbag, Little Bobby
See Crumb, R(obert)

Seabrook, John
See Hubbard, L(afayette) Ron(ald)

Sealy, I. Allan 1951- . . . . **CLC 55**

Search, Alexander
See Pessoa, Fernando (Antonio Nogueira)

Sebastian, Lee
See Silverberg, Robert

Sebastian Owl
See Thompson, Hunter S(tockton)

Sebestyen, Ouida 1924- . . . . **CLC 30**
See also AAYA 8; CA 107; CANR 40;
CLR 17; JRDA; MAICYA; SAAS 10;
SATA 39

Secundus, H. Scriblerus
See Fielding, Henry

Sedges, John
See Buck, Pearl S(ydenstricker)

Sedgwick, Catharine Maria
1789-1867 . . . . **NCLC 19**
See also DLB 1, 74

Seelye, John 1931- . . . . **CLC 7**

Seferiades, Giorgos Stylianou 1900-1971
See Seferis, George
See also CA 5-8R; 33-36R; CANR 5, 36;
MTCW

Seferis, George . . . . **CLC 5, 11**
See also Seferiades, Giorgos Stylianou

Segal, Erich (Wolf)
1937- . . . . **CLC 3, 10; DAM POP**
See also BEST 89:1; CA 25-28R; CANR 20,
36; DLBY 86; INT CANR-20; MTCW

Seger, Bob 1945- . . . . **CLC 35**

Seghers, Anna . . . . **CLC 7**
See also Radvanyi, Netty
See also DLB 69

Seidel, Frederick (Lewis) 1936- . . . . . **CLC 18**
See also CA 13-16R; CANR 8; DLBY 84

Seifert, Jaroslav
1901-1986 . . . . **CLC 34, 44, 93**
See also CA 127; MTCW

Sei Shonagon c. 966-1017(?) . . . . . . **CMLC 6**

Selby, Hubert, Jr.
1928- . . . . **CLC 1, 2, 4, 8; SSC 20**
See also CA 13-16R; CANR 33; DLB 2

Selzer, Richard 1928- . . . . **CLC 74**
See also CA 65-68; CANR 14

Sembene, Ousmane
See Ousmane, Sembene

Senancour, Etienne Pivert de
1770-1846 . . . . **NCLC 16**
See also DLB 119

Sender, Ramon (Jose)
1902-1982 . . **CLC 8; DAM MULT; HLC**
See also CA 5-8R; 105; CANR 8; HW;
MTCW

Seneca, Lucius Annaeus
4B.C.-65 . . . . . . **CMLC 6; DAM DRAM;**
DC 5

Senghor, Leopold Sedar
1906- . . . . . **CLC 54; BLC; DAM MULT,**
POET
See also BW 2; CA 116; 125; CANR 47;
MTCW

Serling, (Edward) Rod(man)
1924-1975 . . . . **CLC 30**
See also AAYA 14; AITN 1; CA 65-68;
57-60; DLB 26

Serna, Ramon Gomez de la
See Gomez de la Serna, Ramon

Serpieres
See Guillevic, (Eugene)

Service, Robert
See Service, Robert W(illiam)
See also DAB; DLB 92

Service, Robert W(illiam)
1874(?)-1958 . . . . . . **TCLC 15; DA; DAC;**
DAM MST, POET; WLC
See also Service, Robert
See also CA 115; 140; SATA 20

Seth, Vikram
1952- . . . . **CLC 43, 90; DAM MULT**
See also CA 121; 127; CANR 50; DLB 120;
INT 127

Seton, Cynthia Propper
1926-1982 . . . . **CLC 27**
See also CA 5-8R; 108; CANR 7

Seton, Ernest (Evan) Thompson
1860-1946 . . . . **TCLC 31**
See also CA 109; DLB 92; DLBD 13;
JRDA; SATA 18

Seton-Thompson, Ernest
See Seton, Ernest (Evan) Thompson

Settle, Mary Lee 1918- . . . . **CLC 19, 61**
See also CA 89-92; CAAS 1; CANR 44;
DLB 6; INT 89-92

Seuphor, Michel
See Arp, Jean

Sevigne, Marie (de Rabutin-Chantal) Marquise
de 1626-1696 . . . . **LC 11**

Sewall, Samuel 1652-1730 . . . . **LC 38**
See also DLB 24

Sexton, Anne (Harvey)
1928-1974 . . . . **CLC 2, 4, 6, 8, 10, 15, 53;**
DA; DAB; DAC; DAM MST, POET;
PC 2; WLC
See also CA 1-4R; 53-56; CABS 2;
CANR 3, 36; CDALB 1941-1968; DLB 5,
169; MTCW; SATA 10

Shaara, Michael (Joseph, Jr.)
1929-1988 . . . . **CLC 15; DAM POP**
See also AITN 1; CA 102; 125; CANR 52;
DLBY 83

Shackleton, C. C.
See Aldiss, Brian W(ilson)

Shacochis, Bob . . . . **CLC 39**
See also Shacochis, Robert G.

Shacochis, Robert G. 1951-
See Shacochis, Bob
See also CA 119; 124; INT 124

Shaffer, Anthony (Joshua)
1926- . . . . **CLC 19; DAM DRAM**
See also CA 110; 116; DLB 13

Shaffer, Peter (Levin)
1926- . . . . . . **CLC 5, 14, 18, 37, 60; DAB;**
DAM DRAM, MST; DC 7
See also CA 25-28R; CANR 25, 47;
CDBLB 1960 to Present; DLB 13;
MTCW

Shakey, Bernard
See Young, Neil

Shalamov, Varlam (Tikhonovich)
1907(?)-1982 . . . . **CLC 18**
See also CA 129; 105

Shamlu, Ahmad 1925- . . . . **CLC 10**

Shammas, Anton 1951-. . . . . **CLC 55**

Shange, Ntozake
1948- . . . . **CLC 8, 25, 38, 74; BLC;**
DAM DRAM, MULT; DC 3
See also AAYA 9; BW 2; CA 85-88;
CABS 3; CANR 27, 48; DLB 38; MTCW

Shanley, John Patrick 1950-. . . . . . . **CLC 75**
See also CA 128; 133

Shapcott, Thomas W(illiam) 1935- . . **CLC 38**
See also CA 69-72; CANR 49

Shapiro, Jane. . . . . **CLC 76**

Shapiro, Karl (Jay) 1913- . . **CLC 4, 8, 15, 53**
See also CA 1-4R; CAAS 6; CANR 1, 36;
DLB 48; MTCW

Sharp, William 1855-1905 . . . . **TCLC 39**
See also CA 160; DLB 156

Sharpe, Thomas Ridley 1928-
See Sharpe, Tom
See also CA 114; 122; INT 122

Sharpe, Tom. . . . . **CLC 36**
See also Sharpe, Thomas Ridley
See also DLB 14

Shaw, Bernard. . . . . **TCLC 45**
See also Shaw, George Bernard
See also BW 1

Shaw, G. Bernard
See Shaw, George Bernard

Shaw, George Bernard
1856-1950 . . . **TCLC 3, 9, 21; DA; DAB;**
DAC; DAM DRAM, MST; WLC
See also Shaw, Bernard
See also CA 104; 128; CDBLB 1914-1945;
DLB 10, 57; MTCW

Shaw, Henry Wheeler
1818-1885 . . . . **NCLC 15**
See also DLB 11

Shaw, Irwin
1913-1984 . . . . **CLC 7, 23, 34;**
DAM DRAM, POP
See also AITN 1; CA 13-16R; 112;
CANR 21; CDALB 1941-1968; DLB 6,
102; DLBY 84; MTCW

Shaw, Robert 1927-1978 . . . . **CLC 5**
See also AITN 1; CA 1-4R; 81-84;
CANR 4; DLB 13, 14

Shaw, T. E.
See Lawrence, T(homas) E(dward)

Shawn, Wallace 1943- . . . . **CLC 41**
See also CA 112

Shea, Lisa 1953-. . . . . **CLC 86**
See also CA 147

Sheed, Wilfrid (John Joseph)
1930- . . . . **CLC 2, 4, 10, 53**
See also CA 65-68; CANR 30; DLB 6;
MTCW

Sheldon, Alice Hastings Bradley
1915(?)-1987
See Tiptree, James, Jr.
See also CA 108; 122; CANR 34; INT 108;
MTCW

Sheldon, John
See Bloch, Robert (Albert)

Shelley, Mary Wollstonecraft (Godwin)
1797-1851 . . . . **NCLC 14, 59; DA; DAB;**
DAC; DAM MST, NOV; WLC
See also AAYA 20; CDBLB 1789-1832;
DLB 110, 116, 159, 178; SATA 29

Shelley, Percy Bysshe
1792-1822 . . . . **NCLC 18; DA; DAB;**
DAC; DAM MST, POET; PC 14; WLC
See also CDBLB 1789-1832; DLB 96, 110,
158

Shepard, Jim 1956-. . . . . **CLC 36**
See also CA 137; CANR 59; SATA 90

Shepard, Lucius 1947- . . . . **CLC 34**
See also CA 128; 141

Shepard, Sam
1943- . . . . **CLC 4, 6, 17, 34, 41, 44;**
DAM DRAM; DC 5
See also AAYA 1; CA 69-72; CABS 3;
CANR 22; DLB 7; MTCW

Shepherd, Michael
See Ludlum, Robert

Sherburne, Zoa (Morin) 1912-. . . . . . **CLC 30**
See also AAYA 13; CA 1-4R; CANR 3, 37;
MAICYA; SAAS 18; SATA 3

Sheridan, Frances 1724-1766. . . . . **LC 7**
See also DLB 39, 84

Sheridan, Richard Brinsley
1751-1816 . . . . **NCLC 5; DA; DAB;**
DAC; DAM DRAM, MST; DC 1; WLC
See also CDBLB 1660-1789; DLB 89

Sherman, Jonathan Marc. . . . . **CLC 55**

Sherman, Martin 1941(?)- . . . . **CLC 19**
See also CA 116; 123

Sherwin, Judith Johnson 1936-. . . **CLC 7, 15**
See also CA 25-28R; CANR 34

Sherwood, Frances 1940-. . . . . **CLC 81**
See also CA 146

Sherwood, Robert E(mmet)
1896-1955 . . . . . . **TCLC 3; DAM DRAM**
See also CA 104; 153; DLB 7, 26

Shestov, Lev 1866-1938. . . . . **TCLC 56**

Shevchenko, Taras 1814-1861 . . . . **NCLC 54**

Shiel, M(atthew) P(hipps)
1865-1947 . . . . **TCLC 8**
See also Holmes, Gordon
See also CA 106; 160; DLB 153

Shields, Carol 1935-. . . . . **CLC 91; DAC**
See also CA 81-84; CANR 51

Shields, David 1956-. . . . . **CLC 97**
See also CA 124; CANR 48

Shiga, Naoya 1883-1971. . . **CLC 33; SSC 23**
See also CA 101; 33-36R; DLB 180

Shilts, Randy 1951-1994 . . . . **CLC 85**
See also AAYA 19; CA 115; 127; 144;
CANR 45; INT 127

Shimazaki, Haruki 1872-1943
See Shimazaki Toson
See also CA 105; 134

Shimazaki Toson 1872-1943 . . . . **TCLC 5**
See also Shimazaki, Haruki
See also DLB 180

Sholokhov, Mikhail (Aleksandrovich)
1905-1984 . . . . **CLC 7, 15**
See also CA 101; 112; MTCW;
SATA-Obit 36

Shone, Patric
See Hanley, James

Shreve, Susan Richards 1939-. . . . . . **CLC 23**
See also CA 49-52; CAAS 5; CANR 5, 38;
MAICYA; SATA 46, 95; SATA-Brief 41

Shue, Larry
1946-1985 . . . . . . **CLC 52; DAM DRAM**
See also CA 145; 117

Shu-Jen, Chou 1881-1936
See Lu Hsun
See also CA 104

Shulman, Alix Kates 1932- . . . . . . **CLC 2, 10**
See also CA 29-32R; CANR 43; SATA 7

Shuster, Joe 1914- . . . . **CLC 21**

Shute, Nevil. **CLC 30**
See also Norway, Nevil Shute

Shuttle, Penelope (Diane) 1947- . . . . . **CLC 7**
See also CA 93-96; CANR 39; DLB 14, 40

Sidney, Mary 1561-1621 . . . . **LC 19, 39**

Sidney, Sir Philip
1554-1586 . . . . **LC 19, 39; DA; DAB;**
DAC; DAM MST, POET
See also CDBLB Before 1660; DLB 167

Siegel, Jerome 1914-1996 . . . . **CLC 21**
See also CA 116; 151

Siegel, Jerry
See Siegel, Jerome

Sienkiewicz, Henryk (Adam Alexander Pius)
1846-1916 . . . . **TCLC 3**
See also CA 104; 134

Sierra, Gregorio Martinez
See Martinez Sierra, Gregorio

Sierra, Maria (de la O'LeJarraga) Martinez
See Martinez Sierra, Maria (de la
O'LeJarraga)

Sigal, Clancy 1926-. . . . . **CLC 7**
See also CA 1-4R

Sigourney, Lydia Howard (Huntley)
1791-1865 . . . . **NCLC 21**
See also DLB 1, 42, 73

Siguenza y Gongora, Carlos de
1645-1700 . . . . **LC 8**

Sigurjonsson, Johann 1880-1919. . . **TCLC 27**

Sikelianos, Angelos 1884-1951 . . . . **TCLC 39**

Silkin, Jon 1930- . . . . **CLC 2, 6, 43**
See also CA 5-8R; CAAS 5; DLB 27

Smith, Alexander 1829-1867 . . . . . **NCLC 59**
See also DLB 32, 55

Smith, Anna Deavere 1950- . . . . **CLC 86**
See also CA 133

Smith, Betty (Wehner) 1896-1972 . . . **CLC 19**
See also CA 5-8R; 33-36R; DLBY 82;
SATA 6

Smith, Charlotte (Turner)
1749-1806 . . . . **NCLC 23**
See also DLB 39, 109

Smith, Clark Ashton 1893-1961 . . . . **CLC 43**
See also CA 143

Smith, Dave . . . . **CLC 22, 42**
See also Smith, David (Jeddie)
See also CAAS 7; DLB 5

Smith, David (Jeddie) 1942-
See Smith, Dave
See also CA 49-52; CANR 1, 59;
DAM POET

Smith, Florence Margaret 1902-1971
See Smith, Stevie
See also CA 17-18; 29-32R; CANR 35;
CAP 2; DAM POET; MTCW

Smith, Iain Crichton 1928- . . . . **CLC 64**
See also CA 21-24R; DLB 40, 139

Smith, John 1580(?)-1631 . . . . **LC 9**

Smith, Johnston
See Crane, Stephen (Townley)

Smith, Joseph, Jr. 1805-1844 . . . . **NCLC 53**

Smith, Lee 1944- . . . . **CLC 25, 73**
See also CA 114; 119; CANR 46; DLB 143;
DLBY 83; INT 119

Smith, Martin
See Smith, Martin Cruz

Smith, Martin Cruz
1942- . . . . . **CLC 25; DAM MULT, POP**
See also BEST 89:4; CA 85-88; CANR 6,
23, 43; INT CANR-23; NNAL

Smith, Mary-Ann Tirone 1944- . . . . . **CLC 39**
See also CA 118; 136

Smith, Patti 1946- . . . . **CLC 12**
See also CA 93-96

Smith, Pauline (Urmson)
1882-1959 . . . . **TCLC 25**

Smith, Rosamond
See Oates, Joyce Carol

Smith, Sheila Kaye
See Kaye-Smith, Sheila

Smith, Stevie . . . . . . **CLC 3, 8, 25, 44; PC 12**
See also Smith, Florence Margaret
See also DLB 20

Smith, Wilbur (Addison) 1933- . . . . . **CLC 33**
See also CA 13-16R; CANR 7, 46; MTCW

Smith, William Jay 1918- . . . . **CLC 6**
See also CA 5-8R; CANR 44; DLB 5;
MAICYA; SAAS 22; SATA 2, 68

Smith, Woodrow Wilson
See Kuttner, Henry

Smolenskin, Peretz 1842-1885 . . . . **NCLC 30**

Smollett, Tobias (George) 1721-1771 . . **LC 2**
See also CDBLB 1660-1789; DLB 39, 104

Snodgrass, W(illiam) D(e Witt)
1926- . . . . **CLC 2, 6, 10, 18, 68;
DAM POET**
See also CA 1-4R; CANR 6, 36; DLB 5;
MTCW

Snow, C(harles) P(ercy)
1905-1980 . . . . **CLC 1, 4, 6, 9, 13, 19;
DAM NOV**
See also CA 5-8R; 101; CANR 28;
CDBLB 1945-1960; DLB 15, 77; MTCW

Snow, Frances Compton
See Adams, Henry (Brooks)

Snyder, Gary (Sherman)
1930- . . **CLC 1, 2, 5, 9, 32; DAM POET**
See also CA 17-20R; CANR 30, 60; DLB 5,
16, 165

Snyder, Zilpha Keatley 1927- . . . . . . **CLC 17**
See also AAYA 15; CA 9-12R; CANR 38;
CLR 31; JRDA; MAICYA; SAAS 2;
SATA 1, 28, 75

Soares, Bernardo
See Pessoa, Fernando (Antonio Nogueira)

Sobh, A.
See Shamlu, Ahmad

Sobol, Joshua . . . . **CLC 60**

Soderberg, Hjalmar 1869-1941 . . . . **TCLC 39**

Sodergran, Edith (Irene)
See Soedergran, Edith (Irene)

Soedergran, Edith (Irene)
1892-1923 . . . . **TCLC 31**

Softly, Edgar
See Lovecraft, H(oward) P(hillips)

Softly, Edward
See Lovecraft, H(oward) P(hillips)

Sokolov, Raymond 1941- . . . . **CLC 7**
See also CA 85-88

Solo, Jay
See Ellison, Harlan (Jay)

Sologub, Fyodor . . . . **TCLC 9**
See also Teternikov, Fyodor Kuzmich

Solomons, Ikey Esquir
See Thackeray, William Makepeace

Solomos, Dionysios 1798-1857 . . . **NCLC 15**

Solwoska, Mara
See French, Marilyn

Solzhenitsyn, Aleksandr I(sayevich)
1918- . . . . . . **CLC 1, 2, 4, 7, 9, 10, 18, 26,
34, 78; DA; DAB; DAC; DAM MST,
NOV; WLC**
See also AITN 1; CA 69-72; CANR 40;
MTCW

Somers, Jane
See Lessing, Doris (May)

Somerville, Edith 1858-1949 . . . . . . **TCLC 51**
See also DLB 135

Somerville & Ross
See Martin, Violet Florence; Somerville,
Edith

Sommer, Scott 1951- . . . . **CLC 25**
See also CA 106

Sondheim, Stephen (Joshua)
1930- . . . . **CLC 30, 39; DAM DRAM**
See also AAYA 11; CA 103; CANR 47

Sontag, Susan
1933- . . . . **CLC 1, 2, 10, 13, 31, 105;
DAM POP**
See also CA 17-20R; CANR 25, 51; DLB 2,
67; MTCW

Sophocles
496(?)B.C.-406(?)B.C. . . . . . **CMLC 2; DA;
DAB; DAC; DAM DRAM, MST; DC 1;
WLCS**
See also DLB 176

Sordello 1189-1269 . . . . **CMLC 15**

Sorel, Julia
See Drexler, Rosalyn

Sorrentino, Gilbert
1929- . . . . **CLC 3, 7, 14, 22, 40**
See also CA 77-80; CANR 14, 33; DLB 5,
173; DLBY 80; INT CANR-14

Soto, Gary
1952- . . . . **CLC 32, 80; DAM MULT;
HLC**
See also AAYA 10; CA 119; 125;
CANR 50; CLR 38; DLB 82; HW;
INT 125; JRDA; SATA 80

Soupault, Philippe 1897-1990 . . . . . . **CLC 68**
See also CA 116; 147; 131

Souster, (Holmes) Raymond
1921- . . . **CLC 5, 14; DAC; DAM POET**
See also CA 13-16R; CAAS 14; CANR 13,
29, 53; DLB 88; SATA 63

Southern, Terry 1924(?)-1995 . . . . **CLC 7**
See also CA 1-4R; 150; CANR 1, 55;
DLB 2

Southey, Robert 1774-1843 . . . . **NCLC 8**
See also DLB 93, 107, 142; SATA 54

Southworth, Emma Dorothy Eliza Nevitte
1819-1899 . . . . **NCLC 26**

Souza, Ernest
See Scott, Evelyn

Soyinka, Wole
1934- . . . . **CLC 3, 5, 14, 36, 44; BLC;
DA; DAB; DAC; DAM DRAM, MST,
MULT; DC 2; WLC**
See also BW 2; CA 13-16R; CANR 27, 39;
DLB 125; MTCW

Spackman, W(illiam) M(ode)
1905-1990 . . . . **CLC 46**
See also CA 81-84; 132

Spacks, Barry (Bernard) 1931- . . . . . **CLC 14**
See also CA 154; CANR 33; DLB 105

Spanidou, Irini 1946- . . . . **CLC 44**

Spark, Muriel (Sarah)
1918- . . . . . **CLC 2, 3, 5, 8, 13, 18, 40, 94;
DAB; DAC; DAM MST, NOV; SSC 10**
See also CA 5-8R; CANR 12, 36;
CDBLB 1945-1960; DLB 15, 139;
INT CANR-12; MTCW

Spaulding, Douglas
See Bradbury, Ray (Douglas)

Spaulding, Leonard
See Bradbury, Ray (Douglas)

Spence, J. A. D.
See Eliot, T(homas) S(tearns)

Spencer, Elizabeth 1921- . . . . **CLC 22**
See also CA 13-16R; CANR 32; DLB 6;
MTCW; SATA 14

Summers, (Alphonsus Joseph-Mary Augustus) Montague 1880-1948 .... **TCLC 16**
See also CA 118

Sumner, Gordon Matthew 1951-.... **CLC 26**

Surtees, Robert Smith
1803-1864 .... **NCLC 14**
See also DLB 21

Susann, Jacqueline 1921-1974....... **CLC 3**
See also AITN 1; CA 65-68; 53-56; MTCW

Su Shih 1036-1101 .... **CMLC 15**

Suskind, Patrick
See Sueskind, Patrick
See also CA 145

Sutcliff, Rosemary
1920-1992 .... **CLC 26; DAB; DAC; DAM MST, POP**
See also AAYA 10; CA 5-8R; 139;
CANR 37; CLR 1, 37; JRDA; MAICYA;
SATA 6, 44, 78; SATA-Obit 73

Sutro, Alfred 1863-1933........... **TCLC 6**
See also CA 105; DLB 10

Sutton, Henry
See Slavitt, David R(ytman)

Svevo, Italo
1861-1928 .... **TCLC 2, 35; SSC 25**
See also Schmitz, Aron Hector

Swados, Elizabeth (A.) 1951-....... **CLC 12**
See also CA 97-100; CANR 49; INT 97-100

Swados, Harvey 1920-1972 .... **CLC 5**
See also CA 5-8R; 37-40R; CANR 6;
DLB 2

Swan, Gladys 1934- .... **CLC 69**
See also CA 101; CANR 17, 39

Swarthout, Glendon (Fred)
1918-1992 .... **CLC 35**
See also CA 1-4R; 139; CANR 1, 47;
SATA 26

Sweet, Sarah C.
See Jewett, (Theodora) Sarah Orne

Swenson, May
1919-1989 ..... **CLC 4, 14, 61, 106; DA; DAB; DAC; DAM MST, POET; PC 14**
See also CA 5-8R; 130; CANR 36, 61;
DLB 5; MTCW; SATA 15

Swift, Augustus
See Lovecraft, H(oward) P(hillips)

Swift, Graham (Colin) 1949- .... **CLC 41, 88**
See also CA 117; 122; CANR 46

Swift, Jonathan
1667-1745 ...... **LC 1; DA; DAB; DAC; DAM MST, NOV, POET; PC 9; WLC**
See also CDBLB 1660-1789; DLB 39, 95,
101; SATA 19

Swinburne, Algernon Charles
1837-1909 ...... **TCLC 8, 36; DA; DAB; DAC; DAM MST, POET; WLC**
See also CA 105; 140; CDBLB 1832-1890;
DLB 35, 57

Swinfen, Ann.................... **CLC 34**

Swinnerton, Frank Arthur
1884-1982 .... **CLC 31**
See also CA 108; DLB 34

Swithen, John
See King, Stephen (Edwin)

Sylvia
See Ashton-Warner, Sylvia (Constance)

Symmes, Robert Edward
See Duncan, Robert (Edward)

Symonds, John Addington
1840-1893 .... **NCLC 34**
See also DLB 57, 144

Symons, Arthur 1865-1945 .... **TCLC 11**
See also CA 107; DLB 19, 57, 149

Symons, Julian (Gustave)
1912-1994 .... **CLC 2, 14, 32**
See also CA 49-52; 147; CAAS 3; CANR 3,
33, 59; DLB 87, 155; DLBY 92; MTCW

Synge, (Edmund) J(ohn) M(illington)
1871-1909 .... **TCLC 6, 37; DAM DRAM; DC 2**
See also CA 104; 141; CDBLB 1890-1914;
DLB 10, 19

Syruc, J.
See Milosz, Czeslaw

Szirtes, George 1948-............. **CLC 46**
See also CA 109; CANR 27, 61

Szymborska, Wislawa 1923- .... **CLC 99**
See also CA 154; DLBY 96

T. O., Nik
See Annensky, Innokenty (Fyodorovich)

Tabori, George 1914-............. **CLC 19**
See also CA 49-52; CANR 4

Tagore, Rabindranath
1861-1941 .... **TCLC 3, 53; DAM DRAM, POET; PC 8**
See also CA 104; 120; MTCW

Taine, Hippolyte Adolphe
1828-1893 .... **NCLC 15**

Talese, Gay 1932-................. **CLC 37**
See also AITN 1; CA 1-4R; CANR 9, 58;
INT CANR-9; MTCW

Tallent, Elizabeth (Ann) 1954- ..... **CLC 45**
See also CA 117; DLB 130

Tally, Ted 1952-.................. **CLC 42**
See also CA 120; 124; INT 124

Tamayo y Baus, Manuel
1829-1898 .... **NCLC 1**

Tammsaare, A(nton) H(ansen)
1878-1940 .... **TCLC 27**

Tam'si, Tchicaya U
See Tchicaya, Gerald Felix

Tan, Amy (Ruth)
1952- .... **CLC 59; DAM MULT, NOV, POP**
See also AAYA 9; BEST 89:3; CA 136;
CANR 54; DLB 173; SATA 75

Tandem, Felix
See Spitteler, Carl (Friedrich Georg)

Tanizaki, Jun'ichiro
1886-1965 ...... **CLC 8, 14, 28; SSC 21**
See also CA 93-96; 25-28R; DLB 180

Tanner, William
See Amis, Kingsley (William)

Tao Lao
See Storni, Alfonsina

Tarassoff, Lev
See Troyat, Henri

Tarbell, Ida M(inerva)
1857-1944 .... **TCLC 40**
See also CA 122; DLB 47

Tarkington, (Newton) Booth
1869-1946 .... **TCLC 9**
See also CA 110; 143; DLB 9, 102;
SATA 17

Tarkovsky, Andrei (Arsenyevich)
1932-1986 .... **CLC 75**
See also CA 127

Tartt, Donna 1964(?)-............. **CLC 76**
See also CA 142

Tasso, Torquato 1544-1595 .... **LC 5**

Tate, (John Orley) Allen
1899-1979 .... **CLC 2, 4, 6, 9, 11, 14, 24**
See also CA 5-8R; 85-88; CANR 32;
DLB 4, 45, 63; MTCW

Tate, Ellalice
See Hibbert, Eleanor Alice Burford

Tate, James (Vincent) 1943- ... **CLC 2, 6, 25**
See also CA 21-24R; CANR 29, 57; DLB 5,
169

Tavel, Ronald 1940-............... **CLC 6**
See also CA 21-24R; CANR 33

Taylor, C(ecil) P(hilip) 1929-1981... **CLC 27**
See also CA 25-28R; 105; CANR 47

Taylor, Edward
1642(?)-1729 .... **LC 11; DA; DAB; DAC; DAM MST, POET**
See also DLB 24

Taylor, Eleanor Ross 1920-......... **CLC 5**
See also CA 81-84

Taylor, Elizabeth 1912-1975 ... **CLC 2, 4, 29**
See also CA 13-16R; CANR 9; DLB 139;
MTCW; SATA 13

Taylor, Frederick Winslow
1856-1915 .... **TCLC 76**

Taylor, Henry (Splawn) 1942-...... **CLC 44**
See also CA 33-36R; CAAS 7; CANR 31;
DLB 5

Taylor, Kamala (Purnaiya) 1924-
See Markandaya, Kamala
See also CA 77-80

Taylor, Mildred D. .... **CLC 21**
See also AAYA 10; BW 1; CA 85-88;
CANR 25; CLR 9; DLB 52; JRDA;
MAICYA; SAAS 5; SATA 15, 70

Taylor, Peter (Hillsman)
1917-1994 ..... **CLC 1, 4, 18, 37, 44, 50, 71; SSC 10**
See also CA 13-16R; 147; CANR 9, 50;
DLBY 81, 94; INT CANR-9; MTCW

Taylor, Robert Lewis 1912-....... **CLC 14**
See also CA 1-4R; CANR 3; SATA 10

Tchekhov, Anton
See Chekhov, Anton (Pavlovich)

Tchicaya, Gerald Felix
1931-1988 .... **CLC 101**
See also CA 129; 125

Tchicaya U Tam'si
See Tchicaya, Gerald Felix

Teasdale, Sara 1884-1933.......... **TCLC 4**
See also CA 104; DLB 45; SATA 32

Tegner, Esaias 1782-1846........ **NCLC 2**

Teilhard de Chardin, (Marie Joseph) Pierre
1881-1955 .... **TCLC 9**
See also CA 105

Temple, Ann
See Mortimer, Penelope (Ruth)

Tennant, Emma (Christina)
1937- .... **CLC 13, 52**
See also CA 65-68; CAAS 9; CANR 10, 38, 59; DLB 14

Tenneshaw, S. M.
See Silverberg, Robert

Tennyson, Alfred
1809-1892 .... **NCLC 30, 65; DA; DAB; DAC; DAM MST, POET; PC 6; WLC**
See also CDBLB 1832-1890; DLB 32

Teran, Lisa St. Aubin de .... **CLC 36**
See also St. Aubin de Teran, Lisa

Terence
195(?)B.C.-159B.C..... **CMLC 14; DC 7**

Teresa de Jesus, St.   1515-1582 ...... **LC 18**

Terkel, Louis   1912-
See Terkel, Studs
See also CA 57-60; CANR 18, 45; MTCW

Terkel, Studs .... **CLC 38**
See also Terkel, Louis
See also AITN 1

Terry, C. V.
See Slaughter, Frank G(ill)

Terry, Megan   1932- .... **CLC 19**
See also CA 77-80; CABS 3; CANR 43; DLB 7

Tertz, Abram
See Sinyavsky, Andrei (Donatevich)

Tesich, Steve   1943(?)-1996...... **CLC 40, 69**
See also CA 105; 152; DLBY 83

Teternikov, Fyodor Kuzmich   1863-1927
See Sologub, Fyodor
See also CA 104

Tevis, Walter   1928-1984 .... **CLC 42**
See also CA 113

Tey, Josephine .... **TCLC 14**
See also Mackintosh, Elizabeth
See also DLB 77

Thackeray, William Makepeace
1811-1863 .... **NCLC 5, 14, 22, 43; DA; DAB; DAC; DAM MST, NOV; WLC**
See also CDBLB 1832-1890; DLB 21, 55, 159, 163; SATA 23

Thakura, Ravindranatha
See Tagore, Rabindranath

Tharoor, Shashi   1956- .... **CLC 70**
See also CA 141

Thelwell, Michael Miles   1939- ..... **CLC 22**
See also BW 2; CA 101

Theobald, Lewis, Jr.
See Lovecraft, H(oward) P(hillips)

Theodorescu, Ion N.   1880-1967
See Arghezi, Tudor
See also CA 116

Theriault, Yves
1915-1983 .. **CLC 79; DAC; DAM MST**
See also CA 102; DLB 88

Theroux, Alexander (Louis)
1939- .... **CLC 2, 25**
See also CA 85-88; CANR 20

Theroux, Paul (Edward)
1941- .... **CLC 5, 8, 11, 15, 28, 46; DAM POP**
See also BEST 89:4; CA 33-36R; CANR 20, 45; DLB 2; MTCW; SATA 44

Thesen, Sharon   1946- .... **CLC 56**

Thevenin, Denis
See Duhamel, Georges

Thibault, Jacques Anatole Francois
1844-1924
See France, Anatole
See also CA 106; 127; DAM NOV; MTCW

Thiele, Colin (Milton)   1920- .... **CLC 17**
See also CA 29-32R; CANR 12, 28, 53; CLR 27; MAICYA; SAAS 2; SATA 14, 72

Thomas, Audrey (Callahan)
1935- .... **CLC 7, 13, 37; SSC 20**
See also AITN 2; CA 21-24R; CAAS 19; CANR 36, 58; DLB 60; MTCW

Thomas, D(onald) M(ichael)
1935- .... **CLC 13, 22, 31**
See also CA 61-64; CAAS 11; CANR 17, 45; CDBLB 1960 to Present; DLB 40; INT CANR-17; MTCW

Thomas, Dylan (Marlais)
1914-1953 ... **TCLC 1, 8, 45; DA; DAB; DAC; DAM DRAM, MST, POET; PC 2; SSC 3; WLC**
See also CA 104; 120; CDBLB 1945-1960; DLB 13, 20, 139; MTCW; SATA 60

Thomas, (Philip) Edward
1878-1917 ...... **TCLC 10; DAM POET**
See also CA 106; 153; DLB 19

Thomas, Joyce Carol   1938- .... **CLC 35**
See also AAYA 12; BW 2; CA 113; 116; CANR 48; CLR 19; DLB 33; INT 116; JRDA; MAICYA; MTCW; SAAS 7; SATA 40, 78

Thomas, Lewis   1913-1993 .... **CLC 35**
See also CA 85-88; 143; CANR 38, 60; MTCW

Thomas, Paul
See Mann, (Paul) Thomas

Thomas, Piri   1928- .... **CLC 17**
See also CA 73-76; HW

Thomas, R(onald) S(tuart)
1913- .... **CLC 6, 13, 48; DAB; DAM POET**
See also CA 89-92; CAAS 4; CANR 30; CDBLB 1960 to Present; DLB 27; MTCW

Thomas, Ross (Elmore)   1926-1995 .. **CLC 39**
See also CA 33-36R; 150; CANR 22

Thompson, Francis Clegg
See Mencken, H(enry) L(ouis)

Thompson, Francis Joseph
1859-1907 .... **TCLC 4**
See also CA 104; CDBLB 1890-1914; DLB 19

Thompson, Hunter S(tockton)
1939- ... **CLC 9, 17, 40, 104; DAM POP**
See also BEST 89:1; CA 17-20R; CANR 23, 46; MTCW

Thompson, James Myers
See Thompson, Jim (Myers)

Thompson, Jim (Myers)
1906-1977(?) .... **CLC 69**
See also CA 140

Thompson, Judith .... **CLC 39**

Thomson, James
1700-1748 .. **LC 16, 29, 40; DAM POET**
See also DLB 95

Thomson, James
1834-1882 ..... **NCLC 18; DAM POET**
See also DLB 35

Thoreau, Henry David
1817-1862 .... **NCLC 7, 21, 61; DA; DAB; DAC; DAM MST; WLC**
See also CDALB 1640-1865; DLB 1

Thornton, Hall
See Silverberg, Robert

Thucydides   c. 455B.C.-399B.C.... **CMLC 17**
See also DLB 176

Thurber, James (Grover)
1894-1961 .... **CLC 5, 11, 25; DA; DAB; DAC; DAM DRAM, MST, NOV; SSC 1**
See also CA 73-76; CANR 17, 39; CDALB 1929-1941; DLB 4, 11, 22, 102; MAICYA; MTCW; SATA 13

Thurman, Wallace (Henry)
1902-1934 .... **TCLC 6; BLC; DAM MULT**
See also BW 1; CA 104; 124; DLB 51

Ticheburn, Cheviot
See Ainsworth, William Harrison

Tieck, (Johann) Ludwig
1773-1853 .... **NCLC 5, 46**
See also DLB 90

Tiger, Derry
See Ellison, Harlan (Jay)

Tilghman, Christopher   1948(?)- ..... **CLC 65**
See also CA 159

Tillinghast, Richard (Williford)
1940- .... **CLC 29**
See also CA 29-32R; CAAS 23; CANR 26, 51

Timrod, Henry   1828-1867 .... **NCLC 25**
See also DLB 3

Tindall, Gillian   1938- .... **CLC 7**
See also CA 21-24R; CANR 11

Tiptree, James, Jr. .... **CLC 48, 50**
See also Sheldon, Alice Hastings Bradley
See also DLB 8

Titmarsh, Michael Angelo
See Thackeray, William Makepeace

Tocqueville, Alexis (Charles Henri Maurice Clerel Comte)
1805-1859 .... **NCLC 7, 63**

Tolkien, J(ohn) R(onald) R(euel)
1892-1973 . . . . **CLC 1, 2, 3, 8, 12, 38;**
DA; DAB; DAC; DAM MST, NOV,
POP; WLC
See also AAYA 10; AITN 1; CA 17-18;
45-48; CANR 36; CAP 2;
CDBLB 1914-1945; DLB 15, 160; JRDA;
MAICYA; MTCW; SATA 2, 32;
SATA-Obit 24

Toller, Ernst 1893-1939 . . . . **TCLC 10**
See also CA 107; DLB 124

Tolson, M. B.
See Tolson, Melvin B(eaunorus)

Tolson, Melvin B(eaunorus)
1898(?)-1966 . . . . **CLC 36, 105; BLC;**
DAM MULT, POET
See also BW 1; CA 124; 89-92; DLB 48, 76

Tolstoi, Aleksei Nikolaevich
See Tolstoy, Alexey Nikolaevich

Tolstoy, Alexey Nikolaevich
1882-1945 . . . . **TCLC 18**
See also CA 107; 158

Tolstoy, Count Leo
See Tolstoy, Leo (Nikolaevich)

Tolstoy, Leo (Nikolaevich)
1828-1910 . . . . . . **TCLC 4, 11, 17, 28, 44;**
DA; DAB; DAC; DAM MST, NOV;
SSC 9; WLC
See also CA 104; 123; SATA 26

Tomasi di Lampedusa, Giuseppe 1896-1957
See Lampedusa, Giuseppe (Tomasi) di
See also CA 111

Tomlin, Lily . . . . **CLC 17**
See also Tomlin, Mary Jean

Tomlin, Mary Jean 1939(?)-
See Tomlin, Lily
See also CA 117

Tomlinson, (Alfred) Charles
1927- . . . . **CLC 2, 4, 6, 13, 45;**
DAM POET; PC 17
See also CA 5-8R; CANR 33; DLB 40

Tomlinson, H(enry) M(ajor)
1873-1958 . . . . **TCLC 71**
See also CA 118; 161; DLB 36, 100

Tonson, Jacob
See Bennett, (Enoch) Arnold

Toole, John Kennedy
1937-1969 . . . . **CLC 19, 64**
See also CA 104; DLBY 81

Toomer, Jean
1894-1967 . . . . . . **CLC 1, 4, 13, 22; BLC;**
DAM MULT; PC 7; SSC 1; WLCS
See also BW 1; CA 85-88;
CDALB 1917-1929; DLB 45, 51; MTCW

Torley, Luke
See Blish, James (Benjamin)

Tornimparte, Alessandra
See Ginzburg, Natalia

Torre, Raoul della
See Mencken, H(enry) L(ouis)

Torrey, E(dwin) Fuller 1937- . . . . **CLC 34**
See also CA 119

Torsvan, Ben Traven
See Traven, B.

Torsvan, Benno Traven
See Traven, B.

Torsvan, Berick Traven
See Traven, B.

Torsvan, Berwick Traven
See Traven, B.

Torsvan, Bruno Traven
See Traven, B.

Torsvan, Traven
See Traven, B.

Tournier, Michel (Edouard)
1924- . . . . **CLC 6, 23, 36, 95**
See also CA 49-52; CANR 3, 36; DLB 83;
MTCW; SATA 23

Tournimparte, Alessandra
See Ginzburg, Natalia

Towers, Ivar
See Kornbluth, C(yril) M.

Towne, Robert (Burton) 1936(?)- . . . . **CLC 87**
See also CA 108; DLB 44

Townsend, Sue 1946- . . **CLC 61; DAB; DAC**
See also CA 119; 127; INT 127; MTCW;
SATA 55, 93; SATA-Brief 48

Townshend, Peter (Dennis Blandford)
1945- . . . . **CLC 17, 42**
See also CA 107

Tozzi, Federigo 1883-1920 . . . . **TCLC 31**
See also CA 160

Traill, Catharine Parr
1802-1899 . . . . **NCLC 31**
See also DLB 99

Trakl, Georg 1887-1914 . . . . **TCLC 5; PC 20**
See also CA 104

Transtroemer, Tomas (Goesta)
1931- . . . . **CLC 52, 65; DAM POET**
See also CA 117; 129; CAAS 17

Transtromer, Tomas Gosta
See Transtroemer, Tomas (Goesta)

Traven, B. (?)-1969 . . . . **CLC 8, 11**
See also CA 19-20; 25-28R; CAP 2; DLB 9,
56; MTCW

Treitel, Jonathan 1959- . . . . **CLC 70**

Tremain, Rose 1943- . . . . **CLC 42**
See also CA 97-100; CANR 44; DLB 14

Tremblay, Michel
1942- . . **CLC 29, 102; DAC; DAM MST**
See also CA 116; 128; DLB 60; MTCW

Trevanian . . . . **CLC 29**
See also Whitaker, Rod(ney)

Trevor, Glen
See Hilton, James

Trevor, William
1928- . . . . . **CLC 7, 9, 14, 25, 71; SSC 21**
See also Cox, William Trevor
See also DLB 14, 139

Trifonov, Yuri (Valentinovich)
1925-1981 . . . . **CLC 45**
See also CA 126; 103; MTCW

Trilling, Lionel 1905-1975 . . . . **CLC 9, 11, 24**
See also CA 9-12R; 61-64; CANR 10;
DLB 28, 63; INT CANR-10; MTCW

Trimball, W. H.
See Mencken, H(enry) L(ouis)

Tristan
See Gomez de la Serna, Ramon

Tristram
See Housman, A(lfred) E(dward)

Trogdon, William (Lewis) 1939-
See Heat-Moon, William Least
See also CA 115; 119; CANR 47; INT 119

Trollope, Anthony
1815-1882 . . . . . **NCLC 6, 33; DA; DAB;**
DAC; DAM MST, NOV; SSC 28; WLC
See also CDBLB 1832-1890; DLB 21, 57,
159; SATA 22

Trollope, Frances 1779-1863 . . . . . **NCLC 30**
See also DLB 21, 166

Trotsky, Leon 1879-1940 . . . . **TCLC 22**
See also CA 118

Trotter (Cockburn), Catharine
1679-1749 . . . . **LC 8**
See also DLB 84

Trout, Kilgore
See Farmer, Philip Jose

Trow, George W. S. 1943- . . . . **CLC 52**
See also CA 126

Troyat, Henri 1911- . . . . **CLC 23**
See also CA 45-48; CANR 2, 33; MTCW

Trudeau, G(arretson) B(eekman) 1948-
See Trudeau, Garry B.
See also CA 81-84; CANR 31; SATA 35

Trudeau, Garry B. . . . . **CLC 12**
See also Trudeau, G(arretson) B(eekman)
See also AAYA 10; AITN 2

Truffaut, Francois 1932-1984 . . . **CLC 20, 101**
See also CA 81-84; 113; CANR 34

Trumbo, Dalton 1905-1976 . . . . **CLC 19**
See also CA 21-24R; 69-72; CANR 10;
DLB 26

Trumbull, John 1750-1831 . . . . **NCLC 30**
See also DLB 31

Trundlett, Helen B.
See Eliot, T(homas) S(tearns)

Tryon, Thomas
1926-1991 . . . . . . **CLC 3, 11; DAM POP**
See also AITN 1; CA 29-32R; 135;
CANR 32; MTCW

Tryon, Tom
See Tryon, Thomas

Ts'ao Hsueh-ch'in 1715(?)-1763 . . . . **LC 1**

Tsushima, Shuji 1909-1948
See Dazai, Osamu
See also CA 107

Tsvetaeva (Efron), Marina (Ivanovna)
1892-1941 . . . . **TCLC 7, 35; PC 14**
See also CA 104; 128; MTCW

Tuck, Lily 1938- . . . . **CLC 70**
See also CA 139

Tu Fu 712-770 . . . . **PC 9**
See also DAM MULT

Tunis, John R(oberts) 1889-1975 . . . **CLC 12**
See also CA 61-64; CANR 62; DLB 22,
171; JRDA; MAICYA; SATA 37;
SATA-Brief 30

Tuohy, Frank . . . . **CLC 37**
See also Tuohy, John Francis
See also DLB 14, 139

Tuohy, John Francis   1925-
  See Tuohy, Frank
  See also CA 5-8R; CANR 3, 47

Turco, Lewis (Putnam)   1934- . . .   **CLC 11, 63**
  See also CA 13-16R; CAAS 22; CANR 24,
  51; DLBY 84

Turgenev, Ivan
  1818-1883 . . . . . .   **NCLC 21; DA; DAB;**
  DAC; DAM MST, NOV; DC 7; SSC 7;
  WLC

Turgot, Anne-Robert-Jacques
  1727-1781 . . . .   **LC 26**

Turner, Frederick   1943- . . . .   **CLC 48**
  See also CA 73-76; CAAS 10; CANR 12,
  30, 56; DLB 40

Tutu, Desmond M(pilo)
  1931- . . . . .   **CLC 80; BLC; DAM MULT**
  See also BW 1; CA 125

Tutuola, Amos
  1920-1997 . . . .   **CLC 5, 14, 29; BLC;**
  DAM MULT
  See also BW 2; CA 9-12R; 159; CANR 27;
  DLB 125; MTCW

Twain, Mark
  . . . .   **TCLC 6, 12, 19, 36, 48, 59; SSC 26;**
  WLC
  See also Clemens, Samuel Langhorne
  See also AAYA 20; DLB 11, 12, 23, 64, 74

Tyler, Anne
  1941- . . . .   **CLC 7, 11, 18, 28, 44, 59, 103;**
  DAM NOV, POP
  See also AAYA 18; BEST 89:1; CA 9-12R;
  CANR 11, 33, 53; DLB 6, 143; DLBY 82;
  MTCW; SATA 7, 90

Tyler, Royall   1757-1826 . . . .   **NCLC 3**
  See also DLB 37

Tynan, Katharine   1861-1931 . . . . . .   **TCLC 3**
  See also CA 104; DLB 153

Tyutchev, Fyodor   1803-1873 . . . . .   **NCLC 34**

Tzara, Tristan
  1896-1963 . . . . . .   **CLC 47; DAM POET**
  See also Rosenfeld, Samuel; Rosenstock,
  Sami; Rosenstock, Samuel
  See also CA 153

Uhry, Alfred
  1936- . . . . .   **CLC 55; DAM DRAM, POP**
  See also CA 127; 133; INT 133

Ulf, Haerved
  See Strindberg, (Johan) August

Ulf, Harved
  See Strindberg, (Johan) August

Ulibarri, Sabine R(eyes)
  1919- . . . .   **CLC 83; DAM MULT**
  See also CA 131; DLB 82; HW

Unamuno (y Jugo), Miguel de
  1864-1936 . . .   **TCLC 2, 9; DAM MULT,**
  NOV; HLC; SSC 11
  See also CA 104; 131; DLB 108; HW;
  MTCW

Undercliffe, Errol
  See Campbell, (John) Ramsey

Underwood, Miles
  See Glassco, John

Undset, Sigrid
  1882-1949 . . . .   **TCLC 3; DA; DAB;**
  DAC; DAM MST, NOV; WLC
  See also CA 104; 129; MTCW

Ungaretti, Giuseppe
  1888-1970 . . . .   **CLC 7, 11, 15**
  See also CA 19-20; 25-28R; CAP 2;
  DLB 114

Unger, Douglas   1952- . . . .   **CLC 34**
  See also CA 130

Unsworth, Barry (Forster)   1930- . . . .   **CLC 76**
  See also CA 25-28R; CANR 30, 54

Updike, John (Hoyer)
  1932- . . . . . .   **CLC 1, 2, 3, 5, 7, 9, 13, 15,**
  23, 34, 43, 70; DA; DAB; DAC;
  DAM MST, NOV, POET, POP;
  SSC 13, 27; WLC
  See also CA 1-4R; CABS 1; CANR 4, 33,
  51; CDALB 1968-1988; DLB 2, 5, 143;
  DLBD 3; DLBY 80, 82; MTCW

Upshaw, Margaret Mitchell
  See Mitchell, Margaret (Munnerlyn)

Upton, Mark
  See Sanders, Lawrence

Urdang, Constance (Henriette)
  1922- . . . .   **CLC 47**
  See also CA 21-24R; CANR 9, 24

Uriel, Henry
  See Faust, Frederick (Schiller)

Uris, Leon (Marcus)
  1924- . . . .   **CLC 7, 32; DAM NOV, POP**
  See also AITN 1, 2; BEST 89:2; CA 1-4R;
  CANR 1, 40; MTCW; SATA 49

Urmuz
  See Codrescu, Andrei

Urquhart, Jane   1949- . . . .   **CLC 90; DAC**
  See also CA 113; CANR 32

Ustinov, Peter (Alexander)   1921- . . . .   **CLC 1**
  See also AITN 1; CA 13-16R; CANR 25,
  51; DLB 13

U Tam'si, Gerald Felix Tchicaya
  See Tchicaya, Gerald Felix

U Tam'si, Tchicaya
  See Tchicaya, Gerald Felix

Vachss, Andrew (Henry)   1942- . . . .   **CLC 106**
  See also CA 118; CANR 44

Vachss, Andrew H.
  See Vachss, Andrew (Henry)

Vaculik, Ludvik   1926- . . . .   **CLC 7**
  See also CA 53-56

Vaihinger, Hans   1852-1933 . . . .   **TCLC 71**
  See also CA 116

Valdez, Luis (Miguel)
  1940- . . . . .   **CLC 84; DAM MULT; HLC**
  See also CA 101; CANR 32; DLB 122; HW

Valenzuela, Luisa
  1938- . . . . . .   **CLC 31, 104; DAM MULT;**
  SSC 14
  See also CA 101; CANR 32; DLB 113; HW

Valera y Alcala-Galiano, Juan
  1824-1905 . . . .   **TCLC 10**
  See also CA 106

Valery, (Ambroise) Paul (Toussaint Jules)
  1871-1945 . . . .   **TCLC 4, 15;**
  DAM POET; PC 9
  See also CA 104; 122; MTCW

Valle-Inclan, Ramon (Maria) del
  1866-1936 . . . . .   **TCLC 5; DAM MULT;**
  HLC
  See also CA 106; 153; DLB 134

Vallejo, Antonio Buero
  See Buero Vallejo, Antonio

Vallejo, Cesar (Abraham)
  1892-1938 . . . .   **TCLC 3, 56;**
  DAM MULT; HLC
  See also CA 105; 153; HW

Vallette, Marguerite Eymery
  See Rachilde

Valle Y Pena, Ramon del
  See Valle-Inclan, Ramon (Maria) del

Van Ash, Cay   1918- . . . .   **CLC 34**

Vanbrugh, Sir John
  1664-1726 . . . .   **LC 21; DAM DRAM**
  See also DLB 80

Van Campen, Karl
  See Campbell, John W(ood, Jr.)

Vance, Gerald
  See Silverberg, Robert

Vance, Jack . . . .   **CLC 35**
  See also Kuttner, Henry; Vance, John
  Holbrook
  See also DLB 8

Vance, John Holbrook   1916-
  See Queen, Ellery; Vance, Jack
  See also CA 29-32R; CANR 17; MTCW

Van Den Bogarde, Derek Jules Gaspard Ulric
  Niven   1921-
  See Bogarde, Dirk
  See also CA 77-80

Vandenburgh, Jane . . . .   **CLC 59**

Vanderhaeghe, Guy   1951- . . . .   **CLC 41**
  See also CA 113

van der Post, Laurens (Jan)
  1906-1996 . . . .   **CLC 5**
  See also CA 5-8R; 155; CANR 35

van de Wetering, Janwillem   1931- . .   **CLC 47**
  See also CA 49-52; CANR 4, 62

Van Dine, S. S. . . . .   **TCLC 23**
  See also Wright, Willard Huntington

Van Doren, Carl (Clinton)
  1885-1950 . . . .   **TCLC 18**
  See also CA 111

Van Doren, Mark   1894-1972 . . . . .   **CLC 6, 10**
  See also CA 1-4R; 37-40R; CANR 3;
  DLB 45; MTCW

Van Druten, John (William)
  1901-1957 . . . .   **TCLC 2**
  See also CA 104; 161; DLB 10

Van Duyn, Mona (Jane)
  1921- . . . .   **CLC 3, 7, 63; DAM POET**
  See also CA 9-12R; CANR 7, 38, 60;
  DLB 5

Van Dyne, Edith
  See Baum, L(yman) Frank

van Itallie, Jean-Claude   1936- . . . .   **CLC 3**
  See also CA 45-48; CAAS 2; CANR 1, 48;
  DLB 7

van Ostaijen, Paul   1896-1928 . . . . . **TCLC 33**

Van Peebles, Melvin
 1932- . . . . **CLC 2, 20; DAM MULT**
 See also BW 2; CA 85-88; CANR 27

Vansittart, Peter   1920-. . . . . **CLC 42**
 See also CA 1-4R; CANR 3, 49

Van Vechten, Carl   1880-1964 . . . . . . **CLC 33**
 See also CA 89-92; DLB 4, 9, 51

Van Vogt, A(lfred) E(lton)   1912-. . . . . **CLC 1**
 See also CA 21-24R; CANR 28; DLB 8;
 SATA 14

Varda, Agnes   1928- . . . . **CLC 16**
 See also CA 116; 122

Vargas Llosa, (Jorge) Mario (Pedro)
 1936- . . . . **CLC 3, 6, 9, 10, 15, 31, 42, 85;**
 DA; DAB; DAC; DAM MST, MULT,
 NOV; HLC
 See also CA 73-76; CANR 18, 32, 42;
 DLB 145; HW; MTCW

Vasiliu, Gheorghe   1881-1957
 See Bacovia, George
 See also CA 123

Vassa, Gustavus
 See Equiano, Olaudah

Vassilikos, Vassilis   1933-. . . . . **CLC 4, 8**
 See also CA 81-84

Vaughan, Henry   1621-1695 . . . . **LC 27**
 See also DLB 131

Vaughn, Stephanie. . . . . **CLC 62**

Vazov, Ivan (Minchov)
 1850-1921 . . . . **TCLC 25**
 See also CA 121; DLB 147

Veblen, Thorstein (Bunde)
 1857-1929 . . . . **TCLC 31**
 See also CA 115

Vega, Lope de   1562-1635 . . . . **LC 23**

Venison, Alfred
 See Pound, Ezra (Weston Loomis)

Verdi, Marie de
 See Mencken, H(enry) L(ouis)

Verdu, Matilde
 See Cela, Camilo Jose

Verga, Giovanni (Carmelo)
 1840-1922 . . . . **TCLC 3; SSC 21**
 See also CA 104; 123

Vergil
 70B.C.-19B.C. . . . . . **CMLC 9; DA; DAB;**
 DAC; DAM MST, POET; PC 12; WLCS

Verhaeren, Emile (Adolphe Gustave)
 1855-1916 . . . . **TCLC 12**
 See also CA 109

Verlaine, Paul (Marie)
 1844-1896 . . . . **NCLC 2, 51;**
 DAM POET; PC 2

Verne, Jules (Gabriel)
 1828-1905 . . . . **TCLC 6, 52**
 See also AAYA 16; CA 110; 131; DLB 123;
 JRDA; MAICYA; SATA 21

Very, Jones   1813-1880 . . . . **NCLC 9**
 See also DLB 1

Vesaas, Tarjei   1897-1970 . . . . **CLC 48**
 See also CA 29-32R

Vialis, Gaston
 See Simenon, Georges (Jacques Christian)

Vian, Boris   1920-1959 . . . . **TCLC 9**
 See also CA 106; DLB 72

Viaud, (Louis Marie) Julien   1850-1923
 See Loti, Pierre
 See also CA 107

Vicar, Henry
 See Felsen, Henry Gregor

Vicker, Angus
 See Felsen, Henry Gregor

Vidal, Gore
 1925- . . . . . **CLC 2, 4, 6, 8, 10, 22, 33, 72;**
 DAM NOV, POP
 See also AITN 1; BEST 90:2; CA 5-8R;
 CANR 13, 45; DLB 6, 152;
 INT CANR-13; MTCW

Viereck, Peter (Robert Edwin)
 1916- . . . . **CLC 4**
 See also CA 1-4R; CANR 1, 47; DLB 5

Vigny, Alfred (Victor) de
 1797-1863 . . . . . . **NCLC 7; DAM POET**
 See also DLB 119

Vilakazi, Benedict Wallet
 1906-1947 . . . . **TCLC 37**

Villiers de l'Isle Adam, Jean Marie Mathias
 Philippe Auguste Comte
 1838-1889 . . . . **NCLC 3; SSC 14**
 See also DLB 123

Villon, Francois   1431-1463(?) . . . . **PC 13**

Vinci, Leonardo da   1452-1519 . . . . **LC 12**

Vine, Barbara . . . . **CLC 50**
 See also Rendell, Ruth (Barbara)
 See also BEST 90:4

Vinge, Joan D(ennison)
 1948- . . . . **CLC 30; SSC 24**
 See also CA 93-96; SATA 36

Violis, G.
 See Simenon, Georges (Jacques Christian)

Visconti, Luchino   1906-1976 . . . . **CLC 16**
 See also CA 81-84; 65-68; CANR 39

Vittorini, Elio   1908-1966 . . . . . . **CLC 6, 9, 14**
 See also CA 133; 25-28R

Vizenor, Gerald Robert
 1934- . . . . **CLC 103; DAM MULT**
 See also CA 13-16R; CAAS 22; CANR 5,
 21, 44; DLB 175; NNAL

Vizinczey, Stephen   1933-. . . . . **CLC 40**
 See also CA 128; INT 128

Vliet, R(ussell) G(ordon)
 1929-1984 . . . . **CLC 22**
 See also CA 37-40R; 112; CANR 18

Vogau, Boris Andreyevich   1894-1937(?)
 See Pilnyak, Boris
 See also CA 123

Vogel, Paula A(nne)   1951-. . . . . **CLC 76**
 See also CA 108

Voight, Ellen Bryant   1943- . . . . **CLC 54**
 See also CA 69-72; CANR 11, 29, 55;
 DLB 120

Voigt, Cynthia   1942- . . . . **CLC 30**
 See also AAYA 3; CA 106; CANR 18, 37,
 40; CLR 13,48; INT CANR-18; JRDA;
 MAICYA; SATA 48, 79; SATA-Brief 33

Voinovich, Vladimir (Nikolaevich)
 1932- . . . . **CLC 10, 49**
 See also CA 81-84; CAAS 12; CANR 33;
 MTCW

Vollmann, William T.
 1959- . . . . . . **CLC 89; DAM NOV, POP**
 See also CA 134

Voloshinov, V. N.
 See Bakhtin, Mikhail Mikhailovich

Voltaire
 1694-1778 . . . . . **LC 14; DA; DAB; DAC;**
 DAM DRAM, MST; SSC 12; WLC

von Daeniken, Erich   1935- . . . . **CLC 30**
 See also AITN 1; CA 37-40R; CANR 17,
 44

von Daniken, Erich
 See von Daeniken, Erich

von Heidenstam, (Carl Gustaf) Verner
 See Heidenstam, (Carl Gustaf) Verner von

von Heyse, Paul (Johann Ludwig)
 See Heyse, Paul (Johann Ludwig von)

von Hofmannsthal, Hugo
 See Hofmannsthal, Hugo von

von Horvath, Odon
 See Horvath, Oedoen von

von Horvath, Oedoen
 See Horvath, Oedoen von

von Liliencron, (Friedrich Adolf Axel) Detlev
 See Liliencron, (Friedrich Adolf Axel)
 Detlev von

Vonnegut, Kurt, Jr.
 1922- . . . . . **CLC 1, 2, 3, 4, 5, 8, 12, 22,**
 40, 60; DA; DAB; DAC; DAM MST,
 NOV, POP; SSC 8; WLC
 See also AAYA 6; AITN 1; BEST 90:4;
 CA 1-4R; CANR 1, 25, 49;
 CDALB 1968-1988; DLB 2, 8, 152;
 DLBD 3; DLBY 80; MTCW

Von Rachen, Kurt
 See Hubbard, L(afayette) Ron(ald)

von Rezzori (d'Arezzo), Gregor
 See Rezzori (d'Arezzo), Gregor von

von Sternberg, Josef
 See Sternberg, Josef von

Vorster, Gordon   1924-. . . . . **CLC 34**
 See also CA 133

Vosce, Trudie
 See Ozick, Cynthia

Voznesensky, Andrei (Andreievich)
 1933- . . . . . . **CLC 1, 15, 57; DAM POET**
 See also CA 89-92; CANR 37; MTCW

Waddington, Miriam   1917- . . . . **CLC 28**
 See also CA 21-24R; CANR 12, 30;
 DLB 68

Wagman, Fredrica   1937-. . . . . **CLC 7**
 See also CA 97-100; INT 97-100

Wagner, Linda W.
 See Wagner-Martin, Linda (C.)

Wagner, Linda Welshimer
 See Wagner-Martin, Linda (C.)

Wagner, Richard   1813-1883. . . . . . . **NCLC 9**
 See also DLB 129

Wagner-Martin, Linda (C.)   1936-. . . **CLC 50**
 See also CA 159

Wagoner, David (Russell)
1926- .... CLC **3, 5, 15**
See also CA 1-4R; CAAS 3; CANR 2;
DLB 5; SATA 14

Wah, Fred(erick James) 1939-...... CLC **44**
See also CA 107; 141; DLB 60

Wahloo, Per 1926-1975 .... CLC **7**
See also CA 61-64

Wahloo, Peter
See Wahloo, Per

Wain, John (Barrington)
1925-1994 .... CLC **2, 11, 15, 46**
See also CA 5-8R; 145; CAAS 4; CANR 23,
54; CDBLB 1960 to Present; DLB 15, 27,
139, 155; MTCW

Wajda, Andrzej 1926-............. CLC **16**
See also CA 102

Wakefield, Dan 1932-............. CLC **7**
See also CA 21-24R; CAAS 7

Wakoski, Diane
1937- .... CLC **2, 4, 7, 9, 11, 40;**
DAM POET; PC 15
See also CA 13-16R; CAAS 1; CANR 9, 60;
DLB 5; INT CANR-9

Wakoski-Sherbell, Diane
See Wakoski, Diane

Walcott, Derek (Alton)
1930- .... CLC **2, 4, 9, 14, 25, 42, 67, 76;**
BLC; DAB; DAC; DAM MST, MULT,
POET; DC 7
See also BW 2; CA 89-92; CANR 26, 47;
DLB 117; DLBY 81; MTCW

Waldman, Anne 1945- .... CLC **7**
See also CA 37-40R; CAAS 17; CANR 34;
DLB 16

Waldo, E. Hunter
See Sturgeon, Theodore (Hamilton)

Waldo, Edward Hamilton
See Sturgeon, Theodore (Hamilton)

Walker, Alice (Malsenior)
1944- .... CLC **5, 6, 9, 19, 27, 46, 58,**
103; BLC; DA; DAB; DAC; DAM MST,
MULT, NOV, POET, POP; SSC 5;
WLCS
See also AAYA 3; BEST 89:4; BW 2;
CA 37-40R; CANR 9, 27, 49;
CDALB 1968-1988; DLB 6, 33, 143;
INT CANR-27; MTCW; SATA 31

Walker, David Harry 1911-1992.... CLC **14**
See also CA 1-4R; 137; CANR 1; SATA 8;
SATA-Obit 71

Walker, Edward Joseph 1934-
See Walker, Ted
See also CA 21-24R; CANR 12, 28, 53

Walker, George F.
1947- .... CLC **44, 61; DAB; DAC;**
DAM MST
See also CA 103; CANR 21, 43, 59;
DLB 60

Walker, Joseph A.
1935- .... CLC **19; DAM DRAM, MST**
See also BW 1; CA 89-92; CANR 26;
DLB 38

Walker, Margaret (Abigail)
1915- ... CLC **1, 6; BLC; DAM MULT;**
PC 20
See also BW 2; CA 73-76; CANR 26, 54;
DLB 76, 152; MTCW

Walker, Ted...................... CLC **13**
See also Walker, Edward Joseph
See also DLB 40

Wallace, David Foster 1962-....... CLC **50**
See also CA 132; CANR 59

Wallace, Dexter
See Masters, Edgar Lee

Wallace, (Richard Horatio) Edgar
1875-1932 .... TCLC **57**
See also CA 115; DLB 70

Wallace, Irving
1916-1990 ..... CLC **7, 13; DAM NOV,**
POP
See also AITN 1; CA 1-4R; 132; CAAS 1;
CANR 1, 27; INT CANR-27; MTCW

Wallant, Edward Lewis
1926-1962 .... CLC **5, 10**
See also CA 1-4R; CANR 22; DLB 2, 28,
143; MTCW

Walley, Byron
See Card, Orson Scott

Walpole, Horace 1717-1797......... LC **2**
See also DLB 39, 104

Walpole, Hugh (Seymour)
1884-1941 .... TCLC **5**
See also CA 104; DLB 34

Walser, Martin 1927-............. CLC **27**
See also CA 57-60; CANR 8, 46; DLB 75,
124

Walser, Robert
1878-1956 .... TCLC **18; SSC 20**
See also CA 118; DLB 66

Walsh, Jill Paton................. CLC **35**
See also Paton Walsh, Gillian
See also AAYA 11; CLR 2; DLB 161;
SAAS 3

Walter, Villiam Christian
See Andersen, Hans Christian

Wambaugh, Joseph (Aloysius, Jr.)
1937- .... CLC **3, 18; DAM NOV, POP**
See also AITN 1; BEST 89:3; CA 33-36R;
CANR 42; DLB 6; DLBY 83; MTCW

Wang Wei 699(?)-761(?)............ PC **18**

Ward, Arthur Henry Sarsfield 1883-1959
See Rohmer, Sax
See also CA 108

Ward, Douglas Turner 1930-....... CLC **19**
See also BW 1; CA 81-84; CANR 27;
DLB 7, 38

Ward, Mary Augusta
See Ward, Mrs. Humphry

Ward, Mrs. Humphry
1851-1920 .... TCLC **55**
See also DLB 18

Ward, Peter
See Faust, Frederick (Schiller)

Warhol, Andy 1928(?)-1987........ CLC **20**
See also AAYA 12; BEST 89:4; CA 89-92;
121; CANR 34

Warner, Francis (Robert le Plastrier)
1937- .... CLC **14**
See also CA 53-56; CANR 11

Warner, Marina 1946-............ CLC **59**
See also CA 65-68; CANR 21, 55

Warner, Rex (Ernest) 1905-1986.... CLC **45**
See also CA 89-92; 119; DLB 15

Warner, Susan (Bogert)
1819-1885 .... NCLC **31**
See also DLB 3, 42

Warner, Sylvia (Constance) Ashton
See Ashton-Warner, Sylvia (Constance)

Warner, Sylvia Townsend
1893-1978 .... CLC **7, 19; SSC 23**
See also CA 61-64; 77-80; CANR 16, 60;
DLB 34, 139; MTCW

Warren, Mercy Otis 1728-1814... NCLC **13**
See also DLB 31

Warren, Robert Penn
1905-1989 .... CLC **1, 4, 6, 8, 10, 13, 18,**
39, 53, 59; DA; DAB; DAC; DAM MST,
NOV, POET; SSC 4; WLC
See also AITN 1; CA 13-16R; 129;
CANR 10, 47; CDALB 1968-1988;
DLB 2, 48, 152; DLBY 80, 89;
INT CANR-10; MTCW; SATA 46;
SATA-Obit 63

Warshofsky, Isaac
See Singer, Isaac Bashevis

Warton, Thomas
1728-1790 .... LC **15; DAM POET**
See also DLB 104, 109

Waruk, Kona
See Harris, (Theodore) Wilson

Warung, Price 1855-1911........ TCLC **45**

Warwick, Jarvis
See Garner, Hugh

Washington, Alex
See Harris, Mark

Washington, Booker T(aliaferro)
1856-1915 .... TCLC **10; BLC;**
DAM MULT
See also BW 1; CA 114; 125; SATA 28

Washington, George 1732-1799...... LC **25**
See also DLB 31

Wassermann, (Karl) Jakob
1873-1934 .... TCLC **6**
See also CA 104; DLB 66

Wasserstein, Wendy
1950- .... CLC **32, 59, 90;**
DAM DRAM; DC 4
See also CA 121; 129; CABS 3; CANR 53;
INT 129; SATA 94

Waterhouse, Keith (Spencer)
1929- .... CLC **47**
See also CA 5-8R; CANR 38; DLB 13, 15;
MTCW

Waters, Frank (Joseph)
1902-1995 .... CLC **88**
See also CA 5-8R; 149; CAAS 13; CANR 3,
18; DLBY 86

Waters, Roger 1944-............. CLC **35**

Watkins, Frances Ellen
See Harper, Frances Ellen Watkins

Watkins, Gerrold
See Malzberg, Barry N(athaniel)

Watkins, Gloria   1955(?)-
See hooks, bell
See also BW 2; CA 143

Watkins, Paul   1964-.............. **CLC 55**
See also CA 132; CANR 62

Watkins, Vernon Phillips
1906-1967 .... **CLC 43**
See also CA 9-10; 25-28R; CAP 1; DLB 20

Watson, Irving S.
See Mencken, H(enry) L(ouis)

Watson, John H.
See Farmer, Philip Jose

Watson, Richard F.
See Silverberg, Robert

Waugh, Auberon (Alexander)   1939-.. **CLC 7**
See also CA 45-48; CANR 6, 22; DLB 14

Waugh, Evelyn (Arthur St. John)
1903-1966 ...... **CLC 1, 3, 8, 13, 19, 27,
44; DA; DAB; DAC; DAM MST, NOV,
POP; WLC**
See also CA 85-88; 25-28R; CANR 22;
CDBLB 1914-1945; DLB 15, 162; MTCW

Waugh, Harriet   1944- .... **CLC 6**
See also CA 85-88; CANR 22

Ways, C. R.
See Blount, Roy (Alton), Jr.

Waystaff, Simon
See Swift, Jonathan

Webb, (Martha) Beatrice (Potter)
1858-1943 .... **TCLC 22**
See also Potter, (Helen) Beatrix
See also CA 117

Webb, Charles (Richard)   1939-...... **CLC 7**
See also CA 25-28R

Webb, James H(enry), Jr.   1946-.... **CLC 22**
See also CA 81-84

Webb, Mary (Gladys Meredith)
1881-1927 .... **TCLC 24**
See also CA 123; DLB 34

Webb, Mrs. Sidney
See Webb, (Martha) Beatrice (Potter)

Webb, Phyllis   1927-.............. **CLC 18**
See also CA 104; CANR 23; DLB 53

Webb, Sidney (James)
1859-1947 .... **TCLC 22**
See also CA 117

Webber, Andrew Lloyd............. **CLC 21**
See also Lloyd Webber, Andrew

Weber, Lenora Mattingly
1895-1971 .... **CLC 12**
See also CA 19-20; 29-32R; CAP 1;
SATA 2; SATA-Obit 26

Weber, Max   1864-1920 .... **TCLC 69**
See also CA 109

Webster, John
1579(?)-1634(?) ...... **LC 33; DA; DAB;
DAC; DAM DRAM, MST; DC 2; WLC**
See also CDBLB Before 1660; DLB 58

Webster, Noah   1758-1843 .... **NCLC 30**

Wedekind, (Benjamin) Frank(lin)
1864-1918 ...... **TCLC 7; DAM DRAM**
See also CA 104; 153; DLB 118

Weidman, Jerome   1913-............ **CLC 7**
See also AITN 2; CA 1-4R; CANR 1;
DLB 28

Weil, Simone (Adolphine)
1909-1943 .... **TCLC 23**
See also CA 117; 159

Weinstein, Nathan
See West, Nathanael

Weinstein, Nathan von Wallenstein
See West, Nathanael

Weir, Peter (Lindsay)   1944- .... **CLC 20**
See also CA 113; 123

Weiss, Peter (Ulrich)
1916-1982 .... **CLC 3, 15, 51;
DAM DRAM**
See also CA 45-48; 106; CANR 3; DLB 69,
124

Weiss, Theodore (Russell)
1916- .... **CLC 3, 8, 14**
See also CA 9-12R; CAAS 2; CANR 46;
DLB 5

Welch, (Maurice) Denton
1915-1948 .... **TCLC 22**
See also CA 121; 148

Welch, James
1940- ..... **CLC 6, 14, 52; DAM MULT,
POP**
See also CA 85-88; CANR 42; DLB 175;
NNAL

Weldon, Fay
1933- .... **CLC 6, 9, 11, 19, 36, 59;
DAM POP**
See also CA 21-24R; CANR 16, 46;
CDBLB 1960 to Present; DLB 14;
INT CANR-16; MTCW

Wellek, Rene   1903-1995.......... **CLC 28**
See also CA 5-8R; 150; CAAS 7; CANR 8;
DLB 63; INT CANR-8

Weller, Michael   1942-........ **CLC 10, 53**
See also CA 85-88

Weller, Paul   1958-.............. **CLC 26**

Wellershoff, Dieter   1925-.......... **CLC 46**
See also CA 89-92; CANR 16, 37

Welles, (George) Orson
1915-1985 .... **CLC 20, 80**
See also CA 93-96; 117

Wellman, Mac   1945- .... **CLC 65**

Wellman, Manly Wade   1903-1986 .. **CLC 49**
See also CA 1-4R; 118; CANR 6, 16, 44;
SATA 6; SATA-Obit 47

Wells, Carolyn   1869(?)-1942 ...... **TCLC 35**
See also CA 113; DLB 11

Wells, H(erbert) G(eorge)
1866-1946 .... **TCLC 6, 12, 19; DA;
DAB; DAC; DAM MST, NOV; SSC 6;
WLC**
See also AAYA 18; CA 110; 121;
CDBLB 1914-1945; DLB 34, 70, 156, 178;
MTCW; SATA 20

Wells, Rosemary   1943-............ **CLC 12**
See also AAYA 13; CA 85-88; CANR 48;
CLR 16; MAICYA; SAAS 1; SATA 18,
69

Welty, Eudora
1909- ...... **CLC 1, 2, 5, 14, 22, 33, 105;
DA; DAB; DAC; DAM MST, NOV;
SSC 1, 27; WLC**
See also CA 9-12R; CABS 1; CANR 32;
CDALB 1941-1968; DLB 2, 102, 143;
DLBD 12; DLBY 87; MTCW

Wen I-to   1899-1946 .... **TCLC 28**

Wentworth, Robert
See Hamilton, Edmond

Werfel, Franz (Viktor)   1890-1945... **TCLC 8**
See also CA 104; 161; DLB 81, 124

Wergeland, Henrik Arnold
1808-1845 .... **NCLC 5**

Wersba, Barbara   1932-............ **CLC 30**
See also AAYA 2; CA 29-32R; CANR 16,
38; CLR 3; DLB 52; JRDA; MAICYA;
SAAS 2; SATA 1, 58

Wertmueller, Lina   1928- .... **CLC 16**
See also CA 97-100; CANR 39

Wescott, Glenway   1901-1987....... **CLC 13**
See also CA 13-16R; 121; CANR 23;
DLB 4, 9, 102

Wesker, Arnold
1932- .... **CLC 3, 5, 42; DAB;
DAM DRAM**
See also CA 1-4R; CAAS 7; CANR 1, 33;
CDBLB 1960 to Present; DLB 13;
MTCW

Wesley, Richard (Errol)   1945-....... **CLC 7**
See also BW 1; CA 57-60; CANR 27;
DLB 38

Wessel, Johan Herman   1742-1785 .... **LC 7**

West, Anthony (Panther)
1914-1987 .... **CLC 50**
See also CA 45-48; 124; CANR 3, 19;
DLB 15

West, C. P.
See Wodehouse, P(elham) G(renville)

West, (Mary) Jessamyn
1902-1984 .... **CLC 7, 17**
See also CA 9-12R; 112; CANR 27; DLB 6;
DLBY 84; MTCW; SATA-Obit 37

West, Morris L(anglo)   1916-..... **CLC 6, 33**
See also CA 5-8R; CANR 24, 49; MTCW

West, Nathanael
1903-1940 ..... **TCLC 1, 14, 44; SSC 16**
See also CA 104; 125; CDALB 1929-1941;
DLB 4, 9, 28; MTCW

West, Owen
See Koontz, Dean R(ay)

West, Paul   1930- .... **CLC 7, 14, 96**
See also CA 13-16R; CAAS 7; CANR 22,
53; DLB 14; INT CANR-22

West, Rebecca   1892-1983 .. **CLC 7, 9, 31, 50**
See also CA 5-8R; 109; CANR 19; DLB 36;
DLBY 83; MTCW

Westall, Robert (Atkinson)
1929-1993 .... **CLC 17**
See also AAYA 12; CA 69-72; 141;
CANR 18; CLR 13; JRDA; MAICYA;
SAAS 2; SATA 23, 69; SATA-Obit 75

Westlake, Donald E(dwin)
1933- .... **CLC 7, 33; DAM POP**
See also CA 17-20R; CAAS 13; CANR 16,
44; INT CANR-16

Woodberry, George Edward
1855-1930 . . . . **TCLC 73**
See also DLB 71, 103

Woodcott, Keith
See Brunner, John (Kilian Houston)

Woodruff, Robert W.
See Mencken, H(enry) L(ouis)

Woolf, (Adeline) Virginia
1882-1941 . . . . . . **TCLC 1, 5, 20, 43, 56;**
DA; DAB; DAC; DAM MST, NOV;
SSC 7; WLC
See also CA 104; 130; CDBLB 1914-1945;
DLB 36, 100, 162; DLBD 10; MTCW

Woollcott, Alexander (Humphreys)
1887-1943 . . . . **TCLC 5**
See also CA 105; 161; DLB 29

Woolrich, Cornell 1903-1968 . . . . . . **CLC 77**
See also Hopley-Woolrich, Cornell George

Wordsworth, Dorothy
1771-1855 . . . . **NCLC 25**
See also DLB 107

Wordsworth, William
1770-1850 . . . . **NCLC 12, 38; DA; DAB;**
DAC; DAM MST, POET; PC 4; WLC
See also CDBLB 1789-1832; DLB 93, 107

Wouk, Herman
1915- . . **CLC 1, 9, 38; DAM NOV, POP**
See also CA 5-8R; CANR 6, 33; DLBY 82;
INT CANR-6; MTCW

Wright, Charles (Penzel, Jr.)
1935- . . . . **CLC 6, 13, 28**
See also CA 29-32R; CAAS 7; CANR 23,
36, 62; DLB 165; DLBY 82; MTCW

Wright, Charles Stevenson
1932- . . . . **CLC 49; BLC 3;**
DAM MULT, POET
See also BW 1; CA 9-12R; CANR 26;
DLB 33

Wright, Jack R.
See Harris, Mark

Wright, James (Arlington)
1927-1980 . . . . **CLC 3, 5, 10, 28;**
DAM POET
See also AITN 2; CA 49-52; 97-100;
CANR 4, 34; DLB 5, 169; MTCW

Wright, Judith (Arandell)
1915- . . . . **CLC 11, 53; PC 14**
See also CA 13-16R; CANR 31; MTCW;
SATA 14

Wright, L(aurali) R. 1939- . . . . **CLC 44**
See also CA 138

Wright, Richard (Nathaniel)
1908-1960 . . . . **CLC 1, 3, 4, 9, 14, 21, 48,**
74; BLC; DA; DAB; DAC; DAM MST,
MULT, NOV; SSC 2; WLC
See also AAYA 5; BW 1; CA 108;
CDALB 1929-1941; DLB 76, 102;
DLBD 2; MTCW

Wright, Richard B(ruce) 1937- . . . . . . **CLC 6**
See also CA 85-88; DLB 53

Wright, Rick 1945- . . . . **CLC 35**

Wright, Rowland
See Wells, Carolyn

Wright, Stephen Caldwell 1946- . . . . **CLC 33**
See also BW 2

Wright, Willard Huntington 1888-1939
See Van Dine, S. S.
See also CA 115; DLBD 16

Wright, William 1930- . . . . **CLC 44**
See also CA 53-56; CANR 7, 23

Wroth, LadyMary 1587-1653(?) . . . . . **LC 30**
See also DLB 121

Wu Ch'eng-en 1500(?)-1582(?) . . . . **LC 7**

Wu Ching-tzu 1701-1754 . . . . **LC 2**

Wurlitzer, Rudolph 1938(?)- . . . **CLC 2, 4, 15**
See also CA 85-88; DLB 173

Wycherley, William
1641-1715 . . . . . **LC 8, 21; DAM DRAM**
See also CDBLB 1660-1789; DLB 80

Wylie, Elinor (Morton Hoyt)
1885-1928 . . . . **TCLC 8**
See also CA 105; DLB 9, 45

Wylie, Philip (Gordon) 1902-1971 . . . **CLC 43**
See also CA 21-22; 33-36R; CAP 2; DLB 9

Wyndham, John . . . . **CLC 19**
See also Harris, John (Wyndham Parkes
Lucas) Beynon

Wyss, Johann David Von
1743-1818 . . . . **NCLC 10**
See also JRDA; MAICYA; SATA 29;
SATA-Brief 27

Xenophon
c. 430B.C.-c. 354B.C. . . . . **CMLC 17**
See also DLB 176

Yakumo Koizumi
See Hearn, (Patricio) Lafcadio (Tessima
Carlos)

Yanez, Jose Donoso
See Donoso (Yanez), Jose

Yanovsky, Basile S.
See Yanovsky, V(assily) S(emenovich)

Yanovsky, V(assily) S(emenovich)
1906-1989 . . . . **CLC 2, 18**
See also CA 97-100; 129

Yates, Richard 1926-1992 . . . . . **CLC 7, 8, 23**
See also CA 5-8R; 139; CANR 10, 43;
DLB 2; DLBY 81, 92; INT CANR-10

Yeats, W. B.
See Yeats, William Butler

Yeats, William Butler
1865-1939 . . . . . **TCLC 1, 11, 18, 31; DA;**
DAB; DAC; DAM DRAM, MST,
POET; PC 20; WLC
See also CA 104; 127; CANR 45;
CDBLB 1890-1914; DLB 10, 19, 98, 156;
MTCW

Yehoshua, A(braham) B.
1936- . . . . **CLC 13, 31**
See also CA 33-36R; CANR 43

Yep, Laurence Michael 1948- . . . . . . **CLC 35**
See also AAYA 5; CA 49-52; CANR 1, 46;
CLR 3, 17; DLB 52; JRDA; MAICYA;
SATA 7, 69

Yerby, Frank G(arvin)
1916-1991 . . . . **CLC 1, 7, 22; BLC;**
DAM MULT
See also BW 1; CA 9-12R; 136; CANR 16,
52; DLB 76; INT CANR-16; MTCW

Yesenin, Sergei Alexandrovich
See Esenin, Sergei (Alexandrovich)

Yevtushenko, Yevgeny (Alexandrovich)
1933- . . . . **CLC 1, 3, 13, 26, 51;**
DAM POET
See also CA 81-84; CANR 33, 54; MTCW

Yezierska, Anzia 1885(?)-1970 . . . . . **CLC 46**
See also CA 126; 89-92; DLB 28; MTCW

Yglesias, Helen 1915- . . . . **CLC 7, 22**
See also CA 37-40R; CAAS 20; CANR 15;
INT CANR-15; MTCW

Yokomitsu Riichi 1898-1947 . . . . . . **TCLC 47**

Yonge, Charlotte (Mary)
1823-1901 . . . . **TCLC 48**
See also CA 109; DLB 18, 163; SATA 17

York, Jeremy
See Creasey, John

York, Simon
See Heinlein, Robert A(nson)

Yorke, Henry Vincent 1905-1974 . . . **CLC 13**
See also Green, Henry
See also CA 85-88; 49-52

Yosano Akiko 1878-1942 . . **TCLC 59; PC 11**
See also CA 161

Yoshimoto, Banana . . . . **CLC 84**
See also Yoshimoto, Mahoko

Yoshimoto, Mahoko 1964-
See Yoshimoto, Banana
See also CA 144

Young, Al(bert James)
1939- . . . . . **CLC 19; BLC; DAM MULT**
See also BW 2; CA 29-32R; CANR 26;
DLB 33

Young, Andrew (John) 1885-1971 . . . . **CLC 5**
See also CA 5-8R; CANR 7, 29

Young, Collier
See Bloch, Robert (Albert)

Young, Edward 1683-1765 . . . . **LC 3, 40**
See also DLB 95

Young, Marguerite (Vivian)
1909-1995 . . . . **CLC 82**
See also CA 13-16; 150; CAP 1

Young, Neil 1945- . . . . **CLC 17**
See also CA 110

Young Bear, Ray A.
1950- . . . . **CLC 94; DAM MULT**
See also CA 146; DLB 175; NNAL

Yourcenar, Marguerite
1903-1987 . . . . **CLC 19, 38, 50, 87;**
DAM NOV
See also CA 69-72; CANR 23, 60; DLB 72;
DLBY 88; MTCW

Yurick, Sol 1925- . . . . **CLC 6**
See also CA 13-16R; CANR 25

Zabolotskii, Nikolai Alekseevich
1903-1958 . . . . **TCLC 52**
See also CA 116

Zamiatin, Yevgenii
See Zamyatin, Evgeny Ivanovich

Zamora, Bernice (B. Ortiz)
1938- . . . . . **CLC 89; DAM MULT; HLC**
See also CA 151; DLB 82; HW

Zamyatin, Evgeny Ivanovich
1884-1937 . . . . **TCLC 8, 37**
See also CA 105

Literary Criticism Series
Cumulative Topic Index

This index lists all topic entries in Gale's *Classical and Medieval Literature Criticism, Contemporary Literary Criticism, Literature Criticism from 1400 to 1800, Nineteenth-Century Literature Criticism,* and *Twentieth-Century Literary Criticism.*

Topic Index

Topic Index

NCLC Cumulative Nationality Index

Nationality Index

ISBN 0-7876-1907-8

90000